THE BOOK
A GLOBAL HISTORY

THE
BOOK

A Global History

EDITED BY

Michael F. Suarez, S.J.

AND

H. R. Woudhuysen

OXFORD

UNIVERSITY PRESS

OXFORD
UNIVERSITY PRESS

Great Clarendon Street, Oxford, OX2 6DP,
United Kingdom

Oxford University Press is a department of the University of Oxford.
It furthers the University's objective of excellence in research, scholarship,
and education by publishing worldwide. Oxford is a registered trade mark of
Oxford University Press in the UK and in certain other countries

© Oxford University Press 2013

First Edition published in 2013
Articles previously published as part of the
Oxford Companion to the Book in 2010

Impression: 1

Published in the United States of America by Oxford University Press
198 Madison Avenue, New York, NY 10016, United States of America

British Library Cataloguing in Publication Data
Data available

ISBN 978-0-19-967941-6

Printed in Italy by L.E.G.O. S.p.A. - Lavis TN

*To Pam Coote from
the ever-grateful General Editors*

Contents

Introduction

Encouraged by the commercial and critical fortunes of *The Oxford Companion to the Book* (2010), its General Editors were nonetheless chastened by the fact that its costliness prevented many from purchasing that two-volume work of 1.1 million words. Seeking a way to disseminate the essays from that compendium of book-historical and bibliographical scholarship, we have now edited *The Book: A Global History*, updating chapters from Part 1 of the *Companion* and adding new essays as well. It is our hope that the publication of this volume will make a valuable collection of bibliographical and book-historical scholarship— ambitious in its scope and innovative in its reach—accessible to a broad audience of general readers and advanced specialists alike. Throughout the planning and production of this vade mecum to the world of the book across myriad times and cultures, it has been our constant ambition to bring to life book-historical studies for students and scholars, librarians and collectors, antiquarian booksellers, and enthusiastic amateurs.

Building on *The Oxford Companion to the Book*, this volume seeks to delineate the history of the production, dissemination, and reception of texts from the earliest pictograms of the mid-4th millennium to recent developments in electronic books. Considering many aspects of 'the book'—a convenient term for any recorded text—the 51 essays comprising *The Book: A Global History* traverse the Inca and the Aztec empires, the European medieval book and the early printing revolution, and the nationalization of the publishing industry and book trades after 1949 in Communist China. We have sought not only temporal comprehensiveness, but broad geographical range as well. In addition to book-historical studies of western European nations and the United States, readers will, for instance, find essays on the history of the book in Byzantium; in the Caribbean islands and Bermuda; in the Czech Republic and Slovakia; in the Baltic States and in the Balkans; in Africa, the antipodes, South America, and the islands of Southeast Asia.

We hope that the gathering of diverse perspectives from many nations in this history will lead readers to forge creative and serendipitous connections more powerful than the boundaries that have traditionally kept them separate. Propinquity may generate productive associations; typographical contiguity might in some felicitous instances help to transcend distances of geography, or even the demarcations of intellectual disciplines. Our hope, then, is not merely to supply information, but to promote new knowledge.

This volume also features topical essays on a wide array of subjects, including censorship, the book in the ancient world, missionary printing, intellectual property, children's books, printed ephemera, Jewish books and manuscripts, the origin and development of writing systems, the book as symbolic object, and the economics of print. The bibliographically inclined may perhaps especially enjoy the chapters on paper, the technologies of printing, editorial theory and textual criticism, bookbinding, and the history of illustration and the processes devised for the reproduction of images in texts.

The use of 'the book' to designate the great diversity of textual forms considered in the 'history of the book', or indeed *The Book: A Global History*, is a kind of synecdoche, a single example to represent the many. Yet, because book history is, necessarily, about far more than the history of books, 'the book' as a category or abstraction encompassing everything from stelae inscriptions to laser-printed sheets is not a formation that comes naturally in English, as it does in French (*Le Livre*; *histoire du livre*) or in German (*Buchwesen*). Naturally, the use of the term 'book' in our title in no way excludes newspapers, prints, sheet music, maps, or manuscripts, but merely suggests a degree of emphasis. Mindful that in every major European language the word for 'book' is traceable to the word for 'bark', we might profitably think of 'book' as originally signifying the surface on which any text is written and, hence, as a fitting shorthand for all recorded texts.

Nevertheless, in several respects, 'the book' label is an unfortunate one. Even when perceived as an archetypal part of a larger whole, the Western codex, much less the printed book, is not really an adequate emblem of many material manifestations of text—say, ink-squeeze rubbings, or the Dead Sea Scrolls. More importantly still, the phrases 'history of the book' and 'book history' can carry with them the unfortunate idea that this area of study is restricted to texts as physical objects—the province of analytical (or physical) bibliography—whereas, as evidenced in the pages of this volume, it encompasses much more as well.

The Book: A Global History seeks to provide an accurate, balanced, comprehensive, and authoritative view of a large subject that is still evolving, based on the present state of our knowledge. All the essays have accompanying bibliographies; these are meant to direct the reader to the most relevant and useful sources for further study. In most cases, the bibliographies also represent the principal works consulted by the authors themselves. For this revised and augmented edition of the essays from the *Companion*, three new contributions have been provided to cover: Censorship; Intellectual Property and Copyright; and The History of the Book in the Caribbean and Bermuda. The essay on the Electronic Book has been extensively revised to reflect changes in this fast-growing field. Some new illustrations have been added. Many of the revised essays incorporate minor changes and corrections, including additions to their bibliographies, but the majority continue to reflect the essential state of knowledge concerning their subject-matter around the time that the *Companion* went into production.

We have not ordinarily translated the titles of works in major European languages other than English, but have provided translations where relevant for languages more likely to present significant difficulties for the majority of our readers. Throughout this volume, book titles follow the capitalization rules of the languages in which they are given. References to other essays are to their numbers and take the form of e.g. (*see* 17, 42). We have included URLs (Uniform Resource Locators, or Web addresses) whenever particularly important and reliable resources are to be found on the World Wide Web. Undoubtedly, some of these will migrate or expire over time, but we nevertheless believe that, when judiciously used, the Web is too valuable an asset for research and teaching to neglect merely because a small number of sites will present future difficulties, many of which can be remedied.

Inevitably, despite our best efforts, this volume will suffer from omissions—some because we were unable to discover a body of rigorous scholarly writing on a subject, others because of the constraints of time and page length in editing and producing a one-volume book of this kind, and still others because we have been too ignorant to know what was missing. Whatever merits *The Book: A Global History* does have are chiefly due to the expertise and generosity of our 58 contributors, hailing from 15 different countries. More and more, book history is a global enterprise. We present these essays in the hope that they will engender in diverse readerships from around the globe more capacious understandings of books and their fascinating histories.

MICHAEL F. SUAREZ, S.J.
H. R. WOUDHUYSEN
Charlottesville and Oxford
11 March 2013

Editors and Contributors

Editors and Contributors

General Editors

Michael F. Suarez, S.J. is University Professor and Director of Rare Book School at University of Virginia. He is co-editor of *The Cambridge History of the Book in Britain, Volume V, 1695–1830* (2009), co-general editor of *The Collected Works of Gerard Manley Hopkins*, 8 vols (2006–), and editor-in-chief of Oxford Scholarly Editions Online (oxfordscholarlyeditions.com).

H. R. Woudhuysen is Rector of Lincoln College, Oxford and a Fellow of the British Academy. He has edited *The Penguin Book of Renaissance Verse* (1992) with David Norbrook; *Love's Labour's Lost* (1998) and, with Katherine Duncan-Jones, *Shakespeare's Poems* (2007) for the Arden Shakespeare third series. His book *Sir Philip Sidney and the Circulation of Manuscripts, 1558–1640* was published in 1996.

Contributors

Charlotte Appel is Assistant Professor of early modern history at Roskilde University, Denmark. Her principal research interests are the history of books, reading, and education, as well as church history.

Scott E. Casper is Professor of History, University of Nevada, Reno, where he studies and teaches 19th-century American history. He is the author of *Sarah Johnson's Mount Vernon: The Forgotten History of an American Shrine* (2008) and co-editor of *A History of the Book in America, Volume 3, The Industrial Book, 1840–1880* (2007).

Daven Christopher Chamberlain obtained degrees in Chemistry (Bath) and Paper Physics (Manchester). He worked at Arjowiggins Research and Development for seventeen years, first as a research scientist, later as Head of Testing and Printing. Currently he is editor of *The Quarterly* (Journal of the British Association of Paper Historians) and of *Paper Technology* (Journal of the Paper Industry Technical Association).

Brian Cummings is Anniversary Professor of English at the University of York. He is the author of *The Literary Culture of the Reformation: Grammar and Grace* (2002) and *Mortal Thoughts: Religion, Secularity, and Identity in Shakespeare and Early Modern Culture* (2013), as well as the editor of *The Book of Common Prayer: The Texts of 1549, 1559, and 1662* (2011).

Christopher de Hamel is Donnelley Fellow Librarian, Corpus Christi College, Cambridge. He was for many years responsible for sales of illuminated manuscripts at Sotheby's. He has published very extensively on medieval manuscripts and book collectors.

Jeremy B. Dibbell is Librarian for Rare Books and Social Media at LibraryThing, where he is head of the Libraries of Early America project. He is also at work on a history of the book in Bermuda.

Cristina Dondi is the Secretary of the Consortium of European Research Libraries (CERL), a member of the History and of the Modern Languages Faculty of the University of Oxford, and one of the editors of the catalogue of incunabula of the Bodleian Library. Her research focuses on the history of printing in Italy in the 15th century and on liturgical texts, both manuscript and printed.

J. S. Edgren is Editorial Director of the Chinese Rare Books Project, an online union catalogue based at Princeton University.

Lukas Erne is Professor in the English Department at the University of Geneva. He is the author of *Shakespeare and the Book Trade* (2013), *Shakespeare's Modern Collaborators* (2008), *Shakespeare as Literary Dramatist* (2003), and *Beyond 'The Spanish Tragedy': A Study of the Works of Thomas Kyd* (2001), and the editor of *The First Quarto of Romeo and Juliet* (2007) and *Textual Performances: The Modern Reproduction of Shakespeare's Drama* (2004).

Patricia Lockhart Fleming is Professor Emeritus, Faculty of Information, University of Toronto, where she served as founding director of the collaborative graduate programme in book history. She is co-general editor and co-editor of volumes 1 and 2 of *History of the Book in Canada (Histoire du livre et de l'imprimé au Canada)* (3 vols, 2004–7).

John L. Flood is Emeritus Professor of German in the University of London, Past President of the Bibliographical Society, and specializes in German book history. His publications include *The German Book 1450-1750* (1995) and *Poets Laureate of the Holy Roman Empire* (2006).

Eileen Gardiner is co-director of ACLS Humanities E-Book and president and co-founder of Italica Press. She holds a Ph.D. in English literature with a specialization in medieval comparative literature, and is the editor of Hell-on-Line.org.

Vincent Giroud is a Professor at the Université de Franche-Comté. He has taught at the Sorbonne and at Johns Hopkins, Vassar, Bard, and Yale, where he also served as curator of modern books and manuscripts at the Beinecke Library.

Paul Goldman is Honorary Professor, School of English, Communication, and Philosophy, Cardiff University. He is the author of works on 19th-century British art and illustration including *Beyond Decoration: The Illustrations of John Everett Millais* (2005), *Looking at Prints, Drawings and Watercolours: A Guide to Technical Terms*, 2e (2006), *Master Prints Close Up* (2012) and, co-edited with Simon Cooke, *Reading Victorian Illustration 1855-1875: Spoils of the Lumber Room* (2012).

Abhijit Gupta is Associate Professor of English, Jadavpur University, Kolkata, and Director, Jadavpur University Press. He is the co-editor of the *Book History in India* series.

Bridget Guzner was Curator of the Hungarian and Romanian Collections of the British Library, responsible for the selection and acquisition of current and antiquarian material, exploring, and describing the collections. Her research interests continue to include all aspects of Hungarian and Romanian printing and publishing, as well as the history and development of the British Library's collections.

Michael Harris worked at Birkbeck College, London University. His main research interest is in the history of print generally and of newspapers in particular. He founded a major conference on book-trade history, which continues to be held in London and has been involved in editing and contributing to the annual publication of the papers (30 titles). He is currently working on a full-length study of printed serials published in London on either side of 1700.

Neil Harris teaches bibliography at the University of Udine. He currently specializes in the history of Italian Renaissance publishing and in the field of early book cataloguing.

Paul Hoftijzer holds the P. A. Tiele Chair in book history at Leiden University. He publishes on the history of the Dutch book in the early modern period.

Leslie Howsam is the author of *Cheap Bibles* (1991) and *Old Books & New Histories* (2006). Her 2006 Lyell lectures discussed research on the correspondence of historians and publishers. She is University Professor at the University of Windsor in Canada.

Clare Hutton is Lecturer in English at Loughborough University, and the editor of volume 5 of *The Oxford History of the Irish Book* (2011).

Jana Igunma is Curator of Thai, Lao, and Cambodian Collections at the British Library. She graduated from Humboldt-University, Berlin in Southeast Asian History (1996), Library and Information Science (2003), and worked as curatorial assistant for Thai, Lao, Cambodian, and Burmese Collections at the Staatsbibliothek zu Berlin.

Andrea Immel is Curator of the Cotsen Children's Library at Princeton University. She co-edited the *Cambridge Companion to Children's Literature* (2009) and *Childhood and Children's Books in Early Modern Europe 1550-1800* (2005), and contributed chapters to the *Cambridge History of the Book in Britain*, volumes 5 and 6.

Craig Kallendorf is Professor of Classics and English at Texas A&M University. He is the author of *The Other Virgil* (2007), *The Virgilian Tradition: Book History and the History of Reading in Early Modern Europe* (2007), and several book-length bibliographies of Virgil, as well as the co-editor of *The Books of Venice / Il libro veneziano* (2009).

Peter Kornicki is Professor of East Asian studies at the University of Cambridge. He is the author of *The Book in Japan* (1998), has published catalogues of early Japanese books in European libraries, and is working on Japanese, Korean, and Vietnamese editions of Chinese texts.

Elisabeth Ladenson teaches French and Comparative Literature at Columbia University. She is the author of *Dirt for Art's Sake* (2007) and *Proust's Lesbianism* (1999).

María Luisa López-Vidriero is Director of the Real Biblioteca (Madrid) and Co-Director of the Instituto de Historia del Libro y de la Lectura.

†Harold Love (1937-2007) was an Australian literary

historian, critic, and editor. Among his many publications are *Scribal Publication in Seventeenth-Century England* (1993); *English Clandestine Satire 1660–1702* (2004); and *Attributing Authorship* (2002). He also produced editions of Thomas Southerne (with R. J. Jordan; 2 vols, 1988); John Wilmot, earl of Rochester (1999); and George Villiers, 2nd duke of Buckingham (with R. D. Hume; 2 vols, 2007).

Beth McKillop has been Keeper of Asia at the V&A since 2004. Earlier a Curator in the British Library, she researches the MS and book history of Korea. Her publications include *Korean Art and Design* (1992).

Adam D. Moore, an Associate Professor in the Philosophy Department and Information School at the University of Washington, works on the ethical and legal issues surrounding intellectual property, privacy, and information control. He is the author of two books, over 30 articles, and has edited two anthologies.

Ian Morrison Tasmanian Archive and Heritage Office, previously Curator of Special Collections at the University of Melbourne, is a past editor of the *Bibliographical Society of Australia & New Zealand Bulletin* (now *Script & Print*) and has published widely on aspects of Australian book and library history.

James Mosley is Visiting Professor in the Department of Typography and Graphic Communication, University of Reading. He was Librarian of St Bride Library, London, from 1958 until 2000. He has written and lectured widely on the history of printing type and letter forms.

Andrew Murphy is Professor of English at the University of St Andrews. He is the author, most recently, of *Shakespeare*

for the People: Working-class Readers, 1800–1900 (2008) and *Shakespeare in Print: A History and Chronology of Shakespeare Publishing* (2003).

Ronald G. Musto is co-director of ACLS Humanities E-Book and co-publisher of Italica Press. He holds a Ph.D. in History, specializing in 14th-century Italy.

Niall Ó Ciosáin teaches in the Department of History, National University of Ireland, Galway. His current research focuses on the relationship between literacy, print, and language shift in the Celtic language areas in the 18th and 19th centuries.

Carl Olson is Professor of Religious Studies at Allegheny College. Besides numerous essays published in journals, books, and encyclopaedias, his latest books include the following: *The Different Paths of Buddhism: A Narrative-Historical Introduction* (2005); *Original Buddhist Sources: A Reader* (2005); *The Many Colors of Hinduism: A Thematic-Historical Introduction* (2007); *Hindu Primary Sources: A Sectarian Reader* (2007); and *Celibacy and Religious Traditions* (2007); *The Allure of Decadent Thinking: Religious Studies and the Challenge of Postmodernism* (2013).

Devana Pavlik is a librarian who was from 1983 to 2003 the curator of Czech, Slovak, and Lusatian Collections in the British Library. In retirement, she continues with her research into Czech and Slovak publishing.

David Pearson Director, Culture, Heritage and Libraries at the City of London, has worked and published extensively on the post-production history of books, with particular reference to bookbinding and book ownership.

Alexis Politis is Professor of Modern Greek Literature at the University of Crete. His main research interests are in the history of modern Greek literature (especially of the 19th century), the history of mentalities, folksongs, and the history of Greek printing and publishing.

Andrew Robinson is the author of some 25 books in the arts and sciences. They include *The Story of Writing: Alphabets, Hieroglyphs and Pictograms* (1995); *The Man Who Deciphered Linear B: The Story of Michael Ventris* (2002); *Lost Languages: The Enigma of the World's Undeciphered Scripts* (2009); *Writing and Script: A Very Short Introduction* (2009); and *Cracking the Egyptian Code: The Revolutionary Life of Jean-François Champollion* (2012).

Ekaterina Rogatchevskaia is Lead Curator of East European Studies, British Library. She has published widely on early Russian literature, Russian émigré literature, and the history of the British Library Russian collections.

Shef Rogers is a Senior Lecturer in English at the University of Otago, Dunedin, New Zealand. He is completing a bibliography of English travel writing 1700–1800 and is working with four Otago colleagues to compile a one-volume history of the book in New Zealand.

Eugenia Roldán Vera is Professor-Researcher at the Department of Education of the Centre for Advanced Research and Studies (DIE/CINVESTAV), Mexico. Her fields of research are the history of education and the history of the book in 19th- and 20th-century Latin America. She is the author of *The British Book Trade and Spanish American Independence* (2003).

Geoffrey Roper is a bibliographical consultant. He was head of the Islamic Bibliography Unit at Cambridge University Library, 1982–2003, and editor of *Index Islamicus* and of the *World Survey of Islamic Manuscripts*.

Joan Shelley Rubin is Professor of History at the University of Rochester, specializing in American culture since 1865.

Emile G. L. Schrijver is Curator of the Bibliotheca Rosenthaliana, one of the Special Collections at Amsterdam University Library and the editor-in-chief of *Studia Rosenthaliana*. He has published extensively on Jewish books, in particular on Hebrew manuscripts of the post-medieval period, and has contributed to numerous exhibition and auction catalogues.

Karen Skovgaard-Petersen is Senior Researcher, Curator of Rare Books in the Department of Manuscripts and Rare Books, The Royal Library, Copenhagen. Her fields of research are early modern historiography, and early modern book and library history.

Claire Squires is Professor of Publishing Studies and Director of The Stirling Centre for International Publishing and Communication at the University of Stirling.

Christine Thomas was formerly the Head of Slavonic and East European Collections in the British Library. She has published on the history of Russian printing, the formation of the Russian collections of the British Museum Library, and on Slavonic early printed books. She is also editor of *Solanus: International Journal for Russian and East European Bibliographic, Library, and Publishing Studies*.

M. Antoni J. Üçerler, S.J. Director of Research, Center for the Pacific Rim University of San Francisco. His main area of research is the history of Christianity in Japan and China and missionary printing in Asia and the Americas.

Andrew van der Vlies teaches in the School of English and Drama at Queen Mary, University of London. He is author of *South African Textual Cultures* (2007) and editor of *Print, Text and Book Cultures in South African* (2012).

Aleksandra B. Vraneš is Professor of Philology, University of Belgrade, and President of the Serbian Library Association. Her fields of interest include library science, bibliography, ethics in science, and the methodology of research. Her publications include *Serbian Bibliography in Periodicals: From Orphelin to 1941* (1996), *Basis of Bibliography* (2001), *Academic Libraries* (2004), and *From the Manuscript to the Library: Dictionary* (2006).

Marcus Walsh is Kenneth Allott Professor of English Literature, University of Liverpool. He has written on Swift, Johnson, and Sterne, biblical scholarship, and the history and theory of editing.

Jürgen M. Warmbrunn, Ph.D., is a Slavicist, historian, and academic librarian with a particular interest in East European and Baltic library history and book culture. He is Deputy Director of the Herder-Institut, Marburg, a centre for historical research on East Central Europe, and Director of the research library of the Herder-Institut.

Alexis Weedon holds a UNESCO chair in New Media Forms of the Book and is Head of Journalism and Communications at the University of Bedfordshire. Specializing in publishing economics, quantification, and cross-media production, she is co-editor of *Convergence* and author of *Victorian Publishing* (2003).

Edwin Paul Wieringa was educated in Indonesian Languages and Literatures at the University of Leiden (MA 1988, Ph.D. 1994). Since 2004, he has been Professor of Indonesian Philology and Islamic Studies at the University of Cologne. He is the author of a two-volume *Catalogue of Malay and Minangkabau Manuscripts in the Library of Leiden University* (1998, 2007).

N. G. Wilson, FBA Fellow and Tutor in Classics (Emeritus), Lincoln College, Oxford, is a specialist in Greek palaeography, the transmission of texts, and the history of scholarship.

Janet Zmroczek is Head of European Collections at the British Library. Her research interests include the history of the British Library Polish and Baltic collections and the cultural, social, and literary activities of the Polish community in 19th-century Britain. Her articles on these subjects have been published in a range of British, European, and American scholarly journals.

List of Abbreviations

1. Bibliographical abbreviations

Altick	R. D. Altick, *The English Common Reader* (1957; 2e, 1998)
BC	*Book Collector*
BH	*Book History*
Bischoff	B. Bischoff, *Latin Palaeography*, tr. D. Ó Cróinín and D. Ganz (1990)
BJRL	*Bulletin of the John Rylands University Library of Manchester*
BLJ	*British Library Journal* (*see also* eBLJ)
BLR	*Bodleian Library Record*
BMC	*Catalogue of Books Printed in the XVth Century now in the British Museum* (11 vols, 1908–2007; vols 1–9 repr. 1963)
BSANZ	*Bibliographical Society of Australia and New Zealand*
CHB	*The Cambridge History of the Bible* (3 vols, 1963–70): 1: *From the Beginnings to Jerome*, ed. P. R. Ackroyd and C. F. Evans; 2: *The West, from the Fathers to the Reformation*, ed. G. W. H. Lampe; 3: *The West, from the Reformation to the Present Day*, ed. S. L. Greenslade
CHBB	*The Cambridge History of the Book in Britain*, 3: *1400–1557* (1999), ed. L. Hellinga and J. Trapp; 4: *1557–1695* (2002), ed. J. Barnard et al.; 5: *1695–1830* (2009), ed. M. F. Suarez, S.J., and M. Turner; 6: *1830–1914*, ed. D. McKitterick (2009)
CHLBI	*The Cambridge History of Libraries in Britain and Ireland*, ed. P. Hoare (3 vols, 2006)
DEL	P. Fouché et al., eds., *Dictionnaire encyclopédique du livre* (4 vols, 2002–11)
DLB	*Dictionary of Literary Biography*
Gaskell, NI	P. Gaskell, *A New Introduction to Bibliography* (1972, repr. 1974)
GJ	*Gutenberg-Jahrbuch*

GW	*Gesamtkatalog der Wiegendrucke* (1925–)
HBA	*A History of the Book in America*, 1: *The Colonial Book in the Atlantic World*, ed. H. Amory and D. D. Hall (2000); 2: *An Extensive Republic: Print, Culture, and Society in the New Nation*, ed. R. A. Gross and M. Kelley (2010); 3: *The Industrial Book, 1840–1880*, ed. S. E. Casper et al. (2007); 4: *Print in Motion: The Expansion of Publishing and Reading in the United States, 1880–1940*, ed. C. F. Kaestle and J. A. Radway (2009); 5: *The Enduring Book: Print Culture in Postwar America*, ed. D. Nord et al. (2009)
HBC	*History of the Book in Canada/Histoire du livre et de l'imprimé au Canada*, ed. P. L. Fleming and Y. Lamonde (3 vols, 2004–7)
HDHB	*Handbuch deutscher historischer Buchbestände in Europa* (4 vols, 1999–2000)
HLB	*Harvard Library Bulletin*
ISTC	Incunabula Short-Title Catalogue
LaB	*La Bibliofilía*
LGB	*Lexikon des gesamten Buchwesens*, ed. S. Corsten et al., 2e (1985–)
McKerrow,	R. B. McKerrow, *An Introduction to Bibliography for Literary Students* (1927)
Middleton	B. Middleton, *A History of English Craft Bookbinding Technique*, 4e (1996)
OBS	Oxford Bibliographical Society
ODNB	*The Oxford Dictionary of National Biography*
PAAS	*Proceedings of the American Antiquarian Society*
PH	*Publishing History*
Reynolds and Wilson	L. D. Reynolds and N. G. Wilson, *Scribes and Scholars*, 3e (1991)

Rose	J. Rose, *The Intellectual Life of the British Working Classes* (1991)	SQ	*Shakespeare Quarterly*
SB	*Studies in Bibliography*	TQ	*The Quarterly* (Journal of the British Association of Paper Historians)

2. Other abbreviations

AD	*anno Domini*	Gk	Greek
BC	before Christ	in.	inch(es)
BCE	before the Common Era	km	kilometre(s)
BL	British Library	Lat.	Latin
BnF	Bibliothèque nationale de France, Paris	LC	Library of Congress
Bodleian	Bodleian Library, Oxford	lit.	literally
c.	*circa*; cent(s)	m	metre(s)
CE	Common Era	mm	millimetre(s)
cm	centimetre(s)	MS(S)	manuscript(s)
d.	died	no.	number
d.	penny, pence	NS	new series
Dr	Doctor	r	recto
e	edition (e.g. 2e, 'second edition')	r.	reigned, ruled
ed.	editor(s)	repr.	reprint(ed)
edn	edition	rev.	revised (by); reviewed by
et al.	*et alii* (and others)	Revd	Reverend
f.	and following	*s.*	shilling(s)
ff.	and following (plural)	sig.	signature
fig.	figure	St	Saint
fl.	*floruit*	tr.	translated by, translation, translator
fo.	folio	v	verso
fos.	folios	vol.	volume
Fr.	French	vols	volumes

Thematic Studies

ᨳ 1 ᨲ

Writing Systems

ANDREW ROBINSON

1 The emergence of writing

Without writing, there would be no recording, no history, and of course no books. The creation of writing permitted the command of a ruler and his seal to extend far beyond his sight and voice, and even to survive his death. If the Rosetta Stone did not exist, for example, the world would be virtually unaware of the nondescript Egyptian king Ptolemy V Epiphanes, whose priests promulgated his decree upon the stone in three scripts: hieroglyphic, demotic, and (Greek) alphabetic.

How did writing begin? The favoured explanation, until the Enlightenment in the 18th century, was divine origin. Today, many—probably most—scholars accept that the earliest writing evolved from accountancy, though it is puzzling that such accounts are little in evidence in the surviving writing of ancient Egypt, India, China, and Central America (which does not preclude commercial record-keeping on perishable materials such as bamboo in these early civilizations). In other words, some time in the late 4th millennium BC, in the cities of Sumer in Mesopotamia, the 'cradle of civilization', the complexity of trade and administration reached a point where it outstripped the power of memory among the governing elite. To record transactions in an indisputable, permanent form became essential.

Some scholars believe that a conscious search for a solution to this problem by an unknown Sumerian individual in the city of Uruk (biblical Erech), c.3300 BC, produced writing. Others posit that writing was the work of a group, presumably of clever administrators and merchants. Still others think it was not an invention at all, but an accidental discovery. Many regard it as the result of evolution over a long period, rather than a flash of inspiration. One particularly well-aired theory holds that writing grew out of a long-standing counting system of clay 'tokens'. Such 'tokens'—varying from simple, plain discs to more complex, incised shapes whose exact purpose is unknown—have been found in many Middle Eastern archaeological sites, and have been dated from 8000 to 1500 BC. The substitution of two-dimensional symbols in clay for these three-dimensional tokens was a first step towards writing, according to this theory. One major difficulty is that the 'tokens' continued to exist long after the emergence of Sumerian cuneiform writing; another is that a two-dimensional symbol on a clay tablet might be thought to be a less, not a more, advanced concept than a three-dimensional clay 'token'. It seems more likely that 'tokens' accompanied the emergence of writing, rather than giving rise to writing.

Apart from the 'tokens', numerous examples exist of what might be termed 'proto-writing'. They include the Ice Age symbols found in caves in southern France, which are probably 20,000 years old. A cave at Pech Merle, in the Lot, contains a lively Ice Age graffito showing a stencilled hand and a pattern of red dots. This may simply mean: 'I was here, with my animals'—or perhaps the symbolism is deeper. Other prehistoric images show animals such as horses, a stag's head, and bison, overlaid with signs; and notched bones have been found that apparently served as lunar calendars.

'Proto-writing' is not writing in the full sense of the word. A scholar of writing, the Sinologist John DeFrancis, has defined 'full' writing as a 'system of graphic symbols that can be used to convey any and all thought'—a concise and influential definition. According to this, 'proto-writing' would include, in addition to Ice Age cave symbols and Middle Eastern clay 'tokens', the Pictish symbol stones and tallies such as the fascinating knotted Inca quipus, but also contemporary sign systems such as international transportation symbols, highway code signs, computer icons, and mathematical and musical notation. None of these ancient or modern systems is capable of expressing 'any and all thought', but each is good at specialized communication (DeFrancis, *Visible Speech*, 4).

2 Development and diffusion of writing systems

To express the full range of human thought requires a writing system intimately linked with spoken language. For, as the founder of modern linguistics, Ferdinand de Saussure, wrote, language may be compared to a sheet of paper: 'Thought is on one side of the sheet and sound on the reverse side. Just as it is impossible to take a pair of scissors and cut one side of the paper without at the same time cutting the other, so it is impossible in a language to isolate sound from thought, or thought from sound' (Saussure, 111).

The symbols of what may have become the first 'full' writing system are generally thought to have been pictograms: iconic drawings of, say, a pot, or a fish, or a head with an open jaw (representing the concept of eating). These have

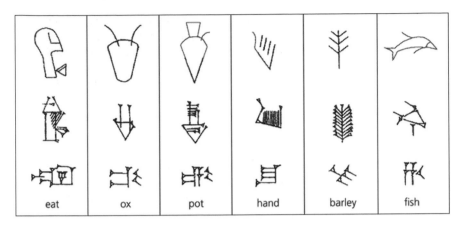

Fig. 1 Some cuneiform (wedge-shaped) signs, showing the pictographic form (*c.*3000 BC), an early cuneiform representation (*c.*2400 BC), and the late Assyrian form (*c.*650 BC), now turned through 90 degrees, with the meaning. Line drawing by Chartwell Illustrators

been found in Mesopotamia and Egypt dating to the mid-4th millennium BC, in the Indus Valley dating to the 3rd millennium, and in China dating to as early as the 5th millennium, according to the (doubtful) claims of some Chinese archaeologists. In many cases, their iconicity soon became so abstract that it is barely perceptible to us. Fig. 1 shows how the Sumerian pictograms developed into the wedge-shaped cuneiform signs that went on to dominate Middle Eastern writing for some 3,000 years.

Yet pictograms were insufficient to express the kinds of words, and their constituent parts, that cannot be depicted. Essential to the development of 'full' writing, as opposed to limited, purely pictographic, 'proto-writing', was the discovery of the rebus principle. This radical idea, from the Latin meaning 'by things', enables phonetic values to be represented by pictographic symbols. Thus in English, a picture of a bee beside the figure 4 might (if one were so minded) represent 'before', and a bee with a picture of a tray might stand for 'betray', while a picture of an ant next to a buzzing beehive full of honey, might (less obviously) represent 'Anthony'. Egyptian hieroglyphs are full of rebuses, for instance the 'sun' sign, ⊙, pronounced *R(a)* or *R(e)*, is the first symbol in the hieroglyphic spelling of the pharaoh Ramesses. In an early Sumerian tablet, the abstract word 'reimburse' is represented by a picture of a reed, because 'reimburse' and 'reed' shared the same phonetic value, *gi*, in the Sumerian language.

Once writing of this 'full' kind, capable of expressing the complete range of speech and thought, was invented, accidentally discovered, or evolved, did it then diffuse throughout the globe from Mesopotamia? It appears that the earliest such writing in Egypt dates from 3100 BC, that in the Indus Valley (undeciphered seal stones) from 2500 BC, that in Crete (the undeciphered Linear A script) from 1750 BC, that in China (the 'oracle bones') from 1200 BC, and that in Mexico (the undeciphered Olmec script) from 900 BC—all dates are approximate and subject to new archaeological discoveries. On this basis, it seems reasonable that the *idea* of writing, but not the signs of a particular script, could have spread gradually from culture to distant culture. After all, 600 or 700 years were required for the idea of printing to reach Europe from China (if we discount the isolated and enigmatic Phaistos disc of *c.*1700 BC, found in Crete in 1908, which appears to be 'printed'), and even longer for the idea of paper to spread to Europe (*see* **10**): why should writing not have reached China from Mesopotamia over an even longer period?

Nevertheless, in the absence of solid evidence for transmission of the idea (even in the case of the much more proximate civilizations of Mesopotamia and Egypt), a majority of scholars prefer to think that writing developed independently in the major civilizations of the ancient world. The optimist, or at any rate the anti-imperialist, will choose to emphasize the intelligence and inventiveness of human societies; the pessimist, who takes a more conservative view of history, will tend to assume that humans prefer to copy what already exists, as faithfully as they can, restricting their innovations to cases of absolute necessity. The latter is the favoured explanation for how the Greeks (at the beginning of the 1st millennium BC) borrowed the alphabet from the Phoenicians, adding in the process signs for the vowels not written in the Phoenician script (*see* **3**). There are many other examples of script borrowings, such as the Japanese taking the Chinese characters in the 1st millennium AD and incorporating them into a highly complex writing system that mixes several thousand Chinese characters with slightly fewer than 100, much simpler, syllabic symbols of Japanese origin. If ever the Rongorongo script of Easter Island—the most isolated inhabited spot on earth—is deciphered, it may shed light on the intriguing question of whether the Easter Islanders invented Rongorongo unaided, brought the idea of writing from Polynesia in their canoes, or borrowed it from Europeans who first visited Easter Island in the 18th century. If Rongorongo could be proved to have been invented unaided on Easter Island, this would at last guarantee that writing must have had multiple origins, rather than radiating from a single source.

3 Decipherment

In ordinary conversation, to decipher someone's 'indecipherable' handwriting means to make sense of the meaning; it does not imply that one can read every single word. In its more technical sense, as applied to ancient scripts, 'deciphered' means different things to different scholars. At one extreme, everyone agrees that the Egyptian hieroglyphs have been deciphered— because every trained Egyptologist would make the same sense of virtually every word of a given hieroglyphic inscription (though their individual translations would still differ, as do all independent translations of the same work from one language into another). At the other extreme, (almost) every scholar agrees that the script of the Indus Valley civilization is undeciphered—

because no one can make sense of its seals and other inscriptions to the satisfaction of anyone else. Between these extremes lies a vast spectrum of opinion. In the case of the Mayan hieroglyphic writing of Central America, for example, most scholars agree that a high proportion, as much as 85 per cent, of the inscriptions can be meaningfully read, and yet there remain large numbers of individual Mayan glyphs that are contentious or obscure. No absolute distinction exists by which a script can be judged to be deciphered or undeciphered; we should instead speak of *degrees* of decipherment. The most useful criterion is that a proposed decipherment can generate consistent readings from new samples of the script, preferably produced by persons other than the original decipherer.

In this sense, the Egyptian hieroglyphs were deciphered in the 1820s by Jean-François Champollion and others; Babylonian cuneiform in the 1850s by Henry Creswicke Rawlinson and others; Mycenaean Linear B in 1952–3 by Michael Ventris; and the Mayan hieroglyphs by Yuri Knorozov and others in the 1950s and after—to name only the most important of the successful decipherments. This leaves a number of significant undeciphered scripts, such as the Etruscan script from Italy, the Indus Valley script from Pakistan/India, Linear A from Crete, the Meroitic script from Sudan, the Proto-Elamite script from Iran/Iraq, Rongorongo from Easter Island, and the Olmec, Zapotec, and Isthmian scripts from Mexico. They may be resolved into three basic categories: an unknown script writing a known language; a known script writing an unknown language; and an unknown script writing an unknown language. The Mayan hieroglyphs were until their decipherment an example of the first category, since the Mayan languages are still spoken, and the Zapotec script may be, too, if it writes a language related to modern Zapotec; Etruscan writing is an example of the second category, since the Etruscan script is basically the same as the Greek alphabet, but the Etruscan language is not related to Indo-European or other languages; while the Indus Valley script is an example of the last category, since the script bears no resemblance to any other script and the language of the civilization does not appear to have survived (unless, as some scholars speculate, it is related to the Dravidian languages of south India).

In each undeciphered case, the techniques used in successful decipherments have been applied, with varying results. Ventris—perhaps the most ingenious of all the decipherers, since he alone had no help from a bilingual aid like the Rosetta Stone—gave a masterly summary of the science and art of decipherment:

> Each operation needs to be planned in three phases: an exhaustive *analysis* of the signs, words, and contexts in all the available inscriptions, designed to extract every possible clue as to the spelling system, meaning and language structure; an experimental *substitution* of phonetic values to give possible words and inflections in a known or postulated language; and a decisive *check*, preferably with the aid of virgin material, to ensure that the apparent results are not due to fantasy, coincidence or circular reasoning. (Ventris, 200)

4 Classification of writing systems

Europeans and Americans of ordinary literacy must recognize and write around 52 alphabetic signs (26 capital letters and their lower-case equivalents), and sundry other signs, such as numerals, punctuation marks, and 'whole-word' semantic signs, for example +, =, &, %, £, $, which are generally called logograms or analphabetics. Japanese readers, by contrast, are supposed to know and be able to write some 2,000 signs, and, if they are highly educated, must recognize 5,000 signs or more. The two situations, in Europe/America and in Japan, appear to be poles apart. In fact, however, the different writing systems resemble each other more than at first appears.

Contrary to what many people think, all scripts that are 'full' writing (in the sense defined by DeFrancis above) operate on one basic principle. Both alphabets and the Chinese and Japanese scripts use symbols to represent sounds (i.e. phonetic signs); and all writing systems mix such phonetic symbols with logographic symbols (i.e. semantic signs). What differs between writing systems—apart from the forms of the signs, of course—is the *proportion* of phonetic to semantic signs. The higher the proportion of phonetic representation in a script, the easier it is to guess the pronunciation of a word. In English the proportion is high, in Chinese it is low. Thus, English spelling represents English speech sound by sound more accurately than Chinese characters represent Mandarin speech; but Finnish spelling represents the Finnish language better than English spelling represents spoken English. The Finnish script is highly efficient phonetically, while the Chinese (and Japanese) script is phonetically seriously deficient—as indicated in Fig. 2.

There is thus no such thing as a 'pure' writing system, that is, a 'full' writing system capable of expressing meaning entirely through alphabetic letters or syllabic signs or logograms—because all 'full' writing systems are a mixture of phonetic and semantic signs. How best to classify writing systems is therefore a controversial matter. For example, some scholars deny the existence of alphabets prior to the Greek alphabet, on the grounds that the Phoenician script marked only consonants, no vowels (like the early Arabic script). Nevertheless, classify-

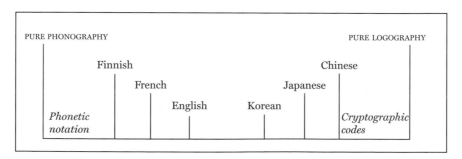

Fig. 2 A schematic diagram of phonography and logography in writing systems adapted from publications by John DeFrancis and J. Marshall Unger. Line drawing by Chartwell Illustrators.

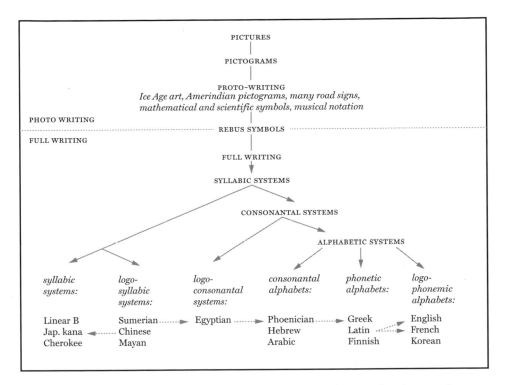

Fig. 3 The classification of writing systems from *The Story of Writing* (Thames and Hudson: 1995). © Andrew Robinson. Line drawing by Chartwell Illustrators.

ing labels are useful to remind us of the predominant nature of different systems. The tree shown in Fig. 3 divides writing systems according to this criterion, not according to their age; it does *not* show how one writing system may have given rise to another historically. (The broken lines indicate possible influences of one system upon another, for example Chinese characters on the Japanese syllabic 'kana'.) Thus, the Phoenician script is labelled a 'consonantal alphabet', with the emphasis on its consonants and without significant logography, in contrast to the 'logo-consonantal' system of Egyptian hieroglyphs, where logography dominates but there is also a phonetic element based on the consonants—24 signs, each representing a consonant. The tree's terminology is self-explanatory, except perhaps for 'phonemic': the phoneme is the smallest contrastive unit in the sound system of a language, for example the English vowel phonemes /e/ and /a/ in *set* and *sat*, and the consonantal phonemes /b/ and /p/ in *bat* and *pat*.

5 The origin of the alphabet

If the emergence of writing is full of riddles, then the enigma of the first alphabet is even more perplexing. That the alphabet reached the modern world via the ancient Greeks is well known—the word 'alphabet' comes from the first two of the Greek letters, alpha and beta—but we have no clear idea of how and when the alphabet appeared in Greece; how the Greeks thought of adding letters standing for the vowels as well as the consonants; and how, even more fundamentally, the idea of an alphabet occurred to the pre-Greek societies at the eastern end of the Mediterranean during the 2nd millennium BC. The first well-attested alphabets belong to ancient Ugarit, today's Ras Shamra on the coast of Syria, where a 30-sign cuneiform alphabet was used in the 14th century BC; and to the Phoenicians in Canaan in the late 2nd millennium BC, who used 22 consonantal letters.

Scholars have devoted their lives to these questions, but the evidence is too scanty for firm conclusions. It is not known whether the alphabet evolved from the scripts of Mesopotamia (cuneiform), Egypt (hieroglyphs), and Crete (Linear A and B)—or whether it struck a single unknown individual 'in a flash'. Nor is it known why an alphabet was thought necessary. It seems most likely that it was the result of commercial imperatives. In other words, commerce demanded a simpler and quicker means of recording transactions than, say, Babylonian cuneiform or Egyptian hieroglyphs, and also a convenient way to note the babel of languages of the various empires and groups trading with each other around the Mediterranean. If so, then it is surprising that there is no evidence of trade and commerce in the early alphabetic inscriptions of Greece. This, and other considerations, have led a few scholars to postulate, controversially, that the Greek alphabet was invented to record the oral epics of Homer in the 8th century BC.

In the absence of proof, anecdote and myth have filled the vacuum. Children are often evoked as inventors of the alphabet, because they would not have had the preconceptions of adult writers and their elders' investment in existing scripts. One possibility is that a bright Canaanite child in northern Syria, fed up with having to learn cuneiform and hieroglyphs, borrowed from the hieroglyphs the familiar idea of a small number of signs standing for single consonants and then invented some new signs for the basic consonantal sounds of his own Semitic language. Perhaps the child first doodled the signs in the dust of some ancient street: a simple outline of a house, Semitic 'beth' (the 'bet' in 'alphabet'), became the sign for 'b'. In the 20th century, Rudyard Kipling's child protagonist in 'How the Alphabet Was Made', Taffimai, designs what she calls 'noise-pictures'. The letter 'A' is a picture of a carp with its barbelled mouth wide open; this, Taffimai tells her father, looks like his open mouth when he utters the sound *ah*. The letter 'O' matches the egg-or-stone shape and resembles her father's mouth saying *oh*. The letter 'S' represents a snake, and stands for the hissing sound of the snake. In this somewhat far-fetched way, a whole alphabet is created by Taffimai.

To quote an earlier poet, William Blake wrote in *Jerusalem*: 'God…in mysterious Sinai's awful cave / To Man the wond'rous art of writing gave'. A small

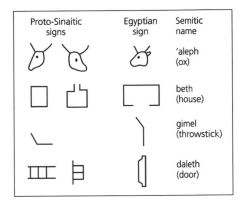

Proto-Sinaitic signs		Egyptian sign	Semitic name
			'aleph (ox)
			beth (house)
			gimel (throwstick)
			daleth (door)

Fig. 4 The proto-Sinaitic theory of the origin of the alphabet. Line drawing by Chartwell Illustrators

sphinx in the British Museum at one time seemed to show that Blake was right, at least about the origin of the alphabet. The sphinx was found in 1905 at Serabit el-Khadim in Sinai, a desolate place remote from civilization, by the famous Egyptologist Flinders Petrie. He was excavating some old turquoise mines that were active in ancient Egyptian times. Petrie dated the sphinx to the middle of the 18th Dynasty; today, its date is thought to be *c*.1500 BC. On one side of it is a strange inscription; on the other, and between the paws, there are further inscriptions of the same kind, plus some Egyptian hieroglyphs that read: 'beloved of Hathor, mistress of turquoise'. Similar inscriptions were written on the rocks of this remote area.

Petrie guessed that the unknown script was probably an alphabet, because it comprised fewer than 30 signs (out of a much larger number of text characters); and he thought that its language was probably Semitic, since he knew that Semites from Canaan—modern Israel and Lebanon—had worked these mines, in many cases as slaves. Ten years later another distinguished Egyptologist, Alan Gardiner, studied the 'proto-Sinaitic' signs and noted resemblances between some of them and certain pictographic Egyptian hieroglyphs. Gardiner now named each sign with the Semitic word equivalent to the sign's meaning in Egyptian (the Semitic words were known from biblical scholarship) (*see* Fig. 4). These Semitic names are the same as the names of the letters of the Hebrew alphabet—a fact that did not surprise Gardiner, since he knew that the Hebrews had lived in Canaan in the late 2nd millennium BC. However, although the names are the same, the shapes of the Hebrew letters are different from the proto-Sinaitic signs, suggesting that any link between them cannot be a straightforward one.

Gardiner's hypothesis enabled him to translate one of the inscriptions that occurred on the sphinx from Serabit el-Khadim as 'Baalat'—in English transcription with the vowels spelt out. (Hebrew and other Semitic scripts do not directly indicate vowels; readers guess them from their knowledge of the language, as explained in 'The family of alphabets' below.) Gardiner's reading made sense: Baalat means 'the Lady' and is a recognized Semitic name for the goddess Hathor in the Sinai region. Accordingly, the inscription on the sphinx seemed to be an Egyptian-Semitic bilingual. Unfortunately, no further decipherment proved tenable, mainly because of lack of material and the fact that many of the proto-Sinaitic signs had no hieroglyphic equivalents. Scholarly hopes of finding the story of the Exodus in these scratchings were scotched. Nevertheless, it is conceivable that a script similar to the proto-Sinaitic script was used by Moses to write the Ten Commandments on the tablets of stone.

It is still not known whether Gardiner's 1916 guess was correct, plausible though it is. For some decades after Petrie's discoveries in Sinai, the inscriptions were taken to be the 'missing link' between the Egyptian hieroglyphs and the cuneiform alphabet at Ugarit and the Phoenician alphabet. But it seems unconvincing that lowly—and presumably illiterate—miners in out-of-the-way Sinai should have created an alphabet; prima facie, they seem to be unlikely inventors. Subsequent discoveries in Lebanon and Israel have shown the Sinaitic theory of the alphabet to be a romantic fiction. These inscriptions, dated to the 17th and 16th centuries BC—a little earlier than the proto-Sinaitic inscriptions—suggest that the people then living in the land of Canaan were the inventors of the alphabet, which would be reasonable. They were cosmopolitan traders at the crossroads of the Egyptian, Hittite, Babylonian, and Cretan empires; they were not wedded to an existing writing system; they needed a script that was easy to learn, quick to write, and unambiguous. Although unproven, it is probable that the (proto-)Canaanites were the first to use an alphabet.

In the late 1990s, however, the picture was further complicated by new discoveries in Egypt itself; and a revised version of the Gardiner theory now seems plausible. In 1999, two Egyptologists, John Coleman Darnell and his wife, Deborah, announced that they had found examples of what appeared to be alphabetic writing at Wadi el-Hol, west of Thebes, while they were surveying ancient travel routes in the southern Egyptian desert. The date of the inscriptions is c.1900–1800BC, which places them considerably earlier than the inscriptions from Lebanon and Israel, and makes them the earliest known alphabetic writings.

The two short inscriptions are written in a Semitic script and, according to the experts, the letters were most probably developed in a fashion similar to a semi-cursive form of the Egyptian script. The writer is thought to have been a scribe travelling with a group of mercenaries (there were many such mercenaries working for the pharaohs). If the Darnell theory turns out to be correct, then it appears that the alphabetic idea was after all inspired by the Egyptian hieroglyphs and invented in Egypt, rather than in Palestine. This latest evidence is by no means conclusive, however, and the search for more alphabetic inscriptions in Egypt continues.

6 The family of alphabets

From its unclear origins on the eastern shores of the Mediterranean, writing employing the alphabetic principle spread—westwards (via Greek) to the Romans and thence to modern Europe, eastwards (via Aramaic, in all probability) to India and thence to Southeast Asia. By the 20th century, as a consequence of colonial empires, most of the world's peoples except the Chinese and Japanese were writing in alphabetic scripts. These employ on average between 20 and 40 basic signs; the smallest, Rotokas, used in Papua New Guinea, has 12 letters, the largest, Khmer, used in Cambodia, has 74 letters.

The western alphabetic link between the Greeks and the Romans was Etruscan—as is clear from the early Greek letter-forms inscribed on Etruscan objects dating from the 7th century BC, which were then borrowed for early Latin inscriptions. This early acquisition from Greek accounts for the differences between some modern European letter forms and the modern Greek letters, which are based on a later Greek alphabet known as Ionian that became standard in Greece in 403–2BC. The eastern alphabetic link is indicated by the fact that in Mesopotamia, by the 5th century BC, many cuneiform documents carried a notation of their substance in the 22 letters of the Aramaic alphabet, inked onto the tablet with a writing brush. From the time of Alexander the Great onwards, cuneiform was increasingly superseded by Aramaic; it eventually fell into disuse around the beginning of the Christian era, with the last cuneiform inscription dated AD 75. In Egypt, fairly soon after that, the Coptic alphabet (consisting of 24 Greek letters plus 6 letters borrowed from Egyptian demotic script) supplanted Egyptian hieroglyphs; the last Egyptian hieroglyphic inscription is dated AD 394.

The Aramaic script is the ancestor of modern Arabic, the sacred script of Islam, and of modern ('square') Hebrew script, as used in Israel (see **8**). (A second Hebrew script, known as 'old Hebrew', evolved from the Phoenician script and disappeared from secular use with the dispersion of the Jews in the 6th century BC.) The first independent Arab kingdom, that of the Nabataeans, centred on Petra in modern Jordan, spoke a form of Arabic but wrote in the Aramaic script. The presence of certain distinctively Arabic forms and words in these Aramaic inscriptions eventually gave way to the writing of the Arabic language in Nabataean Aramaic script. This was the precursor of the Arabic script, which arose during the first half of the 1st millennium AD and replaced the Aramaic script (see **40**).

Both the Arabic and Hebrew scripts write only the consonants, not the vowels, in their respective Semitic languages, using 28 letters in Arabic and 22 in Hebrew. Thus, the three letters in modern Hebrew that stand for *ktb* or *ktv* can take the meanings: 'katav' (I wrote), 'kotav' (I write, a writer), 'katoov' (written), 'kitav' (letters, script), and even 'kitovet' (address), 'kitoobah' (marriage certificate), or 'katban' (scribe). In practice, however, various additional signs have been developed to aid the reader in pronouncing the Hebrew and Arabic vowels. The commonest of these is a system of dots placed above and below a letter, referred to as 'vowel points' or *matres lectionis* (Latin for 'mothers of reading').

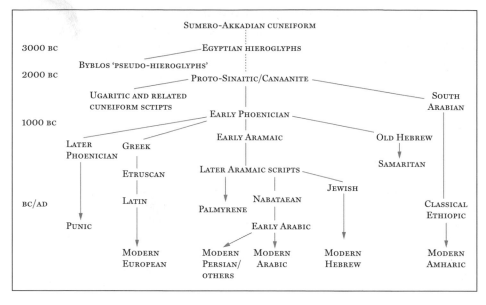

Fig. 5 The evolution of the main European alphabetic scripts adapted from John F. Healey, *The Early Alphabet* (British Museum Press: 1990). © Andrew Robinson. Line drawing by Chartwell Illustrators.

The time chart in Fig. 5 shows the main lines of emergence of the modern alphabetic scripts from the Proto-Sinaitic/Canaanite scripts of the 2nd millennium BC. It does not include the Indian scripts and their Southeast Asian derivatives, since their connection with Aramaic is problematic and, strictly speaking, unproven. (The earliest Indian scripts, leaving aside the undeciphered Indus Valley writing, are Kharosthi and Brahmi, used in the rock edicts of the emperor Ashoka in the 3rd century BC.) Nor does the chart show later alphabets such as the Cyrillic alphabet used in Russia, which was adapted from the Greek alphabet in the 9th century AD (*see* **37**), the Korean Hangul alphabet invented by King Sejong in the 15th century (*see* **43**), or the so-called Cherokee alphabet (really a syllabary), invented by a Native American, Sequoya, in the US around 1821. Also excluded are runes, since the origin of the runic alphabet, in the 2nd century AD or earlier, though clearly influenced by the Roman alphabet, is not known (*see* **28**).

7 Chinese and Japanese writing

If great claims are made for the power of the alphabet, even greater ones attach to Chinese writing. The evident complexity of the system encourages the notion that it operates quite differently from other modern writing systems. The obscurity of its origins—which may or may not have involved foreign stimulus from, for example, Mesopotamian writing—reinforces its apparent uniqueness. The antiquity of the modern Chinese characters, many of which are clearly recognizable in the

Shang 'oracle bone' inscriptions of about 1200 BC, further supports this view, abetted by nationalist pride in the system's exceptional longevity, which exceeds that of cuneiform and equals that of the Egyptian hieroglyphs.

The most important claim is that Chinese characters are 'ideographic'—a word now generally avoided by scholars in favour of the more specific 'logographic'. That is, the characters are thought to be capable of communicating ideas without the intervention of phoneticism or indeed spoken language. Thus, Chinese speakers of Mandarin and Cantonese who do not know each other's 'dialect' and cannot talk to each other are said to be able to communicate in writing through Chinese characters. Some scholars (both Chinese and westerners) have even claimed that the same scenario applies to Chinese, Japanese, Korean, and Vietnamese speakers, whose languages differ greatly but who have shared the use of Chinese characters in their scripts. This, of course, would be inconceivable for equivalent English, French, German, and Italian speakers, who also share one (Roman) script. The implication is that the Chinese writing system works in a completely different way from scripts with a large phonographic component: writing systems are therefore said to come in two fundamental varieties, one ideographic (e.g. Chinese), the other phonographic (e.g. alphabets).

Each of these claims is false. No 'full' writing system, as already explained, can be divorced from the sounds of a spoken language. Written Chinese is based on Mandarin, also known as Putonghua ('common speech'), a language spoken by over 70 per cent of Chinese—hence the myth of the universal intelligibility of Chinese characters. A speaker of Cantonese wishing to communicate in writing with a speaker of Mandarin must learn Mandarin as well as the characters. The characters have both a phonetic and a semantic component, which readers must learn to recognize. The former gives a clue to the pronunciation of the character, the latter to its meaning. Generally, the phonetic component proves a better guide to pronunciation than the semantic does to meaning—contrary to predictions based on the ideographic notion of Chinese.

The Japanese language differs greatly from the Chinese, phonologically, grammatically, and syntactically. Even so, the Japanese based their writing system on the Chinese characters, as remarked earlier. In borrowing the thousands of Chinese signs during the early centuries of the 1st millennium AD, the Japanese altered the original Chinese pronunciation in particular ways corresponding to the sounds of the Japanese language. (Indeed 'kanji', the Japanese word for Chinese character, is an approximation of the Mandarin term 'hanzi'.) Eventually, they invented two fairly small sets of supplementary phonetic signs, the syllabic 'kana' (46 'hiragana' and 46 'katakana')—the forms of which are actually simplified versions of the Chinese characters—in order to make clear how the characters were to be pronounced in Japanese and how to transcribe native words. It would have been simpler, one might reasonably think, if the Japanese had used *only* these invented signs and had abandoned the Chinese characters altogether—but this would have entailed the rejection of an ancient writing system of huge prestige. Just as a knowledge of Latin was until quite recently a *sine qua non* for the educated European, so a familiarity with Chinese has always been considered essential by the Japanese literati.

8 Electronic writing

As the 6th millennium of recorded civilization opened, Mesopotamia was again at the centre of historical events. Where once, at the birth of writing, the

Fig. 6 A clay tablet in cuneiform script from Nineveh, in northern Iraq, written in the 7th century BC, showing part of the epic of Gilgamesh. Associated with Ashurbanipal, king of Assyria, the tablets were identified in 1872 by George Smith in the British Museum's collections. © The Trustees of the British Museum, Dept. of Western Asiatic Antiquities (No. K 3375)

statecraft of absolute rulers like Hammurabi and Darius was recorded in Sumerian, Babylonian, Assyrian, and Old Persian cuneiform on clay and stone, now the Iraq wars against Saddam Hussein generated millions of mainly alphabetic words on paper and on the World Wide Web written in a babel of world languages.

Yet, although today's technologies of writing are immeasurably different from those of the 3ʳᵈ millennium BC, its linguistic principles have not changed very much since the composition of the Sumerian epic of Gilgamesh (*see* **21**). However, the seismic impact of electronic writing and archiving on information distribution and research has polarized the debate about the correct definition of 'writing'. Must 'full' writing depend on a spoken language, as maintained in this essay? Or can it float free of its phonetic anchor?

Although some people persist in thinking that the digital revolution since the 1990s has made little or no difference to what happens in their minds when they actually read, write, and think, others as stoutly maintain that the digitization of writing is radically altering our absorption of knowledge and will at last usher in the ideographic utopia imagined by the philosopher Gottfried Wilhelm Leibniz in the 1690s: 'As regards signs, I see … clearly that it is to the interest of the Republic of Letters and especially of students, that learned men should reach agreement on signs' (Mead and Modley, 58). Moreover, this faith in the increasing intelligence of computers—with their ubiquitous pictographic and logographic icons—chimes with many scholars' growing respect for the intelligence behind ancient scripts. Down with the monolithic 'triumph of the alphabet', they say, and up with Chinese characters, Egyptian hieroglyphs, and Mayan glyphs, with their hybrid mixtures of pictographic, logographic, and phonetic signs. This conviction has in turn encouraged a belief in the need to see each writing system as enmeshed within a whole culture, instead of viewing it simply as a technical solution to a problem of efficient visual representation of the culture's language. Although one may or may not share the belief in the power of digitization, and one may remain sceptical about the expressive virtues of logography, this holistic view of writing systems is surely a healthy development that reflects the real relationship between writing and society in all its subtlety and complexity.

BIBLIOGRAPHY

[British Museum,] *Reading the Past* (1990)

M. Coe, *Breaking the Maya Code*, 2e (1999)

P. Daniels and W. Bright, eds., *The World's Writing Systems* (1996)

J. Darnell, ed., *Two Early Alphabetic Inscriptions from the Wadi El-Hol* (2006)

J. DeFrancis, *The Chinese Language* (1984)

—— *Visible Speech* (1989)

A. Gardiner, 'The Egyptian Origin of the Semitic Alphabet', *Journal of Egyptian Archaeology*, 3 (1916), 1–6

R. Harris, *The Origin of Writing* (1986)

S. Houston, ed., *The First Writing* (2004)

M. Mead and R. Modley, 'Communication Among All People, Everywhere', *Natural History*, 77.7 (1968), 56–63

M. Pope, *The Story of Decipherment*, 2e (1999)

A. Robinson, *The Story of Writing*, 2e (2007)

—— *Lost Languages*, 2e (2009)

—— *Writing and Script* (2009)

F. de Saussure, *Course in General Linguistics* (1983)

J. M. Unger, *Ideogram* (2004)

M. Ventris, 'A Note on Decipherment Methods', *Antiquity*, 27 (1953), 200–6

2

The Sacred Book

CARL OLSON

1 Introduction

Adherents recognize a book as sacred in hindsight after compilers and editors have assembled its parts. A particular book is considered sacred when adherents acknowledge the authoritative nature of the source of the book, which they may believe to be divine or human. When a collection of messages is considered sacred, it is set apart from other types of literature, which are often considered profane or mundane. A sacred book is complete and does not need to be complemented by anything else, although it may invite a commentary to expound its inner meaning. By its very nature, a sacred book represents order, unity, and perfection. A sacred book is also powerful because it can overawe, overwhelm, or inspire a reader or hearer with its message. Although such power is ambivalent because it is both creative and destructive, it also possesses the ability to affect things or persons by forcing them to move or behave in a certain manner, which is indicative of the book's dynamic power to transform people and events. The power inherent within a sacred book contains, moreover, a compulsive aspect because it can coerce and prohibit actions; in short, it exercises control over people and their behaviour. Because of its foundation in an authoritative source—divine or human—readers or listeners are persuaded by the sacred book's message, and they are convinced by its truthfulness to accept it and to live their lives according to its injunctions.

Since a sacred book postulates a fundamental religious message, or makes claims without demonstration, it can function as a performative act in the sense of making something happen, which can assume the guise of faith discovered, knowledge gained, or salvation secured. If to postulate is to take an action that is grounded in a social context, it involves performing a sacred utterance. Lacking material significata (on some levels at least), the sacred book is invulnerable to falsification by reference to natural data within the world. Although a sacred book cannot be falsified by empirical or logical means, it also cannot be objectively or logically verified. Instead of looking at the book as an object that is sacred, it is preferable to concentrate on the sanctity of its religious discourse. It is thus, for instance, not Jesus or the Buddha who are sacred; rather, the discourse proclaiming them respectively divine or enlightened is sacred. This does not preclude the sacred book from being treated with respect and even reverence as a sacred object by its adherents, but it refocuses the notion of the sacred book onto its discourse. Although the sacred book can be discovered in many religious traditions, this essay, for reasons of economy, only considers the formative periods of the major monotheistic traditions (Judaism, Christianity, and Islam), Hinduism, and Buddhism.

Because of the large number of sacred books throughout the world, it is impossible to cover all the worthy candidates. Among the sacred books excluded from this survey are: the *Book of Mormon* revealed to Joseph Smith of the Latter-Day Saints, which shares its status with the Bible for Mormons; the sacred texts of Zoroastrianism: the *Yasna*, *Yashts*, and *Venidad*; the Confucian classics, the products of sages, which include the following five classics: *I-Ching* (Book of Changes); *Shih-Ching* (Book of Poetry); *Shu-Ching* (Book of History); *Li-Chi* (Book of Rites); and *Ch'un-Ch'iu* (Spring and Autumn Annals); the sacred books of Taoism contained in the *Tao Tsang*, a depository of texts that contains such classics as the *Tao Te Ching*, attributed to Lao Tzu, and the *Chuang Tzu*, named for the sage of the text.

2 Formative Judaic tradition

Passed by oral tradition from one generation to another over centuries, the sacred writings of the ancient Jews did not constitute a single sacred scripture: their literature represented a collection of 24 separate books that they came to call the Bible (Gk *biblia*, 'books')—not the Old Testament, which was assembled later by Christians from a prejudicial and theological position. The separate books of the ancient Jews represented a narrative about God's interaction with His chosen people. Within this dramatic narrative, the major themes of Israel's faith were related, which included the promise of the ancient patriarchs to be faithful to their deity, the divine deliverance of Israel from Egypt, divine guidance while wandering in the wilderness, the bestowing of the law at Sinai to the prophet Moses, and the inheritance of the promised land. This narrative is often shortened to and summarized as 'the Exodus event', which depicts God's redemptive work for his people, and not simply a matter of political liberation from servitude. The Exodus event, during which God acted in history, functions as the sign of His revelation and divine presence. Divine intervention for the benefit of His chosen people means that history becomes the acts of God and thus meaningful. Therefore, the narrative of God's active intervention in history informs the Jewish community about what God has done (past), what God is doing (present), and what God will do (future), which unifies the three moments of time into a meaningful configuration.

The ancient Jews referred to their collection of books as *Tanakh*, (*see* 8), a term derived from the first letters of all three divisions: Torah (Law), Nevi'im (prophets), and Kituvim (hagiographa). The initial, most important, and authoritative division is the Torah (Law, also meaning 'instruction', 'teaching'), which includes the so-called Five Books of Moses or the Pentateuch: Genesis, Exodus, Leviticus, Numbers, and Deuteronomy. Scholars refer to the Pentateuch as the Hexateuch, which is derived from the Greek term meaning 'five scrolls' (five books plus Joshua). The Torah represented God's gift to the people of Israel. This gift was, however, conditional upon the people's acceptance of the divine commandments and their obedience to them as the chosen people.

God's scriptural gift to his chosen people was given in Hebrew, a divine language. However, that the Jews lost the language before the Bible was finalized is evident in the Book of Daniel, which was composed in Aramaic. By the post-Exilic period, Aramaic had become the preferred language for translating the Jewish scriptures, and the 2nd century BC marked a time when many Jews read a Greek Septuagint or an Aramaic version. An oral tradition which preceded the Jewish scriptures assumed the form of the scroll (Isa. 34:4) or a roll made of papyrus, leather, or parchment (Jer. 36:14; Ezek. 2:9). Hebrew writing used Canaanite characters, which were eventually replaced with an Aramaic form of script known as the 'square script'. The process of writing was accomplished by using metal implements for the hard surfaces of stone and metal. A stylus was used for writing on clay or wax, a brush for various materials with paint or ink, and a reed pen with ink.

The prophetic literature is divided into the earlier prophets of Joshua, Judges, Samuel, and Kings, while the later prophets are Isaiah, Jeremiah, Ezekiel, and the twelve minor prophets. Finally, the mixed collection called Ketubim (writings) includes works such as the Psalms, the Song of Solomon, and the moral stories of Job, Ruth, and Esther. The writings also include the wisdom of Proverbs and Ecclesiastes, and the historical Ezra-Nehemiah and Chronicles, with both sets of works representing two texts in a single collection. The final collecting, fixing, preservation, and canonization of the Pentateuch occurred during the Babylonian Exile (Ezra 7:14, 25), which was a period centuries removed from the events recounted in the books.

Modern biblical scholars view the Pentateuch as a composite work representing several major traditions that have been artfully woven together. Scholars have identified four main literary strands, signified by the letters J, E, D, and P. The J literary contribution represents the earliest source originating from the period of the early monarchy (950 BC), whereas the E sources can be dated to the time of the Northern Kingdom (about 750 BC). The D literary strand's best example is the book of Deuteronomy, which dates from the period of the Southern Kingdom (about 650 BC or even later). The P source refers to priestly influence, and dates from the time of the fall of the nation in 587 BC. The entire Pentateuch assumed its present shape around 400 BC. The Pentateuch's written stage was preceded by at least three centuries of oral transmission, and it came to be recognized as the written Law (Torah). The prophets and hagiographa became canonized after the destruction of the Second Temple.

Along with the written Law, Jews recognized an oral law that was developed by the Pharisaic teachers and their successors. The oral law took the form of scriptural exegesis. Rabbinic law was summarized in the Mishnah, while the *gemara* consisted of reports of broad discussions about the Mishnaic text, which was the basic text of the oral Torah. Dating to around the 3rd century AD and containing the legal teachings of the Tannaim, or earliest rabbinic authorities, the Mishnah is a collection of originally oral laws divided into six orders according to subject-matter, devoid of direct reference to the Pentateuch (written Torah). In addition, Rabbinic Judaism gave birth to the Talmud, containing analysis and elaboration of rabbinic lore (*aggadah*), which is prominent in the collection known as the Midrash that originated in the academies of Palestine and Babylonia. Within the Talmud, legal (*halakhah*) aspects dominate the text.

3 Formative Christian tradition

The early Christian community did not possess its own sacred book, and any such notion would have probably struck its members as strange. It did, however, make use of the Hebrew Bible, although it tended to read predictions of the Christ figure into the text. From the perspective of his followers, Jesus did not bring a scripture. His actions, charismatic persona, and message represent his revelation, or 'Good News', to the faithful. When a Christian scripture began to evolve its development was uneven, because of a lack of self-conscious effort and a consistent deliberation about what constituted a scripture.

The letters of Paul are the earliest extant Christian literature, dating from around the mid-1st century, and preserved and gathered into a collection by its end. These letters were called 'letters to the seven churches', because seven was a symbol of wholeness in the ancient world and in this context implied the entire Church. Although the letters are addressed to particular congregations and their problems, Paul's message is intended for a wider audience, an evolving community, and considers its struggle to survive in the hostile sociocultural environment of the Graeco-Roman world. For his message, Paul claimed that his authority came directly from Jesus, the resurrected Lord and Saviour.

Paul's letters were intended to be read aloud to an audience, which was also true of the Hebrew Bible and other documents of the New Testament. Within the context of the ancient Graeco-Roman world, all reading was performed aloud, as Paul instructed his letters should be read (1 Thess. 5:27). The sense of a text was thus to be gained by listening to its being proclaimed. When Paul's letters were read aloud, for instance to a church community, the letters evoked the apostle's presence.

In contrast to Paul's letters, the Gospels are more narratives and interpretations of the life and teachings of Jesus. The word 'gospel' is derived from the Greek word *evangelion*, which means 'good news'—in the New Testament this becomes the good news of salvation, rather than its prior meaning associated with the welfare of the emperor. The authority of these texts was grounded in the words and deeds of Jesus, which were preserved by memory and transmitted orally. The Gospels were composed by anonymous authors, who named their works after a disciple of Jesus, and they consisted of Mark (composed *c*.65–70), Matthew and Luke (*c*.80–90), and John (*c*.90–100). In an effort to collect and codify various traditions about Jesus and sayings attributed to him, each Gospel writer sought to interpret the meaning of Christianity for his specific constituencies. The anonymous authors derived their authority from the various communal traditions rooted in the teaching and deeds of Jesus. During their formative period, the Gospels were considered valuable historical testimonies; it was not until later that they were considered scripture. The traditions about Jesus were preserved by memory and circulated orally.

If the four Gospels are compared with each other, striking differences emerge between John and the synoptic (meaning that they present a common view) Gospels. Few of the events in Jesus' life recorded, for instance, in the synoptic Gospels are discovered in John. Besides missing events, the location and chronology of Jesus' ministry are different in John, along with style and language. The close literary relationship of the synoptics reflects another problem associated with their similarities. There is general agreement among scholars that Mark is the earliest and that Matthew and Luke used it as a foundation for their Gospels. In addition, the writer of Mark was not precisely an author but rather a redactor, connecting units of an oral tradition. Scholars tend to agree that much of Mark is discovered in Matthew and Luke: the arrangement and sequence of material support a theory of dependence on Mark, and numerous parallel passages indicate that Matthew and Luke tried to improve on Mark's literary style and language. Material missing in Mark is also found in Matthew and Luke. What accounts for the absent material in Mark? Scholars have rejected the possibility that they borrowed from each other, and have concluded that it would be more reasonable to assume they used an independent source. German scholars dubbed this source *quelle*, which was abbreviated to 'Q'. This means that Matthew and Luke used two sources: Mark and Q. Scholars think that Q was probably a written document because of the verbal agreements between the two Gospels. Scholars also tend to think that Q (dated around 50 AD) existed prior to Mark. In addition to Mark and Q, Matthew and Luke both had access to oral or written traditions independent of Mark: these are called the M and L sources.

Scholars arrived at this general consensus about the Gospels by using three types of criticism: source, form, and redaction. Source criticism examines the origins of the texts, whereas form criticism is a discipline that goes behind the written sources to examine the period of the oral tradition. Redaction criticism is an analysis of the editorial work in relation to sources.

In addition to the four Gospels and the letters of Paul, what came to be called the New Testament also included the Acts of the Apostles, letters of Peter, James, and Jude, and the Book of Revelation, which was attributed to John, author of the Gospel. As the Christian Church developed, numerous prescriptive lists of authentic texts existed in many Christian assemblies (*ekklesiai*). These various lists were called canons (Gk *kanones*, 'measures', 'standards'), so called because connected with criteria associated with authenticity. The formation of the fourfold Gospels occurred, for instance, by the late 2nd century, and was generally accepted by the faithful in the 3rd. The Gospels gained scriptural status as a group rather than as individual texts—a development suggesting that their authority was grounded in their collective nature.

If the early period of the primitive Christian Church emphasized the oral nature of Jesus' message, why were the Gospels committed to writing? New Testament scholars have offered several plausible reasons for a turn to writing the Gospels. The death of the apostles, or those closest to Jesus during his life, induced a fear about losing the tradition of Jesus. The developing Church wanted to know how to deal with persecution by learning from Jesus. The primitive Church also struggled to define and understand itself separately from Judaism. And it wondered how it could appeal to the Gentiles without losing its original Jewish identity. Finally, the problem associated with the delay of the *parousia* (second coming of Jesus) and the end of the world served as motivating factors in committing Jesus' message to writing.

Although Christianity was an apocalyptic sect within Palestinian Judaism and Jesus was a Palestinian Jew, the world of the New Testament was dominated by Greek language and culture; the language itself had been transformed from classical Attic Greek into *koinē* (common) or Hellenistic Greek, which became the language of the New Testament. Using material such as papyrus, parchment, or wooden tablets, Christians preferred the codex (book-like form), previously used for letter-writing and record-keeping, over the scroll employed in Judaism or for Greek literature. Scholars have offered several reasons for the adoption of the codex, such as economy, compactness, convenience, ease of reference, or usage of an already familiar medium and practical means of communication. A four-Gospel codex was used to preserve the best-known and most widely accepted texts for everyday usage as handbooks for the Christian community.

As New Testament texts gained canonical status, the issue of a sacred language never really developed because Christian scripture spread quickly and into a variety of vernaculars. This situation changed when Jerome translated the Bible into Latin during the 4th century. The Latin version of the scriptures became the sacred language of the Roman Catholic Church until Martin Luther, a former Catholic priest turned Protestant reformer, translated the Bible into German with the purpose of making the text more accessible to ordinary people in the 16th century.

4 Formative Islamic tradition

Fifteen years after his marriage to an older woman, the prophet Muḥahmmad, then 40 years old, began to have strange experiences in a cave on Mount Hira, located outside the city of Mecca in Arabia. Some experiences came to him as visions, others as vivid dreams, and some as words on his heart, without his imagining that he had heard anything. An early vision was that of a glorious being standing erect in the sky, who Muhammad thought was God. Muḥammad later interpreted a voice which spoke to him from behind a veil as being an angel that he finally identified with the angel Gabriel.

When he received his first revelation (96.1–5), Muḥammad was commanded by the heavenly messenger to speak, and he refused at first. After a second command, he asked what he should recite; at the third command, he spoke the 96th *sūra* of the Qur'ān. The term 'recite' (*iqra*) is derived from the same Arabic root as *Qur'ān*, which implies a verbal revelation that is closely related to inspiration. Although the command to recite implies that public worship was to be instituted, when Muḥammad began his public preaching in 613 and presented himself to the people of Mecca as God's messenger, his message was met with opposition. Yet he eventually won adherents to his message about the power and goodness of God, the coming final day of judgement, the need to respond to God with gratitude and worship, and his own vocation as the final prophet.

The process of revelation is called *wahy* in Arabic; it embodies the connotation of verbal inspiration through the mind or heart (26.193–5). Muslims believe that the revelation of the Qur'ān is based on a 'heavenly book' that is preserved in the presence of God, and it is called the 'Mother of the Book' (43.1–4) (*see* **40**). The aim of the revelation (6.19) is intended to be a warning to hearers, and what is revealed is the order (*amr*) or command of God. The command is revealed in Arabic in order to facilitate understanding. The best way for a person to receive the message is to memorize it, a practice that keeps the revelation in one's mind.

According to the orthodox understanding of its origin, the Qur'ān represents the eternal word of God in book form. The prophet Muḥammad was not the author of the uncreated word; he was only its recipient. In fact, Muḥammad is referred to as 'the illiterate prophet' (7.157–8) in order to emphasize that it would have been impossible for him to compose it. The Qur'ān was revealed periodically over a period of about twenty years, not all at one time. The angel Gabriel gave the words of the revelation, although Muḥammad did not write the words himself. There are Islamic traditions that refer to others writing the revelation on available material—such as stones, bones, parchment, leather, palm leaves, and the hearts of men—which led to diverse writings inviting assembly into a coherent collection. According to a traditional account of the collection of the pieces of the revelation, after the battle of Yamanah, not long after Muhammad's death, many reciters of the revelation were killed. 'Umar ibn al-Khattāb, who was to become the second caliph, became alarmed about preserving the contents of the revelation, and suggested to Abū Bakr, the first caliph, that it be collected and written down. Zayd ibn Thābit, who was commissioned by Abū Bakr, began to collect the revelation, and the efforts that he initiated led to four early collections in different locations; but none of these texts has survived. Because of serious differences among these four collections, the third caliph, 'Uthmān, urged an end to disputes caused by textual variations by commissioning a revised text. A guiding principle in resolving disputed versions was the preference given to the Quraish tribal dialect of the prophet Muhammad.

There is a twofold separation of the Qur'ān into a ritual division of 30 approximately equal portions; it is also divided into 114 *sūras* (a term of Syrian origin, meaning 'writing' or 'text of scripture'). As a general rule, the title of a *sūra* has no reference to the subject matter of the text. The heading is instead taken from some prominent term in the *sūra*, such as 'The Bees' (16) or 'The Cave' (18). Each *sūra* is dated to either the Meccan or Medinan period, according to where the prophet was living at the time of the revelation. With the exception of *sūra* 11, all *sūras* begin with the *bismillah* phrase: 'In the name of God, the Merciful, the Compassionate'. In 29 of the *sūras*, this is followed by mysterious letters or a letter of the alphabet. Each *sūra* is divided into verses (*āyāt*, 'sign'). The *sūras* are written in rhymed prose in verses without metre or definitely fixed length; they end with a rhyme or assonance. The Qur'ān itself acknowledges the composite nature of the *sūras* when it refers to the piecemeal nature of its delivery (17.106).

Within the *sūras*, Allah speaks often in the first person singular (51.56). Sometimes God is referred to in the third person, and some passages are clearly spoken by angels (19.65), but only in a few passages does Muhammad actually speak (27.93). The orthodox position is that the Qur'ān is the literal word of Allah, because it is believed that God is speaking through the angels and the prophet.

A puzzling feature of the Qur'ān to outsiders is its doctrine of abrogation, which stipulates that a later verse might nullify an earlier one. This doctrine fits into a cultural context in which people accepted the existence of spirits and a satanic being that might have deluded Muhammad into believing that he had received a revelation when in fact he received a demonic message. Such a false passage could be corrected by a later revelation that nullifies the earlier revelation and replaces it with a corrected version in some cases.

The revelation was given in Arabic, or the language of God, according to Muslim tradition, and it was collected in the form of the codex. Arabic presented linguistic challenges for readers because of a lack of vowel signs, diacritical marks, and other orthographic signs, which were necessary in order to differentiate similarly formed consonants. The Qur'ān's language is pre-Islamic Arabic.

A non-revelatory body of literature distinct from the Qur'ān is the *ḥadīth* (a term that embodies the connotation of something 'new', 'coming to pass', and 'occurrence'). It developed to mean 'tradition' in the form of a brief report about what the prophet said, did, approved, or disapproved, although it may also include information in Arabic and preserved in codices about his companions. Besides its textual aspect, the *ḥadīth* consisted of a transmissional chain (*isnād*), such as the following example: A says that he heard it from B, who received it on the authority of C, who said this on the authority of D that the prophet said. These reports were accepted as authoritative secondary sources of Islam by the middle of the 9th century. Scholars collected, sifted, and systematized the traditions until six collections became authoritative. When deciding which reports were authentic, scholars focused on the transmissional chain in an attempt to assess the character and reliability of the transmitters' memories. They also considered the continuity of the transmission and whether or not each link in the transmission was strong and whether any links were broken. The *ḥadīth* is considered coeval and consubstantial with the *sunnah* (lit. 'travelled path') of the prophet, which embodies his exemplary conduct. The prophetic *sunnah* represents reports of Muḥammad's being asked to decide a problem for which no precedent existed. It thereby represents a living tradition for each generation of Muslims, and serves as the norm of the community in the sense of functioning as agreed social practice and social consensus (*ijmā'*). It is possible to differentiate *sunnah* and *ḥadīth* because the latter represents a report and something theoretical, whereas the former is the same report after it acquires a normative quality and becomes a practical principle as the non-verbal transmission of tradition. Besides the revelation, the Islamic tradition thus recognizes the *sunnah*, or exemplary conduct, of the prophet as a standard for behaviour.

5 Formative Hindu tradition

Ancient Indian religious literature can be distinguished as the revealed (*śruti*) and that which is remembered (*smṛti*). The revealed literature includes the Vedas, whereas the remembered body of literature includes the following: Dharma Sūtras (approximate dates of composition 600–200BC), the epic *Mahābhārata* (composed between approximately 300 BC and AD 300), the epic *Rāmāyaṇa* (composed between 200 BC and AD 200), and Purāṇas, which began to be composed around AD 400 (*see* **41**).

The Vedic literature consists of four collections: Rig, Sāma, Yajur, and Atharva. Each of these collections of hymns is further divided into four revealed (*śruti*) sections: Saṃhita (*mantra* or sacred formula/utterance collection), Brāhmaṇa (theological and ritual commentary), Āraṇyaka (forest or wilderness texts), and Upaniṣad (speculative and secret philosophical texts). It is believed that divine beings revealed this literature orally to ancient sages (*rishis*), who heard them, preserved them within their memory, and passed the revealed hymns on to further generations by oral transmission. Eventually, the revealed hymns were written down in order to preserve and protect them from faulty memory and the vicissitudes of time. Although some Vedic seers attached their names to poems, readers should not construe this signature as a claim of authorship. It is merely an acknowledgement of the identity of the person who received the revelation. The divinely revealed origin of the Vedas gives this body of literature an unquestionable authenticity and authority over other bodies of literature that historically followed it.

The Rig Veda is the oldest collection of verses, consisting of 1,028 hymns, arranged in ten books called *maṇḍalas* (circles). Parts of Books 1 and 10 are the latest additions to the entire corpus followed by Book 9, which embodies hymns recited during the Soma sacrifice. The other books (2–7) are designated the family collections because they were preserved within family clans that memorized and transmitted them for future generations. Book 8 contains several more short family collections, representing the literary products of ancient sages or their patrilinear descendants. In fact, the various books are arranged according to author (i.e. family or clan), deity, and metre. In addition, hymns to specific deities are arranged according to length, with the longest at the beginning of the book. If hymns are of equal length, the hymn with a longer metre is placed first.

It is possible that the Rig Veda antedates the introduction and common use of iron, which means that its origin can be dated to around 1200 BC. According to internal textual evidence, the Vedas originated in northern India and spread to the Punjab and more eastern regions between *c.*1500 and *c.*400 BC. Members of the Angirasa and Kāṇva clans formed the bulk of its poets, who treated the hymns as the clans' private property. In time, Vedic schools called *Śākhās* (branches) developed to control and protect the transmission of texts, which usually resulted in a school adhering to a specific text. These various schools created an interpretive body of literature as reflected in various Brāhmaṇic and *sūtra* types of literature.

The Sāma Veda, for instance, represents material drawn from the Rig Veda with the exception of 75 hymns. This collection of hymns is named for the chants (*sāmans*), which represent the earliest written form of music in Indian history, and is recited during the Soma sacrifice. As the priests recite these verses during the rite, they modify the verses. Finally, the Sāma Veda consists of two parts: an actual text (*arcika*) and the melodies (*gāna*).

The sacred formulas (*mantras*, lit. 'instruments of the mind') repeated by priests in rituals form the bulk of the Yajur Veda, or third Vedic collection. The sacred formulas are arranged according to ritual usage, not numerically. By reciting the sacred *mantras* (syllables, words, or verses), the chanter expresses eternal wisdom and the pre-existent sacred word itself. There were four major types of *mantra* chant: ṛcs, *yajuses*, *sāmans*, and *atharvans*, which conformed respectively to each of the major Vedic collections. The importance of *mantras* can be partially grasped by examining Hinduism's two types of speech. The first type was that of the Asuras, or demonic beings: it was without form or order, uncontrollable and inarticulate, similar to the nature of the demonic forces of existence. The Vedic *mantra* was its exact opposite.

The Atharva Veda, or fourth Veda, consists of a collection of hymns focusing on magical and healing rites. In addition, there are hymns related to harmful sorcery and to speculative subjects; others are concerned with rites of passage (e.g. initiation and marriage); there are also two appendices. In sharp contrast to the Rig Veda, the collection begins with short works and increases to longer hymns.

Ancient Indian deities gave the Vedic poets a visionary insight that was conceived as a heart/mind transmission from a superior party to another inferior receiver. After receiving it from higher beings, the poet recites/chants the hymn. By orally reciting a hymn, the poet sends his inner spirit back to the realm of the divine beings who originally inspired the poet. Moreover, the uttering of a hymn about a particular deity sends that hymn back to its source, completing the cycle.

Because the ancient Vedic schools represented a priestly family or clan from a specific geographical area, tribe, or kingdom, and the schools distinguished themselves by their ritual procedures and pronunciation of words, there was no single or original canon of texts established and authenticated by an authoritative body of religious leaders. What we have are plural textual canons of different schools. Thus, the Vedic canon was a collective entity of Vedic texts used by various schools. Vedic literature became a canon by about 400 BC. There is evidence that it was acknowledged by the two grammarians: Pāṇini and Patañjali around 150 BC. Prior to this acknowledgement, the Vedas were also mentioned in the Pāli canon of Buddhism around 250 BC.

Attached to each of the four collections of the Vedas were Brāhmaṇas that explained the complex ritual system. Texts were added to various Brāhmaṇas to explain further the esoteric aspects of the rites. Some of these additional texts were called Āraṇyakas, others were called Upaniṣads, although there was no sharp distinction between these new kinds of text. In addition to treating the ritual system, these esoteric texts also engaged in forms of cosmological and metaphysical speculation. Much like the four Vedas, these esoteric teachings were preserved orally for generations before assuming a written form. As with the Brāhmaṇic texts, particular Upaniṣads are associated with one of the four collections of the Vedas. The Aitareya and Kauṣītakī Upaniṣads are directly connected, for instance, with the Rig Veda, whereas the Kaṭha and Maitrāyanī Upaniṣads are associated with the Black Yajur Veda, and the Bṛhadāraṇyaka and Īśa Upaniṣads with the White Yajur Veda.

The Hindu religious tradition acknowledges the existence of 108 Upaniṣads, but it is generally agreed that there are thirteen major texts. Although it appears that the Upaniṣads evolved from the Āraṇyakas (forest texts) and it is difficult to distinguish between them, the oldest Upaniṣads are the Bṛhadāraṇyaka and Chāndogya. The Aitareya, Taittirīya, and Kauṣītaka followed these texts historically. This second group was subsequently followed by the composition of the following examples: Kena, Īśa, Kaṭha, Śvetāśvatara, Praśna Muṇḍaka, Mahānārayana, Māṇḍūkya, and Maitrī. After the appearance of these thirteen major texts, many later Upaniṣads manifested a sectarian character by focusing on deities such as Śiva and Viṣṇu.

The meaning of the term *Upaniṣad* suggests sitting down near a teacher to receive secret instructions characteristic of an intimate student-teacher relationship. In addition to being secret and personal, the teaching context was characterized as relational and dialogical. Overall, the Upaniṣads are not the result of a single mind, but rather represent the pedagogical efforts of many ancient Indian teachers during a historical period of great social, economic, and religious change.

The Upaniṣads are called *Vedānta* (not to be confused with the historically later philosophical school of thought), because they represent the deepest secrets of the Vedas. Although the Upaniṣads develop some notions of the Vedas, they also introduce new ideas (at least in a primitive form) that shape Indian religious culture, and they transform some of the old notions into something fresh and innovative, such as karma (law of cause and effect), rebirth, immortal self (Ātman), ultimate reality (Brahman), and path to liberation (*mokṣa*).

A prevalent theme in the Upaniṣads is the importance of knowing. Although there are some Upaniṣads that discuss the centrality of devotion to a deity and the necessity of divine grace for salvation, such as the Śvetāśvatara Upaniṣad, most Upaniṣads emphasize the importance of knowledge for attaining liberation, which is to be recovered, because the truth—the object of knowledge—is always present; it has been merely lost, and needs to be recovered and rediscovered. This is not an empirical or rational mode of knowledge, but instead an intuitive insight into the true nature of reality, which is a self-validating, transcendent, and infinite kind of knowledge.

The claim that the Vedic hymns were revealed oral literature suggests that the poets did not create the hymns themselves. They saw or heard the hymns from a deep, mysterious force, and received these messages with their mind and/or heart, which enabled them to grasp the true nature of things. The subtle structure of knowing symbolized by the human mind represented a transformative force that could effect change, produce desired results, and establish connections between humans and divine beings. Likewise, the human heart, which was considered similar to the mind, enabled a person to see what was not normally observable or knowable by ordinary social beings. These gifted, visionary poets were able to receive the revelation because they possessed an insight (*dhī*) or ability to see concealed truths. Once they possessed their visions, the poets were able to express these truths in the perfect language of Sanskrit, which allowed them an opportunity to conform themselves to the divine forces giving the messages. The visionary message received by the inspired Vedic poets also enabled them to view the cosmos as an integrated totality held together by a hidden structure (*ṛta*) that was closely associated with the truth (*satya*) and *tapas* (creative heat), that ushered into being the cosmos and continuously renewed life. Therefore, the inspired Vedic poets were in close touch with the very fabric of the cosmos and the creative forces that sustained it.

These Vedic poets were also the masters and custodians of Sanskrit, which was the language of the revealed hymns and thereby sacred. Sanskrit was inextricably linked with the inspired poets because it was associated with perfection. Sanskrit embodied *brahman*, a mysterious and hidden power that was not only contained within the words of the sacred language, but also functioned to hold the universe together. The power of *brahman* was revealed to the visionary poets. This was considered a sacred power that was directly associated with the sanctity of the scripture preserved in Sanskrit. Nonetheless, the scripture's sanctity was not directly related to its intelligibility to either its hearer or its reciter. The words' holiness was more probably inversely related to their comprehensibility. In other words, strange, mysterious, and unintelligible terms were considered more powerful. Moreover, the sanctity of a term was not something extra added to a word; rather, the holiness of a term was intrinsic to the word.

The importance of poetic inspiration and knowledge is further evident in the Sanskrit term *veda*, because it possesses the root meaning of 'to see', 'vision', and 'knowing'. A master of the *veda* is a person able to see that which is concealed. In short, such a person can witness the eternal, powerful, divine forces of the universe. When the term *veda* is used as a noun, it signifies sacred knowledge. Becoming master or recipient of the *veda* is a transforming experience, because knowing the truth radically changes a person. This points to the powerful nature of knowledge—a conviction that runs like a thread throughout Indian cultural history.

Because of its nature and ramifications, revealed literature takes precedence over literature based on human memory. When there is a discrepancy between the two bodies of literature, a person must rely on revealed literature for guidance because it possesses greater authority than remembered literature. Holding revealed literature in higher regard than remembered literature because of its source in divine revelation and inspiration does not imply that the meaning of revealed literature is readily apparent and easy to discern. Scholarly commentaries are necessary to elicit a hymn's meaning. Within the history of Indian culture, there is a long tradition of textual commentary and interpretation by learned individuals.

The revealed and remembered bodies of literature originated within the cultural context of an oral tradition, which means that the hymns of the Vedas were passed down from one generation to the next via oral transmission after the particular hymns were memorized. In this sense, much of Indian classical literature is related to memory, regardless of its revealed nature. In order to enhance memory and preserve the sacred hymns, priestly scholars devised elaborate methods to assist memory, and particular persons specialized in specific groups of texts to enhance the accuracy of their oral preservation. A person might, for instance, memorize each odd-numbered word of a hymn or every even-numbered term to enhance the correct transmission of the hymn.

Emphasis on the oral nature of ancient Indian sacred literature necessarily implies that scripture is not something written that can be reified. This suggests that scripture in India is not a well-defined entity with clearly established boundaries. The significance of and emphasis upon the oral transmission of hymns can be partially understood by the traditionally negative attitude towards writing in Indian culture. According to the ancient *Aitareya Āraṇyaka* (5.5.3), which originates in an esoteric section of a ritualistic Brahmanical text, the activity of writing is designated as ritually polluting and a person thus stained should avoid reciting the Vedas along with other polluting actions such as eating meat, seeing blood or a dead body, or after sexual intercourse. This attitude helps to explain the traditionally low social status of scribes in the culture.

Despite this negative attitude towards writing and the emphasis on oral transmission that continues into the present, the Vedas were written down around 1000 BC, according to Alberuni (973–1048), a learned scholar of Indian culture of his time period, in Kashmir. In the north, the earliest Indian MSS were composed on palm leaves using black ink; in the south, a stylus was used to scratch letters onto a leaf, which was subsequently blackened with soot. In Kashmir, birch bark was used, whereas other plant materials were used occasionally in Assam. Leather or parchment was avoided because their use involved the killing of animals and pollution, although Kashmiri Brahmins bound their birch bark books with leather. The words of the Vedas were written in the *devanāgiri* script (literally, the writing of the 'city of the gods').

6 Formative Buddhist tradition

There is basic agreement among scholars of Buddhism that an extraordinary and charismatic man lived around the 6th to 5th centuries BC in India, during a period of profound political, social, and economic change. This man is Siddhārtha Gautama, who became known as the Buddha (enlightened one). Distressed by the fundamental problems of human existence, he discovered a solution to these difficulties, spent his life wandering from one place to another teaching, established a monastic community that preserved and expounded his teachings for future generations, and died at around the age of 80. A substantial literature based on his teachings evolved after his death (*see* **41**). Much of this claims to capture his actual teachings that were preserved in an oral tradition two centuries before being written down on pieces of bark, palm leaves, or other available material.

Because the Buddha gave instructions in local dialects, it would be inaccurate to refer to an original Buddhist language, although the closest thing was probably Old Māgadhī, which was the primary language for his teaching.

Pāli preserves Old Māgadhī, and it was the language used by missionaries when they took the Buddha's message to Sri Lanka, where it became accepted as a textual language. According to Sinhalese chronicles, writing of the Pāli canon began in the middle of the 1st century BC because of the decline of reciters, war, and famine; the monastic community preserved the canon on wood products bound together by leather strips.

The religious message contained in this literature is not very complicated: the Buddha provides some simple summaries of his basic teachings. These summaries were called the *dhamma* (Sanskrit *dharma*). The first summary of his teaching and analysis of human existence is embodied in the Four Noble Truths: (1) all life is suffering; (2) ignorant craving is the cause of suffering; (3) the attainment of *Nibbāna* (Sanskrit *Nirvāṇa*) ends suffering; (4) the Eightfold Path is the means of attaining the goal. This path is an interdependent way of wisdom, ethical/moral action, and meditation. The other summary of the Buddha's teachings is contained in the three marks of existence: (1) impermanence due to the cycle of causation that creates a constant state of flux; (2) suffering; (3) non-self. Since everything within the world is subject to the cycle of causation, there is nothing within the empirical realm that is permanent. Moreover, there is nothing permanent about the self, ego, or soul to which humans can cling. The Buddha's basic teaching is that it is important to cut out our love of self, which functions as a means of keeping us confined to this realm of suffering, cyclic causation, ignorance, rebirth, and suffering. The teachings are intended to carry a person to a non-empirical realm beyond the cycle of causation and rebirth, freedom from ignorant craving, and liberation from suffering. This transcendent state of *Nibbāna*, which represents the exact opposite of the characteristics of the world, can only be achieved while one is alive, with an enlightened person gaining a permanent state of liberation after death.

After the Buddha's death, a series of councils sought to establish the authenticity of his teachings and to create a canon of sacred literature. Buddhism was able to thrive, find stability, and expand within the social, political, and cultural context created by the Mauryan Dynasty (322–183BC), which advocated tolerance and support for many religious groups. King Aśoka gave royal support for Buddhism, converting to it late in his life. He transformed it into a missionary religion, which helped it to expand to countries in South Asia, and north to Central Asia and into China, whence it spread to Korea and then to Japan.

Ancient Buddhism traces the origin of its scripture to the personal insights of a human being. Moreover, as the historical Buddha became more revered and exalted in the minds and hearts of his followers, his words became a sacred body of literature due to its origin in the utterances of this historical person. There is thus nothing divinely unique about Buddhist scripture—it is not something that occurred once in history. From the Buddhist perspective, its scriptures are facts about the nature of human existence and the world: they are not the revelation of some deity. This lack of uniqueness should not be construed as a negative characteristic. Rather, Buddhists have tended to place the Buddha's teachings within a broader context because his discourses, based on his personal religious quest and discovery, occurred repeatedly during the lives of previous Buddhas. The historical Buddha merely rediscovered what was known by prior enlightened beings. Thus, the achievement of the historical Buddha represented an awareness of an eternal body of truths that had also been realized by prior figures. This type of belief undermines any possible claim about the uniqueness of the Buddha's achievement. Consequently, what the Buddha taught is fundamentally the same as that taught by other, prior Buddhas. This teaching is always present as a realized possibility for others. Furthermore, the long line of sequential teaching by Buddhas of the past means that enlightenment is not merely an ever-present possibility, but an actuality. The possibility and actuality of enlightenment suggest that there is always the potential for a newer awakening to the eternal truth that can take place within the Buddhist community. Moreover, this suggests that a sacred Buddhist text possesses no intrinsic value. It is only valuable if someone uses it as a guide. Once such a person attains enlightenment, the sacred text can be abandoned and even rejected because it possesses no further utility.

The Buddhist attitude towards scripture is grounded in its understanding of language, which it views as an impermanent human product. Since it is a basic Buddhist philosophical presupposition that everything within the world is impermanent, the impermanent and non-absolute nature of language means that it does not possess an enduring structure or metaphysical status. Lacking any intrinsic value, words are only valuable in an instrumental way. Thus, the value of words resides in their ability to accomplish something.

During the formative period of the historical evolution of Buddhism, its literature was organized into two baskets: *Vinaya-piṭaka* (basket of monastic discipline) and *Sutta-piṭaka* (basket of discourses). According to tradition, this occurred at the first council at Rājagṛha, the capital of Magadha, immediately following the Buddha's death around 486 BC when monks met to recite from memory the words of the Buddha. In order to assure accuracy, the monks chanted the remembered teachings in unison. The teaching (*dhamma*) of the Buddha was called *āgama* (lit. 'that which has been transmitted'). After a period of oral transmission from teacher to disciple, the teachings were collected and organized into *suttas* and *gāthās* (verses). Around the 2ⁿᵈ century BC a third basket was added, the *Abhidhamma-piṭaka* (basket of additional teachings). Before these three collections were written down to preserve them, oral reciters preserved them through memory, typically by specializing in a particular subject-matter.

The basket of monastic discipline contains the rules and precepts that guide monastic life. This basket of literature is divided into three major categories: *Sutta-vibhanga, Khandhaka,* and *Parivāra.* The first category consists of the *Pāṭimokkha* and its 227 rules, which are arranged according to the degree of seriousness of violating them. The *Pāṭimokkha* developed from a simple confession of faith made by monks and nuns into a basic code used to guarantee proper monastic behaviour. After it became established in this way, it functioned as a monastic liturgy. Monks and nuns periodically chanted these rules within their respective communities as entire groups, which worked to unify the communities and functioned as a reminder of the rules that bound them together. The group recitation of the *Pāṭimokkha* occurred twice a month in connection with fast days (*Poṣadha*) that were historically connected to the religious significance of the new and full moon days in ancient Indian religion. Certain literary features were added to the text as it evolved historically. These included introductory and concluding verses praising monastic virtue and discipline. An introduction (*nidāna*) to the text functioned to summon the monastic community together, and served as a means of conducting the proper confessional procedure. Finally, after each category of violations, the text contained an interrogatory procedure with the purpose of determining violators of the monastic code and distinguishing pure from impure members.

The *Sutta-vibhanga* can be literally translated as 'analysis of a *sutta*' (thread/ text). (The root derivation of the term *sutta* or *sutra* connotes the warp of a woven cloth, metaphorically suggesting that the teachings were made into phrases that could be memorized.) The text in this case is the *Pāṭimokkha*, which forms the basis of the regulations for monastic life. There are four parts to the *Sutta-vibhanga*. The initial part is a narrative or narratives that present the actual human circumstances for a particular rule. Secondly, there is the actual rule. Then, there is a commentary on each term of the rule. It concludes with a narrative indicative of any mitigating circumstances, which exemplify exceptions to the rule, and may also relate any changes that could be made regarding punishments. This last aspect suggests the introduction of some latitude into the monastic code. Flexibility is also evident in the use of terms such as 'grave offence', 'light offence', or 'offence of improper conduct'. This introduction of elasticity probably reflects the historical development of the *Pāṭimokkha* into a fixed and closed body of rules. If new rules became inadmissible into the code of conduct, monastic communities discovered that they needed some suppleness in order to respond properly to new incidents that were without much precedent in the established code.

In contrast to the *Sutta-vibhanga*, the *Khandhaka* represents a broader body of rules that serves as a supplement to the basic rules of the *Pāṭimokkha*. The *Khandhaka* also deals with broader issues of communal disharmony and actions by the larger monastic order, along with procedures for the ceremonial life of the community and regulations for dealing with a schism or the threat of a split within the order. It also treats more mundane issues like the use of shoes and leather objects, proper and improper clothing, correct and incorrect behaviour during probationary periods, procedures for settling disputes, and rules specifically for nuns. Finally, the third major category is the *Parivāra*, which is a collection of auxiliary texts of different dates or origin.

The discourses of the Buddha are contained in the *Sutta-piṭaka*, *piṭaka* (basket) connoting something that is capable of holding items. Besides its connection to the metaphor of weaving, the term *sutta* (Sanskrit, *sūtra*) refers to the thread or thong of leather or string used to hold the pages of a text together. In this metaphorical sense, the *sutta* suggests something that binds pages of a discourse together. A *sutta* follows a specific form that starts with the words 'Thus have I heard. At one time...'. This introduction is followed by the name of the location of the discourse, which is followed in turn by a list of names of those in the audience, and concludes with the sermon of the Buddha. This basic format of the text suggests particular historical circumstances after the death of the Buddha. At that time, monks gathered to share and recite from memory the sermons that they had heard and could remember. The disciples of the Buddha were attempting to construct the authentic tradition in order to establish the actual teachings and orthodox tradition. Specifically, the disciples were concerned to transmit accurately their enlightened master's teachings. They were not concerned about proving or verifying his statements: they thought that any person listening to the message could either accept or reject it.

The *Sutta-piṭaka* texts are arranged according to length. Among the five major collections of these texts are the long sayings (*Dīgha-nikāya*), middle-length sayings (*Majjhima-nikāya*), works connected by their contents (*Saṃyutta-nikāya*), texts arranged by numerical groupings of items (*Aṅguttara-nikāya*) in an ascending order culminating with a list of eleven things, and a collection of minor works (*Khuddaka-nikāya*). This Pāli canon became fixed and closed by 100 BC.

The final basket to be added historically to the Pāli canon was the *Abhidhamma-piṭaka*, the prefix *abhi* meaning 'above'. This prefix suggests what is beyond or superior to the *dhamma* (doctrine/teaching) that it is analysing. The meaning of the term *Abhidhamma* implies that it possesses more authority than the explanations to be discovered in the *suttas* themselves. Thus, this basket consisted of scholastic analysis of material from the *Sutta-piṭaka*, suggesting that its meaning embodies 'understanding the teachings' or 'analysis of the teachings'. This basket of frequently technical literature probably originated from lists of doctrinal topics that were used to collect and preserve concepts and teachings of the Buddha. This literature reflects an excellent example of Buddhist scholasticism that attempted to analyse the teachings of the Buddha from a variety of viewpoints.

After the establishment of the *Tipiṭaka* (triple basket), learned monks wrote commentaries on the texts. During the 5th century AD, Buddhaghosa consolidated, for instance, previous commentaries, and wrote five commentaries on the *Nikāya* texts. This great Buddhist scholar also composed several works on the *Abhidhamma* literature. Other scholars followed in the footsteps of Buddhaghosa with their own commentaries.

7 Brief comparison of the five traditions

Each of the five religious traditions considered here uses its sacred book in a performative way in order to make something happen by the reciting of words.

The ritual repetition of the monastic regulations periodically by Buddhist monks, for instance, is a performative function of scripture because it unites the members of the monastery into a brotherhood. The performative nature of *mantras* in Hinduism and Buddhism and prayer in the monotheistic traditions are indicative of the performative aspects of the sacred book that embody *mantras* and prayers. The oral performance of Paul's letters evoked his presence in the early churches. It is also obvious that the psalms of the Hebrew Bible were to be read aloud. Similarly, rabbis of Judaism, Muslim mullahs, and Qur'ānic reciters performed their scriptures.

The sacred language of ancient Hinduism is Sanskrit, Arabic for Islam, and Hebrew for Judaism; but there is no single sacred language for Buddhism or Christianity, although Latin played such a role for some centuries for the Catholic Christian tradition. By surveying the historical expansion of Buddhism throughout the east, it is possible to find that it used the languages of different cultures: Pāli, Tibetan, Sanskrit, Chinese, Korean, Japanese, and others. Beliefs about the impermanent nature of language and lack of a divine revelation within the religious tradition probably formed the context for the use of many languages in Buddhism. Contrary to common presuppositions, the multiple languages for Buddhist scripture did not compromise its authenticity or authority.

These religious traditions also exhibited differences with respect to the issue of the canon, the authoritative and official body of writings of a religious tradition. From a cross-cultural perspective, a canon can be considered closed, as in the cases of Judaism, Islam, Christianity, and Hinduism. In the Muslim tradition, the revelation to the prophet Muḥammad ended with his life, and it was accepted as the final perfect revelation. The Qur'ān anoints itself as scripture and confirms its own canonicity, whereas other traditions experienced a long process before individual tradition reached the status of a canon. With respect to Judaism, there can be levels of the canon formed by Talmudic, legal, ritual, and exegetical commentary. In order for a religious literature to reach canonical status, there must be a strong social consensus about the formation of scripture, and the gradualness of this process has been indicated. In the cases of Buddhism and Christianity, a social consensus was reached by a series of learned councils. Muslims call themselves, Jews, and Christians 'People of the Book' because the three sacred books had the same source, even though the books are very different. Nonetheless, the Qur'ān and the Hebrew Bible have eternal and invariable heavenly prototypes. Muslims stress the uncreated nature of their text and Jews the created nature of it, whereas the Christ himself is seen as the uncreated Word.

In each of the five religious traditions, the original oral nature of their scriptures played an important role in their historical development into sacred books. This process included making decisions about what was authentic and trustworthy—and what was not. The major criterion for inclusion into a canon was whether or not a discourse of the Buddha, for instance, or a saying attributed to Muḥammad, could be traced directly to that figure, or to one or more authoritative witnesses.

These five religious traditions manifest differences with respect to revelation. For Jews and Muslims, scripture is revelation, whereas Christians encounter revelation in scripture. Hindus are closer to the Jewish and Muslim understanding of the relationship between revelation and scripture, while Buddhist scriptures are sacred because of their source in a historical person who achieved enlightenment, which is the source of his authority. This suggests that a sacred book depends on its source, and often a long historical process, until it reaches social consensus and canonicity.

The revelations of the three monotheistic religions represent a historical act that occurred at a particular time and place. There is no divine revelation in Buddhism, although the Buddha did achieve enlightenment within history. For the Vedic sages, their inspiration was an internal process occurring within the mind or heart of an individual sage, who initiated the process of inspiration by ascending and calling upon the gods for assistance, whereas God takes the initiative in the monotheistic traditions.

There are some important differences between writing and the oral transmission of a text. Writing claims an authority the oral cannot, although such authority does not end the importance of the oral tradition, as is evident in Judaism. Writing encourages textual features that make language an object of aesthetic awareness and an artefact to be decoded, which are features that go beyond the oral text. Finally, writing renders possible the creation of a history different from that produced by an oral tradition.

BIBLIOGRAPHY

R. Alter, *The Art of Biblical Narrative* (1981)
J. Barr, *Holy Scripture* (1983)
A. Cole, *Text as Father* (2005)
F. M. Denny and R. L. Taylor, eds., *The Holy Book in Comparative Perspective* (1985)
W. Eichrodt, *Theology of the Old Testament*, tr. J. A. Baker (2 vols, 1961, 1967)
E. Frauwallner, *The Earliest Vinaya and the Beginnings of Buddhist Literature* (1956)
J. Gonda, *The Vision of Vedic Poets* (1963)
— *Vedic Literature* (1975)
B. A. Holdrege, *Veda and Torah* (1996)
M. Levering, ed., *Rethinking Scripture* (1989)
K. R. Norman, *Pāli Literature* (1983)
C. Olson, ed., *Original Buddhist Sources* (2005)
— *Hindu Primary Sources* (2007)
L. Patton, ed., *Authority, Anxiety, and Canon* (1994)
E. F. Peters, *The Monotheists* (2003)
S. Pollock, *The Language of the Gods in the World of Men: Sanskrit, Culture, and Power in Premodern India* (2006)
G. von Rad, *Old Testament Theology*, tr. D. M. G. Stalker (2 vols, 1962, 1965)
C. K. Roberts and T. C. Skeat, *The Birth of the Codex* (1987)
M. Witzel, ed., *Inside the Texts Beyond the Texts: New Approaches to the Study of the Vedas* (1997)

3

The Ancient Book

CRAIG KALLENDORF

1 Introduction

While the main line of descent traces the printed book in the West back through the medieval codex to the scrolls of ancient Greece and Rome, it is important to remember that these latter civilizations arose after, and alongside, a number of other ancient cultures that also had writing. Although it is likely that writing arose independently in the Near East, China, and Central America, Greece and Rome interacted regularly with the cultures of Mesopotamia, Egypt, the Germanic tribes, and Israel, so that a full consideration of the book in the ancient world must take into account all of these areas and their interrelationships.

The earliest writing is logographic (picture writing), beginning with a simple drawing (pictogram), then developing to a sign that represents a number of concepts associated with the original object (ideogram). When the sign represents the sound of an object's name, the logogram has become a phonogram; only when the sign comes to represent consonants, or consonants and vowels, does the system become phonetic. Most early writing systems were mixed, and some have remained that way (*see* **1**).

2 Mesopotamia

By the 4th millennium BC, ancient Mesopotamia had developed the world's first fully developed writing system, a mixed approach of some 2,000 logograms (later reduced to about 800), somewhat over 100 phonograms, and some semantic indicators and syllabic signs. By 2800 BC the signs in this system had taken on a characteristic wedge shape that was easily impressed into the wet clay in which they were usually written, giving the system its name: cuneiform (Lat. *cuneus*, 'wedge-shaped'). This system was developed initially by the Sumerians, but by the middle of the 3rd millennium BC it had been adapted to Akkadian, which became the common language of the Near East, and it was later taken up by the Elamites, Hurrians, Hittites, and Persians.

Ancient Mesopotamian writing is occasionally found on stone, seals, metal weapons and craft objects, leather, and the wax tablets that were ubiquitous in the ancient world for note-taking, letter-writing, etc. The classic Near Eastern book, however, was made of clay. The most common shape was oblong, flat on the top with a convex underside, written on while wet with a reed in horizontal rows, starting at the top-left corner on the flat side and continuing to the lower-right corner, then on to the convex side if necessary, where the writing then went from right to left. The tablets were dried in the sun, or kiln-fired in later periods. Important documents were sometimes put into a protective clay envelope. Several tablets could be joined together to make books, which were collected into libraries. The largest of these was the Ashurbanipal (r. 668–27 BC) Library at Nineveh; the archive at Ebla was notable for its systematic organization, and that of Nippur for its catalogues.

Writing was taught in palace, temple, and home; because the system was complex, the literacy rate remained fairly low (2–5 per cent), but scribes came from a variety of classes, ranging from petty bookkeepers to high officials. A significant part of all cuneiform finds are tied to writing instruction (e.g. word lists), and examples of various literary genres also survive, often as schoolboy exercises. Best known are the *Enuma Elish* ('When on High…'), the Babylonian creation poem, and the Gilgamesh epic. Editions of the literary classics were not illustrated, although mathematical figures and diagrams were entered on documentary tablets, and even the legal Code of Hammurabi (1780 BC) contains a picture of Shamash, the god of justice. Books of magic, medicine, and technology, along with maps, astronomical calculations, and building plans, survive, but 90 per cent of what the ancient Mesopotamians wrote is economic and administrative.

3 Egypt

Beginning around 3000 BC, Sumerian influence on Egypt appears to have stimulated a mixed writing system which eventually evolved into around 600 logograms, 100 phonograms, and 24 alphabet-like signs that represent one consonantal sound. In addition to the formal version of this script, called hieroglyphs (Gk *hieros*, 'sacred' and *glyphein*, 'to carve'), two non-pictorial scripts derived from it—hieratic and demotic—also appeared, to meet the demand for symbols that were faster and easier to write.

The Egyptians wrote on wooden tablets, ostraca (pottery sherds), linen mummy wrappings, monuments, and temples, even occasionally on animal skins, but most often on papyrus, which came from the marshy delta of the lower Nile. The precise details of the production process remain debatable, but it is commonly agreed that the stalks of reeds were opened out and sheets of papyrus were placed on top of one another at right angles, then pressed so that their sap would hold them together. Sheets were next dried and bleached in the sun, then pasted together into scrolls. The pen was cut from the same reed, with its tip pounded into a sort of brush initially, then cut into a split nib in Hellenistic times. Black ink alternated with red to distinguish a second section of text, especially a heading, from which the term 'rubric' (Lat. *ruber*, 'red') is derived. Egyptian scrolls had wide margins, with hieroglyphics being written initially in vertical rows from right to left, generally on the inside only of a roll without handles. The outside of the roll sometimes contained the title, the author's name, and a summary or the opening words of the text, information that could also be written inside as a colophon. The Egyptian book bequeathed several things to its successors: writing in columns, illustrations to accompany a text, and rubrication for headings, titles, and colophons.

In the Old Kingdom, prayers and lists of a deceased person's accomplishments written on tomb walls evolved into catalogues of virtues and maxims that were transferred to papyrus as 'Instructions to the Dead', to which hymns, prophecies, and warnings were later added. Short stories and ballads, then historical inscriptions and narrative poems became common in the New Kingdom, with non-literary writings like astronomical texts, calendars, magical incantations, treatises on practical medicine, and court proceedings being copied as well. The best-known genre, however, is the Egyptian Book of the Dead, which contained burial ceremonies, prayers for the deceased, and speculations about what life beyond the grave held. Illustrations, which were added separately and are sometimes not integrated perfectly with the text, show scenes like the weighing of the deceased's soul and the presentation of the deceased to Osiris by Horus.

4 The Hebrew book

The earliest Hebrew writing goes back to the 15th or 14th centuries BC and is found on metal, pottery bowls, and an ostracon used as an abecedary. By the 10th century, royal records were being kept, and Deuteronomy 6:4–9 presents an early commandment that sacred texts were to be written on doorposts (*mezuza*) and in boxes bound on to the head and arms (*tefellin*). The Bible also refers to seals and signet rings that go back to the 8th century BC, and writing on ivory goes back to the same period, while the earliest fragments of the Bible (Num. 6:24–6) are found on two silver scrolls that date from slightly later. Inscribed stones with the teachings of Moses were displayed publicly (Josh. 8:32), and Ezekiel was commanded to write on pieces of wood (Ezek. 37:15–20). Baked clay ostraca were used for receipts, lists, tax records, and drafts. The Dead Sea Scrolls, fragments found between 1947 and 1956 in caves near Qumran, include the earliest surviving biblical texts written on animal skins.

The Jewish religion has its basis in the Torah, which kept the Hebrews together through exile and persecution; no other book has survived as long with the same physical form and textual stability, nor does any other religious book come with such constraints on its layout, materials, and preparation. The Torah contains the Pentateuch, the first five books of the Bible. It is written on parchment, on the flesh side only, in 248 to 252 columns, with two or three columns per sheet. Mistakes can be corrected, but too many errors condemn the page to the genizah, the burial ground for damaged, worn, or error-filled Torahs. The sheets are sewn together at the end, and each end is attached to a roller. In addition to the Torah, the other parts of the Old Testament (the Prophets and the Hagiographa, or sacred writings) are important, as is the Talmud, the effort to harmonize the Torah with the commands of everyday life. The Talmud was passed down orally until the 4th or 5th centuries AD, so it is written in codex form, since this was what was common when the text was committed to writing (*see* **8**).

Parchment appears to have been used in Hebrew scrolls before it was used widely elsewhere in the Graeco-Roman world. Word spacing and justified margins also first appear regularly in Hebrew books.

5 Greece

5.1 *The physical book*

A good number of charred Greek MSS have been recovered from Herculaneum, and thousands of papyrus fragments have emerged from the graveyards and rubbish dumps of Egyptian towns like Oxyrhynchus. This material has generated fragments of previously lost books by Alcman, Herodas, Menander, Aristotle, and Philodemus, while lines from other lost works have survived in florilegia, but what has perished is still immeasurable: over 95 per cent of Sappho, over 90 per cent of Sophocles, and almost all astronomical works prior to Ptolemy, for example.

Writing in ancient Greece evolved through several forms. The Minoan civilization on Crete was contemporary with those in Mesopotamia and Egypt and similar to them in many ways, producing writing on a number of surfaces in two distinct types of pictogram, then in two cursive syllabic scripts. Linear A, found mostly in Crete in the 17th and 16th centuries BC, was engraved on stone, metal, and clay pottery. From around 1600 to 1200 BC mainland cities like Mycenae and Pylos rose to power as well, producing an official script, Linear B, that was related to Linear A but different from it. When the Mycenean civilization was destroyed around 1200 BC, the knowledge of writing perished with it. Around the middle of the 8th century BC, the Greeks borrowed an alphabetic writing system from the Phoenicians, who also served as intermediaries in the papyrus trade (the Phoenician port of Byblos may have provided the Greeks with their word for book, *biblos*), adapting it to their language. This script began in a monumental version, which evolved into a rounded, more compressed uncial form as a bookhand, then into a cursive form for business purposes.

Within a few generations the Greeks were writing on a variety of surfaces: coins, introduced by the Lydians *c.*630 BC; bronze weapons and utensils; seals, of ivory or stone; gems; and stone slabs, for laws and treaties. Wax tablets, held together by thongs into groups of two (*diptycha*), three (*triptycha*), or more (*polyptycha*), were used for note-taking and schoolwork. Pottery often contained the names of figures in a story or the people to whom the vessels were to be given, and ostraca were inscribed in the assembly with the names of political leaders whom the Athenian citizens wished to send into temporary exile (i.e. to ostracize). Parchment, named from an early production centre in Asia Minor (Lat. (*charta*) *Pergamena*, '(paper of) Pergamum'), was used as well, but not extensively during the classical period. The main writing surface for the ancient Greeks was papyrus, obtained (directly or indirectly) from Egypt and written on with a pen (*kalamos*). Writing was in columns, sufficient for 16–25 letters in prose or a line of poetry, with 25–35 lines per column and two or three columns per sheet, on one side only except for private note-taking. No space was left between words, and there was no systematic punctuation system, although marks like the *paragraphos*, a horizontal stroke indicating a change of speakers in drama or a break in sense in prose, are sometimes found. Standard 20-foot rolls could be glued together into scrolls of up to 100 feet in length, although anything over 35 feet (the length of two or three books of the *Iliad*) was rare because it was so hard to handle. The scroll could be preserved with saffron or cedar oil and its edges were sometimes coloured; often it had a single handle (*omphalos*), around which the papyrus was rolled. Basic information like the name of the owner, the size and source of the text, and perhaps the price could

Engraving of a lost piece of Roman sculpture (*c.*100 AD) of rolled and ticketed scrolls from Neumagen, near Treves, in C. Browerus and J. Masenius, *Antiquitatum et Annalium Trevirensium Libri XXV* (Lyons, 1670). The Bodleian Library, University of Oxford (A 16.2, 3 Th)

either hang from the middle of the lower edge or be added in a note at the end of the text (colophon), where it would be equally accessible, since scrolls were generally not rewound for the convenience of the next reader. The scroll could then be covered with fabric or leather and stored in a bucket, case, or on shelves.

5.2 Book trade

Initially 'publication' in the Greek world meant an author reading from a single roll containing his works. This was succeeded by copying for and among friends, but there was no copyright: an author 'published' a book by seeing to it that correct copies, which were prized more highly than unauthorized ones, were in circulation. In the 6th century BC the tyrant Pisistratus organized competitive recitations of Homer, whose works he also had edited and copied, and later Lycurgus required that an official copy of the works of the three great tragedians be placed in the public record office of Athens. By the 5th century BC a book trade existed in Athens. A semi-circular recess in the marketplace (the orchestra) had been set aside for booksellers, and Plato says that a second-hand copy of the works of the philosopher Anaxagoras could be had there for one drachma, less than a day's wage for an unskilled worker.

5.3 Reading

By the 6th century BC Athenian graffiti show that writing was common, and by 490 BC vases showed people reading from scrolls of literary authors. The average Athenian male citizen knew his alphabet, girls could get enough of an education to run a household, and slaves were also sometimes literate. With wealth and leisure, education could continue, from the elementary level through more advanced study of language, composition, history, and myth, to the *gymnasia* that eventually spread Greek physical and intellectual values throughout the Hellenized world. People wrote letters, contracts, and wills, and court cases depended on written documents.

It is not safe, however, to assume that people in ancient Greece read in precisely the same way that modern Europeans do. The fact that texts were written without word division (*scripta continua*) made vocalization almost imperative, so that reading aloud remained normative throughout Greek culture. In time, some Greeks developed the ability to read silently, in a process that is tied to the rise of Socrates' *daimonion*, the inner voice that would later be called one's 'conscience'. Aristophanes' *Knights* (produced in 424 BC, when Plato was 5 years old) has a scene in which a character reads silently, confusing another character who does not recognize this practice, confirming that it was by no means ubiquitous.

5.4 Libraries

The tyrant Pisistratus, an early book collector himself, founded the first public library in Athens, although the books were carried off by Xerxes when he sacked the city in 480 BC. No public libraries are mentioned in the 5th and 4th centuries, but significant private collections were alluded to by Xenophon in the first half of the 4th century BC, and Aristotle's library in particular was notable for its size and breadth. After the death of Alexander the Great, the Ptolemies in Egypt developed a plan to set up a research institute (a Museum) with a small group of residential scholars and substantial library resources to support their work. Books were collected from throughout the Greek world for the Alexandrian Library, and no expense was spared: after having left fifteen talents (a huge sum) on deposit to borrow the official copy of the plays of the three tragedians, the library opted to forfeit the sum in order to keep the original. The result was the greatest library the world had ever known—by one estimate it contained at least 400,000 books in the main collection, with the 3rd-century catalogue (the *Pinakes*) of Callimachus alone taking up 120 scrolls. The other major Hellenistic library was founded by the Attalids, with the holdings of the Pergamum Library being large enough that, in the 1st century BC, Mark Antony supposedly gave 200,000 books from it to Cleopatra. Other cities often had libraries suited to their special strengths: in Rhodes, a centre for rhetorical studies, the library of the local gymnasium was rich in speeches and works of politics and history. Inscriptions show that these libraries depended heavily on their donors.

5.5 Textual criticism

Since Greek scrolls were copied by hand, the threat of textual corruption was always high. This threat was addressed in a systematic way by scholars associated with the library in Alexandria, with Zenodotus, Aristophanes, and Aristarchus developing a system of critical signs like the *obelos*, a horizontal stroke in the left margin that signalled a verse as spurious. These same scholars advanced the principle that the best guide to an author's usage is what can be found in his other works. Actors' interpolations were identified in Euripides, and the metrical patterns in Pindar were understood well enough to allow for emendation. The earliest fragments of Homer that have emerged from the sands of Egypt are not significantly different from the textual tradition that derives from Alexandrian scholarship, suggesting that Zenodotus and his successors did their job well. (*See also* **4**, **20**.)

6 Rome

6.1 The physical book

Books were present early on in Rome: it is said that in the 6th century BC Lucius Tarquinius Superbus eventually purchased the magical records in the Sibylline Books, which were written on linen (*libri lintei*), as were the consular records of the 5th century BC that are also mentioned by Livy. Other writing materials were used in early Rome as well. The Latin word for 'book', *liber*, serves as a reminder that the inside bark of trees (the root meaning of the word) was written on, while Virgil mentions writing on leaves. Inscriptions were made on stone and coloured, usually in red, sometimes in gold. Wax tablets had a variety of uses, from note-taking to deeds and tax receipts, to the production of prose summaries, then first drafts for poetic composition. In the empire, discharged soldiers received a bronze diptychon called a *diploma*, awarding them citizenship, land, and the right to marry. Inscriptions are also found on mosaics, coins, pottery, and gems. Parchment was known, but its use was widespread only among the Jews, then the Christians.

From the early republic the basic Roman book was the papyrus scroll, developed along the Greek model. The papyrus was attached to a rod (*umbilicus*) of ivory, ebony, even gold, with handles (*bullae* or *cornua*); the scroll was held in the right hand and unrolled with the left. Originally only one side was written on, and mistakes could be scraped off—indeed, entire MSS, called *codices rescripti* (*palimpsesta* in Greek), were scraped or washed off and reused, with several important texts (e.g. Cicero's *De Re Publica* and the 2nd-century BC *Institutiones* of Gaius) surviving only as the lower text on a palimpsest. Illustrated books are found only from the 4th century AD, but their existence before that can be inferred: Vitruvius refers to the drawings that accompanied his work, and it is known that the biographical studies of Varro were accompanied by 700 portraits. Travellers' itineraries required maps (e.g. the Peutinger Table). Several famous Virgil MSS (e.g. Vat. lat. 3225 and 3867, the Codex Romanus) exemplify the achievements of late Roman illumination.

A variety of writing styles were employed. Square capitals (*capitalis quadrata*), used during the first five centuries after the birth of Christ, began as inscriptional lettering, but were quickly transferred to papyrus. Slow and therefore expensive to produce, they offered an elegant contrast of thick and thin strokes with pronounced serifs, or finishing strokes. Rustic capitals, common on monuments from Iberia and the Near East, on less formal public notices, and in many of the earliest surviving MSS of Roman literature, are a more compact majuscule script that originated in square capitals but shows some cursive influence as well. Uncial (Lat. *uncia*, 'one-twelfth of a foot', i.e. an inch, a derisive term applied to these letters by Jerome, who claimed that such large writing was wasteful) results from a rounding-off of square capital forms, with several distinctive new shapes (e.g. a, d, e, and m) evolving from cursive influence; this script flourished from approximately 300 to 900 among the Christians, who preferred it as a new form of writing that was free of pagan overtones. Under greater pressure from cursive, parts of letters came to be left off and ascenders and descenders were exaggerated, resulting in the first true minuscule script: half-uncial or semi-uncial, which appeared in the 5th century AD and flourished in the 6th, again primarily for Christian works. Punctuation was spotty; word division was initially found in inscriptional square capitals, disappeared under Greek influence, and eventually reappeared, beginning in cursive MSS.

6.2 Book trade

A Roman author began the process of publication with a *recitatio*, a public reading, designed to introduce a new work. Virgil and Horace quickly achieved a level of attention which they found embarrassing, and the practice got even more out of hand in the empire, with the younger Pliny complaining that there was a recitation almost every day. There were advantages to the system: a 'bravo' from the audience must have encouraged the author, critics could point to defects while they could still be easily corrected, and the audience had its appetite whetted. Patronage was a key part of the Roman literary system, with Maecenas, Augustus' unofficial minister of culture, being the most famous example of a wealthy man who financed the production and distribution of literature in exchange for having the work dedicated to him.

The primary responsibility for getting a work circulated in written form lay with the author, although precisely how this happened has become debatable. The traditional explanation holds that a writer could have the work copied by his own slaves or could rely on a large-scale 'publisher', someone like Cicero's friend and correspondent Atticus (110–32BC). Atticus and other publishers like Q. Pollius Valerianus, Tryphon, Atrectus, Secundus, and the Sosii brothers had readers dictating to scribes, who produced copies that were disseminated all over the Roman world. The author and his publisher agreed how the book would look (e.g. what type and colour of wrapping the scroll would have), but there was no copyright protection and the author received no royalties: the advantage of using a publisher was that a writer would not have to have more copies produced under his own supervision, at his own expense. Booksellers (*librarii*) were concentrated near the forum and often specialized, some in rare items, some in contemporary authors, and some in antiquarian goods. Recently, however, parts of this picture have been challenged. W. A. Johnson has noted that the consistent way in which scrolls were prepared suggests a professionalized training among scribes. R. J. Starr and others have urged that the picture of mass-production scriptoria be replaced with one focused on a series of concentric circles, in which an author made copies for his friends, who had copies made for their friends, with the personal connection to the author being gradually dissolved, but with a bookshop coming into play only as a last resort in aristocratic circles (although it may well have been the first, indeed only, choice for lower-class readers). Cicero and Atticus, according to this argument, may well have had copying done in house, but this was not the norm; more commonly, someone who needed a copy made would resort to a *librarius*, seen here primarily as a copyist who was relatively indifferent about whether the original came from the customer, the handful of books in his stock, or a library.

6.3 Reading

Although the upper classes took more care to educate their children than the lower classes, education was not simply a function of class, as the number of writers of humble origin confirms: Terence came to Rome as a slave, and Augustus' freedman Hyginus became librarian at the Palatine library and wrote learned encyclopaedic works. Books were necessary, as one might expect, at every level of Roman education. The alphabet, then syllables, and basic reading were taught at the beginning, on wax tablets, then later on writing boards. At the secondary level, under the *grammaticus*, grammar and the interpretation of literature were taught, in Greek and Latin, with reference to many school texts. The third level focused on rhetoric and required both theoretical treatises and sample speeches, and the final level, philosophy, again required access to many books.

Most reading was still done aloud, which required one to learn when to breathe, to raise or lower the voice, and to gesture; it had its physical component, so that reading was commonly positioned in medical books among those exercises that promote good health. Some reading was silent, but usually for texts, like a letter, that did not seem to lend themselves to public consumption. Catullus and Cicero were the first to distinguish kinds of reader, adding to the aristocrats and the teachers traditionally associated with them a new, broad middle group that read more for pleasure than utility, that preferred a simple style, and that was indifferent to the physical qualities of the book. Among them were government employees, soldiers, merchants, tradesmen, and an increasing number of women—indeed, Ovid was especially conscious of this last group. The extensive use of writing within the military suggests that especially in the empire, some level of literacy was widespread, but the poor spelling and grammar of many of the graffiti in Pompeii warn that many of the 'new readers' had absorbed little beyond the basics.

6.4 Libraries

The first significant private libraries came to Rome as the spoils of war: in the 2nd century BC Aemilius Paulus brought back the books of Perseus, king of Macedonia, and Sulla looted from Athens the library of Apellicon of Teos, which included many of Aristotle's books. It quickly became fashionable to have a library in noble villas, with aristocrats like Cicero having books at home but also freely using the libraries of their friends. The library in the Villa of the Papyri in Herculaneum, probably owned in the 1st century BC by Caesar's father-in-law, L. Calpurnius Piso, exemplifies this trend, although its focus on philosophers from Epicurus to Philodemus was probably atypical.

Julius Caesar's plans for a public library in Rome were not carried out, so that it fell to G. Asinius Pollio to found the first public library in Rome. Augustus founded two more, in the Temple of Apollo on the Palatine and in the Portico of Octavia at the Campus Martius. Later emperors built others; beginning with Trajan, libraries were often incorporated into the public baths, until by AD 350 there were 29 in Rome. Libraries were built in the provinces as well, often with the aid of wealthy donors like the younger Pliny, who endowed the library in his native Como. The eastern provinces had a number of famous libraries (e.g. the library of Celsus at Ephesus and, in Athens, the libraries established by Pantainos—built between AD 98 and 102—and by Hadrian), but curiously, the western half of the empire outside Italy has only two securely attested libraries, at Carthage in Tunisia and Timgad in Algeria.

Roman libraries were laid out differently from Greek ones. The Greek library generally contained books in Greek only, stored in small rooms that basically served as stacks and opened onto a colonnade where readers consulted the scrolls. Roman culture was bilingual, so libraries were divided into two sections, one for books in Greek and one for Latin. Scrolls were stored in wooden book-cases (*armaria*), with the centre of the room kept free for readers. Libraries were generally open in the mornings only, but borrowing was occasionally permitted.

6.5 Textual criticism

The initial transmission of texts in ancient Rome was casual, with Cicero complaining that his speeches were mangled and the plays of Plautus being adapted freely by actors. Stability began with the early grammarians. Varro, for example, established a corpus of genuine Plautine plays and worked on the interpretation of obsolete or difficult words. Adoption as a school text helped to preserve a work but also subjected it to poor copying and second-rate scholarly intervention. Among a group of 1st-century AD scholars, the most famous was M. Valerius Probus, who applied Alexandrian methods, correcting transcription errors, punctuating, and adding critical signs for Virgil, Horace, and Lucretius. Later, Fronto and Gellius studied the early republican authors, attempting to recover readings from old MSS to correct the texts. From late antiquity some 27 subscriptions—formulaic expressions at the end of a book indicating the circumstances under which it was revised and copied—attest to the interest of such important families as the Nicomachi and the Symmachi in correcting and preserving key works of Roman culture like the first decade of Livy's histories.

6.6 From roll to codex

The term *codex* was originally the Roman name for the wooden tablet notebook. Before the end of the 1st century AD, the Romans began replacing the wood with parchment, and Martial indicates that standard authors were available in this format in his day. Papyrus was not an appropriate substitute for wood in the codex format, since folding and sewing weakened it at the key point, the spine. Parchment had not worked well for scrolls, since it made the MS too heavy, but it was admirably suited to the codex.

The rise of the parchment codex is linked to the rise of Christianity: all of the Christian works found in 2nd-century AD Egypt are in codex form, while 98 per cent of the non-Christian works are not. A number of reasons have been suggested for this. Initially Christianity spread among the lower and middle classes, who had known the codex as a school notebook, a notepad, or a professional manual. It was easier to find a passage in a codex than in a scroll—an important point for a new religion in which textual authority was important. In addition, the parchment codex was free from the pagan overtones that went with the papyrus scroll. Whatever the reason, by the 4th century AD large bibles like the Codex Sinaiticus were being produced in codex form, which ended up being the dominant model even for pagan texts as antiquity came to an end.

7 Runes

The earliest known example of writing in runes comes from the Danish island of Funen during the second half of the 1st century AD. Often inelegant, runes are associated with peoples not known for their cultural achievements in other areas.

Runes are alphabetic, though without taking full advantage of that system (e.g. consonants do not double) (*see* **1**). They seem to be drawn from the Roman alphabet, adapted to a non-Latin language: five 'unnecessary' letters (K, Q, X, Y, and Z) are used for phonemes and language clusters that have no Latin equivalent, while one rune has no equal in the Roman alphabet. Runes began in the Romanized centres of northern Germany and spread from there, appearing on high-prestige artefacts to record the owner's or giver's name. The only function that goes beyond this is naming a spear 'Prober', which may indicate a certain awareness of the metaphorical but does not suggest magical overtones. The most likely explanation is that runes were developed from Roman writing in the 2nd century AD by Germanic people who had had some contact with the Romans, to mark the donor or maker, ownership or function. Objects so marked became a good way to indicate group membership and forge alliances, something for which the Romans themselves at the same time used language.

8 China

The earliest writing in China appeared *c.*1200 BC in Anyang, the last capital of the Shang dynasty (*see* **1**, **42**). It is sometimes said that this writing was stimulated by contact with Mesopotamia, but there is no archaeological evidence to confirm this assumption. Early Chinese writing appears as a fully developed system, and reasoning from analogy suggests that what has been found at Anyang must be a later version of a writing system whose lost early stages would have resembled early Mesopotamian tablets and Linear A and B remains. Here the problem may revolve around the fact that some writing materials survive longer than others. Early Chinese writing is also found on bones (as souvenirs of royal hunts), turtle shells (as records of the delivery of goods), jade and other precious stones (as marks of ownership), and pottery, but not on the mats of wood or bamboo slips which served as books from the 5th century BC. Letters written on silk were mentioned by writers several centuries before the time to which the earliest surviving examples can be dated. If the early stages of Chinese writing also appeared on surfaces as fragile as these, their disappearance would make sense.

Early Chinese script is often said to be pictographic, but here, each character is part of a real writing system with both a signifier and a signified; in addition, many Chinese pictographs could represent more than one word, so that by evoking a sound as well as an image, they were used as phonograms as well. Abstract signs exist, as do compounds, but only one quarter to one third of the approximately 4,500 surviving signs have been deciphered. These symbols appear most often on animal bones that were heated and cracked for the purpose of divination, with the date and the name of the diviner given first, then the question to which an answer was desired; occasionally the answer is present as well. Fewer examples survive of the bronze ritual vessels in which the elite presented offerings to their dead ancestors, with the name either of the person who commissioned the bowl or of the dead ancestor written on it.

Chinese books written on thin slips of wood begin to be found with some regularity in excavations from the 2nd century BC. The slip (*ce* or *jian*), generally made of bamboo, is 9–9 ½ inches long and a quarter- to half-an-inch long, with one column per side but often with writing on both sides. Writing in vertical columns seems to be an accommodation to the shape of the bamboo slip. Fan-fold paper books and scrolls became common beginning in the 2nd century AD. The book was covered with a case, a title was pasted on the corner of the cover, and the book was stored vertically. Characters were formed with a hair brush— an appropriate instrument for writing on silk and bamboo, but one which also helped stimulate the straightening of the curves in the old characters, so that their resemblances to pictorial symbols diminished. Chinese writing was linked to painting through calligraphy, so that by the 3rd century AD the traditional concern for careful letter-making had been extended to book illustration. Imperial edicts and government reports in turn were written on rectangular tablets (*fang*), and writing is also found on triangular prisms (*kie*).

Among the earliest Chinese books is the Book of Odes (*Shijing*), some 300 poems depicting life in the 8th and 7th centuries BC. The works of Confucius (*c.*551–479BC) were also copied frequently. Around AD 100 Xu Shen wrote a lexicon, and Cao Pei (AD 187–226) produced an encyclopaedia. The Chinese also had scholars investigating the authenticity of works, revising and collating texts, and commenting upon early books at roughly the same time as the Alexandrian scholars were active in the West. Emperor Wu-ti (157–87/6BC) set up a body to collect and copy books, and in 26 BC Liu Xiang organized a thorough survey of the book holdings in the Chinese empire.

9 Mesoamerica

Beginning as early as 500 BC, the peoples of Mesoamerica created writing systems in isolation from the Old World (*see* **1, 48**). The earliest of these scripts in particular remain difficult, if not impossible, to read; as iconic, hieroglyphic systems, they preserved a sense of union between spirit and matter that is fundamentally non-European.

A system of prewriting begins with the Olmec civilization around 900 BC. Mesoamerican writing proper began in the glyphic markers of personal identity: people were identified by signs in headdresses, and captors differentiated from captives by gestures and positioning. Initially the headdresses were lexemic, with signified and signifier still coupled, but beginning around 900 BC the lexical identifier was separated from the representation of the body associated with it. This separation remained porous throughout the scripts of Mesoamerica, however, making them iconic in ways that resemble Egyptian hieroglyphs more than cuneiform and early Chinese writing, which moved towards abstraction more quickly and definitively. Actual writing, in which language is represented graphically, detached from the body of the referent, and arranged sequentially to accommodate greater syntactic complexity, appeared around 500 BC in the Zapotec area of Oaxaca, Mexico, but unfortunately much of it cannot be understood with certainty. A handful of texts also survive from the first few centuries after Christ from the area in and around the Isthmus of Tehuantepec. This writing contains relatively few icons; whether it is decipherable or not remains debatable.

The best-known and best-understood Mesoamerican writing is Mayan, for which thousands of texts ranging from the time of Christ to the 16th century survive. The earliest examples remain difficult to decipher, but examples from the classical period contain comprehensible symbols that changed over time. Mayan script was a relative latecomer in Mesoamerica, using the dating system and column format that had become standard in the other scripts by this time. The earliest examples appear on small objects like carved greenstones and heirlooms, with a tendency for one glyph to fill a block first, then for the block to contain several glyphs. Mayan writing is often said to be tied to the administrative and propaganda needs of the complex society from which it originated; but given the relatively small number of people who could read, this assumption is difficult to prove.

The Mayan script remained tied to the society in which it was created and closed to external influences, ultimately dying with the Spanish conquest. Beginning about AD 350–450, however, the civilization around Teotihuacan began to exert its influence, using an open script that was easily adaptable to the languages and cultures with which it came in contact. The more open writing systems continued among the indigenous peoples of Mexico even after the conquest, appearing in court documents alongside Spanish, then eventually giving way to the Roman script of the Europeans.

BIBLIOGRAPHY

L. Avrin, *Scribes, Script, and Books* (1991)

T. Birt, *Das antike Buchwesen in seinem Verhältniss zur Litteratur* (1882)

H. Blanck, *Das Buch in der Antike* (1992)

W. G. Boltz, *The Origin and Early Development of the Chinese Writing System* (1994)

E. H. Boone *et al.*, eds., *Writing Without Words* (1994)

L. Casson, *Libraries in the Ancient World* (2001)

G. Cavallo, *Libri, scribi, scritture a Ercolano* (1983)

—— 'Between *Volumen* and Codex: Reading in the Roman World', in *A History of Reading in the West*, ed. G. Cavallo *et al.*, tr. L. G. Cochrane (1999; French original, 1995)

E. Chiera, *They Wrote on Clay*, ed. G. C. Cameron, 2e (1969)

J. Černý, *Paper and Books in Ancient Egypt* (1952)

P. T. Daniels *et al.*, eds., *The World's Writing Systems* (1996)

O. A. W. Dilke, *Roman Books and their Impact* (1977)

D. Diringer, *The Book before Printing* (1982)

R. W. V. Elliott, *Runes* (1989)

[Galleries Nationales du Grand Palais,] *Naissance de l'écriture* (1982)

H. Gamble, *Books and Readers in the Early Church* (1995)

J.-J. Glassner, *The Invention of Cuneiform*, tr. and ed. Z. Bahrani *et al.* (2003; French original, 2000)

A. Grafton *et al.*, *Christianity and the Transformation of the Book* (2006)

W. Harris, *Ancient Literacy* (1989)

S. D. Houston, ed., *The First Writing* (2004)

M. A. Hussein, *Origins of the Book* (1970)

W. A. Johnson, *Bookrolls and Scribes in Oxyrhynchus* (2004)

F. Kenyon, *Books and Readers in Ancient Greece and Rome*, 2e (1951)

T. Kleberg, *Buchhandel und Verlagswesen in der Antike* (1967)

R. Pfeiffer, *History of Classical Scholarship from the Beginnings to the End of the Hellenistic Age* (1968)

M. Pope, *The Story of Archaeological Decipherment* (1975)

R. Posner *et al.*, *The Hebrew Book* (1975)

Reynolds and Wilson

C. H. Roberts *et al.*, 'Books in the Graeco-Roman World and in the New Testament', in *CHB* 1

W. Schubart, *Das Buch bei den Griechen und Römern*, 3e (1961)

D. Sider, *The Library of the Villa dei Papiri at Herculaneum* (2005)

R. J. Starr, 'The Circulation of Literary Texts in the Roman World', *Classical Quarterly*, 7 (1987), 213–23

J. Svenbro, *Phrasikleia* (1993)

E. Turner *et al.*, *Greek Manuscripts of the Ancient World*, 2e (1987)

B. L. Ullman, *Ancient Writing and its Influence* (1963)

G. Vermes, *The Dead Sea Scrolls* (1977)

D. J. Wiseman, 'Books in the Ancient Near East and in the Old Testament', in *CHB* 1

4

The History of the Book
in Byzantium

N. G. WILSON

In the early years of the 4th century AD, the literary world of Greece and Rome experienced the completion of a revolution that had begun some 200 years earlier: from now on the form of the book was no longer the scroll (Lat. *volumen*), with the text arranged in a series of columns on one side of the papyrus only, but the codex, with pages. The new format had advantages. If one were searching for a particular passage, it was often quicker to find the right page, even if pages were not numbered and had no running titles or headings, than to unwind a scroll to the appropriate point, and the use of both sides of the leaves meant that more text could be written on a given quantity of papyrus or parchment, which now became available as an alternative. This increased capacity ought to have facilitated the preservation of a large proportion of the vast range of Greek literature, especially as papyrus had traditionally been inexpensive and probably still was. Evidently, however, the book trade was not sufficiently organized to deploy the necessary resources. What can now be read is a minute percentage of what was still available then, even despite the loss of a number of early texts. The codex format, however, if the margins were fully used, did permit the preservation of material culled from a wide variety of secondary literature, i.e. ancient scholarly monographs and commentaries, almost none of which have descended as independent texts.

During the millennium of its existence the extent of the Byzantine empire fluctuated greatly, but even after the loss of political control it retained varying degrees of cultural influence in such areas as southern Italy, Sicily, Egypt, the Levant, and the Balkans. From the beginning of the period parchment was adopted with increasing frequency as a more durable, if more expensive, writing material than papyrus. Various scripts were in use for literary texts. Of these, the most calligraphic is the type generally known as biblical uncial or majuscule, seen at its best in the Codex Sinaiticus of the Bible, which can be dated to the middle of the 4th century; but, despite its name, the use of this script was not confined to biblical texts. With the decline of the empire resulting from the Arab conquests, book production suffered; it is not clear, however, to what extent the loss of Egypt in 641 affected the supply of papyrus nor, supposing that it did, whether this was the only or the major factor leading to reduced production. Very few books (or fragments) survive that can plausibly be dated to the second half of the 7th century or any time in the 8th. When signs of a revival appear c.800, it seems likely that the Byzantines were no longer using papyrus in large quantities, but that they were soon able to avail themselves of the introduction of paper, now being produced in the Levant. Nevertheless, information about the supply and price of writing material at this date is almost entirely lacking. A likely conjecture is that shortages led to experiments with styles of script that had hitherto been used in documents rather than literary texts and that could be written with smaller letters. One of these experiments was eventually found to be satisfactory and generally adopted; it has been suggested that this adaptation of cursive script with numerous ligatures combining two or three letters was invented or popularized by monks of the Stoudios monastery in Constantinople, which was noted for its scriptorium from the 9th century onwards. Uncial was gradually abandoned except for a few luxury copies of texts destined for liturgical use.

Book production was determined to a very large extent by religious requirements: copies of the Bible, liturgical texts, lives of saints and sermons by the Cappadocian Fathers and St John Chrysostom survive in considerable numbers. There was also a steady production of texts for use in school, most of which were the classics of ancient pagan literature. Some of these have come down to us in numerous copies, but this is not true of all—the frequently made assumption that each pupil owned a copy of every text in the syllabus is by no means secure. Members of the professions needed their manuals and specialized treatises; higher education, however, was much less well organized than in western Europe and did not develop a pecia system to provide students with copies of

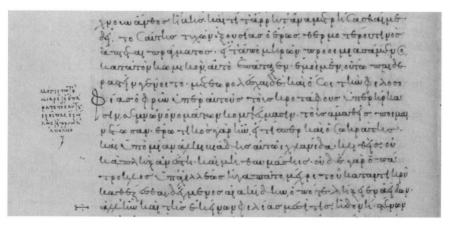

Marginal note by Archbishop Arethas (c.860–c.940) expressing his disgust at Lucian's apparent confession of homosexuality in his Amores. © The British Library Board. All Rights Reserved. Harley. 5694, fol 97v.

essential texts. An educated class that read literature for pleasure scarcely existed. Books seem to have been very expensive. The prices paid by the bibliophile Arethas *c.*900 for a few admittedly calligraphic copies on good-quality parchment prove that a year's salary of a low-ranking civil servant would hardly suffice for the purchase of half-a-dozen volumes. Costs may have been reduced as the production of paper increased; paper was fairly widely used in Byzantium as early as the 11th century, though it probably all had to be imported (*see* **10**). Yet the re-use of parchment in palimpsests continued and was not confined to remote or backward regions of the empire—a fact demonstrating that cheap and readily available writing material could not be taken for granted. In these circumstances, one would expect most scribes to save space by using the comprehensive set of abbreviations that was available for grammatical inflections and certain common words or technical terms. For marginal commentaries the use of the abbreviations was an unavoidable necessity, but generally scribes did not resort to this solution for the main text. They tended to use the abbreviations at the end of a line to achieve justification of the margin, which may be a hint that on aesthetic grounds they preferred to avoid them elsewhere.

Scribes were not organized as a guild. It is clear that many individuals made their own copies rather than employing a professional. There were some professionals, as can be seen from the occasional colophon in which the writer describes himself (women copyists are almost unknown) as a calligrapher; it was possible to earn one's living in this way, but probably not many did so. Some large monasteries (e.g. the Stoudios monastery) had a scriptorium and presumably accepted commissions from external customers; many colophons state that the copyist was a monk. Colophons by Greek scribes are not as frequent or informative as those found in Armenian MSS, however, and so we know relatively little about Greek scribes. A further consequence of this is that it is often impossible to determine in which part of the empire a book was written, because there are only a limited number of cases in which the script gives a clear indication, whereas with Latin MSS it is usually not very difficult to identify the country of origin, and sometimes much greater precision about a MS's provenance can be achieved.

A tantalizing glimpse of the workings of a scriptorium is provided by the rules drawn up for the Stoudios monastery by St Theodore (759–826). There is mention of a chief calligrapher, who is responsible for assigning tasks fairly, preparing the parchment for use, and maintaining the binder's tools in good order. There are penalties for him and for monks who misbehave or fail to perform their duties, e.g. if a scribe breaks a pen in a fit of anger. Inter alia the scribe is required to take care over spelling, punctuation, and diacritics, to stick to his own task, and not to alter the text he is copying. What is not stated is whether a scribe was expected to copy a certain number of pages each day, and how much the house charged external purchasers. There is no reference to illuminators, but scanty evidence from other sources suggests that they may have had independent workshops.

Calligraphy does not appear to have been appreciated in Byzantium as an art in the same way as in some other cultures; but the use of the term by scribes is proof that some clients had a high regard for their services, and many extant MSS are marvels of elegant script with a uniformly high standard maintained for several hundred pages—a striking example is the Euclid written for Arethas in 888 by Stephen the cleric (who as it happens does not call himself a calligrapher in the colophon). It is also clear that, for biblical and other religious texts, there was an expectation that formal script would be used, and generally such books, even if not elegantly written, exhibit a presentable standard of penmanship. This requirement went hand in hand with a conservative tradition characteristic of Byzantine culture: an archaizing tendency detectable in the early years of the Palaeologan period (*c.*1280–*c.*1320) led to the production of many copies, mainly but not exclusively of religious texts, that at first sight look a good deal earlier and as a result used to be incorrectly dated to the 12th century. Nevertheless, schoolteachers and other professionals making copies intended primarily for personal use were often content to write a less formal hand with many cursive elements and abbreviations; these scripts too have often been wrongly dated. In many cases, there is enough individual character in them to permit identification of the writer. A very neat example of this type of script with extremely lavish use of abbreviations is seen in various volumes penned by Eustathius, the lecturer at the patriarch's seminary in the capital, who *c.*1178 became archbishop of Salonica. Much less legible is the protean hand of a 12th-century grammarian called Ioannikios, who can be identified as the scribe of nearly twenty extant MSS, containing predominantly works by Galen and Aristotle, some of which were probably commissioned from him by the Italian translator Burgundio of Pisa.

Circulation and trade are topics about which information is inadequate. The 6th-century lawyer and historian Agathias speaks of bookshops in the capital and there are occasional later references to booksellers. Yet it is curious that a society which attached great importance to the written word and devoted care to the education of imperial and ecclesiastical administrators capable of drafting documents in formal archaizing prose has left so little record of this and other related matters. It is fairly clear, however, that a desire to obtain unusual texts could not normally be satisfied by a visit to a neighbouring shop, even if one lived in the capital of the empire.

The Byzantines called themselves Romans, but understood that they were custodians of the Greek literary heritage; in most of their own writings they did their best to imitate the language and style of the Greek classics. One has to ask how far they succeeded in preserving the stock of Greek literature they had inherited in late antiquity. Already by this date a number of classical texts were no longer in circulation; the destruction of the library at the Serapeum in Alexandria in 391 will no doubt have led to further losses. Though there is very little historical evidence on these matters, it seems that the emperors never succeeded in maintaining a substantial library comparable to those found in the great cultural centres of the ancient world; a monastery with a collection of several hundred volumes such as St John on Patmos was unusually well provided for (an inventory made in 1201 lists 330 items), and a library of fewer than 100 books might be reckoned perfectly satisfactory. The Byzantines would have needed much greater resources than they disposed of in order to conserve a high proportion of the texts that were still extant. For a time they had partial success: Photius in the middle of the 9th century was still able to locate—it is not known how or where—copies of many important works, especially historical texts that no longer survive today. Probably the copies he consulted were already unique, and if they were not texts of orthodox theological content, there was always a risk that they might be discarded by a reader anxious to make a palimpsest copy of some work of seemingly greater relevance (a notorious example is the palimpsest in which liturgical texts have been written over unique treatises by Archimedes, fragments of the Athenian orator Hyperides, and a hitherto unknown commentary on Aristotle's *Categories*). Copies of rare works that had not suffered such a fate or been destroyed by accident mostly disappeared in 1204 when the Fourth Crusade sacked Constantinople. After that date, the range of works available was essentially the same as can now be read in earlier medieval copies. When the Turks took the Byzantine capital in 1453, there were few if any texts, the loss of which we should now regret, lurking in the libraries in Constantinople.

BIBLIOGRAPHY

[Dumbarton Oaks Colloquium,] *Byzantine Books and Bookmen* (1975)

N. Wilson, 'The Libraries of the Byzantine World', *Greek Roman and Byzantine Studies*, 8 (1967) 53–80 (repr. with addenda in *Griechische Kodikologie und Textüberlieferung*, ed. D. Harlfinger (1980), and further addenda (in Italian translation) in *Le biblioteche nel mondo antico e medievale*, ed. G. Cavallo (1988)

—— 'The Manuscripts of the Greek Classics in the Middle Ages and Renaissance', *Classica et Medievalia*, 47 (1996), 379–89

—— *The Oxford Handbook of Byzantine Studies* (2008), 101–14, 820–5

5

The European Medieval Book

CHRISTOPHER DE HAMEL

1 The Dark Ages

For more than a thousand years, between the adoption of the codex as the normal format for MSS in the late Roman empire and the invention of printing in Europe around 1450, all Western books were copied by hand. This is the period that is now called the Middle Ages. Medieval Europe evolved out of the collapse of the Roman empire (Rome finally fell in 476) and emerged in the early kingdoms of Lombardy and in the provinces of Germany, Frankish Gaul, Visigothic Spain, and Anglo-Saxon England. This era is intimately tied up with the history of Christianity, which is a literate religion, like Judaism and Islam. Books—manuscripts (MSS)—were essential to Christianity's success and consolidation. The Scriptures, with written commentaries and interpretations, were fundamental to medieval religious life, and the Christian liturgy was inconceivable without readings and recitations from books. Every church and monastery in Europe inevitably required and used books of some kind. Moreover, Christianity entered into a world where books had been known and valued. The nostalgic and lingering respect for Greek and Roman classical learning survived through the Middle Ages, carrying an uneasy sense that ancient knowledge was somehow unusually special and was even intellectually superior to that of later times. This theme winds in and out of the history of Christian book culture, sometimes in direct conflict and often in an uneasy partnership. The earliest adherents of Christianity grew up in a civilization familiar with Greek and Latin texts of poetry, philosophy, history, and science. Early Christian writers such as Boethius (*c*.480–*c*.524) and Cassiodorus (*c*.490–*c*.580) worked and wrote within this tradition. Boethius was the author of commentaries on Aristotle as well as a work on the Trinity. Cassiodorus, a former Roman civil servant, assembled the *Variae*, a collection of imperial laws, before establishing a monastery near Naples and compiling works on the Psalms and other Christian subjects. Christianity and classical learning were not necessarily contradictory, and the books that emerged around the Mediterranean show debts to both cultures.

A crucial legacy of early Christianity in a Roman context was the invention and adoption of the codex format. Books in the ancient world had mostly been produced on continuous scrolls, but the codex was ideal for texts that needed constant consultation at different places, especially law and the Bible. Biblical texts, such as gospel books, psalters, and the letters of St Paul, are among the most fundamental of early medieval MSS, for they were used in the liturgy as well as in private study. With these came the biblical commentaries, homilies, and explanations of theology and the religious life with which the ever-expanding Christian Church prepared and defended itself against the assaults on the Roman empire from beyond its fragile borders. Many primitive MSS were prepared, probably mostly by monks, of patristic authors such as Ambrose of Milan (*c*.339–97), Jerome (*c*.345–420), Augustine of Hippo (354–430), Gregory the Great (*c*.540–604), and Isidore of Seville (*c*.560–636).

Early Christian books from southern Europe in what are sometimes called the Dark Ages are usually squarish in shape, on parchment (papyrus gradually died out, except in Egypt), and are commonly written in uncial script or rustic capitals, generally with enlarged opening initials often in an orange-red colour, and sometimes with pictures in rather sketchy painterly styles not unlike those of ancient Roman frescos. There must have been sites of book production in places like Ravenna, Lyons (a major Roman town in Gaul), and in Rome itself. On the fringes of the old Roman empire, from former provinces such as Gaul and Spain, informal cursive scripts developed too, derived from the bureaucratic hands of regional imperial administration. Some of these eventually become very distinctive of certain areas, such as Visigothic minuscule in Spain, Beneventan minuscule in southern Italy, and a variety of localizable Merovingian cursive hands in France.

By the late 6th century, the papacy had consolidated its position sufficiently to institute a new, Christian form of Roman imperialism. Gregory the Great sent missionaries to England in 597 bringing, according to Bede, 'all the books that would be necessary' for the conversion of the English. The Roman monks, working northwards in Britain, encountered the Irish or Celtic Christians coming south, carrying their own very different style of books. The ultimate sources of Irish Christianity and MS decoration are elusive, but perhaps both had reached the Western Isles through northern Africa, where the ornament of Coptic books resembles some aspects of what is now known as the Irish or 'insular' style, with its half-uncial script, large interlaced initials, and carpet pages formed of the extremely elaborate decorative interlace of swirling plant stems and incorporating dragons and birds. Famous examples are the Book of Durrow, late 7th century (Dublin, Trinity College, MS 57), the Lindisfarne Gospels, early 8th century (London, BL, Cotton MS Nero D. IV), and the Book of Kells, c.800 (Dublin, Trinity College, MS 58). In the course of the 7th and 8th centuries, the Irish and Roman strands of Christianity merged in Britain, and books were created in a fusion of the two styles. A good example is the Vespasian Psalter (London, BL, Cotton MS Vespasian A. I), made probably in Canterbury, which included innovations like historiated initials, or pictures enclosed within letters. Some MSS created in England, such as the Codex Amiatinus (Florence, Biblioteca Medicea Laurenziana, cod. Amiat.1), a vast single-volume bible in uncial script, are as sophisticated and as classical as anything made in southern Europe.

From England, then, Christianity and insular books moved with missionaries like Willibrord and Boniface to Germany and to other parts of northern Europe. Descendants of the old insular styles are found in MSS made in monasteries and churches founded in Cologne, Fulda, St Gall, Freising, Würzburg, and elsewhere. By the 8th century, there were certainly major centres of book production across southern Germany and Austria; in France at Luxeuil, Autun, Corbie, Fleury, and St-Denis, for example; and in Italy in Monte Cassino, Lucca, Bobbio, Rome, Verona, and elsewhere. The earliest surviving book lists—such as that of St-Wandrille in France in the time of Abbot Wando (742–7)—include gospel books, saints' lives, monastic rules, history, collections of letters from Augustine and Jerome, sermons, and biblical commentaries. The volumes themselves doubtless varied immensely from crowded little tracts in cramped cursive scripts to stately volumes with zoomorphic decoration and bindings ornamented with jewels and precious metal.

2 Carolingian Europe

Charlemagne (c.742–814) took control of the vast Franco-German dominions in the late 8th century. He brought Alcuin (c.740–804) from England to establish a palace library and to reform education in the court. Under circumstances that are hard to document but are graphically visible in the MSS, the script was standardized into a new and (to modern eyes) extremely legible round style, known as Carolingian (or Caroline) minuscule. By the early 9th century, most books being made in Charlemagne's empire conformed to a remarkably consistent style, often beautifully laid out with spacious margins prepared according to mathematically precise proportions. Some books had very fine pictures, modelled (probably deliberately) on late antique prototypes. Devotional books made for the royal family and other principal figures of the Church and nobility sometimes had large initials or even whole pages executed in burnished gold. Some very grand books were evidently commissioned for use as symbolic gifts within the royal families, such as the Dagulf Psalter commissioned by Charlemagne for the pope (Vienna, Österreichisches Nationalbibliothek, Cod. 1861).

There were centres of book production in the great monasteries in Aachen, Tours, Auxerre, St-Amand, Reichenau, and elsewhere, making books for their own use and sometimes also for outsiders. The monastery of St-Martin in Tours, for example, produced Latin bibles for export, such as the spectacular and massive First Bible of Charles the Bald, written *c*.846 (Paris, BNF, ms. lat. 1). Major MSS were made in and around Rheims, including the Utrecht Psalter, *c*.820–40, which has dynamic and frenzied drawings clearly derived from ancient Roman models (Utrecht, University Library, MS 32). It is commonly associated with Ebo (d. 851), archbishop of Rheims 816–35, who had previously been court librarian in Aachen. Another book from Rheims is the vast Bible of San Paolo fuori le Mura—still in the monastery of that name on the outskirts of Rome—*c*.870, perhaps brought to Italy by Charles the Bald at the time of his coronation by the pope in 875. The 9th century is the first period from which MSS survive from France, Italy, and Germany in any reasonable quantity, including the earliest copies of many classical texts. The handsome appearance of many Carolingian books is a reflection of European prosperity and an evident desire for order and legibility.

In England, however, book production fell off dramatically during the Viking invasions of the 9th century. In a reversal of Charlemagne and Alcuin, Alfred the Great, king of Wessex 871–99, brought scholars from France—such as Grimbald of St-Bertin (d. 901)—to revive learning in England. The Carolingian script was promoted in England, especially in Winchester under Aethelwold, bishop 963–84, and was also practised in Canterbury, Abingdon, and Worcester. Important Anglo-Saxon books include the Benedictional of St Aethelwold himself (London, BL, Add. MS 49598); the Eadui Gospels, early 11th century, signed by the Canterbury scribe Eadui surnamed Basan, 'the fat' (Hanover, Kestner Museum, WM. xxi[a] 36); and the Harley Psalter, copied in mid-11th-century Canterbury from the 9th-century Utrecht Psalter, mentioned above (London, BL, Harley MS 603).

The Carolingian legacy was taken up by the Ottonian emperors in Germany, and magnificent MSS were made for Otto III, emperor 983–1002, including a gospel book of quite exceptional splendour in a lavish jewelled binding (Munich, Bayerische Staatsbibliothek, Clm. 4453). Centres such as Bamberg, Reichenau (probably), Trier, and Echternach produced books with very fine illumination, including work by the important Trier artist of the late 10th century known as the Master of the Registrum Gregorii. Some Ottonian imperial MSS were written in gold on purple parchment, a symbolic device believed to go back to the libraries of the emperors of ancient Rome and Constantinople.

In the meantime, MSS were being made in monasteries and churches in Greece and the eastern Mediterranean (*see* 4). Most Greek texts of the Middle Ages were religious, rather than the secular texts of the ancient world. The most common were the different parts of the Bible (the original language of the New

Testament) and patristic and liturgical books. Some were finely illuminated, such as the 6th-century Vienna Genesis (Vienna, Österreichisches Nationalbibliothek, Cod. theol. gr. 31). From 726 until about 842, the period of Iconoclasm, MS illustrations were banned in the eastern empire. Until about the 9th century, most Greek MSS were written in uncial script; minuscule was adopted especially following the initiative of Theodore of Stoudios (759–826), who refounded the monastery and scriptorium of Stoudios in Constantinople in 799.

3 Romanesque Europe

In western Europe, religious life was reformed under Gregory VII, pope 1073–85, whose papacy marked the beginning of a century or more of vigorous monastic fervour, the building and re-endowing of many Benedictine houses, and the foundation and spread of new orders, including the Cluniacs, Augustinians, Cistercians, and Carthusians. This was a most intensive period of book production in European monasteries and priories. Library inventories and very large numbers of surviving Romanesque books attest to vigorous attempts to make monastic collections as comprehensive as possible. Chronicles often record that an abbot or bishop had given great sets of books, which may often mean that the benefactor had sponsored their production in high-profile campaigns of building up libraries. Some records survive, showing monasteries seeking exemplars from elsewhere and lending books to each other. After the Norman Conquest of England in 1066, MSS and scribes were sent from Normandy to English cathedrals, and strong cultural links with French Benedictine monasteries such as Jumièges and Mont-St-Michel are reflected in books made for English cathedral priories, especially Christ Church in Canterbury, Exeter, and Durham. Echoes of Norman forms of script and decoration can be seen too in late 11th-century books made in Sicily, similarly occupied by the Normans from about 1060. A generation later, remarkable homogeneity may be observed in Cistercian MSS. Their austere and elegant style, with prickly script and monochrome initials, may have begun in the mother house of Cîteaux in Burgundy, but the style is easily recognizable in Cistercian books made as far away as monasteries of the order in eastern and southern Europe. The centralized administration of the Cistercian houses has left clear traces in the books they made.

The number of texts in circulation at any period was cumulative. Each generation added new authors and titles to an ever-expanding corpus of required books. The librarian of a late 11th-century monastery might want copies of the Bible—including one of the new, vast many-volumed lectern bibles initially popular in Italy—with the fundamental biblical commentaries, such as Gregory on the books of Ezekiel and Job, Augustine on the Psalms and John, Jerome on the Prophets, Ambrose on Luke, and Bede on Acts. He would want basic theology and philosophy, such as the *Consolatio Philosophiae* of Boethius and Augustine's *De Civitate Dei*, and some works of Carolingian authors such as Claudius of

Turin (d. *c*.827), Rabanus Maurus (d. 856), Pascasius Radbertus (d. 865), and Remigius of Auxerre (d. *c*.908); monastic rules and canons of church councils; early Christian history, including Eusebius, Orosius, and perhaps Bede, and selected saints' lives; some mathematics, music, and science; basic medicine (a herbal perhaps); a few classical texts used for teaching grammar, such as Virgil; and liturgy, of course. It is a good list, but ultimately a finite one. By the early 12ᵗʰ century a monastery would want all these books, and many more, for there were new texts now by Lanfranc (d. 1089), Anselm of Canterbury (d. 1109), Ivo of Chartres (d. 1115), Anselm of Laon (d. 1117), and many others. By the second quarter of the century, learning had begun to move away from the exclusive monopolies of the monasteries, into the schools which eventually evolved into medieval universities, and into the domain of literate laity, both aristocratic and administrative. The number of authors had multiplied further, including Gilbert of Nogent (d. 1124), Rupert of Deutz (d. *c*.1129), Gilbert of Auxerre (d. 1134), Peter Abelard (d. 1142/3), Hugh of St-Victor (d. 1142), William of Malmesbury (d. *c*.1143), Bernard of Clairvaux (d. 1153), Gilbert de la Porrée (d. 1154), William of Conches (d. *c*.1154), Thierry of Chartres (d. *c*.1155), Zachary of Besançon (mid-12ᵗʰ century), and Peter Lombard (d. 1160). There was an almost relentless stream of new titles in the lists of desiderata, in theology, history, politics, geography, natural history (bestiaries, for example), liturgy (missals rather than the older sacramentaries), and the first ancient Greek works translated into Latin from Arabic intermediaries. At the same time, monasteries were increasingly being expected to produce books for lay patrons as well, including luxury psalters. It was too much. What was laudable and mostly achievable for many monastic scriptoria in 1050 was simply impossible a century later. This has significant implications.

The mid-12ᵗʰ century was probably the most important watershed in medieval European book production. It affected what books looked like and how they were made. These two points can be taken in turn. Before the 12ᵗʰ century, monks would generally read books aloud to themselves, from end to end, slowly meditating and ruminating on the text. A monk could spend several months or even years studying a single book and could still hope to master most of his monastery's library in a lifetime. By about 1150, however, the number of works in circulation had rapidly become far too great for any person to manage. New kinds of books were therefore devised: glossed texts with selected marginal quotations for quick reference, encyclopaedias (such as Peter Lombard's *Sententiae* for theology and Gratian's *Decretum* for canon law), concordances, florilegia, digests, and indexes. Scribes devised ways of looking things up, with devices such as alphabetical order, chapter numbers for the Bible and other texts, tables of contents, coloured paragraph-marks, running titles along the top of pages, sometimes even folio numbers, all of which were the result of a sudden excess of knowledge. This phenomenon has some parallels with the information explosion of the 21ˢᵗ century, with innovations in the ways of searching texts. For the first time, books became resources to be consulted, frequently at speed, rather than merely to be read at leisure. The changes were also due to an increase in the lay readership of books, including literate administrators and lawyers. Unlike monks, these were often people in a hurry. A MS of about 1200, usually in two columns, bristling with many carefully graded coloured initials, its margins packed with forms of apparatus for rapid reference, is very different in appearance from a typical book of 150 years earlier, commonly written as a single column of dense text, elegant but austere, with few initials and scarcely any division between words and almost none between paragraphs.

It is reasonable to assume that most MSS earlier than the 12th century were copied by monks (and sometimes nuns), or at least by members of the Church, mostly in leisure time or in periods set aside among other daily duties of the religious life. Where there is historical or architectural evidence, it seems that scribes commonly worked in the cloisters, where the light was good. Sometimes several monks collaborated on a single book, writing and decorating different sections of the (still unbound) volume. The script and the associated decoration were often executed by the same people. All this began to change around 1100. The sudden and rapid increase in the number of books meant that many monasteries simply no longer had the resources or the time to keep up. Some were also under additional pressure to supply luxurious devotional books, like psalters, for local lords and their families. The first evidence emerges of professional scribes, called in by a scriptorium to help with book production, and of secular artists and craftsmen, who evidently travelled from place to place, employed to decorate and illuminate books. A well-known and documented example in England is Master Hugo, whose name suggests that he was not a monk, who was engaged for various artistic projects at Bury St Edmunds Abbey in the 1130s, including the illumination of the Bury Bible (Cambridge, Corpus Christi College, MS 2). It may be that the increased professionalism and specialization of artists might help explain the increasingly lavish quality of many 12th-century books, often using expensive pigments, such as lapis and burnished gold. Probably too this marks the gradual transference of the place of working from the cloister, which was open to the weather (which would make manipulating gold leaf almost impossible), to some dedicated studio indoors.

By the mid-12th century, professional scribes and illuminators were beginning to set up commercial and urban businesses independent of monasteries. The earliest city in which this certainly occurred was probably Paris, where potential clients were attracted by the royal court and by attendance at the schools of Notre-Dame and St-Victor, forerunners of the university. There were probably also professional workshops at Sens and possibly at Troyes in France within the 12th century, and at Bologna and Oxford by about 1200. The secular book trade in western Europe is well documented in the 13th century. With certain notable exceptions (like the work of Matthew Paris, monk of St Albans), few MSS were still being made in monasteries or churches by 1250. A late medieval monastery, wanting a book (for many did, of course), would usually have resorted to a professional craftsman, or urban workshop.

4 Script and decoration

The style of medieval script and book illumination varied immensely through-out the 1,500 years or so of the Middle Ages. The graceful and spacious Carolingian minuscule, first adopted around 800, gradually became heavier with the passage of time, losing its roundness (except in Italy) and fusing laterally about the 1180s into what is usually called 'Gothic' script, or 'textura'. This, in turn, split off into formal display hands, beautiful to look at but slow to write, and the quick cursive scripts of many less grand late medieval books. These hands too constantly diverged and re-crossed, spawning their own unexpected descendants, reflected in the intriguing medieval term *lettre bâtarde* of the 15th century. Pictorial styles too in MSS conform to the general trends of other contemporaneous arts and architecture. Close parallels can be found between jaunty 7th-century MS decoration of northern Europe and barbarian metal-work and enamels; between sombre and monumental 12th-century miniatures and Romanesque wall-paintings; between sparkling 13th-century illumination and Gothic stained-glass windows, infused with blue and red; between grace-ful 14th-century Italian book illustration and the panel paintings and frescos of the early Renaissance; and between the homely, engaging, and sometimes comic miniatures of southern Netherlandish books of around 1500 and the paintings of the Flemish primitives, from the Van Eycks to the Bruegels. That is as one would expect. Often, in fact, they were the same actual craftsmen, working in different media.

Most MSS are transcribed from other MSS, and absorb something of their exemplars and of their creator's own time. The lines of textual transmission can be immensely complicated, for a book may be copied from one source and cor-rected or corrupted against several others, wisely or carelessly, or may have been taken from a very recent exemplar or one which was already many centuries old, or both. The lines of textual descent are predicated by—and are sometimes actually evidence of—trade routes and cultural exchanges of extreme and fasci-nating complexity. The universality of Latin, the principal language of most west European MSS before (and even after) the 13th century, accorded an inter-nationalism to the book trade which it has never really recovered, even today.

If the differences in physical appearance of medieval books had to be catego-rized, it would not be that styles change over various periods and places of pro-duction, for that is obvious and as expected, but that the books vary according to their kind of text, even at the same period. This is crucial, and is more marked in MSS than in any period of printed books. A missal, the most formal of liturgi-cal books, would be of a very different size and shape from a utilitarian cartu-lary, for example, and would be written in a very different script and ornamented in an entirely different way. These would both, in turn, be quite unlike a volume of classical poetry, probably in a tall narrow format with the first letters of each line slightly separated to the left of the text block, or a heavy lectern bible, in two columns marked for public reading, or a genealogical chronicle, strung together like washing on a line, or a pocket-sized book of friars' sermons in tiny abbreviated script, and yet all might have been made at the same period, perhaps even by the same scribe. The hierarchy of MSS, like much of medieval social life, was very pronounced.

5 The Gothic book trade

The best-documented early professional book trade was in Paris. This was mainly, but not exclusively, because of the emerging university, which had been formed into a legally distinct corporation by about 1215, attracting students and literate laity from all over Europe. Many booksellers, or *libraires*, were established in the rue Neuve Notre-Dame, the street created around 1164 leading directly out from the west door of the cathedral on the Île de la Cité (now a pedestrian precinct, with the medieval street-plan marked on its flagstones). Here second-hand books could be bought, and new MSS could be commissioned. The actual work was subcontracted. The parchmenters, scribes, and illuminators often lived on the left bank, in the rue des Ecrivains (already so named by 1209) and the rue Erembourg de Brie, both in the parish of St-Séverin beside the rue St-Jacques, which runs south from the Petit Pont. The names of many such workers are recoverable from documentary sources such as taxation records—at least before 1307, when registered booksellers secured exemption from the *taille*, or royal tax. No fewer than 58 booksellers and 68 parchmenters are known by name from 13th-century Paris.

The university exercised considerable control over the book trade in Paris, ostensibly to prevent over-charging and exploitation of a market on which scholarship depended. From 1275, as far as we know, booksellers were first licensed by swearing oaths of obedience to the university, against the security of a bond of 100 *livres*, limiting the profits which they might make in the buying and selling of books. No one except a sworn bookseller, however, could legally practise his trade in Paris, apart from market traders offering used books valued at no more than 30 sous. There were also strict regulations governing the hiring out of peciae. The registered booksellers would own unbound exemplars of specific university textbooks, checked and confirmed as accurate (or meant to be) by the university authorities. These they would then hire out in separate sections, a gathering or pecia at a time, so that students or others could copy out the texts themselves, rather like a lending library for scribes. When one section had been copied, the borrower would return the pecia to the bookseller, collect the next in sequence, and so on. It meant that many scribes could in theory be making their own copies of the same book at once, and each transcript was taken directly from a corrected and approved exemplar. These official exemplars are listed in the university regulations of 1275 and repeated in 1304.

Something very similar, although so far not as well documented, occurred in the University of Bologna, where there were also official pecia lists, mainly for law books, in which that university was supreme. Sometimes the MSS themselves still contain discreet notes in the margins where the scribe has jotted down the number of the pecia being copied, which is clear and satisfying evidence of a book being made in a university context. There are huge numbers of extant 13th- and 14th-century MSS from the university towns of Europe. Those from Paris include many texts of scholastic theology and biblical commentary. Among these are works by the great Dominican masters (such as Hugh of St-Cher, d. 1263, Thomas Aquinas, d. 1274, and Albertus Magnus, d. 1280), and the Franciscans, including Bonaventure (d. 1274), Duns Scotus (d. 1308), and Nicholas of Lyra (d. 1349). There were also textbooks of mathematics and science, especially new Latin versions of Aristotle, derived from medieval translations into Arabic. MSS from Bologna included books of Roman law, both secular and religious, often with extensive commentaries. The corpus of civil law was centred on the late Roman legal codes of Justinian and its various imperial supplements. Canon law included huge compilations of papal or episcopal letters known as decretals, of which the best-known collections circulated under the names of Popes Gregory IX (1234), Boniface VIII (1298), and Clement V (1317).

With notable exceptions, university MSS are often big, chunky volumes, written on brownish parchment in highly compressed and abbreviated bookhands, decorated with simple trailing initials in red and blue, and with wide margins crammed with readers' notes and glosses. Some have small sparkling illuminations, evidently by professional artists. Apart from those made in Paris and Bologna, there are recognizably university books attributable to Montpellier, Toulouse, Oxford, and Padua, and later to Cambridge, Erfurt, and elsewhere.

The principal university towns were a focus not merely for students, but also for royal and ecclesiastical administrators, wealthy aristocratic families, and communities of urban friars (or, put differently, the great administrative and religious cities were not merely a focus for civil servants, noblemen, and friars, but also for universities). It is very clear that the early book trade in Paris, Bologna, and Oxford, especially, was not only catering for an academic market but also had a local clientele that was both lower and higher than the university in the hierarchy of customers. At the bottom end—this is not insulting: they would ask to be there—were the friars. The Dominican and Franciscan convents in Paris, Bologna, and Oxford were among the largest and oldest in Europe. Friars were mendicants, travelling and preaching in public. Their books had to be small and portable. There evolved quite rapidly a distinctive class of MSS of appropriate texts, such as sermon collections, theological florilegia, treatises on virtues and vices, and guides to confession. These are written on very thin parchment in minute scripts, within bindings that were often of limp parchment or leather, rather than great pieces of wood, all small and light enough to slip into a pocket or mendicant's travelling pouch. It is from this direction that we must look at 13th-century Latin bibles. These little one-volume portable bibles represent one of the supreme success stories of book production in the Middle Ages.

They are extremely common. Almost for the first time, they contained the entire Bible, from beginning to end, as we know it now, in a single volume. The components are in a standard and logical order (something almost unknown before 1200); they are divided into chapters and are supplied with alphabetical indices of Hebrew names. The whole volume can fit into the palm of one's hand. Bibles of the 13th century are often illuminated with tiny historiated initials, no bigger than the smallest of fingernails, marking the beginning of each of their 84 or so books and prologues. They are sometimes called 'university bibles', but it is increasingly clear that their inspiration, format, and extraordinary success were due to the patronage of the Dominicans and Franciscans. So many were made in the 13th century that they evidently furnished the need for Latin bibles for the rest of the Middle Ages, in copies sold and resold for hundreds of years. Bibles as physical books have hardly evolved in shape, size, and arrangement ever since: many of the innovations designed for the friars by the booksellers of Paris in the 1230s are still found in any traditional modern printed bible today.

6 Lay literacy

If the small-format friars' bibles represent the first moment of the mass publication of popular books in Europe, there was also a constantly increasing and important market for books at the other end of the social spectrum. The relentless advance of lay literacy is a consistent theme throughout most of the history of Europe in the last thousand years, even now. The Ottonian and Carolingian emperors had owned books. By the late 12th century, some exceedingly grand MSS were being made for members of the European royal houses—such as gospels for Henry the Lion, duke of Saxony (c.1188, Wolfenbüttel, Herzog August Bibliothek, Cod. Guelf. 105 Noviss. 2° and Munich, Clm. 30055), and psalters for Geoffrey Plantagenet, son of Henry II of England (c.1190, later owned by Louis IX, Leiden, Bibliotheek der Rijksuniversiteit, MS. lat. 76A), Ingeborg of Denmark, wife of Philippe Auguste (c.1195, Chantilly, Musée Condé, ms. 9), and Blanche of Castile, wife of Louis VIII (c.1200, Paris, Bibliothèque de l'Arsenal, ms. 1186). These are illuminated MSS of extraordinary splendour, filled with dozens of full-page pictures, and they must have been phenomenally expensive to make. They are eclipsed, however, by even more extravagant copies of the *Bible moralisée*, of which four principal sets were made for Louis IX and members of his family in France, c.1220–c.1240 (Vienna, Österreichische Nationalbibliothek, cod. 2554 and cod. 1179; Toledo Cathedral and New York, Pierpont Morgan Library, M. 240; and Oxford, Bodleian Library, MS Bodley 270b, Paris, BNF, ms. lat. 11560, and London, BL, Harley MSS 1526–7). It is hard to convey the extreme opulence of these vast, illustrated, royal MSS, originally with more than 13,000 pictures each, in brilliant colours and shimmering burnished gold. The precise circumstances of their production are still unclear, but they were doubtless the work of professional artists, even if the books were not actually made in the kind of workshop to which the public would normally have access.

Fashions trickle downwards. Literacy moves sideways. The 13th-century booksellers of Paris, who were coordinating the production of textbooks for students and bibles for friars, were also selling illuminated psalters and other luxury books to the lesser aristocracy and upper middle classes. It is not always easy to identify the original patrons, for heraldry was not yet as precise or as widespread an art as it became in the 14th century, and lay literacy frustratingly seldom extended to writing names on endpapers. Furthermore, many psalters have survived only because they were later given or bequeathed to religious communities, for which (as careful examination reveals) they were not originally intended. In the course of the 13th century, psalters for the possession and private devotion of the laity became more and more common. A smaller format and the numbers and subjects of the pictures became more routine.

The proliferation of lay psalters was not restricted to Paris, and clear clusters of production can be identified in places like Artois (perhaps in St-Omer), Bruges, Oxford, Alsace (probably in Strasbourg), Würzburg, Regensburg, and elsewhere. The usual format was a calendar at the front, listing the saints' days for the year, followed by a sequence of full-page pictures; then came the psalter itself, with the 150 psalms, usually divided into eight sections, each marked with a large initial, continuing without a break into the biblical canticles, and a Litany; at the end was the Office of the Dead followed by additional prayers to the Virgin Mary and the saints. The supplementary section at the very end gradually assumed ever-greater importance, consistent with the growing cult of the Virgin. It evolved into a series of eight daily occasions for devotion to the Virgin, with selections of appropriate psalms and short hymns. These were named 'hours' after the eight daily services of the monks: Matins, Lauds, Prime, Terce, Sext, None, Vespers, and Compline. By the third quarter of the 13th century this part had become so extensive that, as the metaphor goes, the tail began wagging the dog. For many clients, the whole psalter became superfluous and so scribes omitted it, leaving instead a calendar, the new Hours of the Virgin, the seven Penitential Psalms with Litany, and the Office of the Dead. This was the book of hours, the most famous and the most common MS of the last part of the Middle Ages. It was entirely a lay creation, for private use at home.

A second major result of increasing lay literacy was the production of MSS in the vernacular. With a few and rare exceptions (most notably in late Anglo-Saxon England), almost all books made in Europe before about 1180 had been in Latin. Although it was no longer spoken as a native tongue, Latin was the language of formal education and of the Church. By the early 13th century, however, literacy was beginning to overtake learning, at least among the classes who could afford illuminated MSS. The first booksellers in Paris also undertook MSS of literary romances, either in verse or prose, often loosely linked to the recurring themes of chivalry, which are the war and fall of Troy, the court of King Arthur (including the popular *Lancelot* romances), and the wars of Charlemagne against the Saracens. The allegorical *Roman de la Rose* was begun by Guillaume de Lorris around 1230–35 and finished by Jean de Meun in the early 1270s. Vernacular texts of simple science or self-improvement included the *L'Image du monde* (1246) of Gossuin de Metz, the *Livres dou trésor* (1266–8) of Brunetto Latini, the *Livre de Sydrach: La Fontaine de toutes sciences* (*c*.1270), and others.

There were also translations of classical and religious texts, including the popular *Bible Historiale*, translated by Guyart des Moulins in the early 1290s (revised in 1312) from the 12th-century *Historia Scholastica* of Peter Comestor. All these were produced in fine MSS for an aristocratic and upper middle-class market, often richly illuminated and illustrated in accordance with the client's wealth or desire to impress his family or neighbours. Similar texts were produced in the Holy Roman Empire, in the different dialects of German. A famous example is the Manesse Codex of Middle High German romantic verse, written probably on the Swiss side of Lake Constance in the early 14th century (Heidelberg, Universitätsbibliothek, Cod. Pal. Germ. 848). Devotional texts were quite often copied in the German vernacular, a fact that has some interest for the history of spirituality. It can be argued that the professionalism of the book trade had considerable significance in the spread and stabilization of vernacular languages. The dominance of the Tuscan dialect in Italy is commonly attributed to the enormous success and circulation of Dante's *Divina Commedia*, composed between 1308 and the author's death in 1321, which survives in more than 600 MSS from the 14th century alone. MSS of the *Vite dei Sancti Padri*, translated into Italian by Domenico Cavalca (d. 1342), are far more common than the original text had been in Latin. In England, the development of the vernacular was complicated by the existence of two spoken languages, as well as written Latin. People of Norman descent and the major landowners—those likely to commission MSS—all spoke French, or its Anglo-Norman dialect. The peasants and lower bourgeoisie spoke Middle English, but would seldom have been literate or wealthy enough before the late 14th century to own books. The result is that the very grandest aristocratic books made in England, like the famous and lavishly illustrated 13th- and early 14th-century Apocalypses, are mostly in French. The finest of all were probably made for the English royal family, who spoke French exclusively, including Cambridge, Trinity College, MS R.16.2, and Oxford, Bodleian Library, MS Douce 180. Not until the publication of the *Canterbury Tales* after Chaucer's death in 1400 had the English language really moved up the scale far enough to have become socially acceptable.

It is reasonable to assume that by the mid- to late 13th century most countries of western Europe had organized facilities, if not settled urban workshops, for the writing and illuminating of books. In England, the best evidence of a secular book trade is from Oxford and, as in Paris, MSS attributable to that centre include not only academic texts but also friars' one-volume bibles, lay psalters, and works of vernacular literature. The illuminator who signed two MSS 'W. de Brailes' (Cambridge, Fitzwilliam Museum, MS 330, and London BL, Add. MS 49999) is generally accepted as being William de Brailes, documented in Oxford between 1238 and 1252. It is likely that there was some kind of commercial book production in Salisbury, York, Westminster, perhaps Lincoln, and (but not certainly) Cambridge, all within the 13th century. The first documented book-seller in London is, curiously, as late as 1311. Later still, London came to dominate English book production, as decisively as Paris did in France. Until that happened, some illuminators probably still travelled from place to place, picking up work and moving on. Others may have been members of the households of their employers, as doubtless the scribes and illuminators of Edward I were in Westminster Palace, or wherever the court was in residence. The Bohun family, major patrons of book production in 14th-century England, employed at least two illuminators at Pleshey Castle in Essex, both Augustinian friars (they probably doubled as family chaplains)—John de la Teye, recorded in 1361 and 1384, and Henry Hood, recorded in 1384 and 1390.

Unlike medieval France and England, Italy was still a mass of small independent principalities, dukedoms, and republics, associated only loosely by proximity to each other and by a similar language. There was none of the centralized administration that helped concentrate the French book trade in Paris, or that of the Holy Roman Empire in Prague and Vienna. Even the papacy was exiled from Rome, and the best-documented trade in MS production for the papal court is at Avignon, in southern France, where the popes lived from 1309 to 1377. Certain regions of Italy developed characteristic styles of illumination. Bologna has already been mentioned, and the dominance of legal studies at its university brings it as near to a cultural capital as any by 1300. Very fine bibles and liturgical books, as well as legal MSS and secular romances, are all attributable to Bologna in the late 13th and early 14th centuries. The early Bolognese style, however, is remarkably similar to that of MSS from Padua and Venice, and without supporting evidence, illumination from those three cities is not always easy to separate. Central Italian MSS are usually recognizable, especially Umbrian book production (Perugia was clearly a principal place of production). Southern Italy produced fine books too, particularly Naples. A spectacular example is the hunting book of Frederick II, *De Arte Venandi cum Avibus*, illuminated in Naples *c.*1258–61, with about 660 miniatures (Rome, Biblioteca Vaticana Apostolica, cod. Pal. lat. 1071). Although the evidence is scanty and still in need of research, it is likely too that Liguria was important for book production before 1300, and Genoa may yet prove to have been a major centre.

7 The late Middle Ages and the Renaissance

By the 14th century Italy had already embarked on that cultural rollercoaster later known as the Renaissance. One practical result of the new recognition of the human being as a free and individual spirit is that the names of artists and illuminators begin to be recorded in considerable numbers, and the distinctive hands of specific painters can be recognized, rather than the mere workshop styles by which medieval artists had tried to conceal their personal traits. Some Italian illuminators are extremely famous, and were already celebrated in their own time. Others have modern names assigned from distinctive pieces of work.

In Bologna, a series of illuminators are designated after work on dated guild statutes as the Masters of 1285, 1311, 1314, 1328, and so on, to the Master of 1446. There are also: Nerio, early 14th century; the prolific Nicolò di Giacomo di Nascimbene, documented 1345 to c.1403, known as Nicolò da Bologna; and the Master of the Brussels Initials, c.1400, named after his work in France on the Brussels Hours of the duc de Berry (Brussels, Bibliothèque Royale, MSS 11060-1). In Siena, there are Lippo Vanni, *fl.* c.1340–c.1375, and Sano di Pietro (1405–81). In Florence, many illuminators are known, including Pacino do Bonaguida, also a panel painter, early 14th century; the 'Maestro Daddesco' (*fl.* c.1320–c.1360), a sobriquet that may conceal the identity of more than one illuminator, named from similarity of style to the work of the panel painter Bernardo Daddi (d. 1348); the Master of the Dominican Effigies (*fl.* c.1325–c.1355); don Silvestro dei Gherarducci (1339–99), also a panel painter and a monk, prior of Camaldoli from 1398; don Simone Camaldolese; Lorenzo Monaco (c.1370–c.1424), perhaps originally from Siena, also a monk from 1390 at the Camaldolese monastery of Santa Maria degli Angeli in Florence; Zanobi Strozzi (1412–68), who worked also with Fra Angelico; ser Ricciardo di Nanni, *fl.* 1445–80; Bartolomeo d'Antonio Varnucci (1410–79); Francesco d'Antonio del Chierico (1433–84); Gherardo di Giovanni (c.1446–97); Monte de Giovanni (1448–1532/3); and Vante di Gabriello di Vanti Attavanti (1452–1520/25, known as Attavante).

Many MSS were produced in Milan and other places in Lombardy. Important illuminators there included Giovannino de Grassi (d. 1398, documented in Milan from 1389, illuminator of the Visconti Hours: Florence, Biblioteca Nazionale Centrale, Landau Finaly cod. 22); Michelino da Besozzo (*fl.* in Pavia, 1388 to after 1450); the prolific and engaging Master of the *Vitae Imperatorum*, early to mid-15th century; the Master of the Franciscan Breviary, *fl.* c.1440–c.1460, and the related Master of the Budapest Antiphoner, *fl.* c.1444–c.1450, named after Budapest (Orságos Széchényi Könyvtár (library of the National Museum), c.l.m.ae. 462); the Master of Ippolita Sforza, *fl.* 1450–75; Cristoforo de' Predis, *fl.* c.1450–87; Giovan Pietro Birago, from about 1490 to c.1518 (also in Brescia); and the Master 'B.F.', as he signs himself (*fl.* c.1495–c.1545). In Rimini there was Neri da Rimini (*fl.* c.1300–c.1338); in Perugia, Matteo di ser Cambio (c.1320–1424); and in Verona, Felice Feliciano (1443–c.1480), Liberale da Verona (1445–c.1529), Francesco Dai Libri (c.1450–c.1506), and his son Girolamo Dai Libri (c.1475–1555). These last three are especially known for monumental choirbooks.

Illuminators in Venice included Cristoforo Cortese from the last decade of the 14th century until his death in 1445, and the Master of the Putti (*fl.* c.1466–74), who also worked on printed books. Important names in Naples are Gioacchino di Giovanni de' Gigantibus, *fl.* 1450–85, born in Rottemberg in Bavaria (he also worked in Rome); Matteo Felice, *fl.* 1467–93; and Cola Rapicano and Cristoforo Majorana, both second half of the 15th century. Their style, not surprisingly, seems almost indistinguishable from MSS from Catalonia, across the sea in

Spain. Perhaps they travelled. Ferrara and Este court patronage attracted illuminators who worked elsewhere too, including Taddeo Crivelli (*c*.1420–30 to *c*.1476–9, also known in Bologna), Giorgio d'Alemagna (d. 1479), documented in Ferrara 1441–62 and in Modena 1473–6; Guglielmo Giraldi, recorded 1441–94; Franco dei Russi, *fl.* 1455–*c*.1482, born in Mantua but documented in Ferrara, Padua, Venice, and Urbino; Girolamo da Cremona, documented 1460–83 in Ferrara, Padua, Mantua, Siena, Florence, and Venice; and Cosmè Tura (*c*.1430–95). Rome and the papal court seduced many of the best illuminators of all, but not really until the mid-15th century. They included the master scribe and Renaissance book designer from Padua, Bartolomeo Sanvito (1435–1511), and his sometime collaborator, Gaspare da Padova (*fl. c*.1466–*c*.1493, also called the Master of the Vatican Homer), and several of the last great practitioners of MS illumination, including Antonio da Monza, *fl. c*.1490–*c*.1518, from Lombardy, and one of the most famous of all, the Croatian Giorgio Giulio Clovio (1498–1578), painted by El Greco, eulogized by Vasari.

Although there were certainly regional styles of book illumination in 14th-century France (Metz and Cambrai come to mind), Paris continued to dominate the northern book trade and to attract the best craftsmen. It was by far the largest city in medieval Europe. Identifiable illuminators included Honoré d'Amiens, recorded 1289–1312, who was working for the royal family by 1296. Among his MSS was the Breviary of Philippe le Bel (Paris, BNF, ms. lat. 1023). Another illuminator was Jean Pucelle (d. 1334, documented from *c*.1319), known for the two-volume Belleville Breviary (Paris, BNF, ms. lat. 10483–4) and the tiny Hours of Jeanne d'Évreux (New York, Metropolitan Museum of Art, The Cloisters, Acc.54.1.2). He and his workshop clearly had some business association with the Dominicans, especially with the royal convent of Poissy, downstream on the Seine. French royal patronage achieved its greatest height in the commissions of Charles V (1338–80, king of France from 1364) and his successor Charles VI (1368–1422, r. from 1380), and Charles VI's younger brothers, Jean, duc de Berry, and Philippe le Hardi, duke of Burgundy (1342–1404), and, in time, Philippe's own son and successor, Jean sans Peur (1371–1419). The king and the royal dukes all formed magnificent libraries, many of which are documented in detailed inventories, with histories and chronicles, chivalric romances, allegories, texts of theology and saints' lives, classical texts, moral instruction, poetry, music, politics, warfare, hunting, and alchemy—many of them in specially commissioned translations into French—together with bibles (sometimes also in French), breviaries and missals, and the increasingly popular books of hours, in which they seem to have competed in luxury and refinement. Those made for the duc de Berry include a psalter, *c*.1380, illuminated by André Beauneveu (Paris, BNF, ms. fr. 13091), the *Petites Heures*, *c*.1390 (ibid., ms. lat. 18014), the Brussels Hours, *c*.1400, by Jacquemart de Hesdin and others (Brussels, Bibliothèque royale, ms. 719 (11060–1), the *Grandes Heures*, 1409 (Paris, BNF, ms. lat. 919), and the two supreme MSS painted by the Limbourg Brothers: the *Belles Heures*, 1408–9 (New York, Metropolitan Museum of Art,

The Cloisters, Acc.54.1.1), and the greatest of all, the *Très Riches Heures*, left unfinished at the duc's death in 1416 (Chantilly, Musée Condé, ms. 65). MSS in the royal and ducal collections often had dozens or even hundreds of miniatures, and they were bound in coloured leather or textile, fitted with enamelled and jewelled clasps. Books were clearly a very visible part of a courtly culture; they were exchanged as New Year gifts, and were displayed, shared, and copied. Aspiring authors presented dedication MSS in the hope of further publication under royal patronage. Naturally this affected the fashion for book collecting in France. Stately libraries were formed by noblemen and upwardly mobile courtiers. Wealthy visitors to Paris returned home with MSS or an ambition to own them. Books of hours, at the very least, became almost essential possessions in families of almost any means or literacy.

The Parisian book trade—still principally located around the rue Neuve Notre-Dame—enjoyed a golden period in the decades on either side of 1400, producing many of the most refined and beautiful MSS of the Middle Ages. Some of the illuminators are known only from their best-known books, such as the Master of the *Épître d'Othéa*, the Master of the *Cité des Dames*, the Master of Berry's *Claires Femmes*, the Egerton Master, and the Harvard Hannibal Master. Others—like the Boucicaut Master (named after a very large book of hours made for the maréchal de Boucicaut, Paris, Musée Jacquemart-André, ms. 2), and the Bedford Master (named after a book of hours in London, BL, Add. MS 18850, and a breviary in Paris, BNF, ms. lat. 17294)—can be identified with some plausibility. The former was perhaps Jacques Coene, documented in Paris, 1398–1407. The latter was almost certainly Haincelin de Haguenau, documented in Paris from 1403 and still active in the 1420s. Each of these illuminators had assistants and followers (and probably often family members) producing MSS, especially books of hours, to well-practised formulas and in considerable quantities. Most MSS were presumably commissioned by clients from the booksellers in advance; some artists may even have prepared books on speculation, in anticipation of a ready market.

This halcyon period ended quite suddenly in 1420, when the English armies of Henry V, having defeated the French at Agincourt in 1415, now occupied Paris. For 30 years, business came to a virtual halt in the capital. A few illuminators remained, catering to the new rulers, including the Bedford Master, who is named after his patron, the duke of Bedford, English regent in France from 1422 until his death in 1435. Most illuminators left Paris and established themselves in the provinces. This exodus marks the beginning of a widely scattered book trade which became the principal characteristic of MS production in France in the last 80 years of its life. Artists and scribes arrived from Paris, many of them evidently bringing experience and recognizable pattern-sheets with them. They set themselves up in Rouen (the most famous workshops there are associated with the Master of the Geneva Latini, also called the Master of the Échevinage de Rouen); and in Tours (where the painters included Jean Fouquet, no less, outstanding illuminator of the

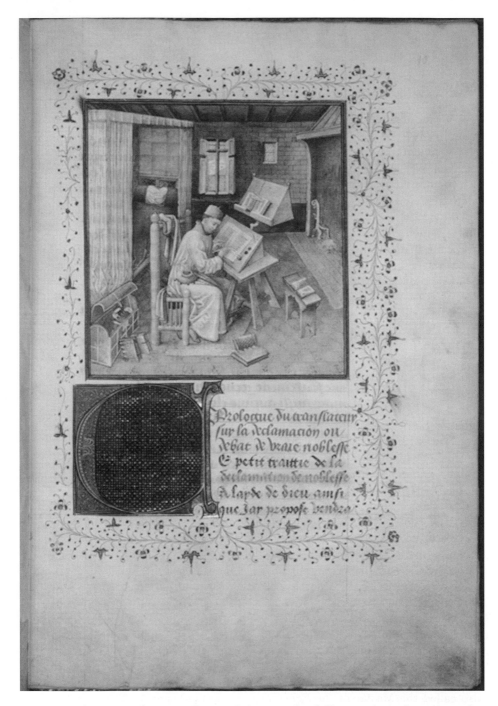

The 15th-century scribe Jean Miélot at work, from *Le Débat de l'honneur*: he employs pens, a stylus, book weight, book desk, and inkhorn, with a book chest behind him. The MS was made for Philip the Good; this miniature may be by Jean le Tavernier. Royal Library Brussels (MS 9278, fo. 10r)

now-dispersed Hours of Etienne Chevalier, mostly in Chantilly, Musée Condé, ms. 71, Jean Poyer, and Jean Bourdichon, court illuminator to Anne of Brittany and Louis XII); in Bourges (Jean Colombe, who finished the *Très Riches Heures* of the duc de Berry); Poitiers (Robinet Testard); Lyons (the Master of Guillaume Lambert, and Jean Perréal); Nantes; Angers; Rennes; Dijon (probable location of the Master of the Burgundian Prelates); Besançon; and Amiens (birthplace of Simon Marmion). Most of these cities were still making MSS until at least the end of the century. By the 1460s, illuminators were drifting back to Paris. The best-known artists there are Maître François, mentioned in 1473, and Jacques de Besançon, who was in the rue Neuve Notre-Dame from 1472 to 1494. Some flashy and unrefined books were still being written and illuminated by hand in Paris in the 1520s, but the book trade there never really regained the unsurpassed dominance it had enjoyed a century earlier. The relatively late arrival of printing in Paris (1470) is some indication of how far the business of book production in the capital had slipped in European importance.

The political turmoils of 15th-century France undoubtedly played into the hands of the book trade in The Netherlands, southern and northern. By the Treaty of Arras in 1435, the dukes of Burgundy moved the seat of their vast dominions to Flanders. Grand and aristocratic MSS were made in towns such as Lille and Valenciennes, but it was the bourgeois merchant towns that profited most. Bruges, still with shipping access to the open sea, was exporting huge numbers of books of hours to England by the middle of the first half of the 15th century. By 1450, at least as many books of hours for the English market were prepared in Bruges as were made in all of England itself. Very many MSS were sold locally too. The trade was highly organized and illuminators were required to be members of the painters' and saddlemakers' guild of Saint Luke. Alliances with England—including the marriage of Edward IV's youngest sister, Margaret, to Charles, duke of Burgundy—brought Edward himself to Bruges, when forced into exile in 1470–71. He stayed there with a local businessman and major book collector, Louis de Gruuthuse (c.1427–92), who convinced his guest to begin commissioning his own luxurious MSS. This event marks not only the true beginning of the English royal library, but also the consolidation of Bruges as the principal centre of the book trade in the southern Netherlands.

William Caxton, aiming for an exclusively English market, established his first press in Bruges, not England, in 1475. With nearby Ghent, where a prominent MS patron was the late duke's illegitimate son, Raphael de Mercatellis (c.1437–1508), Bruges dominated MS production in northern Europe for 50 years, until at least 1530. A distinctive 'Ghent/Bruges' style included borders formed of naturalistic flowers scattered in *trompe l'œil* designs across painted gold grounds, sometimes with snails and insects rendered with extreme precision. Miniatures, often set in realistic, hazy landscapes, reflect the paintings of the Flemish primitives, such as Jan Van Eyck (who had almost certainly contributed to MSS himself) and Gerard David. The great MS illuminators of Bruges and its environs included the Vienna Master of Mary of Burgundy (painter of Vienna, Österreichische Nationalbibliothek, Cod. 1857), Alexander Bening (d. 1518, known from c.1469) and, above all, Simon Bening, who was famous across Europe.

In the northern Netherlands, there was almost no book illumination before 1400. Utrecht, like Bruges, became important from about the 1430s, with painters such as the Masters of Zweder van Culemborg and the supreme, but not prolific, Master of Catherine of Cleves, illuminator of the eponymous book of hours (New York, Pierpont Morgan Library, M. 917 and M. 945). Later in the century, distinctive styles of Dutch illumination and coloured penwork point to notable production in Delft, Haarlem, and almost certainly Zwolle, in the eastern Netherlands. At its boundaries, the Dutch style merges with that of the Rhineland, in a line of book production from Cologne at least as far south as Mainz. Although there are exceptions, it is striking to note the strong religious themes of many northern Netherlandish and Rhenish MSS of the very end of the Middle Ages, dominated by books of hours (often in the vernacular), breviaries, psalters, choirbooks, and large institutional bibles. It is a setting that not only anticipates the religious Reformation of the 16th century but also, and more importantly in the present context, it is a world known and exploited by Johann Gutenberg and his colleagues in Mainz in the 1450s.

This was not the case in Italy. Choirbooks and bibles were certainly still being illuminated in the Italian Renaissance courts, often of princely grandeur (and unexpected secularism), but the distinctive theme was humanism, the Renaissance, and a return to the books and texts of classical antiquity, which is where this essay began. The Florentine humanists, such as Niccolò Niccoli and Poggio Bracciolini, reinvented and promoted a neat, rounded script, resembling Carolingian minuscule but believed by them to be an authentic classical style, ornamented with 'white-vine' initials, as Roman in appearance as the capitals on marble columns. The joyful and infectious rediscovery of classical learning is a familiar tale, and was fed by forays into ancient and neglected monastic libraries and by the exodus of Greek learning into the West following the fall of Constantinople to the Turks in 1453. Italian humanistic MSS are immediately recognizable, wide-margined, elegant, and graceful. The illuminators, many of whom are cited above, supplied appropriate initials and borders, with white vine interlace inhabited by putti, classical urns, butterflies, and—especially in Rome and Naples—long-tailed parrots. MSS are frequently signed and often dated by their scribes. Booksellers, such as Vespasiano da Bisticci, of Florence, created libraries of such books for the princes and collectors—the Medicis, Estes, Gonzagas, Sforzas, and the popes—and for visitors to Italy. When printing was introduced into Italy, around 1465, the early typographers recognized this new and last manifestation of MS handwriting and copied it, later calling it 'Roman' or, in its cursive form, 'italic'. That moment, more than dynasties or battles, marks the cultural end of the Middle Ages.

···

BIBLIOGRAPHY

J. J. G. Alexander, *Medieval Illuminators and their Methods of Work* (1992)

F. Avril and N. Reynaud, *Les Manuscrits à peintures en France, 1440–1520* (1993)

Bischoff

M. Bollati, ed., *Dizionario biografico dei miniatori italiani: secoli IX–XVI* (2004)

L. E. Boyle, *Medieval Latin Palaeography* (1984)

R. Clemens and T. Graham, *Introduction to Manuscript Studies* (2007)

C. de Hamel, *A History of Illuminated Manuscripts*, 2e (1994)

A. Derolez, *The Palaeography of Gothic Manuscript Books* (2003)

N. R. Ker, *English Manuscripts in the Century after the Norman Conquest* (1960)

T. Kren and S. McKendrick, eds., *Illuminating the Renaissance: The Triumph of Flemish Manuscript Painting in Europe* (2003)

E. A. Lowe, *Codices Latini Antiquiores: A Palaeographical Guide to Latin Manuscripts Prior to the Ninth Century* (12 vols, 1934–71)

J. Plummer with G. Clark, *The Last Flowering: French Painting in Manuscripts, 1420–1530: From American Collections* (1982)

R. H. Rouse and M. A. Rouse, *Manuscripts and their Makers: Commercial Book Producers in Medieval Paris, 1200–1500* (2 vols, 2000)

—◌ **6** ◌—

The European Printing Revolution

CRISTINA DONDI

1 Introduction

Printing with movable type, a European invention of the mid-15th century, revolutionized the making and use of books. The innovative nature of the invention and its implications were felt and discussed from the 15th century onwards; however, a comprehensive and systematic analysis of the phenomenon is largely a product of book history as a distinct discipline. In the 20th century, authors such as Marshall McLuhan, Lucien Febvre and Henri-Jean Martin, and Elizabeth L. Eisenstein proposed the idea of a European printing 'revolution' as an all-encompassing intellectual, social, scientific, economic, religious, and cultural revolution. Their arguments, methodologies, and conclusions have been challenged by later scholars (especially in the case of Eisenstein by Needham [review], Grafton, and Johns). Although many bibliographers and book historians now understand printed texts and MSS as coexisting, and even sometimes having a mutually complementary relationship—especially during the incunable period—it is a fact that within a generation the role of the MS book and of manuscript culture was fundamentally changed. The continuing existence of

MS publication, in certain fields, is a historical phenomenon amply documented by Harold Love (*see* **15**).

2 MS production and use in Europe in the second half of the 15th century

The appearance of typographic printing coincided with a period when the production of books in MS was everywhere on the increase and the book market, as a consequence, was rapidly expanding. MS production peaked in the late 1460s in Germany and in the early 1470s in France and Italy, entering into decline immediately afterwards. For the average book user of the second half of the 15th century, the printed book gradually took the place of the MS as a natural vehicle for text (*see* **5**).

The reasons for the increasing demand and production of books lie in a number of interrelated factors, chiefly the spread of literacy in urban centres. This process had begun in the 13th century with the foundation of new lay schools next to the religious ones generally attached to cathedral chapters. In Italy, humanist schools were opened for scholars and *scuole d'abbaco*, where teaching was carried out in the vernacular, were founded to train merchants. New universities were established (ten in Germany between 1402 and 1498), and existing ones grew substantially.

Participants in this spread of literacy were part of an expanded middle class, lay professionals who were neither members of the aristocracy nor artisans or peasants. This class included civil servants employed at the numerous lay and religious courts of Europe, such as ambassadors, judges, bailiffs, and their secretaries; professionals such as lawyers, notaries, physicians, and university professors; and even schoolteachers, merchants, and traders.

Many clergymen and members of monasteries and convents were traditionally also purchasers of books. Reformed congregations—e.g. Windeshcim among the Augustinian Canons; Monte Cassino, Bursfeld, and Melk among the Benedictines; the Observant Franciscans; the Reformed Dominicans; the Fratres Vitae Communis, and Christian humanists of the Netherlands—emphasized university education for their members, rebuilt their libraries, produced new literary works in both the vernacular and Latin to instruct the laity, and paid more attention to the uniformity of their liturgical texts. Naturally, such congregations attached great importance to their book collections.

3 The technical invention

The need to reproduce small images quickly, or to reproduce images with text, was evident by the beginning of the 15th century: representations of saints, with or without accompanying text, and playing cards were reproduced by woodcut. Blockbooks produced using the same method appeared around the middle of the century, their letters carved in woodblocks.

Screw-driven olive and wine presses were common at the period. Punches, with letters and symbols cut in relief on their ends, were used by seal and coin engravers and by goldsmiths to mark their wares to satisfy guild regulations; the mechanical precision necessary for matrix and mould production was also needed to make arms, armour, clocks, and watches. By the middle of the 15ᵗʰ century these skills were concentrated in large cities. Belonging to this milieu, the first printers, such as Erhard Ratdolt in Augsburg and Venice, Nicolas Jenson in Venice, Bernardo Cennini in Florence, and Filippo da Lavagna in Milan, were expert metalworkers and jewellers able to cut their own punches (*see* **11**).

Typographic printing was introduced by Johann Gutenberg around 1450 in Mainz. The first printing experiments—indulgences and Donatus' antique Latin primer, *Ars Minor*—appear to have been conducted on materials small in size and of saleable interest, often ecclesiastical and educational in nature. The first substantial book printed with movable type is the 42-line or Gutenberg Bible. The work of Gutenberg at Mainz was continued by other printers in the city, Johann Fust and Peter Schoeffer.

After the first wave of printer-typographers, printing enterprises were undertaken by individuals familiar with the book as an object, such as scribes (Schoeffer in Mainz, Antoine Vérard in Paris), schoolteachers (the early printers of Verona, Brescia, Mantua, and Treviso), priests (Lorenzo Morgiani in Florence), and stationers and binders (Benedictus Hectoris in Bologna).

Between 1460 and 1470, printing expanded in Germany—at Strasbourg (1459–60), Bamberg (*c.*1459), Eltville (1464), Cologne (*c.*1465), Basel (1468), Augsburg (1468), Nuremberg (1470), and Beromünster (1470)—and in Italy: at Subiaco (1465), Rome (1467), Venice (1469), Foligno, Naples, Milan, and Trevi (1470–71). By 1480 the industry extended even further: to Paris (1470) and Lyons (1473), Barcelona (*c.*1473), Louvain (1473, Dirk Martens and Johannes de Westfalia), Cracow (1473), Gouda (1477, Gheraert Leeu), and Westminster (1476, William Caxton). Altogether, presses were set up in more than 100 towns between 1471 and 1480, in almost 90 further places between 1481 and 1490, and in approximately 50 more towns between 1491 and 1500.

The social groups responsible for the increase in the demand for books also became directly involved in their production and use. The many university graduates and humanists who gravitated towards centres of learning found employment as advisers, editors, and correctors. The spread of literacy and the increased affordability of books secured them new users, further expanding the market. From its very beginnings, clergymen and religious welcomed and participated in the development of printing. Finally, the wealth of the merchant classes brought the capital investment necessary for the new craft.

For the first time, a group of literate merchants, later defined as publishers, were willing to invest in book production as a commercial activity. The great increase in the quantity of circulating books, made possible by the new method of mechanical production, resulted in the availability of a larger variety of titles, to more people, in different locations, generally at a cheaper price.

The establishment of printing in about 250 towns, most of which hosted more than one printing office, is characterized by an enormous amount of entrepreneurial experimentation. A more detailed analysis of the presses' output and period of activity would show that a number of cases involved the work of an itinerant printer or of temporary or short-lived establishments. Printers moved in and out of a profession not yet perceived as such, nor yet clearly defined by regulations, statutes, or guilds; they moved around, sometimes following an invitation, often because they felt they had exploited a limited market's capacity. Surviving business contracts, records of legal disputes, wills, and colophons are the main sources of evidence for this migratory working pattern.

There appears to have been a division between the commercially successful printers, who tended not to move, and the itinerant ones, pushed towards the exploration of new markets and opportunities by the absence of medium- to long-term prospects in the small towns, villages, or isolated abbeys and university towns where they stopped to operate. Why some printers did not succeed in establishing themselves even in large centres is a question that has to be analysed case by case. Finally, a comparison may be drawn between the high level of mobility shown by the early printers and that of professions such as teachers and university professors, whose wandering habits were determined sometimes by their fame, sometimes by economic need.

The unique socio-economic-cultural circumstances surrounding the establishment of printing offices and their subsequent activities varied from place to place and from printer to printer: proximity to the papal curia or to paper mills; the involvement of humanists, university professors, or schools; favourable trading location; the local commercial tradition; access to patronage or commissions—all played a determining role. Scholar printer-publishers, such as Aldus Manutius in Venice and Johann Froben and Johann Amerbach in Basle, were very influential. They were driven by the desire to make available to the international scholarly community works that they deemed important—chiefly classical for Aldus, biblical and theological for Froben and Amerbach—in philologically sound and aesthetically pleasing editions.

4 The physical appearance and textual content of early printed books

The MS lies behind each phase of the history of early printing, not only as a source for texts, but also as a model for the printed book's physical appearance, as reflected in choice of type, format, layout, initials, and rubrication. Types reproduced the scripts most widely used at the time. Gothic textura type had special variants according to different locations (more square in northern Germany and The Netherlands, rounder in southern Germany and Italy) and different uses (for liturgical works, legal and school texts, etc.). Roman, like italic (from 1501), was developed for classical texts, bastarda and Schwabacher founts were cut for printing French and German vernacular works. In the 16th century, a simplification of letterforms was brought about by the growth and organization of the typefounding business, by the commercialization of matrices, and by the spread of specialist punch-cutting as a profession (e.g. by Robert Granjon). The only technical difference in the production of printed over MS books, beyond the use of types and a press, lies in the process of the imposition of the pages to be reproduced on an unfolded sheet. This involved casting off the printer's copy to determine which parts of it would come where on the respective sheets.

During the 15th century, three types of MS were prevalent: the academic book, generally written in two columns on folio pages, for theological and legal works, and normally confined to library use; the humanistic and student's book, of medium (quarto) to small format; and the popular book, whether lay or religious, generally quarto or smaller (in Italy, even pocket-size). Each had its natural continuation in printed form. Data from the incunabula Short-Title Catalogue (ISTC) shows continuity with the period before printing was introduced: 8,662 editions in folio (29 per cent, although the incidence is concentrated more in the first decades of production and falls away in the last twenty years of the 15th century); 15,195 editions in quarto (52 per cent); 3,020 in octavo (10 per cent, mostly printed in the last two decades and increasing after 1501); and 232 in sextodecimo.

The use of large capital initials, paragraph marks, rubrication (titles, running heads, running volume numbers, etc.), decoration, and illustration was introduced gradually to the set page. During the first decades, printing offices drew on the same craftsmen employed by the MS book trade as rubricators, illuminators, and scribes. Far from finding themselves with less work, they saw their skills required as never before for finishing printed books. It is possible to determine whether a printing office had in-house decorators or regularly employed the services of a nearby artist, by examining copies of the same edition or of a number of editions and analysing their handiwork. Generally, rubrication was carried out at point of sale, sometimes near the place of production before distribution (Jenson in Venice, Anton Koberger in Nuremberg). Substantial illumination was mostly added after distribution (with the exception of presentation copies), at the owner's request.

From the 1480s, there appears a substantial increase in the printed component of the page and a falling-off in the need for hand-finishing: woodcut initials and borders, printed running heads, and page or folio numbers are the inevitable consequence of more sophisticated textual articulation, increased press runs, and economic policies. The use of hand-applied colour disappears almost entirely in the 16th century, its visual appeal replaced in part by engravings. The appearance of the printed book had initially been determined by the reading public's habits and tastes, which had developed during the MS period; but from the 16th century onwards, the exigencies of printing would eventually change that public's taste and perceptions.

Books were almost always sold unbound. Most bookshops were, however, able to bind items according to the customer's requirements. There were instances of large-scale importers (e.g. Schoeffer in Mainz) who supplied the binding before offering it for retail. Bindings were provided before distribution only occasionally. Dedication copies sometimes received such bindings, as did books intended for markets known not to be capable of providing them, as was the case for the Glagolitic Breviary, printed in Venice *c.*1491 for the churches of Dalmatia.

A large percentage of the books printed in the first 50 years of printing contained works used during the Middle Ages, particularly within the ecclesiastical and academic worlds, such as bibles and liturgical books, patristics, theology and philosophy, law and science, certain Latin classics (Cicero and Virgil) and vernacular ones (Dante, Petrarca, and Chaucer). However, the publication of works relating to contemporary events or written by contemporary authors is a clear sign of the extent to which printing quickly became a common aspect of 15th-century society. Such works included the writings of the humanists, of authors such as Sebastian Brant and Girolamo Savonarola, diplomatic and funeral orations, *sacre rappresentazioni*, indulgences, and calendars.

An analysis of the titles available to the late 15th-century market has been prepared by Hermand *et al.*, using data from the 1998 illustrated ISTC. It shows that almost one third of the total output was in the category of literature, of which 53 per cent were lay texts and 47 per cent religious. Law supplied almost 15 per cent of the total, evenly divided between civil and canon law. Liberal arts (dialectic, grammar and philology, music, and rhetoric) accounted for almost 11 per cent; theology slightly more than 10 per cent; and liturgy almost 9 per cent. Ephemera (advertising, heraldry, practical astronomy and astrology, commerce, guides, documents pertaining to political and administrative life) supplied slightly more than 6 per cent of the total; history (including biography and hagiography) comprised more than 5 per cent, of which 51 per cent was lay history and the rest religious. Philosophy represented almost 5 per cent; medicine more than 3 per cent. Scientific subjects—alchemy, astronomy and astrology, geography, mathematics and geometry, optics, physics, and natural sciences—account for almost 3 per cent of the total. The smallest categories, each comprising less than 1 per cent of the total output (by numbers of titles, not by sheets, nor ens), are the Bible (text only), and works pertaining to the mechanical arts, such as agriculture, architecture, the art of war, cookery, and dance.

Classical texts, distributed among these categories, represent more than 9 per cent of the total. This percentage can be further broken down according to periods of publication, production within large geographical areas, or according to locale. More than 30 per cent of the total Italian output is made up of editions of the classics, almost 17 per cent of which were printed in Venice alone. In France, classics constituted 7 per cent of the total publication; in Germany more than 6 per cent; in Belgium almost 7 per cent; and in The Netherlands approximately 12 per cent. At present, it is not possible to offer data for the percentage of medieval or contemporary authors published in the 15th century, as a biographical profile of all authors is not yet available.

Continuity with MS production is also evident where language is concerned. Out of some 29,000 editions recorded in the online version of the ISTC database (consulted April 2007), almost three-quarters were printed in the ancient languages: 21,122 were printed in Latin (72 per cent), 154 in Hebrew, 65 in Greek, and 14 in Church Slavonic. As for modern languages, 3,141 editions were printed in German (10 per cent), 2,391 in Italian (8 per cent), 1,611 in French (5 per cent), 566 in Dutch (1 per cent), 421 in Spanish (1 per cent), 234 in English, 134 in Catalan, 33 in Czech, 11 in Portuguese, 2 in Swedish, one edition each in Breton, Danish, Frisian, Provençal, and Sardinian. The editions for which no percentage figure is supplied together represent 3 per cent of the total.

If a country's vernacular output is related to its total output, the extent of modern-language printing by geographical areas can be better understood. In Germany, a total of 9,859 editions were printed, of which 2,897 (29 per cent) were German texts. In Italy, 2,374 of 10,417 editions were in Italian (22 per cent); in France, 1,485 out of 5,167 editions were in French (28 per cent); and in the Low Countries, 554 out of 2,328 editions were in Dutch (23 per cent). Spain shows a higher rate of vernacular printing: of the 882 editions known to have been printed in Spain, 336 were in Spanish (38 per cent). In England, for which more elaborate calculations were carried out by Hellinga, 395 editions are known, of which 63 per cent of the total production was in English, against 9 per cent in legal French, and only 28 per cent in Latin (*BMC* 11.43). Coq observed that at centres where printers had limited commercial power, such as at Florence, or with a number of French and English presses, they tended to specialize in the production of vernacular texts, while the great export centres, such as Venice, published primarily in Latin for a wider European readership.

5 The contribution of the Church and religious orders

From its beginning, members of the Church were very actively involved with the new medium. They acted as benefactors (Nicholas of Cusa, Cardinal Johannes Bessarion, Pope Sixtus IV), as editors and correctors (Franciscan and Augustinian editors of liturgical texts, mathematics, logic, and literature), as authors of lay as well as religious works (Werner Rolewinck), as translators (Niccolò Malermi of the Camaldoli order translated the Bible into Italian), as printers (Benedictines in Augsburg, Erfurt, Subiaco near Rome; Augustinian Hermits in Nuremberg; Cistercians in Zinna; the Dominican nuns of Ripoli at Florence; Fratres Vitae Communis in Marienthal, Rostock, Brussels, and Cologne; Franciscans of Santa Maria Gloriosa in Venice), and finally, as book users and owners, both privately (Jacopo Zeno, bishop of Padua, Cardinal Grimani in Venice) and institutionally (the Dominicans of San Marco in Florence). The preservation of thousands of incunables for posterity has to be credited in large part to the libraries of religious institutions.

6 New aspects

Unlike writing a MS, a private individual could not casually print a book, nor could a printer produce a book by himself without establishing a printing office. Moreover, printing required capital investment, principally for the purchase of paper. In addition, it generally required some knowledge of the subject to be printed, to help in the selection and correction of what was printed. Finally, printing called for marketing knowledge: although texts were initially produced with an ideal customer in mind, in order to be profitable a diverse range of buyers had to be reached. In sum, what distinguishes the production of printed books from that of MSS is the necessary collaboration of individuals, each contributing his or her own skills or assets. Behind the publication of most editions lay the joint efforts of artisan printers, financial backers, commercial dealers, and scholars. Never before had these different segments of society worked so closely together.

The 15th-century printer normally operated in an office where a team of people with different skills was assigned to various aspects of the technical process. The few exceptions, such as wandering printers, would necessarily have had to find support wherever they temporarily set up a press: for example, the assistance of members of an aristocratic household might be needed, or of monks and lay brothers if the printer had been called to print a liturgical book in a monastery.

Financial backing frequently came from the commercial sector, quite often from the Church, occasionally from the aristocracy. The financier would generally supply the cost of paper—equal to approximately half the total investment required to produce a book—and could also have an important role relating to the distribution of copies. The number of sheets per copy and the total press run had to be calculated in advance so as to buy enough paper; sufficient money had to be set aside for that part of the investment. Press runs in the 15th century varied substantially according to the technical and financial capabilities of the printers and publishers. Among the important elements in determining the print run were: production costs, anticipated demand, ability to reach the market, the work's genre, and the printing office's commercial practices. For the first two decades, the typical press run seems to have been between 200 and 300 copies: 180 for the 42-line bible, 275 to 300 for the editions of Conrad Sweynheym and Arnold Pannartz in Rome. Yet, there are exceptions: 1,025 copies of Pliny were printed (on commission) by Jenson in Venice in 1476; 930 copies of the Bible were printed by Leonardus Wild, also in Venice, in 1478. Antonio Zarotto in Milan always produced around 1,000 copies.

A mistake in the calculation of the print run could compromise the business, and the great variety of runs in this period seems to reflect the search for a balance between conflicting needs. Numbers grew substantially—sometimes to above the level of 1,000 copies—when there were better prospects for distribution, either because the edition had been commissioned or because of the work's great popularity. The popular sermons of Roberto Caracciolo were printed by Mathias Moravus in Naples in 1489 in 2,000 copies. In 1492, Bartholomaeus Ghotan in Lübeck produced 800 paper copies and sixteen vellum copies of the *Revelations* of St Birgitta, commissioned by the monastery of Vadstena, Sweden. The work of Savonarola was printed in Florence in 1500 in a run of between 2,000 and 3,000 copies.

The printer's reader or proof corrector, a key figure in the process, had to be an educated person. Different publications demanded different skills from the corrector. He prepared the text for the compositor, marking corrections, spaces to leave blank, and parts of the text to omit. The liberty a compositor ultimately took with a text should not be underestimated: to justify the right-hand margin, he might vary the number and width of blank spaces, introduce or expand abbreviations, intervene in the spelling and punctuation, and sometimes even alter the text. This sort of compositorial intervention is often investigated by analytical bibliography.

Printers frequently used correctors to oversee their editions: Giovanni Andrea Bussi was the editor of Sweynheym and Pannartz's classical editions in Rome. When German printers arrived in Italy, they were helped by local humanists in the selection of works that passed into print; humanists did the same for the presses established in the university towns of Bologna and Paris. The corrector's new professional role involved turning MS into print, paying especial attention to the text's linguistic features.

A further round of collaborative effort is evident at the editorial level. A 15th-century edition commonly contained much more than what was announced in the title. Other works by the same author, by different authors, and excerpts from anonymous works, may all be found before or after the principal work. Moreover, the paratext might contain a number of letters from and to the editor, and verses in praise of the author, of the text, of the editor, or of the printer are also quite commonly present; their authors were generally contemporaries of the editor—perhaps a student, a colleague, or a local worthy. This historical evidence is, in part, what makes each edition unique—yet it is habitually ignored. The exact content of the surviving *c.*29,000 editions published in the last 50 years of the 15th century is still not known, despite the important position they occupy within the transmission of the West's cultural heritage.

It is erroneous to assume that incunable editions of any given text were all similar, depending ultimately on the *editio princeps*. In cases where an edition's position within the textual transmission of incunabula (often of the 1470s) has been established, results have shown substantial variation, as would be expected in editions published in different places and, therefore, most probably based on different MSS. In this respect the work of the Leonine Commission on the early editions of Thomas Aquinas, and of Lotte Hellinga on the tradition of Poggio Bracciolini's *Facetiae*, are exemplary. In later years, a successful or influential edition of a frequently reprinted text, not necessarily the first edition, tended to be reproduced again and again: the main text would be retained, the paratext often changed and additional material inserted. These later editions may appear to be of little philological importance; nonetheless, for someone pursuing 'the study of texts as historical phenomena reflecting social, intellectual, and economic circumstances in which they were produced' (Jensen, 138), they have an important bearing on the transmission and reception of the specific text during the Renaissance. The establishment of an editorial stemma, still carried out too rarely, allows the fundamental distinction to be drawn between those texts that were based on previous editions and those based on a MS exemplar.

The fact that print caused so many more texts to become widely available had the effect of stimulating their critical assessment. MSS gained a new significance as independent sources of earlier authority, a basis for collation, or simply a better alternative to already printed versions. Indeed, the work of 16th-century scholars such as Desiderius Erasmus broke away from the established textual tradition by returning to earlier MSS, which provided fresh evidence for the study of the Bible and the Church Fathers. The wider availability of texts in print did much to foster this critical spirit.

7 Distribution

To distribute their new product, printers initially relied on the same commercial networks in place during the MS period, one that centred on the stationer's shop, traditionally the supplier of writing materials and books. The famous Florentine bookseller and stationer Vespasiano da Bisticci—purveyor of grand MSS to the likes of the Medici of Florence, Federico da Montefeltro of Urbino, and Matthias Corvinus, king of Hungary—refused to accept the new invention of printing with movable type and ended his commercial activities in 1478. His main rival in Florence, Zanobi di Mariano, managed to stay in business as he started to deal in printed books as well. In Florence, the number of stationers' shops rose from 12 to 30 during the first half century following the advent of the printing press. The stationers were immediately involved in the new business of printing: by finishing or selling books, occasionally by becoming typographers themselves, but in particular by editing and publishing. Knowing the public's taste and with an established clientele, their contribution to printing was in many instances essential, if never generally substantiated by large financial investments.

The production and distribution of MSS took place almost invariably for local markets, but a successful printer had to have established networks of distribution that went far beyond the boundaries of the town where the printing actually took place. The need to move from a known public to an unknown, potentially larger one strengthened the printer's connection with merchants and traders. The printed book entered the market as a saleable commodity, one not dissimilar to others that were traded in the Middle Ages and during the early modern period. The book trade made the transition from a local to an international business; but because the book was usually not an essential possession, this trade had its own peculiarities. Surviving documents testify to the many problems encountered by the early printers. Relying on the work of agents and on a network of warehouses and bookshops, they only gradually achieved a stable trading pattern, developing a tendency to share risks and costs by creating joint business ventures. The establishment of a family business with branches abroad (e.g. the Giunta and Giolito firms) was one natural way of ensuring reliable distribution across borders. The circulation of many thousands of printed books throughout Europe—a further new aspect in the transmission of knowledge and information—was inherent in the rise of printing.

8 The Venetian success

The largest and most successful place for printing in the 15th century was Venice, which boasted a cosmopolitan, entrepreneurial, and merchant tradition, the rich libraries and widespread learning of the patriciate and the religious orders, and a large population of professional and non-professional readers. The 233 presses set up in the city before 1500—some transient, others among the most distinguished in Europe—offered the Italian and international markets a full range of printed products.

The state maintained a non-interventionist attitude. After granting a five-year privilege to Johannes de Spira in 1469, which expired with the printer's death in 1470, privileges were issued only ad hoc for specific publications, the first to Marcantonio Sabellico in 1486. Until well into the following century, printers were not required to join a guild or conform to established regulations, as was common in most other longer established professions. However, from the very beginning printers in Venice joined confraternities, which helped their integration into the city's social network, bringing obvious benefits.

The first ten years of Venetian printing were dominated by foreign printers, working alone or in syndicates; their success was determined by their advanced distribution networks (often by exploiting their links with fellow foreign traders), as well as by the production side of the business. The following two decades saw the establishment and consolidation of Italian firms, such as Arrivabene, Giunta, Torresani, Scotto, Aldus, and many others. Venetian printers and publishers became market leaders in the production (often on commission and, therefore, at low risk) of missals and breviaries for dioceses and religious orders throughout Europe. Many technical innovations originated in Venice, something that again reflects the city's attention to different cultures as a potential market: Glagolitic type for the Slav communities, type for musical notation (for whose invention Ottaviano de' Petrucci obtained a privilege in 1498), and Greek printing for Greece (Venice being the leading place of publication for such works until the 19th century), as well as Armenian, Hebrew, and Arabic types (*see* **8, 40**).

Of the 1,123 Venetian editions represented in 1,387 copies now in the Bodleian, 481 (34 per cent) were distributed and used in the 15th and 16th centuries in Italy; almost the equivalent number, 446 (32 per cent), ended up being used either in England (183, 13 per cent) or in Germany (263, 19 per cent). Indeed, England and Spain remained dependent on the importation of foreign books until the following century (see Ford, Needham, 'Customs Rolls'). Latin textbooks used in schools arrived in England mostly from Germany and the Low Countries, until English printers started to print them towards the end of the century. Textbooks for university students and teachers and for professionals came from Italy, mainly Venice, which was only challenged in the field by Lyons towards the end of the century. Research on this fundamental aspect of the international book trade, and its impact on economic and intellectual history, can be advanced by the discovery and study of archival documents and by the physical examination of the thousands of surviving incunabula.

9 Loss and survival

From the Renaissance to the present day, incunabula have been lost in very large quantities: 'a single copy is by far the commonest survival state for incunable editions' (Needham, 'Late Use', 36). From archival and early bibliographical sources, we know of the existence of editions printed before 1500 that do not survive today in even a single copy; more editions must have existed of which we know absolutely nothing. To assess when and how, and possibly why, the loss of incunabula occurred is as important as understanding how, where, and why copies managed to survive to this day. Scholars such as Needham and Harris have recently engaged with this problem.

Among the direct or indirect agents that destroyed editions and copies are reckless consumption—common with school books, some popular vernacular literature such as romances, and, occasionally, devotional books such as books of hours—and obsolescence (typically the publication of more complete and up-to-date works on the same subject). Survival rates are also affected by a book's physical size (small-format books, or books with few leaves are more likely to be lost), its language (Greek and Latin works were more highly valued than vernacular ones), and provenance (institutionally owned books are more likely to survive than individually owned books). Titles may be lost to war, political and administrative changes (notably the secularization of religious institutions and the dispersal of their libraries), censorship, and occasional floods and fires.

10 The outlook now

At the present time, the great majority of known incunable editions have been included in the ISTC. Practically all 15th-century editions have been surveyed and included in some form of national, local, or subject catalogue. However, the historical evidence, which is so important for contextualizing each edition and each copy, is far from being systematically recorded: copy-specific information from thousands of incunabula in US and Italian libraries is still lacking. For many other European libraries, what there is remains patchy.

No serious analysis of the impact of printing on Renaissance and early modern society can be comprehensive until the historical information is gathered from the extant books to assess where and when they were used, by whom, and how. As with archaeological objects, scholars need to interpret the material clues they retain (decoration, binding, MS notes), and identify ownership inscriptions, which may be contemporary or from later periods, institutional or private, male or female, lay or religious. Much has been discovered and published since Febvre and Martin half a century ago attempted a similar analysis, but much remains to be done.

BIBLIOGRAPHY

BMC

C. Bozzolo *et al.*, 'La Production du livre en quelques pays d'Europe occidentale aux XIVᵉ et XVᵉ siècles', *Scrittura e civiltà*, 8 (1984), 129–76

A. Carelli *et al.*, 'I codici miscellanei nel basso medioevo', *Segno e testo*, 2 (2004), 245–309

H. Carter, *A View of Early Typography up to About 1600* (1969; repr. with an introduction by J. Mosley, 2002)

D. Coq, 'Les Débuts de l'édition en langue vulgaire en France: publics et politiques éditoriales', *GJ* 62 (1987), 59–72

E. L. Eisenstein, *The Printing Press as an Agent of Change* (2 vols, 1979)

L. Febvre and H.-J. Martin, *The Coming of the Book* (French original, 1958; tr. D. Gerard, 1976)

M. L. Ford, 'Importation of Printed Books into England and Scotland', in *CHBB* 3

F. Geldner, *Inkunabelkunde* (1978)

E. Ph. Goldschmidt, *Medieval Texts and Their First Appearance in Print* (1943)

A. Grafton, [review of Eisenstein,] *Journal of Interdisciplinary History*, 11 (1980), 265–86

N. Harris, 'Sopravvivenze e scomparse delle testimonianze del Morgante di Luigi Pulci', *Rinascimento*, 45 (2005), 179–245

L. Hellinga, 'The Codex in the Fifteenth Century: Manuscript and Print', in *A Potencie of Life*, ed. N. Barker (1993)

X. Hermand *et al.*, 'Les Politiques éditoriales dans l'Europe des imprimeurs au XVᵉ siècle: un projet de recherches, en cours', *Archives et bibliothèques de Belgique*, 87 (2009), 75–82

R. Hirsch, *Printing, Selling and Reading 1450–1550*, 2e (1974)

ISTC

K. Jensen, 'Printing the Bible in the Fifteenth Century: Devotion, Philology and Commerce', in *Incunabula and Their Readers*, ed. K. Jensen (2003)

A. Johns, *The Nature of the Book* (1998)

H.-J. Martin *et al.*, eds., *Histoire de l'édition française* (4 vols, 1982–6)

P. Needham, [review of Eisenstein,] *Fine Print*, 6 (1980), 23–35

—— 'The Customs Rolls as Documents for the Printed-Book Trade in England', in *CHBB* 3

—— 'The Late Use of Incunables and the Paths of Book Survival', *Wolfenbütteler Notizien zur Buchgeschichte*, 29 (2004), 35–59

P. Nieto, 'Géographie des impressions européennes du XVᵉ siècle', in *Le Berceau du livre: autour des incunables*, ed. F. Barbier, *Revue française d'histoire du livre*, 118–21 (2004), 125–73

A. Nuovo, *Il commercio librario nell'Italia del Rinascimento*, 3e (2003)

7

The Book as Symbol

BRIAN CUMMINGS

'Books are not absolutely dead things,' wrote John Milton in 1644 in *Areopagitica*. A book is a physical object, yet it also signifies something abstract, the words and the meanings collected within it. Thus, a book is both less and more than its contents alone. A book is a metonym for the words that we read or for the thoughts that we have as we read them. At one level, like any domestic object, a book takes on the imprint of its producer and its users. Old books have further value as containing the presence of many other readers in the past. Yet, more than other objects, a book is felt to embody not only a physical memory but also a record of past thoughts. The book contains both its reader and its author. In Milton's more poetic terms, books 'contain a potency of life in them', because they 'preserve as in a vial the purest efficacy and extraction of that living intellect that bred them'. The book thus achieves a further mystery, of transforming what appears to be purely immaterial and conceptual into something with a concrete form. It is therefore not entirely extravagant for Milton to claim that a book possesses 'a life beyond life'. Destroying a book, then, Milton says, is like an act of homicide—indeed it is worse than that, since a book encloses the life of more than one person and exists in more than one time. Paradoxically, regardless of the material survival of a physical copy or artefact, a book is something immortal and imperishable.

Curtius found the origin of the idea of the book as a sacred object in the ancient Near East and Egypt, where the production of books was cultic and their possession restricted to a priestly caste. Writing is a mystical act, and scribes are accorded a corresponding status as its masters and interpreters. The ancient Egyptian word for the script now known as hieroglyphs meant 'words of god'. The earliest inscriptions in the tombs of kings acted not only as a literary record but also as physical totems for the pharaoh to avert danger in the afterlife and to communicate with the gods. In contrast, Curtius asserted, in classical Greece there was 'hardly any idea of the sacredness of the book' (Curtius, 304). Indeed in the notorious formulation in Plato's *Phaedrus* (274C–276A), writing is purely functional, and fails even to perform properly that function. Knowledge exists in the mind of the philosopher: writing is a mere aide-memoire, and an untrustworthy and ephemeral one at that. Only in the Hellenistic period do the Greeks acquire a 'culture of books'. In the later grammarians, indeed, things come full circle, and Homer, in whose writing no figure of the book appears, comes to be regarded as a sacred writing. Roman literature repeats the pattern, favouring the idea of a *rhetor* as a speaker not a writer, until the birth of the codex produces a new configuration of sensibility.

The material form given to a book has a great deal to do with the symbolic value that is ascribed to it. The Greek word *Pentateuch*, which the Christian Church used to describe the most sacred part of the ancient Scriptures, the Jewish Torah, means literally the 'five containers' in which the scrolls of the text were kept. The scroll early became a metaphor for what the scroll contained—and perhaps in an extended sense also for the mystery of the relation between the physical text in which God's words were contained and the spiritual sense of what those words were taken to mean. The laws given to Moses were written on stone tables, which in turn are taken to stand as the embodiment of divine ordinance. The law is then said to be 'written with the finger of God' (Exod. 31:18). Those who are of God are written into His 'book' (Exod. 32:32); those who have sinned are blotted out. Job reinvents the metaphor to refer to the engraving of an iron pen in lead (with wonderful anachronism, but in the same spirit of applying new media to God's work, the Authorized Version translated this as 'printed in a book', Job 19:23). At other times God writes in wax. But most of all, God discloses Himself in a scroll, the dominant written technology of the ancient world. God bears witness to His purposes in a scroll (Isa. 8:1). At the end of time, 'the heavens shall be rolled together as a scroll' (Isa. 34:4).

These Hebraic metaphors carried over into the Greek New Testament. In the vision of the end of the world in Revelation, 'the heaven departed as a scroll when it is rolled together' (6:14). The passage of time in the created world is conceived as a book which opens and which finally is closed. It is here that what Curtius calls 'the magnificent religious metaphorics of the book' reach their symbolic apotheosis. God's entire intervention in creation is imagined as a book. Just as Ezekiel begins his life as a prophet by eating the book of the divine word (Ezek. 3:1), so it is as a book that St John the Divine imagines the enunciation of the apocalypse (Rev. 5:1). When the dead come before God at the end of things, the books are opened, 'and whosoever was not found in the book of life was cast into the lake of fire' (Rev. 20:15).

It is not difficult to see how the symbolic meaning of the book might translate also into the mystical value of the book as artefact. The idea within the Kabbalah of the secret significance of the very letters in which the Torah is transcribed has been traced back to the 1st century BC. The idea of a magical power inscribed into the very letters of the text finds graphic form in the tradition of illuminating letters. The Lindisfarne Gospels and the Book of Kells are now among the best-known artefacts in the Western world, with their extravagant extensions of the individual letter of Scripture to fill out a whole page in a dazzling display of line, colour, and gilt. The metamorphosis of script into abstract geometry or equally into zoomorphic improvisation transforms the book into an object that is hard to summarize in terms of mere text, even though the initials retain their function at the literal level. The book is a figure of itself as much as it is a figure for the contents that it represents.

The book as symbol, then, can be seen to mediate between a number of features of the life of books, both material and abstract. The sense of the book as a sacred object gives rise to a particular kind of artefactual production which manifests in physical form the status of the book as an object. Even in its textual form, the book becomes more than itself, a visual representation not only of the contents within but of the idea of the book altogether. At least in the case of the Semitic religions of Judaism, Christianity, and Islam, this valorization of the book at least partly occurs because of the continual skirmish with iconoclasm. An extraordinary side-effect of this has been the tendency in all three religions towards what can only be described as fetishistic practices of preservation or worship of the material form of the sacred book. The incorporation of the holy book into ritual—the raising of the book, or the carrying of it in procession, or the kissing of the book or kneeling before it—is only the most obvious example of this. Equally widespread is the use of portions of text or even of whole books as amulets or talismans. Hebrew inscriptions worn as amulets are very ancient. Particularly fascinating are the *kimiyah* or 'angel-texts'—names of angels or extracts from the Torah written out on parchment and then encased in a silver or other precious container and worn around the neck or elsewhere on the body. Miniature copies of the Qur'ān were copied using a special script known as *ghudar* or 'dust'—so tiny as to be practically illegible—and encased in small jewelled boxes. Although Christian theology often frowned on the use of talismans, the practice of burying a copy of Scripture with the dead was retained. A beautiful example is the Stonyhurst Gospel—placed inside the coffin of St Cuthbert at Lindisfarne in 698, and discovered intact inside when the saint's body was translated to Durham Cathedral in 1104. Later archbishops wore it round the neck during ceremonial occasions. Hugh Amory has documented a case of a native American being interred with a medicine ball partially made with a page from a printed bible.

Alongside this exceptional investment in the preservation of the book perhaps also should be placed the corresponding urge to destruction. The practice of book burning goes back at least to the Qing dynasty in China in the 2nd century BC. In Christianity, burning physical books is virtually synonymous with the pronouncement of bans on heretical ideas. The books of Priscillian of Ávila were burned in 383, and those of Nestorius within a generation. The simultaneous combustion of the heretic's works with the consumption of his body on the stake was a material symbol of the purging of abstract ideas: Jan Hus was burned with his books at the Council of Constance in 1415, and the same council ordered Wyclif's bones to be exhumed and burned alongside his writings. Such practices survived the Reformation and transferred into nascent Protestantism: Michael Servetus was burned at Geneva in 1553 with several portions of manuscript and one of his printed works bound around his waist. In the new confessional divisions, the Bible itself came under threat: Tyndale's New Testament was burned in England in the 1520s by official order. In such turmoil, a book could be found miraculously to survive even as the authorities strove to extinguish it. Just as Pedro Berruguete's 1480 painting (now in the Prado) of such proceedings against the Cathars showed St Dominic's works preserved intact alongside the charred detritus of the Cathar texts, so John Foxe reports a burning of Tyndale's Testaments in 1526 in which the precious books simply refused to catch fire.

The power of the book as a sacred object is bound up with its capacity to be rendered as a symbol. When Dante comes to the summit of heaven, he learns that all the leaves (the loose gatherings, *quaderni*) that have been scattered by sin are now bound together in one volume by love: *Legato con amore in un volume* (*Paradiso*, 33.86). Shakespeare frequently has recourse to the image of the world as a book. In *Hamlet*, the book of memory becomes the symbol of a person's mortality; *Macbeth* abounds with metaphors of the book as the repository of time and a figure for death.

At iconic moments in the history of the 20th century, the power of the book as symbolic object has been especially apparent. In 1933, the Nazis infamously burned 'degenerate' books in Berlin's Opernplatz. Conversely, in China during the Cultural Revolution, Mao's 'Little Red Book' was carried on the body or held aloft in staged acts of ideological affirmation. Disseminated on a scale to rival even the great religious sacred texts—740 million are believed to have been printed between the first publication in 1961 and the height of the Cultural Revolution in 1969—the 'Little Red Book' gained its value largely from its status as a political icon. Even as the book is demystified and deconsecrated in the modern world, its symbolic value endures. (*See also* **2**, **8**, **40**.)

....

BIBLIOGRAPHY

H. Amory, 'The Trout and the Milk: An Ethnobibliographical Talk', *HLB* NS 7 (1996), 50–65

E. R. Curtius, *European Literature and the Latin Middle Ages* (1953)

J. Milton, *Areopagitica* (1644)

8

The Transmission of Jewish Knowledge through MSS and Printed Books

EMILE G. L. SCHRIJVER

1 Introduction

A beautiful yellow bookcase stood in the house of my deceased grandfather. On the lower shelf were the Holy Scriptures and its commentaries; above these were prayer-books, and what the soul is in need of otherwise; above these were books of customs and of Jewish law; and above these was the Talmud. Like gold coins that shine from a leather purse the golden names of the tractates shone on the leather spines of the Talmud.

This is one of the earliest childhood memories of Samuel Agnon (1888–1970), the first and only Israeli to win the Nobel Prize for Literature (1966). It shows, above all, a young child's fascination with the religious books of his grandfather, but upon further reading it becomes clear that Agnon's fascination would develop into deep piety in the course of his youth:

When my father or grandfather were in the house I would sit there and study. When, however, my father and grandfather were in the store, I taught my hand the art to write the books of the Talmud. At times, I would trace the frame of the title-page or the contours of the first letters of the Talmud, and I would write myself a *Mizrah* [a wall decoration indicating the east] with those. Had, in those days, someone told me that there exist more beautiful images than these, I would not have believed him...My grandfather, of blessed memory, left many things...but hardly anything survived in the hands of his children, as the enemy came and plundered everything. But this Talmud was preserved and I still study from it, and at times, when I am writing my stories to kindle the hearts of Israel to the service of the Blessed One, I take a volume from the shelves and read in it and establish a bond with our sages, of blessed memory, and with their holy words.

These quotations from Agnon underline the central role played by the book in traditional daily Jewish life. At least since the Middle Ages Jews have identified strongly with their traditional literature and have laid great emphasis on studying these texts through MSS and printed books in Hebrew and Aramaic and in all other languages employed by Jews in the Diaspora. Agnon's words also stress the importance of the book in religious education, and it may perhaps be said that in a way the history of the Jewish book is a chapter in the history of Jewish education. Here an attempt will be made to present the history of Hebrew books by concentrating on the role they played in the transmission of Jewish knowledge.

2 Transmission of the Hebrew Bible

The central book in Jewish tradition is obviously the Pentateuch, the Torah (*see* **2**). It is traditionally written as a scroll and read on Shabbat in synagogue in a yearly or three-yearly cycle. The writing of the Torah scroll is guided by set rules which were laid down in a number of treatises, the most famous being the extra-canonical Talmudic tractate *Soferim* (Scribes). This tractate served as the starting point for a number of commentators and legislators who expanded on it, the first and foremost being the great medieval scholar Moses Maimonides in his legal code *Mishneh Torah*. The high esteem for the holy craft of writing Hebrew Scriptures is actually already clear from the Babylonian Talmud. In the tractates *Eruvin* and *Sota* two similar passages occur, wherein Rabbi Ishmael, a 2nd-century CE sage, is quoted as saying to a learned scribe:

> 'My son, what is your occupation?' I told him, 'I am a scribe', and he said to me, 'Be meticulous in your work, for your occupation is a sacred one; should you perchance omit or add one single letter you would thereby destroy all the universe.' (*Eruvin*, 13a)

The first surviving biblical texts are found in the scrolls discovered from 1947 onwards in eleven caves near Khirbet Qumran (south of Jericho), the Dead Sea Scrolls. The greater part of these finds have been published in the last few decades, and they provide a treasure trove of information on early Jewish book culture and the transmission of the text of the Hebrew Bible. For this introduction, two of the most interesting texts among the Dead Sea Scrolls are the so-called Genesis Apocryphon and the Isaiah scroll, both found in Cave 1. Although of a completely different literary character, both provide a fascinating glimpse into the textual variety that existed in these earlier days of the transmission of the Hebrew Bible.

After the period of the Dead Sea Scrolls the textual transmission of the Hebrew Bible is much more blurred because of the absence of written source material. This absence is the result of natural decay, of the hostile destruction of Jewish books, and most probably also of the prominence of the oral tradition within Judaism, which may have been responsible for a general reluctance to write down religious texts.

It was exactly during these dark days of textual transmission that the so-called *Masoretes* developed detailed systems of vowel and diacritic signs that were meant to counter the threat of faulty copying that existed in the Jews' largely oral culture. The systems, of which various forms exist, were included in later bible codices and in the large majority of early printed editions.

The first bible codices emerge as late as the early 10th century: these are indeed the earliest dated Hebrew MSS of the medieval period. The codices were all copied in the Orient, which is most probably the result both of the presence of the necessary knowledge of its textual intricacies and of the favourably dry climatological circumstances under which they have been kept there in the centuries that followed. The most prominent early bible codices are the Moses ben Asher Codex, the Leningrad Codex, and the Aleppo Codex.

The Moses ben Asher codex contains the earliest date mentioned in a colophon of a Hebrew MS, 895 CE. Now housed in the Karaite Synagogue of Cairo, it was copied in Tiberias and contains the text of the Prophets. A detailed codicological analysis of the MS published by Glatzer in 1988, however, has proved quite convincingly that the codex, with its colophon, was copied at least a century later from an older exemplar. Since then a MS with fragments of the text of Nehemiah, kept in the Genizah Collection of Cambridge University Library and written in Da Gunbadan, Persia, in 904, is considered the earliest known dated Hebrew MS. The earliest dated Hebrew MS larger than a fragment is a codex of the Latter Prophets with Babylonian vocalization, finished in 916, now held in the National Library of Russia in St Petersburg.

The National Library of Russia also holds another early codex of the Hebrew Bible, copied in 1008 (MS Firkovich B 19A). This text, also known as the Codex Leningradensis, has served as the basis for the two most important critical editions of the 20th century, the Biblia Hebraica of Rudolf Kittel, first published in 1906, and the Biblia Hebraica Stuttgartensia, first published in 1966. Facsimile reproductions of the MS appeared in 1971 and 1998.

The Aleppo Codex is another early, undated MS of the Hebrew Bible. It is now kept in the Ben Zvi Institute in Jerusalem and was copied more than a millennium ago by Solomon ben Buya'a and vocalized most probably by Aaron ben Asher. The synagogue in Aleppo, Syria, where it had been for centuries, was burned down in 1947 and about one third of the MS was lost. Its remaining part was smuggled to Israel a few years later.

The Jewish preoccupation with the quality of textual transmission is also evident from the high regard accorded to a number of old codices with apparently exceedingly correct biblical texts, which still existed during the Middle Ages but have since disappeared. The most famous is the so-called Hilleli Codex. In his chronicle *Sefer Yuhasin*, written around 1500, Abraham Zacuto reported that the MS was still in existence, but since then no trace of it has been found. Its legendary status confirms the Jewish obsession with a correct text, and, as Zacuto put it, 'all other codices were revised after it'.

3 Oral and written transmission

The oral transmission of Jewish knowledge is best known through the concept of the written and the oral Torah, which were both received by Moses on Mount Sinai and assigned equal value as expressions of Divine Revelation. The oral laws were written down for the first time around the year 200 CE in the so-called *Mishnah*. The oral traditions that were developed around this *Mishnah* were once again written down in the course of the 4th and 5th centuries CE in the so-called *Gemara*, which, together with the *Mishnah*, constitute the Talmud. Two versions of the Talmud exist: a smaller Palestinian version, and a much more elaborate one, the Babylonian Talmud, the version most commonly referred to. This tradition of orality persisted well into the high Middle Ages and even afterwards and, as already indicated, it may account in part for the lack of early medieval written sources.

It is especially the so-called halakhic or legal literature that provides a fascinating glimpse into the specific nature of Jewish textual transmission. The Israeli scholar Israel Ta-Shma coined the term 'open book' for this:

> A long and intensive review of the medieval Hebrew book indicates that quite often books were not meant by their authors to serve as final statements, but rather as presentations of an interim state of knowledge or opinion, somewhat like our computerized databases, which are constantly updated and which give the user a summary of the data known at the time of the latest updating. In a similar way, the medieval book was sometimes conceived of as no more than a solid basis for possible future alterations by the author himself. There were many reasons—some philosophical and psychological, others purely technical—for this profound phenomenon, which can give rise to serious problems as to finality, authorship and authority of a given work. (Ta-Shma, 17)

A fine example of this, among many others, is Isaac ben Moses of Vienna's (c.1180–c.1250) halakhic code *Or Zarua*. This is a huge work, containing abundant halakhic as well as historical material. There are explicit references within the text to the author 'of blessed memory', and to later additions by the author himself, which prove that both during his life and afterwards paragraphs were added to it. One may even doubt whether he ever considered his composition as finished at all. It has been suggested that the author constantly added to his own words in the margins of his own MSS of the text, and that these additions were included in subsequent versions of it. The same process may account for the inclusion of his students' notes.

Interestingly, the very layout of halakhic MSS, especially in the Germanic lands, confirms the open-book nature of texts like *Or Zarua*. In these MSS 'central' texts are often surrounded by all sorts of smaller, commentary-like texts in creative ad hoc layouts. These surrounding texts would afterwards be incorporated into the next, equally authoritative MS witness of the text.

There are, as well, many testimonies of scribal intervention, correction, and editing, especially in colophons. An interesting example is the colophon of the famous Leiden University MS of the Palestinian Talmud, the only surviving complete medieval MS of this work. The scribe reports that he saw himself as forced to correct the text according to the best of his knowledge, since his copy was full of mistakes. He apologizes for any mistakes of his own. The Leiden MS was finished on Thursday, 17 February 1289 in Rome:

> I, Jehiel, son of Rabbi Jekutiel, son of Rabbi Benjamin Harofeh, of blessed memory, have copied this Talmud Yerushalmi…and I copied it from a corrupt and faulty exemplar and what I was able to understand and comprehend I corrected to the best of my knowledge. And I am fully aware that I did not reach at all the corruptions and faults I found in that copy, and not even half of them. And may therefore the reader of this book who will find corruptions and faults therein judge me according to my merit and not blame me for all of them. And may the Lord, in His mercy, forgive me my sins and cleanse me from my errors, as it is said [Ps. 19:13]: 'Who can be aware of errors, clear me of unperceived guilt.' (Leiden University, MS Or. 4720 (Scal. 3), vol. 2, fo. 303ᵛ)

It is important here to emphasize a particular characteristic of Hebrew books of the Middle Ages. This characteristic also permits a more generic focus on textual transmission during the Jewish Middle Ages, i.e. not on biblical or halakhic texts only, but on literary texts as they appear in medieval MSS. As a result of the comparatively very high level of literacy among Jewish men (and a few women), more than half of all the extant medieval Hebrew codices are the product of the work of a learned copyist who copied for his own use, and not of a professional scribe. It goes without saying that this has had a strong influence on the nature of textual transmission, which was formulated by Malachi Beit-Arié as follows:

> Contrary to what one might expect, the high ratio of user-produced manuscripts and the critical reproduction of texts in Jewish society did not necessarily improve the transmission of literary works by eliminating their scribal mistakes and restoring their authentic versions, but often engendered scholarly modifications, revisions and re-creations of the copied text that may very well have distorted and transformed the original work…Versions created by learned copyists on the basis of several exemplars or by scholarly conjecture…mixed inextricably disparate channels of transmission or conflated different authorial stages of the text and were dominated by personal choices and judgments. (Beit-Arié, *Unveiled Faces*, 65–6)

Beit-Arié's position is that of a modern scholar here. In most cases, earlier users of the 'distorted' and 'transformed' MSS he describes must have considered the texts before them as authoritative and reliable textual witnesses and have worked with them as such. A striking example of the problems involved here is provided by the text of the *Mishnah*—which, as already indicated, together with the so-called *Gemara* constitutes the text of the Talmud—as it is preserved in the only known complete medieval MS of the Babylonian Talmud, now in the Bavarian State Library in Munich (Cod. Hebr. 95). Copied in Paris in 1343, its Mishnaic text shows significant textual differences, far beyond the realm of variant spellings or even wordings, from MSS that are considered to represent a reliable textual tradition of the *Mishnah* (such as the famous Kaufmann *Mishnah* MS in the Hungarian Academy of Sciences in Budapest). The rarity of medieval MSS, even fragments, of the Talmud is generally believed to be the combined result of its enormous size, the strength of oral transmission within Judaism, and, notably, Christian aggression, which resulted (for example) in book burnings in Paris in 1242 and, in 1553, in the prohibition against printing the Talmud in Italy. It is therefore difficult to make any final statement about the reliability of the transmission of the text of the Babylonian Talmud. And yet, in the light of the relative quality of its Mishnaic text, it is hard to believe that the text of the Gemara as it appears in the only known complete medieval MS of its text represents anything else but one of Beit-Arié's 're-creations of the copied text that may very well have distorted and transformed the original work'.

In spite of the active copying by individuals, books were generally rare during the Jewish Middle Ages. As a result, scholars and students saw themselves forced to borrow books, often, to make copies for their own use in the process. In the Talmudic academy of Rabbi Israel ben Petahiah Isserlein (1390–1460), the spiritual leader of 15th-century Austrian Jewry, it was customary for students who possessed books to study them during the day, whereas students without books would borrow them to study at night. It is therefore not at all surprising that the lending of books was considered a great merit. In the medieval Ashkenazic *Sefer Hasidim*, or Book of the Pious, it is even stated that when lending books one should prefer a student who uses them on a daily basis over someone who does not. It further states that the greater the number of copies taken from a book, the greater the merit of the owner, and that a fear of possible damage inflicted on a book should never prevent one from lending it. The most striking expression of this attitude is the statement that one should rather sell a book to a Christian who lends it to others, than to one's brother, who does not do so. This general lack of books—in the Middle Ages a larger collection of MSS consisted of some dozens of volumes—would only come to a halt after the invention of printing; even then the relative poverty of the great majority of Jews prevented most of them from building more substantial collections.

4 From MS to printed text

Between 1469 and 1473 the first six Hebrew books were printed by three printers, Obadiah, Manasseh, and Benjamin of Rome. The most likely order of production of these books was established by Offenberg in *BMC* 13 (2005) on the basis of careful typographical and paper analyses of the holdings of the BL and the Bibliotheca Rosenthaliana in Amsterdam. This analysis does not permit a more precise dating of the individual books.

1. David ben Joseph Kimhi's dictionary *Sefer ha-shorashim*;
2. Solomon ben Abraham ibn Adret's collection of responsa;
3. Rashi's (Solomon ben Isaac) Commentary on the Pentateuch;
4. Levi ben Gershom's Commentary on the Book of Daniel;
5. Nathan ben Jehiel of Rome's Talmudic dictionary *Arukh*;
6. Moses ben Nahman's Commentary on the Pentateuch.

It must be emphasized that the world's second specialist in the field, Shimon Iakerson of St Petersburg, in his catalogue of the Hebrew incunabula in the Library of the Jewish Theological Seminary of America in New York (2004–5), is less certain about the exact order of printing. A quick look at the nature of the first six texts ever printed in Hebrew is interesting: two dictionaries, three bible commentaries, and a book of rabbinical responsa (replies to questions about Jewish law); no bibles, no prayer books, no Talmud, no scientific books. Although this would soon be corrected in the course of the 15th century—rather unexpectedly, Avicenna's medical *Canon* printed in Naples in 1491 is the largest of all Hebrew incunabula—and other genres would appear in print as well, the rarity (for example) of copies of the earliest editions of Rashi's commentaries is a clear indication of the popularity of Bible commentaries. Offenberg has even gone so far as to assume that more early editions have existed, of which no copies remain.

The six Rome imprints precede the book that many non-specialists continue to quote erroneously as the first printed Hebrew book, Solomon ben Isaac's commentary on the Pentateuch; finished on 17 February 1475 in Reggio di Calabria, it is the first printed Hebrew book mentioning a date. There were at least 140 Hebrew books printed in the incunable period. These books were produced by approximately 40 presses active in Italy, Spain, and Portugal, and by one in Turkey.

After the expulsion of the Jews from the Iberian peninsula at the end of the 15th century, Italy became the primary centre of Hebrew printing in the Mediterranean world, with Venice, Mantua, Sabbioneta, and Cremona having the most important presses. A particularly significant chapter in the history of the transmission of Jewish texts is the activity of the famous Venetian press of Daniel van Bomberghen, a Christian printer from Antwerp. He had close contacts with Christopher Plantin; his cousin Cornelius van Bomberghen was one of Plantin's partners. Van Bomberghen (just 'Bomberg' in Hebrew) established his printing press in Venice in 1516 and was active there until his return in 1548 to Antwerp, where he died in 1553. He published first-class editions of the *Biblia Rabbinica*, i.e. the Hebrew Bible with relevant translations and commentaries, and of the Palestinian and Babylonian Talmudim. For his 1522–4 edition of the Palestinian Talmud he claimed to have used a number of MSS in order to achieve the best possible text. Although it is not entirely certain that he really used more than the one MS that is now known as the Leiden MS (its colophon was quoted earlier), his text shows an awareness of textual criticism and a sense of editorial responsibility that would remain the standard for many generations. His was also one of the first printing offices in which Jewish and non-Jewish specialists worked closely together—an example that would soon be followed in other centres of humanist printing such as Basle, Constance, and Isny.

Other important centres of Hebrew printing in the Mediterranean area were Constantinople and Salonika. An interesting aspect of the history of Hebrew printing in the Balkan lands (*see* **38**) is the sale of books in weekly instalments of one or more quires, which would be sold after the Shabbat service on Saturday night. This phenomenon, certainly the result of limited funds, may account for the high number of incomplete surviving copies of books published in these cities. Important centres of printing in the Ashkenazi world were Prague, Cracow, and Augsburg. In these a relatively high number of books for everyday use, especially prayer books, were produced: with these, the issue of textual criticism does not seem to have been very prominent (at least judging from the title-pages). Further Humanist centres of Hebrew printing were Paris, Geneva, Antwerp, and, later, Leiden.

Starting in the second half of the 16th century and on into the 18th century in Italy, the censors of the Office of the Inquisition used to check and expurgate the large majority of Hebrew books in private and community collections. They would often even charge the Jews for their 'holy' work. The Inquisition's special attention to the activity of the Italian Jewish printing presses found its most dramatic expression in the prohibition in 1553 against printing the Talmud. This led to a dramatic decrease in Hebrew book production in general and to all sorts of Jewish self-censorship, either through the active changing of texts in order to make them 'clean' for the Inquisition, or through the decision simply not to print certain works that would not avoid the censors' criticism.

The 17th century is the century of Amsterdam. The first Jew to print Hebrew in Amsterdam was Menasseh ben Israel, who started printing in 1627. Other important Amsterdam Hebrew printers were Immanoel Benveniste, Uri Fayvesh ben Aaron Halevi, David de Castro Tartas, and the members of the printing dynasties of Athias and Proops. Although most printers did have a number of major projects through which they would try to establish their name, judging from their productions most Amsterdam printers were willing to print any book that came with proper funding and reliable rabbinical approbations. For their special projects, however, they would invest considerably, either with their own or with external funds, and would do their utmost to produce the best possible text. An interesting case in point are the two competing Yiddish translations of the Bible that were printed more or less simultaneously in 1678 and 1679. The printer Uri Fayvesh ordered Jekuthiel ben Isaac Blitz to make a Yiddish translation. The translator appeared not to be able to deliver the quality that one of the partners in the project, the printer Joseph Athias, had expected. Athias therefore decided to withdraw from the project, ordering a better translation from Joseph ben Alexander Witzenhausen and publishing it himself. Although both editions were printed in press runs of more than 6,000 copies, neither was a commercial success. On a more general level it may be stated that the Amsterdam printing business, with its vast international network of authors and readers, its high-quality output, and its close contacts with the surrounding non-Jewish world, constituted the last stage in the industrialization and professionalization of Hebrew printing.

5 The emergence of publishing

The second half of the 18th century was dominated by a major development in the intellectual history of Jewish Europe. The Jewish Enlightenment, or Haskalah movement, would dominate the world of the book in the late 18th and early 19th centuries and, alongside more traditional presses that catered for the needs of the religious communities, would become responsible for a series of new, critical editions of traditional Jewish texts, textbooks, satirical works, and a number of influential journals. The most important journal was *Ha-me'asef* (the Gatherer), issued originally by the Society of Promoters of the Hebrew Language and published in various places between 1784 and 1811. The journal soon became the voice of the Jewish Enlightenment. Haskalah goals included getting Jews to adopt the German language and to give up Yiddish, to assimilate into the local culture, and, for literary use, to write biblical ('classical') Hebrew instead of what they considered the inferior Rabbinic Hebrew. The best way to implement these ideals was by means of education. Interestingly, fables were considered especially effective for education, which explains why *Ha-me'asef* contains no fewer than 55 fables.

In the course of the 19th and in the beginning of the 20th century ever more belles-lettres were published, both in Hebrew and in Hebrew and Yiddish translations. This illustrates the continuing emancipation of the Jewish intellectual classes, as well as the development of what has been called 'a vigorous, effective, and dynamic publishing apparatus' (Grunberger, 124). Emerging Zionism was an influential factor as well, since it stimulated the publication of historical novels that connected contemporary Jews with their historical ancestors. One publisher has been particularly important in the development of this 'publishing apparatus', Abraham Leib Shalkovich, or Ben-Avigdor. He started off in Warsaw with a series of 'penny books' in 1891, and established two conventional publishing houses, one in 1893 and one in 1896. Ben-Avigdor formulated his deeper motivation as follows:

> Upon examining the poverty of our Hebrew literature in all its aspects, we recognize that one of the main factors preventing it from developing as it should is the absence from our midst of well-financed publishers who could pay authors and scholars a just recompense for their labor...(Grunberger, 120)

Ben-Avigdor's and a number of his successor's efforts paved the way for the development of a national, modern Hebrew literature, publishing the works of such authors as Hayyim Nahman Bialik (1873–1934) and Saul Tchernichovski (1875–1943).

The emigration of these authors and many of their colleagues to Palestine in the first decades of the 20th century signalled the emergence of Palestine as the centre of Hebrew literature. This shift to Palestine was further strengthened by the major political events of the 20th century, the rise of Communism in Eastern Europe, the mass destruction of European Jews by the Nazis, and the foundation of the State of Israel in 1948. Modern Israeli authors such as Abraham Yehoshua (1936–), David Grossman (1954–), and Amos Oz (1939–), are published in Israel and widely translated, read, and appreciated in all modern languages. Oz's monumental and highly erudite novel *A Tale of Love and Darkness* (2004) recounts his own family saga and covers Jewish history and intellectual life of the 19th, 20th, and 21st centuries: while writing about himself and his family, he is also telling the story of the Jews. As such his work is both an integral part of a millennium-old tradition and a worthy representative of the promising future of the Hebrew (for which now read Israeli) book.

....

BIBLIOGRAPHY

S. J. Agnon, *Das Schaß meines Großvaters* (1925)

M. Beit-Arié, *Hebrew Manuscripts of East and West* (1993)

—— *The Makings of the Medieval Hebrew Book* (1993)

—— *Unveiled Faces of Medieval Hebrew Books* (2003)

M. Glatzer, 'The Aleppo-Codex: Codicological and Paleographical Aspects', *Sefunot*, 4.19 (1988), 167–276 (in Hebrew)

Z. Gries, *The Book in the Jewish World, 1700–1900* (2007)

M. W. Grunberger, 'Publishing and the Rise of Modern Hebrew Literature', in *A Sign and a Witness*, ed. L. S. Gold (1988)

M. J. Heller, *Printing the Talmud* (1992)

—— *Studies in the Making of the Early Hebrew Book* (2008)

B. S. Hill, *Incunabula, Hebraica and Judaica* (1981)

—— *Hebraica (Saec. X ad Saec. XVI)* (1989)

S. Iakerson, *Catalogue of Hebrew Incunabula from the Collection of the Library of the Jewish Theological Seminary* (2 vols, 2004–5)

S. Liberman Mintz and G. M. Goldstein, *Printing the Talmud* (2005)

A. K. Offenberg, *Hebrew Incunabula in Public Collections* (1990)

—— *BMC* 13: *Hebraica* (2005)

D. W. Parry *et al.*, eds., *The Dead Sea Scrolls Reader* (2004)

R. Posner and I. Ta-Shma, eds., *The Hebrew Book* (1975)

B. Richler, *Guide to Hebrew Manuscript Collections* (1994)

E. G. L. Schrijver, 'The Hebraic Book', in *A Companion to the History of the Book*, ed. S. Eliot and J. Rose (2007)

C. Sirat, *Hebrew Manuscripts of the Middle Ages* (2002)

I. Ta-Shma, 'The "Open" Book in Medieval Literature: the Problem of Authorized Editions', *BJRL* 75 (1993) 17–24

E. Tov, *Textual Transmission of the Hebrew Bible* (1992)

—— ed., *The Dead Sea Scrolls on Microfiche* (1993)

Y. Vinograd, *Thesaurus of the Hebrew Book* (1993)

Missionary Printing

M. ANTONI J. ÜÇERLER, S.J.

1 Introduction

The history of printing and the history of the book would be incomplete without an understanding of the key role played by printing presses that were established by missionaries, Roman Catholic and Protestant, in countries throughout East and Southeast Asia, Oceania (*see* **46, 47**), Africa (*see* **39**), the Middle East (*see* **40**), and the Americas (*see* **48, 49, 50, 51**). The missionaries soon discovered that both the propagation of Christian doctrine and the inculcation of its ethical precepts could be greatly aided by the mass production and distribution of books and pamphlets. The earliest missionary presses were established in the 16th and 17th centuries and were linked for the most part to the Roman Catholic religious orders—Franciscans, Dominicans, Augustinians, and Jesuits—that were engaged in activities throughout the New World and Asia.

Protestant missionary presses first appeared on the Asian scene in India in the 17th century. Over the following 100 years, foundations such as the London Missionary Society, the British and Foreign Bible Society (BFBS), and the American Board of Commissioners for Foreign Missions were established on both sides of the Atlantic. A common characteristic of their method of evangelization was the strategic use of the printing press.

Missionary printing has taken place throughout the world from the 16th century onwards. This essay provides a preliminary sketch of the most significant developments in South, Southeast, and East Asia: for the Americas, *see* **48, 49, 50, and 51**.

2 India

The story of missionary presses begins on the west coast of India 46 years after the Portuguese first conquered and established a strategic commercial entrepôt in the port city of Goa in 1510. João Nunes Barreto, the patriarch designate of Ethiopia, brought a printing press from Portugal to Goa on 6 September 1556. This press was originally destined for use in Africa, but in view of strained relations between the missionaries and the Emperor of Abyssinia, it remained in Goa. One of the Jesuits who accompanied Barreto to India was Juan de Bustamente (also known from the 1560s as João Rodrigues), who became master printer at the Jesuit College of St Paul. The press was first used on 19 October 1556, when lists of theses (*conclusões*) in logic and philosophy were printed as broadsides for students of the College to defend publicly (Wicki, iii. 514, 574). The following year saw the publication of the first book, a compendium of Christian doctrine, composed several years before by Francis Xavier for the catechesis of local children.

Juan Gonsalves (or Gonçálvez), another Spanish Jesuit, is credited with having produced in Goa, in 1577, the earliest metal type in Tamil. Pero Luis, a Brahmin and the first Indian Jesuit, and João de Faria, who helped to improve the fount, assisted Gonsalves. The result was the first book printed with movable type in an Indian language, namely an emended version of Xavier's original Tamil catechism, revised by Henrique Henriques, who was the first systematic lexicographer of the language. The 16-page booklet was produced in Quilon (Kollam) in 1578. The colophon on the last page includes text printed from the type made in Goa the previous year. Another catechism (*Doutrina christã*) by Marcos Jorge, originally published in Lisbon in 1561 and 1566, was translated into Tamil and printed with Faria's type in Cochin on 14 November 1579 (Shaw, '"Lost" Work', 27). A guide to how to make one's confession (*Confessionairo*) and a collection of the lives of the saints (*Flos Sanctorum*) in Tamil followed in 1580 and 1586 respectively. All these books were prepared in accordance with instructions issued in 1575 by Alessandro Valignano, who was responsible for all Jesuit missions in Southeast and East Asia between 1573 and 1606 (Wicki, x. 269, 334). He would also play a crucial role in the beginnings of missionary printing in China and Japan.

The first publication in an Indian language other than Tamil was printed in Konkani some time before 1561 at the College of St Paul. In a letter from Goa on 1 December 1561, Luís Fróis reports that a printed summary of Christian doctrine was read to the local people 'in their own language' (Wicki, v. 273; Saldanha, 7–9). No copy of this work (probably a small booklet) is known to have survived. There are copies, however, of the books written by Thomas Stephens, an English Jesuit and pioneer in the study of Indian languages. The first was his 'Story of Christ' (*Krista purāna*) in literary Marathi, printed in 1616, 1649, and 1654. The second work was a Christian doctrine (*Doutrina christam em lingoa bramana canarim*) in Konkani, the language spoken by the Brahmins in Goa; it was printed posthumously in 1622 (Priolkar, 17–18). Stephens also composed the first missionary printing grammar of Konkani, which came off the press in 1640. Although the missionaries had made attempts to produce Indian type in Marathi-Devanāgarī script or 'lengoa canarina' as early as 1577, they gave up their efforts on account of the difficulty of producing so many matrices. As a result, they printed Stephens's works in Roman transliteration only (Wicki, x. 1006–7). A total of 37 titles in Portuguese, Latin, Marathi, Konkani, and Chinese were printed between 1556 and 1674 (Boxer, 1–19). The promulgation of a decree in 1684 by the Portuguese authorities in Goa banning the use of Konkani, in a move to root out all local languages, brought Roman Catholic missionary printing in India to an abrupt end. Two centuries would pass before it could be revived.

Meanwhile Bartholomew Ziegenbalg, a Lutheran from Germany and the first Protestant missionary in India, travelled in 1706 to the Danish East India Company's coastal mission at Tranquebar (Tharangambadi), north of Nagappattinam, where he soon became proficient in Tamil. A library of Jesuit publications, including Henriques' grammar, was available to Ziegenbalg, who found them useful in avoiding pitfalls in the translation of his own works. He wrote to Denmark requesting a printing press in 1709. His Danish patrons then appealed to the Society for Promoting Christian Knowledge in London, which shipped a press to India in 1712. On 17 October of that year, a Christian doctrine in Portuguese and Tamil was printed in roman letters. Many other works followed and were printed with Tamil type, which he arranged to be cast in Germany on the basis of drawings he had prepared. The type was produced at Halle in Saxony and sent to India in 1713 with Johann Gottlieb Adler, a German printer who established a type foundry in Porayur just outside Tranquebar. Ziegenbalg's translation of the New Testament into Tamil was printed in two parts (1714–15) with a new smaller typeface cast by Adler. A second edition followed in 1724, with further editions in 1758, 1788, and 1810 (Rosenkilde, 186). To counter the constant shortage of paper and ink, Ziegenbalg also helped establish a local paper mill and a factory to produce ink.

After Ziegenbalg, the most famous Protestant missionary printer in India was William Carey, who founded the Baptist Missionary Society in 1792 and arrived in West Bengal the following year. In 1800, he succeeded in establishing a missionary press at Serampore (Shrirampur), a Danish settlement 20 km north of Calcutta (Kolkata), which was supervised by his fellow missionary and printer, William Ward. Carey then published the Gospel of Matthew, the earliest imprint produced with Bengali type. The following year saw his first complete translation of the New Testament in that language. Working with his fellow missionary, Joshua Marshman, and with learned Indian converts, he produced further translations of the Bible into Sanskrit, Hindi, Oriya, Marathi, Assamese, and many other languages. The Serampore press, in operation until 1855, became the most prolific Christian printing concern in India, producing works in more than 40 different languages and dialects (*see* **41**).

3 China, Malaysia, and Singapore

The Chinese stage on which missionaries made their appearance in the 16th century was very different from that of India. Most significant was the integrity of China's territory, free from any form of colonial coercion that might include foreign attempts to control or censor the printed word. Although records show evidence of the use of movable type made from an amalgam of clay and glue as early as the 11th century, the technology that dominated the Chinese world of printing until the 19th century remained xylography or woodblock printing, first employed in China around AD 220 (*see* **42**). The bureaucracy of the Middle Kingdom, which was based on a highly centralized civil service examination, depended on the ready availability and wide distribution of books. This in turn created the need for thousands of printers and bookshops throughout the realm. Thus, when Michele Ruggieri and Matteo Ricci, the first two Italian Jesuit missionaries to compose works in literary Chinese, wished to have their books published, they turned to their friends among the literati, who made arrangements to have the printing done either in their own private printing office or by another local printer.

In a way similar to their counterparts in India, the missionaries in China concentrated their early efforts on producing summaries of Christian doctrine. In 1584, they succeeded in printing at Zhaoqing Ruggieri's *Tianzhu shilu* (The True Record of the Lord of Heaven), the earliest translation of a catechism into Chinese.

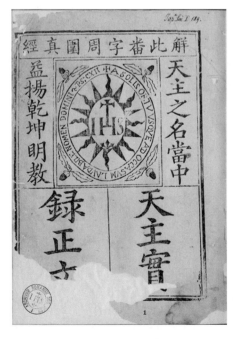

Jesuit printing in China: Michele Ruggieri's *Tianzhu shilu* (The True Record of the Lord of Heaven), printed at Zhaoqing in 1584. © Institutum Historicum Societatis Iesu (Rome).

The *Tianzhu shiyi* (The True Meaning of the Lord of Heaven), a completely revised catechism in dialogue form, was composed by Matteo Ricci and printed in Peking (Beijing) for the first time in 1603. These catechisms, which encompassed a wide range of genres, mark the beginning of the prolific production of works composed in Chinese by several generations of missionaries and printed throughout China on private presses and at printing offices using woodblocks. In addition to expositions of Christian doctrine and liturgical texts, there were works introducing adaptations of Western classical books in the humanities—especially in moral philosophy—as well as numerous scientific treatises on astronomy, mathematics, physics, and geography. In this enterprise the foreign missionaries were often aided by erudite Chinese converts, the most prominent of whom were Xu Guangqi, Yang Tingyun, and Li Zhizao. Approximately 470 works on religious and moral topics composed by missionaries in China and Chinese Christians were printed between 1584 and 1700. Another 120 titles dealt with the West and science (Standaert, 600). These books represent an extraordinary bridge between the canons of classical literature in China and Europe, and they provide both the East and the West with a literary window into each other's ancient cultures and traditions.

The first Protestant missionary in China was Robert Morrison, who arrived in Canton (Guangzhou) in 1807 as a member of the London Missionary Society (LMS). Together with his fellow missionary, William Milne, he subsequently founded the Anglo-Chinese (*Yingwa*) College in the 'Ultra-Ganges Mission' in Malacca (Melaka) in 1818 and completed a translation of the Bible into Chinese in 1819 (printed in 1823). The mission press of the LMS, however, began operations in Malacca as early as 1815. Among the early imprints of 1817 are 'The Ten Commandments' and 'The Lord's Prayer' in Malay, produced in Arabic-Jawi script (Rony, 129). From Malacca, Milne sent Thomas Beighton in 1819 to establish a school for the education of Malays and Chinese in Penang and to work as a printer. Samuel Dyer, Morrison's former student and also an LMS member, arrived in Penang in 1827. An expert in punchcutting, he worked on a new steel typeface for Chinese characters.

In Singapore, the BFBS had been printing works in Malay since 1822, just three years after Sir Stamford Raffles founded the free trading post. There were also other mission presses that produced a variety of imprints in the 1830s and 1840s and were administered by the LMS and the American Board of Commissioners for Foreign Missions (ABCFM). Two men deserve special mention in this regard. The first is Benjamin Peach Keasberry, a pioneer in Malay education who had perfected his printing skills at Batavia (Java). He learned the language from Abdullah bin Abdul Kadir (or Munshi Abdullah), the father of modern Malay literature, who helped him to produce a new translation of the New Testament into Malay (after the earlier partial Amsterdam and Oxford editions of 1651 and 1677). The second was Alfred North, a Presbyterian minister from Exeter, NH, who was head of the printing division until 1843, the year the American Mission in Singapore was closed. When the 1842 Treaty of Nanking allowed the British to take up residence in China, Walter Henry Medhurst established a new LMS Press in Shanghai, which soon became the most prolific in modern China, printing works in English, Chinese, and Malay on a wide range of topics, sacred and secular. An accomplished polyglot and pioneer lexicographer, Medhurst also published numerous dictionaries, including the first English–Japanese, Japanese–English vocabulary, printed in Batavia in 1830.

4 The Philippines

Dominican missionaries, who would lead early missionary printing in the Philippine archipelago, built their church and convent of San Gabriel among the Chinese merchants in the Parián, or market district of Manila after their arrival in 1587. The missionaries soon set about preparing Christian texts for the native Filipino as well as the mixed Chinese (or *sangley*) populations. A number of catechisms circulated in MS as early as the 1580s. Some time before 20 June 1593, Gómez Pérez Dasmariñas (governor, 1590–93) authorized the printing of two Christian doctrines, one in Spanish and Tagalog, and another in Chinese. The Tagalog text was prepared by the Franciscans working under Juan de Plasencia, whereas the Chinese doctrine was composed by the Dominicans supervised by Juan Cobo. Both were printed with woodblocks prepared by a Chinese convert and printer, Geng Yong (or Keng Yong), whose Spanish name was Juan de Vera. Cobo composed another summary of Christian doctrine along with a synopsis of Western natural sciences (*Shilu*), which was printed posthumously in 1593. It is noteworthy that Cobo mentions having read Ruggieri's printed catechism of 1584 (Wolf, 37).

Other devotional works followed in movable type between 1602 and 1640 from the Binondo (or Binondoc) quarter of Manila. Of these, the first imprint was probably a booklet with the mysteries of the rosary, printed in 1602, composed by a Dominican, Francisco Blancas de San José, who set up the press at the convent. This was followed by a pamphlet containing the ordinances of the Dominican Order in the Philippines (*Ordinationes Generales*) and another treatise by Blancas de San José, entitled *Libro de las quatro postrimerías del hombre en lengua tagala, y letra española*. Both were printed by Juan de Vera in 1604–5. Other works, printed by de Vera's brother, Pedro, began to appear in 1606. He printed a grammar, *Arte y reglas de la lengua tagala* (1610), compiled by Blancas de San José, and a book in Tagalog to teach the native population Spanish. Pedro de Vera printed these works in Abucay, part of Bataan province where Tomas Pinpin and Domingo Laog, regarded as the first native Filipino typesetters and printers, were active for several decades. The Franciscans also had a press as early as 1606, but no evidence remains of its productions prior to 1655, after which it was transferred to Tayabas (Quezon) in 1702 and to Manila in 1705. The Jesuits, on the other hand, established a press in 1610 at their college in Manila, and the Augustinians were printing at their own convent in Manila as early as 1618. Thus, several hundred titles were published at missionary presses in the Philippines before the 19th century.

5 Japan

The story of missionary printing in Japan is linked to Alessandro Valignano, who was also instrumental in early printing in India. The Jesuits, who first landed in Japan in 1549, soon realized the need for books in order to carry out their work, especially among the learned elites. Unlike China, Japan during the so-called era of Warring States (1467–1568) did not provide them with a readily accessible network of printers on whom they could rely. Valignano therefore instructed Diogo de Mesquita, a Portuguese Jesuit, to procure a press in Europe and to have Japanese typefaces cut in Portugal or in Flanders. The press was acquired in Lisbon in 1586 and first used to print a small booklet, *Oratio Habita à Fara D. Martino*, in 1588 in Goa. There, a number of young Japanese, including Constantino Dourado and Jorge de Loyola, learned punchcutting from Bustamente, the master printer at the College of St Paul. The press was employed again later that year in Macao to print *Christiani Pueri Institutio*, a popular treatise in Latin by Juan Bonifacio, before it reached its destination further east.

The first imprints of the new Jesuit mission press were prepared at their college at Kazusa in 1590–91 and included summaries of Christian doctrine, broadsides with prayers, and an abridged version of saints' lives (*Sanctos no gosagueo no uchi nuqigaqi*). This last work was the first book printed in Japanese with movable type. These early imprints employed roman script with a few unsuccessful attempts to produce Japanese type. Other works printed with roman type include the *Feiqe no monogatari* (Tale of the Heike) (1592), a translation of Aesop's *Fables* (*Esopo no fabulas*) (1593), as well as the trilingual Latin–Portuguese–Japanese dictionary of 1595. A Japanese–Portuguese dictionary (*Vocabulario da lingoa de Japam*) and the first grammar of Japanese (*Arte da lingoa de Japam*) were printed between 1603 and 1608. Major improvements to the wooden type were made in the early 1590s; metal type of high quality in cursive script (*sōsho*) was finally perfected in 1598–9 and used in the printing of several important works, including a translation of the *Guía de peccadores* by Luis de Granada and the *Rakuyōshū*, a Chinese–Japanese dictionary.

The Jesuits and their converts were instrumental in effecting a number of innovations in printing in Japan, including the first recorded use of movable type to print in Japanese itself (as opposed to the romanized form of the language); the introduction of furigana (i.e. hiragana or katakana, syllabic characters printed in a smaller fount, to indicate the correct reading of the individual Chinese characters); the carving of two or more characters on a single piece of type; and the use of hiragana-script ligatures. By 1600, the Jesuits had handed over the day-to-day operations of the press—which had been moved from Kazusa to Amakusa to Nagasaki—to a prominent Japanese Christian layman, Thomé Sōin Gotō. Another layman, Antonio Harada, began printing Christian works in Miyako (Kyoto) in 1610 at the latest. It is uncertain whether he used traditional woodblocks or movable type in his printing office. When the missionaries were expelled from the country in 1614, the press was shipped to Macao, where it was unpacked in 1620 to print an abridged grammar of Japanese composed by João Rodrigues 'Tçuzzu' ('the Interpreter'). Although some sources claim that the press was subsequently sold to the Augustinians in Manila, no conclusive evidence can be adduced to identify the press used in the Philippines with that of the Jesuits from the Japanese mission.

In the aftermath of Toyotomi Hideyoshi's invasion of Korea, where movable type had been in use since the 13th century (*see* **43**), the Japanese regent brought back Korean printing materials in 1592. As a result, the Emperor Goyōzei and Tokugawa Ieyasu published a number of books between 1593 and 1613 using both wooden and copper type (*see* **44**). Whether either of these two independent developments in the history of Japanese movable-type printing exerted any influence on the other remains unclear.

After Japan closed her doors to the West in 1639, missionary printing ceased altogether. It would begin again in earnest only in the 1870s in Nagasaki and Yokohama, under the aegis of prominent members of the Foreign Paris Missions (MEP) in Japan, including Bernard Petitjean, Pierre Mounicou, and Louis Théodore Furet. Even before the proclamation of religious freedom by the Meiji government in 1873, the French missionaries had succeeded in printing catechisms in Japanese as early as 1865.

6 Conclusion

As Europeans began to travel to all corners of the earth beginning in the 15th century, they were determined not only to conquer new lands but also to spread their faith. From Johann Gutenberg they had learned the power of the printed word, and were determined to use this revolutionary new technology to Christianize Asia. The impact of these efforts varied depending on a number of circumstances. The two most significant variables were the ability to wield control as a colonial power (e.g. in the Philippines, but not in Japan or China) and the pre-existence of a widespread print culture (e.g. in China), or lack thereof (e.g. in India and Malaya).

This summary account of missionary printing in Asia also suggests that the principal difference between Roman Catholic and Protestant presses was the emphasis placed by the former on the exposition of Christian doctrine and the printing of catechetical treatises, and the early concentration by the latter on the preparation of partial or complete versions of the Bible in local languages. In either case, the missionaries made efforts to learn the local languages and pioneered the production of numerous dictionaries and grammars.

....

BIBLIOGRAPHY

C. R. Boxer, *A Tentative Check-List of Indo-Portuguese Imprints, 1556–1674* (1956)

C. J. Brokaw, 'On the History of the Book in China', in *Printing and Book Culture in Late Imperial China*, ed. C. J. Brokaw and K. Chow (2005)

T. F. Carter, *The Invention of Printing in China and its Spread Westward*, 2e (1955; repr. 1988)

A. Chan, *Chinese Books and Documents in the Jesuit Archives in Rome* (2002)

C. Clair, *A Chronology of Printing* (1969)

H. Cordier, *L'Imprimerie sino-européenne en Chine* (1901)

T. Doi, 'Das Sprachstudium der Gesellschaft Jesu in Japan im 16. und 17. Jahrhundert', *Monumenta Nipponica*, 2 (1939), 437–65

W. Farge, *The Japanese Translations of the Jesuit Mission Press, 1590-1614* (2002)

R. P. Hsia, 'The Catholic Mission and Translations in China, *1583-1700*', in *Cultural Translation in Early Modern Europe*, ed. P. Burke and R. P. Hsia (2007)

J. Laures, *Kirishitan Bunko: A Manual of Books and Documents on the Early Christian Mission in Japan*, 3e (1957; repr. 1985)

J. Toribio Medina, *Biblioteca hispano-americana (1493-1810)* (7 vols, 1898–1907)

—— *Historia de la imprenta en los antiguos dominios españoles de América y Oceanía* (2 vols, 1958)

J. Muller and E. Roth, *Aussereuropäische Druckereien im 16. Jahrhundert* (1969)

D. Pacheco, 'Diogo de Mesquita, S. J. and the Jesuit Mission Press', *Monumenta Nipponica*, 26 (1971), 431–43

J. Pan, 'A Comparative Research of Early Movable Metal-Type Printing Technique in China, Korea, and Europe', *GJ* 73 (1998), 36–41

—— *A History of Movable Metal-Type Printing Technique in China* (2001)

A. K. Priolkar, *The Printing Press in India* (1958)

W. E. Retana, *Orígenes de la imprenta filipina* (1911)

A. Kohar Rony, 'Malay Manuscripts and Early Printed Books in the Library of Congress', *Indonesia*, 52 (1991), 123–34

V. Rosenkilde, 'Printing at Tranquebar', *Library*, 5/4 (1949–50), 179–95

M. Saldanha, *Doutrina Cristã em língua concani* (1945)

E. Satow, *The Jesuit Mission Press* (1898)

D. Schilling, 'Vorgeschichte des Typendrucks auf den Philippinen', *GJ* 12 (1937), 202–16

—— 'Christliche Druckereien in Japan (1590–1614)', *GJ* 15 (1940), 356–95

G. Schurhammer and G. W. Cottrell, 'The First Printing in Indic Characters', *HLB* 6 (1952), 147–60

J. F. Schütte, 'Drei Unterrichtsbücher für japanische Jesuitenprediger aus dem XVI. Jahrhundert', *Archivum Historicum Societatis Iesu*, 8 (1939), 223–56

—— 'Christliche japanische Literatur, Bilder, und Druckblätter in einem unbekannten vatikanischen Codex aus dem Jahre 1591', *Archivum Historicum Societatis Iesu*, 9 (1940), 226–80

G. W. Shaw, 'A "Lost" Work of Henrique Henriques: The Tamil Confessionary of 1580', *BLR* 11 (1982–5), 26–34

—— *The South Asia and Burma Retrospective Bibliography* (1987)

N. Standaert, ed., *Handbook of Christianity in China* (2001)

R. Streit and J. Dindinger, *Bibliotheca Missionum* (30 vols, 1916–75)

M. A. J. Üçerler and S. Tsutsui, eds., *Laures Rare Book Database and Virtual Library*, www.133.12.23.145:8080/html/, consulted Apr. 2008

J. Wicki, ed., *Documenta Indica* (18 vols, 1944–88)

E. Wolf, 2nd, *Doctrina Christiana: The First Book Printed in the Philippines. Manila 1593* (1947)

10

Paper

DAVEN CHRISTOPHER CHAMBERLAIN

1 Introduction

Paper is a sheet material consisting of overlapping vegetable fibres that bond together to form a compact mat. Its origin can be traced to China, where a court official named Cai Lun is said to have invented it *c.*AD 105. Paper remained exclusive to the Middle East and East Asia until around 1151, when there is evidence of its being made in Spain during the Moorish occupation. Slowly, the craft spread across Europe, from Italy in 1276 to France in 1348, Germany in 1390, and eventually into England by 1495.

Each sheet of paper bears physical signs of the manufacturing process it has undergone. Coupled with analysis of its constituents, these can be used to provide evidence of provenance. This essay presents information on paper as an historical source; although it is chiefly concerned with occidental manufacture from its inception to the present day, its generalities can be applied, with due consideration, to paper from any period or origin.

2 Paper manufacture

Paper can be made from all manner of vegetable fibres, in a process that has remained largely the same for two millennia. Early Asiatic papermakers used various specially harvested and prepared plants as their fibre sources. By contrast, the first European papermakers used textile waste, cordage (rope), and other pre-processed material. It was only in the 18th century that occidental papermakers and scientists investigated raw plants for their papermaking potential; full commercialization of suitable materials did not start until at least the 19th century.

Regardless of which source of fibrous raw material is used, the same basic steps are followed to turn it into paper. The first process involves cleaning and purification. For rags and cordage this means cutting them into small pieces, dusting them to remove fine matter, cleaning, and softening. The earliest cleaning method involved steeping in water and allowing them to rot partially, and then washing them. Adding alkali, such as lime, helped to speed the disintegration, though this was banned at various times because of the detrimental effect it could have on fibre quality. More recently, processing involved boiling the shredded textile with alkali. The shade of the pulp produced by these methods depended upon the initial textile colour and water quality; by the 1790s, to improve colour and to remove dyes, chemical bleaching was applied in papermaking.

Processing of raw plant matter follows a similar path, except that the unwanted constituents need to be dissolved rather than washed away. Strong alkali or acid is used as a chemical treatment, sometimes following a retting (or soaking) stage in which biological pre-treatment softens the fibres. Again, bleaching may follow before the pulp is ready for use.

Plant or textile fibres prepared in this way are still not suitable for papermaking; they need mechanical treatment to separate the individual fibres, modify their length, alter their flexibility, and increase their surface area to promote bonding. In the earliest European mills, this process was performed using either kollergangs or stamping mills. Kollergangs were large millstones set on their rims, running in a stone trough; they twisted and crushed batches of fibres without cutting them, in a way similar to milling grain or pressing oilseed. The other process involved pounding the wet fibres with large wooden hammers shod with nails; these 'stampers' tended to flatten fibres and break their outer layers, resulting in more fibrillation than kollergangs. Both processing methods resulted in a strong, very long-fibred pulp. The main change in macerating techniques occurred in the late 17th century, when the Hollander beater was introduced. This processed larger batches of fibre faster than either of the previous machines, and by the late 18th century its use was widespread. It could produce in hours what took days in a stamper or kollergang; however, there was a trade-off. The rapid processing resulted in more stress to the fibres, causing significant breakage and a consequent reduction in their length and strength; there were also more fibres of varying length, including many very short fibres. In the late 19th century, as continuous machine production became dominant, the last fibre-processing method, refining, gained prominence. Beating is a batch process, whereas refining is continuous, with the fibres being fed by pipeline through a series of rotating barred discs or cones; the end result is more homogeneous than beating, with much more uniform fibre lengths.

After mechanical processing, the fibre suspension is diluted to the required consistency, mixed with chemicals, and introduced to the forming stage. In a handmaking operation, the vatman uses a mould to scoop a quantity of the

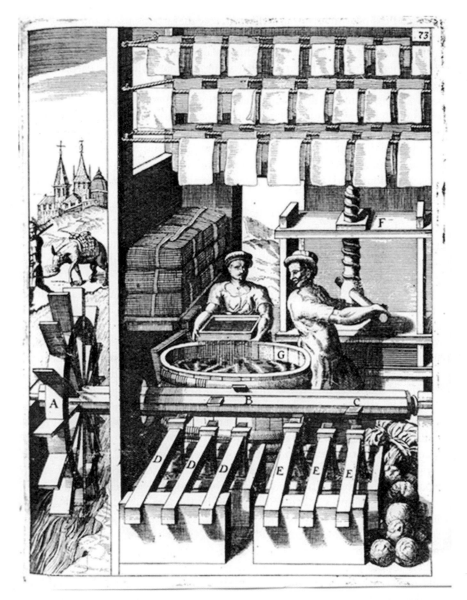

Hand papermaking from G. A. Böckler's *Theatrum Machinarum Novum* (Nuremberg, 1661). With water-powered hammers, the linen rags are pulped. The vatman stands at the vat with a mould; the coucher presses the post; the drying sheets hang on ropes above, ready to be sized, calendared, gathered into reams, and packaged. Courtesy of Alan Crocker

stock, which drains through the porous wire mesh at the bottom to form a sheet. This is then passed to a second worker, the coucher, who transfers the wet fibre mat on to a textile, usually of felt, to support it during the next process, pressing. A stack of alternating wet mats and felts, called a post, is introduced into a mechanical press, which expels much of the surplus water. Pressing may be repeated further times with the paper sheets placed together rather than with felts interleaved, before they pass to the drying stage.

The still-damp sheets are then separated from the pile in 'spurs' of four or five, which are dried as a group, as this produces a flatter sheet than if they are dried singly, when excessive curl and cockling can result. The commonest drying method involves draping the spur over ropes in lofts, where air flow regulated by louvres allows them to dry over a period of days. Other methods include pegging the spurs by the corners and hanging them in a loft, and 'sail drying', where the spurs are laid horizontally upon canvas. Draping the sheets over ropes results in a 'back', and pegging produces localized compression at the corners; both of these methods leave tell-tale signs in sheets.

If sized paper was required, it was made traditionally in a separate process: the dried waterleaf (unsized) sheet was passed through a solution of size, such as animal glue or starch, before being pressed and re-dried. The sheets were then left in stacks to mature, during which time the dried-in stresses relaxed and flattened. By contrast, some modern hand-mills have employed reactive sizes, that are mixed with the fibres prior to forming; in such cases the sheets are fully sized after drying and do not pass through a separate sizing process.

The machine manufacturing process is very similar to that outlined above. The macerated fibre is diluted and mixed with required additives, including sizing chemicals, after which it passes to a moving mesh on which it drains, then through a press section, where it is supported by felts. On early machines the pressed wet web was wound on to a drum, then slit by hand, and the wet sheets were taken to a drying loft; in 1820, however, steam-heated drying cylinders were invented, which allowed the web to be dried prior to reel-up. During this process, the web is pressed against the heated cylinders by stretched textiles, which help maintain contact between paper and hot surface, and exert restraint that helps counteract lateral shrinkage.

Finally, it should be noted that some sheets are made from a multitude of layers. They can be formed from plies brought together in the wet state and glued or pressed to form a single entity, or from previously dried sheets glued together to form a board. Multi-ply sheets made on hand-moulds are usually of board weights; those made on paper machines could be of board or paper weights. A recent invention in machine manufacture allows the various furnish fractions to be separated, then recombined at the forming stage to create a multi-layer product in which the properties of the outer plies are tailored to the needs of the final paper, while the inner section contains cheaper components.

An example of this is a printing paper whose outer layers consist of virgin chemical wood fibre, and the inner layer of cheaper recycled fibre.

Although this description of the process of fibre preparation and sheet formation, as practised over almost 900 years, is highly simplified, it should be obvious that practices have developed so much during this period that clues will reside in each sheet to aid its identification. The following sections describe various ways that such clues may be read.

3 Sheet structure

The heterogeneous nature of paper can be observed by holding a sheet to a light source and looking at its cloudy appearance; this is known as formation. It is a measure of how evenly the various furnish components are distributed throughout the sheet. Distinction depends mainly upon the fibres, their length, and how well they were macerated and individually separated; it also indicates the degree of their dilution and agitation prior to forming. The presence of undispersed fibre bundles, filler agglomerates, dirt, and other contaminants will also be disclosed by looking through the sheet, as will any fault caused during forming, pressing, or sizing operations—air bubbles and pinholes, which disturb formation, and bloom of sizing, which gives a milky sheen to the sheet.

The condition of the mould is also apparent at this point. For example, Bower has noted a case where a sheet showed a preponderance of fibre in the centre compared to the edges; he attributed this to poor attachment between the mesh and frame of the mould, resulting in sagging of the forming surface.

If one sheet is being compared with another, the degree of similarity between them may also be ascertained. In general, if they have been machine-made, the inter-sheet variability will be much less than for hand-made paper. Furthermore, in machine-made papers, especially those made by modern machines, the presence of dirt should be minimal, because efficient cleaners are used before the forming stage; however, a notable exception is with sheets made from recycled fibre, which may have dirt as a contaminant even with current methods.

Looking through the sheet will also reveal the impression of any relief surface upon which the wet fibre mat was laid prior to drying, or that was pressed into the damp or dry web or sheet after forming; these include: watermarks; wire or mesh impressions; laid (wire) and chain lines; and press, felt, rope, and emboss marks. This last group are formed by compaction of the sheet rather than by lateral movement of mass.

Wire marks are the imprint of the mesh through which the water drained as the sheet was formed; they are further enhanced during couching, when the wet sheet is pressed against a textile material and the wire is pushed into the wet fibre mat. The shape of the mark will not be an exact representation of the original wire, because the sheet shrinks as it dries. This is especially significant for machine-made paper, where lateral shrinkage is high—especially at the web edges—typically leading to the formation of a diamond-shape for the wire mark.

Even two hand-made sheets from the same batch can also appear dissimilar, however, if they experience different degrees of shrinkage during drying.

The gross nature of the forming surface will also be visible during drying. In particular, the presence of laid and chain lines will be apparent; wove moulds only became available after 1756. Shadows around the laid lines give information on the barring pattern under the forming mesh, including the presence of tranchefiles, which were added at the edges of deckles to improve drainage. Papers made on Fourdrinier machines have laid lines imparted by a dandy roll pressing on to the felt side of the sheet; on cylinder machines and in hand-made products, these lines come directly from the forming wire and are a feature of the wire side of the sheet. A patent for a dandy roll to impart laid lines was granted in 1825; before that date, all paper from Fourdrinier machines was wove.

Felt marks come from the textile on which the wet sheet is couched. They are enhanced during pressing, when both sides take on some of the surface characteristics of the felts. Sometimes this is exacerbated by using heavily textured fabrics for the final pressing, which impart specific characteristics to the sheet surface. For example, some sheets are given a 'linen' finish by pressing against a coarse-textured fabric with a square weave. Alternatively, some machine-made papers are textured on-machine by having various materials attached to the press fabrics; this is called felt-marking. Use of a textured sleeve on a press roll produces a press-mark.

Prominent wire and felt marks are typically not found on very modern machine-made papers, as recent industrial developments have resulted in machine clothing that minimizes marking of the finished sheet. Rope marks come from the cord over which wet sheets were draped during drying. Occasionally, hairs from the rope can also be found embedded in this area. Emboss marks are imparted to a plain wove material when dry, by passing the sheet through a calender (a machine for smoothing or glazing paper) containing a textured roll.

In hand-made paper, watermarks from adjacent sheets may transfer when they are pressed without intervening felts. This is more likely with bulky sheets, and is generally less problematic with lightweight papers. Hand-made sheets more commonly suffer from occasional random imperfections, such as the slur of laid lines, caused by the coucher slipping during the act of couching, or spots of water from the vatman's hands flicking on to the newly formed sheet.

Marks made while the sheet was still very wet, such as laid and chain lines and watermarks, are permanent. Although some relaxation may occur during humidification or re-wetting, such as happens during wet conservation treatment, they remain largely unchanged because their formation involved physical displacement of fibre. By contrast, marks made when the sheet was drier, such as emboss marks, can be removed almost completely by wetting or humidification. One way of differentiating a 'true' watermark from those formed in the press section, or by printing or embossing techniques, is by imaging, using beta-radiography rather than optical techniques; only a 'true' watermark is visible to radiographic processes.

This discussion concerns the distribution of materials within the plane of the sheet. There also tends to be stratification of material through the thickness of the sheet, however, though this is less obvious during simple visual inspection. Microscopic examination shows quite conclusively that fine materials tend to be concentrated more at the top and in the middle of the sheet, with far less at the surface that contacted the mesh of the forming stage. This is most notable on machine-made paper—especially that made on fast, modern machines where high suction is used to remove water rapidly during sheet formation. The construction of multi-ply sheets is also only revealed by microscopic investigation.

4 Watermarks

Watermarks are one of the main means of identification for assessing paper provenance. Technology follows a simple chronology whereby early examples consisted of bent pieces of wire, tied to the mould face by thinner bits of wire that leave sewing dots. When watermarking was first started on Fourdrinier machines (c.1826), the same procedure was used, with bent wire being tied to the dandy roll cover in a similar manner. Embossed mould covers were invented c.1848; these allowed the development of more complex watermark designs, with a wider optical density range, resulting in complex pictures that are known as light-and-shade or shadow marks. Eventually, this technology was transferred to dandy roll covers. By 1870, soldering was introduced as a means of attaching the bent wire that formed the simple binary watermark image; soldering often replaced sewing because it was quicker. Finally, in more recent years electrotyping was developed as a means of mass-producing the raised designs for binary watermarks; these images could be attached either by sewing or soldering.

Watermark imagery and design are also important. Before the 19th century, watermarks were simple binary line-marks that Dard Hunter divided into four main categories: simple images, such as crosses or circles; human forms and works, such as heads and hands, keys and pottery; animals, including mythological beasts; and flora and images from nature. Eventually, some items from the second category, depicting human creativity, became synonymous with various paper sizes: beakers and pots (pot), and the fool's cap (foolscap). By the era of machine-manufactured watermarks, only these images were commonly in use. Some decades later, the trademark was devised: manufacturers, stationers, and latterly customers, introduced named grades of paper to the marketplace, the most famous being Conqueror from Wiggins Teape. Today, trademarks and geometric designs are undoubtedly the commonest form of watermarks from machine-makers; by comparison, hand-makers produce all manner of images, the main requirement being that the design is not too intricate to reproduce and that the image can be fixed to the mesh cover without danger of removal or fouling during normal working practice.

Many catalogues have been produced in which the general imagery of watermarks can be studied. However, it must be remembered that many of these catalogues (such as Charles Moïse Briquet's or Edward Heawood's) were developed from rather limited sources, and that altogether they contain only a small portion of the whole canon of marks produced since the earliest Western examples, from Fabriano, Italy, in *c*.1282. Furthermore, most watermark publications contain simple tracings that supply insufficient detail for full identification.

Countermarks, often found associated with watermarks, give added information such as dates, mill, and maker identification. Their uses have varied through history, but they are probably the main method by which papers from certain periods are assigned to specific mills. However, the best any watermark or countermark can actually do is identify the original mould or dandy cover used to make a specific sheet, since both are portable and can be used at sites other than their origin. Cases in point include the removal of dandy rolls used to mark postage stamp paper, from Chafford Mill to Roughway Mill in 1878, and the various mills from which Whatman watermarks originate, especially prior to the opening of Springfield Mill in 1807.

Dates in countermarks are another common source of problems, since the apparently simple information they convey may not always be correct. For example, a French ordinance of 1741 required all paper makers in the country to include a date in the countermark; many manufacturers complied by using the date '1742' for a number of years, since it was not stated in the original directive that the date should change every year. A similar order, this time containing the stipulation that dates should change annually, was issued in England, in 1794. This should mean the date in English paper from this period is more reliable; Kelliher, however, has highlighted an intriguing publication printed in 1806 on paper dated 1807. In addition, Hunter described the case of Joseph Willcox, an American hand-maker known to have continued using a mould dated 1810 many decades later. In sum, then, the date in a countermark must be treated with as much caution as any other mark in a sheet.

The formal comparison of watermarks and countermarks can be performed on two levels. Superficial comparison requires the imagery and countermark information in the sheet under examination to agree with either a catalogue picture or other reference sheet of paper. For catalogue images, exact agreement is rarely possible, because most published images are low-quality reproductions. Detailed comparison requires the exact size, orientation, position relative to chain and laid lines and sheet edges, and points of attachment, to be assessed and recorded. These permit greater certainty as to the similarity or differences between two sheets. They also allow the identification of twins, which are pairs of moulds used in tandem to make a single post of paper. Information regarding points of wear and signs of repair to the mould should also be sought. During the working life of a watermark design, parts are subject to abrasion and wear, with sharp edges becoming rounded; Allan Stevenson analysed the chronology of paper used in the *Missale Speciale* by looking at such deterioration. Parts may occasionally need to be removed and replaced; for example, it was common to change the last digit in a date when this became necessary.

Lastly, the watermark's clarity should be noted. The thickness of wire used for producing the image, and its cross-sectional shape, have a bearing on this, as do the condition both of the mould and of the furnish. Good watermark quality requires a short-fibred, well-beaten stock, which is able to conform closely to the watermark design during couching. Insufficient beating—and hence a preponderance of long fibres—significantly affects clarity.

5 Surface characteristics

The sheet surface carries a huge amount of information about its manufacture and processing. Initial investigation can be performed by holding the sheet up to a diffuse light source and viewing it by glancing illumination.

The first features to be noted are whether the individual fibres can be seen, and how glossy the surface looks. If no fibres are visible, the sheet has been coated; this can be confirmed by rubbing the surface with a fingernail or coin, so that the affected area becomes polished and more glossy. If no coating is present, the fibres and filler materials should be visible as shiny filamentous or particulate constituents of the surface. For paper made on a fast machine, especially of Fourdrinier design, the fibres will tend to align in the direction of travel on the forming wire; this allows the grain direction to be assessed. Slower machines, such as cylinder moulds, show less obvious orientation, and hand-made paper shows little or none.

For uncoated papers, the degree of gloss shows whether the surfaces have been calendered, or for older papers, subject to friction- or plate-glazing. Generally this is performed in a paper mill; however, John Baskerville developed a secret process that involved hot-pressing a sheet after printing, which also resulted in a glazed appearance. A gloss finish can also be imparted to embossed paper; however, embossing leaves a gloss effect only in the troughs of the pattern, whereas the other methods only polish the peaks, while the deep parts of any surface pattern remain matt. Finally, if only one surface is gloss, and the other is both matt and rough, the sheet has been machine-glazed—formed on a paper-machine and pressed against a large highly polished cylinder to smooth one surface preferentially.

If a coating has been applied, several other factors can also be deduced by using low-angle illumination. The degree of gloss is a measure of calendering; highly glossed papers have been super-calendered, while matt papers tend to be calendered lightly. Secondly, the relative thickness of coating can be deduced by whether any fibre shapes are visible. If none can be seen, the sheet has probably had two or three applications of coating; where they are partially visible a single application is more likely; if they are fully visible, but are indistinct, it is likely a thin coating—applied by a size-press or other applicator—which is termed a 'lick-coating', is present. Finally, the method used to apply the coat may be discernible in some circumstances: a series of well-defined evenly spaced lines, running mainly in the machine direction, indicates a wire-wound bar applicator (introduced in the mid-1980s); defects such as thin, straight scratches, again running parallel to the sheet grain, suggest a blade applicator. Other methods can be deduced by microscopic examination.

Careful observation of the surface by glancing illumination from diffuse light will often show the wire side, on which a repeating pattern of geometric marks should be visible; turning the paper whilst viewing it helps to highlight their presence. The side to which the watermark was applied should also be apparent by this method; on hand-made and cylinder-mould-made paper, this will also be the wire side, while on paper from a Fourdrinier machine it will be the felt side.

Visual observation reveals much information about the surface, but detailed measurement, especially of repeating marks, is only possible using image capture and mathematical analysis; the basic methodology for this is described by I'Anson.

6 Other characteristics

First, the type of paper should be noted, because grades were introduced to the market at different times: for example very thin India paper was introduced into Europe *c.*1750; coated paper was produced and patented in 1827, as was transparent paper.

The weight of a paper can be gauged by hand, as can other aesthetics, often grouped together as 'handle'. These are judged by gripping the sheet firmly, shaking it, and listening to the timbre of the rattle. Assessing paper by this method requires some experience, but it can give information on the degree of beating, possible furnish composition, and extent of surface sizing, all of which contribute to sheet bonding and rigidity. The process used for cleaning fibres may also have a bearing on handle: Bower attributes the softness of 18th-century French papers to their makers' use of alkali, rather than soap, to clean rags before maceration.

Colour should be examined. In most early cases this was a compromise between the collection of rags used, their treatment during pulping, and water quality. Indeed, water quality may vary with the season: heavy rains churn up sediment, making it impossible at times to produce white paper. The colour of early handmade sheets was never very uniform; even colouration only became possible after synthetic dyestuffs were introduced, along with full chemical bleaching.

Determining the size of the original sheet is difficult, but it can be estimated by carefully measuring the existing trimmed sheet. First, a book's gathering that corresponds to a single sheet needs to be identified; the orientation of chain lines in bound, laid paper helps determine this. In a sheet folded in half, the chain lines run parallel to the fold and book spine, producing a folio. A second fold, perpendicular to the first, will produce chain lines running perpendicular to the spine, and thus a quarto. A third fold restores the original orientation, producing an octavo, and so on. Once a single sheet has been identified, any watermark and countermark can be noted, and their relative positions in the sheet assigned. This should allow the sheet's original dimensions to be estimated from a knowledge of common commercial sheet sizes, taking into account the trimming that is necessary during the book-binding process, and the fact that printing papers were generally slightly larger than their equivalent writing-paper sizes, in addition to being more softly sized.

Finally, the edges of the sheet give information on sheet formation and finishing. Rough borders can be a sign of deckle edges, as from a hand-mould or cylinder-mould machine; equally, however, they could be due to having been torn, in an attempt to simulate the raw edges of a mould. A deckle edge from a hand-mould is generally not straight, and shows an uneven gradation of fibre at the very edge; cylinder-mould machines produce much straighter edges, with a wide fringe of thin fibre at the edge; torn edges are generally straightest and show a preponderance of fibrous filaments along the entire edge. Cut edges can be due to guillotining, die-cutting, or slitting and chopping of the web on a sheeting machine. Guillotined or die-cut edges tend to have a pronounced slur caused by the blade pushing through a mass of sheets; this can be felt by gripping a sheet between thumb and forefinger and pulling it so that the edge is drawn though the digits. Guillotine blades also tend to slice at an angle, which can leave a diagonal scratch on the book edge; die-cutters only move perpendicular to the sheet. Slitting produces a finish known as 'mill' edges.

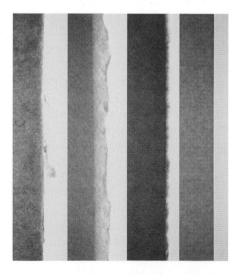

Sheet edges (from left to right): hand-made; machine-made cylinder mould; hand-torn; guillotined or cut edge. Courtesy of Daven Chamberlain

7 Composition

Analysis of the furnish used for a particular paper requires both specialist knowledge and equipment, but is often necessary to verify what has been deduced from visual observation.

Fibre analysis is the most obvious point at which to start. For occidental papers made prior to the 1750s this should yield only linen or hemp, perhaps with some non-vegetable fibre included, such as wool. Cotton only started to make headway thanks to the introduction of mechanized cotton spinning in the last quarter of the 18th century. By 1800, straw was used; wood in various forms was introduced by 1845, but did not become popular until much later; esparto was used from 1857, with bagasse (refuse from sugar-making) added c.1884. Pulping methods for wood can sometimes be assigned by means of stain tests: soda wood came first; mechanical groundwood next, from 1851; sulphite from 1872; kraft from 1884, with various semi-mechanical methods starting in the early 20th century. The exact date for the introduction of any fibre is subject to revision, as early trials certainly antedate the years given, which are when their use was commercialized.

Sizing chemistry is probably of next greatest importance. Early papers used gelatine or starch, which was applied as a post-manufacturing surface treatment; smell will often allow gelatine to be detected, and iodine will indicate the presence of starch. The introduction of machine manufacture coincided with a new method, internal sizing, which used rosin precipitated on the fibre surfaces by alum prior to sheet formation. For machine-made papers, however, coating with starch is also a common post-forming treatment, accomplished at a size-press; in addition, some specialist machine grades produced into the second half of the 20th century were 'tub-sized' by running the waterleaf web through a vat of gelatine solution prior to drying and reel-up. Synthetic internal sizes, such as Alkyl Ketene Dimer (AKD) and Alkyl Succinic Anhydride (ASA), were introduced in the 1950s and 1980s, respectively; these are very popular today in most modern mills.

Inorganic pigments were added to paper from the early 19th century, although they were at first used mainly as cheap extenders to the fibre, and as such were viewed with suspicion by many papermakers and customers. Indeed, concern about their detrimental effect on paper strength was so great that in some countries they were banned. In England, for example, before c.1800 no pigments could be added, since they were considered adulterants. However, the benefits of adding some amount of pigment were eventually recognized: pigments increase opacity and improve ink transfer during printing; they also increase ink hold-out, maintaining it at the surface and decreasing its penetration into the sheet during printing, resulting in a better-printed image. The earliest (c.1820) common filler was barium sulphate; gypsum was added soon after, while clay, which had been tested before barium sulphate, was used from 1870.

Titanium dioxide, calcium carbonate, and various zinc compounds all came into use during the early 20th century.

The final class of major additives worth assessing are colourants and optical whiteners. Early papers used the intrinsic fibre colour, or natural dyestuffs, such as ultramarine or indigo, or coloured earths like ochre. Indeed, James Whatman II is credited with the innovation of adding blue dyes to 'whiten' paper, when in 1765 he started to use indigo; however, continental makers from the 16th century had already developed this practice, adding smalts (an oxide of cobalt), indigo, or even small amounts of blue rag to the furnish for the same reason. Synthetic dyestuffs became available after W. H. Perkin's pioneering work— aniline dyes were used from around 1870, with synthetic pigments added by 1901. Optical brightening agents, which fluoresce under ultraviolet light and give paper a bluish tinge, were introduced around the 1950s, and are particularly common in modern papers, where they are used to enhance whiteness. Indeed, fluorescence due to use of such reagents was a major factor in Julius Grant's exposure of the Hitler Diaries as fraudulent; these chemicals were not introduced to the paper industry until after the Führer's death.

Compared to these four classes, other additives are minor. However, detailed chemical analysis can also reveal traces of bleach residues, formation aids, biocides, fungicides, adhesives, and anti-foam agents, to name but a few chemicals that might be added, intentionally or otherwise, to the furnish. These minor additives, alongside detailed analysis of trace elements found as contaminants in pigments, can be used to provide a paper's chemical 'fingerprint', which may be unique to a locality, mill, or even batch, and which is useful for comparing with other samples of unknown origin.

8 Provenance

Determining the provenance of paper is a complex problem that can be approached on a number of different levels, all with varying degrees of certainty.

If there is no sheet for comparison, assessment involves comparing watermark images with those contained in catalogues or trade listings. Inspection of the surface, looking for coatings or telltale signs of various production processes, should also be undertaken. By these means it may be possible to pinpoint a probable period of manufacture. Chemical and fibre analysis can then be used to identify whether the constituents match those anticipated for the date and origin suggested by visual inspection.

Comparison with a sheet of known origin is far more successful, and is capable of yielding a more exact identification. In this case, visual or instrumental comparison of the two sheet surfaces, markings, structures, and chemistries can be undertaken. In particular, for watermarked paper, an exact comparison of the watermark shape, placement, attachment points, and general quality can be made. However, in many ways this is actually a more difficult analysis to undertake than when no comparison sheet exists, because there is the temptation to look for exact replication of all aspects of the two sheets. Yet, as has been suggested, papermaking is not a wholly controllable process. For sheets made on the same machine or mould at different times, variations in furnish or process conditions can alter appearance significantly. For sheets made from the same batch, differences can also exist for legitimate reasons. Even more importantly, storage and treatment conditions can have a significant bearing on how a sheet looks: two identical sheets, subject to different handling, can appear quite dissimilar.

To conclude, determining provenance is not an exact science. A great deal can be done to analyse paper as bibliographical evidence, but the sheet is only one part of the story and should never be used alone. Evidence from other sources such as printing, typography, and binding should be included, before experience comes into play. Experience, intuition, and judgement must all be used in the final analysis of how the paper helps to determine the provenance of a work of which it is but one part.

....

BIBLIOGRAPHY

J. Balston, *The Whatmans and Wove (Velin) Paper* (1998)

S. Barcham-Green, 'An Illusive Image: Some Thoughts about Watermarking Handmade Papers', *TQ* 62 (2007), 1–9

P. Bower, *Turner's Papers* (1990)

—— *Turner's Later Papers* (1999)

—— 'Watermark Catalogues and Related Texts: A Personal Recommendation', *TQ* 56 (2005), 42–4

B. L. Browning, *Analysis of Paper*, 2e (1977)

N. Harris, *Analytical Bibliography*, www.ihl.enssib.fr/siteihl.php?page=55&aflng=en, consulted June 2007

D. Hunter, *Papermaking: The History and Technique of an Ancient Craft*, 2e (1978)

S. I'Anson, 'Identification of Periodic Marks in Paper and Board by Image Analysis Using Two-Dimensional Fast Fourier Transforms, Part 1: The Basics', *Tappi Journal*, 78.3 (1995), 113–19

—— 'Part 2: Forming and Press Section Marks', *Tappi Journal*, 78.7 (1995), 97–106

H. Kelliher, 'Early Dated Watermarks in English Papers: A Cautionary Note', in *Essays in Paper Analysis*, ed. S. Spector (1987)

B. J. McMullin, 'Machine-Made Paper, Seam Marks, and Bibliographical Analysis', *Library*, 7/9 (2008), 62–88

D. W. Mosser *et al.*, eds., *Puzzles in Paper* (2000)

S. Spector, ed., *Essays in Paper Analysis* (1987)

A. H. Stevenson, *The Problem of the Missale Speciale* (1967)

S. Tanner and D. Chamberlain, 'Chafford Mill: A Short History', *TQ* 57 (2006), 37–43

11

The Technologies of Print

JAMES MOSLEY

1 Introduction

Printing was introduced to a world in which the status of the book and its makers was changing. A professional book trade existed well before printing with movable types was introduced in Europe during the 15th century. The pecia system allowed students at the universities of Bologna, Padua, and Paris in the 12th century to hire an authenticated text, or a part of it, to be copied either by themselves or by professional writers. During the early 15th century, Vespasiano da Bisticci of Florence acquired a reputation as an employer of professional calligraphers and miniature painters who made beautiful manuscript books for rich clients. Such systems and professions point to the opportunities that encouraged the emergence in the 15th century of the printer and publisher who—gambling on the likelihood that a market existed for multiple copies of texts—was willing to invest in the materials and labour necessary to make many identical books (in advance of sales) by mechanical processes.

The terms that were eventually adopted in modern European languages for the 'printing' of texts and pictures had a long history: words (such as 'impression' and 'stampa') typically signified the application of pressure, most often to leave a visible mark. As Shakespeare writes in the Prologue to *Henry V*: 'Think when we talk of horses, that you see them / Printing their proud hoofs i' th' receiving earth.' Indeed, the principle of using an engraved stone to make repeated characters in a soft material, such as clay, is displayed in many surviving early artefacts, from official Mesopotamian seals (3rd millennium BC) to Roman bricks and tiles stamped before they were fired with their makers' names.

2 Origins

In the Middle Ages, western books and documents were commonly written on vellum, a prepared animal skin; although some printed books were also made on vellum, there is no doubt that paper (a product consisting of vegetable fibres reconstituted in the form of thin white sheets of a uniform size and thickness (*see* **10**) was necessary for the development of printing in the West. By the 13th century, paper was sufficiently common in western Europe that a decree forbidding its use for the writing of public records was issued in 1231 by the German Emperor Frederick II.

Techniques for making paper evolved in China and spread along the land routes that brought silk and other goods to the West. The traditional date for the invention of paper made from mulberry bark, hemp, and rags is the start of the 2nd century AD (although some scholars maintain that the actual date is between 200 and 100 BC); by the 3rd century, such paper was commonly used in China to write documents. In 1276, paper mills were operating at Fabriano in Italy, and in 1390 the first paper mill in Germany was established at Nuremberg.

It is not known whether awareness of the processes used in China and neighbouring countries to make multiple copies of books had penetrated to the West before a complete system for printing books evolved in Germany *c.*1450. These, briefly, were the stages of their development in the East (*see* **42**, **43**, **44**, **45**). By the 7th century, inked relief seals, cut on wood and pressed by hand, were used in China to authenticate documents written on paper. Ink-squeeze rubbings were made to provide multiple paper copies of the Confucian texts that were cut on stone and displayed in temples for public reading. A sacred Buddhist text, the Diamond Sutra (868), a scroll made up of strips of paper pasted together, is the earliest datable instance of the use of engraved relief wood blocks to print many copies of an extensive text and an image with ink. The technique of woodblock printing that finally evolved to make printed books required several steps. The text was written by a professional calligrapher on thin sheets of paper and pasted in reverse on a block of wood, so that the writing was visible. Superfluous wood was cut away, leaving a facsimile of the reversed text in relief. Ink was dabbed on the block, and sheets of paper were pressed to it with stiff brushes, thus transferring an image of the writing to the paper. The paper, which tended to absorb the ink, was printed on one side of the sheet only, folded and sewn into books. Until western methods were introduced in the 19th century, this was the usual method of printing texts and pictures in China and neighbouring countries. In 12th-century Korea, movable types reproducing Chinese characters were made from wooden patterns by casting with copper in sand (*see* **43**); such separate types continued in use to some extent in the East, but without displacing engraved woodblocks. The reasons for the very limited use of movable types in the East, compared with the rapidity of their adoption in the West, are complex. The high respect accorded to calligraphy in China, Korea, and Japan, the fluidity and complexity of the forms of Chinese characters when written by hand, and the very large number of characters probably all contributed.

The mid-15th century 'invention of printing' in the West involved the bringing together of several techniques, devices, and materials. Some of these had long existed but others, such as the paper and the ink, were relatively recent. There may have been several experimenters working at about the same time. Procopius Waldfoghel, born in Prague and established in Avignon in the 1440s, is named in contemporary documents as using a process of 'artificial writing' employing alphabets made in steel, but his method did not necessarily involve the printing of texts. During the 16th century, a claim was made on behalf of Laurens Janszoon Coster of Haarlem as the inventor of printing, but none of the surviving early fragments of printing that originate in the Low Countries bears Coster's name, nor are there convincing biographical details. In the *Cronica van Koellen*, the 'Cologne Chronicle', printed by Ulrich Zell (1499)—in which there is some reference to a 'prefiguration' of printing in the Low Countries—unequivocal credit for the invention of printing with movable type in the West is given to Johann Gutenberg (d. 1468), whose life is well documented; the claim is not seriously disputed today (but see modifications to the traditional account of Gutenberg's invention in the work of Paul Needham and Blaise Agüera y Arcas). From 1454, when the folio Gutenberg Bible of 1,200 pages is known to have been in production, and when the texts of indulgences were also printed on single sheets, a technology existed for the making of multiple copies of books and other documents of an acceptable quality. The use of similar techniques spread very rapidly to European countries, and, although MSS continued to be important (*see* **15**), printed texts gradually began taking the place of handwritten ones.

Gutenberg was born *c.*1400 into a patrician family in Mainz with interests in banking, but there is no evidence that he had direct contact with the technologies of making coins or working in precious metals. In the 1430s he was compelled for political reasons to move to Strasbourg, where he became involved in a partnership that made cast-metal items. Later he returned to Mainz, where he borrowed money from Johann Fust, a lawyer, to develop a project described in legal documents as *werck der bücher* ('the work of books'). In 1455 Fust foreclosed on the debt and took over the materials developed by Gutenberg. Peter Schoeffer, Gutenberg's former business partner, joined Fust and married his daughter; the names of Fust and Schoeffer appear on several of the earliest printed books beginning in 1457. Schoeffer inherited the business, remaining an important and an active printer in Mainz until his death in 1502/3. Gutenberg stayed in the same district until his death, still in possession of the printing materials mentioned in his will; yet he is not named in any printed book as its maker.

Gutenberg's partnership in Strasbourg, which became the subject of acrimonious litigation in 1436, produced, among other goods, mirrors cast in metal for sale to pilgrims. It is sometimes suggested that experiments towards the making of type and the printing of books began in Strasbourg before Gutenberg returned to Mainz. There is no direct evidence to support this idea, but if the mirrors were made from lead or an alloy using lead, their makers may have developed some of the expertise that would be needed for making type. The earliest surviving fragments of printing that can be associated with Gutenberg appear to date from about 1450, and make use of a type that is less well finished and printed than that of the folio bible (the so-called 42-line bible) known to have been in production in 1454. This bible and the large 1457 psalter, bearing the names of Fust and Schoeffer, are the products of a printing system capable of making fine books that would command a high price, even if some of its elements may still have needed refinement. The constituents of that system are type, ink, paper or vellum, and a press for making an impression on them.

Paper had long been in use in Europe for the writing of correspondence and documents, and to some extent for books, as a substitute for the more durable vellum. However, whereas eastern paper was written on with a writing brush on one side of the sheet, western paper had been adapted to the use of a relatively hard quill pen to write with a liquid, water-based ink on both sides of the sheet. The materials of paper were still vegetable fibres, mostly in the form of rags, discarded woven linen that had served as clothing or for domestic use. To prevent the penetration of the surface by the liquid ink, the sheet was made relatively hard and firm in its substance, an effect sometimes reinforced by adding size (a diluted solution of colloids made from animal skin and bones) to its surface.

The ink used on metal type was a thin film of stiff, coloured varnish, made by boiling and sometimes setting fire to one of the drying oils, generally linseed or walnut: the process was too dangerous to be carried out in a confined urban space. The substance set firmly and permanently, even without exposure to air. To make black ink, soot was added to the clear varnish; red or other pigments made coloured ink. In fact, printing ink is a version of the oil paint that had become widely adopted by European painters by about 1400.

In order to make a satisfactory print on the hard-surfaced paper that was designed for use with the pen, it was necessary to soften its fibres (by dampening it) and to apply firm pressure. After the sheets were printed, they were hung up on poles or lines to dry. The drying sheets, dangerously flammable, must have been one of the most common sources of the fires that destroyed the premises of many printers during the hand press period.

The printing press was no doubt derived from the screw presses that had evolved in the period of the late Roman empire. They were routinely used for pressing out the juice of grapes and also for squeezing the surplus water from newly made paper. It seems likely that such presses would have been adapted for delivering the pressure needed to make a sharp, clear impression from pages of inked type on paper.

The element that was wholly new (if the possibility can be discounted that news of the Korean practice of some centuries earlier had penetrated to Europe) was the making of 'movable type': a supply of small metal blocks bearing letters and signs in relief, from which multiple impressions could be taken.

How the early types were made is a subject that has been much discussed, although no definitive conclusions have been reached. It is possible that a slow process requiring much hand finishing, or dressing, was used initially (perhaps by sand casting, as was done in Korea). Whatever the first system may have been, it was quite rapidly succeeded by one in which relief steel punches, filed and engraved with the form of the letter, were hardened and used to stamp impressions in a softer metal, copper, to make matrices. Matrices were used together with a type mould that formed the body of the type. As later surviving examples demonstrate, such moulds were simple hand-held devices, formed from two L-shaped pieces that slid against each other to open and close later-ally. Accurate castings about one inch high could be made from a sequence of matrices of letters, with each letter being the same height from top to bottom, but varying according to the different widths required for narrow letters such as 'i' and wide ones such as 'M'. Eventually, the manual processes for making types and assembling them into words and lines were mechanized, and alternative methods of placing words and images on paper were devised. Nonetheless, until the second half of the 20th century, most printed texts were produced using printing surfaces cast in lead alloys from matrices stamped with punches.

3 The hand press period, 1450–1830

The analysis of early fragments of printing attributed to Gutenberg has sug-gested that some early types may have been made in ways that do not corre-spond with traditional methods. However, the comparison of multiple scanned images of the pages of different copies of the Gutenberg Bible has revealed that the setting of its type was often altered during the course of printing, sometimes in ways that are hardly visible to the eye. The latter observations confirm beyond doubt that this work was set with and printed from single movable types.

The method of printing at the hand press seems to have undergone a slow evolution. It can be shown that, at least until the later years of the 15th century and often long after, the dominant technique was printing by formes, in which the first and last pages of one side of a single sheet or of a gathering made up of several inset sheets (the outer forme) were set in type and printed before the other side of the sheet (the inner forme) or those that came inside the section. The process of casting off copy to determine on which page it should come required painstaking calculation, and the compositors who set the type fre-quently needed to alter the text—shortening it by resorting to abbreviations, contractions, or omissions, or expanding it by adding various kinds of spacing such as quads or leading—in order to maintain the continuity of the text in the formes which were set and printed later. This technique of printing by formes may help to explain one enduring feature of the traditional wooden press: its platen (the wooden or metal plate that delivers pressure to the paper) is the size of only one folio page, or half the full forme of type that was later placed on the press.

Some slight qualifications aside, there was a long period from the 1480s until around 1800 when the technology of printing was very stable. Type was made by hand and was set, formed by hand into words, lines, and pages. Presses were operated by hand at a rate that did not—indeed could not comfortably—exceed a certain speed. Paper was made, sheet by sheet, by hand: the maximum width of the mould, and therefore of the sheet it made, was limited by the maker's natural arm span, typically about 30in. or 76cm.

The earliest datable image of a printing office is a woodcut in a book printed in 1499. During the first part of the 16th century, representations of the printing office were symbolic of the trade, and appear on several title-pages. The images differ in some small details, but, taken together, they confirm that, once established, the equipment and the actions of the printers did not essentially change until 1800 or so. At that point, slight alterations that had begun as refinements of traditional methods and materials gave way to radical developments as printing was mechanized, production speed increased, and the unit cost of books fell.

During the hand press period, printing offices were generally normal houses, like the work places of weavers, joiners, and other tradesmen. The printer, with his family and apprentices, occupied some of its rooms, and the presses and type occupied others. Some printing offices were designed to impress visitors, such as the new Clarendon Building (completed 1713) of the Oxford University Press, but these were exceptions. Most premises were like that of printer and novelist Samuel Richardson, whose medium-size London printing office in Salisbury Square was also his dwelling, until the weight of the stock of type began to threaten the building's structure, compelling him to move.

The office's equipment comprised one or more presses and a quantity of type. The type was held in open type cases, subdivided in divisions each of which held multiple sorts of one character. These smaller compartments of the case varied in size according to the frequency with which each letter, number, or mark of punctuation was used, the letter 'e' being the largest of them. The compositor or type setter who had learned the arrangement or lay of the case could pick up each letter without looking at it. Early images show compositors sitting at their work; later it became usual to stand. In some countries, there was a single case, holding both capital and minuscule letters, but in France, and countries such as Britain which followed French practice, capitals and minuscules had a case each, arranged one above the other, so that capital letters became known as upper case and the minuscules as lower case. Whatever its configuration, the case, which held 20–30lb of type (9–14kg), was commonly (like the papermaker's mould) no more than an arm-span wide, so it could be readily lifted and placed on a frame at a convenient height for setting.

The compositor held a composing stick, a tool that allowed several lines of type to be set to a given width. The copy or text for setting was placed where it

Printers and compositor in a Dutch printing office: engraving after a drawing by P. Saenredam for P. Schrijver's *Laure-kranz voor Laurens Koster* in Samuel Ampsing's *Beschryvinge ende lof der stad Haerlem* (Haarlem, 1628). Coster was wrongly supposed to anticipate Gutenberg as the inventor of printing. The Bodleian Library, University of Oxford (Douce A. 219, opposite page 392)

could be seen clearly, sometimes held in a special device called a visorium, or simply placed on the right-hand side of the upper case, which in France or England held the small capitals that were needed only occasionally. The compositor picked up letter after letter and placed them one at a time in the stick, putting

A composing frame with two sets of cases of type: the upper case lies at a steeper angle than the lower case. By permission of Oxford University Press

spaces between words, and working from left to right, reading the line in the stick to check that it was correct. To justify or fill each line, the spaces were added or reduced between words until the line filled the stick firmly. The lines were transferred from the stick to a galley, an open tray, until there were enough for a page. The page of type was tied up with thin cord and placed with other pages on a large flat imposing stone. A chase, an open iron frame, was placed over the pages, along with furniture, pieces of wood cut to size, which filled it exactly and made up the forme for printing. Wooden quoins or wedges were driven against long wedge-shaped sidesticks or footsticks to hold pages and furniture together. If properly assembled, the locked-up forme—made from some thousands of pieces of metal type—was solid and could be safely picked up and placed on the press.

The press in use until the early 19th century was a structure about six feet (two metres) high, made of a solid wood (oak was favoured), and consisting of two uprights with lateral beams. The lower beam received the force of the impression and, accordingly, was fixed; it supported rails on which the carriage, a flat surface bearing the forme, slid in and out under the platen, a solid, flat piece of wood or metal that hung from the screw, which delivered the impression and worked in the beam above. The screw appears in early images to have been wooden, but later was normally made of iron or brass, as was the platen (except in Britain, where it was commonly of wood). The platen hung

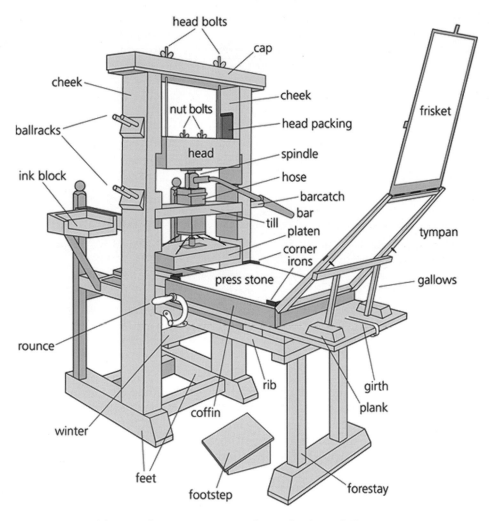

Diagram of the parts of a common press. Line drawing by Chartwell Illustrators

from the hose, a box or framework that served to keep the platen steady while the screw turned within it. A bar set in the screw turned it in an arc of about 90 degrees when pulled, lowering the platen by about half an inch (1.2cm) on to the tympan and the forme beneath it.

The stiff ink was worked out evenly on a flat surface with a pair of leather balls stuffed with wool; the ink balls transferred a thin film to the type of the forme. The tympan, a hinged framework with vellum or cloth stretched tightly over it (as the name implies), was attached to the carriage. The sheet of paper to be printed was fixed on the tympan with adjustable points that pierced it and gave an exact location for the second impression on the reverse of the sheet.

A layer of cloth designed to spread the impression filled the space evenly within an inner tympan that fitted into the outer one. The frisket, a light wrought-iron frame covered with paper, from which spaces for the pages were cut, was hinged over the tympan; it held the paper to it as it was brought down over the inked forme and protected the areas of the paper which were not to be printed from being soiled. A rounce or windlass brought the carriage beneath the platen and out again.

Two men worked the press: the puller, who placed the paper on the tympan, wound the carriage under the platen, and pulled the bar; and the beater, who worked out the ink and applied it to the forme. They were paid for a notional production of 250 sheets in the hour, one every 15 seconds or 2,500 impressions in a ten-hour working day. Printing office accounts confirm that this output could be achieved, but the figure does not reflect stops for any reason, nor the preliminary time spent in making ready (preparing the press for printing by pasting paper on the tympan or beneath parts of the text or wood cuts to make them print evenly). The text was sometimes corrected during the course of printing, which meant unlocking the forme to remove type and make the necessary changes to it: this was known as stop-press correction. The viscous ink on the balls could sometimes extract a loose piece of type, which was reinserted. For all these reasons, as well as the vagaries of human labour, the daily target of 2,500 impressions per press crew was seldom reached. The second side of the sheet was printed from another forme, made up within a chase that was the same size as the first one.

A proof sheet was printed by placing the made-up forme on the press and pulling one or more impressions. To make corrections, it was necessary to loosen the quoins and thus to unlock the forme. If a passage needed to be inserted or deleted, the text in question might overrun the page or cause it to be too short, and many succeeding pages might need to be altered. Late in the 18th century, in order to reduce this need, the practice began of pulling proofs on long slips of paper from type that was held in a long galley (hence galley proofs), and of making corrections before the type was made up into pages.

This was the equipment of the printing office during the hand press period. The basic unit was one press and one frame, and a case or cases of type. The only essential difference between big and small offices was that the large ones had more presses and type and thus could manage the flow of work more efficiently.

3.1 Materials

Paper was bought by the printer from the mill or from an agent ahead of production. The most expensive single element in the cost of printed books, paper also represented the highest risk, since it could not generally be reused once printed. Another consumable commodity was ink, which could be stored in barrels, and was commonly bought from specialist makers.

Unlike paper and ink, type was not wholly consumed by production. However, type gradually wore out in use or was damaged (known as type batter) and needed to be replaced: this was done at a rate that reflected the printer's standards and the economics of his operation. Surviving records from the early 16th century show that some printers bought sets of matrices for the types they used and a mould to go with them, hiring a specialist founder or caster to make a fount or 'casting' from them—at this date a *fount* (Fr. *fonte*, from *fondre*, 'to melt, cast') was the quantity of type made at one session of casting. This commercial practice was common even in major printing offices such as Christopher Plantin's in Antwerp, which had a big collection of matrices for roman and italic as well as many special types for scholarly and liturgical printing. By the 18th century, the founts held by some major printers weighed half a ton or more. From the later 16th century, specialist typefoundries were established in the principal centres of printing, and it became more usual for printers to buy all their founts of type.

Type was cast by hand. First, the matrix for each letter was placed in succession in a two-part mould, which expanded or contracted to suit the letter's width. Next, a ladle was used to pour molten metal into the mould; a rapid upward thrust of the hands while holding the mould ensured that the metal reached the image of the type stamped in the matrix before it cooled. The process of typefounding involved diecasting in an alloy of lead, a cheap and plentiful metal with a low melting-point, which enabled it to be safely used with hand-held devices. The alloy itself was complex, sometimes including more or less tin to aid the flow, and invariably a quantity of antimony, which not only toughened the metal and gave a sharper cast but eliminated shrinkage after casting.

Punches were cut with files and gravers in steel that had been annealed or softened. The punches were then hardened and tempered in order to survive the hammer blow of striking; each punch would serve to make many sets of identical copper matrices. For bigger types, matrices were sometimes struck in lead from punches cut in brass, or were made in brass by casting replicas from big steel punches. The choice of the style of types was governed by the same conventions as styles of writing. Gothic scripts were used for the vernaculars of the northern languages; gradually, however, the use of the new humanistic upright and cursive forms (roman and italic) spread from Italy and tended to displace the gothic forms, except in Germany. New fashions in typography were influenced by shifts in calligraphic styles. When they were used to cast type by hand, copper matrices did not noticeably wear out. Thus, there is a long period from the second half of the 16th century to the first half of the 18th century when the same types, derived from matrices struck from the same punches, were used by many printers in different European countries.

3.2 *Illustration*

Images were cut on wood at an early date and used with type to make illustrations or decorations, and sometimes even whole words. Large words on

A box of John Fell's pica italic matrices, with some steel punches for larger capitals beneath them. By permission of Oxford University Press

title-pages were commonly cut in wood. Block printing, which combines images and text cut on a single block of wood, appears to have been introduced during the later 15th century as a simpler imitation of the new books that had been made by using movable type. Any close-grained wood (e.g. apple or pear) could be used, but fine-grained boxwood was especially favoured for smaller images. At an uncertain date, possibly towards the end of the 17th century, engravers began to work on the end grain of the wood, a technique that sometimes achieved finer detail. Its products are known as wood engravings rather than woodcut illustrations (*see* **18**).

By the 17th century, however, the woodcut was increasingly supplanted by images made in a wholly different medium and printed on a different kind of press: the incised or etched copper plate. The making of printed images from copper plates developed at about the same date as printing from type, but the first intaglio prints were circulated independently and were not incorporated in printed books. To print the fine engraved line, the plate was inked and its surface wiped clean again. When the inked plate, the dampened paper, and a cloth blanket were passed between the two cylinders of a rolling press, the pressure of the rollers and the blanket transferred the ink held in the recessed engraved line to the paper. Since the rolling press applied much greater pressure than the press used for type, its operation was correspondingly slow. The pressure also caused wear to the plate, limiting the number of images that could be made before it needed to be re-engraved. The early market for copperplate engravings was generally for independently published images sold singly, such as maps, reproductions of paintings, and satirical prints. During the 17th and 18th centuries, however, intaglio prints became widely used for illustrations in books, as well as for adding ornaments and decorative initials to sheets already printed from type. The combination of intaglio and letterpress called for coordination between two different kinds of printer, because the letterpress printer appears rarely to have had the means to print from plates.

3.3 *Preserving and duplicating the text*

During the hand press period, type was commonly set for only a sheet or two of a book, and then distributed back in the case after the sheet was printed; thus the same type was used several times in the course of printing a book. Very few printers had enough type to set the whole of a text or, if they had, could afford to leave the type idle while waiting to read and correct one work and finding a press free to print it. If a work sold well, the printing of a new edition required the setting, proofing, and correction of the whole text again.

Nevertheless, if a book had a large or reliable market, the heavy financial burden of buying and printing all of the paper at once to produce a large edition could be reduced by spreading it over time, using the return from the sale of the first printing to buy new stock. With enough type, the whole text could be kept in standing type for years and reprinted many times. There are a few documented cases where this is known to have been done.

Towards the end of the 17th century, a means was found of casting duplicate plates from whole typeset pages; several works, including bibles, were printed from such plates in The Netherlands. This method of duplication was used from a very early period to make reproductions of woodblocks. Most casts of typeset pages were probably made from a mould of fine plaster, although a German work of the 1690s describes a method employing papier mâché. The practice lapsed for some time, although it may well have continued unobtrusively—if such techniques are well used, there is no easy way of detecting them. At the end of the 18th century, however, interest in the duplication of already composed text revived strongly. Experiments with various processes resulted in one, developed by the Didot family, called *stéréotypie*, or stereotyping in English. Another name coined at the same time, and mostly applied to the duplicating of wood-engraved illustrations and ornaments, was 'clichage', known in English as 'dabbing'; its product, the cliché, passed into French and English as a metaphor for phrases repeated unthinkingly.

Reintroduced in the 19th century, papier mâché moulds were sometimes used to make stereotyped casts of the pages of books. Since these moulds were light and relatively durable compared with those of fragile plaster, they could be more safely and easily stored, and were sometimes sent to distant printers to make duplicate plates for printing the same text somewhere else.

3.4 Improvements to existing technology

During the second half of the 18th century, shifts in taste and economic prosperity, which expanded the market for books, encouraged greater aesthetic refinement of the printed page. John Baskerville, a rich Birmingham industrialist, former professional writing-master, and printer, sought to make books in which the type would reflect the elegance of the work of professional calligraphers; his pages show a smoothness resembling the paper of prints from plates that had passed through the rolling press. This effect was achieved partly by pressing the printed sheets between smooth, heated plates, but also by using James Whatman I's new wove paper, which was made in a mould constructed from a fabric of woven brass wires so fine that they left no visible mark.

The expanding market for more visually elegant books led to further improvements to existing technologies and materials. The conventional wooden printing press was adapted in ways that enabled it to deliver a more powerful and consistent impression. Around 1800, Charles Stanhope, 3rd earl Stanhope, designed a cast iron press (the Stanhope press), using a system of linked levers to increase its power. Many other iron hand presses using similar systems were developed during the 19th century (e.g. the Columbian and the Albion). They had greater power and durability than the wooden hand press, and were capable of more refined presswork, but they did not print significantly faster. Other improvements in existing processes, such as the aquatint, a means of printing graded tones from a copper plate, assisted the production of expensive books or

Wood engraving by Thomas Kelly of printers and compositors at work using a Columbian press in an English printing office of the 1820s or 1830s. The St Bride Foundation.

of single prints for sale to collectors. Nonetheless, they did not affect the basic processes of printing.

3.5 Lithography

The growing market for separately sold prints and for illustrated books encouraged the development of a new method for placing letters or images on paper. Lithography, the first truly innovative reproduction system to appear for several centuries, would ultimately supersede both relief (letterpress) and intaglio (copperplate) printing. Its development into a practical process lay in the understanding of chemical reactions, a field of scientific research that developed rapidly at the end of the 18th century. Words or images—indeed both together—were drawn with greasy crayon on a polished block of absorbent limestone. The stone was dampened with water, then received an application of printing ink that adhered to the areas drawn with the crayon but was repelled by the dampened parts, which remained clean. The inked image on the stone could then be transferred to paper by putting pressure on it using a specially designed press. Lithography, or 'stone writing', was initially conceived as a means of transferring handwritten texts or drawings to paper without the intervention of typesetting or copying by professional engravers. Its inventor, Alois Senefelder, seeking a means of copying music, hit by accident on the rare variety of limestone, found at Solenhofen in Bavaria, that most suited the method. In time, a metal plate of zinc was developed as a substitute for the heavy and fragile stone. Other developments included a specially treated paper on which text could be written, and the image transferred to the stone. Later in the 19th century, another chemical process, photography, would enable both images and typeset text to be transferred to the stone or plate. A further process, initially designed for printing on tinplate employed for packaging, used a rubber cylinder interposed between the plate and the printing surface. This method enabled the image to be offset and transferred more efficiently to the surface to be printed. This technique was subsequently developed for lithographic printing on paper. During the second half of the 20th century, offset lithography displaced other processes to become the normal method of printing text and images in books and periodicals and on posters and packaging.

4 Mechanization

The mechanization of printing was largely driven by the possibilities offered by the development in Britain of new power-driven machinery, which enabled the rapid printing of larger quantities of material by fewer workers. Consequently, the unit cost of the printed item was reduced. During the first decades of the 19th century, methods of mass production were applied to the printing of newspapers and journals, most significantly with the printing in 1814 of *The Times*—the newspaper with the largest daily circulation—on a steam-powered machine. *The Times* needed to print some 7,000 copies of the complete four-page newspaper overnight, something that was hardly possible with the use of the hand press. Using hand press technology, the outer forme for pages 1 and 4 (consisting only of advertisements) was printed during the previous day, and the inner forme for pages 2 and 3 (with news and comment) was printed during the night. At *The Times*, multiple copies of this inner forme were set so that the printing could be completed at several hand presses, whose individual output could not exceed 300 impressions in an hour. This arrangement of contents, with advertisements on the front and back pages and news and comment across the centre spread, survived in newspapers long after the technical need for it had ceased.

With the advent of the new printing machine, the sheet was placed on a rotating iron cylinder under which the flat bed carrying the type, inked automatically with rollers, was carried to and fro. It was invented by Friedrich König of Saxony, an engineer who had established a partnership in London in order to develop his machine with the use of British venture capital. The initial speed of impression was 1,000 copies an hour. One of the early investors in König's machine was *The Times*'s proprietor John Walter. However, disagreement with his English investors led König to leave England and set up his own factory at Würzburg with his business partner, Andreas Bauer. König's design was further developed during the 1820s by English engineers, notably the partnership of Applegath and Cowper, who introduced the principle of printing a second impression and delivering a sheet printed on both sides.

A comparable search for venture capital and for purchasers of machinery motivated the Parisian engineer Nicolas-Louis Robert to bring his designs for a paper-making machine to Britain. In this case, the critical innovation was to abandon the mould that made single sheets of paper, and to pour the pulp in a

First made c.1860 at Otley, Yorkshire, by the River Wharfe, for over a century the 'Wharfedale' cylinder press was used for all kinds of printing: from F. J. F. Wilson and D. Grey, *A Practical Treatise Upon Modern Printing Machinery and Letterpress Printing* (1888). The Bodleian Library, University of Oxford (25835 d. 3. fig. 22)

controlled stream on to a long, continuous, rotating band of woven wire. As the pulp dried out, it became paper, which was cut into separate sheets or stored in a roll at the so-called dry end of the machine. Machine-made paper was made and sold from the first decade of the 19th century.

Such innovations transformed the economics of newspaper and periodical printing at a period when the rapid growth in the population and urbanization of industrial nations was expanding markets greatly. Some of the fastest machinery developed at the time employed a principle that was well understood but difficult to apply in practice: namely, passing a continuous band of paper between two cylinders, one bearing the inked text and images, the other applying pressure. After printing, the paper was cut and folded. This process avoided reversing the direction of the heavy flat forme of type—as occurred in the cylinder printing machine—which practically limited the speed of output to about 3,000 sheets an hour. Yet such machines remained in use until the later 20th century for book printing that required relatively short runs and used single sheets of paper.

The principle of rotary printing, as printing from cylinders is known, had been employed by calico printers in Lancashire in the 1780s, where multiple colours were printed simultaneously on a continuous 'web' of fabric from engraved copper plates curved to fit cylinders. Ink was added continuously from rollers and the surplus was removed with a 'ductor' or 'doctor' blade against which the plate rotated before transferring the engraved image to the cloth. This practice of printing on a continuous web was adapted in due course to letterpress, lithographic, and intaglio printing on paper.

The basic requirement of rotary printing was the conversion of the flat printing surface of typeset text to the curved surface of the cylinder. A crude compromise was to lock the type in narrow galleys to the external surface of a cylinder with a radius so big that the lack of curvature was less of an impediment to getting a good impression. This was done during the 1840s on a machine designed for printing the *Illustrated London News*, a magazine that sold 250,000 copies weekly. Multiple stations were set up around the periphery of the cylinder, at each of which was an operator feeding a sheet to be printed with the inked surface. When used for newspaper printing, such presses employed very large sheets of paper, which were delivered folded to the purchaser, who either used a paper knife or struggled with the unopened sheet, like the reader shown in Benjamin Robert Haydon's painting *Waiting for 'The Times'* (1831).

The logical development, when the technical difficulties could be overcome, was a rotary press, printing on a continuous web or roll of paper. This was realized in the 1860s and used initially for newspapers, but the arrangement has become normal for high volume printing of any kind. A mould was made from the flat surface of the forme of type in flexible papier mâché (called the flong, from the French *flan*), then dried and curved so that a cast could be made in the form of a half cylinder. Paper from a continuous roll was fed through inked cylinders, to which pairs of such semi-cylindrical casts had been attached. Having been printed on both sides, the paper was cut and folded at the end of the press. In the early 20th century, the casting process and the machining of the plates to fit the cylinders was made faster and more automatic. With the addition of extra printing units, newspapers with more pages could be produced at speeds reaching 80,000–100,000 copies an hour. To speed production still further, multiple moulds could be made and used to cast plates intended for additional presses in the same location or a distant one. Rotary presses fitted with curved stereotype plates were used until the second half of the 20th century for printing newspapers and, in cases where long press runs were required, for magazine and book production.

4.1 Electrolytic processes

The electrotype, developed c.1840, would for some purposes supersede the cast stereotype, both for the duplication of typeset texts and for the reproduction of wood engravings. In electrotyping, a wax impression was taken from the surface to be duplicated. Then, having been coated with fine graphite to make the surface conduct, the wax was immersed in a bath of copper sulphate solution; as a current was passed through it, particles of copper built up gradually. The resulting copper shell, backed with lead to give it solidity, was capable of a very fine reproduction of the original. It became the standard practice for publishers to keep the original blocks of wood-engraved illustrations (such as those engraved by the Dalziel brothers after Sir John Tenniel's drawings for Carroll's *Alice's Adventures in Wonderland*, 1865) and to supply electrotypes ('electros') to the printer. As they wore out, these were replaced with new plates made from the original wood blocks. Whether stereotyped or electrotyped, plates were made for all books that were frequently reprinted, such as reference works and popular series of inexpensive classic texts.

4.2 Machines for typecasting

Using the traditional hand mould, between 3,000 and 5,000 types could be cast in a working day, depending on the type's body size. In the smaller sizes, equivalent to 10 or 12 point (points are the unit of linear measure for type), the metal solidified as fast as the caster could throw in the metal and open the mould to eject the type. At the beginning of the 19th century, a significant improvement to the hand mould was introduced. A lever at the side enabled the caster to raise the matrix and eject the cast type without opening the mould. This device is credibly said to have raised the daily production by hand to as many as 8,000 small types. Another mechanical aid was the expedient of fixing a pump to the pot containing molten metal, so that the hand mould could be rapidly and more evenly fed. The powered injection of the metal also made it easier to cast finely ornamented types, introduced to rival the lettering drawn by lithographers, who competed for the more elaborate and profitable work of letterpress printers.

In the 1830s, David Bruce, who had emigrated from Scotland to the US where he became a typefounder, invented a machine that incorporated the two halves of the type mould. Using cams mounted on a single shaft, the machine brought the halves together in front of a pump nozzle, mounted on a metal pot, at the moment when it discharged a jet of metal. This 'pivotal' typecaster worked by hand or by power, producing 6,000 pieces of the smaller-bodied types in an hour. They were not finished types, however; as in hand-cast type, the work of breaking off the tang or jet of surplus metal, ploughing the foot, rubbing the edges, and undercutting kerned sorts, had to be done before the type was ready for use. In the 1880s, a new generation of more complex typecasting machines (Barth in the US, Küsterman in Germany) was developed that also cast type in the larger sizes, and delivered the type finished for printing.

The most significant single invention in the field of typefounding was the pantographic machine punchcutter, patented in 1885 by Linn Boyd Benton, an American typefounder. The principle of a rotating cutter, mounted on a pantographic frame and tracing the outline of a relief pattern, had been used since the 1830s to cut big types in wood for use on posters. Its application to the making of steel punches made possible the realization of typesetting machines that changed the market for type for hand setting. It also made possible the creation of types from a drawn alphabet, without the intervention of the hand punchcutter.

4.3 Mechanized typesetting

Much attention was given during the second half of the 19th century to the development of machines for setting type. There were two different approaches to the problem. The first system, widely used, stored cast type and delivered it as unjustified text to a composing stick, where a compositor inserted spaces and justified the line by hand. Such a composing machine, with a keyboard similar to that of a piano, was produced by Young & Delcambre in the late 1840s. More sophisticated machines of this kind were marketed successfully and used well into the 20th century.

The second system, which overtook the first, was for a machine that cast a new printing surface. Several machines of this kind were invented and produced between the 1880s and World War I, but only two of them effectively survived; these divided the larger part of the market between them during the 20th century. In 1887, the Linotype machine was launched by Ottmar Mergenthaler, a German immigrant to the US. A supply of brass matrices was stored in a magazine, from which they were released by keyboard in sequence to form the line of text. The words having been spaced with wedges, the line was cast as a solid bar or slug, the 'line of type' to which its name referred. At first, the Linotype was bought for newspaper composition, but in the US it eventually came to dominate the machine composition of text for all printed matter, including that of books.

A decade later, in 1897, Tolbert Lanston, who as a clerk had seen the potential of punched cards for sorting data, invented the Monotype machine. Its keyboard was separate and freestanding: the operation of the keys punched holes in a paper tape that recorded the characters and added a code to calculate the line's spacing. The tape was read by an automated casting machine, which cast each character and space separately and delivered lines that were ready for placing on the printing machine.

The casting of separate type enabled corrections to lines cast on the Monotype to be made by hand. In the Linotype, a line needing correction was reset and recast. This could be done quickly, however, and Linotype slugs were more stable than single types when they were made up into formes on the composing stone. Accordingly, the Linotype, together with some related machines, retained its hold on the market for newspaper and periodical composition. For the composition of books, the Monotype, which was capable of certain typographical refinements, was often favoured.

4.4 Photomechanical processes

During the later 19th century, highly complex processes were developed for the reproduction of images, some of which had a profound effect on printing processes generally. The principle was simple, although in practice great technical skill was needed. A photographic image of a black-and-white drawing was printed on to a zinc plate with a substance that formed a resist, and the rest of the metal was etched away to leave an accurate relief facsimile of the drawing, ready for printing, without the intervention of a professional engraver to interpret it on wood (*see* **18**).

During the 1880s, images for reproduction in books and magazines (a fast-growing market) were increasingly derived from photographs, but these were necessarily interpreted by professional wood engravers who simulated the continuous tone of the photograph by creating the perceived shades of grey with the skilled use of their tools. The mechanical reproduction of photographs was achieved by breaking up the image with a regular screen of fine crossed lines to create half-tones (comprising dots of varying size) and etching the image in relief on copper. The drawback of the half-tone block was that properly printing its fine detail required the use of a specially prepared smooth paper, ideally one that was coated with china clay, and known as 'art paper'.

Similar techniques were employed to treat photographs to produce a printing surface for lithographic or intaglio printing. The latter process led to the development of photogravure, printed either from flat etched plates or from copper cylinders from which both photograph and text could be printed on large web-fed rotary presses. The process of photogravure printed on rotary machines, which at that date produced a denser image than either letterpress or offset lithography, enabled the production of large-circulation pictorial magazines in the years between the two world wars; it was also used for some books of photographs.

4.5 Colour printing for the commercial and popular market

To print in more than one colour, the same sheet must be printed repeatedly; this adds to the cost and demands accuracy in placing the paper, so that the colours print over each other in register. During the 19th century, multiple colours were increasingly used to increase the effectiveness of new kinds of printing: e.g. posters and packaging, and books for children (*see* **17**). In the 20th century, that market would also include large-circulation periodicals. At first, colours were mixed by specialist printers to make tints that worked in harmonious combinations. With the development of colour theory at the end of the 19th century, processes were introduced that could reproduce all possible colours from the superimposition of three successive printed colours (cyan, magenta, and yellow). However, with experience it became evident that, in addition to the three colours, an additional black printing was needed to give added density to dark hues, thus making a four-colour process.

4.6 Photocomposition of text

A system for setting type by photography was patented in Britain in 1896, and experimental devices for small-scale typesetting were invented and used during the 1930s. It was not until after World War II, however, that systems for text setting were manufactured and marketed on any scale.

One obstacle to the use of photography was that letterpress relief printing was still the dominant means of producing texts. The product of photocomposition was an image on film; using it for letterpress printing required the making of an etched relief on zinc or magnesium, an expensive process that risked some loss of quality. Although photogravure was too small a part of the market, offset lithography was more promising. It generally employed text that had been set in metal, then photographed to make the lithographic plate, so direct photocomposition of the text could eliminate this detour. It is not surprising, therefore, that the early photocomposing machines were designed and made in the US, where offset lithography was gaining a steadily increasing share of the market for printing. For printing books, the process had an additional advantage over letterpress, one that it shared with photogravure: photographs could be printed alongside text on the same paper, rather than segregated in a separate section of plates.

Some early photocomposing or filmsetting machines were based on existing machines for making metal type, and produced by their manufacturers in order to gain a share of the future market. Such machines included the Fotosetter of Intertype (makers of a version of the Linotype) and the Monofoto, made by Monotype. In these, photographic negatives were, in effect, substituted for the brass matrices in which metal had been cast; a beam of light created the text, letter by letter, building up lines and pages on film that was then developed. The most innovative machine, designed from first principles rather than adapted from existing models, was the Photon (called the Lumitype by its French inventors, Higonnet and Moyroud, and marketed under that name in France). On the Lumitype, letters were picked out in rapid sequence from images on a spinning glass disk with an electronic flash and the capacity for multiple sets of types or fonts. (During the middle years of the 20th century, the designs of the printing types sold by typefounders or provided by the makers of composing machines were widely known as typefaces. With the development of photocomposition and digital typography, for which many of the older designs were adapted and redrawn, the term 'font'—the US spelling of the term more commonly spelt 'fount' in Britain—became routinely used for individual designs.)

The first generation of these machines all posed the same problem: to make a correction, it was necessary to set a new line or paragraph and physically strip it into the existing film. It became apparent that the only way of working around this difficulty was to read and correct the text before, rather than after, the type was set and almost ready for printing, as had hitherto been the practice. In the new generation of typesetting machines, the text was entered on a keyboard, coded for such instructions as size of type and bold type and italics, and held on magnetic tape in order to permit correction and alteration that could be viewed on a screen and checked on an intermediate print. The computer had entered the printing office and, within a generation—having irrevocably altered the relationship of author, publisher, and printer—it would change the meaning of 'text'. During the 1970s, a third generation of typesetting devices moved away from photocomposition on film, substituting the generation of type in digital form.

4.7 Digital typography

The Apple Macintosh computer, with its mouse and GUI (Graphics User Interface), was launched in San Francisco on 24 January 1984, a date that is often cited as marking the beginning of the digital revolution in printing and publishing (*see* **21**). In addition to the Apple Macintosh computer ('Mac'), four other products marketed in 1984 and 1985 may together be seen as having initiated the practices that ultimately became a normal part of the process of making books and all kinds of printed matter. The page description language Adobe PostScript enabled the integration of text and images on a range of different computers and printers. The LaserWriter, introduced in 1985, was a laser printer with a raster image processor that incorporated the Adobe PostScript interpreter. Macropedia's Fontographer was a program for drawing new digital fonts, and for adapting existing ones. Aldus PageMaker was a program that facilitated the setting of type, the handling of images, and their placing on a page. Thus, the design and assembly of a publication's parts—originally the printer's responsibility and, during the 20th century, increasingly shared with a design or production department within a publisher's office—could now be performed by one person with a small computer on a desk. By providing their text in digital form, authors became the primary typesetters of their own books. The advent of the electronic book was in many respects an outgrowth of these new, computerized production technologies.

5 Conclusion

The printed book as an object has not changed radically since its introduction in the 15th century. To be sure, the varieties of its form are now very great indeed, with images integrated into text, an abundance of colour, and a wide range of formats. Yet, in order to convey straightforward texts, lines of black words are still placed on white paper, arranged in a sequence of pages, and made up into a

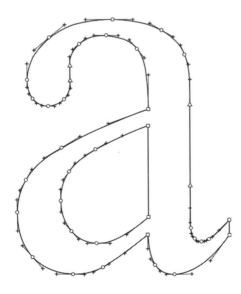

The 'a' of a TrueType font of Times Roman, with all the points that govern its Bézier curves and straight lines. Courtesy of Professor James Mosley. Line drawing by Chartwell Illustrators.

book that can be placed at a comfortable distance for reading. The shapes of the letters may vary from time to time under the influence of changing preferences, but many types in current use are derived directly from those created during the 20ᵗʰ century for machine composition in metal. Indeed, it is generally agreed that—although the appearance of offset lithography is subtly different from that of letterpress printing—digital types and typesetting have on the whole enhanced the look of printing without altering it noticeably.

Nevertheless, the underlying technical processes employed to produce the printed page have changed tremendously. The widespread use of metal type had effectively ceased by about 1980: such type is now employed only rarely, to make special kinds of books. Words are still generally placed on paper with ink, but carbon particles (or toner) fused by an electrostatic process are more likely to be used to generate copies of digitized books that are printed on demand. So too, many works are designed to be read directly from a screen without ever being printed on paper. The processes of making and diffusing texts are still developing in directions that are not easy to predict.

....

BIBLIOGRAPHY

B. Agüera y Arcas, 'Temporary Matrices and Elemental Punches in Gutenberg's DK Type', in *Incunabula and Their Readers*, ed. K. Jensen (2003)

J. M. Funcke, *Kurtze Anleitung von Form- und Stahlschneiden, Erfurt 1740*, intro. J. Mosley (1998)

Gaskell, *NI*

R. Gaskell, 'Printing House and Engraving Shop, a Mysterious Collaboration', *BC* 53 (2004), 213–51

R. E. Huss, *The Development of Printers' Mechanical Typesetting Methods, 1822–1925* (1973)

G. A. Kubler, *A New History of Stereotyping* (1941)

McKerrow, *Introduction*

J. Moran, *Printing Presses* (1973)

R.-G. Rummonds, *Printing on the Iron Handpress* (2 vols, 1997)

R. Southall, *Printer's Type in the Twentieth Century* (2005)

M. Twyman, *Early Lithographed Books* (1990)

12

The Economics of Print

ALEXIS WEEDON

1 The economic value of a book

Four essential factors determine the economic value of a book: its worth as literary property, the cost of its manufacture, regulatory and institutional controls, and its price in the market. The history of the book trade can be read as the economic development of these four key areas. Tracing the development of these factors, this essay's chief focus is on 19th-century Britain, when commercial and technological innovations changed the economic status of the book from a luxury item to an affordable product for the majority of the British population (*see* **22b**).

2 The Stationers' Company and early institutional structures of the British book trade

Even before the invention of printing, book production was regulated through the craft guild of the Company of Scriveners in the City of London. By the mid-16th century the guild controlled the economic organization of book production, which was limited to London. The technical importance of printing and its economic advantage over hand copying gradually gave printers status and influence within the guild. However, printing increased the demand for paper which was imported by wealthy merchants—stationers—who were effectively the capitalists of the trade and held greatest sway within the Company. In 1557, the Stationers'

Company was granted a Royal Charter giving it corporate legal status and the right to self-regulation. The Company gained powers to regulate apprentices and apprenticeships and to seize illegal books, and it prohibited printing by non-members. This largely confined printing to London, centralizing the trade until the end of the 17th century (*see* **22a**).

The Company's custom of recording permission to print a book—a practice inaugurated in part to forestall adverse competition between its members—became regularized, and in 1559 the Stationers' Register became the authoritative record within the trade of who had the right to print copies of a work. By Elizabeth I's reign, registration had become the mechanism for recording the legal right to publish a work, and in 1637 this was confirmed in law.

Certain characteristics of the book business in Britain are evident in the early history of the Stationers' Company: there is a strong institutional structure focused on London, an economic interdependence between the elements of the trade that emphasized their mutual business interests above rivalries, and a mechanism to assign and record the right to print copies of books. The Stationers' Register and patents were early forms of copyright protection. Patents had been assigned by Henry VIII, and they gave the right to print the most profitable books to particular court favourites and their appointed printers. This concentrated economic power in an oligarchy, as the lucrative trade in educational and religious books (ABCs, almanacs, catechisms, psalters, and primers) was given to a few favoured members of the Company. Protests ensued, and as a result the patents were shared more widely amongst the members and became jointly owned property. In 1603 this arrangement was formalized into the Company's English Stock. The Stock was divided into shares with a notional capital of £9,000. Fifteen Court Assistants purchased shares of £320 each, 30 Liverymen purchased shares worth £160, and 60 freemen or yeomen purchased shares worth £80 each. In the early 17th century, shareholders received a remarkable annual dividend of around 12.5 per cent. A large proportion of these co-owners were booksellers and paper merchants who had the capital to invest in the English Stock. The long-term effect of this arrangement was to separate the printing and publishing functions of book production—an outcome that was crucial to the parallel development of the printing industry and of publishing houses in the 19th century.

In 1637, however, the book trade was still small. There were approximately 26 active printing offices in London, and a printer might have two or three hand presses with a couple of journeymen and an apprentice. Essentially, they were small-scale family businesses. By 1730 the size of typical printing offices had increased, while the biggest firms became very large indeed: Jacob Tonson and John Watts, for example, employed over 50 men. In the 1750s, Samuel Richardson had three such establishments with more than 40 men in each. These were printing and bookselling enterprises, fuelled in part by the growing popularity of the novel and the 18th-century circulating library market.

The Printing Act (1662) confirmed the main elements of the trade after the chaos of the Civil War: it was almost exclusively confined to London, limited the number of presses, and ratified that entry in the Stationers' Register was the proof of copyright ownership. The only significant change was that a Licenser, responsible for books and newspapers, replaced the Elizabethan system of approval by two religious or educational authorities.

The Civil War stimulated literacy and a growth in demand for news conveyed through print. In 1668, to gain access to this new market, the trade published the first term catalogues, or lists of new publications for booksellers. It was a significant innovation, which later became the basis of the national bibliography. During this time, wholesalers came to play a key part in the distribution of books. To recoup the expense of manufacture, copy-owners sold a portion of their press run at a discount to wholesalers, who then sold them on to booksellers. Significantly, the discount was calculated on the notional retail price of the book, foreshadowing the rise of the Net Book Agreement (1900), which regulated book prices for nearly the whole of the 20th century.

3 The origins of legal copyright

In 1695, the Printing Act lapsed and the value of English Stock declined, thereby eroding the control of the Stationers' Company over the trade. Copy-owners feared the loss of protection of their copyright and an increase in piracy, so they replaced the institutional control of the Stationers' Company by trade agreements directly with members of congers, associations of booksellers or printers who increased their power in the market by pooling their resources in a kind of joint-stock partnership. Such associations not only helped to ensure greater financial stability for their members, they also extended their range of distribution and provided a measure of protection from piracy. Such amalgamations of businesses are indicative of the tightness of the trade and the mutuality of interests in the production and sale of books. Similarly, shared ownership of a book was kept within the group of shareholders through trade sales. When shares in copyrights became available for sale, often through the estate of a former copy-owner, an auction was typically conducted exclusively for members of the book trade. After the legal protection of the Printing Act lapsed in 1695, this form of trade protection was all that was available until the first Copyright Act came into being.

During the 18th century, various legal remedies were tried to regulate the trade, including laws on copyright, trade protectionism, and taxation. The lapse of the Printing Act was also the end of licensing, and taxes on printed matter, introduced in 1711 and later extended, became the means of regulating access to print. They continued until the mid-19th century. By raising the price of newspapers and print, they effectively circumscribed their readership, excluding the poorer classes. Taxes could be claimed back on books sent abroad, however; for some publishers such as H. G. Bohn, this had the unintended benefit of supporting the growing export trade in books. The 18th century saw the first copyright Act—'for the Encouragement of Learning' (1710)—which gave protection to copy-owners of existing literary property for 21 years and of all new copies after the Act for 14 years. However, it was somewhat hastily drafted, and hence badly worded, leaving open the notion of perpetual copyright. Copy-owners were anxious about the extent of the protection it gave, especially after the initial 21 years had expired, and were concerned about the threat of imported books from emerging centres of printing in Edinburgh and Dublin. Thus, the booksellers put pressure on the government to protect the trade, and in 1739 the Crown passed an act that prohibited the import of English books. It was not to last, and in 1774 a legal judgement ruled that this protectionism was illegal, effectively ending the stranglehold of the London trade. This case (Donaldson vs Becket) was significant for another reason: it ruled against perpetual copyright. From then on copyright acts have set and adjusted fixed terms for copyright protection.

Authors hardly featured in the 1710 copyright Act, although they soon began to see how it gave them more of an economic stake in their work. In the 18th century, the author typically received a lump sum for the number of sheets the work would fill in exchange for its copyright. By 1800 limited-duration copyright was an economic reality, and profit-sharing agreements gradually became more common. During the 19th century the Society of Authors campaigned for royalty agreements so that writers might share in the financial reward of their success. Publishers turned their attention to creating markets within a growing and increasingly literate population. Some were able to make a good living from out-of-copyright books. For example, Bohn's Libraries became renowned for their quality and affordability and opened up a market for other such series, which included books in copyright. Other publishers, such as Smith, Elder, & Co., paid highly for the right to publish fashionable works and to capture the tide of popular interest in a genre or author.

4 Nineteenth-century economic history and innovations in the book trade

Industrialization and the consequent economic prosperity of 19th-century Britain significantly changed the costs of book production. Steam-powered machines revolutionized printing and paper manufacture (*see* **10, 11**). The growth in population and improvements in general welfare and education increased the market for print, and there was an unprecedented growth in output. Print was the first mass media, and in the second half of the 19th century printed matter became ubiquitous—it was on hoardings in the street and on packaging in shops and homes (*see* **16**). Booksellers and newsagents supplied a burgeoning number and variety of books, newspapers, and periodicals. This was the result of falling manufacturing costs, increased demand, and a freedom from the institutional and regulatory controls that had hitherto restricted access.

The market for books expanded as the population grew and the proportion of adults able to read also increased. Market growth meant that, from the 1860s to the 1890s, the industry was financially under pressure to increase productivity without raising costs. This drive for greater economy was achieved though a reduction in the factor costs of production, including: the price of paper, the mechanization of printing, the development of lithography, and limiting composition costs through the use of stereotyping, or taking plate moulds of set type.

Nevertheless, the book trade was not immune from the ups and downs of the economy. Some declines were peculiar to the trade, such as the crisis of 1826 when Archibald Constable, Sir Walter Scott's publisher, and a number of other publishers and printers failed. Yet, the trade recovered by the 1830s. Other crises were international: following the Napoleonic wars, there were economic downturns in 1819, 1829–32, 1837–42, and 1847–8; similarly, optimism in the revival of trade after the American Civil War was short-lived. The 1864–6 monetary crisis in Britain was perhaps the most severe: it had been caused by a number of London discounting houses borrowing short and lending long. Several failed, including the greatest of the lenders, Overend, Gurney, & Co, pushing many businesses that relied on bills of exchange into bankruptcy, including Samuel O. Beeton, husband and publisher of Mrs Beeton. The ensuing financial emergency continued until 1867, reaching its most critical point on 12 May 1866, when the bank lending rate soared to 10 per cent. It was not to reach that level again until the outbreak of World War I.

J. Barnes has argued that such monetary crises spurred innovation in publishing. Certainly, many successes arose from experiments begun in economic depression. For example, Charles Knight and the Society for the Diffusion of Useful Knowledge (SDUK) launched the Library of Useful Knowledge in the turbulent post-Napoleonic era. Each fortnightly issue cost 6d., and sales, often to the working or lower-middle classes, sometimes reached 20,000 per issue. Another publisher who profited from economic downturns was Tegg & Son. It dominated the remaindering market, and during 1825–7 made a successful business from buying at 'vastly reduced prices the copyrights of works that had not sold well or whose proprietors had gone bankrupt' (Barnes, 235). Innovative formats were another method of stimulating the market, as W. H. Smith found when he began his first railway bookstall in the depression of 1848. He tempted middle-class readers with the earliest of many railway libraries; Routledge, Henry Colburn, and other publishers followed. The success of Smith and his competitors was fuelled by a 19th-century vogue for publishers' series or 'libraries', which supplied a market for self-education, for book collecting, and, in the latter half of the century, for schoolbooks.

The success of a format could also bring its own difficulties, however. When J. M. Dent launched Everyman's Library in 1904, he set aside £10,000 to finance it. The initial volumes sold so well that he reprinted, tying up much of his capital in stock. Dent's bindery did not have enough space to cope with the demand, so he moved his works to Hertfordshire, installed his printing machinery in the basement, and built new houses for his workers. These expenses cost him an additional £20,000, compelling him to go to his papermakers and to his bank for credit. As a major customer with a secure business, he was able to get it, but as Barnes has pointed out: 'innovation depends on solvency, whether the times are prosperous or hard' (Barnes, 239).

From 1876 to 1886 there was a considerable increase in the quantity of books produced in Britain. Economic historians have shown that the depression of 1873–96 had been of greater political than economic significance; although Britain lost her predominant position as the leading manufacturing country and growth was not as rapid as before, the economy also slowed in the US and Germany. Britain came to take a new pivotal role in international trade and financial services. In the publishing industry, trade to the empire was strongest during periods of colonial expansion. Customs figures for the declared value of book exports indicate that there was a strong early market in India from the 1820s to the 1840s (*see* **41**). In the early 1850s, however, Australia became a significant consumer of British books: by 1868 the weight of books being shipped to Australia was five times greater than the weight to India (*see* **46**). The export trade suffered reversals in the Australian financial crises of 1883 and 1890. Exports to British North America (later the Canadian Federation) grew in the late 1860s, so that by 1868 the tonnage to North America was double the Indian trade (*see* **49**). From the 1890s, however, British publishers felt the effects of competition from indigenous publishing houses and sought to establish branches abroad to handle their trade in the colonies. Macmillan, for instance, opened offices in India in 1901. Their export trade had been developing over several decades, and from 1873 they had been designing specific editions for the Indian market. Similarly, William Collins & Sons opened a warehouse and showroom in Sydney, Australia, in 1874, and in New Zealand in 1888, and the firm also had travellers in India seeking out markets in Bombay, Calcutta, Madras, and Colombo. Such expansion was a typical feature of the internationalization of British book publishing.

5 Reducing the cost of paper

On the manufacturing side of book production—paper and printing—capital investment in printing equipment was needed initially to fund powered presses from the 1830s to the 1850s, and subsequently to replace those presses with improved versions. From the 1860s printers, such as William Clowes, were investing in patents and were experimenting with composition machines and new photographic and platemaking processes. Similarly, in the papermaking trade, the Fourdrinier machine and its later improvements substantially increased output.

The invention of the papermaking machine had a profound effect on the book trade (*see* **10**). As early as 1804, the Fourdrinier brothers registered a patent for such a machine; their invention was subsequently modified and improved by others. By 1825, over half of all paper in England was made by machine. Machine-made paper had the advantages of speed, flexibility, size, and quality. Testifying to the significance of the Fourdriniers' invention, the book printer George Clowes explained the knock-on result of machine-made paper for the whole of the printing industry: it 'has effected a complete revolution in our business; where we used to go to press with an edition of 500 copies, we now print 5,000' (Plant, 331). Clowes's works at that time was the biggest and most modern in the country; it printed on double-sized paper at a time when only about a fifth of book paper used was double. By 1886, however, this figure had risen to three-quarters. Quad papers succeeded double and by 1906 were the norm. This doubling-up of sheet sizes corresponded with the increase in the size of presses.

In the 30 years following 1866, paper costs were reduced by approximately two-thirds. This substantial decrease had a significant effect on cost of production. Contemporary sources explaining the decline in the cost of paper as a proportion of book manufacturing in the 19th century as a whole cite the earlier abolition of duty and the use of esparto grass and wood pulp in the manufacture of paper as two major causes. However, other variables also effected this fall: the mechanization of the process of paper manufacture; the availability and affordability of the raw materials for paper; and more economical presses and imposition schemes. Probably all these factors contributed to helping printers reap the benefits of mechanization, and ensured the more economical use of larger presses.

6 Mechanization of printing

Although Clowes had already experimented with steam power in his printing office in 1823, it was a while before the printing machine itself was commonplace. Before 1820, the steam press was in use by five London printers: *The Times*, Charles Baldwin, Andrew Strahan, Richard Taylor, and Richard Bensley. Not all of these had double-size presses, and it was not until 1828 that the use of double sheets for book work was possible though the introduction of the improved Applegath and Cowper machine. *The Times* had printed its 29 November 1814 edition on König's steam press, and later used Applegath and Cowper's improved version, which could print double-sized sheets at the rate of 1,000 an hour, four times the speed of the hand presses. Throughout the 1830s and 1840s, other printers began to install steam engines and invest in powered presses. Steam-powered double-platen presses manufactured first by Hopkinson and Cope, then produced to an improved design by Napier, generally came into use during the 1830s. Running at up to 800 impressions per hour, their maximum size was double royal. This increased capacity fuelled experiments in cheap periodicals. Following the Library of Useful Knowledge, for example, the SDUK published its famous *Penny Magazine* and *Penny Cyclopaedia*. This was a boom period in periodical publishing. In 1836, Dickens published *Pickwick Papers* in part numbers. The novel was so successful that Chapman & Hall, Dickens's publishers, had to use stereotypes to print multiple impressions. The stereotyping process enabled type to be cast to fit a curved surface, and this led to faster cylinder and rotary presses coming on to the market. During the 1860s and 1870s, the Napier steam presses were replaced by these fast, but initially less accurate, single-sided cylinder presses. Wharfedales, used in book work, could take the much larger quad demy sheets. In 1858 *The Times* moved to using stereoplates on cylinders; ten years later, taking advantage of the mechanization of paper manufacture, it dispensed with sheets and employed a rotary press that could take a continuous web of paper. This measure doubled its printing capacity.

Such machines made labour more productive. Both the double platens and the double royal Wharfedales used two operators, but the latter's output was greater. The operators were usually boys, overseen by a machine-minder who made ready the press—that is, imposed the forme and put it on the press, adjusted the height of the type by inserting overlays, and packed cuts where necessary. When reprinting a work, fitting stereoplates saved time, as the initial labour of levelling the type was preserved in the cast. This reduced the making-ready, and hence production costs. Often some repair work was needed to the stereoplates, but it usually amounted to no more than a few shillings' worth of labour. Such savings meant that it was cost-effective to reprint in shorter runs, though the effort of setting up the press and washing it down afterwards resulted in the fact that the unit cost for editions of fewer than 500 was markedly higher than for editions above that number. This partly explains why, from the 1860s to the 1880s, the most frequent quantity printed was 1,000 books.

As machining, make-ready, and paper costs varied over the century, so too did the unit cost for printing a book. Unit costs fell when the initial fixed set-up cost could be divided among a larger number of books. As more books were printed, the fraction of the set-up cost was reduced until it was less than the combined cost of paper and machining for each unit. At this point the optimum press run was reached. By the 1890s, the optimum run for the publisher was as high as 30,000 copies, although this was obviously not the longest possible print run. It was not unusual for cheap fiction, for instance, to be printed in numbers of 100,000 or more on cylinder presses, although most quality book work was done on sheet-fed machines. Above the optimum press run, the unit cost consisted of the price of the paper, running the machine, and the wages and overtime of the machine-minder and his boys. For magazine publishers, such as Newnes, using faster perfecting cylinder and rotary presses, much longer press runs were economical, but initial set-up costs meant that runs had to be over 5,000 to be cost-effective. Publishers used these new, highly economical technologies in the penny market. Newnes, John Dicks, and others published editions of popular works, often printed in double columns, magazine-style, on cheap paper; they cost a few pence and were read by the working classes.

Chatto & Windus publish *Choice Humorous Works of Mark Twain* (1873); it was followed by a series of stereotype reprints, all produced by Ballantyne, Hanson, & Co. The publication ledger shows the growing importance of documenting and controlling costs. Chatto & Windus Archives

Although in the 40 years between 1836 and 1876 the average cost of machining gradually rose at a rate of approximately 7 per cent each decade, between 1876 and 1886 the average cost fell by 29 per cent, and in real terms by nearer half; it remained low until the turn of the century. The fall in paper costs after the abolition of the paper tax, then the replacement of the platen-powered presses by the larger cylinder ones in the 1860s and 1870s, meant that the real reduction in the cost of machining came after the beginning of the fall in paper costs. The percentage fall in the expense of machining cannot be wholly attributed to the incremental increase in paper size. The new machinery was more economical.

7 The wages of compositors and cost of composition

The main reason for the fall in the cost of book production was the move from double- to quad-sized paper and presses, and the use of stereoplates. Composition, for nearly the whole of the 19th century, meant hand composition. Experiments with mechanical means for the selection of type and its distribution were on the whole unsuccessful. When labour was plentiful, the main concern was the amount of available type. With the spread of stereoplates and typecasting machines in the 1850s, the quantity of type became less of a problem, and what concerned publishers and printers more was the extent of revisions which added to the rising cost of labour. Correction represented on average 35 per cent of the composition costs of books between 1836 and 1916, although the proportion varied considerably from title to title. The occasional text needed complete resetting, whereas others needed very little alteration.

Throughout the 19th century wage levels gradually increased, making labour more expensive. The main period of rising wages was from 1869 to 1876. However, compositors' wages did not rise so sharply. Bowley's and Wood's studies show that compositors' average wages—which in 1800–1810 had been much higher than their fellow workers in cotton factories, the building trade, and the shipbuilding and engineering industries—were by the 1880s at a similar level. Although there were wide geographical differences in the wages of union labour, non-union labour, and piece-work, a comparison of compositors' earnings with Wood's calculation of the mean wage of the period shows that compositors' wages were falling relative to those of other wage earners. Rates of pay and employment levels varied considerably from county to county, causing concern among the typographical societies. In the crisis of 1826, for example, many compositors lost their jobs, and every London printing house allegedly had notices saying that compositors and pressmen need not apply. Even two years later, 800 out of 3,500 compositors and pressmen in the capital were out of work.

With the mechanization of paper manufacture and the adoption of printing machines, the labour-intensive work of composition was the next logical task to mechanize. However, typographical associations and print unions, which were concerned for the continuing employment of their members and for industry standards, resisted the introduction of composing machines. Their concern over quality was echoed by the printers. The Linotype machine used in America for book work had been gradually introduced into newspaper offices in Britain in the late 1870s, but the printer W. C. K. Clowes judged that although the Linotype was the right principle, 'at present he did not think it was the machine for book-work' (Southward, 82). Clowes's firm invested in Monotype machines when they came into commercial use in 1897, pioneering many of their own modifications. The interval between the technology's invention and its perfection meant that any effect on wages and employment patterns for compositors was deferred until the 20th century, when World War I pushed both prices and wages higher.

When printers moved to an industrialized system of setting and printing, replaced double- with quad-sized presses, and bought machine-made paper, they passed on to publishers the benefits of large-scale manufacturing through the reduction of basic unit costs. By adopting stereoplates, which conserved labour and allowed for a more flexible mode of production, they enabled publishers to tailor their product more effectively to the market. The most significant factor in the reduction of unit costs, however, was the reduction in paper prices (combined with its greater availability).

8 Types of publishing firm

At the end of the 19th century, the newspaper and publishing industry consisted mainly of family businesses and partnerships. In the book trade, partnerships were often turned into family businesses when partners were bought out or lists were sold, and the business was handed down to the founder's sons and grandsons. Printers apprenticed their sons to their clients' businesses, and publishers found their sons places in fellow publishers' and printers' firms. In this manner, the trade was close-knit. However, after the trade crisis of 1866–7, it became increasingly common to adopt the form of a limited liability company and retain the family's interest through their shareholding and by holding seats on the corporation's board.

The publishing industry became an increasingly attractive field for investment, not least because the taxes on knowledge that had inhibited the growth of newspapers were abated, political control of the press was relaxed, and prosperity increased. The spread of industrialization, which affected printers and paper manufacturers, caused some concern to producers of books for export as by the mid-century European countries began to emulate Britain and became able to manufacture paper more cheaply. The commissioning and sale of books—the province of publishers and booksellers—was largely dependent on trading conditions in Britain and abroad. Tariff barriers were imposed to differentiate markets, and this affected both supply factors and, to a lesser extent, distribution; however, there were no barriers within the empire, and publishers' colonial editions appear to have sold in good numbers. Perhaps more significant to the trade was the gradual extension of copyright protection. Although copyright law varied throughout the century, efforts to gain international agreements within Europe (by way e.g. of the Berne Convention) and, most significantly for British publishers, with the US, eventually paid off.

The economic, political, and legal framework that dictated the structure of the newspaper industry also affected book and magazine publishing, though not to the same extent. The mid-century pressures for political reform stimulated the proliferation of newspapers throughout the country. Politics, legal reform, and growing urbanization were agents of change. In the same way as the 19th-century book, periodical, and general publishing firms, so too was the newspaper industry built largely on the model of the family business. Ties between the industries were close, as Lee has stated: 'Newspaper proprietors had customarily been recruited from the ranks of printers and publishers, and the tradition of proprietorship was deeply rooted and long-lived' (Lee, 84).

In the book publishing industry, family firms and partnerships predominated. Such firms were typically valued prior to changing hands, which was either when a firm was being handed on to the next generation, or when a partner left and wanted to release his equity in the stock and good will. As sons (rarely daughters) came into the trade, they were placed in friends' firms to learn the business, sometimes becoming partners, or else setting up partnerships independently when of age. Thus, a close study of 19th-century imprints often leads to tracing the kinship of publishers. Firms tied by blood, friendship, or the supply chain were also linked through capital investment, long-term loans, shares, and bills of exchange. Towards the end of the century, it became usual in both industries to adopt some form of joint-stock company, which necessitated returning a balance sheet with accurate statements of turnover and capital.

The registrations and returns of joint-stock companies were recorded annually in the parliamentary blue books that also noted if they had been wound up or were still in operation at the time they made their return. Although some 18th-century newspapers were organized as joint-stock companies, the real expansion came after the Companies Acts of 1854 and 1862, which offered the security of limited liability. From 1856, the details of their corporate finances were recorded in the blue books. Shannon has shown that the early companies invariably made a loss, causing many investors to be understandably cautious of the new system. Certainly, it seems that many printers and the vast majority of publishing companies remained in private hands. Lee has counted some 420 newspaper companies formed between 1856 and 1885. Only 247 'book, magazine, journal, art or general publishing or bookselling' companies were registered in the same period: 38 in the first decade, 58 in the second, and 151 in the third. This rate of increase was below that of newspaper companies; yet, it reflected the expansion of joint-stock companies at the time. 'Infant mortality' in the first decade was 38 per cent among publishing companies, compared with 20 per cent among newspaper companies, though such early corporate demises too fell swiftly to 7 per cent and 10 per cent in the following two decades, slightly above Lee's newspaper figures of 7 and 6 per cent.

In contrast with the newspaper trade, the number of publishing companies formed remained relatively low until the mid-1870s. In the early 1880s, the rate of formation increased as it did in the newspaper trade, with 26 new companies in 1885. It appears that the economic reversals of the mid-1860s did not affect the number of publishing companies registering, although it does seem to have made them more reluctant to submit returns and more cautious about estimating the company's liability.

Much of the capital held by publishing companies is tied up in their copyrights, in contrast with printers, who invest in machinery and presses. Nevertheless, the industries were closely intertwined, and many of the companies' statements describing their 'object or business' cross the boundaries between printer, publisher, and newspaper proprietor; for example, the Kilgore Newspaper and Publishing Company Ltd included as its business 'newspaper and general printing & publishing'. Book printers such as Clowes partially or wholly owned copyrights as well as holding shares in publishing companies. By 1883, however, categories used in the returns make the distinction between newspaper proprietors and printers and publishers, and this may well reflect an increase in the industry's specialization. From the blue books, it is evident that a larger percentage of publishing than of newspaper companies were medium to large (with a nominal capital £10,000 or above), although in the potentially dangerous period between 1866 and 1875 they were more cautious, and limited their liability to lower amounts. It seems too that more of the nominal capital was called in at this time than during the decades before or after.

Many companies were, of course, established to buy an existing enterprise, and a number of firms were formed for the purpose either of turning partnerships and family businesses into private companies or of buying copyrights in order to establish their own business. Between 1856 and 1865, 70 per cent of publishing companies had fewer than ten shareholders. This pattern was reversed in the following (economically troubled) decade when the risk was spread among a greater number of shareholders. Many of these larger companies were educational suppliers or providers of Christian literature ranging from newspapers to schoolbooks. Others were stationers, printers, or periodical publishers first and foremost, and listed publishing or bookselling as a part of their business. By the end of the 1880s there were many more moderate-to-large businesses whose main object was publishing and bookselling, such as Isbister & Company Ltd (1879) with £32,000 nominal capital and 18 shareholders; Chapman & Hall Ltd (1880) with £150,000 nominal capital and 104 shareholders; and Collins & Sons Ltd (1880) with £200,000 and 17 shareholders. All these publishers called on a fair proportion of their nominal capital: Isbister called in 90 per cent, Chapman & Hall 70 per cent, and Collins 88 per cent.

The hegemonic structure of the publishing industry was challenged by public investment in companies, alternative distribution systems, foreign competition in colonial markets, and ultimately by the reduction in the unit cost of the book. These factors led to a restructuring of the book trades, a phenomenon that had important commercial and cultural implications. Fundamental structural changes paved the way for the future direction of the publishing industry and became integral to 20th-century developments in the horizontal integration of the industry, by which smaller firms merged to form larger publishing houses that commanded a greater market share.

9 The 20th century

The growth in book production in the 50 years before World War I was higher than the growth in the reading public—a 'catching-up' after the setbacks of the mid-1860s. The increase in reading and book buying mirrored the rate of rising literacy. With World War I, both production and labour costs became more expensive. At the same time, however, composition machines—commonly Monotype machines for books and Linotypes for periodicals—were deemed of acceptable quality.

Price structuring, which from the 1870s had become a significant force in differentiating the fiction markets and had taken on greater significance after the collapse of the three-decker novel market, led to greater price specialization among publishers. In the 1920s and 1930s, some publishers concentrated on cheap reprint editions (e.g. Newnes, Rich, & Cowan) and others on inexpensive tie-ins with films—such as the Readers Library. In the middle price range Hodder & Stoughton sold genre fiction at 6s. and their 'yellow backs' at 2s. or 2s. 6d. Increasingly, authors' contracts were for specific editions or price bands;

other rights were sold separately. It was also the era of Penguin's successful launch into the sixpenny market.

The great depression of the 1930s saw some lasting innovations. In 1932 Harold Raymond of Chatto & Windus initiated book tokens. Often given as gifts, the tokens were exchanged towards the purchase of a book, and customers usually spent more than the value of the tokens. The scheme thrived in the difficult economic times of the 1930s and consolidated membership of the Booksellers' Association, since the bookseller had to be a member to claim his proportion of the value of the token. Similarly, the Left Book Club and Book Society's book club, the British counterparts to the Book-of-the-Month Club and the Literary Guild in America, had considerable success, as they were able to offer new titles more cheaply by buying in bulk for their membership.

From the 1890s, literary agencies had grown to become a separate and profitable business. In 1935, Curtis Brown, the international literary agent, wrote that the days of the 'good, kind, old-fashioned publisher who used to take over all of his author's rights and re-sell at 50 per cent' had gone. Successful literary properties commanded 'so many widely varied markets and such intricate contracts' that successful authors needed a business manager (Brown, 239–40). In the 1920s, serialization rights and translation rights usually brought in a lump sum, while royalty agreements for the differently priced book editions were often on a percentage return, depending on how many were sold. Options on novels and plays were eagerly sought as a source of stories for films; such rights could bring in a fixed amount, or be related to box office receipts. Agents found a business niche in negotiating and monitoring such contracts for a return of 10 per cent commission on what they brought the author.

World War I and then World War II profoundly affected the book trade. They imposed, if only for the duration of the conflicts, constraints which the trade had been free of for more than 50 years, ranging from restrictions on what could be published to shortages of labour and paper. However, the industry also supplied news of the war, propaganda, explanatory material, and advice through pamphlets and books. Stereoplates which had been stored for years in printers' warehouses were melted down in the war effort, signalling the end of an era— and a welcome new beginning for those who wanted to put Victorian literature and its values behind them. The Census of Production revealed that the monetary value of the paper, print, and stationery trades increased by £3,481,000 between the first (1907) and the fourth (1930) censuses. Inflation accounts for some of the rise, but not all. The number of titles published annually rose, causing murmurings of 'over-production' from those in the trade. The four essential factors in the value of a book were well embedded, however. Copyright law was underpinned through international agreement; the printing and book-manufacturing industries were mechanized and competitive; the professional associations representing the booksellers, publishers, and authors cooperated in their members' economic interests; and, significantly, the financial basis of this close-knit industry, the Net Book Agreement, had survived the two world wars.

BIBLIOGRAPHY

Altick

J. Barnes, 'Depression and Innovation in the British and American Book Trade, 1819–1939', in *Books and Society in History*, ed. K. Carpenter (1983)

A. L. Bowley, *Wages in the United Kingdom in the Nineteenth Century* (1900)

A. C. Brown, *Contacts* (1935)

D. C. Coleman, *The British Paper Industry, 1495–1860* (1958)

S. Eliot, *Some Patterns and Trends in British Publishing, 1800–1919* (1994)

J. Feather, *A History of British Publishing* (2006)

R. Floud and D. N. McCloskey, *The Economic History of Britain since 1700* (1994)

E. Howe and H. E. Waite, *The London Society of Compositors* (1948)

D. Keir, *The House of Collins* (1952)

A. J. Lee, *The Origins of the Popular Press in England, 1855–1914* (1976)

B. R. Mitchell, *British Historical Statistics* (1988)

C. Morgan, *The House of Macmillan (1843–1943)* (1943)

A. E. Musson, *The Typographical Association* (1954)

M. Plant, *The English Book Trade* (1939; 3e, 1974)

J. Rose, *The Intellectual Life of the British Working Classes* (2001)

R. S. Schofield, 'Dimensions of Illiteracy, 1750–1850', *Explorations in Economic History*, 10 (1973), 437–54

H. A. Shannon, 'The First Five Thousand Limited Companies', *Economic History*, supplement to *Economic Journal*, 2 (1932), 396–424

—— 'The Limited Companies of 1866–1883', *Economic History Review*, 4 (1932–4), 290–316

J. Southward, 'Machines for Composing Letterpress Printing Surfaces', *Journal of the Society of Arts* (20 Dec. 1895), 74–84

A. D. Spicer, *The Paper Trade* (1907)

J. Sutherland, 'The Book Trade Crash of 1826', *Library*, 6/9 (1987), 148–61

S. S. Unwin, *The Truth about Publishing* (1926)

D. Vincent, *Literacy and Popular Culture: England, 1750–1914* (1989)

—— *The Rise of Mass Literacy: Reading and Writing in Modern Europe* (2000)

A. Weedon, 'The Press and Publishing: Technology and Business 1855 to 1885', in *We, The Other 'Victorians'*, ed. S. C. Bizzini (2003)

—— *Victorian Publishing: The Economics of Book Production for a Mass Market, 1836–1916* (2003)

G. H. Wood, 'Real Wages and the Standard', in *British Economic Growth 1688–1955*, ed. P. Deane and W. A. Cole (1962)

Censorship

ELISABETH LADENSON

Literary censorship—the suppression of works either pre- or post-publication—is grounded in the conviction that books have the capacity to influence beliefs and behaviours. Political and religious writings have always attracted the attention of censors and would-be censors, and the depiction of sexuality—with its powerful implications for social and religious mores—has also consistently provided fodder for individuals, organizations, and government bodies interested in upholding a particular moral standard by suppressing the production and dissemination of books. Doubtless the most important events in the history of literary censorship were the invention of the printing press in the 15th century and the advent of widespread literacy beginning in the 18th century and continuing apace throughout the 19th and into the 20th centuries. Books (including pamphlets and newspapers) have always been viewed as ideal vehicles for the circulation of potentially dangerous information and ideas, so that the greater availability of books themselves, and the means to decipher them, inevitably gave rise to efforts to limit their capacity for pernicious influence. Although systematic state-sponsored censorship measures are largely a phenomenon of the early modern and modern worlds, the history of literary censorship is nonetheless almost as long as that of literature itself.

1 Censorship in the classical world

The first sustained argument for literary censorship is to be found in Plato's *Republic* (*c.*380 BC). Here, in one of the early signal ironies of a history replete with irony and paradox, Socrates, who was to be put to death (and indeed already had been at the time of publication) on charges of corrupting the young and offences against religion, argues that in the ideal republic the works of poets should be suppressed—on much the same grounds as those on which he himself, as it happened, was to be accused. By the same token, Socrates anticipates the arguments that were to be repeated at regular intervals by proponents of censorship in a large variety of cultural climates: youth, and especially future rulers, should be protected from the bad examples on display in the works of the great poets and their followers. Nor does he allow the idea that some stories are to be understood allegorically. Using logic that would be wielded to good effect by the French Imperial Prosecutor in the trial of Gustave Flaubert's *Madame Bovary* in 1857, to take one prominent example among many, Plato's Socrates maintains that readers cannot be trusted to distinguish truth from fiction or figurative from literal representation, and must therefore be shielded from all possible ambiguity. He further establishes an argument that would hold currency until the mid-20th century: that literary merit should be seen as an exacerbating rather than an exculpatory factor in judging the potential dangers of a work. This point is made in Book III, in which he discusses Homer's depiction of the underworld in the *Odyssey* (Book XI), singling out for particular disapproval the famous lines in which the shade of Achilles tells Odysseus that he would rather be a field-hand in life than a king in the realm of the dead. Such passages, according to Socrates, are dangerous not because they lack poetic charm, but precisely because they are so rich in it: the beauty and pathos of Achilles' speech rendering all the more persuasive its harmful message that slavery is preferable to death.

Many of the themes that would prove central in debates and censorship trials over the centuries are present in the *Republic*, articulated by a figure who has frequently been portrayed as a martyr to the very cause—freedom of ideas—against which he effectively argues here, in a work written by the most influential philosopher in the Western tradition. Among the elements of the works of Hesiod and Homer which Socrates identifies as representing pernicious influences on the young are the foundational myths of Uranus and Cronus recounted in the *Theogony*, since these stories depict paternal castration and paedophagy as the original methods of divine conflict resolution. Similarly, various episodes from the *Iliad* and *Odyssey* are cited as offering examples of unworthy behaviour, including quarrelling among the gods, and heroes ostentatiously lamenting the deaths of friends and relatives, rather than merely celebrating their valour and glory. Also singled out for opprobrium are representations of gods and supposedly worthy men alike engaging in various basic forms of unseemly comportment, notably laughing, weeping, and allowing themselves to be carried away by drunkenness, gluttony, and lechery. None of these forms of behaviour provides acceptable models for future leaders, nor, in consequence, can such depictions be accurate, as gods and heroes cannot have engaged in ignoble conduct. Portrayals of this sort by the great epic poets, along with those of the 4th-century tragedians, must therefore not be allowed in the ideal republic.

It should be noted that Socrates, or Plato, cites at length the offending passages in the *Republic* itself, its audience presumably deemed capable of reading or listening to them without undue harm. This too is characteristic of later arguments for censorship, one of the basic assumptions of which is that the putatively corruptible subject is generally conceived as being inherently different from both the author of the polemic and its target audience. Here, the immediate interlocutors are friends and students of Socrates, and the readership of the work would have comprised other philosophically inclined, educated citizens, while those to be shielded from harmful literary influences are the young, future ruling-class of a hypothetical ideal society. In France under the *ancien régime*, it was in a similar spirit that specially expurgated versions of classic works were produced *ad usum Delphini*, for the education of the Dauphin. Starting in the 18th century and continuing well into the 20th, however, the vast majority of censorship initiatives construed the vulnerable audiences as comprising women, children, and the working classes.

Plato's own works, especially the *Symposium* with its drinking-party framework and extended discussions of same-sex love, were repeatedly expurgated and at times suppressed entirely, or else accompanied by commentaries asserting the allegorical nature of such passages, as for instance in the first complete translation by Marsilio Ficino in the late 15th century. In antiquity, literary works tended to be suppressed on an ad hoc basis rather than as the result of systematic policies as became the case in later eras. Julius Caesar, and his successor Augustus, did, however, add the category of *famosi libelli* (defamatory or libellous works) to the *lex maiestatis* under which crimes against the majesty of the Roman people—and thus naturally their leaders—were prosecuted, with sentences ranging from deportation and confiscation of property to execution. According to Suetonius, the emperor Domitian, known for his campaigns to improve public morals, not only had the historian Hermogenes of Tarsus (not to be confused with the later Greek rhetorician of the same name) put to death for certain allusions in his *History*, but had the scribes who had copied out the work crucified as well, to make sure its ideas would not be repeated elsewhere; the work itself was publicly burned. Pythagorean writings had already been burned by order of the Senate as early as 181 BC.

Doubtless the most famous censorship case in imperial Rome was the banishment of Ovid by Augustus in AD 8 to Tomis in Boeotia, by the Black Sea in what is now Romania. The reasons and circumstances for this event have never been satisfactorily elucidated. Ovid himself, who spent the rest of his life lamenting his exile and vainly trying to regain favour, attributes his banishment to *carmen et error* (a poem and a mistake). At least one element of his crime seems to have been the licentious tone of the *Ars Amatoria*, all copies of which were removed from public libraries; he may also have been implicated in an adultery scandal involving the emperor's granddaughter. Following the spread of Christianity, the pagan literature of antiquity became a frequent object of expurgation and suppression, while works by Plato, Virgil, and even Ovid himself were (along with Hebrew scriptures) reinterpreted as allegorical anticipations of Christianity. More recently, in the 19th and 20th centuries, unexpurgated editions of certain Greek and Latin works viewed as licentious, especially Aristophanes' comic play *Lysistrata* and the *Satyricon* by Petronius, were regularly seized as obscene material in the US and the UK, often in opulent bibliophile re-editions, along with such Renaissance standbys as Rabelais, Boccaccio's *Decameron*, and Marguerite de Navarre's *Heptameron*.

2 Ecclesiastical censorship

During the Middle Ages, MSS were mostly copied out by monks and chiefly confined to devotional works (*see* 5). Control of the production and dissemination of books was therefore for the most part under direct control of the Church, the censor's job to read and correct the work of scribes. This did not, of course, prevent some theological approaches from being deemed unacceptable by ecclesiastical authorities. In 1120, for instance, Peter Abelard's *Theologia 'summi boni'* was found to be heretical by the Synod of Soissons and the book was burned in public. Once the printing press and movable type became widespread, the possibilities for dissemination of unorthodox ideas naturally aroused concern in the Church, leading to the establishment of the *Index Librorum Prohibitorum*. The first edition of this list was published in 1559, at the behest of Pope Paul IV. A more comprehensive *Index*, backed by the doctrinal weight of the Council of Trent, followed in 1564 and served as the basis of subsequent listings. The *Index* itself was eventually suppressed in 1966, by which time its identification of works forbidden to Catholics carried mostly symbolic weight, rather than the full force of censorship that had marked its beginnings. Its final version featured some 4,000 works dating from the late 16th century to the 1950s, written in Latin, Greek, Italian, French, English, German, Spanish, Portuguese, Dutch, and Hebrew. Consisting for the most part of theological treatises, it also included, in addition to the usual suspects such as Voltaire and Rousseau (39 and 5 titles, respectively): Spinoza, Descartes, Diderot and d'Alembert's *Encyclopédie*, Kant, John Stuart Mill, and Edward Gibbon's *Decline and Fall of the Roman Empire*. Also featured are some perhaps more surprising choices, such as Samuel Richardson's *Pamela*, Laurence Sterne's *Sentimental Journey*, Hippolyte Taine's *Histoire de la littérature anglaise*, and Pierre Larousse's *Grand dictionnaire universel du XIXe siècle*. Authors whose *opera omnia* were forbidden include Benedetto Croce, Anatole France, Thomas Hobbes, David Hume, Maurice Maeterlinck, and Émile Zola; for others, *omnes fabulae amatoriae* are cited, for example D'Annunzio, Dumas (both *père* and *fils*), George Sand, Stendhal, and Eugène Sue. Balzac is present for his early corpus published under the pseudonym Horace de Saint-Aubain; Flaubert's *Madame Bovary* and *Salammbô* appear, but not his other works, while his now-forgotten friend Ernest Feydeau is singled out for his works; Victor Hugo is represented by *Notre-Dame de Paris* and *Les Misérables*. The list features relatively few 20th-century works—although the writings of Jean-Paul Sartre and André Gide were added in 1948 and 1952, respectively—but includes many 19th-century French novels, which the Anglophone press as well as the Vatican long held up as epitomizing subversive indecency. One of the last authors to be added to the *Index* was Simone de Beauvoir, whose *The Mandarins* and *The Second Sex* were prohibited by the Vatican in 1956.

3 From church to government censorship

The development of religious censorship was directly linked to the invention of movable type, and by the end of the 15th century papal authority decreed that all books should be submitted for approval before publication. Canon law provided for the two basic types of censorship: a-priori scrutiny of works pre-publication, and a-posteriori condemnation of published works. Throughout the early modern era, European governments employed both means of suppressing books, with the state often working in conjunction with the Church in Catholic countries. A-priori vetting was instituted by governments across Europe during this period, with particular vigour in Italy and Germany. Religious censorship varied from one country to the next, with France tending to be suspicious of papal decrees, for instance, whereas in Spain the Inquisition controlled the circulation of books from the 1480s into the early 19th century. In 1521, François I declared that all theological works were to be submitted for a-priori authorization to the University of Paris, and a further ordinance of 1566 stated that no new book was to be published in France without an official seal of approval. The eventual development of copyright may be traced in some respects to these forms of censorship. In England, pre-publication licensing was required from 1538; the Stationers' Company was incorporated by royal warrant in 1557, and the 1662 Licensing Act, enforced by this guild, was enacted 'for preventing the frequent Abuses in printing seditious treasonable and unlicensed Bookes and Pamphlets and for regulating of Printing and Printing Presses'. In 1641, Parliament abolished the Court of Star Chamber, and John Milton published his *Areopagitica* in 1644 as a (vain) plea for greater freedom of the press. The Licensing Act was finally allowed to lapse in 1695, and was not subsequently renewed.

Despite the end of the licensing system in England, the 18th century saw frequent prosecutions of authors, printers, and booksellers, in Britain as on the Continent. Many of the great works of French Enlightenment literature as it has been handed down to us, including some of the major works of Voltaire and Rousseau, were able to circulate only in clandestine form during the 18th century— a thriving international illicit book trade characterizes this period. The best known of the royal censors under Louis XVI, Malesherbes, regarded the *philosophes* with a relatively indulgent eye, and even wrote a tempered argument for freedom of expression, *Mémoire sur la liberté de la presse* (1790) (after which he was guillotined for his defence of the king before the Convention). Throughout Europe before the 19th century, censorship, in both a-priori and a-posteriori forms, was directed mainly towards political and religious offences.

4 Pornography and obscenity

The word 'pornography' was coined towards the end of the 18th century, meaning literally 'prostitute writing'; it was at the time mainly used for works whose salacious character tended to be masked by sociological enquiry into the lives and working conditions of prostitutes. (The French writer Restif de la Bretonne wrote such works under the pseudonym 'le Pornographe'.) In England, the category of obscene libel was little used before the 19th century, the vast majority of prosecutions being reserved for seditious and blasphemous libel. There were, however, some notorious exceptions. Editions of works attributed to John Wilmot, earl of Rochester (e.g. *Sodom: or, The Quintessence of Debauchery*, 1685) and to the late-Renaissance Italian author Pietro Aretino, such as *Sonnetti lussoriosi* with its salacious illustrations, dating from 1527, occasioned repeated obscenity prosecutions. In Catholic countries, the celibacy of the clergy provided an irresistible target for writers who, especially in France in the late 17th century, produced many works neatly combining blasphemy with what would later come to be called pornography. A number of these books, especially Michel Millot's *L'Escole des filles* (1655), Nicolas Chorier's *L'Académie des dames* (1680, a Latin version having appeared some twenty years earlier), and Jean Barrin's *Vénus dans le cloître, ou la religieuse en chemise* (1683), were quickly translated into English and became the subject of frequent criminal prosecutions in England and elsewhere. Despite—and also, obviously, because of—their clandestine nature, such works received a great deal of attention. In his diary in 1668, for instance, Pepys recounts his purchase, 'for information's sake', of a plain-bound copy of *L'Escole des filles* which he duly burns after reading the 'mighty lewd book'. The reading habits of Richardson's heroine in *Pamela* (1740–1) include only pious and edifying works, whereas Shamela's library in Henry Fielding's 1741 parody prominently features a copy of *Venus in the Cloister*, along with 'Rochester's poems'; nonetheless, it was Richardson's novel which figured on the Vatican's *Index*. John Cleland's *Memoirs of a Woman of Pleasure*, generally known as *Fanny Hill*, originally published in 1749, became perhaps the most often-censored book in English, capping its career with a 1966 US Supreme Court case. Although its initial appearance had resulted in warrants for the arrest of its author, publisher, and printer, the majority of proceedings against purveyors of the novel, pornographic in every sense of the term, took place long after its author's death.

5 Bowdlerization and its legacies

At the end of the 18th century in England, with governmental fear of spreading revolutionary fervour, Thomas Paine was the author whose works, specifically *Rights of Man* and *The Age of Reason*, printers and booksellers were most often prosecuted for disseminating, on the grounds of seditious libel and blasphemous libel respectively. By the beginning of the 19th century, pre-publication vetting of works by governmental bodies—censorship in the strictest sense of the term—had been abolished in many countries, leading to repeated declarations of complete freedom of the press by successive regimes, which has never, however, meant post-publication impunity. As Sir William Blackstone wrote in his 1769 *Commentaries on the Laws of England*, 'The Liberty of the Press is indeed essential to the nature of a free State; but this consists in laying no *previous* restraints upon publications, and not in freedom from censure for criminal matter when published' (Blackstone, 151).

The 19th century turned its attention from blasphemy and sedition to obscenity and indecency, terms with ever-widening application and which tended to be deployed with deliberate vagueness. Women, children, and the increasingly literate working classes—servants in particular—were seen as being in need of protection from literary corruption. In addition to obscenity prosecutions, this period was marked by the publication of expurgated versions of classic texts dating from less fastidious periods, for family consumption. This process continues to be known as Bowdlerization after its most famous practitioner, the Rev. Thomas Bowdler, who explains in the preface to his 1818 *Family Shakespeare* that his intention is 'to exclude from this publication whatever is unfit to be read aloud by a gentleman to a company of ladies', or a father to his family, without having to worry about 'words or expressions which are of such a nature as to raise a blush on the cheek of modesty'. Several plays proved impossible to expurgate adequately, however, with the result that Bowdler was forced to omit *Measure for Measure*, *2 Henry IV*, and *Othello*, about which he wrote, 'the subject is unfortunately little suited to family reading'. His final, posthumously published effort was an expurgated version of Gibbon's monumental *Decline and Fall of the Roman Empire*, the original edition of which (1776–89) had elicited controversy for what were perceived as attacks on Christianity, and in which passages depicting the Empress Theodora's wilder moments had been written in Latin—the six-volume work remained a mainstay of the *Index Librorum Prohibitorum*. Even before Bowdler began his expurgation campaign, Charles and Mary Lamb had already produced their *Tales from Shakespeare* for children (including decorous accounts of *Measure for Measure* and even *Othello*) in 1807. The 1830s saw publication of a multi-volume *Family Classical Library*, following Bowdler's example and featuring 'those Authors, whose works may with propriety be read *by the youth of both sexes*'.

The proliferation of volumes of tales from the Bible during the 19th century may also be seen as part of the same effort to provide palatable versions of works at once indispensible and problematic. The Bible presented a particular problem, since it could obviously be neither ignored nor suppressed, and yet a large number of the stories in the Old Testament contained material guaranteed to raise many a blush on the cheek of modesty. Moreover, direct allusions to the indecency of Scripture were themselves liable to accusations of blasphemy, as Matthew Gregory Lewis discovered in 1796 when he published *The Monk*. This novel in the tradition of Horace Walpole's and Ann

Radcliffe's popular gothic tales featured such extravagantly sadistic variations on the genre (rapes in burial vaults, etc.) that it earned accolades from the marquis de Sade himself, who deemed it 'supérieur, sous tous les rapports, aux bizarres élans de la brillante imagination de Radcliffe' (Sade, 42). Contemporary commentators, including Samuel Taylor Coleridge (who, along with Jeremy Bentham, had supported freedom of expression in debates on the subject), agreed that the novel was obscene and unfit for public consumption. What earned their particular opprobrium, as well as threats of libel proceedings, was not so much the book's obscenity per se as the blasphemous story of a mother who allows her daughter to read the Bible only in an expurgated version she herself prepares, because of her conviction that 'Many of the narratives can only tend to excite ideas the worst calculated for a female breast: every thing is called plainly by its name; and the annals of a brothel would scarcely furnish a greater choice of indecent expressions' (Lewis, 206–7). Lewis was able to avoid prosecution only by quickly producing an expurgated version of his own book.

In 1822, a man named Humphrey Boyle, shop assistant to Richard Carlile, who was himself in prison for publishing Paine's *The Age of Reason* and other deist works, was tried for selling a pamphlet alleging the Bible to be an obscene libel. During the trial he insisted on reading aloud passages from Scripture, starting with the story of Lot and his daughters; this was greeted with outrage and the courtroom was hastily cleared of ladies and boys. Despite (or, again, perhaps precisely because of) this convincing demonstration of his point, Boyle was sent to prison for eighteen months on a charge of blasphemous libel.

Many of the obscenity prosecutions from the early 19th century well into the 20th were instigated by various anti-vice organizations, starting with the Proclamation Society established by William Wilberforce in 1787, which succeeded the Society for the Reformation of Manners and was the first such body to be specifically concerned with the suppression of obscene and profane literature. The Society for the Suppression of Vice, founded in 1802, became the best known and most effective of these organizations, along with the National Vigilance Association which superseded it in 1885. At its inception, the Society for the Suppression of Vice, which became known as the 'Vice Society', was dedicated to a variety of laudable aims, including the prevention of cruelty to animals and the punishment of those who seduced women and children into prostitution, but it was not long before the pursuit of literary indecency had all but eclipsed its other causes. The Vice Society movement became powerful towards the end of the 19th century in the US, most notably with the New York Society for the Suppression of Vice, founded by Anthony Comstock in 1873, and, five years later, with the New England Watch and Ward Society. France had its own late 19th-century crusader against literary indecency, the Senator René Béranger, derisively known as *Père-la-pudeur*, as well as its own vice society, the Cartel d'Action Sociale et Morale, founded by Protestants in the 1880s and active in highly publicized prosecutions involving works by Henry Miller and

Boris Vian in the 1940s, thanks to the efforts of its indefatigable president Daniel Parker.

6 The Obscene Publications Act and modern literature

The mid-19th century inaugurated an era of obscenity proceedings involving hundreds of books, many of them destined to become classics. In England, the Lord Chief Justice, Lord Campbell, concerned about what he memorably termed 'a sale of poison more deadly than prussic acid, strychnine, or arsenic', that is, the thriving London pornography trade then centred in Holywell Street, proposed what became the Obscene Publications Act of 1857. It made the sale of obscene materials a statutory offence, and was, Lord Campbell explained, 'intended to apply exclusively to works written for the single purpose of corrupting the morals of youth and of a nature calculated to shock the common feelings of decency in any well-regulated mind' (Thomas, 261–3). In order to drive home this point, he brandished a copy of Alexandre Dumas's *La Dame aux camélias* and assured his peers that, however repulsive he might find such works, they could only be stopped by the force of public opinion, whereas the target of his measure was gross pornography only. Lord Campbell's emphatically stated intentions notwithstanding, the Obscene Publications Act ended up being used over the course of the following century precisely against a variety of books along the lines of Dumas *fils*'s novel about a whore with a heart of gold.

In 1868, Lord Chief Justice Cockburn, Campbell's successor, in a case called Regina vs Hicklin concerning the appeal of a ruling about an anti-Catholic pamphlet, established a de facto definition of obscenity. Lord Cockburn declared: 'I think the test of obscenity is this, whether the tendency of the matter charged as obscenity is to deprave and corrupt those whose minds are open to such immoral influences and into whose hands a publication of this sort may fall' (Thomas, 264). This standard, which became known as the Hicklin rule or test, remained the extremely broad criterion according to which allegations of obscenity were judged until it was finally superseded by the Revised Obscene Publications Act of 1959. The 1959 Act did not, in fact, substantially change the basic idea of obscenity as that which depraves and corrupts, so much as make it less absolute, decreeing that works must be taken as a whole rather than inculpated on the basis of passages taken out of context, and allowing for mitigating factors such as historical interest and literary merit.

Meanwhile, in France under Napoleon III, during the same year in which the Obscene Publications Act was passed in England, two of the foundational works of modern literature were put on trial. *Madame Bovary*, Flaubert's first published novel, had appeared in six instalments in the *Revue de Paris* in the autumn of 1856. Maxime du Camp, one of the journal's editors and a friend of the author, insisted on making cuts in the work, including the suppression of an entire scene, in an attempt to ward off censorship. Du Camp's actions not only enraged Flaubert, but attracted the very governmental attention he had sought to avoid. The author, a *Revue* editor, and the printer were all charged with offences against morals and religion (*outrage à la morale publique et religieuse et aux bonnes moeurs*), under a law created in 1819 during the Restoration.

The Imperial Prosecutor, Ernest Pinard, argued that the novel contained no admirable characters, and presented no moral compass to guide the reader; because it was likely to be read by girls and women, what he characterized as its denigration of marriage and its glorification of adultery were destined to corrupt the morals of its vulnerable audience. Flaubert's lawyer, also assuming that literature must be morally edifying, argued that the book was in fact highly moral, demonstrating as it did the very dangers alluded to by his opponent. The tribunal returned a verdict of 'acquittal with blame', suggesting that the defence of depicting vice in the service of virtue—the standard argument of similarly accused authors, at least since Boccaccio in the epilogue to his *Decameron*—was not sufficient, but that while the author was not entirely innocent, he was not entirely guilty either. The novel was then published in volume form, with the excised passages restored.

A few months later, the same Imperial Prosecutor argued against Charles Baudelaire for his collection of poems *Les Fleurs du mal*. With the (somewhat irrelevant) exception of light song lyrics by the Bonapartist Pierre-Jean Béranger, prosecuted under the Restoration, legal proceedings against lyric poetry were all but unheard of in France (whereas in England Shelley's *Queen Mab* was repeatedly prosecuted, and Swinburne's *Poems and Ballads* was withdrawn by its initial publisher for fear of prosecution). As in Flaubert's case, the accusations against Baudelaire included offences against religion, but the prosecution concentrated most heavily on his volume's alleged indecency. Six poems, all of which featured female sexuality, were found to be in violation of the 1819 law; the publisher had to cut them out of remaining copies, in what Baudelaire described as a surgical operation.

In 1866 he and his publisher Auguste Poulet-Malassis, who had moved to Brussels to escape repeated prosecution, brought out *Les Épaves*, which included the six condemned poems as well as a number of new pieces, with a striking allegorical frontispiece by Félicien Rops; this volume occasioned further legal proceedings when it was imported into France. Baudelaire spent the rest of his life producing new poems, often more violently sinister than those that had been removed, for new editions of the *Fleurs du mal*. Although the collection, including the six offending poems, began to be republished during World War I, the condemnation was not formally overturned by a French court until 1949.

Both Flaubert's novel and Baudelaire's poems had been accused of excessive realism, casualties of the larger conflict raging throughout the 19th century and well into the 20th. This continuing debate, fuelled by rapidly increasing literacy rates and the rise of the novel as a largely feminine genre, centred on the question of whether the proper aim of art is to provide uplifting moral guidance by example or, rather, to depict the realities of life, however sordid. The

Freighted with allegorical significance, Félicien Rops' 1866 etching for the frontispiece to Charles Baudelaire's *Les Épaves* ('scraps' or 'jetsam') provided some indication of the forbidden fruits that lay within the limited edition. Musée Rops

art-for-art's-sake aestheticism which had filtered into French literary circles through German Romanticism was not an admissible line of defence in the courtroom, nor was the notion that artistic merit might be seen as a mitigating factor, and indeed this was not taken seriously until the mid-20th century, when obscenity statutes in various countries were finally modified accordingly. In *Le Rouge et le noir* (1830), Stendhal had likened the novel to a mirror carried along a road, noting that the mud and detritus thus exposed to view should be blamed not on the mirror but on those responsible for upkeep of the road. This perspective was not shared by the authorities in any country much before the 1950s, and the French realist novel in particular was the subject of countless obscenity proceedings on both sides of the Channel throughout the rest of the 19th century. In the late 1880s, an elderly London bookseller named Henry Vizetelly was repeatedly tried, and eventually jailed, for publishing obscene libel in the form of some of the first translations of a number of French realist novels, including an expurgated translation of Zola's *La Terre*. Indeed Zola's name came to be a byword for obscenity in England, supplanting that of Rabelais and taking its place alongside that of Sade.

The 1920s and 1930s saw a great number of obscenity proceedings in England, many of them incited by the National Vigilance Association (an organization which was also adept at inciting publishers to withdraw books in fear of punitive lawsuits), and helped along by the moral zeal of Sir William Joynson-Hicks, known as 'Jix', who served as Home Secretary 1924–8. This period was marked most notoriously by the publication of James Joyce's *Ulysses* in France (1922) and D. H. Lawrence's *Lady Chatterley's Lover* in Italy (1928), as well as the trial of Radclyffe Hall's *Well of Loneliness* in England (1928). The *Well of Loneliness* trial was notable for the magistrate's refusal to hear testimony from the many prominent literary figures who had turned out to support the cause of what Virginia Woolf referred to in her diary (31 August 1928) as Hall's 'dull, meritorious book'. It also provided an exemplary demonstration of how literary censorship is meant to work. When Hall's publisher lost his case and the book was suppressed in England, no further novels sympathetic to the cause of homosexuality appeared for several decades (meanwhile, its American publisher, also prosecuted, won on appeal and the book circulated freely in the US). As E. M. Forster had discerned when he refused to attempt publication of *Maurice*, written in 1914, during his lifetime, the world would not be ready to accept stories of non-pathological, non-suicidal homosexuals for a very long time (*Maurice* was finally published almost 60 years later, after Forster's death in 1970).

The *Well of Loneliness* and almost all other books banned in England were immediately reissued in France, notably by Jack Kahane's Obelisk Press, later taken over by his son Maurice Girodias who also founded the Olympia Press, which also published a heady mixture of written-to-order pornography and serious fiction unpublishable in English-speaking countries. (In 1955, Girodias was to bring out Vladimir Nabokov's *Lolita*, causing an international controversy and paving the way for its publication in the US and the UK three years later.) During the 1920s and 1930s, writers such as Lawrence, Joyce, and Henry Miller turned directly to publishers like Kahane on the Continent for the books they knew could not openly be printed in England or America, causing something akin to a reprise of the 18th-century international trade in underground books. *Ulysses*, however, was published in America after eleven years of clandestine importation of the original edition, and Random House won its case thanks to Judge John M. Woolsey's memorable finding that Joyce's novel was not an example of 'dirt for dirt's sake', its sexual content reassuringly 'emetic' rather than aphrodisiac. Judge Woolsey's exoneration of *Ulysses* coincided with the repeal of Prohibition pronounced during the same week in December 1933, which allowed for the somewhat misleading conclusion that Americans were now definitively free both to read and to drink as they saw fit. While Joyce's difficult novel was able to circulate freely in America and England from the mid-1930s, both *Lady Chatterley's Lover*, with its frequent and detailed sex scenes and liberal use of four-letter 'Anglo-Saxon' terms, and *Tropic of Cancer*, with its exuberant stream-of-consciousness vulgarity and similarly ubiquitous profanity, continued to be banned in English-speaking countries for some 30 years.

Once the 1959 Revised Obscene Publications Act was passed, allowing for expert testimony and the consideration of literary and other forms of merit, the practice of censorship began to change quickly. The immediate effect of the revised law was that Penguin Books took the chance of publishing what had already become Lawrence's most famous novel, occasioning the most publicized literary trial since the *The Well of Loneliness* debacle in 1928. Regina vs Penguin Books was an unequal match, during which the defence called 35 expert witnesses, including members of the clergy, prominent writers, critics, medical experts, and educators, while the prosecution called no witnesses, conceding from the start that Lawrence was a great writer and the novel held some merit. The jury quickly returned a verdict of not guilty, eliciting applause in the courtroom and ushering in a new era, as Philip Larkin observed in his famous poem 'Annus Mirabilis': 'Sexual intercourse began/In nineteen sixty-three... Between the end of the *Chatterley* ban/And the Beatles' first LP'.

The era of routine literary censorship in the West came to an end during the 1960s, a period which coincided not only with societal upheaval but, it should be noted, with the rise of television and the gradual eclipsing of literature as a major social force. In the US, *Tropic of Cancer* was published by Grove Press in 1961, leading to a host of local prosecutions and, eventually, a Supreme Court case in 1964 which found that the work had sufficient merit to be published. Remarkably enough, two of the last major literary obscenity cases in the West involved books dating from the 18th century. In 1966 the US Supreme Court heard a final *Fanny Hill* case, making Cleland's woman of pleasure safe at last for public consumption. In France, after some 150 years of clandestine circulation in the country and elsewhere, an enterprising young publisher brought out the complete works of the marquis de Sade in 26 volumes, in a long-term project begun in 1947. Despite a court ruling that several of the books were indeed obscene, the publisher did not withdraw them, and Sade's works are now widely available in various 'classic' editions including Gallimard's venerable Pléiade collection, printed on bible paper.

....

BIBLIOGRAPHY

W. Blackstone, *Commentaries on the Laws of England: A Facsimile of the First Edition of 1765–1769* (1979)

P. S. Boyer, *Purity in Print*, 2e (2002)

A. Craig, *The Banned Books of England and Other Countries* (1937; repr. 1962)

R. Darnton, *The Forbidden Best-Sellers of Pre-Revolutionary France* (1996)

E. de Grazia, *Girls Lean Back Everywhere: The Law of Obscenity and the Assault on Genius* (1992)

Index on Censorship, www.indexoncensorship.org, consulted Mar. 2013

W. Kendrick, *The Secret Museum: Pornography in Modern Culture* (1987)

E. Ladenson, *Dirt for Art's Sake: Books on Trial from Madame Bovary to Lolita* (2007)

M. G. Lewis, *The Monk* (1907)

S. Marcus, *The Other Victorians* (1966)

C. Rembar, *The End of Obscenity* (1968)

D. A. F. Sade, *Les Crimes de l'amour*, ed. M. Delon (1987)

D. Thomas, *A Long Time Burning* (1969)

14

Concepts of Intellectual Property and Copyright

ADAM D. MOORE

Intellectual property is generally characterized as non-physical property that is the product of cognitive processes and whose value is based upon some idea or collection of ideas. Typically, rights do not surround the abstract non-physical entity; rather, intellectual property rights surround the control of physical manifestations or expressions. Intellectual property protects rights to ideas by protecting rights to produce and control physical instantiations of those ideas.

Legal protections for intellectual property have a rich history that stretches back to ancient Greece and further. As different legal systems matured in their protection of intellectual works, there was a growing refinement in the understanding of what it was that was being protected. From the ancients to the Enlightenment, several strands of moral justification for intellectual property have been offered: namely, personality-based, utilitarian, and Lockean. This essay will discuss all of these topics, focusing on Anglo-American and European legal and moral conceptions of intellectual property.

1 History of intellectual property and copyright

One of the first known references to intellectual property protection dates from 500 BC, when chefs in the Greek colony of Sybaris were granted year-long monopolies for creating particular culinary delights. In this case, caterers or cooks who invented new recipes were given exclusive rights to produce the dish for one year, the purpose of this grant being to encourage others to be inventive. There are at least three other notable references to intellectual property in ancient times—these cases are cited in Bruce Bugbee's formidable work *Genesis of American Patent and Copyright Law*. In the first case, Vitruvius is said to have revealed intellectual property theft during a literary contest in Alexandria. While serving as judge in the contest, Vitruvius exposed the false poets who were then tried, convicted, and disgraced for stealing the words and phrases of others.

The second and third cases also come from Roman times (1st century AD). Although there is no known Roman law protecting intellectual property, Roman jurists did discuss the different ownership interests associated with an intellectual work and how the work was codified—for example, the ownership of a painting and the ownership of a table upon which the painting appears. The Roman epigrammatist Martial also makes reference to literary piracy; in this case, Fidentinus is caught reciting the works of Martial without citing the source:

> Rumor asserts, Fidentinus, that you recite my works to the crowd, just as if they were your own. If you wish they should be called mine, I will send you the poems gratis; if you wish them to be called yours, buy my disclaimer of them. (Martial, *Epigrams*, cited in Bugbee, 167, n.15)

These examples are generally thought to be atypical; as far as is known, there were few institutions or conventions of intellectual property protection in ancient Greece or Rome. From Roman times to the birth of the Florentine Republic, however, there were many franchises, privileges, and royal favours granted surrounding the rights to intellectual works. Bugbee distinguishes between franchises or royal favours and systems of intellectual property in the following way: franchises and royal favours restrict access to intellectual works already in the public domain; thus these decrees take something from the people. The protection afforded to an inventor or author of a new original work by a system of intellectual property, on the other hand, deprives the public of nothing that existed prior to the act of invention.

One of the first statutes that protected authors' rights was issued by the Republic of Florence on 19 June 1421, to Filippo Brunelleschi, the famous architect. This statute recognized the rights of authors and inventors to the products of their intellectual efforts; it also built in an incentive mechanism for the creators of intellectual property that became a prominent feature of Anglo-American intellectual property protection. For several reasons, including Guild influence, the Florentine statute of 1421 issued only the single patent to Brunelleschi. The basis of the first lasting patent institution of intellectual property protection is found in a 1474 statute of the Venetian Republic. This statute appeared 150 years before the Statute of Monopolies (1624), the first statutory expression of English patent law and, hence, widely regarded as the beginning of a statutorily regulated intellectual property regime in that country. The Statute of Monopolies, in many respects, was a forebear of the copyright legislation passed by the English Parliament 85 years later: the rights of inventors were recognized, an incentive mechanism was included, compensation for infringement was established, and a term limit on inventors' rights was imposed.

In 1486 in Venice, however, Marcantonio Sabellico was granted what might be considered the first copyright for his history of the Venetian Republic, *Decades Rerum Venetarum*. Sabellico was given exclusive control over the publication of this book, and anyone found to violate this award was to be fined 500 ducats. Peter of Ravenna was awarded a similar grant for his *Phoenix* in 1491.

In France, a system of privileges was adopted as early as 1498, when rights to produce copies were granted for new books, maps, translations, and works of art, although these privileges were not necessarily offered to the original authors or producers of the work in question. Grants to authors and artists for writings, musical compositions, and designs were also found in Germany as early as 1511. Throughout the 15th and 16th centuries, there were various levels of protection for literary works in Europe—most enacted at the local level. By the mid-1500s, the arrival of printing in hundreds of cities across Europe (*see* **6**) created local incentives for safeguarding the ownership of copies, but most forms of protection during this period were less than true copyrights as the notion of intellectual property today would be understood.

Instead, local guilds most often assumed responsibility for protecting their members' properties by policing against piracy, both within and beyond their own ranks. In England, the Stationers' Company, formally incorporated by royal charter in 1557, was active in this regard, especially in London. The pre-publication censorship of print in England—from the reign of Henry VIII to the Printing Act of 1662 (13 & 14 Car. II c. 33), also known as the Licensing Act—proved highly useful in establishing legitimate ownership of copies, because the Stationers' Company regarded the registration of a copy in the Company's Register as conferring legal entitlement to publish that copy.

Following the definitive lapse of the Licensing Act in 1695, An Act for the Encouragement of Learning (also known as The Statute of Anne or The Copyright Act) was passed by Parliament in 1709 to take effect in 1710. Widely considered to be the first statute of modern copyright, it begins:

> Whereas Printers, Booksellers, and other Persons have of late frequently taken the Liberty of Printing, Reprinting, and Publishing...Books, and other Writings, without the Consent of the Authors or Proprietors...to their very great Detriment, and too often to the Ruin of them and their Families: For Preventing therefore such Practices for the future, and for the Encouragement of Learned Men to Compose and Write useful Books; May it please Your Majesty, that it may be Enacted...(8 Anne c. 19)

The law gave protection to the owner of a 'copy', originally the author, but typically the bookseller, by granting fourteen-year copyrights, with a fourteen-year renewal possible if the author was still alive. Works already in print were entitled to protection for 21 years, with no possibility of renewal.

In the landmark case Millar vs Taylor (1769), the inherent rights of copy owners to control their copies, independent of statute or law, was affirmed. Instead of viewing literary property as mere legal rights created by a legislative body or sovereign, Millar affirmed the perpetual moral and common law rights of authors, who might, in turn, assign some of these rights to another party through the sale of their copies. Five years later, the Millar decision was overruled in Donaldson vs Becket (1774). In Donaldson, the court held that the Statute of Anne superseded the inherent rights of authors and copy-owning booksellers. Protections and remedies were limited to what was prescribed by positive law. Nevertheless, the practice of recognizing the rights of authors, as such, had begun. Other European countries, including Belgium, The Netherlands, Italy, and Switzerland, followed the example set by England. Various more recent international treaties, such as the Berne Convention (1886) and the Trade-Related Aspects of Intellectual Property Rights (TRIPS) Agreement (1994), have expanded the geographical scope of intellectual property protection to include most of the globe.

2 The domain of copyright and literary property

At the most practical level, contemporary understandings of literary property are largely delineated in Anglo-American copyright law, in the law of ideas, and in the moral rights granted to authors and inventors within the continental European doctrine. Although these legal institutions do not constitute an exhaustive list, they nonetheless provide a rich starting point for understanding literary property. Accordingly, we shall take up each of these three areas in turn.

2.1 Copyright

The domain of US copyright protection is original works of authorship fixed in any tangible medium of expression (17 U.S.C. § 102 (1988)). Works that may be copyrighted include literary, musical, artistic, photographic, architectural, and cinematographic works; maps; and computer software. For something to be protected, it must be 'original'—the work must be the author's own production; it cannot be the result of copying (Bleistein vs Donaldson Lithographing Co., 188 U.S. 239 (1903)). A further requirement that limits the domain of what can be copyrighted is that the medium of expression must be 'non-utilitarian' or 'non-functional' in nature. Utilitarian products, or products that are useful for work, fall, if they fall anywhere, within the domain of patents. Finally, rights only extend over the actual concrete expression and the derivatives of the expression—not to the abstract ideas themselves. For example, Einstein's Theory of Relativity, as expressed in various articles and publications, is not protected under copyright law. Someone else may read these publications and express the theory in other words and even receive a copyright for that particular expression. Some may find this troubling, but such rights are outside the domain of copyright law. The individual who copies abstract theories and expresses them in other words may be guilty of plagiarism, but cannot be held liable for copyright infringement.

There are five exclusive rights that copyright owners enjoy, and three major restrictions on those rights. The five rights are: the right to reproduce the work; the right to adapt it or derive other works from it; the right to distribute copies of the work; the right to display the work publicly; and the right to perform it publicly. Under US copyright law, each of these rights may be individually sold, separately from the others, by the copyright owner. All five rights lapse after the lifetime of the author plus 70 years—or, in the case of works for hire, the term is set at 95 years from publication or 120 years from creation, whichever comes first. Aside from limited duration (17 U.S.C. § 302), the rules of fair use (17 U.S.C. § 107) and first sale (17 U.S.C. § 109(a)) also restrict the rights of copyright owners. Although the notion of 'fair use' is notoriously hard to define, it is a generally recognized principle of Anglo-American copyright law that it allows anyone to make limited use of another's copyrighted work for such purposes as criticism, comment, news reporting, teaching, scholarship, and research. The 'first sale' rule prevents a copyright holder who has sold copies of a protected work from later interfering with the subsequent sale of those copies. In brief, the owners of copies can do what they like with their property, short of violating the copyrights previously mentioned.

2.2 Protecting mere ideas

Beyond the regime of copyright, there is a substantial set of case law that allows individuals to protect mere ideas as personal property. This system of property is typically called the 'law of ideas'. A highly publicized case in this area is Buchwald vs Paramount Pictures (13 U.S.P.Q. 2d BNA 1497 (Cal. Super. Ct. 1990)), concerning the Eddie Murphy movie *Coming to America* (1988). The law of ideas is typically applied in cases such as this one, where individuals produce ideas and submit them to corporations expecting to be compensated. In certain instances, when these ideas are used by the corporation (or anyone) without authorization, compensation may be required. Such was the court's finding in the Buchwald case, and Paramount Pictures was required to compensate Buchwald for providing the idea that subsequently became a film. Before concluding that an author has property rights to the idea(s), courts require the idea(s) to be novel or original (Murray vs National Broadcasting Co. Inc., 844 U.S. F.2d 988 (2nd Cir. 1988)) and concrete (Hamilton Nat'l Bank vs Belt 210 F.2d 706 (D.C. Cir. 1953)). Compensation is offered only in cases of misappropriation (Sellers vs American Broadcasting Co. 668 F.2d 1207 (11th Cir. 1982)).

2.3 Droits morals: continental systems of intellectual property

Article 6bis of the Berne Convention articulates the notion of 'moral rights' that are included in continental European intellectual property law:

> Independently of the author's economic rights, and even after the transfer of the said rights, the author shall have the right to claim authorship of the work and to object to any distortion, mutilation or other modification of, or other derogatory action in relation to, the said work, which would be prejudicial to his honor or reputation. (Article 6bis, Berne Convention)

The doctrine protects the personal rights of creators, as distinguished from their economic rights, and is generally known in France as '*droits morals*' or 'moral rights'. These moral rights consist of: the right to create and to publish a work in any form desired; the creator's right to claim the authorship of his work; the right to prevent any deformation, mutilation, or other modification thereof; the right to withdraw and destroy the work; the prohibition against excessive criticism; and the prohibition against all other injuries to the creator's personality. Much of this doctrine has been incorporated in the Berne Convention; as Martin Roeder, commenting on the doctrine of the creator's moral rights, affirms:

> When an artist creates, be he an author, a painter, a sculptor, an architect or a musician, he does more than bring into the world a unique object having only exploitive possibilities; he projects into the world part of his personality and subjects it to the ravages of public use. There are possibilities of injury to the creator other than merely economic ones; these the copyright statute does not protect. (Roeder, 557)

It should be noted that granting moral rights of this sort goes beyond a mere expansion of the rights conferred on property holders within the Anglo-American tradition. Although many of the moral rights listed above could be incorporated into copyright and patent law, the overall content of these moral rights suggests a new domain of intellectual property protection. This new domain of moral rights stands outside the economic- and utilitarian-based rights granted within the Anglo-American tradition. This is to say that, independent of social and economic utility—and sometimes in conflict with it—authors and inventors have rights to control the products of their intellectual efforts.

Arguments for intellectual property rights have generally taken one of three forms. Personality theorists maintain that intellectual property is an extension of individual personality. Utilitarians ground intellectual property rights in social progress and incentives to innovate. Lockeans argue that rights are justified in relation to labour and merit. Although each of these strands of justification has its weaknesses, there are also strengths unique to each.

3 Personality-based justifications of intellectual property

Personality theorists such as Hegel maintain that individuals have moral claims to their own talents, feelings, character traits, and experiences. In this sense, individuals are self-owners. Control over physical and intellectual objects is essential for self-actualization—by expanding our selves outward beyond our own minds and mixing these selves with tangible and intangible items, we both define ourselves and obtain control over our goals and projects. In his *Elements of the Philosophy of Right* (1821), Hegel argued that the external actualization of the human will requires property. Property rights are important in two ways according to this view. First, by controlling and manipulating objects, both tangible and intangible, our will takes form in the world, and we obtain a measure of freedom. Individuals may use physical and intellectual property rights, for example, to shield their private lives from public scrutiny and to further their own goals and projects. Secondly, in some cases our personality becomes fused with an object—thus moral claims to control feelings, character traits, and experiences may be expanded to both tangible works, such as a novel or screenplay, and to intangible works, such as a new, more cost-effective method for producing a commodity, or even the imagined plot for a new novel or screenplay.

3.1 Problems of personality-based justifications of intellectual property

There are at least four problems with this view. First, it is not clear that we own our feelings, character traits, and experiences. Although it is true that we have possession of these things or that they are a part of each of us, an argument is needed to establish the relevant moral claims. Secondly, even if it could be established that individuals own or have moral claims to their personality, it does not automatically follow that such claims are expanded when personalities are expressed in tangible or intangible works. Perhaps this sort of expression— one where the author's personality becomes a part of an artefact—should be viewed as an abandonment of personality. Moreover, misrepresenting an intellectual work (assuming there are no moral rights to these expressions) might change the perception of an author's personality, but it would not in fact change his or her personality. Thirdly, assuming that moral claims to personality could be expanded to tangible or intangible items, an argument justifying property rights would still be needed. Personality-based moral claims may warrant nothing more than use rights or prohibitions against alteration. Finally, there are many intellectual innovations in which there is no evidence of a creator's personality—a list of customers or a new safety-pin design, for example. Given these challenges, personality-based theories may not provide a strong moral foundation for legal systems of intellectual property.

3.2 The personality theorist's rejoinder

Even if the force of these objections is acknowledged, there does seem to be something intuitively appealing about personality-based theories of intellectual property rights. Suppose, for example, that Mr Friday buys a book—the only copy of a long-lost Crusoe original. Friday takes the book home and alters some of the text. The additions are so clever that Friday decides to display the altered work in a library exhibition. There are at least two ethical worries to consider in this case. First, the alterations by Friday may cause unjustified economic damage to Crusoe. Secondly, and independent of the economic considerations, Friday's actions may damage Crusoe's reputation. The integrity of the book has been violated without the consent of the author, perhaps causing long-term damage to his reputation and his standing in the community. If these claims are sensible, then it appears that the existence of personality-based moral 'strings' attaching to certain intellectual works is being acknowledged. By producing intellectual works, authors and inventors put themselves on display, so to speak, and incur certain risks. Intellectual property rights afford authors and inventors a measure of control over this risk.

To put the point in a different way, it is the moral claims attached to personality, reputation, and the physical embodiments of these individual goods that justify legal rules covering damage to reputation and certain sorts of economic losses. Moreover, personality-based theories of intellectual property often appeal to other moral considerations. Hegel's personality-based justification of intellectual property rights included an incentive-based component as well. Perhaps the best way to protect these intuitively attractive personality-based claims to intangible works is to adopt a more comprehensive system designed to promote progress and social utility.

4 The utilitarian incentives-based argument for intellectual property

In terms of 'justification', modern Anglo-American systems of intellectual property are typically modelled as incentive-based and utilitarian (Machlup; Hettinger; Moore, 2001). On this view, a necessary condition for promoting the creation of valuable intellectual works is granting limited rights of ownership to authors and inventors. In the absence of certain guarantees, authors and inventors might not engage in producing intellectual property. Thus control is granted to authors and inventors of intellectual property, because granting such control provides incentives necessary for social progress. Although success is not ensured by granting these rights, failure is inevitable if those who incur no investment costs can seize and reproduce the intellectual effort of others. Adopting systems of protection such as copyrights, patents, and trade secrets may aid in an optimal number of intellectual works being produced, and a corresponding optimal degree of social utility. Coupled with the theoretical claim that society ought to maximize social utility, this is a simple yet powerful argument for the protection of intellectual property rights.

4.1 Problems of the utilitarian incentives-based argument

Given that this argument rests on providing incentives, a critique would need to illustrate better ways, or equally good ways, of stimulating production without granting private property rights to authors and inventors. It would, for example, be better to establish equally powerful incentives for the production of intellectual property that did not also require initial restricted use guaranteed by rights (Machlup; Moore, 2001). One alternative to granting intellectual property rights to inventors as incentive is government support of intellectual labour (Hettinger). Such a measure could take the form of government-funded research projects, with the results immediately becoming public property. The question becomes: can government support of intellectual labour provide sufficient incentive to authors and inventors so that an equal or greater quantity and quality of intellectual products are created compared to what is produced by conferring limited property rights? Better results might also be had if fewer intellectual works, but of a higher quality, were distributed to more people.

Unlike the current government-supported system of intellectual property rights, reward models may be able to avoid the problems of allowing monopoly control and restricting access, and at the same time provide incentives to innovate. In this model, innovators would still labour sedulously, seeking to profit from their work, and governments would not have to decide which projects to fund, nor determine appropriate rewards before a work's 'social value' was known. Funds necessary to pay the rewards could be drawn from taxes or from collecting percentages of the profits of these innovations. Reward models may also avoid the disadvantages of monopoly pricing, and obstructions to further adaptation and innovation.

Finally, empirical questions about the costs and benefits of copyright, patent, and trade secret protection are notoriously difficult to determine. Economists who have considered the question indicate that either such determinations are perilously inexact, or that other arrangements would be better (Machlup). If we cannot appeal to the progress-enhancing features of intellectual property protection, then the utilitarian can hardly appeal to such progress as justification.

4.2 The utilitarian rejoinder

The utilitarian may well agree with many of these criticisms and still maintain that intellectual property rights, in some form, are justified—a system of protection is better than nothing at all. Putting aside the last criticism, all of the worries surrounding the incentive-based approach appear to focus on problems of implementation. A government could tinker with its system of intellectual property, cutting back on some legal protections and strengthening others (Croskery). Perhaps it could include more personality-based restrictions on what can be done with an intangible work after the first sale, limit the term of copyrights, patents, and trade secrets to something more reasonable, and find ways to embrace technologies that promote access while protecting incentives to innovate. The utilitarian might also point to the costs of changing the current system of intellectual property.

5 Lockean justifications of intellectual property

A final strategy for justifying intellectual property rights begins with the claim that individuals are entitled to control the fruits of their labour (Hettinger; Himma, 2006; Moore, 2001). Labouring, producing, thinking, and persevering are voluntary pursuits, and individuals who engage in these activities are entitled to what they produce. Subject to certain restrictions, rights are generated when individuals mix their labour with an unowned object. The intuition is that the person who clears unowned land, cultivates crops, builds a house, creates a new invention, or writes a book obtains property rights by engaging in these activities.

A more formal version of Locke's famous argument is that individuals own their own bodies and labour—i.e. they are self-owners. When an individual labours on an unowned object, the labour becomes infused in the object, and for the most part, the labour and the object cannot be separated. It follows that once a person's labour is joined with an unowned object, assuming that individuals exclusively own their bodies and their labour, rights to control are generated. Writing a book is a good case in point; the author takes an unowned, commonly held entity—language—and applies labour to it, thus producing a sequence of words and ideas that the author justly owns and has the right to control or to sell (say, to a publisher). The central Lockean idea is that there is an expansion of rights: individuals each own their labour and when that labour is mixed with objects in the commons (i.e. the natural and cultural resources available to all, or the vast majority, of people in society), individual rights are expanded to include these goods.

5.1 Problems of Lockean justifications

Locke's argument is not without difficulties. Waldron argued that the idea of mixing one's labour is incoherent—actions cannot be mixed with objects. In *Qu'est-ce que la propriété?* (1840), Proudhon argued that if labour was important, the second labour on an object should ground a property right in an object as reliably as the first labour. Nozick asked why labour-mixing generated property rights rather than a loss of labour. Waldron has argued that mixing one's labour with an unowned object should yield more limited rights than rights of full ownership. Finally, if the skills, tools, and inventions used in labouring are social products, then perhaps individual claims to title have been undermined (Hettinger).

5.2 The Lockean rejoinder

Among defenders of Lockean-based arguments for private property, these challenges have not gone unnoticed (Moore, 2001, 2012). Rather than rehearsing the points and counterpoints, a modified version of the Lockean argument might be considered—one that does not so easily fall prey to the objections mentioned above.

Let us imagine that, after years of effort, Smith creates a highly original and entertaining work of fiction. Would anyone argue that Smith does not have at least some minimal moral claim to control the story that he has created? Suppose that Jones reads a selected extract from Smith's story and desires to purchase access to the entire work. Is there anything morally dubious about an agreement between them that grants Jones a limited right to have access to Smith's story, provided that Jones does not publish it himself? It must be remembered that Jones can decide without compulsion that he does not wish to agree to Smith's terms, and that Jones is free to read something else, or to create his own literary work. Arguably, part of the moral weightiness of the agreement between Smith and Jones relies on the fact that Smith holds legitimate title to the story because it is the outcome of his labour. The evident legitimacy of such moral claims and contracts between two parties known to each other may provide the foundations for legal protections of intellectual works on a broader scale (Moore, 2012).

6 General critiques of intellectual property and copyright

Putting aside the strands of argument that seek to justify moral claims to intangible works and the particular problems that opponents of these views offer in reply, there are several more general critiques of the rights to control intellectual property to consider.

6.1 Information wants to be free

Many have argued that the non-rivalrous nature of intellectual works—that is, that the use of a work by one individual does not limit the use of that same work by others—grounds a prima facie case against rights to restrict access. Because intellectual works are not typically consumed by their use and can be used by many individuals concurrently (making a copy does not deprive anyone of personal possessions), there is a strong case against moral and legal intellectual property rights (Jefferson, 3, art. 1, sect. 8, clause 8, document 12; Hettinger). One reason for the widespread pirating of intellectual works is that many people think restricting access to these works is unjustified.

The weak point in this argument is the assumption that the non-rivalrous nature of intellectual works justifies a presumption in favour of access. Yet sensitive personal information, like a diary, provides a case in point. Moore argues that just because this information can be used and consumed by many individuals concurrently, it is false to claim that a prima facie moral claim to maximal access is established. This argument applies as well to violent films, pornography, information related to national security, personal financial information, and private thoughts; each is non-rivalrous, but this fact does not by itself generate prima facie moral claims for access and use. Moreover, it is by no means clear that unauthorized copying does no harm to the owner, even in cases where the individual who has appropriated the owner's property without tendering compensation would not have purchased a copy legitimately—i.e. for the required fee—and thus is not denying the owner economic compensation that would otherwise have been received. Unauthorized copying creates risks that owners must bear without their consent (Moore, 2012).

6.2 The free speech argument against intellectual property

According to some, protecting or creating intellectual property rights is inconsistent with our commitment to freedom of thought and speech (Hettinger; Waldron). Hettinger argues that intellectual property 'restricts methods of acquiring ideas (as do trade secrets), it restricts the use of ideas (as do patents), and it restricts the expression of ideas (as do copyrights)—restrictions undesirable for a number of reasons' (Hettinger, 35).

Two sorts of reply have been offered to this kind of worry. The first notes that it is the incentives found in providing limited protection that foster the creation and dissemination of information—a system of intellectual property protection may cause restricted access in the short run, but over time, the commonly held supply of thought and expression available to the public at large is enhanced. Secondly, it is not at all clear that free speech as a social value is so presumptively weighty a good, or so determinative a principle, that it nearly always trumps other competing values (Moore, 2012).

6.3 The social nature of information argument

A growing school of thought maintains that information is a social product, and that enforcing access restrictions unduly benefits authors and inventors, effectively diminishing the common good of society at large. Because individuals are raised in societies that endow them with knowledge which these individuals then use to create intellectual works of all kinds, the building blocks of intellectual works—knowledge—should be understood as a social product. Hence, individuals should not have exclusive and perpetual ownership of the works that they create, because these works are built upon society's shared knowledge. Allowing rights to intellectual works would be similar to granting ownership to the individual who placed the last brick in a publicly financed dam. The dam is a social product, built up by the efforts of hundreds; knowledge, upon which all intellectual works are built, is built up in a similar fashion.

Many of those in the modern copyleft or creative commons movement echo these sentiments. In the US, Creative Commons, a non-profit organization (founded in 2001) at the vanguard of the copyleft movement, seeks to increase the number and range of works that are freely available to others, so that those works may be legally shared and used for individual enjoyment and the enlargement of the public good. Creative Commons licences, issued free of charge to the public, replace the standard 'all rights reserved' assertion of copyright management with a 'some rights reserved' declaration, thereby allowing each creator of a work to yield some rights to the public without compensation, while retaining others. This attempt at establishing a more reasonable and flexible copyright regime that more equitably balances the creator's rights with the common good, has, despite some criticisms, gained considerable momentum; in 2011, more than 100 Creative Commons affiliates were at work in more than 70 legal jurisdictions from Argentina to Vietnam.

Beyond challenging whether the notion of 'society' employed in this line of reasoning is clear enough to carry the weight that the argument demands, critics have questioned the view that societies can be *owed* something, or that they can *own* or *deserve* something (Nozick; Moore, 2012). In 1855, Lysander Spooner wrote:

> *What* rights society has, in ideas, which they did not produce, and have never purchased, it would probably be very difficult to define; and equally difficult to explain *how* society became possessed of those rights. It certainly requires something more than assertion, to prove that by simply coming to a knowledge of certain ideas—the products of individual labor—society acquires any valid title to them, or, consequently, any *rights* in them. (Spooner, 3.103)

Finally, even if a defender of this view can justify societal ownership of general pools of knowledge and information, it could be argued that the use of this collective wisdom has already been rewarded by paying for education and the like (Moore, 2001, 2012).

7 Conclusion

Protecting the intellectual and literary creations of authors and inventors has a rich history stretching back to the Middle Ages and earlier. In most cases, sociopolitical contexts and economic forces active at the time played an important role in shaping these early rules. Many of these same forces drive the current debate. Content providers want protection as a matter of right and economics. Content consumers, on the other hand, desire access. The proliferation of digital technology has highlighted the tensions between advocates on both sides. The history, arguments, and challenges surrounding the current debates concerning copyright and intellectual property may help to adapt existing institutions, or to create new intellectual property regimes, that most appropriately balance the competing interests of content creators and consumers.

BIBLIOGRAPHY

B. Bugbee, *Genesis of American Patent and Copyright Law* (1967)

P. Croskery, 'Institutional Utilitarianism and Intellectual Property', *The Chicago-Kent Law Review*, 68 (1993), 631–57

E. C. Hettinger, 'Justifying Intellectual Property', *Philosophy & Public Affairs*, 18 (1989), 31–52

K. E. Himma, 'Justifying Intellectual Property Protection: Why the Interests of Content-Creators Usually Wins Over Everyone Else's', in *Information Technology and Social Justice*, ed. E. Rooksby (2006)

—— 'The Justification of Legal Protection of Intellectual Rights', *San Diego Law Review*, 50 (2013)

—— 'Toward a Lockean Moral Justification of Legal Protection of Intellectual Property', *San Diego Law Review*, 49 (2012), 1105–81

J. Hughes, 'The Philosophy of Intellectual Property', *Georgetown Law Journal*, 77 (1997) 88–9, 287–366

T. Jefferson, *The Writings*, ed. A. A. Lipscomb and A. E. Bergh (20 vols, 1904–5)

L. Lessig, *Free Culture* (2004)

F. Machlup, *Production and Distribution of Knowledge in the United States* (1962)

R. Merges, *Justifying Intellectual Property* (2011)

A. D. Moore, *Intellectual Property and Information Control* (2001; repr. 2004)

—— 'A Lockean Theory of Intellectual Property Revisited', *San Diego Law Review*, 49 (2012) 1069–103

R. Nozick, *Anarchy, State, and Utopia* (1974)

Primary Sources on Copyright (1450–1900), http://copy.law.cam.ac.uk/cam/index.php, consulted Mar. 2013

P.-J. Proudhon, *Qu'est-ce que la propriété?* (1840)

M. Roeder, 'The Doctrine of Moral Right: A Study in the Law of Artists, Authors and Creators', *Harvard Law Review*, 53 (1939–40), 554–78

N. Shaler, *Thoughts on the Nature of Intellectual Property and its Importance to the State* (1878)

L. Spooner, *The Law of Intellectual Property*, in *The Collected Works of Lysander Spooner*, ed. C. Shively (6 vols, 1971)

J. Waldron, 'From Authors to Copiers: Individual Rights and Social Values in Intellectual Property', *Chicago-Kent Law Review*, 68 (1992–3), 841–87

15

The Manuscript after the Coming of Print

HAROLD LOVE

1 Introduction

A century ago there were still many inky-fingered individuals, who in Britain were called clerks, whose job was to prepare handwritten records—usually in large volumes called ledgers—of transactions in business, the law, and science. Their forerunners had been active since the first stylus incised the first clay tablet. Much of their work, like that of Melville's Bartleby, Gogol's Akaky Akakevich, and Flaubert's Bouvard and Pécuchet, was the soul-destroying creation of duplicate records. In Shaw's *Misalliance*, a copy-clerk is driven to attempted murder by the monotony and pointlessness of his job. Most inscriptional tasks have now moved via typewriting to the computer. Handwriting today is used to create evanescent records such as shopping lists, lecture notes, or postcards; to fill in crosswords and sudokus; or to complete questionnaires. Even the personal letter is most likely to pass by email. Only the sometimes threatened demise of the keyboard seems likely to modify this situation.

Certainly, there cannot be many important cultural records in the Western world that are conveyed solely by means of handwriting. Under Soviet rule, *samizdat* copies of dissident texts were circulated in typed copies for works in Russian and in handwritten copies for works in Western languages—this was not a question of choice, but dictated by the limitations for that purpose of the Cyrillic typewriter. In China and Japan, where writing systems are much less amenable to keyboarding, the handwritten exemplar retains its prominence, though its multiplication is likely to be performed by the photocopier. Thus that miracle of technology, the Japanese automatic pencil with extrudable eraser, used with the same upwards and downwards alternation as the ancient stylus writing on wax tablets. But a century and a half ago, work by a handful of major writers and thinkers was still being circulated in MS as a matter of preference. The verse of Emily Dickinson and Gerard Manley Hopkins received nearly all its circulation in this way, as did the lucubrations of many humbler authors who sought no audience beyond immediate friends and family, or whose themes were unacceptable to the press. The Brontës' juvenilia are a far from unique example of a family writing exclusively for its own enjoyment. The handwritten work was still prized as a gift to a friend or close relative. Travellers would send letter-diaries to their loved ones with a list of others to whom they were to be circulated, who might in turn make personal copies. Someone requiring an out-of-print book, especially one from an earlier century, would see nothing unusual about making a handwritten copy: many antiquarian records passed in this way from scholar to scholar. At universities, well-off students would buy MS books summarizing the lectures of their professors. Poorer students earned money by inscribing these. And then as now, there were calligraphers, creators of writing as a thing of beauty.

2 From the Enlightenment to the 16th century

A century earlier still, the Europe of the Enlightenment witnessed the closing stages of a tradition of professional MS book production that had been maintained unbroken since the Middle Ages. In countries subject to draconian state censorship, philosophically heterodox and politically oppositional texts were still copied for sale by scribes working for booksellers. While surreptitious publication through the press was certainly common, the handwritten copy of a suspect work retained a cachet that made it a desirable form of luxury product. It was also written to order with sale assured. Music circulated principally through MS, or through a mixed mode in which partbooks might need to be consolidated into a handwritten score, or a published score supplemented by handwritten parts. J. S. Bach in his lifetime published only a relatively small body of music, chiefly for the keyboard. His liturgical and instrumental music with few exceptions remained in MS; and yet much of the latter was widely circulated through copies and copies of copies. Work by his more popular contemporary, Telemann, travelled in MS to all corners of Europe. In early 18th-century Britain, there was a covert market in sumptuously bound folio and large-quarto volumes of MS satires and lampoons, some with their contents arranged in alphabetical order so as to constitute a kind of secret history of the nation since the Restoration of Charles II. Country parsons might purchase collections of MS sermons to see them through the year; lawyers might buy professionally written collections of writs, precedents, or reports.

Moving even further backwards, to the early 17th century, we find scribal production still competitive with the press whenever the ability to create large numbers of copies in a short time was not an issue, or when there were obstacles to the printing of a given work. In Britain, one of these obstacles was the reluctance of many authors, especially women, to have their works appear as articles of sale—what Saunders christened 'the stigma of print', though unwillingness gave little protection when booksellers were free to print any fortuitously encountered MS without permission. Yet, Donne was able to restrict the printing of his poems during a lifetime in which they circulated freely in MS, often in large collections. Carew's and, later, Rochester's verse first appeared in print immediately after their deaths, in pirated editions based on already current MS anthologies. Sidney may never have seen any of his writings in printed form. Writers would woo patrons with works in MS, which were seen to possess a greater exclusivity than print: Shakespeare's Sonnets give every appearance of such an origin.

At a time when Parliament jealously guarded the privacy of its deliberations, there was a roaring trade in sessional diaries and the texts of speeches—either noted down, reconstructed from memory by fellow members, or provided by the members themselves to entrepreneurial scriveners. From the same agencies came a wide variety of political commentaries of a kind often unwelcome to the Crown. The tracts of the great antiquary Sir Robert Cotton fall into this category. John Selden, too, circulated a number of his writings only through the scribal medium. After his death, his free-speaking *Table Talk*, compiled by his chaplain Richard Milward, was reproduced for sale by a scriptorium, not being judged fit for the press until after the Glorious Revolution. One body of early 17th-century material of this kind is linked by the easily recognizable hand of Beal's 'Feathery Scribe'. Even plays, when withheld from the press by acting companies, might be acquired in MS, Middleton's *A Game at Chess* being a famous example. Ralph Crane, a scribe with links to Shakespeare's company, left several play transcripts apparently made for readers.

All these British practices had their counterparts in continental Europe. In addition, there was a lively international exchange of scientific, alchemical, and astrological MSS in Latin. Alchemy, as an occult science, was particularly hostile to the press. Latin epigrams originally exchanged between the statues of Pasquino and Marforio in Rome, or celebrating or burlesqueing Louis XIV's rebuilding of the Louvre, travelled both singly and in bulk along mazelike channels of erudite correspondence. Religious persecution encouraged organized scribal circulation of oppositional writings—in England, Catholic and Puritan, in France, Huguenot and Jansenist. In Spain and Italy, where the Inquisition reigned and suspicious books were confiscated from travellers, what penetration there was of Protestant, heterodox, and freethinking texts was largely through MS. To move even further into the past is to arrive at the Reformation and then to the founding decades of print in the late 15th century, prior to which all texts circulated in either oral or handwritten form. For monks and nuns of that transitional age, copying remained a regular duty prescribed under the rule of St Benedict. For many scholars and churchmen of a humanist persuasion, the beauty of a fine hand and the exclusiveness of a handwritten Horace or book of hours outweighed considerations of price and convenience. In other fields of text production, there is a surprising (but on reflection perfectly predictable) confluence of the media. David McKitterick has pointed to the prevalence of printed books with handwritten elements and of handwritten works containing printed components. Nor were printed books and MSS rigidly shelved apart from each other as happens in today's libraries. Instead, they might well be bound together into larger assemblages, now usually dismembered. It was also common for printed books to be heavily annotated and interleaved by their owners. The note-taking scholars studied by Blair worked in order to return print to MS in the form of vast accumulations of excerpts. Manuals were available on how information was to be assigned to and retrieved from these.

3 Production and dissemination

Reversing the direction of this passage through time, the process by which the handwritten word perpetuated its ancient traditions in the face of competition from the press needs to be considered. It did this chiefly by specialization. Once a bible, a Latin grammar, or the text of a royal proclamation could be reproduced more cheaply and in a shorter time by a printer than by a scribe, there was little point in trying to compete in that field; but in the case of a smaller text, these advantages were not so pronounced and might be offset by others. A scribe could make several copies of a 1,000-word document during the time taken up by the cumbersome print processes of casting off, setting, proofreading, presswork, and collating; in cases where fewer than 50 copies were required, print publication might well prove wasteful. (Even today, as Amory has observed, a large part of print production remains unsold, and much that is sold unread.) A handwritten copy could also claim a greater exclusivity, which often led to it being more carefully read and preserved. It was a much better way of reaching a narrow niche audience. Scribal technology was cheap and portable.

A bundle of quills, a supply of paper and ink, sufficient light, and a table was all that was required to set such work in motion. The time of a clerk came cheaply enough. A team of scribes, gathered together in a scriptorium or contracting individually to write batches for a bookseller or scrivener, was also capable of quite high levels of output when that was necessary. Even for scribal editions of 100 or more documented in the 17th century for newsletters, the economic advantages were probably pretty equally balanced with those of print. Organized production of this kind minimized the textual deterioration that is the bane of seriatim copying while permitting changes to be made at any time to a master copy—a luxury denied the press. Serial publication could also be a way of exploiting otherwise underused labour. Legal offices employed large numbers of clerks whose regular duties would peak when courts were in session and decline during vacations. To take on copying for booksellers offered a solution. Professional scribal services could also be engaged by an aspiring but print-shy author—although this could prove dangerous, since the scribe or scrivener by retaining an extra copy was in a position to commence production on his own behalf. It was usually safer for authors wishing to distribute a text in MS to entrust production to a secretary, family member, or reliable amanuensis—or to copy it themselves—though many were reluctant to have their words appear in their own, recognizable handwriting.

The other mode by which texts proliferated in MS was through copies successively made by readers. It is astounding with what rapidity and in what quantities this method could spread a short work. The fact that each was in effect an 'edition' of one could lead, as mentioned earlier, to rapid textual change. Yet there were also disciplines of textual recuperation (not least emendation), well known to experienced transcribers, and for a popular piece there might well be more than one copy available for consultation. The fragile 'separates', often transported in pockets, in which these texts passed suffered an enormous loss rate, since apart from simple wear and tear, paper was in constant demand for domestic uses. Instead, what has generally survived are copies made from these separates in personal miscellanies and often misnamed commonplace books. The surviving MS heritage of a really popular short piece is usually a mixture of both reader-inscribed and professionally written separates (when any survive at all), copies from personal miscellanies, and copies in scribal anthologies compiled for sale.

Once in the hands of the professionals, a piece might first be gathered into a 'linked group' or relatively small sub-collection that then became absorbed into larger and larger collections whose relationships can be established by a study of the order of their contents. In many cases, the larger collections reveal an aspiration to comprehensive record-keeping of an antiquarian kind. English examples include the MS records (published by Notestein and Relf) of the proceedings of the 1628 Parliament and the collections (mentioned earlier) written c.1700 of political satires and libertine lampoons dating from 1660, some of which extend to over 600 pages and have their contents dated and in chronological order. These large and expensive volumes were intended for the homes of wealthy buyers, where their chances of survival were greatly enhanced, though the 9th earl of Derby did hide a volume of potentially treasonable satires in a chimney, where it was only found when the house was demolished. What began as topical, quickly became historical and was respected as such in a medium that antiquarians were often more at home with than they were with the press.

By the early 18th century, the professional arm of scribal publication still enjoyed the advantages of efficiency over very short runs, rapid response time, flexibility in its handling of texts, freedom from censorship, and controlled availability. These were enough to keep a small cadre of booksellers' scribes at work for some decades (just how long would need to be determined by a systematic survey of surviving MSS that has yet to be attempted). MSS of this kind were certainly expensive, but so too were printed books. Yet professional chirographical bookmaking had undoubtedly retreated to an assemblage of niche markets that was to be further eroded by advances in printing—particularly the arrival of the steam press in the early 19th century and a concurrent sharp decline in the cost of printing paper (*see* **10, 11**)—and then by the transfer of many scribal functions from the male clerk to the female typist. Music copyists survived longer, but even they nowadays are to be found at a computer keyboard. The theatre prompter continued with his copying of promptbooks and actors' 'sides' until well into the 19th century, by which time, in Britain, most of the standard repertoire could be acquired in cheap multiple sets from various booksellers such as Lacy's, French's, and Dicks's. What continued, as already mentioned, was the preparation and circulation of texts by their authors in small handwritten editions or single copies circulated under supervision. A vast amount of writing between the 18th and 20th centuries still reached its readers in exactly this way, sometimes because it was not acceptable to the press, but more often because that was the way authors or transcribers preferred it.

One not atypical career was that of Roger North (1653–1734), a prolific author of biographies and works on music, whose magnum opus is his vast historiographical *Examen*. North continually returned to and revised his writings and held many in multiple copies; yet, he seems to have had no desire to see them in print. Those that did appear were published in edited form by family members after his death. This may have been what he wanted, but it makes more sense to see that family as his intended audience, or to classify him as an author who wrote primarily for himself with no particular desire for readers, except just possibly a generalized 'posterity'. Around 1703 Celia Fiennes opened her account of her travels: 'As this was never designed, soe not likely to fall into the hands of any but my near relations, there needs not much to be said to excuse or recommend it' (Fiennes, 1). Newton's alchemical and theological writings were preserved for private use in careful MS copies: only his scientific ones went to the press. Perhaps the purest examples of composing for personal gratification are writers of diaries. In many recorded cases, the diary, however laboriously compiled, is destroyed before death, having always been intended for the writer alone. There are also cases of writing consciously performed for ritual sacrifice. At Spenser's funeral, fellow poets threw elegies into the grave, together with the quills with which they had been written. D. G. Rossetti buried MS poems with his wife, Elizabeth Siddal, but later thought better of it and had them retrieved.

Moreover, it should not be forgotten that for many writers the preferred form of publication was performance. This was the norm in the ancient world, when the public reading was the means by which most work became known, and only a small proportion was ever available in published form. In the theatre, this has always been the case. Shakespeare is often held to have had little concern for any written dissemination of his plays, though this view has recently been challenged. Clearly, there have always been authors in other genres who preferred the classical tradition. Kafka saw hardly any of his work in print during his lifetime, but he enjoyed reading it aloud to his circle of close friends. Kafka's first printed texts were largely compiled by one of those friends (Max Brod) from his disorganized MSS after his death. Members of the clergy have always devoted a great deal of their energy to the writing of sermons, often on a weekly basis. Although those by recognized stars of the pulpit—or those produced for some shining occasion—might then be printed or recorded in shorthand, and some might be lent or sold on to colleagues, the vast bulk were discarded, if not immediately after delivery, at least on the retirement or death of their authors. Most academic and public lectures suffered the same fate. In some cases those of great philosophers, such as Wittgenstein, or writers, such as Coleridge, and scientists are known only from the notes taken by their students or members of their audience.

Other writers were keen to be read, but wanted to choose by whom and under what circumstances—what Ezell has conceptualized for early modern Britain as 'social authorship'. This would include the more literary stratum of letter writers, such as Horace Walpole. He cultivated correspondence as an art form intended for preservation, but always directed to particular recipients and their immediate circles, with whom they would be assumed to share the pleasures of the epistolary text. It is most unlikely that Walpole foresaw the accumulative passion of Wilmarth S. Lewis. Hopkins, mentioned earlier, circulated new work through the post to a small circle of friends who were mostly fellow poets. For him, as for many other non-professional writers of his and earlier times, authorship was a vital means of intellectual and aesthetic exchange. Thomas Campion's Latin epigrams contain several pieces chiding fellow neo-Latin poets for refusing to circulate their verse except to intimates. In the 18th century, the works of his distinguished successor Anthony Alsop had to be retrieved after his death from copies sent to friends.

For some writers, the management and circulation of their MSS required them to acquire the skills of both the librarian and the publisher. Bach must have filled a good-sized room of his home in Leipzig with the scores and parts for his cantatas alone. In other cases, one detects an almost fetishistic devotion to the handwritten word, often evident in the care involved in its presentation and preservation. Emily Dickinson is one famous example of a hoarder and decorator of her MSS. Other writers surprise by the care taken with their MSS, even when intended for the press. Kipling would write in a special Indian ink on a sheet of high-quality paper and tie the sheets together with a ribbon. It was clearly the initial inscription, not the printed outcome, that represented for him the perfect embodiment of the imagined word.

4 Conclusion

The transition of textual work from the handwritten word to various forms of mechanical and electronic reproduction did not, in many cases, make much difference either to the attitudes of the worker or to how the product was used by its purchaser; but there are ways in which the effect of the 'meaningful surface' of MSS differs from that created by typography or electronography. The most ambitious attempt to theorize those differences is that of the Jesuit scholar

Walter J. Ong, for whom the chirographic text embodies a presence-rich 'secondary orality', anchoring it firmly in the world of human interaction. In contrast, the printed text reduces language to a 'thing-like status' and living knowledge to 'cold non-human facts' in a way that is inherently authoritarian. Certainly, there are degrees of overlap in both cases. A perfectly formed Renaissance italic hand or a flawlessly rounded 19th-century copperplate achieves a suppression of individuality far greater than that of the freewheeling typography of Sir Roger L'Estrange's late 17th-century *Observator*s with their idiosyncratic intermingling of capitals, italic, and black letter and free use of brackets and of capitalization for emphasis. Yet Ong's general point is a fair one. There is something remote and impersonal about a well-constructed typographic page that is the price it exacts for permitting us to read it at high speed. Few reading experiences can, on the other hand, be more intense than that of a great poem or musical work written out in the script of its creator. The late Patrick O'Brian's last, uncompleted novel was brought out in an edition with a reproduction of the MS and a type transcript on facing pages. The MS is a corrected working draft, not a fair copy, but instinct with the human face of authorship. The corresponding typography, by contrast, is sober and inexpressive, but of course much clearer—and one suspects that most readers of the volume quickly revert to it once they become engrossed in the narrative.

BIBLIOGRAPHY

H. Amory, 'The Trout and the Milk: An Ethnobibliographical Talk', *HLB* NS 7 (1996), 50–65

P. Beal, *Index of English Literary Manuscripts*, vol. 1: *1450–1625* (2 parts); vol. 2: *1625–1700* (2 parts) (1980–93)

—— *In Praise of Scribes* (1998)

A. Blair, 'Note Taking as an Art of Transmission', *Critical Inquiry*, 31 (2004–5), 85–107

S. Colclough, '"A Grey Goose Quill and an Album": The Manuscript Book and Text Transmission 1820–1850', in *Owners, Annotators and the Signs of Reading*, ed. R. Myers *et al.* (2005)

M. Ezell, *Social Authorship and the Advent of Print* (1999)

C. Fiennes, *The Journeys*, ed. C. Morris (1947)

E. Havens, *Commonplace Books* (2001)

H. Love, *Scribal Publication in Seventeenth-Century England* (1993)

—— 'Oral and Scribal Texts in Early Modern England', in *CHBB* 4

A. F. Marotti, *Manuscript, Print and the English Renaissance Lyric* (1995)

D. F. McKenzie, 'Speech–manuscript–print', in *New Directions in Textual Studies*, ed. D. Oliphant and R. Bradford (1990)

D. McKitterick, *Print, Manuscript and the Search for Order, 1450–1830* (2003)

W. Notestein and F. H. Relf, *Commons Debates for 1629* (1921)

P. O'Brian, *The Final Unfinished Voyage of Jack Aubrey* (2004)

W. J. Ong, SJ, *Orality and Literacy* (1982)

J. W. Saunders, '"The Stigma of Print": A Note on the Social Bases of Tudor Poetry', *Essays in Criticism*, 1 (1951), 139–64

H. R. Woudhuysen, *Sir Philip Sidney and the Circulation of Manuscripts, 1558–1640* (1996)

16

Printed Ephemera

MICHAEL HARRIS

1 Introduction

The category of ephemera forms an elusive, sometimes contentious, element in the output of print. The aim of this essay is not to attempt to describe everything that can be identified as ephemera, but rather to trace the category's porous boundaries and, in particular, to suggest how different forms have, over time, changed in their relationship to the book. Ephemera challenges definition, and studies have tended to locate the material at the fringes of everyday life. The general sense of marginality is reinforced by the flux of advertisements and notices, concerned for example with pizza delivery and weight-loss clinics, which clog up the postal services. Indeed, whatever the extent of the electronic revolution (*see* **21**), it has not undermined, and in many respects has multiplied, the variety of fugitive or ephemeral print.

Implicit in the definition of printed ephemera as marginal is the notion of a great sea of flimsy print continuously washing up against the sturdy breakwaters of the book—that the book and the printed non-book are two aspects of the same thing. In this notion, the book, as the codex, identified by its binding, its bulk, and its capacity and manufacture for indefinite preservation, is a distinct entity. It is a pragmatic view that has clear benefits to the individuals and institutions seeking to construct a library and preserve its contents. One of the problems with the dialectic between ephemera and books, however, is that the book, though obviously distinct on the shelf, is itself an inherently insecure component of print culture. The book as a form is usually placed at the top of a hierarchy of print, standing at the pinnacle of a pyramid of output that broadens out to the flat base of printed ephemera. However, this seems less than realistic, given the ephemeral nature of many books; moreover, their own boundaries with other forms are often insecure, blurring and fading over time. Within print culture, there has been a continuous process of reassessment, which (mainly through collection) has brought a range of non-book material into a new conceptual alignment with the book and suggested the limitations of the current use of the term 'ephemera'.

2 Some definitions

As currently formulated, ephemera are usually identified in terms of their physical characteristics. Their primary form is as a single piece of paper, although this can be extended to a sheet folded into a limited, but not usually defined, number of pages. However, this is not a hard and fast rule over the historical period of print; telephone directories or railway timetables may also be identified as ephemera in book form on the basis of their content. Typically unbound though often in wrappers, ephemera were usually limited to a day-to-day use and had disposal or destruction as their likely end. This applied particularly to the enormous category of printed advertisements. Even so, the characteristic of disposability has its own problems. Printed ephemera were sometimes produced to be collected and even preserved. This was the case, for example, with cigarette cards as well as with the memorials of such historic events as the battle of Blenheim, the death of Nelson, or the Great Exhibition of 1851. The durability of ephemera through a growing range of individual collections is discussed below.

If the physical characteristics of material lumped under the heading of ephemera are hard to identify, establishing the chronology of ephemeral print's production is equally problematic. Much writing on the subject has emphasized the material's production side. In this context, the business of the jobbing printer and developments in printing and paper technology are crucial (*see* **10, 11**). Both these elements offer a way into the history of the subject and a framework for its analysis; however, they also create a tendency to push the development of forms of ephemeral material into the 19th and 20th centuries, which become, by implication, an age of ephemera. Nobody suggests that such material was not produced before 1800; but the almost total loss of many or most of the early forms—whose rarity is marked by the high commercial value of such items as advertisements for night soil removal—has created some distortion. Similarly, a historical focus on the business organization of printers engaged in the mixed production of books, serials, and jobbing printing has done little, if anything, to augment our understanding of the ephemeral materials themselves.

The modern chronology of the output of ephemeral print must be weighed against the huge scale of material produced across the early modern period. One factor that drove the increase in printed ephemera was the erratic but continuous move from MS to print (*see* **15**). From the early 17th century, serial information,

The spread of ephemera and display types: playbills, posters, and broadsides painted by John Orlando Parry in his *London Street Scene* (1835), also known as *The Posterman*. Courtesy of Alfred Dunhill Museum and Archive

including news, moved from handwritten copies to a printed equivalent. For other kinds of pragmatic material, both freely distributed and paid for, it is extremely difficult to follow the process that changed their character. Advertisements in late 17th-century newspapers indicate that several members of the book trade specialized in the production and supply of printed forms geared to tax collection and other kinds of bureaucratic organization. By 1700, print was the natural medium for handbills and posters, at least in London, and the lines of serial print were beginning to extend across the nation. When Ned Ward visited the Royal Exchange in 1699 during the course of his ramble, he found the pillars and every available wall space covered with posters and advertisements, the bulk probably in printed form. There are no pictorial representations of this scene complete with its burden of fly-posting. In fact, the general exclusion of ephemeral print is a feature of illustrations of London's built environment at this time. Set against this are the views offered in 19th-century prints. In this period, the fascination with the output of the developing technology of print, combined with a growing interest in the lower levels of print culture, supported the production of some striking images depicting the mass of print displayed in public spaces.

Across the entire modern period, a huge and expanding volume of print in all its forms was in circulation. In the attempt to get some sort of bibliographical control over the composition and character of ephemera, scholars have undertaken a process of listing. This has usually been done by constructing sequences made up of main physical forms and of the themes around which ephemeral print has clustered, for example, business, transport, leisure and entertainment, and home life. The *Encyclopedia of Ephemera* originally compiled by Maurice Rickards, and edited and completed by Michael Twyman, offers a long alphabetical list made up of categories and describes, among other items, 'Fly-paper', 'Quack advertising', 'Telephone card', and 'Zoëtrope strip/disc' (an early method of creating the illusion of movement through revolving pictures). If the *Encyclopedia* does not define the field, at least it makes a heroic attempt at laying out an impressive range of representative samples and at providing a useful, inevitably selective, series of bibliographies. An underlying problem with this and alternative listings is that they tend to create an artificial homogeneity in which all the selected non-book materials have an equivalent importance. An alternative approach maintains the interest in form, but focuses on the ways in which the separation of blocks of material has come about, in particular through the process of collection.

In its raw state, printed ephemera can be seen as a huge and alarming heap of materials—the trivial and the profound, the commercial and the exhortatory—jumbled together in the context of the confused variety of everyday life. Supply-side analysis emphasizes this diversity and invariably highlights the technology of production and its relation to what could be done in the printing office. Ephemeral print cannot be defined through the character of the organization or business through which it was produced, however. Any analysis of collecting ephemera, on the other hand, begins with the idea of consumption and indicates the ways in which the conditions for the identification and classification of non-book materials were created. Across the entire period in which the proliferation and diversification of print was taking place, collectors began to offer a gloss on the meanings and uses of an apparently inchoate mass of individual items. Through their intervention, large areas of what is still included with printed ephemera have moved out of the shadowy hinterland of the trivial and disposable to another level where a new set of definitions is required. A few examples follow, each of them having a flexible link to the general category of street literature.

3 Collecting ephemera: ballads, chapbooks, almanacs, and newspapers

The street was and remains one of the most dynamic sites for the dispersal of ephemeral printed products. During the Victorian period, the average metropolitan *flâneur* could expect to be offered dozens of printed items, advertisements, and handbills during a stroll along Oxford Street in London. In the 17th and 18th centuries, huge quantities of handbills—medical, political (in vast numbers during elections), or commercial—were passed around the streets of

London and its suburbs; much of the material was entirely free, and so it remains in the 21st century. The wastage was almost total and the survival of single copies, used as bookmarks or wrapping paper, is almost miraculously unusual. The same can be said of posters, which were once a prominent feature of the urban environment but have since largely disappeared. Even so, some of the materials distributed at street level have survived to become part of the historical printed archive.

All of the street-based material noted above was free and instantly disposable, and hence had an exceedingly short life expectancy. At the same time, within the flow of street-based print was to be found the commercial presence of paid-for material, such as ballads, almanacs, newspapers, and chapbooks; these represented a significant link between the respectable book trade and the popular consumer. Such products satisfy the definitions of ephemerality: their distribution matched the output of handbills in scale and informality, and their survival was just as uncertain. They formed part of the retail process that ran through the street. The presence of this paid-for material and of its hawkers as part of the notorious hyperactivity of the London streets took on a respectable visual dimension through the publication of a series of images representing a cross-section of street traders. From the 1690s, the most frequently reprinted images were those produced by Marcellus Laroon the elder. His lifelike portraits of street dealers, probably from around Covent Garden, published in *The Cryes of the City of London Drawne after the Life* (1687), included some of those whose uncertain livelihood was drawn from the open-air sale of ephemeral forms of print. They included a pair of ballad sellers, an almanac dealer, a newspaper seller and a pedlar whose tray, filled with 'knicknackatories', probably contained a selection of chapbooks. It is this range of generally disposable material that provides the focus of what follows.

Ballads, chapbooks, almanacs, and newspapers were issued under the direction of core members of the book trade working within the orbit of the Stationers' Company. The trade had a presence in the street through the booths and stalls long established in London, while at least some of the hawkers were full or part-time employees of booksellers. Despite these formal arrangements, the products the hawkers sold were, in form and character, intended for the medium of the street, and as such were cheap, short term, and disposable. Though they were produced in very large quantities, their survival was far from assured. Indeed, at the point of purchase and use, it was hard to distinguish them from the other paper items that ebbed and flowed within most urban centres. The question is: how did some components of this material take on an aggregate status over time that has required a different formulation in relation to the book?

The first collectors of ephemeral print were attracted to the street-based, popular character of the material. Individuals—influenced by a variety of cultural and commercial motives—began the process of gathering and preservation, which gradually gave elements of ephemera a place within contemporary private and public collections. Collectors' ideas about popular print were inevitably affected by changing social, political, and economic forces. However, the initial impulse to accumulate and safeguard this material formed part of a more general phenomenon of collecting that, during the 17th century, characterized the activities of the endlessly curious and acquisitive sector of middling society known as virtuosos.

The cultural importance of this amorphous group in the construction of what has been described as a bourgeois public sphere was manifested most fully in the social environment of the coffee house. Such public spaces helped develop the shared interests of its patrons, most notably through serial print, which formed an integral part of coffee house culture. That culture gave rise to the circumstances in which individuals collected and preserved forms of printed material that would otherwise have been destroyed (often by being put to other uses, such as wrapping food or doing service in the lavatory) along with the mass of free promotional material handed about in the street. Collectors in the 17th and 18th centuries created the conditions for an expanded interest in ephemeral print, which is only now moving into the mainstream of respectable scholarship.

Indeed, the act of collecting became a mechanism for repositioning cultural value of the slight and disposable literature of the streets: this is most evident with regard to two popular forms, ballads and chapbooks. Both were produced on a substantial scale at very low cost, and as such might have been thought unlikely to form part of the collecting interests of the book-centred library owner within the social elite. Ballads and chapbooks were published during the 17th century under a monopoly grant by a group of publishers, partners in the Ballad Stock, organized through the Stationers' Company. However, because the grant did not prevent the intervention of others in this profitable and accessible area of the market, the ballad became the focus of long-running commercial struggles. The broadside ballad was printed in black letter on one or both sides of the sheet, usually in double columns, and sold for 1d. Ballad verse, often related to current events and combining information with entertainment, was usually printed under a woodcut pictorial heading. The scale of output was vast: about 3,000 titles were recorded in the Stationers' Register during the 17th century; many were frequently reprinted and press runs were large. At his death in 1664 one publisher, Charles Tias, had about 37,500 ballad sheets at his house and shop on London Bridge. Such materials were eminently disposable. Although, among the lower social levels, their short-term destruction might be delayed because such publications were commonly used for decoration or to teach reading, their ultimate fate was almost certain.

The same might be said of chapbooks, which increased in number over the 17th century and probably overtook ballads in the scale of their distribution. Sold on the street, chapbooks came in a range of formats varying from duodecimos of 4 pages to quartos of 24 or more; the books sold for between 2d. and 6d. Also published by partners in the Ballad Stock and their competitors, chapbooks reached a prodigious level of output. For example, a 1707 inventory of the goods of the publisher Josiah Blare identified his holdings of 31,002 'great and small books', kept in his shop at the sign of the Looking Glass on London Bridge. Blare was one of the group of printers and publishers involved in the chapbook market: the identity of members of the group is often obscure, but they may have numbered around twenty. Their commercial activity suggests the distribution of an enormous volume of material, mostly produced in London and sold throughout the nation by long-distance pedlars, commonly called chapmen, as well as urban hawkers and colporteurs. The chapbook was cheap, ubiquitous, and highly ephemeral. Copies from the 17th and 18th centuries have survived in very small numbers; by the 19th century, the form and its sellers, as recorded by Henry Mayhew, were disappearing as new social and economic conditions overtook the street trade.

A scattering of ballads and chapbooks, along with other kinds of ephemeral print, would have survived in miscellaneous private and public collections; however, because these holdings were constantly dislocated by death or changes in collecting policy, the historical analysis of print relies heavily on the survival of focused accumulations of such material by private individuals. The most important of the early collectors was Samuel Pepys, whose broad interest in printed material extended to the products hawked around the streets of London. His collection of ballads, which he added to the collection made by John Selden, contained at his death 1,775 sheets bound up in volumes and organized by subject. His collection of chapbooks numbered 215 titles, in a variety of formats, bound in eight volumes classified according to trade usage as 'Penny godlinesses', 'Penny merriments', and 'Vulgaria'. Pepys's collection of street literature comprises only a very small part of the total output, but it represents a means by which the ephemeral literature of the period can begin to be identified and assessed. The collection remained intact and passed, at the death of his heir in 1724, to his old college, Magdalene at Cambridge, where it has remained. As one historian put it, 'The convoy of wagons which took the 3000 books and their twelve presses to Cambridge was a sealed train carrying Pepys's reputation to posterity' (*ODNB*). Among the books in the presses or book cases were the popular ephemeral items he had so carefully preserved.

Another important collector of street literature was John Bagford, a shoemaker turned bookseller, antiquary, and pioneering bibliographer. From his base in Holborn in London, he supplied the leading collectors of the day, including Pepys and the omnivorous Robert Harley, with ballads and more conventional forms of print. His own interests as a scholar centred on a never-completed history of printing and printed books. His own collecting was geared to this project: he acquired a large quantity of title- and other pages from derelict books (later used by Joseph Ames for his *Typographical Antiquities*), as well as a steady flow of black-letter ballads published from the Restoration onwards. At his death, the two volumes of ballads were acquired by Harley; they subsequently passed through a series of private collections, including that of John

Ker, the 3rd duke of Roxburghe, before the British Museum Library purchased the collection, now in four volumes, in 1845.

Ballads had been entering the principal public collections from early in the 18th century, as libraries acquired quantities of other material in which many forms of ephemeral print were embedded. The collections of Anthony Wood, Richard Rawlinson, Francis Douce, and Thomas Percy were among those acquired by the Bodleian Library in Oxford. By the 19th century, institutions secured a critical mass of material (not always permanently), creating the conditions for research into it. The formation of societies (such as the Percy Society) and the publication of lists and bibliographies of street ballads began to move this genre of ephemera into a new relation with the printed archive.

A related category of highly ephemeral street literature was the almanac. Possessing a broader social appeal, it stood midway between recurrent forms, produced to supply an apparently continuous demand, and serial commodities, such as the newspaper. Among the most perennial products of print culture, the almanac was constructed around the calendar of saints' days and holidays laid out in the preliminaries to the Bible or to the Book of Common Prayer. By the mid-17th century, it was produced and sold either as a small-format leaflet of up to 24 pages or as a folio broadside printed on one side of a sheet for public display. The Stationers' Company held the monopoly for the calendar, and it licensed production of a changing list of almanacs under approximately fifteen different titles. These were sold in November each year in very large quantities. By the 1660s, an annual total of 300,000 to 400,000 copies were printed, enough for one in every three families in the nation. The numbers exceeded the production of even ballads and chapbooks, suggesting a pattern of consumption that reached far across the social scale. The Stationers' commercial interest in this huge output was sustained throughout the 18th century and defended by a continuous and partially successful rearguard action against a variety of street-level interlopers.

The almanac was essentially ephemeral. Owners would most likely have got rid of it at the end of the year it covered, which meant the almost inevitable destruction of most copies. Aside from the earliest issues, out-of-date almanacs were not sought out by collectors; the relocation of this highly disposable form from the street to the library was tied to changing characteristics of its content and use. First, the calendar was supplemented by an increasing amount of material on a range of practical or entertaining subjects. Predictions of all sorts, the dates of local fairs, historical lists, timetables for gardeners, and medical information became part of the genre's collective and individual appeal. Such material did not lose its currency every year, and it became common for all of the Stationers' Company almanac titles to be bound up together in a decorative binding to be added to the library shelf. Some stationers themselves may have sold cumulative volumes in book form as a commercial enterprise. Secondly, from the late 17th century it became increasingly common for copies to be interleaved with blank pages for use as a diary or a personal record of events. This practice extended from the middling and elite to shopkeepers and farmers—indeed, to anyone with business to transact. Many surviving 17th- and 18th-century diaries were entered in the convenient framework of the almanac. The ephemeral form therefore took on a dual character, both as a throwaway item and as a durable component of the library. Nowadays, this duality can be identified in the publication of *Old Moore's Almanac* on one hand and *Whitaker's* and *Wisden Cricketers'* almanacs on the other.

The transmission of street materials through collections, and the potential duality of such items, also characterize the newspaper. The most complex of the forms still (curiously) considered as printed ephemera, the newspaper poses a number of problems aggravated by the tendency to conceive of ephemera as constituting virtually all non-book print. The difficulty of locating the newspaper within the printed archive is related to the defensive position adopted by librarians hoping to secure themselves from the onset of an avalanche of print. Newspapers' demands in terms of collection, storage, and access are, it must be admitted, almost too much to bear. But problems also arise from the difficulty of conceptualizing an alternative to the established hierarchy of book-down print. The idea that the newspaper is simply a disposable item along with, say, a knitting pattern, railway ticket, or bumper sticker is, regrettably entrenched.

Although the *Encyclopedia of Ephemera* is a useful guide to a wide range of obscure material, it nevertheless does have some significant limitations that reflect common problems in the study of ephemeral print. Ballads, chapbooks, and almanacs each have an entry, as does the newspaper. Its entry states that 'a study of the subject as a whole is virtually impossible', then provides a series of sub-headings: 'First and last issues', 'Mastheads', 'Headlines/front pages', 'Commemoratives', 'Improvised newspapers', 'Mock newspapers', 'Language minority newspapers', 'Ships' newspapers', and 'Curiosities'. The entry embodies the idea of the newspaper as a heap of discrete copies and fits it into a conventionally subordinate position in the hierarchy of print. There is no doubt that, at the point of consumption, the newspaper is an entirely ephemeral product. Created for the day, or some other limited period, it is produced for immediate use and, to some extent, predicated on equally immediate disposal. Its content is as current as possible and its format, geared to cheapness and the exigencies of competition, has a built-in disposability. This sense of immediacy is heightened by the presence of an increasing load of advertising of all sorts. After fulfilling their initial purposes, newspaper copies were applied to a range of mixed and largely non-literary purposes. By the early 18th century, these conventionally included lighting pipes, lining pie dishes, and fulfilling the needs of the jakes. As the scale of output grew and costs fell (following the repeal of mid-19th-century taxes), the newspaper began to manifest itself more clearly as litter. Victorian commuters arriving at the main London stations left behind huge quantities of cast-off copies to be thrown away or recycled. In this context, the association of newspapers with printed ephemera seems hard to resist.

However, the notion of instant disposability misses the point. To its early producers, the newspaper was a collectable form. Pages were numbered consecutively from issue to issue, and annual indexes and cumulative title-pages were often given away to encourage people to collect them. The inescapable fact about the newspaper is that it is a serial product and, in this respect, cannot be disposed of. Throw one away and the periodical flow will bring another one along behind. Periodicity is the mechanism and time the dimension within which the newspaper functions; these are the core characteristics that put the form at the heart of print culture. Continuously present since the first such London publication in 1620, the proliferation and expansion of newspapers have overtaken and dwarfed all the other forms of print put together. The numbers themselves are complex, and indeed alarming. By 1700, about 30 serial titles were in publication, producing a yearly total of more than 1,400 issues. If each is taken to have been printed in the low average of 300 copies per issue, the total annual output would have amounted to just below half a million copies. In 1750, the proprietors of the London titles, with the representatives of a widening circle of local papers, purchased about 7.5 million tax stamps, a number rising annually. The acceleration of output in the 19th century—linked directly to developments in the technology of print (*see* **11**), as well as to the repeal of taxes—ushered in the mass market of the next century. The *Daily Mail* became the first Fleet Street paper to achieve circulation of a million copies for a single issue. At the same time, the newspaper moved beyond the orbit of the relatively conventional and sluggish book trade into its own industrial system. It was a sign of the times when, in 1937, the book trade's much-venerated business organization was retitled the Worshipful Company of Stationers and Newspaper Makers.

Despite this remarkable growth in output, the status and importance of the newspaper remained contested issues. At the end of the 19th century, for example, the idea of the newspaper press as the Fourth Estate was undermined by forms of commercialism rooted in the populist techniques of the new journalism. This undermining promoted the newspaper's identification with ephemera. The fact that there is still no general, comprehensive history of English newspapers suggests that the process by which the newspaper was brought into the orbit of collectors and collections was more problematic than in the case of the less bulky and challenging forms of street print.

Collections of newspapers began to be formed in the mid-17th century when their importance as a contemporary record of events was first recognized. At the outbreak of the English Civil War, the bookseller George Thomason was pressed by Charles I in 1640 to compile an archive of contemporary materials by collecting newsbooks and related current materials as they appeared. Thomason continued the work until the Restoration, by which time he had collected some 30,000 tracts bound up in more than 2,000 volumes. Thomason died without receiving his commercial reward, but his cumbersome collection remained intact, passing through a variety of hands before its purchase in 1762 for the library of George III. It subsequently formed a part of the king's gift of that library to the British Museum.

The wholesale collection of newspapers by a private individual became an increasingly hopeless enterprise; nonetheless, during the late 17th century, runs of the *London Gazette* (1665 to date) were occasionally advertised for sale to the public, and the binding up of selected titles seems to have remained fairly common. A few individuals have succumbed to the mania of general newspaper collecting. For the most part, however, private collections have usually had a specific purpose. Charles Burney—schoolmaster, book collector, and noted classical scholar—maintained an interest in the theatre, filling 400 volumes with newspaper cuttings, playbills, and prints on theatrical matters. From 1781, he filled a further 700 volumes with a retrospective collection of newspapers obtained at first from coffee houses. Similarly, the antiquary and printer John Nichols developed a particular interest in biography, publishing obituaries in the *Gentleman's Magazine* of which he was the proprietor. By the time of his own death, he had built up a collection of newspapers that filled 238 volumes. Such projects indicated the engagement of a later generation of middling virtuosos with the serial publication of news and information. At the same time, from the 18th century, increasing numbers of people developed more limited collections of cuttings, adapted to their own personal use and assembled as part of their private record-keeping.

Although the personal collection of newspapers remained a fairly quixotic enterprise, a semi-automatic accumulation of this material was taking place in London and across the kingdom. From the late 17th century, the tendency for newspapers to pile up in public spaces (such as coffee houses), where access was offered to large numbers of readers, created drifts of serials. Without an active policy of disposal, serial collection was almost unavoidable. When, in the 1850s, Peele's coffee house and hotel in Fleet Street attempted to sell its runs of major titles dating back to the 1770s, the collection weighed about six tons. It was eventually sold as waste. In political departments, lawyers' offices, and businesses and institutions of all sorts, the steady increase in semi-automatic collection continued to take place.

However, for the newspaper and related serials to become more closely identified with the printed archive, a great deal more than the isolated action of individuals and casual, often unwitting, accumulation by institutions was needed. A major development in the formation of a comprehensive and systematic collection came when the British Museum was established in 1753. Even so, the process by which newspapers were incorporated into the library was long and painful. As with other forms of non-book material, the initial intake was both retrospective and marginal to the concerns of the Trustees. The Thomason collection of newsbooks and related items entered the library through royal bequest. Similarly, in 1818, the reluctant acceptance of the Burney newspapers was predicated on the purchase of his huge library of classical texts in book form. The Trustees refused to buy the Nichols newspapers, and, although some part eventually came to the British Museum, the bulk was not acquired by the Bodleian Library until 1865, the same year that the library's Hope Collection of Newspapers—formed by John Thomas Hope (1761–1884) and bequeathed to the Bodleian by Frederick William Hope (1979–1892) had its first published catalogue.

During the early decades of the 19th century, the British Museum library became partially reconciled to housing the current output of newspapers, and made arrangements with the Stamp Office to receive copies of papers deposited at Somerset House in London for tax purposes. As the volume of output increased, conflict arose among British Museum officials over the handling of newspapers within their book-centred collections. As the whole collection was extended and overhauled, Anthony Panizzi's appointment led to disagreements over the purchase of foreign newspapers (and over much else as well). In 1873, however, as the arrangements for taking in current titles were becoming problematic, the legal requirement for the deposit of books was extended to newspapers. The huge build-up in library holdings that accompanied this decision rapidly filled the Museum's newspaper reading room, initially opened in 1885. The imbalance between the scale of the collections of newspapers and of books was becoming critical, and, at the end of the century the Trustees sought powers to disperse the foreign and local papers to their places of origin. A bill in 1899 proposing this measure failed, and a new solution was devised to remove the threat of the rising tide of newspapers and related materials. Land in Hendon at Colindale in North London was purchased; in 1910 it became the base for what is now the British Library Newspaper Library. It was a symbolic as well as an actual separation. On one hand, the split tended to emphasize the division between print in serial and book form. The two could not easily cohabit in a library setting, and the division lent credence to the idea of non-book ephemera. On the other hand, the creation of the Newspaper Library gave a new emphasis to the whole range of serial output as part of the national collection. Over time, the relocated material became a focal point within the printed archive, with its own storage and reading space as well as a specialist staff, and increasingly sophisticated mechanisms for collection and access.

4 Other collections

This sort of redefinition through collection and integration gave serials, along with other forms of street material, a distinct identity. The notion of 'printed ephemera' could no longer accommodate materials that had become major elements in the printed archive. At the same time, from the 19th century, the view of what material was collectable and susceptible to cultural analysis had expanded. The vast, amorphous heap of print—generated over five centuries and relating to nearly every form of human activity—began to take on a clearer definition. The very act of identifying such selected elements within material generally regarded as ephemeral created a mechanism for the continuous reassessment of its value and use.

Pepys had included tobacco labels and trade cards in his London collection, and Bagford had a variety of similar scraps in his volumes. By 1800, a widening spectrum of individuals was becoming involved in collecting ephemeral material. Grangerizing, the extra-illustration of books, encouraged publishers to produce, and collectors to seek out, printed materials, drawn from an eclectic range of sources, to augment and personalize their volumes. Such items might include not only pictures of people and of places, but also oddities such as the printed labels once sold by booksellers and printers at winter fairs on the ice of the frozen river Thames. Contemporary and historic material was also sought after during the middle-class vogue for making scrapbooks and albums. Increasingly, more focused collections of ephemeral printed pieces were also assembled around such items as playing cards, bookplates, stamps, matchbox labels, bill heads, and trade cards, some of which came to be housed in major libraries.

The recognition in the 19th and early 20th centuries of the cultural and historical value of the vast and increasing range of print led to a more generalized identification of the scale and character of printed ephemera. This shift of perspective was encouraged by the creation of huge, open-ended collections in Britain and America. In England, the main line of interest was generated by John Johnson, 'printer, ephemerist, and classical scholar' (*ODNB*). Johnson started working at the Oxford University Press in 1915 and, in 1925, was appointed printer to the university, a post he held until his retirement in 1946. His contribution to the Oxford Press was considerable, but his long-term achievement as a collector of printed ephemera was equally great, if not greater. Taking an entirely open-ended approach, he sought out every form of fugitive print that was part of the 'paraphernalia of our day-to-day lives' and destined for the waste-paper basket after use (*ODNB*). His huge collection came to include more than a million items, mainly dating from the 18th century to his final cut-off date of 1939, though he had 16th-century material as well. It has been incorporated with several large specialist collections of watch papers, valentines, cigarette cards, and bank notes, which have remained intact as subsets within the collection. Johnson himself devised 700 headings for his material, which was already well known by the 1930s. Holbrook Jackson described it in *Signature* in 1935 as 'a Sanctuary of Printing' (*ODNB*).

Part of Johnson's definition of ephemeral print was that it included anything a library would not accept as a gift; the Bodleian Library adopted a position in relation to anything identified as ephemera that echoed the British Museum's response to the newspaper. Collections that included ephemera—such as those accumulated by Robert Burton, Wood, and Thomas Hearne—had long been identified as acceptable acquisitions. However, even in the 1930s a policy of exclusion continued to be applied, and moves were made to clear out calendars, advertisements, and modern illuminated items such as certificates and commendations as unwanted ephemera. The John Johnson collection, as it became known, remained in a semi-detached state in two rooms at Oxford University Press. It was only in 1968 that the Bodleian was reconciled to its existence and the whole mighty accumulation was transferred to new accommodation within the library under a specified curator, in the first instance the scholar and librarian Michael L. Turner.

The metamorphosis of the John Johnson collection both represented and contributed to a flowering of interest in the fugitive output of the press, both as an area of research in its own right and as an increasingly integrated component of academic studies. The collection offered a line of systematic access to the many varieties of print. General studies of the material in it started in the 1960s, and the collection itself has contributed directly to the flow of published information, most recently through a catalogue of its holdings of commercial ephemera (*A Nation of Shopkeepers*, 2001).

In 1975, Maurice Rickards set up the Ephemera Society in London; subsequently, national groups have been formed in America (1980), Australia (1985), and Canada (1988). Exhibitions, lectures, and publications have ensued. At the same time, a wide range of academic and other institutions have become involved in assembling and organizing their own collections. The *Encyclopedia* (2000) provided a list of 116 known holdings and, in a few cases, including Reading University and the Rare Book School at the University of Virginia, courses on printed ephemera have been incorporated into the study of the history of the book. Part of this spread of interest in all areas of fugitive print has been the formation of an international network of ephemera dealers. In England, one of the most active was Andrew Block, who first opened a shop in northwest London early in the 20th century where he sold penny comic books for a halfpenny. In many parts of the world, ephemera fairs in various guises now run in tandem with their book-centred equivalents. Digitization is beginning to change the subject and its study.

5 Conclusion

'Printed ephemera' is an unstable concept, one that shifts according to the chronology of print, the circumstances of production and consumption, and the status of forms within established collections. The separation of books from the rest of the printed archive and the privileging of the codex—not only as a product intended to be preserved and stored, but also as the primary mechanism for cultural formation—seem increasingly untenable. Major libraries have become more aware of the value and interest of alternative varieties of print, and many artificial boundaries have begun to blur. Books are, in many cases, created from the materials that were produced and distributed in forms usually identified as ephemeral. The ebb and flow of their content in and out of serial publications, for example, gives print a much more fluid character than the serried rows of volumes on the library shelf seem to suggest. Similarly, books are surrounded by concentric circles of print relating to every aspect of their production, sale, and ownership, without which their content can hardly make sense. Book history has moved towards an interest in the reception and social context of print, making the issue of daily experience—and, therefore, of ephemerality—an integral part of its remit. It seems increasingly realistic to consider the products of the press as stretched along a spectrum of print, within which the book has (in physical terms at least) a modest place. In many ways the serial form has primacy in such a reconfiguration, mainly through the force of periodicity and the nature of a continuous sequence of production and consumption. The term 'printed ephemera' still has a value, but it should be used with care.

....

BIBLIOGRAPHY

[Bodleian Library, Oxford,] *The John Johnson Collection: Catalogue of an Exhibition* (1971)

—— *A Nation of Shopkeepers* (2001)

B. Capp, *Astrology and the Popular Press* (1979)

F. Doherty, *A Study in Eighteenth-Century Advertising Method* (1992)

J. W. Ebsworth, ed., *The Bagford Ballads* (2 vols, 1876–8; repr. 1968)

G. K. Fortescue *et al.*, eds., *Catalogue of the Pamphlets, Books, Newspapers and Manuscripts Relating to the Civil War, Commonwealth and Restoration Collected by George Thomason, 1641–1661* (2 vols, 1908)

M. Harris, 'Collecting Newspapers', in *Bibliophily*, ed. M. Harris and R. Myers (1986)

A. Heal, *The Signboards of Old London Shops* (1957)

L. James, *Print and the People, 1819–1951* (1976)

J. Lewis, *Ephemera* (1962)

ODNB

M. Rickards, *Collecting Printed Ephemera* (1988)

—— *The Encyclopedia of Ephemera*, ed. M. Twyman et al. (2000)

S. Shesgreen, ed., *The Criers and Hawkers of London* (1990)

M. Spufford, *Small Books and Pleasant Histories* (1981)

M. Twyman, *Printing, 1770–1970* (1970; repr. 1998)

E. Ward, *The London-Spy*, intro. R. Straus (1924)

T. Watt, *Cheap Print and Popular Piety, 1550–1640* (1991)

17

Children's Books

ANDREA IMMEL

1 Introduction

The children's book—a work conceived, produced, and marketed for the consumption of a young audience—appeared relatively late in the history of the western European printed book. Although its development is thought to be symptomatic of the so-called discovery of childhood, the emergence of the children's book after the invention of printing in the late 15th century cannot be understood without reference to the history of European education. Improvements in children's reading materials are sparked by educational reforms and by advances in cognitive psychology, as well as by shifts in literacy rates or by sociopolitical change. Similarly, the evolution of literary works reflecting the way childhood experiences help form children's minds elevated the status of leisure reading. This much-expanded role for imaginative literature in the 19th century became a powerful stimulus to develop the children's market across genres. Finally, advances in the technologies of book production—especially methods for reproducing images and manufacturing edition bindings—made it possible to transform the presentation and packaging of text for children via the codex and related non-book products (*see* **11, 18, 19**). With the development of an extensive network of special collections of historical children's print and material culture, a comprehensive history of the children's book has become feasible. This essay is intended as a prolegomenon to the enterprise. Focusing on the English-speaking world—the home of one of the oldest and most diverse traditions of publishing for children—the following discussion identifies a range of issues with which a full history of the children's book might engage.

2 Origins and development

Most accounts of Western children's books begin with the genre's 'invention' in the mid-18th century; the dramatic increase in production of juvenile books after that date is said to demonstrate that children were being taken seriously as an audience with special requirements. Nevertheless, previous generations of children not only learned to read, but became highly literate, without such luxury of choice. Examining evidence about children's reading experiences before 1700 contributes to the identification and contextualization of forces that subsequently shaped the genre. To understand the shift in attitudes regarding the child reader's requirements—specifically the displacement of the classical curriculum by new kinds of books—consideration must be given to the changes that occurred long before the 18th century in the cultural construction of childhood, educational provision, class dynamics, family structure, and printing technology.

The long history of the children's book properly begins with the invention of printing, by which time parts of English society had been collectively literate for around a century. Many children learned to read at home, instructed by either a parent or an employer. Because literacy had long been linked with religion, learning the alphabet was an act of devotion. After mastering letters, children were taught how to combine letters into syllables, and syllables into words, then encountered their first texts: basic Latin prayers such as the Paternoster and Creed, the psalms, and the hours. At this stage, boys destined for the ministry, trade, or administration attended school to learn Latin grammar; other children learned to read in their mother tongue. Ballads and *chansons de geste* might be given to children to spark their interest in reading, although the practice was generally frowned upon. Social reading—that is, reading aloud to an audience—was a favourite form of entertainment and edification (at least in wealthy households). In a society where books were relatively uncommon, the ability to read was highly variable, and works were often intended for audiences of all ages.

During the late 15th and 16th centuries, much of what children read had been in circulation before the invention of printing. By modern standards, few concessions were made to children as readers. Production was dominated by didactic works, including Latin grammars (by Donatus and others), courtesy literature or conduct books (e.g. Robert Grosseteste's *Puer ad Mensam*), moral instruction (e.g. *Disticha Catonis*), or anthologies (e.g. Geoffroy de la Tour Landry's *Book of the Knight of the Tower*, which William Caxton printed in 1484). In time, illustrated abridgements and adaptations of adult texts intended to teach children began to appear. Notable examples include Charles Estienne's series of illustrated booklets based on Lazare de Baïf's scholarly treatises on Roman antiquities, including *De Re Vestiaria Libellus* (Paris, 1535), and Hans Holbein's picture bible, *Icones Historiarum Veteris Testamenti* (Lyons, 1547). Desiderius Erasmus, Cordier, and Vives attempted to enliven Latin instruction with colloquial dialogues about experiences in the classroom, schoolyard, and street in which the child's voice can be plainly heard. Narrative vernacular fictions were aimed principally at adults, but children almost certainly enjoyed the many works in wide circulation that featured the adventures of young characters, from saints' lives to didactic romances such as the *Seven Sages of Rome*. Some of those popular works, among them the Robin Hood ballads, *Bevis of Southampton*, and *Guy of Warwick*, continued to circulate in chapbook adaptations, picture-book versions, and retellings well into the 19th century.

The most notable 17th-century works for children were produced by Puritans and dissenters, who distinguished little children from youth in order to accommodate their actual capabilities and to ensure that children would not be excluded from God's grace should they die before becoming capable of true faith. Yet the Puritans also shaped texts in ways that respected children's autonomy and preserved their freedom of conscience. The result was revolutionary works whose pedagogy was surprisingly child-centred. For example, the *Ludus Literarius* (1612) of John Brinsley, Master of Ashby-de-la-Zouche School, incorporates progressive teaching techniques for the youngest learners. Among the most influential Western children's books was the *Orbis Sensualium Pictus* (1658) of Johann Amos Comenius, an advocate of universal education who used his years of pedagogical experience to develop the book's method of teaching Latin via a pictorial encyclopaedia. In *A Token for Children* (1672), the minister James Janeway held up young saints who died before reaching adolescence as examples for the emulation of his readers, while Bunyan composed emblems for children on familiar, homely subjects.

The rise of the modern children's book is generally seen as coinciding with the Enlightenment, when advances in science, technology, and manufacturing held out the promise of rationally restructuring society for the improvement of mankind. Educational issues were central to discussions of moral and political philosophy during the period; John Locke held that education was the best means of ensuring the continuity of prevailing values from generation to generation, and Jean-Jacques Rousseau argued that education should transform society by effecting radical change in the attitudes and behaviour of young people. Early childhood was increasingly viewed as the critical stage of life for shaping the future adult, so that ensuring the quality of elementary instruction took on a new urgency. Yet Isaac Watts is a rare example of an important early 18th-century author who condescended to write for young people and to put his name on the title-pages of his books: most preferred anonymity, regarding themselves as philanthropists laying the foundations on which a mind could be built. By the 1790s, well-educated literary women such as Anna Letitia Barbauld, Sarah Trimmer, Ellenor Fenn, Lady Fenn, Maria Edgeworth, and Mary Wollstonecraft carved out a space where women writers might exercise their talents in the nation's service. Idealistic (and shrewd) entrepreneurs such as John Newbery, John Harris, and Joseph Johnson ensured that they also turned a profit. Enterprising book-, map-, and print-sellers drove the expansion of the juvenile market, developing an unprecedented range of illustrated materials adapted from existing print formats—from the harlequinade to the jigsaw puzzle and board game—for the pleasurable instruction of children.

The market for children's books expanded and diversified exponentially during the 19th century, due to the ever-increasing numbers of young British subjects being tutored privately at home or educated in Sunday or board schools. Children's publishers who entered the market's fray during this period battled for hearts, minds, and money. Publishers claimed their part of the market by identifying a constituency and providing it with suitable material at a reasonable price, while keeping an eye on the competition. The Religious Tract Society, Edwin J. Brett, publisher of the blood-and-thunder magazine *Boys of England*, and Henry Cole, in his attempts to elevate the imagination and taste of young readers with the Home Treasury series, all did this. Such major authors as Ruskin and Thackeray wrote original books for children, and continental writers such as Heinrich Hoffmann and Hans Christian Andersen attained international reputations in translation. Similarly, writers from Captain Marryat to Frances Hodgson Burnett produced narrative fiction (tract, historical novel, school or adventure story, *Kunstmärchen*, etc.) for periodicals or as separate volumes, and in the process earned handsome livings and won popular acclaim, even celebrity. At the same time, enterprising publishers such as Routledge and Frederick Warne built up extensive backlists of toy books, consisting chiefly of material in the public domain, such as fairy tales and nursery rhymes, reprinted with stylish illustrations (usually without acknowledgement to the artists) and colourfully repackaged in eyecatching covers, thanks to the technological improvements in book production. A parallel trend was the reprinting of modern classics as series of school prize books.

By World War I, the children's book had developed into a diverse, complex subsystem of fiction and non-fiction genres that paralleled the adult book world. Youngsters in Western industrialized nations could now be provided with specialized books through to their adolescence. Readers could be categorized by age (and by class, sex, ethnicity, disability, and religion as well) to assist in the production of materials that drew young people into appropriate reading communities. These might reflect the educational priorities of institutions or represent groups of varying tastes or socioeconomic classes. This period also marked the beginning of the literary institutionalization of children's books as a genre. Public lending libraries and publishing houses organized children's departments. National and international prizes, such as the Newbery, Caldecott, Carnegie, Hans Christian Andersen, and Astrid Lindgren awards, recognizing achievement in children's books, were established, along with specialized journals to review new publications and analyse contemporary trends (e.g. *The Horn Book*; 1924–) or to provide a forum for academic criticism of children's literature (e.g. *The Lion and the Unicorn*; 1977–). Collectors began to take a serious interest in antiquarian children's books, and major collections were created in public and research libraries (e.g. the Osborne Collection in Toronto, the Opie collection in the Bodleian, and the National Art Library, Victoria & Albert Museum).

With institutionalization has also come the increasing commercialization of children's classics—and relatively short-lived fads such as the Goosebumps series—by international corporations (e.g. Walt Disney Enterprises) and publishers (e.g. HarperCollins, Scholastic) on a scale not envisioned by the Victorians. Dr Seuss, Potter's Peter Rabbit books, Milne's Winnie the Pooh stories, C. S. Lewis's Chronicles of Narnia, and J. K. Rowling's Harry Potter series have all become the basis for literary brands. These books are then periodically repackaged, exploited for merchandizing spin-offs, adapted for television and film versions, and promoted through highly sophisticated interactive websites.

3 Children's texts as printed books

In the late 17th century, the growing interest in the workings of the human mind stressed the training of the senses, rather than the memory, and led to a new emphasis on the visual aspect of children's books. The relations that have persisted since the 18th century between educational, artistic, technological, and commercial considerations have allowed great creative scope in the presentation of material to the child reader. A book's intended audience can be discerned usually from its packaging: the younger the reader, the more features are used to interpret, decorate, or promote the text. As the child matures, the book incorporates fewer such elements.

Children's books have been sold in edition bindings since the late 17th century; the materials of the binding and its decoration typically distinguish a book for younger readers from one for older children, or a school book from one for leisure reading. During the 18th century, school books for vernacular reading instruction, such as James Greenwood's *London Vocabulary* (1711?), were typically bound in tanned sheepskin stretched over boards (with or without endleaves), in undyed canvas boards, or in sheepskin with a row of scallops stamped parallel to the spine. Colourful embossed Dutch gilt-paper wrappers or boards are the hallmark of 'entertaining little books' for younger children, such as *The History of Little Goody Two Shoes* (1765). Works of serious fiction, history, natural history, and school anthologies would be edition bound in sheep- or calfskin (plain or sprinkled), with panelled gilt spines similar to those for adult bindings.

In the 19th and 20th centuries, artists and publishers followed much the same formula, but took advantage of new materials and technologies. The upper cover often featured a striking illustration to attract the readers' eye, while the lower cover served some promotional purpose, typically featuring book lists or blurbs. Walter Crane's four series of toy books—Aunt Mavor's Toy Books, Routledge's New Sixpenny Toy Books, Walter Crane's Sixpenny, and Shilling Toy Books—all feature distinctive cover designs and advertisements for the publisher. Crane also adapted his style to what he was illustrating, using

wrappers for the socialist *The Dale Readers: First Primer* (1899) and decorated cloth for Mrs Molesworth's fantasy *The Tapestry Room* (1879) and Otto
Goldschmidt's *Echoes of Hellas* (1887–8).

Like bindings, the text block is not purely utilitarian, but may be adapted to
meet the audience's special requirements or add a playful element. Durability,
for instance, was crucial. The first untearable book was the hornbook, a wooden
paddle upon which a printed leaf was mounted under a thin layer of horn, from
which children learned their letters. Later, printers used pages of cloth, cardboard, plywood, and plastic that can withstand rough treatment by very small
children: those printed on fabric are known as rag or cloth books, while those
on heavy card stock are called board books. The leaves of the text block may be
folded in various ways. The battledore, an 18th- and 19th-century alternative to
the hornbook, consists of a sheet folded into two panels and a narrow flap, similar to an envelope that has been opened up. The accordion-pleated strip, called
a panorama or leporello, displays collections of images (familiar domestic
objects, for instance) accompanied by minimal text. The folded strip can also
advance the narrative, as in Aliquis's *The Flight of the Old Woman Who Was
Tossed Up in a Basket* (1844). Shaped books are those where the text block is
die-cut in the shape of the figure on the cover, such as Lydia Very's *Little Red
Riding Hood* (1863). To create changing pictures, flap-transformation and split-
leaf books have leaves that are divided vertically into graduated pages, as in
John Goodall's Paddy Pork series, or horizontally into multiple sections as in
Walter Trier's *8192 Crazy People* (*c.*1950). Holes may also be cut through the
text block and integrated into the story line, as in Eric Carle's *The Very Hungry
Caterpillar* (1969).

Modified text blocks are almost always found in works where illustrations
are integral to their concepts. A survey of the history of children's book illustration is beyond this essay's scope (*see* **18**), but brief mention may be made of the
ways visual schemata in children's books become instructive: by training the
eye to observe and analyse, by stimulating the imagination, by encouraging the
assimilation of information, and by teaching children how to interpret images
in different formats and styles. For example, grids filled with small illustrations
are traditionally associated with the teaching of vocabulary and grammar. The
pictorial language of isotypes (pictographic images), such as those by Gerd
Arntz in *Die bunte Welt* (1929), helps children to visualize enormous quantities
of specific things. Numbered tableaux depict animals, things, people, activities, etc., and their respective categories are explained in commentaries on facing pages. This layout, originated by Comenius, looks forward to the
object-lesson books of the 19th century. Such illustrations lend themselves to
visual play (sometimes called the armchair scavenger hunt) in which children
search for objects described in the text, which are concealed in the illustration's
complex compositions. Henry Anelay's *The Mother's Picture Alphabet* (1862) is
a sophisticated Victorian example. In the 20th century, the so-called hidden
picture puzzle-book has developed into a category in its own right, with popular

series such as *I Spy* by Jean Marzollo and Walter Wick, or Martin Handford's *Where's Wally?*

Illustrations in children's books may also be designed to direct artistic play. Colouring and drawing books allow children to copy figures or colour the outlines for models, while patterns for making paper toys are featured in Ebenezer Landells's *Girl's Own Toy-Maker* (1859). The activity book, developed in response to the 19th-century educator Friedrich Fröbel's art curriculum, is frequently consumed in the creation of objects for recreation or display. Paul Faucher's Père Castor series, issued between 1930 and the 1960s, is the most ingenious and distinguished of the activity book genre. Faucher's illustrators, many of them émigrés who had been members of the 1920s Soviet avant-garde, conceived illustrations that could be cut out to make stained-glass windows, magic lantern slides, tangrams, masks, and model gardens.

Related to the activity book are publications in which the illustrations include cut-out figures that engage the child in dramatic play. The earliest examples are the S. and J. Fuller paper doll books issued in the 1810s: the head of the main character can be inserted on six or seven costumed figures, reflecting his or her changing circumstances during the story's progress. A slot book, such as Else Wenz-Viëtor's *Nürnberger Puppenstubenspielbuch* (1919), consists of backgrounds printed on cardboard pages in which slits are cut for the insertion of figures. Nancy Pritchard White's *Nursery Rhyme Puppet Book* (1957) is conceived as a miniature theatre, complete with scripts, sets, and puppets.

Illustrations may also try to bring the other senses into play as in a scratch-and-sniff book. Dorothy Kunhardt's *Pat the Bunny* (1940) encourages preschool children to touch the pages, by stroking, for example, a piece of sandpaper cut in the shape of Daddy's unshaven cheek. Sound was added to books as early as 1865: *The Speaking Picture Book* featured a sound box with nine cords which, when pulled, produced animal noises. Sound recordings may accompany books, whether on phonodisc (e.g. Ralph Mayhew's Bubble Book series, 1917–22) or cassette (e.g. the 1990s Children's Classics from the Stars series produced by Rabbit Ears Productions), or a compact disc (e.g. John Lithgow's 2004 *The Carnival of the Animals*). In movable and pop-up books mechanical illustrations use sophisticated paper-engineering in order to create the illusion of movement and passage of time, to metamorphose an image, or to reveal the differences between the insides and outsides of things and bodies. Almost anything can now be grafted on to a codex to encourage a more interactive reading experience, as the title of David A. Carter's *Jingle Bugs: A Merry Pop-up Book with Lights and Music!* (1992) suggests.

4 The MS book

The almost exclusive focus of the history of the children's book on the printed work has led to the neglect of the long tradition of MS books made by and for youngsters. Whatever the period in which they were produced, the majority of surviving MSS for children are instructional. The most common MSS are those created by a parent or relative (usually a mother or aunt) for a particular child's use: for example the 1814 *Cayer d'instruction pour Alfred, Bourdier de Beauregard* (published by Charles Plante in 2007), a charmingly illustrated compendium of the things encountered within the vicinity of the family chateau by Alfred's uncle, the artist C. P. Arnaud. Many MSS of this type were never intended to circulate outside the family circle. Perhaps the most extensive of these MSS are the 400 reading instruction aids created by Jane Johnson, a minister's wife, for her children in the early 1740s, complete with hand-lettered picture cards illustrated either with cut-outs from engravings or her own lively drawings: these now are in the Lilly Library of Indiana University. Sometimes women published MSS that proved effective in the school room in the hope that others with less time or experience teaching young children would find them helpful. Lady Fenn made books for her nephews, with text composed of cut-out letters and accompanied by her pictures, one of which was the precursor of her easy reader *Cobwebs to Catch Flies* (1783–4), which remained in print for 80 years.

At the other end of the spectrum are instructional MSS commissioned from professional artists for children from privileged backgrounds. The contents and quality of the illuminations in certain books of hours, such as the Winchester Hours, Use of Sarum, *c*.1490 (Pierpont Morgan Library, MS M.487), suggest that they were intended for the religious instruction of young children. Sumptuous works, such the Medici Aesop of *c*.1480 (New York Public Library, Spencer MS 50) compiled for little Piero de' Medici by his tutor, the Florentine humanist Angelo Poliziano, were also produced for foreign language teaching. Similar works have been created in the 20th century: the Rose family have commissioned a series of Haggadahs by famous artists for use in family observances of Passover.

The other most important category of MS book is that created as a gift to a child for leisure reading. Like instructional MSS, they are most often produced by parents or close family friends, sometimes for a particular occasion or as a consolation for an extended separation between parent and child. A notable example is John Lockwood Kipling's album of drawings and photographs, *Picture Bubbles Blown for Ruddy by Papa*, produced for Rudyard and his little sister in 1868. Many famous children's books originated in such private productions, whether first conceived as a bedtime story (Helen Bannerman's *Little Black Sambo*), as a story spun out to pass the time during a summer's outing (Lewis Carroll's *Alice's Adventures in Wonderland*), as a picture letter to amuse a sick child (Potter's *Tale of Peter Rabbit*), or as a Christmas present (Heinrich Hoffmann's *Struwwelpeter*).

Children themselves are great makers of MS books, both for their own pleasure and to fulfil assignments. For instance, Jane Austen and her sister Cassandra wrote and illustrated *A Short History of England* while they were children. The juvenilia of famous writers tend to attract the lion's share of attention, but books made by children who did not attain great distinction later in life also deserve study as a legitimate form of literary production. Commonplace books or family magazines made by young people have attracted serious scholarly attention. More ephemeral works—including scrapbooks like the one assembled by Frederick and Amelia Lock (Princeton University Library, Cotsen 20613), the MS describing everyday occupations by the young cousins of the novelist Frances Burney (Pierpont Morgan Library, MS MA 4166), or the frequently elaborately decorated copy books of apprentices or pupils in writing schools—can be studied as forms of children's self-expression. Such MS books are also testimony to the ways, aside from reading, that children assimilate print culture during work or leisure.

5 Defining the children's book

Defining children's books primarily by audience still raises points of contention a century after the genre's integration into the print networks for publication, consumption, and reception. Compared with most other readers, dependent children have relatively little control over what they read; most of their critical early experiences with books are mediated by the adults who create, publish, distribute, assign, teach, and pay for them. That youngsters need assistance and guidance is indisputable, but they must also be granted agency appropriate to their own development. This tension between adult and child is at the forefront of modern discussions of the genre's definition.

There is consensus that it is too imprecise—because too inclusive—to define a children's book simply as any text that a child happens to read. Youngsters may not restrict their reading to works approved by adults, but range into forbidden territory—chapbooks, ballads, blood and thunders, series fiction, comic books, and manga. Although accounts of childhood reading, almost always reconstructed later in life, may be highly selective or wildly inaccurate, it is clear that children often read indiscriminately, including works far above their capabilities (Gibbon 'rioted' in his father's library; Benjamin Franklin relished speculative divinity and Nathaniel Crouch's sixpenny compilations). Children may also 'adopt' adult works not intended for them, the most famous examples being *Robinson Crusoe* and the first two books of *Gulliver's Travels*.

Central to the definition of the children's book is the traditional desire to inculcate good reading habits as the best way to exploit educational opportunities and to secure a productive and fulfilled future. Thus, the book stands both as the primary means of instruction and as a potent symbol of literacy, promising the possession of cultural capital and the prospect of social advancement. Yet at the same time the school book also represents compulsory reading, to be associated with the regimentation of the classroom. Often, in the elementary school book, cultural expectations, social realities, and teleologies underlying developmental psychology collide. A book adopted for use in a system of national compulsory education is likely to promote the values of the established religion, ruling class, or dominant ethnic group. To minorities, however, school books may look more like instruments of colonization or hegemony than disinterested conveyers of knowledge.

Countervailing such concerns is the powerful image of the solitary child engrossed in a book, cultivating the pleasures of the imagination. Predicated on oppositions between private and public, reason and the imagination, instruction and delight, this construction of the young reader embodies the Romantic paradigm of childhood reading articulated by Wordsworth in Book 5 of *The Prelude* (1805). Attempting to lift the child above the clash of cultural politics, the Romantics privileged such genres as fairy tales, poetry from popular oral traditions, and chapbook abridgements of medieval chivalric romances as true children's books. This narrowly belletristic definition of the children's book has discouraged the careful contextualization of much writing for children, encouraging instead the dismissal of 'didactic' works—including fictions as diverse as Maria Edgeworth's tales, Hesba Stretton's tracts, or Charlotte Yonge's novels—because the authors' designs upon the child are considered too transparent. It has also helped to reinforce a bias against books that were popular with previous generations of children, but which no longer connect with a contemporary audience. Once a children's book is no longer read by its primary audience, it is usually discarded as a curiosity, whose appeal is difficult to conceive.

Given the complexity of the issues surrounding children's books, it may be impossible to arrive at a definition of the genre that allows educators, parents, and critics confidently to sort the sheep from the goats. For example, is a book such as Edgard Tytgat's illustrated version of Perrault's *Le Petit Chaperon rouge*, published by Cyril Beaumont in an edition of 50 copies in 1918, a book for children or adults? The status of Rosemary Wells's board book *Max's First Word* (1998), designed to be read to very small children by an adult or older child, is similarly unclear. Textbooks are generally composed with an eye both to the ideal student, who is supposed to master its contents, and to instructors, who must convey its matter to classes of widely diverging backgrounds and abilities. Because so many books for young readers are arguably cross-written texts (i.e. composed for a multi-generational audience), it may beg the question to put too high a priority on purity or exclusivity in defining the genre. If the children's book is a form that lends itself to hybridity and experimentation in ways whereby boundaries between audiences are constantly subverted, then that reality should be accepted, rather than explained away. That the lines between child and adult readers are frequently blurred should be regarded as normal, rather than an aberration, and perhaps one of the deepest wellsprings of creativity.

BIBLIOGRAPHY

G. Adams, 'The *Medici Aesop*: A Homosocial Renaissance Picture Book', *The Lion and the Unicorn*, 23 (1999), 313–35

B. Alderson, 'Novelty Books and Movables: Questions of Terminology', *Children's Books History Society Newsletter*, 61 (July 1998), 14–22

—— and F. de Marez Oyens, *Be Merry and Wise* (2006)

—— and A. Immel, 'Children's Books', in *CHBB* 6 (2009)

C. Alexander and J. McMaster, eds., *The Child Writer from Austen to Woolf* (2002)

G. Avery and J. Briggs, eds., *Children and Their Books* (1989)

B. Bader, *American Picture Books from Noah's Ark to The Beast Within* (1976)

S. Bennett, *Trade Bookbinding in the British Isles 1660–1800* (2004)

E. Booth and D. Hayes, 'Authoring the Brand: Literary Licensing', *Young Consumers*, 7 (2005), 43–5

R. Bottigheimer, *The Bible for Children* (1996)

F. J. H. Darton, *Children's Books in England* (1999)

K. Drotner, *English Children and Their Magazines, 1751–1945* (1988)

M. O. Grenby, 'Chapbooks, Children, and Children's Literature', *Library*, 7/8 (2007), 279–303

A. Horodisch, '*Die Geburt eines Kinderbuches im 16. Jahrhundert*', *GJ* 35 (1960), 211–22

F. Hughes, 'Children's Literature: Theory and Practice', *English Literary History*, 45 (1978), 542–61

P. Hunt, ed., *Children's Literature: An Illustrated History* (1995)

B. Hürlimann, *Three Centuries of Children's Books in Europe* (1968)

A. Immel, 'Frederick Lock's Scrapbook: Patterns in the Pictures and Writings in Margins', *The Lion and the Unicorn*, 29 (2005), 65–86

—— 'Children's and School Books', in *CHBB* 5

L. Marcus, *Minders of Make-Believe* (2008)

J. Morgenstern, 'The Rise of Children's Literature Reconsidered', *Children's Literature Association Quarterly*, 26 (2001), 64–73

N. Orme, *Medieval Children* (2001)

A. Powers, *Children's Book Covers* (2003)

K. Reynolds and N. Tucker, eds., *Children's Book Publishing in Britain since 1945* (1998)

A. Richardson, *Literature, Education, and Romanticism* (1994)

J. Shefrin, *Neatly Dissected* (1999)

C. Sommerville, *The Discovery of Childhood in Puritan England* (1992)

J. I. Whalley and T. R. Chester, *A History of Children's Book Illustration* (1988)

18

The History of Illustration and its Technologies

PAUL GOLDMAN

1 Introduction

The impulse to illustrate text is of great antiquity and antedates the printed book by thousands of years. It is known that there were books written on wood in China datable to about the 13th or 14th century BC, and it may be assumed that at least some of these were illustrated. The age and fragile nature of the materials has meant that enormous quantities of material, whether illustrated or not, have been lost from the classical periods of Greece and Rome and most other early civilizations, with the notable exception of ancient Egypt. There, the relative durability of papyrus and the fact that items were deliberately and carefully buried has ensured some remarkable survivals. Among the more regularly illustrated works was the Egyptian Book of the Dead: one of the most celebrated examples is the British Museum's Hunefer Papyrus, datable to about 1300 BC.

During the 2nd century AD, as the codex began to be introduced, radical changes in the somewhat static style of illustrative designs might have been expected, but there were few striking developments, at least in the early years. Notable illustrated MS codices from about the 4th century AD are the Milan *Iliad* (Milan, Ambrosiana) and the Vatican Virgil. Of necessity, these books were illustrated by hand but, within perhaps as little as three centuries, the first technology to produce designs that could be multiplied had been discovered and successfully employed. This was the making of woodblocks for the printing of both text and image together; it was in use in China by the 7th century AD—initially, it appears, for printing on textiles. Although this process was also current at about the same time in Egypt, it seems not to have developed there to encompass illustration. The blockbooks of China, then, antedate by several hundred years the Western printing of books from movable type, which was discovered, apparently independently, without knowledge of the Oriental achievement. The Diamond Sutra (British Library)—arguably the earliest dated printed book (AD 868)—contains a remarkable woodcut frontispiece. The printing was done by rubbing the paper against the block, since there appears to have been no handpress in this period.

Both Byzantine and Western MS illumination developed from at least the 6th century AD, attaining ever higher levels of artistry and refinement. Among the outstanding MSS of this period are the Book of Kells (Trinity College, Dublin), datable to about the end of the 8th century, and the Lindisfarne Gospels (British Library), datable to about 710. All such works may be seen as vehicles for illustration, albeit entirely hand-drawn and illuminated. In Europe, printing from woodblocks was known by the 12th century, but it was originally employed only for stamping designs on to textiles. The earliest surviving prints on paper are not datable before the final years of the 14th century.

2 The age of woodcut

Among the earliest European woodcuts to bear a date is a Madonna of 1418, but it is probable that the somewhat crude surviving image-prints of religious subjects date from the final years of the preceding century. These were probably sold as devotional images within churches, or were distributed by travelling chapmen. Although not requiring a press, block printing produced books that combined text and illustrations and helped pave the way for illustrated books printed with movable type. A notable example is the *Biblia Pauperum*, produced in The Netherlands and datable to the middle of the 15th century. Other similar books, mostly of a devotional nature, were printed at about the same time, but almost inevitably the names of their authors, artists, and woodcutters remain unknown. Such books continued to be produced into the 16th century and, when superseded by books printed in a press, their cuts went on being reused for illustrations, sometimes for hundreds of years.

Woodcuts were employed almost as soon as books began to be printed from movable type. It is now believed that Peter Schoeffer's Mainz Psalter of 1457 was the first printed book in the West to contain woodcut decoration—remarkably, some of these cuts were printed in colour. It is possible, however, that the book's colour initials were printed either directly from wood or, conceivably, from metal cast from wood, so that the Psalter could be viewed as a type of illustrated book. The earliest true woodcut-illustrated books seem to have been produced at Bamberg by Albrecht Pfister. The first of these was probably Ulrich Boner's *Der Edelstein* (1461), notable also on account of its being apparently the earliest dated book in the German language. Pfister printed some nine editions of five books; most copies of these rare books are hand-coloured. Ulm and Augsburg also saw rapid development in the publication of books illustrated with woodcuts: two especially significant works were the Cologne Bible of about 1478–9, and Hartmann Schedel's *Weltchronik*, better known as the Nuremberg Chronicle, of 1493. Michael Wolgemut and Wilhelm Pleydenwurff are known to have contributed designs for the *Chronicle*, which perhaps marks the starting point for book illustrations undertaken by major artists, with their contributions being recorded. Wolgemut is significant for another reason: he was the master of Albrecht Dürer, one of the greatest woodcut designers for book illustration. Among his achievements in this regard are the *Apocalypse*, the *Great Passion*, the *Life of the Virgin*, and the *Little Passion*, which were all published between 1498 and 1511. Despite their thin textual content, they should be viewed not merely as vehicles for a genius, but as genuine illustrated books. Dürer's contribution to the medium also seemed to signal the decline in the hand-colouring of woodcuts in books—his work never required hand-colouring.

The other major designer of woodcut illustration in this period was Hans Holbein, arguably the only artist in Europe to rival Dürer. Most of Holbein's work was done in Basel, where the blocks were cut, although many of the books themselves were printed in France. The various cities with which he was associated indicate that the trade in his books was international. The Trechsel brothers of Lyons printed the *Icones Historiarum Veteris Testamenti* (1547), largely derived from Christoph Froschauer the elder's folio Bible (Zurich, 1538), containing Holbein's designs. In the same year the firm also published the celebrated and influential *Dance of Death*.

The great advantage of woodcut (a relief method of printmaking) was that illustration and text could be printed together in the same press—a feature not provided by intaglio and printing from metal. Generally, with 15th- and 16th-century European woodcut printing, artists such as Dürer and Holbein drew designs that were then cut by members of guilds; hence the cuts were not, strictly speaking, autograph. This division of labour was to be repeated in the 19th century, especially in England, where large firms employed wood engravers to interpret artists' drawings. In both cases, the names of the woodcutters and the wood engravers were only occasionally recorded.

3 The age of metal

Following the advent of the woodcut, copper engraving and etching were the two most important techniques for producing images for illustrations. Both were intaglio methods and used a press exerting heavy pressure to force the dampened paper into the lines holding the ink, and hence transfer them to the surface. Etching had been invented first as a means of decorating armour, and the earliest dated print from an etched plate is of 1513 by Urs Graf. Although engraving on metal had been used by the Greeks,

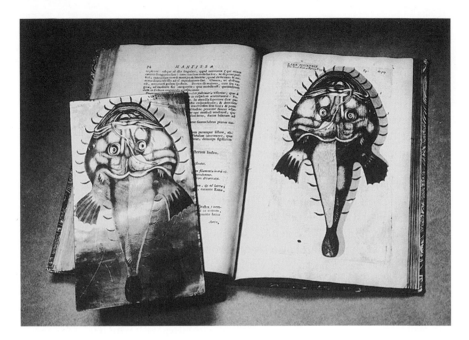

A copper plate and its print: *Rana piscatrix* ('The Toad Fish or Fishing Frog') from Walter Charleton's *Exercitationes de Differentiis et Nominibus Animalium* (Oxford, 1677). By permission of Oxford University Press

Etruscans, and Romans to ornament items such as bronze mirror-backs, it was not until the 15th century that goldsmiths in Germany employed engraved copper plates, initially to record their designs. The earliest such impressions were made in the 1430s, some 50 years after the first Western woodcuts. Many leading artists in Italy, Germany, and The Netherlands took swift advantage of the new techniques, chiefly to produce single-sheet prints. The benefits of sharper lines and enhanced delicacy also encouraged publishers to explore the medium for their own purposes. However, unlike woodcuts, which can be printed at the same time as letterpress, engravings and etchings—both requiring separate, individual printing—had to be inserted into books when they were bound. This was, inevitably, a slower and more laborious process.

Antwerp became an important centre for book production largely through the entrepreneurial French printer Christopher Plantin, who operated his press there from 1535 until his death in 1589. Illustrated books and separate engravings printed in Antwerp circulated in large numbers throughout Europe, and Plantin ensured the success of his engravings by employing many of the finest practitioners. Books by authors such as Alciati with engravings of emblems (his *Emblematum Liber* was first published in 1531) proved enduringly popular. In 1568 Plantin produced what is generally considered to be his most important publication, an eight-volume polyglot bible which contained both copper engravings and woodcuts. Also highly significant was Hieronymus Natalis's *Evangelicae Historiae Imagines*, posthumously published at Antwerp in 1593–5: its engravings were chiefly the work of the three Wierix brothers, who both designed and engraved the plates.

Peter Paul Rubens, himself an Antwerp man, was responsible for some of the most distinguished designs for title-pages that emanated from Plantin's press, then run by his friend Balthasar Moretus I who was also Plantin's grandson. Although making drawings for book illustrations was essentially a part-time activity for Rubens, he produced several which included allegorical figures and motifs, often depicting complex iconographic ideas. One of the most important of such books is the *Breviarium Romanum* of 1614, in which the engraving work was entrusted to Theodoor Galle.

In France too, especially in the two main publishing centres of Paris and Lyons, copper engraving was becoming popular for illustrations. The greatest Lyons publisher in the mid-16th century was Jean de Tournes, and from his shop in 1561 came *L'Apocalypse figurée*, with engravings by Jean Duvet, a faulty though undeniably charming draughtsman, much influenced by Italian mannerist artists, notably Pontormo and Rosso Fiorentino.

Etching also began to find favour with French publishers, and a leading illustrator in the medium was Jacques Callot, celebrated for his disturbing plates on the subject of war, *Les Petites Misères* (1632) and *Les Grandes Misères* (1633). Issued in *carnet* or notebook form, their relative lack of text renders their status as illustrated books doubtful. His two books of emblems—*Vie de la Mère de Dieu* (1646) and *Lux Claustri* (1646)—belong more securely to the category.

In England at around the same time, Wenceslaus Hollar dominated etching and was responsible for more than 2,500 plates. Some of these were for books, and the 44 he made for Virgil's *Georgics* after Francis Clein's designs constitute what was probably the most ambitious illustrated volume yet published in the country. Commissioned by the publisher John Ogilby, it appeared in 1654. Such was the success of this luxurious publication that Ogilby followed it with an edition of Aesop in 1665 for which Hollar etched 58 plates, once again based on drawings by Clein. The year 1688 saw a significant fourth edition of Milton's *Paradise Lost*, printed by Miles Flesher for Jacob Tonson. This work contained just twelve engraved plates of which eight were after John Baptiste de Medina. The unsigned images for Books 1 and 2 were of most significance, however. Now revealed to have been derived from prints by old masters, they form a bridge between those artists and the future generation of Blake and Fuseli.

Just as the Goncourts understood the 17th century in France as 'the century of the frontispiece', so too did they name the 18th 'the century of the vignette'. However, nearly all of the finest productions were made between 1750 and 1780; and it is fair to say that almost no major illustrated books appeared in the country during the first half of the century. Among the finest was La Fontaine's *Contes et nouvelles*—published at Paris in 1762 and commissioned by the Fermiers

Généraux, which formed 'the first financial company in the kingdom'; the Goncourts called the edition 'the great monument and triumph of the vignette, which dominates and crowns all the illustrations of the age' (Ray, *French Illustrated Book*, 31, 54, 55). Charles Eisen made 80 designs for the book, considered to be some of the most vivacious and accomplished he ever drew. There were also 53 tailpieces and four vignette-fleurons by Pierre-Philippe Choffard which complement the more earthy plates by Eisen.

Another equally distinguished but utterly different venture was the appearance of one of the most ambitious and successful travel books ever published. This was *Voyage pittoresque ou Description des royaumes de Naples et de Sicile*, published in Paris between 1781 and 1786, with outstanding designs by several important artists, notably Fragonard and Hubert Robert. The entire undertaking was really the brainchild and the obsession of Jean-Claude Richard, abbé de Saint-Non. He visited Italy for the first time in 1759 and the country, and especially Rome, entranced him. He then devoted his life and most of his wealth to ensuring that this large-scale project was completed to his satisfaction. It is far more than a mere topographical record, since the plates are full of drama, including sections devoted to volcanoes—the plate by Robert of Vesuvius erupting in 1779 is especially striking. Some of the plates were engraved after Saint-Non's own designs, and something of his devotion to creating this book can be gauged by his motto: 'What flowers are to our gardens, the arts are to life.'

In 18th-century England, black-and-white illustration in books became increasingly sophisticated with the growing mastery of the various metal techniques. In the first half of the century, the *Opera* of Horace illustrated by John Pine deserves special note. The book appeared between 1733 and 1737 and is significant because both text and designs were engraved. A pupil of Bernard Picart, Pine created a unity in the volume which is elegant and pleasing, and his use of the vignette makes it virtually the only English production worthy to be compared with the books that were shortly to be produced in such abundance on the other side of the Channel.

Several later works also demand mention: one of the most significant involved the reproduction, in various forms of engraving, of oil paintings. This was the Shakespeare (1791–1804) commissioned by John Boydell, an entrepreneurial and influential printseller in London. He launched his grandiose scheme in 1786 and invited most of the leading artists of the day to paint large canvases on subjects from the plays. Among those who contributed were Reynolds, Benjamin West, Fuseli, Romney, William Hamilton, Northcote, Opie, Wheatley, and Wright of Derby. Boydell's intention was to promote the British school of history painting and encourage a choice of serious subjects by native authors. The idea was first to exhibit the paintings in his own gallery and then, in order to recoup some of the enormous sums involved, to produce engraved versions for a monumental publishing enterprise. Although the project was an abject failure and was mercilessly lampooned by Gillray in his 1791 cartoon, *Alderman Boydell or a Peep into the Shakespeare Gallery*, it was important as a showcase for most of the current metal techniques. It is, for example, one of the few books in which mezzotint was extensively employed. This essentially tonal method had been first mentioned by the German Ludwig von Siegen in 1642; it was mastered by Prince Rupert, who developed the required 'rocking' tool at around the same time. Its principal virtue is a remarkable softness of texture, enabling it to imbue 'colour' to fabrics, especially satin, so that it was used to great effect in the reproduction of portraits, particularly those of Reynolds and Gainsborough. Its chief drawback is the limitation of numbers—only comparatively few impressions can be taken before the plate begins to deteriorate, thus rendering it unsuitable as a method for illustrating books.

Perhaps the greatest book to combine anatomy and art published in England in the mid-18ᵗʰ century is *The Anatomy of the Horse* by George Stubbs, which appeared in 1766. Technically complex—involving various intaglio methods—the 24 plates were intended not only for artists and designers, but for farriers and horse dealers. Additionally, the book demonstrates that illustration could be used for works of imaginative literature and for non-fiction. From the earliest years of printing, science, medicine, and invention, as well as virtually every other subject based on observations that needed recording, provided ideal matter for illustration in Europe and beyond.

William Blake is an isolated genius in the field of illustration. His first significant original work (until late in life he worked as a reproductive engraver) was *Songs of Innocence* of 1789, in which both the text and the illustrations were etched in relief and coloured by hand. He followed this with several more 'Illuminated Books' before the turn of the century; later came two monumental achievements, produced by this method, *Milton* (1801–8) and *Jerusalem* (1804–20). Although Blake had disciples (notably Samuel Palmer), he created no school of illustration. His extraordinary and technically complex publications remain unrivalled and unchallenged, and his unique method of printmaking was rarely emulated.

Turner and Constable, though both primarily painters in oils, nevertheless saw the opportunities illustrated books offered to disseminate their ideas. Turner made nearly 900 designs for reproduction: in his middle years, the larger plates were chiefly produced in the form of copper engravings, but later in life he made many smaller drawings (often vignettes) which appeared as steel engravings. This is a confusing term, since steel is so hard that it is almost impossible to engrave. Instead, where steel was used, the lines were almost invariably etched, although they were laid in the regular manner of a copper engraving. Since Turner was trained in the workshop of the mezzotint engraver John Raphael Smith, he understood the art of engraving almost better than the engravers did themselves, and hence was painstaking in ensuring his watercolours were reproduced in black-and-white prints to the highest possible standards. One of his best books is *Picturesque Views on the Southern Coast of England*, which appeared in parts between 1814 and 1826. Employing several brilliantly talented engravers, notably W. B. and George Cooke, the book encouraged an interest in the beauties of the country in much the same way as William Daniell's *A Voyage Round Great Britain*, which was published at almost exactly the same time. Constable's paintings were splendidly recorded in mezzotint by David Lucas in *Various Subjects of Landscape, Characteristic of English Scenery* (1833). The artist's aim was to bring for himself the same kind of recognition Turner had obtained on the publication of his *Liber Studiorum* (1807–19). In this he was unsuccessful, for both the part-issue (1832–3) and the book itself both sold poorly.

4 Advances in colour

Stipple engraving, which involves a large number of dots as opposed to lines, and aquatint (a variety of etching) are two essentially tonal techniques, which were important, since both could be printed in colours, and also could have colour added by hand. Stipple was never ideal for use within books, however, although one or two notable examples were produced. Perhaps the most magnificent work containing early English stipple colour-printing is *Imitations of Original Drawings by Hans Holbein*, which was published in folio between 1792 and 1800. Francesco Bartolozzi provided all but four of the numerous plates, which are highly sophisticated essays in the form, faithfully recording the appearance of the original designs in the Royal collection.

Perhaps the greatest master of the aquatint method was Goya, but his disturbing plates such as the *Caprichos* (1799), although intended to be issued in sets or in albums, scarcely qualify as illustrations in the accepted sense, since there is little textual matter. Additionally, he did not employ colour with aquatint. In Britain, however, aquatint, which had been pioneered in France in the 1760s, began to be increasingly used for volumes of topography, travel, sport, and humour.

The Microcosm of London (1808–10) combined a detailed record both of the interiors and exteriors of the major buildings in the city and of the animated figures which bring them to life. The architectural drawings were the work of Auguste Pugin and the people were the responsibility of Thomas Rowlandson—arguably the greatest British comic draughtsman, who drew in an inimitable cursive style. The aquatint plates were undertaken by several of the finest practitioners of the period after the designs of the two artists. These volumes, like so many others conceived and executed on a grand scale, were routinely broken up, in order for the plates to be sold separately. Complete volumes are scarce today, but individual plates taken from them appear frequently on the market. Rowlandson was himself an accomplished etcher and aquatinter, and his masterpieces in this manner are probably the three volumes devoted to the travels of that aged pedant, Dr Syntax, published between 1812 and 1821. Although William Combe's text is tedious in the extreme, Rowlandson's quirky images remain forever fresh and amusing.

Aquatint, as its name suggests, imitates watercolour closely, and its rise in popularity coincided, not surprisingly, with the development of the English school of watercolour painting, which was one of the richest and most distinguished movements in the history of art. Travel, botany, and sport were just three of the subjects for which coloured aquatints proved ideal.

Between 1814 and 1825 Daniell produced eight volumes of one of the most sumptuous of such colour-plate books. For *A Voyage Round Great Britain* (with a diverting text by Richard Ayton), Daniell both drew the original designs and made the aquatints from them. The result is a view of the country which is gentle and harmonious: most, if not all, industrial ugliness is rendered with restraint and delicacy. In many such books, the plates were first printed in just two colours and were then augmented by hand-colouring, invariably meticulously done. Almost none of the names of these talented colourists, who often were women, are recorded.

Flowers too attracted the aquatint artists: arguably the most outstanding printed specimen of the time is Robert John Thornton's *The Temple of Flora* (1807), which formed the concluding section of the author's *New Illustration of the Sexual System of Linnaeus*. Although the grandiose nature of the publication seems somewhat risible today, the quality of the plates, exquisitely coloured and finished, after both Thornton and Philip Reinagle (and others), is staggering, and the volume as a whole is a tour de force.

The love of sport, so much a British obsession, was a further area suitable for the attentions of the aquatinters. In 1838, R. S. Surtees published *Jorrocks's Jaunts and Jollities*, with delightful monochrome etched plates by Phiz (Hablot Knight Browne), but it was with the second edition of 1843, published by Rudolph Ackermann, and containing broadly comic colour aquatints by Henry Alken, that the book became celebrated. Alken continued to use aquatint far longer than most other artists, but he was unable to prevent the relentless march of lithography, which by the late 1830s began to dominate colour illustration.

5 The age of stone

Lithography was invented, or perhaps more correctly, discovered in 1798 by Alois Senefelder in Munich. This was the first entirely new printing process since the invention of intaglio in the 15th century, and provided great opportunities to use colour in books, together with a hitherto unmatched softness and delicacy of texture. Lithography proved particularly suitable for large books, especially in Britain for topography and travel, while in France the technique was used to illustrate major works of Romantic literature in which artists such as Daumier, Delacroix, Gavarni, and Géricault chiefly employed black and white.

Delacroix found inspiration in *Faust*; his version, with a translation by Albert Stapfer, appeared in 1828. (Goethe himself was pleased with the lithographs.) Although it initially met with a hostile reception from a public astounded by the daring, fantastic medievalism of the designs, the book created a distinguished tradition in French illustration. Daumier, however, was perhaps the greatest artist to use lithography, and much of his best work appeared in periodicals. It is in *La Caricature* (1830–35) that many of his most memorable satires can be sampled: of the 91 images he made for it, 50 were published in the last year before its suppression. The scenes in which he epitomized the oppressive practices of the July Monarchy were especially acerbic.

In contrast, the colour lithographed books in Britain at the same period dealt in the main with very different topics. In *The Holy Land* (1842–[45]), completed by *Egypt and Nubia* (1846–9), David Roberts produced probably the most remarkable and imposing of English travel books illustrated by lithography. The prints were the work of Louis Haghe, and they were almost exactly the same size as Roberts's deft watercolours. The combination of topographical accuracy, aesthetic sensitivity, and delicate colours ensured enormous popularity for these volumes and, needless to say, most fell victim to 'breakers'. Edward Lear similarly published several important books of his tours: in *Views in Rome and its Environs* (1841) he produced panoramic lithographs of a large size, concentrating more on the countryside than the monuments of the city itself; *Illustrated Excursions in Italy* (1846) combined lithographs and wood-engraved vignettes. His more celebrated *Book of Nonsense* (1846) used lithography both for text and image. Lithographic colour printing, or chromolithography, provided Owen Jones, an architect and ornamental designer, with a suitable medium for his work: perhaps his greatest achievement using it is *The Grammar of Ornament* (1856). His ideas proved influential on the design of wallpapers, carpets, and furnishings, and his approach to book illustration culminated in the work of William Morris.

6 The age of wood engraving and mass production

At the end of the 18ᵗʰ century and in the early years of the 19ᵗʰ, Thomas Bewick was the first leading exponent of wood engraving. Not only did he illustrate delightful books—chiefly of natural history, such as *A General History of Quadrupeds* (1790), with vignettes frequently drawn from life—but he was an influential teacher. Among his pupils were William Harvey, John Jackson, and Ebenezer Landells. Luke Clennell was also taught by Bewick, and one of his best books is undoubtedly Samuel Rogers's *The Pleasures of Memory* (1810), for which he engraved 34 delicate vignettes after Thomas Stothard.

Wood engraving, like the woodcut of a previous age, had the same advantage over all other methods of printmaking: blocks could be set up and printed with the letterpress at the same time. This led in mid-19ᵗʰ century Britain to the mass production of illustrated books and, in a significant expansion of activity, of periodicals. Etching, which was very much the province of comic artists such as George Cruikshank and Phiz, was coming to the end of its life as a mass method of communication, but one of its last gasps was also, paradoxically, hugely influential. This occurred when Phiz was asked to take over the illustration of some 'Sporting Sketches' by Charles Dickens, following the death of the originator of the project, Robert Seymour, who had completed just seven designs before his suicide. Phiz contributed 35 etched plates to what Dickens termed merely 'a monthly something', which became *The Posthumous Papers of the Pickwick Club*. Issued in parts (or numbers) from 31 March 1836 to 30 October 1837, the work has genuine claims to being the first illustrated English novel of stature. In other words, it is probably the first such publication where original illustrations accompany a true first edition, as opposed to a reprint.

A wood-engraved block and its print: TypR-2 (1), Houghton Library, Harvard University. Engraved block of 'The Night Heron' from Thomas Bewick, Wood Blocks for the *History of British Birds*, 57-1418a, Houghton Library, Harvard University. Wood Engraving of 'The Night Heron' from Thomas Bewick, *History of British Birds*, Newcastle: E. Walker, 1804, volume II, page 43.

Wood engraving soon began to overtake etching in Britain and in France, both on account of its convenience and because of the excellence of the engravers. Across the Channel, a landmark was *Paul et Virginie* (1838), published in Paris by Curmer. This lavish edition of Bernardin de Saint-Pierre's classic tale of natural love in Mauritius was illustrated with numerous wood engravings—after artists such as Tony Johannot, Paul Huet, Isabey, and others—that integrated happily with the text. Equally significant is the fact that most of the engravers were English, demonstrating their superiority in the field. Within a year, an English translation was published in London by W. S. Orr in almost as fine an edition, although it lacked four of Curmer's plates. Other English publishers soon followed, bringing to the public the wood-engraved illustrations of artists such as Grandville and Gigoux in English-language editions.

Stylistically, many British artists of the 1840s betray the influence of German designers such as Julius Schnorr von Carolsfeld and Moritz Retzsch. A notable publication in this manner was Samuel Carter Hall's *The Book of British Ballads* (1842, 1844), which was notable for a consciously Teutonic layout—where the designs often encircle the text or run in panels next to it—and was the sole work with illustrations by the uniquely disturbing Richard Dadd.

The year 1848 saw the foundation in London of the Pre-Raphaelite Brotherhood, and although the movement itself was short-lived, its influence on illustration was momentous. In 1855, Routledge published *The Music Master* by the Irish poet William Allingham, with wood engravings after John Millais,

Dante Gabriel Rossetti, and Arthur Hughes. Almost at a stroke a new kind of illustration, which was powerful in execution, intellectual in approach, and essentially realistic in the way faces and bodies were depicted, came to the fore. Rossetti's beautiful image 'Maids of Elfen-Mere' set the standard, not only encouraging other Pre-Raphaelites, such as Holman Hunt and Edward Burne-Jones, to make increasingly bold designs, but also spurring the group known today as the 'Idyllic School' to produce distinguished work. Among these practitioners were George John Pinwell, John William North, Frederick Walker, and Robert Barnes. In 1857, Edward Moxon published an edition of Tennyson's poems, now known as the Moxon Tennyson, containing designs by Millais, Rosssetti, and Hunt in the new style, and others by artists such as J. C. Horsley and William Mulready, still highly reminiscent of the 1840s. The book was a commercial failure, partly because of its lack of artistic unity, but it was a significant achievement. From this date, there was an explosion in the publication both of illustrated books and also of periodicals. Three of the most important magazines for illustrations in the 1860s were the *Cornhill Magazine*, *Good Words*, and *Once a Week*. The wood engraving for them was largely undertaken by large London firms, notably the Dalziel brothers and Joseph Swain. The names of the highly skilled people who worked at speed and often overnight to meet deadlines are rarely recorded. Many of them are likely to have been women who worked in a sweatshop economy. Long press runs from wood engravings were often achieved by the use of metal electrotypes, which were faithful facsimiles of the boxwood blocks.

In *The Pencil of Nature* (1844–6), W. H. Fox Talbot produced the first published book illustrated photographically. It was not until the 1880s that photomechanical processes such as line-block, half-tone, and photogravure began to supplant wood engraving, then in decline.

The subject of illustrated children's books is so vast that it can only be touched on here (*see* 17). By the latter half of the 19th century, more and more books were being published specifically for children to enjoy and read on their own. It was soon realized that colour was an essential ingredient for them, and sophisticated effects were achieved by artists such as Randolph Caldecott, Kate Greenaway, and Walter Crane.

7 The book beautiful, *livre d'artiste*, and the private press

As a reaction to the decay in production values prevalent in the 1880s, William Morris began a movement to produce beautiful books that were consciously medieval both in style and means of production. Paradoxically, however, in his Kelmscott Press books he did not entirely outlaw mechanical means for producing them. Other presses that made illustrated books of distinction included the Vale and Eragny presses, vehicles for Charles Ricketts and Pissarro respectively. By definition, their books were published in limited editions and were aimed at wealthy collectors. At about the same time in France, the concept of the *livre d'artiste* (artist's book) emerged, led by entrepreneurial publishers such as

Ambroise Vollard. These were luxury publications, containing woodcuts and lithographs by major artists such as Bonnard, Rodin, Pablo Picasso, Henri Matisse, and Dufy. Similar publications appeared also in Germany and Austria featuring artists of the stature of Paul Klee and Franz Marc.

Significant and striking though these volumes are, they are fundamentally portfolios of master prints: they are not books in the traditional sense and are certainly not designed for reading. Since the impressions were not invariably bound in, they encouraged the removal and framing of individual sheets. In Britain in the 1920s and 1930s, a few books were published containing original copper engravings, etchings, and even pochoir designs (hand-coloured through stencils). However, it was in autograph wood engraving that the British private press movement excelled. The Golden Cockerel Press was one of the best; it hosted the talents of, among others, Robert Gibbings, Clifford Webb, and Gwenda Morgan. Towards the end of the century several private presses—notably Whittington, Gwasg Gregynog, and the Fleece—continued to thrive using original wood engravings, invariably printed from the wood and published in limited editions and to very high standards.

8 Contemporary illustration and the digital revolution

While the limited edition artist's book continued to flourish throughout the 20th century and beyond, perhaps most notably in the US and UK, becoming ever more experimental and avant-garde, nearly all non-fiction trade books were routinely illustrated by photographic means. The only genre of imaginative book to attract illustration today as a matter of course is that of young children's books, while works aimed at teenagers, such as J. K. Rowling's Harry Potter series, remain unillustrated. Some publishers like the Folio Society still commission new illustrations for their high-quality reprints. Such books are printed in commercial numbers, though theoretically limited, and hence are available relatively inexpensively.

With digital technology, the appetite for illustrated books seems inexhaustible, as the means of meeting it becomes simpler both for the self-publisher and for the professional. In the world of the adult trade novel, an interesting development has been the recent use of digital images by writers such as W. G. Sebald and Michel Houellebecq. Their skilful combining of word and image may presage developments soon to come.

BIBLIOGRAPHY

D. Bland, *A History of Book Illustration* (1958)

A. M. Hind, *An Introduction to a History of Woodcut* (1935)

P. Hofer, *Baroque Book Illustration* (1951)

C. Hogben and R. Watson, eds., *From Manet to Hockney: Modern Artists' Illustrated Books* (1985)

S. Houfe, *Fin de Siècle: The Illustrators of the Nineties* (1992)

G. N. Ray, *The Illustrator and the Book in England from 1790 to 1914* (1976)

—— *The Art of the French Illustrated Book 1700 to 1914* (1982)

F. Reid, *Illustrators of the Sixties* (1928)

J. Selborne, *British Wood-Engraved Book Illustration 1904–1940* (1998)

T. Watt, *Cheap Print and Popular Piety, 1550–1640* (1991)

J. I. Whalley and T. R. Chester, *A History of Children's Book Illustration* (1988)

～ 19 ～

Bookbinding

DAVID PEARSON

1 Introduction

Books have needed outer covers and a means of holding them together for as long as they have existed, partly to keep their pages in the intended order, and partly to provide protection. Bookbinding embraces all the techniques that have evolved to achieve these ends, including the materials and structures employed, and the many ways in which the covers have been decorated. It is a subject of study in its own right, with an extensive literature; bookbindings have been admired and collected for their artistic qualities, but their intrinsic interest goes beyond this. Before mechanization was introduced in the 19th century, all book-bindings were individually handmade objects and the choices exercised in deciding how elaborate or simple a binding should be became part of the history of every book. The introduction of paperback binding, coupled with rising exploitation of the pictorial possibilities of outer covers, is a significant element in modern publishing history and in the dissemination of books to ever greater markets during the 20th century.

2 Early history

Papyrus, which could be glued together into long scrolls that might be stored in protective wooden cases, was the preferred writing medium in ancient Egypt and its use spread across the Graeco-Roman world during the pre-Christian era (*see* **3**). The codex—the form of the book as we know it—emerged from this tradition during the first few centuries AD when leaves of papyrus began to be folded and sewn into leather covers. Structures like this, originating in the near east, known from the 2nd century, are particularly associated with the emerging Christian sects; they gradually replaced scrolls as the preferred method for recording and storing texts during the succeeding centuries.

The Roman statesman Cassiodorus (*c*.490–*c*.580), in his *Institutiones* (written *c*.560), refers to bookbinders trained to produce bindings in various styles, and an 8th-century English MS illustration is generally believed to depict him with his nine-volume Bible, bound as recognizable codices with decorated covers. The Stonyhurst Gospel, made *c*.700, is the oldest surviving European decorated binding; with folded and sewn quires, covered with decorated leather over boards, it brings together essential characteristics that would remain constant in bookbinding practice for the following millennium and more.

3 Western bookbinding structures (pre-mechanization)

Most bookbindings made in Europe between *c*.800 (when the sewing style developed) and 1800 conform structurally to a standard model, sometimes called flexible sewing. The leaves are folded into gatherings which are sewn through the central folds on to a number of supports running horizontally across these folded edges. The projecting ends of the supports are laced and secured into stiff boards, which are then covered with an outer skin (typically leather or parchment, but possibly paper or fabric); this is decorated to create the finished product. Additional leaves (endleaves) are commonly added at each end of the text block before attaching the boards; the spine is rounded; endbands may be added at head and foot; and the leaf edges are trimmed with a sharp blade (sometimes called a plough) to create an even surface. In bookbinding terminology, the construction stages are known as forwarding, and the decoration as finishing.

These processes remained essentially constant throughout the medieval and handpress periods; the relatively few changes that evolved over time were commonly associated with a wish to expedite or economize on labour and materials as more books came to be produced. Once printing was established, the double-thickness sewing supports typically used in medieval bindings gave way to single ones, and various techniques were developed to speed up sewing by running the needle between gatherings as it ran up and down the spine. An alternative practice widely used for pamphlets and

The basic structural features of a European bookbinding in the medieval and hand press periods. Line drawing by Chartwell Illustrators

temporary, cheap bindings was stabbing and stab-stitching, running a thread through the whole text block near the spine edge.

4 Post-mechanization structures

Bookbinding practices, like all other aspects of the book-production and distribution industries, underwent major changes during the 19th century. Towards the end of the 18th century, rising leather costs, combined with ever-growing book production, led to greater experimentation with cloth and paper as alternative materials. During the 1820s and 1830s, books were increasingly issued with cloth-covered boards, secured to the text block using glued strips of canvas, rather than laced-in sewing supports. Cloth covers, decorated and lettered, could be prefabricated and case binding quickly became established as the standard technique. Whole editions of books therefore began to be issued in identical bindings, another major change from the practice of the handpress era.

These essential structural features of casebound books have continued largely unchanged to the present time, although the processes involved have undergone progressive mechanization (see section 8, below). While many 'hardback' books still conform to this style, modern books often rely on glue rather than sewing to hold them together, an alternative (and cheaper) binding technique that dates back to 1836 when William Hancock was granted a patent for what were then called caoutchouc bindings. After gathering the text block in the usual way, the spine folds were cut off (leaving each leaf a singleton, not attached to any other) before being coated with a flexible rubber solution that when set held all the leaves together. As the rubber perished over time, the leaves fell out, and the technique was largely abandoned commercially around 1870. It was revived in the 20th century and the introduction of new thermoplastic glues from about 1950 onwards led to increased production of what are variously called unsewn or perfect bindings, much used particularly for paperback books. The failure of the glue over time remains a problem, and bindings based on sewing continue to provide the strongest and most permanent structures.

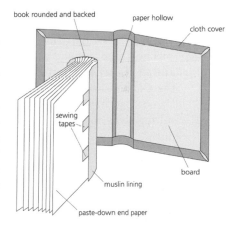

Diagram of the structural features of a modern casebound book ready for casing in (adapted from Gaskell, *NI*). Line drawing by Chartwell Illustrators

5 Non-Western bookbinding structures

The earliest codex bindings, from North Africa and the surrounding area, followed a different sewing technique using a chain stitch sewn across the gather-

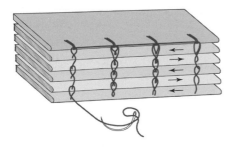

Coptic sewing differs from western flexible sewing technique in that the quires are sewn together with a chain stitch, rather than being sewn on to separate sewing supports run across the spine. Line drawing by Chartwell Illustrators

ings, instead of running the thread up and down the quires. This method, sometimes called Coptic sewing, was initially used across Europe, but was abandoned there in favour of flexible sewing around the beginning of the 9th century. The Coptic method continued to be used in the Near East, including the Byzantine and Islamic cultures where bookbinding flourished throughout the Middle Ages and beyond. Coptic sewing produces books that open well, but whose spines tend to become concave over time, and whose board attachment may be weaker than that produced by Western methods of laced-in supports.

In Asia, a variety of binding styles developed, influenced by the shapes and characteristics of the writing materials. In India and other parts of Southeast Asia, palm leaves, cut into long thin strips, were commonly held together with string passed through holes in each leaf, fastened at each end to a wooden cover; this *pothi* format, an ancient tradition, remained in common use down to the 19th century (*see* **41**). Chinese and Japanese binding (*see* **42**, **44**) evolved differently, following the invention of paper in China around AD 100 and its widespread adoption for documentary purposes (although bamboo and wood, in thin strips tied together, were also used, and *pothi*-type structures using paper leaves are known in China from the 7th century onwards).

The Chinese made extensive use of scrolls during the first millennium AD and their earliest printed books (using block printing) were scroll-based, like the Diamond Sutra (dated to 868). The concertina format, made by pasting sheets together in one long continuous sequence, but folding it rather than rolling so as to create a rectangular book-shaped object when closed, was a natural evolution from the scroll, and began to emerge during the Tang dynasty (618–907). During the Song dynasty (960–1279), scroll-based formats were increasingly replaced by ones based on folded leaves, more like Western book structures. Various kinds of stitching techniques are known to have been used, as well as paste-based ones such as butterfly binding, in which single bifolia are pasted together at the spine fold. The bifolia would typically be printed or written on one side only, leaving alternate blank openings corresponding to the pasted folds. By folding the other way, and binding along the open edge rather than the folded one, it was possible to create a book of continuous text without blanks, and it was this development, together with the emergence of

Thread, four-hole, or Japanese binding: this characteristic binding format developed in China during the Ming period and has been extensively used in East Asia. Line drawing by Chartwell Illustrators

new sewing methods, around the 12th–14th centuries that led to the format most commonly recognized today as a typical oriental binding. Sometimes called four-hole binding or Japanese binding (although it developed in China), such books are sewn through the open folds that make the spine edge, stabbing through the whole text block and running the thread over the head and tail as well as round the back. This format became established during the Ming dynasty (1368–1644) and has continued in use, although Western bookbinding methods also became increasingly common in East Asia after the 19th century.

6 Materials used in bookbinding

In European practice, leather-covered boards were the typical choice, over many centuries, for bindings intended to be permanent. From the earliest times to the end of the Middle Ages, boards were usually made of wood (in England, oak or beech), cut in thin slices with the grain running parallel to the spine. During the 16th century, wood was gradually replaced by pasteboard and other paper-based boards, being both lighter and cheaper, as books became smaller and more numerous. Millboard (made from waste hemp materials) was introduced in the 17th century and strawboard (based on pulped straw) in the 18th. Modern bookbindings typically use some kind of machine-made paper-based cardboard. Medieval bindings commonly had metal clasps across their edges to prevent the vellum leaves from cockling, a tradition which died out (other than for ornamental purposes) during the 16th and 17th centuries as pasteboard and paper replaced wood and vellum.

Leather used for bookbinding has come from a range of animals, prepared in different ways. Leather is made from animal skins either by tanning—treating the dehaired skin with tannic acid—or tawing, when the chemical used is potassium aluminium sulphate (alum). The former creates a smoother, harder leather which can take and retain impressed decoration. Medieval bookbinders typically used tawed leather, made not only from domestic animals but from deerskin and sealskin. In most European countries, tanned leather replaced tawed for bookbinding during the 15th century, although tawed pigskin continued to be popular in and around Germany into the 17th century.

Tanned calfskin, dyed a shade of brown, is the covering material most commonly found on post-medieval British bindings. Calf produced a durable but lightweight leather, with a smooth and pleasing surface. Tanned sheepskin, which has a coarser grain and is less hard-wearing, was used for cheaper work. Tanned goatskin was the leather of choice for the best-quality bindings; it was increasingly used in Europe from the 16th century onwards, having been developed for bookbinding by Islamic craftsmen in the Near East well before then. Most of the goatskin used in England during the hand press period was imported from Turkey or Morocco and, hence, was commonly called 'Turkey' or 'Morocco'.

Vellum or parchment, made by soaking calfskin or sheepskin and drying it under tension, without chemical tanning, was also extensively used as a covering material in early modern Europe, often for cheaper bindings when a vellum wrapper, without boards, might provide sufficient protection for a pamphlet or small book. In Britain, the use of vellum for binding work dwindled after the mid-17th century, except for stationery binding, but it continued to be much used in Germany and the Low Countries well into the 18th century. Paper, or paper over thin boards, was also sometimes used for cheap or temporary bindings, and this practice increased as time progressed; there are a few extant examples of printed-paper wrappers from the early centuries of printing (there must once have been very many more, which have perished), but 18th-century pamphlets in wrappers of blue or marbled paper are relatively common. Towards the end of that century books increasingly came to be issued in paper-covered boards, a trend that continued throughout the 19th century with a growth in printed paper covers. During the hand press period, paper or card-based binding options were generally more common in continental Europe than in Britain; wrappers of rough plain card (sometimes called cartonnage) began to be used in Italy during the 16th century and can also be found from France or Germany around that time and later.

The use of fabric as a covering material dates back to medieval times, originally as a luxury option, using velvet or embroidered textiles. Many elaborately decorated velvet bindings from the 16th and 17th centuries survive, and in early 17th-century England there was a vogue for devotional books with embroidered linen or satin covers. The use of fabric as the default option for bindings dates from the early 19th century, when binders began to experiment with cotton cloth, although rough canvas was used for schoolbooks and similar cheap household books from c.1770. Cloth was quickly established during the second quarter of the 19th century as a standard covering material for the prefabricated binding cases which were then transforming bookbinding production. Bookcloth is typically cotton-based, coated or filled with starch or an equivalent synthetic chemical to make it hardwearing, water-resistant, and capable of being blocked with lettering or pictorial designs.

7 Bookbinding decoration

Decoration has long been the aspect of bookbindings and their history that has attracted most interest, both among those who were producing and owning them at the time of their creation and among their successors. The outside of a book is its first and most immediately visible aspect, the part that can be seen even when it is closed and on a shelf: it thus bears the greatest potential to attract or impress users. Down the ages, handsomely decorated bookbindings have been commissioned, collected, valued, sold, and displayed, appreciated not only for their beauty but for the statements they may make about the importance of the book's contents, or the status of the owner. Much of the published literature on bookbindings is dedicated to these kinds of bindings, but it is important to recognize that all bindings have some kind of decoration, however minimal, and that it is worth studying and understanding the full range of options produced over the centuries.

Bookbinding decoration, like every other kind of art form, has always been subject to ever-shifting tastes and fashions, and each generation had its own ornamental vocabulary within which patterns and styles were created. A 16th-century binding will look different from an 18th-century one because the tool shapes and layout designs belong distinctively to their own time. This applies to plain bindings as well as fancy ones; bookbinders always offered their customers a range of options from the simplest and cheapest to the most luxurious and expensive, with many possibilities in between. Understanding the full picture allows one to recognize bindings of all kinds, to place them within the spectrum of options available, to compare them with other bindings of their time, and to interpret the choices that were made in their creation.

The development of bookbinding design, like all aesthetic fashions, is a process of continual change, dependent partly on the potential of the materials available and partly on the creation and dissemination of new artistic ideas. Styles typically began in one place and spread across continents; English bookbinding was influenced by what was being produced in France and Holland, which in turn was influenced by designs from Italy or other European artistic centres. Across Europe, countries developed variations and characteristics of their own, but at any one time there was a broad commonality of design conventions. In America, where bookbinding began soon after European settlers arrived (the first North American bookbinder is recorded in 1636), styles and techniques followed European, particularly British, models. Bookbinding tools always belonged within the wider ornamental fashions of their time—the neo-classical motifs of 18th-century bindings, for example, are mirrored in contemporary architecture, woodwork, and other decorative arts—but usually with a distinctive twist of their own, making them recognizably intended for binding decoration.

Tanned leather bindings have usually been decorated by building up patterns with heated metal tools, leaving a permanent impression in the surface. Tools may be small individual stamps, large blocks, or wheels with an engraved design around the rim, and are run along a cover to create a continuous line of ornament (fillets and rolls). For greater visual impact, tools can be applied through a thin layer of gold leaf, leaving a gilt rather than a blind impression; this was an Islamic invention, known from at least the 13th century, and many handsome gilt-tooled bindings from Persia and North Africa survive from the 14th and 15th centuries. The technique travelled to Italy and Spain in the 15th century, and gilt-tooled bindings began to be produced in quantity all over Europe from the 16th. The great majority of the countless thousands of tanned leather bindings produced during the hand press period carried some degree of blind- or gilt-tooled decoration, varying from a few lines or simple tools to elaborate designs.

At the top end of the market, skilled craftsmen like Jean de Planche, Samuel Mearne, or Roger Payne produced striking and sophisticated bindings; many examples, showing the ways in which styles developed by time and place, will be found in the extensive literature on bookbinding.

Decorative effects on leather bindings could be further enhanced by using inlays or onlays of differently coloured leather, or by applying paint as well as tooling. Leather could also have patterns cut into it (*cuir ciselé*); this was popular in and around Germany in the late medieval period, but was otherwise uncommon in binding practice. Many of the decorative techniques used on leather were also shared with vellum bindings. Decoration was commonly placed not only on covers and spines, but on board edges, using narrow rolls; leaf edges were usually coloured or sprinkled, or gilded in the case of better-quality bindings. Spine-labelling, using lettered leather labels, became common from the late 17th century; before then, books might have their titles written on their leaf edges or elsewhere, reflecting different storage methods before it became common practice to shelve books upright, spine outwards.

Medieval leather bindings, typically covered with tawed rather than tanned leather, were often largely undecorated, although a vogue for tool-stamped, tanned leather bindings developed in the later 12th century. Special bindings of the Middle Ages tended to rely on other techniques, using covers of ivory, enamel, or jewelled metalwork, made separately and nailed on to the wooden boards. Many medieval abbeys and large churches had treasure bindings like this for bibles and important devotional books, although relatively few have survived.

A 16th-century strapwork binding: brown calf, gold tooling, and black paint. The lower cover of Xenophon's *La Cyropédie* (Paris, 1547), bound for Edward VI. © The British Library Board. All Rights Reserved. (C.48.fol.3)

A 19th-century decorated binding: according to contemporary advertisements, L. M. Budgen's *Episodes of Insect Life* (London, 1849), published under the pseudonym 'Acheta Domestica', was 'Elegantly bound in fancy cloth' and sold for 16 s. The Bodleian Library, University of Oxford (189 a.42 cover)

The introduction of cloth as the standard covering material for bindings, in the second quarter of the 19th century, saw attention rapidly paid to developing its decorative capabilities. Gold blocking on cloth began in 1832, initially for spine lettering, but quickly adapted to be applied to covers as well. Experimentation during the following decade with abstract and pictorial designs, using gold and coloured inks, led to the production from mid-century of a wide variety of striking publishers' bindings in decorated cloth. This tradition declined towards the end of the century, as dust jackets evolved; these became increasingly common from the 1880s, initially with printed text but gradually becoming the more pictorial and actively designed covers we are familiar with today. The story of dust jackets and pictorial covers for paperbacks belongs more to design history than bookbinding history, but the importance of these contemporary methods of drawing attention to books by their covers is self-evident.

The growth of machine-made cloth binding in the 19th century led to a corresponding decline in the making and decoration of leather bindings, although the trade never died out. A reaction against a feeling that artistic standards in bookbinding had fallen was initiated in the 1880s by T. J. Cobden-Sanderson, whose beautifully crafted bindings, produced to his own designs, inspired a revival of interest in handcrafted bookbinding. A tradition of fine bookbinding flourished in many countries during the 20th century; in England, the formation of the Guild of Contemporary Bookbinders in 1955 (subsequently renamed Designer Bookbinders) provided a focus for

A 20th-century binding by Edgar Mansfield, an influential figure in the development of the Designer Bookbinder movement in the later 20th century: blind-tooling on yellow goatskin. The upper cover of H. E. Bates's *Through the Woods* (London, 1936). © The British Library Board. All Rights Reserved. (C.128.f.10)

this movement, within which numerous contemporary binders have continued to produce bindings combining the highest quality of craftsmanship with artistic flair, and experimentation with the possibilities of bookbinding as an art form.

Nineteenth- and 20th-century bookbindings commonly have decoration on their covers or dust jackets that reflects the content of the book. This is a modern development; throughout the medieval and hand press periods, bookbinding decoration was normally abstract, with no attempt to use designs to represent content. There are exceptions, but they are very few in proportion to the bulk of what was produced.

8 The bookbinding trade

Bookbinding was generally carried out as a professional activity within the broader umbrella of the book trade. During medieval times, some bookbinding was undertaken within monasteries as a logical adjunct to the writing and copying of MSS, but as soon as a secular trade in making and selling books developed (around the 12th century), binders emerged as one subset alongside parchment makers, scribes, and stationers.

The organization of binding work varied a little from country to country according to local custom, but throughout the early modern period binders generally entered the trade through apprenticeship to an established practitioner, followed by formal membership of a guild or similar trade association. In England, there was never a separate bookbinders' guild, and London binders (where much of the trade was concentrated) belonged to the Stationers' Company, which also embraced printers and booksellers. Binders were typically the poor relations within this framework, in terms of both earnings and social status, and many binders who succeeded financially did so by diversifying their activities into selling books, stationery, or other wares. The relationship between booksellers and binders in the early modern period—the extent to which binders had independent business relationships, or were employed by the booksellers—is not well documented. It is increasingly recognized that books were often bound before being put on sale, but there is little evidence to suggest that edition binding in any deliberate sense was carried out much before the 19th century. Selling books ready-bound seems to have been more common in Britain than in continental Europe, where the tradition of issuing

books in paper wrappers, to be bound to a customer's specification, continued well into the
20th century.

Before the 19th century, binderies were typically small establishments run by a master with
a handful of assistants (who might be apprentices, journeymen, or members of his family;
women were often involved in some of the
operations, such as folding and sewing). In
France, there was a recognized distinction
between forwarders (*relieurs*) and finishers
(*doreurs*); in Britain, Germany, and elsewhere
these roles were less formally identified,
although individuals within workshops are
likely to have specialized. Representations of
European binding workshops between the 16th
and 18th centuries, of which a number survive,
commonly show something between two and

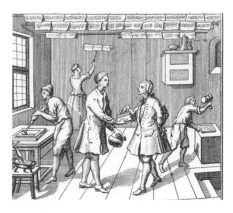

An 18th-century binder's workshop: a relatively
small number of people carry out the various
operations involved in forwarding and finishing; from C. E. Prediger, *Der Buchbinder und
Futteralmacher*, vol. 2 (1745). Private collection.

eight people at work in one or two rooms carrying out the various activities of
sewing, beating, covering, and decorating involved in binding production.

All this changed during the 19th century, when the trade was gradually transformed by mechanization. Growing book production, the development of cloth
casing, and the invention of machines to carry out binding processes led to
binderies becoming much bigger operations with factory-like assembly lines.
During the first half of the century, many of the operations such as folding, sewing, and attaching cases were still carried out by hand, but the second half saw
the introduction of steam-powered folding machines (from 1856), sewing
machines (from 1856), rounding and backing machines (from 1876), case-mak-
ing machines (from 1891), gathering machines (from 1900), and casing-in
machines (from 1903). Many of these were first introduced in America. Bookbinding today, for the great majority of the books issued through normal publishing trade channels, is carried out as an automated industrial process, whose
capacity has been enhanced since the 1950s by the development of new fast-
drying inks and glues.

9 The collecting, study, and importance of bookbindings

Bookbindings play an important functional role in the life of every book, but
their impact and potential to affect the values associated with books goes beyond
this. The statement that a luxuriously bound book can make about the importance of its contents, or its owner, is a tradition that stretches back through
generations of wealthy bibliophiles to the treasure bindings displayed on medieval altars. Queen Elizabeth I liked her books bound in velvet; her royal library
presented a rich and colourful display to impress visitors, and drew together a

collection of books that she found individually satisfying to look at and to handle. Less wealthy owners have also taken active delight in the aesthetic satisfaction which bindings can bring. Samuel Pepys recorded in his diary (15 May 1660) that he purchased books 'for the love of the binding', and had many of his books rebound to create a uniform image. Finely bound books have often been created as gifts, sometimes in the hope of influencing potential patrons. The admiration and expense of fine bindings have also generated criticism; Gabriel Naudé lamented 'the superfluous expenses, which many prodigally and to no purpose bestow upon the binding of their books…it becoming the ignorant only to esteem a book for its cover' (Naudé, 61). Many early purchasers were at least as concerned about functionality as decoration—they wanted their books sound and well made, without missing leaves—and wealthy owners did not necessarily have fancy bindings.

Early bookbinding practice is not well documented; contemporary manuals or archival sources on binders and their lives are relatively scarce before the 19th century. The bindings themselves constitute the largest body of evidence for exploring bookbinding history. The serious study of the subject began in the late 19th century, initially with a focus on the artistic qualities of fine bindings, maturing into a tradition of comparative study of surviving bindings to identify sets of tools used together, from which workshops and their dates of operation may be deduced. Bindings can therefore be attributed to particular binders, times, and places. Towards the end of the 20th century increasing attention was paid to structural aspects as well as decorative ones, with a growing emphasis on the full range of bindings produced, the plain and the everyday as well as the upmarket and the fine. The idea of systematically collecting bindings for their own sake is similarly a relatively recent development, and a number of important collections of fine bindings were formed in the 20th century.

Bookbinding studies have in the past been regarded as having a rather peripheral role in the overall canon of historical bibliography, compared with printing and publishing history, or work more directly focused on textual or enumerative bibliography. Bookbindings have been thought to be incidental to and unconnected with the works they cover, and the past emphasis on fine bindings has lent the subject an art-historical flavour that can veer towards dilettantism. More recent developments in book history, concerned with the ways that books were circulated, owned, and read, have created a framework in which it is easier to see bindings as an integral part of that whole. It is now widely recognized that the reception of works is influenced by the physical form in which they are experienced—an area where bindings play an important role. A reader's expectations may be conditioned by the permanence, quality, or other features of a book's exterior. Bindings may reveal ways in which books were used—how they were shelved or stored, how much wear and tear they have received—and the rebinding of books by later generations of owners may reflect changing values (contemporary bindings of Shakespeare are typically much simpler than the elaborate gilded goatskin in which 19th-century owners rebound early editions of his works). Cheap and temporary bindings, or bindings whose internal structure shows corner-cutting techniques, may indicate likely original audiences.

More obviously, knowledge of binding history allows us to recognize when and where bindings were made, and therefore where they first circulated. In the early modern period, books were not necessarily bound and first sold where they were printed, as printed sheets often travelled significant distances before being bound. Imprints should not be taken as an indicator of place or date of binding, for which decorative, structural, and other material evidence, interpreted by comparison with other bindings, is a surer guide. Bindings may also incorporate direct evidence of early ownership, in the form of names, initials, or armorial stamps on the covers or spine, practices that have been common in Europe since the 16th century.

BIBLIOGRAPHY

D. Ball, *Victorian Publishers' Bindings* (1985)

C. Chinnery, 'Bookbinding [in China]', www.idp.bl.uk/education/bookbinding/bookbinding.a4d, consulted Mar. 2006

M. M. Foot, *The History of Bookbinding as a Mirror of Society* (1998)

E. P. Goldschmidt, *Gothic and Renaissance Bookbindings* (1928)

D. Haldane, *Islamic Bookbindings* (1983)

H. Lehmann-Haupt, ed., *Bookbinding in America* (1941)

R. H. Lewis, *Fine Bookbinding in the Twentieth Century* (1984)

Middleton

G. Naudé, *Instructions Concerning Erecting a Library* (1661)

H. M. Nixon, *English Restoration Bookbindings* (1974)

Nixon and Foot

J. B. Oldham, *English Blind-Stamped Bindings* (1952)

D. Pearson, *English Bookbinding Styles 1450–1800* (2005)

N. Pickwoad, 'Onward and Downward: How Binders Coped with the Printing Press before 1800', in *A Millennium of the Book*, ed. R. Myers *et al.* (1994)

E. Potter, 'The London Bookbinding Trade: From Craft to Industry', *Library*, 6/15 (1993), 259–80

J. Szirmai, *The Archaeology of Medieval Bookbinding* (1999)

M. Tidcombe, *Women Bookbinders 1880–1920* (1996)

20

Theories of Text, Editorial Theory, and Textual Criticism

MARCUS WALSH

1 Issues for textual scholarship and theory

The book as a form has enabled the expression, transmission, and multiplication of knowledge. Written words are more stable than speech. Printed words are more stable and, equally important, more replicable than spoken or written words. Nevertheless, the permanence of the book is undercut regularly by various processes of change.

Texts have been embodied in a number of physical forms: handwritten on papyrus, vellum, or paper (*see* **10**), or scribally copied (occasionally derived in both cases from oral dictation); printed in hand-set type, machine-set type, or stereotype; composed at a keyboard, electronically processed, and output to an electronic printing device; or electronically processed and sent as a file direct to a local visual display or to the World Wide Web. Texts are products of human agency, composed by individuals and copied and processed—in MS, printed, and electronic forms—by a variety of technologies, all embodying human crafts and decisions.

Through these processes, texts are subject to innumerable types of variation and mistake. A dictating voice may be misheard; an author's or a scribe's hand may be illegible and, hence, misread. Transcription always involves change and error, as well as a conscious or unconscious process of editing. Composition (the setting of type) adds technically specific issues: the wrong case, the wrong fount, the turned letter. Performance texts may be transcribed or printed from faulty memorial reconstruction. Type and typeset formes are subject to 'batter', type movement, and loss. Etched or engraved plates are prone to wear and damage.

Authors emend and revise, before, during, and after the publication process. A text may be subject to imposed change, censorship by the publisher, by external authority, or self-censorship. Unique MSS may be lost, destroyed, or damaged by interpolation, fire, flood, or vermin. Transmission from any medium to another—printed, photographic, electronic—may be affected by various types of interference. Electronic texts have their own characteristic modes of variation: misconversion between character sets, or locally unintended effects of global search and replace operations (*see* **21**).

Theorists of text and of editing have thus confronted many practical questions: the construing of foreign letter forms (e.g. Greek or Hebrew) and historical scripts (e.g. secretary hand); consideration of the errors that might arise from misconstruction during the production process; the practices of printing houses and compositors; the possible priorities and relations among multiple witnesses of a text; the historical bibliography of printed texts; and lexical and semantic change.

There are larger issues of philosophical definition and choice, arising from conceptions of textual identity, textual meaning, and textual function. Conceptions of textual editing vary in the regard paid to diplomatic and bibliographical evidence, and to considerations of putative authorial intention and semantic coherence. Should editors base their work on the assumption that the text replicates the words intended by the author? Or should they assume that the text reflects a broader process of interaction among or negotiation between the original author (or authors), sponsors, publishers, printers, and audience? Should editors privilege a particular source document, and, if so, should that document be a MS or a copy of a printed edition? Should they consciously present the text in relation to contemporary audience tastes? These alternatives—variously prioritizing the author, the documentary witness, the sociological circumstances of production, or taste as a principle of authority—respond to different disciplinary and social sources and functions in the edition. For most of the 20th century, literary scholarship, particularly in English, privileged the author and used bibliographical and critical processes in order to reach a putative authorial text hidden or corrupted by subsequent error. Historians, by contrast, have generally preferred diplomatic editions (i.e. a text faithfully transcribed from its appearance in a particular document) or a type- or photographic facsimile of a particular document. In recent years, some theorists have advocated a more sociological approach to editing, and sought textual versions reflecting the complexities of social production. For centuries, texts have been adapted according to the perceived taste or capabilities of their target audience. Alexander Pope, for example, purged Shakespeare of comic improprieties in his 1723–5 edition, and Thomas and Henrietta Maria the Bowdler produced an expurgated *Family Shakespeare* (1818).

2 Early classical and biblical textual scholarship

Textual study and textual editing began with the most ancient Western texts: the Greek classics and the Bible (*see* **2, 3**). Classical textual scholarship originated, as far as is known, in the Alexandrian Library, in the 2nd and 3rd centuries BC. Here, scholars undertook the huge task of ordering some hundreds of thousands of MSS—none of them original authorial documents—to produce from fragmented and widely diverse copies more reliable and complete texts of authors such as Homer. Scholars developed a system of marginal critical signs for such apparent errors as incorrect repetitions, interpolations, misorderings of lines, and spurious lines or passages. Corrections were normally not entered in the text itself, but made and justified in extended scholia. Here, already, is an editorial practice founded on the exercise of critical judgment, in relation to issues of authorial style and usage.

After the decline of Alexandrian scholarship, the copying and editing of Greek and Latin literary MSS continued at Pergamum, where Crates (*c.*200–*c.*140BC) examined and emended the text of Homer, and at Rome, where Aelius and Varro worked on issues of authenticity and textual corruption in the writings of Plautus and of others. In the later Roman empire, Hyginus wrote on the text of Virgil, M. Valerius Probus applied Alexandrian methods to the texts of Virgil, Terence, and others, and Aelius Donatus and Servius commented on Terence and Virgil. After the empire's fall, classical texts continued to be copied in monastic scriptoria. Although textual activity lapsed from the 6th to the 8th centuries, a marked renaissance occurred in the Carolingian era and the 11th and 12th centuries.

In the Renaissance, the classics of Rome and Greece were rediscovered, collected, edited, and annotated by a succession of scholars, from Francesco Petrarca and Poggio Bracciolini onwards. Lorenzo Valla (1406–57) and Angelo Poliziano were key figures in the development of textual criticism and historical scholarship. Valla influentially demonstrated, from linguistic and historical evidence, that the Donation of Constantine was a forgery, and wrote a ground-breaking study of Latin usage, the *Elegantiae Linguae Latinae* (1471). Poliziano used Greek sources to illuminate Latin texts, and argued for the superior authority of the earliest MSS. Aldus Manutius's press issued a stream of Latin and Greek texts edited by a team of scholars, including Marcus Musurus, who used the best available MSS and applied their linguistic knowledge to amend the MSS for the printer. Francesco Robortello edited Longinus (1552) and wrote the first developed study of the methodology of textual criticism, *De Arte Critica sive Ratione Corrigendi Antiquorum Libros Disputatio* (1557), which insisted on palaeography, usage, and sense as criteria for emendation. Major textual scholars in France and The Netherlands—notably Lucretius' editor Denys Lambin; Manilius' editor Joseph Justus Scaliger; Tacitus' editor Justus Lipsius; Gerardus Joannes Vossius; and Daniel Heinsius—made significant contributions both to the methodology of editorial emendation and to essential areas of knowledge for informed editing, including chronology, the usage and lexis of the ancient languages, and literary contexts.

The earliest biblical textual scholars also had to deal with a plethora of non-original documents. The New Testament existed, in whole or in part, in some

5,000 Greek MSS, as well as in Latin versions and patristic quotation. St Jerome, author of the Vulgate Latin translation, was apparently conscious of the problems that arise in MS transcription, including the confusion of letters and of abbreviations, transpositions, dittography, and scribal emendation. Humanist textual scholarship antedated printing. Valla, for instance, amended the Vulgate on the bases of the Greek original and patristic texts (1449; published by Desiderius Erasmus, 1505). The first printed bibles, by Johann Gutenberg and other presses, were in Latin. The Hebrew Old Testament was not printed until 1488, at the Soncino Press; and the first Greek New Testament, the Complutensian Polygot, was printed in 1514 but not published until 1522. It was narrowly beaten to the market by Erasmus's edition, which, despite being hurriedly edited from the few MSS readily to hand, became the basis of the *textus receptus* that would dominate for four centuries, underlying Robert Estienne's editions (1546 and 1549), Beza's Greek testaments (1565–1604), the Authorized Version (1611), and the Elzeviers' Greek testament (1624).

3 After the Renaissance: beginnings of rational methods

In France, Richard Simon's monumental study of the Old and New Testaments was the first full-scale analysis of the textual transmission of an ancient text. Investigating Greek MSS of the New Testament and surveying printed texts from Valla onwards, Simon examined critically the inconsistencies and repetitions of the Old Testament, especially of Genesis, imputing them not to the first penmen, but to scribal error. In England, Walton's polyglot Bible (6 vols, 1655–7) included for the first time a systematic apparatus of variant readings. John Fell issued a small-format Greek Testament with apparatus giving variants from dozens of MSS (1675). John Mill undertook an extensive study of the text of the New Testament; his examination of numerous MSS and printed editions culminated in an innovative edition (1707) with enormously detailed prolegomena, listing some 30,000 variants.

However, the overwhelmingly significant figure of the time, for European and English textual method, was Richard Bentley (1662–1742). In his *Dissertation upon the Epistles of Phalaris* (published in the second edition of William Wotton's *Reflections upon Ancient and Modern Learning*, 1697)—one of the most devastating interventions in a long and pugnacious scholarly career— Bentley emphatically demonstrated that the letters attributed to the ancient tyrant Phalaris were spurious, and thus demolished Sir William Temple's adduction of Phalaris as evidence for the superiority of ancient writers. Bentley's argument was based on extraordinarily extensive literary, etymological, and historical evidence. His imposing scholarship and formidable methodology are in evidence throughout his editions of Horace (Cambridge, 1711; Amsterdam, 1713) and Manilius (1739). Familiar with the MS tradition, Bentley was aware of the distance of all surviving documents of classical writings from their originals. He was prepared both to diagnose errors that had, through many possible routes, entered the text and to make emendations with or without the MSS' supporting authority. For Bentley, editorial choices, though informed by the documentary tradition, must advert to the sense of the text, as constrained by cultural and linguistic possibility: 'to us reason and common sense are better than a hundred codices' (note on Horace, *Odes*, 3. 27. 15).

Bentley also contributed to New Testament editing, publishing *Proposals for Printing a New Edition of the Greek Testament* (1721), to be based on the Vulgate and the oldest MSS of the Greek text, in both English and European libraries. He intended thereby to produce a text, not identical with the irredeemably lost original autographs, but representative of the state of the New Testament at the time of the Council of Nicaea (AD 325)—thus obviating a huge proportion of the tens of thousands of variants amongst later, and generally less authoritative, MSS. On the basis of his collations he claimed: 'I find that by taking 2,000 errors out of the Pope's Vulgate, and as many out of the Protestant Pope Stephens' [i.e. Estienne's 1546 New Testament], I can set out an edition of each in columns, without using any book under 900 years old, that shall...exactly agree.' Aware that he was treading on sensitive ground, Bentley took a more reverent approach to the extant documentary witnesses, avowing that 'in the Sacred Writings there's no place for Conjectures...Diligence and Fidelity...are the Characters here requisite' (Bentley, *Proposals*, sig. A2^v).

Bentley's work had a huge effect on classical editing in Europe and England, where his numerous disciples included Jeremiah Markland (1693–1776) and Richard Porson. His influence also extended into the expanding field of the editing of secular, modern, and early modern literary writing, particularly to Lewis Theobald. For Theobald—editor of Shakespeare (1733) and the critic, in *Shakespeare Restored* (1726), of Pope's earlier, aesthetically driven edition of the playwright's works—the Shakespearean textual situation resembled that of the ancient classics. No 'authentic Manuscript' survived, and 'for near a Century, his Works were republish'd from the faulty Copies without the Assistance of any intelligent Editor...*Shakespeare*'s Case has...resembled That of a corrupt *Classic*; and, consequently, the Method of Cure was likewise to bear a Resemblance' (Smith, 74, 75). Theobald, as an 'intelligent' editor, was prepared, like Bentley, to venture conjectural emendation and to do so through careful reasoning based on a remarkably thorough knowledge of his author's writings, language, and broader cultural and linguistic context. The 'want of Originals' may require us to guess, but 'these Guesses turn into Something of a more *substantial* Nature, when they are tolerably supported by *Reason* or *Authorities*' (Theobald, 133). Theobald's 18th-century successors followed him in their almost universal agreement that textual choices should be made on the basis of interpretive, as well as documentary, arguments. Nevertheless, as the century wore on, editors more fully recognized the status and authority of the folio and quarto texts, found better access to copies of both, and benefited from increasing understanding of Shakespeare and his times. Critical divination became a less significant part of an editor's methods: 'As I practised conjecture more, I learned to trust it less,' Samuel Johnson famously wrote in the Preface to his 1765 edition (Smith, 145).

Theobald and Johnson, for all their textual care, followed the *textus receptus* of Shakespeare, based on the Fourth Folio and inherited through the publishing house of Tonson, which owned the Shakespearean copyright. In a significant move, Edward Capell not only bypassed traditional textual corruption, but applied a sophisticated editorial practice. Having collected virtually all the early printed editions of Shakespeare, Capell proceeded to collation, adhering 'invariably to the old editions, (that is, the best of them) which hold now the place of manuscripts' (Shakespeare, 1. 20). From those early editions, he chose one as the 'ground-work' of his own text, never to be 'departed from, but in places where some other edition had a reading most apparently better; or in such other places as were very plainly corrupt but, assistance of books failing, were to be amended by conjecture' (Capell, i). Capell's use of the earliest texts, his relatively sophisticated understanding of textual authority, and his willingness to apply conjecture where the documents were demonstrably corrupt (i.e. resistant to interpretation by appeal to contextual knowledge) anticipates key features of the Greg–Bowers position in 20th-century textual theory.

The most important contribution to classical and biblical editing was the extended formulation of stemmatics by Karl Lachmann (1793–1853), and his forerunners F. A. Wolf, K. G. Zumpt, and F. W. Ritschl. For textual traditions where the original MSS are lost, even sophisticated practitioners lacked a clear and overriding principle for understanding relations amongst derivative MSS (and printed texts), and were thus limited in the extent to which they could provide bibliographical arguments for editorial choice. Lachmann's genealogical method transformed classical editing, and retains some value today. The editor, by this method, begins with a process of *recensio*, analysing the MS evidence and constructing a *stemma codicum*, a family tree of surviving MSS deriving from an archetype. The enabling principle is that 'community of error implies community of origin', i.e. if two or more MSS share a set of 'variants', they may be assumed to derive from a common source. MSS that can be shown to derive from other extant MSS may be excluded from editorial consideration. From the extant later MSS, it is possible to reconstruct an archetype, usually a lost but sometimes a surviving MS. On the basis of the *recensio* results, an editor may construct a text (*examinatio*), choosing between witnessed readings on the basis of the *stemma*, and making conjectural changes (*emendatio*) at points in the text where the MS tradition fails to provide a credible authorial original.

Lachmann's procedure provided some solid methodological ground for textual editing where originary documents were lost. Nonetheless, it has several limitations. It assumes that each witness derives from only one exemplar, although scribes since antiquity have attempted to improve their work with readings from second or further sources, producing conflated, or contaminated, texts. It assumes that a derivative text can only produce new errors, not introduce corrections. Constructing the guiding stemma also involves judgements about the number and nature of variant readings. Lachmann's method assumes a single authoritative source, not allowing for such complexities as authorial revision. Joseph Bédier alleged that textual critics overwhelmingly construct stemmata with two branches, which does not constitute a historically probable result; in his own work, Bédier rejected eclectic choice among witnessed readings and preferred the conservative policy of selecting a 'bon manuscrit', chosen on such grounds as coherence and regularity, minimally amended.

At the beginning of the 20th century, the most forceful theoretical writings on classical textual editing were those by A. E. Housman. Their lasting import is in no way weakened by their frequent acerbity. For Housman, Lachmann's method was essential; it had properly removed from consideration 'hundreds of MSS., once deemed authorities' (*Manilius*, 1. xxxiii). Nonetheless, textual criticism 'is not a branch of mathematics, nor indeed an exact science at all. It deals with a matter...fluid and variable; namely the frailties and aberrations of the human mind, and of its insubordinate servants, the human fingers' ('Application', 69). Its subject is to be found in 'phenomena which are the results of the play of the human mind' (*Confines*, 38). Textual problems are individual; they require particular solutions. Textual criticism cannot be reduced to hard rules and fixed procedures; it requires 'the application of thought'. Housman had particular contempt for editors who, bewildered by the rival merit of multiple witnesses, retreated from critical judgment into reliance on 'the best MS.' Such a method 'saves lazy editors from working and stupid editors from thinking', but it inevitably begets 'indifference to the author himself', whose original words may not be found in such a MS (*Manilius*, 1. xxxii; *Lucan*, vi). Nor can it be assumed that the correction of obvious errors in a single witness will restore authorial readings: 'Chance and the common course of nature will not bring it to pass that the readings of a MS. are right wherever they are possible and impossible wherever they are wrong' (*Manilius*, 1. xxxii). It is the textual critic's responsibility to identify error, on the basis of the most extensive knowledge of 'literary culture', grammar, and metre, and by the exercise of 'clear wits and right thinking' (*Confines*, 43). The knowledgeable editor will know enough to recognize possible readings, and find 'that many verses hastily altered by some editors and absurdly defended by others can be made to yield a just sense without either changing the text or inventing a new Latinity'. However, Housman was equally alert to the dangers of 'the art of explaining corrupt passages instead of correcting them' (*Manilius*, 1. xl, xli). Behind all these propositions stands Housman's invariable insistence that textual editing should start with the author's thought.

4 Twentieth-century theories and practices of textual editing

As secular classics became increasingly the focus of scholarship in the humanities at the start of the 20th century, so a new methodological sophistication was applied to their textual criticism. The so-called New Bibliography was developed by R. B. McKerrow and W. W. Greg. McKerrow was first to use the phrase 'copy text'. The concept of using a particular text as the basis of an edition was not new, but in McKerrow's thinking it is specifically theorized as the text that best represents the author's intentions. In his earlier work, McKerrow argued that the editor should accept such later texts as incorporated authorial revisions and corrections (Nashe, 2. 197). Subsequently believing that a later edition would 'deviate more widely than the earliest print from the author's original manuscript', he argued that editors should base their text on 'the earliest "good" print', and insert 'from the first [later] edition which contains them, such corrections as appear to us to be derived from the author'. Even at this stage, however, McKerrow's position remained essentially conservative. Resisting eclectic choice, he insisted that where a later edition contained demonstrably authorial substantive variants the editor must adopt them all: 'We are not to regard the "goodness" of a reading in and by itself... we are to consider whether a particular edition taken *as a whole* contains variants from the edition from which it was otherwise printed which could not reasonably be attributed to an ordinary press-corrector, but... seem likely to be the work of the author' (McKerrow, *Prolegomena*, 18). McKerrow's position remains here perilously close to the 'best MS' approach.

New Bibliographical theory reached its classic development in Greg's influential article 'The Rationale of Copy-Text'. Here Greg, in answer to McKerrow, mounted a powerful argument for critical editing. Rejecting 'the old fallacy of the "best text"' (Greg, 'Rationale', 24), by which an editor thinks himself obliged to adopt all the readings of his exemplar, he distinguished between substantive readings ('those namely that affect the author's meaning') and accidentals ('such in general as spelling, punctuation, word-division... affecting mainly... formal presentation') (p. 21). He argued that 'the copy-text should govern (generally) in the matter of accidentals, but that the choice between substantive readings belongs to the general theory of textual criticism and lies altogether beyond the narrow principle of the copy-text' (p. 26). In Greg's recommended procedure, the editor (where extant texts 'form an ancestral series') normally chooses the earliest text, which will 'not only come nearest to the author's original in accidentals, but also (revision apart) most faithfully preserve the correct readings where substantive variants are in question' (pp. 22, 29). Having chosen the copy text, the editor will follow it regarding accidentals. Where there is more than one text of comparable authority, however, 'copy-text can be allowed no over-riding or even preponderant authority so far as substantive readings are concerned' (p. 29). For Greg, as for McKerrow, the editor seeks the author's intended text, and is thus obliged to 'exercise his judgement' rather than fall back on 'some arbitrary canon' (p. 28). By applying critical discrimination amongst substantive readings in the quest for authorial readings, Greg belongs to an English lineage that includes Bentley, Housman, and Theobald.

It is an exaggeration to say that all subsequent textual critical theory consists of footnotes to Greg; nonetheless, a high proportion of writing on the subject over the last half century has elaborated and developed Greg's thinking, or positioned itself in opposition to his tenets or their implications. Greg's rationale continues to provide a vital framework for editors working on English literary texts. Greg's most notable expositors and followers have been F. T. Bowers and G. Thomas Tanselle. Greg's expertise (like McKerrow's, and that of their ally A. W. Pollard) lay chiefly in the field of 16th- and 17th-century literature, but Bowers insisted that Greg's was 'the most workable editorial principle yet contrived to produce a critical text that is authoritative in the maximum of its details...The principle is sound without regard for the literary period' (Bowers, 'Multiple Authority', 86). Indeed, Bowers's own extraordinary editorial output included authors from Marlowe and Dekker, through Dryden and Fielding, to Whitman, Crane, and Nabokov. The Modern Language Association of America adopted the Greg–Bowers position as the basis for its *Statement of Editorial Principles and Procedures* (1967), which guided the work of the Center for Editions of American Authors (established 1963). Bowers's major statements of bibliographical and editorial principle and method may be found in *Principles of Bibliographical Description* (1949), *On Editing Shakespeare and the Elizabethan Dramatists* (1955), *Textual and Literary Criticism* (1959), and *Bibliography and Textual Criticism* (1964).

A major predicate of the work of McKerrow, Greg, Bowers, and Tanselle is that the goal of literary editorial enquiry is the text intended finally by the author. In an age where the concept of authorial intention, or rather its knowability and reconstructability, has itself come under serious attack, this predicate has required sophisticated justification. A key document in this process has been Tanselle's 'The Editorial Problem of Final Authorial Intention', which draws on an extensive range of theoretical writing, including E. D. Hirsch's *Validity in Interpretation* (1967). Editors, Tanselle suggests, 'are in general agreement that their goal is to discover exactly what an author wrote and to determine what form of his work he wished the public to have'. Editorial choice depends upon a critical determination of intended authorial wording and meaning: 'of the meanings which the editor sees in the work, he will determine, through a weighing of all the information at his command, the one which he regards as most likely to have been the author's; and that determination will influence his decisions regarding variant readings' (Tanselle, 'Editorial Problem', 167, 210).

Authorial intention as a basis for textual editing is nevertheless a complex 'problem', and it has been interrogated from many points of view. Some have seen the privileging of authorial intention not as a rational choice, but determined by ideologies of individualism. Morse Peckham has complained that to privilege authorial intention is a form of 'hagiolatry', attributing to the author divine inspiration or charisma (Peckham, 136). Others, such as Greetham, have represented the project of reconstruction of an authorially intended text as an impossible Platonizing attempt to find a nonexistent ideal, a 'text that never was' (Greetham, *Theories*, 40). Texts raising particularly complex questions of intention and revision have given rise to significant shifts or innovations in the editorial paradigm. One controversial exemplar has been George Kane and E. Talbot Donaldson's edition of the B-text of *Piers Plowman* (1975), in which the editors insistently privileged the interpretation of variants based on internal evidence, rather than prior recension. Another, yet more contested, has been Hans Walter Gabler's edition of Joyce's *Ulysses* (1984), in which a clean 'reading' text was printed in parallel with a synoptic text and its apparatus, which documented in detail the diachronic processes of Joyce's alterations. The necessity of extensive textual apparatuses that provide full evidence for editorial deviations from the documentary witnesses has exercised both critical editors and their opponents. Issues raised by authorial revision, already present in writings within the Greg–Bowers tradition, have been a continuing matter of editorial concern. Authorial revision may produce distinct versions, of which no conflated edition can be properly representative. This argument—persuasive in the case of *Piers Plowman* and unimpeachable in the case of Wordsworth's *Prelude*, which grew from a two-book poem (1799) to a thirteen-book poem (1805)—has had force too for less obviously extensive revisions. In Shakespearean textual criticism, it has resulted in discrete editions of the 1608 quarto *History of King Lear* and the 1623 Folio *Tragedy of King Lear*. Parker has argued that relatively small-scale authorial revisions may have partly or wholly unintended consequences for large-scale textual meaning. Greg's textual discriminations have come under fire, as mechanisms of selection and control, in recent arguments for 'unediting' that dismiss cases for textual choice (on interpretive or bibliographical grounds) as arbitrary and ideologically driven, and prefer previously rejected texts, readings, and variants.

The argument for unediting may arise out of an informed insistence on bibliographical particularity, which conscientiously eschews semantic reading and the editorial process of discrimination arising from it (as with Randall McLeod), or from a rejection, itself ideologically compromised, of the historical reliance of critical editors on evidence and reason (as with Marcus). The radical scepticism of postmodern theory has also found its way into textual thinking. Goldberg, for instance, has argued that the multiple forms taken by texts mean 'that there is no text itself...that a text cannot be fixed in terms of original or final intentions'. Hence, Goldberg concludes, 'no word in the text is sacred. If this is true, all criticism that has based itself on the text, all forms of formalism, all close reading, is given the lie' (Goldberg, 214, 215). This is a conclusion that, taken seriously, would disable not only the Greg–Bowers rationale but all text-based academic disciplines, and the book itself.

One of the most significant movements in text critical theory of the last three decades has been a sense amongst some thinkers—notably D. F. McKenzie and Jerome J. McGann—that the Greg–Bowers line reduced bibliography and textual editing to 'a sharply restricted analytic field' in 'desocializing' the understanding of textual production. Rejecting authorial autonomy and the possibility of an uninfluenced intention, McGann insisted that 'literary works are fundamentally social rather than personal or psychological products, they do not even acquire an artistic form of being until their engagement with an audience has been determined...literary works must be produced within some appropriate set of social institutions' (McGann, *Critique*, 119, 121, 43–4). Those social institutions include scribes, collaborators, editors, censors, the printing office, publishers, and the theatre. The production of the literary work, as well as its meanings, is significantly shaped, on this account, by multiple human agents and the forms of presentation with which those agents endow the work. The social argument has been persuasive for many areas of textual work—especially for modern Shakespeare editors, who would shift the emphasis from the book focus of the Greg–Bowers school towards the negotiation amongst playwright, playhouse, players, and audience.

The extent and consequences of these challenges are real, though it has been argued that the breadth and flexibility of the Greg–Bowers position has not always been fully comprehended and that it remains a competent rationale. It has not been refuted by the historical facts of authorial revision and distinct versions, or the social circumstances of literary creativity and production; none of these factors is wholly new to the debate. As Tanselle puts it, 'critical editors interested in authors' final intentions are not trying to mix versions but to recreate one...critical editors...all must rely on surviving documents...and strive to reconstruct from them the texts that were intended by particular persons (whether authors alone, or authors in collaboration with others) at particular points in the past' (Tanselle, 'Textual Criticism and Literary Sociology', 120, 126).

The book-based edition itself faces a challenge from the most consequential recent development in textual criticism: the exploitation of computational resources (*see* **21**). A straightforward and powerful example is the full-text electronic database (e.g. Early English Books Online or Eighteenth-Century Collections Online), which provides users with facsimile pages of an astonishing range of early books. More complex, multimedia hypertextual resources are available on the World Wide Web. Though the printed critical edition has been itself a hypertext of a sophisticated kind, it is certainly true that electronic hypertext can do much that the book cannot. Electronic memory allows for the presentation of multiple particular versions of the text of any particular work. Hyperlinks enable flexible connections among those texts, and among an essentially unlimited range of contexts, in video, audio, and textual formats. Software applications allow for seemingly infinite varieties of search and comparison among the resources of the hypertextual database. There are parallels and synergies here with postmodern tendencies in recent contemporary critical theory. Major hypertextual archives (e.g. the Rossetti Archive at the University of Virginia) already exist, and a number of writers—Landow, Lanham, McGann (*Radiant Textuality*)—have begun to develop the theory of hypertext, mostly in positive terms.

Electronic forms are inherently inclusive, and are thus powerful and valuable in themselves. However, either they do not make discriminations, or they make discriminations in hidden and unarticulated ways. Because of their very plenitude, hypertext archives are not editions. Books are crafted objects, embodying critical intelligence, made by the normally irreversible decisions of their authors, printers, and publishers. The book-based scholarly edition embodies its maker's ethical choices amongst texts, variants, and understandings. Harold Love has argued that 'the electronic medium with its infinite capacity to manufacture increasingly meaningless "choices" and its unwillingness to accept closure is almost by definition post-ethical or even anti-ethical' (Love, 274–5). Editors and textual critics, as they embrace some of the pleasures of an electronic future, will need more than ever to create central and transparent roles for agency, responsibility, and critical intelligence.

BIBLIOGRAPHY

J. H. Bentley, *Humanists and Holy Writ* (1983)

R. Bentley, ed., *Q. Horatius Flaccus* (1711)

—— *Proposals for Printing a New Edition of the Greek Testament* (1721)

F. Bowers, 'Some Principles for Scholarly Editions of Nineteenth-Century American Authors', *SB* 17 (1964), 223–8

—— 'Multiple Authority: New Problems and Concepts of Copy-Text', *Library*, 5/27 (1972), 81–115

E. Capell, *Prolusions; or, Select Pieces of Antient Poetry* (1760)

W. Chernaik *et al.*, eds., *The Politics of the Electronic Text* (1993)

T. Davis, 'The CEAA and Modern Textual Editing', *Library*, 5/32 (1977), 61–74

P. Delany and G. Landow, eds., *Hypermedia and Literary Studies* (1991)

J. Goldberg, 'Textual Properties', *SQ* 37 (1986), 213–17

A. Grafton, *Defenders of the Text* (1991)

D. C. Greetham, *Scholarly Editing* (1995)

—— *Theories of the Text* (1999)

W. W. Greg, 'The Rationale of Copy-Text', *SB* (1950–51), 19–36

A. E. Housman, ed., *M. Manilii Astronomicon* (5 vols, 1903–30)

—— 'The Application of Thought to Textual Criticism', *Proceedings of the Classical Association*, 18 (1921), 67–84

—— ed., *Lucan Bellum Civile* (1926)

—— *Selected Prose*, ed. J. Carter (1961)

—— *The Confines of Criticism*, ed. J. Carter (1969)

G. Landow, *Hypertext* (1992)

R. A. Lanham, *The Electronic Word* (1993)

H. Love, 'The Intellectual Heritage of Donald Francis McKenzie', *Library*, 7/2 (2001), 266–80

L. Marcus, *Unediting the Renaissance* (1996)

R. Markley, ed., *Virtual Realities and their Discontents* (1996)

J. McGann, *A Critique of Modern Textual Criticism* (1983)

—— *The Beauty of Inflections* (1985)

—— *Textual Criticism and Literary Interpretation* (1985)

—— *The Textual Condition* (1991)

—— 'Textual Criticism and Literary Sociology', *SB* 44 (1991), 84–143

—— *Radiant Textuality* (2001)

D. F. McKenzie, *Bibliography and the Sociology of Texts* (1986)

McKerrow, *Introduction*

R. B. McKerrow, *Prolegomena for the Oxford Shakespeare* (1939)

R. McLeod, 'UN *Editing* Shak-speare', *SubStance*, 10 (1982), 26–55

Metzger, *The Text of the New Testament* (1992)

G. Most, 'Classical Scholarship and Literary Criticism', in *The Cambridge History of Literary Criticism*, vol. 4: *The Eighteenth Century*, ed. H. B. Nisbet and C. Rawson, (1997)

T. Nashe, *The Works of Thomas Nashe*, ed. R. B. McKerrow (5 vols, 1904–10; 2e, rev. F. P. Wilson, 1958)

H. Parker, *Flawed Texts and Verbal Icons* (1984)

M. Peckham, 'Reflections on the Foundations of Modern Textual Editing', *Proof*, 1 (1971), 122–55

Reynolds and Wilson

W. Shakespeare, *Mr William Shakespeare his Comedies, Histories, and Tragedies*, ed. E. Capell (10 vols, 1767–8)

P. Shillingsburg, *Scholarly Editing in the Computer Age* (1996)

D. N. Smith, ed., *Eighteenth Century Essays on Shakespeare*, 2e (1963)

G. Tanselle, 'Greg's Theory of Copy-Text and the Editing of American Literature', *SB* 28 (1975), 167–230

—— 'The Editorial Problem of Final Authorial Intention', *SB* 29 (1976), 167–211

—— 'The Editing of Historical Documents', *SB* 31 (1978), 2–57

—— 'The Concept of *Ideal Copy*', *SB* 33 (1980), 18–53

—— 'Recent Editorial Discussion and the Central Questions of Editing', *SB* 34 (1981), 23–65

—— 'Classical, Biblical, and Medieval Textual Criticism and Modern Editing', *SB* 36 (1983), 21–68

—— 'Historicism and Critical Editing', *SB* 39 (1986), 1–46

—— *A Rationale of Textual Criticism* (1989)

—— 'Textual Criticism and Deconstruction', *SB* 43 (1990), 1–33

—— 'Textual Criticism and Literary Sociology', *SB* 44 (1991), 83–143

L. Theobald, *Shakespeare Restored* (1726)

U. von Wilamowitz-Moellendorff, *History of Classical Scholarship*, ed. H. Lloyd-Jones (1982)

W. Williams and C. Abbott, *An Introduction to Bibliographical and Textual Studies* (1999)

F. Wolf, *Prolegomena to Homer 1795*, tr. A. Grafton *et al.* (1985)

21

The Electronic Book

EILEEN GARDINER AND RONALD G. MUSTO

1 Definition

An electronic book (also e-book, ebook, digital book) is a text-, acoustic-, and image-based publication in digital form produced on, published by means of, and readable on computers or other digital devices. E-books are presented visually or aurally, as with the audio book, which repurposed text on a page into an aural medium—a precursor to, and limited exemplum of, electronic publishing's potential. Components other than text have been considered by some as enhancements, including multimedia (sound, images, film/video/animated graphics). By others, these very features define the essence of the electronic book. The e-book and its definition are still a work in progress, emerging from the history of the printed book and evolving technologies. This essay is thus an attempt at an historical survey and not a guide to current innovations or future trends in a rapidly evolving digital realm. In this context, it is less useful to consider the book as object—particularly as commercial object—than to view it as cultural practice and process, with the e-book as one manifestation of this practice.

2 History

This brief history of e-books covers the period from 1945, when visions of e-books are first found in print, to early 2013, when many false starts have been supplanted by a model that has resulted in e-books (content), e-readers (devices), and readers (audience) on a scale that could guarantee sustainability.

2.1 Print antecedents

From the mid-1970s, text- and image-based publications were being produced by computer. The first developments took place in the newspaper industry, and the book business followed. Some segments of the book industry, particularly scholarly publishing and other economically marginal areas, had experimented in the 1970s and 1980s with author-generated books. Following complex instructions from their publishers, authors would produce camera-ready copy that could be used to create plates for printing. When authors began to have desktop computers, they produced copy that could compete with the quality of typeset pages. Within ten years, books were being produced on desktop machines, and innovators in book production had harnessed the power of these small computers to produce books inexpensively from electronic MSS or by simple rekeying, using word-processing software—the era of desktop publishing had begun. By the early 1990s, these capacities were expanded by sophisticated page-makeup programs like PageMaker (later InDesign) and Quark.

Large commercial publishers had invested heavily in the traditional forms of production and were slow at first to adopt new methods. Typesetters, however, were often using computers, even before the publishers who contracted work out to them were aware of it. From the mid-1990s publishers understood the power of exploiting this technology themselves, which had a significant impact on the cost and speed of book production and resulted in the nearly fourfold growth in the number of US titles produced annually between 1994 (52,000) and 2004 (195,000).

The files used to produce books could be read on a computer screen, but paper was still the medium of presentation. Electronic files alone were not enough to initiate a revolution in reading. Many factors had to be in place before the era of e-books arrived.

2.2 Digital development

In July 1945 Vannevar Bush, a pioneering engineer in the development of analog computing, published an article in which he introduced the Memex: a hypothetical instrument to control the ever-accumulating body of scientific literature. He envisioned an active desk that performed as a storage and retrieval system. A Memex user would consult a book by tapping a code on a keyboard, bringing up the text. The Memex had many features that are now familiar components of e-books: pages, page turners, annotation capability, internal and external linking, and the potential for storage, retrieval, and transmittal. However, Bush imagined that all this would be accomplished through the medium of microfilm.

It would be another twenty years before the development of one of the essential elements of the electronic book: hyperlinking. In 1965 Ted (Theodor Holm) Nelson first published the terms 'hypertext' and 'hypermedia'. These two aspects of hyperlinking were developed by teams of engineers working throughout the

1960s and 1970s. On 9 December 1968, Douglas Engelbart made a presentation, now known as 'The Mother of All Demos', of the oNLine System (or NLS), developed at the Stanford Research Institute. This event introduced many of the elements of today's digital world: e-mail, teleconferencing, video-conferencing, and the mouse. Most importantly for the future of the book, it demonstrated hypertext and introduced the 'paper paradigm', which embodied the current standard experience of a computer: windows, black text on white background, files, folders, and a desktop.

At the same time, Andries van Dam was working with colleagues at the Brown University Center for Computer & Information Sciences, developing the Hypertext Editing System, unveiled in April 1969. This spawned a variety of hypermedia and hypertext experiments during the 1970s and 1980s. Between 1978 and 1980, students at the Massachusetts Institute of Technology produced the first significant hypermedia application, the Aspen Moviemap, which used a stop-frame camera to create an interactive map of Aspen, Colorado, based on actual photos. These experiments culminated in the development of HyperCard at Apple Computer by Bill Atkinson in 1987. Apple released this software as freeware on its new Macintosh computer. Content creators immediately embraced the program's promise.

Although many early works have no doubt been lost, one has long endured. In 1988, Brian Thomas, along with Philip A. Mohr, Jr., released *If Monks Had Macs*...from their company, riverText. It was first published as a collection of games and serious ideas constructed in HyperCard using the pre-print metaphor of a monastic library, complete with music and the sound of a cloister's fountain. It came on 800K diskettes as Macintosh freeware, thus establishing an early precedent that would resonate in the later open-access movement. It also included what Thomas said 'might be called the first real or widely read e-book', *The Imitation of Christ*, one of the first bestsellers of the Gutenberg revolution (*see* **6**). *If Monks*...also included an introduction to the White Rose, a clandestine group of young German students who were hunted down and summarily executed for distributing anti-Nazi pamphlets they printed on a secret press.

The choices in *If Monks Had Macs*...were prophetic: its metaphors of pre-print MS, early print, and samizdat-like marginal publishing not only introduced a new medium, but set the intellectual and cultural paradoxes within which the e-book still operates: an essentially nonlinear, multiple medium that most readers and producers approach with the cultural apparatus developed for the codex. It was also both retrospective and prescient in terms of production and distribution: like early print, it was created and circulated outside the mainstream of academic and large business institutions.

In 1993, the small independent firm, Italica Press, published its first e-book, also on HyperCard on two 800K diskettes: *The Marvels of Rome for the Macintosh* was an electronic edition of the celebrated medieval guide to the city. In a 1994 review, *Architronic* remarked: 'It is an enjoyable demonstration of the future of HyperCard programming, when interactive layers will make innovative approaches to thinking about texts possible.' In 1995, *If Monks Had Macs...* was commercially released by Voyager, which had previously released an annotated, disk-based version of the Beatles' *A Hard Day's Night*—a marvel of electronic publishing, if only a curiosity of cinema.

2.3 The CD-ROM

Although tours de force, these early experiments were cumbersome, slow, and nearly unviewable. Things began to change with the introduction of the CD-ROM in 1987. Already in use in the music industry by 1982, the CD-ROM was first widely integrated into consumer computers as a storage device in the 1991 Apple Macintosh. A CD could hold nearly 800MB and was far more convenient to handle, store, and transport than an 800K or 1.4MB diskette. By 1992, the first e-book titles began to arrive on CD-ROM, again as freeware, but intended to encourage consumers to purchase computers with new CD-ROM drives.

By 1993, 4 million CD-ROM players had been sold in the US market; large publishing firms, which had hesitated to enter the market as long as e-books were diskette-based and limited in size, now jumped in. CD-ROM book sales reached nearly $1 billion by 1994, with more than 8,000 titles, ranging from the Bible to reference and business books, and from fiction to children's literature. Bookshop chains were encouraged to set aside CD-ROM sections for the new e-books, and the industry began to float the first of many pronouncements of the end of print. By late 1994, however, sagging sales and a stagnating user base of individual computer owners with CD-ROM drives (5 million)—coupled with a widespread discontent within the library community over the difficulty of cataloguing, and providing storage and access for, the new medium—sent CD-ROM titles tumbling from most publishers' lists. The Library of Congress's decision not to catalogue CD-ROMs confirmed their end for all but large reference collections, archival use, or supplemental material in textbooks, instructors' manuals, or study guides. By the late 1990s, most narrative titles on CD had become audio books: a return not to the codex but to pre-codex oral traditions.

2.4 The World Wide Web

Although disk-based e-books proved as ephemeral to the development of the electronic book as block printing and the block book in the ultimate development of the print revolution, the lessons learned during the years of developing digital content were not lost. Large corporate investments in the digitization of content, improvements in delivery software, and the vital experience in conceptualizing hypertext and in obtaining and then protecting digital rights, had profound effects on the development of the e-book, even if the largest stakeholders ultimately decided to stand on the sidelines and await further signs of progress.

The invention and growth of the World Wide Web was particularly important for e-books, because the Internet provided enormous advantages in storage, retrieval, and delivery. Yet, the first library of e-books antedates this techno-logical leap by almost 25 years. In 1971, Michael Hart at the University of Illinois began Project Gutenberg (PG) by creating electronic texts of small, public-domain works, beginning with the Declaration of Independence, the Bill of Rights, and the US Constitution. These were hand-keyed: a labour-intensive, and volunteer, effort. When the capacity of storage media increased, PG digitized larger books, including *Alice's Adventures in Wonderland*, *Peter Pan*, and the Bible; and with the development of affordable optical character recognition (OCR) technology by the mid-1990s, PG could rely on a speedier processing method, which eventually had nearly the same level of accuracy as rekeying. This pioneer initiative continues on 40 mirror sites with thousands of books that can be read on any computer, personal digital assistant (PDA), smartphone, or reading device.

3 Scale and commercialization

Technologically, commercially, and culturally, the e-book remained essentially a digital version of print; yet by 2003 virtually all content was being produced digitally, either originally created or retrospectively converted. To accomplish this conversion, most enterprises relied either on automated digitization or on the low wages and long working hours of thousands of centres in the Global South (primarily in India), where an enormous new workforce could produce encoded text, images, and links. This raised ethical and economic issues that were virtually nonexistent for the print book, which grew out of the highly skilled guild and other craft enterprises of the late Middle Ages and remained the realm of expert and relatively well-compensated craftsmen.

As early as the 1980s, computer servers were developed with the capacity to store and distribute digital content consistently and widely; from 1991, Gophers and listservs began to establish networks of both scholarly and non-commercial communication. With the emergence of CompuServe and AOL in 1995, widespread commercial delivery systems had begun to take advantage of the web's broad interconnectedness, and its ability to store and serve up content independent of client machines and physical media like diskettes or the CD-ROM.

The development of independent web-browsing software took these disparate elements and brought the possibilities of the e-book one step forward. There were several early examples, but Mosaic, the first 'user-friendly' browser, was not released until 1993. It was developed at the National Center for Supercomputing Applications (NCSA) at the University of Illinois at Urbana-Champaign. Mosaic changed the face of the Internet with the integration of text and image in the same window. Marc Andreessen, the leader of the team that developed it with funding from the National Science Foundation, soon turned Mosaic into a commercial venture that developed into Netscape; Netscape introduced Navigator in 1994. In the same year, Microsoft introduced Explorer, also based on Mosaic. In 1993 there were 500 web servers, and by 1994 there were 10,000; by

June 2007 there were over 125 million websites, and by March 2012 644 million (according to Netcraft)—the shift from counting servers to sites reflecting an enormous growth and change in hosting, from discrete peripheral networks to colossal aggregated data centres.

Such developments meant that libraries of e-books emulating PG began to appear with frequency in the late 1990s. Some mimicked libraries of printed materials by providing a searchable catalogue of available works; others featured searchability of the full text across the collection. Some, such as netLibrary, offered digital downloads; others, including Perseus, Questia, ACLS Humanities E-Book, and Oxford Scholarship Online, afforded online access through institutional or individual subscription. A commercial avatar of PG appeared in the Google Book venture, which promised vast amounts of content free to users. Its liberal approach to copyrighted material, particularly 'orphan works', proved controversial, and the project became mired in a continuing negotiation—with authors, publishers, and courts—known as the 'Google Book Settlement'. The Internet Archive's Text Collection navigated the same waters, but successfully restricted its content to out-of-copyright works in a wide variety of e-book formats, and as of 2012 could deliver nearly 3 million public domain books to readers. Large, print booksellers (e.g. Barnes & Noble and amazon.com), publishers with their own online stores, and dedicated online electronic booksellers favoured a retail model—selling one e-book at a time.

4 Characteristics

Certain characteristics of e-books seem unlikely to change, as they are determined either by cultural habitus or the physiology of reading. These are associated with the codex: title, contributors, table of contents, list of illustrations and tables, front matter, chapters, pages (or screens), page or paragraph numbers (or location numbers), running heads, book marks, annotations, back matter (index, glossary, references, notes, bibliography, etc.), copyright notice, cataloguing information, and International Standard Book Number (ISBN). Although these elements have the same taxonomies in print and electronic media, they may sometimes have a different form and function. For instance, the table of contents in an e-book, instead of being on its own page or pages, may be located in a separate cell next to the text and viewable throughout the book. 'Pages' or 'screens' need not be all the same size and can function organically in relation to the relative size of portions of the text. A page might contain a paragraph or as much as a whole chapter, although for ease of reading and navigation, the chapter is often broken into subsections, each presented on a separate page. In an e-book, pages, paragraphs, or locations are often numbered for identification and referencing. Annotations need not be either footnotes or endnotes. They can appear in a separate (pop-up or parallel) window, giving the reader the opportunity to look at the text and the annotation simultaneously.

They can also appear in the separate window with all the other notes, so that the reader can see them in context. Cross-references hyperlinked within a book can bring a reader to other locations in the text, as well as to reference materials, such as glossaries, dictionaries, and gazetteers.

Such fluidity more closely resembles the process of reading embedded in medieval manuscript culture than the standardized industrial product of print culture. There are several advantages to e-books over their print counterparts. Convenience is one. Having neither weight nor volume, electronic books are easy to store and transport. They offer greater flexibility in format: colour, size, fonts, layouts are all tremendously variable, even within the parameters of good taste, again more closely resembling manuscript variation than print uniformity. They offer a richer reading experience through hyperlinking to sound, video, images, and text. E-books can also incorporate a remarkable timeliness: they can be scripted to gain access to current information from online resources, or information can be updated on devices as required.

In 2000, in a remarkable exploration of the possibilities of this model, Simon & Schuster published online and available for download a novella, *Riding the Bullet*, by one of its star authors, Stephen King. At a price of $2.50, and at the same time offered for free by some online booksellers, 400,000 downloads on the first day reportedly froze servers at SoftLock. This traditional book in electronic form made little use of digital enhancements within the narrative itself, unlike the work of writers who employ electronic authoring tools, from the pioneering work of Michael Joyce and his *Afternoon: A Story*, published in 1987 using Storyspace, to J. R. Carpenter's HTML-based *City Fish*, published in 2010 on Luckysoap. The most advanced uses of electronic capabilities in nonfiction are evident in some of the work of ACLS Humanities E-Book, which incorporated sound, video, and databases into a small subset of TEI-encoded e-books within its collection of more than 3,000 monographs in the humanities. In the future, the distinction between the 'book' and other digital media may change or become blurred, but currently the e-book paradigm that generated the established base of e-book readers is a traditional linear print book readable on digital devices. Change in book culture has come about not by solitary, exemplary projects, but through accumulated critical mass. The light bulb has eclipsed the wonder show.

5 Reading practices and authorship

To understand what components of an e-book make it a 'book' is only half the subject at hand. The other half is to understand what components make it electronic. By definition, it is in digital form: produced on, published by, and readable on a computer or other device, but special attributes accrue to the book by this form. The principal feature of an e-book is hyperlinking, or moving seamlessly from one place to another designated place or 'target' by clicking on text or image (hypertext and hypermedia respectively). Most of the navigation features of e-books are the result of hyperlinking, whether the table of contents, annotations, cross-references, bookmarks, or other resources. A related capability is scripting: like hyperlinking, scripting initiates an action, but rather than simply bringing the reader to another place, it can trigger complex automated actions simultaneously, such as opening additional windows, playing music or video, enlarging images, and enabling readers' responses, including annotation in verbal, aural, or video format.

Searchability is another key feature of the e-book and functions both within the given work or external related resources to identify word or other object occurrences. Searching does not simply replace an index, but augments it, since indexes provide a sense of the topics, questions, and concerns of the text, regardless of the keywords an author uses. Here one encounters one of the chief issues in electronic publishing: authorial intention and control over the reader's experience of the text. Hyperlinking, non-linear and multipolar connections, and vast quantities of supplemental materials open up myriad paths to reading and interpretation: deconstruction and reassembly of an author's argument and ultimate sense may be central to the online experience; authorial voice and point of view are contested far more actively than in print.

The e-book also allows a publisher or distributor to control access to a title in ways unimagined even by the *Index Librorum Prohibitorum*. It can encrypt the book and apply a digital-rights management (DRM) scheme to any book, chapter, article, image, video clip, or sound file. It can control printing, copying, and alterations. It can—depending on legal protocols—track usage, preferences, even the rate of reading. In addition, it can set off years of debate over open access and freedom of the Internet.

6 Coding: approaches and functions

All e-books rely on systems of encoding text and images to deliver consistent and reliable results to a reader. Although it is possible to create e-books from proprietary software packages—for example, word-processing programs, page-makeup programs, extensions of such programs, or hypertext programs—this approach relies on having the proper software to read the e-books installed on the end-user's machine. Solutions to this issue take various forms. The earliest and perhaps still most universal has been ASCII (American Standard Code for Information Interchange). Because of its universal readability, sites such as PG began with, and still make available, ASCII versions of their texts, in addition to other formats. Another solution has been the various versions of 'portable document format' or PDF files first developed by Adobe for its Acrobat software in 1993 and adopted by other commercial and open-source content creators (Common Ground, Envoy). PDFs allow content to be shared with other devices regardless of platform or software. As PDF software has evolved, it has enabled creators to incorporate not only text and images, but multiple viewing options, searchability, sound, music, video, hyperlinking, scripting, and annotation. The chief limitation of collections of PDF documents, however, remains the lack of cross-searchability among titles.

The development of the Web went hand in hand with the creation of its fundamental component, Hypertext Markup Language, or HTML. This coding language is the universal engine of the Web and allows most of its basic functions. Although simple to learn and deploy, HTML has certain drawbacks, most noticeably a lack of predictable results in formatting and presenting anything but basic design layouts and text formats. To refine HTML, various other approaches have been employed, including adaptations to its parent SGML (Standard Generalized Markup Language) and the adoption of the newer XML (Extensible Markup Language). XML is currently the standard for e-book development because it offers greater control over text, images, and other e-book components. Also, and more importantly, it establishes the overall structure of e-books in an open-source, replicable, scalable, and predictable manner.

The basic language structure of XML is also a subset of SGML and was developed in the 1980s (with the most recent version, P5, published in 2007) for the parsing, presentation, and preservation of early texts. From SGML derived the conventions of the TEI (Text Encoding Initiative) consortium, from which derive most document architectures (document type definitions or DTDs). Developers continued to create sophisticated variations on page layout, hypertext, and parsing programs, but the widespread international adoption of TEI in the world of libraries, archives, and publishing has seemed to assure its place. The complexity of TEI may weigh against it, however, as publishers, devices, and platforms—such as ePub, mobi (azw), iBooks, and Kindle—incline towards a variety of formats that easily support digital rights management (DRM), images, tables, text wrap, sound, and hyperlinking. Because files in a variety of text and page-layout formats could easily be exported or converted into these distributable e-book formats, publishers and content developers have been able to create a critical mass of material quickly and economically.

7 Models and aesthetics

E-books are extremely adaptable and functional; when the proper coding language and syntax are applied, they can be formatted and designed to mirror the best print traditions and practices. Yet, this very comparison with print models raises issues of technological dependence and transition; every new model of digital innovation for the book seems to look back to historical precedents from the age of the codex and early print. After Johann Gutenberg's revolution, the various forms of book production—MS, block printing, or movable type—coexisted for almost two centuries with no readily apparent fitness of any one mode to survive the others.

Ultimately, movable type outstripped both the MS and the block book for reasons which are obvious today but which, at the time, seemed its very weaknesses: standardization; the reorganization of the page to clearly defined zones of type, margin, and image; the inflexibility of its glossing and other annotation systems; the paring down of de luxe features such as elaborately decorated or illuminated capitals, flourishes, colouring, variation of typeface and point sizes; and even limitations on the physical dimensions and media of the book—all in the name of sustainability. In the end, however, movable type's modularity offered convenience, economy, and consistency.

In the same way, the creation of standardized online tools and coding modules today may limit the creative freedom of website authors, whose works remain unique artistic creations, akin to the artist's book: beautiful works, like those by Pablo Picasso or Henri Matisse, that are not intended to be duplicated, but stand alone to present us with the freshness of the state of the art. Like the MSS of the classics and scriptures with their manifold textual variations, multiple forms of mise-en-page, and apparatuses bemoaned by Renaissance scholars and printers, these websites—like those produced by the Institute for Advanced Technology in the Humanities (IATH) at the University of Virginia and by Columbia University Press in their Gutenberg-e project—lack common standards and common norms for reading and review. These characteristics make such websites unamenable to common publishing or scholarly practices of fixed revisions and editions. Although often collaborative, these websites are also frequently individually maintained. Like the MSS scattered in monastic libraries throughout Europe that the humanists sought to recover and transform into standardized print before they disappeared, websites are also difficult to sustain and preserve.

Although by no means determinative, these lessons and precedents of the codex's past remain cogent in the digital realm. As in print, the best e-books are formatted with sufficient borders around the text block and a line length constrained by the eye's gaze—not more than ten to twelve words per line. While online choices are more limited, fonts and sizes are applied with the same care: primarily serif for text and sans serif for display. Colour is used sparingly in text, as it may distract from the flow of reading.

New and old technology: the iLiad Reader marketed by Libresco. Just as the characteristics of newspapers changed people's reading habits and the railway revolutionized the distribution of print, so e-books may change how, what, when, and where material is read. Courtesy of Libresco.com

Apart from coding languages, editorial skills, and historical precedent, some of the more significant disadvantages of e-book production in its first decade were aesthetic, perhaps chiefly as a result of the limitations of available reading devices. The electronic 'substrate', or surface that substitutes for paper, did not enhance the reading experience. Both the texture and lighting of most screens were mediocre. In addition, the space of the reading display was often small, and it was usually horizontal (or 'landscape'), whereas the print book and its cultural habitus customarily favoured a vertical (or 'portrait') format.

Presentation and reading remained highly dependent on the device and software used. Two alternatives appeared possible: devoted readers and PDAs with dedicated software, as against conventional computers with web browsers and other general-reader software. PDAs constrained the format and potential of e-books, whereas computers offered more user-friendly display space, usability, and compatibility.

Between 1999 and 2002, a concerted effort was launched to capture the term 'electronic book' or 'e-book' and associate it with the devices themselves rather than with content. This effort emanated from a 'book as object' perspective, particularly 'the book as commercial object', weighing mass and price against cultural practice. The market saw the rapid rise and decline of the devices—Franklin eBookMan, Gemstar and RCA eBooks, PalmPilots, RocketeBooks, all missing the mark.

What emerged from the first efforts to produce such devices was the development of e-book reader software, such as Adobe, Microsoft, Palm, Mobipocket, and Kindle. Initially, many were device-specific; but as desktop and laptop computers became the most widely used reading devices, browsers began to function seamlessly with reader software, thus piggybacking on an installed base of available devices, which also had the advantage of not being single-purpose or dedicated. Each year brought new efforts, and the technologies improved, so that the electronic reader might one day function like a full computer while emulating or improving upon the look and feel of the attractively bound codex.

After these device experiments around the turn of the millennium, readers were used to the recurring introduction and market failure of small, hand-held, e-book readers. In late 2007, however, a new wave began with devices that proved sustainable, in part because they were supported by the publication of sufficient e-books to attract a significant audience. In retrospect, perhaps it is only too obvious that online booksellers would be in the forefront of that wave, because they had the corporate capacity to handle sales of both books and devices, and were entrepreneurial enough to develop, create, or promote user-friendly e-book readers, platforms for e-book distribution, and formats for e-book conversion.

The first such device to market was the Kindle, launched on 19 November 2007, the product of the Internet bookseller amazon.com. The first generation of this dedicated reading device was approximately 5 x 8 inches—a very standard book size—with a greyscale display and a 250MB storage capacity, enough for approximately 200 unillustrated books. It was followed by a second-generation device with 1.4GB storage, which could hold almost eight times as many books; a larger DX version—measuring approximately 7 x 10 inches, again a very standard book size—also appeared. New generations, with a variety of new and improved features, followed approximately every year, with Kindle 3 in July 2010, Kindle 4 in September 2011, and Kindle 5 in September 2012. In the earlier versions, connectivity to the device was provided by the proprietary Whispernet, but Wi-Fi replaced Whispernet in the third generation.

In November 2009, two years after Amazon introduced the Kindle, another major bookseller with a very significant web presence, Barnes & Noble, introduced its e-reader, the Nook. Like the Kindle, the Nook originally had a greyscale display; connectivity was via Wi-Fi and 3G. Enhancements over the next four years kept pace with other developments in the e-reader world in terms of colour display and capacity.

Five months after the premiere of the Nook, on 3 April 2010, Apple released its first iPad, the device that 'changed everything'. As small as a dedicated reader, the iPad could do, or would come to do, almost everything that laptop or desktop computers would accomplish for all but the more intense users of computing power.

Each of these major new devices used specific platforms for creating e-books and delivered files using different distribution platforms. The Kindle employed the Kindle Direct Publishing platform, converting ePub files to azw format based on Mobipocket. The newer Kindle Fire reader uses a Kindle 8 format; a Kindle app delivers the files to readers. The Nook also uses ePub files, uploaded into the PubIt! platform. These are readable in the proprietary Nook app. Apple's iBook app reads files created in a proprietary ePub. Although these file formats, platforms, and apps will continue to develop and improve, the coincidence of these three devices significantly changed the entire e-book landscape. Their success was virtually guaranteed by the collaboration resulting from an almost absolute necessity that app readers be device-neutral and usable on anything from a smartphone to a tablet or desktop computer. As was the case with earlier devices, the tablet has been the object of both high praise and criticism as it has reopened the door to standardized, mass-market reading, marginalizing more 'hand-crafted' solutions to interface, delivery, and reader experience.

8 State of the art: three visions

In March 1999, Robert Darnton described a highly complex model for the scholarly e-book as a six-layered pyramid, with the most easily intelligible level of material at the top (the author's historical interpretation of the archive), and the material becoming broader and heavier with primary sources and learned commentary as the reader delved towards the bottom. The e-book was a self-contained construct produced by author and reader together, with comments, interpretive essays, and exchanges all holding up the first layer of text at the top.

Darnton's concept had an immediate and profound impact and became an important theoretical model. He also considered the culture of reading in the electronic environment, believing that 'the computer screen would be used for sampling and searching, whereas concentrated, long-term reading would take place by means of the conventional printed book or downloaded text'.

In 2001, Clifford Lynch of the Coalition for Networked Information offered his own definition of the e-book: 'just a large structured collection of bits that can be transported on CD-ROM or other storage media or delivered over a network connection, and which is designed to be viewed on some combination of hardware and software ranging from dumb terminals to web browsers on personal computers to the new book reading appliances'. Lynch wondered if the tradition of the book, as either cultural practice or commercial object, would be discarded in favour of some new model. Lynch's bare-boned and catholic definition reflected his thoroughgoing familiarity with the field and its most important players. He dared to look forward to the end of print culture.

At the same time, and with greater fanfare, the editor and publisher Jason Epstein offered in the *New York Review of Books* his own vision of the e-book and its future: most digital files will be printed and bound on demand by ubiquitous ATM-style 'Espresso' machines. Epstein's view was utopian, not because of any grand vision of a digital future, but precisely because of its negation of technological and cultural developments. Like Thomas More's original *Utopia*, it was as much a critique of current practice and a nostalgic glance at a lost past as a blueprint for the future. Epstein's Espresso technology depends upon an alliance of publishers that essentially links the future of the e-book to that of print, relying on myriad physical points of sale and assuming a widespread ability to provide retail delivery.

9 Conclusion

With the e-book well into its second decade, all options have continued to remain viable, ranging from scanned print, to print on demand, digital downloads, and born-digital works existing on and delivered through the World Wide Web. While tablet-based publication has attained the level of an industry standard, and is moving towards becoming a cultural standard, issues of open access, edition and version, copyright, and innovation have remained problematic. The delivery of moderately enhanced print-first books in digital format has become well accepted, widespread, and commercially viable. More experimental, highly encoded productions remain the purview of a small portion of potential creators and readers. Through the cumulative impact of both commercial and theory-driven e-books, enormous changes had already occurred in the culture of reading and production: the electronic realm is firmly rooted; an entire generation has been educated and reared on various electronic formats; and the amounts of data, including the book produced in electronic form, have long overwhelmed that produced by print.

The efflorescence of the electronic book complicates and enriches our understandings of books and reading. What is a book? Is it a product, a process linking author and reader, or a cultural habit open to any number of iterations? If a series of discrete cuneiform texts recording grain or cattle stocks were placed in some edited order inside a container, would they constitute a 'book'? Can we reasonably consider all the MS books and other documents, catalogued and uncatalogued, in an archive to be one large book? Are games, telephone directories, interactive narratives, or the results of data mining, meaningfully conceived as books? What roles do the author, the reader, and the medium play in our evolving understandings? For example, do the ever-changing content, bookmarks, and hyperlinks in an iPhone constitute a new, irreplicable book? Have we reached a stage in the development and organization of information where human agency is becoming increasingly irrelevant to the creation and consumption of objects of knowledge? Or will individual choice and taste become all important? The radical dismemberment and reassociation of content in the digital realm compels us to consider these questions in a new light, with a newly focused urgency. As Clifford Lynch notes, physical objects and cultural practices inevitably stand together in a dynamic dialogue. Are all these forms of communication part of the future of 'the book' in which we still play a role, assume an agency, or are they part of some other future?

BIBLIOGRAPHY

V. Bush, 'As We May Think', *Atlantic Monthly*, July 1945, www.theatlantic.com/magazine/archive/1945/07/as-we-may-think/303881, consulted Mar. 2013

C. M. Christensen, *The Innovator's Dilemma: When New Technologies Cause Great Firms to Fail* (1999)

R. Darnton, 'The New Age of the Book', *New York Review of Books*, 46 (18 Mar. 1999), www.nybooks.com/articles/546, consulted Mar. 2013

D. Edgerton, *The Shock of the Old: Technology and Global History since 1900* (2006)

D. Englebart, 'The Demo', www.inventinginteractive.com/2010/03/23/the-mother-of-all-demos, consulted Mar. 2013

J. Epstein, 'Reading: The Digital Future', *New York Review of Books*, 48 (5 July 2001), www.nybooks.com/articles/14318, consulted Mar. 2013

M. Hart, 'The History and Philosophy of Project Gutenberg', www.gutenberg.org/wiki/Gutenberg:The_History_and_Philosophy_of_Project_Gutenberg_by_Michael_Hart, consulted Mar. 2013

C. Lynch, 'The Battle to Define the Future of the Book in the Digital World', *First Monday*, 6.6 (June 2001), www.firstmonday.org/htbin/cgiwrap/bin/ojs/index.php/fm/article/view/864/773, consulted Mar. 2013

'Mosaic: The First Global Web Browser', www.livinginternet.com/w/wi_mosaic.htm, consulted Mar. 2013

V. Mosco, *The Digital Sublime: Myth, Power, and Cyberspace* (2005)

M. Naimark, 'Aspen Moviemap', www.naimark.net/projects/aspen.html, consulted July 2007

Regional and National Histories of the Book

22a

The History of the Book in Britain, *c.*1475–1800

ANDREW MURPHY

1 Origins

The history of the book in Britain begins, in fact, on the Continent. In 1471, the Kent-born merchant William Caxton travelled from Bruges to Cologne, where he formed a partnership with the printer and punchcutter Johannes Veldener. Having mastered the art of printing, Caxton returned to Bruges in the following year, probably accompanied by Veldener and by an assistant, Wynkyn de Worde. At Bruges, the merchant set up a press and issued the first English-language printed book, the *Histories of Troy* (1473/4), his own translation of Raoul Le Fèvre's *Le Recueil des histoires de Troyes*. Caxton eventually returned to England (probably in 1476) and established a press in the precincts of Westminster Abbey, assisted again by de Worde. The first piece of printing to be completed at Caxton's English press was an indulgence produced for the abbot of Abingdon—an early indication of how important jobbing printing would prove to be within the trade. In 1477, Caxton issued the first printed edition of *The Canterbury Tales*. In the same year, he published *The Dictes or Sayengis of the Philosophres*, an 11th-century Arabic work by Mubashshir ibn Fatik, Abu al-Wafa, which had been translated (from a French-language version) by Earl Rivers, brother-in-law of Edward IV. Over the course of his career, Caxton published works by Boethius, Cato, Cicero, Higden, Lydgate, Virgil, and others.

On Caxton's death in 1492, de Worde took over the business. A native of Alsace, he was typical of the printers who helped to expand the trade in its earliest decades. Government legislation in 1484, intended to restrict the conditions under which aliens could conduct business in England, specifically exempted printers and other members of the publishing trade from its terms in order to promote the growth and development of the industry at a time when few natives had the necessary training or equipment to set themselves up as printers. De Worde soon found himself competing for business against the Normans Richard Pynson and Guillaume Faques (who changed his name to William Fawkes and was appointed King's Printer in 1503), along with the Belgian William de Machlinia and his partner Johannes Lettou, who may have been a Lithuanian. Gradually, more native printers entered the trade, and in 1534 the government repealed the exemption that foreign printers had enjoyed since the 1484 Act.

As the trade expanded, competition caused printers to move towards specialization. De Worde, one of the first to recognize the value of the textbook trade, aimed a substantial percentage of his output squarely at the grammar school market. Pynson (who succeeded Fawkes as King's Printer in 1506) specialized in legal printing, producing volumes of statutes, law codes, and handbooks for lawyers. Other identifiable popular classes of books in the first century of printing included herbals and medical works, most notably Sir Thomas Elyot's *Castel of Helth*, issued in several editions from 1539; translations of the classics, such as Arthur Golding's version of Ovid's *Metamorphoses* (first four books, 1565; fifteen books, 1567); chronicles and histories (e.g. Holinshed's *Chronicles of England, Scotlande, and Irelande*, 1577) and ephemeral works of various kinds, including ballads, almanacs, and pamphlets purporting to provide the last words of executed criminals. Religious publishing was also particularly important in the period.

2 The Stationers' Company

Over time, the publishing trade became more highly organized. A trade company for scribes, illuminators, and those involved in the binding and sale of MS books had existed in London since 1403. The earliest printers tended not to affiliate themselves with this company, largely because they were generally based in parts of the capital that lay beyond the City of London's jurisdiction. This was Caxton's situation, as his original base in Westminster was not within the City boundaries (and, in any case, having started life as a merchant, he was a long-standing member of the Mercers' Company). As time went on and more printers began to locate themselves within the city (particularly in the area around St Paul's), the Stationers' Company gradually came to be the publishing trade's representative organization. The Company's importance was recognized in 1557, when Queen Mary granted it a charter establishing it as a fully fledged corporation. The charter decreed that printing was to be confined to those who were freemen of the Company, thus giving them, as Peter Blayney has put it, 'a virtual monopoly of printing in England' (Blayney, *Stationers' Company*, 47). In return for the powers granted to it, the Stationers' Company was expected to play a role in what amounted to government censorship. Company officers were empowered to search the premises of all printers and other members of the trade and to seize any seditious or heretical material. The Company regulated publishing and enforced an early system of copyright (though the word itself is an 18th-century coinage) by requiring that new titles be registered in advance of being printed.

By the close of the 16th century, the Stationers' Company was beginning to lay the groundwork for consolidating the rights in certain standard works into a portfolio controlled by its most senior members. A royal grant by James I in 1603 added to this portfolio a further range of works, including books of private prayers, psalters, psalms, and almanacs. The 'English Stock', as it became known, confirmed the prosperity of the Company, although the running of the scheme also had the effect of alienating many among the most junior ranks of the profession, who felt excluded from the profits generated by the staple works that formed the core of the English Stock. Efforts in the early decades of the 17th century to create a Latin Stock and an Irish Stock proved unsuccessful.

At the same time as the Stationers' Company was consolidating its power, the book trade itself was also undergoing a process of division and specialization. When Caxton printed a book, he bore the up-front costs—such as buying paper—himself (though he also relied on the frequent support of aristocratic patrons). He then printed the book using his own press and sold at least some copies directly to the buying public. As the 16th century progressed, these three aspects of the book trade—financing the production costs, producing the book, and selling it—gradually diverged into the distinctive roles of publisher, printer, and retailer. At the end of the century, there was still a high degree of overlap between the three, and it was not uncommon for individual members of the trade to serve, effectively, as publisher-printers: purchasing the rights to print a book, financing the costs, and then printing it themselves. Thus, the title-page for Edmund Spenser's *The Shepheardes Calender* (1579) indicates that it was 'Printed by Hugh Singleton, dwelling in Creede Lane neere vnto Ludgate at the signe of the gylden Tunne, and are there to be solde.' Increasingly, however, title-pages came to bear a standard formula, which indicated that a book was printed 'By X for Y.' Thus, for example, when Thomas Middleton's *Micro-cynicon* appeared in 1599, the title-page noted that it had been 'Imprinted at London by Thomas Creede, for Thomas Bushell' and that it was 'to be sold' at Bushell's 'shop at the North Doore of Paules Church'. Here Bushell was the publisher, employing Creede as his printer; by now, the publisher's address was being provided largely for the benefit of those seeking to buy copies of the book wholesale (Blayney, 'Publication', 390).

Early in the 17th century, Thomas Bodley prevailed upon the Stationers' Company to enter into an unusual agreement with Oxford University. He set himself the task of resuscitating the University's library and oversaw the opening of a new building—named in his honour—in 1602. Bodley had considerable success in convincing antiquarians, scholars, and other benefactors to donate books and MSS to the library. He also persuaded the Stationers' Company to arrange for the library to be provided with one free copy of every work registered at Stationers' Hall. Although the library's holdings increased considerably as a result of Bodley's efforts, in truth the collection remained quite limited by modern standards. Almost half a century after it had opened its doors, the Bodleian held a mere 15,975 volumes (Benson, 113). The Oxford holdings were not, however, unusually small: all British universities had very limited collections at the time. Beyond the universities, libraries tended to be smaller still and were mostly confined to religious institutions of one sort or another. The high cost of books throughout this early period tended to restrict private ownership of significant numbers of books to those with substantial incomes.

3 Beyond London

The concentration of power in the hands of the Stationers' Company had the effect of retarding the development of printing elsewhere in the country. Some printing had been carried out at the abbey of St Albans late in the 15th century, where the output of the Press at St Albans included the *Book of Hawking* (compiled 1486). There were also early attempts to establish publishing enterprises in the English university towns. Theodericus Rood began printing at Oxford in 1481 and Johann Siberch commenced work at Cambridge in 1519; neither venture was particularly successful. In the 1580s, Joseph Barnes and Thomas Thomas carried out some printing at, respectively, Oxford and Cambridge, but it was not until the late 17th century in Oxford and the very early 18th century in Cambridge that the university presses were established in something approximating their modern form. At Oxford, the key figure was the vice-chancellor John Fell, who put into practice the kind of ambitious scholarly publishing project that Archbishop Laud had originally envisaged earlier in the 17th century. At Cambridge, Richard Bentley, Master of Trinity College, advanced the University Press as a serious business concern from the beginning of the 18th century. Notable volumes published by the Press at this time included Bentley's own edition of Horace (1711) and the second edition of Newton's *Philosophiæ Naturalis Principia Mathematica* (1713). In 1662, York was also granted the right to have printers operate there.

The development of printing in other parts of Britain was similarly fitful. Wales lacked the concentrated population necessary to sustain a native industry. In the early modern period, the largest town in the principality was Carmarthen, with a population of just 2,000. A clandestine Catholic press operated fleetingly from a cave in Little Orme in 1587, but the first successful printing press in Wales was not established until 1718, when Isaac Carter set up a business in Trefhedyn in Cardiganshire. From the early 18th century onwards, a reasonably well-rooted print industry did take hold in the principality. Outside Wales, however, a relatively vigorous tradition of Welsh-language publishing had been established long before this period. In 1546, Edward Whitchurch published *Yny Lhyvyr Hwnn y Traethir* in London. Written by John Prise, secretary of the King's Council in Wales and the Marches, the book was aimed partly at popularizing the basic tenets of the Christian faith; it included an alphabet, basic Welsh reading lessons, and a selection of prayers and other elementary religious texts. The Welsh scholar William Salesbury published a Welsh–English dictionary in the following year; he also wrote Protestant polemics in both languages. A Welsh New Testament was published in 1567 and a Welsh Bible in 1588. The success of the Reformation in Wales played a significant role in establishing a Welsh-language publishing tradition. Williams, for example, has observed that the widespread use of Welsh translations of the scriptures 'enabled the Welsh, alone among the Celtic-speaking peoples, to move on—to some degree at least— from the oral and manuscript tradition of the Middle Ages to the printed-book culture of the sixteenth and seventeenth centuries' (Williams, 49).

The first printer to operate in Scotland was Andrew Myllar, who seems to have been born in Fife and to have studied at the University of St Andrews (without completing his degree). Myllar learned the art of printing in Rouen, and on returning to Scotland entered into a partnership with Walter Chepman. Granted a printing patent by James IV in 1507, the two men set up a press in Edinburgh. Their publications included a *Book of Good Counsel to the Scots King* (1508), poems by Dunbar and Henryson and, perhaps most famously, the *Breviarium Aberdonense* (1509–10). Through the middle decades of the 16th century, Scottish imprints remained relatively uncommon, but, in the 1570s, Thomas Bassandyne and Alexander Arbuthnet collaborated in producing an English-language Bible that was widely used throughout Scotland. Like its southern neighbour, Scotland had its royal printers, with Robert Waldegrave, printer of the Martin Marprelate tracts, serving James VI in this capacity from 1590.

The first work printed in Scots Gaelic was the *Foirm na nUrrnuidheadh*, a translation by John Carswell of the Book of Common Order (generally known as 'Knox's Liturgy'), published by Robert Lekpreuik in 1567. The text has an interesting 'archipelagic' context, in that, as Mac Craith has noted, Carswell chose 'classical common Gaelic as his medium, with relatively few concessions to Scotticisms' (Mac Craith, 143), signalling that the book was intended for Irish speakers as well as speakers of Scots Gaelic.

Attempts to foster the Protestant Reformation in Ireland through publications in the Irish language were less than convincing and met with little success. Elizabeth I provided funding for the casting of a fount of Irish type in 1567, but the first Irish printed work did not appear until 1571, when a trial piece entitled *Tuar Ferge Foighide* (a religious ballad by Philip Ó hUiginn) was produced. Shortly afterwards, Seán Ó Cearnaigh (John Kearney) printed the *Abidil Gaoidheilge agus Caiticiosma*, a Protestant primer. These proselytizing efforts prompted a Catholic counter-move in which Irish Franciscan friars initiated a programme of Irish-language publishing from a base located first at Antwerp and, subsequently, at St Anthony's College in Louvain. The Franciscans commissioned a fount that more closely matched the distinctive characteristics of the Irish alphabet.

4 MS circulation and playbooks

In addition to continental printing ventures, the MS circulation of texts—particularly Geoffrey Keating's *Foras Feasa ar Éirinn* (1634/5)—also remained an important part of Irish-language textual culture until the end of the 18th century. The Irish tradition was not, however, exceptional in this, and, as Harold Love, Woudhuysen, and others have shown, MS circulation remained an important part of the textual scene in England as well (*see* **15**). From the closing decades of the 16th century onwards, a dual culture developed whereby literary works, in particular, often circulated both to a coterie MS audience and to a broader and more anonymous print audience. Shakespeare's sonnets may serve as an emblematic instance here. In his *Palladis Tamia* (1598), Francis Meres praised his contemporary for his work in the theatre, and commented favourably on Shakespeare's 'sugred sonnets', then in circulation only among the poet's 'private friends'. These private texts became a public commodity a little more than a decade later when Thomas Thorpe—with or without the poet's consent—published *Shake-speares Sonnets* (1609), thus circulating the poems to a wholly new audience. For some writers, MS circulation was the dominant mode of publication for much of their work. Indeed, although Donne's poetry was well known within his own extended social network during his lifetime, a substantial collection of his poems was not issued in print until 1633, two years after his death.

The persistence of MS circulation also highlights the fact that many of the pieces now considered masterworks of the English Renaissance may not have had such elevated status (at least from a publishing point of view) in their own time. This is particularly true of Renaissance drama. In the early 20th century, some bibliographical scholars plotted scenarios in which unscrupulous publishers sought out bit-part actors and paid them to reconstruct the text of popular plays from memory so that they could rush them into print (as 'bad' quartos) and turn a quick profit. Blayney challenged this view in 1997, arguing that the publishing and reprint histories of Renaissance plays indicate that they were unlikely to have made any publisher's fortune. Thus, *Hamlet*, which in its first 25 years appeared in no more than four editions (excluding the First Folio collection of 1623), might be contrasted with Arthur Dent's *Sermon of Repentance* (first published in 1582), which achieved nineteen editions over an equivalent span of time (Blayney, 'Publication'; Farmer and Lesser; Blayney 'Alleged Popularity').

5 Religious publishing

Dent's outselling of Shakespeare by a factor of almost five to one (not even taking into account that the press runs of the *Sermon* were probably larger than of *Hamlet*) draws attention to the central importance of religious material to the publishing trade in this period. The output of the majority of publishers in the first century or so of printing was heavily dominated by religious works of one sort or another. Indeed, in his influential study of English books and readers, Bennett estimated that, in this period, 'printers, as a body, gave something like half their output to this side of their business' (Bennett, 65). Once the Reformation—with its emphasis on reading scripture in the vernacular—firmly took hold in England, there was a high demand for English-language bibles, prayer books, and catechisms. In 1571, the Convocation of Canterbury ordered that a copy of the Bishops' Bible (first published in 1568) should be placed in every cathedral and, if possible, in every church. It was subsequently issued in scores of editions. The Authorized Version of the Bible, first published in 1611 under the sponsorship of King James I, was one of the signal achievements of the early modern era.

If the state sponsorship of Protestantism helped to drive forward vernacular religious publishing, then the emergence towards the end of the 16th century of more radical types of Protestant belief, which were opposed to what they perceived as the compromising doctrines and policies of the state Church, had the effect of accelerating such publishing still further. The Marprelate tracts provide an early example of this process. The pseudonymous Martin Marprelate took 'ecclesiological battle out of the study and into the street' (*ODNB*). The Marprelate attacks on the episcopacy first began to appear in 1588, clandestinely printed by Waldegrave. The pamphlets' wit and energy generated considerable public interest, as did the cat-and-mouse game that the producers of the tracts played with the authorities. The first pamphlet was printed at East Molesey, near Kingston-on-Thames. For the second, Waldegrave moved to Fawsley House in Northamptonshire, after which he moved again, this time to Coventry, where two further works were produced. Then, Waldegrave bowed out and John Hodgkins took over as printer, working at Wolston Priory. Hodgkins subsequently moved the operation to Newton Lane, near Manchester, but here he and his workmen were finally arrested by the earl of Derby's men and taken to London to be tortured and imprisoned. (Nevertheless, one final tract was produced at Wolston Priory.) The anti-episcopal polemics prompted a number of replies and counter-attacks from the government side, indicating how printed matter tends to generate still more print.

6 Copyright and control

The battles between the Puritans on one hand and the government and the state Church on the other did not come to an end with the silencing of the Martinists. Religion and politics became ever more closely entwined in the run-up to the Civil War, prompting further pamphlet exchanges that persisted throughout the War and Interregnum. This period witnessed an extraordinary efflorescence in the number of titles published, as indicated by the remarkable collection of some 22,000 printed items gathered together by the bookseller George Thomason between 1640 and 1661 (preserved in the British Library). As the

Thomason collection's large number of newsbooks indicate, the era has become closely associated with the emergence of the newspaper as a distinctive form in Britain.

The structures of authorization and control instituted by the government authorities and the Stationers' Company in the mid-16ᵗʰ century fractured irretrievably in the face of the proliferation of publishing activity prompted by the Civil War and its aftermath. Throughout the Interregnum, Parliament struggled to reimpose some form of order and control on the publishing trade, but with steadily diminishing results over time. In the wake of the Restoration, an attempt was made to return to the status quo. An Act passed in 1662 sought to reinstate the old order, with one notable innovation: the appointment of an official surveyor and licenser of the press. This role was initially filled by Sir Roger L'Estrange, who claimed to have suppressed more than 600 publications during his licensing career. The 1662 legislation was renewed in 1664 and 1665, lapsed in 1679, was revived in 1685, and then finally lapsed again without any further renewal in 1695. Government authorities seem not to have been unduly troubled by the loss of the licensing provisions that had been included in the legislation. Treadwell has noted that, in 1693, the Jacobite printer William Anderton was tried and executed under the law of treason—suggesting that, in taking forward the case, the government was seeking to reassure itself that 'there were other and more effective means than licensing to control the press' (Treadwell, 776).

The lapsing of the 1662 legislation signalled the final shattering of the mid-16ᵗʰ century dispensation that had granted such a high degree of control over the publishing trade to the Stationers' Company. With the geographical and other limitations on printing effectively withdrawn in 1695, the number of presses increased both in London and throughout the country. As Treadwell has noted, London had about 45 printing offices in 1695, but by 1705 that number had risen to close to 70. During that ten-year period, printers set up presses in numerous towns including Bristol (1695), Shrewsbury (1696), Exeter (1698), and Norwich (1701). The Stationers' Company never really recovered from the loss of power that resulted from the lapse of the licensing Act, and it would never again be quite the same force in British publishing.

From the late 17ᵗʰ century onward, many leading publishers avoided relying on the Company to protect their interests; instead, they banded together into smaller-scale, semi-formal trade alliances. Thus, when Richard Royston—who had himself served as Warden and Master of the Company—drew up his will in 1682, he advised the beneficiaries that new editions of the works to which he held the rights should be undertaken by six or eight members of the trade (Blagden, *Stationers' Company*, 174–5). The logic of his proposal implied that multiple investors would have the effect of spreading the risk of any new undertaking; such a plan would also help to draw in potential competitors and thereby guard against possible rival editions, at a time when the enforceability of ownership rights could not be legally guaranteed.

The kind of collaboration that Royston proposed became standard practice in the 18th century (extending even into the early decades of the 19th), and the groups of publishers which came together in such arrangements were known as 'printing congers'. The title-page of Samuel Johnson's *Dictionary* (1755) indicates that it was printed for 'J. and P. Knapton; T. and T. Longman; C. Hitch and L. Hawes; A. Millar; and R. and J. Dodsley.' Such ad hoc conglomerations were essentially joint-stock companies; each member bought shares in a book and divided the profits according to his initial investment. Such joint ventures spread the financial risk of publishing; for a large work such as the *Dictionary* in two substantial folio volumes, a considerable amount of capital was required. Another tactic adopted by publishers to minimize the investment risk involved in undertaking larger-scale projects was to seek out subscribers who paid (or sometimes part-paid) for their copy of a new work in advance, with their names then being included among the list of subscribers in the opening pages of the book. Lewis Theobald's edition of Shakespeare's *Works* (1733), issued in seven octavo volumes, included a subscription list running to just under 430 names, headed by the Prince of Wales and the Princess Royal.

In the wake of the definitive lapse of the 1662 Act in 1695, the publishing trade persistently lobbied Parliament to pass some form of legislation that would afford legal protection of their interests. What emerged from this process was an Act for the Encouragement of Learning, by Vesting the Copies of Printed Books in the Authors or Purchasers of such Copies (8 Anne, c. 19), passed by Parliament in 1709 to take effect in 1710. Feather has observed that, to the trade, the legislation 'represented a substantial victory, granting them the rights they sought while not reimposing the irksome requirements of pre-publication censorship' (Feather, 5). The Act, however, contained a set of far-reaching provisions, whose implications seem not to have been fully registered by the publishing trade when it was passed. The legislation introduced a modern concept of copyright as being vested in the author and, crucially, restricted in duration. Copyright on works already in print was to be limited to 21 years; new works were to be protected for 14 years, renewable for a further 14 if the author were still alive. The copyright provisions of the Act were a radical departure from standard practice within the industry. Traditionally, authors sold their work outright to a publisher, who then owned the rights to reproduce the text in perpetuity. The 'property' of a book was, therefore, treated in much the same way as real property: publishers could buy and sell such rights and they could pass them on in their wills.

The London publishing trade largely ignored the time limitations introduced by the 'Statute of Anne', or 'Copyright Act', as it is commonly called, and proceeded as if copyright continued to be perpetual. Throughout the 18th century, trading in shares in the most lucrative titles continued, even beyond the point when the new legislation dictated that these shares had effectively been rendered worthless. Thus, for example, when the Tonson publishing firm—one of the foremost London houses of the 18th century—was wound up following the death of Jacob Tonson III in 1767, the rights held by the company were sold at auction for £9,550 19*s*. 6*d*., despite the fact that the copyright on many of the 600 lots being offered for sale had expired. A notable example is the Tonson rights in Shakespeare, which fetched £1,200 at the trade sale, even though Shakespeare's works had effectively been out of copyright for more than three decades (Belanger, 195; Blagden, 'Trade Sales', 250).

The London trade's insistence that the 1710 Act had not changed the traditional practice of perpetual copyright did not go unchallenged over the course of the century, however. Some less well-established members of the trade in England did, from time to time, attempt to assert their entitlement to print works whose copyright had expired. In general the London publishing elite were able to counter such moves, either by exploiting the law courts' uncertainty over the issue or by simply buying off the publishers concerned. A more determined challenge developed, however, from outside England. In the 18th century, Scottish and Irish publishing came into their own and the number of printers operating in both countries increased very considerably. Some, such as the Foulis brothers, who were based at the Glasgow University Printing Office, aimed at producing work of the very highest quality; others, such as Patrick Neill of Belfast, had rather more fleeting and less ambitious careers in the trade. The Scots and the Irish undercut their London rivals and often exported their wares into the English market. English publishers complained bitterly of piracies, with the novelist Samuel Richardson, himself a printer, railing against cut-price editions of his work, which arrived from Dublin virtually before he had finished printing them himself in London (Ward, 18–20).

However, the more significant battle to be fought in the 18th century was not over works such as Richardson's, which were still in copyright, but rather over those works where copyright had lapsed, but which the London trade still treated as if they were private property. It was a Scottish publisher, Alexander Donaldson, who forced the issue of the unrestricted reprinting of these works, setting up a branch of his Edinburgh firm in London and challenging the established trade all the way to the House of Lords. In 1774, the Lords confirmed Donaldson's assertion that the time limits placed on copyright by the 1710 Act effectively negated traditional practice. The 1774 ruling in Donaldson vs Becket had the result of dramatically opening up the publishing trade in Britain. As Mark Rose has observed, the 'works of Shakespeare, Bacon, Milton, Bunyan, and others, all the perennials of the book trade that the booksellers had been accustomed to treat as if they were private landed estates, were suddenly declared open commons' (Rose, 53). W. Forbes Gray has characterized the ruling as 'the Magna Charta of literary property', since it helped to establish the notion of a 'public domain' of works that were available to any publisher who wished to produce an edition at a competitive price (Gray, 197).

Among those who took immediate advantage of the new dispensation was John Bell, proprietor of the 'British Library' bookshop on the Strand in London. In 1776, Bell initiated his 'Poets of Great Britain Complete from Chaucer to

Churchill', a series running to a total of 109 volumes, priced at 1s. 6d. each. He also launched 'Bell's British Theatre' in 21 volumes, published in 6d. weekly numbers, or parts (Altick, 54). These volumes were inexpensive by the standards of the 18th century, and Bell's efforts prompted others, such as John Cooke and James Harrison, to enter the field with competitively priced series of their own. As a result books became cheaper, and a much wider range of works became available to the less well-off sectors of society (athough St Clair has argued that this range narrowed progressively as the limits on copyright were extended over time).

One other legacy of the 1710 Copyright Act was the formalization of the entitlement of certain libraries to receive copies of new publications without charge—and this was not altered by the 1774 Lords' decision. Where Bodley, in a private arrangement, had persuaded the Stationers' Company to supply his Oxford library with one copy of every book registered at Stationers' Hall, in 1662 this agreement was extended by law to include Cambridge University Library and the Royal Library. The Act further extended and codified the arrangement, with the four Scottish universities, the library of Sion College in London, and the Faculty of Advocates' Library in Edinburgh gaining legal deposit status. The range of institutions benefiting from this provision was narrowed early in the 18th century, but it is in the 1710 Act that the seeds of the great copyright deposit collections can be found. The British Museum was established in 1753; four years later, it took possession of the Royal Library collection, which served as the foundation of what has since become the British Library. The Faculty of Advocates' Library formed the starting point of the National Library of Scotland collection.

Outside these great libraries, more modest institutions were slowly beginning to emerge, dedicated to scrving the needs of the general reader. In 1725, Allan Ramsay opened the first British circulating library, in Edinburgh. Sixteen years later, the miners of Ramsay's own birthplace, Leadhills, in Lanarkshire, came together to establish the Leadhills Reading Society, setting up a library and assembling a significant collection of books on a wide variety of topics. Local initiatives of this kind proliferated throughout Britain during the course of the 18th century, serving the needs of less well-off general readers until the institution of the public lending library system from the middle of the following century.

7 Conclusion

In the closing decades of the 15th century, Caxton offered his customers a luxury product, of interest largely to wealthy members of the aristocratic circles in which he moved. In the centuries that followed, books remained expensive commodities, with prices held artificially high, partly as a result of the restrictive practices employed by a London-based publishing elite. The 1774 Lords ruling was an early step towards making books less expensive and more readily available to a wider social spectrum. As the 18th century drew to a close, further steps in this direction were being taken.

If Caxton could have been plucked from his Westminster printing office and dropped into its late 18th-century equivalent, he would have been able to work as a compositor or printer with very little adjustment. The common presses being manufactured in the 18th century differed very little from the first press that Caxton had brought with him from the Continent in the mid-1470s (*see* **11**). In the final years of the 18th century, however, printing technology began to change. In 1727, the Edinburgh goldsmith William Ged began experimenting with stereotype printing—taking impressions of the completed formes of type and using the moulds to produce metal plates that could be used repeatedly, without the need for recomposition. Ged never managed to make the process commercially viable (largely because of the resistance of typefounders and compositors who feared for their livelihood), but at the very end of the century, Charles Stanhope, earl Stanhope revived the technique, eventually making it a commercial success and opening the way for extended press runs and cheap reprints. The earl also, around 1800, introduced the iron Stanhope press, which significantly reduced the amount of labour involved in the printing process. If Caxton could have stood on the threshold of the 19th century and looked forward, he would have seen a future that would surely have astonished him: the hand-crafted printed book of his day gradually turning into a genuinely mass-produced object passing into the hands of even some of the poorer members of society.

BIBLIOGRAPHY

Altick

T. Belanger, 'Tonson, Wellington and the Shakespeare Copyrights', in *Studies in the Book Trade in Honour of Graham Pollard*, OBS, NS 18 (1975)

H. S. Bennett, *English Books and Readers 1475 to 1557*, 2e (1969)

C. Benson, 'Libraries in University Towns', in *CHLBI* 2

C. Blagden, 'Booksellers' Trade Sales 1718–1768', *Library*, 5/5 (1950–51), 243–57

—— *The Stationers' Company: A History, 1403–1959* (1960)

P. W. M. Blayney, 'The Publication of Playbooks', in *A New History of Early English Drama*, ed. J. D. Cox and D. S. Kastan (1997)

—— *The Stationers' Company before the Charter, 1403–1557* (2003)

—— 'The Alleged Popularity of Playbooks', *SQ* 56 (2005), 33–50

H. Carter, *A History of Oxford University Press* (1975)

B. Cunningham, *The World of Geoffrey Keating* (2000)

A. B. Farmer and Z. Lesser, 'The Popularity of Playbooks Revisited', *SQ* 56 (2005), 206–13

J. Feather, 'The Publishers and the Pirates: British Copyright Law in Theory and Practice, 1710–1755', *PH* 22 (1987), 5–32

W. F. Gray, 'Alexander Donaldson and His Fight for Cheap Books', *Judicial Review*, 38 (1926), 180–202

R. G. Gruffydd, 'The First Printed Books, 1546–1604', in *A Nation and its Books*, ed. P. H. Jones and E. Rees (1998)

H. Love, *Scribal Publication in Seventeenth-Century England* (1993)

E. W. Lynam, *The Irish Character in Print, 1571–1923* (1968)

M. Mac Craith, 'The Gaelic Reaction to the Reformation', in *Conquest and Union*, ed. S. G. Ellis and S. Barber (1995)

D. McKitterick, *A History of Cambridge University Press* (3 vols, 1992–2004)

A. J. Mann, *The Scottish Book Trade 1500–1720* (2000)

M. Plant, *The English Book Trade* (1939; 3e, 1974)

J. Raymond, *The Invention of the Newspaper* (1996)

M. Rose, *Authors and Owners* (1993)

W. St Clair, *The Reading Nation in the Romantic Period* (2004)

M. Treadwell, 'The Stationers and the Printing Acts at the End of the Seventeenth Century', in *CHBB* 4 (2002)

R. E. Ward, *Prince of Dublin Printers* (1972)

G. Williams, 'The Renaissance and Reformation', in *A Nation and its Books*, ed. P. H. Jones and E. Rees (1998)

H. R. Woudhuysen, *Sir Philip Sidney and the Circulation of Manuscripts, 1558–1640* (1996)

The History of the Book in Britain, 1801–1914

LESLIE HOWSAM

1 A book culture

Print was the principal medium of written communication in Britain during the 19th and early 20th centuries. In that era of rapid population increase and concentrated industrial, urban, and imperial expansion, MS circulation was minimal and broadcasting lay in the future. Along with periodicals and newspapers, books and pamphlets constituted the material culture of print in a rapidly changing society. Much of that change was painful, and for many the experience of reading was a source of comfort or consolation; for others it was an opportunity to acquire useful knowledge or adhere to a system of belief. Men and women of all social ranks were readers, writers, and publishers, but a passion for the acquisition of literacy was particularly conspicuous in the working class. William Lovett (1800–1877) characterized his 'life and struggles' in terms of 'the pursuit of bread, knowledge and freedom'. In printing offices and booksellers' shops, and on the streets where vendors cried their wares, ideas and arguments jostled together. Evangelical religious enthusiasm, liberal political economy, and radical egalitarianism were only the most prominent of many competing ideologies. Pious people of the middle class eschewed the theatre and frivolous amusements, but enjoyed respectable novels read aloud in the family circle, while conduct books taught young people how to behave in polite society. Meanwhile, more secular spirits sought to break free of the prevailing culture's unofficial censorship by seeking out cheap, sometimes disreputable, editions of works of science and politics as well as of fiction and poetry.

Literacy measured by the ability to sign one's name (which normally implied at least minimal skills with reading) sat at about 50 per cent in 1801 and had risen to almost 100 per cent by 1914. Percentages, however, are of less interest than the way in which people used their literacy: for maintaining relationships with family at a time of increasing social mobility; for engaging with the natural world, with employers and colleagues in factories and other workplaces; and for engaging with religion or politics. The balance of work and leisure changed too, as the economic misery of the Napoleonic wars (until 1815) and their aftermath (until about 1850) gave way to a period of relative prosperity. Governments mandated a reduction in working hours for adults as well as educational provision for children. Both policies affected the practices of writing and publishing books, as well as the experience of reading.

The spread of reading and the dissemination of print can be credited both to broad socio-economic forces and to specific technological and cultural changes. Religious and political ideals competed vigorously and prosperity increased unevenly. At the same time, the mechanical capacity of printing and bookbinding equipment improved, along with readers' ability to illuminate their books or journals by something stronger than candlelight. As a society, Britain had been moderately pious, but people's reading of bibles and tracts increased significantly as a result of the evangelical publishing activities of the British and Foreign Bible Society and the Religious Tract Society. Strict sabbatarianism gave rise to Sunday newspapers and to programmes of respectable reading for boys and girls. Similarly, the secular utilitarian ideologies of free trade and political economy, espoused by the Society for the Diffusion of Useful Knowledge (SDUK), were widely promoted in its *Penny Magazine* and other publications. At the other end of the political spectrum, radical political ideas circulating in the first two decades of the 19th century grew out of a profoundly literate working-class culture, steeped in the notion of human rights expounded by Paine in *Rights of Man*. Despite the variety of ideologies in the politics of reading, all these people and organizations shared two things: they believed in the power of print to create change, and they were deeply suspicious of merely entertaining literature.

The book trade was based in the growing urban centres of Britain, primarily in London and Edinburgh. Indeed, there were strong business and personal relationships between publishers in the two cities. Yet printing, bookselling, and circulating libraries all flourished in Wales, and in Scottish and English provincial cities and towns as well. In the comfortable middle class, as among the struggling labourers, books were the mass medium through which culture was constructed. Children learned from print both directly and indirectly (*see* 17). Women readers, and indeed writers, found in books and periodicals a respectable place from which to approach the wider world, despite the social constraints that operated throughout most of the period. Men and boys could explore their masculinity and women and girls their femininity, and Britons of both sexes and all classes could use print to position themselves in relation to the imperial and colonial possessions that their nation claimed.

2 Economics

From the consumers' and producers' points of view, the economics of the book in Britain went through a dramatic transformation (*see* **12**). Identified in the first half of the 19th century as a luxury commodity (short press runs offered at high prices), the book became a commonplace cultural product (manufactured on an industrial scale and priced for middle- and working-class budgets). This distinction is complicated, however, by two major exceptions. Commercial circulating libraries (of which Mudie's was the largest) purchased the expensive volumes and rented them to readers at a manageable rate; and various publishers circumvented the high cost of a complete book by making it available to readers on a week-by-week or monthly basis. Bible and tract societies saw social utility in collecting penny subscriptions until a book was paid for, and Dickens's first publishers, Chapman & Hall, discovered the benefits of selling books in numbers, or parts. They could always be collected up and repackaged as a new edition—or various editions—after the author had finished the tale and the first cohort of readers had followed in his or her wake.

In the early decades of the 19th century the rate of publication rose, from a few hundred titles annually at the beginning, to 3,000 or 4,000 by the mid-1840s. New technologies (*see* **11**) meant new economies of scale for the book trade, and entrepreneurs also took advantage of changes in the banking and insurance sectors. In 1814, *The Times* first used a steam press to print the newspaper, and although the use of steam for book printing was not commonplace until later, the new technology was perceived as a watershed. In the 1840s there arose a 'passionate argument about the future of publishing and bookselling' (Raven, 321). The debates revolved around intellectual property and taxes on knowledge, often pitting the interests of publishers against those of authors and of readers. The Copyright Act of 1842 extended protection of an author's rights to 42 years (or seven years after his or her death, whichever was greater). Yet it was publishers and star authors, more than readers or the majority of writers, who benefited most from the change. Further legislation concerned international copyright, but British authors remained unprotected in the colonial and American markets for most of the century. The British government derived income from the book trade by means of the stamp tax. Increasingly, this was seen to stifle the freedom of the press and the circulation of knowledge. The last stamp tax was repealed in 1855 and the excise tax on paper in 1861.

The economics of the book in the second half of the 19th century have been succinctly characterized: 'the period from 1846 to 1916 saw a fourfold increase in production and a halving of book prices' (Weedon, 57). By 1914 there were some 10,000 titles a year being published, and prices for books had plummeted from the luxury level into the range of modest family budgets. The circulating libraries, which had benefited from the three-decker format when prices were high, now forced it out of the market. The publishing business, which for most of the 19th century had been one where powerful individual literary entrepreneurs were succeeded by their sons and nephews, now began to be reorganized as limited-liability companies.

3 Production and publishing

As in other parts of the industrialized world, most of the technologies of book production in Britain advanced dramatically between 1800 and 1914. Paper made by hand from rags gave way to paper made by machine, and, later, from esparto grass and, eventually, wood pulp as raw material (*see* **10**). The craft of setting movable type by hand, which had changed little since William Caxton's time, was supplemented by making stereotype (from the 1820s) and later electrotype (from the 1890s) plates that captured whole pages at once. Yet composition itself was not mechanized until the introduction of Linotype in the 1870s and Monotype in the 1890s. Hand presses remained ubiquitous in local printing offices and for small jobs for many years, but the larger printers adopted steam presses by the 1830s and 1840s. Twyman has characterized the transformation of illustrations (first from copper and later from steel engravings, then electrotype) as a complex and multilayered process (*see* **18**). At the end of the century, photography was in use and colour was enriching printed pages for the first time. The practice of supplying expensive books in flimsy paper covers or boards, so that they could be rebound for the purchaser's private collection, began to give way to edition binding in the 1830s (*see* **19**). Leather was used only for bibles and special works, while the use of book cloth for a whole edition could be made attractive with colour and design. Over the course of the century, the cost of labour as a proportion in the cost of producing a book increased, while that of raw materials decreased.

The culture of book production was transformed along with the technology. During the first quarter of the 19ᵗʰ century, the bible and tract societies were among the few publishers interested in keeping the price of books low. Their concern was with saving souls, while a few other specialists in cheap books churned out reprints of the classics for the school and popular working-class markets. The leading London firms, meanwhile, provided luxurious volumes for the leisured upper-class reader and used copyright law to protect their investment in works. The firms included the Rivington, Longman, and Murray families as well as Richard Bentley and others in London. Blackwood & Sons, the Chambers brothers, and William Strahan operated in Edinburgh. These booksellers—the term was still in use whether or not the firm engaged in the retail trade—were conservative men of business to whom the luxury price of two guineas for a work in quarto seemed appropriate. Charles Knight likened their strategy to that of fishmongers who destroyed their stock in the late afternoon, rather than reducing its price after servants had purchased enough for the gentry's midday meals. Like reprinting in cheap editions, this policy would have allowed the fish merchants to take advantage of a second class of customers, poorer families preparing supper, without any risk to the market earlier in the day. Similarly, the top London and Edinburgh publishers were slow to recognize that the market for reprinted works of literature in cheap editions would not spoil that for fresh originals in good bindings at high prices. Exacerbating the effects of this commercial outlook, the price of paper was high during the

Napoleonic wars, and printing and bookbinding (*see* **19**) remained labour-intensive crafts. Even stereotype was only practical for those few works that would be very widely circulated. These included not only spiritual and educational books, but the novels and poetry of Sir Walter Scott, whose influence on book prices was profound. His popular novels, beginning with *Kenilworth* in 1821, were the first to achieve the exorbitantly high price of 31s. 6d. and to expand to three volumes. A noticeable but brief dip in booktrade fortunes occurred in 1826 when the firm of Constable went bankrupt despite owning the profitable copyrights to Scott's works as well as publishing the *Edinburgh Review* and the *Encyclopaedia Britannica*.

During the 1830s and 1840s, the book trade's leaders maintained their conservative approach, but experiments in social engineering by means of print culture were nevertheless under way. Railway books and booksellers appeared later, along with trains and stations. Under Knight's leadership, the SDUK published series of works in both 'useful' and 'entertaining' knowledge, issued in affordably priced part-issue format, rather than full-scale volumes. Later, they developed their periodical, the *Penny Magazine*; in *Crotchet Castle* (1831), Thomas Love Peacock captured the SDUK's timeliness when he caricatured it as the 'Steam Intellect Society'. Knight campaigned vigorously for the stamp duty on paper to be repealed. The tax, determined by the Stamp Act, was also the focus of working-class political activity, which flourished in the 1830s as a campaign for the publication and sale of *The Poor Man's Guardian* and other unstamped periodicals. It was in 1836 that the formidable partnership of Chapman & Hall as publishers and Dickens as author initiated *The Pickwick Papers* and hit upon the idea of part-issue. The combination of a negligible unit price and a cliffhanger ending proved irresistible. This format became part of the infrastructure of publishing and remained so until the 1870s, when magazine serialization and one-volume reprints took over.

Dickens's huge income from authorship in mid-century was scarcely typical; also unusual were the complex business, literary, and indeed social relationships with his publishers that Patten has recorded. Most authors had to be content with a modest one-off payment for the copyright, so that if their work became popular it was the publisher who benefited. The usual alternative method of payment, a system of half-profits, was equally unsatisfactory for authors. There were numerous instances of unfair accounting practices by publishers that occasioned vociferous objections, both from individual writers and from the Society of Authors. The system of paying a percentage royalty, popular in the US, was slow to be adopted in Britain. Meanwhile, publishers acquired works for their list not only in the form of new MSS by unknown (and untried) authors, but by purchasing stereotype plates and producing reprints. By the 1860s, the practice of reprinting was finally reducing the price of books. Publishers issued 6s. editions of works they had originally published at much higher prices. Sometimes this happened quickly, but in other cases so slowly that the crusade for cheap literature continued to flourish.

The railway boom of the 1840s and 1850s transformed the distribution of books and periodicals and affected patterns of publishing and of reading. W. H. Smith and other booksellers profited from the railway novel that could be purchased at a station stall and that could be consumed comfortably on a train journey. The leading publisher here was Routledge. Their shilling Railway Library editions, known as yellow backs, were bound in coloured paper and furnished with an illustration on the upper cover and advertisements on the lower. Smith and Routledge, however, never competed directly with the major publishers that had survived from the 18th century into the Victorian age. Macmillan & Co. was different. Founded in 1843 at Cambridge, it moved to London in 1858 and became a leading publisher with a general list that included history, literature and criticism, and science (with periodicals such as *Nature*), as well as heavyweight new books and cheap reprints of older ones. Alexander Macmillan once told a correspondent, 'I don't think that *paying* things need be done in a slovenly way', a remark that combined his commercial ambitions with his literary and bibliophilic ones (Freeman Archive 1/7, fo. 495). Although his 'tobacco parliaments' were at the very centre of London's literary culture, Macmillan was also one of the Victorian publishers most active in reaching out to customers and colleagues throughout the British world, establishing offices not only in the colonies but in North America.

The book culture at the turn of the 20th century was very different from the mid-Victorian trade. The three-decker novel format came to an end, while the penny dreadful flourished. A Society of Authors was founded in 1883 to protect its members' literary property. Authors' literary agents began to undertake the filtering services previously handled by publishers' readers. A Net Book Agreement in 1890 ensured that price competition would not damage the infrastructure of the trade. New firms and new series appeared: John Lane founded the Bodley Head in 1894, establishing ambitious aesthetic standards for the book trade; and J. M. Dent initiated Everyman's Library in 1906. Everyman offered Edwardian readers many of the works, as standards or classics, that had been seen as risky a few decades earlier. Philological and literary scholars combined forces to initiate the *New* (later *Oxford*) *English Dictionary*, while other men of letters joined together to produce and publish the *Dictionary of National Biography* under the auspices of George Murray Smith in 1900.

4 Circulation and preservation

Authors, readers, and publishers have been seen as the three central constituencies in the culture of books from 1800 to 1914, but the institutions of circulation and preservation—periodicals, booksellers, and libraries both public and private—were essential supporters of their interdependent relationship. The periodical press benefited even more than the book trade from the changes in technology, literacy, and leisure that characterized the period (*see* **16**). North estimates the quantity of text published in periodical form to have been at least

100 times that appearing between the covers of books. Moreover, book and periodical formats became closely interrelated. An alternative to the part-publication of novels was publication in the weekly or monthly issues of a periodical; once a literary work was brought to completion in a periodical, it could be reissued in one or more volumes. Several major publishers maintained their own periodicals, employing their authors on them, in order to manage this policy: W. M. Thackeray, for example, served as editor of the *Cornhill Magazine*. Conversely, some historians, cultural critics, and other non-fiction authors sought contracts with publishers for volumes of their collected essays, works that had first appeared in periodical form. The periodical has been identified, by Beetham and Brake among others, as a hybrid form that was enormously influential in the print culture of Victorian Britain.

Periodicals arrived through the postal system, or were purchased alongside books or newspapers. Books could also be ordered from the publisher (or the circulating library) to be delivered by post to the country; cities and provincial towns had bookshops, where sellers were entitled to discounts on set prices. In the earlier decades of the 19th century, street vendors supplemented the established shops, particularly for politically radical pamphlets and evangelical tracts. In rural areas, colporteurs carried print from house to house. Especially when the price of new books was exceptionally high, second-hand bookshops and market stalls were a crucial source for working-class and lower-middle-class readers.

Libraries ranged from the small number of great copyright libraries, through the innovative subscription-supported London Library, to modest and well-meaning local institutions as well as private collections large and small. State-funded public lending libraries were slow to develop, despite the support of Edward Edwards and the passage of enabling legislation in 1850. Mechanics' institutes were furnished with libraries that provided much of the material for the reading lists of working-class autodidacts. In both public and mechanics' institute libraries, the provision of fiction was discouraged. Meanwhile the commercial circulating libraries, whose existence was so central to the structure of the publishing trade, filled the need for entertainment. By the late 19th century, however, readers and writers were increasingly frustrated by the restrictions imposed by Mudie's and other circulating libraries, which many perceived as a form of censorship.

5 Subjects and genres

The 19th century saw the appearance of a rich body of fiction and poetry that has become part of the English literary canon. Among the principal authors of the day were Austen, Scott, the Brontës, Tennyson, the Rossettis, Dickens, Elizabeth Gaskell, Thackeray, Trollope, George Eliot, Meredith, Gissing, Stevenson, Hardy, and Wilde. In the history of the book, however, these great names take their place among the vast number of unknown writers who contributed to the market for fiction and poetry. Those categories, in turn, exist in relation to religion, history, philosophy, science, and all the other subdivisions of the publishing trade's vast output. The material is difficult to count and categorize, partly because it so far outpaced that of the 18th century and partly because the sources from which statistical and subject analysis can be drawn were not consistently organized throughout the period.

Religion, not fiction, was still the dominant subject of the early 19th century, although literary writing was already growing fast. Bibles, tracts, and commentaries made up some 20 per cent of the books published between 1814 and 1846. The second- and third-largest categories were almost equal: a catch-all, combining works on geography, travel, history, and biography came in at 17 per cent, while fiction and juvenile literature measured about 16 per cent. A little over half of the latter category, 8.9 per cent or 3,180 entries over 32 years, constituted novels, romances, and tales as distinct from moral tales and books for children. Poetry and drama, however, were a separate category in the booktrade press's calculations. They were sixth at about 8 per cent, after education (12 per cent) and the jumble of arts, science, mathematics, and illustrated works (9 per cent). Works on medicine and law amounted to 6 per cent and 4 per cent respectively. Another unhelpful combination category was politics, social science, economics, and military and naval (4 per cent—but some works that would now be included under those headings no doubt found themselves in geography, travel, and so forth). Finally, works of logic and philosophy, and belles-lettres amounted to only 1 per cent; a further 3 per cent of works defied categorization as miscellaneous (Eliot, *Patterns and Trends*, 44–6). These figures must be treated with caution, however, as they are based on counting titles only, and take into account neither the sizes of works (best measured by counting sheets), nor the extent of press runs. In the absence of edition quantities, especially, such numbers can be used only as general markers.

Another snapshot of the reading public's preferences in terms of genre and subject is available for the end of the period, 1870–1919. By then, the fiction and juvenile category was highest at 23 per cent, followed by religion (only 16 per cent), geography, travels, history, and biography (down to 12 per cent) and education (11 per cent). The awkward 'miscellaneous' now amounted to 19 per cent, with arts, science, mathematics, and illustrated works falling to 8 per cent and poetry and drama rising to 7 per cent. Meanwhile logic, philosophy, and belles-lettres rose to 5 per cent. Medicine and law both sat at 3 per cent, with their declining percentage share being attributed to the rise of other categories rather than to any decline in interest or rate of publication. The portmanteau category of politics, social science, economics, and military and naval also came in at 3 per cent of all the many titles published and recorded by the trade (Eliot, *Patterns and Trends*, 46–53). Now it was fiction, or more broadly literature, that was the subject of most new books, not religion.

Percentages can be deceptive: they create artificial disconnections between ways of knowing the world that were tightly twisted together. Religion and science, for example, are often regarded as competing ideologies in the mid-19th century, and Darwin's ideas are seen to counter those of the Bible. A more complex and more interesting perspective is provided by Secord's scholarly examination of the authorship, production, distribution, and reception of all the variations of a single work of evolutionary science that encompassed and challenged religion (as well as phrenology) and that prepared the minds of readers for Darwin's ideas.

School books and textbooks were part of the 11 or 12 per cent of the titles reckoned as education, but their numbers accounted for a much larger proportion of the total quantity of volumes in print, because their print runs tended to be substantially larger than those for most other kinds of books. Longmans and others began publishing textbooks in the 1830s; Macmillan, George Bell & Sons, and the Cambridge and Oxford university presses all started to compete with them in the 1860s; changes in education law and financing in 1870, 1882, and 1902 greatly increased the demand. School books were exported to the colonies and to the US. Profit margins were small, but the global English-language market was reliable. Boards of Education in Britain and the colonies ordered about 60,000 copies of the compendia known as 'readers' or reading books in a single year, 1860–61 (Weedon, 128).

6 Reading

Scholars from a variety of academic disciplines and cultural commentators of all political stripes have weighed in on the subject of the British reading public between the Napoleonic wars and World War I. Had Britons become irresponsibly frivolous addicts of sensational trash by the end of the century, as Leavis insisted, or were they serious autodidacts devoted to the classics, as J. Rose has maintained? Although a Reading Experience Database is seeking to collect the transitory and precious evidence, there may ultimately be no satisfactory way to measure or to characterize, for a whole nation, so private and intimate a process as reading. Because many books and newspapers were very widely read, however, the communal aspects of the experience and influence of reading are factors that scholars dare not overlook.

The autodidact experience is important in the early 19th century, when educational provision was spotty and unregulated. Working-class autobiographies disclose how difficult it was to find affordable and engaging reading material. Even the poorest homes had copies of the Bible and Book of Common Prayer, *The Pilgrim's Progress* and, sometimes, *Paradise Lost*, although it is not clear how often or how intensively those works were read; probably they formed part of most children's preparation in the skills of literacy. The possession and reading of other books depended on chance, on the works of history, science, fiction, or philosophy that happened to be available from a second-hand bookseller or in a mechanics' institute library. Cheap reprints increased the access of humble people to books, but, as St Clair has argued, that access was shaped—and drastically limited—by publishers' control over intellectual property. In the mid- and

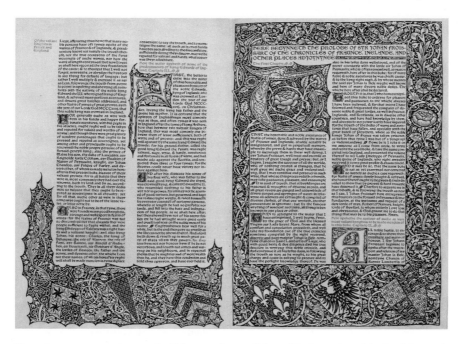

The private press movement: the Kelmscott Press edition of Froissart (1897) in Lord Berners's translation. Printed after W. Morris's death in two limited editions of eight and two leaves, the latter on vellum. The red printing, elaborate borders, and initials provide a luxurious display. © Sothebys

late 19th century, cheap editions of the 'old canon' of authors were more affordable than contemporary books.

As is invariably the case, throughout the period the material book and the cultural experience of reading it were intertwined. In 1800 literacy was restricted, and only a limited range of engaging reading material was available. Yet as the century progressed, new formats and cheaper prices created new markets and found new readers. By the 1860s publishing had become a major enterprise: books and periodicals were taken for granted as a cultural necessity. In 1914 the stereotype plates that had by that time provided millions with access to novels and poetry at modest prices were melted down to make munitions, and the people who had been brought up on them took their universal literacy into the trenches.

....

BIBLIOGRAPHY

Altick

J. J. Barnes, *Free Trade in Books* (1964)

—— *Authors, Publishers, and Politicians* (1974)

M. Beetham, 'Towards a Theory of the Periodical as a Publishing Genre', in *Investigating Victorian Journalism*, ed. L. Brake *et al.* (1990)

B. Bell, 'New Directions in Victorian Publishing History', *Victorian Literature and Culture* (1994), 347–54

L. Brake, *Print in Transition, 1850–1910* (2001)

N. Cross, *The Common Writer* (1985)

A. C. Dooley, *Author and Printer in Victorian England* (1992)

S. Eliot, 'The Three-Decker Novel and its First Cheap Reprint, 1862–94,' *Library*, 6/7 (1985), 38–53

—— *Some Patterns and Trends in British Publishing 1800–1919* (1994)

—— 'Patterns and Trends and the NSTC', *PH* 42 (1997), 79–104; 43 (1998), 71–112

J. Feather, *A History of British Publishing*, 2e (2006)

N. N. Feltes, *Modes of Production of Victorian Novels* (1986)

—— *Literary Capital and the Late Victorian Novel* (1993)

D. Finkelstein, *The House of Blackwood* (2002)

E. A. Freeman Archive, John Rylands University Library

A. Fyfe, *Industrialised Conversion* (2000)

—— 'Societies as Publishers', *PH* 58 (2005), 5–42

G. L. Griest, *Mudie's Circulating Library and the Victorian Novel* (1970)

L. Howsam, *Cheap Bibles* (1991)

—— 'Sustained Literary Ventures', *PH* 32 (1992), 5–26

—— *et al.*, 'What the Victorians Learned', *Journal of Victorian Culture*, 12 (2007), 262–85

E. James, ed., *Macmillan* (2002)

J. O. Jordan and R. L. Patten, eds., *Literature in the Marketplace* (1995)

M. E. Korey *et al.*, *Vizetelly & Compan(ies)* (2003)

R. G. Landon, ed., *Book Selling and Book Buying* (1978)

P. Leary, 'Googling the Victorians', *Journal of Victorian Culture*, 10 (2005), 72–86

Q. D. Leavis, *Fiction and the Reading Public* (1932)

W. Lovett, *Life and Struggles* (1876)

P. D. McDonald, *British Literary Culture and Publishing Practice, 1880–1914* (1997)

J. North, 'Compared to Books', in *The Waterloo Directory of English Newspapers and Periodicals*, www.victorianperiodicals.com, consulted Sept. 2007

R. L. Patten, *Charles Dickens and His Publishers* (1978)

M. Plant, *The English Book Trade* (1939; 3e, 1974)

J. Raven, *The Business of Books* (2007)

J. Robson, ed., *Editing Nineteenth Century Texts* (1967)

Rose

M. Rose, *Authors and Owners* (1993)

W. St Clair, *The Reading Nation in the Romantic Period* (2004)

J. Secord, *Victorian Sensation* (2000)

J. Shattock and M. Wolff, eds., *The Victorian Periodical Press* (1982)

P. L. Shillingsburg, *Pegasus in Harness* (1992)

J. A. Sutherland, *Victorian Novelists and Publishers* (1976)

—— 'The Book Trade Crash of 1826', *Library*, 6/9 (1987), 148–61

J. Topham, 'Scientific Publishing and the Reading of Science in Nineteenth-Century Britain', *Studies in the History and Philosophy of Science*, 31 (2000), 559–612

M. Twyman, *Printing, 1770–1970* (1970; repr. 1998)

D. Vincent, *Bread, Knowledge and Freedom* (1981)

—— *Literacy and Popular Culture* (1989)

R. K. Webb, *The British Working-Class Reader* (1971)

A. Weedon, *Victorian Publishing* (2003)

J. H. Wiener, *The War of the Unstamped* (1969)

The History of the Book in Britain from 1914

CLAIRE SQUIRES

1 The 20th-century book

What might be distinctive about the book in 20th-century Britain, the publishing industry that produced it, the book trade that circulated it, and the readers that consumed it? The most iconic books of the period, as well as the most indicative of the book's relationship to wider society, were Penguin paperbacks. They were cheaply priced and appealed to a mass readership; in addition to fostering innovation in design and being creatively marketed, the series took advantage of developing distribution channels. There is nothing more characteristically 20th-century, or more British, than the Penguin. As historians of Penguin know, however, the launch of the company in the 1930s drew as much from continuity and revival as it did from change and revolution. The post-1914 period has similarly been one of upheaval, but also of evolution: in production techniques; business practices; the culture of publishing; and in books themselves, both in form and in content.

Indeed, a history of the book in 20th-century Britain could be told through some of the publishing industry's individual products and book series, which demonstrate changes and continuities from the preceding era. For a large part of the 20th century, British books continued to exist under a legislative framework that curtailed their production and sale. Radclyffe Hall's *The Well of Loneliness* was banned in the 1920s for obscenity; Joyce published *Ulysses* overseas. Later in the century, Penguin's publication, in 1960, of Lawrence's *Lady Chatterley's Lover* successfully challenged the Obscene Publications Act, seemingly ushering in a period of freer social mores and publication practices, although the controversies surrounding Rushdie's *The Satanic Verses* in the 1980s and 1990s demonstrated that freedom of speech remained contested. In a different vein, J. M. Dent began production of the first Everyman's Library books (themselves modelled on earlier reprint series) in the opening decade of the century. These were marketed for the growing population of newly literate readers, which Penguin also sought in the 1940s with its Penguin Classics. Another instance of change is the global phenomenon of the Harry Potter series in the 1990s and 2000s. J. K. Rowling's stories illustrated the overwhelming commercial potential of the British book, founded on packaging, brand management, rights sales, merchandizing, and relations with other media. Yet, some 100 years earlier, Beatrix Potter's Peter Rabbit books employed the same sorts of strategies to foster their international success.

These examples afford a view of only a few of the patterns and progressions of the British book in the 20th and early 21st centuries. The following sections offer a more comprehensive survey, through an examination of the relationships between British publishing, society, and the rest of the world; its own internal business and culture; and its readers and consumers.

2 Empire, export, and globalization

The shape of a nation's publishing industry reflects and affects the nation itself; the many shifts in British history have no small bearing on book-trade history. At the start of the 20th century, the industry was built upon imperial lines. It was structured around independent, largely family-run, companies; industrialized in terms of production and distribution; and catering to the new mass markets engendered by the Education Acts of the previous century.

In 1914 Britain had the world's largest empire, its vast territories spread throughout the globe. British publishing followed suit, providing books for the empire. Copyright legislation protected publishers' property overseas, and the printing offices that had been established originally for colonial and missionary communications now brought a wider print culture to the colonies. Subsequently, publishing companies such as Oxford University Press, Heinemann, Longman, and Nelson set up branch offices and subsidiaries in Africa, Australia, Canada, New Zealand, and Asia, though the management of these enterprises tended to remain firmly with the British base (*see* **39**, **46**, **49**, **47**, and **41**, respectively). The British book was widely exported, and British publishers benefited greatly from international trade. Educational publishing was central to the building of the Empire, and in the development of the colonies.

Although World War II inevitably disrupted the patterns of colonial publishing, after 1945, the British government strongly encouraged reconstruction. At the end of the 1940s, 29 per cent of the value of British publishers' book sales derived from exports. By the end of the 1960s, this figure had climbed to almost half of all British publishing revenue. As the empire began to crumble, and successive nations won their independence and joined the Commonwealth, the export trade faced a serious threat. Many decolonized nations worked towards establishing indigenous publishing enterprises, although for many countries, problems with infrastructure, investment, and a lack of skilled workers and of publishing education, made local publishing problematic. For British publishers, however, the greater threat came in terms of international competition from the increasingly powerful US publishing industry and from an attack on trade agreements and conventions that safeguarded British interests. Territorial rights in the English language were traditionally drawn upon colonial lines, with Britain publishing exclusively throughout the Commonwealth. The Australian and New Zealand markets became particularly contentious, as readers wanted access to inexpensive US editions. The US successfully challenged the British Commonwealth Market Agreement in 1976, and protected markets were forced open, driving down British profits and the value of export sales. Nonetheless, the exclusive territorial rights specified in contracts meant that worldwide English-language publishing continued to operate along neo-colonial lines, even if the profits derived by Britain were much diminished. The post-colonial era was neither one of completely unfettered free trade nor one which saw the uncomplicated rise of local publishing industries.

In the second half of the 20th century, global economic and business development extended into the publishing industry. A succession of conglomerations produced ever-larger and more internationalized companies, frequently with multimedia portfolios. At the beginning of the 21st century, some of the biggest British publishing groups were ultimately owned by foreign companies: Hodder Headline (originally Hodder & Stoughton), Little, Brown, and Orion (Hachette); Macmillan (Holtzbrinck); and Random House and Transworld (Bertelsmann). Yet the relationship between global ownership and publishing patterns is complex. In the 21st century, British writers and publishers remained important originators and producers of cultural material, with intellectual properties widely translated elsewhere. Although their global dominance was unprecedented, the Harry Potter books demonstrated how the British publishing industry could foster publishing on an extraordinary international scale.

3 Wartime

As with every other area of civilian life, the two great armed struggles of the 20th century had their impact on the British book trade. World War I seriously depressed book production, with title output falling by 1918 to its lowest level since 1902. The book trade lost key workers, first to voluntary recruitment and then to conscription (publishers were not exempted from national service). The cost of raw materials—crucially, that of paper—rose dramatically as imported supplies were restricted, and the cost of books duly followed the upward trend. By 1918, the industry was seriously depressed.

A similar pattern occurred during World War II, although with arguably even greater effects. Publishers had their access to paper stocks rationed as foreign importation was banned. The Book Production War Economy Agreement, negotiated by the Publishers Association, imposed low production standards as a paper-saving measure. Books produced under the Agreement had thin, low-quality paper covered with small, closely set type. These challenges to the trade were exacerbated by aerial bombardment. During the Blitz, several publishers, including Unwin, Ward, Lock, & Co., Hodder & Stoughton, and Macmillan, were bombed, losing business records and stock. The wholesaler Simpkin, Marshall, which supplied many of Britain's booksellers, received a direct hit. As a consequence, demand far outstripped publishers' capacity to supply. The issues of supply continued well beyond 1945, and the editor Diana Athill's description of the 'book-hungry days' of the 'post-war book famine' was not exaggerated (Athill, 34).

Wartime inhibited publishers in terms of content, sometimes with overt government censorship. The Defence of the Realm Act (DORA) of 1914 affected many areas of life, including publishing and the dissemination of information. The Act meant that some publishers engaged in self-censorship by deciding not to publish potentially controversial works, while others (including the pacifist publisher C. W. Daniel) were prosecuted for publishing books dealing with subjects such as homosexuality and conscientious objection.

Wartime publishing also presented publishers with opportunities, however. In World War I, companies responded to the changed environment by publishing works relating to the new social and political conditions: pamphlets assessing current affairs; novels with wartime themes; periodicals with articles on the war effort. In the years before and during World War II, publishers' output similarly reflected the changing times. Penguin's 'Specials'—midway between books and pamphlets—were produced rapidly to cater for readers eager for information about the precarious days through which they were living (titles included a guide to identifying combat planes). Penguin also developed schemes to supply books to the troops via the Forces Book Club and to prisoners of war.

During both world wars, some companies operated by publishing works in partnership with, or on behalf of, the government. In 1914–18, these included veiled propaganda, such as patriotic novels from mainstream publishers (including Hodder & Stoughton, T. Fisher Unwin, and Macmillan), arranged under the auspices of the propaganda department at Wellington House. In World War II, OUP played a vital role in government printing and publishing by secretly producing, distributing, and even creating propaganda and informational materials, leading it to be dubbed 'Printing House Number One' by the Admiralty. Although the primary impetus was patriotism, incentives to produce such materials also ranged from the financial to (in World War II) the granting of additional paper rations.

The commercial legacy of both wars was—like much in industrial Britain—depression. The book trade suffered from downturns in production figures; disabled organizational structures; continuing problems with the supply of raw materials; and the knock-on effects of a broader economic malaise. The conservatism of the 1920s and 1930s did not bode well for publishing innovation, although the growing provision of education and the vision of a small number of key interwar publishers— George Allen & Unwin, Victor Gollancz (and his Left Book Club), and Penguin among them—militated against this. Paper rationing remained in place until 1949. The prewar output of more than 17,000 new titles in 1937, after reaching the low of *c*.6,700 in 1943, would not be surpassed until the early 1950s. Depression and austerity were threats to the reconstruction of a strong national publishing industry in both postwar periods. Still, there were opportunities—pre-eminently, the waves of educational reform—which were eagerly seized by some sections of the book trade.

4 Education, access, and the reading public

Substantial British educational reform began in the 19th century, with the 1870 Education Act establishing the principle of free and compulsory primary-level education. In 1902 similar legislation was applied to the provision of secondary-level education, and by 1944 school attendance was made compulsory and free for all children under 15. From the 1960s there was a rapid expansion of the university sector. Publishers sought to cater for this newly literate and expanding mass readership. The ubiquity of the reprint series in the 19th and 20th centuries was indicative of a close marriage between educational reform, literacy, and publishers' lists. World's Classics and Penguin Classics would, in later editions, include critical apparatus such as introductions and footnotes or endnotes, increasing their pedagogic usefulness. From the 1930s onwards, the rise and success of the paperback was intimately connected with universal literacy and the production of affordable, quality literature and non-fiction for all. Many of Penguin's non-fiction Pelicans appealed to readers' self-educative tendencies, and a certain earnestness in the post-1945 book-buying public was echoed by a seriousness in publishing programmes, discussed and analysed in works such as Richard Hoggart's *The Uses of Literacy* (1957)—itself a Pelican title.

Yet, as Hoggart's book emphasized, leisure and entertainment were also important factors in shaping the nature of publishers' output. Between the wars, popular fiction flourished, with genres such as westerns, detective, and romance novels having widespread appeal. Emblematic of the popularity of genre fiction is the decision in the 1920s by the general publishing company Mills & Boon to specialize in romance. Interwar critics of the mass reading public, such as Q. D. Leavis in *Fiction and the Reading Public* (1932), expressed deep concerns about the direction publishing and literature was taking, proclaiming that 'novel-reading is now largely a drug habit' (Leavis, 19). The anxieties displayed by some in the 19th century about the subversive dangers of a newly literate audience developed in the 20th century into fears about the deterioration of literary quality in a democratized marketplace. The ambivalence of the book trade, caught between the demands of capitalism and those of culture, would continue to cause consternation throughout the 20th century. Geoffrey Faber, publisher of high-modernist authors including Eliot and Pound at his eponymous company, articulated his disdain for a market-focused breed of publishers whom he perceived to be publishing for the 'herd'. Carey has advanced the polemical argument that, as a result of the reading public's expansion, modernist writers intentionally retrenched their art in order to exclude new readers, and to extract themselves from the marketplace. Nevertheless, other historians of the period have maintained that the modernists were as keen to situate themselves in the market as more obviously popular writers, promoting their authorial personae and collaborating and negotiating with publishing intermediaries to produce their work.

Publishers keen to cater to the new reading public did not only have to compete among themselves, however. The increasing numbers and distribution of newspapers and periodicals were in themselves competition for the book (*see* **16**). The development of new technologies led to a widening of cultural and leisure pursuits: in the early 20th century, radio and cinema; post-World War II, television; and at the end of the century, computers and the World Wide Web. Each of these developments presented real threats to reading as a leisure pursuit and—particularly with the Internet—as a source for information. Yet, at the beginning of the 21st century, the production of print-based books remained buoyant: the development of other mass media, including the advent of the electronic book (*see* **21**), posed a threat, but also presented opportunities. Cross-media interactions created a vibrant market in subsidiary rights, as publishers, authors, and literary agents negotiated deals to turn literary content into film and television versions, and new media spawned spin-off publishing activities. Contrary to the expectations of some more pessimistic commentators, new media in the 20th century could also enhance the publishing trade.

The push towards mass education and literacy in Britain developed alongside the growth of public lending libraries. The 1850 Public Libraries Act enshrined the principle of such libraries, but they did not take substantial hold until the end of the 19th century and the opening decades of the 20th. At the beginning of World War I, 60 per cent of the British population had access to a public library; by the mid-1930s such access had become near-universal. Commercial circulating libraries were also widespread in the first half of the 20th century, but these largely disappeared after World War II, as the public library system strengthened. Towards the end of the 20th century, however, the public library system suffered from funding cuts and diminishing borrower figures.

Shifting moral attitudes and the changing shape of British society during the 20th century both influenced and was influenced by the materials produced by publishing companies. Throughout the course of the century, the legislative framework and judicial activity surrounding the content of books underwent radical changes with the gradual arrival of a more permissive society. However, although bold and progressive publishers such as Calder & Boyars continually pushed at social and political boundaries, the courts' role in censorship and publishers' attendant fear of prosecution meant that material about certain topics still struggled to be disseminated.

The *Lady Chatterley* trial gave rise to words much repeated in histories of British publishing. The jury was asked by the prosecution whether Lawrence's work was one that they 'would approve of your young sons, young daughters—because girls can read as well as boys—reading this book...Is it a book that you would even wish your wife or your servants to read?' (Rolph, 17). The assumption of upper-middle-class male mores was rejected, and Penguin was vindicated. The second half of the 20th century was undeniably a freer environment for the book, although legislation that could be invoked to censor books continued: the Official Secrets Act; Section 28 of the Local Government Act 1988 (which curtailed the 'promotion' of homosexuality within schools); and the Incitement to Racial and Religious Hatred Act 2006. The desire to establish a free society continued to be in conflict with a desire to protect some groups within it.

5 The business of books

The foundations of the 20th-century book business had been laid at the end of the previous century. The Society of Authors, the Booksellers Association, the Publishers Association, and the literary agent, all had their origins in the late 19th century. Their establishment pointed towards a more organized, professionalized industry. As the 20th century wore on, this modernity intensified, as the industry became increasingly corporate and globalized.

The shape of the British publishing industry had already changed substantially in the previous century, with existing and new companies gaining in size, and developing diverse lists. From 1914, several new companies joined their ranks, which, in addition to Allen & Unwin, Gollancz, and Penguin, included firms established by émigrés: André Deutsch, Paul Hamlyn, and Weidenfeld & Nicolson, for example. In the 1960s, a concerted wave of mergers and acquisitions began to reform the national publishing industry, with ever-larger publishing groups being subsumed into global corporations, whose interests were much broader than publishing alone. By the beginning of the 21st century, British publishing had come to be dominated by a very small number of very large publishing groups: Bertelsmann, Hachette, HarperCollins (News International), and the Pearson Group.

Nonetheless, the second half of the 20th century also allowed for diversity and innovation. The feminist publishers of the 1970s and 1980s, pre-eminently Virago Press, shook up the male-dominated industry by revising gatekeeping policies, by publishing many more books by and about women (both reprints and originals), and by encouraging exclusively or predominantly female staffing. New computer-based technologies such as desktop publishing and print-on-demand meant that smaller companies could be quickly established, with a much lower threshold of required technical expertise. Apart from the wartime periods, annual British book-title production saw a relentless increase—from under 10,000 new titles at the beginning of the 20th century to over 100,000, and rising, at its end.

With all-encompassing changes in organization, structure, and technologies in the 20th century came transformations in the culture of publishing. Publishers became increasingly market-focused, with a concomitant shift in emphasis from the editorial function of publishing houses to their accounting, marketing, and sales departments. Publishing, which had once been seen as an 'occupation for gentlemen', as the title of Frederic Warburg's memoir affirms, had always been more mercantile than some of its participants would have wanted to admit. Yet the growth of the mass market, and the activities by which publishers sought to develop their share of it, meant that, as the 20th century progressed, Warburg's distaste for the 'tradesman' and publishing as a business would come to be deeply anachronistic. At the beginning of the 21st century, British publishers—and their global parent companies—demanded a strong return on investment, and viewed their operations as businesses first, and purveyors of culture and information second.

The Net Book Agreement, established at the very beginning of the 20th century, but dissolved in its final years, symbolically brought to an end the argument that, compared to other goods, 'books are different', a phrase that was used in an unsuccessful challenge to the agreement in the 1960s. Heavy discounting practices followed the NBA's dissolution. In the competitive environment of the 1990s and 2000s, with chain superstores, supermarket selling, and online retailing, independent booksellers struggled for survival in a market in which price was a key marketing weapon.

At the turn of the new century, the need for publishers to reach their markets nurtured a promotional culture in which authors could become heavily involved with their books' marketing through literary festivals and meet-the-author events in bookshops, schools, and libraries. The category of authorship expanded to encompass a substantial celebrity book market, which was reliant on the practice of ghostwriting to deliver autobiographies and novels. Literary prizes have proliferated, with the long-established James Tait Black Memorial Prize joined in the second half of the century by (among many others) the Booker, Whitbread, and Orange. Reading groups spearhead sales in the general trade market, while in the 2000s a televised book club, Richard and Judy, became the single most effective maker of bestsellers.

Meanwhile, technological advances have led to rapid changes in the sectors of educational, STM (Science, Technical, and Medical), and reference publishing, with digital publishing pushing new business models (*see* **21**). The nature of some market sectors has rendered book publishers into information providers, with their products barely recognizable as the traditional codex. As these technological developments have progressed, however, a reverse trend can be perceived in the enduring activities of private presses. Their use of hand presses in a globalized, digital environment is undoubtedly nostalgic; nevertheless, the continued resilience of the printed British book in the 21st century suggests that it is far from dead.

The landscape of post-1914 British publishing, and the books that it produced, have thus undergone a series of rapid transformations. These developments have frequently been organic rather than schismatic, growing out of 19th-century trends. Yet, for all its continuities, the British book in the 20th and early 21st centuries has proved itself distinctive: thoroughly engaged with deep changes in society, heavily market-oriented, and occasionally iconic both in form and in content.

....

BIBLIOGRAPHY

D. Athill, *Stet* (2000)

E. de Bellaigue, *British Book Publishing as a Business since the 1960s* (2004)

C. Bloom, *Bestsellers* (2002)

P. Buitenhuis, *The Great War of Words* (1987)

J. Carey, *The Intellectuals and the Masses* (1992)

G. Clark and A. Phillips, *Inside Book Publishing*, 4e (2008)

P. Delany, *Literature, Money and the Market* (2002)

J. Feather, *A History of British Publishing*, 2e (2006)

D. Finkelstein, 'Globalization of the Book 1800–1970', in *A Companion to the History of the Book*, ed. S. Eliot and J. Rose (2007)

R. Hoggart, *The Uses of Literacy* (1957)

A. Jaffe, *Modernism and the Culture of Celebrity* (2005)

M. Lane, *Books and Publishers* (1980)

Q. D. Leavis, *Fiction and the Reading Public* (1932)

J. McAleer, *Popular Reading and Publishing in Britain, 1914–1950* (1992)

I. Norrie, *Mumby's Publishing and Bookselling in the 20th Century*, 6e (1982)

A. Phillips, 'Does the Book Have a Future?', in *A Companion to the History of the Book*, ed. S. Eliot and J. Rose (2007)

J. Potter, *Boys in Khaki, Girls in Print* (2005)

—— 'For Country, Conscience and Commerce', in *Publishing in the First World War*, ed. M. Hammond and S. Towheed (2007)

L. Rainey, *Institutions of Modernism* (1998)

C. H. Rolph, ed., *The Trial of Lady Chatterley* (1961)

Rose

J. Rose, 'Modernity and Print I: Britain 1890–1970', in *A Companion to the History of the Book*, ed. S. Eliot and J. Rose (2007)

—— and P. J. Anderson, eds., *British Literary Publishing Houses 1881–1965* (1991)

C. Squires, 'Novelistic Production and the Publishing Industry in Britain and Ireland', in *A Companion to the British and Irish Novel 1945–2000*, ed. B. Shaffer (2005)

—— *Marketing Literature* (2007)

J. A. Sutherland, *Bestsellers: Popular Fiction of the 1970s* (1981)

A. Travis, *Bound and Gagged* (2000)

F. Warburg, *An Occupation for Gentlemen* (1959)

J. P. Wexler, *Who Paid for Modernism?* (1997)

23

The History of the Book in Ireland

NIALL Ó CIOSÁIN AND CLARE HUTTON

1 From the coming of print to the Great Famine

Although Ireland had a rich MS culture throughout the Middle Ages, it was not until 1551 that the first printed book was produced there, and very little was printed for a century thereafter. It has been estimated that, in 1640, one title was printed in England for every 8,800 people, whereas in Ireland the figure was one for every 190,000. One reason for this is that printing was an urban phenomenon, and Ireland was an overwhelmingly rural country. Its towns were mainly seaports trading with England and, to a lesser extent, with continental Europe. Imported books dominated the market: as late as 1700, only 20 per cent of books bought in Ireland were produced there; of the rest, 75 per cent came from England and 5 per cent from Europe. Ireland was England's largest market for book exports, surpassing both Scotland and Virginia. Most book imports came into Dublin, the capital, but there was also substantial traffic into the south and west, to Waterford, Cork, Limerick, and Galway.

Another reason for the slow development of printing in Ireland was that, as in England, the legal structure of the trade was effectively a monopoly. Printing was introduced by the state and, until 1732, was restricted to the holder of the patent of King's Printer. The first to occupy that office was Humphrey Powell of London, who came to Dublin and produced the first book printed in Ireland, the Book of Common Prayer, in 1551. Powell is one of only two known printers in 16th-century Ireland. The other, William Kearney, was also a state printer; between them, they are known to have produced eight works, four of which were broadsides.

The royal patent was granted in 1618 to the London Stationers' Company, who intended to continue importing their Irish stock as well as producing books in Dublin, but the venture was not a success, and the Company sold the patent in 1639 to William Bladen. However, the lengthy civil war and the political fragmentation of the 1640s led to a considerable expansion of printing: presses were established for the first time in Waterford, Kilkenny, and Cork. The full monopoly was restored in 1660 and granted to John Crooke, although he allowed other printers to work under licence from him.

The King's Printer's exclusive rights ensured that Ireland's printed output would be entirely Anglican and overwhelmingly in the English language. The vast majority of the population, however, remained Roman Catholic; most of them spoke Irish, although English was well established among the Catholic commercial and political elite. Catholic books, mainly devotional, were imported from Europe; they were not produced in any numbers in Ireland until well into the 18th century. The King's Printers did produce a few books in Irish, including a New Testament in 1602, but this was not followed by other religious works and was not part of a successful Reformation.

From the early 18th century, however, the Irish economy as a whole began to expand and rural areas became more commercialized. The consequent increase in the domestic market for consumer goods, along with the growth in literacy, created a network of distributors and customers for the book trade. This trend was reinforced by a long period of political stability, in contrast to the wars of the 17th century. The Dublin book trade expanded continually throughout the 18th century; and while the capital retained its overwhelming dominance in book production, the century also saw the establishment of printers and booksellers in provincial towns. Whereas in the 1690s printers were active outside Dublin only in Cork and Belfast, in the 1760s there were presses in some 16 towns, and by the 1790s in 34. The majority of these, however, produced newspapers and jobbing printing; significant quantities of books were manufactured only in Cork, Belfast, Newry, Limerick, and Waterford.

In Dublin, expansion began during the 1680s and was rapid after 1700. The number of booksellers increased from 25 in 1700 to 65 in the 1790s. By mid-century, some specialist sellers had emerged. Although the office of King's Printer continued to exist, its privileges had effectively disappeared by the late 17th century. A printers' and stationers' guild, the Guild of St Luke the Evangelist, was established in 1670, but it was confined to Dublin and even there had little effect in regulating the trade, functioning principally as a political club. One feature of the stationers' guild, typical of 18th-century Ireland in general, was that full membership was restricted to adherents of the state Church. Catholics were permitted to have a type of sub- or quarter-membership. This did not inhibit the activities of Catholic printers, however; and since the vast majority of the population outside the towns was Catholic, printers and booksellers serving this market flourished in Dublin, particularly after 1750. Ignatius Kelly and Patrick Wogan, among others, made fortunes from devotional books, schoolbooks, and chapbooks produced for a mainly rural market.

The 18th-century Dublin book trade's most distinctive feature, however, was that it was a reprint trade. The British Copyright Act of 1710, which protected literary property in a printed work, did not apply to Ireland, and throughout the century many Dublin booksellers were active in reprinting works already published in London. They were typically able to procure sheets of new books from London quickly enough to be able to produce a Dublin edition within a month or two of its initial publication. Labour costs in Dublin were lower and copyright costs did not have to be paid, making these editions cheaper than the originals. They also tended to be in smaller formats and of inferior quality. Until 1739 these reprints could legally be exported to Britain and, after 1783, to the US. Their principal market was domestic, however, and although there are suggestions that Dublin reprints may have been smuggled into Britain after 1739, the level of port surveillance meant that the numbers of books may have been very small. Certainly, domestic reprints dominated the Irish market; the private libraries of Irish elites tended to contain Dublin reprints of authors such as Samuel Johnson or Gibbon, rather than the original London editions.

One consequence of the lack of copyright in Ireland was that Irish authors, such as Sheridan and Goldsmith, had their work published in London, initiating a trend that continued long after the reprint trade had ended. The main exception was Jonathan Swift, whose political pamphlets of the 1720s and 1730s won him national fame, and whose works were published by George Faulkner, the leading printer of mid-18th-century Dublin.

The buoyancy of the Dublin book trade came to a sudden end at the close of the 18th century. The later 1790s saw serious difficulties in procuring paper; although there were some paper mills in Ireland, most of the paper used was imported. War with France after 1793 cut off much of this supply, and an increased duty imposed in 1795 meant that Dublin-produced books no longer had a price advantage over London imprints. The reprint industry came to an end with the 1801 Act of Union, through which British copyright law was immediately extended to Ireland. The effect was dramatic: the publication of books in Ireland fell by three-quarters in the early decades of the 19th century. At the same time the economy as a whole continued to grow, with war even accentuating agricultural prosperity, and domestic demand for books remaining high. The result was a huge increase in imports, whose annual value rose from an average of £650 in 1780 to about £6,500 in 1810. This phenomenon reinforced the trend of Irish writers publishing their works in London; during the first half of the 19th century, the only prominent Irish author to be published initially in Dublin was William Carleton.

Some Dublin booksellers survived by becoming agents for London publishers. Others emigrated, resulting in a substantial movement of personnel to the US. This emigration had begun already in the 1760s, and gathered pace with increased contact between the Irish and American trades after 1780. The largest migration came at the turn of the century, produced by economic downturn and political crisis; by the early 19th century, at least 100 booktrade workers had settled in America, mainly in Philadelphia and New York. Many continued their reprinting activities, including Mathew Carey, who in the early 19th century was the most successful publisher in the US.

The effect of the Act of Union was felt principally at the top of the market. Among the more popular readership, however, the Act had less impact, and a number of developments in the early 19th century provided a good deal of business for printers and publishers. From about 1810 onwards, and particularly in the 1820s and 1830s, a series of Protestant evangelical societies was active in rural Ireland, constituting what has been called 'the Second Reformation'. Although they produced very few converts, these organizations had a major impact by establishing schools (for which they provided textbooks), and by subsidizing and distributing vast amounts of religious and moral literature, all of which was printed in Dublin. The Catholic response, which included setting up rival schools, along with a mass Catholic political movement in the 1820s, also stimulated popular publishing. The state responded to both groups by establishing a national education system in 1831, ensuring a continued and vibrant business in schoolbooks.

In provincial towns, where the market was local and not dependent on reprints, the effect of Union was not felt very strongly; indeed, printing and publishing in places such as Cork, Limerick, and Belfast was at its height in the decades after 1810. Belfast was the home of one important innovation in book marketing in the 1840s: Simms & M'Intyre's Parlour Library, which packaged popular novels in a single volume costing 1s. In the towns of the south and southeast, more Irish language publishing occurred during these decades than any other.

Printing in Irish effectively ceased for decades after the Great Famine of the late 1840s, which devastated Irish-speaking areas. The famine was also a turning point for printing and the book trade in Ireland more generally. Printing in provincial towns declined, and the trade began to centre on Dublin. Technological advances such as steam printing (*see* **11**) demanded substantial investment, which favoured larger firms in the capital; improvements in communications, particularly the spread of railways, enabled the Irish rural market to be centrally supplied. In Dublin, the combined effect of the Famine and a commercial crisis in 1847 resulted in a series of bankruptcies of printers and publishers.

2 1850 to the early 21st century

One publisher to survive the profound cultural, social, and economic upheaval of mid-19th century Ireland was James Duffy, who published the immensely popular and successful 'Library of Ireland' in Dublin between 1845 and 1847. This series of monthly shilling volumes included newly commissioned works of nationalist history and literature and was designed, in Duffy's words, to appeal to the 'increased education and Nationality of the People'.

McGlashan & Gill, established in 1856 by Michael Henry Gill, a Catholic who worked as the printer for the Protestant stronghold of Trinity's Dublin University Press, followed the example set by Duffy and published titles that appealed more or less exclusively to the local market. As Printer to the University, a post he held until 1875, Gill was able to establish a strong position in the market, coming to his new business with an intimate knowledge and experience of all aspects of the book trade, a solid contact list, and an awareness of the gaps in the market which the University Press could not hope to fill.

By the late 19th century, Gill & Son (as it became) was one of the firmer fixtures within the Irish book trade, with a printing works that backed on to the firm's shop on Dublin's main thoroughfare, O'Connell Street, and which sold missals, prayer books, religious statues, priests' vestments, and candles alongside the firm's publications. Duffy and Gill had earlier shown evidence of their interest in the intellectual revival of Irish culture, through the publication of titles such as Eugene O'Curry's *Lectures on the Manuscript Materials of Ancient Irish History* (Duffy, 1861) and John O'Donovan's annotated translation of *The Annals of the Kingdom of Ireland by the Four Masters*, a large and beautiful parallel text edition in seven quarto volumes, expertly printed by Gill at the University Press (1848–51). By the early 1890s, however, when W. B. Yeats and his peers wished to gain support for their attempts to rejuvenate Irish culture more generally, the editorial response from Irish publishers was decidedly lacklustre. The dynamism and energy associated with the house of Duffy faded quickly when its founder died in 1871. By the 1890s, the publishing arm of the business was doing little more than issuing reprints of titles published decades earlier. Under the guidance of Gill's son, Henry, nationalist and stridently Catholic literature had come to dominate the firm's lists, this being, perhaps, the inevitable consequence of the increasing public confidence of the Catholic Church, which both Duffy and Gill had done much to engender in the 1860s and 1870s.

With such fixed and limited horizons, and in the face of such strong competition from London, the Irish publishing industry had little to offer aspiring and serious authors. Production values were generally poor, distribution networks were dwarfed by those of the London firms, and the chance of an author being paid a competitive rate was all but nonexistent. That the Irish publishing industry was revived in the early decades of the 20th century, and in the face of such inauspicious circumstances, is testimony to the vigour and nationalist commitment of Yeats's generation, which became increasingly aware that it was culturally incongruous for a separatist literary movement to be dependent on the support of British publishers.

In 1903 Yeats, with his sister, the printer and artist Elizabeth Corbet Yeats, established the Dun Emer Press (later known as the Cuala Press), a private press which published limited and expensive first editions of Yeats's works and those of his friends. Maunsel & Company, established in Dublin in 1905 by a group of literary enthusiasts, also did much to promote the literature of the Irish Literary Revival and the thinking behind the more general cultural revival and political upheavals that took place in Ireland in the period leading up to the foundation of the independent Irish Free State (1922). Yet Maunsel was undercapitalized and poorly managed, and despite achieving standards of literary and typographical excellence, it was bankrupt by 1925. The Talbot Press, founded in 1913 as the cultural imprint of the Educational Company of Ireland (established

1910), ran on a smoother basis. It served some contemporary authors by subsidizing cultural publishing with the steady profits made by the publication of school textbooks, a sector of considerable importance to the Irish publishing business throughout the 20th century.

The status of the Irish language was also transformed by the cultural revival of the early 20th century, with the production of works in Irish growing from perhaps two or three books per decade in the late 19th century to ten or twenty per year in the 1900s. The Irish language movement was self-consciously and deliberately attempting to create a new literature, a new print culture, and a new readership. In the realm of typography, a choice had to be made between using roman type or Gaelic type. The vast majority of books in the early 20th century used Gaelic type, chosen probably as a sign of the distinctiveness of Gaelic culture. This meant that a printing trade that had functioned almost exclusively in English needed to procure new founts, as well as compositors and proofreaders with the ability to deal with them.

The period leading up to the outbreak of World War II was particularly difficult for publishers in both the Irish Free State and the six counties of what had become, with Partition in 1920, Northern Ireland. Those who survived the violence and political instability accompanying the War of Independence and the Civil War found themselves working in a climate of reaction and cultural caution which developed as the 1920s wore on, culminating, in the Irish Free State, in the Censorship of Publications Act (1929). This notorious Act saw many works by leading writers of British, American, and Irish modern fiction being prohibited for being 'indecent and obscene'. Censorship was a significant feature of Irish literary culture up to 1967, when the government finally responded to the palpable shift in public opinion and amended legislation to allow prohibitions on books to lapse after twelve years, a development which, applied retroactively, immediately lifted the ban on over 5,000 titles.

The impact of the 'Economic War', a tariff dispute between Britain and Ireland from 1932 to 1938, was considerable, with Irish producers generally suffering more than British consumers. As British publishers found the books that they wished to export to Ireland becoming subject to duties, the British authorities retaliated by imposing prohibitive taxes on Irish books, including those crossing the border to Northern Ireland. This levy added to the difficulties which censorship had already put in place, and the only significant Irish publishing firms to survive were Gill and Talbot, who worked with caution and diplomacy, serving the steady indigenous religious and educational markets while firmly rejecting anything that threatened to upset the pieties of Irish public life. The deterioration of the international situation in 1939 further disrupted business, with military censorship, paper shortages, and printing firms finding that it was impossible to get replacement parts for their machines.

Under the Irish Free State (Constitution) Act of 1922, Irish was recognized as the state's national language, and Irish became compulsory in schools. The new government set up its own publishing venture, An Gúm (The Scheme) in

1927. By the mid-1930s it had published more than 400 works, including original material in Irish, modern versions of older Irish classics, and translations of foreign novels, particularly novels in English. In some respects the state's support for Irish-language publishing went hand in hand with its enthusiasm for censorship: both initiatives involved the desire to control and direct the evolution of national book culture. By reducing the supply of largely imported literature, the government inadvertently provided a fillip to the commercial fortunes of the Irish publishing sector, as domestic production expanded to fill the gap. Moreover, the two publishing houses established in the 1940s—a period of intense difficulties for those in the book trade—reflected the Catholic and Gaelicizing tendencies of the State's founders. The Cork-based Mercier Press, founded in 1944, was committed to publishing books that explored 'spiritual and intellectual values over material ones', while Sáirséal agus Dill, established in 1947, was an Irish-language publishing house that issued over 100 titles before the death of its founder, Seán Sáirséal Ó hÉigeartaigh, in 1967.

From 1949 to 1957, the Republic of Ireland's annual economic growth rate was only 1 per cent, easily the lowest in western Europe. Unemployment was high, and there was mass emigration. Most significant authors continued to seek publication primarily in London, and there was little innovation or dynamism within the Irish book trade, which largely served a limited indigenous market with works that could only achieve a local sale. The one exception to this general pattern was the Dolmen Press, a small literary publishing house founded by Liam Miller in 1951. A literary enthusiast who was committed to the value of publishing Irish literature in Ireland, Miller's list would eventually include works by writers such as Thomas Kinsella, Flann O'Brien, and John McGahern, whom he numbered as friends. Miller's first interest, however, was book design: he was inspired by the private press ideal espoused by the Cuala Press, and, with his wife Josephine, he printed many of the works on a hand press. Unfortunately, however, Dolmen was not run on a secure financial basis and did not survive beyond Miller's death in 1987.

In the period 1958–64, following the introduction of new economic policies in the Republic, annual growth shot forward to 4 per cent. Paperback publishing boomed, making access to a wide range of literature easy and affordable. In a dramatic reversal of cultural policy, the government in the Republic became increasingly helpful to both English-language publishers and authors. The Arts Council (An Chomhairle Ealaíon) began to provide grants for individual titles as well as interest-free loans, and profits arising from 'original, creative' work by writers 'solely resident in Ireland' became exempt from income tax in 1969, a move that made the Republic something of a writers' haven. In 1967, the Irish University Press was established, inspired by the worldwide expansion of the university sector, the market for reprints, and the tax-free status of the Shannon Industrial Estate, where the press established a vast modern printing office. The dramatic collapse of this venture in 1974 had one unexpected consequence: it left a large number of talented young editors, production staff, and promotions people out of work. A number of these went on to found their own publishing businesses, mostly small, editorially led and owner-managed literary presses publishing books on issues of Irish interest; by the early 1980s there was considerable energy in the sector.

The escalation of violence in Northern Ireland from 1969 provided another paradoxical boost to the culture of the Irish book, to the extent that the violence generated responses in the form of histories, autobiographies, polemics, fiction, drama, and poetry. In recent decades, Belfast's Blackstaff Press, established in 1971 and given crucial financial support by the Arts Council of Northern Ireland, has been an important outlet for material of this kind. The Gallery Press, founded in 1970, and now operating from County Meath, in the Republic, is also a significant force in Irish publishing. However, Gallery, like Blackstaff, would long ago have faded from the scene had it not been for significant sponsorship from both the Irish Arts Council and the Arts Council of Northern Ireland.

The contours of Irish life began to change decisively in the mid-1990s, during a period of very rapid economic growth. The 'tiger' years, which saw Ireland become a normal European economy, now appear to have been a period of 'catch-up' rather than the miracle they seemed at the time. Publishers have shared in the increased wealth, and Irish authors are no longer so likely to seek initial publication overseas, owing to the growing size and professionalism of the Irish publishing industry, a more general confidence in Irish business, and—in an ironic sign of globalizing times—the presence of Penguin Ireland and Hodder Headline Ireland, two publishing conglomerates, which set up offices in Dublin in 2003.

BIBLIOGRAPHY

C. Benson, 'Printers and Booksellers in Dublin 1800–1850', in *Spreading The Word: Distribution Networks of Print 1550–1850*, ed. R. Myers and M. Harris (1990)

R. C. Cole, *Irish Booksellers and English Writers, 1740–1800* (1986)

R. Gillespie, *Reading Ireland: Print, Reading, and Social Change in Early Modern Ireland* (2005)

—— and A. Hadfield, eds., *The Oxford History of the Irish Book*, vol. 3: *The Irish Book in English, 1550–1800* (2006)

M. Harmon, *The Dolmen Press* (2001)

C. Hutton, ed., *The Irish Book in the Twentieth Century* (2004)

—— *The Oxford History of the Irish Book*, vol. 5: *The Irish Book in English, 1891–2000* (2011)

V. Kinane, *A Brief History of Printing and Publishing in Ireland* (2002)

L. Miller, *The Dun Emer Press, Later the Cuala Press* (1973)

J. H. Murphy, ed., *The Oxford History of the Irish Book*, vol 4: *The Irish Book in English, 1800–1891* (2011)

N. Ó Ciosáin, *Print and Popular Culture in Ireland, 1750–1850* (1997)

J. W. Phillips, *Printing and Bookselling in Dublin, 1670–1800* (1998)

M. Pollard, *Dublin's Trade in Books, 1550–1800* (1989)

W. Wheeler, 'The Spread of Provincial Printing in Ireland up to 1850', *Irish Booklore*, 4.1 (1978), 7–18

24

The History of the Book in France

VINCENT GIROUD

1 Introduction

The history of the book in France reflects the peculiar dynamics between culture and power that have characterized the country throughout its history. These dynamics take two principal forms. The first is a constant trend towards centralization, resulting in the supremacy of Paris, always but never successfully challenged. The second is a long tradition, beyond regime changes, of state intervention or control in cultural matters. Yet this situation also carries contradictions and paradoxes, including the perpetual gap between cultural policies, stated or implemented, and a reality that, through inertia or active resistance, counters them.

2 The MS age

Books, in France as everywhere else, preceded printing. By the 2nd century AD in Gaul, dealers in codices were established in the major Roman cities of the Rhône valley (Vienne, Lyons), indicating that Latin literature was distributed in the country. In the 4th century, as Christianity spread, intellectual centres focusing on the dissemination of sacred texts were formed around the great figures of the period, such as Martin in Tours and Marmoutiers, and Honorat on and off the Mediterranean coast. Three centuries later, under the Merovingian kings, came the first wave of monastic foundations, some in the main cities (Paris,

Arras, Limoges, Poitiers, Soissons) but many in isolated areas, mostly in the northern half of what is now France. The majority were founded between 630 and 660: Luxeuil, near Besançon; Saint-Amand, near Valenciennes; Jouarre, near Meaux; Saint-Bertin, near Saint-Omer; Saint-Riquier, in Picardy; Fleury (now Saint-Benoît), on the Loire near Orléans; Jumièges, on the Seine south of Rouen; Chelles, to the northeast of Paris; Corbie, near Amiens. These, along with cathedral schools in the cities named above, as well as Arles, Auxerre, Bordeaux, Laon, Lyons, Toulouse, and others, became and remained the principal centres of book production in the country until the creation of universities in the 13th century. Their scriptoria were among the most important of medieval Europe. While many of these made books for the monastery's use, some became book production centres, specializing—like modern publishing houses—in certain types of MS. Commentaries on the Fathers of the Church came from Corbie, didactic texts from Auxerre and Fleury-sur-Loire. Saint-Amand was famous for its gospels and sacramentaries. Saint-Martin in Tours became a leading producer of large, complete bibles, of which the Bible of King Charles the Bald (823–77), now in the Bibliothèque nationale de France (BnF), is an outstanding example. On becoming abbot of the recently founded Cluny in 927, Odon brought with him 100 MSS; their number grew to 570 by the end of the 12th century. The second wave of monastic foundations—in the 11th century, especially under the impulse of St Bernard—resulted in an increase in MS production and in new networks for their dissemination, with the Grande Chartreuse (1084), Cîteaux (1098), and Clairvaux (1115) forming important libraries.

The university of Paris, created in 1215, while opening up the territory of learning beyond the confines of monasteries and cathedral schools, produced an immediate demand for books—as did the foundation by Cardinal Robert de Sorbon, in 1257, of a college for poor theology teachers that was to bear his name. By the late 13th century the Sorbonne, enriched by donations, had (for the time) a large library. In 1338 it contained 1,722 volumes, 300 of them publicly accessible (though chained against theft) in the main reference room (*grande librairie*), the remainder locked up in the *petite librairie*, from which they could be made available for consultation and circulation. In addition to academic libraries, a book trade appeared, with stationers operating workshops in the Latin Quarter to furnish students and teachers with copies of MSS. Laymen, responsible to the university's religious authorities, ran the pecia system: for a fee, students or professional copyists could borrow MSS established from a model copy (the exemplar) previously checked by university commissions. The dealers (*libraires-jurés*), affiliated to the university, were to check the new copies for completeness and accuracy. Like the monasteries before them, universities acquired specialisms—Paris in theology and Orléans in civil law—differences that were reflected in the libraries and book trades flourishing around those two centres. With the development of biblical exegesis in the 12th century, new types of bible, incorporating commentaries (some running to fourteen volumes), became a Parisian specialty in the 13th century, as did one-volume 'pocket bibles'.

Another speciality, recorded by Dante in the *Divina Commedia* (*Purgatorio*, 11.80–81), was illumination, with workshops such as that of the Limbourg Brothers producing luxury volumes of which the spectacular books of hours of the period remain celebrated examples.

Although lay books *par excellence*, books of hours and psalters were both in Latin; a genuine vernacular literature appeared in the 12th century, both in the *langue d'oc* spoken in southern France and the *langue d'oïl* spoken in the north. At first the transmission of these texts was oral. Thus, there are no early MSS of the 9th-century *Chanson de Roland*, which began to be written down in the early 11th century. Of the five verse novels of Chrétien de Troyes (*fl.* 1170–85), the most important writer of his age, there are no MSS before 1200. As early as the 13th century, the most widely disseminated French work was the allegorical, didactic *Roman de la Rose* (first part *c.*1230, second part *c.*1270): about 250 complete copies are preserved. Troubadour poems started being collected only during the 14th century. By then, Christine de Pisan, the first real woman of letters, operated the equivalent of a small private scriptorium to disseminate her poems.

Considering that only about 10 per cent of the French population was literate in 1400, books were used and enjoyed by a privileged minority. An even smaller minority within that minority, the first French book collectors, appeared at that time. The famous image of King Charles V among his books, like a monk (BnF, Fr. MS 24287), was a political statement of sorts. The king's library, to be sure, was as much an ancestor of the BnF as a private library. It also served as a model for the aristocracy, a model not only followed but surpassed by some members of the royal family, who were truly the first French bibliophiles—especially Jean, duc de Berry (the king's brother) and their cousin Philip the Good, duke of Burgundy: both owned some of the most expensive books of their time. The 15th century also marks the beginnings of urban patronage, characteristic of the rise of an identifiable bourgeoisie, with well-known instances in Bourges and Rouen.

Humanism, as has often been pointed out, came to France as a result of the sojourn of the popes in Avignon (1309–78), which brought Petrarch (Petrarca) and Boccaccio to the country, while Poggio Bracciolini toured abbeys (Cluny) and cathedral schools (Langres) in search of MSS of classical authors. Avignon became one of the earliest centres of paper production in France (Champagne was another) as the new material began to replace parchment. It also figures in the immediate prehistory of the invention of printing, as a certain Procopius Waldfoghel formed an association with local scholars and printers in 1444 to develop a system of 'artificial writing' about which nothing else is known. Other prototypographical experiments may have taken place in Toulouse around that time (*see* **6**, **11**).

3 The coming of print

Printed books were introduced into France before printing was established in the country. Johann Gutenberg's associates Johann Fust (who died in Paris in 1466) and Peter Schoeffer brought their productions to the French capital, where they were also available through their representative, Hermann de Staboen. Once Johann Heynlin and Guillaume Fichet had established the first French printing press in a Latin Quarter house owned by the Sorbonne, the new technology spread fairly quickly to the provinces. Guillaume Le Roy printed the first book in Lyons in 1473. Presses are recorded at Albi in 1475; at Angers and Toulouse in 1476; at Vienne and Chablis (the northern Burgundy wine village) in 1478; in Poitiers in 1479; at Chambéry and Chartres in 1482; at Rennes and two other Breton cities in 1484 (the first work in the Breton language was printed as early as 1475); at Rouen in 1485; at Abbeville in 1486; at Orléans and Grenoble in 1490; at Angoulême and Narbonne in 1491. Save for a few ephemeral undertakings, like the one Jehan de Rohan ran in his Breton château of Bréhant-Loudéac in 1484–5, most were permanent establishments. Leaving aside the Alsatian region, which was politically and culturally part of the Germanic world, there were presses in about 30 French cities by 1500.

Lyons was not a university town but a major commercial centre with frequent contacts with northern Italy and Germany. It soon became the second most active city for printing in France and, in the 1490s, the third in Europe. Books were sold at its four annual fairs. Of its emergent prosperous, progressive merchant class, Barthélémy Buyer, Le Roy's patron, was an outstanding example. Paper mills operated in Beaujolais nearby and in not-too-distant Auvergne. By 1485 Lyons boasted at least twelve printers, most of them coming from Germany, such as Martin Huss from Wurtemberg, whose *Mirouer de la rédemption de l'humain lignaige* (1478) is the first illustrated book printed in France (using woodcuts from Basel). To the same Huss is owed the first known representation of a printing office, in the 1499 *Grande danse macabre*, a powerful image showing the emissaries of death grabbing the compositor, pressmen, and corrector caught in the middle of their respective tasks. Also in Lyons, Michel Topié and Jacques Heremberck printed Bernhard von Breydenbach's *Sainctes peregrinations de Jerusalem* (*Peregrinatio in Terram Sanctam*), the first French book illustrated with engravings (the plates copied from the woodcuts of the 1486 Mainz edition). Half the titles printed in French before 1500 originated from Lyons, including the very first, the *Légende dorée* which Le Roy issued in 1476.

Although Lyons to a great extent showed the way, Paris was already the capital of the book in France and, after Venice, the second most active publishing centre in Europe in the 15th century. Printers and booksellers soon congregated in the southeastern part of the Latin Quarter, especially along the rue Saint-Jacques (where Ulrich Gering and his associates set up shop after Heynlin left the Sorbonne). Paper and parchment dealers were situated further east, in the Faubourg Saint-Marcel. The book trade established itself mostly along the river and on the Île de la Cité. Most of the early Parisian printers came from abroad, especially the German-speaking world. The first 'native' printing office, the Soufflet Vert, was opened in 1475 by Louis Symonel from Bourges, Richard Blandin from Évreux, and the Parisian Russangis; Pasquier Bonhomme, who printed the first French book issued in the capital, probably set up his press in that same year. The university's presence influenced the types of book first printed in the city: pedagogical works like Gasparino Barzizza's letters and spelling manual, Fichet's *Rhétorique*, classical authors in particular favour in schools (Cicero, Sallust), or works popular in the legal and clerical professions, like Montrocher's *Manipulus Curatorum*. The city's long association with illuminated MSS was also a factor: a large part of the Parisian 15th-century output (700 of the 4,600 incunables that originated in France) was printed books of hours, produced at times with blank spaces left so that they could be decorated by hand. These were the specialty of Jean Du Pré and Pierre Pigouchet and, after them, Antoine Vérard, who before becoming a prolific and successful printer ran a workshop of copyists and *enlumineurs*. The continued prestige enjoyed by MSS also explains some of the typographical characteristics of many French incunables: the preference for the so-called gothic bastarda type, closest to late medieval calligraphy (whereas Gering and his colleagues had initially used an elegant roman type cast from Italian models); and the taste for elaborately decorated initials also reminiscent of illumination (which recur in French books well into the 17th century).

Other printing cities in France were often university towns, like Angers and Tours. In most cases, however, the Church was the promoter, the resulting products being books needed for religious services: breviaries were printed at Troyes and at Limoges, and copies of a missal and psalter at Cluny. The patronage of the Savoy court played an important role in Chambéry, where Antonine Neyret issued his *Livre du roy Modus*, the first French hunting book, in 1486.

Much 15th-century book production was targeted at the academic world or the Church, while books of hours and chivalric romances were favoured by the rich bourgeoisie. Literature as it might be understood now—including many reprints of the *Roman de la Rose* and rare editions of the greatest poet of the previous generation, François Villon (*fl.* 1450–63)—represented a small percentage of the trade's output. Yet more popular forms of printing appeared and spread in the shape of small pamphlets printed in French in gothic type, ranging from current news to practical handbooks; many have not survived.

Naturally, the political powers viewed the invention of printing with movable type with interest and encouraged it. There are signs that Heynlin was protected by Louis XI (r. 1461–83); the Italian campaigns of his son Charles VIII in 1495–8 (their spoils leading to the establishment of royal MS collections in Amboise) spurred the spread of humanism in France.

4 The 16th century

Paris, with 25,000 titles, and Lyons, with 15,000, continued to dominate French printing in the 16th century, while Rouen established itself as the country's third printing centre (with Toulouse fourth). The proportion of titles printed in French grew rapidly, the balance relative to Latin tilting towards the vernacular in the 1560s. At the same time, humanism brought to France an unprecedented interest in Greek texts: Gilles de Gourmont printed the first French book in Greek in 1507, while François I gathered at Fontainebleau the best collection of Greek MSS in western Europe, appointing as its curator Guillaume Budé.

Between 1521, when the Paris faculty of theology condemned Luther and obtained from the Paris parliament the right of control over all religious publications, and 1572, the year of the St Bartholomew Massacre, printing was intimately connected with the spread of the Reformation in France, with the king acting at first as an arbiter. His sister, Marguerite de Navarre, protected the reformist circle formed around Guillaume Briçonnet, bishop of Meaux. The king himself defended the biblical scholar Jacques Lefèvre d'Étaples, whose translation of the New Testament was issued by Simon de Colines in 1523, two years after the faculty of theology had banned biblical translations. But he was powerless to prevent the execution of Louis de Berquin, the translator of Desiderius Erasmus, in 1529, and turned to repression when Lyons-printed broadsides attacking the Catholic mass were posted in 1534, an indirect cause of the condemnation and execution of Antoine Augereau in the same year. For a while, early in 1535, printing was banned altogether. Then came a series of regulations destined to establish royal control over all printing-related matters: the institution of copyright deposit (the Edict of Montpellier, 1537), the regulation of the printing professions and the creation of the post of *Imprimeur du Roi* (1539–41), and the tightening of censorship in 1542. More such measures were adopted by Henri II. The Ordinance of Moulins (1566) made general the obligation to obtain a privilege, to be granted exclusively by the Chancery. The success of these repressive measures is attested by Étienne Dolet's execution (1546) and the departure of Robert Estienne for Geneva following the deaths of François I (1547) and Marguerite (1549).

The first half of the 16th century, heralded by the publication of Erasmus's *Adagia* at Paris in 1500, is dominated by the great humanist printers: in Paris Jodocus Badius Ascensius, Geofroy Tory, Colines, Guillaume Morel, Michel de Vascosan, and above all the Estiennes; in Lyons Sebastianus Gryphius, Dolet, and Jean de Tournes. The dissemination of humanism was also facilitated by entrepreneurs like Jean Petit, the most prominent French publisher of the age, who issued over 1,000 volumes between 1493 and 1530. While the 'archaic', gothic appearance of the previous period was still widespread, humanist printers favoured roman types such as the one Estienne used for Lefèvre's revisionist *Quincuplex Psalterium* (1509)—thus typographic innovation, soon to be codified by Tory in *Champfleury* (1529), typically accompanied progressive thinking. It led to the work of the great French typographers Claude Garamont, Robert Granjon, and the Le Bé dynasty in Troyes, suppliers of Christopher Plantin's Hebrew types. One of the most admired typographical achievements of the period is *Le Songe de Poliphile*, a French version of the *Hypnerotomachia Poliphili*; printed by Jacques Kerver in 1546, it also marked the apogee of the French Renaissance illustrated book with its beautiful woodcuts, attributed to Jean Goujon and Jean Cousin.

Lyons, having neither a university nor a parliament, enjoyed greater political freedom, at least until the early 1570s, to the point of becoming a Calvinist city in 1562–72. At least fifteen editions of the Bible in (banned) French translation appeared there between 1551 and 1565. In 1562 de Tournes published at Lyons the first edition of Marot's translation of the Psalms completed by Beza, 'the most ambitious publishing project of the 16th century' (Chartier and Martin, 1. 321) for which nineteen Parisian printers were contracted (two, Oudin Petit and Charles Périer, were victims of the St Bartholomew Massacre), as well as many in the provinces. After 1572, Geneva (where de Tournes's son and successor moved in 1585) replaced Lyons as the principal centre of dissident religious texts printed in French (*see* **27**).

This ideological effervescence was accompanied by an extraordinary literary flowering: Rabelais (*Pantagruel* and *Gargantua*, first printed at Lyons in 1532 and 1534), the Lyonnais Maurice Scève (*Délie*, 1544), du Bellay (*Défense et illustration de la langue française*, 1549 and many later editions), Ronsard (*Les Amours*, two editions in 1552), the other poets of the Pléiade group, and Montaigne, whose *Essais* were first printed at Bordeaux. André Thevet popularized voyages of discovery with his *Singularitez de la France antarctique* (1557). Ambroise Paré fostered the renovation of surgery with his *Cinq livres de chirurgie* (1572)—its Huguenot printer, Andreas Wechel, left Paris for Geneva that same year—and Androuet du Cerceau's *Plus excellents bastiments de France* (1566–79) promoted the canons of the Fontainebleau School.

Montaigne's library (described in *Essais*, 2. 10) is that of a cultivated reader of wide intellectual curiosity; it differs from that of a bibliophile like Jean Grolier, earlier in the century, with his particular interest in bindings. The 16th century can rightly be called the golden age of French binding, with names like Étienne Roffet (named Royal Binder in 1533), Jean Picard, Claude Picques, Gomar Estienne (no relation of the printing dynasty), and Nicolas and Clovis Eve (the latter active during the 1630s). Progress was also made in printing music, first by Pierre Haultin, then by Pierre Attaingnant of Douai (*fl.* 1525–51), who became the first royal printer of music, to be succeeded by Robert Ballard, whose family retained the office for more than two centuries.

The Wars of Religion, for all their human cost, resulted in relatively little destruction of books (the main casualties were in the libraries of Cluny, Fleury, and Saint-Denis). They generated, on both sides, a mass of propaganda and counter-propaganda (362 pamphlets printed at Paris in 1589 alone). On the Catholic side, they resulted in a revival of liturgical and patristic literature at the end of the century, often involving—in Paris and in Lyons—groups of printers operating as 'companies' to share the publication of particular works. Another, long-term consequence of the Counter-Reformation, the establishment of Jesuit schools throughout the country, produced a rise in literacy and fostered the development of new printing centres in medium-sized cities such as Douai, Pont-à-Mousson, and Dole.

5 The 17ᵗʰ century

Historians of the book who regard the 16ᵗʰ century, especially the reign of Henri II (1547–59), as the apogee in French book arts from both a technical and an aesthetic standpoint, view the 17ᵗʰ century as a period of decline. This applies to the number of titles printed (not, however, to the total output), with Parisian production dropping to 17,500 titles (excluding pamphlets). Lyons, meanwhile, kept its provincial supremacy in absolute terms, but declined in proportion, challenged by other cities, especially Rouen. The development of the paper industry, discouraged by heavy taxes, was further slowed down by the growing shortage of rags, which led to a serious crisis until the 1720s. The quasi-medieval organization of the book trade stifled initiative. Despite Denys Moreau's attempts under Louis XIII, and with the exception of Philippe Grandjean's efforts at the end of the century, the triumph and ubiquity of Garamond type did not stimulate typographical innovation. Nor is the period particularly notable for its illustrated books, though significant exceptions include Jean Chapelain's *Pucelle* with engravings by Abraham Bosse after Claude Vignon (1656) and, in the later period, Israel Silvestre's and Sébastien Leclerc's festival books documenting Versailles's grandest occasions.

The 17ᵗʰ century is notable for other reasons. First, books and reading habits—the result of a higher literacy rate, which by 1700 averaged 50 per cent—became more general. This applied to men more than to women, to cities more than to the countryside, and to the areas north of a line going from Saint-Malo to Geneva (known as the 'Maggiolo line' after the author of a survey in the late 1870s) more than to western, southwestern, and southern France. Beyond the prestigious collections formed by Jacques-Auguste de Thou, Cardinal Mazarin, Louis-Henri de Loménie, comte de Brienne, Jean-Baptiste Colbert, and the Lamoignons, private libraries, even of modest size, became normal among the growing merchant and legal professions in Paris and most French towns. In the lower echelons of society, the spread and lasting success of the Bibliothèque bleue, which made Troyes the fourth most important printing city in 17ᵗʰ-century France, is a signal phenomenon, highlighting the growing role of non-conventional channels (such as itinerant pedlars) in book distribution.

The second notable factor is the bolstering of political controls over all matters relating to the printing and selling of books after the period of unrest following the relatively liberal reign of Henri IV (1589–1610). Richelieu (prime minister 1624–42) and his successors, suspicious of provincial printing, allied themselves with the Parisian printing oligarchy (Sébastien Cramoisy and Antoine Vitré, among others), rewarding them with privileges (and privilege extensions) for lucrative publications in exchange for their docility: Vitré was thus among the publishers who denounced the poet Théophile de Viau for freethinking in 1623. Censorship was taken away from the universities and concentrated in the hands of the chancellor, a policy reinforced when Pierre Séguier was appointed to the chancery in 1633. The Imprimerie royale, installed in 1640 at the Louvre, with Cramoisy as its first head, both conferred prestige and exercised control. Even the Académie française (1635) was intended partly as a group of royal censors. Similar strictures on the rise of newsletters were maintained by granting an exclusive privilege to Théophraste Renaudot's *Gazette de France* (1631).

As controls grew, however, so did the inability of the authorities to enforce them, as shown by the massive pamphlet literature, printed and disseminated throughout France, that accompanied the revolt known as the Fronde (1649–52)—more than 1,000 titles are recorded in its first and final years, many of them personal attacks on Mazarin, the prime minister, so that the term *mazarinade* was coined to describe them (he himself collected them). Among many glaring indications of the failures of the privilege system is the example of Sully (prime minister under Henri IV), who did not bother to apply for one when publishing his memoirs in 1638. A longer-term phenomenon with far-reaching implications in the publishing world was the Jansenist crisis, which began in 1643 when Arnauld and his Port-Royal allies protested against the papal condemnation of Jansen's *Augustinus*, attacking the Jesuits in return. Not only did the ensuing conflict lead to a vast number of publications, largely unauthorized, on both sides, it also destabilized the Parisian printing establishment. The paradoxes of this period are typified by the fact that Pascal's publisher, Guillaume Desprez, went to the Bastille for printing the immensely successful *Provinciales* (1656–7)—he was also to publish the posthumous *Pensées* (1669)—but became rich in the process.

The policies of Louis XIV—genuine 'cultural policies' ahead of their time—also reveal both great determination to control print and ultimate powerlessness to do so. His measures included the creation of more academies (1663–71), the incorporation of writers (Boileau, Racine, La Fontaine) into an all-encompassing system of court patronage, the reduction and eventual limiting of the number of authorized printers, and imposing a cap on the number of provincial printing offices. In 1667, powers to enforce book controls and exercise censorship were given to the Lieutenant of Police. In 1678–9, local privileges were suppressed: some parliaments, like Rouen, had taken advantage of their relative autonomy to encourage local business. While these policies, though repressive enough, were unsuccessful in stemming the spread of 'bad' books, their chief victim was provincial printing. By the most conservative estimates, at the end of Louis XIV's reign Paris produced 80 per cent of the national output. Another unintended consequence of French absolutism was the prosperity of foreign printers of French books, who now contributed 20 per cent of the total, a proportion that peaked at 35 per cent in the middle of the 18th century.

The first decades of the 17th century had seen the triumph of the religious revival launched by the Counter-Reformation, St Francis de Sales's *Introduction à la vie dévote*, first printed at Lyons in 1609, being its most famous title. It is contemporary with another publishing phenomenon, the success of Honoré d'Urfé's 5,000-page novel *L'Astrée* (1607–24), the 'first bestseller of modern French literature' (Chartier and Martin, 1. 389). The baroque and classical periods are characterized above all by the enormous development of the theatre, as shown by the careers of Corneille, despite the Académie's strictures on *Le Cid* (1637); Molière, despite his brush with censorship; and Racine. Typically, printer-publishers (like Augustin Courbé and Claude Barbin) formed groups to issue plays and divided the imprint between themselves. Meanwhile, clandestine reprints appeared almost immediately, originating in the provinces (such as Corneille's native Rouen) or abroad (especially from the Elzeviers). The success of these piracies also revealed the vast appetite of the market. Barbin, the leading literary publisher of the day, was also responsible for La Fontaine's *Fables* (first edition, 1668) and Mme de La Fayette's novel *La Princesse de Clèves* (1678), published anonymously. In 1699 his widow issued Fénelon's *Télémaque*, which was pirated twenty times that year and went through innumerable editions. Among the century's other notable productions are the first French world atlas, Nicolas Sanson's *Cartes générales de toutes les parties du monde* (1658); the Port-Royal *Grammaire* (1660–64) and *Logique* (1662); and the founding text of French art history, André Félibien's *Entretiens sur les plus excellens peintres anciens et modernes* (1666–88).

6 The 18th century

The early 18th century is dominated by the figure of the Abbé Bignon (1662–1747), appointed in 1699 by Chancellor Pontchartrain, his uncle, to be in charge of all book policies (the title *Directeur de la librairie* became official only in 1737). Bignon was, in fact, a sort of 'minister of literature' (to use Malesherbes's phrase, though he claimed there was no such thing). He organized a countrywide publishing survey in 1700 and spearheaded the development of provincial academies, while proving an inspired leader of the Bibliothèque royale from 1719 until 1741. Although the number of censors increased (there were close to 200 by 1789), and despite a few well-known cases such as the banning of Voltaire's *Lettres philosophiques* in 1734 (they had first come out in English the previous year), Bignon's influence and that of his successors was largely a moderating one. In fact—and this is one of the many paradoxes of the late *ancien régime*—the agents of the repressive policies were chiefly animated by pragmatism. To counter the growing number of illicit imports of French books printed in Germany or Holland, Bignon created a system of 'tacit' or oral permissions to legitimize provincial piracies. Chrétien Guillaume de Lamoignon de Malesherbes, director of the Librairie in 1750–63, was a friend of the *philosophes* and pursued this trend, protecting Jean-Jacques Rousseau and tipping off the printers of the *Encyclopédie* against possible arrest. But he was caught in another French 18th-century paradox: although the monarchy was largely sympathetic to the Enlightenment, it had to contend with other traditional sources of censorship, the Church and parliaments, whose interventions (generally after publication) eventually turned into embarrassments for the Crown, as in the case of Helvetius' *De l'esprit* (1758–9).

In 1764, only 60 per cent of the books printed in France were 'legal'. Of the 'illegal' works, most were banned religious books (Protestant, Jansenist, or otherwise unorthodox). The rest were unauthorized provincial reprints, political satires, or pornographic literature (which boomed in the 18th century, the marquis de Sade being one example of this trend among many). A large number of the century's 'great books'—*Candide* may be the most famous—were for one reason or another illegal. The absurdity of this situation, denounced by Diderot in his *Lettre sur le commerce de la librairie* (1763), was partly remedied in 1777 when Miromesnil, Keeper of the Seal, modified the privilege system to legitimize a large portion of provincial, clandestine productions, while recognizing for the first time that literary property belonged to the author. Ultimately, to paraphrase Tocqueville (Malesherbes's great-grandson) in *L'Ancien Régime et la révolution*, the real winners were men of letters, propelled to the rank of major political figures of international stature.

Against this backdrop, the French 18th century rivals the 16th for its accomplishments in the arts of the book. Their prestige was such that Louis XV, as a child, was initiated into printing, while the regent and the marquise de Pompadour published their efforts as amateur book illustrators. Some of the great painters of the age—Oudry, Boucher, Fragonard—contributed to the genre, along with the more specialized book illustrators Charles-Nicolas Cochin, Charles Eisen (his most celebrated work was the 1762 'Fermiers Généraux' edition of La Fontaine's *Contes*), Hubert-François Gravelot, and Jean Michel Moreau le Jeune. Louis-René Luce and the Fournier family renewed typography early in the period, while the Didots brilliantly interpreted neo-classical taste during the latter half. Technical innovation came to the paper industry as well: the Annonay mills near Saint-Étienne made the names of Canson, Johannot, and Montgolfier famous, while to the south of Paris the Essonnes mill, purchased by a Didot, became the country's most technologically advanced by the last years of the *ancien régime*. Equally esteemed for their technical mastery and decorative brilliance, the Deromes, Padeloups, and Dubuissons produced bindings of unsurpassed elegance. The enlightened aristocracy and princes of the Church—François-Michel Le Tellier, Joseph Dominique d'Inguimbert, the duc de La Vallière, the prince de Soubise, the marquis de Méjanes, the marquis de Paulmy—formed bibliophilic collections, some of which are now the great treasures of Parisian or provincial libraries. There was an expanded market for ambitious editorial projects: the *Encyclopédie*, naturally, the Oudry-Jombert *Fables* of La Fontaine, and Buffon's *Histoire naturelle*, printed by the Imprimerie royale (1749–89). Printed across the river from Strasbourg, the Kehl edition of Voltaire's works (1785–9), launched by Charles-Joseph Panckoucke before the writer's death in 1778, was brought to completion by Pierre Augustin Caron de Beaumarchais amidst many difficulties, and sold out despite two concurrent piracies. Panckoucke typifies the growing contemporary awareness of the publisher's role, distinct from the printer's. The book trade also acquired greater professional autonomy. These advances were paralleled by the growth and success of book auctions. There were between 350 and 400 book dealers in Paris in 1789, most of them established in the traditional area around Notre-Dame and along the river, but many migrating to the Palais-Royal area. Some doubled as *cabinets de lecture* (small lending libraries), institutions that remained in favour throughout the first half of the following century. Meanwhile, the first genuine public libraries appeared: in 1784 there were eighteen in Paris, beginning with the Bibliothèque royale, open twice a week to 'everyone', and sixteen in the provinces; some had begun as private collections, others as religious or institutional collections, others prefigured municipal libraries.

7 The Revolution and afterwards

One of the first initiatives of the Revolution was to abolish royal censorship and to proclaim the freedom of writing and printing, both included in the Declaration of the Rights of Man of 26 August 1789. The office of the Librairie and even copyright deposit, seen as a repressive measure, were terminated, along with printers' and all other guilds. The copyright legislation adopted by the Convention in 1793 (a maximum protection of ten years after the author's death) advanced many titles into the public domain. The nationalization of church properties (decreed in November 1789), the confiscation of works belonging to émigrés and (after 1792) the royal collections, followed by the libraries of all suspects under the Terror of 1793–4 (coinciding with a de facto re-establishment of censorship), displaced vast numbers of books and MSS. To a considerable extent, this benefited the Bibliothèque nationale (BN) and future municipal libraries. The revolutionary book world, especially in Paris, has been aptly compared to a 'supernova' (Hesse, 30), growing to nearly 600 *libraires* and printers, most of them small, precarious units, while 21 traditional houses, having lost their clientele, went bankrupt in four years. The explosion of periodicals and ephemera was accompanied by a decline in book production, and piracy was rife. Among the many worthy projects launched during that short period, the last king's librarian, Lefèvre d'Ormesson, started a 'Bibliographie universelle de la France' in 1790. He was guillotined in 1794. The same fate was met that year by Malesherbes and by Étienne Anisson-Duperron, head of the Imprimerie royale, where he had been a strong promoter of technical innovation.

The Napoleonic system, so much of which has survived in modern France, restored stability through an approach that was, in fact, the opposite of the free-market model favoured in the first stages of the Revolution. In the short term, its chief beneficiaries were municipal libraries, which in 1803 received (theoretically on deposit) the revolutionary spoils stored in warehouses: many such libraries were actually born out of this decree. In the long term, the chief victims of the Napoleonic system were arguably universities: not only had they lost their libraries, abolished in 1793 (not to be formally re-established until 1879), but they were regimented once and for all into a state educational structure that gave them neither the opportunity nor the funds to build research collections comparable to their British, Dutch, German, and, later, American counterparts. (Strasbourg, the only possible exception, is largely indebted in this respect to its having been under German rule between 1871 and 1918.) Until 1810, the surveillance of publications was left to the police, headed by the notorious Fouché, an arrangement that induced a self-censorship even more effective than outright repression. Nor was there any hesitation to resort to repression when necessary: in 1810, Fouché's successor, Savary, was directed to seize and destroy the entire edition of Mme de Staël's *De l'Allemagne*; its author was exiled. The new set of rules established in 1810 remained in place more or less until 1870. They officially reintroduced censorship, reduced the number of Parisian printers to 60 (later increased to 80), and made authorization to print or sell books subject to a revocable licence or *brevet*. Tight control was exercised by a Direction de la librairie, which proved so zealous that Napoleon had to dissociate himself from it publicly. A more positive and longer-lasting creation was the future *Bibliographie de la France*, reviving d'Ormesson's plans. Characteristically, the Imprimerie nationale ('Impériale' for the time being) grew enormously, involving more than 150 presses and 1,000 printers by 1814. A splendid product of state intervention, the *Description de l'Égypte*, documenting the scientific aspects of Bonaparte's 1798–9 expedition, was commissioned in 1802. The last of its 21 volumes (13 comprising plates), issued in 1,000 copies, came out in 1828.

The period associated with Romanticism witnessed what has been termed 'the second revolution of the book', namely, the appearance of a mass market. This was made possible by the progress of literacy as well as by technical innovation. Mechanization affected the paper industry, printing (with some resistance among workers, as a case of Luddism in the 1830 Revolution attests), and binding (*see* **11**). Stereotyping became enormously important—Didot, in particular, exploited and systematized the discoveries of 18th-century pioneers such as François-Joseph-Ignace Hoffmann and L.-É. Herhan. Lithography made possible large press runs of high-quality illustrated texts, while the coloured woodcuts manufactured by Pellerin in Épinal not only remain forever associated with this Vosges city but also played a key role in the dissemination of the Napoleonic legend. Large printing plants flourished: Chaix in Paris, which prospered by printing railway timetables; or, in Tours, the equally famous Mame, specializing in religious literature, a field dominated by the figure of the Abbé Migne. Another mark of progress was the birth of 'industrial' distribution methods, facilitated after 1840 by the spread of railways and the growth of modern publicity methods. One consequence of these developments was the separation of the functions of printer and publisher—still often united in the first decade of the century (as in the case of the Didots), but almost universally kept apart by its end. On the other hand, the tradition of publishing houses owning and operating a bookshop remained alive throughout the century and beyond. Typographically, the only innovator was the Lyonnais Louis Perrin and his *augustaux*, inspired by Roman inscriptions, which in 1856 became the 'Elzévir' type popularized by Alphonse Lemerre's imprints.

Balzac, a sometime printer himself, has left in his 1843 novel *Les Illusions perdues* a memorable account of the book world of the 1820s—from the traditional, family operation of David Séchard in Angoulême, threatened locally by enterprising, commercially minded competitors, to the new type of Parisian publishers and dealers, for whom poetry and the novel were above all a commodity to be bought and sold. The year 1838 typifies the liveliness of the book world: Louis Hachette, a successful supplier of primary school textbooks now in great demand following Guizot's 1833 education laws, opened a branch in Algiers; the first novel to be serialized in the popular press, Dumas's *Le Capitaine Paul*, appeared in *Le Siècle*; Labrouste drew the plans for the new Bibliothèque Sainte-Geneviève; and Gervais Charpentier launched his 'Bibliothèque Charpentier', which genuinely prefigures the modern paperback, and whose modest price (3.50 francs) compensated for its dense typography. The 'Charpentier revolution', as it has been called, which did away with the elegant 'Didot style' that had dominated the previous 40 years, was quickly imitated. Bourdilliat & Jacottet dropped the price of their books to 1 fr., as did Michel Lévy, publisher of *Madame Bovary* (his brother Calmann later headed his house). By 1852, only fifteen years after the line from Paris to Saint-Germain opened, Hachette acquired the monopoly on French railway station bookstalls, creating a 'Bibliothèque des chemins de fer' the following year. Other successful careers of the period resulted in the establishment of long-lasting houses: Dalloz, Garnier, Plon, Dunod, Larousse. The mechanization of wood engraving led to a boom in children's literature. Although the best-known names remain those of the comtesse de Ségur (a Hachette author) and Jules Verne (published by Hetzel), the phenomenon also benefited provincial publishers.

French Romanticism is associated above all with poetry and the novel, and to a lesser extent the theatre; but the greatest success of the period was a religious essay, Lamennais's *Paroles d'un croyant* (1834). Its sales were boosted by its being immediately added to the *Index Librorum Prohibitorum*, a fate it shared with Renan's even more successful *Vie de Jésus* (1863), which sold more than 160,000 copies in its first year. The 'consecration of the writer' (Bénichou) in 19th-century France reached its apex with Hugo's state funeral in 1885. This development began with the founding of the first writers' associations: the Société des auteurs in 1829, followed by the Société des gens de lettres in 1837. Decades before the Berne Convention on copyright of 1886, these organizations were instrumental in securing the first bilateral agreement against piracy (with Belgium, 1852), and in having copyright extended to the surviving spouse (1866). Similarly, progress was achieved in the book world (including unionization) as a result of the founding of the Cercle de la librairie in 1847.

The general trend towards democratization that characterizes the 19th century had implications for the illustrated book, which had largely been a de luxe affair in the previous century. Although Delacroix's lithographs for the second edition of Nerval's translation of Goethe's *Faust* (1828), today considered a landmark in book illustration, were a commercial failure, the technique was popularized in the 1830s by a new kind of illustrated press (*Le Charivari*, *La Caricature*), where Honoré Daumier and, especially, J. J. Grandville published their work. Grandville dominated the illustrated book of the 1830s and 1840s, much as Gustave Doré did in the 1850s and 1860s. A celebrated achievement of the Romantic period remains the 1838 *Paul et Virginie* published by Léon Curmer, with woodcuts and etchings by Tony Johannot, Louis Français, Eugène Isabey, Ernest Meissonier, Paul Huet, and Charles Marville. The greatest monument of the time, however, and one of lithography's most beautiful products, is the series of *Voyages pittoresques et romantiques de l'ancienne France* edited by Charles Nodier and Baron Taylor, published by Didot in ten parts, each devoted to a French province, between 1820 and 1878. Géricault, Ingres, the Vernets, and Viollet-le-Duc, among others, participated in the project. Seven years after H. F. Talbot's *Pencil of Nature*, the French 'photographic incunable' (Brun) was Renard's *Paris photographié* (1853). Nevertheless, its appearance was anticipated by the two photographic plates—reproduced via the process invented by A. H. L. Fizeau—that were included in *Excursions dagueriennes* in 1842.

Since the French Revolution put large quantities of early and rare books on the market, the 19th century was the golden age of French bibliophilia, with

A bookworm, by J. J. Grandville, from *Scènes de la vie privée et publique des animaux* (Paris, 1842) by P.-J. Stahl (P.-J. Hetzel) and others. The Bodleian Library, University of Oxford (Vat. FR. III. B. 4053, opposite page 327)

Nodier, creator of the *Bulletin du bibliophile*, as its patron saint and J.-C. Brunet its founding father. The Société des bibliophiles françois was established in 1820. Among the collections dating from the period, few can match in splendour the one formed (largely in England) by the duc d'Aumale and now preserved at Chantilly.

Considering their rapid rise at the end of the *ancien régime*, French libraries should have enjoyed a golden age in the 19th century as well. With exceptions— the Arsenal under Nodier (though more as a salon than from a professional viewpoint) and Sainte-Geneviève—they did not. Even the Bibliothèque nationale suffered from comparative neglect until space problems forced the renovation begun in the 1850s and completed in the 1870s. Municipal libraries, consolidating their revolutionary gains, did relatively better. Compensating in part for the lack of public investment, lending *cabinets de lecture* flourished in the early 19th century (more than 500 operated in Paris) and several different types of library appeared during the period, especially small, specialized institutional libraries established by learned societies, such as the Société de l'histoire du protestantisme français; chambers of commerce (created throughout the country between 1825 and 1872); and religious institutions (some of these were confiscated, once more, at the 1905 separation between Church and state). As a result of the parallel rise in industrialization and literacy, a growing concern for popular libraries manifested itself during the Second Empire. The Société Franklin, founded in 1862, devoted itself to this effort. The École des Chartes, possibly the century's greatest legacy to librarianship, was founded in 1821 in order to train palaeographers and archivists. It was moved in 1897 to the new Sorbonne buildings.

The period 1870–1914 confirmed and accelerated the trends of the second book revolution. Although around 6,000 titles were printed in 1828, the figure had risen to 15,000 by 1889 and grew to about 25,000 by 1914. The growth was particularly spectacular in the newspaper and periodical press, finally liberalized by the law of 29 July 1881. Newspapers reached a circulation they were never again to equal: Milhaud's *Petit Journal* was selling more than a million copies by 1891. In 1914, *Le Petit Parisien* was issued in 1.5 million copies, with *Le Matin* and *Le Journal* not far behind at 1 million each. After a relative decline in the 1870s, this boom affected nearly all sectors, perhaps most especially the novel. Thus, if the initial volumes of the Rougon-Macquart series sold moderately, the success of *L'Assommoir* in 1876 propelled Zola (a Charpentier author) to the highest print runs of any novelist in his generation (55,000 copies for the first printing of *Nana* in 1879). Yet these figures pale before those achieved by the book that has become synonymous with Third Republic ideology, the *Tour de la France par deux enfants* by 'G. Bruno' (nom de plume of Mme Alfred Fouillée). Published by Belin in 1877 and read by generations of schoolchildren, it sold more than 8 million copies over the course of a century. Another popular genre of the pre-1914 period, detective fiction, was born in 1866, when Émile Gaboriau's *L'Affaire Lerouge* was serialized in *Le Soleil*. Its leading exponents in the early 20th century were Maurice Leblanc (his hero, Arsène Lupin, described as a 'gentleman burglar') and Gaston Leroux with his Rouletabille series.

New publicity methods soon affected literary publishing. They were used by the young Albin Michel to launch his first title, Félicien Champsaur's *L'Arriviste* (1902), and by Arthème Fayard (a house founded in 1857) for its collections 'Modern Bibliothèque' (note the missing 'e' in the adjective) and 'Le Livre populaire', which had considerable success before 1914, thanks to a policy of combining large print runs (100,000 or more) and low royalties.

At the other end of the spectrum, French bibliophilia continued to flourish at the fin de siècle, as the names of the prince d'Essling, Édouard Rahir, and Henri Béraldi (founder of the Société des amis des livres in 1874) testify. French bibliophiles of the period, however, do not seem to have had much contact with the pictorial avant-garde of their age, which left disappointingly few traces on the book arts of the time. Little notice was given to such landmark works as Manet's illustrations to Stéphane Mallarmé's version of Poe's *The Raven* (1875), *L'Après-midi d'un faune* (1876), and Poe's *Poèmes* (1889)— also in Mallarmé's translations—nor to Lautrec's two remarkable productions, Clemenceau's *Au pied du Sinaï* (1898) and Jules Renard's *Histoires naturelles* (1899). The foresightful Ambroise Vollard tried to redress the situation at the end of the century. Mallarmé's death in 1897 having interrupted his tantalizing project of *Un coup de dés* illustrated by Odilon Redon, Vollard's first two books, Verlaine's *Parallèlement* (1900) and Longus' *Daphnis and Chloé* (1902), were both illustrated by Bonnard. Now considered the first masterpieces of the modern artist's books, they were poorly received at the time. (Vollard printed them both at the Imprimerie nationale, an institution then in such turmoil that the French Parliament debated its abolition.) Vollard's example inspired another pioneer, Daniel-Henry Kahnweiler, whose first book, Apollinaire's *L'Enchanteur pourrissant* (1909), with Derain's subtly 'primitivistic' woodcuts, is another landmark; his *Saint Matorel* (1911), derided by contemporary *livres à figures* collectors, inaugurated Pablo Picasso's glorious association with the illustrated book.

8 After 1914

After the expansion of the late 19th and early 20th centuries, the period beginning in 1914 was, in France as elsewhere, a time of crisis and renewal. World War I, during which restrictions halved paper supplies, was followed by a short boom in publishing during the 1920s. The so-called *années folles* were well attuned to the development of modern methods of book promotion. One of their early beneficiaries was Pierre Benoît's novel *L'Atlantide*, a 1919 bestseller (a term soon adopted by the French) published by Albin Michel; the Académie française awarded it the Grand Prix du roman it had established the previous year. This new importance of literary prizes in the publishing world was signalled, also in 1919, by the controversy that ensued when the Goncourt went to Proust's *À l'ombre des jeunes filles en fleurs* in preference to Roland Dorgelès's war novel *Les Croix de bois*. (A different kind of controversy had surrounded the creation of the Femina Prize in 1904—its all-female jury was a response to the Goncourt Academy's perceived misogyny.) The Renaudot Prize, founded in 1926, was soon seen as open to the avant-garde: its early laureates included Céline and Aragon, whose publisher Denoël thus came close to rivalling Gallimard and Grasset. A fifth prize, the Prix Interallié, was created in 1930 and first awarded to Malraux's *La Voie royale*. After more than three-quarters of a century, the same five prizes continue to dominate the French literary landscape.

If the late 19th century had seen a gap between bibliophilia and the artistic avant-garde, the first half of the 20th saw the triumph of the *livre de peintre* or *livre d'artiste* (artist's book), with strong innovators following in Vollard and Kahnweiler's footsteps: Albert Skira and Tériade in the 1930s and 1940s, Iliazd (Ilia Zdanevich), Pierre Lecuire, Pierre-André Benoît, among others, in the 1950s and after. By contrast with their 19th-century predecessors, Henri Matisse and Picasso, arguably the century's two most important painters, were each involved in many book projects; Picasso throughout his career (he illustrated more than 150 books), Matisse for a relatively short period in the final part of his, both with magnificent results. No satisfactory discussion of their art—or of the art of the book in France between 1930 and 1970—can ignore their achievements in this field.

The 1920s and 1930s were a time of typographical success, led by the Imprimerie nationale and epitomized by the success of the Futura (or 'Europe') type launched by the foundry of Deberny & Peignot. The same decades also witnessed a renaissance of bookbinding design in France (which had begun in the art nouveau period), marked by the achievements of Henri Marius-Michel, Victor Prouvé, and Charles Meunier. An even more impressive group—under the aegis of dealers like Auguste Blaizot and collectors gathered in the association Les Amis de la reliure originale—was the generation of Paul Bonet, Henri Creuzevault, Georges Cretté, and Pierre Legrain. They were succeeded, after World War II, by the outstanding trio of Georges Leroux, Pierre-Lucien Martin, and Monique Mathieu. Their successor, Jean de Gonet, has been remarkable both for his efforts to democratize original bindings by using industrial leather ('revorim') and because, unlike them, he operated his own workshop rather than being strictly a designer.

World War II, when the country was occupied for more than four years, had dramatic consequences for the book world. Censorship was imposed by the Nazis (the notorious 'Otto list'); shortages of paper more than halved production; 'Aryanization' measures affected individuals (such as the general administrator of the BN, Julien Cain, who was sacked by Vichy and later deported by the Nazis) and publishing houses—although Nathan managed to sell its shares to a group of friends, Calmann-Lévy was purchased and run by a German businessman and Ferenczi was put into the hands of a collaborator. The first two publishers were later revived, but the third never regained its prewar status. Yet, paradoxically, the four years of occupation coincided with a literary flowering, reading having become by necessity the chief cultural activity. The years following liberation confirmed the emergence of a new literary generation—that of Beauvoir, Camus, Queneau, and Sartre—which recaptured the kind of prestige enjoyed by 18th-century *philosophes*, a prestige reflected in their publisher, Gallimard.

For all its aberrations, the Vichy period also marked a return to the long French tradition of intervention in cultural matters, following the relative disengagement that had characterized most of the Third Republic. From this point of view, there was a continuity with the Fourth and Fifth Republics. Already in the 1930s, particularly in the shadow of the Depression, there was a growing concern that the state was not doing enough to support libraries or the book trade and that a *politique de la lecture* was in order. This was accomplished through a variety of government agencies working sometimes in harmony, at other times in competition. The cultural division of the ministry of foreign affairs, established in the early 1920s, subsidized French book exports (and was quickly accused of favouring Gallimard authors). A Caisse nationale des lettres, with representatives of the profession, was created in 1930 with a view to granting loans and subsidies—it became the Centre national des lettres in 1973 and the Centre national du livre in 1993. It too has not been immune to charges of favouritism. In the wake of the liberation, a Direction des bibliothèques et de la lecture publique was created within the education ministry (with Cain at its head). Since school libraries were not part of its responsibilities, it focused instead on the creation of a network of lending libraries called Bibliothèques centrales (renamed 'départementales' in 1983), which helped to reduce the cultural gap not only between Paris and the provinces but also between large cities and rural areas. School libraries began to receive serious attention in the 1970s. University libraries, however, remained (and still are) the poor relations of the French educational system, even as the French student population doubled over the same decade. The overwhelming success (particularly with students) of the Bibliothèque publique d'information at the Pompidou Centre, which opened in 1977, showed how keenly the lack of research facilities with open stacks and late and Sunday hours was being felt.

The Mitterrand government that came to power in 1981 proclaimed ambitious cultural policies (the official portrait of the president showed him with an open copy of Montaigne in his hands). One of its first measures was the imposition of a 5 per cent cap on book discounts, with a view to protecting independent bookdealers. The Direction du livre (created in 1975) and BN were placed under the authority of an expanded ministry of culture headed by Jack Lang. More subsidies were indeed available, but to what extent any of the official measures have affected continuing economic or cultural trends is debatable. The most enduring legacy of the Mitterrand years and, significantly, the most controversial of his *grands projets* remains the new, high-tech BnF, opened in 1996 after his death and named after him.

Economically, the trend towards greater corporate amalgamation, beginning in the 1950s, led, after the economic crisis of 1973, to the formation of three publishing giants: Hachette, which throughout the century had grown as both publisher and book distributor; the Groupe de la Cité, formed in 1988 and including Larousse, Nathan, the Presses de la Cité, Bordas, and the 4-million-member France-Loisirs book club; and Masson, the medical publisher, which had grown by absorbing Colin in 1987 and Belfond in 1989. The three became two when Masson Belfond was absorbed by CEP/Cité/Havas in 1995—to be resold to a different group six years later. Behind these two groups are larger financial entities, Lagardère for Hachette, Vivendi-Universal (originally a water-supply company) for the other. Following Rizzoli's purchase of Flammarion, only five major Parisian firms, which themselves had absorbed smaller houses, remained independent by 2005: Albin Michel, Calmann-Lévy, Fayard, Gallimard, and Le Seuil. According to 2002 statistics, 80 per cent of all French book production came from the top 15 per cent of a total of 313 publishers. The same statistics revealed a significant decline of the workforce in the publishing sector (about 10,000, down from 13,350 in 1975), while the number of titles published (20,000) is lower than the figure for 1914. A very small number of titles represent a high percentage of the total sales, not necessarily at the lower end: Marguerite Duras's *L'Amant* in 1984 and Yann Arthus-Bertrand's photographic album *La Terre vue du ciel* in 2000 both sold more than 1 million copies each. Corporate mergers have also affected the book trade, with large chains like FNAC (itself now controlled by a major financial group) or non-traditional outlets ('hypermarkets') occupying a position of growing importance. Despite remarkable exceptions like Actes Sud—which, however, eventually opened offices in Paris—the trend towards amalgamation has reinforced the position of the capital, which at the beginning of the 21st century controlled about 90 per cent of production. One could qualify this picture, however, by stressing the viability of small or medium-sized specialized houses, such as L'Arche, devoted almost entirely to the theatre; or the relative health of religious publishing, dominated by the three Catholic houses of Bayard, Le Cerf, and Desclée de Brouwer.

Culturally, the most important event in French book history between 1945 and the advent of the Internet was the launching of the 'Livre de poche' series by Hachette and Gallimard (1953). This comparatively belated French answer to Penguin Books deeply affected book-buying and reading habits—a 20th-century equivalent of the 'Révolution Charpentier' in the 19th. Gallimard and Hachette were 'divorced' in 1972, when Gallimard created the Folio collection to reissue titles from its own considerable list.

Another notable postwar change has been the growth of children's literature and the parallel development of children's libraries since the first, 'L'Heure joyeuse', was opened in Paris in 1924 by a branch of the American Relief Committee. A landmark in this respect was the creation of the association La Joie par les livres in 1963. A private initiative, it led to the opening of a model children's library in the Paris suburb of Clamart in 1965. In addition to specialized houses like L'École des loisirs (also established in 1965), many of the major publishers (Gallimard for one) opened a children's department.

In a different sphere, the postwar period saw a resurgence, followed by a gradual decline, of censorship on moral grounds: Olympia Press and J.-J. Pauvert, publisher of Sade and *L' Histoire d'O*, were prosecuted in the 1940s and 1950s, while the suppression of Bernard Noël's *Le Château de Cène* was met with a public outcry in 1973. In popular literature, where detective fiction has continued to flourish, perhaps the most striking phenomenon has been the spread of comic books to the adult population, exemplified by the success of Goscinny and Uderzo's Astérix series in the 1970s. The 'bande dessinée' is now a respectable genre with its museum and annual festival in Angoulême.

Traditional forms of book culture, however, are still very much alive at all levels. Evidence for this can be found at the academic level by the vitality of 'l'histoire du livre' (launched by the publication in 1957 of Lucien Febvre and Henri-Jean Martin's *L'Apparition du livre*); at the bibliophilic level by the health of book collecting, nourished by the seemingly endless supply of material at auction or through the outstanding antiquarian book trade; and, in the population in general, by the qualitatively important place books and reading continue to occupy in the collective perception the French have of their own culture.

....

BIBLIOGRAPHY

F. Barbier, *Histoire du livre* (2000)

P. Bénichou, *The Consecration of the Writer, 1750-1830*, tr. M. K. Jensen (1999)

[Bibliothèque nationale de France,] *En français dans le texte: dix siècles de lumières par le livre* (1990)

R. Brun, *Le Livre français* (1969)

R. Chartier and H.-J. Martin, eds., *Histoire de l'édition française* (3 vols, 1982)

A. Coron, ed., *Des Livres rares depuis l'invention de l'imprimerie* (1998)

DEL

L. Febvre and H.-J. Martin, *The Coming of the Book*, tr. D. Gerard (1997)

C. Hesse, *Publishing and Cultural Politics in Revolutionary Paris, 1789-1810* (1991)

H.-J. Martin, *Print, Power, and People in 17th-Century France*, tr. D. Gerard (1993)

P. Schuwer, *Dictionnaire de l'édition* (1977)

M.-H. Tesnière and P. Gifford, eds., *Creating French Culture* (1995)

25

The History of the Book in the Low Countries

PAUL HOFTIJZER

1 The Roman period to the Middle Ages

The region that is now roughly The Netherlands, Belgium, Luxemburg, and the upper part of northwestern France first came into contact with written culture during the Roman period (1ˢᵗ–4ᵗʰ century AD). Archaeological evidence is scarce, but certainly in larger Gallo-Roman settlements, writing for administrative, commercial, and educational purposes appears to have been used on a regular basis. How much of this practice survived the onslaught of the Migration Period is uncertain, but by the 6ᵗʰ century writing returned at least in the southern Netherlands. In the north, the former border region of the Roman empire, MSS did not appear until the 8ᵗʰ century. The first codex ever seen there may well have been the book with which the English missionary Boniface tried to defend himself, when he and his 52 companions were slain by heathen Frisians at Dokkum in 754.

For the next few centuries, ecclesiastical and monastic sites, of which the densest concentration was found in the south, were the main centres of book production and consumption in the Low Countries. The books were almost exclusively liturgical and theological works, but there is also evidence for the transmission of classical texts. The 8ᵗʰ-century bishop Theutbert (Theodard) of Utrecht, for instance, possessed a MS of Livy copied two centuries earlier. Little remains of the earliest work of local scriptoria documented at important Benedictine abbeys such as Echternach, Elno, St Omer, and Arras. Most MSS in the libraries of churches and monasteries would have been acquired from elsewhere in any case.

The era of Charlemagne (742–814) and his immediate successors—whose policies of political, religious, and cultural reform created more stability in northwest Europe—strongly promoted the making and use of books, aided by the introduction of the Carolingian minuscule, the dominant form of writing until its ultimate replacement by gothic-style scripts in the 13th century. Various schools and traditions existed next to each other, such as the large, sumptuously illuminated books produced at the court of Charles the Bald (823–77) and the more soberly executed work of monastic scriptoria, which were strongly influenced by English and Irish models. This receptivity of Netherlandish MS production to influences from other regions would remain one of its characteristic features.

During the 10th and 11th centuries, when Viking raids still ravaged the Low Countries, MS production was at a low. The 12th century, however, saw the height of Romanesque illumination, which, although remaining traditional in its concepts, combined a newly found vitality with great plasticity. Bookmaking was still the prerogative of the monasteries, but the Benedictines now had to share their dominance with new monastic orders, such as the Cistercians and Premonstratensians. The main centres of production were located in the present border region with northern France, in Flanders, and along the Meuse valley. Of the output of scriptoria in the north, particularly those at the Benedictine abbey of Egmond and the cathedral school of Utrecht, only a few specimens have survived.

As in architecture, sculpture, and painting, the arrival of the Gothic style in MS production was closely connected to the emergence of cities. Reading and writing turned into a normal feature of many aspects of city life; the making of books became an activity for professional lay artists working for a predominantly urban clientele. This is not to say that monastic scriptoria dwindled, but their output decreased in relative terms. As the Low Countries during the high Middle Ages swiftly developed into one of the most densely populated and urbanized areas of Europe, the production and use of MSS in cities all over the region expanded substantially. Religious and theological books remained of primary importance, but more and more works on worldly subjects, such as law, medicine, astrology, and history, as well as literary compositions and schoolbooks, were becoming available. In book illumination, highly expressive and elaborate styles emerged, with a typical Netherlandish tendency towards naturalism and realism.

This development reached its peak during the 15th century. The flowering of urban society was reinforced by the incorporation of a large part of the region into the dominions of the dukes of Burgundy, who, having huge resources at their disposal, sought to affirm their power and status by cultural means. In this cross-fertilization of urban and courtly culture, MS making thrived as never before. Ghent and Bruges in particular became the leading centres for the production of luxurious MSS of the highest quality after the fashion of Flemish mannerism. Many of these MSS found their way into collections of highly placed patrons and bibliophiles in the Low Countries as well as abroad, especially in France and England. The names of the artists involved are often unknown; they are referred to by such titles as the 'Master of Mary of Burgundy' or the 'Master of the Dresden Hours'. Their highly specialized art continued well into the 16th century, as can be seen in the work of one of the most accomplished illuminators from Bruges, Simon Bening. At Louvain, which had become the seat of the first university of the Low Countries in 1425, several *librarii* were soon active in the copying and selling of more functional academic texts.

The new impetus was also felt in the northern Netherlands, which for a long time had lagged behind the far more prosperous south. Under the influence of the spiritual renewal of the Devotio Moderna and the establishment of the court of the Counts of Holland in The Hague, a remarkable regional flowering occurred. In their striving for piety and spirituality, the Devotionalists attached great value to reading and writing and were very active in copying MSS—for their own use as well as on commission. A large part of their work consists of books of hours, intended for private devotion and for that reason often written in the vernacular. The courtly milieu of the counts of Holland, who had close connections with the neighbouring bishopric of Utrecht and the dukedom of Guelders, proved a fertile environment for the production of exquisite illuminated MSS, the most famous of which is the Hours of Catherine of Cleves (*c.*1440), made by an unknown master.

Under these circumstances, it is not surprising that printing arrived early in the Low Countries. Precisely when, however, is impossible to say, as no dated or otherwise identifiable printed material has survived from before 1473. What now is called 'Dutch prototypography'—fragments of anonymously printed schoolbooks and religious and humanistic works (once attributed to Laurens Janszoon Coster)—in all likelihood dates from *c.*1470 and may well be associated with one punchcutter-printer. Of even older origin are a series of xylographic prints or woodblock-printed books, but again nothing is known about their maker(s).

Most early printers in the southern Netherlands were active in major cities such as Ghent, Bruges, Brussels, Louvain, and Antwerp, while in the north they worked in smaller towns such as Utrecht, Deventer, Zwolle, Gouda, Delft, Leiden, and Haarlem. They had as a rule learned their craft in Germany or northern Italy. Their printing offices were small and often still combined the entire process of book production and distribution, from casting type to selling books. Although catering for a regional and supraregional market, they very much depended on local conditions for their survival. The economic depression and political instability in the northern Netherlands during the last decades of the century were the cause of a series of bankruptcies and the migration of businesses to the south, particularly to Antwerp.

Early Netherlandish book production, which amounts to some 2,200 editions before 1501, was mainly religious in character, with an emphasis on works connected to the Devotio Moderna movement. Educational centres such as

Deventer, which had a famous Latin school, and the university town of Louvain specialized in schoolbooks and classical and humanist texts. The dominant language was Latin, books in Dutch amounting to only 25 per cent of the total. The common typeface—for Latin texts as well—was a formal gothic letter (textura); roman faces were only used occasionally. A large percentage (40 per cent) of Netherlandish incunables are illustrated with woodcuts, sometimes of exceptional artistic quality.

2 1500–1700

During the 16th century, printing in the Low Countries came into its own. As humanism became the driving force of intellectual life, first in the south and in the second half of the century also in the north, education, and consequently literacy, were considerably enhanced. Large quantities of textbooks for use in the region's growing number of primary and secondary schools were printed. Supplementing the canon of established classical and medieval knowledge, new scholarly works on a wide range of subjects were published. Although literary expression was still very much the domain of older traditions of medieval drama, rhetoric, and romance, new forms of poetry and prose, inspired by Italian and French Renaissance models, gained popularity, first in Latin, soon also in Dutch. The book trade eagerly tapped into these new trends.

The Reformation provided an equally potent incentive to book production. From the 1520s onwards there was a growing demand for Protestant books, from treatises by Luther and other, often more radical reformers to editions of the Bible in the vernacular. The first complete Dutch edition of the Bible, which was partly based on Martin Luther's German translation, appeared from the Antwerp press of Jacob van Liesveldt as early as 1526. Many others would follow. The so-called 'Souterliedekens', rhymed translations of the Psalms in Dutch, set on the melodies of secular songs, were very popular too. First published in Antwerp in 1540, they were reprinted over and over again. Although the Catholic Church and the secular authorities reacted vehemently against the Reformation movement by putting increasingly severe sanctions on the making, selling, and reading of heretical works, the storm could not be calmed. Motivated by religious zeal as much as by commercial gain, some printers did not hesitate to risk their lives by producing Protestant books, often working underground or from exile in places such as Emden just across the border in Germany. A typical example is the Antwerp printer and bookseller Adriaen van Berghen. Having been convicted in 1535 for selling heretical books from his stall in Antwerp, he fled to Holland, where he lived in various places until he finally settled in Delft. When, in 1542, his house was found to contain a stock of forbidden books, he was banned from the city, but this relatively mild punishment was overturned by the Court of Holland and he was beheaded soon after in The Hague.

The undisputed centre of the 16th-century Netherlandish book trade was Antwerp. The city on the Scheldt was a magnet for printers and booksellers from other places, because of its large population, booming economic conditions, and excellent connections to European markets. Book production in Antwerp shows all the characteristics of early capitalist enterprise, such as the participation of external investors, the diversification of production, and adaptation to a mass market. All this can best be seen in the activities of the most renowned printer and publisher of the period, Christopher Plantin. At the height of his career, in the 1570s, he ran a fully equipped typefoundry, a printing office with sixteen presses, and a bookshop with sales all over Europe. His output of some 1,500 publications ranged from the impressive eight-volume polyglot *Biblia Regia* (1568–72) and ponderous scholarly works to elegant emblem books, small-format editions of classical writers, schoolbooks, and pamphlets. Other Antwerp book trade entrepreneurs chose to concentrate their activities on a specific genre, for instance music books, the speciality of the firm of Jean Bellère, maps and atlases, pioneered by Gerard Mercator and Abraham Ortelius, books for the Spanish market, the business of Martinus Nutius, or all sorts of prints and engravings, made in the workshops of Hieronymus Cock and his successors the Galle family.

Works in Latin were now printed in a wide range of roman and italic faces in all sizes, designed by the best French and Flemish punchcutters such as Claude Garamont, Robert Granjon, Guillaume Le Bé, and Hendrik van den Keere. For vernacular books, a growing number of gothic types were available, including the elegant civilité letter. In book illustration, high-quality images were often executed by etching or engraving (*see* **18**). Bookbinding followed the fashion of neighbouring countries, especially France, but during this and later periods, frugal Netherlandish taste on the whole did not allow for much luxury in external ornamentation. The most commonly used type of binding was made of plain, unadorned vellum (*see* **19**).

The combination of religious oppression, social and political unrest, and outright war in the second half of the 16th century proved fatal to the cohesion of the Low Countries. Within twenty years the Dutch Revolt—started in 1568 as an uprising against the autocratic rule of Philip II of Spain—divided the region into two political entities: the Roman Catholic southern Netherlands, which remained first under Spanish, then Austrian Habsburg rule, and the northern provinces which became an independent, predominantly Protestant republic. Thousands of religious and economic refugees left the south. Many temporarily went to England and Germany, but in the end most found a permanent home in the newly created United Provinces. Among them were scores of printers and booksellers, the majority of whom settled in the rising cities of Holland and Zeeland: Amsterdam, Haarlem, Leiden, Rotterdam, Dordrecht, Gouda, Delft, and Middelburg. Bringing with them technical skills and commercial expertise, they greatly invigorated the book trade in the north.

Apart from immigration—a phenomenon that would recur on a huge scale at the end of the 17th century when large numbers of Huguenot refugees arrived from France, among them again many printers and booksellers—there were other factors that contributed to the success of printing and bookselling in the Dutch Republic. A loose confederation of seven provinces, of which Holland was the most powerful, the country lacked central political authority, while its largest and most powerful city, Amsterdam, at times acted like a state within a state. A situation existed in which censorship was by no means absent, but could only be practised in a limited manner. Even the system of privileges, which in other countries served as a means of preventive government control, in the northern Netherlands remained confined to its primary function as a protection of publishers' copyrights. Combined with long-established traditions of tolerance, these realities earned the Dutch Republic a reputation for being a country where the printing of books that were forbidden elsewhere was openly permitted. As the English naturalist John Ray wrote in his travel journal in 1633: 'The People say and print what they please, and call it Liberty' (Ray, 54). Indeed, during the 17th and 18th centuries many controversial foreign authors, from Galileo to Descartes and from Johann Amos Comenius to Jean-Jacques Rousseau, published their work more or less freely in the United Provinces. Even the most hated of religious sects, the Socinians, had their writings printed without too much difficulty in Amsterdam in a splendid multi-volume *Bibliotheca Fratrum Polonorum* (1665–9).

The book trade in the Dutch Republic equally profited from favourable economic conditions. A good network of roads and waterways made transport easy and inexpensive. Thanks to low interest rates and a well-developed financial market, capital was readily available, and there was abundant skilled labour in all branches of bookmaking. The absence of strict external and internal economic regulation prevented excessive monopolies and market protection. In most cities, restrictive guilds of printers and booksellers did not come into existence until the second half of the 17th century, and their rules were not on the whole very strict. Following in the wake of other merchants, booksellers developed extensive international networks for the distribution of their books. They regularly visited the semi-annual book fairs at Frankfurt and later at Leipzig in order to exchange their latest publications, but also to act as middlemen for colleagues in other countries. Some booksellers had agents and even branches in strategically located cities such as Paris, London, Florence, Vienna, Gdańsk (Danzig), and Copenhagen. The home market was no less important, thanks to high literacy levels among men and women and a flourishing cultural and intellectual climate. The foundation of new universities in Leiden (1574), Franeker (1585), Groningen (1614), and Utrecht (1636), which all soon attracted many students from abroad, created opportunities for specialized scholarly publishers: thanks to the use of Latin as the language of academic communication, they could easily reach an international clientele. The most famous Dutch academic publishers, the Elzeviers in Leiden, were active for well over a century and had branch offices in Amsterdam, The Hague, and Utrecht.

Because competition was fierce, Dutch printers and publishers were constantly trying to strengthen their position by finding new niches in the market.

A stereotype plate (1) believed to have been made by the process invented by Johann Müller and the corresponding page of a Dutch bible printed by Müller's sons and Samuel Luchtmans at Leiden in 1718. © The British Library Board. All Rights Reserved (C.37.l.3*)

A 17th-century Dutch bookshop from two drawings by Salomon de Bray, c.1625: the shop, probably in Haarlem, sold prints, pictures, and globes as well as bound books and books in sheets. On the left in the upper picture an assistant is binding books. Collection Rijksmuseum Amsterdam (M RP T 1884 A 290/291)

For example, newspaper publishing in various languages and various forms (including the coranto) became a separate branch of publishing as early as the second decade of the 17th century. Amsterdam firms such as the Blaeu family and Johannes Janssonius in the 17th century, and the Mortier and van Keulen families in the 18th, applied themselves to the publication of high-quality maps and atlases. Jewish printers, often financed by external backers, specialized in the bulk production of religious texts for Jewish communities in Germany and eastern Europe (see 8). In the 1680s, French-language scholarly journals, carrying book reviews, were introduced, thanks to the contribution of immigrant Huguenot publishers, editors, and journalists. Examples of this highly successful genre include the *Nouvelles de la République des Lettres* (Rotterdam, 1684–7), edited by Pierre Bayle, and the *Bibliothèque choisie* (Amsterdam, 1703–13) of Jean Le Clerc.

There were also technological innovations, such as the application of an improved hose in printing presses (an invention attributed to the Amsterdam printer Willem Jansz Blaeu) and the introduction of forms of stereotype printing by the Leiden Lutheran minister Johann Müller, c.1710. The widespread use of smaller formats was made possible by the introduction of compact, yet highly legible roman typefaces. These founts, cut by Christoffel van Dijck and others, also found their way to other countries, especially England. The most important innovation in the second-hand book trade was the printed auction catalogue. The first such catalogue appeared in Leiden in 1599 for the auction by Louis Elzevier of the library of the statesman-scholar Marnix de Sainte-Aldegonde; within a few decades they were common all over the country.

The large number of auction catalogues from the 17th and 18th centuries that have survived are proof of a very lively book culture in the Dutch Republic. Reading vernacular books was a fairly normal practice among upper- and middle-class sections of the population, and many people, certainly in the cities, owned small to medium-sized book collections. Their contents ranged from religious texts—above all the Bible, but also sermons and treatises of an often moral and pious nature—to practical and educational works, books on history and travel, and a wide variety of literary genres: farcical and anecdotal texts, non-fictional prose, poetry, song books, plays, emblematic works, etc. In addition, newspapers, broadsides, pamphlets, chapbooks, almanacs and more ephemeral printing, much of which has not survived, were consumed in vast quantities (*see* **16**). Most of these publications were acquired through regular bookshops, but there also existed a thriving itinerant book trade in spite of restrictions enforced by local booksellers' guilds. Some cities had municipal libraries, although access was normally restricted to the members of the elite. Private book collections of true bibliophiles were relatively scarce, perhaps partly because of the absence of a strong aristocracy and court. Nevertheless, important libraries were created by individuals such as Joannes Thysius, Adriaan Pauw, Hendrick Adriaansz van der Marck, the Meermans, and Bolongaro Crevenna.

3 1701–1900

That the book trade in the Dutch Republic was vulnerable became apparent from the end of the 17th century onwards. The succession of continental wars seriously affected international sales, while at the same time competition grew from other countries—France, England, and the German states. Also, the decline of Latin as the scholarly language of the republic of letters and the growing importance of vernacular languages in Europe presented a significant barrier to this Dutch-speaking nation. Even the mass production of pirated editions of foreign bestsellers, which for a long time was one of the mainstays of the early modern Dutch book trade, lost much of its ground, as can be seen in relation to the printing of English bibles. The huge flow of copies of the Authorized Version with the original London imprint from Amsterdam to Britain in the 1670s and 1680s was reduced to a trickle by the middle of the 18th century. Only the piracy of French bestsellers continued to thrive; but here too, competition from other countries, in particular the southern Netherlands and Switzerland, was fierce. Attempts to redress this downward spiral—by the introduction of commission trading and a system of trade correspondents, or by the reduction of entrepreneurial risk through subscription publishing and the collaboration of multiple publishers—were not sufficient. As the Leiden bookseller Elie Luzac observed in his *Hollands rijkdom* (The Wealth of Holland) published in 1783, when the Dutch Republic was torn apart by political crisis: 'Elsewhere they now have paper of the same quality but cheaper than ours; they print as well but cheaper than we and they produce type as good as ours but cheaper; and although we may have political hackwriters in abundance, our Dutch book trade lacks serious works of scholarship' (Luzac, 4. 425–6).

In stark contrast to the north, the book trade in the southern Netherlands during the 17th and 18th centuries experienced a period of prolonged decline. To the drain of talent and skills at the end of the 16th century were added economic and cultural stagnation and the strict supervision of the printing press by the Catholic Church and the secular authorities. In order to survive, printers and publishers adopted various strategies. The Plantin-Moretus firm, for example, concentrated its activities on the publication of luxurious and expensive works and on the mass production of all sorts of Catholic Church books intended for the global Spanish market, for which they enjoyed a royal privilege. Some firms, like the Verdussen family of Antwerp, tried to cut back on expenses by outsourcing their printing or restructuring their distribution, while others concentrated their efforts on the manufacturing of cheap devotional booklets, images of saints, tales of chivalry, romances, almanacs, catchpenny prints, plays, and songs, all in the vernacular and aimed at the domestic market. Piracy and the printing of illicit, particularly French, books provided another route of escape. In the 18th century, Brussels, capital of the Austrian Netherlands, and the autonomous cities of Liège and Bouillon hosted numerous printing offices working exclusively for the French market. Between 1774 and 1783, the French-born publisher Jean-Louis de Boubers at Brussels, for example, printed a splendid collected edition of Rousseau's works in twelve illustrated volumes with the false imprint 'Londres', but, needless to say, without the consent of the author, nor of any legitimate publishers.

The transitional period from the 18th to the 19th century was a bleak era for publishing and bookselling in both the northern and southern Netherlands. In addition to the deep economic depression, repeated changes in the political regime of the two countries, growing censorship, and the seemingly endless Napoleonic wars all had a devastating impact on the book trade. Yet there were some redeeming features. Under the influence of the Enlightenment, the emancipation of the middle classes brought about the participation of a greater element of the population in cultural and political life. Many local and national societies and reading circles were founded for the active or passive pursuit of science and literature, and these initiatives stimulated publishing and the consumption of books. The collapse of the political system of the *ancien régime* gave birth for the first time to a free, critical, and opinion-forming periodical press. However short-lived it may have been, it set an example for the future. Where the book trade, under harsh economic circumstances, had become increasingly protective of vested interests, the step-by-step abolition of the guild system contributed to a much-needed liberalization of the market. Finally, the issue of copyright was gradually being addressed by a succession of laws that better protected the rights of publishers and, to a limited extent, of authors.

In 1815 the Congress of Vienna decided to restore the political unity of the Low Countries through the creation of the Kingdom of the Netherlands, headed by the son of the last Dutch stadtholder, King William I (1772–1843). It was an artificial construct destined to fail from the start. Despite some successes in the economic and social sphere, the north and south had been separated too long to be able to form a coherent national community. The Belgian Revolt of 1830 and the ensuing independence of the southern Netherlands under the royal House of Saxe-Coburg meant that each of the two countries would go its own way. A long and difficult process of recovery began, in which more general social developments, such as the growth of the population, the centralization and democratization of government, the liberalization and industrialization of the economy, educational reform, and the emancipation of the underprivileged directly correlated with changes in the world of books. It is worth noting, for example, that printing and publishing for a mass audience in The Netherlands did not come about until the second half of the 19th century. This was the era when, among many other factors, the mechanization and industrialization of production in printing and related activities finally got off the ground (*see* **11**), the old stamp duty on newspapers and journals was abolished (1869), the quality of primary and secondary education was drastically improved, working hours of labourers were reduced and their wages increased, and the first steps were taken on the road to the liberation of women.

Annual book production in The Netherlands in this period rose from a few hundred titles at the beginning of the 19th century to some 3,000 by 1900. Foreign-language publication having come to an almost complete standstill, publishers now aimed entirely at the vernacular market. In relative terms, religious books began to lose ground to other genres. Literary works found their way to the public in an increasing variety of guises, as original or translated individual pieces, but also in the shape of serial publications, anthologies, and contributions to journals and almanacs. They were, moreover, printed in various forms and formats for different readerships. The highly popular *Nederlandsche Muzenalmanak* (1819–47), for instance, could be had in five different versions at prices ranging from three and a half guilders for a copy on ordinary paper, bound in cardboard, to seven and a half guilders for a fine paper copy, bound in satin with a slipcase. At the same time, there was a growing demand for non-specialist books on a wide range of topics—science, medicine, biology, history, and art. Moreover, thanks to innovative techniques in book illustration—such as wood and steel engraving, and lithography and photography—new types of publications came on the market, including children's books, illustrated magazines, and practical handbooks (*see* **17, 18**).

The organization of the Dutch book trade changed with the times. The branch organization Vereeniging ter Bevordering van de Belangen des Boekhandels (the ancestor of the present Koninklijke Vereniging voor het Boekenvak) was founded in 1815 as a national successor to the local guilds. It was established first and foremost to combat piracy, but gradually took on other tasks as well, such as the regulation and improvement of the trade, the compilation of an annual bibliography of newly published books, the publication of a trade journal (*Nieuwsblad voor den boekhandel*), the organizing of trade fairs, and even the provision of a professional library and documentation centre in Amsterdam (the present Library of the Royal Netherlands Book Trade Association (KVB). A prominent role in these activities was played by the Amsterdam publisher and antiquarian bookseller Frederik Muller. Book distribution was modernized by the creation in 1871 of a central distribution office in Amsterdam, the Bestelhuis, which organized the now generally accepted commission trade. The traditional figure of the bookseller, who combined both publishing and bookselling and often ran a printing office as well, slowly disappeared. Instead, printing, publishing, and modern and antiquarian bookselling became separate activities. The foundation of separate organizations for publishers (Nederlandse Uitgevers Bond, 1880) and booksellers (Nederlandse Boekverkopers Bond, 1907) is an indication of this process of occupational diversification and professionalization. At the other end of the spectrum, by 1866 Dutch typesetters had already achieved a national trade union (Algemene Nederlandse Typografen Bond)—the first such organization in The Netherlands—which successfully campaigned for a reduction of working hours and higher wages in the printing industry. Finally, in 1881, a modern Copyright Act was issued to protect the rights of native authors and publishers, although it would take until 1912 for the Dutch government to sign up to the international Berne Convention of 1886.

In Belgium, the modernization of printing, publishing, and bookselling was a much longer-drawn-out affair. The main obstacle was the linguistic division of the country between French- and Flemish-speaking regions. French had long been the language of the political and cultural elite of southern Netherlandish society, which in effect meant a lasting dependence on the powerful publishing industry in France. Authors preferred to have their work issued by French publishers, as it guaranteed them better terms and conditions and a larger audience. The Flemish-speaking population, on the other hand, had become culturally backward and provincial. The volume of Flemish books produced at the beginning of the 19th century consisted of little more than, as the Antwerp author Domien Sleeckx recalled in his autobiography, 'almanacs, schoolbooks, church books, and similar pious writings' (Simons, 1. 18–20). It took the protagonists of the Flemish Movement (Vlaamse Beweging), which started as a band of romantic writers and intellectuals after Belgian independence, much time and effort before they were able to use the printing press as an instrument for the promotion of their ideals. The problems they encountered may be illustrated by the publishing history of the first edition (1838) of the most famous Flemish book of the 19th century, the nationalist historical novel *De leeuw van Vlaanderen* (The Lion of Flanders) by Hendrik Conscience. As no publisher dared to take the risk of issuing it, the book was printed at the author's own expense; to his relief, he had (barely) found a sufficient number of people willing to subscribe to it. (Nearly a third of the subscribers came from The Netherlands.) The novel's eventual success convinced one entrepreneur, Joseph-Ernest Buschmann, of the viability of setting up a publishing firm in Antwerp that specialized in Flemish literary works; throughout the second half of the 19th century, however, it would remain difficult for Flemish writers to get their work published. Although in 1893 a Dutch book trade and publishing company, De Nederlandsche Boekhandel, established itself in Antwerp with the aim of promoting Flemish literature, leading Flemish literary authors by that time had their books published in The Netherlands because in all respects—editorial attention, typography, remuneration, readership—they were better served there than in Flanders.

4 The modern era

It has been said, with some exaggeration, that the modern era in The Netherlands did not begin until after World War II. To an extent this observation also holds true for the book trade. With the exception of a handful of more enterprising firms—Albert Willem Sijthoff in Leiden, the Enschedé family in Haarlem, Martinus Nijhoff in The Hague, Elsevier in Amsterdam—publishing and book-selling up to the 1950s could be characterized as insular and conservative in their method, scope, and ambition. Most publishing and bookselling businesses were small in size and family-owned. They stuck to their traditional ways and shied away from innovation. Moreover, the rigid segmentation (*Verzuiling*) of society along the lines of religious and political groupings dominated publishing and bookselling. Firmly believing in the principle of 'sovereignty within one's own community', Catholic and Protestant publishers supplied their co-religionists with their own children's literature, schoolbooks, magazines, and newspapers. Even in smaller Dutch towns, it was quite normal up to the 1960s to find one bookshop for Catholics and another for Protestants. On a lesser scale, socialists and communists practised similar forms of media control.

In the prewar years, the demand for books and other reading matter grew enormously, however. Whereas in the 19th century readers often had been dependent on subscription libraries and on reading rooms to quench their thirst for reading, the improved economic situation of a large part of the population now made it possible to buy books as well. Demand was stimulated by idealistic publishers such as the socialist Arbeiderspers and the humanistic Wereldbibli-otheck, which offered good books at a low price. Reading was also actively promoted by initiatives such as the annual Boekenweek (Book Week), first organized in 1932. Each year a renowned author was invited to write a short novel which was given away free in bookshops when customers spent a certain amount of money on other items during the Boekenweek.

In Flanders, the situation was rather different. The catastrophe of World War I—as far as books are concerned, best symbolized by the burning of Louvain University Library by the Germans—was followed by a period of new nationalist confidence and optimism, during which several important publishing houses were founded, such as De Sikkel (1919), Standaard Uitgeverij (1924), and Manteau (1932). It seemed that Flemish publishers were finally able to free themselves from the Dutch stranglehold. A further indication of the increased self-awareness was the creation in 1929 of the branch organization Vereniging ter Bevordering van het Vlaamse Boekwezen, the counterpart of the Dutch Vereeniging ter Bevordering van de Belangen des Boekhandels, in order to represent better the economic interests of Flemish publishers.

World War II did not stop this development. During the Nazi occupation, Flemish publishers enjoyed remarkably more freedom than their colleagues in the north. This was due in part to differences in their administrative situations. Whereas The Netherlands had a civic government under complete German control, Belgium was governed by a somewhat more tolerant German military administration. But it also had to do with the affinity felt in certain circles of the Flemish Movement for National Socialism. Either way, while in Belgium book production remained relatively unhindered and stable, in The Netherlands there was harsh censorship and, partly also because of a serious paper shortage, a sharp drop in production. In 1944 only 965 titles were published, against 3,370 in the first year of the war. At the same time, restrictions on Dutch publishing resulted in a flurry of illegal printing activities. All kinds of illicit newspapers, books, and pamphlets were printed, mostly in limited press runs. One of the best-organized illegal publishers was De Bezige Bij in Amsterdam. The revenues of its publications, such as the famous poem *De achttien doden* ('The Eighteen Dead') by Jan Campert and the news-sheet *Vrij Nederland*, were used to support people in hiding and to finance the Resistance movement.

Although the end of the war did not bring about the radical change to the old political system desired by many, in both countries a process of reorientation and modernization in many spheres of society soon got under way. The book trade was no exception to this development, although it must be said that changes in Belgium, where the situation remained complicated by the country's linguistic divisions, were slower and less comprehensive than in The Netherlands. Within a few decades, publishing changed from a supply-oriented to a demand-driven industry, resulting in an ever-growing number of books and other publications. By 1980, some 15,000 titles were published annually in The Netherlands alone, a number that by the end of the century would rise to approximately 18,000. The majority of this output consisted of 'general books', including popular fiction and non-specialist works.

In this far more competitive market there was a constant drive for cost reductions, both in production and in management. The introduction of new typesetting (photo, computerized), printing (offset), and binding (paperback) techniques made it possible to handle larger print runs at a lower cost, thereby fulfilling the growing demand of the reading public as well as stimulating it. This development can best be illustrated by the unparalleled success of the paperback. The first paperback pocket-book in The Netherlands appeared in 1951 as part of the Prisma series of classic literary works from the Utrecht publishing firm Het Spectrum. Print runs of individual volumes soon reached 250,000 or more. The formula was immediately copied, so that by the 1960s most publishers had their own paperback series in a wide range of genres, including literature, popular science, leisure, dictionaries, and children's books.

Rising costs and the increased scale of production necessitated organizational reforms. Mergers and takeovers succeeded each other rapidly, both nationally and internationally. In the 1970s and 1980s in particular, firms like Elsevier and Kluwer expanded at breakneck speed, both eventually becoming world leaders in their fields. In the course of these events, quite a few Belgian publishers who did not have the necessary financial resources were swallowed by more affluent Dutch publishers, thus counteracting the trend set in Flanders during the interwar period. The few houses that survived as independent enterprises by and large were modest-scale publishers of educational and academic books, such as Brepols in Turnhout and Peeters in Louvain.

Similar processes of rationalization, concentration, and commercialization can be observed in book distribution. The Dutch Bestelhuis was transformed by a collective effort of the various branch organizations in 1973 into the Centraal Boekhuis, which took care of the storage, distribution, and transport of the constantly growing volume of books. Independent bookshops joined trade syndicates to strengthen their position in relation to publishers. The downside was that bookshops became much more uniform. The first Dutch book club had been founded in 1937, but the great success of this means of distribution came in the 1960s and 1970s, when two more book clubs were created. Together they achieved a temporary market share of no less than 20 per cent. A characteristic feature of the Dutch book trade was the fixing of book prices, a collective agreement among publishers and retailers enforcing uniform pricing, with the intention of guaranteeing a varied supply of books. One undesired effect, however, was overproduction. At the same time, new collective initiatives were adopted by the various branch organizations of the book trade. Book promotion was now organized centrally by the Commissie Collectieve Propaganda van het Nederlandse Boek (CPNB), which has both a commercial and cultural purpose and is responsible for the Boekenweek. In 1960 the Stichting Speurwerk betreffende het Boek was founded, which gathers much-needed statistical information.

In libraries in Belgium and The Netherlands, the postwar trend has been towards professionalization, increases in scale, and automation through the integration of new information technologies. More than its counterpart in Brussels, the Koninklijke Bibliotheek (KB) in The Hague has deliberately taken on the role of national library: it has set up new projects in centralized cataloguing (Nederlandse Centrale Catalogus; Short-Title Catalogue, Netherlands); acted as a voluntary deposit library for Dutch publishers; and promoted preservation and digitization. In 1998 the KB initiated the Bibliopolis-project, an electronic history of the book which integrates existing and new information systems in the field of Dutch book history. In university libraries, electronic access for all members of the academic community has become a key notion, while there is a growing awareness of the importance of special collections in teaching and research. Public libraries, which experienced an enormous expansion of readers in the 1950s and 1960s, have been liberated from concentrating on specific groups of users, and in both countries now cater to about a quarter of the population, offering a varied supply of materials and services.

BIBLIOGRAPHY

H. Furstner, *Geschichte des niederländischen Buchhandels* (1985)

J. P. Gumbert, *The Dutch and Their Books in the Manuscript Age* (1990)

H. Hasquin, ed., *La Belgique autrichienne, 1713-1794* (1987)

W. Gs. Hellinga, *Copy and Print in the Netherlands* (1962)

L. Hellinga-Querido *et al.*, eds., *The Bookshop of the World: The Role of the Low Countries in the Book-Trade 1473-1941* (2001)

P. G. Hoftijzer and O. S. Lankhorst, *Drukkers, Boekverkopers en Lezers in Nederland tijdens de Republiek* (2000)

P. Janssens, *België in de 17de Eeuw*, vol. 2: *De Cultuur* (2006)

E. Luzac, *Hollands rijkdom* (4 vols, 1780-3)

J. H. Marrow *et al.*, *The Golden Age of Dutch Manuscript Painting* (1989)

P. F. J. Obbema *et al.*, *Boeken in Nederland* (1979)

J. Ray, *Observations Topographical, Moral, & Physiological Made in a Journey Through Part of the Low-Countries* (1673)

P. Schneiders, *Nederlandse Bibliotheekgeschiedenis* (1997)

L. Simons, *Geschiedenis van de Uitgeverij in Vlaanderen* (2 vols, 1984-7)

M. Smeyers, *Flemish Miniatures from the 8th to the mid-16th Century* (1999)

M. van Delft and C. de Wolf, eds., *Bibliopolis: History of the Printed Book in the Netherlands* (2003), www.bibliopolis.nl, consulted Feb. 2008

L. Voet, *The Golden Compasses: A History and Evaluation of the Printing and Publishing Activities of the Officina Plantiniana* (2 vols, 1969-72)

26

The History of the Book in Germany

JOHN L. FLOOD

1 Introduction

Historically, 'Germany' is difficult to define in geographical and political terms. The Roman province of Germania covered only the southern part of what we now call Germany; the area north and east of the Danube, Main, and Rhine was never part of the Roman empire. Whereas around 1200 Germany was thought of as extending 'from the Rhine to Hungary'—and Hoffmann von Fallersleben in the 1840s saw it as stretching 'from the Maas to the Memel, from the Etsch to the Bælt'—modern Germany's borders are more narrowly drawn: the Etsch, the river Adige, is now in Italy, and Germany's eastern frontier is at the Oder. In political terms, German history is essentially the painful story of various German states, sometimes pulling together, sometimes pulling apart, united only by the German language. After 843, the Frankish empire (which under Charlemagne had comprised what is now France, much of Germany, Switzerland, and part of Italy) was divided into three, in essence creating France, Germany, and the buffer state of Lotharingia in between—sowing the seed of future conflicts. Even this 'Germany' was not a unity: the 'Holy Roman Empire of the German Nation' remained a loose conglomeration of territories and municipalities under the notional direction of the Holy Roman Emperor until its dissolution in 1806. Austria then became a nation in its own right (*see* **32**). Whereas countries like Britain and France have for centuries had national capitals exerting a powerful cultural influence, it was not until 1871 that Berlin became the capital of the newly established German Reich. The 20th century saw this unity torn asunder and, in 1990, reassembled.

Yet even today, Germany, though it again has a national capital, is a federation of territories, at least some of which (Bavaria and the Hanseatic City of Hamburg, for instance) are exceedingly proud of their own history and distinctive cultural traditions. The regional diversity of Germany helps to explain the relative decentralization of the German book trade and the lack of a single national library. Against such a background the German language—spoken also in Austria, parts of Switzerland, and in some areas of Belgium, and, in earlier times, also used where French (e.g. Alsace) and Slavonic languages now hold sway—has (despite marked regional differences) been a major factor for cultural unification. German book history likewise transcends national boundaries; hence, this survey will address the German-speaking area of past and present Europe as a whole.

2 The Middle Ages

The history of the book in Germany must begin with the early monastic scriptoria. Two of the most important were those at Fulda, where the monastery was founded in 744 by the English missionary Wynfreth (St Boniface), 'Apostle of the Germans', and St Gall in Switzerland. It is at St Gall (founded 613) that the oldest German book is preserved, the so-called *Abrogans* (Codex 911), a small late 8th-century glossary giving the German equivalents of words from the Old Testament; *Abrogans* ('humble') is the first word in the list. This modest book encapsulates something of the monastic endeavours of the Carolingian period to express Christian terms and other concepts from the world of late antiquity in the vernacular. Indeed, the struggle between Latin and the vernacular would play a major part in the history of the book in Germany. Other early monastic scriptoria, mostly dating from the 8th century, include Freising, Reichenau, Murbach, Corvey, Regensburg, Salzburg, and Tegernsee. As elsewhere in Europe, they chiefly produced works of theological interest—but also literary, scientific, and medical MSS—either for their own use or for exchange. By 1200, there were about 700 monastic houses in German-speaking areas, but by then towns were becoming more important, and the emerging secular culture led to the spread of knowledge beyond the cloister's confines. Monastic scriptoria could no longer satisfy the demand for books, so increasingly they were produced by lay scribes, and MSS began to be disseminated through the developing trade in commercial centres and university towns. MS production peaked in the 15th century, when we also find secular scriptoria such as Diebold Lauber's at Hagenau (near Strasburg), which produced illustrated MSS of German literary texts on a commercial basis. Bookbinding now became a lay occupation, too. The turn of the 14th century saw the earliest German paper mills, the first built near Nuremberg in 1389 by the merchant Ulman Stromer, who had learnt the technique in Lombardy (*see* **10**).

3 The 15th century

Roman Germania created a number of major towns in southern and western Germany—Cologne, Mainz, Trier, Strasburg, Augsburg, Regensburg, and

Vienna—that would for centuries play important roles as administrative, ecclesiastical, cultural, and commercial centres. Several of them were significant in the rise of the printed book in the 15ᵗʰ century. Johann Gutenberg from Mainz, the inventor of printing with movable type, spent several years experimenting at Strasburg in the 1430s and 1440s. His achievement was to have combined many pre-existing elements—printing, punchcutting, the press, paper—into a single effective technical process (*see* **6, 11**). He invested a considerable sum of borrowed money in developing the technique at Mainz in the early 1450s, and though in effect he bankrupted himself, he completed the printing of the two-volume Latin Bible now known as the Gutenberg Bible or the 42-line Bible (from the number of lines of text on the page) by August 1456 at the latest.

Printing soon spread to other towns, in Germany and beyond. From Mainz it was introduced to Bamberg, an important bishopric, *c.*1459; here Heinrich Keffer completed the 36-line Bible by 1461. Initially, the principal centres were generally commercial cities where capital, suitable texts, and readers could be found. At Strasburg, where Gutenberg's invention was introduced in 1459–60, early printers included Heinrich Eggestein, Johann Mentelin, Johann Prüss, and Johann Grüninger. Cologne (where printing was introduced in *c.*1465), a city of 35,000 inhabitants, was the largest German printing centre in the 15ᵗʰ century, especially for theological books. Here the most productive printer was Heinrich Quentell; the leading publisher was Franz Birckmann, whose business extended into The Netherlands and Burgundy, and who also had a shop at St Paul's in London. At Augsburg, the first printer was Günther Zainer in 1468. The foundation of the University of Basle in 1460 led to this city's early importance as a printing centre from 1468–70, associated with famous humanist printer-publishers like Johann Amerbach, Johann and Adam Petri, Johann Froben, Andreas Cratander, and Johann Oporinus. At Nuremberg (1470), the leading publisher was Anton Koberger, who had 24 presses working for him.

The all-pervasiveness of the Church and of Latin meant that the book trade throughout Europe was international in scope, relatively little being published in the vernacular. Latin would predominate in the German book market for at least two centuries. Until the Reformation at least, printing did not much favour contemporary writers, publishers preferring the well-tried texts of the past. Among the few contemporary authors whose works were regularly printed in the first decades of printing were Sebastian Brant, whose *Narrenschiff* (Ship of Fools, 1494) became an international success once it had been mediated through Latin into French and English; and the Ulm physician Heinrich Steinhöwel, whose many translations from Latin were printed by Johann Zainer, the first printer at Ulm from 1472 onwards.

The introduction of printing did not mean a sudden break with the MS tradition. As elsewhere in Europe, the handwritten book and the printed book coexisted for some time (*see* **15**). A phenomenon particularly characteristic of The Netherlands and Germany in the mid-15ᵗʰ century was the production of

Blockbooks, mostly short devotional texts (*Biblia Pauperum, Apocalypse, Ars Moriendi*), with text and illustrations carved into blocks of wood, inked, and transferred to paper by rubbing; the method was still being used for ABCs and similar works in the 1520s. Though the earliest typographic books were modelled on MSS, in time their appearance changed. The folio format inherited from MS culture increasingly gave way to the handier quarto and octavo. The title-page came into regular use and subsumed the function of the colophon. The abbreviations and ligatures familiar from the MS age largely disappeared from printing founts. In scholarly books, footnotes replaced marginal notes. And although outside Germany roman typefaces predominated, books in German were generally printed in gothic and books in Latin in roman.

Of the *c.*27,000 different books printed in the 15th century, about 11,000 were produced in Germany, with only about 4 per cent in German. Yet works in German figured among the earliest books printed: one of Gutenberg's first trial pieces was a German poem on the Day of Judgment, and in 1461 Albrecht Pfister printed Johannes von Tepl's *Ackermann von Böhmen* and Ulrich Boner's *Edelstein* at Bamberg (these two were the first typographic books to contain illustrations, with 5 and 203 woodcuts respectively). It was Augsburg, however, that was particularly noted for books in the vernacular: G. Zainer, Johannes Bämler, Anton Sorg, and Schönsperger played leading roles, each often bringing out works that one of the others had already published. Though perhaps initially not a place that one associates particularly strongly with vernacular books, several notable German works appeared in Strasburg as early as 1466–80, including Johann Mentelin's 1466 Bible (the first printed bible in any vernacular) and his 1477 editions of the Arthurian romances *Parzival* and *Titurel*. Strasburg's output in this field certainly expanded around 1500 and especially in the early 16th century, when printers like Johann Grüninger, Hans Knobloch, and Bartholomaeus Kistler established reputations for illustrated works. Books in German were also printed at Basle, Nuremberg, Heidelberg, Ulm, and smaller towns like Urach, Esslingen, and Reutlingen; further north, printers at Leipzig, Cologne, Lübeck, Magdeburg, and Stendal issued books in Low German, which was then still the mother tongue of virtually everyone in that area.

Among the chief glories of early German printing were the illustrated books, particularly from Augsburg, Strasburg, Nuremberg, and Ulm. They included devotional works (Cologne Bibles, *c.*1478; Zainer's 1472 edition of the *Golden Legend* with 120 woodcuts, the first illustrated book from Augsburg), classics (the illustrations in Grüninger's 1496 Terence are constructed from 85 interchangeable woodcut components), practical handbooks (Bämler's 1475 Augsburg edition of Konrad von Megenberg's *Buch der Natur*, containing the earliest known printed botanical illustrations), chronicles (including Ulrich von Reichenthal's *History of the Council of Constance*, Augsburg, 1483; the *Chronicle of the Saxons*, Mainz, 1492; and Koberger's Latin and German editions of Schedel's Nuremberg Chronicle, Nuremberg, 1493, with 1,809 woodcuts), travel accounts (Bernhard von Breydenbach's *Peregrinatio in Terram Sanctam*,

Part of the Psalms in German from the first vernacular translation of the Bible, printed at Strassburg by Mentelin not after 1466 (*GW* 4295). The Bodleian Library, University of Oxford (Auct. Y 4.2)

Mainz, 1486), herbals, didactic works (Brant's *Narrenschiff*, Basle, 1494), heroic poems (*Heldenbuch*, Strasburg *c.*1479), chivalric romances (*Tristrant*, Augsburg 1484; *Wigoleis vom Rade*, Augsburg 1493), and other popular narratives. More incunabula illustrated with woodcuts were produced in Germany than anywhere else, and this tradition continued into the 16th century, which saw the woodcut develop into a major art form in the hands of artists like Albrecht Dürer, Lucas Cranach, Hans Holbein, and Hans Burgkmair.

By the early 16th century, the market was already oversupplied with books. In 1504, Koberger in Nuremberg lamented that trade was not what it had been, even the Latin Bible Amerbach had printed for him at Basle between 1498 and 1502 (*GW* 4285) proving unsaleable. As books became more plentiful, humanist scholars began to form significant private libraries. Examples include those of Amplonius Ratinck at Erfurt, Hermann and Hartmann Schedel and Bilibald Pirckheimer at Nuremberg, Sigismund Gossembrot and Konrad Peutinger at Augsburg. The library of Beatus Rhenanus survives, still intact, at Sélestat in Alsace.

4 The 16th century

Gutenberg's 42-line Bible was the first of 94 Latin bibles printed in Europe in the 15th century. Of these, no fewer than 57 appeared in German-speaking towns. Germany led the way in printed vernacular bibles too, long before the Protestant Reformers, in asserting the priesthood of all believers, contended that all Christians had the right and duty to explore scriptural truth for themselves. Starting with Mentelin's edition of 1466, ten German bibles were already on the market by 1485 when the archbishop of Mainz attempted to ban their printing. By the time Martin Luther published his New Testament translation—based on Desiderius Erasmus's Greek text instead of the Latin Vulgate—at Wittenberg in September 1522, fourteen editions of the complete Bible had appeared in High German (at Strasburg, Augsburg, and Nuremberg) and four in Low German (at Cologne, Lübeck, and Halberstadt). The first edition of Luther's New Testament quickly sold out, and a revised edition (with Cranach's woodcuts altered for reasons of censorship) appeared in December 1522; there were many reprints, authorized and unauthorized. Its popularity was such that already in 1527 Hieronymus Emser published at Dresden a rival, 'Catholicized' version of Luther's translation, even though he believed that reading the Bible should be restricted to scholars. Luther's complete Bible translation (based on Hebrew and Greek sources), first published in 1534, has influenced the German literary language just as much as the Authorized Version has influenced English. By the time of Luther's death, at least 355 editions of his translation, or parts of it (Pentateuch, Prophets, Psalms, New Testament, Apocrypha, etc.), had been published (chiefly at Wittenberg, Augsburg, Strasburg, Nuremberg, Basle, Erfurt, and Leipzig), with at least 90 more in the Low German version (mainly from Magdeburg, Wittenberg, Erfurt, Lübeck, and Rostock).

The press was undeniably a significant factor in the success of the Reformation, but printing, especially in the vernacular, would not have developed as rapidly without its stimulus. In 1525, 60 per cent of everything printed in Germany was in German, but this was a passing phase: for the rest of the century, printing in German was about 40 per cent. Luther himself saw printing as 'the greatest and latest gift of God, for by this means God seeks to extend the cause of true religion to the ends of the earth and to make it available in all languages'. Already by 1500, printing had been attempted in some 60 German-speaking towns and was well established in most of them; but with the torrent of pamphlets issued after 1517 the industry soon spread to a multitude of small, relatively unimportant towns—some 160 in all by 1600, and 330 by 1700. The main centres of Protestant publishing included Wittenberg, Nuremberg, Frankfurt, and Strasburg, while Catholic books were chiefly produced in Cologne, Ingolstadt, Munich, and Dillingen. By 1530, some 10,000 pamphlets had appeared, totalling nearly 10 million copies, and many more were issued throughout the century. Broadly speaking, these aimed to influence public opinion both on burning social and political issues (such as the Peasants' War and the threat of Turkish expansion) and especially on matters concerning religion and the Church (for instance, Henry VIII's quarrel with Luther). Some 70 per cent of titles published between 1520 and 1526 debate the fundamental importance of the Scriptures for the laity. By 1520, 32 tracts by Luther had been published in more than 500 editions, and within a few years a quarter of all German publications appeared under his name. Before he died, more than 3 million copies of his writings, excluding his Bible translations, had been printed.

The Reformation, and all it entailed, inevitably encouraged reading and stimulated book production generally: a wider range of books was being published, not least in the fields of literature, medicine, and technology. It is, however, difficult to quantify this precisely. Given the lack of exact information about the number of printing offices, the titles they published, and indeed the vague definition of 'book' (whether, for instance, proclamations, pamphlets, and calendars are included), estimates are largely speculative. It has been claimed that in the 16th century 150,000 items were published in Germany, while estimates for the 17th century range between 85,000 and 150,000, and for the 18th century between 175,000 and 500,000.

With the growth of the book trade, patterns of business had to change. Whereas MSS were mainly produced on commission, printing was generally a speculative business, stocks being produced in the hope of finding customers for them. Distribution thus acquired a new importance. Until the 18th century, book fairs, principally at Frankfurt and Leipzig, played a major role. Frankfurt, in the centre of Germany and readily accessible by river, was important for the distribution of scholarly books in Latin throughout Europe; books were certainly being traded there in the 1480s, decades before its first press was established. Leipzig, too, lay on major north–south, east–west trade routes. These fairs, held twice a year, around Shrovetide or Easter and at Michaelmas, provided the best opportunity for publishers to sell books in quantity to other book dealers. The book trade expanded so greatly that a guide to what was on offer became a desideratum. The initiative was seized by the Augsburg bookseller Georg Willer, who in the autumn of 1564 issued his first Frankfurt catalogue, *Novorum Librorum, quos Nundinae Autumnales Francofurti Anno* 1564 *Celebratae Venales Exhiberunt, Catalogus*; thereafter it appeared twice yearly. Books were listed first by language (Latin and Greek, then German) and within each group by subject: theology, law, medicine, the liberal arts. So successful were Willer's catalogues that he soon had rivals. In 1598, the Frankfurt Council decided to ban the publication of private fair catalogues and to issue its own—a sensible precaution, given surveillance by the Catholic-orientated Imperial Book Commission (established in 1569 to prevent the circulation of seditious and defamatory material). Issuing an official catalogue not only enabled the council to demonstrate to the emperor that it was being vigilant, but helped it exercise stricter control of the trade by keeping a watch on the observance of printers' privileges and ensuring that copies of books were deposited as required. The official catalogue (Mess Catalog) appeared—latterly somewhat fitfully—until about 1750. A catalogue was issued at Leipzig, too, but there it remained in private hands, being first published by Henning Grosse in 1594 and then by his successors until 1759. Because the Leipzig fairs followed those held at Frankfurt, the Leipzig catalogues generally listed the same books as the Frankfurt ones, though they often included a (sometimes substantial) section of 'books not shown at Frankfurt'. As the first regularly appearing bulletins of recent publications, these catalogues long remained essential reading for scholars. The curators of the Bodleian Library at Oxford consulted them to select books, though from 1617 they used the London bookseller John Bill's own English version of the Frankfurt catalogue. In 1685, Jean-Paul de La Roque, editor of the *Journal des savants* in Paris, remarked that until then German books had been known in France only through the Frankfurt fair catalogues. The catalogues represent a useful, if far from comprehensive, indicator of the book trade in the early modern period. Their purpose was to advertise and to generate interest, not to serve as comprehensive bibliographical aids: it is reckoned that they include only about 20–25 per cent of the books actually available. Their focus is primarily on books of scholarly interest, especially in Latin, with a potential for wide geographical dissemination, while small works, books of sermons, prayer books, university theses, and calendars scarcely feature. Fuller coverage was attempted by early efforts at cumulative bibliography such as Conrad Gessner's *Bibliotheca Universalis* (Zurich, 1545), Johannes Cless's *Unius Seculi Elenchus Librorum* (Frankfurt, 1602), and Georg Draud's *Bibliotheca Classica* (Frankfurt, 1611) and *Bibliotheca Exotica* (Frankfurt, 1625).

5 The 17th century

The Thirty Years War (1618–48) had a devastating effect on Germany: one third of the population is believed to have perished. The economic downturn affected the quality of books, inferior paper and narrow types being used to reduce costs. (The Endters of Nuremberg were one of the few firms still producing fine books.) During the 1630s, the number of titles listed in the fair catalogues was little more than a third of what it had been in 1619, and even after the cessation of hostilities, slow economic recovery—exacerbated by plague, food shortages, and a prolonged cold spell (the 'little Ice Age')—meant that it was decades before the prewar level was reached again.

Although Vienna and Munich publishers effectively had a monopoly in the Catholic domains of the Habsburgs and the Wittelsbachs, the centre of gravity of the book trade shifted from the south to the centre and north. Even though the Lutheran Reformation had spent its force by the mid-16th century, the Protestant book trade maintained its ascendancy over German intellectual life. The Frankfurt fair, however, lost its dominant role. Many dealers, especially foreigners, failed to resume their activities there after 1648, the restrictions imposed by the Jesuit-dominated Imperial Book Commission proving serious disincentives. The attempts of the Commission and the *Index Librorum Prohibitorum* to control books were largely ineffective, however, in part because their workings were arbitrary. Titles sometimes appeared on the *Index* simply because their authors were non-Catholics. Books in the vernacular were particularly targeted because they were intended for a wider public. One might have expected the Catholic authorities to permit Protestant books dealing with internal theological quarrels as revealing the inadequacies of their cause, but these too appeared on the *Index*. Often it sufficed for a book to have been printed in a Protestant town for it to be listed.

Between 1680 and 1690, publishing at Frankfurt collapsed, and Leipzig moved quickly into the forefront of the German book world. This city was favoured by its accessible position in central Europe and the privileges that the Saxon government bestowed on the trade fairs (and the liberality with which the city council interpreted them), as well as by the importance of its university. The business acumen of members of the book trade there was also a major factor in its success. It was a member of the Leipzig trade, Philipp Erasmus Reich, a partner of the firm of Weidmann (founded 1680, later Weidmann und Reich), who would eventually put an end to the Frankfurt fair by closing his Frankfurt warehouse in 1764 and encouraging others to do likewise.

As yet there was no attempt to enlarge the reading public by drawing in the bourgeoisie or the lower classes. Commonly, households might possess a bible, Luther's catechism, an almanac, perhaps a herbal or other household medical book, a guide to letter writing, and a popular religious book, but hardly ever any imaginative literature. A great deal of popular religious writing, described on title-pages as 'useful' or 'edifying', was published. In the early 18th century, one of the most widely read books was still *Vom wahren Christenthum* by the Pietist Johann Arndt, first published in 1605. Yet, such reading ensured that literacy was reasonably widespread, especially in Protestant areas.

Among the characteristic forms of publication in the 17th century were popular, illustrated political broadsides. Thousands still survive, not only dealing with the war (the demise of Tilly, for instance, or Gustavus Adolphus of Sweden as the saviour of Lutheranism) but treating such topics as the Dutch struggle for independence from Spain, the Gunpowder Plot, and hatred for the Jesuits. Another ubiquitous form of ephemeral publication was booklets of occasional verse, often in Latin, marking birthdays, name-days, marriages, promotions, retirements, deaths, and other significant events—well over 160,000 funeral booklets alone survive. The year 1609 saw the appearance of the first two regularly numbered and dated German newsbooks, the forerunners of modern newspapers: the Wolfenbüttel *Aviso, Relation oder Zeitung*, and the Strasburg *Relation aller Fürnemen und gedenkwürdigen Historien*. The first German daily newspaper was the *Neueinlaufende Nachricht von Kriegs- und Welthändeln*, published by Timotheus Ritzsch at Leipzig on 1 January 1660; this became the *Leipziger Zeitung* in 1734 and ceased publication only in 1921.

The artistic talents that helped adorn early printed books became rarer after the mid-16th century, and woodcuts more workaday and less imaginative. The 17th century saw increasing use of engraving. Among the best-known examples are Johann Philipp Abelin's *Theatrum Europaeum* (21 vols, 1635–1738) and various topographical works of Matthäus Merian (1593–1650) from Basle, who took over the Frankfurt business of his father-in-law, Johann Theodor de Bry, in 1624.

6 The 18th century

In the 17th and early 18th centuries, the book market was still dominated by the old-fashioned polyhistor penning enormous tomes (often still in Latin) for a restricted scholarly public. Theology was particularly strongly represented. In 1650, 71 per cent of the books in the Leipzig catalogues were in Latin; in 1701, 55 per cent; but in 1740, only 27 per cent; in 1770, 14 per cent; and only 4 per cent in 1800. The proportion of books produced in Latin was higher in university towns such as Jena and Tübingen than in commercial centres like Augsburg and Hamburg. The catalogues also show (notwithstanding their limitations) that the proportions of books in the categories of 'religious literature for the layman' (devotional works, sermons) and 'imaginative literature' (including novels, drama, and poetry) were inverted between 1740 and 1800—the former representing nearly 20 per cent and the latter barely 6 per cent of the total books on offer at the earlier date, and under 6 per cent and more than 21 per cent respectively at the end of the period. In general, the book trade expanded fourfold during the 18th century. The mid-century saw the emergence of the popularizing writer who made knowledge available in German for a wider readership. The numbers of books in the fields of philosophy, philology, pedagogy, natural sciences, and economics increased to some 40 per cent, while belles-lettres grew almost tenfold, from 2.8 per cent in 1700 to 21.5 per cent in 1800. At this date, theology represented only about 13 per cent of the total.

By about 1740, the position of writers was changing and the potential public for imaginative literature was expanding. In the 17th century, there had not yet emerged a profession of letters as such. Writers had depended on their main occupations or professions for any social respect they enjoyed; anyone hoping to live by his pen was invariably doomed to contempt and poverty. Writers had been primarily scholars: professors, schoolmasters, or clergymen. Aristocrats would have considered it unseemly to be seen as dependent on their pens, and bourgeois writers would emphasize that their writing was merely the product of their leisure hours. In the 18th century, the role of aristocratic literary patrons declined, and that of the commercial publisher grew.

An important development in the 18th century was the emergence of the novel. Earlier, novels had been of a learned character, intended not for popular consumption but rather for aristocratic or scholarly readers well acquainted with the events and personalities of ancient and contemporary history, classical mythology, and the works of ancient philosophers and poets. A good example is *Die Römische Octavia* by Anton Ulrich, duke of Braunschweig-Wolfenbüttel (1633–1714). Such novels primarily reflected the absolutist court ideal, and served as vehicles for moral or political ideas of the kind young noblemen were expected to imbibe. In the 18th century, however, a market developed for travel novels, love stories, ghost stories, novels about knights and robbers, and more besides. The epistolary novel became fashionable, Goethe's *Werther* (1774) becoming the best-seller of the century, with authorized editions far outnumbered by piracies and translations. Translated works were also attractive to publishers, who did not need to pay authors an honorarium, only a translator's fee. Foreign authors popular in Germany included Richardson, Sterne, and (earlier) Defoe. Three translations of *Robinson Crusoe* (1719) appeared within a year: one translation saw five editions in 1720 alone. *Crusoe* precipitated a flood of German imitations, the best of which was Johann Gottfried Schnabel's four-volume *Insel Felsenburg* (1731–43), in which four shipwrecked travellers seek to live in harmony in an ideal social community that contrasts sharply with contemporary German society. This novel, frequently reissued and reprinted in pirated editions, came to be found next to the Bible in all pious middle-class homes. Another, later excrescence of the craze for 'Robinsonades' was *Der schweizerische Robinson* (1812)—written by Johann David Wyss of Berne—known to generations of English readers as *The Swiss Family Robinson*.

Numerous distinguished publishing houses emerged in the 18th century. At Stuttgart, Johann Friedrich Cotta is famous for his 60-volume Goethe edition. At Leipzig, Johann Gottlob Immanuel Breitkopf (1719–94) became renowned for innovations in printing complicated music from movable type; the firm's successor, Breitkopf & Härtel, established in 1796, remains one of the leading names in music publishing. Another Leipzig firm was Georg Joachim Göschen (1752–1828), whose most prominent authors were Schiller, Goethe, and

Wieland. His Wieland edition, printed in roman instead of 'monkish' Fraktur, failed to be the pioneering success it might have been because other printing houses considered it too expensive to re-equip themselves with roman types, and the public was too inured to reading German in Fraktur to want to change. Johann Friedrich Unger at Berlin, who published Goethe, Schiller, and also the early Romantics—including August Wilhelm Schlegel's translations of Shakespeare—was likewise interested in typography. He helped promote Firmin Didot's roman letter in Germany but, faced with continuing opposition to roman, he devised a lighter gothic type, the 'Unger-Fraktur', intended to assist foreign readers unfamiliar with the traditional Fraktur then still generally in use; Unger's type extended the life of Fraktur in Germany.

The growth of the reading public in the 18th century led to reorganization of the book trade. Whereas previously the publisher-bookseller had dominated, with trade being conducted on an exchange basis largely through the book fairs, from the mid-18th century publishing and bookselling evolved into separate activities. The advantage of the exchange system, with printer-publishers and booksellers trading books primarily according to the quantity of paper involved, had been that it obviated the need to hold considerable capital in the form of cash; moreover, it facilitated trade between the various territories in the empire (with their different currencies) as well as the international trade in Latin books. The disadvantages were that many booksellers found themselves sitting on a wide-ranging, unspecialized collection of sometimes quite unsaleable books, without adequate liquid capital to finance new ventures or pay authors who increasingly wanted to be paid in money, not in books.

The lack of an effective central government in Germany meant that publishing was still carried on under exclusive regulations in each individual state. This perhaps worked well enough while the book market was relatively small, but became problematic as it expanded. The most urgent needs were for a general system of copyright and for measures to prevent the production of cheap, shoddily printed unauthorized editions in other territories. Such piracy was not only widely tolerated but, in some states, even encouraged. The demise of the Frankfurt fair and the inconvenience of the long journey to Leipzig meant that piracy particularly flourished in many south German towns, printers there seeing this as a legitimate response to the monopolies and higher prices of Leipzig publishers. The pirate publishers—who paid no authors' fees, printed only successful works, and often used the cheapest paper—contributed in no small measure to making books cheaper and thereby encouraging reading. One of the worst offenders was Johann Thomas von Trattner in Vienna, who was abetted even by the imperial court; he employed fifteen presses in a large-scale operation to produce cheap reprints. His leading opponent was Philipp Erasmus Reich in Leipzig, who in 1764 attempted to form a protective organization and found support in most of the large towns in northern Germany, as well as in Nuremberg and Ulm. Leipzig publishers abandoned the old exchange system and began to insist that booksellers pay in cash and maintain no right to return unsold books. While this had some positive effects—publishers flush with cash were now able to contemplate new projects and authors could expect larger fees—it also meant that readers faced higher prices for books. In 1773 the sale of unauthorized editions at Leipzig was prohibited, but the pirates resorted to selling their wares through travelling salesmen who visited localities where books had previously been a rarity. In the absence of central government, there was little authors or publishers could do to remedy the situation. Even after the end of the Holy Roman Empire in 1806, little changed: in 1815 the kingdoms of Württemberg and Bavaria both expressly permitted the reprinting of 'foreign' books, that is, those published beyond their own narrow confines. It was not until well into the 19th century that general protection could be guaranteed. The first work granted full copyright protection, recognized throughout Germany, was Cotta's Goethe edition (1827–30).

One manifestation of the 18th-century Enlightenment was a tremendous growth in the publishing of encyclopaedias and reference works and an explosion in the publication of journals and almanacs. The first major German encyclopaedia was Johann Heinrich Zedler's 68-volume *Grosses vollständiges Universal-Lexicon aller Wissenschaften und Künste* (Halle and Leipzig, 1732–54). It was innovative in two respects: it was the first such work written by a team of editors, each responsible for a particular field of knowledge, and it included biographies of living persons. The first German periodical, the *Acta Eruditorum*, launched at Leipzig in 1682, was a scholarly journal in the mould of the *Philosophical Transactions* of the Royal Society of London; but Christian Thomasius's *Monatsgespräche*, published from 1688, marked the beginning of a new age with articles on a wide range of topics and reviews of new publications, presented to a broader public in German. By the mid-18th century, hundreds of similar weeklies and monthlies were appearing, mostly in university towns like Halle, Leipzig, and Jena, but also in Frankfurt, Berlin, and Hamburg, addressing themselves not to a scholarly public but to the bourgeoisie, and aiming to instruct in a pleasant and entertaining way. The earlier part of the century also saw the launch of imitations of English moral weeklies: *Der Vernünfftler* (1713), *Der Patriot* (1724), and others were modelled on Addison and Steele's *Tatler* (founded 1709) and *Spectator* (1711). Then came more specifically literary journals such as Friedrich Nicolai's *Allgemeine deutsche Bibliothek* (1765–1806) and Christoph Martin Wieland's *Teutscher Merkur* (1773–1810), emulating the *Mercure de France*. Others fostered interest in foreign literature, such as Johann Joachim Eschenburg's *Brittisches Museum für die Deutschen* (1777–80). Noteworthy, too, are some early journals for women readers, including Johann Georg Jacobi's *Iris* (1774–6), Christian Gottfried Schütz's *Akademie der Grazien* (1774–80), and many others, most of them short-lived. By publishing texts and reviews, these journals encouraged a love of literature and sharpened readers' critical faculties.

Altogether 2,191 journals of all kinds began publication between 1766 and 1790—three times as many as in the previous 25 years. The resonance they found may be gauged from the lively debate engendered by Moses Mendelssohn's and Immanuel Kant's discussion of the question 'What is Enlightenment?' in the *Berlinische Monatsschrift* in 1784. Particularly influential was the *Allgemeine Literatur-Zeitung*, published six times a week by Bertuch in Jena, which reviewed the latest German and foreign books. Bertuch also published the *Journal des Luxus und der Mode*—one of the earliest illustrated magazines—which remains a valuable source of information about men's and women's fashions and the domestic scene around 1800. Another of Bertuch's ventures was *London und Paris*, published until 1815, which informed readers about the social scene in the British and French metropolises. While *London und Paris* merely reported on the French political scene following the Revolution, other journals—such as J. F. Unger's *Deutschland*, with its pronounced republican sympathies, and the conservative *Wiener Zeitschrift*—more actively espoused politics of various hues. By contrast, with *Die Horen* Friedrich Schiller strove 'to unite the politically fragmented world under the flag of truth and beauty'. It called forth a wave of new literary journals, which, though generally short-lived, testified to the vitality of the Romantic Age. The most important of these was *Athenaeum* (1798–1800), edited by Friedrich and A. W. Schlegel.

Almanacs, catering for almost every profession, interest, or taste, were a special feature of 18th-century German publishing. Examples include the *Gothaischer Hofkalender* or *Almanach de Gotha*, first published in 1763, and Schiller's *Historisches Kalender für Damen*, published by Göschen (1790–94). They contained contributions by leading writers and poets and were often illustrated by well-known artists such as Daniel Nikolaus Chodowiecki.

Germany had always been well supplied with libraries, but access was generally privileged. Many religious houses held significant collections, often splendidly housed (as at Ottobeuren, Kremsmünster, Melk, Einsiedeln, St Gall, Schussenried, and Admont). The 17th century had been the age of the great private and court libraries, among them those of the Elector Palatine at Heidelberg, Duke August of Braunschweig-Lüneburg (1579–1666) at Wolfenbüttel, the imperial court library at Vienna (founded 1493, now the Austrian National Library), and the Royal Library at Berlin (founded 1661). Several towns had old-established Ratsbibliotheken, municipal libraries intended for the use of city councillors and other worthies. Such collections had existed since the late 14th century in Nuremberg and Regensburg, while Lüneburg, Braunschweig, Hanover, Leipzig, Lübeck, Hamburg, and Frankfurt followed in the 15th, with others founded in the 16th, often as a direct consequence of Luther's encouragement of town councils to enhance library provision. A few libraries actually called themselves 'public', but they were generally poorly stocked and had extremely restricted opening hours—the one in Bremen was accessible only fortnightly on Wednesdays, for example. Even university libraries were hardly user-friendly: those at Leipzig and Halle were open for only four hours a week, and it was considered a real novelty when Göttingen, on its foundation in 1734, opened its library every day to staff and students and allowed them to borrow books—from the outset, this library was conceived as a research facility. As the reading habit grew, so too did demand for access to books. This resulted in the establishment of lending libraries and 'reading societies', which in turn stimulated the demand for more books. A lending library open to all-comers had been founded in Berlin as early as 1704, but only somewhat later did these proliferate: Braunschweig had one in 1767, Hanau 1774, Munich 1774, Schwäbisch Hall 1784, Giessen 1785, Stuttgart 1791, Bamberg 1795, and Breslau 1800, for instance. One enterprising Leipzig book dealer, Sommer, sold bargain-priced 'starter collections' of up to 500 volumes to people wanting to establish libraries. Reading societies (*Lesegesellschaften*) were established in many towns: 13 by 1770, a further 50 by 1780, and about 370 more by 1800. The one at Stralsund, founded in 1779, specialized in lighter fare such as novels, plays, and poems, but others provided more generally for philosophy, theology, history, and geography. These societies aimed to give members—mostly the better-educated middle class—the opportunity to read as inexpensively as possible. Books and journals might be circulated among members or made available in a common reading room. Contemporary observers, critical of a perceived 'mania' for reading, advocated attempts to direct readers towards what was 'useful', with the aim of fostering good Christians, obedient subjects, and committed workers. A notably successful example of such 'improving' reading-matter, aimed at countryfolk, was Rudolf Zacharias Becker's *Noth- und Hülfsbüchlein für Bauersleute* (1788); by 1811 a million copies had been produced, many of which had been foisted by territorial princes on their unsuspecting subjects. Other works were targeted at women, servants, children, and young people.

Great libraries have at all times been threatened with plunder and dispersal. The Palatine library at Heidelberg was removed to the Vatican in 1623; Gustavus Adolphus took many books from Catholic libraries to Sweden at about the same time (*see* **28**). Napoleon is said to have looted 10,000 incunabula from libraries on the west bank of the Rhine; about 100 Jesuit libraries were closed in Germany alone in 1773. From 1783, 1,300 monastic libraries were confiscated, and hundreds more were secularized around 1803. Their MSS and incunabula substantially enriched court and university libraries—thus, what is now the Bavarian State Library (which holds the second largest collection of incunabula in the world) at Munich became the largest German library in the 19th century. About this time, a number of smaller universities were also closed and their collections were amalgamated with other university libraries. Germany, being decentralized, still has no true national library; instead, it relies on a collaborative network of state and university libraries.

7 The 19th century

The 19th century saw decisive developments in book production. New inventions reduced production costs, and increasing literacy created further demands for books. The writing profession expanded considerably. As early as 1777, Georg

Christoph Lichtenberg asserted, 'There are assuredly more writers in Germany than all four continents need for their wellbeing', and in 1785 it was claimed that 'the army of German writers' was 5,500 strong. By 1800, no fewer than 10,648 Germans were calling themselves writers, a figure that, by 1900, rose to 20,000 and included hundreds of women writers, 70 per cent of whom wrote under male pseudonyms. The number of bookshops grew from 300 to 5,000 during the century, and the annual output of titles increased from 3,906 in 1800 to 14,039 in 1843, and 24,792 in 1900. The number of periodicals and newspapers grew from under 1,000 around 1800 to 5,632 in 1902, with the real growth coming in the last third of the century. Music publishing increased by 250 per cent between 1871 and 1900. Growth was further fostered by improvements in communications (railways, telegraph, telephone) and the emergence of railway bookstalls, department stores, and mail order. Series for travellers began to appear in the 1850s (such as F. A. Brockhaus's *Reisebibliothek für Eisenbahn und Schiffe*, 1856–61) on the model of George Routledge's Railway Library (1848). The 19th century was the heyday of serial novels, marketed through itinerant booksellers. Late in the century, there were an estimated 45,000 men peddling books to 20 million readers throughout Germany and Austria. The 19th century also saw the foundation of the earliest book clubs, offering subscribers new books at advantageous prices. The earliest, apparently, was the Verein zur Verbreitung guter katholischer Bücher, founded in 1829. The Litterarischer Verein in Stuttgart, founded in 1839, specialized in scholarly editions of older literary works, many of which have still not been superseded. Later, 20th-century book clubs included the Büchergilde Gutenberg and the Deutsche Buchgemeinschaft, both founded in 1924. Among the newcomers after World War II were the Wissenschaftliche Buchgesellschaft with 140,000 members, originally designed to reissue standard works of scholarship that had become unobtainable since the war, and the Bertelsmann Club (with some 4.7 million members and 300 branches in Germany alone).

Among the inventions that led to cheap editions were wood-pulp paper—achieved as a practical process by Friedrich Gottlob Keller in 1843—and the steam press, devised by Friedrich König. Steam-driven presses were first put to use by *The Times* in 1814 and employed for the printing of books by Brockhaus at Leipzig in 1826. Planographic lithography, invented by Alois Senefelder in 1798, represented a major step forward in the reproduction of illustrations. The advantages such innovations conferred went hand in hand with improvements in the organization of the book trade, especially through the Börsenverein des deutschen Buchhandels, established at Leipzig in 1825 and soon embracing publishers, wholesalers, and retailers of books throughout the German-speaking world. In 1887, the Börsenverein introduced a net price agreement, saving smaller booksellers from being undercut by unscrupulous profiteers. Though the German states lagged behind England and France in introducing copyright laws, the grand duchy of Saxe-Weimar was the very first, in 1839, to incorporate the principle of a 30-year term of protection after the author's death. Copyright was confirmed throughout Germany in 1871 and internationally by the Berne Convention in 1886.

An important issue in publishing during the first half of the 19th century was the struggle for freedom of the press. Political journalism expanded spectacularly during the century (200 titles in 1800; 1,012 in 1847; 1,300 in 1862; 2,427 in 1881; 3,405 in 1897; and 4,221 in 1914). Restrictions were somewhat less irksome in Saxony than in Metternich's Austria, but everywhere publishers fought courageous battles against censorship and police control. Concessions were made in 1848, but rescinded in 1851—the situation improving only in 1874, when censorship was finally abolished, though even then the writings of many social democrats were banned (2,592 items between 1878 and 1918).

One vigorous campaigner in the battle for freedom was the Leipzig publisher Reclam, remembered today above all for Reclams Universalbibliothek, a series he founded in 1867 (and still going strong) which brought to the masses the works of writers of all periods in good, cheap editions. Reclam had already had a remarkable success with an inexpensive twelve-volume edition of Shakespeare in 1858, reprinted six times within a year and followed by editions of 25 individual plays in 1865. The Universalbibliothek was inaugurated with Goethe's *Faust*, but the most popular title has proved to be Schiller's *Wilhelm Tell*, with well over 2 million copies sold. By 1892 the series comprised 3,000 titles. The texts were reliable but produced as economically as possible—Reclam was one of the first German publishers to use stereotypes extensively. The paper-covered editions were available singly, and for half a century the price was kept at 20 pfennigs a copy, thus enabling even the most impecunious to gain access to great literature. In 1917 Reclam started selling titles through vending machines on 1,600 railway stations, in hospitals, and even on transatlantic liners. So immediately recognizable was Reclam's design that during the two world wars, propaganda pamphlets made up to look like Reclams were disseminated among German front-line troops.

Other successful 19th-century Leipzig publishers included Karl Christoph Traugott Tauchnitz. Around 1816, he produced cheap editions of the Greek and Latin classics employing the stereotype process, which he was the first to use in Germany. In 1837, his nephew Christian Bernhard Tauchnitz established his own business, which became famous for its Collection of British and American Authors, founded in 1841: this eventually comprised some 5,400 titles. Tauchnitz secured the goodwill of authors by voluntarily paying them a royalty and undertaking not to sell the books in Britain or its empire. Another Leipzig publisher was Teubner, renowned for editions of the Greek and Latin classics, as well as mathematical books and other scholarly works. Teubner, like Cotta and others, sometimes co-published works with Black, Young, & Young of Tavistock Street, London. F. A. Brockhaus, who originally worked under Teubner, established his reputation with his *Conversationslexikon* (1812), which in its present form, *Brockhaus Enzyklopädie* (21e, 2005–6), is still the leading German encyclopaedia. The early success of the *Conversationslexikon* demonstrated the tremendous potential for sales among the middle classes. In 1984 Brockhaus amalgamated with Bibliographisches Institut, Mannheim, publisher of *Meyers Enzyklopädisches Lexikon* (9e, 1971–9), which originated in Meyer's *Großes Lexikon für die gebildeten Stände* (52 vols, 1839–55). Another well-known firm linked with Leipzig, though only after relocating there in 1872, was Baedeker, publisher of the renowned series of travel guides; the firm began when in 1832 Karl Baedeker acquired the Koblenz publisher Friedrich Rähling and with it J. A. Klein's *Rheinreise von Mainz bis Köln* (1828).

The early 19ᵗʰ century saw the founding of three influential literary journals: *Zeitung für die elegante Welt* (1801–59), August von Kotzebue's *Der Freimüthige* (1803–56), and, most important of all, Cotta's *Morgenblatt für gebildete Stände* (1807–65). The huge growth in publishing is reflected in the need for reviews like the Heidelberg *Jahrbücher der Literatur* (1808–72) and the *Wiener Jahrbücher* (1818–49), while the more popular end of the market was catered for by J. J. Weber's enormously successful *Pfennig-Magazin* (1833–55), modelled on the English *Penny Magazine*. Another of Weber's ventures, launched in 1843, was the *Leipziger Illustrierte Zeitung*, modelled on the *Illustrated London News*. As censorship restrictions were relaxed, ever more periodicals and magazines came on to the market. The *Berliner Illustrierte Zeitung*, which started with an edition of 14,000 copies in the 1890s, had sales of more than a million copies by 1914. Then there were family magazines like *Die Gartenlaube* (from 1853) and *Westermanns illustrirte Monatshefte* (from 1856), both of them long-lived. The satirical journal *Simplicissimus* was founded in 1896. Although they were the forerunners of the magazines we know today, they were not scandal sheets, but were published to inform and educate a broader reading public.

8 The 20ᵗʰ century

Throughout the 19ᵗʰ century Leipzig publishers led the field in Germany, though the quality of their typography, paper, illustrations, and binding was often far from outstanding. The turn of the century, however, saw growing interest in book design based on the traditions of earlier periods. William Morris's Arts and Crafts movement resonated in Germany, where like-minded people tried to link new artistic forms with an appreciation of materials and craftsmanship to create a harmonious combination of type, paper, illustration, and binding. Notable examples of this trend were the magazines *Pan* and *Jugend* (from which the term *Jugendstil* derives). A number of private presses on the English model were founded, such as Carl Ernst Poeschel's and Walther Tiemann's Janus-Presse (1907); the Bremer Presse (1911), influenced by T. J. Cobden-Sanderson; and the Cranach-Presse, established by Harry Graf Kessler who emulated the Kelmscott and the Doves presses. After about 1910, the decorative, flowing forms of *Jugendstil* increasingly contrasted with the hard, broken forms of Expressionism—among whose exponents as book illustrators were

Oskar Kokoschka, Max Beckmann, Ernst Barlach, and Alfred Kubin. The growing number of design-conscious mainstream publishers included Anton Kippenberg of the Insel-Verlag in Leipzig, Eugen Diederichs at Düsseldorf, and Hans von Weber, who founded his Hyperion-Verlag in Munich in 1906.

The momentous political events that overwhelmed Germany in the 20th century inevitably affected the book trade. In 1922–3 it was devastated by galloping inflation. Soon after Hitler's appointment as chancellor, one of the most notorious episodes took place when nationalistically minded students set fire to thousands of Jewish, socialist, and other 'un-German' books in various university towns on 10 May 1933. The works of Freud, Marx, Heinrich Mann, Kurt Tucholsky, and hundreds of others were ceremoniously burnt. These events presaged tighter control of the production and distribution of written material. Authors wanting to continue publishing were obliged to join the Reichsschrifttumkammer, established under the aegis of Goebbels's Reichsministerium für Volksaufklärung und Propaganda in September 1933. Publishers and booksellers were made to toe the line in the same way. Thus, in 1934 the Jewish firm of Ullstein was 'Aryanized'. While a small number of Jewish publishers such as the Schocken-Verlag were initially tolerated, from the end of 1938 all Jewish businesses were forbidden. Lists of prohibited books and authors were drawn up, but these were not divulged to the book trade, so that booksellers needed to be extremely circumspect in selecting their stock. The works of émigré authors such as Thomas Mann and 'decadent' writers such as Robert Musil and Joseph Roth were forbidden, and books were removed from libraries or placed under restrictions. Concomitant with such repressive measures were various initiatives to promote officially approved works—couples getting married were presented with Hitler's *Mein Kampf*.

World War II and the postwar division of Germany inevitably had enormous consequences for both library provision and the book trade. Many libraries were destroyed (15–20 million books were lost), though precautions had been taken to evacuate some major collections: the Prussian State Library's stock of 3 million books and 71,600 MSS was dispersed from Berlin to some 30 sites throughout the country. After the war, some material returned to the original building on Unter den Linden in East Berlin, while other parts of the collection formed the nucleus of a new library in West Berlin; much valuable material has still not yet returned from Cracow (Poland). Following the fall of the Berlin Wall in 1989, the two libraries were unified, administratively, though not physically. As for publishing, output—which had stood at 24,792 new titles in 1900, 34,871 in 1913, and 37,886 in 1927—fell to 20,120 in 1938 and 5,304 in 1944. Leipzig, the centre of the industry, was largely destroyed by bombing in December 1943: Reclam's stock was lost, and though their printing works survived unscathed, the equipment was taken by the Russians as war reparations in 1946. After the war, the Occupying Powers (Britain, France, USA, and the Soviet Union) initially forbade the production and dissemination of printed material, confiscated National Socialist and militaristic literature, and introduced censorship.

Gradually, the Four Powers issued licences and German publishing burgeoned again, though developments varied somewhat in the different zones of occupation. The first licence for the publication of books in the British Sector of Berlin was granted on 3 October 1945 to Walter de Gruyter Verlag, whose roots go back to 1749. In the German Democratic Republic (GDR), the former Soviet Zone of Occupation, almost all publishing firms passed into state control. Thus, long-established firms like Breitkopf & Härtel, Brockhaus, Insel, and Reclam at Leipzig, and Niemeyer at Halle, were taken into state ownership as *Volkseigene Betriebe* (VEB), while the same firms re-established themselves as private companies in the West—Breitkopf & Härtel at Kassel, Brockhaus at Wiesbaden, Insel at Frankfurt, Reclam at Stuttgart, and Niemeyer at Tübingen. The West German publishing industry recovered so quickly that the expectations of Swiss publishers that they would be able to step into the breach were scarcely realized (*see* **27**). West German output increased from 14,094 titles in 1951, to 42,957 in 1971, and 63,679 in 1986. In the GDR, production grew from 1,998 in 1949 to 6,471 in 1985, and publishing was affected by tense power struggles between authors, publishers, the political leadership, and the State Security Service (the 'Stasi'). Since the reunification of Germany, considerable reorganization of the publishing industry has taken place. In 2004, German publishers issued 86,543 titles in 963 million copies. Recent years have seen increasing tendencies towards globalization, in which German publishing houses such as Bertelsmann and Springer play major roles. Bertelsmann, which today operates in 63 countries and has 95,000 employees, with a turnover of 17.9 billion euros in 2005, was founded as a small publisher of bibles and religious literature at Gütersloh in 1835. After 1850 it broadened its range, and during World War II it became a leading supplier of reading matter to soldiers at the front. Its premises were destroyed in 1945, but in 1946 it began afresh, receiving a licence to publish from the British Military Government. It launched its book club in 1950, moved into gramophone records in 1958, collaborated with AOL to promote multimedia in 1995, acquired the New York publisher Random House (which includes such well-known names as Chatto & Windus, Bodley Head, Jonathan Cape, and Virago) in 1998, and entered into partnership with Sony Corporation to produce music and videos in 2004. Similarly, Springer-Verlag, which was part of the Bertelsmann empire from 1999 to 2003, began in 1842 as a Berlin bookshop founded by Julius Springer, who published a few political and general magazines. Today Springer, based at Heidelberg, is a world leader in the fields of science, medicine, economics, engineering, architecture, construction, and transport.

One of the most obvious changes in the appearance of German books since the middle of the 20th century, the abandoning of Fraktur, is a legacy of National Socialism. German texts had customarily been printed in gothic types since the 16th century, partly rejecting foreign (especially Italian) influence, partly from national pride, and partly from Lutheran rejection of Roman Catholicism. In 1794 the Berlin publisher Nicolai described gothic type as a truly national script that would encourage a wider national ethos. When the Brothers Grimm began publishing their *Deutsches Wörterbuch* in roman type in 1852, some critics were fiercely hostile. After the creation of the Reich in 1871, support grew for Fraktur as a truly German script—Bismarck claimed he would refuse to read a German book that was not printed in gothic type, for 'a German word in Latin letters is as alien as a Greek word in German letters'—and the Reichstag was petitioned on the matter, though in 1911 it decided not to proceed. But the continuing preference for gothic typefaces deterred foreign readers—even conservative Sweden had increasingly adopted roman, largely under the influence of Carolus Linnaeus (1707–78), who induced the government to abolish customs duty on Dutch roman type. For scholars and scientists hoping to reach an international readership, Fraktur was an obstacle, so books intended for such an audience were often printed in roman. Yet domestic readers preferred Fraktur as being more legible and easier on the eyes. In the 1930s, the National Socialists were inclined to enforce its use as an expression of the Nordic soul—only with difficulty were they persuaded by the ministry of transport that it would be unsafe to use Fraktur for road signs at the time of the Berlin Olympic Games in 1936. However, the matter was settled once and for all when on 3 January 1941 Hitler declared gothic type to be a Jewish invention and ordered that henceforth roman should be the norm. 'A century from now,' he said, 'our language will be *the* European language. Countries to the east, north, and west of us will learn our language in order to be able to communicate with us. The prerequisite of this is the replacement of so-called gothic script by the script previously known as Latin script and which we now call normal script.' Thereafter, editions of *Mein Kampf* and of the party newspaper, *Völkischer Beobachter*, were duly printed in roman, and very soon this ousted Fraktur almost entirely except for ornamental purposes. The last major newspaper to adopt roman was the *Neue Zürcher Zeitung*, in 1946.

A recent development that initially occasioned great controversy and even led to lawsuits before the Federal Constitutional Court at Karlsruhe, but which ultimately has had little effect on the appearance of books, was the spelling reform ratified by the governments of Germany, Austria, and Switzerland in 1996, introduced in 1998 and, in theory, finally implemented in 2005. A final important development concerns recent progress towards the creation of a proper German national library. As indicated earlier, Germany essentially relies on a collaborative network of state and university libraries with particular responsibilities for research-level provision. There is still no national library in the sense of a single institution with a comprehensive collection embracing both current titles and historical depth. The Deutsche Nationalbibliothek, established in its present form in 2006, brings together under a single umbrella two physically separate institutions: the Deutsche Bücherei, founded in Leipzig in 1912, and the Deutsche Bibliothek, set up in 1946 at Frankfurt-am-Main. Its task is to form, catalogue, and conserve a complete collection of all material published in German since 1913, including material in German or relating to

Germany published outside its borders, translations of German works, and editions of German émigré authors published between 1933 and 1945. Publishers are required to deposit two copies of each book with either the Leipzig or the Frankfurt branch, one copy then being transmitted to the other location, thus building up two parallel collections (a wise precaution given the turmoil of the 20th century). The total holdings ran to *c.*27 million items in 2011.

BIBLIOGRAPHY

N. Bachleitner *et al.*, *Geschichte des Buchhandels in Österreich* (2000)

J.-P. Barbian, *Literaturpolitik im 'Dritten Reich'* (1995)

——*Literaturpolitik im NS-Staat. Von der Gleichschaltung bis zum Ruin* (2010)

F. Barbier, *L'Empire du livre* (1995)

B. Bischoff *et al.*, eds., *Das älteste deutsche Buch* (1977)

S. Corsten, ed., *Lexikon des gesamten Buchwesens*, 2e (1987)

V. Dahm, *Das jüdische Buch im Dritten Reich*, 2e (1993)

O. Dann, *Lesegesellschaften und bürgerliche Emanzipation* (1981)

M. U. Edwards, *Printing, Propaganda, and Martin Luther* (1994)

R. Engelsing, *Analphabetentum und Lektüre* (1973)

J. Eyssen, *Buchkunst in Deutschland vom Jugendstil zum Malerbuch* (1980)

E. Fischer and S. Füssel, eds., *Geschichte des deutschen Buchhandels im 19. und 20. Jahrhundert: Die Weimarer Republik 1918–1933* (2012)

S. Fitos, *Zensur als Mißerfolg* (2000)

H. Flachmann, *Martin Luther und das Buch* (1996)

J. L. Flood, '"Omnium totius orbis emporiorum compendium": The Frankfurt Fair in the Early Modern Period', in *Fairs, Markets and the Itinerant Book Trade*, ed. R. Myers *et al.* (2007)

—— and W. A. Kelly, eds., *The German Book, 1450–1750* (1995)

M. Giesecke, *Der Buchdruck in der frühen Neuzeit* (1991)

[Gutenberg-Gesellschaft and Gutenberg-Museum,] *Blockbücher des Mittelalters* (1991)

J. Ing, *Johann Gutenberg and his Bible* (1987)

G. Jäger, *Geschichte des deutschen Buchhandels im 19. und 20. Jahrhundert*, pts. 1 and 2, *Das Kaiserreich 1871–1918* (2001–3)

F. Kapp and J. Goldfriedrich, *Geschichte des deutschen Buchhandels* (4 vols, 1886–1913; repr. 1970)

A. Kapr, *Johann Gutenberg*, tr. D. Martin (1996)

H.-J. Künast, 'Getruckt zu Augspurg': *Buchdruck und Buchhandel in Augsburg zwischen 1468 und 1555* (1997)

H. Kunze, *Geschichte der Buchillustration in Deutschland: Das 15. Jahrhundert* (1975); *Das 16. und 17. Jahrhundert* (1993)

J. Lehnacker, *Die Bremer Presse* (1964)

A. Martino, *Die deutsche Leihbibliothek* (1990)

B. Müller, ed., *Zensur im modernen deutschen Kulturraum* (2003)

U. Neddermeyer, *Von der Handschrift zum gedruckten Buch* (1998)

U. Rautenberg, ed., *Buchwissenschaft in Deutschland* (2010)

F. Ritter, *Histoire de l'imprimerie alsacienne au XVe et XVIe siècles* (1955)

H. Sarkowski, *Springer-Verlag: History of a Scientific Publishing House* (1977)

G. K. Schauer, *Deutsche Buchkunst 1890 bis 1960* (1963)

R. Schenda, *Volk ohne Buch* (1977)

W. Schmitz, *Deutsche Bibliotheksgeschichte* (1984)

R. W. Scribner, *For the Sake of Simple Folk: Popular Propaganda for the German Reformation* (1981)

P. Stein, *Schriftkultur* (2006)

L. Tatlock, ed., *Publishing Culture and the 'Reading Nation': German Book History in the Long Nineteenth Century* (2010)

T. Verweyen, *Bücherverbrennungen* (2000)

A. Ward, *Book Production, Fiction, and the German Reading Public 1740–1800* (1974)

L. Winckler, *Autor—Markt—Publikum* (1986)

R. Wittmann, *Geschichte des deutschen Buchhandels*, 2e (1999)

C. Woodford and B. Schofield, eds., *The German Bestseller in the Late Nineteenth Century* (2012)

27

The History of the Book in Switzerland

LUKAS ERNE

1 The Middle Ages

Medieval book production in Switzerland chiefly took place in monastic scriptoria. The St Gall Abbey Library, the country's oldest library, preserves a unique collection of books from the Carolingian period, many of exceptional beauty, with important miniatures and bindings. The abbey is known to have had a scriptorium as early as the 8th century, and the first known scribe, Winithar, was active in the years 761–75. From the 10th to the 12th centuries, newly founded monasteries (including the Benedictine houses at Einsiedeln, Engelberg, and Muri) acquired and produced significant collections of theological literature. In the 13th and 14th centuries, Zurich saw the production of splendidly illustrated MSS in German, made for the aristocracy or rich citizens, most notably the Manesse Codex. Apart from medieval books produced in Switzerland, a few modern libraries house collections consisting chiefly of MSS produced elsewhere. For instance, the Bongarsiana collection, in the Burgerbibliothek in Berne, comprises an important collection of medieval codices, the St Gall Abbey Library houses significant illustrated Irish MSS from the 8th century, and the Bibliotheca Bodmeriana in Cologny near Geneva, founded by Martin Bodmer, contains a number of outstanding works, including the earliest dated MS (1308) of Guillaume de Lorris and Jean de Meun's *Roman de la Rose*.

2 The early modern period

Situated on the borders of Germany and France, on the banks of the Rhine, Basle was ideally placed to become one of Europe's early centres of book production. The Council of Basle (1431–49) brought about important traffic in books from abroad, and the foundation of the country's oldest university (and university library) in 1460 testified to the city's intellectual life. Berthold Ruppel, who had worked with Johann Gutenberg in Mainz, introduced the printing trade to Basle in the 1460s; it rose to considerable significance by the 1480s, with more than 70 printers at work by the turn of the century. Among the important incunables produced in the city was Sebastian Brant's *Narrenschiff* (Ship of Fools, 1494), printed by Johann Bergmann von Olpe, easily the most popular book in German before the Reformation.

Around 1500, humanism and the Basle book trade enjoyed a fruitful relationship which resulted in important works of biblical philology, the Church Fathers, Greek and Latin classics, and neo-Latin literature. Many of these books were of the highest typographic quality, some of them illustrated by leading artists of the time, among them Hans Holbein the younger. Important printers active in Basle at the time include Johann Amerbach, Johann Petri, and Johann Froben, who collaborated on major printing projects up to 1511. Froben's printing house, in which a Latin bible was produced as early as 1491, became a centre of humanist book production (with books printed in Latin and Greek, as well as Hebrew) to which (among others) the humanist scholar Beatus Rhenanus contributed. Froben's close ties to Desiderius Erasmus, who lived in Basle in 1514–15 and from 1518 to 1529, led to the publication of almost half of Erasmus's first editions by Froben. The Basle book trade, with its solid network of agents abroad, was also of importance for the rapid spread of Martin Luther's ideas: as early as 1518, Froben published a Latin edition of his works, followed by a second edition the following year, while Petri published Luther's *Septembertestament* in December 1522, just three months after its original publication.

Although Basle was the earliest and most important centre of book production, the first dated printed book in Switzerland, Johannes Marchesinus's *Mammotrectus super Bibliam* of 1470, names not Basle but Beromünster as the place of printing. Other dated incunabula were produced in Burgdorf (1475), Zurich (1479–82), Rougemont (1481), Promenthoux (1482), Lausanne (1493), and Sursee (1499–1500), but since these books were the work of itinerant printers, the locations tell us little about the significance of these places for the early book trade. The place that did become another early centre of book production before the end of the 15th century was Geneva, where printing started in 1478, with the *Livre des saints anges*, printed by Adam Steinschaber (a rare copy of which belongs to the British Library's strong collection of incunables printed in Geneva). Louis Cruse (from 1479), Jean Belot (from 1497), and Wigand Köln (from 1521) were the chief Geneva printers in the following decades; but the Geneva book trade would no doubt have remained in the shadow of that of Lyons if it had not been for the Reformation. Called to Geneva by Guillaume Farel, Jean Girard (from 1536; d. 1558) became the chief printer of the works of Calvin. As the Protestant Rome, Geneva saw the publication of many important works of reformed religion, particularly bibles and psalters, although the first French

Protestant translation of the Bible (1535), by Pierre-Robert Olivétan, was printed in Serrières (now part of Neuchâtel), by Pierre de Vingle. This translation was revised under the influence of Calvin, leading to the publication of the important versions of 1560 and 1588, both printed in Geneva. An Italian translation of the Bible was also printed in Geneva, in 1555, as was, in 1560, the famous English Geneva Bible as well as the first translation of the New Testament into Romansh, the fourth national language, by Jachiam Bifrun. In the 1550s a number of significant French printers escaped from religious persecution by going to Geneva, including Jean Crespin, Conrad Badius, and the Estienne family, Robert and his eldest son, the great scholar-printer Henri Estienne (whose five-volume *Thesaurus Graecae Linguae* was published at Geneva in 1572–3), establishing work of unprecedented quantity and quality in the Geneva book trade.

Owing to the Reformation, Zurich became the third centre of book production in Switzerland from the 1520s. Hans Hager printed a number of works by Ulrich Zwingli as well as an early edition of Luther's translation of the New Testament. Christoph Froschauer, who published most of Zwingli's writings, printed superb books, including the so-called Froschauerbibel (1524–9), the first Swiss folio Bible, and the Zürcher Bibel (1531). Froschauer was also long believed to be the printer of the Coverdale Bible (1535), although current scholarly opinion calls this into question. Along with humanism, the Reformation was thus the chief motor of the Swiss book trade in the early modern period. Literacy among the population remained low, however, and the proportion of people reading regularly was probably no higher than 2 per cent before and 4 per cent after the Reformation. Publishers therefore did not primarily aim at local sales, and the book fairs in Frankfurt, Leipzig, Paris, and Lyons remained of great importance for the dissemination of books produced in Switzerland. This may also explain why throughout the 16th and 17th centuries books printed in Switzerland—contrary to other European countries—mostly continued to appear in Latin rather than in the vernacular.

3 The 17th and 18th centuries

In the 16th century, the Catholic parts of Switzerland produced less than 1 per cent of the country's total output, and in Fribourg printing even remained prohibited until 1584. In the 17th century, however, the Counter-Reformation led to sustained book production in Catholic parts of the country, in particular in Einsiedeln, Lucerne, and St Gall. In Einsiedeln Monastery a printing office was founded in 1664, in which massive, multi-volume works of theology and history were printed. At the same time, the Thirty Years War (1618–48) and its consequences hampered the development of the book trade, until the following century when Enlightenment doctrines led to a significant increase in the demand for secular literature. From early on, the book trade in Switzerland had been catering for an international market, but this proved particularly true in the latter half of the 18th century, when Swiss-French publishers in Geneva, Lausanne, Neuchâtel, and Yverdon flooded the international market with piracies of recently published literary and philosophical works, notably the *Encyclopédie* (1751–72), but also political and anti-clerical tracts, as well as erotica and porno-graphic literature. Of particular importance was the Société Typographique de Neuchâtel, founded in 1769, whose archives have survived largely intact and constitute an invaluable source of information about the book trade and intellectual life of the 18th century, as demonstrated, most notably, in Robert Darnton's *The Business of Enlightenment*.

4 From the 19th century to today

In the course of the 19th century, reading spread thanks to newly founded lending libraries, reading groups, and book societies. For instance, the Geneva Société de lecture was founded in 1818 and acquired as many as 30,000 books within the first twenty years of its existence. In the course of the 20th century, book produc-tion in Switzerland increased from about 1,000 titles to almost 14,000 per year. Just over four-fifths of the books published at the end of the 20th century appeared in one of the national languages: 59 per cent in German, 18 per cent in French, 3 per cent in Italian, and 0.6 per cent in Rhaeto-Romanic, much of the rest being published in English. Yet these account for only about 30 per cent of the books on sale in Switzerland, with roughly 70 per cent being of foreign origins. Among Swiss publishing houses established in the 20th century are Slatkine and Droz, both based in Geneva, founded in 1918 and 1924, respectively. In the mid-20th century, Switzerland became a centre for high-quality colour book production thanks to publishers such as C. J. Bucher, Conzett & Huber, and Albert Skira.

With regards to book preservation, a number of public or private libraries today house important collections, notably the chief university libraries, the Public Library of the University of Basel, the City and University Library of Berne, the Cantonal and University Library of Fribourg, the Library of Geneva, the Public and Cantonal Library of Lausanne, the Public and University Library of Neuchâtel, and the Zurich Central Library. The Swiss National Library in Berne, founded in 1895, collects all publications relating to Switzerland and also houses the Swiss Literary Archives, created in 1989, following the Swiss writer Friedrich Dürrenmatt's donation of his MSS to the Confederation. The Swiss Federal Archives, which build on the archives of the Helvetian Republic founded in 1798, have similarly been housed in Berne since the early 19th century. Several museums display aspects of the history of the book, including the Basler Papiermühle, the Swiss Gutenberg Museum of Fribourg, founded in 2000, and the new museum of the Bibliotheca Bodmeriana, inaugurated in 2003.

BIBLIOGRAPHY

J. Benzing, *Die Buchdrucker des 16. und 17. Jahr-hunderts im deutschen Sprachgebiet*, 2e (1982)

D. Bertholet, *Suisse Romande terre du livre* (2006)

P. G. Bietenholz, *Basle and France in the Sixteenth Century* (1971)

A. Bruckner, *Scriptoria Medii Aevi Helvetica* (14 vols, 1935–78)

E. Büchler, *Die Anfänge des Buchdrucks in der Schweiz*, 2e (1951)

T. Bürger, *Aufklärung in Zürich* (1997)

P. Chaix, *Recherche sur l'imprimerie à Genève* (1954)

R. Darnton, *The Business of Enlightenment* (1979)

—— and M. Schlup, eds., *Le Rayonnement d'une maison d'edition dans l'Europe des Lumières* (2005)

R. Diederichs *et al.*, eds., *Buchbranche im Wandel* (1999)

J.-F. Gilmont, *La Réforme et le livre* (1990)

P. L. van der Haegen, *Der frühe Basler Buchdruck* (2001)

U. Joerg and D. M. Hoffmann, eds., *La Bible en Suisse* (1997)

P. Ladner, ed., *Iter Helveticum* (5 vols, 1976–90)

E. C. Rudolphi, *Die Buchdrucker Familie Froschauer in Zürich, 1521–1595* (1963)

P. F. Tschudin, *Handwerk, Handel, Humanismus* (1984)

B. Weber, ed., *Cinq siècles d'imprimerie à Genève* (1978)

M. E. Welti, *Der Basler Buchdruck und Britannien* (1964)

28

The History of the Book in the Nordic Countries

CHARLOTTE APPEL AND KAREN SKOVGAARD-PETERSEN

1 Introduction

When surveying the history of the book in the Nordic countries, a balance needs to be struck between the region as a whole and its individual countries (Sweden, Denmark, Finland, Norway, Iceland, Greenland, and the Faroe Islands). Among the most important unifying factors is language. Swedish, Danish, and Norwegian are closely related and still mutually intelligible, whereas Icelandic and Faroese have stayed closer to Old Norse. Finnish belongs to a different language group (Finno-Ugric), as do the Sami languages, spoken in the north of the Scandinavian peninsula. Greenlandic is an Inuit language. Many people in the outer regions have also been able to communicate in Swedish, Norwegian, or Danish.

The present survey, emphasizing the relationship between book and society, cannot do justice to the region's richness and variousness. Even though societal developments have often been similar or directly shared, different geographical and natural conditions have created diversity across the extensive region and its populations. These numbered in total 24 million people in 2000, compared to 2 million around 1600. Moreover, international orientations have varied (from Finland in the east to the Atlantic Islands in the west), and borders and political alliances have often changed.

2 The Middle Ages

The great majority of medieval books once found in the Nordic countries have disappeared completely. Some were worn out, and some vanished after the Reformation because of general neglect and contempt. Others were lost in fires, notably in Copenhagen (1728) and Åbo/Turku (1827). Among those that have been preserved are a number of invaluable Icelandic codices. Furthermore, numerous fragments have survived as binding material (e.g. *c.*10,000 leaves or sheets representing *c.*1,500 books from Finland), adding considerably to what is known about Nordic medieval book culture.

With the missions and the establishment of churches in the 10th–12th centuries, Scandinavia became part of Christian European culture, being introduced to parchment books and to the Latin language and alphabet. Reading and writing were not entirely new phenomena. Runes (*see* **3**) had been used for inscriptions on metal, stone, and wood since around AD 200. After the Latin alphabet was introduced, runes remained in use for short inscriptions; in some areas, as indicated by outstanding finds from Bergen, west Norway (*c.* 1100–1400), they may even have become more common for everyday purposes.

The earliest Nordic book production can be traced to Lund, a Danish episcopal seat from *c.*1060 and a Scandinavian archdiocese from 1104. Monarchs worked closely with church leaders, and Lund was an important centre of both learning and politics in the 12th century, particularly while Absalon was archbishop (1177–1201). He commissioned the writing of Saxo Grammaticus' *Gesta Danorum*. The Norwegian archbishopric of Nidaros (Trondheim), founded 1153, occupied a similar position. Here the legend of St Olav, Norway's royal saint, was given its written form, an Olav liturgy established, and national historical writing cultivated. By contrast, the establishment of the Swedish archdiocese in Uppsala (1164) did not result in a national historiography, probably owing to the Swedish monarchy's weaker position.

In the 12th and 13th centuries, collections of books were established in connection with churches, particularly cathedrals and monasteries. These were Latin libraries, containing liturgical books, bibles, collections of sermons, schoolbooks, and, to a lesser degree, classical authors and books on secular subjects such as medicine. Book production took place in the scriptoria of larger ecclesiastical institutions, although in Iceland there was considerable involvement by lay landowners. Among local ecclesiastical productions were books about the lives and miracles of local saints, annals, and registers of donations.

European influence was also evident in the field of law. Legal books in Latin were imported, providing additional inspiration for the composition of provincial laws in the vernacular. As early as 1117/18, Icelandic laws were recorded in writing. Many vernacular laws from the 12th and 13th centuries bear witness to strong royal powers in mainland Scandinavia; in 1274 King Magnus Lagabøtir ('Law-amender') promulgated a legal revision that provided a uniform law for the whole of Norway.

In Iceland and Norway, the vernacular was central, even within ecclesiastical administration. Here, an extraordinary narrative literature in Old Norse emerged during the 13th and 14th centuries. Hundreds of sagas were recorded in writing, some of them based on oral traditions known in other Scandinavian areas as well. The Icelanders' sagas, e.g. *Njál's Saga*, and Snorri Sturluson's

Heimskringla, are justifiably famous. The *Edda* poems are important sources of Nordic mythology. An outstanding treatise is the *King's Mirror*, written in Norway *c*.1250. As early as *c*.1150, the establishment of a written standard of Old Norse was discussed theoretically in the so-called *First Grammatical Treatise*.

In Sweden and Denmark, book culture was primarily a Latin phenomenon until the 14th century, when the vernacular, including Low German, became more common in law books and legal documents, medical manuals, and devotional books. Continental romances were translated at noble courts. Particularly in towns, the need for reading, writing, and accounting increased, as did the number of schools, scriptoria, and administrative archives. The introduction of paper *c*.1350 contributed further to more widespread and informal use of writing (private letters, copies of documents) (*see* **10**). Books and documents of particular importance, however, were still written on locally produced parchment.

Around 1500, the majority of books proper were presumably liturgical and devotional volumes in Latin. The richest library was the Swedish monastery of Vadstena, which housed the Order of the Most Holy Saviour, instituted by St Birgitta. The library comprised *c*.1,400 books, of which *c*.500 are still extant (in Uppsala and Stockholm).

In order to obtain a university education, increasing numbers of young Scandinavians went abroad. Only in 1425 did it become possible to obtain a bachelor's degree at Lund; the first—and for centuries the only—Scandinavian universities opened in Uppsala (1477) and Copenhagen (1479).

3 1500–1800

During the early modern period, Nordic countries were divided politically in two. The kingdom of Sweden also comprised Finland, while the Danish-Norwegian king ruled Denmark, Norway, Iceland, the Faroe Islands, and Greenland, as well as the mainly German-speaking duchies of Schleswig and Holstein. Post-Reformation Nordic book history is well documented thanks to comprehensive national bibliographies. The first books were printed in Denmark in 1482 and Sweden in 1483 by the German Johann Snell, following invitations from the bishops of Odense and Uppsala. Imported printed books had been on the scene earlier, however. The Dutchman Gotfred of Ghemen settled briefly in Copenhagen, but otherwise most early 16th-century printers were itinerant Germans. Throughout the early modern period, many craftsmen and tradesmen emigrated from or were trained in Germany. German trends and techniques were followed closely: black letter was used for vernacular texts, whereas gotico-antiqua roman type became the standard for books in Latin; likewise, bookbindings displayed German influence in the use of decorative roll tools, many of them imported.

After the Lutheran Reformation, the Swedish and Danish kings sought to control imported and domestic publications. A royal printing press, Kungliga Tryckeriet, was founded in Stockholm (1526), establishing an effective monopoly for almost a century. In Denmark, two or three presses were active simultaneously, but with a few exceptions, they were situated within the city walls of Copenhagen, effectively tied to the government through privileges and commissions. In both countries, the Crown ordered and financed important publications, including the first full bibles in the vernacular (Sweden, 1540–41; Denmark, 1550) and national hymnals. Privileges were also given for the printing of homilies, prayer books, and other literature regarded as useful or edifying by the authorities.

The first book produced for Finland was the *Missale Aboense* (1488), printed by Bartholomaeus Ghotan in Lübeck; during the 16th century, almost all books for Finnish use were printed in Stockholm. Of special importance was Mikael Agricola, who translated the New Testament (1548) and composed several religious books in Finnish.

In Iceland, the Catholic bishop invited a Swedish printer *c.*1530 to Hólar; after the Reformation (1550), Hólaprent remained the only Icelandic printing press. Many bishops were involved in the production of vernacular religious books. In the late 17th century, the press was moved to the other episcopal see, Skálholt (where Icelandic sagas were also printed), but later returned to Hólar. Much literature continued to be copied and read in MS. Danish was the language of the administration, and many Icelanders read books in Danish.

Copenhagen had three printers *c.*1600, ten *c.*1700, and twenty *c.*1800. A few provincial presses (Elsinore, Sorø, Aarhus, and Odense) operated for short periods, but provincial printing offices were not established on a more permanent basis until the 1730s, when they often centred on a local newspaper. In 1643, Tyge Nielsen came to Christiania (Oslo) as Norway's first printer. This was the only Norwegian town with a permanent printing office until printing began in Bergen (1721), followed by Trondheim (1739); many authors on the west coast continued to use Copenhagen presses. The Danish and Norwegian book markets formed a whole, not least because Danish was used as the written language in both countries.

Sweden had one (royal) printing house in 1600, but seventeen in 1700, six of them in Stockholm. Other towns with presses were Uppsala (from 1618), Västerås, Strängnäs, Kalmar, Linköping, and Gothenburg. In 1642, the first complete bible in Finnish was printed in Stockholm; in the same year a press was established at the new Finnish Academy in Åbo. Another two presses were founded later in the 17th century, in Åbo and Viborg.

The increasing number of printers weakened direct royal control, but governmental and ecclesiastical influences remained strong due to official privileges and censorship regulations. Everyday censorship was fairly lax, but enforced vehemently as soon as suspicions arose. Apart from confessionally dubious books, most attention was directed at criticism of the king (in Denmark particularly after the introduction of absolutism in 1660–61) and at the new medium of the regularly published newspaper, in Denmark from 1634 and in Sweden from 1645.

The Danish and Swedish governments continued to support the printing of religious and educational books, as well as laws and statutes. Political pamphlets became increasingly important, especially in Sweden, in connection with its numerous 17th- and early 18th-century wars. After 1658, when Denmark lost the southern parts of the Swedish peninsula, the printed word (especially Swedish catechisms) was used in a campaign to 'Swedenize' former Danish subjects.

Book production and the book trade became increasingly differentiated during the 17th century. Bookbinders formed special guilds, obtaining in Sweden a monopoly for the selling of bound books. Some of Stockholm's printing houses— Ignatius Meurer, Henrik Keyser, Georg Gottlieb Burchardi—developed into important publishing firms with strong international relations. In Copenhagen, major booksellers, such as Joachim Moltke and Daniel Paulli, became the most important publishers. At international book fairs, they exchanged scholarly books in Latin with their European colleagues.

Rising production is indicated by extant imprints. According to the bibliography *Bibliotheca Danica*, fewer than twenty different publications survive from the years 1500–1509, 368 from 1600–1609, and 1,164 from 1700–1709. The balance between titles in Latin and Danish fluctuated (though was often close to being equal), until Latin became confined to academic titles during the 18th century. However, press runs as well as multiple editions indicate that many more copies of books were printed in the vernacular from the late 16th century onwards. Popular religious and entertaining titles were printed in runs of 1,000 or 2,000 copies. Many such editions have not survived.

New genres appeared (household manuals, devotional titles for female readers) along with older ones (chapbooks, ballads). Such items, usually printed in octavo or even smaller formats, sometimes contained woodcuts. Copper engravings (from *c.*1600) were confined to more expensive folios. Both Denmark and Sweden saw the appearance of such magnificently illustrated publications as Samuel Pufendorf's *De Rebus a Carolo Gustavo Gestis* (1696) and *Flora Danica* (1761–1883).

Popular literacy was stimulated by many factors. After the Reformation, the teaching of the catechism was given high priority, and clergymen encouraged 'reading in books' to strengthen children's rote-learning. Seventeenth-century reading campaigns were supported by bishops and kings, most directly through the Swedish Church Law of 1686. The rising trade in ballads and 'harmful' stories—an unintended consequence of increasing literacy standards—was opposed by the same authorities.

By the mid-18th century, according to the extraordinarily detailed information of Swedish and Finnish parish registers, more than 90 per cent of adults could read the required religious texts in print. Writing, by contrast, remained more closely tied to professional needs. Standards in the rest of Scandinavia, Iceland, and—a few decades later—Greenland were probably as high. In Norway and Denmark, governmental regulation was gradually intensified, and more formal schools were established following legislation in the 1730s. In the early 19th century, national laws concerning compulsory school teaching for all children were issued across the region.

Local book supplies varied considerably with population density and infrastructure. In most towns, especially along the coasts, books were permanently available (e.g. in the numerous small-scale Danish boroughs with typically 1,000–5,000 inhabitants and between one and four binders selling books). People in southern Scandinavia's rural areas and along the Norwegian west coast also had frequent contact with urban book markets. Further inland and further north, however, deliveries were few and far between. In addition to the religious context of reading instruction, this meant that for many Nordic people the world of books was confined to a limited selection of (mainly devotional) literature.

Readers interested in a wider range of books had to acquire these in a capital or university city. The populations of Stockholm and Copenhagen grew significantly, from 10,000 and 20,000 inhabitants respectively in 1600 to c.60,000 in 1700. Dutch booksellers were present in Copenhagen from the 1630s and in Stockholm from 1647 (Johannes Janssonius, the Elzevier family). Foreign books were also imported by university booksellers. Traditional bookselling in churches ceased, but around 1700 more booksellers and publishers opened shops with their own premises.

In the 18th century, the acquisition of colonies led to a boom in Pietist missionary printing. In Copenhagen, a special press was established in 1714 (from 1727, Vajsenhuset) for both missionary and domestic education. For some years, a printing press was also installed in the colony of Tranquebar, India, and in the West Indies. Swedish missionary publications were printed for North America (including books in the Indian Lanape language). In 1755, the New Testament was translated into Ume-Sami, and a Swedish–Sami dictionary was published (1780) to assist missionary work. Hans Egede brought a Pietist mission and Danish religious books to Greenland in the 1720s. The Bible was translated into Greenlandic, thus profoundly shaping the written and printed language. The first book was printed in Greenland in 1793, but traditional MS publication survived in this small population until well into the 19th century.

Enlightenment ideas came to Stockholm and Copenhagen at a time when the capitals were experiencing flourishing trade and rising standards of living and education. A key figure was the history professor, playwright, and essayist Ludvig Holberg (1684–1754), regarded as the first Norwegian-Danish author to become rich from the sale of his books. From the 1740s, new societies and journals, particularly concerned with economics and science, were established with royal support.

In the world of libraries, significant developments took place during the early modern period. Medieval clerical book collections were dissolved or destroyed after the Lutheran Reformation, and Protestant church libraries remained modest, although some cathedral libraries and cathedral schools could boast fine collections. From the late 16th century, extensive libraries were built up by nobles (Heinrich Rantzau, Magnus Gabriel de la Gardie, Karen Brahe, Otto Thott), some of whom invested in exquisite uniform bindings by trendsetting bookbinders inspired by French and English fashions (e.g. the Reusner, Bergman, and Boppenhausen families).

Probate inventories and the new trend for public book auctions (from the mid-17th century) provide documentation for the many scholars and wealthy merchants who owned major libraries. One private collector, P. F. Suhm in Copenhagen, famously opened his library to the public (1778). The universities, particularly Uppsala and Copenhagen, had considerable collections. The two royal libraries expanded from the mid-17th century, primarily by incorporating private collections and war booty; and bookbinders were attached to the courts. Legal deposit was formally introduced in Sweden in 1661 and Denmark in 1697. Public access to the National Library of Sweden in Stockholm was granted from 1713; the Royal Library in Copenhagen gave limited access to scholars, but otherwise remained closed to the public until 1793.

The first commercial lending library appeared in Copenhagen in 1725. From the mid-18th century, a variety of private and institutional libraries were established across Scandinavia, in provincial towns and the country. Moreover, private ownership of books became generally more common. One remarkable Norwegian peasant, Sivert Knuddssøn Aarflot, even turned his collection into a public lending library.

The market for books changed from the mid-18th century. Newspaper production took permanent hold, especially in towns. Major firms expanded and modernized their businesses, helped by the abolition of old regulations in the different crafts. Among the leading names in Stockholm were Peter Momma, Elsa Fougt, and Lars Salvius, the latter reorganizing Swedish bookselling by commissioning provincial booksellers. Similar changes took place in the Danish and Norwegian markets thanks to Gyldendal (Copenhagen, 1770-). In the 18th century, Finland endured frequent periods of war and Russian occupation, forcing Finnish book production to move to Stockholm; Jacob Merckell and, later, the Frenckell family dominated the Finnish book trade.

The Enlightenment increasingly challenged censorship. It was relaxed considerably in Sweden (1766), where freedom of the press became relatively well secured. In Denmark, censorship was abolished during J. F. Struensee's short rule (1770–71), but controls were gradually re-established and tightened in 1799.

4 1800–2000

After the Napoleonic wars, the Nordic political landscape was radically transformed. In 1814 Norway was separated from Denmark and made subject to the Swedish king until 1905. Iceland, Greenland, and the Faroe Islands remained with Denmark; Iceland achieved independence in 1944, and home rule was established in the Faroes and Greenland in 1948 and 1979, respectively. After wars with Germany, Denmark lost Schleswig-Holstein in 1864. Finland, an autonomous grand duchy of Russia 1809–1917, was subject to strict censorship at a time when such control was being dismantled in Sweden, Norway, and Denmark (1810, 1814, 1849) in connection with new democratic constitutions. Around the mid-19th century, liberalization, including the abolition of guild monopolies in trade and manufacturing, was occurring all over Scandinavia.

At the same time, history, mythology, and language were cultivated intensely as part of the formation of national identities. In the 'new' nations—Norway, Finland, Iceland, the Faroes, and Greenland—language became a major issue. Two Norwegian written language forms, *bokmål* (relatively close to Danish) and *nynorsk* (based on western Norwegian dialects with elements from medieval Norse), were created, the latter as a reaction against former Danish rule. Today both are recognized as official written languages (*bokmål* being more commonly used).

In Finland, Swedish remained the cultural and administrative language for much of the 19th century, but Finnish gradually gained ground, achieving equal legal status in 1892. Both languages are now officially recognized (Swedish being a minority language). In Iceland, the nationalist movement stressed continuity with medieval Norse. An active language policy strove to replace old and new borrowings from foreign languages with Icelandic words.

The general interest across Scandinavia in national history and popular culture gave rise to numerous important and popular collections of ballads and tales. Examples include the Swedish ballads edited by Geijer and Afzelius, the Norwegian tales collected by Asbjørnsen and Moe, and the monumental Finnish national epic, the *Kalevala*.

Popular religious revivalist movements profoundly influenced 19th-century developments. In Norway, the lay preacher Hans Nielsen Hauge (1771–1824) achieved a tremendous following by distributing huge quantities of religious tracts across the country. In Denmark, N. F. S. Grundtvig (1783–1872) became the unofficial head of a nationally oriented, non-puritan, religious revival, inspiring the establishment of 'folk high schools' (*folkehøjskoler*), exam-free boarding schools for adults in the countryside. Although preferring the 'living word' to 'bookish learning', these schools motivated generations to further study across Scandinavia and, along with other religious movements of more puritan origin (especially in Norway and Sweden), made inventive use of printed materials such as newsletters, recruiting pamphlets, and edifying tracts.

New publication strategies were explored by the many recently established societies, associations, political parties, trade unions, cooperatives, temperance societies, and sports clubs. The resulting explosion in jobbing printing and small editions was assisted by lower printing costs and improved distribution channels (new railway systems revolutionized the transport system, especially

Illustrations of runic stones from the Danish scholar Carl Rafn's 'Runic Inscriptions in which the Western Countries are Alluded to', in *Mémoires de la Société Royale des Antiquaires du Nord, 1848-9* (Copenhagen, 1852); the variety of languages is notable. Private collection

in the vast, less densely populated areas of Scandinavia). At the same time, major industries and retail concerns began to print catalogues, and even small shops used print for advertising.

Newspapers were perhaps the single most important media of the 19th and early 20th centuries, stimulating democratic developments and vice versa. From c.1830, they could be printed faster and more cheaply, resulting in a dramatic increase in print runs and diversity. In Sweden, L. J. Hierta founded the politically influential *Aftonbladet* in 1830; by 1900, the country had c.120 newspapers. In Finland (where the oldest still-published newspaper is *Åbo Underrättelser* (1824–)), both Finnish and Swedish-language newspapers became important organs of public debate. The Atlantic regions saw their first periodicals in the last half of the 19th century: Iceland's *Þjóðólfur* (1848), Greenland's *Atuagagdliutit* (1861–), and the Faroese *Dimmalætting* (1877–). The first Faroese printing press was established in 1852, when a short-lived attempt at newspaper publishing was made.

From the late 19th century, new political parties were formed, all with their own newspapers. Several Danish provincial towns had four different daily papers, representing different parties. Norway had an abundance of local newspapers and, despite declining readerships, remains—like Finland, Iceland, and Sweden—among the leading newspaper nations worldwide.

As elsewhere in Europe, the book industry in the Nordic countries changed following the introduction of new printing and manufacturing technologies *c*.1830 (*see* 11). Hitherto, Nordic countries had mainly used imported paper, producing it on a small scale (mainly in Sweden). However, after the development of wood-based paper, Finland and Sweden (and to a lesser extent Norway), with their large areas of forest, developed significant paper industries. In 2000, Finland was the second largest exporter of paper, after Canada (*see* 10).

During the 19th century, publishing and the book trade were organized along still recognizable lines. Professional bodies were established. Danish book prices became fixed in 1837—a principle that was relaxed only in about 2000—and regulations were made against the unauthorized sale of books. Of the numerous publishing companies founded in the mid-19th century, many existed well into the 20th century. C. A. Reitzel (1789–1853) published the period's most celebrated Danish authors, including Hans Christian Andersen and Kierkegaard. The largest and most influential firm, however, was Gyldendal, not least because of its dynamic director Frederik V. Hegel (1817–87).

For most of the 19th century, the Norwegian book market remained strongly influenced by Danish interests. Prominent authors such as Ibsen and Bjørnstjerne Bjørnson published their books with Gyldendal, Copenhagen. Under its director William Nygaard (from 1888), Aschehoug gave ample opportunity to authors to publish with a Norwegian firm, but it was not until Gyldendal had set up an independent Norwegian company (1925) that it became a matter of course for authors to publish in their own country. Both Aschehoug and Gyldendal Norsk Forlag have remained important elements in Norwegian literary life.

In Finland, a significant role was played by the Finnish Literature Society (1831), which initiated several publications, including the *Kalevala* and Aleksis Kivi's *Seven Brothers*. Major firms did not emerge until the last decades of the 19th century. Werner Söderström's publishing house supported Finnish-language literature, but for moral reasons refrained from publishing modern realism. He was soon rivalled by the more liberal publishing house Otava (1890). Both are prominent in the contemporary Finnish book market.

In Sweden, the early establishment of a free press stimulated the rapid expansion of publishing across the country. One particularly influential house was that of Bonnier, which published Strindberg's works and grew during the 20th century into a major media group.

Technical, economic, and social developments made books widely affordable. Entertaining literature was consumed in large quantities, and new foreign novels by e.g. August Lafontaine, Scott, Dickens, and Dumas were translated. Some were serialized in newspapers, others launched in cheap editions, often through subscription sales, by major publishing houses.

One successful enterprise (1897–1918) was the Danish-Norwegian series *Frem* (in Swedish, *Ljus*), with *c*.170,000 subscribers in the three countries. It published articles relating to history and science and could be bought in inexpensive instalments. Exceptionally large press runs were also reached by the 'crown' and 'half-crown' editions of classical bestsellers. Such developments arrived later in Scandinavia than in many other parts of Europe; pocketbook series similar to Penguin's were only introduced in the Nordic countries after World War II. By the 1970s, book clubs had acquired a dominant position in the market for popular literature.

Another important phenomenon in the decades around 1900 was the multivolume encyclopaedia (e.g. the Danish *Salmonsen's Leksikon*). In the 1970s, the publication of extensive encyclopaedias and reference works boomed in Finland. Major national encyclopaedic projects were completed in Sweden and Denmark around 2000.

Lending libraries existed in all Nordic countries from the mid- or late 19th century. In rural districts, they were often established within individual parishes; in towns, many were run by societies and organizations. The first public libraries appeared in the 1880s, and during the 1920s and 1930s, the young welfare states took over full responsibility for municipal libraries. Much money was spent to supply the same variety of books to all citizens, irrespective of location. Local branches were set up in small communities, and mobile libraries introduced. From the 1960s, comic books were made available in libraries, followed by tapes, videos, CDs, DVDs, and free Internet access. Special departments for children's books are found in all public libraries.

Since the 1960s, children's literature has achieved an important position in the Nordic countries, being recognized for both educational value and literary quality. Books by numerous authors (especially Astrid Lindgren) have been widely read by children in all parts of the region, possibly providing more shared reading experiences than any other works of Nordic literature.

In other respects, Nordic book culture has become increasingly international. During the late 19th century, professional standards and artistic aspirations were raised through French and English influences (e.g. Rasmus Fr. Hendriksen, and later Akke Kumlien). Around this time, German Fraktur gradually disappeared as a standard type. Aesthetic concerns were also manifested in bookbinding, with Sweden's Gustaf Hedberg and Denmark's Anker Kyster as pioneers. Early 20th-century Scandinavian typography was strongly influenced by Modernism (Hugo Lagerström, Steen Eiler Rasmussen). In the 1940s and 1950s, British axial typography prevailed in fiction (C. Volmer Nordlunde) and Swiss asymmetry in textbooks (Viggo Naae, Karl-Erik Forsberg). From the 1960s onwards, both lines were typographically improved (Erik Ellegaard Frederiksen, Carl Fredrik Hultenheim, Poul Kristensen), and increased legibility became a major desideratum (Bror Zachrisson). Late 20th-century typographers excelled in imaginative book cover design (Austin Grandjean).

Since World War II, the majority of translated books have come from English-speaking countries; from the late 20th century, globalization and higher standards of English proficiency have resulted in Scandinavians buying and reading increasing numbers of books in English. However, some 'book traffic' has also gone the other way. Several 20th-century Nordic authors have had their works translated into English and other languages, including Nobel prize-winners Selma Lagerlöf, Knut Hamsum, and Sigrid Undset and crime fiction writers Maj Sjöwall, Per Wahlöö, and Henning Mankell. According to UNESCO's 1998 World Culture Report, the Nordic countries are among the nations with the highest numbers (per capita) of library books and book titles published annually.

BIBLIOGRAPHY

GENERAL

P. Birkelund *et al.*, eds., *Nordisk Leksikon for Bogvæsen* (2 vols, 1951–62)

Royal Library, Denmark, www.kb.dk/en/index.html, consulted Sept. 2007

National Library of Finland, www.lib.helsinki.fi/english/, consulted Sept. 2007

National Library of Iceland, www.bok.hi.is/id/1011633, consulted Sept. 2007

Nordisk tidskrift för bok- och biblioteksväsen (1914–2006; from 2001, *Nordisk tidskrift för bok- och bibliotekshistoria*)

National Library of Norway, www.nb.no/english, consulted Sept. 2007

National Library of Sweden, www.kb.se/ENG/kbstart.htm, consulted Sept. 2007

DENMARK

Bogvennen (1893–)

C. Bruun, *Bibliotheca Danica, 1482–1830* (6 vols, 1877–1914); 2e (5 vols, 1961–3)

H. Ehrencron-Müller, *Forfatterlexikon omfattende Danmark, Norge og Island indtil 1814* (12 vols, 1924–35)

A. Frøland, *Dansk Boghandels historie 1482–1945* (1974)

Fund og Forskning i Det kongelige Biblioteks samlinger (1954–)

Grafiana (1997–)

I. Ilsøe, 'Printing, Book Illustration, Bookbinding, and Book Trade in Denmark, 1482–1914', *GJ* 60 (1985), 258–80

K. B. Jensen, ed., *Dansk Mediehistorie* (4 vols, 1996–2003)

L. Nielsen, *Dansk bibliografi 1482–1600* (3 vols, 1919–35); 2e (5 vols, 1996)

—— *Den danske bog* (1941)

E. Petersen, ed., *Living Words and Luminous Pictures* (1999)

FAROE ISLANDS

M. Næs, *Fra spadestik til global udfordring* (2005)

FINLAND

T. Boman *et al.*, eds., *Bibliografi över Finlands bokhistoria 1488–1850 före 1991* (1993)

Fennica: The National Bibliography of Finland, www.fennica.linneanet.fi, consulted Sept. 2007

C.-R. Gardberg, *Boktrycket i Finland* (3 vols, 1948–73)

K. K. Karlsson, *Finlands handpappersbruk* (1981)

A. Perälä, *Typographischer Atlas Finnlands 1642–1827* (2 vols, 2000)

[F. W. Pipping,] *Förteckning öfver i tryck utgifna skrifter på Finska* (1856/7)

GREENLAND

K. Oldendow, *Groenlandica: Conspectus Bibliographicus* (1967)

ICELAND

B. S. Benedikz, *Iceland* (1969)

H. Hermannsson, *Catalogue of the Icelandic Collection Bequeathed by Willard Fiske* [1960]

S. Nordal, ed., *Monumenta Typographica Islandica* (6 vols, 1933–42)

NORWAY

J. B. Halvorsen, *Norsk forfatter-lexikon 1814–1880* (6 vols, 1885–1908)

H. Pettersen, *Bibliotheca Norvegica (1643–1918)* (4 vols, 1899–1924; 2e, 1972–4)

C. Sciøtz and B. Ringstrøm, *Norske førsteutgaver, en hjelpebok for samlere av skjønnlitteratur*, 2e (2006)

H. L. Tveterås, *Den norske bokhandels historie* (4 vols, 1950–96)

SWEDEN

Biblis (1957–97; 1998–)

Bokvännen (1946–97)

J. Brunius, ed., *Medieval Book Fragments in Sweden* (2005)

I. Collijn, *Sveriges bibliografi intill år 1600* (3 vols, 1927–38)

—— *Sveriges bibliografi, 1600-talet* (2 vols in 1, 1942–6)

K. E. Gustafsson and P. Rydén, eds., *Den svenska Pressens historia* (5 vols, 2000–03)

H. Järv, ed., *Den svenska boken* (1983)

D. Lindmark, *Reading, Writing, and Schooling, 1650–1880* (2004)

H. Schück, *Den svenska förlagsbokhandelns historia* (1923)

Svensk bibliografi 1700–1829 (SB 17), www.kb.se/hjalp/english, consulted Sept. 2007

The History of the Book in the Iberian Peninsula

MARÍA LUISA LÓPEZ-VIDRIERO

1 Early printing

Printing arrived late in the Iberian Peninsula, towards 1472 in Spain and 1487 in Portugal; the region's surviving incunables are characteristically archaic in style. The introduction and subsequent development of the printing press in Spain did not follow the pattern typical in the rest of Europe for three principal reasons: the political organization of Spain into multiple kingdoms; the fact that no one city was identifiable as the national capital; and the coexistence of two main languages, Castilian and Catalan.

Although Saragossa, Logroño, Barcelona, Valencia, and Seville were leading printing centres, the Castilian presses (Salamanca, Burgos, Alcalá de Henares, and Toledo) were especially important in Spain's typographical map. As printing began to develop, Castile was enjoying a golden moment of political and cultural hegemony; the printing press played a crucial role in the policy of national unity promoted by the Catholic Monarchs (1474–1516). Just as the Habsburg and Bourbon dynasties would later, the *Reyos Catholicos* used the press as an instrument for developing both the theory of statecraft and its practical application.

The advent of printing called for the reorganization of bookselling and the circulation of MSS, requiring the introduction of edicts to regulate the book as a commercial and intellectual product. These legislative measures attempted to bring authorized printed materials on to the market during escalating conflicts in 16th-century Europe. Widespread censorship became one of the gravest intellectual and civil problems of the period. A law of 1502 regulated the intervention of the Crown in the printing industry and tried to resolve conflicts over the importation of 'false and defective' printed books. This was the first of many such measures that were to run alongside developing religious problems in Spain and Europe. Thus, a proclamation of 1558 established administrative and doctrinal control based on a complex formalized system, reinforced by the appearance in 1559 of expurgatory indices and lists of forbidden books drawn up by Fernando Valdés, Inquisitor General 1547–66. The reign of Philip II (1556–98) saw increasingly severe legislation: originally it attempted to regulate the printed book as a commercial object, but finally it consisted of a complex web of measures treating the book as an intellectual and ideological product. The consequences were decisive for controlling the publication of spiritual and liturgical literature for laymen.

Imports, opportunism, and service to the Church—already observable in the earliest Spanish incunable, Juan Parix's *Sinodal de Aguilafuente* (Segovia, 1472)—are three of the chief characteristics of early Spanish printing. The use of roman type in the first product of the Spanish press distinguishes it from the gothic type employed in most early Spanish printing. This peculiarity reveals Spain's dependence on foreign models for its printing: prominent workshops employed foreign experts, including Parix, Heinrich Botel, Paul Hurus, Mathaeus Flander, Peter Brun, Nicolaus Spindeler, and Johannes de Salsburga, as printers. Before coming to Spain, European journeymen printers (principally Germans) passed through Italy and France; as a result, they stocked the type cases of their new Spanish offices with founts collected on their travels, their work reflecting their native customs and preferences.

Parix's Spanish output illustrates other printing tendencies. His second series of printed books—e.g. Escobar's *Modus Confitendi* (1471-2), and Pontanus' *Singularia Iuris* (c.1473)—all demonstrate the desire to open up broader geographical markets. These works, associated with university studies, tested possible demand for establishing production centres close to towns where the *studia generalia* (the great medieval universities) flourished. The Church and the universities were the driving forces of publishing and printing in Spain; they provided the texts and a guaranteed market for printers and stationers. They also financed many editions of religious books.

From 1475, gothic and roman types were both employed in Spanish incunable printing, but gothic dominated production well into the 16th century. Gothic type remained in use for legal printing, and it appeared in popular productions such as broadsides until well into the 18th century. Spanish gothic founts reveal the foreign influence in type design, and, to a certain extent, that influence lies behind the typographical features common to Castilian black-letter types.

Three stages of Castilian printing can be distinguished. From 1472 to 1478, there are records of only fifteen printing offices, of which nine had a printer whose name is known. Spanish printers worked in Seville and Valencia; in the rest of Spain, presses were run by foreign master printers. The names of most printers working in the northern Castilian Meseta remain unknown, except for

Parix (at Segovia and perhaps also at Salamanca). Both the language of the works produced (seven in Latin, five in vernaculars) and the types employed (eight in roman, four in gothic) reflect the need to meet the demands of a precise and ready market in the midst of manifest technical limitations.

From 1480 to 1490, presses were distributed more widely. In Castile, they extended over both Mesetas. Printing took root in urban centres with established markets. Workshops were set up in university and commercial towns: Salamanca, Valladolid, Toledo (Juan Vázquez), Huete (Álvaro de Castro), Burgos (Fadrique de Basilea), and Zamora (Antonio de Centenera, focusing on university courses at Salamanca). Almost all the printers of the day used a particular international gothic type, even at Coria and León. The quality of the editions improved, incorporating native engraving and wood engraving. In *Los doze trabajos de Hércules* (Zamora, 1483), for example, Centenera considerably advanced the illustration of literary works, a practice that would flourish in the 16th century.

From 1491 to 1500, native gothic types were improved and new, foreign types also appeared. The gothic designed by the brothers Baptista and Gregorio de Tortis, for example, became fundamental to Hispanic typography. Fadrique de Basilea at Burgos, the anonymous printing office at Salamanca, and Peter Hagembach in Toledo, all used these Venetian typefaces. At Valladolid, Juan de Francourt employed a new gothic typeface of Parisian design for *Tratado de confesión* (1492), *Ordenanzas reales de la audiencia y chancillería de Valladolid* (1493), and Díaz de Toledo's *Notas del relator* (1493). Publishing output grew and became more refined: page design began to be richly ornamented, and illustrated editions appeared from workshops whose importance grew. These years also witnessed the appearance of Arnao Guillén de Brocar, one of the principal printers during the reign of the Catholic Monarchs. He was active or had a commercial presence in Pamplona (Navarre), Logroño (Rioja), Alcalá de Henares, Burgos, Toledo and Salamanca (Castile), Seville (Andalusia), and Saragossa (Aragon).

By European standards, 15th-century Spain had a small printing output, although its presses produced more than Belgian or English workshops. Spanish printing was competitive chiefly because more than half of its publications were in the vernacular (Castilian and Catalan). In this respect, Spain led Europe. Spain's production of liturgical and legal texts was also the highest in Europe. The geographical radius of its printing activity is equally significant: only a quarter of Spain's output emerged from Catalonian and Valencian presses. The Castilian cities, with good communications, relied on long-established commercial fairs and a civic elite active in the import and export business. Castile's commercial prosperity and the growth of its governmental administration and universities ensured that printing became a permanent industry.

The Catholic Monarchs' legal measures to stimulate printing and the book trade were potent weapons in their establishment. Printers' exemption from military service and the reduction of taxes on book imports served to encourage the book trade and turn it into an attractive mercantile sector. These measures also included incentives for citizens to enter the trade, and for foreign printers to consider Spain, and later Portugal, countries with favourable employment prospects, especially during the European economic crisis towards the end of the 15th century.

Seville was well suited to immigrant German printers, and in 1490 a group of them was invited to make the city a typographical centre. The aim was for them to collaborate with the *studia*, a typical arrangement in other European university cities. However, an analysis of Sevillan production shows that publications there went beyond academic matters. Meinardus Ungut and Stanislaus Polonus came from Naples and formed a printing company in Seville to meet the official aim of producing editions of works on civil and ecclesiastical law that previously had been scattered and inaccessible. *El libro en que están compiladas algunas bulas*, printed by Polonus years later in Alcalá de Henares (1503), testifies to the aim of publishing a legal canon to standardize juridical and legislative provision.

Sevillan printers produced the highest proportion of vernacular books in all Spain. Across a broad range of genres—medicine and law, liturgical works, and translations and adaptations of the classics—only a third were in Latin. Moreover, a national literature was developing that included histories of Castile, vernacular devotional works, and books for entertainment. The publication of Ludolf of Saxony's *Vita Christi*, translated by Ambrosio Montesino and printed by Polonus at Alcalá de Henares (1502, 1503), was subsidized by the government, despite its being a religious work. It demonstrates the Spanish monarchy's desire to rival the magnificent illustrated edition (in four volumes, printed by two Germans) financed by the Portuguese monarchs in 1495.

The introduction of printing in Portugal, however, was not associated with royal power, but rather with the Jewish community (*see* **8**). Works printed in Hebrew were the first to appear from 1487 (*Pentateuco*, printed by Samuel Gacon in Faro); these were set in imported types, easily obtained by an international community with commercial ties to Paris, Livorno, Genoa, Naples, Antwerp, and Amsterdam. The type designs found in these incunables reflect a desire to embellish the biblical text. The quality of their execution may be explained by collaboration, before the arrival of printing, between an important centre of Luso-Hebraic calligraphers and the probably Jewish school of xylography connected to local scriptoria. The neighbouring paper mills established in 1411 helped foster the emergence of the main Hebraic printing offices at Faro, Lisbon, and Leiria. The seven incunables from the first press (1489–92) in Lisbon—that of Rabbi Eliezer Toledano—employ characters and ornamental borders closely related to those created in Hijar (Aragon) by the Hebrew printer Eliezer ben Alantansi (1485–90). The similarity of name and typeface suggests that this printer possibly migrated. Between 1488 and 1495, printing moved from the coastal region to the interior of Portugal, and the spread of Judaic and Christian bibliography connected with biblical exegesis lasted until the decree expelling the Jews in 1497. The last Hebrew press was that of Samuel Dortas in Leiria, ending its activities in 1496 with three editions of Abraham Zacuto's *Almanach Perpetuum*, now with the text in Latin. These firms began printing in Hebrew, but later in Latin, Castilian, and Portuguese. In Spain, the crisis facing Hebrew printing had already occurred in 1492, the year of the expulsion, causing the disappearance of the presses of Juan de Lucena (1475) at La Puebla de Montalbán (Toledo), Solomon Alkabiz (1476–82) at Guadalajara, and those at Zamora and Hijar that had provided synagogues' liturgical needs, including exegetical readings.

Portuguese incunables, both Latin and vernacular, reveal the importance of the Church and the Crown in such titles as: *Tratado da Confissom* (Chaves, attributed to Randolfo, 1489); *Constituições do Bispado do Porto* (Rodrigo Álvares, 1497); and *Breviarium Bracarense* (Braga, 1494), printed by Johann Gherlinc, an immigrant from Barcelona, where he operated 1486–9. Ludolf of Saxony's *De Vita Christi*, translated into Portuguese by the Alcobaça Cistercians, is a fine example of foreign participation in Portuguese typography. In 1495, the Germans Nicolaus of Saxony and Valentinus of Moravia (who adopted the Portuguese name Valentim Fernándes under the protection of João II) produced this emblematic work in four volumes, decorated with woodcut borders, chapter-headings, and engravings of German provenance. Fernandes was the first to be granted the royal privilege to print and sell Marco Polo's *Travels* (1502).

2 From the 16th century to the Baroque period

During the 16th century, Portuguese printing progressed slowly. The Lisbon presses remained in foreign hands: Jakob Cromberger, a member of a German family established in Seville; Germão Galharde, a Frenchman; and Giovanni Petro Buonhomini (active 1501–14), an Italian who also worked in association with Fernándes, using the name of João Pedro de Cremona. With João Álvares (1536–c.1587), originally holding the privilege of printer to the University of Coimbra, a group of native printers emerged. Luís Rodrigues (Lisbon 1539–49) improved typography and added the use of italics. In 1564 António Gonçalves, assistant to Duarte Nunes de Leão, obtained his licence and devoted the greater part of his output to religious and moral works; in the *Espejo del Principe Christiano* he appears as printer to the archbishop of Lisbon. The *editio princeps* of *Os Lusíadas* (1572) marks the start of a prolific epoch in Rodrigues's workshop. Camões's influence—based on his experience on the Malabar coast—is reflected in editions from 1573: *Sucesso do Segundo Cerco de Diu* (1574) and *História da provincia de sãta Cruz* (1576). António Ribeiro (1574–90), was the King's Printer from 1580; António Álvares, was printer to the archbishop of Lisbon; and Francisco Correia, the royal printer and printer to Cardinal Don Enrique, rented his printing office from Johannes Blavius in 1564 and continued printing in Lisbon until 1581. From the middle of the century, Lisbon again depended on important foreign master printers. Among these were: Blavius, from Cologne who settled in Lisbon between 1551 and 1563, and Pedro Craesbeeck, a Flemish disciple of Plantin's, who established his Lisbon printing office in 1597 and produced a fundamental work for the history of the Portuguese language, *Origem da Lingua Portuguesa* (1605) by Nunes de Leão. Craesbeeck and his son António held the title of royal printer until it passed to the Frenchman Miguel Deslandes.

The period of Portugal's annexation to Spain (1580–1640) had repercussions for written culture and for the activities and allegiances of the printing trades. Lourenço de Anvers, printer to the duke of Bragança, and Valente de Oliveira both printed periodicals, *gazetas*, and *mercúrios*. Domingo Lopes de Rosa and António Olivares, through minor and occasional publications, supported the Portuguese political cause. During the 16th century, Spanish presses published works in Portuguese: liturgical books commissioned by the Braga diocese at Salamanca, legal works, and the Manueline *Ordenações* at Seville (Cromberger, 1521, 1525). With the Annexation, both countries published significant works of imperial policy. Political events and permeable frontiers explain the phenomenon of 'flying printers' between Spain and Portugal (e.g. Tanco de Frejenal).

The early years of the 16th-century Spanish printing scene brought increased attention to Seville, where works including Juan del Encina's *Cancionero* and Nebrija's *Introductiones* represented contributions to national literacy and linguistic history. An active family enterprise began with Jakob Cromberger in 1503. The intellectual circle surrounding Seville cathedral and the city's academy—Pedro Núñez Delgado, López de Cortegana, and Jerónimo Pinelo—had their books printed by Cromberger, his son Johann, and above all by the latter's widow, Brígida Maldonado, who supervised the printing of Juan de Cazalla's works (*Lumbre del alma*, 1542), as well as *Doctrina Cristiana* and the *Confesionario* by Domingo de Valtanás (1544). The Crombergers printed the first Spanish translations of Desiderius Erasmus (*Querella de la paz* (1520), *Enchiridion* (1528?), *Los coloquios* (1529), and *La lengua* (1533, 1535, 1542). Spanish Erasmianism had another active printing office in Castile, that of Miguel de Eguía, Brocar's son-in-law. Eguía's press at Alcalá de Henares, a university city and focus of intellectual reform, issued the monumental Complutensian Bible (1514–17). In 1529, Eguía also printed an anonymous edition of the *Diálogo de Doctrina Christiana* by Juan de Valdés, whose condemnation by the Inquisition prompted his journey to Italy.

The reformers, including Juan and Alfonso de Valdés, exemplified the supporting role of European presses in the spread of Erasmianism: the *Diálogo de Lactancio* or *Lactancia*, together with the *Diálogo de Mercurio y Carón*, were printed in Spain in 1529. In 1531 the Inquisition banned the publication, and Juan and Alfonso de Valdés appeared in the indexes of prohibited books at Milan and Venice in 1554, and at Portugal in 1581. The *Lactancio* was printed on its own (bearing a false imprint) in Spanish at Paris in 1586. Another edition (*Dialogo en que particularmente se tratan las cosas acaecidas en Roma*,

Oxford: Joseph Barnes, 1586), was produced by Antonio del Corro, whose Protestantism obliged him to leave Spain. At the insistence of the earl of Leicester, he was appointed theological censor at Christ Church, Oxford (1578–86); he founded the Spanish Protestant Church. Queen Elizabeth I's protection enabled Spanish exiles to continue their intellectual work; English presses played a fundamental role in publishing books written by Spaniards persecuted for religious and political motives. Spain, for its part, supported English Catholics and, through the Jesuits, encouraged a secret press for the English mission and the establishment of another press in the English College at St Omer to produce Counter-Reformation works for distribution among recusants.

There were also other reasons for European countries to involve themselves energetically in the market for Spanish books. The consequences of the Council of Trent (1545–63) were decisive. The *Nuevo rezado* required the immediate and huge production of liturgical books beyond the capacity of the Spanish presses. Philip II granted the right to print these books to foreigners who possessed the necessary technical and economic means. Christopher Plantin, appointed chief King's Printer in 1570, was the great beneficiary of this measure that proved so adverse for the national book industry. The fact that the Spanish monarchy had possessions outside the Iberian Peninsula explains why presses in the Low Countries (Brussels and Antwerp) or in Italy (Milan and Naples) should have produced Spanish works for sale not only in Spain and America, but for the European trade. From the 15th century, Spain's principal book imports were Latin works from Italy and Germany. There was considerable European involvement in the Spanish book trade, including the financing of occasional publications.

At the beginning of the 16th century in Catalonia, Venetians such as the bookseller Francesco de Moris represented and acted on behalf of a wide network of booksellers from Venice and from Genoa; the latter were also active in the paper trade. In Valencia, Giovanni Battista Riquelme and Lorenzo Ganoto, both merchants from Savona, financed the *Suma de todas las crónicas del mundo* (printed by Gorge Costilla in 1510) and the *Cancionero General* (printed by Christoph Kaufmann in 1511). In Castile, Francesco Dada and Giovanni Tomasso Favario financed Andrés de Burgos in 1505 to print Encina's *Cancionero* on his Burgos presses. Melchior Gorricio subsidized Hagembach's editions in Toledo. From the 1520s, the companies of bookseller-stationers who were related to the great printing houses of Italy or Lyons (Giunta, Portonariis, Boyer) turned from controlling book imports to book production and publishing through their Castilian sub-offices in Salamanca or Valladolid. They maintained an active presence in the fairs at Medina del Campo; the Giunta family set up in Saragossa, Burgos, Salamanca, and Madrid; Guillaume Rouillé, the outstanding Lyons publisher, created a powerful commercial network. The Lyons publishers—the Cardon brothers, Philippe Borde, and Claude Rigaud— strongly supported Catholic reform by financing Jesuit and Dominican authors in the Iberian Peninsula.

Royal, noble, and patrician book-collecting in Spain provides an excellent vantage point for observing the vitality and shape of the book trade. As the collections and rare items belonging to individual bibliophiles became available, three exceptional libraries were created: the Columbine Library, the Casa del Sol library, and the Royal Library of Philip II, also known as the Escorial Library. The Columbine Library in Seville houses the collection of the humanist Hernando Colón (1488–1539), son of Christopher Columbus, while the Casa del Sol library in Valladolid, which is essential for studying the Anglo-Spanish book trade, contains the holdings of the count of Gondomar, who served as Philip III's ambassador in London (1613–18, 1620–22).

The poor quality of paper and ink and the worn types of many later 16th-century books testify to the generally low standards of bookmaking at a time when the world of Spanish letters was reaching its zenith. Although Spanish presses were generally undistinguished, production was increasing considerably, religion, history, law, and cartography being the dominant subjects. Closely linked to Spanish political and economic development during the reigns of the later Habsburg monarchs, there was a proliferation of minor printing in the form of news-sheets, *arbitrios*, and reports. Post-Tridentine spiritual practices led to an increase in sermons and devotional literature consonant with the new urban religious sensibility and sociability. Nevertheless, the printing industry and book trade began to decline in the last quarter of the 16th century. The lack of technical resources and skilled operatives became evident, especially in the early decades of the 17th century, when the wish to publish in Spain still existed. But the decisive causes of the decline were religious and civil censorship, interventions by the Inquisition, royal privileges permitting monopolies of sales and of printing liturgical books, together with the lack of essential materials and means. The shortage of trained professionals is palpable: around 1640 in Madrid there were only ten printing offices with some 50 master printers and pressmen, and 45 people in the bookselling trade.

Madrid, a great printing centre from 1560 to 1580, also boasted the Imprenta Real (Royal Press), set up by an agreement between Philip II and Juan de Junta (a Florentine printer belonging to the Giunti family, who had started printing at Salamanca). In contrast with more ordinary productions, this workshop's output represented the splendour of the Baroque, creating outstanding illustrated books with characteristic architectural title-pages—portico and altarpiece—designed by important Spanish and foreign artists, especially Flemish engravers (Pedro Perret, Juan Schorquens, Jean de Courbes, Juan de Noort, Pedro de Villafranca), such as João Lavanha's *Viaje a Portugal de Felipe III* (1622). The works of great Spanish authors of the Golden Age—Góngora's *Soledades* (1635) and his *Polifemo* (1629)—were set in type at the Imprenta Real as well as at other Madrid printing offices. Under Juan de la Cuesta's imprint (1604–25) appeared Cervantes's *Don Quixote*, part I (1605) and *Novelas ejemplares* (1613), Lope de Vega's *Arcadia* (1610) and *Jerusalén conquistada* (1609), and Ercilla's *Araucana* (1610). Luis Sánchez, who had the best pressmen and was also a publisher and bookseller, printed Pedro Mexía's *Silva de varia lección* (1602).

The printing office visited by Alonso Quijano (*Don Quixote*, part II, chapter 62) has been identified with the outstanding firm in Barcelona at that time, owned by Sebastián Cormellas. His presses were divided between two establishments, one in El Call and the other in Plaça de Sant Jaume. Before Don Quixote's fictional arrival, he had already brought out *Lazarillo de Tormes* (1599), *Guzmán de Alfarache* (1599), and Montemayor's *La Diana* (1614). The Prologue to *Quixote*, part I, reconstructs in masterly fashion the complexity of the Spanish book during the Golden Age.

On the Spanish Levante, Valencia maintained its leading place as a printing centre; a number of its successful families—Mey, Macé, and Gárriz—demonstrate the benefits to be obtained from the printing trade. In Aragon, the Dormer, Larumbe, and Lanaja families maintained a high level of book production at Saragossa. Seville continued as the main Andalusian centre; the widow of Nicolás Rodríguez is associated with a typical illustrated genre, the festival book, which reproduces ephemeral architecture (e.g. Torre Farfán, *Las Fiestas de S. Iglesia de Sevilla*, 1671). In Old Castile, the presses remained active at Valladolid, the capital of Spain under Philip III between 1601 and 1606, with established printing offices (Fernández de Córdoba) and printers such as Luis Sánchez, who operated there and in Madrid, and Godínez de Millis who also had premises at Medina del Campo.

3 From the Enlightenment to the 20th century

The Spanish and Portuguese Enlightenment modernized the legal, industrial, and economic aspects of the printed book. Lisbon reflected this vitality: the number of booksellers swelled to 750, mostly of Portuguese origin. A similar increase occurred among the printers, especially from 1756 onwards. Until José I's death in 1777, the marquis of Pombal's political programme, most notably the expulsion of the Jesuits in 1759, promoted this noteworthy growth. In Spain, a change of dynasty began to take place in 1700 with the death of Charles II. The house of Bourbon entered Spain with Philip V (born at Versailles in 1683), who reigned 1700–1746. Thus began a process of profound modernization and accommodation with the European Enlightenment, which would reach its apogee during the second half of the century and the reign of Philip's nephew Charles III (1759–88). New legislation supported efforts to promote the commercialization of the book, but the measures sharply divided different sectors of the book trade. In 1752, legislation against the import of books failed because of fierce opposition from Spanish booksellers; but the law of 1754, promulgated by Ferdinand VI (1746–59), successfully regulated trading in imported books. It demanded a special royal authorization for works in Spanish by native authors, and imposed a tax by the Council of State on every foreign printed book imported for sale. The bookbinders opposed imports because they took away their business, and in 1778 they succeeded in obtaining a legal measure that allowed the import only of unbound books, those in paper wrappers, or those with old bindings. The government's strategy of attempting to break the centuries-old dependence of Spanish booksellers on foreign products was designed to promote domestic production by making it difficult to import books and by fostering local trade associations. Between 1758 and 1763, Madrid saw the creation of the Royal Company of Printers and Booksellers, which principally used Joaquín Ibarra y Marín's printing office. In 1759 the Compañía de Impresores y Libreros de Valencia was formed, followed four years later by the Royal Company of Printers and Booksellers of Madrid. Supported by the government, this limited company aimed to recover parts of the market traditionally dependent on foreign presses.

With Charles III came approval for the free pricing of books, the first measures to control periodical publications, and recognition of the exclusive rights of authors and their heirs. Responsibility for censorship rested with the cultural institutions of government, such as the royal academies. A law of 1768 enshrined the intervention of the Inquisition in the printing of books. The Imprenta Real collaborated with other institutions such as the Royal Academy of Fine Arts, producing such publications as *Retratos de los españoles ilustres* (1791), a monumental work that engendered pride in the Spanish Enlightenment. This attitude was reflected in the publication of Juan Sempere y Guarinos's six-volume bibliography *Ensayo de una Biblioteca española de los mejores escritores del reynado de Carlos III* (1785–9).

Education was to be encouraged and national pride recovered by publishing the country's historical sources as well as the classical and contemporary works essential for enlightened thought. These texts were to be translated into Spanish by great authors who would help to create a national consciousness and restore the purity of the language. This initiative is represented by such publications as: *Los Diez libros de Architectura de M. Vitruvio Polione, traducidos y comentados por Don Joseph Ortíz y Sanz* (1787) and Conyers Middleton's *La vida de Cicerón*, translated by Nicolás de Azara (1790). The Biblioteca del Palacio Real, founded in 1711, collaborated in this undertaking as a supplier of texts and as a publishing house. Nicolás Antonio's national bibliography—*Bibliotheca Hispana Nova* (Ibarra, 1783–8); *Bibliotheca Hispana Vetus* (widow and heirs of Ibarra, 1788)—is a product of that cooperation. One indication of Spain's resurgent importance is the fact that both John Baskerville (*Specimen of the Word Souverainement in 11 sizes*, 1766) and Giambattista Bodoni (1776) travelled to Madrid to present samples of their types for the royal press.

The state also sought to make Spanish de luxe publishing competitive throughout Europe. Books of quality emerged from the Madrid workshops of Ibarra, Antonio de Sancha, and Benito Cano, and from printing offices in Valencia run by Antonio Bordazar (active 1701–40), Benito Monfort y Besades, José Orga, father and son (1744–1808), and Salvador Fauli (1742–1800). The engravers from the Academy of Fine Arts worked for these printers on editions that are justly famous today, such as a Sallust (*Conjuración de Catalina y Guerra de Yugurta*, translated by the Infante Don Gabriel Antonio, son of Charles III, 1772), and the *Quixote* of the Academy (edited by the Real Academia Española, 1780), both printed by Ibarra. Bodoni was appointed royal printer, in part because the dukedom of Parma was linked to the Spanish royal family. Typography and the allied book arts improved considerably, to some extent because government grants to printers, engravers, and binders allowed many to have professional training in Paris or London. The type specimen books of the era—by Antonio Espinosa (1766, 1771, and 1780), Gerónimo Antonio Gil (1774), the convent of San José in Barcelona (1777 and 1801), the Palacio Real (1787), the Royal Press (1788 and 1799), the widow of Eudal Paradell (1793), and Francisco Ifern (1795)—bear witness to typographical advances mainly concentrated in Madrid, Barcelona, and Valencia. One of the most interesting and wide-ranging of contemporary bookmen was Antonio de Sancha; a bookseller, printer, publisher, and binder. Among the re-editions of the Spanish Golden Age published by the elder Sancha is the poetic anthology *Parnaso español* (1768–78), a nine-volume compilation of the best Castilian poets illustrated with their portraits. His son Gabriel produced the exquisite volumes of both parts of *Quixote* (1797–8, 1798–9).

The chronicles of Spanish history were republished in monumental style by the academic movement: the *Crónica de Juan II* (Valencia: Monfort, 1779), for example, rivalled in political design the handsome edition printed by Brocar in Logroño in 1517. The Spanish monarchy's links with the Kingdom of the Two Sicilies and the dukedom of Parma widened the ambit of Spanish printing to Italy. From the middle of the 18th century until the death of Ferdinand VII (1833), Spanish binding also enjoyed a period of splendour; and although French and English influences were manifest, royal binders such as the Sanchas, Gabriel Gómez, Carsí y Vidal, Santiago Martín, and Antonio Suárez Jiménez developed techniques in which the mosaic, 'cortina', Valencian, and Spanish tree calf styles stood out.

From 1808 political problems—royal exile, the Peninsular War (1808–14), constitutionalism, and Ferdinandine absolutism—delayed until the 1840s the modernization of printing that had taken place in the rest of Europe. Nevertheless, the period of transition between the *ancien régime* and modern society is of great interest for publishing history. Spain, an invaded country that was developing a parliamentary system of government, adopted new uses for printed material, including propaganda, ephemeral patriotic literature, and newspapers. The mechanization of book production had a special impact on Madrid and above all Barcelona, which, impelled by Catalonian industrial development, became a powerful urban printing centre during the 19th century. Towards the end of the century, the *indianos*, or rich colonists returning from America, provided capital, brought new marketing techniques, and favoured the launch of a book industry that relied on the collaboration of the magnificent *noucentisme* artists.

Espasa-Calpe, a remarkable Spanish publishing house that connects the 19th and 20th centuries, employed a business model favoured by industrial societies. Espasa, the family imprint (Barcelona, 1860), formed an association with Salvat (1869–97) and captured the market in translations of French books. The firm launched a magazine of high quality (*El Mundo Ilustrado*), bought the rights of Brockhaus & Meyer (1905), and the plates of *Meyers Großes Konversations-Lexikon*. Later, with a committee of 33 editors and more than 600 collaborators, the firm published the *Enciclopedia Espasa*. In 1925, now merged with Calpe and assisted by a favourable contract with Papelera Española, the national paper-making company, Espasa opened an innovative, all-embracing bookshop in the Gran Vía in Madrid. La Casa del Libro was stocked with their older flagship series of scholarly texts: Clásicos Castellanos and their more popular Colección Austral, launched in 1937 by their Buenos Aires office during the Spanish Civil War.

The Second Spanish Republic (1931–6) brought in a policy of promoting books and of integrated publishing that supported education and the diffusion of culture. Intellectuals associated with the Institución Libre de Enseñanza (Free Institute for Teaching) and members of La Generación del 27 (The Generation of 1927) founded important periodicals: the *Revista de Occidente*, directed by the philosopher José Ortega y Gasset between 1923 and 1936; *Litoral*, edited by Emilio Prados and Manuel Altolaguirre; *Gaceta Literaria*, edited by José Bergamín between 1933 and 1936; *Caballo Verde para la Poesía*, edited by Neruda; and *Octubre*, founded by Rafael Alberti and María Teresa León. They also published books of high quality via private presses (Manuel Altolaguirre-Concha Zardoya). Silverio Aguirre was the Madrid printer most involved with the Silver Age authors, and Signo the most representative publisher.

Argentina and Mexico, countries that welcomed the Spanish Republican exiles from 1939, provided continuity for this intellectual publishing movement (Losada, Emecé, Séneca, and *Sur*) (*see* **48**). In postwar Spain, poetry magazines such as *Garcilaso* or *Vértice* were the heirs, albeit under a Fascist banner, of the aesthetics and high standards of 1930s printing. The annual publishers' prizes awarded by Nadal (1944) and Planeta (1952) encouraged literary publishing. Editorial Aguilar promoted high production values with its three differently sized series, 'Obra Completa', 'Crisol', and 'Crisolín', all printed on India paper and bound in leather. In Valencia, María Amparo and Vicente Soler (Tipografía Moderna) launched their exquisitely produced series for bibliophiles, 'La fonte que mana y corre' (1945–75). Collaboration between Amparo-Soler and the bibliophile Antonio Rodríguez-Moñino saw the launch of Editorial Castalia in Madrid and its flagship series in 1969, Clásicos Castalia, which has since proliferated in series for all ages of reader: Castalia Prima, Castalia Didáctica, and Escritoras Madrileñas, to name a few. This collaboration gave continuity, in the midst of the dreary postwar Spanish publishing scene, to the Republican tradition of careful critical editing.

Francisco Pérez González created the publishing house Taurus in 1955, with Gutiérrez Girardot and Miguel Sánchez. Later on, Santillana, under Jesús Polanco's direction, consolidated and gave security to the publishing industry. Juan Salvat joined the family firm in 1955 and ran Salvat Editores until 1992, when it was sold to Hachette. He introduced door-to-door selling of weekly parts or fascicles; his programme for revolutionizing the distribution system was adopted by Circulo de Lectores and Grupo Zeta. In 1959, Germán Sánchez Ruipérez founded Anaya, which became a leader in educational texts and is now incorporated into the Santillana Group. Beatriz de Moura founded Editorial Tusquets in 1969 after working at Lumen, created by Esther Tusquets. Their series 'Marginales' and 'Cuadernos Ínfimos' became essential for short-story readers and authors. Jorge Herralde founded Anagrama in 1969 and created the prizes Ensayo (best essay, 1973) and Herralde de Novela (best novel, 1983). Carlos Barral and Jaime Salinas, promoters of the Formentor Prize at the end of the 1950s, internationalized Spanish publishing at Seix Barral and introduced the Latin American Boom writers at Alfaguara. Alianza Editorial (with its pocket editions designed by Daniel Gil), Siglo XX, Taurus, and Cuadernos para el Diálogo, were all symbols of progressive quality of popular publishing in the late Francoist era.

....

BIBLIOGRAPHY

A. Anselmo, *Origens da imprensa em Portugal* (1981)

—— *História da edição em Portugal*, 1 *Das origens até 1536 (1991)*

P. Berger, *Libro y lectura en la Valencia del Renacimiento* (1987)

Bibliografia Geral Portuguesa, Século XV (2 vols, 1941–2)

BMC 10

J. Delgado Casado, *Diccionario de impresores españoles (Siglos XV–XVII)* (1966)

—— and J. Martín Abad, *Repertorios bibliográficos de impresos del siglo XVI* (1993)

V. Deslandes, *Documentos para a história da tipografia portuguesa nos séculos XVI e XVII*, ed. A. Anselmo (1988)

J. Domínguez Bordona, *Manuscritos con pinturas* (1933)

M. Fernández Valladares, *La imprenta en Burgos, 1501–1600* (2005)

C. Griffin, *The Crombergers of Seville* (1988)

—— *Journeymen-Printers, Heresy, and the Inquisition in Sixteenth-Century Spain* (2005)

F. Guedes, *Os livreiros em Portugal e as suas associações desde o século XV até aos nossos dias* (1993)

[*Leituras,*] *O livro antigo em Portugal e Espanha, séculos XVI–XVIII/El libro Antiguo en Portugal y España, Leituras*: *Revista da Biblioteca Nacional*, 3.9–10 (2002)

M. L. López-Vidriero and P. M. Cátedra, eds., *El libro antiguo español* (3 vols, 1992–6)

J. P. R. Lyell, *Early Book Illustration in Spain* (1926)

M. de la Mano González, *Mercaderes e impresores de libros en la Salamanca del siglo XVI* (1998)

F. J. Norton, *A Descriptive Catalogue of Printing in Spain and Portugal, 1501–1520* (1978)

M. Peña Díaz, *Libro y lectura en Barcelona, 1473–1600* (1995)

—— *El laberinto de los libros: historia cultural de la Barcelona del Quinientos* (1997)

W. A. Pettas, *A History and Bibliography of the Giunti (Junta) Printing Family in Spain, 1526–1628* (2005)

J. V. de Pina Martins, *Para a história da cultura portuguesa do Renascimento: A iconografia do livro impresso em Portugal no tempo de Dürer* (1972)

Real Biblioteca (Madrid), *Encuadernaciones de la Real Biblioteca*, www.encuadernacion.realbiblioteca.es, consulted May 2008

The History of the Book in Italy

NEIL HARRIS

1 Introduction

Histories of the book in Italy, especially those assessing the impact of printing, often follow a predictable and all too conventional narrative pattern. They open with the German printers—who began publishing the works of antiquity at Subiaco in 1465 and at Rome in 1467—before switching to Venice in 1469, where yet more German printers and a French goldsmith cut the first roman types. They usually describe the extraordinarily rapid spread of printing through the Italian cities: Trevi and Foligno in 1470; Bologna, Ferrara, Florence, Milan, Naples, and Treviso, and possibly Genoa, Perugia, and Verona in 1471; Cremona, Fivizzano, Mantua, Mondovì, Padua, and Parma in 1472. Indeed, by 1500, presses had operated in almost 80 localities. They next offer detailed accounts of Aldus Manutius from 1495 onwards: his recovery of the Greek and Latin classics, his design of roman type, and his pocket-sized texts in italic. If space allows, they might say something about Venetian publishing's Renaissance dominance and praise its illustrated books, before jumping to an account of the unique visual achievement of Giambattista Bodoni in Parma at the end of the 18th century. The conclusions of such standard accounts often comment on modern publishing in Italy, on the rise of Milan, and (perhaps) on the bestseller *all'italiana* in the 1950s and 1960s. None of this is wrong, since the salient facts are correct; even so, such a view is at best superficial, and the same pattern can be seen in a different light.

Rather than begin with the itinerant typographers, it may be useful to glance at the state of the book trade in Italy just before the advent of printing. The chief figure is the Florentine bookseller Vespasiano da Bisticci, who organized on a huge and costly scale the copying and decoration of MSS for such clients as Cosimo de' Medici and Federico da Montefeltro. Late in life, Vespasiano included in his memoirs a spiteful jab at the printing press, which was putting traditional bookmakers like himself out of business. His jaundiced claim that Federico would never have allowed a printed text in his collection is unfounded, but revealing. It shows that it is misleading to apply to Italy the idea—intrinsic to Lucien Febvre's and Henri-Jean Martin's French concept of the history of the book—of a sharp rupture between printing and the MS tradition (*see* **15**), since, if anything, the two for a while flourished and intermingled.

In 1949, Roberto Ridolfi defined early printers as 'gente di necessità intesa alla moneta' ('people who are obliged to deal with money') (Ridolfi, 6). The German artisans, who hauled their possessions over the Alps on the back of a mule, had their eyes on a book market where fabulous sums were being paid for illuminated MSS on vellum. Italy was also undergoing a cultural revolution (characterized as 'the Renaissance' by 19th-century scholars) that consisted initially in the rediscovery of ancient Greek and Roman works. This innovation was prompted in part by the Council of Ferrara and Florence in 1438, which attempted a conciliation between the Western and Orthodox churches; although the council ultimately failed, it did establish a direct acquaintance with Greek culture and language, up to that time known to Italian intellectuals principally through medieval Latin. The subsequent fall of Byzantium (Constantinople) in 1453 precipitated a migration of Greek scholars, often with MSS in their baggage, who scraped a living in Italy through teaching. With its position athwart the Mediterranean, governing trade between West and East, with the wealth of its great banking families, and the influx of outside revenue ensured by the Catholic Church, 15th-century Italy (albeit fractured into feuding and sometimes warring states) was the richest and culturally fastest-moving 'country' in Europe. It was ripe, therefore, for a new way of making books.

2 The introduction of printing

Recent years have seen a lively discussion about the Parsons fragment, comprising eight leaves belonging to an octavo edition in Italian of the *Leiden Christi* (Passion of Christ), a popular German work circulated widely in northern Europe in the 15th century. Discovered in 1925 by the Munich bookseller Jacques Rosenthal, the fragment was described by Konrad Haebler in 1927, before disappearing the following year into the collection of the Louisiana bibliophile Edward Alexander Parsons (1878–1962); it was forgotten until 1998, when it resurfaced and was sold at auction by Christie's in London. The bibliographical excitement it generated stemmed from the large rotunda type, whose sorts have been filed to make them fit together, suggesting an early date of printing. Since its metal-cut illustrations were used in southern Germany c.1459–61, the edition may have been printed soon afterwards, almost certainly in Italy; linguistic analysis suggests that the translation was done in or near the triangle formed by Parma, Bologna, and Ferrara. If the assumptions about the date and place are correct, the fragment is unquestionably the first surviving printed Italian artefact. (This same rationale acknowledges, however, that other texts may have been produced even earlier and have been entirely lost.) Following its purchase for the Scheide collection in Princeton, the fragment was connected to a document written in Bondeno, near Ferrara, in February 1463, containing an agreement between a German priest, Paul Moerch, and his compatriot, Ulrich Purschmid (or Bauerschmid), from Baisweil, near Augsburg. The agreement refers to making terracotta figures of a Pietà and of a Virgin and Child; it also discusses shaping formes to produce a Latin grammar ('formam unius Donati'), a child's psalter ('formam unius Psalterii puerorum'), and an ABC for learning purposes ('formam unius Tabule puerorum'). It has been argued that the fragment and the agreement are closely related, so that the dawn of printing in Italy should be antedated to Bondeno, c.1463 (Scapecchi). Yet, however beguiling at first sight, the presumption is a dangerous one. In Latin, *forma* designates any surface used as a matrix, while the agreement as a whole suggests that Purschmid's expertise is in ceramic rather than casting in metal. Moreover, rudimentary printing techniques were employed in Italy in the pre-Gutenberg era. A Venetian document of 1441 talks of 'carte da zugar' and 'figure stampide' (playing cards and printed images); another of 1447 mentions 'alcune forme da stanpar donadi et salterj' ('some formes to print grammars and psalters')—two of the three items in the Bondeno document (Cecchetti). Although the 1463 agreement may well refer to a primitive process in which sheets were impressed on one side only from a surface moulded in relief, no verdict is yet possible on the Parsons fragment. Nonetheless, it does support the observation that, following the spread of printing north of the Alps, German artisans (who financed their move by printing small, easily sold books) might plausibly have arrived somewhere in the Po valley.

Unless an earlier example comes to light, it must be concluded that datable printing began in Italy when Conrad Sweynheym and Arnold Pannartz set a press up in Subiaco, a small town 70 km east of Rome. Why they settled there, at the Benedictine monastery of Santa Scolastica, unfortunately remains unknown. Their first printed text was a Donatus, which has been lost. The first to have survived, in some twenty copies, was Cicero's *De Oratore*; the edition is undated, but a copy once in Leipzig, now in Moscow, bears a note written on 30 September 1465. This was followed by a Lactantius in October and, in 1467, by Augustine's *De Civitate Dei*. Thereafter, they sensibly shifted business to Rome. The ups and downs of their subsequent enterprise are delineated in the prefaces and dedications of their editor, the bishop designate of Aleria, Giovanni

Andrea Bussi. Far from enjoying an overwhelming success, a combination of factors—including a policy of issuing large, humanist-orientated works, the overprinting of such sure sellers as Cicero, and competition from other Germans such as Ulrich Han (who in the meantime had gravitated to Rome)—ensured that, by the early 1470s, there was a book glut (Bussi). The early publishers' pecuniary embarrassment is symptomatic of a wider difficulty: they failed to harness the dynamics of an expanding but largely unknown market.

The standard view of Italian book history states that, by 1500, printing had gained a foothold in numerous cities; what is generally not mentioned is how often that foothold was lost. Usually, a press was set up and operated for a short period of time (sometimes producing only a single edition), before moving elsewhere. One example is Treviso, where printing was introduced by Geraert van der Lys in 1471; some eleven presses worked there until 1494, after which printing was extinguished until 1589. Geraert also inaugurated printing at Udine in 1484, where it lasted for a couple of years; the next press did not appear there until 1592. Unlike Germany, where printing, once established, in most cases persisted, in Italy it failed to take root just about everywhere. Only five Italian cities (Rome, Venice, Ferrara, Milan, and Bologna) maintained unbroken publishing activity up to and including the 16th century. In another five (Florence, Naples, Parma, Modena, and Turin), printing had a false start, but was introduced a second time and afterwards proceeded steadily. In another two (Brescia and Siena), the new *ars* ran well during the 15th century, once under way, but suffered major setbacks in the 16th century. To understand why the printing seed was often sown but rarely flowered, one episode is particularly instructive, because those involved went to court and left a sheaf of documentation. These legal records tell the story of the partnership between Johannes Vurster, who in 1473 introduced printing at Modena, and a local paper merchant, Cecchino Morano, who saw in it a chance to expand his business. The two turned out several large books aimed at nearby Bologna University, but failed to find a market. In 1476, after being sued by his partner and narrowly escaping imprisonment, Vurster fled town, leaving behind him a shop full of unsold volumes (Balsamo). Although supporting evidence of this quality is generally lacking, it is plausible that many such early ventures regularly teetered on the brink of financial disaster and sometimes plummeted into the abyss. After all, the foreign prototypographers lacked both the local market knowledge needed to distribute what they printed (hundreds of copies of the same book) and the depth of capital necessary for a more gradual sales policy. Although printing failed to establish itself in 85 per cent of the places it touched, one city rapidly triumphed over all the others: Venice.

3 Venice

Introduced by John of Speyer in 1469, printing in Venice burgeoned extraordinarily in just a few years. According to the *Incunabula Short Title Catalogue*

(ISTC), Venice produced some 3,500 known editions, putting Italy as a whole—with some 9,900 impressions—just ahead of Germany's 9,300, and far exceeding France's 4,500 items. Venice outstripped Paris, its main European rival, by 25 per cent, and issued double the number of editions produced by Rome, its principal Italian competitor. Yet the editions do not tell the full story. In Venice, half the recorded output was in folio format and only 9 per cent in octavo or smaller; in Paris, folio represented only 12 per cent, quarto 58 per cent, and octavo the rest; in Rome, folio stood at 15 per cent, quarto 68 per cent, octavo 17 per cent, while many items there were orations confined to a single sheet of paper or less. In other words, most Venetian books were big and those of other centres were conversely small. Although the distribution of books has been much disturbed over the course of centuries, censuses of 15th-century books conducted in outlying European districts show the extent of Venice's penetration: 23 per cent of incunabula now in Poland were printed in Venice, 27 per cent in Spain, 28 per cent in Hungary, 33 per cent in Portugal.

Venice's dominance inside Italy grew constantly, and the city acted as a publishing magnet, attracting other enterprises. Among the presses that disappeared from Treviso, several reappeared in its powerful neighbour a year or so later. Precise counts are never possible, but it is estimated that some 230 printing businesses were active in Venice before 1501. In simple terms, Venetian books were better. Not only were they better designed and better printed, they also used better paper and were usually the first to employ illustrations and paratextual elements, such as indexes. At the same time they were less expensive. Not surprisingly, therefore, booksellers and customers in cities all over Europe accorded their preference to Venetian products, so that local printers had to fall back on narrower markets. William Caxton's patriotism was genuine, but by publishing mostly in the vernacular, he tacitly admitted his inability to compete with the elegant Latin imprints of Nicolas Jenson and the like. The technical superiority of Venice appears above all in her printers' mastery of the more complex typographical procedures, such as liturgical texts in red and black. The existence, sometimes fragmentary, of breviaries and missals 'ad usum Sarum', for the diocese of Salisbury, bears witness to commissions received from the far-off English market. Once the industry was well established, continuity with the tradition of hand decoration was translated into supremely elegant woodcut illustrations, inspired by major artists such as Mantegna, which again increased the product's marketability. Likewise, European music printing, in which the staves, the notes, and sometimes the words required separate impressions, was dominated by Venetian firms, beginning with Ottaviano de' Petrucci in 1501 and followed later in the century by Antonio Gardano and Girolamo Scotto.

The question why this happened in Venice is rarely asked. Naples possessed a larger population, Florence was at the height of its Renaissance glory, while Rome boasted the luxury and splendour of the papal court. Italian cities such as Milan and Ferrara had ruling dynasties offering patronage, while Bologna,

Padua, and Pavia had flourishing universities. Albeit with a mountain range at its back, a city such as Genoa shared many similarities with Venice: a maritime republic, with a papermaking industry at nearby Voltri, and an almost identical political system, in which a doge was elected by a hereditary aristocracy. Yet printing there took several attempts to get off the ground, establishing itself securely only in 1534. What Venice had on a greater scale was a highly ramified mercantile and financial organization, definable as a predisposition to risk, based on the lucrative but financially dangerous trade with the Middle East and East Asia. Even before the time of Marco Polo, luxury commodities such as silk and spices had passed through Venice for distribution elsewhere in Europe. The economy of the city revolved around the *sortes* (shares) purchased in trading ventures, which, if successful, recouped the original investment several times over; if the ship failed to return, as in Shakespeare's *The Merchant of Venice*, the participants lost some or all of their money. The system involved society at all levels, even very small investors, such as widows and orphans; this induced a mentality in which Venetians instinctively grasped the economics of the new publishing business, where a raw commodity (paper) was transformed into a value-enhanced, finished product (printed text) that required further monies in order to distribute it and ensure a profit.

As far as an early concentration of capital is concerned, Jenson's career provides valuable insights. Known today for the marvellous *mise-en-page* of his editions and for a roman type surpassed only by Aldus, he was the front man for a publishing consortium that included the merchant-bookseller Peter Ugelheimer (Nuovo). The annals of his output can be read in ISTC, but a project worth undertaking would be an exhaustive census of surviving copies to establish what proportion were printed on vellum and how many were rubricated and/or illuminated. In the one edition subjected to such an inquiry, the 1478 folio Roman Breviary, 24 of the 45 known copies are vellum and almost all exhibit hand-added decoration of the first order (Armstrong). Publishing in the long term went in the opposite direction, as large, high-quality, hand-embellished, polychrome books on parchment (which approximated MSS) were replaced by small, sometimes shoddily printed, monochrome books on paper. Nonetheless, the luxury, high-cost product filled something more than a niche market; holding its own up to the beginning of the 16th century, it was fully exploited by Jenson, who was followed by Aldus and emulated in Paris by Antoine Vérard.

A book industry which produced vastly more than the local market could ever have absorbed had to export on a large scale. Venice's other great advantage was its pre-existent distribution network, allowing it to send goods via water along the Adriatic seaboard and through a system of rivers and canals covering the whole of northern Italy, as well as by road, with trains of mules that crossed the Alps into Germany and France. This same network was exploited in parallel by the paper and textile trades, with which the book trade had many affinities—some publishers are also known to have been cloth merchants. The concentration of commercial expertise from elsewhere in Italy ensured furthermore that, once the publishing industry was fully established, few in it were bona fide Venetians. The places of origin of the city's printers, proudly declared in the colophons of its Renaissance imprints, mostly form a pinpoint map of the Po valley, with a grouping of dots around Brescia and the Italian lakes (Toscolano on Lake Garda was also the heart of the Venetian papermaking industry) and, further off, the Piedmont town of Trino.

Venice's bookshops and printing offices were concentrated between the Rialto and St Mark's Square; from the Renaissance to the 18th century, travellers' accounts speak of a vast emporium, where buyers spent hours browsing in dozens and dozens of shops. An early measure of this intense bookselling activity is the *Zornale* of Francesco Maggi, which from 1484 to 1488 provides a record of each day's sales: entries are concise, usually no more than the title, but the ledger scrupulously records prices, which can be compared to other commodities, and the nature of the purchases. Although most items are sold singly, sometimes a buyer takes two, three, even up to twenty books together. At the same time, the book trade perceptible through the *Zornale* remains conservative; for all the speed with which Italian printers mastered the technology, their prime concern was to transfer the textual heritage of the Middle Ages into the new medium. As Victor Scholderer observed in 1935, 'while Italian incunabula form the most varied and interesting body of books of their class, the culture which they reveal is so fully elaborated as to appear to a large extent static' (*BMC* 7. xxxvii). Rather curiously, when the shake-up came, it was produced largely by a return to an even greater antiquity.

4 Aldus

The importance of being Aldus, to misquote Oscar Wilde, is undeniable. After that of Johann Gutenberg, his name is probably the best known in the whole of book history. On the other hand, although Gutenberg's claim to fame is established by his invention of the printing press, why precisely has Aldus gained such renown? After all, he was a latecomer to the profession; in 1495, when he opened shop, over 200 other presses had already worked or were working in Venice. While rivers of ink have been lavished on his achievement—and there is no doubt that there was an achievement—its nature is not always clear; indeed, it is necessary to remember that the first, and most diligent, purveyor of the myth of Aldus was Aldus himself. After his death in 1515, the Aldine brand was assiduously marketed for the rest of the century, first by the Torresani family, later by his direct heirs, so that, matters of *pietas* apart, the legend must have been good business. Consequently, the whole story abounds in pitfalls: even today some bibliographical writers assert that Aldus launched a 16th-century proto-paperback revolution with low-cost, octavo-format classics, despite the fact that his enchiridions were expensive by contemporary standards, so much so that it was profitable to counterfeit them in Lyons.

A proper assessment of Aldus would concentrate on his personality as a schoolteacher and on the fact that, like another remarkable typographical innovator, John Baskerville, he came to printing late in age by Renaissance terms, in his mid-40s. He did so in the guise of a frustrated intellectual, one who had failed to succeed as a humanist or as a scholar in the mould of his teacher, Battista Guarino. Education, therefore, was the lynchpin of the Aldine project, because he aimed not only at recovering the texts of classical antiquity, but at finding readers for them. He was the right man at the right time, but he also found the right collaborators: Torresani and the aristocrat Pierfrancesco Barbarigo, whose deep purses financed the enterprise; Francesco Griffo, whose extraordinary eye and hand produced the required typefaces; Marcus Musurus and Pietro Bembo, whose intellectual prestige and editorial abilities guaranteed the quality of the texts. The central idea was that the study of Greek and, to a lesser extent, Latin should be at the heart of the educational canon; however, the correct printing of Greek, with its numerous combinations of breathings and accents, presented a considerable obstacle. The first individual to overcome these challenges successfully, Aldus placed at the core of European pedagogical thinking the concept that the education of young gentlemen and of governing elites should be based on the intensive study of a remote dead language. The net outcome was that, for 400 years, students sweated over Aeschylus and Sophocles in the classroom, becoming adults who shared a common *forma mentis*.

Focusing on Aldus's part in this intellectual upheaval allows Italy's role in book history to be better defined. Most of the high moments in the canonical interpretation sketched out in the introduction of this essay have common ground in the same element: in a word, design. Early in 1496, after issuing his first books set entirely in Greek, Aldus published *De Aetna* with a new roman type that elaborated upon and strengthened Jenson's already remarkable character of 1470, and that, with refinements, culminated in the unreadable but visually splendid *Hypnerotomachia Poliphili*. The type's subsequent versions, remodelled by Claude Garamont, culminate in Stanley Morison's Times New Roman (1932), the common default character on today's computer screens. Yet, it remains recognizable as Aldus's offspring. Much the same is true of italic; the first Aldine design of 1501 may have no direct modern progeny, but nobody has ever questioned the significance of his innovation.

5 An interlude with factors and causes

By the end of 1500, the Italian publishing industry (mostly in Venice) had taken on a recognizable physiognomy that in many respects would remain unaltered until the fall of the Venetian Republic in 1797. However, its dominance and success simultaneously held the seeds of its own decline, one that would last for centuries. At the cost of some simplification, five interrelated factors are examined in this digression: political structure, new world exploration, religious reform, national language, and readership.

During this period, Italy had no single dominant political entity. The peninsula was broken into small states, of which the two strongest, Venice and the papacy, depended on the election of a gerontocrat ruler. In Venice, the doge was little more than a figurehead: real power generally rested with the faceless aristocrats of the Council of Ten. The system ensured political continuity, but constrained initiative, since the favoured policy was to hedge, block, and wait for the problem to go away. The papacy did elect a real ruler, but usually at an advanced age: an energetic figure, such as Julius II (r. 1503–13), could mould events, but reigns were so short that enemies rode out the storm. The political set-up meant, therefore, not only that there was no single central market represented by a capital (such as Paris or London), but also that, when by the late 18th century the book industry needed vigorous institutional measures, the Italian states were too weak and too divided to supply them.

The second event contributing to the long-term decline of the Italian publishing industry was the discovery of America in 1492 and of the sea route to the East in 1497–9, which gradually shifted the balance of power in Europe from the Mediterranean to the more dynamic nations along the Atlantic seaboard, gradually nullifying Venice's role as an entrepôt for trade with the Orient. The third historical consideration is the religious metamorphosis caused by the success of Protestant reform in northern Europe and by its failure in Italy. The long-term outcome of the Reformation was a gradual closing of the frontiers to the Italian book, linked also to the decline of Latin as a universal means of communication.

Although these first three factors were external to the book trade, the two remaining were internal, and require lengthier treatment, starting with the national language. From the 16th to the middle of the 20th century, an averagely educated Italian was expected to master two languages, apart from what was spoken at home, through schooling and reading. The first was classical Latin (often with the rudiments of Greek)—a dead language, but necessary to understand the importance of Italy's cultural heritage. The second language was Italian, which at that time was neither dead nor living. Outside school, the average Italian employed a dialect whose range of intelligibility varied considerably. In the north and in Tuscany, the same dialects covered large regions; in the agricultural and poverty-stricken regions of the south and in the islands, however, linguistic zones were more restricted, meaning that people living in one village could hardly talk to those 20 miles away. Italian's growth into a national spoken language is that of an artificial tongue, to some extent an ideology, that was largely book-disseminated. Its progress originated in two key periods. First, in the 14th century, three works written in Tuscan vernacular—Dante's *Divina Commedia*, Francesco Petrarca's *Rerum Vulgarium Fragmenta*, and Giovanni Boccaccio's *Decameron*—set new literary standards and started the long, slow march of European modern languages. Secondly, in the 16th century, Bembo decreed in his *Prose della Volgar Lingua* (1525) that the norm for written Italian should be Petrarca in poetry and Boccaccio in prose. To some extent, he only expressed as theory what had been posited previously by others, such as Fortunio's *Regole Grammaticali della Volgar Lingua* (1516), and what Venetian printers were already doing. What made the difference was his authority as a nobleman, as an editor, and as an author, who in 1539 received a cardinal's hat, in modern parlance 'for services to literature'. Bembo and his fellow theorists were not, however, concerned with whether the establishment of a single written norm would lead to a unified spoken language. That process would not occur for another four centuries, when other media were introduced.

The application of a Tuscan norm based on the literature of the Trecento (i.e. writers of whom the youngest was 30 years older than Chaucer) was facilitated by the example of Renaissance masterpieces such as the *Cortegiano* (1528). Written by the Mantuan career diplomat and papal nuncio Baldassarre Castiglione, the archetypal conduct book went through several drafts in order to obtain the right linguistic patina; it was seen through the press in the author's absence by a Venetian corrector, Giovan Francesco Valier, whose final emendations are visible in the printer's copy kept by the Aldine press and given to Jean Grolier. The case of the Ferrarese poet Ludovico Ariosto is even more interesting, since his *Orlando Furioso* (1532) continues an earlier poem, the *Orlando Innamorato* by Matteo Maria Boiardo, first published in 1482–3 in a lost *editio princeps*, with a third book added in 1495 (Harris). Telling the story of the paladin Roland—who falls in love with the beautiful but evil-intentioned Angelica and thus forsakes his duty to Charlemagne and to Christendom—Boiardo's story enthralled 15th-century readers with its breathtaking adventures and spectacular sword fights; however, it was written in a Po valley cadence, whose rhymes offended the ear of Italian purists. The first version of Ariosto's continuation, in 40 cantos, published in 1516 was a half-way stage that maintained dialect forms and rhymes; a partial revision appeared in 1521, followed by a fully-fledged Tuscanized definitive edition, with the addition of six cantos, in 1532. The 287 press variants and a cancellans sheet described by Conor Fahy show the author fiddling with the text up to and even after the last possible moment. The virtuosity of the outcome was hailed as a triumph, and its stature as Italy's Renaissance chef-d'œuvre has rarely been questioned; it also proved to be a commercial success for publishers such as Giolito and Valgrisi, who turned out editions in multiple formats augmented with illustrations, commentaries, and other sorts of paratext. In the 1580s it was temporarily eclipsed by the *Gerusalemme Liberata*, initially entitled *Il Goffredo*, which contained a poetical, allegorical account of the First Crusade that profoundly influenced other European writers. Its author, Torquato Tasso, can claim to be the first genuine pan-Italian writer, since in childhood he travelled widely and thus avoided growing up speaking a local dialect. All these writers, who grappled with the task of creating literary works in what was effectively a foreign language, are comparable to a novelist such as Conrad, who wrote in English, his third language after his native Polish and after French.

The last factor bearing on the history of the book in Italy is the absence of a solid middle-class readership. The term 'middle-class' here is a deliberate anachronism, designating a numerically consistent body of users who see the book as an instrument for self-improvement and as an expression of their own upward aspiration. Since Italy had enjoyed a higher level of urban literacy than elsewhere in Europe during the early Renaissance and has never since lacked erudition nor scholars, to speak of the absence of a whole class of readers appears to be a contradiction. Nevertheless, this is what happened and, though the causes were many and complex, the key moment in this literacy-failure probably occurred in 1559, when the first Roman *Index Librorum Prohibitorum* banned the Bible in Italian. Quite independently of the sacred text's content and import, the Bible is a large book and therefore its removal from circulation had important and damaging consequences for the general standard of literacy. Before that date, reading the scriptures, even by those who knew little or no Latin, was fairly widespread in Italian society. The earliest *volgarizzamento* of the Bible by Nicolò Malermi had appeared in Venice in 1471. The 16th century saw further translations, especially that by Antonio Brucioli (1532) which seemed tainted with heresy. The Catholic Church's fears about uncontrolled and uncontrollable reading of the biblical text thus resulted in a wider clampdown on the circulation of ideas. From 1559 (or rather from 1564, when the definitive Tridentine *Index* confirmed the ban), a split emerged in Italian reading practice and habits. At one extreme, an elite educated on the Aldine model consumed works in both quantity and quality; however, because members of religious orders constituted a significant portion of this category, family reading was generally excluded and women were often discouraged from becoming literate. At the other end, readers with minimal formal education sought out and perused texts, sometimes incurring the wrath of the authorities. For example, at Udine in 1584 and again in 1599, a miller, Domenico Scandella (known as Menocchio), was accused of heresy before an Inquisition tribunal, which recorded his reading and what he thought he found there (Ginzburg). The trial has a bibliographical import, since the books Menocchio liked best, such as Mandeville's travels, were second-hand and dated back half a century and more. Otherwise, as a direct consequence of the clampdown, the books of the last third of the 16th century are unappetizing fare and there is little to attract a middle-of-the-road reader. Textual censorship may not have wholly deterred lovers of literature, but episodes such as the *rassettature* of the *Decameron* between 1573 and 1588, in which negative references to the clergy were removed and some tales were substantially rewritten, demonstrate that the conduct of the book trades was materially altered, and not for the better. A sea-change is visible also in the catalogues of firms such as Giolito, which abandoned its predominantly literary output in favour of markedly religious productions. To attribute this metamorphosis merely to publishing timidity is to oversimplify: society was changing, readers were changing, and books merely followed the trend. This crack in social literacy created in the 16th century became a chasm by the 18th century.

6 The 16th century and the supremacy of Venice

The minute tallying of Venetian daily existence in Marin Sanudo's diaries, kept from 1496 to 1533, is silently eloquent when it reaches the last day of 1500. No jubilant throng of printers, publishers, and booksellers gathered in St Mark's Square to cheer the ending of the incunable age and dance into the small hours of the incoming century. This is hardly surprising, since the bibliographical threshold of New Year's Day 1501 is a later demarcation, long recognized as artificial and undesirable; it is, nevertheless, a convenient moment for taking stock (Norton). The ongoing Italian census of 16th-century books (*Edit16*), together with its sister system, Servizio Bibliotecario Nazionale (SBN), shows that, in 1501, slightly more than 200 titles were published in a dozen cities. The lion's share appeared in Venice (64 per cent). Its closest rival was Milan (16 per cent), which had a plethora of small printers and two large publisher-booksellers, Legnano and Nicolò da Gorgonzola. Thereafter came Bologna (7 per cent), mainly with large tomes for university use, then Rome (3 per cent) and Brescia (2 per cent). Reggio Emilia (2 per cent) was surprisingly active, publishing its statutes in that year, while token presences mark the output of Turin, Parma, Pavia, Perugia, Ferrara, and Florence. Centres that temporarily appear dormant, however, such as Modena, may have produced ephemera that have not survived (*see* **16**), or undated imprints that have been classified as possible incunabula. A pattern emerges that remained true up to the 17th century: Venice dominated the trade and other centres struggled to compete. Although important literary works might have a first edition elsewhere (e.g. Sannazaro's *Arcadia* in Naples, or Ariosto's *Orlando Furioso* in Ferrara), subsequent editions invariably migrated to Venice.

This dominance was reinforced by legislation and by the lobbying power of the publishers themselves, who from 1549 were organized in their own guild (Brown). John of Speyer's 1469 monopoly concession was followed by a hiatus, but around the turn of the century requests for privileges came thick and fast. Aldus was especially assiduous: he obtained protection for his Greek texts in 1496 and 1498 and for his new italic type in 1501; the year after, he demanded measures against the counterfeit printing of his octavo editions. The system was open to abuse, so much so that in 1517 the senate, irritated by the number of blanket applications for authors and titles, cancelled all extant concessions and—recognizing the need for tighter controls—in 1545 placed the book trade under the charge of the Riformatori dello Studio di Padova. Like other Italian states, Venice kept its university in a satellite city, Padua, where, owing to the disastrous war of the League of Cambrai (1508–16), all teaching had ceased; in 1528, therefore, this new magistrature was created to reopen the university and oversee its running. Elective by nature and considered prestigious, the Riformatori became the equivalent of a culture ministry with powers over academies, libraries, and the book trade. Printers had to submit any work they intended to publish for approval, and permission followed swiftly—as long as nothing was found against religion, against princes (i.e. other governments), or against morality in general. With the promulgation of the *Index*, the Inquisition's attempts to impose censorship led to bitter disputes, not only with publishers but also with the Venetian authorities, who resented and obstructed Roman interference (Grendler). In 1596 a concordat was signed, however, ratifying a system of double approval, in which the inquisitor verified that the book contained nothing against the Catholic faith. However, owing to frequent—and often justified—complaints about his overstepping his jurisdiction, it became increasingly common to obtain only state approval and to evade church control by a false imprint describing the place of publication (Infelise).

Statistics defining early book output are misleading at the best of times, but evaluating Italian Renaissance production is akin to a blindfold obstacle race. First, a significant percentage of imprints no longer survive. Second, large-scale export at the time and bibliophile collecting in the interim have ensured that approximately half the surviving copies of pre-1601 books—sometimes the sole witnesses of their respective editions—are now found outside Italy. The largest single collection is in London: rough counts suggest that, if the British Library took part in *Edit16*, it would hold just under 40 per cent of the total, whereas the National Central Libraries of Florence and Rome both average fewer than 30 per cent. Third, inside Italy itself, there is no tradition of concentrating early books in a few major collections. Instead, small towns have collections besides which the well-known public library parameter of one book per inhabitant appears almost absurd: Poppi, in Tuscany, with 5,300 inhabitants boasts 500 incunabula, while not-too-distant San Gimignano, with a population of 7,400, owns 1,600 16th-century books. Up to now, therefore, attempts at quantification—such as those constructed on the BL's holdings—have proved inaccurate. However, the existence of electronic media not only simplifies counting, but also offers new opportunities.

At the time of writing, *Edit* 16 lists 6,800 entries for 1501–20 (39 per cent from Venice); 6,300 for 1521–40 (54 per cent); 10,800 for 1541–60 (56 per cent); 16,900 for 1561–80 (43 per cent); and 21,100 for 1581–1600 (34 per cent). The sort of plateau in early production is attributable to the anti-Venetian war and to the subsequent sack of Rome in 1527, accompanied by an outbreak of the plague, so that the century's publishing nadir came in 1529. Otherwise, from 1501, inspired by the Aldine model, Venice reversed its earlier practice of publishing large-format books. According to ISTC, in 1465–80 54 per cent of Italian editions were in folio, 41 per cent were quarto, and 5 per cent were octavo or less; in 1481–1500 these proportions have already shifted respectively to 39, 50, and 11 per cent. By comparison in *Edit* 16, by 1521–40 folio shrinks to 13 per cent, quarto holds at 32 per cent, octavo reaches 52 per cent, and even smaller formats—mainly duodecimo—make themselves known at 3 per cent. In 1581–1600, folio remains constant at 10 per cent, though some titles are large, multi-volume publications; quarto climbs again to 46 per cent; octavo drops back to 31 per cent; and smaller formats make inroads to reach 13 per cent. The objective of resorting to smaller formats was to save paper, which in a Renaissance book could lead to savings of up to a third, though paradoxically the first edition in a new format often employs a greater number of sheets than its immediate pre-decessor. A large work never out of print, such as Boccaccio's *Decameron*, shows a characteristic evolution: after the folio *editio princeps* c.1470 (127 sheets), it reached its maximum size with the Ripoli edition c.1483 (151 sheets), although from 1504 to 1518 a more compact layout reduced the sheets to 63. The first quarto in 1516 contained 91 sheets, reduced to 68 by 1541; the octavo format first introduced in 1525 required 84 sheets, which fell to 56 by 1540; a trial sex-todecimo imprint in 1542 has 23 1 2 sheets, although the first duodecimo in 1550 uses 38 1 2.

In this competitive market, books had to be attractive to buyers and Venice pioneered the innovation of the title-page and the consequent shift of publica-tion-related information from the colophon to the front of the book. Publishers there swiftly caught on to the importance of clearly recognizable brand names. In incunabula, the traditional sign, or mark, of the medieval *stationarius* (stationer)—an orb with a double-cross, hanging over the shop door—appeared as a woodcut printer's device, often with the addition of the proprietor's initials, in conjunction with the colophon. This usage gave way, by the following cen-tury, to a more distinctive publisher's mark that visually identified the book-shop, at times with a pun on the owner's name, as with the Tower (Torresani), the St Bernard (Bernardino Stagnino), and the St Nicholas (Nicolò Zoppino). Other establishments employed an easily remembered symbol, such as the Anchor (Aldus), Cat (Sessa family), Dolphin (Garanta), Lily (Giunta family), Mermaid (Ravani), and Phoenix (Giolito). Publisher-printers were also adept at other tricks, such as modifying the date on the title-page, typical of Giolito's out-put (so that the book would appear to be 'new' for more than a year at a time), or edition-sharing (where the name and mark of one publisher were substituted in press with those of another). This last habit in particular might cause migraines for those who have to catalogue such books, but it reveals substantial alliances within the Venetian industry, especially in the last part of the 16th century, when the market for large editions of patristic authors experienced an upturn after the regeneration of monastic libraries following the Council of Trent and the creation of a network of seminaries to train priests. A consortium of Venetian publishers, therefore, issued editions where each owned a personalized quota, the most striking example being the eleven-volume quarto edition of the works of St Augustine in 1570 (republished in 1584), split between Giunta, Nicolini, Sessa, Valgrisi, Varisco, and Zenaro.

7 The 17th to the 19th centuries: decline, revival, fall, renewal

The number of titles published in Italy peaked in 1588. The publishing crisis that followed—in full swing by the early 17th century—was mainly Venetian and had various causes, some of which have already been noted, such as the introduction (or often return) of printing to minor centres, usually as a service industry catering for local needs; thus, by 1601 presses were solidly implanted in more than 40 localities. In 1606 the jurisdictional conflict between Venice and Rome reached its height, with the interdict, largely disobeyed, forbidding priests from holding religious events in the city. The opposing factions engaged in a pamphlet war, in which Venice's spokesman, the Servite friar Paolo Sarpi, demolished the papal arguments. In retaliation the Church intensified its attack on the economic base of the Venetian industry—the publishing of liturgical texts in red and black—by issuing privileges that favoured Roman editions and encouraging Venetian printers to relocate to Rome. With the trade elsewhere in Europe crippled by the Thirty Years War (1618–48), the final blow for a struggling industry came with the 1630 plague, which decimated the population of northern Italy. In the decade that followed, Venetian output dropped to 20 per cent of its former height, overtaken within the Italian market (albeit temporarily) by Rome and within the international market by Paris. Italian dominance of the European market had always been favoured by the role of Latin as the universal language: around mid-century, a different economic and political hegemony imposed French as the new lingua franca.

By the 18th century, a qualitative split is apparent. The top end of the market was occupied by works of notable, if to modern eyes dusty, erudition: the age's leading intellectual was a librarian, Ludovico Antonio Muratori. Just as the *Encyclopédie* was the most important French book of its time, so its Italian counterpart was the immense assemblage of medieval sources Muratori edited as the *Rerum Italicarum Scriptores* (25 vols, 1723–51). Second place on the scale of importance belongs to his later successor at the Estense Library, Girolamo Tiraboschi, whose *Storia della Letteratura Italiana* (10 vols, 1772–82) imposed a nonexistent national identity on a very existent literature. The publishing trade revived, bolstered by large-scale printing projects and aided both by the decline of traditional rivals Lyons and Antwerp and by the recession caused in France by the War of the Spanish Succession (1701–14). Venice in particular, led by the Baglioni firm, recovered its pre-eminence in the printing of liturgical texts, which were exported mainly to the Spanish dominions in the New World. Another proof of revival was the success enjoyed by what to all intents and purposes was an academic press, set up in the house of a Padua University professor and managed by the printer Giuseppe Comino, with an essentially Aldine programme of Greek and Latin classics in elegant typography. The exclusive market for quality printing also sustained and largely justified the remarkable career of Bodoni, who transformed type design more profoundly

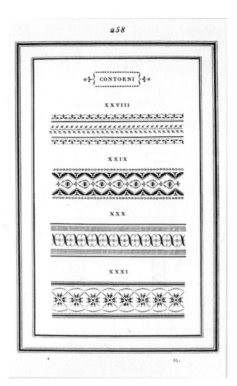

Contorni, printers' ornaments (fleurons or borders), from Bodoni's widow's celebrated type specimen book, *Manuale tipografico* (1818). The Bodleian Library, University of Oxford (Arch. BB. c. 2–3, vol. 2, p. 258)

than anyone since Aldus. But however extraordinary as typographical artefacts, his books are not intended to be read: his best-known publications therefore are his specimens, including the misleadingly titled *Manuale tipografico* issued by his widow in 1818. The steady advance of francophone culture is marked also by editions of the *Encyclopédie* in Lucca (1758–76) and in Livorno (1770–78), as well as by the reprint of the later *Encyclopédie méthodique* undertaken by the Seminary of Padua.

The other end of the market was formed by a large-scale production, often in minor centres, of almanacs, chapbooks, works of popular piety, and so on, much of it anonymous and largely uncharted by bibliographers. To Venetian eyes, the most damaging producer was the Bassano Remondini firm, which, after opening a branch in Venice, attacked the publishing establishment from 1750 onward by systematically undercutting the price of steady-selling works whose privilege had recently expired. Savings were obtained by crowding half as much text again on to the page, with deleterious results for its quality, so that they were accused, rightly, of provoking a lapse in printing standards, in which others followed suit.

The French revolutionary armies that swept through Italy overthrew the Venetian Republic in 1797 and, among other things, turned the book trade inside out. When the dust settled in 1814, much appeared the same, but new ideas were stirring in the north. In particular, there was a growing sense that Italy was more than a geographical expression, and in the Risorgimento (resurgence) that followed, the existence of a national language and literature, however virtual, thrust the country towards unity. The cause was significantly espoused in publishing circles by foreign nationals, such as the Frenchman Felice Le Monnier and the Swiss Giovan Pietro Vieusseux, together with francophone Piedmontese such as Giuseppe Pomba and Gasparo Barbèra, who with their respective series, the 'Biblioteca Italiana' and the 'Collezione Diamante', insisted on the nation's de facto cultural homogeneity. The cities of the north were also more amenable to technological progress; Pomba in Turin was the first to invest in a mechanized printing office, and Milan rapidly became Italy's main publishing centre (Berengo). In the period 1814–1900, book production increased tenfold, leaving aside the growth of newspapers and magazines.

The century was also marked by a search for readers. Now that Italian publishing was confined to Italy, with few opportunities for export elsewhere, the domestic market proved suffocatingly small. The one exception to this rule was music publishing, dominated by Ricordi, for Italian opera ruled the European stage in the period from Verdi to Puccini. In the 19th century, two important factors emerge regarding the question of the absence of a middle-class readership. The first is the failure of the circulating library to take root, presumably because not enough native Italians were willing or able to disburse the sums involved: the one splendid exception, Vieusseux in Florence, was funded by foreign tourists. The second is the meagre fortune enjoyed by that archetypal middle-class genre, the novel, with its obligatory happy ending bringing marital, monetary, and social advancement. The first successful European novel, Samuel Richardson's *Pamela* (1740), was translated into Italian in 1744, whereas the first indigenous attempt, Pietro Chiari's *La Filosofessa* (1753), significantly pretended to be the translation of a French original, made as the sheets came off the press in Paris. Although other titles were produced, for a long time only one was accepted as literature, Manzoni's *I Promessi Sposi* (The Betrothed). Sharing with Richardson a story-line where a young girl is kidnapped in order to be seduced, it involved a significant effort to erase the dialect forms of the first edition and to create the pure contemporary Tuscan of the final version; thus, it established a new standard for the Italian language. The two other most successful fictional works of the 19th century were both aimed at the children's market: De Amicis' *Cuore* (1868) and Collodi's worldwide bestseller *Pinocchio* (1883) (*see* **17**).

Outside the French-reading, educated classes, fictional narrative otherwise struggled with a dearth of readers and with the backwardness of the educational system. For Italy as a whole, 75 per cent of the population was unable to read or write in 1870; in the rural south, this figure reached 90 per cent. Primary schooling became obligatory in 1877, but a lack of resources and the opposition of the clergy meant that the law remained a dead letter in many places; in 1911 the number of Italians with inadequate literacy skills still averaged 38 per cent.

8 The 20ᵗʰ and 21ˢᵗ centuries: two wars, Fascism, and after

In 1901, the Italian book trade presented geographical and cultural anomalies that remain substantially true today. Rome was the political capital; Milan, dominated by the rivalry between Sonzogno and Treves, was the economic and publishing capital; Florence—with the official home of the Italian language at the Crusca Academy, the country's most important libraries, and publishers such as Barbèra, Bemporad, Le Monnier, and Sansoni—was the cultural capital. Although once-glorious Venice had almost disappeared from the map, other cities had publishing houses of considerable standing, such as Utet in Turin and Nicola Zanichelli in Bologna. An important novelty was the arrival of professional booksellers from the German-speaking world, such as Loescher, Ulrich Hoepli, and Leo Samuel Olschki, who took over established firms and subsequently broadened their scope. Beyond the handful of large companies, much publishing was local in character, revolving around a network of bookshop-stationers in small centres. Unity had also left the country with a network of libraries, including those of the universities, belonging to the former Italian states. Although enormously wealthy in terms of manuscripts and valuable printed books, most of these collections had little to offer for a population with low-grade reading skills.

Italy entered World War I in 1915 to settle its outstanding account with the Austro-Hungarian empire, suffered a shattering defeat at Caporetto, and obtained little more than crumbs at the Versailles peace table. Resentment opened the door to Mussolini, who took power in 1922. Fascism was not, as Benedetto Croce subsequently claimed, a Hyksos invasion by an external enemy that had to be borne and resisted; it began as a movement of army veterans, led by a man who started his political career on the left and veered to the right; and it happened with the support, outspoken or silent, of many institutions, including the Catholic Church. In the circumstances, the connivance of publishers, who bowed to the regime or actively profited from it, such as Arnoldo Mondadori and Vallecchi, is comprehensible; it makes the stand of the few who did not, especially Giulio Einaudi and Laterza, all the more admirable. As a totalitarian dictatorship, Fascism strongly exploited publishing as propaganda: from 1926, books had to display on the title-page the year in the Fascist era. The government also imposed a central control on the industry, both by censorship, through what in 1937 became the ministry for popular culture (usually known by its Orwellian semi-acronym Minculpop), and by incentives, including substantial loans to modernize printing works. The central figure and intellectual of a regime otherwise notoriously short of brainpower was Giovanni Gentile, a philosopher, university professor, owner of the publishing firm Sansoni, and driving force behind Giovanni Treccani in producing the *Enciclopedia Italiana*. Though anti-Semitism was not intrinsic to Fascism but borrowed from its nastier stablemate, with the passing of the racial laws in 1938 lists were compiled of Jewish authors and of writers judged 'decadent', who were banned, while publishing houses with Jewish links were taken over (such as Treves) or renamed (such as Olschki, which became Bibliopolis).

Despite the devastation and the chaos brought by World War II, in the aftermath newspapers, publishing houses, and cinema production companies in Italy remained in substantially the same hands. The Christian Democrat party, after the 1946 referendum transformed Italy into a republic, won a landslide election victory in 1948 and remained in power for the next 50 years. If the institutions and the government were in the hands of the Right, the intelligentsia was synonymous with the Left, and a heady mixture of economic boom, the expansion of university education, a steep rise in the birthrate, and ideas—sometimes music—from across the Alps, the Channel, and the Atlantic, set a cultural revolution in motion. From 1945 until the 1980s, Italy had the most politicized publishing output in Europe. Although the two publishing giants, Mondadori and Rizzoli, remained middle-of-the-road, thinkers and political activists were catered for by Einaudi and Feltrinelli; university texts were supplied by Il Mulino and Angeli; the dictionary market was covered by Zanichelli and Utet; while specialist academic publishing was the preserve of a renewed Olschki.

In one sense, the paperback revolution had its beginning in Italy in 1932, when Giovanni Mardersteig designed the Albatross Verlag layout in Mondadori's Verona printing works; but otherwise the difficulty of finding a mass Italian readership has continued to trouble publishers. The postwar market was dominated by translations of English-language writers, ensuring steady growth for firms such as Longanesi and Bompiani; more recently, European authors have been catered for by the elegant Adelphi. If the novel is taken as a mirror of the society it depicts, a list of the most successful 20th-century titles whose first edition appeared on Italian soil offers food for thought. The top two works are not Italian at all: *Lady Chatterley's Lover*, which Lawrence self-published in Florence (1928), and Pasternak's *Dr Zhivago* (1957), which Giangiacomo Feltrinelli had smuggled out of the USSR. Third on the list is another triumphant Feltrinelli intuition, *Il Gattopardo* by Tomasi di Lampedusa (1958); fourth place goes to Eco's medieval whodunnit *Il Nome della Rosa* (1980). Further places are occupied by a string of 1960 bestsellers *all'italiana*, including Cassola's *La Ragazza di Bube* (1960), Sciascia's *Il Giorno della Civetta* (1961), and Bassani's *Il Giardino dei Finzi Contini* (1962). Several of these have highly successful film versions; indeed, Italian narrative is closely interwoven with cinema, dominated by the neo-realism of De Sica, who in 1960 filmed Moravia's 1957 novel *La Ciociara*, and the luxuriant imaginings of Fellini, who in the same year made *La Dolce Vita*. Successful cinema versions have also reinforced the genuine popular success of Guareschi's Don Camillo stories (1948); although the anti-communist satire was anathematized by left-wing critics, they have sold in the millions and been translated into 20 languages.

Change has also been manifest in librarianship, where the static network of state-owned and municipal collections—with valuable holdings of rare material, but with little to interest the contemporary user—has been challenged by the genesis of numerous libraries in small urban centres, especially those under communist administrations in Emilia Romagna and Tuscany. Here the example of Einaudi—who donated a library to his family's home town, Dogliani, and published the catalogue as a guide to a model collection (1969)—proved hugely influential.

Through the advent of new media (cinema, radio, and television), a sort of linguistic unity was reached—though even in the 21st century dialect is still spoken in the mountains to the north, in the south, and in the islands. The task begun by the Tuscan writers of the Trecento, continued by Bembo and Manzoni, was rounded off through popular TV culture, whose abundant quiz shows—with long-standing comperes such as Mike Bongiorno—regularly oblige contestants to display their knowledge of the Italian language.

Italy remains a complex, contradictory publishing market, with lots of books, lots of bookshops, lots of book lovers, lots of libraries, and few readers. Obligatory secondary education and the freedom of university access have significantly redrawn the literacy map, especially for women, who form up to 90 per cent of arts faculty students. Nonetheless, there remains an unbridged gap between a highly educated intellectual class, often with impressive personal book collections, such as Umberto Eco, and a vaster general public, whose interests are bounded by the sporting newspapers. Nationwide publishing is mostly controlled by larger media corporations, which sustain this relatively unprofitable activity, almost as a front activity, in order to guarantee the circulation of certain ideas and concepts. The media tycoon Silvio Berlusconi, at the time of writing Italy's third-time prime minister, is also the country's largest publisher by virtue of his ownership of the Mondadori group. Lastly, the economic 'miracle' of the 1960s made Italy the world leader in the field of colour printing, both in product packaging (e.g. Barilla pasta) and in advertising material for the luxury goods industry, which exports worldwide such Italian brands as Versace, Ferragamo, and Ferrari. The availability of this technology has an obvious spin-off in the market for glossy, lavishly illustrated exhibition catalogues, where the leading firm is Electa. Another application for this expertise has been developed by Panini in Modena, which patented collectable cards with pictures of footballers, and which now offers many card albums on diverse subjects, including Harry Potter. In the 1990s, it applied its skill in polychrome printing to make perfect facsimiles of Medieval and Renaissance MSS, most notably the Bible of Borso d'Este, marketed in numbered editions intended for wealthy bibliophiles. The success enjoyed by this and other initiatives shows that in some ways the book market in Italy has little altered in nearly six centuries—or perhaps it is necessary to admit, like the main character in *Il Gattopardo*, that 'for everything to remain the same, everything must change'.

BIBLIOGRAPHY

L. Armstrong, 'Nicolaus Jenson's *Breviarium Romanum*, Venice, 1478: Decoration and Distribution', in *Incunabula: Studies in Fifteenth-Century Printed Books Presented to Lotte Hellinga*, ed. M. Davies (1999)

L. Balsamo, *Produzione e circolazione libraria in Emilia (XV–XVIII sec.)* (1983)

M. Berengo, *Intellettuali e Librai nella Milano della Restaurazione* (1980)

H. F. Brown, *The Venetian Printing Press* (1891)

G. A. Bussi, *Prefazioni alle edizioni di Sweynheym e Pannartz prototipografi romani*, ed. M. Miglio (1978)

B. Cecchetti, 'La stampa tabellare in Venezia nel 1447', *Archivio Veneto*, 29 (1885), 87–91

Edit16 (Edizioni Italiane del XVI secolo), vols A–F (1989–2007), on-line version on SBN site

G. Fragnito, *La Bibbia al Rogo: la Censura Ecclesiastica e i Volgarizzamenti della Scrittura, 1471-1605* (1997)

C. Ginzburg, *The Cheese and the Worms: The Cosmos of a Sixteenth-Century Miller*, tr. J. and A. Tedeschi (1980; Italian original, 1976)

P. Grendler, *The Roman Inquisition and the Venetian Press 1540-1605* (1977)

N. Harris, *Bibliografia dell' 'Orlando Innamorato'* (2 vols, 1988–91)

—— 'Ombre della storia del libro italiano', in *The Books of Venice*, ed. L. Pon and C. Kallendorf (2008)

M. Infelise, *L'Editoria Veneziana nel '700* (1989)

P. Needham, 'Venetian Printers and Publishers in the Fifteenth Century', *LaB* 100 (1998), 157–200

F. J. Norton, *Italian Printers 1501-1520* (1958)

A. Nuovo, *Il Commercio Librario nell'Italia del Rinascimento*, 3e (2003)

B. Richardson, *Print Culture in Renaissance Italy* (1994)

—— *Printing, Writers and Readers in Renaissance Italy* (1999)

R. Ridolfi, 'Proposta di ricerche sulle stampa e sugli stampatori del Quattrocento', *LaB* 51 (1949), 2–9

SBN (Servizio Bibliotecario Nazionale), www.sbn.it, consulted Sept. 2007

P. Scapecchi, 'Subiaco 1465 oppure [Bondeno 1463]? Analisi del frammento Parsons–Scheide', *LaB* 103 (2001), 1–24

G. Turi, ed., *Storia dell'Editoria nell'Italia Contemporanea* (1997)

31

The History of the Book in Modern Greece, *c.*1453–2000

ALEXIS POLITIS

1 The 15th century to 1820

The history of modern Greek books can be divided into two periods: before and after 1820. The early printing of Greek books occurred outside Greek territory, on presses partly owned by Greeks. After 1820, numerous presses operated in the Greek state and in eastern Mediterranean towns.

The first modern Greek book—that is, a book written in the Greek language (though not necessarily in the modern tongue) and printed for the Greek public—is Constantinus Lascaris' grammar (Milan, 1476). Modern Greek society readily adapted to the appearance of printed books, and several Greeks contributed to their development. Greeks cut various typefaces, and in the late 15th century, Zacharias Callierges and Nikolaos Vlastos founded the earliest Greek press. The first Greek books, however, were printed in Italy, and, by the early 16th century, several Italian printers sought to expand into the Orthodox East, starting Greek-interest presses in Venice. Approximately 440 titles had been printed by 1600, mostly for liturgical or educational use; modern Greek literary works were far less numerous.

This pattern persisted during the early 17th century: Greek books were printed by Italian publishers, most appearing in Venice. In 1627, Patriarch Cyril Lukaris attempted to found a press at Constantinople, but ultimately failed; his printer, Nicodemo Metaxàs, was forced to seek refuge on the Ionian Islands. In 1670 the first Greek firm appeared: Nikolaos Glykis bought a Venetian publishing house, which his descendants maintained until 1854. A second Greek press was started by Nikolaos Saros in 1686. Greek publishing almost doubled during this period, bearing witness to significant market demand in the Orthodox East. Liturgical texts, together with religious books, accounted for approximately three-quarters of the output. Only a third of the books were new, the rest being reissues.

In the first half of the 18th century, Venice remained the main centre for Greek books, with output determined by educational and religious requirements. Presses began operating in the semi-autonomous principalities of present-day Romania (*see* **33**) and in Albania (*see* **38**), but the printing office at Moschopolis produced only fifteen books between 1725 and 1755. By the century's end, a press was established on Mount Athos, along with others in Constantinople and Corfu. Little popular literature appeared, although some older works were published, including Georgios Chortatzis's 16th-century *Erophile* and Vicenzos Cornaros's 16th–17th-century *Erotocritos* (1713). After 1750, the coming of the Enlightenment brought rapid change.

The Greek Enlightenment's first book was Eugenios Voulgaris' *Logic* (Leipzig, 1766). By the century's end, the cultural landscape in Ottoman-occupied Greece resembled Europe's: schools proliferated, scientific works were translated, and a small number of people travelled or studied in Europe. This coincided with significant social changes and incipient revolution. As the new merchant class increased in numbers and gained in social power, Rhigas Velestinlis published pamphlets (Vienna, 1797) calling for a national uprising.

These changes are reflected in book production. In the first two decades of the 19th century, the number of books reached approximately 1,400, or 35 per cent of the total national output of 5,000 titles between 1476 and 1820. Simultaneously, the numbers of reprints and of religious books fell. Production in Venice declined proportionally from 80 per cent to 50 per cent, with 25 per cent being printed in Vienna; production in Constantinople, where a press controlled by the patriarchate was founded in 1798, was insignificant.

Qualitative changes were more marked, with books appearing in the fields of philosophy, science (mostly translations), classics, and language instruction; literary output, mostly plays in translation, remained insubstantial. As intellectual circles grew, the Vienna-based periodical *Ermis o Logios* (The Learned Hermes, 1811–21) became a rallying point for progressives, whose leading light was Adamantios Coray.

The formats and press runs of books varied considerably. Ecclesiastical books were generally printed as quartos, school and scientific works in octavo, and popular literature in smaller formats. The normal size of editions seems to have been 500–1,000 copies, but larger numbers were not unknown, particularly for liturgical works and school textbooks.

Bookshops first appeared in early 19th-century Constantinople. Books were sold either by orders placed with general merchants or by colporteurs at trade fairs. However, the mid-18th century saw the advent and growth of subscription publishing: handwritten or printed advertisements for the book were circulated, and once there were enough subscribers, it would be printed, with a subscription list. Most scientific and new books were published in this manner.

Public libraries were similarly lacking. Several monasteries had libraries, typically formed from bequests by monks or prelates; however, they were rarely used. From the early 19th century onwards, however, school libraries were established in Chios, Smyrna, Milies on Mount Pelion, and Kozani. Private libraries were rarer. By the 16th century, several major libraries survived in Constantinople. The Maurokordatos family established a significant library (*c.*1720), gathering printed books from Europe and attempting to collect the entire modern Greek output by copying monastic MSS; the library was broken up *c.*1765. In the early 19th century, several private Greek libraries were established in Europe and on the Ionian Islands, some of which still survive.

2 1821–1900

Between the Greek declaration of independence in March 1821 and the arrival of the first king of Greece in January 1833, centuries-old assumptions were overturned in every part of life. Printing presses donated by European philhellenic committees were established in the newly free state at Kalamata, Missolonghi, Athens, and Hydra. Although a mere 5–6 per cent of all Greek books printed in 1821–30 were produced on free territory, they redrew the ideological landscape. By 1850 there were more than 50 printing offices in Greek territory and the Ionian Islands, primarily in Athens where the government was based; by 1863, there were 35 more. Although few of the presses were long-lived or prolific, the book market was dynamic.

The most important press was owned by an Athenian, Andreas Coromilas, who specialized in school textbooks and literature. In 1833–6, his presses produced 70,000 copies, overshadowing the 29,000 produced by his four major rivals. He introduced stereotyping (1840) and opened a branch in Constantinople (1842). He printed more than 300 titles in all, mostly textbooks, dictionaries, or scientific works. The business survived until 1884.

Athens gradually increased its lead in book production. Of the *c.*9,000 Greek books produced in 1828–63, half were printed there; 500 in Constantinople (5.5 per cent); 450 in Smyrna and Hermopolis (5 per cent); and 600 in Venice (6.5 per cent). In 1864–1900, *c.*32,000 Greek books were produced; Athens's and Constantinople's share of the market increased, while that of the other places fell. Annual book production grew tenfold between 1820 and 1900. As the economy improved and population increased, new and better-organized publishing houses appeared, creating distinctive series (plays, handbooks, pocket books).

At the end of the War of Independence, bookshops run by foreigners appeared on Greek territory (Nafplio, Hermopolis, Athens); their number increased *c.*1840 in Constantinople and in Athens after 1850. By 1877 Athens had 16 bookshops, Constantinople 8, Smyrna 5, and Hermopolis 4, with another 24 in 11 provincial towns.

Subscription publishing, often used by provincial booksellers, retained wide currency. It peaked *c*.1880 with 153,000 named subscribers to 213,000 copies, but declined after 1890, disappearing by the following century. To facilitate ordering, publishers and booksellers printed catalogues, which are now a primary source of information on book distribution from 1860. After 1850, books (particularly novels) were sold by serial publication in numbers with newspapers. Assisted by the foundation of the press distribution agency in 1877, this practice of issuing fascicles was also applied to such books as the second edition of the *History of the Greek Nation* (1892), by Constantinos Paparrigopoulos, and the 79-volume scientific series 'Maraslis Library' (1897–1908).

Before 1821, Coray had proposed creating a central National Library; an initial core collection was assembled at Aegina in 1829. The University of Athens Library was founded in 1838, and housed in a building shared (1842–1903) by the National Library of Greece. The Parliament Library opened in 1845 and grew rapidly thereafter. Other public or municipal libraries either languished or relied on private donations. An attempt to establish a network of school libraries was bogged down by bureaucracy.

3 1901–2000

Between 1901 and *c*.1925, Greek publishing was dominated by Georgios Fexis' firm, founded in 1888. Initially relying on cheap novels, a 'drama library', and similar series, he bought Venice's last publishing house in 1901, producing more than 300 titles in six years about subjects including law, medicine, language learning, modern history, and practical matters.

During the wars of 1912–22, the reading public grew and Greek territory doubled, allowing the creation of several new publishing houses. The most important were Eleftheroudakis (1877–1962), Sideris (1874–1928), Georgios Vasileiou (1888–1932), Zikakis (1883–1925), Ganiaris (1894–1966), and Govostis (1904–58). Several smaller publishers active in the 1920s created literary or philosophical series, translating 19th-century European works and fostering modern Greek literature. Perhaps the best indicator of financial and intellectual vigour was the publication of the *Great Greek Encyclopaedia* (1926–34), a 24-volume work produced by Paul Drandake. Related developments include the creation of the Aspiotis-ELKA graphic design workshop, which produced major art publications until the 1980s, and the foundation of the Gennadius Library (1926). In 1926, Greece's second university was founded in Thessaloniki, followed a year later by the Academy of Athens; both formed noteworthy libraries. This period also saw the publication of the twelve-volume Eleftheroudakis *Encyclopaedic Dictionary/Lexicon* (1927–31), followed by the nine-volume *Major Dictionary of the Greek Language* (1936–50) by Demetrios Demetrakos-Mesiskles.

During World War II, literary publishing blossomed. In the absence of European imports, Greek books gained readers, some books generating queues outside bookshops, and some editions selling out in days. New publishing houses appeared on the scene, including the short-lived Glaros (Seagull), Ikaros, headed by Nikos Karydis, and Alpha, run by Ioannis Skazikis.

The 48-volume 'Basic Library', the first series to anthologize a substantial body of modern Greek literature, appeared between 1953 and 1958. In 1955, Atlantis, the earliest five-colour rotogravure press, was established. State literature and essay prizes were inaugurated in 1958, as was the National Research Foundation's Centre for Modern Greek Research, which has worked systematically on the history of the Greek book.

In the 1960s, the Galaxy Press emerged, producing the first successful series of pocket books featuring quality Greek and foreign literature; its 300 titles were often reprinted, some poetry volumes running to 5,000 copies. Kedros Press, which promoted modern literature, also appeared at this time. The 1967 dictatorship impeded literary activity; in an act of passive resistance, several authors voluntarily stopped publishing until 1970. After that year, there was a miniature publishing boom, comprising small new publishing houses (mostly left-leaning) as well as a new, cheaper series of pocket books: Viper Books (by Papyros Press) numbered 2,650 titles in ten years, selling one million copies in 1971. Other signs of this blossoming include the inauguration of the Modern Greek Library series (by Hermes) and Ekdotiki Athinon's multi-volume *History of the Greek Nation*.

In 1990, books became a trade commodity, sold in supermarkets and attracting the interest of big business. After 1995, most newspapers included a weekly books supplement or dedicated several pages to books. Oddly, the circulation of pocket books dwindled; popular bestsellers appeared in the same format as quality literature, often issued by the same publishing houses. The 21st century has been marked by the establishment of multi-story book 'megastores' (e.g. Eleftheroudakis, Ianos, Fnac) in city centres and suburbs. The explosion in book publishing seems unlikely to abate: the 7,450 titles published in 2001 rose to 9,209 in 2006.

....

BIBLIOGRAPHY

L. Droulia, *History of the Greek Book* (2001) [in Greek]

D. S. Ginis and V. Mexas, *Greek Bibliography 1800–1863* (3 vols, 1939–57) [in Greek]

P. Iliou, *Additions to the Greek Bibliography (1515–1799)* (1973) [in Greek]

—— *Greek Bibliography 1800–1818* (1998) [in Greek]

—— and P. Polemi, *Greek Bibliography 1864–1900* (2006) [in Greek]

A. Koumarianou *et al.*, *The Greek Book 1476–1830* (1986) [in Greek]

E. Legrand, *Bibliographie hellénique: XVe–XVIe siècles* (4 vols, 1885–1906)

—— *Bibliographie hellénique: XVIIe siècle* (5 vols, 1894–1903)

—— *Bibliographie hellénique: XVIIIe siècle* (2 vols, 1918–28)

National Book Centre, www.ekebi.gr, consulted Sept. 2007

National Documentation Centre, www.argo. ekt.gr, consulted Sept. 2007

D. E. Rhodes, *Incunabula in Greece* (1980)

K. S. Staikos, *Charta of Greek Printing* (1998)

—— and T. E. Sklavenitis, eds., *The Publishing Centres of the Greeks* (2001)

—— *The Printed Greek Book, 15th–19th Centuries* (2004) [in Greek]

32

The History of the Book
in Austria

JOHN L. FLOOD

1 Introduction

Given Austria's linguistic and historical ties with Germany, its book culture has inevitably been strongly influenced by its neighbour (*see* **26**). Part of the Holy Roman Empire until 1806, Austria was for centuries dominated by the Habsburgs, who ruled until 1918. Under this dynasty, Bohemia and Hungary were united with Austria in 1526. In 1867 the double monarchy of Austria-Hungary was created, whose multi-ethnic population (51 million in 1910, with 2.1 million in Vienna) embraced not only German-speakers, but also the peoples of most of the now independent states of central Europe. Following World War I, the borders were redrawn, creating the (first) Republic of Austria, with Czechoslovakia and Hungary as independent states. In 1938, Austria was annexed to the German Reich, and in 1945 occupied by American, British, French, and Soviet forces until the Second Republic officially came into being in 1955. Today Austria's population is *c*.8.2 million, of whom 1.6 million live in Vienna.

2 Early history

In the Middle Ages, book culture flourished in such monasteries as Salzburg (then belonging to Bavaria) and Kremsmünster, both 8th-century foundations, and later at Admont, St Florian, and elsewhere.

In 1500, the population of the area corresponding to present-day Austria was about 1.5 million. Vienna had *c*.20,000 inhabitants, Schwaz 15,000, Salzburg 8,000, Graz 7,000, Steyr 6,000, and Innsbruck 5,000. At that date, Vienna's university (founded 1365), was a centre of humanist scholarship. The first printer in the city was Stephan Koblinger, who arrived from Vicenza in 1482 and stayed until at least 1486. Next came Johann Winterburger (active 1492–1519, producing *c*.165 books, including many editions of classical authors), Johann Singriener (1510–45, with *c*.400 books in various languages), and his partner, Hieronymus Vietor. In 1505 the brothers Leonhard and Lukas Alantsee established a bookshop in Vienna. The chief places of printing outside Vienna were Innsbruck (1547), Salzburg (1550), Graz (*c*.1559), Brixen (1564), Linz (1615), and Klagenfurt (1640). Yet, compared with Germany, the book trade in Austria was relatively underdeveloped. Austrian readers were principally supplied by booksellers from southern Germany, especially Augsburg.

In the early modern period, Austria experienced a series of crises. The economy (especially mining) was affected by the geo-strategic shift resulting from the discovery of the New World. Vienna and Graz were besieged by the Turks in 1529 and 1532 respectively, and the Turkish wars flared up again in 1593. Vienna was besieged once more in 1683. From the 1520s there was social unrest among the peasants, and religious life was shaken by the Reformation. The fear of Lutheranism led to censorship being imposed as early as 1528. Unlike in Germany, Protestant printing was never more than peripheral in Austria. The Counter-Reformation brought educational reform and renewal of intellectual life through the Jesuits, who also established printing presses (for example, in 1559 at Vienna), but it also meant the confiscation and burning of Protestant books (for example, 10,000 books at Graz in August 1600). Even in 1712, Salzburg householders had non-Catholic books confiscated during fire inspections of their premises.

Austria was not spared the economic decline associated with the Thirty Years War, and even between 1648 and the Napoleonic era there were more years of war than of peace. Although printer-publishers were found throughout Austria, their importance was generally limited and local; few of them attended the book fairs in Frankfurt or Leipzig. Hence Austrian authors seldom enjoyed European resonance. One exception was the preacher Abraham a Sancta Clara (1644–1709), whose works reached an international audience, chiefly through German reprints produced at Nuremberg and Ulm.

On 8 August 1703, Johann Baptist Schönwetter launched a daily newspaper, the *Wiennerisches Diarium*; renamed the *Wiener Zeitung* in 1780, it became the official gazette of the Austrian government in 1812, and is today one of the oldest continuously published newspapers in the world. In the 18th century, responsibility for censorship in Austria shifted from the Church to the state. Censorship was relaxed under Joseph II (emperor 1765–90), but the Napoleonic wars and the repressive policies of Prince Metternich led to its reimposition. Only after the 1848 revolution did matters improve.

As for the book trade itself, the demise of the exchange system for settling accounts and the insistence of Leipzig publishers on cash payments led to a boom in cheap reprints in southern Germany and Austria. A prominent figure in this regard was Johann Thomas von Trattner, court bookseller and printer in Vienna, who was actively encouraged by Empress Maria Theresa to issue reprints of German books.

3 Modern times

Until 1918, the centres of publishing and literary life in the Austrian empire were Vienna and Prague. Writers associated with Vienna at this time include Hugo von Hofmannsthal and Karl Kraus (founder of the most important critical journal of the early 20th century, *Die Fackel*), while Prague produced Kafka, Rilke, and Franz Werfel.

During the 1930s, competition from German publishers became particularly intense. In 1934 the German government decreed that books sold abroad should receive a 25 per cent price subsidy. For Austria, this meant that German imports were now cheaper than home-produced books. In 1936 the Austrian government retaliated with a 3 per cent surcharge on foreign books, to provide a subsidy for Austrian publishers.

Between 1918 and 1938, some 90 publishing houses were founded in Austria, most of them short-lived, not least because of National Socialist policies following the Anschluss in March 1938. Among them were Phaidon Verlag, established in 1923—which became renowned for its large-format, richly illustrated, but modestly priced art books—and Paul Zsolnay Verlag, also founded in 1923, which specialized in literature. With the annexation, both these firms moved from Vienna to Britain. Phaidon is now an international concern; Zsolnay was re-established in Vienna in 1946. Other Austrian publishers and booksellers emigrated and built up successful businesses in the US: Friedrich Ungar, who founded the Frederick Ungar Publishing Company in 1940; Wilhelm Schab, who set up in New York in 1939; and H. P. Kraus.

The Nazis took immediate steps to control the book trade. Many Vienna publishers and booksellers quickly fell into line, while Jewish firms were liquidated and undesirable books impounded. More than 2 million books were removed from publishers' stockrooms and bookshops; some were retained for 'official' purposes but most were pulped. Books were removed from libraries, too—only the Austrian National Library and the university libraries in Vienna, Salzburg, Graz, and Innsbruck were spared.

In 1945, the Allies imposed various denazification measures. A list of more than 2,000 prohibited books and authors was drawn up, and these were removed from public and private libraries—60,000 volumes from municipal libraries in Vienna alone were pulped. Pre-publication censorship was introduced, and schoolbooks were subjected to especially rigorous inspection.

Given that Leipzig, the centre of the German publishing industry, had been largely destroyed, there was initially great optimism in Austria that Vienna might become the centre of German-language publishing. However, paper was in short supply, printing equipment was antiquated, and the books produced had limited appeal. More new publishing ventures were founded on idealism than on a sound commercial basis. Moreover, in the early postwar years exporting to Germany was prohibited, which meant that the largest potential market was closed to Austrian publishers.

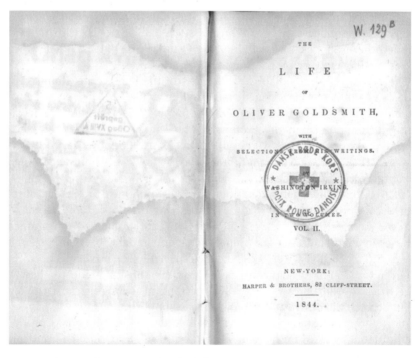

Prisoner-of-war reading: W. Irving's *Life of Oliver Goldsmith* (New York, 1843–4) sent by the Danish Red Cross, examined by camp officials, and marked with a fine hand-printed bookplate as belonging to international prisoners in Oflag XVIIIa in south Austria. Private collection

Austrian publishers' chief problems continue to be that the local market is too small and competition from powerful German rivals too intense. In the 1970s, while Austrian sales to Germany doubled, German publishers quadrupled theirs to Austria. Today, four out of every five books available in Austrian bookshops have been published in Germany, while German bookshops stock barely any Austrian titles. Of *c*.500 Austrian publishers today, more than half are based in Vienna. Two-thirds of them cater purely for the Austrian or regional market. A distinctive feature of Austrian publishing is the number of firms run by state organizations, the Catholic Church, and other institutions. The Österreichischer Bundesverlag (ÖBV), the largest publisher and a state enterprise until it was privatized in 2002, traces its origin to the schoolbook printing works established by Maria Theresa in 1772 to promote literacy. Firms such as Carinthia, Styria, and Tyrolia belong to the Church. Only three Austrian publishers— the ÖBV, the privately owned Verlag Carl Ueberreuter in Vienna, and the educational publishers Veritas in Linz—figure among the 100 largest German-language publishers. The continued independence of Austrian publishers has become more precarious since the country's accession to the EU in 1995.

BIBLIOGRAPHY

K. Amann, *Zahltag: Der Anschluss österreichischer Schriftsteller an das Dritte
Reich*, 2e (1996)

N. Bachleitner *et al.*, *Geschichte des Buchhandels in Österreich* (2000)

A. Durstmüller, *500 Jahre Druck in Österreich* (1982)

H. P. Fritz, *Buchstadt und Buchkrise. Verlagswesen und Literatur in Österreich 1945–
1955* (1989)

M. G. Hall, *Österreichische Verlagsgeschichte
1918–1938* (1985)

—— *Der Paul Zsolnay Verlag* (1994)

—— Hall 'Publishers and Institutions in
Austria, 1918–1945', in *A History of Austrian Literature, 1918–2000*, ed. K. Kohl
and R. Robertson (2006)

—— and C. Köstner, "...*allerlei für die Nationalbibliothek zu ergattern...*": *Eine österreichische Institution in der NS-Zeit* (2006)

A. Köllner, *Buchwesen in Prag* (2000)

J.-P. Lavandier, *Le Livre au temps de Marie
Thérèse* (1993)

LGB 2

33

The History of the Book in Hungary

BRIDGET GUZNER

1 Book culture in the Middle Ages

The earliest Hungarian written records are closely linked to Christian culture and the Latin language. The first codices were copied and introduced by travelling monks on their arrival in the country during the 10th century, not long after the Magyar tribes had conquered and settled in the Carpathian Basin. Written records were primarily created in monasteries; however, legal and other official documents were produced by an ecclesiastical body ('loca credibilia') unique to Hungary. This legal institution continued to operate in convents and chapter houses, issuing certified records in chancery script to laymen and the clergy until 1874. The earliest ecclesiastical library, founded in 996, was that of the Benedictine monastery of Pannonhalma. Its MS holdings included as many as 250 liturgical and classical works by Cicero, Lucan, Donatus, and Cato, but the original library repeatedly fell prey to fire and only one codex survives from it. The cathedral libraries of Pécs (where there had also been a university, founded in 1367 but which closed in 1390), Veszprém, and Esztergom were destroyed following the continuous expansion of the Ottoman empire and the battle of Mohács, where the Turkish army, led by Süleyman I, attacked and defeated Hungarian forces in August 1526.

In the 14th century Hungarian students frequently studied at European universities, especially in Cracow, Vienna, Bologna, and Padua. On their return, they were reported to have owned small libraries, but none of their booklists survives. Information on the origins and subsequent fate of the most significant medieval MSS is scant. The *Gesta Hungarorum* (*c.*1200) chronicles the history of the Hungarians from the beginnings till the Árpáds' conquest of Hungary. Written by the unidentified Magister P. (sometimes referred to as 'Anonymus') during the reign of King Béla III (1172–96), the book had been held abroad since its creation, only to be repatriated to the National Library of Hungary from Vienna in the 20th century. The most impressive historical work of the Hungarian Middle Ages is the chronicle (also called *Gesta Hungarorum*) of Simon Kézai, the court chaplain of Ladislas IV, written in 1282–5. The Leuven Codex of the late 13th century is a collection of MS sermons, including the first fragment of Hungarian literary text, known as *Ómagyar Máriasiralom* (Old Hungarian Lamentations of the Blessed Virgin), written on vellum at Orvieto by Dominican monks, three of whom were Hungarian. The Belgian university of Leuven (Louvain) finally agreed to give it to Hungary in 1982.

The first Hungarian printed book was produced in the Buda printing house of Andreas Hess at Whitsuntide in 1473, at the invitation of and with financial support from the city's provost, Vice-Chancellor László Karai. Hess, who was probably German, had left Rome for Buda—the spiritual and administrative centre of the Empire formed by the famous collector Matthias Corvinus—and proceeded to set up his printing office. Over the next five months, he produced his *Chronica Hungarorum* (also known as the *Buda Chronicle*). He cast his letters from matrices imported from George Lauer's press in Rome, and used the same paper and fount in his second, undated book printed in Buda. It comprised two works: Basil the Great's *De Legendis Poetis* and Xenophon's *Apologia Socratis*, with the colophon '.A: .H. Bude.' at the end of the first work.

Between 1477 and 1480, an unknown printer produced three more incunabula, most likely in Hungary, but at an unidentified place of printing. The first was the *Confessionale* of Antoninus Florentinus, archbishop of Florence; the second, Laudivius Zacchia's *Vita Beati Hieronymi*; and the third, a broadside indulgence granted by Canon Johannes Han to Agnes de Posonio (dated, by hand, 11 May 1480), was discovered near Pozsony (now Bratislava). All three documents were probably printed by a small itinerant press in Hungary from type cast from matrices attributed to the press of the Neapolitan Matthias Moravus.

Popular interest in MSS and books continued after the cessation of the two earliest printing offices. Foreign booksellers in Buda supplied the clergy and the royal court with books printed in Venice or MSS commissioned from Germany. Of nine Buda publishers, only two are known to have been Hungarian. Theobald Feger was the first in Hungary to sell Latin and German editions of Hartmann Schedel's Nuremberg Chronicle, printed by Anton Koberger. The most notable publication of the age, however, was János Thuróczy's (Johannes de Thwrocz) *Chronica Hungarorum*, printed in March 1488 in Brünn (Brno) for János Filipec, bishop of Olmütz (Olomouc). As Filipec's church press had no suitable type for secular works, his printers, Conrad Stahel and Mathias Preunlein, used the gothic founts of missals and a large number of high-quality woodcut illustrations. The *Chronica* was reprinted in June of the same year in

The royal Hungarian book collector, King Matthias Corvinus, depicted in a woodcut illustration to the *Chronica Hungarorum* by János Thuróczy (Johannes de Thwrocz), printed at Augsburg in 1488. © The British Library Board. All Rights Reserved. IB 6664, Page 148.

Augsburg by Erhard Ratdolt with a printer's device designed by Feger. This second edition, dedicated to Matthias Corvinus, was illustrated with more woodcuts, and is still the best-known and most distinguished incunable associated with Hungary, owned by many European and US libraries.

2 The Reformation and the baroque age

For most districts of Royal Hungary, the battle of Mohács (1526) and the subsequent Turkish occupation were followed by 150 years of turmoil, loss of independence, and economic degradation. Hungarian centres of humanist and literary thought were destroyed and Hungarian books came to be printed abroad, mainly in Cracow and Vienna. Thus, the first book printed entirely in Hungarian, an edition of St Paul's Epistles, translated and with a commentary by Benedek Komjáti (a follower of Erasmus), was produced at Cracow in 1533 by Hieronymus Vietor.

The traumatic experience of Mohács was associated with the birth of the Reformation. The reformers' teachings spread in the 1520s, gaining ground in the relatively secure region of Transylvania, the only Hungarian territory to have escaped Turkish occupation. In Braşov, Johannes Honterus (1498–1549), a learned reformer of the Transylvanian Saxons, set up his printing press in the early 1530s and went on to produce more than 35 works in Latin, Greek, and German. Still in Braşov, the first books in Romanian printed with Cyrillic types were attributed to Coresi, the deacon, printer, and editor who promoted vernacular Romanian in church as the official written language. More than 30 of his books were circulated throughout the Romanian lands. Another town that played an important role in the printing of Latin and Hungarian books while upholding Protestant reform was Kolozsvár (Cluj). There, Gáspár Heltai, preacher, writer, and pre-eminent theorist of the Hungarian Reformation, founded a famous printing office (originally, with György Hoffgreff) in 1550. Between 1559 and 1575, it produced 45 works in Hungarian, Latin, and Greek, all enriched with attractive woodcut illustrations. Heltai initially printed religious works, but he later turned to more secular genres: romances, tales, and legends. After his death, his wife continued to print less prestigious but no less entertaining chronicles in verse.

Other printers during the Reformation and Counter-Reformation produced material aimed at serving and supporting Hungarian Protestantism. The most significant of these, Gál Huszár, established his printing office first in Magyaróvár (Mosonmagyaróvár), then in Kassa (Košice). He later settled in Debrecen to print and publish the works of the Reformed bishop Péter Juhász Melius (1532–72). In 1555, Raphael Hoffhalter settled in Vienna, where his printing office produced 123 Latin and Hungarian publications during the following seven years. His Protestantism made him flee, in 1563, to Debrecen, where the quality of his books and engravings surpassed those of his predecessors. Between 1588 and 1590, Bálint Mantskovits established a printing office in

Vizsoly, producing the first complete Hungarian Protestant Bible. The Vizsoly Bible, translated by Gáspár Károlyi, is considered the finest undertaking of 16th-century Hungarian printing.

Under Habsburg domination, there were two noteworthy workshops on Hungarian territory. One was in Nagyszombat (Trnava), the centre of the Counter-Reformation at the time, where the Grand Provost Miklós Telegdi founded his press in 1578 and produced superb examples of baroque printing. The other press was located in Bártfa (Bardejov): its master printer, David Guttgesel, used attractive German types, borders, and ornaments in his Latin, Hungarian, and German books.

Most 17th-century Transylvanian Protestant printers, however, learned their art in workshops in The Netherlands. Ábrahám Szenczi Kertész became acquainted with Dutch book production while studying in Leiden. He founded his printing office in Nagyvárad (Oradea) in 1640 and printed more than 100 books, mostly in Hungarian. János Brewer brought his finely cut Dutch types back from Holland to his press at Lőcse (Levoča) to produce, with his brother Samuel, exquisite editions of Johann Amos Comenius' work, as well as the famous calendars of Lőcse.

Nicholas Kis followed the same pattern, starting his apprenticeship with the Blaeu family in Amsterdam, improving his type designing, cutting, and printing skills. By 1685 he had produced 3,500 copies of his Amsterdam Bible. In 1686 he published the Book of Psalms, translated by Albert Szenczi Molnár, and the New Testament in the following year. His European fame led to commissions from Holland, Germany, England, Sweden, and Poland. His Georgian, Greek, Hebrew, and Armenian types, cut with meticulous expertise, further enhanced his reputation. On his return to Kolozsvár, he brought together municipal and church presses, and in the next nine years published more than 100 finely printed inexpensive books, including the scholarly works of Ferenc Pápai Páriz, the scientist and compiler of a Latin–Hungarian dictionary. Kis strove to stamp out illiteracy and cultural backwardness and to develop a uniform Hungarian orthography.

In Transylvania the princes Gábor Bethlen (r. 1613–29) and György Rakóczi I (r. 1630–48) sought to deprive indigenous Romanians of their national rights and to convert them to Calvinism. The Romanians responded with a developing sense of patriotism, striving to promote their unified literary language. The Romanian New Testament (Alba Iulia, 1648), printed by its translator, Simion Ştefan, Metropolitan of Transylvania, during the autonomous province's golden age, was part of this process. Romanian printing with Cyrillic characters reappeared in 1733 in a calendar printed in Braşov and produced by the schoolteacher Petcu Şoanul. Enlisting the help of experienced Hungarian printers, Bishop Petru Pavel Aaron refurbished the Blaj printing works with new Cyrillic and Latin founts, as well as high-quality materials and typographic equipment, to produce large numbers of Romanian school textbooks and primers. This was a step towards a new age of secular culture.

3 Enlightenment and the Reform era

After the dissolution of the Jesuit order in 1773, the Nagyszombat University and Press, formerly under Jesuit leadership, was moved to Buda in 1777 to be managed by the printer Mátyás Trattner (1745–1828). In 1779, it was licensed to print and distribute textbooks for all Hungarian schools, but it also enthusiastically distributed Reform literature. Reorganizing and expanding production under Sámuel Falka Bikfalvi's direction, Buda's university press employed nineteen typefounders to supply most of the country's presses. Falka's types show the influence of foreign printers and designers, such as Didot and Giambattista Bodoni. As manager of the foundry, Falka renewed his types (much admired by the author Ferenc Kazinczy) while developing and producing beautiful wood and copperplate engravings.

Throughout the 18th century, printing offices opened in Eger, Esztergom, Temesvár (Timișoara), Pécs, Nagykároly (Carei), and Kassa (Košice), but none reached the high standards of the Debrecen or Kolozsvár workshops. By the end of the 18th and the beginning of the 19th centuries, competition among the growing number of printers forced prices and quality down. The development of lithography resulted in the break-up of technical and commercial networks; typographical traditions and aesthetic considerations were disregarded. With the mass production on cheap paper of ephemera, daily newspapers (*see* **16**), books, and journals, typographic standards sank to low levels.

The 19th-century Reform Movement sought to promote Hungary's economic and cultural progress. To eradicate the country's cultural backwardness, Count István Széchenyi (1791–1860) became the founder and sponsor of various projects and reforming institutions, including the Hungarian Academy of Sciences. His political writings, in which he argued that Hungary should remain loyal to the Austrian empire, were mostly printed by the newly founded Trattner-Károlyi Press. Another representative of the Reform Era was the printer and bookseller Gusztáv Emich (1814–69). During his 26-year publishing career he produced 663 works, of which 629 were in Hungarian. His printing and publishing enterprise effectively created the Athenaeum Literary and Joint Stock Limited Printing Company (1868), which by the end of the century had become the best-equipped printing establishment in the country.

Pallas, the country's largest printing and publishing firm, was founded in 1884. It boasted a modern typefoundry, a lithographic press, a bindery, rotary-offset and intaglio printing presses. Besides books, it produced journals as well as commercial and official documents. The eighteen-volume Pallas encyclopaedia (1893–1900) turned the Pallas Literary and Printing Company into Hungary's most prestigious enterprise. As the smaller printing offices gradually replaced their obsolete equipment with modern machinery, they developed advertising techniques and widened their business networks. Towards the end of the 19th century, the spread of literacy increased the demand for books so rapidly that booksellers became publishers. They sponsored Hungarian literature

and produced editions of national classics, large press runs of popular fiction, cheap newspapers, series of complete works, and translations of popular
authors, making contemporary world literature available to a Hungarian readership. By 1895, there were 104 printing offices in the capital, and their products
began to reflect the elements of the eclectic and Art Nouveau styles.

4 The 20th century

The Kner printing and publishing firm at Gyoma, founded in 1882, adopted
the theories and practices of earlier typographers and contemporary designers.
The family business was at its peak in the 1920s. Following losses suffered in the
war, Imre Kner (1890–1945) and Lajos Kozma (1884–1948) revived the typographic traditions of the baroque period, combining them with modern-day
typesetting technology. They produced remarkable works such as the 'Monumenta Literarum' and the 'Kner Classics' series. The Kner Press was the first to
announce the liberation of Hungary following World War II. It continued to
function under the directorship of the designer, printer, and researcher György
Haiman (1914–96), until it was nationalized in 1949.

Between the wars, the traditions of prestigious later 19th-century publishers—
Athenaeum, Révai Brothers, and Singer & Wolfner—in producing important
titles in small editions, with little art or music publishing, were continued.
World War II and the Communist takeover in 1948 changed everything virtually overnight. All publishing houses, booksellers, and printers were nationalized. The new copyright law stripped publishers of their rights; those not closed
down were amalgamated with larger socialist enterprises responsible for publishing within rigidly defined fields. Under the general censorship of the Ministry of Culture, which was ruled by the Communist Party, and the Book
Commission, their main task was to educate the masses. During the 1950s, publishing houses were based on Soviet patterns and integrated into a strongly centralized system. In 1952, the trade licences of 182 booksellers and 153 stationers
were revoked; the subjects assigned to the newly appointed publishing houses
remained unchanged for the following 35 years.

Throughout the 1960s and early 1970s, the political authorities chose which
literary works were to be supported or tolerated, and which to be banned and
their authors silenced by the general Directorate of Publishing. Although this
system of ideological control remained unchanged for more than 40 years, censorship gradually became more relaxed; economic difficulties led to dwindling
state subsidies; and the 1980s began to see a technically developed and intellectually strong publishing industry able to satisfy a readership that was by now
aware of Communism's impending collapse. Samizdat books did not have the
important role in Hungary that they had in other Soviet bloc countries. By the
end of the 1980s, there was little to distinguish samizdat from 'official' publications. The Hungarian Writers' Association became a stronghold of dissent as
well as a centre of political opposition. Its leaders played an important role in

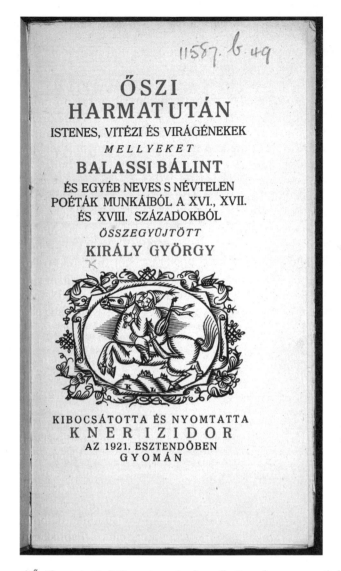

The title page of *Őszi harmat után* ('After autumn dew'), a collection of poems compiled by György Király, printed and published by Izidor Kner at Gyoma in 1921, with Lajos Kozma's woodcut vignette. © The British Library Board. All Rights Reserved. 11587 b 49, title page

the movement that marked the end of dictatorship. In 1987–8, the Europa publishing house produced Koestler's *Darkness at Noon*, Pasternak's *Dr Zhivago*, and, in 1989, Orwell's *Nineteen Eighty-Four,* all in excellent Hungarian translations.

5 Publishing after 1989

In 1989, censorship and state control over publishing were officially lifted. Legally registered companies were free to engage in publishing. Focusing chiefly on bestselling books and popular fiction, huge editions of previously banned literature were distributed by the burgeoning number of publishers and street vendors throughout the country.

After 1993, two of the previously state-owned distributors were privatized and remodelled to meet modern needs. This resulted in the creation of well-appointed large bookshops and the emergence of a balanced book market. Hungary had been one of the earliest European countries to be admitted into the International Publishers Association, hosting the first international conference of publishers in 1913. In 1998, the Hungarian Publishers' and Booksellers' Association (MKKE) joined the prestigious European Publishers' Federation and the European Booksellers' Federation, and in 1999 the country was chosen as guest of honour at the Frankfurt Book Fair, considerably enhancing its standing on the European cultural scene. In the 2000s, Hungarian publishing has been characterized by trends common throughout Europe: growth in sales volume; better quality production; greater variety of titles; expansion of bookshop chains; the establishment of web-based bookstores; and the expansion of electronic publishing.

BIBLIOGRAPHY

J. Fitz, *A magyar könyv története 1711-ig* (1959)

K. Galli, *A könyv története: I. A kezdetektől a 15. század végéig* (2004)

P. Gulyás, *A Könyvnyomtatás Magyarországon a XV. és XVI. században* (1931)

D. Simionescu and G. Buluță, *Pagini din istoria cărții românești* (1981)

34

The History of the Book in the Czech Republic and Slovakia

DEVANA PAVLIK

1 Historical background

Czechs and Slovaks shared their early history in the Great Moravian Empire, a 9th-century Slavonic state along the middle Danube. The first MSS were brought by missionaries promulgating the Church's Latin rite. Liturgical texts in Old Church Slavonic were introduced and copied by the Byzantine mission of Sts Cyril and Methodius who were invited, in 863, to replace the Latin rite with a language understood by the people. For this purpose, they invented Glagolitic script, translating liturgical texts and the Bible into Old Church Slavonic. When Great Moravia collapsed in 906/8 the Czech centre of power grew in central Bohemia, while Slovakia was, until 1918, under the rule of Hungary, whose religious, political, and cultural development it followed. The Czech lands of Bohemia and Moravia came under the dominance of the Holy Roman Empire.

Both the Czech lands and Slovakia were part of the Austro-Hungarian empire until its dissolution in 1918, when they co-founded a democratic state: Czechoslovakia. Until 1945, Czech and Slovak printing, publishing, and book-selling did not markedly differ from the rest of Europe. Fundamental changes came with the Communist takeover in 1948, however, when private firms were either liquidated or transferred into state ownership and centralized. Soviet-style organization of publishing and distribution was enforced, together with strict censorship. Material deemed politically undesirable was withdrawn from libraries. Some free Czech and Slovak émigré publishing continued abroad and was re-energized by the post-1968 wave of exiles. At home, independent underground publishing took off in the 1970s and 1980s, signalling future developments.

The demise of Communism in November 1989 brought complete transformation: with a market economy came the reorganization of the publishing and distribution industries as well as of libraries and archives. Private publishing ventures started practically overnight, and large print runs of suppressed works by dissident Czech and Slovak writers were produced. Translations of the latest fiction and popular non-fiction quickly appeared, satisfying demand for previously inaccessible literature. In 1993, Czechoslovakia was divided along its historical borders into the Czech Republic and Slovakia.

2 The Czech Republic

2.1 Early development

The 11th century saw the founding of monasteries and of cathedral and collegiate chapters that began assembling collections of imported and domestically produced MSS. The earliest evidence of biblical translations into Old Czech comes from the late 11th or early 12th century. Existing Czech texts were finally assembled into the complete Bible around 1380, the Czech translation being the third vernacular rendering of the Scriptures after French and Italian. Surviving MSS include 25 complete bibles, 27 Old Testaments, 35 New Testaments, 22 psalters, 17 gospel books, and numerous smaller fragments. Many are beautiful examples of Czech Romanesque and Gothic book illumination. The most outstanding among the early illuminated examples is the Codex Vysehradensis (1086); the most famous is the Codex Gigas, or Devil's Bible (1204), over one metre high. The foundation of the university at Prague in 1348 and the existence of the archbishopric there encouraged MS production that reached its zenith during the reign of Wenceslas IV (1378–1419), when only Parisian scriptoria outshone Prague's in the beauty of their illuminated codices.

Printing in Bohemia is traditionally thought to have begun in 1468 with *Kronika trojánská* (Trojan Chronicle), the first Czech printed book, and the New Testament (with the unclear inscription 'M.4.75'). Because there is no conclusive evidence, however, the Latin *Statuta Synodalia Arnesti*, printed at Pilsen in 1476, is now regarded as the first book printed in the Czech Republic. The majority of incunables were printed in Prague, but printing also went on at Vimperk in southern Bohemia.

Of the 44 surviving incunabula printed in Bohemia, 39 are in Czech and 5 in Latin. Most Bohemian printers were local craftsmen, but the situation differed in Moravia, where foreign printers worked. Of the 23 extant incunabula produced in the Moravian printing centres of Brno and Olomouc, 2 are in German and the rest in Latin.

Most titles were secular in nature. There were educational works (e.g. Latin grammars, Donatus' *Ars Minor*), legal works (Latin and vernacular), travelogues, legends, and chronicles (e.g. the *Trojan Chronicle*, in two editions; Twinger's *Martimiani* (1488); and the *Chronica Hungarorum* (1488), the first illustrated Brno imprint, printed in Latin). The Severin-Kamp press brought out the first illustrated Prague imprint, the Czech edition of Aesop's *Fables* (1488?). A Czech version of the popular *Legenda Aurea*, known as *Pasionál*, was printed twice, once lavishly illustrated, but it is the unillustrated edition that represents the height of Czech incunabula typography. There were almanacs, calendars, and other works, including *Von den heissen Bädern* (Brno, 1495), Folz's tract on the medicinal value of bathing in natural hot springs.

Sacred incunabula are dominated by biblical texts. The first complete bible in Czech, a folio of 610 leaves printed in double columns of 47 lines with titles in red, was printed in 1488 by Severin-Kamp. An illustrated edition, with 116 locally made woodcuts, was printed a year later in the silver-mining town of Kutná Hora (Kuttenberg) by Martin of Tišnov. The New Testament in Czech was also published in illustrated and plain versions. The Psalter appeared in Czech and Latin; there were also liturgical works, books on church administration, two missals, and a number of contemporary tracts, Catholic and Protestant.

Incunables in the vernacular were printed using Czech bastarda types, the earliest being the most ornate (emulating handwritten forms), the later influenced by rotunda and Fraktur. Textura and rotunda founts were used for Latin works; imported German Schwabacher is found in imprints connected with Prague University.

Several incunabula printers from the kingdom of Bohemia and Moravia distinguished themselves abroad, including Johann Sensenschmidt at Nuremberg and Bamberg, Mathias Grossmann Moravus at Naples, and Valentinus de Moravia, who printed the first book in the Portuguese language at Lisbon.

2.2 The 16ᵗʰ century

The 16th century was the golden age of Czech printing, with 4,400 titles printed. Religious controversies stimulated the growth of printing, driven in part by the rapid production of pamphlets and polemical literature. Humanism began to change the look of the printed book and its contents, and the increasing wealth of burghers brought books to a wider public. As the number of book collectors and readers grew, the libraries of professional men sometimes surpassed those of the nobility. Printing offices were established in many towns; bookselling was promoted through bookshops, markets, and book fairs, and via lists of books in print distributed throughout the country and abroad. In addition to printing in Latin (using Roman types), Czech, and German (using Fraktur and Schwabacher), there was also printing in Cyrillic script: the first bible in Cyrillic was printed in Prague in 1517–19 by Francysk Skaryna. The first book in Hebrew was printed in Prague in 1513, and, by the end of the century, there were several Hebrew presses operating in the city (*see* **8**).

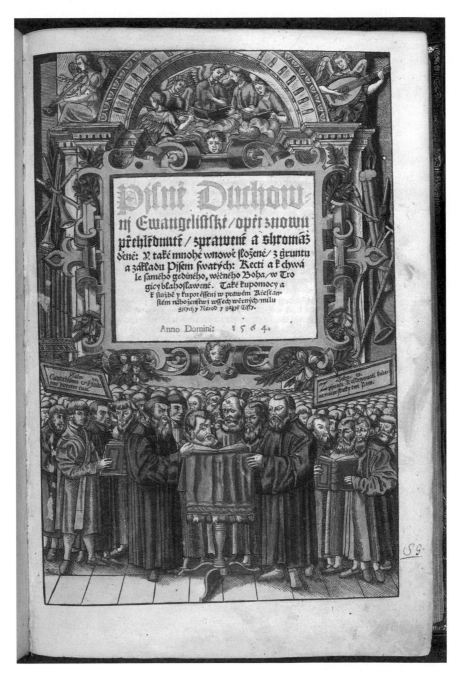

Music and books displayed on the title-page of the Moravian hymnal, *Pjsně Duchownj Ewangelistské* (Ivančice, 1564), generously illustrated with woodcuts; the British Library has a copy partly printed in gold. © The British Library Board. All Rights Reserved. C 36 g 12, title page

A monument of 16th-century Czech language and printing: a woodcut Mauresque from the sixth and last volume of the Kralice Bible (1579–94) incorporates the date of printing in its centre. © The British Library Board. All Rights Reserved. C. 114. n. 18.

Printing presses were established by scholars and intellectuals promoting humanist literature. Most significant was the press of Daniel Adam of Veleslavín, a Prague University professor who took over from the highly successful Jiří Melantrich z Aventina in 1584. Publishing 100 titles, Veleslavín was an enthusiastic promoter of the use of the Czech language in scholarly literature and founded modern Czech lexicography, his best work in this sphere being a monumental Latin–Greek–German–Czech dictionary (1598). He used some 50 different founts, employed high-quality ornaments, and lavished great care on title-pages, typically executed in black and red. The peak of 16th-century printing was achieved at the printing offices of the Unity of Brethren, especially at their Moravian locations in Ivančice and Kralice. Founded soon after 1500, the Unity was among the first printers to spread Reformation ideas. Its imprints are characterized by fine typography and design, and by the high standard of their Czech language. The Unity's six-volume Kralice Bible (1579–94) crowns the impressive sequence of Czech bible printing in this era.

2.3 The 17th and 18th centuries

The victory of the Catholic Habsburgs over the Protestants in 1620 had far-reaching consequences for the development of printing. The Czech language, regarded as a tongue of heretics and rebels, was replaced by German as the official language; printing in Czech was largely confined to prayer books, hymn books, sermons, hagiographies, novels, and folk tales. As exponents of the Counter-Reformation, the Jesuits exercised tight control over printing, which they concentrated in a small number of establishments. The largest of these was their own press at the Klementinum complex in Prague. Lists of prohibited books were compiled, and many books printed in the previous century were taken from their owners and banned and burned. Destroyed books were fast replaced by new material—textbooks, postils (biblical commentaries), hymn books, and homiletic literature—issued in large numbers by the Jesuits.

Many Czech scholars and artists, such as the educationalist Johann Amos Comenius or the engraver Wenceslaus Hollar, went abroad to work and publish, while foreign artists began leaving their mark on the baroque book in the Czech lands. Copperplate engravings replaced woodcuts in book illustration, and large presentation volumes incorporated engraved plates, frontispieces, and title-pages. Marked differences in quality emerged between editions of historical, legal, theological, and scientific works, and cheaply produced editions for the mass market. At the lowest end of the 'paper goods' market were broadsides, numbering some 6,000 items by the end of the 18th century.

The first periodicals appeared after 1658, achieving genuine popularity in 1719 with the *Prager Post*, published twice weekly by Carl Franz Rosenmüller, the best Prague printer of the rococo era, whose press issued historical works by Bohuslav Balbín, Václav Hájek, Gelasius Dobner, and others.

Enlightenment ideas and religious and social reforms introduced in the last part of the 18th century heralded the awakening of Czech national consciousness. Scholarly research into Czech history, the revival of Czech as a literary language, and new discoveries in science benefited from the relaxation of printing restrictions. The Royal Czech Society of Sciences was founded in 1770, and works by such eminent scholars as M. A. Voigt, G. Dobner, R. Ungar, J. Dobrovský, J. Jungmann, P. J. Šafařík, and F. Palacký were published. The publisher who best represented the Czech national awakening was Václav Matěj Kramerius (1753–1808), journalist and translator, who started his renowned *Imperial and Royal Prague Post Newspaper* in 1789. His 'Czech Expedition'—a centre for the publication and distribution of books in Czech, mostly renderings of popular foreign works—issued some 84 titles printed by various presses.

2.4 The 19th century

The first half of the 19th century saw the foundation of many learned societies and libraries, as well as the beginnings of modern Czech literature, especially poetry. The cost of publication, and sometimes distribution, was often borne by authors themselves. In science and the humanities, publishing was subsidized by the Matice česká, founded in 1831, which organized public collections and appeals for donations. With Matice's financial support, scientific illustration and the publication of maps and atlases developed and flourished. It ensured the survival of the *Journal of the Czech Museum*, that started in 1827 and continues to this day, and financed such significant undertakings as Jungmann's five-volume Czech–German dictionary (1835–39) and Šafařík's *Slovanské starožitnosti* (1837).

The second half of the century witnessed considerable developments in the field of Czech belles-lettres as well as science, and a corresponding growth of publishing houses. The largest firm was that of Ignác Leopold Kober (1825–66), which published *c.*300 titles including the first Czech encyclopaedia, the ten-volume *Slovník naučný* (1860–72), edited by František Ladislav Rieger.

Modern book illustration began in the 1860s with the artists Josef Mánes and Mikoláš Aleš. In the 1890s, Zdenka Braunerová pioneered the movement for the book as an aesthetic artefact (see artist's book); her compatriot artists Alphonse Mucha and František Kupka made their name in book art in France. The journal *Moderní revue* became a platform for the Decadent and Symbolist movements. The efforts of late-century graphic artists were summarized by Vojtěch Preissig, who provided the theoretical and practical foundation for the development of 20th-century book design.

2.5 The 20th century and after

The largest publishing house before the foundation of the Czechoslovak Republic in 1918 was that of Jan Otto (1841–1916). It encompassed many fields of knowledge for all levels of readership and price ranges, including prestigious illustrated journals (*Lumír*, *Zlatá Praha*, and *Světozor*) and several ambitious literary series. The firm's efforts culminated in 1888–1909 with the still-unsurpassed 28-volume encyclopaedia *Ottův slovník naučný*.

In typography, great advances were made in the first twenty years of the new century. Important developments in this sphere are connected with the 1908 foundation of the Association of Czech Bibliophiles and with Karel Dyrynk, Method Kaláb, and Oldřich Menhart. Typography was also of great interest to the Czech avant-garde, represented by Josef Šíma, Jindřich Štýrský, and Toyen, together with its theorist, Karel Teige.

During World War II, the seven-year Nazi occupation of Bohemia and Moravia severely restricted freedom of the press. These strictures were partly compensated for by publishing abroad, mainly in England, through the efforts of Czechoslovak forces and the exiled government.

The legacy of 40 years of Communism, 1948–89, with its centralized system of publishing, bookselling, libraries, and archives, meant huge changes when its rule ended. By the close of the millennium, economic changes—the rising cost of living and increasing book prices (the average book price rose by 260 per cent between 1990 and 1995)—resulted in a sharp drop in book sales. However, both the fact that quality publications maintained their value and the continuing vitality of the annual Prague Book Fair testify to a buoyant Czech book culture.

3 Slovakia

3.1 Early development

In Slovakia, the Nitra Gospels, dating to the end of the 11th century, were among the Latin MSS that were copied and kept in monasteries and chapter houses. Lay scriptoria arose at the end of the 14th century.

The first Slovak printed books, the work of an unidentified Bratislava printer, date to 1477–80. Lutheranism influenced the development of the first printing presses: 16th-century printers travelled frequently, forced to change their place of work when harassed for their religious beliefs. They set up in Košice, Šintava, Komjatice, Plavecké Podhradie, and Hlohovec, sometimes printing parts of one book in different towns. The Slovak printer Mikuláš Štetina Bakalár worked in Pilsen in Bohemia. The language of the landlord class and most of the urban population was Hungarian; until the end of the 18th century, a large proportion of Slovakian printing was carried out in Hungarian. Books in Czech for the Slovak-speaking population (standard written Slovak did not develop until the 1780s) were mostly imported from Bohemian and Moravian presses, which were better equipped to produce large volumes such as bibles, postils, and hymn books. Such printing in Slovakized Czech as existed in Slovakia concentrated on popular works, e.g. textbooks and calendars. By the last quarter of the 16th century, printing presses were established in Trnava, Bardejov, and Banská Bystrica. Bratislava grew in importance by the century's end when, during the occupation of a large part of Hungary by the Turks, many government bodies and schools moved there from Buda. The foremost Bratislava printing press, that of the archbishopric, flourished 1608–63. Printing grew in Trnava after the foundation of the university in 1635.

Until 1700, the centre of book production was concentrated in Levoča, mainly in the hands of the Breuer family, who produced some 700 titles by the late 17th century. Most of these were in Latin, but some were in the vernacular, including three editions of Juraj Tranovský's popular hymn book *Cithara Sanctorum* (1636, 1639, 1653) and Comenius' *Orbis Sensualium Pictus* (1685). The first newspaper in Hungary was printed in Levoča and Bardejov in 1705–10; others followed in Bratislava. Košice, the eastern Slovakian metropolis, rose to prominence as a printing centre in the 18th century. The works of Sámuel Timon, printed in Košice in 1733 and 1736, greatly contributed to the national identity of Slovakia, as did Bel's *Compendium Regnorum Sclavoniae* in 1777. The written Slovak language, based on western Slovak dialect, was codified by Anton Bernolák in 1787.

3.2 The 19th century and after

At the end of the 18th century, the Slovak National Revival, together with Enlightenment ideas, spurred the growth of printing, publishing, bookselling, and the founding of libraries. In 1843, Ľudovít Štúr, leader of the revival movement, introduced written Slovak based on the dialect of central Slovakia: this became the language of the revivalists and was accepted as the standard national language. Slovak revivalist printing was provided by the Jelínek Press (Trnava) and Škarnicel Press (Skalica), which issued the acclaimed journal *Slovenské pohľady*. Technical progress in the 19th century brought fundamental changes in printing, publishing, and distribution, facilitating further growth.

In 1870, the Book Printing Holding Association in Turčiansky sv. Martin became the leading printer of Slovak language books and periodicals. Vernacular publishing grew, leading to the foundation of the Booksellers and Publishers Holding Association (1885). The two organizations merged in 1908, representing the bulk of Slovak publishing prior to 1918.

Between the two world wars, Slovakia enjoyed unprecedented economic and artistic development. Many cultural and educational institutions were established or renewed, libraries of all types built, and publishing houses established to issue books in Slovak. The end of Communist rule advanced the Slovak quest for complete independence from the Czechs, which was attained in 1993.

In 2000, the Slovak National Library separated from the cultural body Matica Slovenská. Large publishing firms that survived the transition into the market economy, such as the SPN-Mladé letá, have been augmented by small independent publishers. The skilfully managed Petrus in Bratislava exemplifies current trends. The Bratislava Biennial of Illustrations (started in 1967) is arguably the most important international exhibition of book illustration for children and young adults worldwide. Under the patronage of UNESCO and IBBY, it presents several prizes and has exhibited work from some 90 countries.

BIBLIOGRAPHY

M. Bohatcová, *Česká kniha v proměnách staletí* (1990)

V. Breza, *Tlačiarne na Slovensku 1477–1996* (1997)

HDHB

F. Horák, *Pět století* [Five Hundred Years of Czech Printing] (1968)

I. Kotvan, *Inkunábuly na Slovensku* (1979)

Lexikon české literatury (1985–2008)

V. Petrík, *Slovakia and its Literature* (2001)

M. Strhan and D. P. Daniel, eds., *Slovakia and the Slovaks* (1994)

P. Voit, *Encyklopedie knihy* (2006)

The History of the Book in Poland

JANET ZMROCZEK

1 The foundations and development of book culture

When the Polish King Mieszko I was baptized in 966, his acceptance of Catholicism set the course of Polish cultural history and the development of the Polish book. Evidence suggests that MS books had come to Poland with Christian missionaries from neighbouring countries and farther lands (Ireland and Italy) even before Mieszko's official conversion. Poles themselves began participating in the development of an indigenous book culture only in the 12th–13th centuries; until this time, books were generally imported from abroad, or created by people from other countries. Annals and chronicles recording Polish history may have been written as early as the 10th century, but the first surviving example is the 12th-century *Rocznik Świętokrzyski*, now held by the National Library of Poland in Warsaw.

As Poles travelled more frequently to study at Italian and French universities and more monasteries were established on Polish soil, a greater interest in writing led to the development in the 13th century of a wider network of scriptoria, attracting native Polish clergy. The scriptoria in Silesia were particularly prolific, producing a number of richly illuminated MSS, including the oldest surviving MS containing a full sentence in Polish: The Chronicle of the Cistercian Monastery at Henryków. From the 14th and early 15th centuries, the book began to spread beyond church and court circles, encouraged in part by the beginning of writing in Polish. Important surviving Polish-language MSS of this period include the Sermons from the Holy Cross Mountain Monastery and *Psałterz*

Floriański, a richly illuminated codex containing psalms in Polish, Latin, and German.

Under the Jagiellonian dynasty (1385–1569), Poland, in union with Lithuania, was the largest and most powerful empire in Europe with a truly multi-ethnic population. It encompassed the Korona (Poland proper) as well as Lithuania, Orthodox Ruthenia, and Lutheran Prussia. Thus, German, Lithuanian, Ruthenian, Yiddish, and other minority languages coexisted with Polish, enabling cross-fertilization between diverse cultures. Political and economic prosperity facilitated patronage of the arts and an interest in books among royalty, magnates, and prosperous townsfolk, which led to a flowering of the art of illumination in the 15th–16th centuries, led by Cracow. The *Kodeks Behema*, (*c*.1505–6)—a compilation of statutes, privileges, and laws relating to trade and the guilds of Cracow, illustrated with exquisite miniatures—testifies to this. Cracow, the capital city and a thriving commercial centre, was home to the Akademia Krakowska (precursor of the Jagiellonian University) founded in 1364, where the professors found MS books a vital working tool, which they frequently donated to the Academy's library.

2 Printing to 1600

Printing in Poland began in Cracow, with the arrival of an itinerant Bavarian printer, Kasper Straube, in 1473. Schweipolt Fiol established the second Cracow printing office, subsequently printing the first four books in Cyrillic types (*c*.1490–91). The first printed text in Polish—daily prayers included in the *Statuta Synodalia Episcoporum Wratislaviensium*—appeared in 1475 at the Wrocław (Breslau) printing office of Kasper Elyan (*c*.1435–1486). In the 15th century, there were also printers in Malbork (Jakub Karweyse), Gdańsk (Konrad Baumgarten), and probably Chełmno (the anonymous printer of the sermons of Pope Leo I). However, Polish publishers still often used printers from abroad for more complex commissions, as Polish printers frequently lacked up-to-date types and equipment.

Polish-language printing in Cracow dates from 1503, when the wine merchant Jan Haller established his own printing office, run by the German Kasper Hochfeder. Their *Commune Incliti Poloniae Regni Privilegium*, a collection of Polish legislation compiled by Jan Łaski (1456–1531) was among the first of *c*.250 items printed by Haller in twenty years of work. He also owned one of Poland's oldest paper mills, at Prądnik Czerwony near Cracow, founded *c*.1493. Other prominent printers of early 16th-century Cracow were Hieronymus Vietor, the Szarffenberg family, Florian Ungler, and Maciej Wirzbięta. Both Ungler and Vietor made important contributions to the development of Polish language and its orthography. Ungler printed the first known book in Polish, *Raj duszny* (1513), a prayer book translated from Latin. Ungler's books were richly ornamented and illustrated (e.g. Stefan Falimirz's herbal *O ziołach i o mocy gich* (1534) with 550 fine woodcut illustrations). Vietor, initially a printer in Vienna, developed close links with humanist intellectuals there; his printing office in Cracow contributed to the dissemination of humanist thought. He printed works by Desiderius Erasmus and acquired Greek types to print the Greek writings of the Cracow humanists. Hungarians studying at the Akademia Krakowska also worked with Vietor to publish Hungarian grammars, dictionaries, and religious works. In the later 16th century, Jan Januszowski introduced new types and improved printing processes. His *Nowy karakter polski* (1594), published using his new types, established the rules of Polish orthography. He printed more than 400 titles, including many works by Jan Kochanowski. Wirzbięta printed most of the works of Mikołaj Rej, the first outstanding author writing exclusively in Polish. In the second half of the 16th century, Cracow had twelve printing offices, including one printing Hebraica (*see* **8**). In all, around 4,200 different titles were printed in Poland during the 16th century.

Both Ungler and Maciej Szarffenberg possessed Hebrew types, the latter using them in 1530 to print Phillippus Michael Novenianus' *Elementale Hebraicum*. The first Jewish printing house in Poland was founded in Kazimierz near Cracow in 1534 by the Helicz brothers, who learned the craft in Prague. They enjoyed great success until boycotted by their fellow Jews for converting to Christianity. Another early Hebrew printing house dating from 1547 was located in Lublin. Polish Hebrew printers, like Polish Latin printers, always faced competition from printers abroad, particularly in Italy, Bohemia, Germany, and Holland, since the importing of Hebrew books was unrestricted.

As in much of Europe, the Reformation and Counter-Reformation facilitated the spread of literacy and increased demand for print. Printing spread beyond the capital city to small towns and villages where Protestant printers operated presses under the protection of local landowners. In Poland-Lithuania, Lutheranism held sway in the north, whereas Calvinism, antitrinitarianism, and unitarianism took hold amongst the landed gentry, the magnates of Małopolska, the grand duchy of Lithuania, and even Europe's largest landowners, the Radziwiłłs. At first, Polish-language Protestant literature was printed primarily in Königsberg, where Jan Seklucjan published his New Testament (1551–3) in Polish. The first full text of the Bible in Polish, the *Biblia Leopolita* (1561)—published by Cracow Catholics, printed by the Szarffenbergs—was lavishly illustrated, but relied on older translations.

Meanwhile, the Polish Calvinists were working on a completely new translation, the *Biblia Brzeska* (Brest-Litovsk, 1563). The work of some dozen theologians, writers, poets, and translators led by Jan Łaski (1499–1560), it remains one of the great Polish cultural treasures both for its linguistic beauty and its appearance, though most copies were destroyed when Mikołaj Krzysztof Radziwiłł returned to the Catholic fold. The Catholics realized that in order for them to participate fully in the polemical debates raging at the time, a more accurate translation, drawing on the most recent research, was required. The result was Jakub Wujek's bible (Cracow, 1599). For the next three centuries, it was the canonical text of the Polish Bible. In response, other Protestant bibles appeared in the early 17th century, including the Polish Brethren's New Testament (1606), rigorously translated from the Greek, and the *Biblia Gdańska* (1632), the canonical text for Polish Protestants. No significant translations of the Bible into Polish appeared thereafter until 1965.

3 Relations between Polish and European cultures

In the 16th and 17th centuries, Polish writers, thinkers, and theologians were integrated into mainstream European culture. With Latin as the lingua franca of intellectual life, Poles studied and taught at universities in Italy, France, Switzerland, and Germany; many Protestants sought asylum in Poland, where from 1573 non-Catholics were protected by the state. Publishers in Germany, Switzerland, Italy, The Netherlands, France, and England produced works by Polish writers, many of whom were part of the European intellectual network. For example, Jan Zamoyski, founder of the Akademia Zamoyska, was close to Aldus Manutius in Venice. Several influential works of Polish history (e.g. by Marcin Kromer and Maciej z Miechowa) and treatises on government and politics (e.g. Andrzej Frycz Modrzewski's *De Republica Emendanda* and Wawrzyniec Goślicki's *De Optimo Senatore*) enjoyed great acclaim throughout Europe. In the 16th century, 724 titles by Polish authors were printed abroad, and in the 17th century more than 550.

4 The 17th and 18th centuries

By the mid-17th century, disastrous wars with Sweden and Russia, Cossack uprisings, and internal feuding had brought about the demise of Poland-Lithuania's golden age. Polish printing deteriorated, particularly in the second half of the century, as did cultural, economic, and educational life generally. The victory of the Counter-Reformation stifled much of the open debate that had characterized 16th-century Polish intellectual life. Printing became subject to strict censorship by the Church, which produced indexes of prohibited books; book burning became a public spectacle in Cracow. When Sigismund III moved his capital to Warsaw (1596), Cracow lost its supremacy as a printing centre because the privileges for government printing ceased. When the royal court moved to Warsaw, this privilege passed from the Piotrkowycz family in Cracow to Jan Rossowski, who had been printing in Poznań 1620–24. The Piotrkowycz family eventually donated all their printing equipment to the Akademia Krakowska, which formed its own printing house at the end of the 17th century. Another notable academic printer at this time was the Akademia Zamoyska in Zamość, which benefited from Januszowski's experience and equipment. Itinerant printers profited from the boom in the printing of ephemera, as in the rest of Europe (*see* **16**). A vogue for popular literature also developed, where the quality of the printing mattered little, if at all.

The Enlightenment reached Poland much later than it did western Europe: Polish culture was not revitalized until the 1730s, after the intellectual and institutional stagnation of the previous century. German influences in Gdańsk led to the first learned societies whose aim was to promote the sciences and humanities, and in Toruń, to developments in the study of Polish language and culture. Enlightenment ideas reached Warsaw considerably later, mainly through French influence, though in 1732 Józef Andrzej Załuski announced his intention to form a public library in Warsaw. Poland's last king, Stanisław August Poniatowski, played a pivotal role in the development of intellectual and cultural life via his support for the arts and reform of the state, including the introduction of state control of the educational system with the Commission of National Education. This necessitated an entirely new set of textbooks, since Polish replaced Latin as the language of instruction. New Polish terminology was introduced in mathematics, physics, and grammar; important steps were taken in the codification of the language, which reached fruition with the publication in 1807–14 of Samuel Bogusław Linde's six-volume dictionary of the Polish language. The press began to play an important role in public life with the magazine *Monitor* (1765–84), attracting the most significant writers and thinkers of the day. Warsaw supported eleven printing firms in the latter part of the 18th century. The most ambitious were those of Michael Gröll—who arrived in Warsaw in 1759 via Dresden—and Pierre Dufour, a Parisian who established his printing office in 1775 and produced titles in Polish, Hebrew, and Cyrillic. Their work characterized the new trend for simple, cleaner types and a modern design aesthetic enabled by new type foundries, such as that run by Piotr Zawadzki, a printer, publisher, and bookseller in his own right. Gröll also modernized Polish bookselling practice, holding auction sales, publishing fixed-price catalogues of his own publications, and promoting books by reviews. He also marketed Polish books abroad through firms in Amsterdam, Paris, and Berlin, and presented translations of Polish writers at the Leipzig book fair.

5 Book culture in partitioned Poland

After 1795, when Poland ceased to be a sovereign state and was partitioned between Russia, Prussia, and Austria, the fate of the Polish book was subject to the vagaries of the occupying powers. The printed word became a force that united Poles living in the tripartite partition with their fellow countrymen who sought asylum abroad, and kept a Polish national identity alive. Inside partitioned Poland, conditions varied. During the early 19th century, within the Russian partition, Wilno (Vilnius) was the most important cultural centre, largely because of the university where Polish Romanticism developed (with Adam Mickiewicz playing a central role). Józef Zawadzki, the leading printer in Polish, Lithuanian, and Hebrew, did much to modernize Polish bookselling and publishing: his authors were paid royalties, and he established a chain of bookshops in other cities. Wilno was also home to the Typographical Society, formed in 1818 to promote reading. This early progressive atmosphere came to an end after the November Uprising of 1823. In Warsaw, from 1801 the Society of the Friends of Science played an invaluable role in promoting academic publishing until its closure in 1831. During the later 19th century, without state support, the Polish School Society and the Mianowski Fund supported publishing both for schools and for research and academic communities. Influential private firms included the Glücksbergs for Polish history and literature, and the Arcts for textbooks, music, children's books, and, in the 20th century, dictionaries and encyclopaedias. The other major publisher of reference works was Samuel Orgelbrand, whose 28-volume *Encyklopedia Powszechna* first appeared in 1859–68. Gebethner & Wolff, founded in 1857, was the largest publisher, printer, and bookseller; the firm continued until the Communist authorities closed it in 1960. Among its authors were many of the greatest writers, composers, and historians of the day: Władysław Stanisław Reymont, Henryk Sienkiewicz, Bolesław Prus, Bruckner, and Szymanowski.

A weak economy and intensive Germanization policies subdued the development of Polish cultural life throughout the Austrian partition during the 19th century, though the scope for Polish educational, cultural, and social activities revived after Galicia gained autonomy in 1868, with Cracow and Lvov playing a leading role. Lvov was the site of the Ossoliński Institute; Cracow was home to the Academy of Sciences (founded 1873) and the Jagiellonian University, which regained its Polish identity in the 1870s and thus resumed its role as the centre for academic publishing. Cracow was also at the heart of the revolution in Polish artistic book design encouraged by the Young Poland movement at the turn of the century. The artist and dramatist Stanisław Wyspiański, influenced by William Morris and Walter Crane, sought to bring to his works a unity of form and content that expressed national characteristics with secessionist and symbolist aesthetics. His work with members of the Polish Applied Arts society, Józef Mehoffer and Zenon Przesmycki (founder of the Warsaw journal *Chimera*), laid the foundation for the modern Polish book arts.

In the Prussian partition, particularly strong pressures to Germanize left no infrastructure for higher education or Polish learned societies until the later 19th century, when the Society for Public Education (1872–9) and the Poznań Society of the Friends of the Sciences (1857–) were formed. Poznań was the regional centre for bookselling, printing, and publishing activity, with many bookshops also operating reading rooms and lending libraries. In Silesia and East Prussia, material was also produced for the Polish-speaking population—chiefly popular and religious literature, calendars, journals, and practical manuals.

6 Nineteenth-century Polish publishing abroad

Publishing activity both by Polish exile communities of the Great Emigration after the failed Uprising of 1830–31 and by subsequent waves of political refugees was particularly important. The centre of Polish printing abroad was in

Paris, where many of the great works of Polish Romanticism were first published. In the period 1831–61, some twenty Polish printers were active in eleven French cities, with significant activity also in the UK, Belgium, and Switzerland. The first Polish-language publications in England were pamphlets of the utopian socialist organization, the Grudziąż Commune in Portsmouth. The first Polish book printed in London, Antoni Malczewski's *Marja* (1836), was printed at an English press using Polish types. Stanisław Milewski and Aleksander Napoleon Dybowski opened the first Polish printing office in London in 1837 to publish the journal *Republikanin*. Although the Polish community in Great Britain was small compared to that in France, it was politically very active, and published prolifically for its size, with output intended for readers in the UK community, émigré communities elsewhere, and sometimes in partitioned Poland itself. Radical Poles in London had close links with other such groups, including the Russians; 1853 saw the founding of a joint printing house for the Polish Democratic Society and Herzen's Free Russian Press. Between 1891 and 1903, B. A. Jędrzejowski (Józef Kaniowski) ran a printing office for the Polish Socialist Party in London.

7 The 20ᵗʰ century

When Poland regained independence in 1918, printing, publishing, and cultural life were reinvigorated, but many obstacles remained for the development of reading and book culture. Literacy levels were low (*c.*33 per cent in 1921) and book prices were high. There were approximately 500 publishers in Poland in 1935; overall production in terms of titles had nearly trebled from *c.*3,000 (early 20ᵗʰ century) to *c.*8,700 (1938). Gebethner & Wolff remained the giants of Polish publishing and bookselling, but the Arcts were still influential, as was the Mianowski Fund for the publishing of scholarly works; however, there was still a preponderance of small and medium-sized firms. There were more than 1,000 bookshops, but these were very unevenly distributed, with many in Warsaw and other large cities and few in the eastern and western provinces. In the 1920s–30s, as in the rest of Europe, there was renewed interest in the art of the book in Polish circles. A number of bibliophilic associations emerged to publish journals such as *Ex Libris* (1917–25) and *Silva Rerum* (1925–31) and to support printers with artistic ambitions. These included Jakub Mortkowicz, who distinguished himself in the early 20ᵗʰ century as a literary publisher of writers such as Cyprian Norwid and Stefan Żeromski; he was influential in setting up Polish booksellers' and publishers' associations. Other producers of acclaimed artistic books were Adam Jerzy Połtawski and Samuel Tyszkiewicz. Tadeusz Makowski and Tytus Czyżewski, both working in Paris, were also renowned Polish illustrators.

World War II resulted in huge losses for Polish culture. Under German occupation, schools and bookshops were closed. Printing houses and libraries came under German administration. Polish publishers were forbidden to operate;

three German firms published popular literature, primers, and propaganda in Polish. All Jewish bookshops, libraries, and printing offices were destroyed. Soviet occupiers also removed collections of books and whole libraries from Poland's eastern territories, sometimes burning them as they went. There was wholesale destruction of books deemed undesirable by the occupiers; booksellers, librarians, and private individuals heroically endeavoured to hide their collections and so preserve the national printed heritage. An underground publishing infrastructure developed, far more prolific than that in other occupied countries. It produced more than 1,500 journals and 1,400 book titles. During the war, Poles in exile and in military camps abroad also published extensively, producing some 15,000 titles overall.

Immediately after World War II, with the publishing, bookselling, and library infrastructure all but destroyed, many prewar publishers sought to satisfy the hunger for books sparked by the government's education campaign. From 1946, Communist authorities began exerting control, establishing a system of censorship and assuming control over publication rights for the principal twelve classic Polish authors—required reading in schools and thus the largest sellers. Censorship suppressed the publication of works considered harmful to the interests of the Polish People's Republic, including all mention of Polish–Russian relations and other controversial political issues. In reaction to this, London, sometimes called the Polish capital abroad, became the greatest centre of free Polish publishing. Major London publishing houses included Gryf, Veritas, Oficyna Poetów i Malarzy, the Polish Cultural Foundation, and Odnowa. With print runs as high as 2,000, they flourished until the mid-1970s, when the older generation of Poles began to die and émigré literature lost some of its vitality, though later waves of emigration after the political crises of 1968, 1976, and 1981 led to some revitalization. The Instytut Literacki in Paris was also influential, publishing books and the monthly journal *Kultura*. At times in postwar Poland, there were harsh punishments for possessing émigré literature, and its importation was strictly prohibited. However, as clandestine publishing took off in the late 1970s, new generations of Poles were able to read émigré classics and other independent publications.

In Poland itself, from the late 1940s, private publishers were branded as petty capitalists with no place in the new popular democracy. In 1949–50, printing, bookselling, and distribution were all brought under state control. Before 1950, approximately 300 private publishers were in operation; by 1955, 97 per cent of books were published by 33 publishers heavily centralized in Warsaw. Despite huge subsidies and record press runs, the needs of the reading public were not met. For example, the thirteen-volume *Works* of Stalin was published in a print run of 1.8 million, while textbooks and belles-lettres were in short supply. The state bookseller, Dom Książki, bought the entire print run of every book published, so publishers had no interest in whether a title sold well. Books often cost less than the paper on which they were printed, straining available resources. From 1956, the de-Stalinization of Polish cultural policy led to far

Polish samizdat publishing: George Orwell's *Folwark Zwierzęcy* (*Animal Farm*; Warsaw, 1979), originally translated by Teresa Jeleńska for the League of Poles Abroad (London, 1947), here illustrated by Andrzej Krauze. The stapled binding is noteworthy. © The British Library Board. All Rights Reserved. (Sol. 244 FC)

fewer titles being published—and these in lower print runs—as well as to more realistic publishing programmes and pricing policies.

Publishers' and booksellers' associations were allowed to operate again and seek out new writers. Policies that kept Polish readers isolated from Western ideas and literature were slightly relaxed, although international links were still fostered primarily within the Soviet bloc. However, the 1960s and 1970s were marked by perennial paper shortages and the inability of Polish publishing to satisfy reader demand. Books were often printed on poor paper with low production standards.

In the late 1970s a new phenomenon began to ripple the stagnating waters of Polish state publishing. Samizdat was known to small, select audiences in a number of Communist countries, but in Poland, the phenomenon of independent publishing reached a mass audience. The organizational strengths of Polish oppositional movements such as KOR (the Committee for the Defence of Workers), coupled with assistance from abroad, meant that many independent publishers could work at a professional level, using materials and equipment from official printing houses or smuggled in from abroad. Some titles had press runs reaching more than 100,000. From 1976 to 1989, more than 6,500 books and 4,300 periodical titles were published, printed, and distributed underground. This breaching of the government's control over the media and publishing played a profound role in the collapse of Communist power.

Since the later 1980s the state monopoly had been progressively weakening, and in May 1990 censorship and state control over publishing were officially lifted. The early 1990s saw a production boom, with thousands of new publishers, many short-lived, making the most of the public's hunger for popular fiction in translation, cookbooks, practical manuals, etc. The state publishers were gradually privatized or became cooperatives. Polish readers finally had access to the full range of books, including those by previously banned writers or on taboo subjects. In 1999–2003, the number of book titles published per annum hovered around 20,000. In 2003, not surprisingly, the largest number of titles (500) was published by WSiP, a specialist in textbooks, but a further seven firms produced more than 200 titles each. Of the 20,681 book titles appearing in 2003, just under a quarter were translations. The first decade of the 21st century has been characterized by common global trends: retail book chains, Internet bookselling, and growth in electronic publications.

BIBLIOGRAPHY

B. Bieńkowska, *Książka na przestrzeni dziejów* (2005)
——and H. Chamerska, *Books in Poland* (1990)

Encyklopedia wiedzy o książce (1972)
J. Sowiński, *Polskie drukarstwo* (1988)

$\sim\!\!\!\curvearrowleft\ 36\ \curvearrowright\!\!\!\sim$

The History of the Book
in the Baltic States

JÜRGEN M. WARMBRUNN

1 The independent states

The Baltic States comprise the Republics of Estonia, Latvia, and Lithuania. As the so-called Baltic Sea Provinces, all three states formed part of the Russian empire in the 18th and 19th centuries (except for Lithuania Minor, which was under the governance of Prussia and later of Germany). The three states proclaimed their respective independence in 1918, losing it again in 1940 following the Hitler–Stalin pact and annexation by the Soviet Union. After the outbreak of the war between the Soviet Union and Nazi Germany, the Baltic States were briefly occupied by German troops until the Soviet Union reconquered and annexed the republics within the USSR. Under Soviet occupation, the Baltic States suffered severe population loss through deportation and emigration, the latter resulting in a sizeable output of émigré publications (e.g. in Sweden, Germany, the UK, US, and Australia). Following the establishment of strong pro-independence movements during the second half of the 1980s, Estonia, Latvia, and Lithuania formally declared their independence in 1990 and de facto became independent sovereign states again in 1991. In 2004, they became members of the European Union and NATO.

2 Similarities and differences

The historical and cultural development of Estonia and Latvia has been largely influenced by the presence of a German upper class—originally established under the rule of the Teutonic Order and comprising noblemen, academics, clerics, merchants, and craftsmen—as well as by their long affiliation with Russia and later the Soviet Union. Lithuania in turn has strong historical ties to Poland; the two countries formed a 'Republic of two Nations' (Rzeczpospolita Obojga Narodów) between 1569 and 1795, and share a predominantly Catholic faith. Particularly in Estonia and Latvia, the Reformation played a major role in the spread of books and reading in the vernacular. Latvian and Lithuanian are both Baltic languages and form part of the Indo-European linguistic family, whereas Estonian is a Finno-Ugric language, which in part explains the traditionally strong ties between Estonia and Finland.

Under Soviet rule, the Baltic States' printing and publishing industries were nationalized into large state enterprises and tightly controlled to forestall the publication of dissenting opinions. In Latvia, for example, following a 1965 decision by the Central Committee of the Communist Party of the Soviet Union, the issuing of all newspapers, journals, and other publications was centralized in the Riga Printing House, where editorial staff and production facilities for the whole country were concentrated. During the occupation of the Baltic States, the Soviet authorities nevertheless permitted the publication of a considerable number of works in the three languages.

The library system in the Baltic Soviet republics had been reorganized according to Soviet directives. Since 1990, however, the independent countries have again developed a system of public and academic libraries offering free access to their holdings and information resources. In Estonia in particular, libraries also play a major role in the dissemination of information technology and use of the World Wide Web.

Following the return to independence, censorship was abolished in the Baltic States and a new printing, publishing, and bookselling sector has developed under free market conditions with a wide variety of publishers and booksellers. Estonia and Latvia still have significant Russian minorities, a fact that results in a continuing demand for Russian language publications in those countries.

3 Estonia

Fragments of the first surviving work printed in Estonian come from a catechism printed at Wittenberg in 1535, the Wanradt-Koell Catechism. Printing in Estonia itself developed only in the 17th century: first—from 1631—in Dorpat (Tartu), and later—from 1634, when Cristoph Reusner established his successful enterprise—in Reval (Tallinn). Book publishing in Estonian began in 1637, and periodicals in Estonian followed in 1766. Many printers also worked as booksellers and publishers. From the second half of the 19th century, the numbers of printers and of printed materials in Estonia increased rapidly; towards the end of the first period of independence in 1936, there were 94 printers at work.

The first itinerant booksellers were active in Estonia in the 16th century, while the earliest bookshops recorded in Tallinn and in Tartu date from the 17th.

Initially, books were mainly sold by bookbinders, but later, printers also offered their products for sale. Independent bookshops developed in the 18th century (Gauger in Tartu, von Glehn in Tallinn), often operating subscription libraries simultaneously. In the 19th century the numbers of publishing companies increased, mostly due to the merging of printing and bookselling enterprises.

Publications in Estonian were originally distributed by shops catering for the needs of country people, and later by itinerant booksellers. The first bookshop selling Estonian language publications was established in 1867 by Heinrich Laakmann in Tartu. The publication of titles in Estonian, the official language of the new state, increased enormously following its first declaration of independence in 1918.

The development of libraries in Estonia has been strongly influenced by the country's political and social changes. Tallinn has only a few pre-Reformation fragments from monastic libraries, while the library holdings of the Swedish University in Tartu were taken to Stockholm in 1710. The oldest book collection still to be found in Estonia derives from St Olav's Church in Tallinn. Reading societies in Estonia developed towards the end of the 18th century. In 1825 the Estonian Public Library was founded in Tallinn, and the country's major academic library, the Tartu University Library, was founded in 1802. From the 1860s, libraries catering for the Estonian-speaking population developed in towns and in the country. In 1918 the Estonian provisional government decided to establish a state library, originally designed mainly to meet the needs of government and parliament; by the 1930s, it began systematically to collect all publications in Estonian and on Estonia.

4 Latvia

The first work in Latvian was most likely printed in Germany in 1525, but the oldest surviving Latvian printed text is a Catholic catechism printed at Vilnius in 1585, closely followed by books printed in Königsberg for Latvian evangelical parishes (1586–7).

In 1588, the Riga town touncil established the Riga Town Printing House, owned by Nicolas Mollyn, who also acted as a bookseller. Following a Swedish initiative, a second printing office—the Royal Printing House—was established in Riga by J. G. Wilcken, publishing many books in Latvian and Estonian. In Mitau (Jelgava), a printing office existed from 1666–7, but its importance was later overshadowed by J. F. Steffenhagen's printing company (1769–1919). For the region of Latgale (which came under the control of Russia in 1772 through the First Partition of Poland, and underwent a ban on using roman script), books were mostly printed in Vilnius. Although, by the end of the 18th century, there were printers throughout the country, the first printing office run by Latvians was not opened until 1869. During the country's first period of independence, the number of printing firms increased considerably owing to much higher demand, reaching 108 in 1931.

Vernacular works were mostly sold by itinerant booksellers (colporteurs, or chapmen) who are documented in Riga from the second half of the 15th century. Bookshops traded mainly in conjunction with printers and bookbinders. Of primary importance is the bookseller J. F. Hartknoch, who also ran a publishing firm, maintained close links with western Europe, and published the most prominent Baltic authors of his day, including Kant and Johann Gottfried von Herder. The first Latvian-language publishing firms set up business in 1867 in Riga and Jelgava. The turn of the century saw a huge expansion of the book industry, which continued to flourish during Latvia's first period of independence.

Despite the loss of the famous collection of the dukes of Courland to St Petersburg in 1714, Latvian libraries have a long history, beginning with the foundation, in 1524, of Riga City Library which was based on the libraries of secularized monasteries. In 1885 the Jānis-Misiņš-Library was founded, with the aim of documenting the history of the Latvian book. The library of the University of Latvia (founded in 1909) took over the holdings of the earlier Polytechnic Institute, and the foundation of the National Library of Latvia followed the country's first declaration of independence (1919).

5 Lithuania

Printing, publishing, and bookselling in Lithuania were largely influenced by religious divisions. Duke Albrecht of Prussia brought theologians from Lithuania to Königsberg, where works in Lithuanian intended to strengthen the Lutheran faith were printed. Martynas Mažvydas's Lutheran catechism, printed in roman type in 1547 by Hans Weinreich in Königsberg, is regarded as the first Lithuanian book. Earlier, between 1522 and 1525, the first vernacular editions of the Bible had been printed in Vilnius by Francysk Skaryna. From 1553, printers worked with roman type in Brest-Litovsk. Their printing equipment was later transferred to Vilnius and given to the Jesuits for use in their university by Count Mikolaj Krzysztof Radziwiłł, whose family supported the printing of both Protestant and Catholic books in the 16th and 17th centuries. By 1805 the Vilnius Academic Printing House had produced 3,264 titles, mostly in Latin and Polish, but also in Lithuanian. Among these are the first Lithuanian Catholic books: Mikalojus Daukša's catechism (1595; the unique copy is now in the Vilnius University Library) and *Postilla* (1599), as well as the earliest Lithuanian Dictionary by Konstantinas Sirvydas. The first Lithuanian grammar, however, was printed in Königsberg (1653). Until the 18th century, there were also 33 smaller printing houses working for Catholics, Protestants, and the Orthodox in Lithuania.

Following the uprising of 1863–4, the Russian governor-general banned the printing of Lithuanian books in roman type in an attempt to Russify the country, a move strongly opposed by the nationalist movement, the Catholic Church, and the general population. As a consequence, Lithuanian Catholic books with roman characters were printed in Prussia at Memel and Tilsit and brought illegally over the border by *knygnešiai* (book-bearers).

In 1900, there were 51 printing houses in Lithuania, producing Russian, Polish, and Jewish publications. Once the printing of Lithuanian books in roman type had been legalized again (1904), there was a significant increase in the number of printing offices, which—as in the other Baltic States—flourished, particularly in the first period of independence; between 1918 and 1940, 110 printing companies operated in Lithuania. The Polish printing firm of Zawadzki, successor to the Academic Printing House, was the most productive in Vilnius, combining publishing, printing, and bookselling activities between 1805 and 1940. Because Kaunas was Lithuania's interwar capital, a large number of publishing houses opened there, among them state, university, ministerial, minority, and private commercial publishers.

The existence of book collections in the Roman Catholic monasteries of Lithuania dates back to the 16th century. The library of the Jesuit Academy in Vilnius later became part of the Vilnius University Library, but, following the university's closure, its holdings were taken to Kiev, Kharkov, and St Petersburg. During Lithuania's first period of independence, a central library was founded in the capital Kaunas, but its books and MSS were transferred to Vilnius in 1963 to form the State (today National) Library of Lithuania. Since 1922, Kaunas has also had a university with its own library, which was closed in 1950, but reopened in 1989 following independence. The holdings of the Kaunas Art Institute were among the many losses suffered by official and private libraries in the Baltic States during World War II.

BIBLIOGRAPHY

H. Bosse *et al.*, eds., *Buch und Bildung im Baltikum: Festschrift für Paul Kaegbein* (2005)

K. Garber and M. Klöker, eds., *Kulturgeschichte der baltischen Länder in der Frühen Neuzeit* (2003)

Z. Kiaupa, *The History of the Baltic Countries*, 3e (2002)

L. Kõiv and T. Reimo, eds., *Books and Libraries in the Baltic Sea Region from the 16th to the 18th Century* (2006)

A.-M. Kõll, ed., *The Baltic Countries under Occupation: Soviet and Nazi Rule, 1939–1991* (2003)

P. Lotman and T. Vilberg, eds., *The 20th-Century Libraries in the Baltic Sea Region* (2004)

37

The Slavonic Book in Russia, Ukraine, and Belarus

CHRISTINE THOMAS

1 Early East Slavonic MSS

There is no direct evidence of written documents from East Slavonic lands before the acceptance of Christianity by Prince Vladimir of Kiev *c.*988. From the 11th century, there are twelve extant MSS (seven of them dated) written in Old Church Slavonic in Cyrillic script. The first MSS are the Novgorod Codex (beginning of 11th century), discovered in 2000; the Ostromir Gospels (1056–7); and Sviatoslav's Miscellanies (*Izborniki Sviatoslava*) (1073, 1076). These compendia of works by the Church Fathers, parables, riddles, moral instructions, aphorisms, and citations originated in Kiev in the reign of Prince Sviatoslav. Three of the 11th-century MSS (the Ostromir Gospels, the Sviatoslav Miscellany (1073), and the Chudov Psalter) are richly illuminated and contain decorative woodcut headings made of intertwined letters, known as *viaz'*. All surviving pre-14th- century MSS are on vellum, after which paper came increasingly into use. In Novgorod, archaeologists have unearthed medieval commercial and private texts scratched with a bone stylus on birch bark.

2 The beginning of printing

The earliest Cyrillic books, printed in the Balkans and in Crakow by Schweipolt Fiol, were liturgical and closely modelled on MSS (*see* **38**). They are mostly small folios (without title-pages), with elaborate interlaced woodcut headpieces and initials, a lavish use of red, and with signed gatherings but without foliation. Later products, such as Francysk Skaryna's Cyrillic imprints, were closer to the central European Renaissance tradition and completely alien to Moscow printing, which began only in the 1550s; they influenced the work of some later Ukrainian and Belarusian printers.

Seven undated liturgical books were printed in Moscow in 1553–67 at the Anonymous Press, which was founded at the instigation of Tsar Ivan IV (the Terrible) and Metropolitan Makarii to ensure both the uniformity and the wider circulation of Orthodox liturgical texts. The earliest dated Moscow imprint is the famous 1564 folio *Apostol* (liturgical Acts and Epistles), printed by Ivan Fedorov and Petr Timofeev Mstislavets. It has elegant and well-set type and headpieces of white flowing foliage on a black background, typical of Muscovite MSS and later printed books. In 1565, Fedorov and Mstislavets printed two editions of a book of hours but then, accused of heresy, fled to the grand duchy of Lithuania.

After their departure, printing in Moscow revived in 1568 and continued sporadically until the city's Printing House burned down in 1611, during the Time of Troubles. Five other 16th-century printers are named in surviving Muscovite books: it seems likely that printing expertise came to Muscovy from Poland, with Ukraine and Belarus acting as a conduit. By the end of the century, some twenty editions had been published in Moscow, all Orthodox liturgical texts, the vast majority at one press controlled by Church and state.

3 Printing in 17th-century Moscow

In the 17th century, Moscow became the single greatest producer of Cyrillic books, most coming from the Moscow Printing House (Pechatnyi dvor), reopened in 1614. The House was divided into three 'huts', each under a master printer and with its own proofreading department, forge, carpenter's shop, typefoundry, block-making shop, and bindery. Its output was almost entirely religious in content, the vast majority of its books being large-format liturgical works, though the largest press runs were for smaller-format primers, psalters, and books of hours. In the 1630s the master printer Vasilii Burtsov Protopopov, who had earlier worked with the Belarusian itinerant printer Spiridon Sobol, began to lease two presses in the Printing House. Burtsov broke new ground for Moscow. In 1634 and 1637 he produced primers in two large editions of 6,000 and 2,400 copies, respectively; the 1637 edition had a woodcut of a schoolroom, the first illustration in a Moscow-printed book. His *Kanonnik* of 1641 was the first Muscovite book to have a title-page.

Under Tsar Alexei (r. 1645–76), the Printing House's repertoire became more varied. Alexei, with aspirations to modernize Russia and to create an orderly and efficient realm, not only attempted to standardize church ritual and liturgical texts but instigated, in a limited way, secular printing. He commissioned codes of civil (1649) and canon law (completed in 1653), and a book on infantry warfare (1647), translated from the German of Johann Jacobi von Wallhausen's *Kriegskunst zu Fuss* (1615).

Yet it was the Church, rather than the government, that provided the main impetus for printing: decrees and other government documents were not printed. The energetic Nikon, appointed Patriarch of Moscow in 1652, set the Printing House the task of standardizing and revising liturgical texts, seeking to ensure their accuracy. Church councils in 1654 and 1656 produced his corrected versions and banned earlier texts and liturgical practices. A group of Old Believers rejected these innovations, continuing to copy in MS and to print the pre-reform texts until well into the 20th century.

In 1663, the first Moscow Bible appeared. It incorporated a number of innovations, such as a woodcut frontispiece with the national coat of arms, a portrait of the tsar, a map of Moscow, and Old and New Testament scenes. By the end of the 17th century, about 500 books had been printed in Moscow, almost all religious in content and all in Church Slavonic. The first grammar of the vernacular (Russian) language was printed at Oxford in 1696.

4 Belarusian and Ukrainian printing, 16th–17th centuries

In contrast with Muscovy book culture, the Ukrainian and Belarusian book developed in an environment where Orthodoxy was not the sole religion. However, printing with Cyrillic type in those lands was influenced by the wish of the Ukrainian and Belarusian Orthodox to keep their religion alive. Although most printers were itinerant, some printers and Orthodox merchants had their own presses. Of the presses financed by merchants, the most famous was that of the Mamonich family in Vilnius. Other presses were set up by magnates, such as the hetman Hryhorii Chodkiewicz and Prince Vasyl Kostiatyn of Ostrih (Konstanty Wasyl Ostrogski). At the Ostrih (Ostrog) Press on Kostiatyn's estate, Fedorov printed five books, notably the Bible of 1581 that served as an archetype for the Moscow Bible (1663). The third category of printing houses was those of the Orthodox confraternities whose educational programmes needed grammars and books on poetics, rhetoric, and philosophy as well as polemical works. The most prolific were in Lviv (1591–1788), headed by the distinguished printer Mikhail Slezka, and in Vilnius, established in 1591. A fourth category of presses was the monastery presses. For Belarusian book culture, the most important was that of the Vilnius Holy Spirit Monastery, and, for Ukrainian works, the press of the Kiev Monastery of the Caves, founded in 1616. Throughout the 17th century, this press continued to produce books of very high scholarly and technical standards, especially during the tenure of Petro Mohyla. In the second half of the century, most privately owned presses ceased to exist, and printing was dominated by the monasteries. Although only Vilnius, Kiev, and Lviv developed into major printing and bookselling centres, presses were active in more than 30 locations.

Ukrainian and Belarusian books were closer to mainstream European print-ing tradition than Muscovite books. For example, dates of printing were given in the Western style from the birth of Christ, whereas Moscow followed the Byzantine tradition of dating from the creation of the world. Even religious books contained secular elements: there was some use of the vernacular and wider use of illustrations, title-pages, commentaries, and indexes.

5 Eighteenth-century Russia

The end of the 17th century marked a turning point in the history of Russian printing. In 1698, Peter the Great hired Dutch printers to establish Russian presses for printing maps, charts, and books on technical subjects, and com-missioned the new Civil founts for secular publications. The state supplanted the Church as the main driving force behind printing. In the tsar's new capi-tal, the St Petersburg Press, established in 1711, became the main publisher of government publications, notably the *Vedomosti* (News), the first printed Russian newspaper. A new monastic press was established at the Alexander Nevsky Monastery outside St Petersburg in 1719. The Moscow Printing House (known, from 1721, as the Moscow Synodal Press) expanded, and the quan-tity of religious printing under Peter grew, though not as fast as secular printing.

Twice as many books were published during Peter's reign (1682–1725) as during the whole of the 17th century, with state and legal documents constitut-ing more than 60 per cent of the titles, religious publications totalling less than a quarter, and popular publications (calendars and primers) forming the third largest category. Fewer than 2 per cent of publications were devoted to history, geography, science, and technology; these, intended for a narrow audience, were issued in small print runs. Between 1727 and 1755, the Russian Academy of Sciences press published about half of all new books and over three-quarters of secular books. Its products, including Russia's first scholarly journal, *Commentarii Academiae Scientarium Imperialis Petropolitanae*, were almost invariably in Latin or German, and so were accessible only to a small readership. The Academy bookshop, opened in 1728, sold Russian and foreign books, and from 1735 it issued a catalogue that also circulated in the provinces.

In 1714, the Russian Academy of Sciences Library opened in St Petersburg to all, free of charge; Moscow State University Library and press were established in 1755–6. The 1750s saw the expansion of the periodical press, an increase in the publication of literature translated into Russian, and, to a lesser extent, of original works in Russian. These developments were given impetus by the ini-tiatives of Catherine the Great (r. 1762–96). She supported the founding of the Society for the Publication of Foreign Books (1768–83), which was responsible for the publication of 112 separate translations (including Fielding, Tasso,

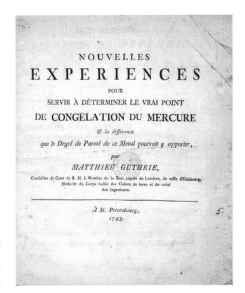

NOUVELLES

EXPERIENCES

POUR

SERVIR À DÉTERMINER LE VRAI POINT

DE CONGÉLATION DU MERCURE

& la différence

que le Degré de Pureté de ce Metal pourroit y apporter,

par

MATTHIEU GUTHRIE,

Conseiller de Cour de S. M. I. Membre de la Soc. royale de Londres, de celle d'Édinbourg,
Medecin du Corps noble des Cadets de terre et de celui
des Ingenieurs.

À St. Petersbourg,
1785.

International science in 18ᵗʰ-century Russia:
the Scottish scientist Matthew Guthrie,
living in St Petersburg, publishes his
account of the freezing point of mercury.
The Bodleian Library, University of Oxford
(G. Pamph. 1821(5))

Jean-Jacques Rousseau, Montesquieu, Voltaire, and selections from the *Encyclopédie*), and became the leading voice for the Russian Enlightenment. In the wake of Catherine's initiation of the journal *Vsiakaia vsiachina* (Odds and Ends, 1769), a spate of short-lived satirical journals, on the model of English periodicals such as the *Spectator*, came into existence, four of them edited by Nikolai Ivanovich Novikov.

6 Private printers in Russia

In the 1770s, leasing agreements were granted to some non-native printers, and in 1771 J. F. Hartung became the first private printer in Russia—for foreign books only. A 1783 decree permitted the free establishment of presses anywhere within the empire, subject to the censorship of local police. Half a dozen independent presses sprang up in Moscow, including Lopukhin's Masonic press, with which Novikov was closely associated. It published some 50 works before being closed down in 1786. By 1801, 33 private presses had opened in Moscow or St Petersburg, publishing over two-thirds of Russian books. Most private printers were from the merchant class; the majority were non-Russian, and largely German-speakers. There was a smaller group of 'intellectual' publishers. For all private publishers, finances were precarious. State monopolies had been granted to institutions (mainly the Academy) for the few profitable types of publication—textbooks, calendars, and almanacs. However, private publishers were able to exploit the growing market for popular adventure stories; the most sought-after was Matvei Komarov's bawdy *Adventures of the English Lord George* (1782).

Only the police, the senate, or the empress had the power to ban books. In the face of the publication of Old Believer texts and a growing number of mystical, including Masonic, works, the Church felt most threatened by relatively unrestricted printing. In 1787 an imperial edict authorized the synod to search all bookshops and publishing houses in the empire. The subsequent 'book raids', especially stringent in Moscow, temporarily paralysed the book trade, although ultimately few books were confiscated. On reopening, bookshops recovered quickly until the outbreak of the French Revolution. In 1790–95 several writers and publishers were arrested, books were confiscated, and printing offices closed down. Imports of French books and newspapers were banned. The first (official) presses had been established in the provinces in 1784; by the end of the century, seventeen provincial capitals had printing offices. The 1795 clampdown provided a stimulus to provincial printing, with a number of printers moving out of the capitals. In September 1796, two months before her death, Catherine issued an edict revoking the right of individuals to operate their own presses. The repression of Catherine's last years was intensified by her son Paul (r. 1796–1801), and by the end of the century, only three active private presses remained.

Alexander I (r. 1801–25) allowed the independent presses, closed under the 1796 law, to reopen. A decree of 1804 established Russia's first systematic censorship legislation, which, although relatively liberal in spirit (operated not by the police but by the ministry of education), introduced the concept of pre-publication censorship. Private publishing, overwhelmingly concentrated in the capitals, revived very slowly, and operated far below the level of the late 1780s. The book market was too small to make unsubsidized publishing a viable enterprise. However, some firms, like that of Semen Ioannikievich Selivanovskii and Ivan Petrovich Glazunov, the most famous representative of the Glazunov dynasty of publishers and booksellers, emerged and were to play an enduring and prominent role. The Academy, kept afloat by its monopoly on calendars, remained the dominant publisher of scholarly monographs and journals. Besides its main journal, *Mémoires de l'Académie* (then in its fifth series), it launched in 1804 the innovative and successful *Tekhnologicheskii zhurnal* (Technological Journal), intended to popularize science. It also continued to publish *Sanktpeterburgskie vedomosti* (St Petersburg News), and produced textbooks for the educational institutions established in the early 1800s.

7 From 19th-century Russia to World War I

In the first half of the 19th century, education expanded and university enrolments grew, stimulating a demand for books among a wider section of society. Printing technology improved, and in the 1830s the first successful commercial publishers and booksellers emerged.

The war against Napoleon had a devastating effect on the trade: the 1812 fire of Moscow destroyed presses (including Moscow University Press), MSS, and thousands of books. The following years saw a steady recovery. The Ekspeditsiia Zagotovleniia gosudarstvennykh bumag, established in St Petersburg in 1818 for the printing of bank notes, incorporated a paper mill, and by the 1820s Russia was producing much of its own paper. In 1812, the first iron press was imported for use by the Russian branch of the British and Foreign Bible Society. The first lithographic presses appeared in St Petersburg (1816) and Moscow (1822). Moscow University Press—which by 1825 had overtaken the Academy in size, with 30 presses—was the main producer of textbooks and modern literature. The skills of a rising school of Russian engravers were used in finely printed books, including about 40 publications devoted to Russian history, commissioned by Nikolai Petrovich Rumiantsev.

Until the 1820s, most elite reading was of works in French, but then a vogue arose for Russian-language almanacs, similar to the gift books fashionable in Britain and the US; they were popular with a new readership of women educated in institutes for aristocratic girls, boarding schools, or at home. The most famous almanacs of the 1820s (e.g. *Poliarnaia Zvezda* (Polar Star) in 1823–5, and *Mnemozina* in 1824–5), featuring some of the best Russian authors of the day, were literary and commercial successes, stimulating interest in native writing. They also played an important part in the professionalization of authorship, since their publishers paid fees to contributors. In the 1820s and 1830s, an increasing demand for home-grown literature was met by the works of such authors as Ivan Krylov and Aleksandr Pushkin, although all writings were severely censored following the failed Decembrist uprising (1825).

Bookshops and fee-based circulating libraries had existed in Moscow and St Petersburg from the mid-18th century, owned primarily by foreigners. The bookshop and library opened in St Petersburg in 1788 by the Russian bibliographer Vasilii Stepanovich Sopikov was a notable exception. After 1812, however, the trade was mostly in the hands of Russians. The most outstanding library was that of the bookseller and publisher Vasilii Alekseevich Plavil'shchikov, founded in St Petersburg in 1815. By the 1820s it had a stock of 7,000 titles and had become a meeting place for writers. Upon his death in 1823, Plavil'shchikov left his bookshop and library to his most valued assistant, Aleksandr Filippovich Smirdin, under whose aegis it became one of the richest in Russia.

Some of Smirdin's publications, such as his two-volume *Novosel'e* of 1833–4, are prime examples of the Didot style of typeface, introduced to Russia by the typefounder Zhorzh Revil'on (Révillon). The press and type foundry of Adol'f Pliushar (Pluchart) was also in demand for fine publications. Other St Petersburg firms that came to prominence include those of the Glazunov family (whose catalogues remain an invaluable bibliographical source), and of Isakov, Bazunov, and Lisenkov. Iakov Alekseevich Isakov was at work from 1829 until his death in 1881, with a lending library for foreign books and an office in Paris for the purchase of French books. One of Smirdin's former salesmen, Fedor Vasil'evich Bazunov, set up the St Petersburg branch of the business, in 1835 (its Moscow branch was run by other family members). After 1854, it expanded

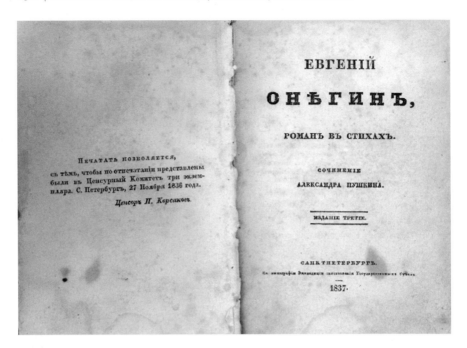

The third edition of Aleksandr Pushkin's *Eugene Onegin* (St Petersburg, 1837), the last for which he read proofs. A thirty-twomo, such miniature books (it is 11cm tall), were a novelty in Russia at the time. The Museum of the Miniature book, Azerbaijan

under Aleksandr Fedorovich Bazunov until its bankruptcy in the early 1870s; the firm also produced useful catalogues.

In Moscow, the leading figures were the bookseller and publisher Aleksandr Sergeevich Shiriaev and the French publisher and printer Auguste Semen, whose press was considered the finest in Moscow. Among institutional publishers, the Academy's repertoire was broadening. From 1834, its *Mémoires* were divided into four specialized subject series, and in 1836 it launched a *Bulletin scientifique* with more concise articles and announcements. Moscow University Press continued its dominance: by mid-century it was still producing a third of all secular Moscow publications. Religious publications were produced in considerable numbers by the Synod Press.

Provincial publishing, which had seen some expansion from the 1820s onwards, continued to develop very slowly, dominated by local government publications. Provincial readership also grew slowly, poor transport making books 10–12 per cent more expensive in the country. In the 1830s, 'thick' encyclopaedic journals began to find a niche, constituting popular and useful reading for country landowners and their families. Urban publishing in the 1830s saw an increasing readership, larger editions, lower prices, and the expansion of periodical circulation. However, the economic depression of the 1840s was followed by the Crimean War and the 'Seven Years' Gloom' (1848–55), with a tightening of censorship in response to European revolutions. A number of booksellers went out of business.

Between 1855 and 1860, there was a striking increase in the number of periodicals: over 150 new titles appeared. The political climate under Alexander II (r. 1855–81) allowed the topic of the emancipation of the serfs to be discussed in print. The abolition of serfdom in 1861, economic recovery, the flourishing of trade and industry, and the growth of the railways resulted in a corresponding upturn in the production and distribution of printed material. Despite intensified censorship (responsibility for censorship passed in 1865 from the relatively enlightened ministry of education to the ministry of the interior), this growth continued into the 1870s. Large-scale capitalist enterprises began to emerge, among them the publishing houses of Mavrii Osipovich Vol'f and Aleksei Sergeevich Suvorin in St Petersburg, and Ivan Dmitrievich Sytin in Moscow. Suvorin and Sytin became leading newspaper proprietors.

The tsar's reforms also resulted in the development of public lending libraries in the 1860s. Charitable literacy committees raised funds for the creation of over 100 local libraries. The publisher Florentii Fedorovich Pavlenkov bequeathed his entire fortune to create more than 2,000 public libraries. Following Alexander II's assassination in 1881, censorship became harsher. Numbers of publications, especially those on political topics, declined; but the end of the 1880s saw an increase in scholarly works, and a government drive for economic growth resulted in a proliferation of agricultural and technological materials. Around the turn of the century there was an expansion in mass market publishing, ranging from Marxist publications to cheap editions of Russian and foreign classics and translations of detective novels.

The material infrastructure for printing expanded and developed; the number both of presses and of technological advances—including the introduction of rotary presses and the mechanization of typesetting—grew (*see* **11**). Educational works became a more important strand in popular publishing. A series of inexpensive editions of Russian classics and Western authors in large print runs was launched by Suvorin, who established retail outlets in many provincial towns. The publishing firm Posrednik (Intermediary), established in 1884 as a joint enterprise of Sytin, Tolstoy, and his disciple Vladimir Chertkov, provided wholesome and edifying booklets for the minority of literate peasants (13 per cent), as did some 50 educational organizations. Catering to the higher end of the educational market were the St Petersburg firm Prosveshchenie (Enlightenment, established 1896), and the German-Russian concern Brokgauz & Efron.

In contrast with the largely utilitarian, mass-produced publications most typical of this time, some lavish illustrated books and magazines also appeared, exemplified by the journals of the World of Art (Mir iskusstva) movement. The work of some of the best illustrators of the period can also be seen in the short-lived satirical journals that sprang up after the 1905 revolution, when censorship was temporarily in abeyance. From 1910 to 1914, Russian Futurist poets and painters collaborated to produce handmade books, with very limited press runs, later to become collectors' items.

The first years of the century up to the outbreak of World War I saw an unprecedented expansion in Russian publishing, with a growing emphasis on the commercial mass market. Whereas between 1801 and 1900, c.2,500 titles had been published, some 400,000 appeared between 1901 and 1916. In 1912 and in 1913, Russia produced nearly as many books as Germany. The outbreak of war caused figures to slump; there was a chronic shortage of paper (the huge growth in Russian output had made the country dependent on imported printing supplies, particularly from Germany) and many presses were forced to close. The chief academic publishers, such as the Academy of Sciences and Moscow University, as well as some of the larger commercial publishing houses, survived the war, and the printing of government patriotic literature, as well as of Bolshevik leaflets and broadsides, continued.

8 Ukraine and Belarus within the Russian and the Austro-Hungarian empires

The 18th century saw a decline in Ukrainian and Belarusian book culture. Russian imperial decrees in the 1720s banning the publication of anything apart from liturgical texts identical to those printed in Moscow and St Petersburg limited the previously distinctive nature of Ukrainian printing. The first work of literature in modern Ukrainian, Ivan Kotliarevs'kyi's burlesque travesty of Virgil's *Aeneid* (in which the Trojan heroes become Cossacks expelled from their homelands by the Russian government), circulated in MS and was eventually published in St Petersburg in 1798. Publications in Ukrainian, or even in the Ukrainian recension of Church Slavonic, were not allowed. No longer permitted to publish new texts, the Kiev Monastery Press did, however, continue to produce books with ornaments and illustrations, including excellent woodcuts by prominent Ukrainian artists. The presses of the Uniate monasteries—at Pochaiv (1734–1914) and at Univ (1660–1770)—on territory that remained part of Poland-Lithuania, became the most productive centres. Printing for the Orthodox in Belarus, also part of Poland-Lithuania, was restricted by the Catholic Church. Publishing continued in the (Uniate) Supraśl Monastery and nine other cities.

As a result of the first partition of Poland, Russia gained more Ukrainian and some Belarusian territories. State presses were opened in Elizavetgrad (1764), Kharkiv (1793), Kiev (1787), and Ekaterinoslav (1793), and in the administrative centres of Belarus (Vitebsk, Hrodna, Mohileu, and Polotsk) for the publication of official directives and reports in Russian.

In the first half of the 19th century, there was still no Ukrainian-language publishing. The Ukrainian-language *Istoriia rusiv*, an anonymous history of the Ukrainians, circulated in MS, as did some other books in the language. Several publishers in Ukraine (notably Kharkiv University Press, founded in

1805) touched on Ukrainian themes. Kiev University Press (founded 1835) published some important historical documents on national history in its four-volume *Pamiatniki* (Monuments, 1845–59), and from 1839 the Odessa Society for History and Antiquities began publication of its journal. In 1836 Ivan Timofeevich Lisenkov, a native of Ukraine, established his publishing and bookselling business in St Petersburg, specializing in Ukrainian authors; and in the 1860s, against a background of increasing national cultural awareness, the scope of Ukrainian publishing in Russia widened somewhat. Panteleimon Aleksandrovich Kulish set up a press in St Petersburg, publishing the works of Ukrainian authors, textbooks in Ukrainian for Sunday schools, and, in 1861–2, the only Ukrainian-language periodical in the empire, *Osnova* (The Base). In East Ukraine, centres of printing included Kiev, Odessa, Chernihiv, and Poltava.

Ukrainian-language printing in East Ukraine was again curtailed by the 1876 Edict of Ems, which authorized the publication of only limited subject matter—historical documents, ethnographic materials, and belles-lettres (subject to approval by the censor)—and also required that permission be sought for the importing of Ukrainian-language publications from abroad (e.g. Prague, Vienna, and Geneva, as well as Western Ukraine). From 1875, some underground revolutionary and populist presses were set up in Odessa, Kiev, Kharkiv, and Ekaterinoslav.

One of the results of the 1905 revolution in Russia was the appearance of Ukrainian- and Belarusian-language magazines, newspapers, and educational societies. New Belarusian publishers began work, two in St Petersburg and three in Vilnius, where one, *Nasha Niva* (Our Cornfield) and its newspaper of the same name, came to embody the early 20th-century Belarusian literary renaissance.

A 1906 law established freedom of publication of books for non-Russian nationalities, including the Ukrainians. The Kiev publisher Chas (Time, 1908–20) made a particularly important contribution to the development of Ukrainian culture, producing works by Ukrainian authors, translations from other languages, and textbooks for a mass readership. Nevertheless, Ukrainian publications were censored more strictly than those in other 'minority' languages of the Russian empire. From 1798 to 1916, only about 6,000 books were published in Ukrainian, and fewer than half of those within the Russian empire.

In Western Ukraine, conditions for publishing became more favourable following the 1867 Austro-Hungarian Constitution. Private and institutional presses were founded in Lviv, Chernivtsy, Peremyshl, and Kolomye; the most influential and long-lasting were those of the Prosvita (Enlightenment) society, established in 1868, and the Shevchenko Scientific Society, which set up a press in Lviv in 1873.

During World War I, most Ukrainian publishing was carried out abroad—in Vienna, Canada, and the US. During the short-lived period of Ukrainian statehood

(1917–21), 78 Ukrainian titles were published in 1917, and 104 in 1918. In 1918–19, the National Library of Ukraine and the Ukrainian Book Chamber (centres for legal deposit and national bibliography) were founded.

9 The Soviet Union

Soon after the October 1917 revolution, all press organs deemed to be counter-revolutionary were closed down. A number of pre-revolutionary publishing houses, including Sytin, were allowed to continue operations. In the civil war years, when publishing reached its lowest ebb, Russian publishers abroad, notably Zinovii Isaevich Grzhebin in Berlin, were enlisted to help supply textbooks for the government's literacy campaign.

The first state publishing enterprises were set up from 1918, among them Vsemirnaia Literatura (World Literature), the State Publishing House, and Kommunist. The most important, the State Publishing House (Gosizdat), established in 1919, was charged with regulation of other publishing bodies, state and private, and after 1921 was producing one third of all books on Soviet territory. The printing industry was nationalized. In 1922, with the foundation of the Soviet Union, bodies equivalent to Gosizdat were established in East Ukraine and Belarus, now designated 'Soviet Socialist Republics'. Moves were made to build up the library network. All significant private book collections were nationalized, benefiting especially the Petrograd Public Library (later National Library of Russia) and the Library of the Rumiantsev Museum (later the Russian State Library). Both had been designated legal deposit libraries in May 1917. The Chief Administration on Publishing Affairs (Glavlit) was established in 1922 and operated as the main organ of censorship until 1990. During the years of the New Economic Policy (1921–9), some relaxation of state control galvanized the publishing industry, leading to a rise in the quantity and quality of publications. By the late 1920s, print runs of a million were not uncommon. Gosizdat, with its subsidies, control over allocation of scarce paper supplies, and right of first refusal of all MSS, retained its favoured position, but private publishers were again allowed to operate. By January 1925 there were 2,055 publishing houses in the Soviet Union, of which around 400 were private. Some of the best avant-garde artists of the time produced remarkable books. Innovation in literature was also tolerated. However, as the 1920s progressed, there was more and more state pressure for 'approved' literature (propaganda, socio-economic and political titles) to be published.

The Soviet government also followed a policy (1925–32) of 'indigenization', promoting the indigenous languages of the Union's non-Russian peoples. There was an initial period of Ukrainianization during which Ukrainian-language book publishing, though state-controlled, increased. A Ukrainian-language-based education system was introduced, dramatically raising the literacy of the Ukrainophone rural population. By 1929 the number of Ukrainian newspapers, of which there were very few in 1922, had reached 373 out of a total of 426 titles published in the republic. Of 118 magazines, 89 were Ukrainian. There was a renaissance of national literature, and book publishing in Ukrainian reached 83 per cent of the total output.

The 1930s brought dramatic strengthening of the powers of censorship, wielded not only by Glavlit but, increasingly, by the Central Committee of the Communist Party and the USSR Writers' Union. In literature, the doctrine of socialist realism ruled. An attempt was made to eradicate duplication and to rationalize publishing; as a result of mergers and restructuring, a number of specialized state publishing houses were formed under the aegis of the Association of State Publishing Houses (OGIZ). There were parallel developments in Ukraine and Belarus. However, duplication and inefficiency remained widespread.

Government sales of rare books and MSS (including the Codex Sinaiticus) abroad for hard currency impoverished Soviet libraries and enriched public and private collections in Europe and North America. The Stalinist terrors of 1934 and 1937–9 resulted in bookshop and library purges: works written by or making reference to condemned people or on forbidden subjects were removed, to be destroyed or placed in libraries' special, restricted-access collections ('spetskhrans'), together with most foreign publications. Writers, bibliographers, and book historians were among those to perish in the purges. In 1939, Western Ukraine (Galicia) was incorporated into the Soviet Union and all its publishing houses were closed down (50 had existed in the interwar period).

World War II brought with it a chronic shortage of paper, the relocation of much publishing away from Moscow and Leningrad, and loss of Soviet control in areas under German occupation. Book production fell from about 40,000 titles in 1941 to about 17,000 in 1944. Rare items from libraries in the western part of the USSR were evacuated to the east, but thousands of books were lost, as a result of bombing or seizure by the Germans, and more than 40,000 Soviet libraries were destroyed. Many libraries managed to function throughout the war, including the Leningrad Public Library (later National Library of Russia), which served readers throughout the 900 days of the siege of Leningrad. There was some underground publishing in the occupied territory of Belarus and Ukraine, and the Belarusian Gosizdat, evacuated to Moscow at the end of 1942, continued to function.

After the war, the Soviet publishing industry recovered relatively quickly: by 1948 output had come close to 1938 levels, and it rose steadily thereafter. The industry retained its prewar structure, and output was very much influenced by the dictates of the Party. Following Stalin's death in 1953, Khrushchev's dismantling of the Stalin cult and selective relaxation of censorship resulted in some liberalization of literature, and diversification in the content of published works. In Russia, a degree of polemical debate appeared in the literary journals, both hard-line (notably *Oktiabr'* (October) and liberal.

Among the latter, *Novyi mir* (New World), edited by Aleksandr Tvardovskii, was in the forefront, publishing Solzhenitsyn's *One Day in the Life of Ivan Denisovich*.

An August 1963 decree initiated a radical reorganization of publishing, printing, and the book trade; by 1964, these had a structure that was to remain in place until the emergence of a market economy in the 1990s. In order to establish more effective government supervision, responsibility for control of the press in the Soviet Union passed to the State Committee for the Press (renamed State Committee for Publishing, Printing, and the Book Trade in 1972), directly subordinate to the USSR Council of Ministers (other republics had separate equivalents). It was charged with reducing the number of publishing houses and rationalizing areas of coverage assigned to those remaining. However, both in the book trade and in library supply, the cumbersome 'administrative command' system, which inhibited publishers' ability to respond to readers' demands, caused a shortage of the books that people wanted to read. Along with samizdat, a thriving black market emerged not only to disseminate dissident and other forbidden literature but also to make up for the shortage of popular and perfectly legal publications.

During the Brezhnev era, known as the 'period of stagnation', the book industries remained stable. In the 1970s and early 1980s, all printing was censored, and the central control of raw materials and printing continued to influence print runs. Authors were paid to a standard formula, according to genre (e.g. fiction or textbook) and length. Perhaps for this reason, the average length of a Soviet book in 1984 was about 136 octavo pages, in contrast with the average 82 pages during the 1930s.

One of the Soviet media's clichés—that the USSR was 'the world's foremost nation of readers'—could in many ways be justified. The book industry had few rivals worldwide in numbers of titles and copies published. Illiteracy had been virtually eradicated, and more than half the population were users of the extensive network of urban and rural libraries. Yet, for seven decades, the book was essentially the ideological tool of a totalitarian state.

The Gorbachev reforms brought about a loosening of state control, initiated from above and seized upon from below. The Law on State Enterprises (1987) allowed some private initiatives, and the Law on the Press and the Media (1990) guaranteed their freedom. The Law also allowed any organization or individual to register as a publisher and establish mass media publications. State publishers were given more leeway to decide what they would publish, and some were leased to collectives. The first private publishing firms, small cooperatives, appeared in 1988, and a considerable number were established in 1989–90, but most were short-lived. A parallel press emerged, producing thousands of semi-legal leaflets and periodicals of every conceivable kind, among them anarchist, feminist, Green, nationalist, and religious.

10 Post-communist Russia

Following the break-up of the Soviet Union in 1991, the collapse of centralized control brought with it a crumbling of state structures. The political and economic crises of 1990 and 1991 brought the publishing industry to its knees. In 1992 there was an all-time slump, with only about 28,000 books being published, but there were already signs of recovery in 1993. In 2000 the Russian Book Chamber registered 56,180 titles (surpassing the previous official record of 55,657 titles in 1977). The Book Chamber record is almost certainly an underestimate because of the failure of some publishers to comply with legal deposit. The shape of the industry also changed: by mid-1993, state houses were producing only 30 per cent of books, and in the ensuing years private publishers took over more and more of the market. By 2000, the seven most prolific publishers were all—with the exception of the state-owned textbook publisher, Prosveshchenie—private firms, less than a decade old. Some of the larger ones— EKSMO, Terra, and Olma-Press—had acquired their own printing plants and distribution systems.

With the demise of the state publishers and the appearance of private houses more responsive to demand, the two most popular genres to emerge were crime and romance novels. In the early 1990s, these were translations of foreign writers, but Russian authors largely superseded them later in the decade. Glossy magazines also began to make an appearance. Another significant growth area was encyclopaedic dictionaries on a wide range of subjects. Scholarly publishing survived, and even flourished, aided by finance from NGOs (non-governmental organizations). Alongside books on previously taboo subjects or by banned authors, works formerly published in centres of Russian publishing abroad—such as Paris, Frankfurt-am-Main, Berlin, Israel, and various cities in the US and Canada—made their first appearance in Russia.

There was considerable democratization in libraries, in spite of difficulties caused by dwindling financial support from the state. By the early 1990s, the considerable task of releasing restricted books from the spetskhrans and entering them in general library catalogues was virtually complete. The 1994 Law on Libraries guaranteed all citizens free access to information through libraries. An Open Society programme, Russian Libraries on the Internet, helped to provide access through the World Wide Web.

11 Post-Soviet Belarus

At the end of the Soviet period, Belarus was probably the most Russified of all the republics, with a weak sense of national identity. At the very time in early 1989 that a law was passed prohibiting cooperative or private publishing, the first private publishers appeared, circumventing the law by purchasing ISBNs from Russian publishers in return for giving them 10 per cent of every print run.

In the early years of independence, up to 1994, the government had a policy of Belarusianizing education and reviving the moribund literary language (kept alive in the diaspora). The works of émigré writers were published. Post-1990, more books, booklets, magazines, and newspapers were published in Belarus: 2,823 books (435 in Belarusian) were produced in 1990 compared with 7,686 (761 in Belarusian) issued in 2000.

In 1995, the Russian language was given official status along with Belarusian. Although the situation in Belarus was not conducive to the development of independent publishing, by 1995 private publishers accounted for some 70 per cent of the nation's total output. The second half of the decade, however, saw a decrease in private publishing. The government repressed the independent press, refused registration to private publishers, and closed down newspapers offering a critical perspective. The state-owned press enjoyed more favourable conditions, although it too was in crisis. The beginning of the 21st century saw a significant growth in numbers: there were 490 publishers in 2002, although 80 per cent of them were orientated towards the Russian-language market.

12 Independent Ukraine

Steady Russification throughout the Soviet period had caused a decline in Ukrainian-language publishing. Although in the 1960s some 60 per cent of the books published in Ukraine were in Ukrainian, by 1980 that figure had decreased to 30 per cent. As a consequence, some Ukrainian-language publishing was undertaken abroad. Following its revival in 1947 in western Europe and in the US, the Shevchenko Scientific Society played an important role in publishing: it issued three multi-volume encyclopaedias of Ukraine and, from 1989, operated in Ukraine. Other key publishing centres were the Harvard Ukrainian Research Institute (founded 1968) and the Canadian Institute of Ukrainian Studies (founded 1976).

Post-independence, political restrictions on publishing were replaced by economic constraints, and publishing grew slowly, from 5,855 books in 1991 to 7,749 in 2000. Russian and Belarusian publishers, who operated under a more favourable tax regime, flooded the Ukrainian market with cheaper Russian-language books, especially in the lucrative area of popular literature. Despite a large number of enterprises (2,000 private and 28 state publishers in 2002), Ukraine produced less than one book per person in 2002, compared to 3.5 in Russia and seven in Belarus. The distribution system broke down, and newly established wholesalers concentrated mainly on popular material. However, in the field of scholarly publishing, both state publishers and institutions, ranging from the Academy and national libraries to small local museums, produced a wealth of historical and bibliographical material on Ukrainian history and culture. Scholarly publishing was assisted by funding from government, NGOs, and Ukrainian centres in the diaspora. The Ukrainian Publishers and Booksellers

Association, established in 1994, became an energetic lobbying body, and the Ukrainian Academy of Printing in Lviv established courses in publishing and bookselling. By the end of the 1990s, there was a substantial improvement in typographical standards and in publishing facilities. Electronic publishing developed quickly, and the Vernads'kyi National Library of Ukraine began an active digitization programme.

BIBLIOGRAPHY

M. R. Barazna, *Belaruskaia knizhnaia hrafika, 1960-1990-kh hadou* (2001)

I. A. Isaievych, *Ukraïns'ke knihovydannia: vytoki, rozvytok, problemy* (2002)

M. N. Kufaev, *Istoriia russkoi knigi v XIX veke* (1927; repr. 2003)

D. Likhachev, ed., *Knizhnye tsentry Drevnei Rusi* (2 vols, 1991–4)

S. Lovell, *The Russian Reading Revolution* (1999)

G. Marker, *Publishing, Printing, and the Origins of Intellectual Life in Russia, 1700-1800* (1985)

E. L. Nemirovskii, *Frantsisk Skorina* (1990)

I. Ohiienko, *Istoriia ukrains'koho drukarstva* (1925; repr. 1994)

M. Remnek, ed., *Books in Russia and the Soviet Union: Past and Present* (1991)

G. P. M. Walker, *Soviet Book Publishing Policy* (1978)

38

The History of the Book in the Balkans

EKATERINA ROGATCHEVSKAIA AND ALEKSANDRA B. VRANEŠ

1 Balkan geography

The Balkans, the region in the southeast of Europe, is geographically bounded by the rivers Sava and Danube in the north; the Mediterranean in the south; the Black Sea, the Sea of Marmara, and the Aegean Sea in the east and southeast; and the Adriatic and Ionian seas in the west and southwest. Although the question is disputed, the countries making up the region are generally taken to include: Albania, Bosnia and Herzegovina, Bulgaria, Croatia, Greece, Macedonia, Moldova, Montenegro, Romania, Serbia, Slovenia, and European Turkey. Geographical position defines the Balkan identity, but the region is diverse politically, ethnically, and linguistically. The book culture of the area is characterized by the coexistence in its history of different ethnic groups (e.g. Celts, Illyrians, Romans, Avars, Vlachs, Germans, Slavs, and Turks), languages (e.g. Latin, Greek, Albanian, various Slavonic and Turkic languages), cultures, religions (e.g. paganism, Catholicism, Orthodox Christianity, and Islam), and political systems (e.g. of the Roman, Ottoman, and Austro-Hungarian empires, and the Soviet bloc).

2 South Slavonic MSS and the beginning of printing

The Balkans could be called the birthplace of Slavonic literacy, which began in the second half of the 9th century with the missionary activities of the brothers Cyril (Constantine) and Methodius, Byzantine Greeks from Thessaloniki. They introduced Glagolitic and later the Cyrillic alphabet, translating parts of the Bible and some service books into the Old Church Slavonic understood by all Slavs. The first Slavonic centres of literacy developed at Ohrid (now in Macedonia) and Preslav (the capital of the first Bulgarian empire; now in Bulgaria). Whereas Ohrid cultivated Glagolitic, Cyrillic became the official script of Bulgaria. Old Church Slavonic gradually assumed vernacular features, laying the basis for the development of other literary Slavonic languages.

Glagolitic script was used in the south Slavonic countries and in Moravia until the 12th century, but then was generally replaced by Cyrillic or Latin, and localized mainly in Croatia. Early examples of Glagolitic script are rare. The first surviving MSS are of the 10th–11th centuries: the Kiev Folia, the Prague Fragments, the Glagolita Clozianus, the Codex Zographensis, the Codex Assemanianus, the Codex Marianus, the Sinai Psalter, and the Euchologium Sinaiticum. Cyrillic script had three main variants: uncial ('ustav', in use during the 11th–14th centuries), half-uncial ('poluustav', 15th–17th centuries), and the cursive script called 'skoropis' (mainly used in documents since the 14th century). The earliest dated Cyrillic MS is the Savvina Kniga. Scholars estimate that about 30 other books survive from the 11th century, although not all of them originated in the Balkans.

Before the 18th century, when Peter the Great introduced Civil founts in Russia (*see* **37**) and the codification of national languages started in some countries, Cyrillic printing—mainly catering for the needs of the Orthodox Church—was widely used. Although the first Cyrillic book was printed by Schweipolt Fiol in Poland, and highly productive presses also existed in Venice, Prague, Vilno, and elsewhere, the Balkans played an important role in Cyrillic printing, the second Cyrillic press beginning production in Montenegro as early as in 1493. Glagolitic printing was localized in Croatia and Slovenia, although Glagolitic presses also operated in Italy.

3 Bulgaria

The Church Slavonic MSS written in the first Bulgarian empire are richly illuminated. The earliest Cyrillic MS of Bulgarian origin is the Codex Suprasliensis. In the 14th century, the Tărnovo school of literature developed a distinct style of handwriting and illumination. One of the best examples of this style is the Gospels of Tsar Ivan Alexander (1356), now in the British Library. The first printed books were produced outside Bulgaria.

The elements of Modern Bulgarian were first evident in Filip Stanislavov's *Abagar* (Rome, 1651). The leading figure in the Bulgarian National Revival

(1762–1878) was Paisius of Hilandar (1722–73), who wrote a Slavonic-Bulgarian history (*Istoriya Slavyanobolgarskaya*). Another person of note was Neofit Rilski, the author of the first Bulgarian grammar (1835). The National Revival made possible the start of printing in Bulgaria. Having bought a press in Belgrade, Nikola Karastoyanov, who had worked previously in Serbia, founded the first printing office in Samokov (1828). Commercial publishing and bookselling are associated in Bulgaria with Khristo G. Danov. The national bibliography was initiated by K. Velichkov in 1897.

Independence from the Ottoman empire meant the revitalization of publishing and bookselling, and there were 80 independent publishers before World War II. In 1939, they produced 2,169 titles with a total press run of 6.4 million copies.

4 Serbia

Serbian book culture also developed using the Cyrillic alphabet and was shaped by Orthodox Christianity, although it later experienced Arabic and Turkish influence within the Ottoman empire. The most productive scriptoria were located in monasteries. One of the earliest South Slavonic Cyrillic MSS, the Miroslav Gospels, written *c*.1185–1190, probably in Kotor (now in Montenegro), was commissioned by Prince Miroslav, brother of Stefan Nemanja (later known as St Simeon), the ruler of the most successful medieval Serbian kingdom of Raška. The richly illuminated gospels are among the most beautiful Slavonic MSS; unsurprisingly, both Montenegrins and Serbs claim them as part of their own written heritage. Stefan Nemanja's youngest son, Rastko Nemanjić (later St Sava), is considered the founder of the independent Serbian Orthodox Church and the author of the *Life of St Simeon*. The father and son were also founders of Hilandar monastery, an Eastern Orthodox monastery on Mount Athos in Greece; following its foundation in 1198, Hilandar was the principal centre for Serbian medieval book culture. During the Turkish rule that began in the 15th century and lasted for over 300 years, Serbian spirituality and national identity were preserved in monasteries, Hilandar taking the lead.

The printed book evolved in parallel with the MS book in the 16th century (*see* **6, 15**). Serbia's first press, which produced the Rujan Gospels (1537), was located at the Rujan monastery, close to the Tara Mountain. Presses were established in the monasteries of Gračanica (producing an Octoechos or prayer book, 1539), Mileševa (three books printed, 1544–57), and the Mrkša Church (two imprints, 1562–6). In 1552, Prince Radiša Dmitrović founded a press in Belgrade, and started working on the gospels. As he died shortly afterwards, the work was continued by Trojan Gundulić of Dubrovnik and Mardarios of the church at Mrkša. After this brief period of activity, Serbian printing declined, religious and historical works being printed at Venice. Zaharije Stefanović Orfelin, a Serbian poet and engraver, established the first Serbian periodical in 1766 and wrote a biography of Peter the Great. In the 19th century, Serbian books were published in Leipzig, Novi Sad (the capital of Voedovina, then under Hungarian jurisdiction), and other towns that were situated in territories belonging to the Austro-Hungarian empire. Matica Srpska played an important role in developing printing in the Serbian language and promoting Serbian book culture. The language reforms introduced by Vuk Stefanović Karadžić contributed to the landmark events in the history of the Serbian book. These included the foundation of the Royal Serbian Press in Belgrade in 1832 and the opening of the National Library of Serbia and of the Serbian Literacy Society, the predecessor of the present Serbian Academy of Sciences and Arts (1892).

During World War I, significant numbers of Serbian books and periodicals were published in France, Greece, and Switzerland. The national book industry quickly recovered, only to collapse again during World War II, when the partisans' illegal presses alone were active.

5 Montenegro

In the 8th and 9th centuries the medieval state of Duklja, a predecessor of the modern Montenegro, was under Byzantine, Serbian, and Bulgarian domination. After the Great Schism in 1054, Duklja became predominantly Catholic. Once Stefan Nemanja made the land part of his state of Raška, he converted the population to Orthodoxy, and Latin cultural advancement was effectively stopped by ending the production of Latin books. Since then, Montenegro's book culture has been closely connected with the Serbian book. The second Cyrillic press—founded in 1493 on the initiative of Đurađ Crnojević, the ruler of the independent principality of Zeta—opened in Montenegro. Although its exact location remains unknown, the press, where the hieromonk Makarije may have worked, most likely operated in Cetinje. The Montenegrin printing tradition was continued in Venice by Božidar Vuković from Podgorica, who had a great influence on Serbian and Montenegrin culture, as well as on the development of printing in other Slavonic countries.

Under Ottoman rule, printing and literary activities were significantly reduced; but one of the first signs of the national revival, Vasilije Petrović Njegoš's *History of Montenegro*, was published in Moscow in 1754. *The Mountain Wreath*, the best-known book by the Montenegrin national poet and philosopher Petar II (Petrović Njegoš), was also published abroad in 1837, although by then he had already established his own press (1834), the second on Montenegrin soil. During a Turkish siege in 1852 its type had to be melted down for bullets, but in 1858 a new press was obtained.

The establishment of a National Public Library in Cetinje was first proposed in 1879, but implemented only in 1893. From 1905, the library started receiving legal deposit copies. By 1912, it had more than 10,000 titles, a large number of incunabula and early printed books, and more than 100 MSS, but the holdings suffered severely from the occupying Austrian troops in 1918. In 1946 the Public Central Library was created at Cetinje, and given its current name in 1964.

The library's major published work was *Crnogorska bibliografija* 1494–1994, a national bibliography.

6 Macedonia

Macedonian book culture developed under Bulgarian, Serbian, and Byzantine influence, reflecting the political landscape of southern Europe. Skopje, Macedonia's capital, became the capital of the Serbian empire in 1346, but from the late 14th century, the region was part of the Ottoman empire for about 500 years.

Important Macedonian books were produced outside the country: Jakov of Kamena Reka (the Stone River) had a Cyrillic press in Venice in 1560s; Hristofor Žefarovik's *Stemmatographia*, containing portraits of Bulgarian and Serbian rulers and images of South Slavonic coats of arms, was published at Vienna in 1741. In the 19th century, when publishing in Macedonia largely depended on the requirements of local schools, Teodosij of Sinai owned a press in Salonica, issuing the first prayer book in a local Macedonian dialect and a short Dictionary. Although Bulgarian, Serbian, and Greek were the languages of instruction, fifteen primers in a local Macedonian dialect were published between 1857 and 1875. The idea of establishing a Macedonian linguistic and national identity was first mooted in 1870, but was delayed during the interwar period, when local dialects were largely banned. The language was standardized and officially recognized in 1944. At present, materials in three main languages—Macedonian, Albanian, and Turkish—are published to serve the needs of the ethnically diverse population. In 2012, more than 100 publishing houses were issuing material in Macedonian, with some twenty publishers catering for the other languages. On average, domestic authors comprised between 15 and 30 per cent of the total production, with the remainder being translations.

7 Bosnia and Herzegovina

Medieval Bosnian literature developed in Bosnian Cyrillic script, a variant of Cyrillic, and in Glagolitic. The oldest work in the Bosnian Cyrillic script is the Charter, a trade agreement between Bosnia and Dubrovnik (1189), issued by the Bosnian Ban (ruler) Kulin; the oldest book in this script is the Service to St Mary (Ofičje svete dieve Marie), printed by Giorgio de Rusconi at Venice in 1512. The two known copies are held at the Bibliothèque nationale and at All Souls College (Oxford).

Cyrillic printing in Bosnia is associated with Božidar Goraždanin. In Goražda (in the east of Bosnia and Herzegovina), he established a press that produced three books in 1519–23. During the entire Ottoman period only four presses operated in Bosnia (three of them in the 19th century), with the total output of four newspapers and 50 book titles.

For a period of more than 300 years no Bosnian press existed, and all printed materials came from abroad. Even the first periodical, *Bosanski prijatelj*, was founded in Zagreb in 1850. However, following an initiative by the Ottoman authorities, the first modern Bosnian printing office was set up in Sarajevo in 1865. By the end of the 19th century, two offices had been established in Mostar: the Press of the Catholic Mission in Herzegovina, started by the Franciscans, and the Herzegovina vilajet ('province' in the Ottoman empire) press. Under Austro-Hungarian rule, publishing grew, and the number of enterprises reached 40, adding German, Hungarian, and Yiddish to the linguistic landscape of Bosnian publishing. During the 40 years of Austro-Hungarian domination, 1,600 titles were published—Bosnia contributed 2,000 titles to book production for the kingdom of the Serbs, Croats, and Slovenes—and in 1945–51 book production reached 1,750 titles. Bosnian companies did fairly well as part of the publishing industry of the Socialist Federal Republic of Yugoslavia, but the 1992–5 war had a devastating effect not only on the local economy, but on the area's cultural heritage, as the National and University Library of Bosnia and Herzegovina in Sarajevo was destroyed.

8 Croatia

The earliest works written on Croatian territory were in Glagolitic script. In their union with Hungary, the Croats were mainly Catholics, but Croatia appeared to be the only European nation given special permission by Pope Innocent IV (in 1248) to use its own language in its liturgy and the Glagolitic alphabet for service books. One of the most beautiful Glagolitic MSS is the Missal of Prince Novak (1368), now held in the Austrian National Library. It contains the famous hymn 'Dies irae' and some musical notation. The earliest Croatian incunabulum, the *Missale Romanum* (1483; its place of printing is unknown), survives in thirteen copies and eight fragments.

The first dated press in Croatia was opened in 1494 at Senj by Blaž Baromić, Croatia's first printer, who learned the art in Venice. The press was active until 1508 and printed seven books. In Rijeka (Fiume), a press was established in 1530 by the bishop of Modruš, Šimun Kožičić Benja. It published six Glagolitic books in two years. Croatian Cyrillic script was used in the Adriatic city-state of Dubrovnik and in Bosnia and Herzegovina; some scholars consider it the same as the Bosnian Cyrillic script, bosanica or bosančica. From the 15th century, the bulk of Croatian literature appeared in Roman script. In the 17th century, only one printing house operated in Zagreb (1664), but during the 18th and early 19th centuries, seven presses were working on Croatia territory. A Venetian printer, Carlo Antonio Occhi, published 50 books at his press in Dubrovnik in 1783–7.

Croatian Romantic nationalism emerged in the mid-19th century to counteract the apparent Germanization and Magyarization of the country. The Illyrian movement attracted a number of influential figures from the 1830s onward, and produced some important advances in Croatian culture and language.

These were promoted by a society, Matica Ilirska (later Matica Hrvatska), formed in February 1842 and based at the National Library of Croatia. After the fall of the absolute monarchy, the publishing industry revived. Matica published the first literary-scientific magazine *Književnik* (1864–6), and from 1869 the main fiction magazine for 19th-century Croatian literature, *Vijenac*.

9 Slovenia

As Slovenia's history includes its being part of the Roman empire, the Holy Roman Empire, and Austro-Hungary, the development of its book culture was considerably influenced by Latin and by German culture. As in the rest of Europe, scriptoria were mainly based in monasteries. For example, in the late 12th century, the Cistercian monastery of Stična produced the *Collectarium*, a collection of religious lives. Overall, 32 codices and five fragments from Stična have survived. Another scriptorium of note is the former Carthusian abbey at Žiče, the largest Carthusian monastery in this part of Europe and the first charterhouse outside Romance-language countries. The monastic library contained about 2,000 MSS, of which only 120 books and about 100 fragments survived.

The first printer of Slovenian origin, Matevž Cerdonis, worked in Padua in 1482–7, but the earliest books in Slovenian, by Primož Trubar, were produced at Ulrich Morhart's press in Tübingen. The Reformation was especially important for Slovenian culture and the development of the language: the first complete Bible in Slovenian, translated by Jurij Dalmatin, was printed at Johann Krafft's press in Wittenberg in 1584. A press on Slovenian soil opened in 1575 at Ljubljana; it belonged to Janž Mandelc, and produced ten books before it closed in 1580. Another press at Ljubljana was in operation from 1678 until 1801. The largest 19th-century publishers were Druzba Svetega Mohoria (1852), Slovenská matica (1846), and Slovenska knižnica (1876–80). The beginning of the 20th century saw several waves of Slovene publishing, closely linked to the nationalist movement. Publishing and other cultural institutions suffered considerably under the German occupation during World War II, although partisans maintained active underground presses.

10 Albania

The Illyrian tribes that populated the territory of present-day Albania were Christianized in the 1st century AD. The country's central position subsequently made it a battlefield between the western and the eastern halves of the Byzantine empire; at some point in history it was administered by the eastern empire, but ecclesiastically dependent on Rome. In the Middle Ages, the population of the southern and eastern parts of Albania became Orthodox Christians, whereas Roman Catholicism remained strong in the north. During the Ottoman rule that lasted until the beginning of the 20th century, the majority of the Albanian population converted to Islam.

The written Albanian language can be traced back to the 14th or late 15th century. Gjon Buzuku's *Meshari* (Missal), published in 1555 at Venice, is the first printed work in the language. The effects of the Reformation greatly advanced the development of Albanian literature and book culture, and in the 16th–17th centuries, original works of poetry, prose, and philosophy were published. In the 18th century, both Christians and Muslims used the Albanian language to maintain their cultural heritage. However, the works of the most notable Albanians were published abroad (e.g. Pjetër Budi's *Rituale Romanum* and *Speculum Confessionis*, or Pjetër Bogdani's *Cuneus Prophetarum*, a parallel-text theological tract in Albanian and Italian). On the other hand, Greek language and culture dominated southeastern Albania. In Voskopojë, a press was set up which produced books in Greek and Aromanian (the vernacular language close to Romanian) in the Greek alphabet. Although Albania was the last Balkan country to gain independence from Ottoman rule, it too had its National Renaissance movement and version of literary Romanticism. The development of printing was, however, slowed because of complications with the Albanian language, which had been written with various alphabets since the 15th century. The roman alphabet for Albanian was standardized in 1909, and a unified literary version of Albanian, based on the Tosk dialect, was established in 1972.

Émigré publishing represented a further distinctive characteristic of Albanian book culture. The Albanians who fled the country because of Enver Hoxha's regime set up their publishing centres in Italy, France, Germany, and the US. In the 1990s, Albanian communities all over the world were enlarged by the Kosovo Albanians, who had produced their printed material in Zagreb, Skopje, and Tirana, but had mostly lost the opportunity to do so at home due to political turbulence.

11 Romania

In the Middle Ages, Romanians lived in two distinct and independent principalities, Wallachia and Moldavia (Moldova), as well as in the Hungarian-ruled principality of Transylvania (*see* **33**). During Ottoman rule, Wallachia and Moldavia had some internal autonomy and external independence, which were finally lost in the 18th century. Christian Orthodox, Latin, and oriental cultures influenced Romania's culture. Tîrgovişte and Braşov became noteworthy centres for early Cyrillic and Romanian printing.

The Romanian language finally established itself as part of written culture in the 17th century. The first collection of laws printed in Wallachia, the *Pravila de la Govora*, appeared at Govora in 1640. Other printing centres of note were Iaşi, where Varlaam's *Cazania* was printed; Alba Iulia (the Bălgrad New Testament, 1648), and Bucharest (the first Romanian Bible, 1688). In the 18th century, new presses were installed in Buzău, the Snagov monastery, and Râmnicu Vâlcea; a third (which had Greek types) began operating in Bucharest. Arab, Greek, and Turkish books were printed in addition to the Cyrillic and Romanian ones.

The first newspaper, *Curierul românesc* (1829), was started by 'the father of Romanian literature', Ion Heliade Rădulescu. Bucharest was also home to the Library of the Academy (1867) and the Central State Library (1955; later the National Library of Romania), while university libraries had been established earlier in Iaşi (1839) and Cluj (or Cluj-Napoca, 1872).

12 The socialist and post-socialist eras

The publishing and bookselling industries in all socialist countries followed the pattern previously established by the Soviet Union: private publishers and printers were closed; the state controlled the production and distribution of printed material; censorship was introduced. This resulted in an unbalanced book market, with overproduction of propaganda and severe shortages in popular literature. Large state subsidies led to unnaturally low book prices. On the other hand, communist ideology contributed to creating a cultural infrastructure of schools, public libraries, book clubs, and so on in all the Balkan countries. Having recovered from the devastation of World War II, most of the communist bloc countries reached their highest book production figures by the 1990s, although problems with distribution were much harder to solve: for example, in 1988, 27 per cent of books published in Bulgaria did not find their way to consumers, as demand for them did not exist.

Different political and economic conditions determined the development of publishing in individual countries. In Bulgaria, publishing and censorship were strictly centralized, unlike in Tito's Yugoslavia, where publishing relied on state giants and on private and small enterprises that balanced self-censorship and profitability. Slovenia was early in learning Western marketing strategies and adopting modern manufacturing techniques.

Not surprisingly, the transition from socialism was difficult, and was accompanied in some cases by military conflict. In Bulgaria, although overall production figures in the early 1990s were lower than at the end of the communist era, the number of publishers grew from 752 in 1993 to 2,000 in 2000, spread equally over the country. In Bosnia and Herzegovina in 1996, 1,800 publishers were operating in the country in a great number of new and well-established places. Romanian publishing activity was still strongly centred around Bucharest, however. In Croatia, 1,828 of more than 3,000 publishers were located in Zagreb, followed by Split with 184 firms. Another common tendency in the transitional market economy was a significant growth of titles produced to satisfy different types of readership, combined with a notable fall in print runs. Many national libraries also found it extremely difficult to exercise their right to receive legal deposit publications during this period. Such problems were partly caused by political and economic instability and partly by the legal ignorance of new participants in the book market. Links between national libraries across the Balkans were broken. In Serbia, there was a clear reduction in materials printed in the non-Serbian languages of the former Yugoslavia. Montenegro and Macedonia, having lost their Serbo-Croatian-speaking market, concentrated on their national readership. The numbers of bookshops in all the countries fell, as very few survived the early years of a market economy. However, the face of bookselling changed dramatically with the introduction of large book chains and online shops, and e-publishing.

....

BIBLIOGRAPHY

M. Biggins, 'Publishing in Slovenia', *Slavic & East European Information Resources*, 1.2–3 (2001), 3–38

—— and J. Crayne, eds., *Publishing in Yugoslavia's Successor States* (2000)

A. Gergova, ed., *Bŭlgarska kniga* (2004)

S. Jelušič, 'Book Publishing in Croatia Today', *Javnost: The Public*, 11.4 (2004), 91–100

G. Mitrevski, 'Publishing in Macedonia', *Slavic & East European Information Resources*, 1.2–3 (2001), 187–209

E. L. Nemirovskii, *Istoriia slavianskogo kirillovskogo knigopechataniia XV–nachala XVII veka* (2003)

I. Nikolic, 'Publishing in Serbia', *Slavic & East European Information Resources*, 1.2–3 (2001), 85–126

D. Tranca, *A General Survey of the Romanian Book* (1968)

The History of the Book in Sub-Saharan Africa

ANDREW VAN DER VLIES

1 MS cultures

Although the printing press did not reach sub-Saharan Africa until colonial administrators and Christian missionaries arrived in the 18th and early 19th centuries, the continent's engagement with writing and the economies of text is much older. Scribal cultures thrived in parts of West Africa on early trade routes across the Sahara, and although knowledge of Arabic seems never to have been widespread, a significant literature in African languages transcribed in Arabic script ('Ajami') developed. Important MS libraries survive in Mali, as well as in Ghana, Côte d'Ivoire, Niger, Senegal, and northern Nigeria—whence early Hausa-language Ajami texts date from the 17th century. Most other West African countries also have significant collections, many in private hands. In East Africa, Arabic MSS survive from the 11th century, although Kiswahili, the lingua franca of the coastal region, is now nearly exclusively written and printed using the roman alphabet.

More than 1,500 languages are spoken in Africa, and many sub-Saharan countries possess an extraordinary linguistic richness (Nigeria's 100 million people speak more than 250 languages; the same number occur among Cameroon's population of 20 million). Despite the difficulty of conveying the complexities of some tonal languages in script, most African languages are now written and printed using the roman alphabet. A few languages—notably Egyptian, Berber, and Nubian in North Africa, and Vai in 19th-century Liberia—developed their own, sometimes short-lived writing systems. The Ge'ez syllabary, developed from a consonantal alphabet, is still the basis for the alphabet in use in many printed works in contemporary Ethiopia—a country unique in sub-Saharan Africa for its history of written literary production dating to the first centuries of the Common Era. Early MSS in Ge'ez, which developed as a literary language between the 3rd and 8th centuries and persists as a liturgical language in the Ethiopian Coptic Church, include translations from Greek and Arabic and an Old Testament with 81 books (to the Catholic Bible's 45 and the Protestant tradition's 39). Most early Ethiopian MSS are theological treatises (e.g. *The Interpretation of Divinity*), lives of saints, and royal chronicles

While copying the MS, two scribes fall into sin: an 18th-century Ethiopian MS of the Smithsonian's *Miracles of the Blessed Virgin Mary and the Life of Hanna (Saint Anne)*, reproduced in E. A. Wallis Budge's facsimile edition (1900). The Bodleian Library, University of Oxford (Aeth. b.1, plate LVI)

(*Kebra-Negast, Lives of the Kings*), although religious poetry and hymns developed in the 14ᵗʰ century. Amharic, the language of the common people rather than the Church and its scribal culture, grew in importance with the ascendancy of the centralizing Shoan dynasty and the influence of Protestant missions in the early 19ᵗʰ century. In 1824, the British and Foreign Bible Society printed a bilingual Ge'ez-Amharic edition of the Gospels; *The Pilgrim's Progress* appeared in Amharic in 1887, and Afä-Wärq Gäbrä-Iyäsus's *Lebb Wälläd Tarik* (A Story from the Heart, one of Africa's first African-language novels) was published in Amharic in 1908. Shortly after a printing press was installed in Addis Ababa in 1911, catalogues of Ge'ez and Amharic MSS were printed. In 1922, the Berhanena Selam Printing Press began publishing Amharic school texts locally. Soon, the power of the press superseded that of the continent's oldest surviving scribal culture.

2 The impact of slavery and evangelism

Seminal 'movements' in the development of African print cultures include slavery, and the forces that opposed and finally achieved its abolition—Christian evangelism, and the mission-facilitated literacy it spread across broad swathes of the continent (*see* **9**). The arrival of print and the book produced ambivalent results in zones of cultural contact: facilitating productive engagements with modernity yet silencing ancient cultures; promoting new forms of knowledge while functioning as a vehicle for organizing site-specific hierarchies of power.

Early Portuguese settlements were established in West Africa in the 15ᵗʰ century, and the European slave trade—which would transport more than 11.5 million Africans to Europe and the Americas between the 16ᵗʰ and 19ᵗʰ centuries—began with a voyage to Portugal in 1441. The slave trade was banned throughout the British empire in 1807, and slavery itself abolished in 1833, although it persisted elsewhere—notably in the southern US—until significantly later in the century. Narratives produced by slaves forcefully removed from their West African homelands in the 18ᵗʰ and early 19ᵗʰ centuries constitute perhaps the earliest works produced in English by black Africans. Emancipated slaves were often engaged by abolitionists to produce anti-slavery memoirs; some were examples of ghostwriting, including those by Briton Hammon (Boston, 1760), James Albert Gronniosaw (Bath, *c.*1770), and Venture Smith (New London, CT, 1798). Philip Quaque, sent for his education from the Gold Coast (present-day Ghana) to Britain by the Society for the Propagation of the Gospel in Foreign Parts, corresponded extensively with the London-based Society on his return to Africa to serve as a minister; his late 18ᵗʰ- and early 19ᵗʰ-century letters offer nuanced engagements with patronage and missionary education. Other notable works in a similar vein include Phillis Wheatley's *Poems on Various Subjects* (1773), Ignatius Sancho's *Letters* (1782), and Ottabah Cugoano's *Thoughts and Sentiments on the Evil and Wicked Traffic of Slavery*

(1787). The most famous remains *The Interesting Narrative of the Life of Olaudah Equiano, or Gustavus Vassa, the African* (1789).

Much of sub-Saharan Africa's indigenous print and publishing history is most deeply marked by the complex consequences of the work of 18th- and 19th-century Christian missionaries. Their idea of the book—and of the Book—as a symbolic marker of a newly configured African engagement with European models of modernity promoted print cultures that interacted with a variety of local cultural attitudes and intellectual traditions, and thus accumulated a range of functions, forms, and symbolic values. Hofmeyr cites a 1931 report in the *Missionary Herald* of a Baptist convert called Ruth, who attached the pages of a bible to a flagpole beside her home in the Belgian Congo, claiming that it marked her family as 'People of the Book', just as the Belgian official flew the Belgian flag when in residence (Hofmeyr, 'Metaphorical Books', 100). The book serves here as literal and figurative flag, a sign of the imbrication of print cultures with local structures of understanding and identification.

Presbyterians were among the first in West Africa to import presses and train local operators, and by the mid-19th century had produced catechisms, lessons, almanacs, and schoolbooks. Other missionary and philanthropic societies followed suit, some importing foreign expertise (the American Colonization Society employed a Jamaican printer in Yorubaland in the late 1850s), and many establishing depots to sell imported texts and produce translations into local languages. The Bremen Mission published Ewe grammars in eastern Gold Coast in the 1850s; others (e.g. the Basel Mission and Wesleyan Methodists) were responsible, in the later 19th century, for early works in languages such as Twi, Ga, and Fante. Missionary activity was fraught with contradictions, often engendering tensions with colonial administrations; in a famous mid-19th century incident in eastern Cape Colony, colonial soldiers melted Lovedale press type to make bullets.

Missions had a widespread effect, influencing European attitudes towards Africa (through tracts and other material about evangelical work in Africa distributed in Europe), and encouraging the export of specially produced material to Africa. The London-based Sheldon Press's 'Little Books for Africa' and similar series found their way to the continent before World War II, when missionary-sponsored journals such as *Books for Africa* also flourished. Accounts including Margaret Wrong's *Africa and the Making of Books: Being a Survey of Africa's Need of Literature* (1934), published in London by the International Committee on Christian Literature for Africa, assessed the economic and practical difficulties of producing affordable books for Africans during the global depression. Paradoxically, restrictions on shipping and imports during World War II boosted local book production, much of it then still mission-controlled. After a decline in the 1930s, Ghana's Methodist Book Depot enjoyed a 60 per cent share of the national educational market by 1950, regularly distributing 500,000 copies of individual textbooks.

Mission presses also facilitated the growth of literate African elites, allowing local writers access to print and distribution networks, and, with the spread of literacy, to audiences for writing in indigenous African, as well as in European, languages. Literary genres encouraged by missionary presses—exemplary lives, conversion narratives, didactic poetry, self-help manuals, and ethnographic accounts—proved highly adaptable by politically pragmatic African writers. The Liberian Joseph J. Walters's *Guanya Pau: A Story of an African Princess* (1891), for example, argued for improving the condition of women, and Jomo Kenyatta's apparently merely ethnographic *My People of Kikuyu and The Life of Chief Wangombe* (1942) offered critiques of European intervention in East African societies. Mission presses dominated book production in many parts of the continent until the mid-20th century (with a handful of foreign-owned or multinational-affiliated presses controlling much publishing activity during the century's second half). Missionary-facilitated print production, with its own complex traditions, necessarily disseminated European institutional and cultural assumptions. Nevertheless, access to the technologies of print also paved the way for the pamphlets, books, and journals that would fuel anti-colonial independence movements.

3 West Africa

The British colony of Sierra Leone served, after 1787, as a home for emancipated slaves from Britain and from colonies such as Nova Scotia; after the abolition of the slave trade throughout the empire, in 1807, it provided refuge for freed slaves from the rest of West Africa. Liberia, too, became a home for former slaves from North America after 1822, the American Colonisation Society having been established in 1816 to facilitate their return. West African intellectuals including E. W. Blyden, Samuel Ajayi Crowther, and J. E. Casely Hayford produced early works central to forging notions of pan-African identity. Crowther's *The Gospel on the Banks of the Niger* (1859) recorded his prescient concern with the importance of written forms in securing the influence of Christianity in the region; his legacy in making the Bible available in Hausa is particularly valuable. Casely Hayford's *Ethiopia Unbound* (1911) was long regarded as the first fictional work in English by an African writer, although credit is now given to the unidentified author of *Marita: or the Folly of Love* (serialized in Gold Coast's *Western Echo*, 1886–8) and to Walters for *Guanya Pau* (1891).

Missionaries and mission-educated Africans were not alone in directing printing and publishing. From the mid-20th century onwards, booksellers operated wherever print flourished, however sporadically; schools, newspaper offices, churches, and clubs all frequently featured small bookshops. There were also notable state interventions, as in the Translation Bureau in Zaria in northern Nigeria, directed by Rupert East. Initially given the task of educating Africans for clerical work in the colonial administration, it soon ran writing competitions, and commissioned works in Hausa, encouraging book production in a roman script— which Ricard noted is called *boko*, from the English 'book', but (not accidentally) sounds like the Hausa for 'trickery' (Ricard, 58–9). Similar enabling work was continued by the Nigerian Northern Region Literature Agency (until 1959), the Hausa Language Board, and, after independence, the Northern Nigeria Publishing Corporation (1967). The state government in Kano later funded a publishing company, Triumph, to produce two newspapers in Hausa (one printed in Ajami). Such vernacular literature bureaux and state-sponsored initiatives operated at various times across the continent, with varying degrees of success. Others in West Africa included the United Christian Council Literature Bureau in Bo, Sierra Leone (1946), and the Bureau of Ghana Languages, Accra (1951).

Oxford University Press Nigeria (now University Press plc) opened in Ibadan in 1949. The Ibadan University Press, the first African university press outside South Africa, followed in 1951. The 1950s saw the foundation of a number of new literary magazines—pre-eminently, perhaps, J. P. Clark Bekederemo's *The Horn* and Ulli Beier and Janheinz Jahn's *Black Orpheus*, both in 1957—and the first significant indigenous publishing ventures (including Onibonoje Press & Book Industries Ltd in Ibadan, 1958). They were joined by increasing numbers of presses, commercial or state-sponsored, both locally and foreign owned, as independence spread across West Africa from Ghana (1957) and French Guinea (1958), to Ivory Coast (Côte d'Ivoire), Upper Volta (Burkina Faso), Dahomey (Benin), Mali, Cameroon, Mauritania, Nigeria, Senegal, Togo (all in 1960), and beyond. In 1961, the influential Mbari press was founded, as well as Longman's Nigerian company, and the African Universities Press in Lagos in the following year. Macmillan opened its Nigerian branch in 1965, when the Nigerian Publishers' Association, Africa's first national book trade organization, was also established (Kenya's was second, formed in 1971, with Ghana's following in 1975). In 1968, UNESCO hosted a regional book development conference in Accra, the first of several such regional initiatives. The International Conference on Publishing and Book Development in Africa was convened at Nigeria's University of Ife in 1973; 1975 saw the establishment of the now-defunct UNESCO co-sponsored Regional Book Promotion Centre for Africa in Yaoundé, as well as the first issue of the influential *African Book Publishing Record*. The Noma Award for Publishing in Africa was established in 1979, the first award going to the Senegalese author Mariama Bâ, for *Une si longue lettre*.

Landmarks in Francophone book production in the region include the establishment of the journal and publishing house *Présence africaine* by Alioune Diop, Aimé Cesaire, and Leopold Sédar Senghor in 1946, and the publication of standard anthologies of African and Caribbean writing, including *Poètes d'expression française* (ed. Léon Damas, 1947) and *Anthologie de la poésie nègre et malgache* (ed. Senghor, 1948). Among early Francophone African publishing houses were the Centre d'édition et de diffusion africaines in Abidjan, the Centre d'édition et de production pour l'enseignement et la recherche in Yaoundé (both 1961), and, more significantly, Éditions CLE in Yaoundé, established in 1963 with German and Dutch church funding; the last remained for many years the only significant African publishing venue for local Francophone writers. However, in 1972, the governments of Senegal, Côte d'Ivoire, and Togo, along with French publishing interests, set up Les nouvelles éditions africaines (NEA) in Dakar, with branches in Abidjan and Lomé. NEA Dakar split from the branches in 1991, and smaller firms such as Éditions Khoudia in Dakar (founded by Aminata Sow Fall, the first female publisher in Francophone West Africa), Les Éditions du livre du sud (Abidjan), Le figuier and librairie-éditions Traoré (both Bamako), and Arpak-gnon (Lomé), have since come to prominence. The devaluation of the Commun-auté Financière Africaine (CFA) franc stimulated indigenous presses, now able to compete with increasingly expensive imports from France.

Between the 1930s and 1960s, vibrant popular print cultures developed, exemplified by so-called market literatures, cheaply published and widely cir-culated works including self-help manuals and popular thrillers, often drawing on local or mission-endorsed narrative models. Another influence was the arrival of cheap Indian pamphlets in the late 1940s (many Nigerian soldiers served in the British army in India and Burma), and of popular American and European detective fiction and comics. The best-known market literature is associated with Onitsha in southeastern Nigeria, whose heyday was from the 1950s to the mid-1970s; pamphlet cultures emerging elsewhere include, since the early 1990s, charismatic Christian publications, and northern Nigerian, Hausa-language 'Kano market literature', often written by women and address-ing domestic issues pertinent to the predominantly Muslim society. There is a similar 'hawkers' literature' tradition in Francophone West Africa.

4 East and Central Africa

Print cultures in the East African states of Kenya, Tanzania, and Uganda devel-oped comparatively later and more sparsely than in West Africa for a number of reasons: the absence of large-scale resettlement of former slaves (as in Sierra Leone and Liberia); the later and less intensive establishment of missions in the region; and the absence of educational institutions for Africans (such as Sierra Leone's Fourah Bay College) until the early 20th century. Indeed, Makerere Uni-versity College, a significant site in the development of a regional community of African writers, was not founded until the 1920s, and was granted university status a decade later. Uganda long enjoyed a vibrant intellectual culture, with elites writing and publishing in Luganda rather than English. In Kenya, how-ever, the case was somewhat different. Kiswahili—a language with significant influence from Arabic, spoken in the coastal regions from Kenya south to north-ern Mozambique—was perhaps the only indigenous Kenyan language with a written tradition in the 19th century. The first book in English by a black Ken-yan, Parmeneo Gĩthendu Mockerie's *An African Speaks for his People*, was pub-lished in London by the Hogarth Press in 1934; Kenyatta's *Facing Mount Kenya* (1938) followed. Early works in Gĩkũyũ were mostly inspired by the oral narra-tive tradition or were accounts of a society under threat from colonial settler religion and government—e.g. the early landmark book by Stanley Kiãma Gathĩgĩra, *Miikarire ya Agikuyu* (*Customs of the Kikuyu*, 1933), published by the Church of Scotland Mission press, Tumutumu. Vernacular presses, newspapers, and book publishing developed widely after World War II. The East African Literature Bureau, run initially by the Church Mission Society's Nairobi bookshop manager, Charles Roberts, was established in 1947 (with offices in Dar es Salaam, Nairobi, and Kampala) to provide development-related material on agriculture, health, and education, as well as fiction, poetry, and anthropologically inspired titles. From its founding to the beginning of the Mau Mau struggle in 1952, it published more than 900,000 volumes, mostly in Kiswahili (41 per cent), but also English (12 per cent), Luganda, Gĩkũyũ, and Dholuo. The Kenya Literature Bureau resumed its operations in 1980, and numerous government or state-sponsored bodies, such as Kenya's Institute of Education and the British Council in Nairobi, have also produced important anthologies and publications in a number of languages.

The influence of educational publishing on book production in East Africa, as elsewhere in Africa, cannot be overestimated. Missionary presses published grammars and school books from the earliest days of printing, and literature bureaux and other government agencies continued the trend. Western publishers were quick to see the potential for books in Africa's large post-independence markets, with educational criteria structuring the field of expectation (including standards of aesthetic judgement) and reception in a perhaps unprecedented manner. Oxford University Press opened its East African branch in Nairobi in 1952; other British firms followed: Longman Kenya, Longman Tanzania, and Longman Uganda in 1965. Heinemann Educational Books established an East African firm in 1968 (this became Heinemann Kenya, and later East African Educational Publishers). Other local publishers, though markedly fewer than in West Africa, operated sporadically throughout the early post-independence period. Significant presses established in the region in the last decades of the 20th century include the Mzumbe Book Project (Mzumbe, Tanzania, 1988), Phoenix Publishers in Nairobi (1989), Fountain Publishers in Kampala, and Mkuti na Nyota Publishers in Dar es Salaam (both 1991). Educational publishing still accounts for up to 80 per cent of the African publishing industry's economic activity.

Elsewhere, book production has faced greater hurdles. A number of presses have existed in the former Belgian Congo (Zaïre; Democratic Republic of Congo)—including Éditions CEDI (1946), Éditions Saint-Paul Afrique (1957), CEEDA Publications (1965), and Les Éditions Okapi (1966)—but despite landmark early works (including Thadée Badibanga's *L'Éléphant qui marche sur les oeufs*, 1931, and Paul Lomami-Tshibamba's *Ngando*, 1948), literary production did not flourish there until the late 1960s, and has been constrained by recent protracted civil conflicts.

5 Southern Africa

Whereas printing arrived in Batavia in 1625, the first press appears to have reached the Dutch East India Company's settlement at the Cape of Good Hope (established 1652) after 1784, when a German bookbinder, Johann Christian Ritter, produced handbills and three almanacs. Repeated requests for a press to serve the official needs of the settlement were refused by the Company's ruling council in Amsterdam until 1795, and were then frustrated by the surrender of the Cape to British rule that year. Some believe an eight-page Dutch translation of a letter from the London Missionary Society (LMS) to believers at the Cape, printed by V. A. Schoonberg in 1799, to be the first 'book' printed at the Cape. A private firm, Walker & Robertson, enjoyed a brief monopoly on printing after August 1800; they issued South Africa's first serial, the *Cape Town Gazette and African Advertiser* (forerunner of the *Government Gazette*), in August 1801. The government took over the press the following October.

Early South African book collections include over 4,000 volumes bequeathed to the Dutch Reformed Church by Joachim von Dessin, a Dutch East India Company soldier at the Cape between 1727 and 1761, and that amassed by Sir George Grey after 1855 (while governor of the Cape Colony), which formed the core of the foundation collection of the South African National Library.

George Greig, Thomas Pringle, and John Fairbairn published the short-lived *South African Commercial Advertiser* in 1824, sparking confrontation with the Cape Colony's governor, Lord Charles Somerset, and igniting a debate about freedom of the press in the colonies. Significant other periodicals between the 1830s and 1880s included the *Cape Monthly Magazine*, the pro-settler *Graham's Town Journal*, and *De Zuid-Afrikaan*, sympathetic to the 'Dutch' proto-Afrikaners. Early Afrikaans-language works include the fascinating case of Abu Bakr Effendi's *Uiteensetting van die Godsdiens* (Exposition of the Religion), compiled in the 1860s as a guide to Islamic law and ritual practice for the Cape's Muslims (predominantly descended from the earlier Malay slave community), printed in Arabic script and published by the Ottoman state press at Istanbul in 1877.

Jan Carl Juta established a commercial publishing firm in Cape Town as early as 1853; it remains the oldest continuously productive publishing house in the country. Commercial English-language publishing began in earnest with Thomas Maskew Miller in 1893. After World War II, local publishing expanded, with Timmins, Balkema, and Struik setting up as trade and Africana publishers. Oxford University Press and Purnell had both entered the local market by the 1960s, and significant local oppositional presses during the apartheid era included the African Bookman, David Philip, Ravan Press, Ad. Donker, Skotaville Publishers, and Taurus. Important journals of the period include *The African Drum* (later *Drum*)—the primary venue for 1950s black writers including Lewis Nkosi, Es'kia Mphahlele, and Can Themba—as well as English-language literary organs such as *Contrast*, *New Coin*, *Ophir*, *Purple Renoster*, and *Classic*, some of which heralded the emergence of a generation of Black Consciousness poets.

As elsewhere in Sub-Saharan Africa, missionary activity played an important role in the development of printing cultures. T. J. van der Kemp, of the

LMS, may have printed a spelling table in a local Khoi language at Graaff Reinet as early as 1801, and *Tzitzika Thuickwedi mika khwekhwenama* (Principles of the Word of God for the Hottentot Nation) at Bethelsdorp *c.*1804. At Kuruman, in the northern Cape, Robert Moffatt translated the Bible into Setswana, acquired a press from the LMS, and published more than 100 items between the 1830s and 1870. Moshoeshoe invited the Paris Evangelical Missions to his mountain kingdom (Basutoland, now Lesotho, annexed by Britain in 1868) *c.*1833; they printed actively from 1841 (at Morija, after 1860), producing a Sesotho New Testament (1845) and *The Pilgrim's Progress* (1872). In time, the first collections of Basotho customs and proverbs were compiled (Azariele M. Sekese's *Mekhoa le maele a Basotho*, 1907), and important early poetry and creative prose published—notably Thomas Mofolo's *Moeti ao Bochabela* (translated as *The Traveller to the East*; serialized 1906) and *Chaka* (1925). As was common practice, the Morija Press vetted indigenous writing for compliance with Christian orthodoxy, a fate that also befell, for example, Solomon T. Plaatje's groundbreaking novel, *Mhudi*, at the Lovedale Press in 1930 (the Heinemann African Writers Series published an unexpurgated version in 1978). Plaatje is also remembered as an influential editor of newspapers—*Koranta ea Becoana*, and *Tsala ea Batho* (or *Tsala ea Bechuana*)—and for his translations of Shakespeare into Setswana.

Scottish missionaries at Chumi and, especially, Lovedale, in the eastern Cape Colony, effectively directed early isiXhosa-language written and printed culture, publishing a primer (1823), *Systematic Vocabulary* (1825), English–isiXhosa Dictionary (1846), isiXhosa Bible (1857), and Tiyo Soga's translation of *The Pilgrim's Progress* (1867). The Wesleyan Missionary Press in Grahamstown also facilitated important early isiXhosa publications, including a grammar (1834) and journal, *Umshumaydi Wendaba* (Publisher of News, 1837–41). Lovedale published newspapers like *Isigidimi SamaXhosa* (The Xhosa Messenger, 1870–88), edited by such leading black intellectuals as John Knox Bokwe, John Tengo Jabavu, and William Wellington Gqoba. By the end of the 19th century, there were two independent weekly newspapers with black editors: *Imvo zabantsundu* and *Izwi labantu*. In Zululand, annexed by the British Crown in 1887, missionary activity and print cultures were hampered by Shaka's expansionary wars of the early 19th century. American missionaries printed elementary educational and religious texts from 1837, an isiZulu grammar (1859), and a New Testament (1865). An isiZulu grammar in Norwegian was published in 1850. Important early newspapers include *Ilanga lase Natal* (The Natal Sun), published first in April 1903, edited by John Langalibalele Dube; a leading writer and educationalist trained in the US, he would later be the first president of the African National Congress. The earliest printed book in the vernacular by a black author was Magema M. Fuze's *Abantu abamnyamalapha bavela ngakhona* (Black People: Where They Come From), written in the late 19th century but published only in 1922. In the early 20th century, R. R. R. Dhlomo and H. I. E. Dhlomo also produced significant work.

In Rhodesia (Zimbabwe), missionary presses published bible translations into Ndebele (1884) and Shona (1907), and there was an active literary bureau in Salisbury (Harare). Post-independence Zimbabwe has been home to a number of energetic publishers, notably Baobab Books, co-founded and run by Irene Staunton in 1987, which regularly published editions (with press runs of c.2,000 copies) of Zimbabwean and other African authors. In 1999, Staunton left to launch Weaver Press.

Printing began in Lusophone southern Africa in 1843, with the first book, verse by the mestizo writer José da Silva Maia Ferreira, published in present-day Angola in 1849. Portuguese contact with this region's Kongo kingdom had begun in 1493; some 1,540 letters between its Christian convert king, Afonso I, and the king of Portugal are among the earliest Lusophone African texts. An early collection of kiMbundu orature (orally transmitted literature), Joaquim Dias Cordeiro da Matta's *Philosophia popular em provérbios Angolenses*, appeared in 1891. From the 1930s, the Lisbon-based House of Students from the Empire proved crucial in the development of nationalist literary and political elites, many of whom returned home to the colonies (Angola, Mozambique, Cape Verde, Guinea-Bissau, and São Tomé e Príncipe) to fight for the independence that would come after the 1974 coup in Portugal. Communist regimes in newly independent Angola and Mozambique established high levels of state control over publishing, the Instituto Nacional do Livro et do Disco (Maputo, 1976) and Instituto Nacional do Livro (Luanda, 1978) enjoying near-monopolies. However, the end of South African-sponsored insurgencies, and increased support for civil society in these countries in the 1990s, allowed a number of autonomous, commercial publishers (e.g. Editora Escolar, Maputo, 1993) to emerge.

Elsewhere in the Southern African Development Community, printing was introduced to Île de France (Mauritius) by the French in 1767, and subsequently reached Madagascar (where the LMS also established a press, in 1826). Madagascar is its own special case, unusual among former French colonies in having been a unified kingdom with a single written language (Malagasy, related to Malay) before colonization. It also possessed a history of writing in Arabic script. Throughout the early 20th century, French colonial policy was to promote the teaching of French, but after the 1972 revolution, Malagasy literary production and printing have been actively encouraged.

6 Book production in Africa today

Africa generates less than 2 per cent of global book production, and remains unable to satisfy its own book needs, importing some 70 per cent of its books from Europe and North America (and exporting about 5 per cent of its output). Economic crises in the 1980s and 1990s hampered many African governments' abilities to fund book development or subsidize publishing, much less stock libraries; weak currencies across the continent have made imports of foreign-produced books and publishing materials prohibitively expensive. Even in South Africa, which has arguably the most developed publishing industry, fewer than 10 per cent of the population have the money to purchase books regularly. Nonetheless, small presses across the continent—more than 200 were active in 2000—continue to produce material in a variety of forms and languages, both African and European, with initiatives such as the African Books Collective, and African Publishers Network, Southern African Book Development Education Trust, and specialist foreign publishers such as James Currey and Hans Zell, seeking to support their endeavours. *See also* **25, 27.**

BIBLIOGRAPHY

African Book Publishing Record

E. A. Apeji, 'Book Production in Nigeria: An Historical Survey', *Information Development*, 12 (1996), 210–14

D. Attwell, *Rewriting Modernity* (2005)

F. R. Bradlow, *Printing for Africa* (1987)

M. Chapman, *Southern African Literatures* (1996, 2003)

N. Evans and M. Seeber, eds., *The Politics of Publishing in South Africa* (2000)

A. Gérard, *African Language Literatures* (1981)

J. Gibbs and J. Mapanje, *The African Writers' Handbook* (1999)

S. Gikandi, ed., *Encyclopedia of African Literature* (2003)

G. Griffiths, *African Literatures in English* (2000)

I. Hofmeyr, 'Metaphorical Books', *Current Writing*, 13.2 (2001), 100–108

—— *The Portable Bunyan: A Transnational History of 'The Pilgrim's Progress'* (2004)

—— and L. Kriel, 'Book History in Southern Africa', *South African Historical Journal*, 55 (2006), 1–19

—— *et al.*, eds., 'The Book in Africa', *Current Writing* 13.2 (2001)

C. Holden, 'Early Printing from Africa in the British Library', *BLJ* 23 (1997), 1–11

D. Killam and R. Rowe, *The Companion to African Literatures* (2000)

L. de Kock, *Civilising Barbarians* (1996)

S. I. A. Kotei, *The Book Today in Africa* (1987)

C. R. Larson, *The Ordeal of the African Writer* (2001)

B. Lindfors, *Popular Literatures in Africa* (1991)

S. Mafundikwa, *Afrikan Alphabets* (2004)

R. L. Makotsi and L. K. Nyariki, *Publishing and Book Trade in Kenya* (1997)

C. R. Namponya, 'History and Development of Printing and Publishing in Malawi', *Libri*, 28 (1978), 169–81

S. Newell, *Literary Culture in Colonial Ghana* (2002)

—— ed., *Readings in African Popular Fiction* (2002)

—— *West African Literatures* (2006)

J. Opland, 'The Image of the Book in Xhosa Oral Poetry', in *Oral Literature and Performance in Southern Africa*, ed. D. Brown (1999)

A. Ricard, *The Languages and Literatures of Africa*, tr. N. Morgan (2004)

A. H. Smith, *The Spread of Printing: South Africa* (1971)

A. van der Vlies, ed., 'Histories of the Book in Southern Africa': *English Studies in Africa*, 47.1 (2004)

—— *South African Textual Cultures* (2007)

B. A. Yates, 'Knowledge Brokers: Books and Publishers in Early Colonial Zaire', *History in Africa*, 14 (1987), 311–40

H. Zell, *Publishing, Books and Reading in Sub-Saharan Africa*, 3e (2008)

40

The History of the Book in the Muslim World

GEOFFREY ROPER

1 The origins of the Arabic book

Arabic is a Semitic language akin to Hebrew and Aramaic. The Arabic script developed from that of ancient Nabataean Aramaic, and reached only a very imperfect state in the pre-Islamic period. Arabic literature (mainly poetry) was then transmitted almost entirely orally. The written language of the period has survived only in the form of inscriptions on stone, but there are a few tantalizing references in early Arabic poetry to writing on palm-bark and parchment, and the use of reed pens. Arabia also accommodated communities of Jews and Christians with a scriptural tradition in which some Arabs participated. Thus, book culture was not completely alien to pre-Islamic Arabs, even though they have left no surviving physical books. The form of the book was at this stage in a state of transition, from the scroll to the codex. By the time the Arabs felt an imperative need to create enduring but portable written texts, in the 7th century, the codex had already emerged as the norm, and it therefore became the prime vehicle for their emerging culture of the book. This need, and its physical expression, resulted from the impact of the new religion of Islam, conveyed through, and embodied in, a great book of revelation in the Arabic language.

2 The Qur'ān: the book seen as divine revelation and redemption

The word *qur'ān* in Arabic means simply 'reading' or 'recitation' but when applied to the founding revelatory scripture of Islam, it may have taken on some of the connotations of the cognate Syriac word *qeryānā*, meaning 'scripture reading' or 'lesson'. In the view of Muslims, the Holy Qur'ān contains the spoken words of the one transcendent God (Allāh), transmitted through the angel Gabriel (Jibrīl) to the Prophet Muhammad, who lived in the Hijaz (western Arabia), *c.*570–632. These words, comprising 114 unequal chapters (*sūras*), each divided into verses (*āyas*), were received over a period of about twenty years. They constitute a variety of material, ranging from passages of sublimely poetical quality to narratives, liturgies, and regulations for personal and communal conduct. Together they are regarded as the final revelation and message of the one true God to humankind, providing the ultimate source of belief and behaviour for all people who submit to Him (Muslims). Islam (literally, 'submission') is therefore, above all, a book-centred religion, in which redemption comes through obedience to a sacred text.

The Qur'ān was also regarded as being derived from a transcendent celestial Book (*Kitāb* or *Umm al-Kitāb*, Mother of the Book), which had previously been revealed to Jews and Christians. Although they were accused by the Muslims of having corrupted their versions of the text, they were nevertheless regarded as the People of the Book (*Ahl al-Kitāb*) and respected as such (*see* **2**).

It is thought that Muhammad, in the final period of his life, started the process of committing the Qur'ān to writing, probably by dictating it to scribes who wrote it down on available materials, such as stones, animal bones, or palm leaves. Oral transmission and memorized versions, however, continued alongside the written texts, which inevitably took varying forms. Eventually a standardized recension emerged, which is traditionally attributed to 'Uthmān ibn 'Affān (d. 656), the third caliph (successor of the Prophet and leader of the Muslim community), who is said to have ordered four or five master copies to be made of the definitive text, to be placed in the main Muslim cities and towns and used as exclusive exemplars. Historically considered, it is likely that the process actually took much longer, and that, although the standard form of the text may go back to the 7th century, its detailed readings were not standardized for a further three centuries. One important reason for this was the fact that the Arabic script contains only consonants and long vowels, and reading and syntax depend on the insertion of short vowels, for which a consistent orthographical system was not devised until later. Early Qur'ān MSS also often lack even the dots that distinguish consonantal letters of the same basic shapes.

Until the advent of a standard printed version in the 20th century, the making of accurate copies of the Qur'ān (*mushaf*, plural *masāhif*—Muslims never speak of them as 'Qur'āns') was a sacred duty, since they embodied both the divine revelation and the indispensible guide to human life. They moreover became reflections of the sublime beauty of the divine word, through the development of Arabic calligraphy, which evolved into the highest art form in Muslim societies. Great care was also taken with the design of Qur'ān copies, including the use of illumination. Nevertheless, educated persons still had to learn the text by heart, and oral transmission continued to be of great importance until the print era, because MSS could not meet the universal demand among Muslims.

Non-Muslims have naturally not shared the Muslim faith in the divine origin and nature of the Qur'ān. European Christians until recent times regarded it as a forgery, created by an impostor. Nevertheless, because of the challenges presented by Islam, they undertook translations of it into Latin, from the 12ᵗʰ century onwards, and later into European vernaculars. They were also responsible for the first printed versions of the Arabic text, starting with the Venice Qur'ān of 1537/8. In the Enlightenment period and later, there was a growing appreciation of its literary merits, and even of its spiritual qualities. Modern ecumenism and multiculturalism have continued this tendency. Meanwhile, from the 19ᵗʰ century onwards, the Qur'anic text was subjected to philological, textual, and historical analysis comparable to the 'Higher Criticism' of the Bible, which cast considerable doubt on the integrity and chronology of the text and highlighted its relationship with pre-Islamic, especially Christian, scriptural traditions and terminology. For Muslims, however, such treatment was anathema.

Whatever view is taken of these matters, it is hardly possible to overestimate the historical role of the Qur'ān as a book that has influenced and even determined the social, moral, and intellectual life, over many centuries, of about one fifth of the world's population.

3 Arabic scribal culture and its legacy

The Qur'ān also transformed Arab society into a pre-eminently literary culture. Because the overwhelmingly powerful revelation had come in the form of a book, textuality became the predominant characteristic of Arab and Muslim cognitive processes, and came to permeate Muslim society. From the earliest stage, it was necessary for Muslims to supplement the Qur'anic text with further sources of authority. The most important of these were the remembered and recorded sayings of the Prophet, known as *Hadīth*s. These were eventually systematized and elaborated, together with the regulations in the Qur'ān itself, into bodies of law, which were carefully recorded in writing and continually copied and recopied to serve the needs of the community and its governing authorities. At the same time, the old Arabic poetic tradition was revived, re-examined, and committed to writing in order to provide insights into the meanings of Qur'anic terminology. This in turn stimulated a new Islamic Arabic poetic and literary movement that produced large numbers of new texts, incorporated into MS books over the following centuries.

In a few decades following the death of the Prophet, the Muslims pushed out of Arabia and conquered vast areas from the Atlantic to central Asia. Many of the populations of these areas adopted Islam, and some, especially among the adjacent territories, also adopted the Arabic language. They thereby entered this new Arabic-Islamic book culture, but at the same time they brought their own literary and intellectual heritage into it. Not only older literary traditions, but also philosophy, science, mathematics, geography, historiography, and other disciplines came to flourish in the Muslim environment, which enthusiastically promoted the acquisition of knowledge and learning as a virtue enjoined by the Prophet. The writing and copying of texts was an essential and integral part of this endeavour; during the 8th–15th centuries in Muslim lands it reached a level unprecedented in the history of book production anywhere. In his *Fihrist*, the 10th-century bibliographer Ibn al-Nadīm al-Warrāq used his knowledge of the trade and of the contents of important collections to list the works of some 4,300 authors whose writings were then available in Arabic; in the 17th century, the Turkish scholar Kâtib Çelebi (Hacı Halife) enumerated more than 14,500 titles of which he had knowledge. Many texts were, of course, copied repeatedly down the generations.

The number of MSS produced is impossible to compute. Today there are more than 3 million MS texts in the Arabic script, preserved in libraries and institutions throughout the world, as well as an unknown but substantial number still in private hands. A very high proportion of these were written within the last 500 years: this reflects the longevity of the scribal tradition, but it is also a result of the destruction which has overtaken much of the earlier written output of Muslim civilizations in the period of their greatest intellectual vigour. Neglect, decay, and accidental loss by fire and flood have been compounded by the deliberate and belligerent destruction of significant parts of the written heritage, both by Muslims and by their enemies. The Mongol devastations of the 13th century are especially notorious, but the phenomenon has continued into the present era: important Islamic MS collections have been wholly or partly destroyed in and after the wars in Bosnia-Herzegovina, Kosovo, Afghanistan, and Iraq in the late 20th and early 21st centuries.

What remains, however, forms a substantial part of the world's intellectual and textual heritage. Not only is this heritage a vital underpinning of Muslim life and thought, but it has also constituted an essential strand of the European philosophical and scientific tradition. This was partly because Muslims inherited, translated, and transmitted the ancient books of the Greeks, Iranians, and Indians. Equally important were the original intellectual contributions of writers such as Ibn Sīnā ('Avicenna'), Ibn Rushd ('Averroes'), Al-Khwārizmī (whence 'algorithm'), and many others, whose books contributed to the development of thought that led to the European Renaissance. Muslim books entered Christian Europe by two routes: some were studied and translated in the medieval period in former Muslim centres in Spain; others were brought later, from the 17th century onwards, as Arabic MS books from Ottoman and other Muslim territories.

4 Physical aspects of the Muslim MS book

Although the earliest Arabic and Muslim writings may have been on bones and palm leaves, the normal materials in the first two centuries were papyrus and parchment. The former entered widespread use after the Muslim conquest of Egypt in the 0640s, but chiefly for letters and documents, rather than books. Literary texts and Qur'anic fragments written on papyrus are extant, however, and there is evidence that some of them were assembled into codices. Parchment was the writing material favoured for Qur'āns, for which durability was more important than portability. Some magnificent specimens, usually in oblong shape, with their width exceeding their height by up to 50 per cent, can be seen in surviving collections.

In the 9th century, a new material was introduced from China, via central Asia: paper (*see* **10, 42**). As a comparatively portable as well as durable medium, this soon became widely adopted both for fine Qur'āns and for more mundane and secular texts. Many centres of paper production were established throughout the Muslim world, and their techniques were eventually transmitted to Christian Europe. Not only was paper convenient to use, transport, and store, it was, most importantly, considerably cheaper than papyrus and parchment, probably partly because of the use of recycled rags as raw material in its manufacture. Whereas an early Qur'ān on parchment is reckoned to have required the skins of about 300 sheep, an equivalent amount of paper could be produced much more rapidly and at much lower cost.

The relative inexpensiveness of paper was a major factor in the explosion of book production and the transmission of knowledge in medieval Muslim societies from the 10th century onwards. Generally, only rulers, officials, and other privileged persons could afford the older materials, but paper put books within reach of a wider class of educated readers. Its availability and use seem also to have been the main reasons for the development of more cursive and legible styles of the Arabic script in that period. It provided a more convenient and readily usable medium for texts other than the Qur'ān, in which functional legibility was more important than hieratic presentation. Later, these styles were themselves calligraphically elaborated and used for fine Qur'āns written on paper.

Further developments in Iran from the 13th century onwards also made available much larger paper sizes, which in turn may have encouraged the development of book illustration (miniatures), as well as more lavishly and monumentally written and illuminated Qur'āns. From the 14th century, higher-quality European (especially Italian) paper rapidly displaced the local product in most Muslim lands. This reliance on imports does not seem, however, to have had an adverse effect on book production.

Because both parchment and paper were, by later standards, relatively scarce and expensive commodities, the practice of reusing them was not uncommon. Arabic palimpsests on parchment exist in a number of collections; paper was also often recycled, both for non-book uses and to make further supplies.

Muslim scribes continued to use the ancient pen made from reed (Arabic *qalam*, from Greek καλαμos), which was already the normal writing implement in the areas where Islam became predominant, and is mentioned in the Qur'ān itself. It consisted of a tube cut from the stem of a carefully selected reed (those from the marshes of Egypt and Iraq were especially favoured), which was matured by soaking in water and then carefully sharpened to an incised point. The shape and position of the incision varied according to the style of script for which it was intended. There were also distinct regional differences in the shapes of the nibs, especially between Spain and North Africa on the one hand and the central and eastern Muslim lands on the other. The craftsmanship involved in preparing pens was considered an essential and integral part of scribal art. Although there are occasional references in Arabic sources to metal pens, and one 10th-century Egyptian ruler is even said to have designed a gold fountain pen, the reed remained the *sine qua non* for Muslim penmanship until the 19th century. Pens were protected by being kept in special cases, incorporating inkwells; the cases were often themselves vehicles for artistic decoration.

The inks used had almost as exalted a status in the literature of penmanship as the pens (one poet called ink 'the perfume of men'). They varied in their recipes. In the earlier period, for writing on parchment, a brownish ink was used, made from combinations of mineral salts and tannins derived from gall-nuts. After the introduction of paper, however, this was found to have a destructive effect, and black inks made from soot and gum (already used on papyrus) were preferred; they were also considered aesthetically superior. Moreover, they were easier and cheaper to prepare, and this too contributed to the efflorescence of MS book culture. Coloured, especially red, inks were quite often used, and the practice of rubrication was widespread, helping to clarify the structures of texts and headings in the absence of punctuation. Gilt and silver also appear in some more prestigious MSS, especially Qur'āns, both for script and illumination.

The Arabic script, under the impetus of the need to write down the divine text of the Qur'ān, quickly developed from its rudimentary beginnings. By elaborating a system of pointing and diacritics, it remedied its deficiencies and emerged as a functional means of rendering and recording Arabic texts, although it never became fully phonetic. At the same time, as the vehicle of the divine message, it attracted a spiritual, even mystical, veneration that inspired the desire to transform it into an object of sublime beauty. Calligraphy therefore became the highest art form in Muslim culture, and a great variety of fine script styles emerged, used primarily, but not exclusively, for writing the Qur'anic text. These ranged from the simple and dignified, even monumental, Kufic of the earlier period to intricate, elaborate, and curvaceous compositions in later times. There were also considerable regional variations, reflecting the different civilizations and patrimonies of Muslims across Asia, Africa, and Europe.

The production of more utilitarian MSS, embodying the huge output of devotional, theological, legal, historical, scientific, and other 'secular' knowledge,

Tawqī' and *riqā'*

اللهم بنورك اهتدينا وبفضلك استغنينا

وفي كنفك أصبحنا وأمسينا أنت الأول فلا شيء قبلك وأنت
الآخر فلا شيء بعدك نعوذبك من الفشل والكسل

ومن عذاب القبر ومن فتنة الغنى والفقر

Muḥaqqaq and *rayḥān*

اللهم بنورك اهتدينا وبفضلك استغنينا

وفي كنفك أصبحنا وأمسينا أنت الأول فلا شيء قبلك
وأنت الآخر فلا شيء بعدك نعوذبك من الفشل والكسل ومن

عذاب القبر ومن فتنة الغنى والفقر

Thulth and *naskh*

اللهم بنورك اهتدينا وبفضلك

استغنينا وفي كنفك أصبحنا
وأمسينا أنت الأول فلا شيء
قبلك وأنت الآخر فلا شيء بعدك
نعوذبك من الفشل والكسل ومن

عذاب القبر ومن فتنة الغنى والفقر

Nasta'līq

اللهم نورك ارتد ينا وبفضلك اسـتـغنينا في

كنفك اصبحنا وامتينا الاول فلاشى قلك

Thulth maghribī

اللهم نورك اهتدينا وبفضلك الاستغنينا وفي كنفك الاصحنا

وامسينا انت الاول ولاشئ قبلك ولت الاخر ولاشئ بعدك نعوذ

بك من العثرا والكــرا وبسوء عذاب الفبر وبرفتة الغنى والفقر

Scribal maghribī

اللهم نورك اهتدينا وبفضلك استغنيناو وكعمك اصبحنا واهسينا انت اله واولاشئ

قلك وانت الاخم ولاشئ بعط نعوذبك من العثا ولكدا وبسوء عذا بـ النقم ومرفتة الفنر والفقر

Qur'anic maghribī

أَللَّهُمَّ نَوِّرْ إِلَى اهْتَدَيْنَا وَبِفَضْلِكَ إِسْتَغْنَيْنَا وَ فِي

كَنَفِهَا أَصْبَحْنَا وَأَمْسَيْنَا أَنْتَ الْأَوَّلُ وَلَا شَيْءَ فَمَا

وَأَنْتَ الْآخِرُ وَلَا شَيْءَ بَعْدَ هَ نَعُوذُ بِهَا مِنَ الْعَثَلِ

وَالْكَسَلِ وَمِنْ عَذَابِ الْقَبْرِ وَمِرْفِتَنَّهِ الْغُنَّى وَالْعَفْرِ

The six classic hands, *al-aqlām al-sittah*, of Arabic calligraphy, with *nasta'līq* and the three *Maghribī* hands. Nour Foundation, New York

required more functional styles of script, designed primarily for legibility and communication. Most Arabic MS books are therefore written in smaller and simpler cursive styles, notably *naskh* (which later became the basis of Arabic typography) and, in the Muslim West, various forms of *Maghribī*. Yet, even in workaday MSS, aesthetic considerations were rarely abandoned altogether, and writing still had sacred connotations, especially since the name of God (Allāh) was always present, if only in the universal opening invocation (*basmala*): 'In the name of God, the Compassionate, the Merciful.'

The complexities of nomenclature for the different script styles, and the lack of consistency and systematic correlation with what appears in extant MSS, has rendered the entire field of Arabic palaeography quite problematic. Much scholarly work remains to be done before a clear picture can emerge of the typology of bookhands and their chronological and geographical interrelationships.

There is one respect in which the more utilitarian bookhands were less practical than the grander Qur'anic scripts: they were rarely vocalized, whereas Qur'anic MSS, from the 10th century onwards, normally carried the diacritic vowel signs (*ḥarakāt*), to ensure the sacred text's correct reading. The absence of these in more mundane texts undoubtedly speeded up their production, and economized on the use of paper and ink; but it inevitably led to ambiguities in understanding and interpretation, and may have played some part in restricting functional literacy to an elite who knew the full phonetic and semantic values of the literary language through oral transmission. This may in turn have reinforced the still-prevailing division between literary Arabic and the unwritten colloquial dialects spoken by ordinary people.

The presence of pictorial illustrations in Muslim MS books was discouraged by Islamic injunctions against figurative representation. Certainly, they are never found in Qur'ān MSS, but they do appear in some 'secular' books to accompany literary, historical, scientific, and occasionally even erotic texts, especially from the 13th century onward. Schools of miniature painting emerged, mainly to cater to the tastes of ruling elites. Miniatures' exquisite beauty has appealed also to connoisseurs, mostly non-Muslims, in recent times, and they have become sought-after collectors' items; they were, however, for the most part extrinsic to mainstream book culture in the Muslim world.

Other features of book design and layout are worthy of note. Except in the humbler 'working' MSS, pages were carefully ruled to ensure regular and equal spacing of lines, and to calibrate texts in terms of page numbers. This was done either with a stylus or, more commonly, with cords assembled in a frame (*misṭara*), which could be used to provide standard rulings throughout a volume. Although some MS pages were designed to provide a comfortable balance between black and white through generous margins and interlinear space, the high cost and uncertain availability of paper in many cases imposed cramped layouts making maximum use of space. Sometimes a virtue seems to have been made of this necessity by dividing the text blocks into columns and/or panels, in some cases with oblique lines of text, arranged in a harmonious manner: poetry MSS offer the best examples of this. Otherwise, margins were often filled with glosses and commentaries, sometimes also written obliquely to the main text. Punctuation was rudimentary, consisting only of circles, rosettes, palmettes, groups of dots, or other devices separating verses of the Qur'ān and occasionally clauses, paragraphs, or sections in other works. Where they do occur, they rarely follow sentence structure in the modern sense.

Gatherings (quires) were often (except in the early period) numbered to assist in assembling them in the correct order, using first alphabetic (*abjad*) numeration and later Indo-Arabic numerals or numbers spelt out as words. The numbering of leaves (foliation) did not become widespread until the 16th century. Catchwords were also used as a method of ensuring correct sequences as early as the 11th century, and became common from the 13th century onwards.

Texts normally ended with colophons, which usually gave the date (and occasionally also the place) of copying and the copyist's name, together with thankful invocations and benedictions, and sometimes a recapitulation of the title and/or author of the work. At the beginning of a MS, title-pages are sometimes found on the blank recto of the first leaf, or incorporated into an illuminated frontispiece, but they are not necessarily contemporary with the rest of the book, and their contents may be inaccurate. Details of author and title are normally located within the first page or two of text, after preliminary pious invocations and, sometimes, other prefatory matter. The text nearly always starts on the verso of the first leaf.

The illumination and decoration of MSS was an important Islamic art form, second only to calligraphy. The finest Qur'āns contain magnificent frontispieces and headpieces (*'unwāns*) with gilt and/or multicoloured abstract, floral, and foliate patterns, as well as text borders, panels for headings, and sometimes interlinear decoration as well. Many lesser MSS were also illuminated, at least at their start. This, and some of the other features previously mentioned, underline the important role of the book in the visual as well as the literary culture of Muslim societies. These features can also provide useful, sometimes vital, evidence for the placing and dating of otherwise unattributed MSS.

One category of MS book in which the Muslim world made a notable contribution to global knowledge is that of maps and atlases. Muslims extended the inherited traditions of Ptolemy and other ancient cartographers to create world and regional maps of an accuracy that was not matched until modern times. This development was driven by the official and administrative requirements of the Muslim empires, but it coincided and interacted with the emergence of the new paper-based book culture from the 9th century onwards. Maps and atlases were, however, produced not to meet any widespread demand, but generally in response to rulers' commissions. Many of these maps were schematic rather than realistically scaled, but they reflected a growing visual sophistication that eventually culminated in such cartographical masterpieces as the world map of the 12th-century geographer Al-Idrīsī and the extraordinary atlas entitled *Kitāb Gharā'ib al-Funūn* (Book of Curiosities) now in the Bodleian Library, Oxford, which has published it on the World Wide Web.

Bookbindings in the Muslim world were also vehicles for artistic finesse (*see* **19**). Although isolated examples are recorded of books in scroll form, the codex

A map of the Gulf of İzmir from a MS dated 1587 of Piri Reis's *Kitāb-i Baḥriyye*: the original work belongs to about 1521 and, like a portolan, describes the Mediterranean for sailors. The Bodleian Library, University of Oxford (MS D'Orville 543, fol. 17r)

was the normal form of the book from the very beginning of the Islamic period, and at first wooden boards, later leather covers, were used to hold the leaves and gatherings together. Bookbinders emerged as specialized craftsmen by the 9th century, when several of their names were recorded. Yet, although the craft clearly enjoyed a certain prestige, its practitioners are predominantly anonymous, and their status is unclear.

Book covers were generally made of pasteboard, often containing recycled MS leaves, and wholly or partly covered with leather, which was also pasted directly on to the spine. This unsatisfactory method often caused bindings to become detached, so many MSS were subsequently rebound. The rear cover was normally extended into a folding flap covering the book's fore-edge. The front cover was usually decorated—in the late medieval period from which most of the earlier surviving examples date—with tooled rectangular panels containing geometric patterns, and borders, sometimes containing Qur'anic quotations. Often, the rear cover was also decorated, with a different design. Gilding was sometimes used. Later, central medallions of various shapes were imposed. In Iran, from the 16th century onwards, there was greater use of gold, with other colours added. Lacquer was also used to create elaborate pictorial compositions on bindings. Inside the binding, the endpapers of books of this later period were sometimes adorned with marbling, using a technique that seems to have originated in Iran and reached its apogee in Ottoman Turkey.

Some MSS, of square or oblong shape, were encased in boxes, often glued to the spine, which served to protect what would otherwise have been a somewhat cumbersome and vulnerable book. Boxes, envelopes, and bags were also used for small portable MSS, especially Qur'āns and prayer books, designed to accompany and to protect travellers.

However important bindings may have become, the central role in the production of MS books was always held by the scribes themselves. The profession of scribe soon became established and honourable in Muslim society, and included people of all levels of education. Professional scribes were sometimes also specialized calligraphers, illuminators, or miniature painters operating in palace workshops, or secretaries working in court chanceries with an exalted status. At the other end of the scale, however, they might be market stallholders offering their services to all and sundry. In between, there were many paid copyists working in libraries, colleges, mosques, and other religious institutions. They were employed by wealthy patrons and book collectors, by scholars with particular needs, or by authors. Many MSS, however, were not written by professionals. Some were written by authors themselves: a number of autograph or holograph copies of Muslim writings survive in libraries. Impecunious writers and scholars also often resorted to copying in order to sustain themselves; students and other readers frequently made copies, in libraries and elsewhere, simply for their own use; such MSS often fall well short of the standards of calligraphy, or even legibility, found in those made for sale or on commission.

Inevitably in traditional society, most scribes, whether professionals or amateurs, were male. Yet there exist a surprising number of references to women performing this role. Some caliphs and other rulers employed female servants or slaves as calligraphers or as secretaries. Poets and writers also sometimes employed bondwomen to transcribe their works; other Muslim women were themselves poets or scholars who produced their own MSS. Even some fine Qur'āns are known to have been copied by female calligraphers, and in 10th-century Córdoba there were reported to be 170 women occupied in writing Qur'āns in the Kufic script. Much later, in 16th-century Iran, a traveller claimed that 'the women of Shiraz are scribes...in every house in this city the wife is a copyist' (Būdāq Qazwīnī, quoted in Déroche, 192). With all due allowance for exaggeration, these references indicate that book production was by no means an exclusively male domain in traditional Muslim societies.

Scribal activity did not entirely displace oral transmission in the diffusion of texts, however. Written books were often created in the first place by copying from dictation or from memory. The right to transmit the text was frequently granted in the form of a licence (*ijāza*) given by the author (or, later, an authorized agent in an established chain of transmission) on the basis of a satisfactory reading from the copy, which had to conform to the orally transmitted and memorized version. This system applied especially to religious or legal texts copied in the environment of a *madrasa* (college), and was prevalent in the 11th–16th centuries, although in some places it continued until much later.

Whatever the immediate source, the maintenance of accuracy has always been a problem in texts reproduced in Muslim MS culture, as elsewhere. Copyists, however well-educated and trained, were always fallible. Sometimes they may have had difficulties reading the source MS, especially if it were in an unfamiliar variety of script. Even if this were not so, they could all too easily lapse into unintentional repetitions, omissions, and other corruptions of the text. Two particular problems arising from the nature of the Arabic script are false transcriptions caused by misreading or misplacing the diacritical points distinguishing different letters (*taṣḥīf*), and by transposing root letters within a word (*taḥrīf* or *ibdāl*). Although many MSS were checked and edited before being released, the corruption of texts in this way, an inevitable consequence of scribal culture, was a continual source of anxiety and insecurity in a civilization for which the authenticity and integrity of texts was of paramount importance.

Some books, as already stated, were written to order or for the use of the writer. Many others, however, were produced for sale. The occupation of bookseller and stationer (*warrāq*) overlapped with that of scribe. In some ways, this enterprise was comparable to that of publishers in the print era: they received texts from authors, either by dictation or in writing, then transcribed them, or employed others to do so, in sufficient quantities to meet demand, bound them, and sold them at a profit. Occasionally, they restricted the supply in order to keep prices high; sometimes they sold books by auction. As well as trading in copies made by or for themselves, booksellers dealt in copies bought in from elsewhere; they also acted as purchasing agents, seeking out particular titles or genres on behalf of scholars or collectors. Some booksellers were learned or literary men themselves: one of the most famous was the 10th-century scholar-bibliographer Ibn al-Nadīm al-Warrāq. Bookshops tended to cluster in particular streets or quarters of towns, a pattern (common among many trades) that can still be found today in, for example, the Sahaflar market in Istanbul. In some cities, a guild structure existed, with the book trade supervised by a *shaykh* or master.

The high importance and value attached to books and reading in traditional Muslim societies led to the formation of many large libraries. These belonged to rulers, mosques, educational institutions, and private individuals. Although the quantities of volumes that they contained were undoubtedly exaggerated in literary sources, there can be little doubt that they numbered many tens of thousands in the major centres, such as Baghdad, Cairo, and Córdoba. Catalogues of libraries were compiled, and some libraries provided facilities, and even personnel, for making new copies of texts. Many libraries in the Muslim world were established as inalienable endowments (*waqfs*), so that books could not be sold or otherwise dispersed. Yet, borrowing by scholars was generally allowed, and this inevitably led to some losses. Much greater destruction and dispersal, however, resulted from fires, floods, and conflict, often compounded by neglect, misappropriation, and theft—problems that have continued into modern times.

5 The Muslim MS book beyond the Arab world

The Qur'ān gave the Arabic language and script a central importance in Islam. The areas of western Asia, North Africa, and Spain that adopted Arabic became the heartlands of book culture in the heyday or 'classical' period of Muslim civilization, from the 8th to the 13th centuries. As such, they have been the main focus of studies of that culture. But Islam eventually spread over a huge area from the Atlantic to the Pacific, and in later periods other, non-Arab Muslim peoples and empires became predominant. They created their own literary traditions and produced MS books in their own languages; but the powerful influence of Arabic was such that they adopted many Arabic loanwords and, most importantly, the Arabic script, which was adapted to write a variety of languages, most of which are intrinsically unrelated to Arabic. In most of these areas, however, much religious and legal literature was also written in Arabic, and many copies of the Qur'ān were made, always in the original.

Iran had a proud ancient literary tradition and, from the 10th century onwards, in addition to producing magnificent Qur'āns, created a flourishing Persian MS culture. Poetic books were especially noteworthy, and a characteristic oblique and highly artistic form of the Arabic script was developed to write them, known as *nasta'līq* ('hanging script'). Rulers and wealthy patrons often commissioned exquisitely decorated and illustrated MSS, and Persian miniatures have become much-treasured *objets d'art*. Unfortunately, this has led to many of them becoming separated from the texts they were created to illustrate.

Ottoman Turkey became the centre of a large empire that by the mid-16th century included most of the Arab world and much of southeastern Europe. Having inherited the Arabic MS tradition, the Turks both continued it and created a Turkish book culture that also borrowed some elements of the Persian. Ottoman calligraphers became especially celebrated, both for Qur'āns and for more humble MSS executed with great elegance. Istanbul became the greatest centre in the world for Islamic books, and remains the largest repository of them to this day. At the same time, the Ottomans extended Muslim book culture into the Balkans. In Bosnia-Herzegovina especially, many MSS in Arabic, Persian, and Turkish were both written and imported, and were preserved in important libraries. The Bosnian language itself was also written in the Arabic script.

Further east, in India (and south Asia generally) there were many centres of Muslim civilization, especially during the period of the Mughal empire (1526–1857), and many of these also became centres of MS production. Apart from Qur'āns, most books were in Persian, including fine illuminated and illustrated MSS, but from the 18th century onwards, there was also some writing in local vernaculars, especially Urdu. In central Asia, many MSS were likewise in Persian, but with increasing use of regional Turkic languages. In southeast Asia, Arabic Qur'āns were written in quite distinct local styles (similarly, in China), and there was also a significant Malay literature in the Arabic script that developed its own MS traditions. Finally, mention must be made of sub-Saharan Africa, where the advent of Islam in large areas of both east and west brought literacy and a distinctive written culture embodied in characteristic MS books both in Arabic and in African languages, using a distinctive style of the Arabic script (*see* **39**). Some of these were preserved in libraries; many more have emerged from private collections in recent years.

6 The longevity of the Muslim MS tradition

Most surviving Muslim MSS date from the 16th century or later. This is only partly due to the loss of older ones. The writing of books by hand continued as the normal method of textual transmission for far longer in the Muslim world than elsewhere. The late arrival of printing was as much the consequence as the cause of this state of affairs. A number of more fundamental reasons can be identified.

One is the extreme reverence felt by Muslims for the handwritten word. Not only was writing regarded as a quasi-divine and mystical activity, but the beauty of the cursive Arabic script aroused an almost physical passion, akin to human love. Annemarie Schimmel has identified numerous passages of Muslim poetry in which books and writing are likened to bodily characteristics of the beloved that arouse desire. Given such feelings, even if they were directed by poetic conceits, it is not surprising that Muslims were reluctant to abandon the handwritten book. Another factor was the widespread engagement of large sections of the educated population in book copying (and associated trades). Many wholly or partly earned their living by it. There was thus a substantial vested interest in retaining this method of production, whatever its limitations. A third reason, arising from the other two, was that Muslims felt supremely comfortable with MSS, which they regarded as an integral part of their culture and society. Even when economic and other conditions created a substantial rise in demand for books among emerging classes of society, as in 18th-century Egypt, it was felt that scribal production was adequate to cope with this phenomenon.

At the same time, patterns of intellectual and religious authority within Muslim society were closely bound up with book production and the limited transmission of texts. Islam has no ecclesiastical organization, and the status of religious leaders, who had great authority but lacked secular power, depended essentially on their role as scholars and producers of texts. This in turn depended on maintaining the sacred character of writing and a degree of exclusiveness in and control over the creation and distribution of books. Accordingly, Muslims went on writing and copying books by hand until the emergence of new patterns of state authority that were associated with modernizing influences coming partly from outside the Muslim world.

7 The origins of printing in the Arabic script

Printing was practised in the Muslim world as early as the 10th century. Block prints on paper, and at least two on parchment, found in Egypt, survive in several collections, notably in Cairo, Vienna, Cambridge, and New York, and further pieces have emerged from excavations. One in private hands may originate in Afghanistan or Iran. However, no literary or historical testimony to the craft of block printing seems to exist, except for two obscure references in Arabic poems of the 10th and 14th centuries to the use of *ṭarsh* to produce copies of amulets. It has been suggested that this non-classical Arabic term signified tin plates with engraved or repoussé lettering used to produce multiple copies of Qur'anic and incantatory texts for sale to the illiterate poor. Certainly, the style of the surviving pieces indicates that they were not intended to gratify any refined literary or artistic taste, since the script is generally far from calligraphic, and there are even errors in the Qur'anic texts. Some have headpieces with designs incorporating bolder lettering and ornamental motifs, sometimes white on black, which may have been printed with separate woodblocks. Some block-printed patterns have also been found on the endpapers of MS codices. The origin of the processes used is unknown: China or central Asia have been suggested, but there are serious doubts about any connection with Chinese woodblock printing, in view of the marked differences in the techniques and the contrast between these pieces and the luxurious character of other Chinese imports to the Muslim world and their local imitations. A link with the printing of patterns on textiles, also practised in medieval Egypt, cannot be ruled out.

Some scholars have speculated that this Muslim precedent may have played a part in the origins of European printing several centuries later. No evidence of any such link has yet emerged, and definitive answers to this and other outstanding questions concerning medieval Arabic printing must await further discoveries and research.

Muslim block printing of texts seems to have died out in the 15th century, although this or a related technique was evidently employed subsequently to make lattice patterns for use in the decorative arts. There is nothing to suggest that this technique was ever used to produce books or substantial literary texts in any form. These remained the monopoly of scribes in the Muslim world until the 18th century, and the origins of Arabic typography and printed-book production must be sought not in the Muslim world itself, but in Europe.

Arabic script, being cursive, presents problems quite unlike those of the Roman, Greek, and Hebrew alphabets which preoccupied the first few generations of European typographers. Not only is a higher degree of punchcutting skill required—especially if calligraphic norms are to be imitated—but matrices must be justified even more minutely if the breaks between adjacent sorts are to be disguised. The compositor likewise must constantly avoid using the wrong letter form. Moreover, as well as different initial, medial, final, and isolated sorts for each letter, an abundance of ligatures is also needed for pairs or groups of letters. If vowel signs (*ḥarakāt*) are required—for Qur'anic and certain other texts—then even more sorts are needed, as well as huge quantities of quadrats and leads to be interspersed between the vowel strokes. A full Arabic fount can therefore contain over 600 sorts. This makes it an expensive investment, and economic factors alone have therefore impeded the development of Arabic typography, as compared with its European counterparts.

Arabic printing with movable type originated in Italy in the early 16th century. The first book was the *Kitāb Ṣalāt al-Sawāʿī* (Book of Hours), printed by the Venetian printer Gregorio de Gregorii at Fano (or possibly in Venice) in 1514 and sponsored by Pope Julius II for the use of Arab Melkite Christians in Lebanon and Syria. The type design is inelegant, and it was set in a clumsy, disjointed manner. Rather better was the typography of Alessandro Paganino, who printed the whole text of the Qur'ān in Venice in 1537/8, probably as a commercial export venture. Nevertheless, it was still so remote from calligraphic norms as to make it quite unacceptable to the Muslims for whom it was intended, especially as its pointing and vocalization were inaccurate and incomplete; it also contained errors in the Qur'anic text. Italy remained the main home of Arabic printing for the rest of the 16th century; it was in Rome that Robert Granjon produced his elegant Arabic types in the 1580s, which for the first time achieved calligraphic quality, with their liberal use of ligatures and letter forms derived from the best scribal models. They were used principally in the lavish editions of the Tipografia Medicea Orientale between 1590 and 1610, and they set the standard for nearly all subsequent work. Their influence is notable in the Arabic founts of the Dutch scholar-printer Franciscus Raphelengius and his successor, Thomas Erpenius, who produced many Arabic texts with his more practical and workmanlike founts in the early 17th century, and whose type-styles were much used or copied in Germany, England, and elsewhere. A more elegant and beautiful fount was commissioned by the French scholar-diplomat François Savary de Brèves: it was evidently based on Arabic calligraphy seen while he was French ambassador in Istanbul between 1592 and 1604, and/or in MSS in Rome, where the types were cut before 1613. It was later used both there and at the Imprimerie royale in Paris in the mid-17th century, and again in the Napoleonic period. Subsequently it provided a model for other types, notably that of the Congregatio de Propaganda Fide, which had a monopoly on Arabic printing in Rome from 1622 onwards, and that of the monastic presses of 18th-century Romania (*see* **33**).

There was a steady flow of Arabic printed books from most of the European centres of learning during the 17th–19th centuries. After Granjon, other leading typographers, such as William Caslon I and Giambattista Bodoni, were also involved in the design of Arabic founts. As well as Orientalist editions, the European presses produced biblical and other works for use by Christians in the Middle East, and some polemical literature written with the futile aim of converting Muslims. There were also some 'secular' texts intended as a commercial export commodity for sale to Muslims. These seem to have met at first with some resistance, and were seized and confiscated, but the Ottoman sultan in 1588 issued a decree forbidding any such interference. Nevertheless, these exports of European printed books in Arabic achieved little commercial success, although some copies were used by Muslims, as is shown by owners' inscriptions in them.

8 Arabic-script book printing in the Muslim world

Printing in the Muslim world originated in the non-Muslim communities living there. Hebrew typographic printing started in the Ottoman empire in 1493, and in Morocco in 1515; Armenian types were used from 1567 in Turkey, and from 1638 in Iran; Syriac type was used for both Syriac and Arabic in Lebanon in 1610; Greek books were printed in Istanbul from 1627; roman types appeared in Izmir in the 17th century. Yet typography in the Arabic script of the Muslim majority was not used in the Muslim world until the 18th century: before then, the few such printed books in use were imported from Europe.

Why was book printing not adopted by Muslims for more than 1000 years after it was invented in China and 250 years after it became widespread in western Europe (in spite of its use by non-Muslims in the Muslim world)? The reasons for this delay must be sought both in the nature of Muslim societies and in the supreme religious and aesthetic role accorded to the written word within them. Some indications of the profound Muslim attachment to MS books and scribal culture have already been given, and there can be no doubt that this was the main reason for the reluctance to embrace printing. Some more specific reasons can also be adduced.

The use of movable type seemed to be the only practical method of printed-book production before the 19th century. This involved creating punches and matrices and casting individual types for all the letters and letter combinations of the Arabic alphabet, in their different forms; then, the compositor had to reassemble these separate sorts to create lines of text and pages of a book. As far as Muslims could see, this was done without regard to the intrinsic subtleties of the processes of calligraphic composition, and its relation to underlying aesthetic and 'spiritual' considerations. Such segmentation and mechanization of the sacred Arabic script seemed tantamount to sacrilege in the eyes of devout Muslims. The production of the Qur'ān by mechanical means was considered unthinkable, but other texts bearing the name of God (as nearly all did) were also regarded by most scholars and readers as not to be violated by the methods of mass production. Rumours were also spread of the use in printing of ink brushes made from hogs' hair, which would automatically defile sacred names; other rumours circulated about impure inks, which might also have the same effect.

Apart from these considerations, the mass production of books by printing challenged the entrenched monopolies of intellectual authority enjoyed by the learned class (*'ulamā'*), and threatened to upset the balance between that authority and the power of the state. This was indeed one important reason why printing was eventually sponsored, in the 18th and 19th centuries, by modernizing rulers. They wanted to create a new, broader military and administrative class, versed in modern sciences and knowledge, who could bolster the power of the state against both traditional hierarchies within and new threats from outside. The printing press was seen as an indispensable instrument for achieving this new order.

The first printing with Arabic types in the Middle East was at Aleppo in Syria in 1706, by the Christian deacon 'Abd Allāh Zākhir: the first book was a psalter—*Kitāb al-Zabūr al-Sharīf*. The initiative in setting up this press came from the Melkite Patriarch of Antioch, Athanasius Dabbās, who between 1698 and 1705 had spent some time in Romania, where he arranged for two Arabic liturgical books to be printed at the monastery of Sinagovo (Snagov) near Bucharest, under the auspices of the Voivod of Wallachia, Constantin Brâncoveanu. This cooperation was facilitated by the common religious and political interests of Melkites and Romanians, both being semi-autonomous Orthodox subjects of the Ottoman empire. They were intended for free distribution to Orthodox priests in Arab countries, to overcome the shortage and high price of MS service books. Under Patriarchal auspices, and with the cooperation of the Romanians, this activity was transferred to Syria, and Zākhir went on to print in Aleppo an Arabic New Testament (also in 1706) and other Christian works, until the press ceased operation in 1711. He subsequently embraced Catholicism and moved to the Greek Catholic monastery of St John the Baptist at Shuwayr in Lebanon, where he set up a new press which published a long but intermittent series of biblical and theological works from 1734 to 1899. Its early materials can still be seen in the museum there. Another Orthodox Arabic press was established in Beirut at the beginning of the 1750s, again with help from Romania, but it published only two books, in 1751 and 1753.

Arabic printing in the Arab world remained in the hands of Syrian and Lebanese Christians for more than 100 years. They used types modelled partly on local Christian bookhands, but also influenced by the European tradition of Arabic type design, especially that of Orthodox Romania and of the Propaganda Fide Press in Rome. Their output was too small and intermittent to bring about any revolutionary change in book culture, but some observers, such as the French traveller and intellectual C. F. Volney, observed an increase in reading and writing among the Levantine Christians in that period. In his view, however, the press's potential for such improvement was vitiated by the exclusively religious nature of the books printed there.

Meanwhile, the Ottoman Turks revived Muslim printing in Istanbul in the second decade of the 18th century, when İbrahim Müteferrika began printing engraved maps, using copper plates, and probably techniques, imported from Vienna: the earliest extant map is dated 1719/20. This was part of a programme of Westernizing innovations in the Ottoman capital which also led, less than ten years later, to the establishment of Müteferrika's famous book-printing establishment, complete with Arabic types cut and cast locally and modelled on the neat Ottoman *naskhī* bookhand of the period. The first book, an Arabic–Turkish Dictionary, was printed in 1729 in 500 copies and was followed by sixteen others in Ottoman Turkish, in editions ranging from 500 to 1,200 copies, before the press was closed in 1742. They were all secular works—on history, geography, language, government (including one written by Müteferrika himself), navigation, and chronology—because the printing of the Qur'ān and religious texts was still forbidden. Several were illustrated with maps or pictorial engravings. Apart from a reprint in 1756, the press was not restarted until 1784, after which Ottoman Turkish printing had a continuous history until the adoption of the Latin alphabet in 1928.

It has been claimed that the 18th-century Müteferrika press was a failure, that its printed editions were only marginal phenomena in Turkish literary and scholarly culture, and that most of its limited output remained unsold. Recent research by Orlin Sabev into the book inventories contained in Ottoman probate documents of the period has shown, however, that these printed books achieved a considerable penetration among the contemporary educated classes, especially among administrators and officials, and that 65–75 per cent of the press's output was sold or otherwise distributed before Müteferrika died in 1747. Yet it remains true that 18th-century Turkish book printing and its impact was at a very modest level compared with earlier western European incunabula (*see* **6**), and that scribal transmission remained prevalent. Print had not yet become an agent of change in the Muslim world, although the way was now open for it.

Arabic printing in Egypt began with the presses of the French occupation of 1798–1801. Napoleon took from Paris a fount of the 17th-century Arabic types of Savary de Brèves, and from Rome the Arabic founts of the Propaganda Fide Press. However, these were used only for a relatively insignificant output of proclamations, materials to help the French occupiers to learn Arabic, and a treatise on smallpox. All the equipment was removed when the occupation of Egypt came to an end. The continuous history of Arabic printing in that country, and among Arab Muslims in general, dates from 1822, when the first book emerged from the state press of Muḥammad ʿAlī (ruler of Egypt, 1805–48), known as the Būlāq Press, after the place near Cairo where it was situated. This undertaking was started by an Italian-trained typographer, Niqūlā Masābikī (d. 1830); the first presses and types were imported from Milan, and are perceptibly European in style. They were soon replaced, however, by a succession of locally cut and cast founts based on indigenous *naskhī* hands. Although somewhat cramped and utilitarian, rather than calligraphic, they set the norm for Arabic typography, both in Egypt and at many other Muslim Arabic presses elsewhere, for the rest of the 19th century. *Nastaʿlīq* types were also occasionally employed, both for Persian texts and for headings in Arabic works. A *Maghribī* fount was also later created, but little used.

In the first twenty years of the Būlāq Press (1822–42) about 250 titles were published, including some religious and literary works—e.g. the *Thousand and One Nights* (*Alf Layla wa-Layla*)—but most were military and technical books, official decrees, grammars, manuals of epistolography, and translations of European scientific and historical works. After some vicissitudes in the mid-19th century following the death of Muḥammad ʿAlī, the Būlāq Press again became, from the 1860s onwards, the driving force behind a publishing explosion in Egypt. Between 1866 and 1872, it was thoroughly modernized, with new typefounding equipment and mechanized presses imported from Paris, and greatly improved typefaces. By the end of the century it had published more than 1,600 titles, representing about 20 per cent of total Egyptian book production.

As the first press in the Arab world to produce Arabic (and Turkish) books for Muslims, the Būlāq Press occupies a crucial place in Arabic and Muslim book history. Although some of its early output achieved only a very limited circulation, it nevertheless established printing for the first time as a normal method of producing and diffusing texts. Initially, technical and educational works, and, then, historical, literary, and religious titles became available to educated people on an unprecedented scale, despite initial resistance. This access to books in turn helped to create a new reading public and a new public sphere. Nor was the influence of the Būlāq Press confined to Egypt: its books were exported to Turkey, Syria, Lebanon, Palestine, and other Muslim countries, and stimulated the establishment or revival of printing far beyond the Nile valley.

In the first half of the 19th century, many Arabic books were imported into the Middle East by Christian missionaries. Most of these were printed at a British-run press in Malta between 1825 and 1842; they included secular educational works as well as religious tracts. The types were at first brought from England, but in the 1830s a new fount was cut and cast locally from calligraphic models, almost certainly prepared by the famous Arab writer Fāris al-Shidyāq, who had been a scribe in his youth and worked at the Malta press in this period. These set new standards among the Arab (mainly Christian, but also some Muslim and Jewish) pupils who used them, and the tradition was later continued by the American mission press in Beirut, which introduced a new typeface in the late 1840s, again based on calligraphic models: known as 'American Arabic', it has a characteristic attenuated and forward-sloping appearance, and was also used by several other presses in the Arab world. A more orthodox, but clear and workmanlike face, based on Turkish models, was adopted by the press of the Jesuit mission in Beirut about 1870, and also became very popular throughout the Levant (*see* **9**).

Other Catholic mission presses inaugurated Arabic printing in Jerusalem in 1847 and in Mosul in 1856: in both cases, their first founts were brought from Europe (Vienna and Paris, respectively). The first press in Iraq had, however, operated in Baghdad in 1830, using a fount similar to those of the first Persian ones in Iran, established at Tabriz *c.*1817 and Tehran *c.*1823: an elegant Persian-style *naskh*, but with some curious idiosyncrasies, such as the shortened top-stroke of the letter *kāf. Nasta'līq* typography was not and has never been favoured in Iran, despite the prevalence of this style in the scribal tradition (including lithography). It was, however, used in India as early as 1778 and remained in use there, both for Persian and for Urdu, until the mid-19th century; it was later revived in Hyderabad.

In the Middle East, Arabic typography burgeoned from the mid-19th century onwards, with presses starting at Damascus in 1855, Tunis in 1860, Ṣanʿāʾ in 1877, Khartoum in 1881, Mecca in 1883, and Medina in 1885. Most of these used local types in the Istanbul and Būlāq traditions, and many of them produced newspapers as well as books.

From the late 1820s onwards, however, many books and some newspapers, were printed not from type, but by a hybrid method of book production: lithography. This was favoured in many places, especially in Morocco, Iran, and central, south, and southeast Asia, where it almost completely displaced typography for nearly half a century. This phenomenon in Muslim printing history has no counterpart in earlier European experience. Whereas in Europe lithography was used almost entirely for pictorial and cartographical illustration, Muslims used it to reproduce entire texts written by hand. In this way, they could retain most of the familiar features of Islamic MSS, and the calligraphic integrity of the Arabic script, including some styles difficult to reproduce typographically. At the same time, they could also avoid expensive investment in movable types. As a consequence, some of the conscious and subliminal effects of the standardization of text presentation, and the emergence of a new print-induced *esprit de système*, as proposed by Elizabeth L. Eisenstein in relation to early modern

Europe, do not apply to those societies where this method was prevalent (*see* **6**). On the other hand, the low prices and ready acceptability of books printed by this method meant that lithographically reproduced texts—mainly traditional and classical ones—achieved a far wider dissemination. In this way, lithography did much, as Ian Proudfoot has shown, to 'usher in the print revolution' (Proudfoot, 182). At their best, lithographed texts, many complete with pictorial miniatures, could rival well-executed MSS of the period in beauty and clarity; at their worst, they could degenerate into barely legible grey scrawls.

The late 19th and early 20th centuries saw a revival of Arabic typography in the Middle East, with considerable improvements in typefaces, especially in Egypt, where the new founts of Dār al-Maʿārif, and of the Būlāq Press itself from 1902 onwards, set higher standards of clarity and elegance. In 1914, the new fount designed there for Aḥmad Zakī Pasha halved the number of sorts by eliminating many ligatures, while retaining some of the calligraphic features of the older Būlāq types. Later, the introduction of Linotype hot-metal machines further simplified the setting of Arabic-script texts, while inevitably moving the appearance of such works further away from traditional calligraphy and bookhands. However, with the modern decline of metal types and the introduction of photocomposition, latterly computer-generated, the way was opened for a return to calligraphic norms.

Apart from type styles, other features of the early Muslim printed book must be noted. As with earlier European incunabula, the tendency at first was to imitate MS styles and layouts. Words and lines were set closely, paragraphs and punctuation were lacking, the main type area was often surrounded by rules, and glosses or even complete commentaries appeared in the margins. Red ink was sometimes used for headings or key words, following the scribal practice of rubrication. Traditional tapered colophons were common. Title-pages were often lacking, but the verso of the first leaf was commonly commenced by a decorative *ʿunwān* (headpiece), often containing the title and/or *basmala* formula: the earliest were engraved on wood, but later elaborate designs were constructed from fleurons and other single-type ornaments, following a European printing practice whose aesthetic origins lay in the infinitely repeatable geometric and foliate patterns of Islamic art. In the late 19th century, some elaborate pseudo-Oriental designs were used for headpieces and borders, especially in Ottoman Turkey, perhaps reflecting a European rather than an indigenous taste; later still, other European artistic influences, such as the *Jugendstil* (*see* **26**) can be detected in decoration and page-design. By this time, European norms—title-pages, paragraphing, running heads, etc.—had begun to dominate Muslim book production.

Punctuation was another such modern feature. In Muslim MSS, as has been said, it was rudimentary, and it remained so in printed texts until the end of the 19th century. In the 1830s the celebrated Arab writer Fāris al-Shidyāq had become familiar, while working at the Malta press, with European books and literature, and had observed the usefulness of punctuation marks in clarifying the structure and meaning of passages of prose. In 1839, he published at Malta a primer and reading book of literary Arabic, and boldly decided to introduce Western punctuation into it, using commas, dashes, colons, exclamation marks, question marks, quotation marks, and full stops (or periods). He set them out in his introduction, explained their use, and urged that they should be generally adopted in Arabic. This proposal was, however, ahead of its time. In the Muslim world, his appeal at first fell on deaf ears, and he himself eventually gave up the idea. In the second edition of his primer, published at his press in Istanbul in 1881, all the punctuation marks were omitted, as well as his introduction to them. Later, in the 20th century, full punctuation was widely adopted in Arabic.

Fāris al-Shidyāq's Istanbul press (the Jawā'ib Press) introduced other significant improvements to Arabic book design in the 1870s and 1880s. His books look different from those of most other 19th-century Muslim presses. They largely abandoned the marginal commentaries and glosses with which earlier books were often encumbered. In some cases running heads were introduced, repeating the title or number of the chapter or section at the top of each page as an aid to those referring to the book. They nearly all have title-pages, setting out clearly and systematically not only the title itself, but also the name of the author, and such imprint information as the name of the press, the place and date of publication, and whether it is a first or later edition. This practice, as Eisenstein has pointed out, engendered 'new habits of placing and dating' (Eisenstein, 106); it also aided the subsequent development of more precise cataloguing and enumerative bibliography. Another new feature of the print era to be found in most publications of this period is a table of contents, with page numbers, likewise enabling the reader to make more systematic use of the book.

Page layouts at the Jawā'ib Press also set new standards, being generally more spacious and easier on the eye than most ordinary MSS or earlier printed books from the Muslim world. Margins are reasonably wide and, as already mentioned, unencumbered by glosses or commentaries. The spacing between words tends also to be more generous, leaving a better overall ratio between black and white than on most pages either of ordinary MSS, or of Būlāq and early Turkish printed books. These features made them easier to read and therefore more accessible to a wider public. They eventually became standard aspects of 20th-century Arabic book design.

The character of the Arabic script itself has been remarkably unaffected by its use in printed books. Because Arabic writing was and is regarded by Muslims as sacred, the self-imposed task of typographers has nearly always been to reproduce its calligraphic qualities as faithfully as possible. As already noted, this involved the creation of extensive founts containing all the letter forms and combinations. Thus confronted with considerable difficulties and expense, Arab typographers towards the end of the 19th century began to introduce some simplifications, while for the most part successfully retaining full legibility and a degree of elegance. Yet, the Arabic script, unlike the roman, has never really acquired separate typographic norms, either aesthetic or practical, which could permit a decisive breach with its scribal past. Some radical innovators in the 19th and 20th centuries produced schemes to reform the alphabet by creating entirely discrete 'printed' letters, but there was never any serious prospect of their acceptance.

Illustrations in Muslim printed books, until the introduction of modern half-tone techniques at the end of the 19th century, can be divided into two categories. First, woodcuts and engraved or lithographed plates were used in typographic books, mainly for maps, diagrams, and didactic or technical illustrations. These often incorporated perspective, itself an innovation in the visual culture of many areas of the Muslim world. Technical illustrations were sometimes found in Arabic MSS. Before the print era, however, the transmission of technical data in the form of diagrams always depended upon the accuracy of scribes who often regarded them as little more than exotic appendages, frequently misplacing and sometimes omitting them altogether. With the introduction of standard, repeatable, engraved diagrams incorporated into printed books, the presentation of such information became far more accurate and reliable.

The second category of illustration consisted of pictures introduced into the texts of lithographed books; these were often copied from, or in the style of, miniatures in MSS. Such miniatures are a notable feature of Persian lithographed books of the 19th century, where they usually accompany literary works from an earlier period. Although they are broadly in the style of MS miniatures, it has been observed that they belong more to the domain of popular art than to that of the lofty court culture from which illustrated MSS originated. Lithographic miniatures also sometimes feature modern subject matter. A notable example is the depiction, in a work of classical Persian poetry printed at Tehran in 1847, of the process of lithographic printing itself. In an Uzbek lithographed text of 1913 a miniature shows a gramophone of the period.

Both kinds of illustration—in typographic and lithographic books—reproduced pictorial elements in a standard, repeatable form for a much wider readership than that of illustrated MSS, and thus helped to transform the visual and artistic awareness of educated Muslims during the 19th and 20th centuries.

9 Printing the Qur'ān

Apart from short extracts used in medieval block-printed amulets, the Arabic text of the Qur'ān was not printed until the 1530s, when a somewhat inaccurate and defective version was published by Christians in Venice. Subsequent complete editions appeared in Hamburg (1694), Padua (1698), and St Petersburg (1787). This last was personally commissioned by the Russian empress Catherine for the use of her Muslim subjects, and was the first to involve Muslims in its preparation. It represents a curious and unusual amalgamation of European book design, with baroque text borders and ornaments, and traditional Muslim presentation of the vocalized Qur'anic text, with marginal notes on readings and variants. It was later reprinted a number of times, both in St Petersburg and in Kazan (Russian Tatarstan). In the Muslim world itself, however, printing the sacred text remained firmly off-limits until the 1820s or 1830s, when the first editions were published in Iran. The earliest of these may have been typeset (reliable bibliographical information is not readily available), but it was the advent of lithography that gave the impetus to Qur'ān printing because it enabled the all-important MS conventions and aesthetic/theological ethos to be maintained.

A further incentive was also provided by another European non-Muslim edition, greatly superior to its predecessors, edited by the German orientalist Gustav Flügel, and first published by Tauchnitz in Leipzig in 1834. This for the first time provided a convenient and affordable text that was reasonably authentic. It was stereotyped and issued in several subsequent editions, and achieved a considerable circulation, even reaching the Muslim world. However, the verse numbering and some other aspects of this version were not in accordance with orthodox Islamic practice, so there remained a clear need for further Muslim editions. This demand was partly met by subsequent lithographed versions in Iran, India, and Turkey.

In Egypt, the impetus of modernization created a tension between conservatives, who abhorred the idea of profaning God's words with movable types, and more progressive religious educators who wanted to place a copy of the Qur'ān, if not in the hands of every Muslim, then at least of every college pupil. Some attempts were made to publish the text in the 1830s, but the distribution of copies was successfully blocked by the religious authorities. Later, in the 1850s, some were distributed, but only after each individual copy had been read by a Qur'anic scholar and checked for errors, at great expense. From the 1860s onwards, the Būlāq and other Egyptian presses did print more Qur'āns, but generally embedded in the texts of well-known commentaries.

In Istanbul, the Ottoman calligrapher and court chamberlain Osman Zeki Bey (d. 1888) started printing Qur'āns reproducing the handwriting of the famous 17th-century calligrapher Hafiz Osman, using new lithographic equipment capable of an unprecedented, high-quality output. For this publishing venture, he had the express permission of the sultan-caliph—one reason why his editions gained a wide popularity in Turkey and elsewhere. This press also used photolithography, which enabled it to print miniature Qur'āns, small enough to be carried in a locket—no other technique could do this. The Glasgow firm of David Bryce, which specialized in miniature books, produced a rival version around 1900, and Muslim troops on both sides in World War I carried these amuletic miniatures into battle (*see* 7).

By the early 20th century, now that reluctance to accept printed Qur'āns had largely been overcome, the need was felt for a new authoritative version that would do full justice to the demands of traditional Islamic scholarship, in respect of both the shape of the text (i.e. the form of the text as it appears in the early MSS without vocalization and diacritics) and the way it was presented. The lead was taken by scholars at Al-Azhar mosque-university in Cairo, the pre-eminent seat of traditional learning in Islam. After seventeen years of preparatory work, their edition was published in 1924, under the auspices of King Fu'ād of Egypt. It was printed orthographically in such a way that the shape of the original 7th-century consonantal text is clearly presented, but at the same time it included all the vocalization and other indications which are required for understanding the meaning and for correct recitation. It is also meticulously executed in conformity with calligraphic norms. The Cairo Qur'ān quickly established its authority, and was followed by a host of further printed editions reproducing it or based upon it. These have continued to the present day, and even online digitized versions follow the Azhar text.

The ready availability of inexpensive copies of a standard authorized version of the Qur'ān transformed the attitude of many Muslims to the sacred text, and the uses to which they put it. Its function ceased to be primarily ritual and liturgical, and it came to be regarded as a direct source—not necessarily mediated by scholarly interpretation and authority—of guidance and wisdom in human affairs. This idea was reinforced by the abolition, in that same year (1924), of the Islamic caliphate, which had previously been, at least in theory, a religiously ordained but non-scriptural source of authority. The new accessibility and role of the Qur'ān consequently led some believers to adopt fundamentalist attitudes to Qur'anic doctrine, with considerable consequences in the social and political spheres. Others, in contrast, gradually abandoned traditional scholastic and legal interpretations in favour of their own reconciliations of Qur'anic ethics with modern life and politics. This divergence remains an acute feature of modern Islam, reinforced by outside pressures and new sources of authority in what continues to be above all a book-based system of belief.

10 Muslim book culture in the 20th and 21st centuries

By the beginning of the 20th century, printing had largely displaced the writing of MSS as the normal method of transmitting texts in most of the Muslim world. Only in a few remote areas, such as Yemen, did the scribal profession continue to flourish. In the main centres of literary culture, a new civilization of the book emerged, in which texts were readily available for purchase at affordable prices and were relatively easy to read. Newspapers, periodicals, and other serials were also widespread. These developments in turn encouraged and facilitated the spread of literacy. In schools, the availability of printed primers and textbooks revolutionized education, enabling students to embrace reading as an individual, internalized activity, rather than a ritual adjunct of rote learning. Nevertheless, older practices continued in some places where well-educated teachers were in short supply, or where conservatism or ideology rejected the free understanding of texts.

The rapid transition from MSS to printed books and serials as the normal means of transmitting texts had profound effects on the development of Muslim literary cultures. Insufficient research has been done to enable these effects to be measured or to be traced accurately. It seems likely, however, that the much wider dissemination of texts, both new and old, together with the standardization and systematization of their presentation, and their permanent preservation, played a major role in promoting the cultural and national self-awareness that has led to a renaissance of Arabic, Turkish, Persian, Urdu, Malay, and other Muslim literatures in modern times. This new self-consciousness has also had repercussions in the social and political spheres. In the case of Turkish and Malay, the rejection of the Arabic script in favour of the roman alphabet has reinforced their separate literary and national identities.

In the Arab world, the early 20th century saw a revival in Arabic typography: a development subsequently reinforced by the adoption of Linotype machines in major printing offices, as well as by the greater mechanization of the printing presses themselves. These developments permitted considerable increases in the production of books, magazines, and newspapers. Cairo and Beirut remained the principal publishing centres, as well as the main hubs of literary activity, throughout the transition from Ottoman and European rule to full independence and beyond. Both lost ground, however, in the 1970s and 1980s because of declining quality, lack of investment, rising prices in Egypt, and ruinous strife in Lebanon. Other Arab countries have therefore become relatively more important, notably those of the Maghrib (with an important output in French as well as Arabic), Iraq until 1991, and most recently Saudi Arabia. The lack of a well-developed book trade in these countries has, however, hampered development, as have political and religious censorship and restrictions in some cases. As elsewhere, the spread of broadcast and electronic media, especially television, video, and the Internet, has had some adverse impact on the market for printed literature, but this has been largely offset by the rise in rates of literacy. Similar trends are to be found in most other Muslim countries, but there has been a publishing explosion in Turkey and Iran, especially in the late 20th and early 21st centuries.

The advent of electronic texts and the Internet has had a noticeable effect in the Muslim world, as elsewhere (*see* **21**). In some countries, such as Saudi Arabia, governmental controls and restrictions on Internet access have prevented full use being made of the new opportunities for access to texts in global cyberspace. Even where this was not the case, however, language barriers have created problems, because the digitization of the Arabic script was a late development, which at first lacked standardization. Since the widespread adoption of Unicode, however, many websites in Arabic and Persian have been established, some of which provide substantial textual databases, including the Qur'ān, *Ḥadīth*, and other essential Islamic texts, as well as a great deal of secondary material, much of it promoting particular doctrinal, sectarian, and political viewpoints. The Internet has also accelerated a pre-existing tendency to adopt English, rather than Arabic, as an international Muslim language. As in the rest of the world, the long-term effects of the development of electronic textuality on Muslim book culture cannot yet be predicted.

BIBLIOGRAPHY

H. S. AbiFarès, *Arabic Typography* (2001)

G. N. Atiyeh, ed., *The Book in the Islamic World* (1995)

J. Balagna, *L'Imprimerie arabe en occident* (1984)

A. Ben Cheikh, *Production des livres et lecture dans le monde arabe* (1982)

J. M. Bloom, *Paper before Print* (2001)

A. Demeerseman, *Une étape importante de la culture islamique: une parente de l'imprimerie arabe et tunisienne, la lithographie* (1954)

—— *L'Imprimerie en Orient et au Maghreb* (1954)

F. Déroche *et al.*, *Islamic Codicology*, tr. D. Dusinberre and D. Radzinowicz, ed. M. I. Waley (2005)

P. Dumont, ed., *Turquie: livres d'hier, livres d'aujourd'hui* (1992)

E. L. Eisenstein, *The Printing Press as an Agent of Change* (2 vols, 1979)

A. Gacek, *The Arabic Manuscript Tradition* (2001)

W. Gdoura, *Le Début de l'imprimerie arabe à Istanbul et en Syrie* (1985)

Y. Gonzalez-Quijano, *Les Gens du livre: édition et champs intellectuel dans l'Egypte républicaine* (1998)

E. Hanebutt-Benz *et al.*, eds., *Middle Eastern Languages and the Print Revolution* (2002)

N. Hanna, *In Praise of Books: A Cultural History of Cairo's Middle Class* (2003)

F. Hitzel, ed., *Livres et lecture dans le monde ottoman*, special issue of *Revue des mondes musulmans et de la Méditerranée*, 87–8 (1999)

K. Kreiser, ed., *The Beginnings of Printing in the Near and Middle East* (2001)

M. Krek, *A Bibliography of Arabic Typography* (1976)

—— *A Gazetteer of Arabic Printing* (1977)

U. Marzolph, *Narrative Illustration in Persian Lithographed Books* (2001)

—— ed., *Das gedruckte Buch im Vorderen Orient* (2002)

B. Messick, *The Calligraphic State* (1993)

J. Pedersen, *The Arabic Book*, tr. G. French (1984; Danish original, 1946)

I. Proudfoot, 'Mass Producing Houri's Moles, or Aesthetics and Choice of Technology in Early Muslim Book Printing', in *Islam: Essays on Scripture, Thought and Society*, ed. P. G. Riddell and T. Street (1997)

N. A. Rizk and J. Rodenbeck, 'The Book Publishing Industry in Egypt', in *Publishing in the Third World*, ed. P. G. Altbach *et al.* (1985)

G. Roper, ed., *World Survey of Islamic Manuscripts* (4 vols, 1992–4)

O. Sabev, 'The First Ottoman Turkish Printing Enterprise: Success or Failure?', in *Ottoman Tulips, Ottoman Coffee*, ed. D. Sajdi (2007)

P. Sadgrove, ed., *History of Printing and Publishing in the Languages and Countries of the Middle East* (2004)

K. Schaefer, *Enigmatic Charms: Medieval Arabic Block Printed Amulets* (2006)

A. Schimmel, 'The Book of Life – Metaphors Connected with the Book in Islamic Literatures', in *The Book in the Islamic World*, ed. G. N. Atiyeh (1995)

C. F. de Schnurrer, *Bibliotheca Arabica* (1811)

J. Skovgaard-Petersen, ed., *The Introduction of the Printing Press in the Middle East*, special issue of *Culture and History*, 16 (1997)

41

The History of the Book in the Indian Subcontinent

ABHIJIT GUPTA

1 The MS book

The Indian subcontinent is home to more languages than anywhere else in the world. The Indian constitution recognizes 22 official languages, but the number of mother tongues in India exceeds 1,500, of which 24 are spoken by a million or more people. Any history of such a diverse constituency is bound to be selective and incomplete. This is true for the book as well, especially in the pre-print era. Although the first printing with movable type in India occurred as early as in 1556, almost two and a half centuries were to pass before print was able to infiltrate the intellectual world configured by the MS book. This should not be surprising, for the history of the MS book in the Indian subcontinent is a long and highly sophisticated one, dating back to at least the 5th century BC. It is beyond the scope of this essay to treat the MS book in any detail, but it is essential to have an understanding of some of its basic features.

The rise of heterodox movements such as Buddhism and Jainism triggered a movement from orality to literacy in India. Orthodox Hinduism set little store by writing, and its key texts, the Vedas, were memorized and transmitted orally (*see* **2**). A great deal of significance was attached to the spoken word and the performative aspects of the text. There are some technical terms in later Vedic works that might be taken as evidence for writing, but that task was assigned to the clerical caste of *kayasthas* who did not enjoy any great social prestige. On the other hand, the need to transcribe correctly the teachings of the Buddha and

Mahavira led to a widespread MS tradition from the 5th century BC in which authenticity and canonicity were the chief impulses, as opposed to the more prosaic aims of Hindu MS practice. The Jatakas (collections of stories about the Buddha) mention wooden writing boards (*phalaka*) and wooden pens (*varnaka*), and *lekha* or writing as part of the school curriculum. Buddhist MSS were mostly produced in monasteries and universities. When the Chinese traveller Fa Xian visited India in the 5th century CE, he saw professional copyists at work at Nalanda University; two centuries later, another Chinese visitor to the university, Yi Jing, reportedly carried away 400 Buddhist MSS. Similarly, Jain copyists were monks and novices, sometimes even nuns.

The earliest known substrate for recording texts in ancient India is the talipat or writing palm (*Corypha umbraculifera*), which is native to the Malabar coast of southern India and has palmate leaves folding naturally around a central rib. The tree was extensively cultivated, since the leaves were also used for thatching and the sap fermented to make palm wine. It is believed that there was a rich trade in the leaves from the south to the north, but this also meant that the Buddhist scriptoria in Bihar and Nepal were heavily dependent on the availability of the leaf. One of the earliest accounts of the general use of the talipat throughout India is from Xuan Zang, who described it in the 7th century CE. In about 1500 CE, the talipat was supplanted by the palmyra, which was easier to cultivate and commercially more valuable, owing to the range of products it yielded. Reed pens were used with the talipat, while an iron stylus was used with the palmyra. After the grooves were scored, they were smeared with ink and then cleaned with sand. In north India, the bark of birch and aloe seem to have been extensively used, the former in the western Himalayas, the latter in the Assam valley. Birch bark was known as *bhurjapatra*, and is frequently mentioned in northern Buddhist and Brahmanical Sanskrit works (Buhler, 1973). After writing, the finished stack of leaves was strung on a cord through pre-bored holes and protected by a pair of wooden covers. This form of the book—known as the *puthi* or *pothi*—survived until the mid-19th century, with some minor variations. In Nepal, for example, covers of valuable MSS were sometimes made of embossed metal, while Jain MSS were kept in sacks made of white cotton.

Papermaking had been known in China from the beginning of the first millennium CE, but it reached India via the Turks after their conquest of northern India in the early 13th century (*see* **10**). There is some evidence of papermaking in the Himalayan region before this period, especially in Nepal, but it never posed a serious challenge to palm-leaf MSS. With the beginnings of Muslim rule in India, paper became the substrate of choice, as no material other than paper was considered suitable for writing in Arabic, Persian, and Urdu (*see* **40**). The rich traditions of illumination, illustration, and calligraphy in these languages required exceptionally high-quality paper, which sometimes had to be imported from places such as Iran. For bindings, leather and board were used: these could not be used for Hindu MSS. Perhaps the richness and sophistication of the

Mughal MS tradition was one reason why printing failed to make much impact in north India, despite the presentation to the Emperor Akbar of a copy of Christopher Plantin's polyglot Bible in 1580. This historic gift was made when a delegation of Portuguese Jesuits visited the emperor at Fatehpur Sikri (*see* 7). In a richly symbolic response, the emperor had several of the engravings in the Bible copied by his own painters.

Although the Hindu and Muslim MS traditions took somewhat different routes, they were both instrumental in creating highly evolved communication networks. Access to the production and ownership of MSS was restricted in the Hindu and Buddhist traditions, yet the rise of the vernaculars in the second millennium CE saw a much wider diffusion of the culture of writing and reading. The examples of the great Indian epics *Mahābhārata* and *Rāmāyaṇa* demonstrate how new interpretive communities were formed once the Sanskrit hegemony was challenged, and created a kind of 'social memory' mediated by the book. On the other hand, the Islamic MS tradition in India was a direct result of court patronage, and consequently much more opulent. Given the centrality of the Qur'ān to Islam, book arts such as calligraphy and illumination were accorded the highest prestige. Outside court circles, guilds of scribes acted as purveyors of knowledge and information, leading to the creation of a robust public sphere.

The coming of print did not immediately precipitate a battle of books. More often than not the printed book took its cue from the MS book, and for a while there was space for both forms. Ultimately, however, it was the loss of political power to the British that undermined the cultural and social authority of the MS tradition. Under the new political dispensation, the voice of power would henceforth be articulated through print.

2 Early printing: from Goa to the Malabar coast

Print arrived in India by accident. In 1556, King João III of Portugal despatched a group of Jesuit missionaries and a printing press to Abyssinia, at the request of its emperor. When the ship put in at Goa, a Portuguese colony on the west coast of India, news came that the emperor had changed his mind. The Portuguese authorities in Goa had not been particularly keen to introduce printing to the area, but they now found themselves with not just a press but a printer. He was Juan de Bustamante, a Jesuit brother from Valencia, reportedly accompanied by an Indian assistant trained in printing at Lisbon (*see* 9).

The first book to be printed in Goa was *Conclusões e outras coisas*, in 1556. Unfortunately, no copy is extant, a fate shared by most of the early publications from Goa. The first Indian language rendered in the medium of print was Tamil. This might appear odd, given that the lingua franca in and around Goa was Konkani. But the Jesuits, led by Francis Xavier, who died in Goa in 1552, had established an extensive network of Jesuit missions along the Coromandel coast and had baptized more than 10,000 Tamil-speaking Parava fisher-people. A key figure in the new technology was Henrique Henriques, a Portuguese Jew, who produced five books in Tamil script and language, as well as a Tamil grammar and Dictionary. In 1577 Henriques's first book was printed at Goa: *Doctrina Christam, Tampiran Vanakkam*, a translation of a Portuguese catechism of 1539. This book was not only the first to be printed with Indian type, but the first with non-roman, metallic type anywhere in the world. The Tamil type for the book was prepared by the Spaniard Juan Gonsalves, a former blacksmith and clockmaker, with assistance from Father Pero Luis, a Tamil Brahmin, who had entered the Jesuit order in 1562.

Bustamante was asked by the Portuguese Jesuits to set up a press at the College of St Paul in Goa, and it was under the imprint of the college that most of the early publications were issued. Other printers who were active in Goa during this period were João de Endem and João Quinquencio. Their output may be described as modest, having little or no impact outside the immediate circle of missionary activity. Printing was too alien and expensive an activity to elicit more than polite interest locally, while the finished product—the printed book— was regarded as part of the paraphernalia of church ritual. Even within missionary circles, the protocols and potential of printing were only partially appreciated. In the context of Goa, it seems that the printed book was seen solely as a tool for evangelizing. According to Priolkar, 'Printing activity continued to prosper so long as the importance of local languages for the purpose of proselytisation was fully appreciated' (Priolkar, 23). This was reinforced by the Concílio Provincial of 1606, which stated that no cleric should be placed in charge of a parish unless he learnt the local language. Yet Priolkar has argued that this stipulation was steadily undermined through the 17th century, until a decree was promulgated in 1684 which required that the local populace abandon the use of their mother tongues and switch to Portuguese within three years. It is therefore not surprising that printing came to a standstill in Goa at about the same time, in 1674. Another century and a half was to pass before it would reappear, in 1821.

The next significant printing initiative took place in Tranquebar (now Tharangambadi), on the east coast of India, and was triggered by the arrival of the Danish Lutheran missionary Bartholomew Ziegenbalg in 1706. The nearest Jesuit mission at Elakkuricci was less than 50 miles away, and a battle began between the two rival missions to win the hearts and minds of the local people. Ziegenbalg spent long sessions with an Indian pundit learning local language and customs. To his parent body, the Society for Promoting Christian Knowledge, he wrote:

> I must confess that my School-Master…has often put such *Philosophical* Questions to me, as really made me believe…one might discover things very fit to entertain the curiosity of many a learned Head in *Europe*…We hope to bring him over to the Christian Knowledge; but he is confident as yet, that one time or other we will all turn *Malabarians*. (Priolkar, 37)

He sent his emissaries far and wide, to buy up books from the widows of scholarly Brahmins, and left detailed descriptions of the MSS:

> As for the *Outside* of these Books, they are of a quite different Dress from those in Europe. There is neither Paper nor Leather, neither Ink nor Pen used by the Natives at all, but the Characters are by *Iron Tools* impressed on a Sort of Leaves of a Certain Tree, which is much like a Palm-Tree. At the End of every Leaf a Hole is made, and through the Hole a String drawn, whereby the whole Sett of Leaves is kept together. (Priolkar, 39)

Between 1706 and 1711, Ziegenbalg wrote a number of letters to the SPCK asking for a printing press:

> We heartily wish to be supplied with a *Malabarick* and a *Portuguese* printing press to save the expensive charges of getting such books transcribed as are necessary for carrying on this work. I have hitherto employed Six *Malabarick* writers in my house… 'Tis true those books which we get from the *Malabar* heathens must be entirely transcribed; or brought up for ready money, if people will part with them; but such as lay down the grounds of our holy religion, and are to be dispersed among the heathens, must be carefully printed off for this design. (Priolkar, 40)

In a remarkably shrewd move, Ziegenbalg argued that the book's form and content were indivisible, and the 'superior' technology of printing must be employed to confer an equivalent superiority upon Christian teachings. Convinced by his arguments, the SPCK despatched a press to Ziegenbalg in 1711, with a printer, Jonas Finck. After many vicissitudes the ship arrived, but not Finck, who disappeared off the Cape of Good Hope after the ship had been waylaid by the French and diverted to Rio de Janeiro. A soldier was found to work the press, and printing began in October 1712.

The press's crowning work was Ziegenbalg's 1715 Tamil translation of the New Testament—the first such translation in any Indian language. The fount bore a close resemblance to the letters in the palm-leaf MSS, while the language used was a version of demotic Tamil spoken in and around Tranquebar. The type had originally been cast at Halle in Germany, but it became necessary to cast smaller founts for the various publications undertaken by Ziegenbalg. A typefoundry was set up in Poryar, the first in India, and this was followed by the establishment of the first modern paper mill in the country in 1715. With these, the Lutheran mission attained a degree of self-sufficiency in printing, and was no longer entirely dependent on the long supply chain from Germany. This self-sufficiency can be gauged from the press's high output: 65 titles from 1712 to 1720, 52 more in the next decade, and a total of 338 titles for the 18th century. The mission also received requests from the Dutch in Ceylon to print in Tamil and Sinhalese. A press at Colombo was reportedly set up by Peter Mickelsen, one of the casters of Tranquebar's types. The first book printed in Ceylon was an octavo Singhalese prayer book produced in 1737–8 for the East India Company.

And what of the Jesuits? In 1717, the controversial and colourful C. G. Beschi arrived in Elakkuricci near Trichinopoly and stayed there for the next three decades. Despite his meddling in local politics and ostentatious habits, he was unable to raise sufficient resources to take on the well-funded Lutherans and was forced to fall back on palm-leaf MSS. The only weapon in his arsenal was his vastly superior knowledge of Tamil: what ensued was a battle of books—MS versus print, Jesuit versus Lutheran, purity versus contamination—in many ways anticipating the clash between the rival intellectual worlds of MS and print in 19th-century Bengal. Though Beschi poured scorn on his rivals for their imperfect knowledge of Tamil and their flawed translations of the scriptures, he was fighting a losing cause, and soon the Jesuits were in retreat in the region, leaving the field clear for Protestants.

After Tranquebar and Colombo, the scene for printing shifted to Madras (now Chennai). In 1726, Benjamin Schultze set up a branch of the SPCK at Vepery, outside Madras. By the middle of the century, it was under the care of Johann Philipp Fabricius. In 1761, the English under Sir Eyre Coote successfully besieged the French at Pondicherry, and the spoils of war included a printing press seized from the French governor's palace. This press would probably have been used for Jesuit printing, so its loss was a further blow to the Society of Jesus in the region. Coote took the press and its printer to Madras, where Fabricius persuaded him to donate the press to the SPCK, on condition that printing orders from Fort St George—the seat of the Madras presidency—would take precedence over mission work. Soon the SPCK acquired its own press: the English war booty was returned to Fort St George, where it was renamed the Government Press, while the Vepery Press now became the SPCK Press. It was on this press that Fabricius printed his famous Tamil–English dictionary in 1779. In 1793 the Press produced a Tamil translation of *The Pilgrim's Progress*: this was a bilingual edition, with English on the left and Tamil on the right side of every page.

In many ways the fortunes of the Pondicherry press were symbolic of the momentous changes taking place in mid-18th-century India. Coote's military action dealt a decisive blow to French colonial aspirations, leaving the way clear for the British. Just four years earlier, in 1757, Robert Clive had won a historic battle at Plassey in Bengal, defeating the last independent nawab of Bengal, and paving the way for the territorial expansion of the East India Company in India. As centres of administration were set up in the three presidencies of Calcutta, Madras, and Bombay, print became an indispensable component of the engine of colonization. The missionaries, who had thus far championed print, suddenly found their efforts being swiftly outstripped by government printing.

3 Printing in the east: Serampore and Calcutta

If religion was behind the coming of print to west and south India, the initial impulse in Bengal was almost entirely political. In 1778 Nathaniel Brassey

বোধপ্রকাশ শব্দশাস্ত্র
প্রিরিশ্চিনাযুপকারার্থ
ক্রিয়তে হালেদদ্বেজী

A
GRAMMAR
OF THE
BENGAL LANGUAGE
BY
NATHANIEL BRASSEY HALHED.

ইন্দ্রাদয়োপি যস্মাত্ নয়যুঃ শব্দবারিত্রেঃ
পুক্রিয়াভন্য হুৎ ধন্য ছমোবত্ নরঃ কথ°॥

PRINTED
AT
HOOGLY IN BENGAL
M DCC LXXVIII.

The first British use of Bengali founts: N. B. Halhed, *A Grammar of the Bengal Language* (1778). The Bodleian Library, University of Oxford (EE 48 Jur., title page)

Halhed, a civil servant of the East India Company, produced the first printed book in the Bengali language and script, *A Grammar of the Bengal Language*. Initially, William Bolts was asked to design the Bengali type, but his design was not to Halhed's liking. The task was then entrusted to Charles Wilkins, also a civil servant with the Company, who cast the type with the help of Pancānan Karmakār, a smith, and Joseph Shepherd, a seal- and gem-cutter. The printing was carried out on a press at Hooghly, possibly owned by one John Andrews. The Company itself paid for the printing, in a somewhat miserly manner.

By the end of 1800, there were as many as 40 printers working in Calcutta (now Kolkata). This was unprecedented not just in India, but in the whole of south Asia. Although presses in Madras remained mainly in government hands, Calcutta saw a large number of private entrepreneurs open printing offices. The almost overnight rise of the periodical press is also remarkable. In the period 1780–90, seventeen weekly and six monthly periodicals were launched in Calcutta; almost all of the city's printers were connected with the periodical press at some time. Chief among them was James Augustus Hicky, who was the editor of the first newspaper in India, the weekly English-language *Bengal Gazette* (1780), and who went to jail for his fearless—and sometimes scurrilous—criticism of the governing council. As far as book publishing was concerned, Andrews's press had travelled to Calcutta via Malda and had acquired a new name—the Honourable Company's Press—and was now run by Charles Wilkins. This press accounted for a third of all books printed in Calcutta before 1800, including *Asiatick Researches*, the journal of the newly established Asiatic Society. Books and periodicals were, however, not the chief sources of revenue for the Calcutta printing trade. stationery, legal and mercantile forms, handbills, etc. formed the staple of their survival, a further sign that the trade was coming of age. The most characteristic product of the trade was the almanac, with three different calendars: Muslim, Hindu, and Christian. In fact, the trade in almanacs still continues to be a lucrative sector of the Bengali book trade.

Materials and equipment—type, paper, ink, and the presses—had to be imported from Europe. Some type was manufactured locally, notably by Daniel Stuart and Joseph Cooper, who set up a foundry for their Chronicle Press. Along with Bengali, this foundry also made Devnagari and *nastaʿlīq* types, the latter being used for printing in Persian. The availability of paper continued to be a problem. Good-quality paper had to be imported from Britain, while Patna supplied the local handmade variety, which was considerably cheaper. There were several unsuccessful attempts to set up paper mills in Calcutta during this period. John Borthwick Gilchrist, principal of Fort William College in Calcutta and founder of the Hindustanee Press, was not alone in complaining bitterly about the unscrupulous and fraudulent behaviour of printers, referring to 'typographical quicksands, and whirlpools, on the siren shores of oriental literature' and deploring the 'eternal treacherous behaviour' of his Bengali assistants (Shaw, *Printing*, 24–5).

Two events in 1800 were to have a momentous effect on printing in south and southeast Asia. The first was the establishment in Calcutta of the Fort William College to train the British civilians of the East India Company. The second was the establishment of a Baptist mission at Serampore (25 km from Calcutta) by William Carey, an ex-cobbler, who arrived at Calcutta in 1793. His first few years in India were spent in Malda, working for an indigo planter, and learning Bengali and Sanskrit from his *munshi* (language teacher), Rām Rām Basu. His early attempts to set up a mission in British India failed, as the Company was hostile towards missionary activity. Eventually, Carey was permitted to establish his mission in Danish-controlled Serampore (then known as Fredericksnagar), where he was joined by two other Baptists, William Ward and Joshua Marshman. In the meantime Carey had acquired a wooden hand press, thanks to the munificence of George Udny, the indigo planter who had supported Carey and his family.

The Serampore mission was founded on 10 January 1800. In August that year, a Bengali translation of St Matthew's Gospel was published by the press. About the same time, Carey joined Fort William College as a teacher of Bengali and Sanskrit, for a salary of Rs. 500. The same mission that had been refused permission by the government now became a partner in training the future elite of the Raj.

The efforts of Carey and his assistants soon made the Serampore Mission Press the most important centre of printing in Asia. Pancānan Karmakār, the goldsmith trained in type production by Wilkins, was 'borrowed' by Carey from Colebrooke, and then put under virtual house arrest in Serampore. With the help of Pancānan and his son-in-law Manohar, a typefoundry was set up in March 1800. In its first ten years, the foundry produced type in at least thirteen languages. The printing press was in the immediate charge of Ward, who left detailed accounts of its day-to-day running. In a letter of 1811 he wrote:

> As you enter, your see your cousin in a small room, dressed in a white jacket, reading or writing, and looking over the office, which is more than 170 ft. long. There you find Indians translating the scriptures into the different tongues and correcting the proof-sheets. You observe, laid out in cases, types in Arabic, Persian, Nagari, Telugu, Panjabi, Bengali, Marathi, Chinese, Oriya, Burmese, Kanarese, Greek, Hebrew and English. Mussulmans and Christian Indians are busy composing, correcting, distributing. Next are four men throwing off the scripture sheets in different languages, others folding the sheets and delivering them to the large storeroom, and six Mussulmans do the binding. Beyond the office are varied type-casters besides a group of men making ink, and in a spacious open-walled round place, our paper-mill, for we manufacture our own paper. (Koschorke, 59–60)

Not surprisingly, translations of the Bible accounted for the bulk of the publications. Between 1800 and 1834, the Serampore Press printed bibles in almost 50 languages, 38 of which were translated at Serampore by Carey and his associates. There were altogether 117 editions, of which 25 were in Bengali. It seems that the Press supplied bibles to almost all significant Baptist missions in the region, from Indonesia in the east to Afghanistan in the west. From the report for 1813, it appears that a Malay bible in roman characters was in preparation, while a five-volume reprint of the entire Bible in Arabic was being undertaken for the lieutenant-governor of Java. The memorandum of 1816 claims that a Chinese Pentateuch was in the press, and that 'the new moveable metal type, after many experiments, are a complete success'. The 1820 report records the printing of the New Testament in Pashto, and also the setting up of a paper factory: 'After experiments lasting for twelve years, paper equally impervious to the worm with English paper, and of a firmer structure, though inferior in colour, is now made of materials [from] the growth of India' (Grierson, 247).

Perhaps even more significant than the bibles were the Bengali translations of the two great epics *Rāmāyana* and *Mahābhārata*. These were published during 1802–3, and marked the first appearance of the epics in printed form, in any language. The Press also published dictionaries, grammars, dialogues or colloquies, Sanskrit phrasebooks, philosophy, Hindu mythological tales, tracts, and the first newspaper in Bengali, the *Samachar Durpun*. The first number of this twice-weekly, bilingual (Bengali and English) paper was published in May 1818. According to a calculation made by the missionaries themselves, a total of 2,120,000 items of print in 40 languages were issued by the Serampore Press from 1800 to 1832.

Along with the mission's own publications, the Press also filled orders from Fort William College. During the first two decades of the 19th century, the college played a crucial role in producing grammars and lexicons in all the major Indian languages, a task carried out by Indian and European scholars.

Altogether, 38 such works were produced in Arabic, Persian, Sanskrit, Urdu, Braj, Bengali, Marathi, Oriya, Panjabi, Telugu, and Kannada. Another important category was ancient Indian tales and verses, translated for classroom use into modern languages, especially Urdu and Bengali. The college's publications programme had a twofold aim: to produce textbooks for its students, and to encourage scholarly editions of books with no immediate pedagogical value. Besides the Mission Press, two other presses printed for the College. The first was the Hindustanee Press of John Gilchrist, which specialized in Persian-Arabic printing, especially in *nasta'līq*. The second was the Sanskrit Press of Bāburām Śarmmā, the first Indian to own a press in Bengal (he was succeeded by Lallulāl in 1814–15, who was also a teacher at the college). In 1808 the college noted:

> a printing press has been established by learned Hindoos, furnished with complete founts of improved Nagree types of different sizes, for the printing of books in the Sunskrit language. This press has been encouraged by the College to undertake an edition of the best Sunskrit dictionaries, and a compilation of the Sunskrit rules of grammar. (Das, *Sahibs*, 84)

The College's publications did not have much impact beyond the classroom and European circles. This lack was filled by the Calcutta School-Book Society (founded in 1817), which began to commission and publish some of the earliest secular school textbooks in Bengali and English. Its establishment coincided with that of the Hindu College in the same year. For more than half a century, the CSBS published hundreds of titles for 'cheap or gratuitous supply...to schools and seminaries of learning'. Significantly, the Society's charter stated that it was not its design 'to furnish religious books: a restriction however very far from being meant to preclude the supply of books of moral tendency' ([Calcutta School Book Society, iii]). From 1821, the Society was assisted by a monthly grant from the government; a few years later it acquired its own press and depository at Lallbazar. In 1823, the Calcutta Christian Tract and Book Society was set up to supply books to missionary-aided vernacular schools. Within a short time it had published a large number of tracts whose press runs often went into five figures. A similar role was played by the Christian Vernacular Literature Society. But the man who had the most impact on the textbook trade was the scholar and reformer Īśvaracandra Vidyāsāgar. While a teacher at Fort William College, he started the Sanskrit Press in 1847, along with his colleague Madanmohan Tarkālankār. Both men produced Bengali primers which became legendary: the former's two-part *Barṇaparicay* (1855) and the latter's *Śiśuśikṣā* (1849). Their popularity can be gauged from the fact that in 1890, the 149th and 152nd editions (respectively) of the two primers were issued. Vidyāsāgar reformed Bengali typography into an alphabet of 12 vowels and 40 consonants and designed the so-called Vidyāsāgar *saat* or type case, for greater ease of composition.

By the middle of the 19th century, printing had spread to Assam, with Baptist missionaries setting up a press there and starting the first Assamese periodical,

Aruṇoday, in 1846. After a slow beginning, Dhaka exploded into print in the second half of the century, with the Girish Press printing more than 500 titles by 1900. The trade in Bengal had become sufficiently large to require bibliographical control. James Long, a philologist and ethnographer, compiled three bibliographies of printed works in the 1850s, the first of their kind in India. His *Descriptive Catalogue of Bengali Works* (1855) contained 1,400 entries on books and periodicals in Bengali. A high proportion of the titles were accounted for under such categories as textbooks, translations, dictionaries, grammars, law books, and religious literature, but the trade in popular books flourished as well. This was commonly—and often pejoratively—known as 'the Bat-tala trade', in reference to the north Calcutta location where such books were mostly printed. According to Long,

> Few Bengali books are sold in European shops. A person may be twenty years in Calcutta, and yet scarcely know that any Bengali books are printed by Bengalis themselves. He must visit the native part of the town and the Chitpoor road, their Pater Noster Row, to gain any information on this point. The native presses are generally in by-lanes with little outside to attract, yet they ply a busy trade. (Ghosh, 118)

One of the pioneers of this new literature was Gaṇgakiśor Bhattāchārya, considered the first Bengali printer, publisher, bookseller, and newspaper editor. After beginning his life as a compositor at the Mission Press, in 1818 he set up his own Bangal Gezeti Press, and was also responsible for printing the first illustrated book in Bengal, Bhāratcandra's *Annadāmangal*, in 1816.

Tales, light verses, and farces were common examples of Bat-tala printing, and Long recorded with disapproval that many of these dealt with erotic themes, 'equal to the worst of the French school' (Ghosh, 87). Long's reservations notwithstanding, the Bat-tala trade was thoroughly indigenous, unmediated by missionary or reformist values. Yet, it was not until the mid-century that the Bat-tala trade assumed a truly commercial character. In 1857, Long listed 46 presses in the area—along the Garanhata, Ahiritola, Chitpur, and Barabazar roads—which printed a wide range of genres such as almanacs, mythological literature, farces, songs, medical texts, and typographically distinct Muslim-Bengali works. This last category is particularly remarkable for the way in which it retained some of the protocols of the MS book. In fact, many Bat-tala productions show a divided commitment to MS and printed forms of the book, especially in the disposition of the title-page, whose paratextual excess seemed to signal some kind of confusion about proprietorship, authority, and entailment. Although the production values of Bat-tala literature often left a lot to be desired, there is no doubting the energy and vitality of its genres. Bat-tala publications consciously distanced themselves from the moralizing and reformist agenda of print, and dealt unabashedly in subgenres such as erotica, scandals, current events, doggerel, and songs. These proved so irksome to the reformist lobby that they pushed for and, in 1856, succeeded in having an Act passed to prevent the public sale or display of obscene books and pictures. Shortly afterwards, Long reported with some satisfaction that three people had been arrested for selling an obscene book of songs by Dāśarathi Roy, and that 30,000 copies of the book had been sold at the price of four annas. The Supreme Court imposed a fine of Rs. 1,300 upon the vendors, then a considerable sum. This post-publication censorship was in fact the first of a number of official measures to impose some kind of restriction on print—an initiative that would gain urgency after the failed 1857 uprising by the sepoys and the consequent takeover of India by the British Crown. Matters reached a crisis with the furore over the English translation of Dīnabandhu Mitra's *Nīl-darpaṇa* (The Indigo Planting Mirror), a play fiercely critical of indigo planters. Following a successful libel action by the planters, Long went to jail (for a month) for his role in facilitating the translation. It was therefore not surprising that the Indian Press and Registration of Books Act (1867) mandated that all publications in British India be registered. The Act was a watershed in the history of Indian printing and, in hindsight, an acknowledgement that print had truly become a part of everyday life in India.

4 The other presidencies: Bombay and Madras

Printing came to Goa in as early as 1556, but bypassed Bombay (now Mumbai), fewer than 500 miles away. The Marathas of the Peshwa period did not seem interested in printing, although there is some evidence that Bhīmjī Pārekh, a Gujarati trader, set up a press in 1674. After this, there was a hiatus for more than a century until 1780, when Rustom Caresajee printed the *Calendar for the Year of Our Lord for* 1780, a 34-page publication priced at two rupees.

In the last years of the century, the Courier Press was the most important in Bombay. It printed the periodical *The Bombay Courier*, which was probably started in 1791. An advertisement carried by it in 1797 is thought to be the first in Gujarati characters: its type was cast by a press employee named Jijibhāi Chhāpghar. Robert Drummond, who wrote a *Grammar of the Malabar Language* in 1799 and for whom Jijibhāi also cast type, hailed him as an 'ingenious artist who, without any other help or information than what he gleaned from Chamber's Dictionary of Arts and Sciences, succeeded in completing a font of the Guzzeratty types a few years ago' (Priolkar, 73). The first Maratha characters are likewise thought to have appeared in an advertisement in the *Bombay Courier* in July 1802. The first Gujarati press proper was established in 1812 by Ferdunji Mārzābān, who used to visit his friend Jijibhāi at the Courier Press, and was inspired by his example to start a printing office of his own. The first book to be printed by Ferdunji's press was an almanac, in 1814.

As in Bengal, missionaries were quick to appear on the scene. In 1813, although they had been turned away from Calcutta, a group of Americans were allowed by the governor, Sir Evan Nepean, to open a mission in Bombay. A printing office was started in 1816 with a single wooden press and a single fount of Marathi type, acquired in Calcutta, with which an eight-page scriptural tract was produced in 1817. Over the next two decades, the press steadily grew in size until it employed a staff of 25. It had its own typefoundry, which could cast type in at least nine languages, a bindery, and a lithographic press. Thanks to the ingenuity of a young apprentice, Thomas Graham, by the mid-1830s the press was able to produce vastly improved Marathi and Gujarati type. The 1840s also saw the beginning of printing in Mangalore, on the west coast. A mission from Basle was established there in 1836; the first newspaper in Kannada came from its press in 1843.

At the end of the third and decisive Anglo-Maratha War in 1818, British power replaced the Peshwas in Maharashtra. The new regime established the Bombay Education Society, whose task was to produce vernacular textbooks. With the help of a group of *shastris, pandits,* and *munshis* (teachers) the society produced the first Marathi dictionary (*Shabdakosh*) in 1824. The availability of Marathi type was a recurring problem, so a government lithographic printing unit was inaugurated with six machines. Printing by lithography was considerably aided by the discovery in 1826 that the Kurnool stone was particularly suitable for lithographic use. For a period, lithography was preferred over typographical printing in government circles, principally owing to the large size and crude contours of the available type. As far as private initiatives were concerned, the Parsi trading community took the lead in setting up printing presses. Consequently, a commercial print culture in western India first developed in Gujarati, rather than in Marathi. Veena Naregal has suggested that the slow growth of a Marathi print culture was largely due to high-caste repugnance towards the manual labour associated with the print trade.

In the mid-19th century, two men changed the face of Marathi printing. In 1840, Gaṇpat Kṛṣṇājī built a wooden hand press and started experimenting with ink-making and type design. In order to print the Hindu almanacs that were his stock-in-trade, he designed and cast improved type in both Marathi and Gujarati. Until Bhau Mahājan established his press in 1843, Kṛṣṇājī's press was the sole producer of Marathi books outside government and missionary circles. His 'pioneering efforts to publish sacred and "popular" precolonial texts illustrated many trends that were to characterise the emerging sphere of vernacular production' (Naregal, 185). Bhau Mahājan's Prabhakar Press printed progressive periodicals such as the *Prabhakar* and the *Dhumketu*. The task of typographical reform, on the other hand, was carried on by Jāvjī Dādājī, who had started his career by working at the American Mission Press, and later joined the staff of the Indu-Prakash Press. In 1864 he opened a small typefoundry, and he established the Nirnaya-Sagara Press in 1869. Along with his friend Ranojī Rāojī Aru, he set a very high standard for Marathi, Gujarati, and Sanskrit typography.

In keeping with the two other presidencies, Madras became the undisputed centre of 19th-century print culture, although mention must also be made of Maharaja Serfoji II of Tanjore. In his palace in 1805, he set up a press that produced eight books in Marathi and Sanskrit. But it was in Madras that a 'nexus between pundits, printing and public patronage was cemented with the establishment of the College of Fort St George in 1812' (Blackburn, 74). This was followed by the establishment of the Madras School Book Society in 1820, to cater for students in missionary-run schools. The SPCK's Vepery Press continued to be active: along with the Madras Male Asylum Press (established in 1789), it accounted for a major share of periodical printing. At the suggestion of the Vepery Press, the government decided to train local goldsmiths in cutting type. This resulted in the creation of the first Telugu type in India. However, advances in Telugu printing were hampered by confusion over competing renderings: the Telugu used by missionaries, for example, was a mishmash of dialects and styles, to which Hindu scholars paid no attention. This confusion delayed the advent of print in the language by almost half a century.

The founding of the College of Fort St George in 1812 marked the entry of the pundits into the world of printing, and initiated a fascinating encounter between the worlds of print and MS. The publishing history of the Tamil epic *Tirukkurāl* in 1812, for instance, shows how the MS book's editorial and textual protocols were being exploited to arrive at an authentic version for print. With the pundits drafted into teaching at the college, in its first two decades the press produced 27 books, mostly in Tamil and Telugu. More importantly, teachers acquired a familiarity with print that would later be employed in a radical reshaping of literary culture. From the third decade of the century, a number of 'pundit-presses' began to appear, such as the Kalvi Vilakkam, founded by the Aiyar brothers in 1834, Tiru Venkatacala Mutāliyār's Sarasvati Press, and the Vidya-anubalana-yantra-sala or the Preservation of Knowledge Press of the famous Jaffna Tamil scholar Ārumaka Nāvalar, a remnant of which still exists. Many of these presses played an important role in shaping public opinion, especially during the anti-missionary campaigns of the 1840s. Another important development of the period was the rise of journalism in several languages—European and Indian—representing almost all shades of political and social opinion. By the middle of the century, printing in Tamil had encompassed almost all major genres, and a standardized orthography was more or less in place. In 1862, the Revd Miron Winslow of the American Mission Press published his landmark Tamil–English dictionary; three years later, the missionary John Murdoch produced the first bibliography of Tamil printed books. The founts for the dictionary, cut by P. R. Hunt, were a high water mark of Tamil typography.

5 Printing in north India

When printing began to spread westward in the first third of the 19th century, it took the lithographic rather than the typographic route. Lithography was particularly suitable for printing in Urdu and Persian, as it was an inexpensive technology, and 'reproduced the elegant hand of calligraphers, who in turn found cheap employment' (Orsini, 'Detective Novels', 437). The problems associated with the development of Indian types could be bypassed through the new technology of lithography, and by mid-century, Lucknow and Kanpur became the principal centres of lithographic printing in all of South Asia.

That is not to say that there was no typography in Hindi publishing. Printing in Devanagari (the script in which Hindi and many Indian languages is written) dates back to the 17th century, but its appearances were sporadic until the Serampore missionaries began to use Devanagari type to print in a large range of north Indian languages and dialects. Of the 2,120,000 volumes issued from the press in its first three decades, as many as 65,000 were printed in Devanagari. There was a good deal of printing in Devanagari at Bombay as well, but primarily in Marathi and Sanskrit. In Europe too, the rise of Indian studies led to the casting of high-quality Devanagari founts, especially in Germany, where Schlegel and Bopp produced editions of the *Bhagavadgītā* and the *Hitopadeśa* in the 1820s. Thanks to the refinements in Devanagari, printers in Calcutta and Benares (Varanasi) were able print books in the Nepali language as well.

Printing came to Lucknow in 1817 when the Matba-i Sultani, or Royal Press, was established; but printing did not begin in earnest until the coming of lithography in 1830. That year, Henry Archer, superintendent of the Asiatic Lithographic Company in Kanpur, was invited to set up a press in Lucknow. In the beginning, the trade was not commercial, in the sense that books were usually published to an author's or a patron's order. Nevertheless, a score or so of lithographic presses were operating in the city by the 1840s, chief among which was Muṣṭafā Khān's Mustafai Press, which published expensive books as well as popular genres such as *masnavis* and *qissas*. The *quissas*—moral tales, short anecdotes, fables—were first published at Fort William College in Calcutta for pedagogical purposes, but soon became a staple of commercial publishing in Persian and Urdu. A particularly popular title was the *Tuti nāmā* (Tales of a Parrot) of which at least fifteen different editions appeared in Calcutta, Bombay, Madras, Kanpur, Lucknow, and Delhi between 1804 and 1883.

Largely owing to the activities of schoolbook societies and missionaries, printing also spread to nearby towns and cantonments such as Agra, Allahabad, Meerut, and Lahore. A schoolbook society for the North-Western Provinces, with its headquarters at Agra, was set up in 1838. The same year saw the establishment of a missionary schoolbook society in Benares. Two major blows were subsequently dealt to printing at Lucknow, however. In 1849 the Nawab Wajid Ali Shah imposed a temporary ban on printing, as a result of which many firms shifted to Kanpur. This was followed by the sepoy uprising in 1857, leading to further uncertainty in the trade. The one beneficiary of this state of affairs was Nawal Kishore Bhargava of Agra, who in 1858 set up the Nawal Kishore Press at Lucknow, in a field virtually devoid of competition. Munshi Nawal Kishore had started his career as an Urdu journalist and had learnt presswork while employed at the Kohinoor Press of Lahore. In Lucknow, he started by printing in Urdu, but soon became the pioneer of Hindi printing in the city. More crucially, he enjoyed English patronage, which meant that the Press received the lion's share of government custom, especially extremely lucrative textbook contracts. In the 1860s the Press issued cheap editions of famous Hindi classics, in printings of several thousands at a time, followed by Hindi translations of Sanskrit scriptures, and bilingual editions of Sanskrit texts with Hindi commentary. Another important centre of printing in Hindi was Benares, although a fully fledged print culture would develop there only in the 1870s. This was largely brought about by the efforts of the remarkable Bhāratendu Hariścandra, who wrote and published in every possible literary genre in his short but extremely productive life. His lead was followed by the likes of Rāmakr̥ṣṇā Varmā, whose Bharat Jiwan Press (established in 1884) specialized in Brajbhasa poetry, as well as translations of Bengali novels: the latter paved the away 'for the explosion in fiction writing that took place in Benares in the 1890s' (Orsini, 'Pandits', 120).

6 Print and the nation

By the turn of the century, print had spread to almost every part of the Indian subcontinent, with an elaborate network of production and distribution in place. The rise of public libraries and reading rooms created new spaces for the consumption of print. The Calcutta Public Library (established in 1836) showed the way, by involving its subscribers, both Indian and British, in decision-making, especially with regard to acquisitions. The gradual increase in literacy and the formation of new interpretative communities created new tastes and reading habits, as embodied most visibly in the phenomenal rise of the Indian novel. The pioneer in this regard was the Bengali author Bankimcandra Cattopādhyāy, who is credited with having written the first novel in an Indian language, in 1865. The rise of this genre was perhaps the most decisive indication of the extent to which print had penetrated and modified the literary protocols of Indian languages.

The potentially large Indian market now began to attract overseas publishers. The two houses that took the lead in this initiative were Macmillan and Oxford University Press. The rapid spread of education made the textbook market in India highly lucrative, and Macmillan entered it with a splash, taking over Peary Churn Sircar's Books of Reading in 1875 from the firm of Spink, & Co. Macmillan published F. T. Palgrave's famous *Golden Treasury*, and the algebra and geometry of Hall and Knight, and Hall and Stevens, which are still in use. In 1886, the firm ventured into fiction, with 'Macmillan's Colonial Library' and 'Macmillan's English Classics' for Indian Universities. OUP took a more scholarly route, by publishing the monumental 50-volume *Sacred Books of the East* (edited by F. Max Müller), as well as the 'Rulers of India' series, although it set up an Indian branch office only in 1912, in Bombay, under E. V. Rieu. Other British firms following their lead included Longman and Blackie & Son, the latter publishing the ubiquitous Wren and Martin *Grammar*. In the field of distribution, A. H. Wheeler & Co. obtained the franchise for bookselling at railway stations all over India, and became an essential part of Indian travelling experience. Another bookselling giant was Higginbothams Bookstore of Madras; it started as the Wesleyan Book Depot in 1844 and is currently India's oldest surviving bookshop. The Oxford Book and Stationery Company (not connected to OUP), a chain of bookshops run by the Primlanis, set up business in 1920 and opened bookshops in Calcutta, Bombay, and Allahabad which continue to operate.

By the beginning of the 20th century, print had become an integral part of the public sphere and thoroughly indigenous. The competition between traditional and modern knowledge systems was now firmly enacted in the arena of print. There was an enthusiastic collaboration between print and the rise of regional-language literatures, involving figures such as Subramaṇiya Bhārati, Rabindranath Tagore, Fakirmohan Senāpati, and Munsī Premcānd. The beginnings of the freedom movement during this period also saw the emergence of what may be called print nationalism. Print, especially in the periodical press, was widely mobilized in the task of articulating the idea of a nation, and focusing opinion about the evils of colonial rule. The proposed partition of Bengal in 1905, and the *swadeshi* movement in its wake, saw extensive use of print, with leadership provided by men of letters such as Tagore and periodicals such as the *Jugāntar*. Not surprisingly, the hand of the Raj began to come down heavily upon so-called 'seditious' literature, and books were often proscribed and withdrawn from circulation. Raids on bookshops, the interrogation of suspects, and the arrest of authors, publishers, and printers became common. In 1907, Gaṇeś Deśmukh was sentenced to seven years' transportation for distributing a seditious songbook, while the minstrel poet Mukundadās was jailed for three years for performing a *jatra*, or musical drama, critical of the Raj. There were attempts at circumvention, however. After the passage in 1910 of the Indian Press Act, which aimed to prevent the publication and dissemination of seditious literature in all forms, nationalist literature was often circulated via princely states and non-British foreign enclaves such as Pondicherry and Chandannagar. Returning Indian and European sailors provided another conduit for overseas revolutionary literature. The civil disobedience movement brought in its wake the repressive 1931 Indian Press Act, which sought to prevent the distribution of material considered an incitement to violence.

The new century also saw the rise of a number of firms that took the lead in standardizing publishing, and bringing it more into line with international practice. The first attempts to form trade associations took place during this time, notably in the College Street book mart in Calcutta. The passing of the Indian Copyright Act of 1914 ratified the 1911 British Act with minor changes, and helped clarify author–publisher relations. Another notable development was the rise of specialist publishers, leading to the standardization of editorial and scholarly practices, a task initiated by learned societies such as the Nagari Pracharini Sabha of Kasi and the Bangīya Sāhitya Pariṣat in Calcutta. When Tagore set up the publishing arm of his world university, Visva-Bharati, it became one of the first publishing houses in India to adopt uniform editorial conventions. A similar role was played by the South India Saiva Siddhanta Works Publishing Society in Madras.

7 Publishing after 1947

The first two decades after Independence saw the coming of age of a number of young firms. Many of them had been loosely associated with the freedom movement, such as Hind Kitab and Renaissance Publishers, set up to publish the works of the revolutionary M. N. Roy. But the field was dominated by Asia Publishing House of Bombay, founded in 1943 by Peter Jayasinghe, and widely regarded as the first Indian publishing house to be organized along truly professional lines. Over a period of four decades it published nearly 5,000 titles, mostly in the social sciences and politics, and in its heyday was able to maintain branch offices in London and New York. Nevertheless, it may have overreached itself, for its decline in the 1980s was sharp and sudden. Another publisher of serious books was Popular Prakashan, which was started as a bookshop in 1924 but soon went into publishing, and which distinguished itself by issuing the seminal works of the historian D. D. Kosambi in the 1950s. In fact, many firms that had begun life as booksellers and distributors branched out into publishing after Independence, making intelligent use of their networks. Such was the case with Rupa & Co., which was founded in 1936 and became one of the largest wholesalers, distributors, and exporters in India before diversifying into publishing. Allied, established in 1934, took the same route and went into textbook publishing.

In the paperback sector, two firms led the way: Jaico Books, founded in 1946 in anticipation of Independence, was the first publisher of paperbacks in English. Hind Pocket Books, started in 1958 by D. N. Malhotra, began the paperback revolution by printing ten Hindi titles. It published fiction and non-fiction in Hindi, Urdu, Punjabi, and English, and started two book clubs, one for books in Hindi and one in English. But perhaps the most energetic publisher of the period was a late entrant, Vikas Publishing House (established in 1969), which published in a wide range of subjects, at an average of 500 titles every year. A key factor in the firm's success was the access it had to its sister concern, the UBSPD, which had one of the most sophisticated distribution networks in the country. Alternative models of publishing were provided by the Sahitya Pravarthaka Cooperative Society, set up as a cooperative for Malayalam authors, and P. Lal's Writers Workshop in Calcutta, which has published over 3,000 young English-language authors since 1958.

A large part of the publishing market was accounted for by the government and its subsidiaries. In 1954 the government founded the Sahitya Akademi as a national academy of letters, with the mandate of publishing in Indian languages, both in the original and in translations. The Akademi has since published several thousand titles, but its distribution network is practically nonexistent. The National Book Trust was established in 1957 to provide books at cheap prices. Among overseas publishers, OUP India led the field, steadily consolidating its position, while others such as Macmillan, Blackie, and Orient Longman (the post-Independence avatar of Longman) closed their Indian businesses following restrictions on foreign firms' holding equity. OUP was unaffected because it is a department of the University and enjoys exemption from corporate taxes in many countries. Currently, it is India's leading publisher of scholarly and reference books, with a list of more than 3,000 titles. In the 1960s, the United States' PL 480 programme resulted in more than a thousand American college-level textbooks being registered in India at subsidized prices. Some four million books were distributed through this route. American publishers were late to enter the field and when they did so, it was with higher-level textbooks. Prentice Hall set up business in 1963, while McGraw-Hill entered the market in collaboration with the Tata family in 1970.

This was roughly the state of the publishing business until economic liberalization was set in motion in the early 1990s. Penguin India started publishing from 1987, and currently publishes 200 titles annually, with a backlist of 750 titles, making it one of the biggest publishers of English books in South Asia. Macmillan returned to India after a period of absence, and has tried to reclaim the prominence it once enjoyed in educational publishing. The loosening of import and equity restrictions led to the entry in recent years of conglomerates such as HarperCollins, Random House, and the Pearson Group: HarperCollins was the first out of the starting gate, and has recently allied with the India Today group. All this portends an imminent boom in publishing in India, and one not merely restricted to the English language. Penguin has plans to enter into regional-language publishing, a market whose full potential is far from being tapped. India is also in the process of becoming the 'back office' for overseas publications, with increasing volumes of editorial and production work being outsourced to it.

According to the Federation of Indian Publishers, there are more than 11,000 publishing firms in India, some four-fifths of which are publishing in regional languages. Unfortunately, most of them seem unable to break out of their outdated business models. There are some exceptions, of course, such as Ananda, which is the leading publisher of Bengali books, and belongs to the group of companies that includes *Anandabazar Patrika*, the first Bengali daily to have used Linotype. In contrast, English-language and bilingual publishing has seen the entry of a number of independent niche firms, which have brought creativity and energy to publishing. Tara in Madras publishes for the neglected young adult sector, while Kali for Women and Stree have distinguished themselves in women's studies. Permanent Black has set a high standard for scholarly publishing; Seagull is noted for the quality of its theatre and arts books, and Roli publishes expensive art books for an overseas market. Translation is another sector that is beginning to register growth after decades of inexplicable neglect. Thus, with an expanding population, solid businesses, overseas and domestic investment, and a degree of commercial innovation, the future of Indian publishing seems highly promising.

BIBLIOGRAPHY

P. Altbach, *Publishing in India* (1975)

C. Bandyopādhyāy, ed., *Dui śataker bānglā mudraṇ o prakāśan* (1981)

S. Blackburn, *Print, Folklore, and Nationalism in Colonial South India* (2003)

—— and V. Dalmia, eds., *India's Literary History* (2004)

G. Bühler, *Indian Paleography* (1904; repr. 1987)

[Calcutta School-Book Society,] *The Fifteenth Report of the Proceedings of the Calcutta School Book Society* (1852)

R. B. Chatterjee, 'A Short Account of the Company's Trade with the Subcontinent', in *Macmillan: A Publishing Tradition, 1843–1970*, ed. E. James (2001)

—— *Empires of the Mind: A History of Oxford University Press in India Under the Raj* (2006)

R. B. Darnton, 'Literary Surveillance in the British Raj: The Contradictions of Liberal Imperialism', *BH* 4 (2001), 133–76

S. K. Das, *Sahibs and Munshis: An Account of the College of Fort William* (1978)

—— *Encyclopaedia of India Literature* (5 vols, 1989)

K. S. Duggal, *Book Publishing in India* (1980)

A. Ghosh, *Power in Print: Popular Publishing and the Politics of Language and Culture in a Colonial Society, 1778–1905* (2006)

G. A. Grierson, 'The Early Publication of the Serampore Mission Press', *The Indian Antiquary*, (1903), 241–54

A. Gupta and S. Chakravorty, eds., *Print Areas: Book History in India* (2004)

—— *Moveable Type: Book History in India* (2008)

P. Joshi, *In Another Country: Colonialism, Culture, and the English Novel in India* (2002)

B. S. Kesavan, *History of Printing and Publishing in India* (3 vols, 1985–97)

V. Koilpillai, *The SPCK in India* (1985)

K. Koschorke *et al.*, *History of Christianity in Asia, Africa, and Latin-America, 1450–1990* (2007)

J. P. Losty, *The Art of the Book in India* (1982)

M. Mamoon, *Unish shatake dhakar mudran o prakashana* (2004)

V. Narayana Rao, 'Print and Prose: Pandits, *Karanams*, and the East India Company in the Making of Modern Telugu', in *Literary History: Essays on the Nineteenth Century*, ed. S. Blackburn and V. Dalmia (2004)

V. Naregal, *Language Politics, Elites and the Public Sphere* (2001)

Nikhil Sarkār (Śrīpāntha), *Jakhan chāpākhānhā elo* (1977)

F. Orsini, 'Detective Novels: A Commercial Genre in Nineteenth-Century North India', in *India's Literary History*, ed. S. Blackburn and V. Dalmia (2004)

—— 'Pandits, Printers and Others: Publishing in Nineteenth-Century Benares', in *Print Areas: Book History in India*, ed. A. Gupta and S. Chakravorty (2004)

R. Pinto, *Between Empires: Print and Politics in Goa* (2007)

S. Pollock, *The Language of Gods in the World of Men: Sanskrit, Culture and Power in Premodern India* (2006)

A. K. Priolkar, *The Printing Press in India* (1958)

G. Shaw, *Printing in Calcutta to 1800* (1981)

—— 'On the Wrong End of the Raj: Some Aspects of Censorship in British India and its Circumvention During the 1920s–1940s: Part 1', in *Moveable Type: Book History in India*, ed. A. Gupta and S. Chakravarty (2008)

U. Stark, *An Empire of Books: The Naval Kishore Press and the Diffusion of the Printed Word in Colonial India* (2007)

42

The History of the Book in China

J. S. EDGREN

1 The book before paper and printing

Although the early invention of true paper (2nd century BC) and of textual printing (late 7th century) by woodblock printing profoundly influenced the development of the book in China, the materials and manufacture of books before paper and before printing also left some traces. Preceding the availability of paper as a writing surface, the earliest books in China, known as *jiance* or *jiandu*, were written on thin strips of prepared bamboo and wood, which were usually interlaced in sequence by parallel bands of twisted thongs, hemp string, or silk thread. The text was written with a writing brush and lampblack ink in vertical columns from right to left—a layout retained by later MSS and printed books—after which the strips were rolled up to form a primitive scroll binding (*see* **19**). The surviving specimens of *jiance* are mostly the result of 20th-century scientific archaeological recovery, and date from around the 6th century BC to the 3rd century AD.

An important and unusual example of *jiance* was discovered in 1959 at Wuwei county, Gansu province. The text of the classic *Yili* (Book of Etiquette and Ceremonial) was found in a Han dynasty (206 BC–AD 220) tomb. The text-bearing strips, mostly of wood, are exceptionally long: they record the number of each column, as well as displaying the name and number of each section of text when rolled up. On the basis of very early inscriptions and citations in ancient texts, there is good reason to believe that this book form existed four or five centuries earlier than the 6th century BC. The subject-matter of *jiance* ranges from mundane archival documents to important historical, philosophical, medical, and military texts. Some large caches containing thousands of bamboo strips have been discovered in recent decades, and many such texts have not yet been published or made available for study. Because the binding thongs or strings usually disintegrate, some texts have been difficult to put in order. Others found in tombs in humid regions present serious conservation problems.

Although its use began later, silk is mostly contemporaneous with bamboo and wood as an important material for pre-paper MS books. By the early Warring States period (403–221BC), the philosopher Mozi (*fl.* 400 BC) could state that texts written on bamboo and silk or engraved on metal and stone were thus transmitted for posterity. Silk books also took the form of scrolls, and the continuous weaving of textiles allowed for drawings or diagrams accompanying the text. The early Han tomb at Mawangdui, Changsha, Hunan province, contained maps on silk as well as silk books. A highly valuable material, silk was used sparingly. According to the *Hanshu yiwenzhi*, the catalogue of the early Han imperial library, compiled by Ban Gu, only about 25 per cent of its holdings consisted of silk scrolls. In fact, the invention of paper probably came about as an economical alternative to silk.

Script has a history of more than 4,000 years in China, and text was inscribed on objects of diverse materials and forms before and during the development of scroll books of bamboo and silk. The so-called 'oracle bones' used for divination since the mid-Shang dynasty (*c.*1300–1046BC) comprise animal bones as well as tortoise shells with brief texts engraved on their surfaces. Mozi's mention of texts engraved (and also cast) on metal chiefly refers to Shang and Zhou (1046–256BC) bronze ritual vessels; his mention of texts engraved on stone refers to stone monuments such as the so-called 'stone drums' (7th or 8th century BC) still preserved at the Palace Museum in Beijing. The more familiar flat stone tablets with lengthy inscriptions came into being in the Han dynasty. In Chinese culture, the durability of metal and stone serves as a metaphor for the inscriptions' longevity. Furthermore, inscribed seals of metal (bronze, iron, gold) and stone (especially jade), as well as inscribed stone tablets, probably inspired the invention of printing.

Commemorative stone tablets (*bei*) have been erected in China for more than 2,000 years. Chinese stele inscriptions also include tomb inscriptions (*muzhi*), inscriptions on natural stone surfaces, and inscriptions on objects such as Buddhist and Daoist stone sculptures. Engraving of the Han 'stone classics' was undertaken in AD 175–183; the tablets were erected in a public place at the capital Luoyang to allow scholars and students to copy standardized versions of the Confucian classics. Three or four centuries later the technique of ink-squeeze rubbings made from *bei* initiated the primitive duplication of texts that led to the method of xylographic printing.

The *Suishu jingjizhi*, the bibliography of the official history of the Sui dynasty (581–618), includes several ink-squeeze rubbings (*taben*), apparently all in the form of scrolls. Rubbings are also sometimes stored as folded sheets. The earliest extant ink-squeeze rubbing mounted as a primitive scroll is of an inscription commemorating a hot spring entitled *Wenquan ming*. It was written by the

Tang emperor Taizong, and is dated 653. This incomplete scroll discovered in Dunhuang is now in the Bibliothèque nationale de France (BnF). The vertical orientation of most inscriptions engraved on steles is not directly compatible with the horizontal orientation of scroll and of album binding, which eventually became the favoured form of preserving ink-squeeze rubbings. Rubbings made on large sheets of paper must first be cut into columns of text equal to the height of the scroll or album leaf, and then arranged to read from right to left by pasting the strips in the correct order. This is a task more often assigned to a scroll-mounter than to a bookbinder. The album binding, which superficially can be mistaken for the pleated binding, is usually regarded as belonging to the realm of painting and calligraphy rather than of books. Folding albums of painting or calligraphy are called *ceye* (Japanese *gajō*), and are made from single sheets of stiff paper folded vertically in the centre. The sheets are then bound by consecutively pasting the edges parallel to the centrefold until the volume is formed. Covers of wood or textile-covered pasteboard can be attached to the top and bottom surfaces.

Although archaeological evidence shows that paper existed in China two to three centuries earlier, the first formal acknowledgement of papermaking was made in a report to the emperor, in AD 105, by Cai Lun, a eunuch at the Han court. Most importantly, he encouraged the use of a variety of raw materials such as tree bark, hemp, rags, and fishing nets to produce a writing material to replace silk. After its dissemination in China during the first centuries of the Common Era, paper became the dominant material for MS production. Scrolls of paper gradually replaced rolls of silk. The period from Han to Sui witnessed increased circulation of books and the growth of libraries. The introduction of Buddhism to China at about the same time gave added stimulus to these through the promotion of sutra-copying. As the number of translations increased, the Buddhist canon expanded rapidly and demanded countless copies of texts; this is reflected in the hoard of tens of thousands of Buddhist scrolls discovered at Dunhuang, a cave complex in Gansu province, a desert outpost in Chinese central Asia. There, in 1907, while leading a British archaeological expedition from India, Aurel Stein was shown previously sealed caves containing enormous quantities of mostly Buddhist artefacts dating from the 4th to the 10th centuries. Most of the Chinese objects that he acquired entered the British Museum, including thousands of Buddhist MSS in scroll binding, as well as a small number of books in codex forms, and some twenty specimens of Tang xylography. A year later, Paul Pelliot arrived at Dunhuang with a French expedition and acquired a smaller quantity of valuable MSS and several examples of printing, now in the BnF. German, Russian, Japanese, and Chinese teams also collected MSS at Dunhuang. Despite limitations of subject-matter and regional provenance, the magnitude of the discovery, and the fact that the MSS and books had been preserved intact for more than eight centuries, profoundly influenced Chinese textual and bibliographical scholarship. The International Dunhuang Project was established in 1994 at the British Library, where most of the Stein documents are now housed.

In ancient times, textual seals and pictorial seals, cut in relief or intaglio, were used for identification and authentication. Seals were impressed in soft clay, which was allowed to harden and display its text while sealing a document. Malleable clay was suited to the uneven surface of books made of bamboo and wooden slats. The use of silk as a writing material made it possible to apply ink to the surface of the seal and stamp it directly on to the silk. The increased use of paper invited innovations such as the use of vermilion ink—made from cinnabar—to replace black ink from soot, or the use of engraved wooden stamps to replace seals cut in metal or stone. Reproducing a brief text or religious votive image by means of an inked stamp impressed on paper is not far removed from transferring text or illustration by pressing paper on to an inked woodblock. Unlike the relief text of seals cut backward in 'mirror' image for stamping, the intaglio text of steles was cut forward and could be read directly. However, at least one stone inscription cut in reverse exists from the first half of the 6th century, implying that it could be treated as a large printing block. The ink-squeeze rubbing method of duplicating the texts of steles, and their assumption of book forms in imitation of MSS, offered further stimulation to the idea of textual printing.

2 Tang to Yuan (7ᵗʰ–14ᵗʰ centuries)

The actual circumstances of the invention of printing in China are not known; however, Tang dynasty (618–907) references to printing and the corpus of undated specimens of printing from Tang tombs all point to an approximate date no later than AD 700. Thanks to datable specimens of printing, such as the Pure Light Dharani Sutra (*Mugu chŏnggwang tae taranigyŏng, c.*751) from neighbouring Korea and the Empress Shōtoku's printed charms (*Hyakumantō darani,* 764–70) from Japan, printing is known to have spread to both places by the mid-8th century (*see* **43, 44**). Chinese scholars recently have regarded the Pure Light Dharani Sutra as imported into Korea from the Tang capital, Luoyang, but they have not presented satisfactory evidence for this.

There is no doubt that the widespread availability and diverse uses of paper before the 8th century provided the necessary basis for xylographic printing. The corps of artisans skilled at cutting text on seals and steles, as well as workers in decorative architectural wood carving, provided a ready source of labour needed to engrave the wooden blocks for books. The selective inclusion of the names of scribes and block-cutters on the woodblocks used for printing was inherited from the tradition of engraving stone tablets. Among the early single-sheet prints from Dunhuang, a block-cutter is referred to as *jiangren,* a general term for craftsman, together with his personal name.

The names of patrons and publishers also appeared quite early. The *Jingang jing* (Diamond Sutra), published in 868 (on the fifteenth day of the fourth month, i.e. 11 May), is regarded as the world's oldest complete printed book.

The dated colophon by a certain Wang Jie records that he printed the book in honour of his parents. It too was discovered at Dunhuang, and is now in the British Library. In the mid-10th century, large-scale publishing of printed Buddhist texts was sponsored in Hangzhou by Qian Hongchu, fifth prince of the Wu-Yue Kingdom. He published the dharani-sutra text *Baoqieyin tuoluonijing* in 956, 965, and 975, each in a purported edition of 84,000 miniature scrolls. Each version contains a dated colophon before a small frontispiece woodcut clearly stating his aims. The 956 edition was reprinted in Korea in 1007, which provides further evidence of the early transmission of printed texts from China to Korea (*see* **43**). Around the same time as Qian Hongchu's Buddhist activity in eastern China, two officials in other realms independently completed publication of the Confucian classics. Feng Dao published his canon at the National Academy in Kaifeng in 953, and a little later Wu Zhaoyi published his version in the Shu Kingdom (Sichuan), but specimens of neither exist today. Shortly thereafter, printing of the first Buddhist canon was begun in Sichuan in 971 during the Kaibao reign period (968–75). Called the *Kaibao Tripitaka*, its *c.*5,000 volumes were in scroll form, and several are still extant. The first *Tripitaka Koreana* of the early 11th century was based on the *Kaibao Tripitaka*, imitating both its printed style and its scroll binding.

Up to the early Northern Song (960–1127), the majority of published books and prints were either religious or official governmental publications. At the same time, there were ephemeral private publications such as dictionaries, almanacs, and calendars. Nearly all of the above appeared as unbound single sheets or were bound as scrolls or pleated books. By the mid-11th century there was a new-found growth of secular printing and commercial publishing in China due to the relaxation of government restrictions. Traditional Chinese bibliography divides publishers into three general categories: *guanke* (official publishing), *sike* or *jiake* (private publishing), and *fangke* (commercial publishing). Although religious publishing might be taken as a type of private publishing, it deserves a category of its own as a significant form of non-governmental institutional publishing.

Buddhist and Daoist books continued to follow the conventions of scroll and of pleated binding; but to serve the new demands of secular publishing, butterfly binding was conceived, for ease of reading as well as for convenient sales and distribution. In scrolls and pleated books, the right- and left-hand borders of printed sheets were concealed in the course of binding to provide continuous text, but the butterfly binding left all four borders exposed and provided an advanced codex format with conveniently divided units of text. This new format of the Chinese printed book (one leaf to be folded into two pages) that is meant to be bound upright—initially as a butterfly binding, and later as a wrapped-back binding, or a thread binding—is always a 'folio' binding in Western terms. Some MS books followed this model from printed sheets, with bordered and lined stationery, but many were written on blank paper without borders or dividing lines.

Traditional East Asian book forms. **A** (top): scroll binding: 18th-century printed Buddhist sutra (Japan). **B** (2nd from top): pleated binding, 17th-century printed Buddhist sutra (Japan). **C** (3rd from top left): butterfly binding: 16th-century Buddhist MS (Japan). **D** (3rd from top right): butterfly binding: contemporary printed book bound in traditional style (China). **E** (bottom left): wrapped-back binding with original printed title label: 17th-century printed book (China). **F** (bottom centre): thread binding: 18th-century printed book (China). **G** (bottom right): protective folding case, MS title label: early 20th century (China). © J. S. Edgren

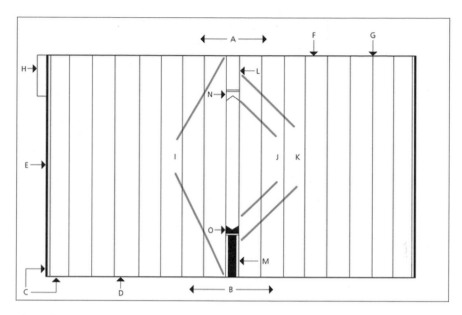

The traditional format of the Chinese printed book (one leaf to be folded into two pages) that is meant to be bound upright as a butterfly binding, a wrapped-back binding, or a thread binding. Some MS books follow this model, with bordered and lined stationery, but many are written on blank paper without borders or dividing lines. Books to be bound as scroll or pleated bindings share a few of the same elements as the traditional format.

The area of the sheet of paper (one leaf) is called *zhimian* (paper face or surface). The woodblock printed area is called *banmian* (block face or surface). The space above the printed area is called (A) *tiantou* (heavenly head or upper margin). It is also called *shumei* (book eyebrow), and the space below the printed area is called (B) *dijiao* (earthly foot or lower margin).

The border lines (upper, lower, left, right) of the rectangular woodblock are called (C) *bianlan*. A single line is called (D) *danbian* or *danlan*; double lines are called (E) *shuangbian* or *shuanglan*. The columns to accommodate vertical rows of text are called (F) *hang*, and the vertical dividing lines between them are called (G) *jie* (boundary lines). The small rectangular box attached to the upper-left or upper-right corner of the woodblock printed area is called (H) *shuer* (book ear), *erge* (ear box), or simply *erzi* (ear).

The column in the centre of the woodblock is called (I) *banxin* (block heart), or *bankou* (block mouth). When the leaf is folded and bound with other leaves as a book, the area is called *shukou* (book mouth). The *banxin* is usually divided into three segments: the middle is called (J) *zhongfeng* (central seam). *Zhongfeng* can also refer to the *shukou*. The upper and lower segments of the *banxin* are called (K) *xiangbi* (elephant trunk). If the space is left blank, it is called (L) *baikou* (white mouth); if it contains a black column of varying width, it is called (M) *heikou* (black mouth). A thin line of black is called *xian heikou* (wire black mouth) or *xi heikou* (fine black mouth); a thick line of black is called *da heikou* (big black mouth) or *cu heikou* (coarse black mouth). Small segments called *yuwei* (fish tails), flat on one side and V-shaped on the other, can appear above the lower *xiangbi* and/or below the upper *xiangbi*. If left blank, they are called (N) *bai yuwei* (white fish tails), and if blank but outlined with double lines, *xian yuwei* (wire fish tails). If they are filled in with black, they are called (O) *hei yuwei* (black fish tails). Line drawing by Chartwell Illustrators

Tang bibliographies in the official histories—arranged according to the quad-ripartite classification scheme of *jing* (classics), *shi* (histories), *zi* (philosophers), and *ji* (literature)—contain an immense variety of titles. These and many other works were available to early Song readers and scholars in the form of original and transcribed MSS. In the 11th century, after exposure to limited categories of printed books, and after laws prohibiting the private printing of certain types of book had been rescinded, the concept of printing and distributing multiple cop-ies of all kinds of text took hold. This stimulating environment encouraged the Song polymath Shen Gua to describe in detail the mid-11th-century invention of printing with movable type made of earthenware. He tells of a commoner named Bi Sheng, who during the Qingli reign (1041–8) made movable type of clay hardened in a kiln. He further explains each step of setting and levelling the type, and finally of printing. It is not known whether this experimental method was used at the time, but Shen's vivid account has influenced later generations throughout east Asia.

Despite resistance from conservative scholars who feared the wide dissemi-nation of faulty texts by private and commercial publishers, the desire for con-venient and cheaper access to texts and the lure of profit from commercial publishing prevailed. Indeed, by all accounts the growth of xylographic print-ing, invented 300 years previously, was surprisingly rapid. A level of demand that exceeded the printed output, and the persistence of respected associations attached to MSS, meant that handwritten books continued to coexist with printed books for a long time. Nevertheless, by the end of the century the cele-brated statesman and poet Su Shi, among others, commented on the prevalence of printed books in society. However, the Northern Song's violent demise has resulted in a paucity today of actual examples of secular books that circulated at the end of this dynasty.

Buddhist books from the late Northern Song have survived much better because they often were published in larger quantities, and because two volu-minous Tripitaka editions were published in Fujian province in the south of China, where the woodblocks were stored for continual use. The first, called the *Chongning Tripitaka*, was begun at the Dongchansi Temple near Fuzhou around 1080, and the second one, known as the *Pilu Tripitaka*, commenced publication at the Kaiyuansi Temple, also in Fuzhou, about three decades later. When completed, each of these Tripitaka editions contained *c*.6,000 volumes in pleated binding form, and nearly complete sets and many individual volumes are held by major libraries. The names of patrons, block-cutters, and printers appear in most of the volumes, providing valuable material for the study of Song Buddhist books. The *Pilu Tripitaka* was not completely published until the mid-12th century, and the woodblocks for individual titles from both Tripitaka editions continued to be made available as a form of printing on demand. Unlike these institutional publications, privately published Buddhist books of the Northern Song often have splendid woodcut frontispiece illustrations. The first Daoist canon was published (1113–18) in Fuzhou at the Tianning Wanshou

Temple under imperial patronage. Unfortunately, the books and woodblocks were transported to the Northern Song capital, and nothing survived its downfall.

In 1127, when Kaifeng fell to the nomadic Nüzhen, founders of the Jin dynasty (1115–1234), the fleeing Chinese were not able to save many printed books. The printing history of other border states such as the Qidan-Liao (907–1125) and the Tangut-Xia (1038–1227)—as well as of the Tibetans, the Uygurs (Uighurs), and the Mongols, all of whom were interactive contemporary with Song China—needs to be included in any comprehensive understanding of Chinese book culture spanning the period from late Tang to Yuan (1279–1368). Among these peoples there survive unique Chinese texts and editions of books imported to those regions from China proper, but no longer extant in China itself. The influence of Chinese printing technology is apparent; indeed, the Uygurs and the Tangut made early use of movable-type technology. In the cases of the Qidan (Khitan), the Tangut, and the Nüzhen (Jurchen), the influence of Chinese institutions and their need to deal directly with China led all of them to publish Chinese-language educational and Confucian texts. More importantly, however, they had a great need for Buddhist texts, usually available in Chinese-language translations, and they reprinted many of them. The Liao and Jin editions of the Tripitaka were both based on the *Kaibao Tripitaka* and were published in scroll bindings. Among these three border groups, the Tangut presents an especially interesting case, because its population in the Xi Xia state contained few ethnic Chinese, and because a great number of its printed books exist. Unlike Dunhuang, Xi Xia imprints discovered in 1908–9 by the Russian P. K. Kozlov at Karakhoto greatly outnumber MSS. The books and documents are housed in the Institute of Oriental Studies of the Russian Academy of Sciences, and the works of art and cultural objects are kept in the Hermitage Museum, both in St Petersburg. After the Xi Xia state was established, it quickly created a complex system of script and, for political as well as practical reasons, published a majority of books in its own language.

The style of printing of Chinese script in the border regions depended upon whether the block-cutter was a non-Chinese native or an ethnic Chinese. In the absence of contemporary models to copy, older styles from the Tang appear in books. In addition to the use of non-Chinese languages and scripts in some of the books produced by these border-state peoples, exotic book forms also were employed. The form known in Chinese as *fanjiazhuang* (Sanskrit clamped binding) refers to *pothi* (Indian palm-leaf MS books) imported to China through Tibet and central Asian territories. Although the horizontal orientation of the palm-leaf books was unsuited to later Chinese books, *fanjiazhuang* was used for Sanskrit and Tibetan books, whose languages were written horizontally, as well as for Mongolian books, which adapted to the form.

After the Southern Song dynasty (1127–1279) established its capital at Hangzhou and gained effective control of all of southern China, it maintained a century-long coexistence with the Jin dynasty in the north. In this relatively peaceful climate, the country prospered and the role of books in society reached new heights. Official publishers at the capital and in the provinces produced editions for the revived political and educational bureaucracies, as well as for the growing number of civil service examination candidates. When their efforts failed to meet demands, commercial publishers eagerly supplied the market with comparable publications. Rong Liulang (12th century) is an example of a commercial publisher who relocated from the former capital of Kaifeng to Hangzhou. The Southern Song civil service network ensured that locations of official publishing were widespread, and in each of these locations and beyond, private and commercial publishers sprang up. The expanding market for books inspired diversity. Although type design in the conventional sense was not an issue, publishers of high-quality xylographic books were sensitive to the calligraphic style of the text. In addition to models derived from the famous Tang masters, contemporary calligraphers served as scribes for texts to be engraved. Like the *kegong* (block-cutters), the scribes' names often were recorded in the books. A unique characteristic of xylographic printing is the ability to produce accurate facsimiles of actual handwriting: this was done for prefaces contributed by famous persons. Another characteristic of Song printed books is the use of many varieties of paper, which presumably were produced near places of publication using local raw materials. The regions around Hangzhou in the east, Sichuan in the west, and Fujian in the south were recognized as the three major publishing centres. In addition to the standard classics, histories, and philosophical works produced for the educated classes, popular publications for a wider audience circulated. Literary editions enjoyed a particular vogue. Thanks to informative prefaces and printers' colophons in many Song books, the distribution of places of publication can be clearly understood, and occasionally the particular circumstances of an edition can be established.

Members of the Chen lineage, headed by Chen Si, published books and ran bookshops in Hangzhou in the Southern Song. Some published the collections of Tang and Song poets with an elegant and distinctive style of printing; their one-line colophons advertised their addresses. An example is the 13th-century edition of the *Tang nülang Yu Xuanji shiji*, the collected poems of the Tang female poet Yu Xuanji, published by the Chen bookshop at the Muqin district in the capital. The last page of text and the one-line colophon are surrounded by more than 40 *ex libris* seal impressions and a couple of collectors' inscriptions. This is a vivid reminder that the proliferation of printed books in the Southern Song stimulated private book-collecting, and that later generations of Ming and Qing book-collectors prized Song editions above all else.

The 1173 edition of *Huaihai ji*, the collected writings of Qin Guan, was published at the local academy of Gaoyoujun in Yangzhou. After the preface, the itemized costs (i.e. sale price) for bound volumes is calculated in great detail:

> The Gaoyoujunxue edition of *Huaihai wenji* [i.e. *Huaihai ji*] accounts for 449 woodblocks [i.e. woodblock surfaces, since blocks usually were cut on both sides],

which together with blank leaves and endpapers uses altogether 500 sheets of paper. *Sansheng* paper at 20 cash per sheet is 10 strings of cash; *xinguan* paper at 10 cash per sheet is 5 strings of cash; *zhuxia* paper at 5 cash per sheet is 2 strings and 500 cash; ink at 1 cash per woodblock is 500 cash; the binding of 10 volumes with dark blue paper at 70 cash per volume is 700 cash; and the fee for labour and materials is 500 cash. (Nihon Shoshi Gakkai, pl. 38)

The currency cited is the familiar Chinese round coin with a central square hole, commonly called 'cash'. A thousand coins can be strung together as a 'string of cash'. The names of the block-cutters responsible are engraved throughout the book.

Under the great Khubilai Khan, the Mongol-Yuan dynasty was exceptional in thoroughness of its conquest of China; nevertheless, it can be said to have inherited the Song Chinese publishing tradition and other institutions intact. Official government publications were issued from the new capital, Dadu (Beijing), and official editions, as well as many Buddhist books, were printed from existing Song woodblocks in the former Song capital, Hangzhou. Private publishers and academies throughout the empire were also very active. The improvement of transportation networks and the growth of commercial publishing—particularly in Fujian province—resulted in the increased use of cheap bamboo paper, which came to characterize inferior popular printing in later periods. The publishers of Jianyang in northern Fujian developed now familiar formats such as *shangtu xiawen* (picture above, text below), in which continuous woodcut illustration ran across the top of the pages, with text placed underneath. They also produced many medical books, popular encyclopaedias, and works of fiction and drama. The travels of Marco Polo included the first decade of the Yuan dynasty, and his book was among the earliest to report on China to the West. Strangely, however, despite his visits to the publishing centres of Hangzhou and Fujian, he failed to mention the existence of printed books in China long before their appearance in Europe.

In the realm of books, one of the outstanding achievements of the Yuan period was the earliest use of two-colour printing. The Buddhist text of the Diamond Sutra with commentary, published in 1341 at the Zifusi Buddhist Temple in Huguang (Hubei province), has a main text of large characters printed in red with a commentary of smaller characters printed in black. The work also contains a two-colour woodcut which demonstrates good registration. This magnificent publication was produced more than 250 years before the wave of two-colour printing in the late Ming.

Influenced by Bi Sheng's invention, at the end of the 13th century a Yuan man named Wang Zhen carved more than 60,000 pieces of wood type for printing projects in Anhui province. His detailed description of the type and his method for printing are all that survive: when he published his major work, the *Nongshu* (Book of Agriculture), in 1313, he used xylography. This choice suggests the difficulty private or commercial enterprises had in using native typography successfully to print texts in a language with many thousands of different characters.

The Qing court in the 18th century, without regard for cost, produced two founts (one bronze, the other wood), each of around 250,000 types, to execute its projects. From the end of the 15th century in China, movable-type printing was carried out on a small scale, but it never successfully challenged xylography as a viable method of printing. The principal investment of the traditional Chinese publisher was in suitable wood to be prepared as printing blocks, the commission of the calligraphic transcription of the text on to thin paper to serve as the pattern for engraving, and the necessary labour to cut the blocks. The printing of a small number of copies, collating, and providing a temporary binding for the volumes, was often performed by the block-cutter. A small outlay for paper and ink for the initial printing was also required. As far as is known, an average initial printing was between 50 and 200 copies, and each subsequent printing may have numbered no more than that. Nevertheless, total print runs were often numbered in the thousands. In the case of certain popular books and religious publications, individual printings of 1,000 or more are not unknown. The cost of paper, ink, and labour would become an extended expense over the blocks' life. This differs from the Western publisher's need to produce the entire edition at once.

3 Ming to Qing (14th–19th centuries)

In 1368, Zhu Yuanzhang declared himself emperor of the Ming dynasty (1368–1644), and China again reverted to native Chinese rule. The Ming capital was established at Nanjing in the south, but the Yongle emperor moved the capital to Beijing in 1420. The first decades of the new regime were rather unsettled, and private and commercial publishing fell into decline. The organs of official publishing were active, however, and the Silijian (Directorate of Ceremonial) took a leading role. Throughout the 15th century, the palace published lavish editions of standard works in large formats. The regional academies published the classics and educational works, and the network of princedoms set up in the early years of the Ming produced more than 500 titles. As the economy improved in the 15th century, the number of booksellers and publishers increased, and more illustrated popular literature and religious tracts, especially in the *shangtu xiawen* format, began to appear.

Imperially sponsored projects in the early Ming were conceived on a grand scale. Three Buddhist Tripitaka editions and a Daoist canon were published in the first 75 years of the dynasty. In 1403 the Yongle emperor initiated his most famous enterprise, the *Yongle dadian*. It was a huge MS compilation ordered as a classified encyclopaedia of extant knowledge, based on citations culled from 8,000 works. It was arranged in 22,877 *juan* (the chapter-like division of traditional books) and bound in more than 11,095 folio-size volumes. Nearly 3,000 scholars and scribes worked full-time to complete the compilation in five years. Printing a work of this size was out of the question, so the encyclopaedia had to be consulted in the imperial library. After centuries of attrition and misfortune, less than 10 per cent of the original exists today. The largest parts are held by the National Library of China, the Library of Congress, the Tōyō Bunko, and the British Library.

By the Jiajing period (1522–66), a significant change had taken place and book-collectors, as well as private and commercial publishers, were laying a foundation for the flourishing of publishing that would occur towards the end of the Ming period. The oldest surviving private library in China was founded in Ningbo in 1561 by Fan Qin, a retired official. The library is called Tianyige, and in time it came to symbolize the ideal private library. The Jiajing era also witnessed increased official publishing, including the activities of the Southern Academy in Nanjing. Jianyang commercial publishers increased their output, and private publishers in the Jiangnan area of central China began producing editions of the highest quality, especially facsimiles based on Song and Yuan editions. Superior editions of the Jiajing period have always been in great demand. The modern Nanjing book-collector Deng Bangshu went so far as to collect 100 Jiajing editions and provide them with a room of their own in his library. He designated the room as Baijingzhai (studio of 100 Jiajing editions), and ordered a special *ex libris* seal to be stamped in each of them.

Beginning in the Wanli reign (1573–1620), improved economic and social conditions, and increased numbers of candidates sitting imperial examinations, led to an unprecedented offering of books that reached readers across a broad spectrum. Two examples embody this 16th-century trend. First, the *Xuanhe bogu tulu*, a magnificent illustrated catalogue of the Northern Song imperial collection of bronze vessels, was published in the 14th century; in the Jiajing period, a full-size facsimile edition appeared in 1528. In the Wanli period no fewer than five new editions, all illustrated, were published in 1588, 1596, 1599, 1600, and 1603. Secondly, the collected works, entitled *Cangming ji*, of Li Pan-long, an official and writer whose poems and essays were greatly admired after his death in 1570, were published in at least ten different editions between 1572 and the early 17th century. A collection of his poetry, published earlier, had at least four editions. Copies of *Cangming ji* also circulated in Korea and Japan, where selections were published.

The period also witnessed the introduction and spread of two important developments in Ming printing: books illustrated with woodcuts and books printed in colour. Suddenly, all China's major works of fiction and drama were available in illustrated editions, and even picture books with minimal text appeared. Polychrome printed books fell into two categories: pictorial and textual. The total colours used on a page or leaf ranged from two to five or six, including black (ink) as one of them. Polychrome textual printing seems to have been limited to the *taoban yinfa* (multi-block) technique, although the 14th-century Diamond Sutra, already described, used the more primitive *shuangyinfa* (double-impression) technique. From around 1615, two lineages (Min and Ling) in Wuxing (Huzhou) published most of these books, in which the main text was printed in black, and punctuation and facsimiles of handwritten annotations and other text appeared in red, blue, and occasionally in one or two additional colours. Fine white paper was used, and these books were undeniably elegant. Polychrome pictorial prints consisted of prints that attempted to imitate the appearance of colourful hand-painted pictures with little or no outlining, as well as narrative pictures with outlined figures containing colours.

A sub-genre of two-colour textual printing is the *yinpu* (seal book), which began to be published in the early Wanli period. Seal books contain collections of seal impressions printed in red, either impressed from actual seals using cinnabar paste or printed in red xylographically, accompanied by seal texts and minimal explanations printed in black. Such books containing the seals of one person or family may be compared with Western books of heraldry. Collections of ancient seal inscriptions suited the growth of epigraphical studies in the Qing. All editions with actual seal impressions were extremely limited.

The best-known of the pictorial books is the *Shizhuzhai shuhuapu* (Ten Bamboo Studio Manual of Calligraphy and Painting), published by Hu Zhengyan from 1633 to 1644, although work may have begun earlier. It took more than a decade to complete and employed the refined *douban yinfa* (assembled-block) technique. His *Shizhuzhai jianpu* (Ten Bamboo Studio Collection of Letter Paper) of 1644 moreover used the *gonghuafa* (blind-printing) technique that produced exquisite small units of embossed surface. Other examples of pictorial colour printing are exceedingly rare; arguably the finest instance—the unique illustrations for the Yuan drama *Xixiang ji* (Tale of the West Chamber) in the Museum für Ostasiatische Kunst, Cologne—was published in 1640 by Min Qiji, the doyen of the Min printers in Wuxing. The recent rediscovery of the Shibui collection of late Ming polychrome editions of erotic picture books will require a reassessment of early colour printing and of the role of pornography in late Ming society—a role which previously was limited to critical accounts of published pornographic fiction.

The renowned Italian Jesuit missionary Matteo Ricci was involved with the earliest polychrome printing of the *Cheng shi moyuan*, a compilation of decorative designs for Chinese moulded ink sticks, published in 1606. The work contains essays and encomiums, including one by Ricci accompanied by his original phonetic transcription—the first published attempt to romanize Chinese. It is likely that Ricci had met the compiler, Cheng Dayue, in Nanjing, and given him original engravings that were copied into *Cheng shi moyuan* as woodcut facsimiles—the first examples of Western graphics to appear in a Chinese publication. Three images were from *Evangelicae Historiae Imagines* by the Jesuit Gerónimo Nadal, and the fourth was an image of the Madonna and Child produced in Japan in 1597 after a Spanish prototype. In a small number of copies of *Cheng shi moyuan*, Cheng Dayue experimented with the *duoyinfa* (multiple-impression) technique to produce polychrome woodcuts; however, the Western ones from Ricci were printed in black only. Beginning with Ricci, a succession of talented Jesuits in China published books in Chinese until their presence was banned in 1724 (*see* **9**). These books included works on theology, geography, history, science, and mathematics. Works such as *Zhifang waiji*, a geography of the world with six folding maps, compiled and translated into Chinese by Giulio Aleni and others and published in Hangzhou in 1623, had a profound effect on the Chinese intellectual class. This publication was the first of its kind in Chinese, and was intended to explain some of the new concepts of cartography and geography introduced by Ricci a couple of decades earlier.

Publishing in the last four decades of the Ming became frenetic. Besides new editions of the classics and standard titles, often hastily edited in the rush to market, dictionaries, primers, textbooks, anthologies, practical handbooks, medical texts, travel guidebooks, artisan pattern books, novels, and plays circulated. Unauthorized editions, plagiarized prefaces, and pirated contents were not uncommon. The growth of titles and subject-matter in this competitive commercial environment encouraged new forms of advertising. Most commercial editions included a separate leaf called *fengmianye* (cover page), folded and printed on one side and attached to the uppermost bound volume of a work. It resembled a Western title-page, and likewise seems to have evolved from the printer's colophon. These cover pages—used since the late 13th century, following the introduction of the wrapped-back binding, but especially popular at the end of the Ming—commonly included the title, author's name, publisher's name, and occasionally a date and a brief statement about the book and its contents. The cover page was fundamentally a commercial advertisement with appended statements by the publisher, and many were bound into the books, preserving their valuable data. The cover page sometimes contained a hand-stamped price or a distinctive seal impression meant as a trademark, and it was common to print pseudo-copyright statements such as *fanke bijiu* ('unauthorized reprints will be investigated'), which were utterly ineffectual. However, it all ended unceremoniously for the most speculative publishers in 1644, when Li Zicheng entered Beijing and the Manchus began their conquest of the entire country.

The first years of the Qing dynasty (1644–1911) included aggressive efforts to stabilize the country: official publishing consisted mostly of moralistic tracts emphasizing the new Manchu rulers' commitment to traditional Confucian values. Scholarly publishers such as Mao Jin continued into the Qing, private publishers cautiously carried out their projects, and commercial publishers tried to survive without the flamboyance they had become used to. As Chinese scholars recovered, they looked inward to try to understand the sources of this transformation of power. At the same time, the Manchu ruling class, recognized for its grasp of military matters (*wu*), was eager to demonstrate its support for civil affairs (*wen*) through promotion of literate culture. During the Kangxi emperor's reign (1662–1722), ambitious scholarly publications were initiated, and the Wuyingdian hall within the Forbidden City was established as the central office for palace publications.

The Kangxi emperor took particular pride in publication of the *Quan Tang Shi* (Complete Poetry of the Tang Dynasty) in 900 *juan* in 1707, which he had commissioned through Cao Yin, head of the salt monopoly at Yangzhou. Over the next decade the palace published two new, classified encyclopaedias plus the eponymous *Kangxi zidian* (Kangxi Dictionary) in 40 volumes. The emperor also ordered the missionary Matteo Ripa to produce the first copperplate prints in China. Completed in 1713 and based on a suite of woodcuts published by the Wuyingdian, 'Thirty-six Views of the Jehol Imperial Gardens' appears to have used both etching and engraving. The greatest enterprise sponsored by the emperor, however, was not completed until four years after his death in 1726. The *Qinding Gujin tushu jicheng* is an enormous classified encyclopaedia of 10,000 *juan*, bound in 5,000 volumes. It is the largest printed book of its kind produced in China; only the MS *Yongle dadian* is bigger. What is most remarkable is that the work was printed from a fount of 250,000 bronze types and is profusely illustrated with woodcut illustrations. Whether these types were cut by hand or cast at the Wuyingdian is still debated. During the emperor's lifetime, the palace also published his collected writings and a large illustrated work commemorating his 60th birthday celebrations in Beijing in 1713.

Later in the 18th century, the Qianlong emperor (r. 1736–95) continued this form of imperial patronage and published even more works, including the *Shisanjing zhushu* (Thirteen Classics) from 1739 to 1747 in 115 volumes and the *Ershisi shi* (Twenty-four Dynastic Histories) from 1739 to 1784 in 722 volumes. The MS compilation called *Siku quanshu* (Complete Library of the Four Treasuries) was unquestionably his greatest achievement. Thousands of works from all over the country were sent to an editorial committee in Beijing for consideration. The emperor's aim was not merely to preserve important extant texts by copying; he wanted to exercise the power of censorship through the committee's review, and lists of proscribed books were issued. The Manchus feared sedition among the majority Chinese population, and they opposed moral turpitude of the sort that was perceived to have led to the fall of the Ming. Names of authors considered critical of Manchu rule were to be deleted from books, and their books and woodblocks were to be burned. In the end, 3,461 titles were selected for inclusion in the *Siku quanshu*, and 6,793 were merely reviewed. Editing and transcription took place between 1773 and 1782. Seven identical MS sets of *c.*36,000 volumes each were produced between 1782 and 1787. The complete bibliographical descriptions for these 10,254 titles were published by the Wuyingdian as the *Qinding siku quanshu zongmu* (Imperially Authorized Annotated Catalogue of the Complete Library of the Four Treasuries), which is still one of the most important Chinese descriptive bibliographies. Another by-product of these activities was the printing of 134 significant titles from the *Siku quanshu*. In 1773 the superintendent of the Wuyingdian, Jin Jian, was appointed to undertake the project. In a persuasive proposal to the throne, which was followed by publication of an illustrated handbook describing the process, Jin recommended that the entire collection, to be named the *Wuyingdian juzhenbanshu*, be printed from wooden types. After the emperor's approval,

253,500 types had to be cut by hand, and the printing of all 134 titles, numbering over 800 volumes, lasted from 1774 to 1794.

The Qianlong emperor's expansion of the palace rare book collections coincided with great interest in book-collecting in society at large. Encouraged by the palace publication projects, many of whose titles were reprinted in the provinces, and buoyed by the improved economy, an upsurge of private and commercial publishing took place in the 18th century, despite threats of censorship emanating from the Qing court. Civil service officials posted throughout the empire were very active, printing local histories and a variety of scholarly works. The Qing period was also noteworthy for the widespread publication of genealogies using native typography. Early in the 19th century, scholars and book-collectors, inspired by the likes of Huang Pilie and Gu Guangqi, produced numerous bibliographical works and published facsimile reprints of Song and Yuan editions.

The 19th century witnessed the beginning of the end of the dominance of xylography in the history of book and print culture in China. Nevertheless, certain events conspired to prolong that demise. In the West, the year 1800 is a convenient (if approximate) date to divide the era of hand printing from the age of machine printing; in China, the corresponding dividing line would be nearly a century later.

By the end of the 1830s, high-quality private publishing began to decline, probably owing to economic downturns and the foreign incursions leading up to the Opium Wars, and followed by the Taiping Rebellion. The Taiping armies left a swathe of destruction across central and southern China in the 1850s. Book collections were destroyed and book production was interrupted for more than a decade. In the wake of the disaster, voluminous reprint collections of new xylographic editions of standard texts were commissioned to replace the losses. A new demand for printed matter came from Protestant missionaries, and although they promoted letterpress printing, they also turned to xylography as a practical and economic means of producing some of their texts. It was not until the end of the 19th century that alternative technologies such as lithography and Western-style movable-type printing began to compete successfully with xylography. As the dynasty declined, their use increased, including reprints of the huge reference work *Qinding Gujin tushu jicheng*. The Shenbaoguan in Shanghai printed a small-format edition with lead type (1884–8), and an official agency, the Zongli Yamen, published a full-size lithographic reprint, printed by Tongwen Shuju (1895–8). These two reprints were in thread binding, but at the turn of the century Western-style bindings began to appear and would soon become the norm. The century, and before long the dynasty, ended amid an outpouring of publications, new in form and content. Journalism, especially pictorial journals and serial fiction, attracted a wide audience. New publishers using lithography and Western-style movable type sprang up everywhere, but especially in Shanghai.

4 The 20th century

The future course of books and publishing in 20th-century China was set in 1897 with the founding of Shangwu Yinshuguan (Commercial Press) in Shanghai. After the abolition of the imperial examinations in 1905, traditionally educated scholars such as Zhang Yuanji (1867–1959) encouraged the publishing of new Western-style textbooks, from which the Commercial Press first gained its reputation. The Zhonghua Shuju, founded in Shanghai in 1912, would become its leading competitor. The first decade of the 20th century also saw the birth of modern libraries in China. Academic and public libraries such as the Peking University Library, the Nanjing Library, and the National Library of China were founded then. The New Library Movement was linked to educational reform and was inspired by the American model. By 1925 the Library Association of China was established, with the reformer Liang Qichao as chairman and Yuan Tung-li as secretary. In 1927 the new organization became a founding member of the International Federation of Library Associations.

Increased political activities after the republican revolution of 1911 greatly stimulated the periodical press. *Qingnian zazhi* (Youth Magazine), also titled *La Jeunesse*, was established by Chen Duxiu in 1915 in Shanghai, where it was published by Qunyi Shushe with support from Yadong Tushuguan. In 1916 the title was changed to *Xin qingnian* (New Youth). The New Culture Movement that followed spawned countless books and periodicals. For the first half of the

The inaugural issue of *Qingnian zazhi* (Youth Magazine) or *La Jeunesse* (September 1915). Private collection

20th century, revolution, foreign invasion, and civil war precluded publishing's peaceful development. Publishers changed names and locations, property was destroyed, and writers used many pseudonyms under threats of censorship and imprisonment. Yet the book survived and flourished.

After 1949, the new Communist government merged and nationalized the publishing industry and book trade. Most of these activities were organized by the distributor Xinhua Shudian. In the 1950s, important publishing projects benefited from government subsidies and from a large pool of talented writers and editors. At the same time, major publishing houses such as Shangwu Yinshuguan and Zhonghua Shuju, as well as the Nationalist government publisher Zhengzhong Shuju, were replicated and set up in exile in Taiwan by former managers and editors who had fled the mainland. During the Cultural Revolution (1966–76) publishing and bookselling in China came to a standstill; but since then they have re-emerged very strongly, and the antiquarian book trade has been aided by a vibrant book auction market. Since 1949, woodblock printing has been extolled as an important Chinese invention and national cultural asset. This historical turn has resulted in the preservation of existing collections of woodblocks and the maintenance of skills such as papermaking, calligraphic transcription, block-cutting, hand printing, and traditional binding.

Like other countries, China has been profoundly affected by the digital revolution. The automation of data brought about by the introduction of computers was first applied to cataloguing and indexing books—catalogues of individual libraries developed into electronic databases. The digitization of texts in China has grown exponentially in recent years without reducing the growth of new print publications, and the natural division between modern books and ancient texts has not disappeared. The digitization of new books, of course, is merely a new form of publication, and the digitization of current publications is fraught with legal issues of copyright. On the other hand, the digitization of ancient books and MSS not only provides access to their texts but is closely related to issues of preservation. The future of Chinese digital books and virtual libraries is as unpredictable as the technology that underlies them.

BIBLIOGRAPHY

C. Brokaw, *Commerce in Culture* (2007)
—— and K. Chow, eds., *Printing and Book Culture in Late Imperial China* (2005)
T. Carter, *The Invention of Printing in China and Its Spread Westward* (1925; rev. edn. 1955)
L. Chia, *Printing for Profit* (2002)
K. Chow, *Publishing, Culture, and Power in Early Modern China* (2004)

J.-P. Drège, *Les Bibliothèques en Chine au temps des manuscrits* (1991)
J. S. Edgren, 'The *fengmianye* (Cover Page) as a Source for Chinese Publishing History', in *Studies of Publishing Culture in East Asia*, ed. A. Isobe (2004)
M. Heijdra, 'Technology, Culture and Economics: Movable Type Versus Woodblock Printing in East Asia', in *Studies of Publish-*

ing Culture in East Asia, ed. A. Isobe (2004)

P. Hu, *Visible Traces* (2000)

International Dunhuang Project, www.idp. bl.uk, consulted Dec. 2007

J. McDermott, *A Social History of the Chinese Book* (2006)

[Nihon Shoshi Gakkai (Japan Bibliographical Society),] *Naikaku Bunko sôhon shoei* (Illustrations of Song Editions in the Naikaku Bunko Library) (1984)

C. Reed, *Gutenberg in Shanghai: Chinese Print Capitalism, 1876–1937* (2004)

T. H. Tsien, *Paper and Printing* (1985)

—— *Written on Bamboo and Silk*, 2e (2004)

K. T. Wu, 'Ming Printing and Printers', *Harvard Journal of Asiatic Studies*, 7 (1943), 203–60

—— 'Chinese Printing Under Four Alien Dynasties', *Harvard Journal of Asiatic Studies*, 13 (1950), 447–523

∽ 43 ∾

The History of the Book in Korea

BETH MCKILLOP

1 Three Kingdoms (*c.*57 BC–AD 668, United Silla 668–935)

In Korea and throughout East Asia, engraved intaglio seals and texts cut on stone steles were precursors of printing as a widespread technology. In neighbouring China, the fixing of classic texts as engraved stone slabs in AD 175 is an important landmark. Early political groupings on the Korean peninsula also recorded texts on stone and later took black-and-white ink-squeeze rubbings on paper from such engraved slabs. Intensive contact with China had led to the spread of Chinese script and knowledge of the Chinese language in Korea by about the 1st century AD. Chinese characters, which have both a semantic and a phonetic element, were used to write Korean words by following their sounds. Educated Koreans also learned to read and write in Chinese. From about the 6th to the 15th centuries, this complex and confusing system of borrowing Chinese script was the only one used to record the Korean language.

The earliest surviving writings using the native transcription system are poems. Texts from the Three Kingdoms period that survive as physical objects include a massive memorial slab—more than seven metres high and engraved with 18,000 seal-script Chinese characters, praising King Kwanggaet'o (who ruled the northern Kingdom of Koguryŏ, AD 391–413)—and an engraved stele (AD 503) from Yŏngil, North Kyŏngsang Province. It is a slab of granite, polished for engraving on three sides; bearing 231 characters of various sizes, in an archaic style, it records the judgement of a dispute about land ownership. The preservation of written words for posterity has been an enduring preoccupation on the Korean peninsula.

Papermaking had probably reached Korea from China early in the Three Kingdoms period, transmitted through the Chinese commandery at Lelang, which ruled the northwest of the peninsula in 108 BC–AD 313. The spread of the Buddhist faith eastwards into Korea in the 4th to 6th centuries brought the need to provide copies of holy writings, required by monks and believers for their devotions and studies. Sponsors supported hand-copying and, later, printing of scriptures; the names of such benefactors are sometimes recorded in colophons or other notes to the texts. During the Three Kingdoms, United Silla, and Koryŏ (918–1392) periods, all such copies were in Chinese characters, since classical Chinese was accepted as the written language of palace, court, and temple. Finely produced temple copies of such texts as the Diamond and Lotus Sutras, stamped images of the Buddha, and copies of incantations and chants were certainly produced in great numbers, although few have survived from before the Koryŏ.

The printed text of the *Mugu chŏnggwang tae taranigyŏng*, (Pure Light Dharani Sutra), a kind of Buddhist incantation, was discovered in October 1966 in the second storey of the Sŏkkat'ap (Sakyamuni Pagoda) at Pulguksa (Pulguk Temple), Kyŏngju. This text was translated into Chinese in 704, and the temple built in 751; thus, the Dharani was printed and then enclosed inside the pagoda, probably to mark the temple's consecration. This small paper scroll, measuring 6.5 × 648 cm, was found in a container for Buddhist relics. Its measurements are approximate, since the early sections are in a poor state of conservation. Each of its twelve sheets of paper contains between 55 and 63 columns of characters; each column has seven to nine characters, measuring 4–5 mm. It was printed on thin mulberry (Korean *tak*) paper from engraved wooden blocks. On the basis of analysis of the graphic style of the characters and the vegetable material used for the paper (*broussonetia kazinoki*), it seems that the Silla kingdom was its probable place of production. The text uses Empress Wu characters, special graphic forms for a small number of terms created in China during her rule (684–705). Given the extent of cultural exchange between Tang China and Silla, it is entirely credible that a text originally cut on to blocks and printed in China could have been re-cut and printed in Korea, to be buried as part of a group of protective holy relics during the consecration of Pulguk Temple.

Another example of the highly developed nature of textual transmission in the Silla period is a fine scroll MS of chapters 1–10 of the Avatamsaka Sutra in the Ho-Am Museum (National Treasure 196 of the Republic of Korea). This document was copied in 754–5 at the behest of High Priest Yŏn'gi Pŏpsa of Hwangnyong Temple, Kyŏngju. The colophon records the date of production, as well as the names and ranks of the nineteen workers who made the copy. They include the sutra copyists, the painter of the cover papers, and the papermakers. The text, in regular sutra-script, is enclosed in a cover of purple-dyed mulberry paper, on which two Bodhisattvas seated in front of a storied, tiled-roof building have been painted in gold. Measuring 14 metres long and 26 cm high, with 34 characters per column, the scroll is composed of 43 sheets of sheer white paper and is rolled around a 24-cm wooden spindle with crystal knobs on both ends.

2 Koryŏ (918–1392)

Woodblock printing of Buddhist texts grew in volume and extent throughout the period of Koryŏ rule, a time of intense devotion to the Buddhist faith. The Korean printing historian Sohn Pow-Key has estimated that more than 300,000 woodblocks for the texts of Buddhist scriptures were cut. The act of sponsoring sutra-copying was believed to gain spiritual merit for the believer.

Pre-eminent among the printing enterprises of the period were the two sets of woodblocks engraved to print the entire known corpus of Buddhist scriptures, the Tripitaka. In both instances, the enterprise was motivated as much by a desire to secure divine protection for the nation against the succession of continental invaders who attacked it—the Khitan in the 11th century, the Jurchen (founders of the Jin dynasty in China) in the 12th century, and the Mongols in the 13th century—as by a pious concern to preserve and record its sacred sermons, Buddhist rules, and treatises. Mindful of the need for divine protection, the court commissioned artisans to select and prepare wood, to copy the carefully chosen and checked texts, to cut the transferred texts in relief on both sides of the blocks, and then to print, using charcoal-based inks, on to locally produced paper.

The Tripitaka was first cut in Korea for printing in its entirety, over a long period between 1011 and 1087; however, the blocks were lost, destroyed by fire during the Mongol invasions of the early 13th century. About 300 printed Tripitaka scrolls (out of some 11,000) survive in the Buddhist temple Nanzenji, Kyoto. Volume 78 of the Avatamsaka Sutra from the same Tripitaka is in the Ho-Am Art Museum (National Treasure 267 of the Republic of Korea). The monk Ŭich'ŏn (1055–1101), fourth son of King Munjong, had travelled to China and collected thousands of Buddhist texts to bring to his native country. He devoted many years to cataloguing the teachings of the different Buddhist schools, and compiled the *Sok changgyŏng* (Supplement to the Canon).

Immediately after the first Korean Tripitaka was lost, the enterprise of cutting a new Tripitaka was undertaken. This re-cut Tripitaka was a project of the highest importance for king and country, the work lasting from 1236 to 1251. The exact number of blocks, made of seasoned woods, has been estimated differently by various scholars. Currently, 81,155 blocks survive: eighteen of the original blocks were lost, 296 were added in the Chosŏn period (1392–1910), and twelve were added during the Japanese occupation (1910–45). The number of blocks has given the name 'P'almangyŏng' (Tripitaka of 80,000) to the 13th-century Tripitaka. The blocks measure 72.6 × 26.4 × 3 cm and are engraved on both sides. The print area, delineated by single-line borders, is 24.5 cm high, and each block has 23 columns of fourteen 27-mm-high characters. The graphic style of the characters is uniform throughout the entire corpus. Each block carries the name of the sutra, the chapter and the folio number. The blocks have been lacquered, and metal reinforcing strips have been applied to the corners to prevent warping. On completion of cutting in 1251, the blocks were used for printing at Namhae, South Kyŏngsang province, and subsequently moved north for storage to a repository on Kanghwa Island.

At the time of the second cutting of the Tripitaka blocks, between 1236 and 1251, the Koryŏ court had fled from the invading Mongols, to take refuge on Kanghwa Island. By the late 14th century, however, even Kanghwa Island was no longer secure against hostile forces. Pirate attacks endangered the security of the scriptures, and there was military unrest throughout the country. This led to the choice of the distant southern mountain fastness of the Haeinsa Buddhist temple as a safe storage location for the precious double-sided printing blocks, which were moved there in 1398. In 1488, decades after the blocks had arrived at Haeinsa, a set of four special buildings was repaired and adapted to protect the blocks. Located higher than the rest of the temple complex, these structures are rectangular wooden-pillared, hipped-roof buildings, set on granite stones, and arranged in a courtyard formation. Rows of slatted windows punctuate the walls, providing natural ventilation and minimizing the spread of damp. The earthen floors of the stores lie on a layer of charcoal, regulating humidity and temperature, and exposed rafters encourage air circulation. The woodblocks are arranged on five-storey shelf structures. Rare survivals of the wooden architecture of the early Chosŏn dynasty, the repositories have proved a well-ventilated and damp-proof environment to safeguard the precious blocks. Between 1967 and 1976, a set of impressions of the Korean Tripitaka was made from these blocks and distributed to libraries and universities in Korea and around the world.

Looking more broadly at book production in Koryŏ, it is notable that scholars and officials paid increasing attention to the teachings of the Chinese philosopher Confucius, and thus required copies of definitive versions of Confucian texts and commentaries by later Chinese scholars. Obtaining books from China was often difficult, because of war or because the Chinese authorities were suspicious of Korea's reasons for seeking copies of Chinese books. Indeed, the Song poet Su Dongpo (1036–1101) wrote several times against the sending of books to Koryŏ. The Korean court was often frustrated in attempts to obtain the goods it needed from China. Gifts of books were sent only with imperial consent, which could not be relied upon. Despite these difficulties, Korean book collecting was so persistent that on three or four occasions during the 10th and 11th centuries, Koryŏ sent back Chinese books that had been lost in Song China and were required there. The Chinese envoy Xu Jing, who visited Korea in 1123, noted in his account of the visit, *Xuanhe fengshi Gaoli tujing* (Illustrated Account of the Xuanhe Emperor's Envoy to Korea), that the 'Royal Library by the riverside stores tens of thousands of books' (Sohn, 'Early Korean Printing', 98).

During the 13th century, experiments with movable type produced works that have since been lost, but are remembered because of the practice of recording printing information in colophons. From this period, three pieces of evidence survive for the use of movable metal type. One is a collection of Buddhist sermons entitled *Nanmyŏng ch'ŏn hwasang song chŭngdoga*, printed on Kanghwa Island in 1239 using blocks cut from a text originally printed using cast movable types. The colophon states:

> It is impossible to advance to the core of Buddhism without having understood this book. Is it possible for this book to go out of print? Therefore we employ workmen to re-cut the cast-type edition to continue its circulation. Postface written with reverence by Ch'oe I [d. 1249] in the 9th moon [of 1239].

The second piece of evidence for 13th-century movable-type printing is a collection of ritual texts, *Sangjong yemun*, which were reprinted *c.*1234 during the Kanghwa Island period, using metal types, to replace an original lost during the flight from Kaesŏng. The colophon clearly states, 'here we have now printed 28 copies of the book with the use of movable metal types, to distribute among the various government offices'; it then expresses the hope that officials will not lose it. The third piece of evidence is a number of excavated individual types from the Koryŏ era, now in Korean museum collections. These types have a metallic composition similar to that of Koryŏ coins. An example is the 1 cm-high character for 'return' (*pok*), now in the National Museum of Korea. Scholars believe that the disruptions of the mid-Koryŏ, when the court moved from Kaesŏng to Kanghwa, stimulated the use of metal types, in order to produce small editions of essential works destroyed during the Mongol invasions. Clearly, Koryŏ printers made significant use of movable type in the mid-13th century.

No dated work printed with movable types survives from the 13th century. For the 14th century, however there is an extant work—the world's earliest—printed by means of metal movable types. *Paegun hwasang ch'orok pulcho Chikchi simch'e yojŏl* (Essentials of Buddha's Teachings Recorded by the Monk Paegun) is a collection of Buddhist biographical and historical excerpts by the Sŏn (Zen) Buddhist master Kyŏnghan (1298–1374), better recognized by his pen name of Paegun. Also known as *Chikchi simch'e yojŏl*, it consisted of two volumes: the lost first volume comprised hymns and poems, and teachings of Buddhist masters; the incomplete second volume is held by the Bibliothèque nationale de France. The surviving volume bears a colophon dating it to the seventh moon of 1377; it notes that the place of production where movable type was used was Hŭngdŏksa, a temple in Ch'ŏngju. The verso of the colophon sheet records the names of two Buddhist believers in charge of printing, Sŏkchan and Taldam, as well as a sponsor, the nun Myodŏk. The volume contains 38 sheets, with a print area of 20.2 × 14.3 cm. There are eleven columns of 18–20 characters. Formerly in the collection of the French diplomat Collin de Plancy (1853–1922), the book was recorded by Courant in *Bibliographie coréenne* (no. 3738) before disappearing from view; it reappeared in a 1972 exhibition in Paris. Hŭngdŏksa was excavated in 1984 during the construction of a housing development, revealing bronze vessels bearing the temple name. Subsequently, the Cheongju (Ch'ŏngju) Early Printing Museum was opened at

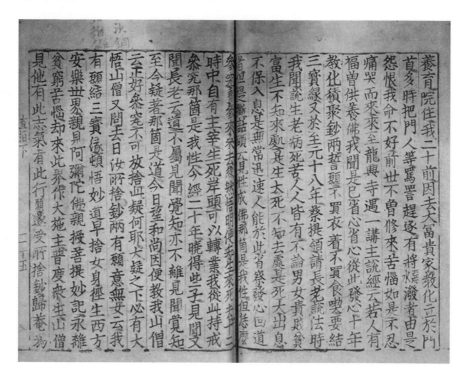

The world's earliest dated printing using movable type, *Paegun hwasang ch'orok pulcho Chikchi simch'e yojŏl* (Essentials of Buddha's Teachings Recorded by the Monk Paegun), printed at Hŭngdŏksa (Ch'ŏngju) in 1377. Bibliothèque nationale de France, Département des Manuscrits (division orientale) (Koreana 7, no. 2)

the temple site to celebrate Korea's contribution to printing and to mark the place of production of this, the world's earliest surviving book printed with metal movable type.

To understand the reasons for the adoption of movable type as a method of printing in Korea, it is useful to think of the disadvantages of woodblock printing in a society where the need for books was confined to a small readership. Cutting wooden blocks is relatively wasteful of materials, and requires that the blocks be stored for reuse, with the ever-present danger of destruction through fire. It is striking that evidence of 13th-century metal movable type dates to the period of the Mongol invasions, when fire destroyed countless buildings and their contents. In China, by contrast, print runs were much larger than the tens of copies normal in Korea; thus, there was little incentive to popularize the use of movable type, because blocks could be used to make dozens of impressions. Sohn has pointed out that, in Korea,

> works printed with metal type were printed in relatively small quantities and include a wide variety of titles. On the other hand, works in great demand, such as calendars, were printed from woodblocks. (Sohn, 'King Sejong's Innovations', 54)

A further consideration must be the availability of raw materials and of skilled metal-working artisans engaged by the foundries of Buddhist temples, which commissioned bronze bells, drums, and utensils for temple services.

3 Chosŏn (1392–1910)

In 1392, after a period of instability and Mongol-dominated rule earlier in the century, the new dynastic house of Chosŏn came to power and established its capital in the centre of the peninsula, in modern-day Seoul. It continued to patronize Confucian studies in an increasingly systematic fashion. The period of Buddhist predominance drew to a conclusion. Indigenous customs and practices had long coexisted with those of the imported religion, but Confucian rites and practices began to exert an ever-stronger influence on family and ritual life. Confucian ideals gradually penetrated beyond the court and aristocratic class. Confucian studies were not an innovation of the Chosŏn period—they had formed the syllabus of the state examinations introduced in Koryŏ in the 10th century—but the early Chosŏn kings and their advisers began to reform social and religious observances and to sweep away heterodox ideas and practices, both those of native Korean origin and the excessive powers of the Buddhist Church. For this, they needed to study many Chinese editions of works of neo-Confucian philosophy. Chosŏn rulers and officials may have known of printing using metal types in Koryŏ times. In the early years of the 15th century, they began attempts to make the technique more efficient.

The third Chosŏn king, T'aejong (r. 1400–1418), is recorded as showing great concern about how books were produced:

> Because our country is located east of China beyond the sea, not many books from China are readily available. Moreover, woodblock imprints are easily defaced, and it is impossible to print all the books in the world using the woodblock method. It is my desire to cast bronze type so that we can print as many books as possible and have them made available widely. This will truly bring infinite benefit to us. (Lee, i. 537)

The types cast at T'aejong's behest, known from the cyclical name of the year 1403 as *kyemi*, were the first of a series of cast types—almost all made of bronze, but including a number of iron, lead, and even zinc types—produced throughout the long rule of the Chosŏn house.

After the 1403 fount, the next casting was in 1420, the *kyŏngja* year. Again, the dynastic annals provide a detailed account of royal involvement, in the person of the fourth king, Sejong (r. 1418–50):

> To print books, type used to be placed on copper plates, molten beeswax would be poured on the plates to solidify the type alignments and thereafter a print was made. This required an excessive amount of beeswax and allowed printing of only a few sheets a day. Whereupon His Majesty personally directed the work and ordered Yi Ch'ŏn and Nam Kŭp to improve the casting of copper plates to match the shape of the type. With this improvement the type remained firmly on the

plates without using beeswax and the print became more square and correct. It allowed the printing of several sheets in a day. Mindful of the Typecasting Foundry's hard and meritorious work, His Majesty granted wine and food on several occasions. (Lee, i. 538)

The resulting page was well proportioned, with characters whose horizontals slope slightly upwards from left to right. This flat-heeled type could be evenly spaced without wax; it represents an important refinement of the use of movable type.

Sŏng Hyŏn (1439–1504) described the processes involved in printing with metal types in *Yongjae ch'onghwa* (Assorted Writing):

> The person who engraves on wood is called the engraver and the person who casts is called the casting artisan. The finished graphs are stored in boxes and the person responsible for storing type is called the typekeeper. These men were selected from the young servants working in the government. A person who reads manuscript is called the manuscript reader. These people are all literate. The typekeeper lines up the graphs on the manuscript papers and then places them on a plate called the upper plate. The graph levelling artisan fills in all the empty spaces between type on the upper plate with bamboo and torn cloth, and tightens it so that the type cannot be moved. The plate is then handed over to the printing artisan to print. The entire process of printing is supervised by members of the office of editorial review selected from among graduates of the civil service examination. At first no-one knew how to tighten up the type on a printing plate, and beeswax was used to fix type on the plate. As a result each logograph had an awl-like tail, as in the *kyŏngja* type. Only after the technique of filling empty space with bamboo was developed was there no longer a need to use wax. Boundless indeed is the ingenuity of men's intelligence.

In 1434, the type known as *kabin* was cast, and enjoyed such popularity that it was recast seven times over hundreds of years. It is a large fount, with characters measuring 14 × 15 mm (compared to 10 × 11 mm for the 1420 fount), and an elegant and lively calligraphic style. This type is narrower at the base than on the printing surface, and was therefore economical to cast. *Kabin* types for Chinese characters were also used in the first work to be printed using both Chinese characters and Korean *han'gŭl* movable types: the *Sŏkpo sangjŏl* (Episodes from the Life of the Buddha) printed in 1449 from a 1447 fount. *Han'gŭl*, an invented syllabic script, was introduced by King Sejong in 1443 to increase the literacy of the population and to represent the sounds of Korean graphically. In the preface to *Hunmin chŏngŭm* (Correct Sounds to Instruct the People), Sejong wrote:

> The sounds of our language differ from those of Chinese and are not easily communicated by using Chinese graphs. Many among the ignorant, therefore, though they wish to express their sentiments in writing, have been unable to communicate. Considering this situation with compassion, I have newly devised twenty-eight letters. I wish only that the people will learn them easily and use them conveniently in their daily life.

The new alphabet was the culmination of years of research by King Sejong and his scholar assistants. The letterforms have a fascinating origin. Consonants are shown in shapes mirroring the position of oral organs during articulation of each sound: the 'k' sound being shown by ㄱ, reflecting the position of the tongue against the roof of the mouth, while the 'm' sound, a square shape, □, imitates pursed lips in forming the sound. Closed vowels are represented graphically using horizontals, and open vowels using vertical lines. The Korean alphabet has always been written syllabically, with groups of letters arranged in discrete squares rather than in long strings, reflecting the phonemic structure of the language. This grouping convention is clearly influenced by the appearance of written Chinese characters. The earliest *han'gŭl* letters, in the 15th and 16th centuries, were upright and angular, but with time the practice of brush writing engendered a more fluent style incorporating curved and weighted strokes. The first publications to reproduce *han'gŭl* were produced from woodblocks, but in the centuries that followed, many works were published using types; Sohn listed fourteen *han'gŭl* founts in his 1982 survey of Korean types, *Early Korean Typography*.

The finest editions continued to be court-sponsored works, supervised by the Office of Paper Production, the Office of Movable Type, and the Office for Woodblock Printing. By the late Chosŏn, private individuals, Confucian academies (*sŏwŏn*), local scholars, and authors all sponsored the printing of books, and some commissioned new types.

Despite the close interest of 15th-century Korean kings in printing technology, the early introduction of cast metal-type printing led neither to an expansion

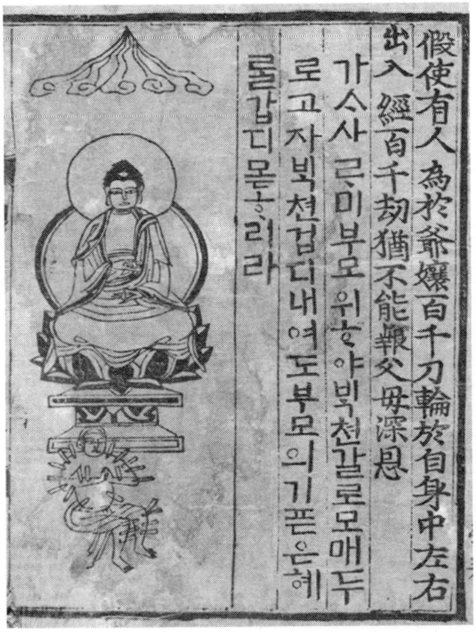

Han'gŭl script from the *Sutra of Filial Piety* in a 16th-century block printing copy. © The British Library Board. All Rights Reserved (Or. 74.b.3)

of publishing nor to demonstrable increases in literacy. The reasons for this lie in the Confucian values that dominated society. With a strong focus on self-cultivation and virtuous leadership, the government encouraged austerity and deplored commerce. According to Confucius, the ideal man should be 'poor yet delighting in the Way, wealthy yet observant of the rites' (*Analects*, i.15). Korean scholar-officials of the Chosŏn fervently upheld this Confucian ideal, depressing the natural growth of markets and the circulation of traded goods. In this restrictive economy, books were printed for use in tightly controlled circumstances. Technical manuals, children's textbooks, lists of medical plants, maps, collections of letters, language primers, and practical and literary works were available to the officials, teachers, and artisans who required them. Gazetteers recorded the topography, products, population, and significant achievements of the various regions of the land. For lower-class people, and for teachers in schools in different regions of the country, popular and philosophical works were produced to promote the Confucian virtues of loyalty, obedience, chastity, brotherly love, and filial piety. Clan associations issued detailed genealogies to allow each generation to trace its family lineage, an important component of Confucian ancestor worship. Candidates for the civil service examinations studied the philosophical and literary texts that formed the syllabus of these gruelling, extended tests.

Despite the restrictive nature of the economy and government control of print, then, tens of thousands of hand-copied and printed books from Koryŏ and Chosŏn times survive in Korean and overseas libraries. The Harvard-Yenching Library catalogue alone lists 3,850 titles. Libraries in Japan contain substantial holdings of rare Korean books. Despite the losses caused by time and by war, the national and former royal libraries in South Korea preserve vast repositories of archival and published material, periodically enriched by donations from private collections. Book reading and scholarship were a vital part of Korean life.

With the advent of Japanese and Western political and economic interests c.1880, modern printing technology was introduced. The *Hansŏng Sunbo/Seoul News* was printed using a Western-style press imported from Japan, associating new technology with the reform movement that flourished briefly in the face of strong conservative opposition from the political elite. Christian missionaries were important carriers of printing innovation to Korea (*see* 9): the Trilingual Press was established in 1885 by a Methodist, H. G. Appenzeller. French Catholics were also active in the late 19th century, and Father E. J. G. Coste supervised the printing and binding of the pioneering *Dictionnaire coréen* in 1880, introducing the first *han'gŭl* founts used by non-Korean printers. Bibles and language-learning aids were among the early publications of the first English press, which printed James Scott's *English and Corean Dictionary* under the supervision of Bishop C. J. Corfe in 1891. *The Pilgrim's Progress*, Aesop's Fables, and *Gulliver's Travels* were other early Western titles published by missionaries in this period.

4 Modern (1910–)

Japan annexed Korea in 1910, leading to a decline in independent publishing. The period 1910–45 was characterized by some cultural enterprises forcefully resisting the Japanese colonial regime, while others accommodated and collaborated with the Japanese. Writing and publishing in the Korean language was constrained, as the colonizers attempted to shape Korean social and cultural identity in ways that supported Japanese imperialist ambitions. For a time, the future of Korean as a medium of formal communication and education was uncertain. It was against this background of struggle and contested nationhood that modern Korea's influential newspaper and book publishing companies were founded. Writers, academic societies, and newspapers all had to contend with military control and close censorship. Resentment against Japan continues to colour both of the modern Korean states' commercial and official publishing enterprises.

Following Japan's defeat in 1945 and the Korean War of 1950–53, the peninsula was divided into a communist north and a capitalist south. Since then, the Korean book has had two principal manifestations, which naturally reflect the separate social systems, market models, and graphic identities of North and South Korea. South Korean books have used a mixed script, with a small number of Chinese characters, particularly for place and personal names. The publishing industry, both academic and commercial, is highly developed and integrated into the international community. Bookshops thrive in the major cities. In addition to print publishing, South Korea has become a world leader since the 1990s in electronic publishing and database creation. Digitized versions of the Korean Tripitaka and the Annals of the Chosŏn Dynasty are pioneering examples of large-scale scholarly digital projects that have revolutionized access to premodern textual sources in the humanities (*see* **21**).

North Korean publishing is dominated by Communist Party doctrine and the cult of the late President Kim Il Sŏng (1912–94) and his son and successor, Kim Jŏng Il (1942–2011). The quality, circulation, and appearance of North Korean publishing in the early 21st century has changed little since the economic crisis that followed the collapse of the international socialist bloc in 1989. Book circulation in North Korea is low, and subject-matter tightly controlled by the state. Nevertheless, a steady stream of fiction, poetry, historical studies, reference books, sheet music, cartoons, and educational textbooks is produced. In contrast to the South Korean practice of mixed Chinese and *han'gŭl* script, in North Korea, no Chinese characters are used. There is very little interaction with publishing outside the country; electronic publishing is closely controlled. Generally, North Korean institutions and individuals are not connected to the World Wide Web. Despite these differences, however, the two Koreas are united by their pride in the 15th-century *han'gŭl* alphabet. They also celebrate Korea's notable achievements in printing culture: the world's earliest datable printed text (*c.*751); the earliest dated work printed with movable type (1377); and the survival of the Korean Tripitaka wood-blocks stored at Haeinsa (13ᵗʰ century).

....

BIBLIOGRAPHY

M. Courant, *Bibliographie coréenne* (3 vols, 1894–1901)

P. Lee, ed., *Sourcebook of Korean Civilization* (2 vols, 1993–6)

B. Park, *Korean Printing* (2003)

Sohn Pow-Key, 'Early Korean Printing', *Journal of the American Oriental Society*, 79 (1959), 96–103

—— *Early Korean Printing* (1984)

—— 'King Sejong's Innovations in Printing', in *King Sejong the Great*, ed. Y.-K. Kim-Renaud (1992)

—— 'Invention of the Movable Metal-type Printing in Koryo: Its Role and Impact on Human Cultural Progress', *GJ* 73 (1998), 25–30

The History of the Book in Japan

P. F. KORNICKI

1 Scribal culture

Japan first became acquainted with both writing and the book from China, at some time in the first half of the first millennium AD. There can be no doubt that Chinese, as the language of Buddhism in East Asia, as the language of the intellectual tradition that is now termed Confucianism, and as the language of scholarly discourse in East Asia, was central to book production in Japan from its beginnings right up to the 19th century.

In all likelihood Chinese texts had been transmitted to Japan by the end of the 5th century, and although the dates and details given in Japanese annals are not reliable, it seems clear that books from China were increasingly valued as gifts in Japan. These would have been Confucian and Buddhist texts, and would have taken the form of rolls or scrolls rather than bound books. Imported works needed to be copied to become accessible, and this was particularly important in the case of Buddhist texts once Buddhism took root in Japan. By the 7th century, therefore, *shakyō*, or sutra copying, was an organized activity, both as a means of reproducing texts for study and devotion and as a pious activity in its own right. In 673, a complete copy of all the Buddhist texts so far transmitted to Japan was made at the Kawaradera Temple for the purpose of preservation, while a sutra copied in 686 was copied primarily to benefit the sponsor's ancestors. By 727, a sutra scriptorium had been established by the government at Nara with a staff of copyists and proofreaders for the production of sutras to be used in government-sponsored temples. Most of these texts were copied in black ink on paper that had been dyed with a yellow preservative, but some were luxury copies in gold letters on indigo paper. In addition, a state library had been established in 702 with a staff of twenty copyists who were supposed to copy Confucian as well as Buddhist MSS; the Confucian texts would have been essential for the newly founded university, since the education system was modelled on that of China and required Chinese literacy.

Most of the MSS produced in the Nara period have long since perished, but recent finds of *mokkan* (wooden tablets used to record bureaucratic texts) and *urushigami* (scraps of paper preserved by lacquer) have over the last 50 years greatly enhanced our knowledge of the texts and the forms of the Chinese language in use in early Japan. A much clearer picture of the Chinese books that were available in Japan at the end of the 9th century is provided by *Nihonkoku genzaisho mokuroku*, a catalogue of extant books compiled at imperial command.

The oldest extant MS produced in Japan is a commentary on the Lotus Sutra which dates from the early 7th century; it is, of course, entirely in Chinese and may indeed have been written by an immigrant from the mainland rather than a native Japanese. By the early 8th century, however, the Japanese had not only written their first Chinese-style chronicle, but also two works in which the Japanese language appears for the first time: *Kojiki* (Record of Ancient Matters) and *Man'yōshū* (Collection of 10,000 Leaves), an anthology of poetry. At this stage the only technique for recording Japanese was, rather clumsily, to use Chinese characters for their sound value alone. In the 9th century, however, this developed into a syllabary of highly abbreviated forms of Chinese characters known as *kana*, which were used to record Japanese texts, such as poetry and, later, prose works such as the poetic diaries of the Heian period (794–1185) and, especially, the *Tale of Genji* and other classic works of court literature. By the late Heian period, woodblock printing was being used in Japan to print various Buddhist texts, but all works of Japanese literature circulated only in MS until the early 17th century, when the first printed editions were produced. The reasons for this exclusion of Japanese writings from the world of print are complex, but they may be summed up as: the domination of printing by Buddhist monasteries; the importance of calligraphy in the preparation of MS copies; and the hermetic court milieu in which Japanese literature was produced and consumed. As a result, large numbers of Heian texts—known now only by name—did not survive the centuries of MS tradition and some, such as the *Tosa nikki* (Tosa Diary) of 935, only survived by chance.

Throughout the Heian period, and indeed right to the present day, the practice of copying sutras for devotional reasons continued. The celebrated scholar and poet Fujiwara no Teika (1162–1241), for example, made many copies of the Lotus Sutra in his own hand for this purpose. Sutra decoration assumed ever more elaborate forms, with frontispieces and beautiful papers—and sometimes the text was superimposed on scenes of secular life. But sutras were also being copied for more scholarly reasons. In the 9th century, six monks were at various times sent to China to procure MSS of Buddhist texts; on their return catalogues were drawn up of the MSS they had managed to acquire. Subsequently, monks came from other temples throughout Japan to copy them and take copies elsewhere. From the 11th century, however, it was increasingly common for printed Buddhist texts to be imported from China or Korea, and from the 12th century Buddhist texts were being printed in Japan, so the imperative to keep making copies by hand weakened, except for devotional purposes.

During the wars of the 12th century and those that followed, many Japanese books were lost: more than half of the 493 works described in *Honchō shojaku mokuroku*, a 13th-century catalogue of Japanese books, are no longer extant. On the other hand, the *Tosa nikki* survived, because the original MS of 935 survived in a palace library until at least 1492 and was copied four times: two 13th-century copies have survived and have made it possible to reconstruct the original text.

Once commercial publishing grew in importance in the 17th century, the scribal traditions, it might be supposed, died away. This was not, however, the case. Scribal production and circulation continued up to the end of the 19th century. This was partly a matter of continuing traditions: sutra copying for devotional reasons continued, and so did the production of luxury editions of classical works of literature with fine calligraphy, which the samurai elite preferred to printed copies. A new practice was making MS copies of printed books, either for reasons of economy, or because of rarity, or as a way of learning the text: this last purpose was recommended, for example, in the case of the *Onna daigaku* (Greater Learning for Women), a moral primer for girls first published in the early 18th century. Another reason for preferring MS over print was to restrict the circulation of new knowledge: innovative medical techniques or new styles of *ikebana* (flower arrangement), for example, generated an income for the initiators, and it was therefore in their interests to restrict circulation by producing MS accounts for the eyes of their followers only. But the most significant reason for the continued circulation of MSS was the censorship legislation of the Edo period (1600–1868), which forbade the publication of scandalous or other matters concerning the samurai class as a whole. As a result, accounts of the samurai rebellion of 1651, or of the sex scandal of 1801 which embroiled women of the shogun's household, could not be printed; although bans were placed even on the circulation of MS versions, there was no effective means of policing this practice—and the heavy demand for works of this kind, often written up in a sensational manner or semi-fictionalized, was met by circulating libraries. This is clear not only from surviving books bearing the seals of these libraries but also from legal documents generated by cases in which circulating libraries were caught with such material in their possession.

In the modern period since 1868, MS production, except for devotional or other private purposes, has diminished considerably. However, it is worth noting that, given the cumbersome nature of the Japanese typewriter, official documents were commonly written by hand until the advent of computer-generated text.

2 Print up to 1600

Woodblock printing is without doubt a Chinese invention, probably of the 7th century, but the oldest extant printed texts in East Asia are to be found in Korea and Japan. The first evidence of printing in Japan is on a stupendous scale: it is reported in the chronicles that between the years 764 and 770 1 million Buddhist invocations (*Hyakumantō darani*) were printed and inserted inside miniature pagodas. This was both an exercise in atonement and a monument to the power of the imperial institution that commissioned this exercise. Large numbers of these pagodas and their printed contents have survived, sufficient to show that at the least 100,000 were produced, if not the full million. But this was decidedly not a case of printing for the purpose of reading; it was rather a ritual act, which has other parallels in the treatment of texts in Buddhism, such as prayer wheels, and the texts were not intended for reading. Nevertheless, it is eloquent evidence of the transmission of printing technology to Japan in the 8th century.

There are some records of similar instances of the devotional printing of sutras in the Heian period, but it is not until commentaries and doctrinal works were being printed (the earliest extant one is dated 1088) that printing for the purpose of producing texts to read is encountered. These were, of course, Buddhist texts in Chinese, as was true of almost all printing up to the late 16th century. Most printing at this stage was conducted in Nara at the Kōfukuji, the family temple of the dominant Fujiwara family, but in the Kamakura period (1185–1333) printing spread to other parts of Japan. The monasteries of Mount Kōya began printing works of esoteric Buddhism and the writings of the monk Kūkai (774–835), such as his *Sangō shiiki* (printed in 1253), a comparative study of Buddhism, Confucianism, and Taoism. Kyoto temples began printing works related to their particular sect of Buddhism, sometimes in the form of facsimile editions of imported Chinese editions. One of the very few works to be printed in the Japanese language in these centuries was *Kurodani shōnin gotōroku* (printed in Kyoto in 1321), a collection of the sayings of the founder of the Pure Land sect of Buddhism in Japan.

Zen temples in Kyoto and Kamakura began printing in the late 13th century, but they were concerned less with the production of sutras than with printing collections of the sayings of Chinese, or occasionally Japanese, Zen masters. In 1367, eight Chinese Zen monks skilled in printing came to Kyoto at the request of Japanese monks and worked for some years as printers. Around a quarter of all the editions produced by Zen temples were of Chinese secular works, starting in 1325 with an edition of a collection of poems by a monk of the Tang dynasty. This, like many other such editions of Chinese works, was a facsimile of an imported Chinese edition.

The first canonical Chinese text printed in Japan was an edition of the Confucian *Analects* printed in the trading community of Sakai, south of Osaka, in 1364, and in 1481 Zhu Xi's commentary on the *Greater Learning* was printed in

Kagoshima. However, given the importance of Confucian texts for elite education, it has to be said that surprisingly few were printed before the 17th century. During the 16th century more and more Chinese secular works were being printed, but these were mostly dictionaries, guides to poetry composition, and medical texts.

Throughout this entire period from the 12th to 16th centuries, very few works of Japanese authorship were printed, with the principal exception of *Ōjō yōshū*, a treatise on the 'essentials for salvation', of which nine editions were printed between 1168 and 1600. The world of print was dominated in fact by Buddhist texts and texts in Chinese, and these required sophisticated Sinological literacy of their readers. There is little sign, therefore, of a book trade or of commercial publication at this stage.

In the late 16th century, Japan was brought into contact with two distinct typographical traditions, those of Europe and of Korea. As early as the 1540s, Francis Xavier had had some of his works translated into Japanese with a view to having them printed, but the printing activities of the Jesuit Mission in Japan did not commence until 1590, when the first European printing press was brought to Japan, to be followed later by others (*see* **9**). Although many of the publications of the Jesuit Mission press were deliberately burnt by Japanese authorities in 1626 in connection with the suppression of Christianity, it is clear that in fewer than 30 years around 100 titles were printed; fewer than 40 survive today, however, many in a single copy. Jesuit Mission printing included annual church calendars and various devotional works and classical authors in Latin—and, remarkably, some devotional works in a romanized transcription of Japanese as well. The casting of a Japanese fount made Japanese publications possible, too, and in 1592 the Jesuits printed part of the *Heike monogatari* (Tale of the Heike) in romanized transcription: this was the first work of Japanese literature to appear in print.

The Korean tradition of movable type (*see* **43**), which goes back to the 13th century, does not seem to have been transmitted to Japan until force intervened: as a result of the Japanese invasion of Korea in 1592–8, printed books were looted and a printing press with type was taken back to Japan and presented to Emperor Go-Yōzei. In 1593, the press was immediately put to use to print a Chinese text, the *Classic of Filial Piety*, the first book to be printed typographically in Japan by Japanese artisans.

In a sense, both of these developments stimulated printing in Japan, the Jesuits by printing Japanese literature and the printers working for the emperor or the shogun by printing secular Chinese works. However, since the Jesuit press was located in Kyushu, far from the centre of political power, and since all Christian missionaries were subject to persecution, it has long been assumed that Korean typography had the greater impact. Recent discoveries have nevertheless suggested that Jesuit printing techniques did have an influence that was subsequently denied by contemporaries for fear of being associated with a banned religion. Whatever the case, it is clear that these developments brought print out of the monasteries and gave it a secular purpose in Japan.

3 Print 1600–1868

In the 1590s, both the imperial household and Tokugawa Ieyasu, soon to be shogun, separately sponsored the preparation of large founts of wooden type and, then, the use of these founts for printing books. The *chokuhan*, or imperial editions, produced 1595–1621, were all secular works—at first Chinese works and then some works of Japanese authorship, such as the first two books of the *Nihon shoki* (Chronicles of Japan). Ieyasu, meanwhile, printed other Chinese secular texts and the *Azuma kagami* (Mirror of the East), a 13th-century Japanese chronicle. By this time, monasteries in and around Kyoto were also experimenting with typography (the oldest surviving imprint dates from 1595), and so were some private individuals, such as the physician Oze Hoan, who printed four Chinese medical works in 1596–7.

The most impressive typographic products of these early years were the so-called Sagabon, books printed in Saga, near Kyoto, between 1599 and 1610. The calligraphy and artistic direction were provided by the arbiter of taste Hon'ami Kōetsu; a merchant intellectual, Suminokura Soan (1571–1632), brought the organizational skills. Together they printed mostly Japanese texts, such as the *Ise monogatari* (Tales of Ise), the first Japanese secular book to be illustrated. Through the use of ligatures, their wooden types sought to reproduce the flow of calligraphy, and aesthetic effects were enhanced by the use of coloured and patterned papers. The art of the Japanese book had its beginnings here.

At what point a book trade can be talked of is unclear. Most of the works mentioned so far seem to have been printed in small numbers, and there is no evidence of commercial distribution. By the 1620s, however, there certainly were commercial publishers in operation, and they were printing for the market.

For the first half of the 17th century, typography and woodblock printing existed in tandem, and sometimes they were used together, as in the case of woodblock illustrations to typographic texts. These were decades of extraordinary productivity as most of the classic works were put into print for the first time. Take the case of the *Tale of Genji*: four typographic editions were printed between 1600 and 1644; in the 1650s the poet Yamamoto Shunshō put out a large-format illustrated edition that went through innumerable reprints and also appeared in other formats; and more than twenty editions of several condensed versions were published between 1651 and 1700. In addition, annotated editions of the *Tale of Genji* and other classics were published, making these difficult texts accessible in a linguistic sense as well. Reprinted classics were far from dominating production, however, and the range of books was vast. Sinological works such as the Four Books of the Confucian tradition, which formed the cornerstone of the education system, were a staple product, but the new printed editions differed from their predecessors and from Chinese editions in

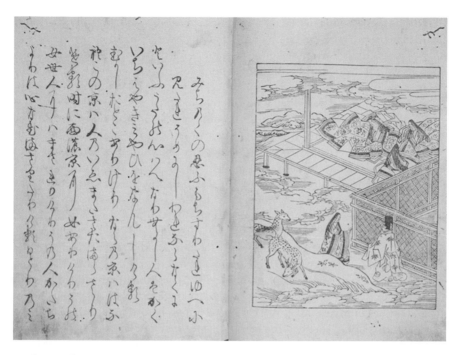

Sagabon production in 1608: *Ise monogatari* (The Tales of Ise). The books were the product of a collaboration between the merchant connoisseur Suminokura Soan and the artist and calligrapher Hon'ami Kōetsu. © The British Library Board. All Rights Reserved (Or. 64.c.36 1v-2)

being equipped with *kunten* (reading marks) which enabled Japanese readers to construe Chinese as if it were Japanese. In addition to these existing texts, there were also many new books, and increasingly books were being written with a view to being printed. These included new works of fiction, letter-writing manuals, and guide-books; most of them took advantage of the one feature that typography could not supply, namely woodblock illustrations, which became an indispensable part of almost all texts until the late 19th century.

By around 1650, however, all commercial publishers had abandoned typography and operated exclusively with woodblock printing. Was this a technological reversion? Why did it happen? For a number of very good reasons, typography could not at this stage compete. First, given the nature of the Japanese language, vast founts of type were needed to represent all the characters and *kana* signs, and since metallic type was too costly to contemplate for this purpose, wooden type dominated, although it was subject to splitting and movement in the frame; by contrast, woodblocks involved much less capital investment. Secondly, woodblocks suited the slower markets of the 17th century, for extra copies could be printed at will over years or decades, whereas typography proved less flexible. Thirdly, by the 1620s most publishers were producing books laden with *kunten* in the case of Chinese texts or, in the case of Japanese texts, with *kana* glosses beside the characters to indicate their pronunciation and thus make texts accessible to those with lower levels of literacy. There can be no doubt that it was far easier to incorporate these glosses in woodblock-printed works, to say nothing of the ease of including illustrations within the text. For commercial purposes, then, typography was dead by 1650, and did not revive until the mid-19th century; a small amount of private publishing continued to use wooden type, but the quantities were tiny.

As woodblock printing resumed its pride of place, publishers began to be more innovative and adventurous in their pursuit of the market. Periodicals and newspapers were unknown, but many types of publication had steady sales and required constant updating. One of these was maps and another was the samurai directories known as *bukan*. The cartographic knowledge acquired by the shogunal government in connection with its assertion of control over all the land of Japan acquired a commercial life of its own as publishers put out large, block-printed maps of cities, provinces, the whole of Japan, and even the world. One of the most significant maps was that of Japan produced in 1779 by Nagakubo Sekisui, a man of humble origins who achieved fame and position by means of his cartographic skills; his map of 1779 was the first in Japan to show lines of latitude and longitude and thus fix Japan's position on the globe in relation to other countries. Like other maps of Japan before modern times, it did not show Hokkaidō, which at the time was not considered part of Japan proper; the many reprints and cheap versions of this map testify to its lasting popularity as the most accurate map of Japan available. All printed maps carried information in the form of text as well, and labelling included the names of prominent officials; to keep them constantly up to date, therefore, it was necessary to make frequent alterations to the printing blocks by excising text and replacing it with plugs of wood on which the new text was cut.

Bukan, on the other hand, were samurai directories—exhaustive lists of officials, giving details of rank, office, heraldic symbols, notional income, and so on. These details were naturally subject to incessant change, and the publishers usually indicated that they revised the texts every month to keep them up to date. The same applied to other such directories, such as the *Yoshiwara saiken*, or guides to the Yoshiwara-licensed quarter listing all the brothels and the courtesans, and the *unjō meiran*, guides to the Kyoto aristocracy. Print made all this knowledge public and indiscriminately available, but its susceptibility to change made these directories and maps a profitable staple for publishers in Edo.

Most publishers sought to produce a wide variety of wares, with Sinology and Buddhist texts at one end and popular fiction at the other, and in between niche publications like medical textbooks, flower arrangement manuals, poetry collections, and so forth. As early as the 1660s, there was a growing sense that printed books had become a flood, and in an attempt to bring order to the undifferentiated mass of books already on the market, the booksellers in Kyoto clubbed together to produce catalogues listing books in print according to a number of categories. The first of these appeared in the 1660s, and it was succeeded every five or ten years for over a century. These catalogues became both

A book- and printseller's premises in the Edo period, illustrated in the first volume of *Edo meisho zue* ('The Famous Places of Edo', 1834–6): the project was initiated by Saitō Nagaaki and illustrated by Hasegawa Settan. © The British Library Board. All Rights Reserved (16114.b.1)

increasingly sophisticated in their classification systems and more detailed, giving even book prices in some cases. It was at this time that some publishers were appending notices at the end of their publications listing other books they had for sale, indicating a growing awareness of the market. By the late 17th century, there were the beginnings of a booksellers' guild in existence in Kyoto, but it was not recognized by the authorities until 1716. This was followed by the acknowledgement of similar guilds in Osaka in 1723 and Edo in 1725; the only provincial guild was that of Nagoya, which was recognized in 1798. The shogunal government was not enthusiastic about the establishment of trade guilds, but perceived them to be a necessary evil in order to limit the scope for copyright disputes. Until the late 19th century, copyright lay with publishers, not with authors, and the most common cause of legal disputes was copyright infringement. The establishment of guilds reduced the number of cases within any one publishing centre, but did not stop disputes between publishers in different cities: thus, when an Osaka publisher put out a collected edition of Tang poetry in 1751, it was found that this replicated a book produced by an Edo publisher, and so he lost not only the copies he had printed but also his printing blocks. The guilds did not prevent such cases occurring, but they did provide a mechanism for resolving inter-city disputes like this. The guilds served one other important function as well, and that was the delegated role of censor.

Until the Edo period, censorship had been virtually unknown in Japan; there were none of the book burnings or systems of control found in earlier ages in China. There were, it is true, two or three cases of books causing offence in Japan before 1600, but these were MSS, and it is not until the Edo period that printed books began to come under scrutiny. What first prompted this scrutiny was not the development of a publishing industry in Japan, but the importation of Chinese books written by Matteo Ricci and other European missionaries in China. By this time Christianity had been proscribed in Japan, but among the imported books was a book by Ricci refuting Buddhism and justifying Christianity, as well as other books that had nothing to do with Christianity except that they were written by missionaries and concerned Europe, such as a study of European irrigation. In 1630, an edict was issued banning 32 named books of this sort, and the list was later extended. By the end of the century, a bureau was in operation in Nagasaki to check the cargoes of all incoming Chinese ships to make sure that they were not carrying any of the proscribed books or similar works. The efficiency of this bureau kept offending books out of the official trade, but could not prevent smuggling; the detailed bureaucratic records now give a good idea of what books were legally imported to Japan and when. This system of import censorship remained rigidly in force until the 1720s when the Shogun Yoshimune, who was a man of scientific curiosity, relaxed the ban to permit books written by Jesuits to enter Japan so long as they were not about Christianity, so that their writings on astronomy could be of benefit to Japanese scholars.

There was no censorship legislation aimed at domestically published books in the first half of the 17th century, but that does not mean that no censorship was exercised. It is clear from a number of book bannings that the two taboo subjects were Christianity and Toyotomi Hideyoshi (1536–98), the hegemon who had preceded Tokugawa Ieyasu and whose heirs were considered by some to have been cheated by Ieyasu. In 1657 in Kyoto and in 1673 in Edo, the authorities at last took cognizance of the rising tide of publications, and of the possibility that some might have undesirable contents, by issuing the first censorship edicts. These were vaguely worded, prohibiting books that depicted the Shogun and the samurai class (whether favourably or not) and books that dealt with matters 'unusual', meaning scandals and sensational events; nothing was said about policing. By 1682, public notice boards were warning people against handling 'unsound' books, but this did nothing to stem the tide, for news-sheets were gaining in popularity, especially after the sensational case in 1703 of the 47 samurai who avenged their master by slaughtering his high-ranking aggressor and were then forced to commit ritual suicide. An Osaka publisher put out a book on these events in 1719, fully aware that punishment would follow, but convinced that if he could sell half his copies good money could be made; he and the author had to spend some time under house arrest as a result, but the book reached the public and MS copies were made to satisfy continuing demand.

It was finally in the 1720s that legislation was issued laying down the guidelines that were to govern censorship for the remainder of the Edo period. In future, all publications were to carry the real names of the author and publisher in the colophon, and the guilds were to be responsible for ensuring that publications by members did not contravene the law. Since the guilds now enjoyed monopolistic publishing privileges recognized by the authorities, they had little choice but to cooperate. Needless to say, these new arrangements did not prevent daring publishers from publishing books without colophons, and erotic books in particular took this strategy, even sometimes ridiculing the law by appending lewd parodic colophons. The major difficulty for the guilds, however, lay in understanding just what constituted 'undesirable' books; for the most part they seem to have erred on the side of caution, but in the 1790s and the 1830s there were crackdowns that caught the guilds unawares and led to punishments not only for the publishers and authors but also for the guild officials responsible.

The censorship system was never effectively policed and many publications slipped under the net, but the timidity of the guilds ensured that few risks were taken with books that went through the normal procedures. On the other hand, some publishers became adept at finding ways around the law, by omitting colophons altogether or resorting to MS publication, for selling books remained their business.

From the early decades of the 17th century, publishers had been striving to make their books more attractive and accessible to readers. One practice that soon became ubiquitous was the inclusion of small *kana* glosses alongside characters to indicate the pronunciation; this initially constituted a service to readers with a limited grasp of characters, but it later became a means for playful or ironic use of the glosses to subvert the sense of the characters. Similarly ubiquitous was the use of illustrations, which formed an indispensable part of all literary works; some authors produced their own illustrations, some made sketches in their MSS to indicate to the artist the kind of illustration required, and others still teamed up with famous artists such as Utamaro (1759–1806) and Hokusai (1760–1849), to produce books in demand both for the text and for the illustrations. Almost all *ukiyoe* (woodblock print) artists undertook book illustration, and so highly was their work regarded that from the middle of the 17th century publishers were already producing *ehon*, books consisting solely or almost entirely of illustrations. By the end of the 18th century the development of colour printing made it possible to print exquisite books like Utamaro's *Ehon mushierami* (Picture Book of a Selection of Insects, 1788) in which close observation made possible by imported microscopes was married with Utamaro's skills as a graphic artist. In the 19th century, artists like Hokusai were as busy with book illustration as they were with single-sheet prints, and Hokusai's illustrations for the historical novels of Kyokutei Bakin were as successful as his own picture books, such as his famous *manga* books.

In the 17th century, books were generally expensive and sales of more than 2,000 indicated a bestselling book. The catalogues produced by the booksellers' guilds in 1681, 1696, and 1709 all provide prices; and although these were subject to variation depending upon the quality of the paper and the covers, they provide a glimpse of the relative cost of books at the end of the century. The *Ise monogatari*, one of the most popular works of classical literature, was usually published with illustrations in two volumes, and these rarely cost more than 2 *monme*; by comparison, the normal daily wage of day-labourers at this time was 1.5 *monme*, so books were becoming more affordable. In the course of the 18th century, some kinds of fiction were being produced in small illustrated booklets with poor calligraphy, and these sold for very low prices. Multi-volume works of fiction, with better calligraphy and finer illustrations, inevitably cost more, but again the price was lower for copies printed on paper of poorer quality.

Readers did not necessarily have to purchase books, however. Diaries, letters, and notations in surviving copies attest to the widespread practice of borrowing books from neighbours. This was particularly common in rural communities or in cities far from Edo or Kyoto where the supply of books could not be relied upon until the 19th century. It was also common for borrowers to make copies by hand of books they did not own, or to hire an amanuensis to do so, and this practice survived until the late 19th century.

A particularly important means of gaining access to books, almost everywhere in Japan, was the circulating library, or *kashihon'ya*. Unlike their European counterparts, these generally consisted of men carrying their stocks around on their backs, visiting their regular customers and collecting payment in arrears. They were definitely operating in Kyoto and Edo by the late 17th century, and it is clear that by the late 18th century they were working in most castle towns throughout Japan and in hot-spring resorts and similar places of leisure. Some of them were independent businesses specializing in book lending, but others were an arm of bookselling firms seeking to extend their customer base by taking books for sale or rent into the rural environs of big cities. For the most part their stock was dominated by current fiction, but they also carried illicit MSS, travel guides, and other non-fiction. The largest of them all, Daisō in Nagoya (founded in 1767), had a stock of 20,000 books with sometimes as many as six copies of a single title in the case of illicit MSS; unusually, Daisō took the form of a shop rather than a delivery service.

Before the Edo period, Japan had made strenuous efforts at various times to maintain the flow of books from the mainland—mostly China, but also Korea. By the early 17th century, the quantity of Chinese works that had already been transmitted to Japan was huge, ranging from Buddhist and Confucian texts to Tang poetry, neo-Confucian texts of the Song dynasty, and the colloquial fiction of the Ming dynasty. This flow of books did not cease in the Edo period, even though there were no direct diplomatic relations between the shogunate and the rulers of the Qing dynasty that assumed power in China in 1644. The trade was conducted at Nagasaki, the only port open to foreign ships, at the initiative of Chinese merchants, and all imports were carefully examined and registered by shogunal officials before being offered for sale. The number of ships varied from year to year, reaching a peak of 193 in 1688, and not all of them carried books.

In the middle of the 19th century, after China's humiliation in the first Opium War (1840–42), imports from China assumed a new importance as Japan sought to avoid China's fate. Particularly important were two works by Wei Yuan on the threats that the Western barbarians posed: they were not only imported, for in the 1850s countless Japanese editions, at first in the original Chinese and then in Japanese translation, were published. These provided information about the Western nations who were encroaching ever more frequently on East Asian waters and about how they might be repulsed—issues which were of prime importance following the arrival in Japan of ships from America and Russia in the summer of 1853.

Of increasing significance, too, were the Dutch books imported into Japan. By the middle of the 17th century, the Dutch were the only Europeans remaining in Japan, the Portuguese and Spanish having been expelled and the English having withdrawn. The Dutch were confined to the man-made island of Deshima in Nagasaki harbour, and were subject to more stringent controls than the Chinese. Knowledge of Dutch was largely limited, in the 17th century, to the official interpreters, who seem to have had little intellectual curiosity. Nevertheless, it was in that century that the flow of books from Holland to Japan began. As early as 1650, the shogunal government had placed an order with the Dutchmen for a book on dissection, and over the succeeding decades there are records of other books being presented to the shogun, including Rembert Dodoens's herbal in the 1618 Dutch edition and a zoological treatise. In the 18th century, interest in Dutch books gradually spread, to some extent with shogunal encouragement, and a school of learning known as Rangaku (Dutch studies) began to make increasing contributions to Japanese intellectual life.

In 1771 Sugita Genpaku, a doctor with an interest in Western science, was shown an imported copy of a Dutch edition of J. A. Kulmus's *Anatomical Tables* and, although he could not read the text, he was impressed by the detailed illustrations. With a group of like-minded scholars, he proceeded to carry out a dissection to test their accuracy, and having concluded that Chinese and Japanese conceptions of the workings of the body were not empirically based like those of Kulmus, he enlisted the help of Maeno Ryōtaku (1723–1803) and others to produce a translation. This was completed in 1774 and published under the title *Kaitai shinsho* (New Book of Anatomy). This book, of which a copy was tactfully presented to the shogun, legitimized Dutch studies and stimulated interest in Dutch books. (It should be remembered, however, that many of these Dutch books were, like the Kulmus, in fact Dutch translations of books published first in other languages.) Thereafter, the Dutchmen were requested to bring more medical and scientific books, and in the 19th century books on military science as well. In this way, a thin but steady stream of imports introduced empirical science to Japan and familiarized Japanese with European science and medicine well before the so-called opening of Japan in 1854.

From the 1850s onwards, it became easier to acquire Western books as foreigners began to settle and trade in the treaty ports of Yokohama and Kobe.

However, the numbers of Japanese with a reading knowledge of any European language other than Dutch was insignificant, and it was only in the late 1870s that proficiency in English, French, German, and Russian grew to the point that it was worthwhile for the Maruzen bookshop in Tokyo to stock some foreign titles.

4 Print since 1868

The Meiji Restoration of 1868 had no immediate effect on print and publication except in the area of censorship, for the first efforts were made in that year to initiate a rigorous system of pre-publication censorship. A new word, *kankyo* (government permission), was introduced to make it clear that the government, rather than the guilds, was now to determine permission to publish. Already in that year news magazines had vigorously opposed the new government—most of them had been banned and closed down before the end of the year. As the government's authoritarian tendencies became clearer in the 1870s and opposition became more strident, the regulations became ever more severe until in 1875 new laws were drawn up on the French model, which held newspaper editors criminally responsible for the contents of their newspapers and made it impossible to publish books deemed to be damaging to public peace or morals. In the same year, the notorious Libel Law made it an offence to publish matters that reflected badly on members of the government, even if they happened to be true.

The technology of commercial print continued to be dominated by woodblock printing up to the 1880s. Metallic movable type had been reintroduced in the 1850s and was favoured for translations of Western books and for new works of fiction, but in the 1880s it became the dominant technology, except for Buddhist sutras, which continued to be printed with woodblocks. Many of the publishers of the Edo period proved unable to cope with the shift in technology and closed their doors in the 1880s, but some, like Murakami Kanbei of Kyoto, weathered the storm and survive to this day.

The government reversed the policy of the Tokugawa shoguns and adopted a public presence in the world of print by launching an official gazette, the *Dajōkan nisshi*, in 1868 to make public the texts of government decrees. At first this was printed with woodblocks, but the government then established in the Ministry of Works an office for the casting of type for the use of the agencies of central and local government and the Imperial University (founded in 1877). Following the government's lead, others founded newspapers, too; the first daily was *Kankyo Yokohama Shinbun* (Government-Permitted Yokohama Newspaper), which was founded in 1870 and switched from woodblocks to typography in 1873.

Circulating libraries continued to flourish in the Meiji period and continued to offer customers the fiction of the early 19th century; some, however, began to advertise newspapers, textbooks, and even books in English on scientific or professional subjects with a view to attracting students at the new educational institutions. Japanese who travelled to the West in the 1860s reported on the provision of public libraries which were free at the point of access; from the

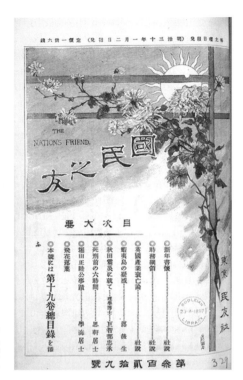

The cover of an 1897 issue of the journal
Kokumin no tomo (The Nation's Friend).
The Bodleian Library, University of
Oxford (Per. Jap. E. 39, cover)

desire to emulate Western practices sprang Japan's first public library, which was established by the ministry of education in 1872. Although this institution started charging fees in 1885, public libraries were founded throughout Japan in the early 20th century. Nevertheless, circulating libraries survived by offering their customers fiction, and later *manga* (comics), for the public libraries disdained to stock these categories of book.

The first decades of the Meiji period saw the emergence of a flood of periodicals, including women's literary journals such as *Jogaku zasshi* (Journal of Women's Learning, 1885–1904) and influential political magazines such as *Kokumin no tomo* (The Nation's Friend, 1887–98). Other new forms of publication were translations of Western writings on law and medicine and translations of Western literature, including the novels of Disraeli and Sir Walter Scott. At the same time, however, the literature of the Edo period had not been forgotten: many works were frequently reprinted typographically, albeit inevitably without the illustrations, testifying to their lasting appeal.

Towards the end of the 1880s, new publishing firms began to replace the older businesses that had failed to adapt to the new world of typography, steam power, and modern business methods. One of these new firms was Hakubunkan (1887–1947), which established a presence with a succession of strikingly new magazines and was soon the leading publishing house in Japan. The first of these magazines was *Nihon taika ronshû* (Essays by Leading Japanese), founded in 1887, in which the issues discussed ranged from literature to medicine and hygiene. In 1894, upon the outbreak of the Sino-Japanese War, Hakubunkan produced the first photo magazine, *Nisshin sensō jikki* (True Record of the Sino-Japanese War), and the following year launched *Taiyō* (Sun), a bestselling general magazine. The firm was also making its mark with major publishing projects, such as an encyclopaedia in 1889 and from 1893 *Teikoku Bunko* (Library of the Empire), a series of 100 volumes containing the major literary works of the Edo period presented without their illustrations as if they conformed to the conventions for current novels.

By the late 19th century, Japanese publishing had caught up technologically with Europe and North America, and the reading public's appetite for new journals was unabated. A number of these have enjoyed remarkable longevity, such as *Chūō Kōron*, (The Central Review), which had its origins in a temperance magazine founded in 1887. In 1899, its name was changed and it became a serious journal containing an offering of literature and comment. It took a liberal stance, and in 1944 was suspended at army insistence following the publication of an article that was judged damaging to the war effort; it resumed publication in 1946. Another was *Bungei Shunjū* (Literary Times), founded by the prominent writer Kikuchi Hiroshi in 1923 and still influential today; it supports the Akutagawa Prize, the most prestigious prize for works of fiction in Japan. There were also important mass-market magazines aimed at women readers, such as *Katei no tomo* (The Family's Friend, from 1903) and *Shufu no tomo* (The Housewife's Friend, from 1917).

In the 1930s, censorship became ever more severe: a left-wing writer, Kobayashi Takiji, was brutally murdered by the police, and all left-wing journals were forced to cease publishing. Under the US occupation, which lasted from 1945 to 1952, wartime censorship controls came to an end, though criticism of the Occupation authorities was not permitted in public media, and left-wingers again came under pressure during the Cold War. Nevertheless, the more liberal atmosphere encouraged a resurgence, and new magazines were launched with information about Western fashions or ways of life.

Two of the leading publishers in Japan today are Kōdansha and Shōgakukan. Kōdansha was founded in 1909 and continues to dominate the Japanese publishing world, although in 2002 it recorded an overall loss for the first time since 1945. Today, it is known for a clutch of serious magazines as well as for its large stable of *manga* magazines. Kōdansha International publishes books in English and other languages on Japanese culture and society, often translated from Japanese originals. Shōgakukan is also active as a publisher of *manga* and, together with a subsidiary, owns Viz Media, which publishes, among other things, English versions of Japanese *manga*. *Manga* remain a prominent feature of popular culture, and have shrugged off accusations that they are violent, sexist, and racist; the rise of the Japanese animation film, or *anime*, has generated new tie-ins for *manga* publishers.

In spite of the popularity of *manga*, they are by no means all there is to Japanese publishing today. Every bookshop stocks large numbers of the small and modestly priced paperbacks known as *bunkobon*, which provide easy access to Japanese literature old and new, to foreign literature in translation, to books on contemporary issues, and so on. Bunkobon were first introduced to the reading public in 1927 when Iwanami Shoten launched their series. Iwanami, which was founded in 1913, is now a respected academic publisher responsible for a number of academic journals; the firm has issued the standard editions of many works of classical Japanese literature and has published several editions of the complete works of Natsume Sōseki (1867–1916), one of the leading novelists of modern Japan.

There is much talk of a crisis in Japanese publishing and of a move away from print—the latter is seen to be behind the decreasing circulation figures of daily newspapers. It is also true that there has been a decline in sales of new books and in the number of bookshops (though there are still more than 8,000). On the other hand, the number of new titles published each year has continued to rise (74,000 in 2002), and when a translation of J. K. Rowling's *Harry Potter and the Goblet of Fire* was published in Japan, the first printing was of 2.3 million copies. This may suggest that Japanese publishing follows global trends, but the globalization of Japanese books still has a long way to go. It may be easier to buy them now in London or Seoul, but while many foreign books are published in Japanese translation, very few Japanese books are translated into other languages, except a handful of literary works into European languages and some academic or political books into Korean or Chinese.

....

BIBLIOGRAPHY

M. E. Berry, *Japan in Print: Information and Nation in the Early Modern Period* (2006)

J. Hillier, *The Art of the Japanese Book* (1988)

P. F. Kornicki, *The Book in Japan* (1998)

—— 'Block-Printing in Seventeenth-Century Japan: Evidence from a Newly Discovered Medical Text', in *Print Areas: Book History in India*, ed. A. Gupta and S. Chakravorty (2004)

—— 'Manuscript, not Print: Scribal Culture in the Edo Period', *Journal of Japanese Studies*, 32 (2006), 23–52

E. May, *Die Kommerzialisierung der japanischen Literatur in der späten Edo-Zeit* (1983)

R. Mitchell, *Censorship in Imperial Japan* (1983)

G. Richter 1997, 'Entrepreneurship and Culture: the Hakubunkan Publishing Empire in Meiji Japan', in *New Directions in the Study of Meiji Japan*, ed. H. Hardacre and A. L. Kern (1997)

H. Smith, 'The History of the Book in Edo and Paris', in *Edo and Paris: Urban Life and the State in the Early Modern Era*, ed. J. McLain *et al.* (1994)

K. Yamashita, *Japanese Maps of the Edo Period* (1998)

The History of the Book in Southeast Asia (1): The Islands

EDWIN PAUL WIERINGA

1 General introduction

The region of insular or maritime Southeast Asia, which today comprises six young nation-states, encompasses not only hundreds of languages and literatures but also quite different cultural and political backgrounds. Indonesia (independence: 1945), Malaysia (independence: 1957), and Brunei (independence: 1984) are countries with Muslim majorities, whereas the populations of East Timor (officially Timor-Leste; independence: 2002) and the Philippines (with the exception of the Islamic South; independence from Spain declared in 1898, but only achieving sovereignty from the US in 1946) are predominantly Roman Catholic. The city-state of Singapore (independence: 1965), previously a British colony and part of Malaysia, is often referred to as a 'Chinese enclave' by its neighbours.

Until the 20th century, the overwhelming majority of the myriad language communities in this region were pre-literate. However, most of them have rich and varied oral traditions. It has been argued that even in the 'literate' societies—such as among the Malay-speaking group—oral habits still persist in written composition. Whereas reading is normally a silent and private activity in present-day Western societies, literature is often still reproduced orally and publicly in maritime Southeast Asia.

This region is home to some of the world's oldest and richest literatures. For example, the earliest inscription in Old Javanese is dated AD 25 March 804, and the first dated poem in Old Javanese idiom, composed in Indian metres, is preserved in a stone inscription, dated AD 856. Probably the longest literary work in the world is found in South Sulawesi: an old Buginese epic, known as *I La Galigo*, telling the story of the mythical ancestors and founders of the local kingdoms. Its size is estimated at *c*.6,000 folio pages.

The history of the book in maritime Southeast Asia is beset with gaping lacunae, not least because writings on perishable materials of plant origin such as palm leaf and bamboo rarely survived the centuries. Most pre-19th-century MSS have fallen victim to unfavourable climatic conditions, while fire, floods, and vermin also have taken their toll. Moreover, the tsunami of 26 December 2004 almost completely destroyed several important library holdings in Aceh, North Sumatra.

2 Writing systems

Three kinds of writing system successively entered maritime Southeast Asia: Indic, Arabic, and roman scripts. For the period before the 16th century, the only reliably dated sources of information are haphazard stone and metal-plate inscriptions. The earliest known inscriptions are in Sanskrit on seven stone pillars in what is now the Kutai region in East Kalimantan, dated to the 4th century, and described as (early) Pallawa script. Pallawa script as found in various parts of the archipelago is a lithic script used for monumental purposes.

By the middle of the 8th century, a rounder and more cursive script, called Kawi or Old Javanese, begins to appear in inscriptions. Apparently, Kawi was intended for writing on palm leaves. Different styles of Indic scripts in the archipelago have been identified, especially for the 13th–15th centuries, but the paucity of inscriptions does not allow an exact reconstruction of the expansion of writing systems.

Around the 16th century, four families of Indic scripts can be distinguished in Indonesia: Batak, South Sumatran, Javanese-Balinese, and Bugis-Makasar. These four related but distinct Indic writing systems are syllabaries, in which the letters represent consonants with the inherent vowel /a/, altered by adding dots or dashes. The interrelationship between them is still shrouded in mystery. In 2002 a Malay tree-bark MS, said to date from the second half of the 14th century, was discovered in Kerinci, South Sumatra. Intriguingly, however, this text—known as 'The Tanjung Tanah Code of Law'—is written in a script strongly resembling 17th- or even 18th-century Javanese script.

Following the advent of Islam in the 13th century, Arabic script was adopted for writing several Austronesian languages (*see* **40**). Malay was almost exclusively written in a modified version of the Arabic script called Jawi, whereas the use of the Javanese version of the Arabic script called Pégon was generally reserved for writing religious texts.

The Europeans, who entered the region in the 16th century, championed the use of roman script. Dedicated to translating the Bible into indigenous languages, Christian missionaries were especially active in employing this script. Its use in printing gave roman script an overpowering advantage, strongly supported in the 19th and 20th centuries by colonial governments. In the 20th century, roman script became the accepted medium for the public sphere throughout the entire region. In the Philippines, Indic syllabaries closely connected to the Indic scripts in Indonesia had been in use before the 16th century, but under the Spanish colonial system roman script rapidly superseded the ancient Philippine alphabets.

3 Dating systems

Ancient systems of chronology—intimately associated with agriculture and astrology—have been identified among several maritime Southeast Asian peoples. These age-old and now obsolete calendars manifest a strong Indian influence. For example, the Batak possess a chronological system imbued with Sanskrit-derived terminology that is used to find auspicious moments. Regional versions of the octaval calendar, a rather simple system based on an eight-year cycle, have enjoyed great popularity among the Muslim communities of maritime Southeast Asia for ages, but nowadays outside Java its workings are forgotten. The modernization process which forcefully set in around the turn of the 20th century has promoted a globalization of time-reckoning: modern printed books bear imprints with dates in the Christian era, whereas Islamic publications follow the calendrical practices of the Middle East.

4 Book forms

Although almost all writings before *c.*1500 are inscriptions engraved in stone or metal (with hardly any surviving MSS), after that date there are only a few inscriptions, but many MSS. In the pre-modern period, two traditions of writing stemming from different cultural sources can readily be discerned: an 'Indianized' tradition, bringing with it a syllabic script and a tradition of using palm leaves; and an Islamic tradition originating in Western Asia, bringing with it an Arabic script and a tradition of writing on paper.

Before paper was introduced, palm leaf was the most popular writing material, and in the Javanese-Balinese tradition its use continues today, especially in Bali. Most widely used are the leaves of the *lontar*-palm (*Borassus flabellifer* or *flabelliformis*); a MS consisting of a bundle of these leaves is also called *lontar*. Both sides of the leaf are incised with a knife, and the script is then blackened with lampblack. The leaves are bound in bundles by string through a central hole. A coin with a hole is knotted at the end of the string, which is then wound around the boards, holding the leaves together. Important texts were kept in wooden boxes, sometimes beautifully painted and carved. The leaf of the *nipah*-palm (*Nipa fruticans*) is thinner than that of the commonly used *lontar*, and is usually inscribed with a pen or writing brush and ink.

In South Sulawesi the common word for MS is *lontaraq*, clearly a borrowing from Javanese/Malay *lontar*. A few extant palm-leaf MSS from this region have a singular shape in that they look like audio or video cassettes: their contents are written on rolled-up palm leaves, and by unwinding the roll the text 'unfolds' before the reader's eyes between the two reels, not unlike a scroll. However, such palm-leaf examples are rare; all other MSS from South Sulawesi, written by the Bugis, Makasarese, and Mandarese peoples, are on paper, almost exclusively European.

In Sumatra, the Batak used the inner bark of the *alim* tree (*Acquilaria malaccensis*) for their folding-book MSS, characteristically folded in concertina fashion. The bark books, generally characterized as 'books of divination', used to be compiled by magicians and healers. However, people outside the priestly circle also crafted MSS, using bamboo to write letters and lamentations. South Sumatran MSS, which are written on bark, bamboo, rattan sticks, and goat or buffalo horn, also reflect an ancient writing tradition that antedates Islam in Sumatra. The oldest specimen of a South Sumatran MS is a tree-bark book in Lampung script containing a version of the Malay *Hikayat Nur Muhammad* (Story of the Muhammadan Light), presented to the Bodleian Library, Oxford, in 1630 (MS Jav. e. 2).

The use of paper is closely associated with the spread of Islam from the 13th century onwards. In this respect it is a telling fact that nearly all Malay MSS have been written on paper, known as *kertas*, a loanword from Arabic. By the 18th and 19th centuries, the high-quality products of European paper mills were eagerly imported in the archipelago. Today, paper is the most widely used material for all writing. With the advent of printing and machine-made paper (*see* **10**), the age-old traditions of MS writing were practically discontinued.

5 Printed books

The introduction of print in the region is intertwined with European colonial involvement. The first book printed in the Philippines was the *Doctrina Christiana en lengua española y tagala* in 1593, explicating basic Roman Catholic teachings in Spanish and Tagalog, written by Friar Juan de Plasencia, and printed with woodblocks (xylography) in Manila. The only known surviving copy is in the Library of Congress (Rosenwald 1302). Until the late 19th century, printing presses were owned and run by Roman Catholic orders. After Spain ceded the Philippines to the US in 1898, English was to become the language of government and education. Books in Tagalog generally have a nationalist outlook.

In the Indonesian archipelago, the Dutch East India Company issued a printed Malay translation of the Bible in 1629, but only from the 19th century onwards would the impact of European printing make itself felt. The puzzling question of the 'delayed' use of printing by Muslims is still unclear. The jealousy of scribes is sometimes mentioned among the reasons for this reticence, as well as an aversion to the mechanical reproduction of books dealing with God's word, but inadequate capital must also have played a considerable role. The invention of lithography by Alois Senefelder around 1797 paved the way for a revolution in the Islamic book world (*see* **40**). Lithographed books ideally fitted the traditional views on the art of book production, carefully preserving the form of MSS, while the newly available technique needed much lower capital investment than printing with movable type.

The British missionary Walter Henry Medhurst (1796–1857) seems to have been the first person to use lithographic printing in maritime Southeast Asia. His lithographic press in Batavia (Jakarta) printed texts in Malay-Arabic, Javanese, and Chinese scripts. The Revd Benjamin Peach Keasberry, who learned about printing from Medhurst, established a printing office in Singapore in 1839, working together with the Malay language teacher and writer Abdullah bin Abdul Kadir Munshi. Abdullah Munshi has been called the 'father of Malay printing'. During the 1840s and 1850s collaboration between Keasberry and Abdullah Munshi resulted in a number of printed Malay books, of which Abdullah's own autobiography, *Hikayat Abdullah* (Abdullah's Story, 1849), brought its author lasting fame.

The first known Islamic printed book in the archipelago was an edition of the Qur'ān published in Palembang in 1848. A Malay version of a devotional text in praise of the Prophet Muḥammad was printed in Surabaya in 1853. The third lithographic press in the archipelago was established in the 1850s at the Buginese-Malay court on the island of Penyengat in Riau. By the 1860s, Singapore emerged as the region's Muslim printing centre. Its printing industry was run by a few men from the north coast of Java. In Singapore they were not subjected to the highly restrictive Dutch press laws, and could take advantage of the city's strategic position as the most important assembly point for the increasing number of Southeast Asian pilgrims in transit to Mecca.

At the beginning of the 20th century, however, the Singapore book printers' position was challenged by imported, better-quality products from Bombay (Mumbai) and the Middle East. In 1884, the Meccan-based *ulama* (Islamic scholar) Ahmad bin Muḥammad Zayn from Patani became the supervisor of the Malay press established in Mecca under the auspices of the Ottoman government. Understandably, works of Malay scholars from the region of Patani in southern Thailand were most numerously represented in the Meccan editions.

In the gradual transition from MS to print, two decisive streams of printing activity may be distinguished. On the one hand, Islamic printing mainly reproduced texts belonging to the traditional Arabic-script MS literature. On the other hand, the European and Chinese printing presses created a new Malay literature in roman script. In the 20th century, book production was increasingly based on type. The Dutch colonial government set up its own bureau for popular literature in 1908, known as Balai Pustaka (Institute of Belles-Lettres), which actively attempted to transform Indonesian writing traditions in accordance with modern Western tastes. This institution had a tremendous influence upon the development of the Malay language used in Indonesia, which came to be known as 'Indonesian' (Bahasa Indonesia). The Malay Translation Bureau, established by the British in the Malay Peninsula at about the same time, was far less successful. However, in independent Malaysia the governmental Dewan Bahasa dan Pustaka (Language and Literature Agency), established in 1956, plays a powerful role in promoting Malay as the national language.

Print caused an explosion in the amount of reading material: already in the 1860s the number of books produced by one Singapore printer in one year equalled the estimated number of all Malay MSS extant (*c*.10,000 items). The mass production and distribution of texts greatly augmented the reading audience and broadened its composition. However, the oft-made claim of the so-called 'literacy thesis'—that literacy, the technology of writing and printing, develops a 'modern' mentality, transforming ways of thinking and representations of tradition—is debatable. Although the proliferation of print is generally regarded as the driving force of 'modernity', the fact that the new print media were not exclusively a 'modernizing' domain is easily overlooked. 'Traditionalists', too, crossed the print threshold, indicating that print *per se* did not necessarily change time-honoured thinking and received wisdom. Undeniably, however, print technology was to play a formative role in shaping public

A printing press above a Malay advertisement for the printer in Tanah Abang (a sub-district of Central Jakarta, Indonesia), from Haji Adam's 1926 booklet *Syair Mikraj Nabi Muhammad SAW* ('Poem on the Ascension of the Prophet Muḥammad, peace be upon him'). Private collection Professor E. P. Wieringa, Cologne

discourse and in forging different 'imagined communities' of people sharing the same world view.

....

BIBLIOGRAPHY

B. Anderson, *Imagined Communities* (1983)

T. E. Behrend and W. van der Molen, eds., 'Manuscripts of Indonesia', *Bijdragen tot de Taal-, Land- en Volkenkunde*, 149.3 (1993)

D. D. Buhain, *A History of Publishing in the Philippines* (1998)

P. Herbert and A. Milner, eds., *South-East Asia* (1988)

H. C. Kemp, *Oral Traditions of Southeast Asia and Oceania: A Bibliography* (2004)

A. Kumar and J. H. McGlynn, eds., *Illuminations: The Writing Traditions of Indonesia* (1996)

J. H. McGlynn, ed., *Language and Literature* (1998)

Asmah Haji Omar, ed., *Languages and Literature* (2004)

J. de Plasencia, *Doctrina Christiana en lengua española y tagala* (1593), www.lcweb2.loc.gov/cgibin/ampage?collId=rbc3&fileName=rbc0001_2002rosen1302page.db, consulted Sept. 2007

I. Proudfoot, *Early Malay Printed Books* (1993)

A. Sweeney, *A Full Hearing* (1987)

The History of the Book in Southeast Asia (2): The Mainland

JANA IGUNMA

1 Writing systems

The development of writing and dating systems in mainland Southeast Asia is connected with the spread of Hinduism, Buddhism, Confucianism, and Christianity in this area. The first writing system was *chû' nho'*, Classical Chinese, which was the official writing system when Vietnam was under direct Chinese rule (111 BC–AD 938). In the 13th century, *chû' nôm*, a system based on *chú nho*, was developed to write the Vietnamese language. It consisted of orthodox Chinese characters supplemented by a set of new characters specifically created to write Vietnamese words. The situation was complicated, however, as constant close contact with the Chinese produced layers of Chinese vocabulary in varying degrees of Vietnamese naturalization, and the most highly naturalized words were accepted as Vietnamese. In the 19th century, both *chû' nho'* and *chû' nôm* were replaced by *quôc ngû'*, a system developed by Portuguese Jesuit missionaries in the 17th century based on the Latin alphabet. *Quôc ngû'* is still used to write Vietnamese and several languages of minority subgroups as well.

From the 6th to 8th centuries, a growing Indian cultural influence led to the creation of writing systems based on Indic scripts belonging to the Brahmi family (*see* **41**). Khmer script is known to date back to the 6th century. Among the several styles of Khmer script are *'aksar chrĭĕng* (slanted script), *'aksar chhŏr* (upright script), *'aksar mūl* (round script), and *'aksar khǭ'm* (a variation of round script). Khmer script was also used at the Thai royal court until the late 19th century.

Burmese script, as a descendant of the extinct Mon script, has been attested as early as the 12th century. It is used to write the Burmese language, as well as languages of the Karen, Taungthu, and Mon people in Burma. A variation of Burmese is used to write modern Shan.

Thai script descended from the Brahmi script through its intermediate descendant, Khmer. The development of Thai script is usually attributed to King Ramkhamhaeng in the 13th century. Since then, it has undergone many stylistic changes. In Thailand, Thai script is also used to write Lao and other Tai languages. Historically, most of the Tai groups in Vietnam, Laos, Thailand, and Burma have had their own writing systems based on Indic models of writing.

The Lao script, which exists in different styles (*Lao tham*, *Lao būhān*, modern Lao), can be traced back to the 14th century. It was used to write the Lao language of Laos and northeast Thailand, and Northern Thai as well. Today, it is also employed in writing several minority languages of Laos. Variations of *Lao tham* were used to write the languages of smaller Tai groups such as Tai Lu and Tai Khœn.

2 Dating systems

The traditional Vietnamese calendar followed the Chinese model. Years were recorded using a method of cyclical characters and year designations, marking the divisions into different periods or eras of a ruler's reign. The years, in turn, were divided into twelve lunar months of 29 or 30 days. Over a period of nineteen years, seven intercalary months were added in order to bring the lunar cycle into accord with the solar cycle. In the 20th century, the lunar calendar was replaced by the Gregorian calendar and Christian Era (or Common Era) for official purposes. Modern printed books give an imprint in the Christian Era.

In Burma, government and administrative matters are regulated by the Christian Era and Gregorian calendar. Religious and cultural festivals are determined either by the Burmese Era, which is counted from AD 638, or the Buddhist Era, dating from 544 BC. MSS and older books usually are dated according to the Buddhist Era or the Burmese Era. Modern printed books often give an imprint in the Christian Era and/or the Buddhist Era.

The traditional Cambodian calendar is lunar-solar, in which the months are lunar, alternately having 29 or 30 days. The gap between the solar and the lunar years is resolved by adding, every three or four years, an intercalary month. In Buddhist texts, the Buddhist Era is normally used. In inscriptions and some recent texts, the Saka Era is used, beginning AD 79. Besides that, the Culla Era, dating from AD 639, and the Christian Era are common.

In Thailand, the Buddhist Era was adopted as the official dating system in 1932. Since the beginning of the Bangkok period (AD 1782), the Buddhist Era has been defined as starting at 543 BC. Other eras in use, mainly in MSS and early printed books, are Chunlasakkarāt (beginning AD 638), Mahāsakkarāt (beginning AD 78), and Rattanakōsinsok (beginning AD 1781).

In Laos, the Christian Era, which remains officially in use today, was introduced by the French at the end of the 19th century. Until the mid-20th century, the Buddhist Era (starting 543 BC), the Chunlasakkarāt, and the Mahāsakkarāt eras were also used. Traditionally, the Lao followed a lunar-solar calendar similar to the Cambodian model.

3 Book forms

Palm-leaf MSS and folding books were produced for a variety of purposes in Buddhist monasteries and at the royal and local courts in Burma, Thailand, Cambodia, and Laos. The production of MSS was regarded as an act to gain merit. They provided teaching material and handbooks for monks and novices, as well as Buddhist literature and historical works to read to the lay people during religious ceremonies. MSS were also important for history writing (by demand of the royal or local courts), the transcription of oral tradition, and the production of professional manuals (including for astrologers, healers, fortune tellers, legal specialists, and artists).

The earliest material for producing MSS in these countries was the palm leaf. Most commonly, the *Corypha umbraculifera* was used. The leaves of MSS are mostly 45–60 cm long and 4.5–6 cm wide; shorter ones are 25–30 cm long. There are usually three to five lines of writing on each leaf. Sometimes, small drawings decorate the text. The writing is incised with a metal stylus before lampblack is applied to the leaves, and then wiped off, leaving the black in the incisions only. The leaves are then bound in bundles with a string and preserved in wooden covers, which can be lacquered and gilded, or decorated with an inlay of glass or mother-of-pearl (*see* **19**). Infrequently, a similar type of MS was produced from bamboo stems. Because of the late introduction of printing in Laos, palm-leaf MSS are still produced there today for religious purposes.

Other MSS to be found in Burma, Thailand, Laos, and Cambodia are folding books (Thai/Lao *Samut khoi*, Burmese *Parabaik*). The paper, normally made from the bark of the *Streblus asper*, was folded in an accordion fashion to form a book. Folding books are mostly 30–50 cm long and 10–15 cm wide, but longer ones are up to 70 cm long. The paper is usually a natural cream colour and written on with black China ink and a bamboo pen. Alternatively, the surface could be blackened with lacquer or soot and written on with a white steatite (soapstone) pencil, in yellow ink made from gamboges, or from orpiment mixed with the sap of *Feronia elephantium*. The cover pages often were lacquered and gilded.

Illustrations could be an important part of a folding book. They give a pictorial (and often idealistic) impression of the work's content (or of a topic related to it). Sometimes, however, text and illustrations were unrelated. Lavishly coloured illustrations often accompany folding books on Buddhist themes, especially MSS dealing with the Jātakas and the life of the Buddha, Buddhist cosmologies, treatises on worldly and supernatural beings, and MSS on fortune-telling, astrology, or traditional healing.

Vietnamese MSS were written in standard or cursive calligraphy on paper made from the bark of *Streblus asper*. The size of the paper varied considerably, from an oblong format of *c*.14 × 25 cm to a large format of *c*.22 × 32 cm. If bound, butterfly and thread bindings were used. Vietnamese MSS often contained literary and philosophical works, chronicles, and works on administrative and legal issues.

Lacquered MSS or *Kammavaca*, as they are known in Burma, are among the most sacred of Burmese Buddhist texts. These MSS are still used for monastic ritual, most commonly for ordinations in Burma. Containing rules of monastic service, they include scripts (*khandaka*) on ordination and admonitions to the newly ordained monk. *Kammavaca* consist of a number of unbound 'leaves', made from thin wood or bamboo slices, folded layers of cotton, or thin metal sheets, which are then covered thickly with a few coats of red or brown lacquer to create a smooth, pliant surface. Some rare *Kammavaca* MSS are made from ivory. Normally, gold leaf is applied before the words are painted in a stylized fashion with thick black lacquer. Intervening illustrations are often added. The finished MS is protected by covers of brown or orange lacquered teakwood, also decorated with panels of lively freehand gold leaf or relief-moulded lacquer with glass inlay. When boys enter a monastery for a period (a practice that remains obligatory), parents present the presiding monk with a *Kammavaca* concerning ordination.

4 Printed books

The oldest method of printing in mainland Southeast Asia was woodblock printing (xylography), a limited art confined chiefly to certain temples and villages of northern Vietnam. The beginnings of printing in Vietnam are not precisely known, though it is believed to date back to the 13th century AD, and is especially associated with the efforts of the 15th-century scholar Lương Nhu Hộc. The oldest definitely dated specimen is the 1697 edition of the Great Official History.

The first publishers in Burma and Thailand were missionary presses, which printed biblical texts and teaching materials for Christian communities (*see* **9**). Later, royal and governmental presses printed official papers and materials for administrative purposes; Buddhist institutions printed for the Sangha and lay people; and libraries and public bodies published to promote indigenous literatures and cultures. By the end of the 19th century, Buddhist monasteries played an important role as publishers: their cremation volumes appeared in high numbers and were dedicated to various topics, from Buddhism to linguistics, literature, anthropology, arts, history, and archaeology.

In 1816, the first printing press in Burma was established at Rangoon under the supervision of Adoniram Judson. The press was made and the types cut at the Serampore Mission of the Baptist Missionary Society, where Burmese texts had been printed since 1810. After the British acquisition of Arakan and

Tenasserim, missionary work increased and more presses were established in Tavoy (1837) and Moulmein (1843). These operations pioneered the translation and printing of the Bible in the Karen and Mon languages. King Mindon established the first Royal Printing Press in Mandalay in 1864. By 1870, the Burma Herald Press started publishing law books, moral tracts, and popular Burmese dramas. Among printing ventures that transferred Burmese MS texts into printed forms was the Haddawaddy Press (founded in 1886), which produced nearly 1,000 titles, including the whole Tripitaka in Burmese script. Another important publisher was the Burma Research Society, which did valuable work in editing and publishing old MS texts under the guidance of U Pe Maung Tin (1888–1973).

In Thailand, the first printing press was established in Bangkok by Roman Catholic missionaries in 1836. Interest in publishing was confined mostly to the foreign missionary organizations, which published numerous translations of biblical tracts, commentaries, and catechisms in Thai languages. The royal court first made use of a press in 1839 to publish a royal proclamation banning the opium trade. In 1858, King Rama IV commanded the government to establish its own press to print *The Royal Gazette* (*Ratkitchanuphēk*), as well as administrative papers and records (*čhotmaihēt*), handbooks, laws, travel reports, speeches, and descriptions of the provinces of Thailand.

Thailand's policy of educational modernization in the first two decades of the 20th century required the mass production of teaching materials, textbooks, and teachers' manuals. The Buddhist community produced pedagogical matter in great quantities, including translations of Buddhist scriptures and commentaries from Pāli into Thai. Cremation volumes appeared in large numbers, and often had the character of research papers or speeches dedicated to religious, cultural, anthropological, linguistic, literary, and social topics. During the reign (1910–25) of King Rama VI, the publishing of literary works reached new heights. The king, a dedicated writer himself, translated numerous literary works from Western languages into Thai.

By the end of the 19th century, some commercial publishing houses had been established in Bangkok, and more followed during the first 30 years of the 20th century. Notable publishers include Bradley's Press, Smith's Press, Union Press, Thai Printers, and Sophon Phiphatthanakon Printers, as well as the Siam Society and the Vajiranana National Library.

In 1892, the first Lao/Lanna printing press was founded in Chiang Mai, after a Tham Lao/Lanna typeface had been acquired from the Lampang Presbyterian Mission. For much of its history, the press was the only body printing in the Lao/Lanna languages and *Tham* script. It produced large quantities of bibles, textbooks, and tracts, as well as administrative papers and handbooks.

The French introduced modern techniques of printing in Vietnam, Laos, and Cambodia. Western typographic presses were established in Cochinchina in 1862 and Tonkin in 1883. One of the earliest Vietnamese publishers was Imprimerie de l'Union (founded in the late 19th century), which competed with

French publishing houses in Saigon. After World War I, a large number of publishing houses were established in Hanoi, Huê, and Saigon. In the first three decades of the 20th century, the French made great efforts to rein in publishing in Chinese characters and successfully promoted printing in *quốc ngữ'* and French.

Although a Khmer type had been developed by the end of the 19th century, the first Khmer text to be printed in Cambodia appeared only in 1908. In the 1920s, modernist monks such as the Venerable Chuon Nath and Huot That promoted the publication of a range of texts with the help of Louis Finot. In Laos, the first press to print Lao script was established only in the late 1930s, although a press in Paris had been printing texts in Lao būhān script since 1906. After World War II, organizations such as the Comité Littéraire Lao, the Ministère des Cultes, and the Bibliothèque nationale used photocopying to reproduce texts, whereas the revolutionary Neo Lao Haksat (Lao Patriotic Front) printed large editions of propaganda literature in cave presses until 1975.

BIBLIOGRAPHY

[Cornell University Library,] *The Book in Southeast Asia* (1990)

H. Ginsburg, *Thai Art and Culture: Historic Manuscripts from Western Collections* (2000)

P. Herbert and A. Milner, eds., *Southeast Asia: Languages and Literatures* (1989)

D. E. U. Kratz, ed., *Southeast Asian Languages and Literatures* (1996)

S. F. McHale, *Print and Power: Confucianism, Communism, and Buddhism in the Making of Modern Vietnam* (2004)

E. Rhodes, *The Spread of Printing, Eastern Hemisphere: India, Pakistan, Ceylon, Burma and Thailand* (1969)

B. Siworaphot, *Samut khoi* (1999)

The History of the Book
in Australia

IAN MORRISON

1 Introduction

At the beginning of the 21ˢᵗ century, Australia is among the most urbanized countries in the world, and one of the most sparsely populated. The three major cities of the eastern seaboard—Sydney, Melbourne, and Brisbane—account for nearly half the country's population of 20 million. Similarly, the book trade is dominated by just a few of the more than 200 active publishers. In 2001, six multinationals—Penguin, Random House, HarperCollins, Pan Macmillan, Hodder Headline, and Simon & Schuster—held more than 60 per cent of the general retail market. The largest Australian-owned publisher, George Allen & Unwin, had 9 per cent of the market. Only two other Australian-owned companies—the (now British-owned) travel-guide publisher Lonely Planet and the directory publisher UBD—featured in the top 25. The general retail market is dominated by chain stores and franchises.

Sales data are more ambiguous, however. The educational and general non-fiction markets are dominated by Australian titles, which in 2004–5 outsold imported titles by more than two to one (84.4 million copies, against 39.5 million). Adult fiction, however, is dominated by imported titles, which in monetary terms outsold Australian titles by more than 50 per cent. Translating this data into an accurate account of what Australians read is complicated by the fact that it reports only mainstream commercial outlets: direct retail sales by small publishers, religious bookselling, and subscription publishing by multinationals such as Time-Life Books and Reader's Digest are not included. Further, a 2001 survey found that as many as one third of books purchased are intended as gifts; that few of these gifts are actually read; and that about one third of the books that *are* read are borrowed either from friends or from libraries. It is clear that Australian authorship and subject-matter are valued highly by readers of non-fiction, but are largely inconsequential to readers of fiction.

2 First encounters to the gold rushes, 1788–1850

Australia's foundation legends are products of the European Enlightenment: from reports of explorers, scientists, and settlers, beginning with Dutch landfalls in the 17th century, through the scientific voyages mounted by the French and the English in the 18th century, to the 'heroic age' of land exploration in the 19th century. The eleven convict transport ships that set out from England in 1787 to establish a colony in New South Wales brought books of all kinds and a printing press. Although nobody was found to work the press until 1796 (the first professional printer, George Howe, arrived in 1800), print culture was integral to the colony from the start.

The first book produced specifically for distribution in Australia was a homily directed at transported convicts, Richard Johnson's *Address to the Inhabitants of the Colonies Established in New South Wales and Norfolk Island* (London, 1794). An official account of *The Voyage of Governor Phillip to Botany Bay* was published at London in 1789, and several officers also produced accounts of their experiences. Watkin Tench, John White, John Hunter, and David Collins were all remarkable for their scientific curiosity. Their books went through multiple editions and were widely translated. A number of works attributed to the 'gentleman thief' George Barrington (who had been transported in 1790) were compiled by hack writers from these genuine narratives. Long before Europeans began publishing accounts of the continent, however, the Aboriginal Australians had complex oral cultures stretching back tens of thousands of years, with hundreds of different languages. The subtleties of their encounters with European literacy have only recently begun to be explored. David Unaipon (*Native Legends*, 1929) is justly famous as the first published Aboriginal author, but the first Aboriginal to engage actively with European literacy was the Eora leader Bennelong, who dictated a letter in 1796. In the intervening years, Aboriginal publishing was predominately conducted by white missionaries and fell into two main categories: language books directed at Europeans (starting with Lancelot Threlkeld's 1827 *Specimens of a Dialect of the Aborigines of New South Wales*); and scripture texts and primers for Aboriginals on mission stations. Penny van Toorn has pointed out that categorizing Aboriginal culture as 'oral' and European as 'literate' is oversimplistic, privileging European concepts of what writing *is* and *does* over other sign systems. Aboriginal culture inscribed meanings on message-sticks, as well as on rocks, bark, human bodies, clothing, and ritual objects. European writing appeared, as van Toorn puts it, 'on objects as diverse as Bibles and flour bags', and 'entered Indigenous life-worlds as part of a foreign invasion' (van Toorn, 14).

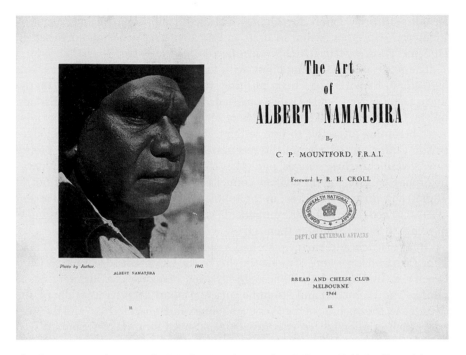

The first monograph on an Aboriginal artist. The Bread and Cheese Club's leading spirit was J. K. Moir, who donated his collection to the State Library of Victoria. The Commonwealth National Library was the forerunner of the National Library of Australia. Private collection

Literacy levels among the 'invaders', who included Irish, Scots, and Welsh, as well as West Indians such as Howe, also varied enormously. The culture of many convicts and common soldiers was primarily oral and highly diverse. Nonetheless, Lieutenant Ralph Clark was able to stage a production of Farquhar's *The Recruiting Officer* with a convict cast in 1789.

Howe's appointment as Government Printer around 1800 marked the beginning of local publishing. He started Australia's first newspaper, the *Sydney Gazette*, in 1803 with a press run of 100 copies. Modelled on the *London Gazette*, it contained official notices, advertisements, and general news. With such a tiny circulation, its survival depended on Howe's government salary and the success of his other business ventures, notably trading in sandalwood. In 1810, Howe replaced the original wooden common press with an iron Stanhope. By 1819, the colony's population had grown to 30,000 and the *Gazette*'s circulation to 400. Howe's publishing activities expanded to include missionary works in Pacific languages, some literary titles, and John Lewin's *Birds of New South Wales* (1813).

The next permanent British settlements in Australia were in Van Diemen's Land, now Tasmania, at Hobart in 1804 and at Launceston in 1806. Hobart's first newspaper, the *Derwent Star*, appeared in 1810. It ceased after a few issues, and only three copies have survived. The *Hobart Town Gazette*, established by Andrew

Bent in 1816, proved more durable, surviving Bent's imprisonment and sacking by Lieutenant-Governor Arthur in 1825. In 1827 Bent's replacement, a free settler, Dr James Ross, started an independent newspaper, the *Hobart Town Courier*.

The 1820s were a turning point, with the settlements' physical dimensions expanding. Explorers had been pushing west, south, and north: in 1812, the known land of New South Wales consisted of a few dozen miles around Sydney, but by 1827 it extended for hundreds of square miles. The Australian colonies were becoming attractive to free settlers. Hobart and Sydney were no longer prison camps on the edge of the recognized world; they had become proper towns, with churches, schools, and other civilized amenities. Military rule was beginning to give way to civilian councils. During the 1820s, 11,200 out of 43,950 new arrivals were free; in the 1830s, free settlers numbered 66,400 out of 117,090 arrivals. Growing numbers of people born in the colonies were now of an age to become parents themselves.

Many convicts and emancipists had a rudimentary education, but few could afford to spend large sums of money buying books. Libraries and learned societies began to form. Although the Philosophical Society of Australasia (Sydney, 1821–3) and the Van Diemen's Land Scientific Society (Hobart, 1829) were stillborn, the decade saw the opening of the Wesleyan Library in Hobart in 1825 and the Australian Subscription Library (forerunner of the State Library of New South Wales) in Sydney in 1826. Independent newspapers were increasing in number, and were less vulnerable to government interference: Bent's defiance had been squashed in 1825; but when Governor Darling imprisoned the proprietors of the *Australian* and the *Monitor* in 1829, the newspapers both continued publishing.

The mid-1820s saw an upsurge of original poetry in Sydney and Hobart newspapers. The first magazine, Robert Howe's *Australian Magazine* (Sydney, 1821), was soon followed by the first book of verse by an Australian-born poet, Charles Tompson's *Wild Notes from the Lyre of a Native Minstrel* (Sydney, 1826) and the first Australian-published novel, Henry Savery's *Quintus Servinton* (Hobart, 1830).

In 1820, there were only two Government Printers, Howe and Bent; ink and paper were expensive, often unobtainable, and seldom of high quality. The limited capacity of colonial printers and the high costs of raw materials ensured that the book trade continued to be dominated by imports, and most Australian writers sought to have their books produced in England. The colonial market was nevertheless substantial: booksellers' and auctioneers' catalogues from the 1840s show between 10,000 and 30,000 books advertised each year. The London publisher Thomas Tegg's sons James and Samuel arrived in 1834. James established a business in Sydney, Samuel settled in Hobart. For most of the following decade, they played a dominant role in the Australian book trade. James published more than 100 titles, including two magazines (*Tegg's Monthly Magazine*, 1836, and *Literary News*, 1837–8), broadside and book almanacs, political and religious pamphlets, literary works, and William Bland's account of Hume and Hovell's expedition to Port Phillip (1837).

During the 1830s, newspaper circulation grew and prices fell; the cover price of the *Australian*, for example, was 9*d*. in 1830; by 1835, it was down to 4*d*. The total weekly output of all newspapers in 1827 was 3,700 copies; in 1836 it was 7,800. Sydney readers could choose from seven titles: the staid *Sydney Gazette*, the radical *Australian*, the once outrageous but now stuffy *Monitor*, the conservative *Sydney Herald*, the eccentric *Sydney Times*, the provocative *Colonist*, and—for business news—the *Commercial Journal*. Only the *Herald* (now the *Sydney Morning Herald*) survived the economic depression of the 1840s, but new papers continued to appear, and the overall effect was of continuing expansion. Hobart too had several newspapers, and a provincial press was emerging in the towns around Sydney, as well as in the new settlements of Moreton Bay (Queensland), Western Australia, South Australia, and Port Phillip (Victoria). Most struggled financially, but their proprietors were motivated more by political power than by financial gain. By the end of the 1850s all the colonies had elected legislatures, and many politicians were newspapermen.

Booksellers were running successful circulating libraries in the 1830s, and athenaeums or mechanics' institutes were established in the larger centres: Hobart (1827), Sydney (1833), Newcastle (1835), Melbourne (1838). By the end of the century, every town of any size had its 'institute'. Free public libraries were slower to develop. The Melbourne Public Library (now the State Library of Victoria) opened in 1856, and the other colonies gradually followed suit: New South Wales (1869), Tasmania (1870), South Australia (1886), Western Australia (1887), Queensland (1890).

3 From the gold rushes to Federation, 1850–1901

The great spur to colonial growth in the 1850s was the discovery of gold in Victoria and New South Wales. Early gold finds had been suppressed by administrators fearful of losing control—a reasonable fear in a penal colony. The influx of free settlers, and the economic downturn of the 1840s, made such news more welcome. It is impossible to overstate the effects of the rushes. Between 1851 and 1861, the population of Victoria grew from 77,000 to 538,000; New South Wales from 178,000 to 350,000; South Australia from 63,000 to 126,000; Queensland from 8,000 to 30,000. Tasmania, however, flat-lined; the end of convict transportation in 1855 combined with the pull of the mainland goldfields to cancel out any population growth from free settlers. Universities, too, were being established—at Sydney (1851), Melbourne (1853), Adelaide (1874), and Tasmania (1890)—although higher education remained the exclusive preserve of a tiny minority until well into the 20th century, and university libraries were accordingly slow to develop.

Inflation soared as employers increased wages to keep tradesmen from the diggings. In 1850, skilled tradesmen could earn 5*s*. or 6*s*. a day; by 1855, compositors on the Melbourne *Herald* were being paid £1 a day. Melbourne, the city hardest hit, embarked on a series of major public works—a Public Library, an Exhibition Building, a University—to bring a sense of order to what was essentially a frontier town devastated by the stampede to the diggings. By the 1890s, Sydney and Melbourne were comparable in size to many European cities. Melbourne's leading newspapers, the radical *Age* and the conservative *Argus*, had reputations that extended far beyond Victoria. International Exhibitions brought Sydney (1879) and Melbourne (1880 and 1888) world attention.

The gold rush also accelerated the growth of non-English publishing. The first German newspaper, the *German Australian Post*, appeared in Adelaide in 1848, and numerous other German-language publications were issued in South Australia and Queensland during the second half of the century. German Moravian missionaries were active in publishing works in South Australian Aboriginal languages. Other non-English publications included the French *Journal de Melbourne* (1858), the *English and Chinese Advertiser* (Ballarat, 1850s), the Welsh *Yr Australydd* (Melbourne, 1866–72), and a Hebrew almanac (Hobart, 1853).

Rapid population growth created a steady market for textbooks and practical treatises, but literary publishing remained fragile. The colonial market was too small to sustain even the most prolific writer. Newspapers were the main outlet for fiction and poetry throughout the 19th century. The country press in particular was extraordinarily literary by 21st-century standards, but it offered only a precarious livelihood. Most colonial writers had other careers—commonly the law or the civil service—or private means. The few who lived by their pens either published in Britain or worked as journalists or newspaper editors.

Given these conditions, the richness and diversity of writing that appeared in the 1860s is remarkable. The instant popular success of the *Australian Journal* (Melbourne, 1865–1962) gave colonial writers a major boost, in morale if not earning power, and the decade saw the emergence of prolific popular writers such as Garnet Walch and R. P. Whitworth. Marcus Clarke and 'Rolf Boldrewood' (Thomas Alexander Brown) began their careers as newspaper columnists, the precocious Clarke writing for Melbourne's *Australasian* and Boldrewood for Sydney's *Australian Town and Country Journal*. Nicol Drysdale Stenhouse, a Sydney lawyer, became the patron of a coterie of intellectuals that included Daniel Deniehy, editor of the *Southern Cross* (1859–60), and the poet Henry Kendall. Kendall and his contemporaries Charles Harpur and Adam Lindsay Gordon are renowned for their poems of the Australian bush, but each was just as at home with European and biblical mythology.

The major book publishers during this period were all based in Melbourne: George Robertson, Samuel Mullen, and E. W. Cole. Several of the larger Melbourne printing firms also became successful publishers. Sands & McDougall, F. F. Bailliere, and Gordon & Gotch all built intercolonial mini-empires based on publishing modest-looking reference books that few could afford to be without. Sands & McDougall's postal directories (published from the 1850s to the 1970s), Gordon & Gotch's *Australian Handbook and Almanac* (1870-1906), and Bailliere's atlases, gazetteers, and directories (1860s to 1880s), have retained their value as sources for historical research.

Among the notable figures in the Sydney trade were: William Maddock (active 1862-96), whose list included practical treatises on topics as diverse as billiards and animal husbandry; William Woolcott and J. R. Clarke (active 1850-95), who published music and scenic views; and J. J. Moore, whose *Moore's Almanack and Hand Book* (1852-1940) quickly established itself as a standard reference work. Unlike its English namesake, the Sydney *Moore's* was a rationalistic compendium of useful knowledge.

The prominent religious publishers were the Catholic Edward Flanagan and J. G. O'Connor (Sydney, 1860s-1880s) and the Anglican Joseph Cook (Sydney, 1850s-1890s). Heterodox publishers included Joseph Wing, publisher of the *Spiritual Enquirer* (Bendigo, 1874-5), the *Reformer* (Melbourne, 1880-83), and numerous spiritualist pamphlets; the atheist Joseph Symes, publisher of the *Liberator* (Melbourne, 1884-1904); and the spiritualist W. H. Terry, publisher of the *Harbinger of Light* (Melbourne, 1870-1956).

Many provincial centres had flourishing printer-publisher-booksellers. Most survived principally as booksellers and jobbing printers; some, notably Ballarat's F. W. Niven (who developed an innovative crisp photolithographic process), played a major part in the industry's development.

South Australian and Tasmanian publishers concentrated on localized almanacs, guidebooks, and technical works. In Adelaide, the major figures were E. S. Wigg (active from 1849) and W. C. Rigby (active from 1859); the firms they established flourished well into the 20th century. Hobart publishing was dominated by the Davies family—proprietors of the *Mercury* newspaper (established 1854)—and the Walches. Besides their *Literary Intelligencer* (1859-1915) and *Tasmanian Almanac* (1862-1980, by far the longest-running Australian almanac), the Walches were significant for promoting the career of the writer and artist Louisa Anne Meredith.

Western Australia and Queensland, both first settled in the 1820s, developed more slowly. Other than government publications, their 19th-century publishing consisted mainly of newspapers and almanacs.

During the 1870s and 1880s, colonial publishers, especially in Melbourne and Sydney, were increasingly active in promoting local authors, but they seldom managed to do more than cover expenses. Writers with serious ambitions looked to Britain. Clarke's *His Natural Life* (1874) and Boldrewood's *Robbery Under Arms* (1888) first appeared as serials in Australian journals, but only achieved 'Australian classic' status after publication in London. The prolific thriller writer Fergus Hume published his first novel, *The Mystery of a Hansom Cab*, in Melbourne in 1886; he returned to England in 1888 and spent the rest of his life there. The careers of such diverse writers as Rosa Praed, Ada Cambridge, and Nat Gould all followed similar trajectories.

To the extent that such writers built their careers on British sales, they might seem irrelevant to Australia. However, the Australasian colonies were, at least in terms of volumes per capita, many British publishers' largest market. The newspaperman James Allen was doubtless bragging when he commented at length in his *History of Australia* (1882) on the wide reading and deep knowledge of contemporary literature, science, and international politics displayed by the people of Victoria; but all the statistical and anecdotal evidence supports the general point that Australians devoured any printed matter they could obtain. British publishers began to produce cut-price 'colonial editions' in the 1840s; by the end of the century, several—notably Cassell & Co. and Eyre & Spottiswoode—had established branches in the colonies rather than rely on agents, and had become part of the local publishing scene.

By the 1880s, colonial publishing was again shifting gears, conscious of the coming centenary of British settlement and of the growing agitation for the Australian colonies' political union. The market for commemorative reference books—such as the *Australian Dictionary of Dates and Men of the Time* (1879), *Cyclopedia of Australasia* (1881), *Picturesque Atlas of Australasia* (1886–9), *Cassell's Picturesque Australasia* (1887–8), *Chronicles of Early Melbourne* (1888), and *Australian Men of Mark* (1889)—seemed inexhaustible. With the success of the aggressively nationalistic Sydney weekly, the *Bulletin*, in the 1880s, it was possible to imagine a future in which Australia had a thriving literary culture all its own.

4 Federation to World War II, 1901–45

By the 1890s, Australian attitudes to Great Britain and the empire were diverse and complex. A series of crises in the Pacific spurred agitation for political union; fears of French and German expansion were exacerbated by reports of Russian plans to attack Melbourne and Sydney. In 1885, Queensland, Tasmania, Western Australia, Victoria, and Fiji formed the Federal Council of Australasia. Sir Henry Parkes, the New South Wales premier and former newspaper proprietor, initiated moves towards full political unification in 1889. Then, leading up to Federation, the Australian colonies contributed troops to Britain's war against Boer separatists in southern Africa. One of the most popular Australian books of this period was the Revd W. H. Fitchett's *Deeds that Won the Empire* (first published as a newspaper serial in 1896), with total sales of more than half a million.

After a decade of negotiations and political campaigning, New South Wales, Victoria, Queensland, South Australia, Tasmania, and Western Australia formed the Commonwealth of Australia in 1901. A strain of populist nationalism—at once egalitarian and xenophobic—found literary expression in the Sydney weekly, the *Bulletin*, which also produced a popular monthly, *Lone Hand* (1907–21). A. G. Stephens, the *Bulletin's* literary editor (1894–1906), had mixed success with his own magazine, the *Bookfellow* (three series: 1899, 1907, 1911–25).

The success of Angus & Robertson and the *Bulletin* in promoting populist, nationalistic writers proved there was a viable market for Australian stories told in an Australian idiom. The New South Wales Bookstall Co.—the first great Australian pulp publisher—offered Australian writers the prospect of a living wage in their own country for the first time. In Melbourne, the bookseller Thomas Lothian began publishing in 1905, setting a more literary tone with poets such as Bernard O'Dowd, John Shaw Neilson, Marie Pitt, and 'Furnley Maurice', as well as the short-lived magazine the *Native Companion* (1907), which published the New Zealand writer Katherine Mansfield's first stories.

When the Berne Convention on international copyright was signed in 1886, Australia was part of the British empire, and the Net Book Agreement of 1900 perpetuated British control of the Australian market. Although Australian writers were free to seek out US publishers, British editions of their works took precedence in their home country—and Australian literary history has been framed largely within the history of British publishing. Although US editions were demonstrably superior in their physical presentation, the quality of their texts, and the financial rewards they gave to authors, they have remained largely unknown to Australian audiences. British 'colonial editions' retained a presence in the Australian market until 1972.

Once the initial euphoria of 1901 had passed, the Commonwealth of Australia continued to cling to the British empire. Between the 1890s and the 1940s, Australian culture became increasingly xenophobic. A defining moment for the new Commonwealth was the Immigration Restriction Act of 1901, which effectively prohibited non-European immigration. The 'White Australia Policy' was not formally abandoned by the Australian government until 1973.

Commemorations such as the sesquicentenary of Sydney in 1938 and the centenary of Melbourne in 1934 saw an upsurge in the collecting of Australiana, especially books from the age of British exploration in the 18th and early 19th centuries. This trend reached its apex when the Melbourne businessman Sir Russell Grimwade acquired 'Captain Cook's Cottage' (actually the home of the navigator's parents after their son had gone to sea) for Melbourne's centenary celebrations. That Cook never saw Melbourne, and may not have seen the cottage, was no deterrent. More importantly, large-scale bibliographies were appearing: the Mitchell Library's *Bibliography of Captain James Cook* (1928); Edmund Morris Miller's *Australian Literature* (1940); and Sir John Alexander Ferguson's *Bibliography of Australia 1784–1900* (1941–69). Sir Edward Ford began the collecting that would eventually lead to his *Bibliography of Australian Medicine* (1976).

A key episode in the development of Australian library services was the scathing report in 1935 by Ralph Munn, of the Carnegie Corporation, and Ernest Pitt, head of the State Library of Victoria. The Munn–Pitt report was a political success in promoting the concept of free, municipally funded public libraries; by the 1960s such libraries had replaced, or subsumed, the vast majority of the subscription-funded mechanics' institutes and schools of arts that had been the standard model of library service since the mid-19th century. Circulating libraries, too, began to decline after World War II, and, although some lingered into the 1970s, they ceased to play a significant part.

Robertson's *Monthly Book Circular* came to an end in 1891, and when Walch's *Literary Intelligencer* closed in 1915 the Australian book trade found itself without a local journal. In 1921, D. W. Thorpe started the *Australian Stationery and Fancy Goods Journal*, forerunner of the *Australian Bookseller and Publisher*.

Art publishing gathered momentum during World War I with Thomas Lothian's production in 1916 of two lavish books, *The Art of Frederick McCubbin* and Ida Rentoul Outhwaite's *Elves and Fairies*. Sydney Ure Smith established two key journals: *Art in Australia* (1916–42), with its tipped-in colour plates, provided a forum for the fine arts; *The Home* (1920–42), although focused on interior design and decoration, included articles about contemporary art, and featured covers by such notable artists as Thea Proctor. *Manuscripts* (1931–5) was another notable art journal, promoting the work of such artists as Margaret Preston, Eric Thake, and Christian Waller, although it also included substantial poetry and prose fiction; later issues included bibliographical notes by George Mackaness.

One of the most striking little magazines of the period was *Vision* (1923–4). Edited by Frank C. Johnson, Jack Lindsay, and Kenneth Slessor, it struck a pose against both the populist balladeers of the *Bulletin* and European modernism, instead struggling to articulate an aesthetic based on youth and vitality. Decorated with Norman Lindsay's erotic drawings of nymphs and satyrs, its stated aim was to make Australia the centre of a new renaissance. Two *Vision* poets—Slessor himself and R. D. FitzGerald—became major figures, but *Vision*, like so many other journals, folded after a few issues. Lindsay's next magazine venture, *The London Aphrodite* (published by his Fanfrolico Press, 1928–9), was deliberately planned to cease after six issues. Johnson, at that stage working in Dymock's bookshop, went on to become a successful paperback publisher.

In 1939, the Sydney branch of the English Association, based at the University of Sydney, started *Southerly*, now Australia's longest-running literary journal. The Brisbane journalist Clem Christesen established *Meanjin* in the following year. Initially a vehicle for Queensland writers, *Meanjin* had achieved a circulation of 4,000 and a national profile by 1943. Published with the patronage of the University of Melbourne from 1945, *Meanjin* developed during the 1950s and 1960s an increasingly internationalist outlook along with an interest in contemporary political events, as well as in literature and art. Since Christesen's retirement in 1974, it has become predominantly an academic journal.

Angry Penguins (1940–46) promoted surrealist art and writing, making it a target for the 'Ern Malley' hoax perpetrated by the conservative poets James McAuley and Harold Stewart. The duped editor, Max Harris, put up a spirited defence of the poetic quality of the fake author's work, but in the face of withering tabloid scorn he had little chance of being taken seriously by anyone who was not already sympathetic. It would be another twenty years before Australian literary editors were comfortable publishing poetry that rejected conventional forms.

5 Since World War II

The end of World War II brought a period of reconstruction. The population boomed—from 7.5 million in 1947 to 10.5 million in 1961. Country towns stagnated, but in the major cities suburban sprawl escalated. Throughout the 1970s and 1980s there was a growing sense of cultural maturity, as writers and artists found it increasingly possible to be based overseas without losing their 'Australianness', or to develop an international profile without leaving Australia.

Higher education expanded dramatically. Until the 1930s, universities were a minor part of the Australian library scene. At that time Australia had just six universities—one in each of the state capitals—and a range of other tertiary colleges. Between 1946 and 1980, thirteen new universities were established. Melbourne's Monash (1958) and La Trobe (1964) were completely new institutions; others, such as the Australian National University (1946) and the University of New England (1954), were developed out of existing regional colleges. A complex series of reconfigurations over the next twenty years saw the number of universities double again, with most having multiple campuses. Many regional centres now have a university campus; some universities have expanded internationally: Monash, for example, has campuses in Malaysia, South Africa, and Italy. The number of students as a proportion of the total population has grown from a few thousand out of 3.7 million in 1901 to around half a million students in a population of 20 million at the end of the century.

The growth of higher education was a major factor in the development of Australian publishing, in particular during the 1960s and 1970s, as income from textbooks gave publishers scope to risk promoting less commercial works—poetry in particular—that they considered culturally important. A precondition for the growth of tertiary education was increasing retention rates in secondary schools. F. W. Cheshire in Melbourne and the Jacaranda Press in Brisbane specialized in secondary-school publishing. Melbourne University Press (which concentrated on non-fiction, including key reference works such as the *Australian Dictionary of Biography*) and the University of Queensland Press (which played a leading role in promoting the work of new poets and novelists, most famously Peter Carey, David Malouf, and Michael Dransfield) became major players in both the general and education markets. Angus & Robertson continued to produce important reference works, notably the ten-volume second edition of the *Australian Encyclopedia* (1958), and Ferguson's *Bibliography of Australia*, the seventh volume of which appeared in 1969.

The Australian branches of Oxford and Cambridge university presses seemed intent on outdoing each other with guides and companions to all aspects of Australian history and culture. Oxford argued, with some justification, that the Australian edition of its *Concise English Dictionary* was a more genuine Australian production than its locally named but American-sponsored competitor the *Macquarie Dictionary*. Cambridge picked up the *Encyclopedia of Melbourne* (2005) when it was abandoned by Melbourne University Press. The small publisher Currency matched the academic presses with its *Companion to the Theatre in Australia* (1985) and *Companion to Music and Dance in Australia* (2003). Another minnow, Australian Scholarly Publishing, produced the first volume of John Arnold *et al.'s Bibliography of Australian Literature* (2001); subsequent volumes were published by the University of Queensland Press. Melbourne University Press added to its stable of reference works with Marcie Muir and Kerry White's *Australian Children's Books: A Bibliography* (1992–2004).

The pace of postwar change and the structures adopted for the expansion of public library services differed from state to state: in Victoria, for example, local lending libraries were run by municipalities, with the State Library completely separate; in Tasmania, local lending libraries became branches of the State Library. However, the broad principle of public funding for library services—a radical innovation when it was proposed by Munn and Pitt in 1935—had become the accepted norm. Professional qualifications for librarians and archivists shifted from a workplace training model to graduate qualifications. Melbourne Teachers' College introduced a programme for school librarians in 1955. John Wallace Metcalfe initiated a postgraduate diploma course at the University of New South Wales in 1960; a master's programme began in 1972. Jean P. Whyte, a Master in Library Studies graduate of the University of Chicago, started a master's programme at Monash University in 1976. By the 1990s, graduate professional qualifications were also becoming a requirement for editors and publishers.

Libraries were becoming conscious, too, of rare or 'heritage' materials, and specialist rare book librarians were beginning to be appointed in the larger institutions. During the 1960s and 1970s, increasing numbers of private individuals gave their collections to them. Among the more significant were: Henry Allport and Sir William Crowther to the State Library of Tasmania; Ian Francis McLaren and Orde Poynton to the University of Melbourne; J. K. Moir to the State Library of Victoria; Father Leo Hayes to the University of Queensland; and Sir Rex Nan Kivell to the National Library.

A Commonwealth Literary Fund had been established in 1908, essentially as a pension scheme for writers and their dependants. In 1973 its functions were taken over by the Literature Board of the Australia Council, which, with a dramatically increased budget, moved to provide fellowships to support writers during their working lives. The Miles Franklin Award, for a published novel portraying some aspect of Australian life, was initiated in 1957; other literary prizes proliferated during the 1970s and 1980s.

The award of the 1973 Nobel Prize for Literature to Patrick White brought international attention to Australian literature. In the decade leading up to the award, a generation of writers that included Randolph Stow, Thea Astley, and

Christopher Koch followed White's lead in rejecting 'dun-coloured realism'. However, White was only able to produce the sort of work he did because he was independently wealthy and did not need to earn money from his writing. In contrast to White was the prolific pulp writer 'Carter Brown' (Alan Yates), who wrote several hundred thrillers during his 30-year career. His early successes in the Australian market enabled him to leave his day-job as an airline publicist, and huge American sales brought him wealth and (at least pseudonymously) fame. The detective novelist Arthur Upfield and the romance writer Lucy Walker were hailed overseas but disdained in Australia—Upfield sought his revenge by casting one of his detractors, the novelist Vance Palmer, as the murder victim in *An Author Bites the Dust* (1948). It was only with Peter Corris's Chandleresque Cliff Hardy in the 1980s that crime writing acquired local critical respectability.

Penguin established a Melbourne office in 1946 and immediately became a major publishing force, selling some half-million books in their first year. George Allen & Unwin established a Sydney branch in 1976; this became the Australian-owned Allen & Unwin in 1990. Meanwhile, small Australian publishers such as Outback Press (1973–80), McPhee Gribble (1975–89), and Fremantle Arts Centre Press (1976–) were discovering writers as diverse as 'B. Wongar', Helen Garner, and Elizabeth Jolley. The arrival of significant numbers of Vietnamese refugees in the late 1970s, along with the Australian government's shift from 'White Australia' to a commitment to multiculturalism, was followed by the flowering of a non-English language press; by the 1990s leading non-English newspapers such as the Greek *Neos Kosmos* and the Italian *Il Globo* were commonly available in metropolitan newsagents. Aboriginal people were recognized as citizens after a referendum in 1967; movements for land rights and reconciliation followed. Magabala Books (established 1974, wholly Aboriginal-owned since 1990) took the lead in promoting indigenous writers; IAD (Institute for Aboriginal Development) Press and the Aboriginal Studies Press soon followed. The mainstream success achieved by the feminist cooperative Sisters (1979–83) encouraged the development of other feminist presses. Gay and lesbian writing began to enter the mainstream commercial market in the 1990s.

The Children's Book of the Year awards instituted by the Children's Book Council in 1946 encouraged the development of critical standards in evaluating writing for children and young adults, although its awards have been frequently criticized for favouring worthy, issues-based books over material that attracts and engages young readers. The Yabba awards (instituted 1985) are selected by children and invariably produce a very different list from the CBC awards.

Creative writing programmes began to proliferate during the 1990s, just as publishers moved away from cross-subsidization and became increasingly reluctant to risk publishing anything that would not pay its own way. Whether in spite of or because of this, a new professionalism in publishing emerged, and a cultural maturity capable of accepting that for most readers of fiction the tag

'Australian literature' is not in itself sufficient reason to buy or read a book. At the beginning of the 21st century, Australian crime, romance, and speculative-fiction writers are finding commercial and critical success both at home and abroad. A generation that includes Shane Maloney, Kerry Greenwood, Garth Nix, and Glenda Larke seems at last to have found forms of expression for an Australianness that needs neither assertion nor concealment.

....

BIBLIOGRAPHY

D. Carter and A. Galligan, eds., *Making Books: Contemporary Australian Publishing* (2007)

W. Kirsop *et al.*, eds., *A History of the Book in Australia*, vol. 1: *To 1890* (forthcoming)

M. Lyons and J. Arnold, eds., *A National Culture in a Colonised Market, A History of the Book in Australia*, vol. 2: *1891–1945* (2001)

C. Munro and R. Sheahan-Bright, eds., *Paper Empires, A History of the Book in Australia*, vol. 3: *1946–2005* (2006)

A National Survey of Reading, Buying and Borrowing Books for Pleasure, Conducted for Books Alive by A. C. Nielsen (2001)

P. van Toorn, *Writing Never Arrives Naked* (2006)

E. Webby, ed., *The Cambridge Companion to Australian Literature* (2000)

The History of the Book in New Zealand

SHEF ROGERS

1 Missionaries and colonies

A narrow, mountainous pair of islands stretching almost 800 miles through the South Pacific, New Zealand possesses a rich and well-documented print heritage despite its geographic isolation. From 1848, would-be colonists could peruse E. J. Wakefield's *Hand-Book for New Zealand* for a recommended list of books on practical topics such as cooking, ornithology, and astronomy. Early settlers, conscious of a non-literate aboriginal population far larger than their own, deliberately recorded their efforts to establish a local print culture. Jim Traue, a former chief librarian of the Turnbull Library, has argued for two histories (aboriginal and colonial) of New Zealand print culture and notes that the country's settler history is typical of other 19th-century colonies: its print history begins with newspapers and periodicals, then only gradually moves to books.

New Zealand's book history is, therefore, very much a history of importation, even for books in Maori. Numerous Europeans (particularly whalers, sealers, and traders from New South Wales) visited in the late 18th and early 19th centuries. Christian missionaries brought books and printing presses to provide religious works for the Maori; they made strenuous efforts to establish a written form of the Maori language and to record Maori oral culture in print (*see* **9**). By 1815, the Church Missionary Society (CMS) had produced a Maori grammar and Maori primers, printed in London and Sydney. In 1830, at the Kerikeri Wesleyan settlement, the Revd William Yate printed Maori hymn sheets and a six-page Maori catechism. The CMS further established the printed word in New Zealand when William Colenso arrived with a Stanhope press in 1834.

Colenso overcame numerous technical problems to produce the New Testament in Maori in 1837 (the Old Testament was not fully translated until 1868) and remained active as a printer in both Maori and English until 1840, one of his last publications being the printed version of the Treaty of Waitangi, New Zealand's founding constitutional document. His ledgers survive in the Alexander Turnbull Library in Wellington, making New Zealand one of the few nations able to produce the account books of its first significant printer.

Nine months after the Treaty of Waitangi, Queen Victoria established New Zealand as a separate Crown colony; organized settlement soon followed. In almost every New Zealand Company community, colonists established printing presses within a year of arrival: sixteen newspapers were founded by 1851, 28 by 1858. The Government created an official Printing Office in Auckland in 1842–7, and in Wellington from 1864, until its privatization in 1989. For many years it was the country's most technically advanced printer, producing parliamentary material, along with numerous major reference works and New Zealand's largest publication, the telephone directory.

2 Newspapers

Population grew rapidly with the discovery of gold in the South Island in 1861. Each new strike seemed as likely to yield a *newspaper* as a nugget, with 181 newspapers founded 1860–79. These mainly English-language newspapers depended heavily upon reprinting material from overseas publications, eagerly resetting stories from newspapers and magazines as soon as a ship berthed. Although it was often cheaper and easier for a newspaper to serialize a syndicated British work, original local writing was also published, especially accounts of inland exploration and of native flora and fauna. This local interest was reflected in the scientific nature of many of the 19th-century pamphlets printed for exchange via the postal services with colleagues internationally. The third governor-general, Sir George Grey, was especially active in collecting and translating Maori songs, while fictional and semifictional accounts of settlers' experiences provided popular topics for early literary efforts.

Newspapers were also the main publishers of printed Maori, other than the religious books imported and printed by missionaries. Although the largest book produced in 19th-century New Zealand was the Maori Bible, most other printed books were in English. The Government Printer continued to produce some works in Maori, but after publication of *The Native School Reader for Standards II and III* in 1886, government policy shifted towards teaching the Maori to read in English, a focus retained in schools until the beginnings of Maori language immersion schools in the late 1970s. Maori only became an official language of New Zealand in 1987, and the first New Zealand publisher specializing in Maori, Huia, was not established until 1991.

3 Publishers commercial and educational

English-language printing and publishing expanded significantly from the 1880s. Distribution improved with the coming of railways between most of the main centres; the new telegraph cable to Australia in 1876 improved the speed of international communication. The major Australian periodical distributor, Gordon & Gotch, gradually expanded from Victoria throughout Australia and into New Zealand at the turn of century, and remained a major periodical supplier (although a subsidiary of PMP Communications since 1992). Booksellers continued to order books independently, under various legal arrangements intended to maintain Britain's dominance over Commonwealth markets. Until World War II, there were no European or American wholesale booksellers in New Zealand; many publishers still find the country too small a market to merit the presence of a wholesaler, locating Australasian offices in Sydney or Melbourne.

Within the country, however, the end of the 19th and the first half of the 20th centuries saw the development of significant bookselling chains that also became successful publishers. First and foremost was Whitcombe & Tombs. The bookseller George Whitcombe and the printer George Tombs, both of Christchurch, merged their businesses in 1882, expanding to Dunedin in 1890, then throughout the country and ultimately overseas to Australia and England. Deriving early success from its educational publishing, Whitcombe & Tombs merged with the Dunedin printing firm Coulls Somerville Wilkie to form Whitcoulls in 1973. The new company dominated publishing until the mid-1980s and remains the country's most significant retail bookselling chain.

Educational publishing continues to dominate New Zealand book production, with millions of copies sold. From 1877, the New Zealand government required all regional authorities to provide public schools, but not books; those remained a cost to students' families. Seeing an opportunity in the market because of the high prices of imported texts, Whitcombe & Tombs began selling, then publishing, school textbooks. The first challenge to the firm's dominance came in 1907, when the government established the *School Journal*, distributed free to primary schools. Only after World War II, however, did the newly formed School Publications Branch of the Education Department begin producing a regular series of publications that gradually eroded Whitcombe & Tombs's textbook market.

Although the average press run for a textbook exceeded 5,000 copies, print runs for more literary works could be as small as a few hundred. Nonetheless, New Zealand's most successful literary publisher, Caxton Press, managed to sustain quite a strong list in this small market. Begun by several like-minded friends from Canterbury University between 1933 and 1935, Caxton quickly established a reputation for high-quality printing of well-regarded writers; but as other literary publishers came on the scene, Caxton returned to its roots as a printer. Similarly, the Dunedin printing firm McIndoe (established 1890) was, under John McIndoe III, a notable publisher from 1956 until the mid-1980s, but then reverted solely to printing. In 2002, it merged with a complementary printing firm to create Rogan McIndoe, but closed in September 2008. Another significant literary publisher, Pegasus Press (1947–86), issued more than 100 volumes of poetry, as well as seven of Janet Frame's novels, and was one of the first New Zealand firms to secure international joint publication agreements and translation rights for its authors. Four university presses, all established since 1960, have developed, in addition to their academic titles, specializations in New Zealand poetry, fiction, history, or natural history. They all subsidize these academic and New Zealand-centred ventures with revenues from traditionally lucrative textbook titles.

Children's publishing, predominantly in English but with a consistent Maori presence, has long been an important part of New Zealand publishing. Edward Tregear's *Fairy Tales and Folk Lore of New Zealand and the South Sea* (Wellington: Lyon & Blair, 1891) is considered the first New Zealand children's book (*see* 17). Whitcombe & Tombs entered the market with Johannes Andersen's *Maori Fairy Tales* in 1908 and developed a series, *Whitcombe's Story Books* (1904–56), with *c*.450 titles—the largest children's book series in the world. With its research into literacy and methods of reading instruction, and the talents of such witty authors as Joy Cowley, Margaret Mahy, and Lynley Dodd (not to mention many captivating illustrators), New Zealand has become a leader in early reading series. Publishers such as Nelson Price Milburn (now an imprint of the Thomson Corporation), Wendy Pye, and Mallinson Rendel maintain New Zealand's reputation in this field.

The New Zealand publisher best known internationally is undoubtedly A. H. & A. W. Reed. Like Whitcombe & Tombs, A. H. Reed found a niche market—religious publications. From the mid-1930s, he became a leading figure in the New Zealand trade, with historical booklets for general and educational markets, sports books, and other popular works on local topics. He was joined by his nephew A. W. Reed in 1925; together, they wrote more than 100 of the approximately 1,000 titles published by the firm.

Such local successes dwindled in the face of faster transport and a global media. By the end of the 20th century, there were no longer any major New Zealand-owned printing companies or bookselling chains. This shift away from local ownership began with the arrival of firms like Collins, Random House, and Longman in the 1960s, though the pace of mergers quickened at the end of the 20th and start of the 21st centuries. Whitcoulls absorbed the Government Printer and was, in turn, taken over by U.S. Office Products; London Books is owned by the Blue Star Conglomerate, owner of U.S. Office Products; and Reed, having changed names and hands at least six times, became part of Reed Elsevier. Smaller independent booksellers and publishers survived, but faced tough competition from the chains' discounts and from increasing use of the World Wide Web for individual orders of less readily available titles. Borders Bookstores opened its first New Zealand branch in Auckland in 1999 and operated a total of five outlets before its Australian parent holding-company, RedGroup, went under in February 2011, enabling the Pascoe Group to return those shops and the Whitcoulls chain to New Zealand ownership.

Despite the dominance of multinationals in its domestic market, New Zealand retains a strong international presence in intellectual publishing. The Royal Society of New Zealand (established in 1867 as the New Zealand Institute) has fostered a range of specialist scientific journals and research programmes. In association with the Government Printer, the Royal Society developed the world's first computer typesetting system in the mid-1970s. Developments in digital printing have further transformed the publishing industry and reduced costs for shorter runs of books. Government support for an upgraded Internet feed has eased electronic exchange of published material in print and film media.

4 Libraries

Although New Zealanders have always purchased relatively large numbers of books, they have also been eager borrowers. The Otago region on the lower South Island supported 116 public libraries and athenaeums between 1872 and 1884 (for an 1881 population of 135,023); the province of Nelson at the top of the South Island sustained eleven institutions holding collectively some 12,000 books in 1874 (for a population of 22,558). The novelist Anthony Trollope, visiting in 1872, commented: 'In all these towns are libraries, and the books are strongly bound and well thumbed. Carlyle, Macaulay and Dickens are certainly better known to small communities in New Zealand than they are to similar congregations of men and women at home' (Rogers and Rogers, 3). British publishers' colonial editions made many current works of fiction available in the colony more cheaply than in London, although booksellers and libraries sometimes had to settle for what arrived rather than precisely what they wanted. Australia provided alternative import sources, predominantly through the New South Wales Bookstall Co. and later Angus & Robertson.

Within two decades of settlement, readers could select from a good range of books and, in the larger towns, from an assortment of subscription libraries. George Chapman's lending library in Auckland held more than 4,000 titles in 1863. Traue has shown, through comparisons with Australia and Britain, that 'within 40 years of settlement New Zealand had more public lending libraries per head of population than any other country in the world' (Traue, 'Fiction, Public Libraries', 86). As with all such comparative statistics, the per capita qualification is crucial; New Zealand's high figures result, in part, from a fairly sparse and dispersed population. Nonetheless, demand was strong and reading widely valued. One reason that colonial New Zealand enjoyed so many libraries was that provincial, and later central, government education boards offered institutions with libraries an annual subsidy of up to £100 to purchase books. From 1877 to 1902, however, this subsidy was made available only if an institution imposed an annual borrowing fee of at least 5*s.*, although most permitted free on-site reading. This stricture discouraged the establishment of free municipal libraries. It also reinforced a Protestant sense of propriety that regarded the reading of fiction as entertainment, and therefore a personal luxury. Later, the influence of the Carnegie Corporation encouraged a move away from lending fees; eighteen institutions benefited from its support, as did universities and other specialist libraries when the Corporation funded overseas training for librarians in the 1930s and 1940s. Even free institutions, however, retain a semblance of the older view, with modest fees ranging from 50¢ to $5 rental for the most popular items, such as detective fiction or current bestsellers. Such fees permit libraries to collect a much broader range of works and still meet the demand for current fiction.

In a country so dependent on importation for the availability of books, libraries play a major role in providing access to them, and few towns of any size lack a public library. The Library and Information Association of New Zealand boasted 459 institutional members in 2006, for a country with only five main cities. Public libraries (as opposed to the earlier subscription services) first came to most small towns in the form of mobile libraries (book vans) operated by the Country Library Service set up by G. T. Alley in 1938. The service continued until 1988, when it was replaced briefly by a mail service, until overtaken by the Internet. In 1942, the government formed the School Library Service, a programme that amalgamated with the Country Library Service to form the first National Library Service in 1945. Meanwhile, copyright legal deposit requirements fed continual growth of the General Assembly Library in Wellington, which, together with the National Library Service, formed the basis of the National Library established in 1965.

The National Library houses the Turnbull Library, one of New Zealand's three most significant heritage collections; the others are the Grey Collection (Auckland City Libraries) and the Hocken Collections (Dunedin). All three— gifts from dedicated collectors interested in the early history of New Zealand— were established between 1882 and 1920, but have been continually expanded by further gifts and bequests to ensure that the country's print heritage is well preserved.

5 Current trends

The small publisher remains the norm in New Zealand: a 2003 report found that only a few multinational publishers, such as Penguin, successfully exported New Zealand titles, while three-quarters of New Zealand publishers together generated just 2 per cent of the total revenue from book exports. Thus, the majority of New Zealand books are just that—books written by New Zealanders for New Zealanders. International distribution, where it occurs, is most likely to be carried out by a multinational publisher, while book production may take place either in New Zealand or overseas, primarily in Asia. Fortunately, New Zealanders continue to borrow and buy books in healthy numbers, and the number of publishers and titles continues to rise, although the average size of print runs is probably dropping.

A small country of slightly more than 4 million people, New Zealand has always been self-conscious about documenting itself. This has resulted in the creation and preservation of much material. Yet, this abundance of sources, the bifurcated strands of New Zealand print history, and uncertainties about the social status of print have also produced, problematically, a certain hesitancy about composing a national history of the book. The exemplary selected studies of aspects of print history in *Book & Print in New Zealand* have sketched out what is known of many aspects of New Zealand print culture, and recent investigations have added greatly to knowledge of Maori newspapers. More detailed bibliographies, such as George Griffiths' *Books and Pamphlets on Southern New Zealand* (2006), acknowledge the significance of the local even as they enumerate a daunting number of potential new sources. Teasing out the strands of local, national, and international history remains a desideratum, one that will probably await the completion of histories in other former colonies, including Australia and Canada. Allen Curnow, New Zealand's most famous poet, memorably characterized New Zealand as a 'small room with large windows', and the publishers, readers, and writers of New Zealand will undoubtedly maintain their tradition of a strong local sense of place mediated by a broad international perspective.

BIBLIOGRAPHY

A. G. Bagnall, *New Zealand National Bibliography to the Year 1960* (5 vols in 6, 1969–85)

J. Curnow et al., eds., *Rere Atu, Taku Manu: Discovering History, Language and Politics in the Maori Language Newspapers* (2002)

Exports of New Zealand Published Books, report for the Ministry of Culture and Heritage (2003), www.mch.govt.nz/publications/book-export/export-nz-books-report.pdf, consulted Mar. 2007

P. Griffith et al., eds., *Book & Print in New Zealand* (1997); online at the New Zealand Etext Centre, www.nzetc.org/tm/scholarly/tei-GriBook.html, consulted Sept. 2007

P. Parkinson and P. Griffith, *Books in Maori, 1815–1900* (2004)

L. Paterson, *Colonial Discourses: Niupepa Maori, 1855–1863* (2006)

H. Price, *School Books Published in New Zealand to 1960* (1992)

A. Rogers and M. Rogers, *Turning the Pages* (1993)

J. Traue, 'The Two Histories of the Book in New Zealand', *BSANZ Bulletin*, 25:1–2 (2001), 8–16

—— 'Fiction, Public Libraries and the Reading Public', *BSANZ Bulletin*, 28 (2004), 84–91

The History of the Book in Latin America (including Incas and Aztecs)

EUGENIA ROLDÁN VERA

1 Pictorial MSS

Before the Spanish conquest, the people of the Americas had a wide range of systems for recording dates, astronomical information, and numerical data. Writing, in the form of pictograms that represent meanings with no relation to sounds, was used by virtually all indigenous groups throughout the continent. Good examples are known from the Olmecs, Zapotecs, Mixtecs, Purépechas, and Aztecs in Mexico, and the Incas in Andean South America. Although these people did use some developing phonetic signs, only the Mayas in Mesoamerica (the region comprising today's Central America, southern Mexico, and central Mexico) developed a method of writing that represents phonetic language, from the 3rd century BC. Theirs was a system that combined logograms, phonetic syllables, and ideograms, and it was significantly more complex than the writing systems of later Mesoamerican civilizations. Both pictographic and phonetic scripts were carved in stones or bones, engraved in metal, and painted on ceramics; some scholars suggest that the still not fully deciphered Inca quipu computing system, consisting in assemblages of knotted strings, was a form of writing in its own right (*see* 1).

In Mesoamerica, information was also recorded on long strips of paper (made of the bark of the amate tree, a variety of the genus *Ficus*), agave fibres, or animal hides, which were folded like an accordion for storage and protected by wooden covers. These were the so-called codices or pictorial MSS, for many the

Americas' first proper 'books', which must have existed at least since the Classical Period (AD 3rd–8th centuries). Codices recorded astrological information, religious and astronomical calendars, knowledge about the Indian gods, peoples' histories, genealogies of rulers, cartographic information (land boundaries, migration routes), and tribute collection. They were stored in temples and schools, and reading them was an activity that combined individual visual decoding with an oral explanation provided by priests or teachers. Other codices seem to have been used as visual mnemonic supports for traditional oral poetry, storytelling, and moral teachings given by parents to their children. Although most of these codices were burnt by the Spanish conquerors and missionaries after 1521, fifteen have been preserved, among them the codices Borgia, Fejérváry-Mayer, Laud, Vindobonensis, Nuttall, Bodley, Vatican B, Dresden, and Tro-Cortesiano. They all date from the 14th–16th centuries and belong to the Maya, Mixtec, Aztec, and other peoples from the Nahua group.

In spite of the large-scale destruction of indigenous culture caused by the Spanish conquest and colonization (16th–early 19th centuries), pictorial MSS remained a widespread form of recording information in Mesoamerica during much of the colonial period. Apart from the introduction of Western painting styles and the use of Spanish paper and cloth in addition to the indigenous amate, the most significant change in the post-conquest codices was the combination of painting with text written in the roman alphabet, which was introduced by the Spaniards. Most of these MSS were used for administrative purposes—they were made by indigenous local authorities as registers of tribute for the colonial rulers and proof of land titles in the context of litigation. Others were commissioned from indigenous scribes—or indigenous students trained in Spanish schools—in the first decades of Spanish rule by missionaries or colonial authorities interested in pre-Columbian thinking and traditions, history, and knowledge about the natural world. Whereas for the Spanish these codices were seen as a means to facilitate Christianization or colonial administration, for the Indians they constituted a way to preserve the memory of their culture. Nearly 430 codices of this sort have been preserved, the most comprehensive inventory of which was produced by Cline (Cline, 81–252). Some paradigmatic examples include: the *Tira de la Peregrinación*, the Codex Xólotl, the *Matrícula de Tributos* (which showed the tribute system of the Mexica empire), the Codex Bourbon and the *Tonalámatl Aubin* (divinatory almanacs), the Codex Mendoza (commissioned by the first viceroy of New Spain, Antonio de Mendoza, to inform the emperor Charles V (King Charles I of Spain) about the history, administration system, and everyday life of the ancient Mexicas), the Codex Badiano (an inventory of medicinal plants), and the Codex Florentino (a compilation of testimonies of the elderly about the divine, human, and natural world of the pre-Columbian Mexicans).

Spanish missionaries drew on the tradition of codices in their effort to convert the indigenous population to Catholicism. They created the genre of pictorial catechisms—known as 'Testerian MSS'—which were small volumes of religious doctrine drawn with mnemonic figures, each of which represents a phrase, word, or syllable of the Christian text in indigenous language. Through them, the Indians were to memorize the dogmas, prayers, and commandments of the new religion, and by means of the images they would be able to communicate to the priests the sins they had committed. On the other hand, Indians also chose to use the roman alphabet to put down in indigenous languages information that had been previously orally transmitted in their cultures; the best examples of such texts come from the Maya region. The *Popol Vuh*, a history of the Mayan people (allegedly based on ancient codices and oral tradition), was secretly recorded (*c.*1550) in Mayan language but in roman alphabet by Indians who had attended Spanish missionary schools. Mayan priests followed a similar strategy in their writing of at least eighteen *Chilam Balam* books, in which they recorded the past, described the present, and stated prophecies for the future. These were collectively written MSS—with the main body of the text in Mayan language, often accompanied by drawings—copied and enlarged during the 16th–18th centuries, and passed down through the generations. This new arrangement epitomized the semantic transformation that took place with the introduction of new writing and reading practices in the colonial period: images, which in pre-Columbian codices were the powerful support for a predominantly oral culture, became a device meant to assist the understanding of written texts.

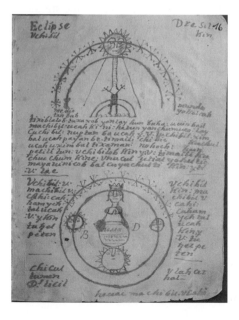

Notes on astronomy from the MS *Chilam Balam de Chumayel* (*c.*1775–1800). The MS relates the Spaniards' conquest of the Yucatán. Princeton Mesoamerican Manuscripts (C0940). Manuscripts Division. Department of Rare Books and Special Collections. Princeton University Library

The persistence of the codex as a form for recording information in later stages of the colonial period is exemplified by the so called *Techialoyan* codices or 'fake' pictorial MSS, produced by some indigenous communities by the end of the 17th and the early 18th centuries. These were the communities' property titles intended to prove their ancient possession of the land; they were drawn in a way that made them appear pre-Columbian and were used in litigation.

2 Book restrictions under colonial rule

The Spanish and Portuguese conquerors brought with them not only the alphabet but also the printed book and, at least to some places, the printing press. The first books to arrive in America were the books of hours taken by Columbus's men to the Caribbean islands, together with chivalric romances— such as the *Amadís de Gaula*, *Cid Ruy Díaz*, or *Clarián de Landanis*—and other fictional literature which contributed so much to feeding the conquerors' imagination and their dreams of glory. Although the Spanish Crown attempted to prohibit the export of non-religious popular literature (of which more than 50 titles in at least 316 editions were printed in Spain during the 16th century) to the New World, its flow was steady throughout the first century of colonial rule.

Spain and Portugal attempted to control the production and reading of books in their colonies, both by issuing exclusive printing and trade rights and through the vigilance of the Inquisition. In 1525, the Spanish Crown gave the Seville-based publisher Jakob Cromberger absolute control over the book trade with New Spain (today's Mexico, parts of the southwestern US, and Central America), a monopoly that was later transferred to his son Johann (Juan). Subsequently, the Spanish Crown granted exclusive publishing rights to selected printers in the colonies, especially for the publication of popular religious books; the rights also tended to inhibit the expansion of print in those territories. The Inquisition was meant to see that none of the books listed in the *Index Librorum Prohibitorum*— mainly heretical works, books of magic and divination and, in the 18th century, works of the French *philosophes*—made its way into the Americas. Yet this form of control was not very strict, and smuggling from Britain and France was common, especially in the last decades of Spanish rule. Furthermore, every book printed in Spanish America had theoretically to be examined by the Inquisition, the *Consejo de Indias*, or the *Real Audiencia* before publication, but this form of censorship was less effective in the control of print than the granting of exclusive printing rights. Portugal's monopoly over Brazil was even stricter, for the colony was treated largely as an agricultural producer, and the production of manufactured goods, including print, was prevented by a series of laws until the mid-18th century.

Nevertheless, during colonial times *c*.30,000 titles were printed in Latin America, the most comprehensive accounts of which can be found in the bibliographies compiled by José Toribio Medina. Of all those titles, 12,000 were produced in New Spain. Indeed, during the 16th and 17th centuries, only the viceroyalties of New Spain and Peru, the richest colonies of the Spanish empire, possessed printing presses. The first printing press of the Americas was established in Mexico City in 1539, by Juan Pablos, a contractor of Johann Cromberger. In Lima, the first printing press was established in 1581, in the charge of the typographer Antonio Ricardo. With the exception of Puebla, in New Spain, and Guatemala City, which acquired their first printing presses in the 17th century (1640 and 1660 respectively), the rest of the Spanish and Portuguese colonial cities had to wait until the 18th or even until the 19th century to acquire a press: La Habana in 1701, Oaxaca in 1720, Bogotá in c.1738, Rio de Janeiro in 1747, Quito in 1760, Cordoba (Rio de la Plata) in 1765, Buenos Aires in 1780, Santiago de Chile in c.1780, Guadalajara and Veracruz in 1794, San José de Puerto Rico in c.1806, Caracas in 1808, La Paz in 1822, and Tegucigalpa in c.1829. In their South American reductions or settlements, the Jesuits attempted to make their own manual printing presses; but they managed this only in some cases. In Paraguay (a territory that comprises today's Paraguay and parts of Brazil and Argentina), they put together a rudimentary hand-made press towards 1705, with which they printed works in Spanish and in the Guarani language.

Peruvian and Mexican publishing in the 16th century was largely dominated by material used for the religious conversion of the Indians—catechisms, doctrines, and primers, as well as dictionaries and grammars of indigenous

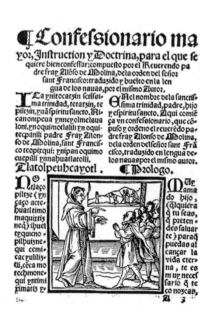

A bilingual book for the conversion of the Indians in the New Spain: the Franciscan priest Alonso de Molina's *Confesionario Mayor en la lingua Mexicana y Castellana* (Mexico, 1569). www.cervantesvirtual.com

languages; prayer books and liturgical works, alongside compilations of laws, were also published from an early date. But none of the chronicles of the conquest or of the works of the missionaries about the history and traditions of the indigenous peoples was published in the Americas. Neither was a single chivalric romance published in the colonies, in spite of the genre's popularity in those territories, thus indicating the efficiency of the Spanish publishers' monopoly over certain kinds of works. In the 17th century, book production increased considerably; in New Spain alone 1,228 titles were published, in contrast with the 179 of the previous century. New genres were added to the works used regularly in Christianization: books about natural history and astrology such as the *Repertorio* by Henrico Martínez (Mexico City, 1606), chronicles of the activities of the religious orders in the respective colonies, and even literary works by authors such as Bernardo de Balbuena, the Mexican nun Sor Juana Inés de la Cruz, and the Peruvian Juan de Espinosa Medrano ('El Lunarejo'). The books imported from Spain were largely literary, with the dominant romances giving way to plays. Most of the books of this period, given their scarcity, high cost, and the low level of the general population's literacy, ended up in the libraries of the universities of Mexico City, Lima, and Santo Domingo, in convents, or in the private libraries of members of the upper-level clergy and government officials.

In the 18th century, the production of print in Latin America increased three-fold compared to the previous century (in New Spain at least 3,481 titles were published), partly thanks to the establishment of printing offices in other colonies. Works of religious doctrine and religious instruction continued to dominate, alongside religious chronicles and some historical and literary works. The main novelty of this century, however, was the emergence of the periodical, in the form of the monthly or weekly *Gacetas*. These publications contained news from the Crown; events in Europe and in the different colonies; notices about the arrival and departure of ships; edicts; and information about deaths, feasts, and lost objects. They became common in the second half of the 18th century and in the first decade of the 19th. The following titles exemplify this trend: *Diarios y memorias de los sucesos principales* (Lima, 1700–1711), *Gaceta de México* (1722, 1728–42), *Gaceta de Guatemala* (1729–31), *Gaceta de Lima* (1739–76), *Mercurio de México* (1741–2, 1764), *Gaceta de La Habana* (1764), *Papel Periódico de La Habana* (1789), *Papel Periódico de la Ciudad de Santafé de Bogotá* (1791–7), and the *Gaceta de Buenos Aires* (1810–21). Some *gacetas* focused specifically on scientific and learned matters, such as the *Mercurio volante* (Mexico City, 1772–3), by José Ignacio Bartolache; the *Gaceta de literatura de México* (1788–95), by José Alzate; and the *Mercurio peruano* (1791–4); these were intended not only for the scientific community but also for the enlightened general reader. A few daily newspapers such as the *Telégrafo mercantil del Río de la Plata* (1801–5) and the *Diario de México* (1805–17) appeared at the turn of the century. It is generally assumed that these periodicals helped form an incipient public sphere: communities of readers were created and provided with a space in which awareness of their own country and of the situation within the Spanish empire was moulded on a daily basis. Such writings also gave shape to a feeling of American (or creole) identity, which was reinforced by another kind of literature imported from abroad: works published by a handful of exiled Jesuits (expelled from the Spanish empire in 1767) about the history, the natural world, and the geography of individual Spanish-American countries. José Gumilla's *El Orinoco ilustrado* (1741–4), Juan José de Eguiara y Eguren's *Bibliotheca Mexicana* (1755), or Francisco Xavier Clavijero's *Historia antigua de México* (1780) are the best examples of this kind of works.

In addition to such developments, educational reforms carried out in the Spanish empire in the last decades of the 18th century resulted in an expansion of basic literacy, thus expanding the market for print. Moreover, changes in maritime trade brought about by the French Revolution and the Napoleonic wars led the Spanish and Portuguese empires to lose some of their monopoly over the Americas. This facilitated the smuggling of French and British books to the colonies, which enlarged the libraries of Spanish-American creole elites and gradually made them more cosmopolitan.

3 Independence and the print revolution

The French invasion of the Iberian Peninsula in 1808 unleashed a political crisis throughout the Spanish and the Portuguese empires that, between 1808 and 1824, eventually led to the independence of all their colonies in America (except Cuba and Puerto Rico). These events were accompanied by a print revolution. The Spanish king's abdication and the dissolution of his empire resulted in the virtual disappearance of the printing monopolies, the end of the Inquisition, and the lifting of restrictions on the import of foreign books and printing presses. The need for rapid information about events in Europe and about the independence movements' development stimulated the publication of periodicals, the appearance of new genres such as flyers and pamphlets, and the opening up of new spaces for public discussion and collective reading. The armies fighting for independence began to use portable printing presses, as they were advancing, to promulgate their manifestos and war reports. Moreover, the liberal 1812 Spanish constitution (endorsed by the colonies that had not yet become independent) established freedom of the press, a measure which was later incorporated into the liberal constitutions of all the newly independent countries—most of them republics. As a result of these developments, a total of 2,457 books and pamphlets were printed in Mexico alone between 1804 and 1820, and over that period the ratio of religious to political titles was inverted from around 80 per cent over 5 per cent in 1804–7, shifting to 17 per cent over 75 per cent in 1820 (Guerra, 288–90). In Venezuela, where the first printing press was introduced in 1808, 71 periodicals were published between 1808 and 1830.

In Brazil, the print revolution corresponded to Rio de Janeiro's rise between 1808 and 1821 as the metropolis of the Portuguese empire. When the royal family fled Lisbon and settled in Rio de Janeiro, the king lifted the ban on printing and established the official *Impressão Régia* (Royal Press) there, which opened with a few presses imported from England. The Royal Press produced roughly 1,200 titles on a variety of subjects over the course of thirteen years. When Brazil declared its independence in 1821 and constituted itself as a liberal parliamentary monarchy (with Dom Pedro, the son of the Portuguese king, as its head), press freedom was declared. As a result, the official printing house's monopoly ended; the number of printing presses grew exponentially; books could be imported without restriction; and local publishing flourished. Haiti, which had obtained its independence from France earlier, in 1804, experienced a similar expansion of print during the liberal regimes of the first two decades of the 19th century. The South American Liberator Simón Bolívar was reportedly provided with a printing press for military use by the Haitian President Alexandre Pétion in 1815.

During the early years of independence, the expansion of print with a more or less free press and a system without exclusive printing rights led to the formation of a rudimentary public sphere. In the painful process of nation-building, the publication of periodicals and pamphlets, the prime genres of the first half of the century, contributed to the circulation of opinion; some 6,000 titles, for example, were published in Mexico between 1821 and 1850. Throughout the continent, a cosmopolitan liberal elite of men of letters who combined political activity, legislation, and literary work played a disproportionate role in shaping local book production. Among the new types of publication were accounts of the wars of independence, personal apologias for political histories, discussions about the best way to organize the new countries, and literary works about the nature of America and about the ideal of pan-American unity. A Mexican, Fray Servando Teresa de Mier, a Cuban, José María de Heredia, and a Chilean, Andrés Bello, were among the prominent members of a group of writers who produced these sorts of work. The first national libraries, sponsored with public funds, were founded in the 1810s and 1820s (of Brazil and of Argentina in 1810, of Chile in 1813, of Uruguay in 1816, and of Colombia in 1823), largely on the basis of the collections of books confiscated from the Jesuits after their expulsion from the Spanish empire in 1767; but these institutions' existence was interrupted throughout the century. However, political instability and economic grievances, as well as the high price of imported paper, hampered the development of profitable and long-lasting publishing industries, and only the so-called 'state presses', funded directly by governments for the publication of official periodicals, were able to survive continuously. Imported books, mainly Spanish editions printed in France or England, largely dominated the newly opened reading markets. These books were sold in different kinds of places (groceries, stalls in the marketplace, haberdashery shops, sugar depots, ironmongers, butchers, or post offices) and in a handful of bookshops, some of which were branches of well-established French booksellers—such as Bossange, Didot, Garnier—or of the London publisher and bookseller Rudolph Ackermann.

British and French novels, together with treatises by European writers (mostly by Jeremy Bentham, Benjamin Constant, Destutt de Tracy, and Montesquieu), formed the majority of imported books. The reprinting of successful foreign works by local printers was also a common practice throughout much of the 19th century; before the Berne Convention on copyright in 1886, there were no bilateral agreements for the protection of publishers' rights between France, Britain, or the US and any Spanish-American country (although some countries signed sporadic individual agreements on an individual basis).

From the 1840s to the 1860s, a handful of local printer-publishers achieved a degree of commercial success thanks to a combination of factors: the beginning of local paper production (in Chile, Brazil, and Mexico); a strategy of market diversification (periodicals, tracts, and coffee-table books), with publications for specific groups, such as women or children; and a policy of securing agreements with foreign publishers. The printer-publishers Ignacio Cumplido, Mariano Galván Rivera, and Vicente García Torres in Mexico and Santos Tornero in Chile are examples of such successful local publishing ventures. Moreover, the emergence of the popular serial novel (*feuilleton*) in newspapers towards the middle of the century changed the reading habits of large parts of the population (*see* **16**). Historians maintain that Brazilian and Mexican serial novels, such as Manuel Antônio de Almeida's *Memórias de um sargento de milícias*, published in the *Correio Mercantil* (1852–3), and Manuel Payno's *El fistol del diablo*, in *Revista científica y literaria* (1845–6), contributed significantly to the growth of the reading public in their countries.

The consolidation of nation-states in the second half of the 19th century, together with gradual economic expansion, gave a new impetus to the publishing industry and shaped the emergence of new genres. This growth was reflected in the increased production of national histories and geographies, the foundation of more national libraries (of Puerto Rico in 1843, of Nicaragua in 1882, and of Mexico in 1867), and the quest for national literatures. Under the influence of romanticism, local book production was dominated by national themes, local landscapes, and regional human types; the colonial past became the subject of the increasingly popular historical novel. José Hernández's *Martín Fierro* (Argentina, 1872–9), which became a bestseller, Jorge Isaacs's *María*, a Cuban anti-slavery novel, (Colombia, 1867), and Ricardo Palma's *Tradiciones peruanas* (1872–1910) are only a few examples of this nationalistic approach.

Moreover, although universal education was made a legal requirement from the early period of independence, considerable expansion of the educational system in most Latin American countries only began in the second half of the century. The growth in numbers of students had the double result of enlarging the reading public and of making textbooks a secure and fast-growing business after 1850—a business that was dominated by foreign publishing houses with branches in Spanish- and Portuguese-speaking countries. Indeed, the incursion of foreign publishers in the Latin American textbook market had started in the 1820s, when Ackermann exported, with limited success, large numbers of secular 'catechisms' of general knowledge (meant for both school and non-school audiences) to all Spanish-American countries. Later in the century, in the 1860s and 1870s, the American D. Appleton & Co. was more successful with exports of books to South America. But it was the French publishing houses Bouret, Garnier, and Hachette with branches for the printing and selling of their publications in Spanish-American countries and Brazil, that became the most important textbook suppliers in the second half of the 19th century and the beginning of the 20th. The expansion in schooling was accompanied by the creation of larger numbers of public libraries (the prime example was in Argentina, where the reformer Domingo Faustino Sarmiento founded more than 100 public libraries after 1868). Towards the last decades of the 19th century, the influence of positivism encouraged the production of national bibliographies—of which the works by the Chilean Medina about all the Spanish-American countries are the foremost examples—and monumental national histories, such as the five-volume work coordinated by Vicente Riva Palacio entitled *México a través de los siglos* (1880), the ten volumes of Vicente Fidel López's *Historia de la República Argentina* (1883–93), and Diego Barros Arana's sixteen-volume *Historia general de Chile* (1894–1902). In terms of literature, the economic stability and relative prosperity of the last two decades of the 19th century favoured the development of modernism, a trend that was influenced by European cosmopolitanism and fascination for the 'Orient'. Most of the works of Rubén Darío of Nicaragua, José Martí of Cuba, José Asunción Silva of Colombia, and Manuel Gutiérrez Nájera and Amado Nervo of Mexico were also published in Latin American countries other than their own, indicating that their movement's cosmopolitanism was paralleled by the internationalization of the literary market. This broadening of the marketplace coincided with a trend across the region towards the professionalization of publishing, which became a separate business from printing and bookselling.

4 The development of the publishing industries in the 20th century

By the early 20th century, the growing Latin American book market was still dominated by French publishing houses—Garnier, Bouret, Ollendorff, Armand Colin, Hachette, Michaud, and Editorial Franco-Iberoamericana—plus some German (Herder), English (Nelson) and American (Appleton) houses. They all specialized not only in translations but in original publications in Spanish and Portuguese, and their superior technology and commercial policies allowed them to make large profits. However, after the outbreak of World War I French book exports to Latin America declined considerably, and Spain began taking over as an important supplier of books to the region. In fact, a few years after the 1898 Spanish-American war, when Spain lost Cuba and Puerto Rico, its last colonies in the continent, the former power tried to deepen its cultural ties with its past colonies, and successive Spanish governments saw in the book trade a vehicle for this. Thus, new international involvement, and the implementation of a fiscal regime more or less favourable for book exports to the region from the late 1910s to the 1930s, led Spain to become a power in Spanish-language publishing. By 1932, Spain's book exports had reached US $1,214,000 (Subercaseaux, 148). Similarly, French involvement in World War I also resulted in a decrease of book exports to Brazil, which in turn favoured Portuguese exports to its former American colony.

On the other hand, the Mexican revolution (lasting from 1910 to c.1920) and the repercussions of World War I generated new intellectual trends across the continent; many thinkers were led to reconsider the cultural uniqueness of Latin America as a region in relation to other parts of the world. In the wake of nationalism and pan-Americanism, new genres flourished, especially novels with a social content and provocative essays. Intellectuals with political positions such as the Uruguayan José Enrique Rodó, the Peruvian José Carlos Mariátegui, the Mexicans José Vasconcelos and Alfonso Reyes, the Dominican Pedro Henríquez Ureña, and the Colombian Germán Arciniegas wrote extensively on the conceptualization of Latin America as a geographic, cultural, and spiritual unity. In parallel with intellectual debate, social reform—the attempt to integrate marginal sectors of the population, including Indians and Africans, into the new idea of the nation—resulted in creating a huge reading public for the first time in the history of those countries.

Although the 1930s were affected badly by the world economic depression, the outbreak of World War II in Europe coincided with the start of industrialization in most Latin American countries, with positive repercussions for the publishing industry. Indeed, the Spanish Civil War (1936–9) and World War II gave the emerging publishing industries of many Latin American countries an unexpected boost. A decrease in European book exports allowed domestic book production to increase, resulting in the creation of new publishing houses throughout the region. After 1945, the book industry followed the rapid pace of economic growth and industrialization, aided by strong government incentives.

In an era of state expansion and support for nationalism, culture was seen to be a government responsibility. In Argentina, Brazil, Colombia, and Mexico, favourable tax regimes for publishers (but not necessarily for booksellers) were inaugurated; in many cases, levies on imported materials for book production were lifted; the budget for public universities—which had their own publishing departments—increased, and the state itself even became the patron of some publishing houses. Prominent examples of state-sponsored publishers include: the Fondo de Cultura Económica, created as a government holding in Mexico in 1934; the National Book Institute in Brazil (1937); and the Mexican Comisión Nacional de Libros de Texto Gratuito (1959), established to publish set works for primary schools in the whole country. In addition, those countries' publishing industries began to acquire the structure of modern enterprises, ruled by market forces: low production costs were achieved through high press runs (especially for pocket books and textbooks), which could be sold in Latin American countries with less developed publishing industries such as Chile, Uruguay, Ecuador, Peru, Bolivia, and the Central American republics. As a result, Mexican book exports grew threefold between 1945 and 1955; by 1967 export levels reached US $11.5 million. Yet the most spectacular growth was experienced by the Argentinian publishing industry, for which the period 1938–55 is known as 'the golden years': its exports went from US $20,000 in the 1940s to nearly US $200 million in the 1960s (Subercaseaux, 147). By 1960 Argentina had some 160 publishing houses, not counting the printing departments of ministries, universities, and public cultural institutions. Brazil, which had started exporting books to Portugal in the late 1920s (mainly through the publishing house Civilização Brasileira), also saw a great increase in that trade between 1958 and 1970, from US $54,000 to US $2.4 million (Hallewell, 208).

By the 1960s, Latin American publishers also helped to expand the population's reading habits by diversifying distribution. Instead of relying only on bookshops (which were still limited in number), they reached out to stationers, post offices, corner shops, and other kinds of popular outlets. This strategy, which was initiated successfully by Monteiro Lobato of Brazil in the 1910s and 1920s, was later put into practice by the Argentinian Editorial Universitaria de Buenos Aires (EUDEBA) and the Centro Editor de América Latina. Among other factors, these measures contributed to the consolidation of the internal market from the 1950s through to the 1970s.

State support came later (reaching its peak in communist Cuba, where all publishing houses were state-related and publishing was controlled by the government) or was limited in other Latin American countries; but on the whole the entire region experienced a growth in book production and consumption during the mid-20th century. It was precisely at this time of the Latin American publishing industry's expansion that literary production grew and came to be recognized internationally as original and characteristically 'Latin American'. With a combination of influences from early 20th-century surrealism, an interest in social topics, and the consciousness of a distinct Latin American cultural identity, poetry and fiction created new kinds of realism, in particular 'magical realism', metaphysical tales, and other kinds of fantastic literature. Pablo Neruda, Octavio Paz, Gabriel García Márquez (all of whom won the Nobel Prize for Literature), Miguel Angel Asturias, Julio Cortázar, Jorge Luis Borges—to mention only the best-known authors—produced their most important works between the 1940s and the 1960s. Their rapid rise to international fame was assisted by the peak in production and international trade reached by Latin American publishing in the period.

Complementing state support for the production and reading of books, UNESCO in 1971 created a Regional Centre for the Promotion of the Book in Latin America and the Caribbean (CERLALC), situated in Bogotá; members of the centre were Argentina, Bolivia, Brazil, Colombia, Costa Rica, Chile, Cuba, Dominican Republic, Ecuador, Guatemala, Nicaragua, Panama, Paraguay, Peru, Spain, Uruguay, and Venezuela. CERLALC's aim was and is to promote the production, circulation, distribution, and reading of books in Latin America. Its design incorporates legal frameworks for free trade in books; it encourages regional governments to sign international conventions concerning copyright and against piracy; it initiates reading campaigns and training for professionals in the book industry. CERLALC also monitors aspects of book production and circulation in most Latin American countries, about which it publishes quantitative material and qualitative essays on its website, and in books, newsletters, and journals. As a result of CERLALC's efforts, a number of Latin American countries issued so-called 'Book Laws' from the 1970s to the 1990s, which (taking as a model the Spanish book law of 1967) attempt to create legal and fiscal frameworks favourable for the production and circulation of books, as well as for the protection of authors' rights. Yet these laws, while tending to privilege author's and publishers' rights, have done little to help booksellers.

Despite such legal measures, in the second half of the 20th century the Latin American publishing industry developed unevenly and suffered important setbacks. Argentina's and Mexico's primacy in the Spanish book trade were somewhat curtailed by Spain's renewal in the 1950s and 1960s; indeed, by 1974 Spanish book exports had reached US $120 million (Subercaseaux, 148). The bloody military dictatorships of the 1950s–1980s that quashed vigorous social movements in Nicaragua, Paraguay, Guatemala, Haiti, Bolivia, Uruguay, Chile, and Argentina imposed tight censorship and control over the importing, production, and reading of a large number of books. Ill-considered policies in other countries ended up affecting the book industry or the business of bookselling: for example, a protectionist national policy towards papermaking in Mexico resulted in higher production costs for books. In addition, the fall in oil prices, precipitating a financial crisis that led to cycles of hyperinflation, devaluation, and economic recession in most of the region during the 1980s actually reduced the population's income, increased book production costs, and led to declining book sales. From 1984 to 1990, for example, Argentina produced 18 per cent fewer titles.

By the mid-1990s, the return of democracy in most Latin American countries and trade liberalization stimulated the circulation of books throughout the region, but it took away some of the direct state support of the publishing sector; in some countries, this resulted in increased retail prices for books. An imported book in Peru in the 1990s, for example, cost 40 per cent more than in its country of origin, because of the high taxes imposed by a government needing to increase its revenues. By 1999, Brazil was publishing 54 per cent of the total number of books in Latin America, Argentina 33 per cent (11,900 titles), Mexico 29 per cent (6,000 titles), and Colombia 11 per cent (2,275 titles) (UNESCO). With the exception of Argentina and Chile, school textbooks were the dominant genre in all Latin American countries.

National unity was now no longer a reliable guide for understanding the publishing industry. A new phenomenon, the result of globalization, was the merging of transnational publishing groups and the integration of Latin American and European publishing houses. Groups such as Planeta, Santillana, Norma, Random House, Mondadori, and Hachette absorbed the most successful publishing houses and operated with branches in six or more countries. Such consolidation led to a reduction in the number of independent publishers, and of publishers with a specific cultural agenda. Most of the conglomerates made their money in the secure textbook market; reduced costs by producing in countries where materials and labour were cheap; published large numbers of editions of established authors and relatively few editions of new works; and aided their distribution by using mass media they also owned. For its part, the Mexican Fondo de Cultura Económica, which still enjoyed government subsidies, became one of the strongest non-textbook publishing houses by opening branches in Argentina, Colombia, Brazil, Peru, Guatemala, Chile, and Spain.

5 Trends and perspectives for the 21st century

In the first decade of the 21st century, the trend towards the transnational merging of large publishing houses has persisted. Spain recovered its dominant position as provider of Spanish-language books: by 2005 it produced 39.7 per cent of all Spanish books sold in Latin America, whereas Spanish-American countries accounted for 40.2 per cent of sales. The biggest Latin American publishers of books in Spanish continued to be Argentina (27.1 per cent), Mexico (19 per cent), and Colombia (16.3 per cent), followed by Peru (6.1 per cent), Venezuela (5.9 per cent), Chile (5.6 per cent), Ecuador (4.3 per cent), Costa Rica (3.8 per cent), and Cuba (2.8 per cent) (SIER). Given that school textbooks were still dominant—with the significant exceptions of Argentina and Chile, where general-interest books still prevailed—and considering that the school population remained stable, the region's book industries continued to thrive. However, the main problem appeared to be distribution: large numbers of books remained unsold, booksellers had few incentives to innovate, and the big publishing groups relied on discount bookshops or supermarkets to sell their products.

Finally, the numerical domination of textbooks in book production was also suggestive of the poor reading habits of the adult Latin American population—a subject that has become a major concern in studies carried out since 2000. Although varied in scope and methodology, these investigations seem to suggest that, in spite of relatively high levels of basic literacy, the number of books read per capita in Latin American countries is very small. According to UNESCO, Mexicans read on average less than 1 book per year (although a government study from 2003 raised that number to 2.9), and only 2 per cent of citizens regularly bought a newspaper; Colombians read an average of 1.6 books, Brazilians 1.8, and Argentinians 4. In countries such as Mexico and Brazil, where there were wide social divisions, there has been a persistent pattern of polarization between groups of the population who read many books each year and groups who read nothing. A study carried out in Mexico in 2001 about the population's reading habits revealed that the most widely read 'book' was the weekly adult comic *El libro vaquero* (The Cowboy Book), of which 41 million copies were bought each year—18 million copies fewer than in 1985. Whether such a decrease indicates a change towards more sophisticated reading habits, declining enthusiasm for what popular adult comics offer, or a decrease in reading altogether awaits further determination.

BIBLIOGRAPHY

Centro Regional para el Fomento del Libro en América Latina y el Caribe (CERLALC), www.cerlalc.org, consulted Aug. 2007

CERLALC, *Producción y comercio internacional del libro en América Latina* (2003)

H. F. Cline, ed., *Guide to Ethnohistorical Sources, Handbook of Middle American Indians*, vol. 14, part 3 (1975)

J. G. Cobo Borda, ed., *Historia de las empresas editoriales en América Latina* (2000)

R. L. Dávila Castañeda, 'El libro en América Latina', Boletín *GC*, 13 (Sept. 2005), www.sic.conaculta.gob.mx/documentos/905.pdf, consulted Aug. 2007

V. M. Díaz, *Historia de la imprenta en Guatemala* (1930)

J. L. de Diego, *Editores y políticas editoriales en Argentina* (2007)

Facultad de Filosofía (UNAM), *Imprenta en México*, www.mmh.ahaw.net/imprenta/index.php, consulted Aug. 2007

A. Fornet, *El libro en Cuba* (1994)

M. A. García, *La imprenta en Honduras* (1988)

F. X. Guerra, *Modernidad e independencias* (1993)

L. Hallewell, *Books in Brazil* (1982)

T. Hampe Martínez, 'Fuentes y perspectivas para la historia del libro en el virreinato del Perú', *Boletín de la Academia Nacional de la Historia* (Venezuela), 83.320 (1997), 37–54

I. A. Leonard, *Books of the Brave*, 2e (1992)

M. León Portilla, *Códices* (2003)

J. L. Martínez, *El libro en Hispanoamérica*, 2e (1984)

A. Martínez Rus, 'La industria editorial española ante los mercados americanos del libro', *Hispania*, 62.212 (2002), 1021–58

J. T. Medina, *Biblioteca hispano-americana (1493–1810)* (7 vols, 1898–1907)

I. Molina Jiménez, *El que quiera divertirse* (1995)

E. Roldán Vera, *The British Book Trade and Spanish American Independence* (2003)

D. Sánchez Lihón, *El libro y la lectura en el Perú* (1978)

SIER (Servicio de Información Estadística Regional), *Libro y desarrollo* (2005), www.cerlalc.org/secciones/libro_desarrollo/sier.htm, consulted Aug. 2007

L. B. Suárez de la Torre, ed., *Empresa y cultura en tinta y papel* (2001)

B. Subercaseaux, *Historia del libro en Chile* (1993)

E. de la Torre Villar, *Breve historia del libro en México*, 2e (1990)

UNESCO Institute for Statistics, 'Book Production: Number of Titles by UDC Classes' (2007), www.stats.uis.unesco.org/unesco/TableViewer/tableView.aspx, consulted Aug. 2007

H. C. Woodbridge and L. S. Thompson, *Printing in Colonial Spanish America* (1976)

G. Zaid, *Los demasiados libros* (1996)

49

The History of the Book in Canada

PATRICIA LOCKHART FLEMING

1 Before printing

Since printing came late to Canada, book historians turn to anthropologists and other scholars to understand its antecedents, the Aboriginal systems of cultural transmission described by European newcomers. These scholars have observed that Native peoples created pictorial records of hunts, warfare, and spiritual life on rock by painting and carving, drew on bark scrolls and animal hides, and kept tallies on wooden slabs and notched sticks. Native allies of the French helped explorers such as Samuel de Champlain to draft maps. On the Pacific shore, cedar totem poles carved with crests announced the ancestry of family or clan, while in eastern North America wampum strings or belts made of shell beads documented events by means of symbols that were read in public performance.

Beginning with Jacques Cartier's voyage up the St Lawrence River in 1534, France claimed the Atlantic region and Quebec, as well as territories around the Great Lakes and further inland. Founded by Champlain in 1608, the city of Quebec was the capital of New France and a centre for trade, civil administration, and missionary activities. Although several of the governors requested equipment for the production of official documents, their proposals failed, leaving New France without a printing press. Forms and bills of exchange were ordered from France or copied locally; proclamations were published orally and circulated in MS. A Huron catechism was printed in Rouen in 1630; a book of ritual for the diocese of Quebec bore a Paris imprint of 1703. It was not until after the conquest of New France, when France ceded the colony to Britain in 1763, that a press was finally set up in Quebec. By that time printing had already begun at Halifax, an Atlantic port founded by the British in 1749 to counter the French, established at Louisbourg on Cape Breton Island.

2 1752–1840

The first press belonged to Bartholomew Green, a Boston printer who died soon after coming to Nova Scotia in 1751. His partner, John Bushell, succeeded him, launching the *Halifax Gazette* on 23 March 1752. Bushell's output was typical of a colonial office: a weekly newspaper, government orders, jobbing printing, and pamphlets such as the rules of a local club of firemen. He printed in English and occasionally in French. His successor, Anthony Henry—who worked at the press in Halifax for more than 40 years—launched two durable almanac series, the second in German to compete with imports from Pennsylvania favoured by the 'foreign Protestants' settled in Nova Scotia by the British. When the Stamp Act of 1765 required newspaper printers to use paper marked with a British tax stamp, Henry first complied but then showed opposition by framing the text with thick black mourning rules, a mockery he may have copied from the New England press. Quebec's first printers, William Brown and Thomas Gilmore, who had come from Philadelphia and founded the *Quebec Gazette/La Gazette de Québec* in June 1764, suspended it for seven months in 1765–6 when the Stamp Act drove up paper prices. Brown, his Neilson nephews, and John Neilson's sons went on to

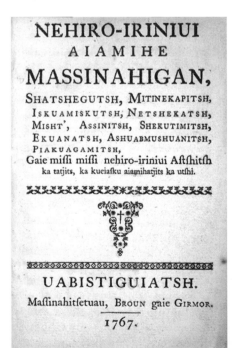

Quebec's first press—founded in 1764 by William Brown and Thomas Gilmore—printed a Montagnais prayer book, *Nehiro-Iriniui* by Jean-Baptiste de La Brosse, in 1767. The Bodleian Library, University of Oxford (Arch. 8° Misc. 1767)

dominate the trade in Quebec for decades. Although their earliest translations have been criticized, their French improved and they ventured into Native languages, completing 2,000 copies of a Montagnais prayer book in 1767. Montreal's first printer, who also came to Canada from Philadelphia, was Fleury Mesplet, a native of Marseilles. As French printer for the Continental Congress, he had printed three letters encouraging the inhabitants of Quebec to join the Americans in rebellion. He packed his press and set off for Montreal in 1776 while the city was occupied by the American army, but when the troops withdrew he was detained. The political turmoil that brought Mesplet to Montreal drove other printers, Loyalists, from a newly independent US. John Howe came from Boston to Halifax, while Shelburne, on Nova Scotia's south shore, attracted printers from New York and Philadelphia. New Brunswick's first printers were Loyalists; its first King's Printer was Christopher Sower III, member of a distinguished printing family in Germantown, Pennsylvania. The first presses on Prince Edward Island and Newfoundland were also Loyalist in allegiance. However, when the province of Upper Canada was created in 1791 to extend British laws and customs to the Loyalists settling present-day Ontario, the first printer at Niagara was not a Loyalist but a native of Quebec, trained there by William Brown. The lieutenant-governor's wife noted in her diary that the French printer Louis Roy did not write good English.

Canada's founding printers shared similar patterns of diversification as booksellers, binders, and stationers. The spread of the press can be mapped by the establishment of newspapers, because most printers in the years before 1840 were also newspaper publishers. Many papers were partisan, some openly political, others allied to a denomination or faction. Government supporters won printing contracts; opponents could face prosecution. In Montreal, Mesplet and the editor of his first newspaper were detained without charge for three years. A Scottish reformer, found guilty of seditious libel at Niagara in 1821, was banned from the province; his publisher was sentenced to a lengthy prison term. At Toronto, Francis Collins served 45 weeks for libel, although he continued to edit the *Canadian Freeman* from his cell. In 1835, Joseph Howe overwhelmed and convinced a Halifax jury with a speech of more than six hours in his own defence against a charge of seditious libel.

Two of the most prominent printers who voiced public demands for government reform in the 1830s were William Lyon Mackenzie of Toronto and Ludger Duvernay of Montreal. The office of Mackenzie's *Colonial Advocate* was vandalized in 1826, but compensation awarded by the court kept him in business. Elected to the House of Assembly in 1828, he continued to attack the government and was expelled then re-elected several times. In 1834 he was Toronto's first mayor; in 1837 he led the rebels who marched on the city but were easily put to rout. Mackenzie escaped to the US, returning in 1849 after an amnesty. Between 1828 and 1836, Duvernay was jailed three times and wounded in a duel because of articles in *La Minerve*. Warned that he was on a list of Patriote leaders about to be arrested in 1837, he left Montreal and lived in the US until

1842. Duvernay was more fortunate than many of his colleagues in Quebec and Montreal—journalists, printers, publishers, and booksellers were jailed or exiled after the Rebellions of 1837 and 1838.

The English writer Anna Jameson declared, during an unhappy visit to Toronto in 1837, that in the absence of books, newspapers were the principal medium of knowledge and communication in the province. Yet books too played an essential role in early Canada. Books were written, published, advertised, reviewed, imported, sold, serialized, bought, borrowed, collected, recited, and read. Ambitious authors writing in English usually looked abroad for publication, since the domestic market for literature was narrow. At home, they circulated poems in MS and tried to find an audience in newspapers and magazines. Subscription publishing brought some books to press, others were subsidized by the author. One bestselling work offered a warning to Canadian publishers whose original editions—not registered in Britain prior to publication, or produced within American jurisdiction by an American citizen—were not protected by copyright. Howe first published Thomas Chandler Haliburton's sketches for *The Clockmaker* in his *Novascotian* in 1835–6. Their positive reception prompted him to issue the series in book form. Within the year, editions published in London, Philadelphia, and Boston were competing for sales, even in Halifax. Haliburton thrived on international success, but Howe suffered professional and financial losses. Estimates of the output of Canadian presses show that most printers minimized risk by printing for government (nearly 40 per cent of imprints before 1821) and by relying on safe religious publication (22 per cent, in 1821–40). Almanacs were steady sellers throughout the period while cookbooks, a genre that would support the publishing ambitions of some small houses in the 20th century, first appeared in French and English in 1840.

On the shelves of bookshops in town or general merchants in the country, modest local imprints were outnumbered by books imported from the US, Britain, and France. Newspaper publishers filled columns with lists of new books for sale at their printing offices. Leading figures such as Neilson and Mackenzie travelled abroad to deal directly with wholesalers, while from the 1830s Édouard-Raymond Fabre, a Montreal bookseller who had learned his trade in Paris, published catalogues of imported stock. Although lists of books on offer provide some indication of what was available for purchase, the published catalogues of subscription and garrison libraries and the first mechanics' institutes bring us closer to the eager readers of novels, memoirs, travel, science, and history.

Recent studies of the book in Canada have taken the year 1840 as the end of the pioneer period. By that date, printers were organizing and their first strike in Toronto had failed; power presses were speeding production; the first major literary magazine was thriving in Montreal, novels had been published in French and English; and Ontario and Quebec were joined in political union. In that year, James Evans, a Wesleyan Methodist missionary in the Northwest, began to print in Cree using a syllabic system that the Aboriginal peoples adopted and still use today.

3 1840–1918

Between 1840 and 1918 Canada settled into its modern borders, lacking only Newfoundland, which joined Confederation in 1949. The population grew from 2.4 million in 1850, 3.7 in 1871, and 4.8 in 1891 to 8.8 million by 1921. Political change was negotiated in print, from responsible government in 1848 to Confederation of the provinces between 1867 and 1905, and the enfranchisement of women starting in 1918. In World War I Canada outgrew colonial status, but the monetary burden was heavy and social division severe when many in Quebec opposed conscription, and suspicion of immigrants spread. Starting in the 1870s, the federal government promoted immigration and settlement of the West. An energetic programme in which print played a central role addressed both the repatriation of Canadians who had moved on to a more prosperous US and the recruitment of newcomers from Britain and the Continent. The Dominion Lands Act of 1872 offered free land to homesteaders lured by thousands of newspaper notices and millions of pamphlets and posters published in more than a dozen languages. Completion of the transcontinental railway from Halifax to Quebec in 1876, and Montreal to Vancouver in 1885, ensured transportation and communication from Atlantic to Pacific. Block settlements were set aside for Mennonites, Icelanders, Doukhobors, and Hutterites. Other communities (such as Ukrainians) took up lands together in certain districts. The railway brought thousands of immigrants to the West—more than 100,000 in 1882, 1883, 1884, and 1903; more than 200,000 in 1907; and 400,000 in 1913.

Although some groups read American newspapers published in their own languages, most were eager to establish a local press. Like the Loyalists in Atlantic Canada a century before, they usually started with a four-page (one-sheet) weekly. An Icelandic paper in 1877 was the earliest in that language in North America. German printing, which began in Nova Scotia in 1787 and continued in Ontario from the early 19th century, dates from 1889 at Winnipeg, a printing centre for many immigrant groups. A Swedish press was established there in 1887, and the first of a flurry of competing Ukrainian newspapers appeared in 1903. A pioneer Yiddish weekly, published in Winnipeg from 1906, was soon joined by others in Montreal and Toronto. Immigrants who settled in urban centres established printing offices: Chinese and Japanese in Vancouver in 1903 and 1907, Arabic speakers in Montreal in 1908, and Italians and Bulgarians in Toronto in 1908 and 1912. In its programme to settle sturdy farmers in the West and to recruit workers for central Canada, the government preferred immigrants from Britain, Germany, and Scandinavia. After the British empire, including Canada, entered the war in 1914, however, Germans and some eastern Europeans were declared enemy aliens. Bilingual schools were closed, recent immigrants interned, and publication, even possession, of printed material in enemy languages was banned until the lifting of restrictions in 1919.

The pockets of ethnic publishing that grew up among mission and commercial presses already established in the West strengthened the regional nature of

Canada's trade during the 19th century. While publishers in Montreal and Toronto defined their ambitions nationally and imagined international success, regional publishers supplied their markets with newspapers, almanacs, textbooks, as well as verse, sermons, history, and politics, of local composition or interest. The westward expansion of the press saw newspapers established at Victoria in 1858; Winnipeg in 1859 (with a French paper across the river in St Boniface in 1871); Battleford, Saskatchewan in 1878; and Edmonton in 1880. In the North, the first gold-rush press at Dawson City, Yukon, in 1898 was preceded by Arctic printing on board the flagships of five expeditions engaged in the search for Sir John Franklin and his crew between 1850 and 1854. Although the mission of shipboard printers was to produce rescue information on coloured paper and silk for release as balloon messages, they amused their isolated readers with an almanac, a weekly newspaper, song sheets, and playbills.

Two firms established in the Atlantic region in the 1820s as booksellers, and conducted within the family for more than a century, exemplify adaptability in the trades. J. and A. McMillan of Saint John, New Brunswick, published poetry and local history, and printed for temperance, religious, and business interests. They operated a bindery, acted as wholesalers, and sold books and stationery. In Halifax, A. and W. MacKinlay's list was similar to McMillan's, with a particularly strong line of textbooks reprinted from Irish and Scottish series. On Prince Edward Island, three generations of the Haszard family sold books and stationery, served as King's and Queen's Printers, and published newspapers, textbooks, an important almanac, and other books of local interest. At its landmark 'Sign of the Book' in downtown St John's, Newfoundland, Dicks & Company, binders and stationers from the 1850s, expanded for the 20th century into printing and publishing. An early venture, *Through Newfoundland with the Camera* (1905), was directed towards an expanding tourist market for guidebooks and souvenirs of spectacular Canadian scenes.

A popular destination for visitors, the city of Quebec was also Canada's most important printing centre before 1840, although Montreal's share increased after 1820. At mid-century, Montreal's population exceeded that of Quebec; as growth slowed in the capital, Montreal boomed, emerging as a national leader in trade, industry, and transportation. Shifts within the population of both cities altered the composition and ambitions of the book trades, narrowing the market at Quebec as English speakers declined from 40 per cent in 1861 to 15 per cent by 1901. In contrast, Montreal francophones were outnumbered by British and Irish immigrants between the 1830s and the 1860s. Both markets were courted by entrepreneurs such as Charles-Odilon Beauchemin and John Lovell. French readers could browse catalogues of Beauchemin's stock or shop at Beauchemin et Valois. He published popular fiction and literary work by contemporaries; children studied Beauchemin textbooks and set off for school with his colourful notebooks. A marker of daily life, the *Almanac du peuple* was owned by Beauchemin from 1855 to 1982, and is still published today.

The founding Beauchemin, Charles-Odilon, began his career in the shop of John Lovell, arguably the most important figure in the book trades in 19th-century Canada. Apprenticed to a printer in 1823, he died 70 years later at the head of a prosperous Montreal firm. An early venture was the *Literary Garland* (1838–51), the first successful literary magazine in Canada as well as the first to pay contributors. In addition to publishing a wide range of trade books in English and French, Lovell was a pioneer printer of Canadian music. His series of textbooks was the first written by Canadians for Canadian schools. He took on lucrative contracts for government printing, and lost money on the massive *Lovell's Canadian Dominion Directory* (1871). As an active reprinter of popular British and American books, he tried to negotiate local and imperial copyright laws. He occasionally resorted to piracy, and shocked the trade in 1871 by building a plant just over the New York state border to print British works for import into Canada as foreign reprints, which had to pay far lower duties to British copyright holders than did Canadian editions.

Around mid-century in Toronto, the book trades grew out of newspaper offices when successful printers and publishers built companies that would remain in business throughout the next century and beyond. Copp Clark, tracing its origins back to the founder's apprenticeship in 1842, took over the *Canadian Almanac* (1848–) and produced maps and scientific works. The firm competed in the lucrative textbook market that expanded in Ontario after the passage of the 1871 School Act. Books authorized for the Ontario system (shaped from 1844 to 1876 by Egerton Ryerson, a Methodist of Loyalist descent) were readily adopted for use in classrooms across Canada. By the 1880s, Copp Clark was one of three publishers sharing a school reader contract that would earn profits for the next twenty years. The others were Gage and the Methodist Book & Publishing House. Finally sold to a multinational in 2003, Gage had opened as the Toronto branch of a Montreal partnership in 1860. In addition to printing, publishing, and bookselling, W. J. Gage operated a paper mill and made a speciality of school notebooks: for the 1898 school season, he had two dozen workers filling orders from all parts of the country. Established by Ryerson in 1829 to publish a denominational paper and sell religious works, the Methodist Book and Publishing House expanded its publishing mandate after the election of William Briggs as book steward in 1878; by the 1890s, it was probably Canada's largest printing and publishing enterprise.

In the 1870s, Toronto's reprint publishers earned a reputation as pirates by exploiting weaknesses in the international copyright system to pick off popular titles for unauthorized reprinting. Under various imprints and at different presses, the Belfords pirated books by the expatriate New Brunswicker May Agnes Fleming, as well as by Trollope, Mark Twain, and others. John Ross Robertson, a prominent newspaper publisher and advocate for copyright reform in parliament in the 1890s, is said to have pirated hundreds of titles for his cheap series in the 1870s and 1880s. Of course, Canadians were not alone in the scramble to supply an expanding market with cheap reading in book and serial form. One of the first local books to attract an international readership was *Black Rock* by Ralph Connor, the pen name of Charles Gordon, a young Presbyterian minister living in Winnipeg. Serialized in 1897 in a denominational paper, the novel was published the following year by Westminster in Toronto and by Hodder & Stoughton in London. Since simultaneous American publication had not been arranged, the book was widely pirated in that country. Gordon remained in Winnipeg, while most of his later works were printed in the US or stereotyped there for the Toronto publisher.

Other Canadian authors followed a similar path, selling verse and stories to American serials and trying to place their fiction in the more lucrative American markets. Marshall Saunders's *Beautiful Joe* appeared in Philadelphia in 1894, while L. M. Montgomery's fifth attempt to find an American publisher for *Anne of Green Gables* (1908) succeeded with Page of Boston. *The White Wampum* (1895) by the Native poet and performer Pauline Johnson was accepted in London by John Lane, and Louis Hémon's *Maria Chapdelaine* appeared in a Paris serial in 1914, two years before the illustrated Montreal edition. Because the French-born Hémon had already published in *Le Temps*, his situation differed from other authors writing in Quebec, whose principal markets remained local serials, almanacs, and school prize books. A notable exception was *Les Anciens Canadiens*, a novel by Philippe-Joseph Aubert de Gaspé published at Quebec by Desbarats in French (1863) and English (1864), and frequently reprinted. Outside government printing offices, translation between the two languages was not common at this time, although Pamphile Le May translated two works into French for Quebec readers: Longfellow's *Evangeline* in 1865 and William Kirby's *The Golden Dog* in 1884.

At the end of the century, a certain stability prevailed in Toronto. Britain had joined the Berne Convention for international copyright in 1886; new copyright laws were in force in Canada and the US, and a reciprocal Anglo-American agreement for the protection of copyrights was signed in 1891. Books took their place among other important commodities such as groceries, hardware, and dry goods in the expanding trade journal empire of Maclean-Hunter with the launch of *Canadian Printer and Publisher* in 1892. *Books and Notions*, published since 1884, became *Bookseller and Stationer* in 1896. New directions at the Methodist Book and Publishing House included publishing Canadian authors and strengthening the agency system. The firm moved cautiously with the Canadian list, publishing at the risk more often of the author than of the house. Robert Service sent $100 to have *Songs of a Sourdough* (1907) printed, and at the age of 92, the widely published Catharine Parr Traill was expected to find 200 subscribers for her new work of natural history. Other books were not accepted until the MS had been placed with a British or American firm. Under the agency system—which prevailed through much of the 20th century—Canadian houses were named exclusive agents for foreign publishers. In some instances they distributed bound books, in others they imported printed sheets, or bought or rented stereotype plates for a Canadian issue, possibly under a local imprint. As the trade developed, foreign firms opened branches in Toronto: Oxford University Press came in 1904; Macmillan opened in 1906. Young entrepreneurs, such as the founders of McClelland & Stewart, left established houses to set up their own companies in the early decades of the new century.

By this time public libraries were an important market for wholesalers and publishers. Starting in the 1880s, the patchwork of subscription, circulating, parish, and mechanics' institutes libraries gave way to tax-supported public libraries. Ontario set the pattern with enabling legislation in 1882. Voted into existence by a majority of citizens, the Toronto Public Library opened in 1884. By 1901, Ontario had 132 free public library boards; by 1921, there were 111 new libraries built with support from the Carnegie Foundation. Thirteen Carnegie libraries in the west included landmark buildings in Victoria, Vancouver, Edmonton, Calgary, Regina, and Winnipeg. Readers living at a distance from libraries and booksellers could supplement the offerings of the local general store by mail order. Eaton's department store, circulating 1.3 million catalogues annually by 1901, began to offer books in the 1880s. With cut-rate prices and low, even free, postage, department stores offered stiff competition to the retail trade. Rural readers could also anticipate visits from pedlars, Bible and tract society volunteers, and agents of subscription publishers. Particularly in south-western Ontario, local firms and branches of American houses outfitted travelling agents with samples of elaborate binding styles available to subscribers who signed up for a religious or topical volume. For everyday reading, almanacs—particularly Quebec's literary and historical series—remained popular. The circulation of daily and weekly newspapers exceeded 1 million copies before the end of the 19th century; and despite an abundance of imported titles, domestic publishers supplied religious and agricultural serials as well as illustrated magazines. The postal rate, reduced to a penny per pound by the end of the century, encouraged the publication and circulation of Canadian periodicals.

4 1918–2000

In the prosperous postwar years, Montreal and Toronto remained the publishing centres for French and English. Although Canada had fought free of its colonial past, the future was in question. Lingering bitterness over conscription, and limits on the teaching of French in schools in Ontario and the West, isolated Quebec from the rest of Canada. New publishing houses in Montreal were largely nationalist, offering popular and patriotic works by French Canadians. In 1920s Toronto, three publishers were investing in books by Canadian authors: McClelland & Stewart; Ryerson Press, established in 1919 to continue the trade list of the Methodist Book and Publishing House; and Macmillan of Canada. The Great Depression, which lingered through much of the 1930s, hit Canada hard, particularly in the West and among immigrants and blue-collar workers. Publishers became more cautious about Canadian MSS, although textbooks and agency sales continued to return a profit. There was fresh competition from book clubs, department stores, and cheap imports—so much activity that a new book trade journal, *Quill & Quire* (1935–), was launched. The establishment by the federal government in 1932 of a public broadcaster, the Canadian Broadcasting Corporation since 1936, was a turning point for book culture in Canada. On radio, and television from 1952, authors found both a market and an audience. After Canada entered the war in 1939, the Canadian Broadcasting Corporation, the new National Film Board, and print in every form from ration books to posters were mobilized.

The occupation of France by the German army in 1940 transformed Quebec into an international centre for French publishing, with Europeans writing in exile and the authorized reprinting of French books. Fides and other major houses were established in Montreal during this period. After the war, when restrictions on paper and other materials were lifted, the publishing trade was ready for change. The great Jack McClelland entered his father's firm in 1946; a year later, the University of Toronto Press issued a catalogue reflecting its new programme; the bookseller Jack Cole published the first Coles Notes in 1948; and the imprint 'A Harlequin Book' was initiated by a Winnipeg publisher in 1949. Canadian librarians formed their national association in 1946, the same year that the Bibliographical Society of Canada was organized. A doubling of university enrolment from 1944 to 1948 spurred the growth of collections and the construction of new libraries for McGill, the University of Toronto, and other institutions.

At the end of the decade, the federal government appointed the Royal Commission on National Development in the Arts, Letters and Sciences, which reported in 1951. Taking a strongly nationalist stance—particularly in 'The Forces of Geography', an introductory chapter documenting the powerful influence of American institutions, media, and books—the commissioners argued for a distinct Canadian culture that would be supported by public funds. They recognized the insecurity of domestic publishing, noting that the fourteen works of fiction in English published in Canada in 1948 competed with some 3,000 from Britain and the US. In addition to funding for media and the arts, they recommended scholarships and aid to universities, and chided the government about the absence of a national library. A key recommendation was the establishment of an arts funding board, the Canada Council, created in 1957. Together with the Social Sciences and Humanities Research Council of Canada (1978), it continues to play a central role in support of authors and publishers. The National Library, now Library and Archives Canada, was established in 1953 but waited until 1967 for a new building. In that same year, the Bibliothèque nationale du Québec, now Bibliothèque et Archives nationales du Québec, was formed.

The celebration in print of the Centennial of Confederation in 1967 was marked by Carl Dair's gift to the nation of Cartier, the first roman fount designed in Canada. Tundra Books began modestly in Montreal with paperback guides to Expo '67. House of Anansi, still a major literary publisher, issued its first title in 1967. In Quebec, writers, and publishers such as Éditions de l'Homme were leaders in the Quiet Revolution that transformed political, social, and cultural life as power shifted in the 1960s from Church to state. This extraordinary decade ended badly in Toronto when major publishers began to fail. As the text-book market, which had sustained the industry for more than a century, was weakened by pedagogical change and increasing competition from foreign branch plants, Gage sold its publishing division to an American educational publisher and Ryerson was bought by McGraw-Hill.

The Ontario government, which had established a Royal Commission on Book Publishing, acted promptly when Jack McClelland offered his company for sale in 1971, loaning almost $1 million and setting up a system for loan guaran-tees. In 1972, the federal government initiated block grants and translation subsidies; other measures followed, including controls on foreign takeovers, assistance with promotion and distribution, and, in 1979, a programme to award funds on the basis of sales. Still crucial to the Canadian-controlled sector, it con-tinues as the Book Publishing Industry Development Program. Other federal grants targeting youth employment and local initiatives supported writers and new presses, including specialists in alternative and feminist materials. Kids Can Press, a leader in the children's industry, began as one of the collectives in 1973. In the West, two seasoned bookmen ventured into publishing: Mel Hurtig, an Edmonton bookseller since 1956, and J. J. Douglas, later Douglas & McIntyre of Vancouver. A publishing renaissance in the Atlantic region took shape around new presses and in scholarly, literary, and popular periodicals.

By the 1980s, every province but Prince Edward Island was funding its writ-ers and publishers. Quebec went further, with a policy giving bookshops wholly owned by Canadians resident in the province the exclusive right to sell to insti-tutions. Together with federal and provincial support programmes, this realign-ment of the trade led to growth and prosperity in the 1980s and 1990s. In contrast, the closing decades of the century were treacherous for the English sector when recessions choked the market and the federal government imposed a tax on the sale of books in 1991. The budgets of granting agencies fluctuated with changes in government, and mergers and takeovers of Canadian-owned firms increased. Concentration on retail bookselling left publishers and distrib-utors vulnerable when the superstore Chapters, having bought up other national chains and squeezed out many independents, demanded stiff discounts and returned books in unprecedented numbers.

In the early years of the 21st century, publishing in English Canada is domi-nated by a handful of multinationals sharing the market with smaller, Canadian-owned presses from every region of the country. New Canadian titles in English, some 12,000 a year, now enter the market with 150,000 from Britain and the US.

BIBLIOGRAPHY

HBC
R. MacSkimming, *The Perilous Trade*, 2e
  (2007)

50

The History of the Book in America

SCOTT E. CASPER AND JOAN SHELLEY RUBIN

1 General

For nearly four centuries, the production and distribution of books has occurred within broader transformations of the American economy. Colonists in British North America depended on London for their bibles and much other reading matter, even as local printers produced many of the secular staples of everyday life. Those colonial printers and their successors in the new United States worked within the craft economy that typified most early American manufacturing. During the nation's industrial revolution of the 19th century, capitalist publishing firms came to dominate an increasingly sophisticated trade that encompassed sometimes complex author–publisher relations, mechanized production processes, and nationwide networks of distribution and credit. Modern business methods and the ascendancy of advertising reshaped publishing and bookselling in the first half of the 20th century, even as publishers sought to preserve the notion of books and literature as a realm apart from the marketplace. Since World War II, American books have more and more become the products of a global economy, where publishing conglomerates and, more recently, the World Wide Web blur the boundaries between nations.

Because the book has never been like most economic commodities, which are utilitarian and for which equivalent substitutes can be found, its meaning has always been linked to the central tensions in American culture. The capitalist market for books has simultaneously promoted broad access to diverse publications and fuelled a persistent concern about the welfare of the nation's literary and spiritual life. Cultural mediators have sought to exert centripetal force on Americans' choices for and their practices of reading from the 17th century to the present day. From Puritan authorities who attempted to guard early New Englanders from worldly publications, to 20th-century cultural figures who hoped to restore the place of 'great books' in America's schools and homes, individuals and institutions have seen the book as a bulwark against spiritual decline and secular democracy. Yet American history has witnessed an ever-expanding array of religious, ethnic, occupational, political, and regional ties, which complicate any unitary definition of national culture. That multiplicity of collective identities, as well as the differences among the intermediaries themselves, has worked to foster a wider range of meanings, purposes, and settings for reading.

2 The colonial period: a transatlantic world of books

2.1 17th-century printing

Printing in America before 1700 was a colonial endeavour in most respects. The first printers were immigrants, some of whose families would remain in the trade for generations, such as the Greens of New England and the Bradfords of Pennsylvania and New York. For lack of manufacturing in the colonies, they imported

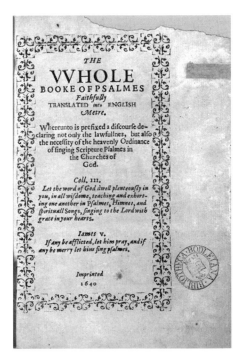

One of the eleven known surviving copies of the Bay Psalm Book, printed by Stephen Day at Cambridge, Massachusetts, in 1640. The Bodleian Library, University of Oxford (Arch. G. e. 40)

their capital goods (presses, type, composing sticks, and other materials) and even their paper, until the establishment of America's first paper mill outside Philadelphia in 1690. Far from London, some Boston and Cambridge printers produced their own almanacs and other cheap books as early as 1640, when the Bay Psalm Book became the first book printed in British North America. The Licensing Act of 1662, however, gave the London Stationers' Company a royal patent on most of the significant works and genres, including bibles, psalters, textbooks, almanacs, and law books. Long after that Act expired in 1695, economic factors posed still greater barriers to indigenous colonial production. Except for identifiably strong sellers, particularly annual almanacs and schoolbooks such as the *New England Primer*, few books justified the risk required for a sufficient press run to meet the costs of capitalization. Importing small quantities of works from England was much more profitable for colonial booksellers.

American printing in the 17th century depended heavily on governmental and clerical imprimatur and patronage. The earliest press was at Cambridge, brought from England in 1638 to serve the needs of Harvard College, the General Court (colony government), and John Eliot's mission to the Massachusett Indians. It was not until after the publication of Eliot's Indian Bible (1661–3) that the Cambridge printers Marmaduke Johnson and Samuel Green began reprinting London pamphlets, a short-lived commercial endeavour that the colonial magistrates may have closed. In 1674, the General Court granted Johnson permission to operate a press in Boston, where printing quickly assumed a different character. While Cambridge imprints were local and ecclesiastical, Boston's diverse productions included histories and biographies, almanacs, practical medical texts, and other works catering to an incipient commercial market.

Printing was slower to originate in Virginia. In 1671, more than six decades after the colony's founding, Governor William Berkeley wrote to the English government about the potentially destabilizing effects of printing and schools: 'But I thank God, there are no free schools or printing [in Virginia], and I hope we shall not have these [for a] hundred years, for learning has brought disobedience, and heresy, and sects into the world, and printing has divulged them, and libels against the best government. God keep us from both!' (Hening, 2. 517). Virginia's laws were published scribally until the early 1680s, when a member of the House of Burgesses imported a press and a skilled printer, William Nuthead, to print them. The governor and council quickly ordered the process to be stopped for lack of authorization, and Nuthead departed for Maryland, becoming that colony's first printer. Pennsylvania's proprietor, William Penn, brought its earliest printer, William Bradford, to the colony to produce Quaker materials. After various disputes with the authorities, Bradford left to become New York's first official printer.

2.2 The 18th-century book trade

If colonial printing began and sometimes ended at the whim of governmental authority, the 18th-century rise of printers in the northern seaport cities betokened a new era of commercial, competitive print culture. Philadelphia, where Benjamin Franklin made his way in 1723, is illustrative. Andrew Bradford, son of William, became Pennsylvania's government printer in the 1710s, but his output remained the typical mix of laws, almanacs, and religious publications. A London emigrant and failed printer, Samuel Keimer, arrived the same year as Franklin, established a competing press, and hired the seventeen-year-old Bostonian as his pressman. Soon Bradford and Keimer were printing rival political pamphlets and almanacs and vying for the most lucrative contracts, from the Society of Friends and the government. After an eighteen-month sojourn in London, Franklin entered the fray. With press and type ordered from London, he and Hugh Meredith opened their own printing office in 1728 and won a Quaker commission that had languished in Keimer's hands. His ambition to publish a rival newspaper to Bradford's *American Weekly Mercury* foiled by Keimer's launch of the *Pennsylvania Gazette*, Franklin satirized Keimer's paper in articles for Bradford's, then bought the *Gazette* when its circulation plummeted. By 1730, Pennsylvania's political wars had cooled and Keimer had departed for Barbados, leaving Franklin indisputably Philadelphia's second printer. John Peter Zenger played the same role in New York, setting up shop in competition with his former master, William Bradford. However, where Franklin printed contributions from all sides of the political debate, Zenger allied his *New-York Weekly Journal* with the council and against the governor—leading to the libel trial that would eventually make his name a staple of journalistic history.

Franklin built his reputation by capitalizing on nearly every niche in an increasingly intercolonial print culture. In addition to the *Gazette* and his *Poor Richard's Almanack*, he published books occasionally at his own risk, generally English works of proven appeal. More often, he printed books and pamphlets for other individuals or for corporate bodies such as the Presbyterian synod or the Library Company of Philadelphia, which he founded in 1731. A significant portion of his business was in the jobbing printing of legal forms and other ephemera. He procured lucrative government contracts to print the laws and proceedings of the Pennsylvania assembly and issues of paper money for Pennsylvania, Delaware, and New Jersey, and he won Pennsylvania's postmastership in 1737. Through partnership arrangements, Franklin helped establish printing offices across the colonies, including his former journeyman Lewis Timothy's office in Charleston, South Carolina. He also set up paper mills (including Virginia's first) to control the supply for his own printing and to assist printers elsewhere. By the 1750s, he was the colonies' largest paper merchant as well as Philadelphia's leading book importer and bookseller. Remarkable both in its own time and in the perspective of his subsequent scientific, political, and diplomatic career, Franklin's life as a printer was an unusually diverse variation on the 18th-century norm. Colonial printers made a living by combining printing and bookselling and by emphasizing jobbing printing and government printing over work on their own account. Only in Boston did a distinctive bookselling trade develop in imports from London and in locally sponsored works. By the 1740s, with the growth of commerce between the colonies, the distribution of domestically printed works went beyond their place of production as men like Franklin and his network of printer-booksellers exchanged works from New England to South Carolina.

The 18th century also witnessed an expanding transatlantic book trade, for imports of British books far outpaced population growth in British North America. It has been estimated that 'America-bound shipments between 1771 and 1774 (inclusive) comprised some 60 per cent of all English book exports' (Raven, 185). New England absorbed the greatest share of these imports in the first half of the century; from 1751 to 1780, other colonies (particularly Virginia and Maryland) accounted for a rising proportion. London wholesalers sent large shipments to colonial traders, including to small general merchants as well as dedicated booksellers and printer-booksellers. The bookshop in Williamsburg, Virginia, for example, counted more imported books than domestically produced ones in its inventory. Booksellers' newspaper advertisements proliferated throughout the colonies. Colonial retailers, such as Williamsburg's William Hunter and Joseph Royle, cultivated relationships with London traders and agents in order to acquire information about new publications and to improve their terms of payment and credit. Distance often led to strained relations, and delayed shipments—and payments—were common. American retailers complained that wholesalers dumped unsaleable London books on the colonial market, or sent books they had not ordered. London wholesalers, moreover, did not typically give American printer-booksellers the same credit terms and discounts that English metropolitan and provincial retailers received. For all the American booksellers' complaints, imports diversified their stock and connected colonists to the cosmopolitan and intellectual worlds of the imperial capital.

2.3 Reading communities and practices

Literacy rates increased in most sections of the colonies during the 18th century, although book ownership (except for almanacs and other cheap books) remained primarily the province of the affluent and the learned. Studies of signature literacy—an imprecise measure of writing ability, which lagged behind reading ability in a society where reading was taught earlier in life—offer several conclusions. Colonists arrived in America with high levels of literacy, compared with contemporary European rates. For example, 69 per cent of male indentured servants emigrating from London between 1718 and 1759 signed their contracts, as did 34 per cent of female indentured servants. Among male German immigrants, required to take loyalty oaths in Philadelphia, 60 per cent signed their names in the 1730s, a rate that rose above 80 per cent after 1760. Increasing literacy rates were the predominant pattern. This was most evident in New England, where 60 per cent of men could sign their names in 1660, 70 per cent by 1710, 85 per cent by 1760, and 90 per cent by 1790. Women's literacy rates began significantly lower (45 per cent in the early 18th century), but narrowed the gap with men's by the 1780s. Elsewhere in the colonies, literacy rates were lower, but increased during the century. Anticipating laws that would become more prevalent in the 19th century, several colonies began to proscribe instruction in writing for African-American slaves, fearing insurrection or escape: South Carolina after 1740, Georgia fifteen years later.

Estate inventories suggest that the typical household library was tiny, containing only a bible or psalter and occasionally a few other books. Bookshops' most frequent customers, learned and wealthy men, purchased mostly British imprints in an era when the financial risk of reprinting London books dwarfed that of importing a few copies. Cheap books—almanacs, chapbooks, primers, psalters, and pamphlets—were the exception, produced locally and vended in large quantities even in the colonial hinterlands. The bookshop at Williamsburg sold 4,000 to 6,000 almanacs a year in the 1750s and 1760s, and Franklin estimated that 10,000 copies of *Poor Richard's Almanack* sold annually around the mid-century. Franklin's Philadelphia partner David Hall calculated that the firm printed 141,257 copies of the almanac and 25,735 more in a pocket size, between 1752 and 1765. Such cheap publications were disseminated not only (or not even primarily) by printers and bookshops, but by chapmen or colporteurs and through general stores. Subscription and circulating libraries also originated in the mid-1700s, offering access to books to members without the cost of purchase.

Especially in emerging colonial cities and towns, reading communities took shape in a variety of social milieus that had English antecedents. In literary salons organized by elite women such as Annis Boudinot Stockton in Princeton, New Jersey, and Hannah Simons Dale in Charleston, South Carolina, women and men circulated their poetry and prose in MS. Coffee houses became centres for the exchange of news among men, as well as meeting places for private societies that practised cosmopolitan ideals of witty writing and conversation. Like the salons, coteries such as the Tuesday Club of Annapolis, Maryland, and the Schuylkill Fishing Club of Philadelphia fostered the emergence of a 'public sphere' separate from official government and religious discourse. Learned institutions also fostered intellectual connections. Colonial America had three colleges (Harvard, William and Mary, and Yale) by the early 18th century and five more by 1770. Pioneering learned and scientific societies included the American Philosophical Society for the Promotion of Useful Knowledge, created in 1769 by the merger of two existing societies. Such institutions subscribed to the transatlantic notion of a 'republic of letters', in which free inquiry would counteract the long-standing effects of church and state control. At the same time, evangelicals, influenced by the mid-century Great Awakening, developed their own reading communities, often based in the libraries and homes of local ministers and fuelled by opposition to worldly urban elites and self-consciously polite culture.

Reading practices differed according to the nature of the work and the purposes that Americans brought to their books. Cheap and ephemeral texts, such as almanacs, newspapers, and pamphlets, might be 'read to death'. For books, the oldest and still strongest meanings were spiritual: whether the Bible, Bunyan's *Pilgrim's Progress*, or Christian biographies, printed works possessed the power to transform the reader's inner self. An alternative, newer mode of reading emphasized secular rationalism, generally against the perceived excesses of evangelical enthusiasm. By the mid-18th century, literary sentimentalism offered a semblance of common ground between the evangelical and rationalist models, blending their shared emphasis on moral formation. The popularity of Samuel Richardson's *Pamela* suggested the emergent power of this model, even as it engendered enduring debates about the potentially pernicious effects of novel-reading.

The Revolution did not immediately transform Americans' reading, although it inspired the first indigenous bestseller, Thomas Paine's *Common Sense* (1776), and helped swell the number of American newspapers from 23 to 58. The war suspended the transatlantic trade in books and most other commodities. Printers struggled to survive, and membership in the trade was marked by high turnover. An emergent colonial reprint business, begun by the Scottish-born Philadelphia printer Robert Bell in the 1760s, collapsed. Instead, the war politicized printers, whose circumscribed output still included newspapers, pamphlets, government documents, and broadsides. Independence freed printers from the royal copyright on bible publication: petitioned by Presbyterian clergymen, a committee of the Continental Congress recommended the publication of an American edition of the Bible. After Congress fled from Philadelphia, the Scottish émigré printer Robert Aitken undertook the venture on his own, producing five successful editions of the New Testament. Unfortunately for Aitken, he decided to print the entire Bible just before the war ended—and the resumption of British imports undercut his initiative with cheaper bibles. As they had a century earlier, economic realities proved more powerful than either political restrictions or their demise.

3 The 19th century: print cultures in the expanding nation

3.1 The emergence of American publishing

In the aftermath of the Revolution, the new nation's publishing trade originated primarily in reprints of familiar works, not in the production of new books written by Americans. Aitken's failure did not deter other printers from attempting American imprints of British books. Thomas Dobson, an Edinburgh clerk, was sent by his bookseller employer to Philadelphia to open a bookshop for imported stock. Dobson diverted much of the proceeds to creating his own publishing enterprise, which included American editions of Adam Smith's *Wealth of Nations* (1788) and the eighteen-volume *Encyclopaedia Britannica* (1789–98). Isaiah Thomas, a Worcester, Massachusetts, newspaper printer, began his publishing career with reprints of small children's books (*see* **17**), then turned to the project that had bedevilled Aitken. Indeed, in the 1790s numerous American printers worked on editions of the Bible. The profusion of bibles, in a variety of formats from folio to duodecimo with market niches for diverse customers, provided the first evidence that American reprints could supplant British imports.

That recognition became the genesis of a publishing trade in the US. Some publishers, such as Dobson, had begun as importer-booksellers. Others, such as the Irish émigré Mathew Carey, started as printers, went into bookselling, and parlayed their capital into publishing (assuming the financial risks of production). Between the 1790s and the 1820s, these publishers devised a variety of mechanisms to address the common challenges of financing, distribution, and competition. At a series of book fairs following the Frankfurt and Leipzig models, held from 1802 to 1806, publishers gathered from around the nation to exchange and sell unbound stock to one another in larger quantities and at greater discounts than ordinary retailers received. Publishing by subscription, a method that in the US dated back to the 18th century, helped ensure sales in advance of production, especially for expensive illustrated or multi-volume works. In collaboration with the itinerant bookseller Mason Locke Weems, Carey used this method to redirect the southern and western markets for such works away from British imports and towards his own productions. Weems's contacts with local retail booksellers in these regions also provided Carey with a network of 'adjutants' for his cheaper books. Co-publication, an arrangement whereby multiple publishers jointly assumed the risks by purchasing a percentage of an edition in sheets, offered an alternative in the 1820s to cut-throat competition for popular British works. Beginning in 1824, publishers promoted trade sales, at which booksellers purchased works at auction. Trade sales helped establish uniform wholesale prices for books, encouraging differentiation within the book trades, with wholesaling and distribution distinct from publishing.

Meanwhile, religious publishers pioneered new forms of mass production and distribution. Non-denominational, evangelical organizations such as the Society for Propagating the Gospel Among the Indians and Others in North-America (founded in 1787) and the Massachusetts Society for Promoting Christian Knowledge (1803) contracted with printers to produce books and tracts, to be distributed to the worthy poor by volunteer travelling agents. The Philadelphia Bible Society (1808) and the New England Tract Society (1814) went a step further, becoming large-scale publishers as well as distributors. Their business model combined economy of scale in production with decentralized, local distribution. Taking advantage of the new technology of stereotyping, the Philadelphia society produced bibles in the tens of thousands; a network of auxiliary societies distributed them across Pennsylvania. The national evangelical publishing concerns founded over the next two decades—the American Bible Society (1815), the American Sunday-School Union (1824), and the American Tract Society (1825)—employed similar methods. These religious publishers stood at the forefront of technological change and mass communication in the US. To produce their huge print runs, they relied upon stereotyping before the commercial publishers did; moreover, by the 1820s the American Bible Society had also invested heavily in steam-powered printing (using the new Treadwell press) and mechanized papermaking (with Fourdrinier machines) (*see* **10, 11**). Even as the societies' nationwide distribution networks launched what would later be recognized as modern communications, their message was explicitly anti-commercial. The book market, they argued, spread the gospel of greed and immorality in the form of vicious literature, which only an equally vigorous programme of religious publishing could combat. The religious societies' early business model proved difficult to sustain. As local auxiliaries lost their energy by the 1840s, the American Tract Society and the American Bible Society employed colporteurs to distribute their books. Although the major national societies continued to prosper throughout the century, their centralized dominance of the field gave way to smaller, denominational publishing concerns.

By the 1830s, commercial firms such as Philadelphia's Carey & Lea and New York's Harper & Brothers exemplified a new mode of publishing. Some of the publishers, including the four Harper brothers, had trained as printers, but most—including New York's G. P. Putnam's Sons, Boston's W. D. Ticknor and J. T. Fields, and Philadelphia's J. B. Lippincott—had never been printers but came to publishing from other businesses. These publishers became book-trade entrepreneurs, coordinating the supply of raw materials and the physical production of printed, bound works. A few publishers conducted most of these operations themselves; most famously, the Harpers erected a seven-storey factory in 1853 after fire destroyed their earlier, more modest operation. Others, such as Ticknor & Fields, built relationships with local firms specializing in papermaking, composition, stereotyping, printing, and bookbinding. By the 1850s, American book publishing was increasingly centralized in New York, Philadelphia, and Boston; Cincinnati had a brief heyday as a western publishing hub. Firms elsewhere were associated with particular genres; for example, Chicago's Rand McNally & Co. became America's leading map publisher late in the century. Yet the eastern cities that gained predominance by the mid-19th century remained the nation's publishing centres through the 20th.

New technologies facilitated the publishers' ascendancy and fostered their distinctive identities in the literary marketplace. Stereotype plates became capital, signifying the right to publish a work and discouraging competitors from the expense of producing their own editions. As case bindings replaced unbound sheets or unadorned boards, publishers created house styles to promote brand identification. Among the first to seize this opportunity, the Harpers produced series such as 'Harper's Family Library', intended for wholesome domestic reading, and 'Harper's School District Library', designed to capitalize on the burgeoning public school movement. Both 'Libraries' were composed of diverse works, mostly by British authors, unified by a common series name and binding. As promoters of American authorship drew upon the 1840s rhetoric of Manifest Destiny, Wiley & Putnam advertised native productions in its 'Library of American Books' series, which included Melville's *Typee*, Hawthorne's *Mosses from an*

Old Manse, and works by Margaret Fuller, Edgar Allan Poe, John Greenleaf Whittier, and William Gilmore Simms. Soon thereafter, 'blue and gold' cloth-bound editions of British and American authors helped Ticknor & Fields create a reputation as America's premier publisher of transatlantic 'high' literature.

At the same time that they were organizing the processes of book production, publishers worked to manage their trade and subvert the potential for ruinous competition. In the absence of international copyright treaties, rival editions of popular British authors could lead to falling book prices as publishers sought to undersell one another. This concern led to the extra-legal but widely understood conventions known as 'the courtesy of the trade'. The primary tenet of trade courtesy stipulated that the first American publisher to announce that it had a foreign work 'in press' won the rights to its publication; other publishers were expected to relinquish any plans to publish it. By a second principle, the 'rule of association', the publisher that initially reprinted a foreign author's work could stake a claim to that author's subsequent works. The system was far from perfect, and participating publishers routinely complained about trade pirates who failed to obey these unwritten rules, such as the publishers of 'mammoth weeklies' in the 1840s and of 'cheap libraries' 40 years later. A boom-and-bust economy exacerbated the precariousness of publishing. J. P. Jewett published the century's best seller, Stowe's *Uncle Tom's Cabin*, in 1852, but suspended payments and went out of business during a nationwide depression five years later. Ticknor & Fields experienced a series of reorganizations over three decades, overextended its resources in the 1860s and 1870s, and ultimately merged in 1878 with another publisher to form what would become Houghton Mifflin Co.

Attempts to organize were more successful in niche publishing markets than in the general trade. The short-lived American Book Trade Association of the 1870s, which included most of the leading publishers as well as dozens of smaller ones, sought to establish uniform discounts to vendors in an effort to regulate prices and combat 'underselling' by agents and retailers. In more specialized areas, consolidation reigned by the end of the century. Schoolbook publishers formed their own Board of Trade in 1870; after its collapse, the four largest firms created a syndicate and eventually merged into the American Book Co., which contemporaries believed controlled 50–90 per cent of the textbook market. Music publishers, who flourished in large and small cities across the nation, formed a Board of Music Trade in 1855 to curtail their own tendencies towards ruthless price-cutting and discounting. By 1890, Boston's Oliver Ditson & Co. had swallowed most of the other leading firms from Philadelphia to San Francisco, achieving a measure of industry-wide control unparalleled in any other part of American publishing.

3.2 Disseminating the industrial book

No matter how effectively they centralized book production, American trade publishers needed to distribute their wares to far-flung customers across a geographically expanding nation. To accomplish this, they created networks to exchange information, goods, and credit. The traditional means of sharing information by letters was supplemented by specialized periodicals, notably the magazine that began as *Norton's Literary Advertiser* (1851) and became *Publishers Weekly* (1873). Advertising was promoted through publisher's lists and catalogues, with posters and flyers for new books, and in newspapers and periodicals. From the 1850s, the major firms' own general-interest magazines (such as *Harper's New Monthly Magazine* and *Putnam's Monthly*) became important venues for reviewing and advertising their books. Books were distributed by express companies and the US postal system, which maintained special rates for printed matter. To coordinate both supply and credit, publishers relied increasingly on wholesale book dealers, known as jobbers. These dealers, such as the American News Co. and A. C. McClurg & Co., distributed publishers' books to booksellers, who received a discount on the stated retail price. Trade sales, which persisted as a forum for auctioning stock, declined in importance by the 1870s as the larger publishing houses and jobbers dispatched travelling agents ('commercial travellers') to visit local retailers. Publishers in specialized areas developed distinct distribution systems: for instance, sheet music and scores were sold primarily in music shops, and schoolbook publishers hired sales agents to secure adoptions by county and state school districts. Especially after the Civil War, subscription publishing firms sent sales agents across the nation and even into remote towns and mining camps to vend their wares. In rural areas where bookshops were few, customers purchased books in general stores, ordered them by mail or by subscription, or borrowed them from libraries and other associations devoted to collective ownership. None of these modes of book distribution offered what bookshops in cities and towns made available: the fullest range of trade publishers' titles. However, unlike 20th-century bookshops, these urban shops were not places for browsing; organized by publisher rather than by subject, the stock was shelved behind the counter, with sales clerks serving and advising readers.

As Americans embraced the pleasures of reading many books just once (what scholars have termed 'extensive reading') alongside the familiar custom of studying the same ones (such as the Bible) again and again ('intensive reading'), the collective ownership of books remained an attractive alternative to individual purchase. Social libraries—voluntary associations founded by members' purchase of shares—blossomed after the Revolution, flourishing until the 1830s. More than 2,100 such libraries were created between 1786 and 1840, but many did not survive their first decade as their collections stagnated and members sought new books elsewhere. Created to shape appropriate reading tastes, social libraries generally did not collect the novels and romance fiction that readers most desired. Commercial circulating libraries, often operated by booksellers, filled that gap, offering readers the opportunity to borrow recent, popular fiction for a fee. Other sorts of libraries, founded for specific segments of urban society such as apprentices, mechanics, and merchants, were torn between their founders' mission to provide morally and socially edifying fare and their fee-pay-ing members' wishes for popular literature. By 1875 the largest of these, the New York Mercantile Library, boasted 160,000 books to cater to its members' tastes. The crusade for 'proper' reading persisted in Sunday school libraries, which increased in number from 2,000 in 1850 to more than 34,000 two decades later, and in the tax-supported school district libraries that began in Massachusetts and New York in the 1830s and 1840s.

Local governments launched the movement for tax-supported public librar-ies, the first being the Boston Public Library (1854). The movement spread slowly, but by 1894, according to one study, there were 566 free public libraries with collections of 1,000 books or more. The earliest professional librarians were men associated with learned libraries, such as Joseph Green Cogswell of New York's Astor Library. Although the Smithsonian Institution's Charles Cof-fin Jewett first imagined the possibility of a national union catalogue based on the published catalogues of many American libraries as early as the 1850s, standardization in cataloguing and collection practices proved elusive. The American Library Association and the *American Library Journal* were founded in 1876, but professional librarianship took several more decades to catch up with the spread of public libraries across the nation.

American learned culture in the first half of the 19th century relied heavily on its better-developed European counterparts. Aspiring scholars studied in Ger-man universities; and scholarly books continued overwhelmingly to be imported from Europe, even as American publishers reprinted European works in most other genres. The transatlantic moorings of learned culture gradually shifted as the US developed its own sites for the production and dissemination of knowl-edge: discipline-specific scholarly periodicals, colleges, seminaries, and research universities along the German model. The US government played a significant role in publishing the fruits of American science and exploration, in such works as the *Smithsonian Contributions to Knowledge* (1848–1916), the seven-volume geological surveys of the 40th parallel (1870–80), and John Wesley Powell's geo-logical and ethnographic studies of the American west. At the same time, com-mercial publishers created niches by catering to the learned professions: Little, Brown, & Co., and Baker, Voorhis, & Co. in law books; Lea & Blanchard (succes-sors to Mathew Carey's firm), William Wood & Co., and P. Blakiston's Sons in medical books.

3.3 Literacy and modes of reading

Across the century, literacy rates rose in tandem with the spread of public schooling, especially in the northeast and northwest (today's midwest). Tax-supported schools dated from the 17th century in Massachusetts because indi-viduals' ability to read the Bible had been central to Puritan theology, but their operation had been sporadic and decentralized. After the Revolution, propo-nents of education added a republican argument (the need for an educated citi-zenry) to the older religious one, and reformers such as Henry Barnard and

Horace Mann proposed statewide school systems to coordinate teacher training and ensure educational standards across economically and ethnically diverse populations. The number of public schools grew rapidly in New England and western states (such as Ohio) populated by New England emigrants. Few southern states or localities established public schooling before the Civil War, both because wealthy planters resisted paying to educate poorer white farmers' children and because populations were widely dispersed. In 1840, the first time the US census enumerated school attendance, 38.4 per cent of white children aged 5–19 went to public or private school for some portion of the year; by 1860, attendance had increased to 58.6 per cent. Beneath these aggregate numbers lay significant regional variation: more than four-fifths of children in New England attended school in 1840, but fewer than one-fifth of children in the south did. Similarly, although literacy was nearly universal in New England, nearly 20 per cent of white southerners reported an inability to read or write. Most southern states proscribed teaching enslaved African-Americans to read or write; an estimated 5–10 per cent of slaves were literate. After the Civil War, when southern states created public school systems and former slaves sought education for themselves and their children, the ability of African Americans to write (and, hence, presumably to read) increased rapidly: from 30 per cent in 1880 to 55 per cent two decades later.

By the mid-19th century, several conceptions about reading predominated in the US. The oldest, grounded in evangelical Protestantism, gained new energy with the Second Great Awakening, the rise of reform movements such as temperance and abolition, and the tract societies' and religious publishers' prodigious output. Evangelicals argued for literacy and reading, but against reading the wrong books: fiction, adventure stories, and irreligious material. A second ideology, linked to the public-school movement, emphasized the civic value of literacy. Equally, mass immigration led educators and civic leaders to proclaim the need to Americanize the 'foreign element'. A third mode—reading for 'self-culture', to use William Ellery Channing's term—sprang from the middle-class emphasis on self-improvement and character development. In such institutions as lyceums, lecture series, and debating societies, women and men sought intellectual and moral improvement from one another and from lecturers and authors such as Emerson. A fourth mode increasingly separated self-improvement from its earlier religious foundation: it had a transatlantic, cosmopolitan vision that developed primarily after the Civil War and prefigured 20th-century literary publishers and book clubs. Books and learning in this model implied or conferred a social and cultural cachet as well as knowledge. Against all these models stood reading purely for pleasure, which expanded with the proliferation of inexpensive books and the spread of libraries. However, commentators continued to lament the corrupting or subversive potential of entertaining reading, especially on impressionable segments of society such as women and the young.

Americans read in a variety of settings and for diverse purposes, connected to individual and collective identities. The widening availability of books, more leisure time (at least within and above the middling classes), and enhanced lighting (oil lamps and, later, electric lights) all increased the opportunities for home reading at night as well as by day. Although elementary instruction moved from households into schools, Americans still probably read more at home than anywhere else. Publishers capitalized on that transformation by marketing books in editions designed for parlour display as well as for everyday perusal. Shared reading experiences, whether the Bible on Sundays or secular works read aloud, reinforced family bonds. In schools and colleges, especially those for young women, reading contributed to the intellectual and political formation of individuals who challenged conventional constraints. Biographies of learned and eminent women encouraged their readers to imagine intellectual and social possibilities outside 'women's sphere', and so did many other genres: belles-let- tres, history, travel literature, even fiction. In the last quarter of the century, the home-study programme of the Chautauqua movement sponsored or inspired thousands of reading circles and study clubs. In these settings, women enjoyed the sorts of opportunities for self-improvement that men had long found in debating societies and mercantile associations.

Depending on the books and the circumstances, reading could strengthen national identity or promote other collective sentiments. For example, reading societies in the north before and after the Civil War instilled a sense of racial and social pride among middle-class African-Americans, who sought at once to assert their membership in the national mainstream and to challenge its assumptions about black people's capacity for education. Foreign-language publications always played a similar, dual role for their first- and second-gener- ation American readers. From their origins in colonial Pennsylvania, German- language presses followed German-speaking Americans as far west as St Louis. Rather than form a unified German-American identity, these presses promoted various senses of belonging such as to religious, literary, and learned groups, as well as to a vernacular culture. For other immigrants, reading promoted both Americanization and home ties. The Yiddish press published editions of European and American books, and America's 23 Yiddish periodicals had a circulation of 808,000 by 1910. For immigrant central and eastern European Jews, as for newly arrived Italians and many others, access to American printed works in their native languages became a tool for creating ethnic identity and community.

4 1890–1950: modern business and cultural capital

4.1 Trends in publishing and marketing

In some respects, the history of book production, distribution, and consump- tion between 1890 and 1950 is one of continuity with the previous period: the processes of urbanization, industrialization, and technological change that con- fronted publishers with opportunities and challenges had been under way for decades, along with the rise in the educational level of American readers. Within those long-term trends, however, particular developments altered conditions for print producers, mediators, and consumers in the first half of the 20th century. The influx of non-English-speaking immigrants, the growth of mass entertainment, the increase in leisure time for some workers as well as for the middle classes, and new forms of advertising and display simultaneously strengthened and threatened the place of print in American life. More books, produced more cheaply and efficiently, were available to more people, but so was a wider array of competing commodities and diversions. Publishers and readers alike responded by negotiating various compromises between acceptance of modern business values and the preservation of a realm for the book that appeared to be above the market.

By the 1890s, the innovations of the preceding 50 years in papermaking (*see* **10**) and printing (*see* **11**) had dramatically increased American publishers' output. Of course, the term 'publishers' conceals a range of enterprises, including the dime novel paperbacks of Street & Smith, reprint volumes such as George P. Munro's 'Seaside Library', the mainstream fiction issued by established firms like Harper, and the collected editions of venerated American writers produced by Houghton Mifflin in variably priced sets. Slim volumes of verse—the products of self-publishing, or inspired by the Arts and Crafts movement—made poetry available to readers apart from weightier collections from Macmillan or Frederick A. Stokes Co. These various formats in turn created and reinforced differences in the cultural expectations surrounding a given book—whether it seemed ephemeral or permanent, serious or frivolous, entertaining or trashy.

Among the still-powerful trade houses in the first decades of the 20th century were those that had sustained the ethos of the 'gentleman publisher' from their inception: these included Henry Holt & Co., Charles Scribner's Sons, Harper & Brothers, Houghton Mifflin, Putnam, and D. Appleton & Co. They generally remained committed, along with making a profit, to supplying American readers with books that, in the publishers' judgement, possessed literary merit or social utility. Thus, Henry Holt personally oversaw the compilation of *The Home Book of Verse* (1912), edited by Burton E. Stevenson, while putting his resources into such 'serious' authors as Dorothy Canfield Fisher, Robert Frost, John Dewey, and Stuart P. Sherman; Charles Scribner published Henry James, George Santayana, and Edith Wharton, but refused a novel of Arnold Bennett's because of its 'unpleasant sordid details' (Madison, 199). Many of these firms maintained the 'courtesy of the trade' by refusing to lure authors away from their competitors. As had been true for earlier figures such as Fields, however, ideological principles coexisted with, and sometimes served, business priorities. By the turn of the century, the spread of a national market, the volatility of Wall Street, and the aggressive business climate of the late 19th century allowed the book industry to expand, but also heightened the risk that output would fall victim to overproduction, inadequate distribution, or price-cutting at the point of sale. As the older trade publishers, in need of capital, searched urgently for an elusive financial guarantee for their products, they adopted many modern commercial practices they disdained in their role as public servants.

Chief among these was the introduction of professionalization into what had been family-run houses. In 1896 the Harper brothers, out of money, lost control of the company to the financier J. Pierpont Morgan. Subsequently, the entrepreneur Colonel George Harvey, with Morgan's blessing, took over the firm and reorganized it along lines that had already revolutionized railroad operations and steel production: he introduced separate departments for specialized functions and installed middle-level managers to run them. In 1908, under George Brett, the American branch of Macmillan became the first house in the US to establish a separate higher education division. Capitalizing on the concerns of parents and educators, in 1919 Brett also instituted the first children's book department (*see* **17**). At the same time, publishers sold off unprofitable parts of their business: Dodd, Mead, & Co. parted with the firm's bookshop in 1910 and its periodical, *The Bookman*, in 1917. Along with such structural changes, several trade houses vied with cheap reprint libraries by offering their own inexpensive series, such as the 'Modern Student's Library' (Scribner) and 'Everyman's Library' (E. P. Dutton & Co.). They also adopted their competitors' distribution methods, selling books through subscription agents or via the mails. The limited-edition set provided another way in which trade publishers learned to lock customers into a multi-volume purchase—one that carried the promise of literary culture. Such 'gentlemanly' individuals as Holt, Brett, and Houghton Mifflin's Horace Scudder remained committed to fulfilling that promise—hence, their willingness to publish poetry or criticism at a loss—but they did so in part because they understood that distinguishing their firms from reprint houses and producers of cheap fiction had its own marketing value.

In their efforts to rationalize production and distribution, late 19th- and early 20th-century publishers also tried to gain control over the price of books. The imposition of international copyright protection in 1891 and the consequent blow to piracy was one source of price stability. But price-cutting in shops remained a problem for mainstream firms. The usual practice of the period was to offer retail booksellers a 40 per cent discount on trade titles, which they then marked up for sale. By 1900, however, some bookshops and department stores were offering customers a bargain by charging less than the standard markup. To counter that tactic, the American Publishers' Association and the American Booksellers Association devised a 'net pricing system' (modelled on Britain's Net Book Agreement) that prohibited publishers from distributing titles to price-cutters. R. H. Macy's legal challenge to net pricing, which the Supreme Court upheld in 1913, required publishers to accept discounting and the uncertain profits it entailed. Subsequent efforts in the 1930s and 1940s to make retailers observe fair trade contracts proved largely unsuccessful.

Modern advertising methods were also used to increase revenues: instead of relying on sober announcements of a firm's new books for the season, some publishers tried promotional campaigns for particular titles. Both *Publishers*

Weekly and the monthly magazines affiliated with individual publishing houses were sites for such undertakings, although many publishers before World War I remained convinced that books were different from other commodities and that advertising did not result in greater sales. After the war, that attitude persisted in some quarters, but not in others. Such figures as Albert Boni and Horace Liveright (of Boni & Liveright), Richard Simon and Max Schuster (of Simon & Schuster), Alfred A. Knopf, Bennett Cerf, Donald Klopfer, Harold Guinzburg, John Farrar and Stanley Rinehart (of Farrar & Rinehart), and Benjamin W. Huebsch—mainly university-educated, Jewish New Yorkers—founded new houses in the 1910s and 1920s or assumed editorial positions that changed the tone of the book business. The relatively prosperous postwar economy and the attendant growth of mass consumer culture fuelled their success. It was also encouraged by the consolidation of a common school curriculum and the rising numbers of high school and university graduates in the same years: a consequent increase in literacy complemented a growing interest in mastering the specialized knowledge that seemed essential for success.

In this climate, new publishers (benefiting from new business methods) had fewer qualms than their predecessors about treating books as consumer goods. When Simon & Schuster started their firm in 1924, they pioneered a number of effective entrepreneurial techniques. The partners sought authors to create MSS they thought would sell; they allocated more money for advertising than other publishers; they developed a recognizable logo and company identity; and they handled each title as if it were 'a separate business venture'. They also surveyed customers by placing return postcards in their books. In 1927, they promoted Will Durant's *The Story of Philosophy*, as *Fortune* magazine noted, with an 'excitement' that was 'impossible to escape' (Rubin, *Middlebrow Culture*, 246, 249). The campaign included sales incentives for bookshops, direct-mail solicitation, a money-back guarantee, and a series of well-placed advertisements that fed readers' desire for knowledge and prestige. Trade publishers like Schuster still thought of themselves as cultural missionaries, but there was a heightened tension between that ideal and the successful marketing of books.

Similarly, Knopf, who founded his own firm in 1915, distinguished it by his commitment to cosmopolitanism, literary quality, and good design. The Knopfs brought the best contemporary writers to American audiences. Insisting that they believed in publishing meritorious works whether or not they would sell, they were particularly hospitable to European literary modernism. Knopf nevertheless was aggressive in marketing books, stamping a recognizable personality on them: he put men in sandwich boards to publicize Floyd Dell's *Moon-Calf* (1921), was the first publisher to use photographs in testimonial advertisements, and devised slogans that resembled those for household products.

New publishers' openness to modern promotional methods matched a shift in attitude among some typographers and printers. Like their European colleagues, proponents of a streamlined modernist aesthetic hailed machine typesetting as the means to efficiency and beauty. Yet the great American typographers and designers of this period—Carl P. Rollins, Daniel Berkeley Updike, Thomas Maitland Cleland, Bruce Rogers, Frederic William Goudy, William Addison Dwiggins—tended to advocate and practise hand-setting and printing as well as machine production to preserve older printing techniques.

The educational mission of scientific publishers dictated both non-profit or subsidized operations and profit-making enterprises. The audience for certain kinds of technical knowledge was necessarily limited; adjudicating the content of books was the task of scientists, not non-specialist editors. By 1919, Van Nostrand and John Wiley & Sons dominated this field with Macmillan and McGraw-Hill. University presses, founded around the turn of the century as an alternative to commercial houses, accounted for a small share (about 11 per cent) of new scientific titles; over the next twenty years, the proliferation of journals and of publishing programmes sponsored by professional associations furnished additional non-profit outlets for publicizing scientific discoveries. At the same time, both in the interwar years and with greater urgency as the atomic age dawned, trade houses produced volumes of popular science for general audiences.

Similarly, Protestant religious publishing involved a mixture of institutions. Some church-owned publishing firms (e.g. Methodist Book Concern) issued devotional and inspirational texts. Steady sellers, such as Mary Baker Eddy's *Science and Health*, came from church-related publishers. The market for bibles repackaged in a variety of formats expanded, stimulated by non-profit organizations like the Gideons. Some commercial, privately owned presses specialized in Protestant subjects, while trade houses maintained religious departments: at Harper's, its masterful editor Eugene Exman took over in 1935. The 1920s saw a surge of interest in religious titles, which poured forth from all these sources, as well as the invention, in 1921, of Religious Book Week, which broke down the distinction between religious and trade books. Yet some of the most popular volumes, such as Mrs Charles E. Cowman's locally published *Streams in the Desert* (1925), evaded commercial account books, enjoying a kind of hidden life among the devout.

4.2 New mediators for a diverse public

In the interwar period, mediators between producers and consumers of books— book club judges, literary critics and journalists, librarians, and educators— grappled with a set of tensions related to publishers' ambivalence towards commercialism: they sought to juggle a desire to influence large numbers of readers with an awareness that popular appeal would undermine their own stature and the prestige of the book itself.

At the mid-century, publishers distributed directly to readers about half the hardcover books sold in the US. The other half reached purchasers through retail outlets: not only department stores such as Macy's but also large chains like Doubleday, Kroch's, and Brentano's. Independent bookstores such as the Hampshire Book Shop and Sunwise Turn, whose proprietors offered advice about good reading, particularly flourished near university campuses. At the same time, even before the paperback revolution of the postwar years, the sale of soft-cover books and remainders at drugstores and newsstands became common practice.

Within the hardcover trade, however, the book club provided a new method of distribution perfectly attuned to the period's cultural preoccupations. Organizations such as the Book-of-the-Month Club, founded in 1926, sought to satisfy social as well as intellectual aspirations, mediating between 'high' culture and consumer desires. Henry Seidel Canby, the longtime head of the Club's Selecting Committee, undertook a similar role as editor of the *Saturday Review of Literature*, a periodical he helped found in 1924. As part of an effort to widen and to guide the audience for 'serious' novels and non-fiction, Canby and Stuart P. Sherman, his counterpart at the *New York Herald Tribune's Books*, sustained a concern for the craft of writing, taking a dim view of modernist experimentation while adapting literary criticism to the consumer-friendly format of a weekly tabloid.

Librarians, too, balanced acting as cultural authorities against their interest in building systems and institutions that would serve diverse populations and varying standards of taste. At the close of the 19th century, the leaders of the American Library Association felt that they were responsible for stocking their shelves with the 'best' reading. The reformer Melvil Dewey ardently promoted that principle, which implicitly relegated most fiction to an inferior status. The rapid proliferation of local libraries between 1900 and 1920 (thanks in large part to Andrew Carnegie's philanthropy), however, heightened librarians' concern with library science. The ALA's *Booklist*, created in 1905, was designed to help library professionals systematically identify good books for their growing numbers of patrons. In the 1920s and 1930s, library leaders such as Douglas L. Waples sought to establish their authority on civic grounds, arguing that democracy required the nurturing of 'enlightened public opinion'. The ALA's 'Reading with a Purpose' campaign reflected that concern, along with anxieties about mass media and materialism; yet its proponents adopted modern advertising techniques to get across their message. Progressive educators, aware of the 'large foreign element' in schools, joined library professionals in the belief that inculcating good reading habits would prepare the nation's children for adult citizenship. Yet librarians continued to struggle among themselves about how much to oppose the public's overwhelming preference for novels. Despite the official emphasis on 'purpose', that preference led most ordinary working librarians to concentrate on providing information rather than shaping taste.

The individuals who developed the nation's great research libraries after 1900 experienced fewer tensions, because they saw themselves as contributing to the modern advancement of knowledge. That outlook led the Library of Congress in 1901 to create its own classification system, which promised to accommodate new subject areas more flexibly than Dewey decimal classification. The standardization of interlibrary loans in 1917 allowed higher education institutions to share materials readily. Two commercial publishers, R. R. Bowker and H. W. Wilson, produced bibliographies, the *Reader's Guide to Periodical Literature*, and other indices for the library market. Under the administration of Herbert Putnam, the Library of Congress joined in this activity, developing the National Union Catalog in the early 1900s; its publication in the mid-1940s of volumes reproducing its printed catalogue cards was another landmark in LC's nationalization of support to scholars. At roughly the same time, the New York Public Library (second in its holdings only to the Library of Congress) embarked on wide-ranging collection-building. Relatively free of the ideological constraints that animated their less cosmopolitan colleagues, the librarians who built the NYPL (especially its Reference Department, which became the Research Libraries in 1966) were committed to acquisitions that reflected the multiplicity of human experience and the unpredictable needs of future scholars. Their democratic outlook and their devotion to wide collecting distinguished them from their European counterparts. A dedication to comprehensiveness also characterized the major academic libraries (e.g. at Harvard, Yale, Columbia, Cornell, and the University of Chicago); by 1939, each of those had amassed more than a million volumes. In the same years, several individuals—among them Henry E. Huntington, J. P. Morgan, Jr., and H. C. Folger—enriched the possibilities for scholarship by founding repositories (the Huntington Library, the Pierpont Morgan Library, the Folger Shakespeare Library) to house and build upon great private collections.

4.3 Continuity and community in reading

As producers and mediators of books adapted to the burgeoning, diverse consumer culture of the 20th century, their audiences perpetuated established reading practices while simultaneously endowing print with new significance. In the 1930s, the Civilian Conservation Corps popularized the term 'functional literacy' to denote the skill necessary to read the materials pertinent to daily life. By 1947, when the Census Bureau defined 'functional illiterates' as those with fewer than five years of schooling, only 6 per cent of Americans fell into that category, in contrast with 24 per cent in 1910. Book readers were more likely to be from the middle or upper classes than from the working class, and before World War II most people, regardless of income, preferred newspapers and magazines. As Waples and other social scientists had shown in the preceding two decades, a minority of Americans turned to books for self-improvement, pleasure, and (especially during the Great Depression) diversion from daily life. They made meaning by connecting eclectic texts to their experiences within families, religious settings, and classrooms. Although silent reading largely displaced reading aloud as an instructional mode and leisure activity, the social dimension of reading persisted in the 'literary evening' and the book group. For both white and African-American women, literary clubs fostered a sense of identity and empowerment, as well as political activism.

5 1950 to the present: the American book in a global economy

5.1 Consolidating the publishing industry

Although technological innovation, ever-proliferating leisure activities, and a more highly educated population remained part of the book's social environment in the US following World War II, a distinguishing feature of the second half of the 20th century was the repositioning of the book business within a global economy. The war itself contributed to internationalization by involving publishers in efforts to supply American troops abroad with reading material: beginning in 1943, the Council on Books in Wartime, an industry consortium, brought out more than 13,000 titles in lightweight, pocket-size Armed Services Editions. It also oversaw the issuing of Overseas Editions—volumes aimed at building understanding of the US among Europeans. The project stimulated and prefigured the expansion of American publishing into foreign markets in the immediate postwar period. Textbooks and works on scientific and technical subjects dominated the vigorous export trade in the 1950s and 1960s, and the sale of translation rights also increased dramatically. American firms subsequently developed independent subsidiaries abroad—32 by the 1980s. At the same time, European publishers such as Oxford University Press, Elsevier, and Springer opened offices in the US.

The impetus for the internationalization of American publishing was partly political, given the Cold War perception that America needed to strengthen its cultural presence around the world. For the most part, however, the US book industry's global expansion was the result of a quest for greater profits—a fact that underscored its similarity to other businesses. Still, many of the dominant figures in 1950s and 1960s trade publishing maintained a sense of obligation to turn out good books—even though initial printings of non-fiction volumes tended not to make money—and cultivated a personal tone with authors and employees.

The relationship between books and other means of communication changed after 1950. Whereas many publishers had sought to maintain the book's position on higher cultural ground than that occupied by film, radio, and recorded music, the sale of Random House to the Radio Corporation of America in 1965 symbolically recast print as simply one of several forms of entertainment available to the American public. Moreover, by the 1970s the sale of subsidiary rights—not only to book clubs or to the booming paperback houses, but also to Hollywood or television—had become the major source of some firms' revenue, so that, far from fearing competition from other leisure activities, many publishing executives now depended on those activities for their survival.

In the last decades of the 20th century, media conglomerates—several based in Europe—continued to absorb formerly independent publishers, both exclusively trade operations and those houses with mass-market paperback divisions. Scribner merged in 1984 with Macmillan, which was in turn bought by

Paramount nine years later; Bertelsmann purchased Bantam, Doubleday, and Dell in 1986; Rupert Murdoch acquired Harper in 1987. Christian publishing was not exempt from this pattern: Zondervan became part of HarperCollins in 1988. More recent industry mergers include Viacom's purchase of Paramount in 1994, the amalgamation of its publishing interests under the name of Simon & Schuster, and Simon & Schuster's reorganization as part of CBS Corporation in 2006. In 2002, the eight largest firms controlled more than half of American book sales. At the same time, the production of new titles, especially in categories such as religion and fiction, increased sharply: between 1992 and 1997 the book industry grew at a rate of 34 per cent.

The industry's volatility increased the pressure on editors to sign up titles that would make money, with a corresponding expansion of the role of the literary agent. Owners of the new conglomerates, indifferent to editorial freedom and cultural ideals, required high profits from each book and a concentration on big sellers. Paperback publishers, who in the 1970s and 1980s had discovered the lucrativeness of issuing original titles in such genres as romance fiction, contributed to the competitive atmosphere by bidding up the cost of reprint rights as well. The rise of media conglomerates has been blamed for a marked decline in American publishing, measured by the quality of the industry's product. The complaint echoed the lament of designers and typographers, adjusting to the development in the 1970s of photocomposition and offset printing, that labour-saving automation was destroying aesthetic standards.

Some observers have challenged those assumptions, arguing that the book business needed to overcome inefficiencies. Moreover, independent publishers have retained a significant economic and cultural role into the 21st century. According to the Book Industry Study Group, the number of small firms in 2005 was higher than ever. There is room, still, for the limited edition of poetry and for fine printing, typified by the Black Sparrow and the Arion presses; even within the trade, houses such as Knopf strive for excellence in design. The spread of identity politics in the 1960s created niche markets for houses publishing Hispanic and African-American literature (such as Arte Publico and Broadside Press). Evangelical publishers market works in Spanish to reach their multicultural followers. Outside the commercial sector, university presses and other entities such as the New Press, which André Schiffrin founded in 1990, uphold their mandate to bring new knowledge to the reading public. Even the disaffected former Random House editor Jason Epstein conceded in 2001 that, in absolute numbers (rather than as a percentage of total output), more 'valuable' books were being published than ever before. Yet these trends and the diversity they preserve do not counteract the disproportionate influence of the media giants on the choices available to American readers.

Although internationalization and mergers also affected scientific and educational publishing, the nature of the subjects and their exponents exerted a visible effect on the content of books. In the 1980s many smaller companies disappeared; by the end of the decade, Macmillan, Harcourt Brace Jovanovich, and Simon & Schuster owned close to half of the textbook trade. Subsequently, the British conglomerate Pearson, which acquired Simon & Schuster's educational operation in 1998, controlled more than one quarter of American textbook production. Yet the stifling of variety has resulted as much from local as from global forces. State-wide adoption committees, especially those in Texas and California, have long wielded power over publishers by requiring that they comply with rules about representations of race, gender, environmental issues, 'lifestyles', and similar matters. The most controversial of such stipulations has concerned the presentation of evolution versus creationism. In the 1960s and 1970s, federally funded innovative books for use in biology, physics, and social studies courses provoked attacks from conservative groups because of their ostensible 'humanism' and cultural relativism. Left-wing critics, often at odds with one another, have likewise been vocal in assailing the depiction of African-Americans as either idealized or too realistic, too separate or too integrated. The result, some educators charge, is a reduction of the average American textbook to a bland, inoffensive, lowest common denominator calculated to win the biggest market. However, scientific thought has also produced books that serve and reflect the priorities of scientists themselves: reference works such as the *Science Citation Index* (now online and part of Thomson Corporation); texts for advanced study synthesizing new research (e.g. James Watson's *Molecular Biology of the Gene*, 1965); and trade books such as James Gleick's *Chaos* (1987) and Stephen Hawking's *A Brief History of Time* (1988), popularizing the activities of the scientific community for lay readers. Even as the scholarly journal, in digitized form, became entrenched, by the 1990s, as the primary means for the circulation of scientific knowledge, the science book had its place in laboratories and living rooms alike.

5.2 Transforming bookselling and libraries

In the postwar period, the forces of consolidation were also at work within institutions disseminating books to readers. The Book-of-the-Month Club became part of Time Inc. in 1977 (later Time-Warner Books); Bertelsmann became its sole owner in 2007. At the same time, the Selecting Committee virtually vanished from club advertising and was disbanded in 1994. With it went the idea that distance from commercialism was worth maintaining. Yet the Club's reorganization as part of a conglomerate arguably led to less homogenization as its executives, aiming to reverse declining membership, gave up the pretence of choosing the 'best' books for all in favour of targeting particular type of volumes at niche markets.

Retail bookselling developed against the backdrop of postwar suburbanization, evolving from a mix of department store, drugstore, independent, and chain outlets to a business dominated by a few national chains. In the 1960s and 1970s, Waldenbooks and B. Dalton opened in suburban shopping centres throughout the country. The distinguishing feature of those shops was that their proprietors believed they could sell books in the same way that Kmart, which bought Waldenbooks in 1984, sold socks. Using computer technology, they centralized inventory control. After Crown Books introduced consistent discounting in 1977, both Waldenbooks and B. Dalton followed suit. Independent bookshops responded by imitating the informal atmosphere the chains were creating. At the same time, some stores cultivated specialized clienteles: political activists, children, New Age believers. In the 1990s, the superstore chains (Barnes & Noble and Borders were the largest) supplanted mall shops and dealt a fatal blow to many independents. Operating in huge spaces, the superstores welcomed readers with cafes, book talks, discounts, and vast selection. In 1997 the two biggest chains had 43.3 per cent of bookshop sales: by then both publicly traded companies, they wielded unprecedented power over publishers in matters such as pricing and display.

In cultural terms, the consolidations in the book business entailed a repudiation of the genteel aura that had once surrounded Brentano's or Scribner's. The function of the bookseller as supplier of literary guidance was largely a casualty of this process; the connection between buying a book and affirming one's 'literariness' grew weaker as well. Arguably, however, the rise of superstores was less detrimental to American culture than was the wave of mergers among publishers: purchasing books became unintimidating and the bookshop a more prominent feature of the retail landscape, encouraging buying of and conversation about books, if not more reading.

Other mediators emerged to guide readers in choosing books. The relocation of literary critics to academia in the 1950s and 1960s reduced the role of the generalist 'man of letters'. Yet, the more educated readers leaving the nation's burgeoning universities expanded the audience for the purveyors of expertise in the *New York Review of Books* (founded in 1963) and other specialized journals. The creation of amazon.com in 1995, which inaugurated large-scale Internet retailing, seemed to transfer authority from the critic to the ordinary reader. Despite the loss of face-to-face contact, those who ventured to explore Amazon's website found personalized recommendations and customer reviews to guide their purchases. In 1996, Oprah Winfrey (the ordinary reader writ large) created bestsellers and revived older titles by choosing them for Oprah's Book Club on her television talk show. The American Library Association joined with Winfrey and the publishing industry to donate the club's selections to community libraries nationwide.

That intervention on the part of librarians to shape America's reading habits, however, was something of an anomaly by the 1990s. In the years following World War II, library professionals moved even further away from their commitment early in the century to influence readers. The proponents of libraries as information centres rather than book repositories began to be heard. An infusion of federal money, much of which went into computerization, enhanced the emphasis on librarianship as information science. Although libraries continued to acquire books, in the political climate of the 1960s and 1970s the predominant vision of the institution was of an organization providing its 'customers' with knowledge leading to jobs, justice, or a good used car; it also served as a meeting place. The affinities with postwar consumer culture (and hence with the ethos of publishing and bookselling) were clear: the new public library accommodated users looking for a particular item of information, not necessarily for self-cultivation. As with bookshops, this trend did not necessarily signal cultural decline: it got more people into the building, fostered community, and increased book circulation. Within research libraries, the picture was gloomier: budget crises curtailed book purchases in the 1970s. Throughout the succeeding decades, the growth of online databases and inter-library loans continued to reduce the place of periodicals and scholarly monographs in university collections. Undergraduates had to be reminded that the stacks—not just the Internet—contained resources for their work.

5.3 Modern American reading

Greater knowledge and pleasure remained among the chief goals of reading in the postwar period, but the political and cultural developments of those years created opportunities for readers to use books in historically specific ways. The growth of 'speed-reading' among managers and executives testified that the mastery of voluminous printed information seemed increasingly necessary for success in the corporate sector. Conversely, in the 1960s the spirit of the New Left, itself a product, in part, of its participants' youthful brush with existentialist writers, found expression in reading groups devoted to explorations of radical thought. Similarly, women activists in the 1960s and 1970s drew support from feminist works that, if not necessarily discussed collectively, nevertheless sustained social connections by assuring individuals that they were not alone in their discontent. By the 1980s, women's literary clubs typically stood aloof from reform agendas; like their predecessors, however, club members derived a sense of community from reading with others.

As the imperatives of personal growth and self-help became more pervasive in American culture, therapeutic language became a hallmark of readers' remarks about the role of books in their lives. Among the thousands of respondents to the former poet laureate Robert Pinsky's invitation to reflect on their 'favorite poem', for example, many people spoke of works as wellsprings of insight and healing. Yet encounters with the book still led readers outside the self, into what one subscriber to the Book-of-the-Month Club called 'enhanced intellectual or spiritual understanding of the meaning of life' ([Library of Congress,] *Survey of Lifetime Readers*, 6).

Throughout the second half of the 20th century, investigators (building on librarians' and sociologists' studies in the interwar period) conducted periodic surveys to determine Americans' reading habits. Animated by concerns over the teaching of reading in public schools, and worried about the nation's future prosperity, researchers repeatedly raised alarms about the fall in the number of citizens who regularly read books. The National Endowment for the Arts reported that literary reading had dropped in almost every demographic category between

1982 and 1992; in 2004 and again in 2007, the NEA declared that even more precipitate declines jeopardized the prospects for a rich civic life. Yet those who do read books continue to remake texts in the light of their own needs, aspirations, and locations, and to enrich American culture in the process.

5.4 The future of the book

The impact of digitization on the processes of production, distribution, and reading are easy enough to specify in broad outline. In the 1980s and 1990s, the development of editing and design software transformed the preparation of MSS for publication. In the same period, the birth of desktop publishing and the use of lasers rather than film to reproduce images, followed in the early 1990s by the introduction of digital printing presses, enabled producers to tailor press runs and books themselves to specific markets. This new world of print-on-demand promises to eliminate the costs of overproduction and overstocking; ordering a book can mean requesting not merely that it be sent to a retailer but, rather, that it be moved from screen to page. The digital revolution has also allowed publishers of conventional books to construct web sites featuring 'podcasts' with their authors, distribute textbook supplements electronically, and streamline office and inventory operations. Similarly, the advent of online reference works and electronic catalogues, together with the creation of digitized databases and document collections, enlarged the scope of library holdings and offered patrons greater access and convenience. As already noted, Internet bookselling, complete with its mechanisms for customer feedback, simplified distribution and facilitated direct contact between author, publisher, distributor, and reader.

The rapidity of these changes led publishers and entrepreneurs in the 1990s to predict—and to invest money in—the dominance of the e-book (*see* **21**), especially for scholarly monographs. The prospect was particularly appealing to academic presses because, by 2000, university libraries, faced with the rising costs of periodicals, were buying only about a quarter as many volumes as they had in the 1970s. Commercial publishers—notably Simon & Schuster and Random House—put sizeable funds into e-book development. The bestselling novelist Stephen King tested the waters in 2000 by arranging to sell a novella exclusively to readers who paid $2.50 to download it over the Internet; there were 400,000 requests for it on the first day alone. Yet, in its 2001 report, the *Bowker Annual* declared that hopes for electronic publishing had given way to 'business realities': consumers were not rushing to curl up with hand-held screens in place of physical books (*Bowker Annual*, 2002, 18). By the same token, the non-profit History E-book Project, an attempt to issue new and out-of-print scholarship electronically along with university presses' publication of print versions, struggled to secure sufficient subscriptions from libraries to sustain itself, although it has subsequently achieved stability under the auspices of the American Council of Learned Societies. Nevertheless publication of books in conventional printed form (at least initially) remains the widely shared preference of academic historians. They are much more enthusiastic about the research possibilities digitization has generated, including the Google Book Project, which is scanning thousands of works in university libraries and making some entire texts available for online searching.

If the future of the book does not lie exclusively in the electronic format, perhaps the advent of the digital age will ensure the preservation of diversity in American publishing. Epstein's reflections on the triumph of commercial over literary values in the current book industry end with that hope; he envisions the Internet and related technologies as forces liberating authors and readers from the tyranny of profit-minded publishers and booksellers. Whether or not Epstein's prophecy proves true, the book is sure to remain connected, as it has always been, to the tensions between democracy and refinement, materialism and spirituality, at the heart of American culture.

BIBLIOGRAPHY

T. Augst and K. Carpenter, eds., *Institutions of Reading* (2007)

B. Bailyn and J. B. Hench, eds., *The Press and the American Revolution* (1981)

R. W. Beales and E. J. Monaghan, 'Literacy and Schoolbooks', in *HBA* 1 (2000)

M. Benton, *Beauty and the Book* (2000)

Bowker Annual of Library and Book Trade Information (1991, 2002)

R. H. Brodhead, *Cultures of Letters* (1993)

R. D. Brown, *Knowledge Is Power* (1989)

K. E. Carpenter, 'American Libraries', in *HBA* 2

—— 'Libraries', in *HBA* 3

S. E. Casper, *Constructing American Lives* (1999)

—— *et al.*, eds., *Perspectives on American Book History* (2002)

W. Charvat, *The Profession of Authorship in America*, ed. M. J. Bruccoli (1968)

J. D. Cornelius, 'When I Can Read My Title Clear' (1991)

L. A. Coser *et al.*, *Books: The Culture and Commerce of Publishing* (1982)

P. Dain, 'The Great Libraries', in *HBA* 4

J. P. Danky and W. A. Wiegand, eds., *Print Culture in a Diverse America* (1998)

C. N. Davidson, ed., *Reading in America* (1989)

K. C. Davis, *Two-Bit Culture* (1984)

DLB 46, 49

J. Eddy, *Bookwomen* (2006)

J. Epstein, *Book Business* (2001)

S. Fink and S. S. Williams, eds., *Reciprocal Influences* (1999)

J. Gilreath, 'American Book Distribution', *PAAS* 95 (1985–6), 501–83

J. N. Green, 'The Book Trade in the Middle Colonies', in *HBA* 1

—— 'English Books and Printing in the Age of Franklin', in *HBA* 1

—— and P. Stallybrass, *Benjamin Franklin, Writer and Printer* (2006)

P. C. Gutjahr, *An American Bible* (1999)

—— 'The Perseverance of Print-Bound Saints', in *HBA* 5

M. Hackenberg, ed., *Getting the Books Out* (1987)

D. D. Hall, *Worlds of Wonder, Days of Judgment* (1989)

—— *Cultures of Print* (1996)

—— ed., *A History of the Book in America* (5 vols, 2000–2010)

W. W. Hening, *The Statutes at Large; Being a Collection of all the Laws of Virginia* (13 vols, 1819–23)

B. Hochman, *Getting at the Author* (2001)

W. L. Joyce *et al.*, eds., *Printing and Society in Early America* (1983)

C. F. Kaestle *et al.*, *Literacy in the United States* (1991)

M. Kelley, *Learning to Stand and Speak* (2006)

H. Lehmann-Haupt *et al.*, *The Book in America*, 2e (1951)

[Library of Congress, Center for the Book and Book-of-the-Month Club,] *Survey of Lifetime Readers* (1990)

E. Long, *Book Clubs* (2003)

B. Luey, 'The Organization of the Book Publishing Industry', in *HBA* 5

E. McHenry, *Forgotten Readers* (2002)

C. A. Madison, *Book Publishing in America* (1966)

L. J. Miller, *Reluctant Capitalists* (2006)

E. J. Monaghan, *Learning to Read and Write in Colonial America* (2005)

G. F. Moran and M. A. Vinovskis, 'Schooling, Literacy, and Textbooks', in *HBA* 2

M. Moylan and L. Stiles, eds., *Reading Books* (1996)

D. P. Nord, *Faith in Reading* (2004)

C. Pawley, *Reading on the Middle Border* (2001)

J. A. Radway, *Reading the Romance* (1989)

—— *A Feeling for Books* (1997)

J. Raven, 'The Importation of Books in the Eighteenth Century', in *HBA* 1

E. C. Reilly and D. D. Hall, 'Customers and the Market for Print', in *HBA* 1

R. Remer, *Printers and Men of Capital* (1996)

A. G. Roeber, 'Readers and Writers of German in the Early United States', in *HBA* 2

J. S. Rubin, *The Making of Middlebrow Culture* (1992)

—— *Songs of Ourselves* (2007)

B. Ryan and A. M. Thomas, eds., *Reading Acts* (2002)

J. Satterfield, *The World's Best Books* (2002)

A. Schiffrin, *The Business of Books* (2000)

D. Sheehan, *This Was Publishing* (1952)

J. H. Shera, *Foundations of the Public Library* (1949)

D. S. Shields, *Civil Tongues and Polite Letters in British America* (1997)

B. Sicherman, 'Ideologies and Practices of Reading', in *HBA* 3

L. Soltow and E. Stevens, *The Rise of Literacy and the Common School in the United States* (1981)

C. Z. Stiverson and G. A. Stiverson, 'The Colonial Retail Book Trade', in *Printing and Society in Early America*, ed. W. L. Joyce *et al.* (1983)

L. I. Sweet, ed., *Communication and Change in American Religious History* (1993)

G. T. Tanselle, *Guide to the Study of United States Imprints* (2 vols, 1971)

J. Tebbel, *A History of Book Publishing in the United States* (4 vols, 1971–81)

I. Thomas, *History of Printing in America* (2 vols, 1810)

J. B. Thompson, *Books in the Digital Age* (2005)

C. Turner, *Marketing Modernism* (2003)

J. L. W. West III, *American Authors and the Literary Marketplace since 1900* (1988)

W. A. Wiegand, *The Politics of an Emerging Profession* (1986)

M. Winship, *American Literary Publishing in the Mid-Nineteenth Century* (1995)

—— 'The Rise of a National Book Trade System in the United States, 1880–1920', in *HBA* 4

E. Wolf, 2ⁿᵈ, *The Book Culture of a Colonial American City* (1988)

L. C. Wroth, *The Colonial Printer* (1931)

R. J. Zboray, *A Fictive People* (1993)

N. Zill and M. Wingler, *Who Reads Literature?* (1990)

51

The History of the Book in the Caribbean and Bermuda

JEREMY B. DIBBELL

1 Historical background and overview

Printing was slow to arrive in the Caribbean islands and Bermuda: the passage of a century or more between settlement and the establishment of a press was not uncommon, and some of the smaller islands were without a printing press well into the 20th century. Among the factors responsible for this trend were the islands' close connections with—and reliance on—the European colonial powers; their relatively small populations and physical areas; the shifting geopolitical status of the islands, which served to impede institutional development; and restrictive colonial or local policies and customs. This notwithstanding, the region remains one of the most understudied geographical areas in terms of book history, and much work remains to be done to expand our current understanding of print and book culture in the Caribbean.

Prior to the establishment of presses, material for printing, such as laws, proceedings of local legislatures, and other local productions, was sent abroad, to be printed at presses either in the European or North American cities, particularly New York. In later years, the presses located in the larger Caribbean population centres such as Jamaica, Barbados, and Antigua supplied their smaller neighbours. Before the advent of print on some islands, including Bermuda, MS newsletters are known to have circulated in the early years of the 18th century.

The earliest confirmed printing operation in the Caribbean islands was Robert Baldwin's firm, established at Kingston, Jamaica in the early part of 1718. There was a press in Cuba by the early 1720s, and in Barbados in about 1730. St Domingue (Haiti) may have had a press as early as 1725. There were presses in St Kitts around 1747, Antigua in 1748, and Dominica, Guadeloupe, and Grenada in 1765. A newspaper was started in St Vincent around 1767; at approximately the same time, printing was begun in Martinique. St Croix's first press began operation in 1770, and Joseph Stockdale brought printing to Bermuda in 1784, the same year John Wells set up his press at Nassau in the Bahamas. Trinidad had a press by 1786; there was a newspaper in St Eustatius in 1789, and there may have been a small printing office in Curaçao in the late 1790s. There was a press on St Bartélemy from 1799 until 1819. What is now the Dominican Republic had a press by 1801, Puerto Rico by 1806, and St Thomas in 1809. It was not until 1845 that the Turks and Caicos Islands had their own newspaper. Aruba had no press until the late 19th century, and no press is known to have been in operation on St Martin, St John, Tortola, Anguilla, or the other small islands before the second half of the 20th century.

Presses were established for a variety of sometimes overlapping reasons. In several cases, the local residents and government sought a printer and supported the establishment of a press: Jamaica's Robert Baldwin and Bermuda's Joseph Stockdale appear to have immigrated at the urging of island governments. In contrast, the French colonial government issued several *brevets d'imprimeur* in the 1720s for printers in St Domingue and Martinique, but the local governments seem to have prevented the printers from setting up shop. The first presses in Antigua and Barbados were commercial ventures, as were the second and third presses in Jamaica and other locations. Several presses were established following changes in colonial control, or by loyalist refugees from the American mainland (John Wells's press at Nassau, for example). In some cases, presses were subsequently set up to print rival newspapers or to provide an alternative to the existing, established press: these included the pro-government second press in Bermuda, pro-emancipation printing offices in Jamaica and Trinidad in the 1830s, Catholic presses on several islands, and the press set up by Samuel Nelmes on Grand Turk in 1845 to advocate separation from the Bahamas.

Even with the significant linguistic, legal-political, and economic variation between the islands in the region, once presses were in operation their early outputs tended to be quite similar, and the products likewise can be compared to those of provincial presses in Britain and North America. A weekly newspaper, usually printed on one sheet and sometimes with additional sheets as supplements, tended to be the norm for island presses; the papers were very likely to contain plaintive missives from the printer begging for payment of subscriptions or advertising fees. Subscriptions were costly, and with the already-small population base, many newspapers failed to thrive, or appeared briefly during times of political or economic strife, only to fade away quickly. Almanacs, at first broadsheets and then later in pamphlet or book form, were a common production in the Caribbean islands until the 19th century, when production generally shifted to Britain. More substantial periodicals generally did not last long, due to competition from imported publications, a limited local audience,

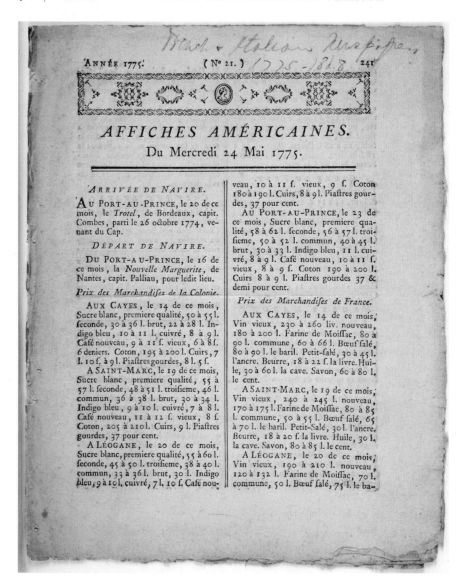

Latest prices for sugar, indigo, coffee, and cotton from the colony; and of wine, flour, salted beef, butter, oil, and soap from France: the 24 May 1775 issue of *Affiches Américaines*, a French-language newspaper printed in Haiti from 1764 to 1791. Courtesy American Antiquarian Society

and high production costs. Printers eagerly sought contracts from local governments to print proclamations, laws, records of legislative sessions, and votes; their dependence on this support often made printers more compliant to the demands of local officials than they might otherwise have been. As in other areas, jobbing printing of blank forms, official documents, handbills, and other ephemeral matter was a key element of the printer's business; unfortunately, much of this material has not survived. Relatively few books were printed on the islands, and of those, medical, agricultural, and other practical books were more commonly produced than literary works (though there are several notable exceptions). There were relatively fewer sermons and religious tracts published in the region than elsewhere, and most of those produced were concerned with slavery.

Given the wide range of colonial powers active in the Caribbean, a diversity of languages was at play from the very beginning. Printed matter in most colonies tended to appear in the language of their mother countries, but as the islands were occupied by, or transferred to the control of, different European colonizers, and as local Creole languages and dialects developed, the lingua franca was adjusted accordingly, and bilingual and sometimes even trilingual publications began to appear. In 18th-century Grenada, newspapers were printed in French and English; in the middle decades of the 19th century, Papiamento newspapers and pamphlets (sometimes in combination with Dutch, Spanish, and other languages) were printed in Curaçao and Aruba. The first books published in St Croix were a Creole ABC and grammar, sponsored by Moravian missionaries. Creole languages continue to be spoken and printed in certain islands at the present time.

Roderick Cave has compared the mobility of Caribbean printers to that seen in 15th-century Europe (Cave, 12). Juan Cassan printed on Grenada and Trinidad; Matthew Gallagher is known to have printed on Dominica, Grenada, and Trindad; William Smith printed on Dominica and St Vincent. The movement of printers extended beyond the region, as many of them trained in England, Scotland, France, or the American mainland. William Brown, who was apprenticed with William Bradford and William Dunlap in Philadelphia, printed on Barbados from 1760 until 1763, then went to Quebec; the first two printers on Barbados, David Harry and Samuel Keimer, had both previously worked in Philadelphia as well. Benjamin Franklin dispatched first Thomas Smith and later (after Smith's death in 1752) his own nephew, Benjamin Mecom, from Philadelphia to Antigua. Thomas Howe, an early St Kitts printer, taught his son George to print; in 1800 George became the first trained printer in Australia. By the early years of the 19th century, local ownership of presses became more common.

There is evidence that both slaves and free blacks were occasionally employed as pressmen and even compositors, at least in Jamaica, Antigua, and St Vincent. The common practice of widows managing printing offices was in evidence in this region as well: in Jamaica, Robert Baldwin's widow Mary managed the press from Robert's death in 1722 until after 1734, and the widow of Jean Bénard printed the *Gazette de la Guadeloupe* in 1788. When Joseph Stockdale died in 1803, his three daughters managed the business and printed the newspaper until 1816. Printers on the islands frequently shared publications with each other as sources of news, and several opened separate reading rooms to provide access to newly arrived newspapers and other printed matter.

Printing equipment and paper were imported from Europe and, later, America; Caribbean printers were quick to adopt iron hand-presses when they became available, as the tropical climate wreaked havoc on wooden presses. There was a lithographic press at Bermuda by 1821, when the governor there attempted to circumvent the newspapers and began printing his own proclamations. Over the course of the 19th century, the quality of Caribbean publications tended to decline, as the islands' economies faltered and the original equipment wore out.

Caribbean printers typically sold books and other general merchandise in their shops, while general grocers often stocked imported books and other printed matter. Cave describes a typical stock of books: 'some standard schoolbooks, a range of medical and law books, history, biography, and political treatises for the man of affairs, charts and pilots for the mariner' (Cave, 27). Books comprised a significant portion of imports to the region: Giles Barber calculated that for the period 1700–80 books exported to the Caribbean region represented roughly a quarter of total British book exports, with Jamaica alone importing nearly as many books as New York over the course of those decades. Literary publications formed no small part of the stock: newspaper advertisements reveal that plays, novels, and periodicals were commonly available alongside the more utilitarian titles. By the middle of the 19th century, American books were often imported into the region, a trend which continues into the 21st century.

The first libraries in the region were those of ecclesiastical institutions in the early Spanish colonies, including one begun in 1523 at the Santo Domingo convent in Puerto Rico. Thomas Bray's Society for Promoting Christian Knowledge dispatched small religious libraries throughout the English Caribbean in the early years of the 18th century, and the organization later funded and supplied schools for slave and free black children in several islands during the 1790s, Bermuda's being the most successful. Social and subscription libraries were not uncommon, although these often failed after their original founders passed from the scene. Commercial, religious, and small local libraries were available in some islands by the middle of the 19th century, but it was not until the late 19th and early 20th centuries that more widespread local and national libraries were established across the region, including five funded by Carnegie grants (in Barbados, St Lucia, Grenada, St Vincent, Dominica, and Trinidad).

2 Press controls

Control over the press by local or colonial governments varied markedly. Throughout the region, a combination of rewards (in the form of government contracts) and threats was often used to keep printers and editors in line. An editor was deported from Trinidad in 1790 for printing articles about the French Revolution, and a later governor on that island made his views on press coverage clear by requesting the temporary loan of the handle of the printing press when the editor gave offence. Libel charges against editors were not infrequent. The English-controlled islands had what would be considered the most press freedom, but even there significant pressure was brought to bear when situations seemed to warrant it.

In the French islands, a royal *brevet d'imprimeur* was required for any printer, and, even following the Revolution, the government kept a firm control over the output of any press. Pre-publication censorship was enforced, and printers, booksellers, and editors all had to pay licence fees until 1827. An 1848 decree abolished censorship prior to publication, but that step was revoked in 1852 and censorship continued until 1863. Newspapers containing political content still had to obtain prior approval, however, and J. A. Lent notes that 'administrative authorities had a right to warn the press, to suspend newspapers during certain times, to suspend papers with or without warning by proportion of general surety, and to hand press offenses over to correctional tribunals' (Lent, 172). Censorship was generally the rule rather than the exception in Haiti as well, and a journalist was even executed there in 1820. Rules were similar in the Spanish and Dutch colonies. The Danish islands (now the US Virgin Islands) were governed by a 1779 law establishing censorship and the granting of subsidies to royal-approved publications, which continued until 1916–17.

In Cuba, by contrast, the government has owned and controlled the media, publishing, and bookselling industries since the time of the Revolution. Concerted literacy campaigns and the rapid establishment of a nationalized publishing system beginning in the early 1960s contributed to the development of a dynamic graphics industry, making possible the explosive growth of poster art, for decades a major component of Cuban print culture.

3 Recent trends

Literacy rates in the Caribbean grew sharply in the 20th century; while Haiti's rate remains in the 50–60 per cent range, the other islands report literacy rates above 85 per cent. Yet, as has generally been the case throughout their history, the Caribbean islands suffer from a relative dearth of books. Bookshops must import the bulk of their stock from the US and Europe, which greatly increases the cost to consumers. Similarly, purchasing books from abroad means paying what are often exorbitantly high shipping rates. While there was a brief heyday of West Indian fiction publishing in the middle decades of the 20th century by such houses as Heinemann and Longman, for the most part it has remained a fact that authors must look abroad to find a wide reading audience. Small speciality or academic publishers for books of local or regional interest have been established on several islands; the Leeds-based publisher Peepal Tree Press specializes in works by Caribbean authors, and the multinational publisher Macmillan has a dedicated Caribbean imprint. Self-publishing, particularly for fiction and poetry titles, has been common in the region for decades, and many authors are now turning to electronic publishing as an outlet.

Public libraries have and continue to play an important role in the region, providing reading material and other resources to island residents. Regional cooperation among libraries and archival repositories is becoming increasingly common and widespread: in 2004, a large group of national and university libraries from around the area founded the Digital Library of the Caribbean (dLOC), an extensive repository for digitized materials of local and regional interest from partner institutions. Like their counterparts around the world, 21st-century librarians, booksellers, authors, and readers from the Caribbean region are navigating their way through the rapid changes taking place in the world of books and reading. Regardless of what the future holds, the region's diverse and complex history offers much untilled, fruitful ground for scholars of print culture and history, the reading experience, and bibliography.

BIBLIOGRAPHY

G. Barber, *Studies in the Booktrade of the European Enlightenment* (1994)

R. Cave, *Printing and the Book Trade in the West Indies* (1987)

G. Frohnsdorff, *Early Printing in Saint Vincent* (2009)

J. A. Lent, *Mass Communications in the Caribbean* (1990)

B. F. Swan, *The Spread of Printing: The Caribbean Area* (1970)

Index

This index consists of a consolidated alphabetical list of entries for people, companies, and titles of works mentioned in this work. Entries are arranged in letter-by-letter sequence. Page numbers in italics refer to figures. Dates for individuals have been taken from standard reference works such as *ODNB* and Oxford companions, but in such a huge field it has not proved possible to ensure the accuracy of a great number of such dates.